'illuminating, wry and exhaustive'
Newsday (USA)

'The third (and allegedly final) edition of Michael Gray's pioneering tome...
runs to a colossal 900 pages and confirms once again Gray's position as the doyen
of Dylan scholars...even in its initial modest form, [it] was profoundly significant...
a revelation...thrilling...The third edition of Gray's lifetime study displays
an almost insane degree of scholarship...an intellectual tour de force.'
Uncut (London)

'*Song & Dance Man* in its original form appeared in 1972 and shook up the world of
rock music criticism as much as Dylan himself shook up the twee folk scene of early
1960s Greenwich Village...All of that original volume and its 1981 update are
included here, along with a host of new chapters...The book has therefore grown up
with its subject...What is truly refreshing about Gray [is] his fine and unpretentious
tone even when he is going into detail about poetic techniques or references...a
cohesive and enlightening volume that actually makes you want to hear over-familiar
songs again. Great criticism, literary or popular, should inspire the reader to return to
the original and re-evaluate. Gray's *Song & Dance Man III* is a delight...definitive.'
bibliomania.com

'This major update of a seminal work deserves to be read and studied by anyone
with even the slightest interest in song lyrics and it's essential as a storehouse of
knowledge on folk, country and blues records.'
Folk Roots (London)

'a marvelous work of literary archaeology, cool analysis, and inspired guesswork'
Asahi (Tokyo)

'The original *Song & Dance Man* was a pioneering piece of rock scholarship...
Written with great intelligence and passion...the result was the first important book
about a rock artist's output, not just their life... But these 250 pages are merely a
fragment of the 900-page monster which Gray has [now] unleashed...magnificent...
soaked in insight...gems of perception on almost every page.'
Record Collector (London)

'Fascinating, scholarly and very readable...an absolute must for Dylan admirers...
The longest and most relevant chapter for *Blueprint* readers ["Even Post-Structuralists
Oughta Have the Pre-War Blues"] is...packed solid with informative and enthralling
reading. I cannot congratulate Gray enough for this outstanding chapter...[a] very
important study. A thoroughly enjoyable and informative book by an author who
writes knowledgeably, with style and with great insight – very highly recommended
to all.'
Blueprint (UK)

'Gray's monumental study...dissects Dylan's songs to reveal their literary and
musical origins...His precision identifies the essence of Dylan...Michael Gray writes
exuberantly, critically and is never lost for a judgement... His evaluations are
refreshing and accurate.'
Der Bund (Switzerland)

'This is a wonderful book…A monumental work of detailed scholarship, this…sets a benchmark of critical excellence…Composed with passion and consummate artistry…essential.'
The Bridge (UK)

'Gray remains passionate about his subject. His writing is both scholarly and readable. This is an entertaining, educational, funny, infuriating book…His opinions are strong, and he delivers them with surgical precision…*Song & Dance Man III* is a must-read for Dylan enthusiasts and a fun, literate exploration for the casual fan.'
Dirty Linen (USA)

'Michael Gray showing why he is the heavyweight champion of Dylanology'
Write Angles (UK)

'Indispensable…His research is formidable, and his knowledge encyclopedic…great cogency, confidence and authority…a quite splendid critic…Gray can explain *how* the text [of a Dylan song] works poetically. It's a rare gift…at the heart of this book is some of the finest critical writing ever done about Bob Dylan.'
Stephen Scobie, University of Victoria, Canada, and author of *Alias Bob Dylan*

'serious Dylan criticism…sober and intricate analyses…monumental'
Bryan Appleyard, *Sunday Times* (London)

'This is a generous book…solid analysis…lucid discussions…Like few other books about Dylan, this one will stay at hand for a long, long time.'
On the Tracks (USA)

'I've reaped inestimable enjoyment leaping and lingering through this wonderful tome. I love the blues chapter. I love the book!! I greatly enjoy the style of writing, one of well researched passionate abandon, and there is no need to catalog the innumerable insights provided.'
Peter Narváez, Professor of Folklore, Memorial University, Newfoundland, Canada

'It is the most penetrating and clear-headed work on his work ever done – a monumental achievement.'
David Hajdu, author of *Positively 4th Street*

'This brilliant work establishes itself at once as *the* book on its subject, the one to which all those in the field will refer for many years to come.'
Aidan Day, Professor of English, Edinburgh University

MICHAEL GRAY

SONG & DANCE MAN III

The Art of Bob Dylan

continuum
LONDON • NEW YORK

Continuum
The Tower Building, 11 York Road, London, SE1 7NX
370 Lexington Avenue, New York, NY 10017–6550

First published 2000 by Continuum
by arrangement with Bayou Press Ltd

Reprinted 2000 (twice), 2001, 2002

British Library Cataloguing-in-Publication Data
A catalogue record for this book is available from the British Library.

ISBN 0-304-70762-7 (hardback)
     0-8264-5150-0 (paperback)
     0-8264-6382-7 (paperback – special edition)

Library of Congress Cataloging-in-Publication Data
Gray, Michael.
     Song & dance man III : the art of Bob Dylan / Michael Gray.
          p.   cm.
     Rev. ed. of: The art of Bob Dylan.
     ISBN 0-304-70762-7 (hb.)—0-8264-5150-0 (pb)—0-8264-6382-7(pb)
     1. Dylan, Bob, 1941– —Criticism and interpretation. I. Gray,
Michael. Art of Bob Dylan. II. Title. III. Title: Song and dance
man three. IV. Title: Art of Bob Dylan.
ML420. D98G7   1999   99–42572
782.42164′092—dc21   CIP

Typeset by ensystems Ltd, Saffron Walden, Essex
Printed and bound in Great Britain by Bath Press

to Sarah:
the main ms

I think of myself . . . as a song & dance man.

Bob Dylan, 1965

Never trust the artist. Trust the tale.

D. H. Lawrence, 1923

Contents

Thanks and Acknowledgements   ix
Preface   xvii
Notes on the Recording and Release Information   xxiii

Introduction: An Album-by-Album Guide to Dylan's Work   1

1. Dylan and the Folk Tradition   17

2. Dylan and the Literary Tradition   45

3. Dylan and Rock Music   85

4. Dylan's Use of Language: Towards Complexity   122

5. Dylan's Use of Language: Towards a New Simplicity   159

6. Lay Down Your Weary Tune: Drugs and Mysticism   194

7. The Coming of the Slow Train   206

8. Well I Investigated All the Books in the Library . . .   249

9. Even Post-Structuralists Oughta Have the Pre-War Blues   268

10. Closin' the Book on the Pages and the Text?   380

11. Yonder Comes Sin: The Retreat from Evangelism   391

12. Every Grain of Sand   400

13. Groom Still Waiting at the Altar?   426

14. Jokerman   464

15. Bob Dylan, Blind Willie McTell and 'Blind Willie McTell'   517

16. Oh Mercy . . . the Second Half of the 1980s   548

17. Nursery Rhyme, Fairy Tale and "Under The Red Sky"   634

18. Good as He's Been in a World Gone Wrong?   703

19. Time Out of Mind   785

20. There Is Only Up Wing an' Down Wing   835

    Bibliography   879
    Index   897

(The Album-by-Album Guide updates and extends that in the previous edition of this book; Chapters 1–7 reproduce the chapters of that edition, with new annotations; Chapters 8–20, the Bibliography and Index are wholly new for the present edition.)

Thanks and Acknowledgements

THANKS, for help towards one or more editions of this book, to: 'Jailhouse John' Alexander; the American Arts Documentation Centre at Exeter University, especially David Horn (now at the Institute of Popular Music at Liverpool University); Karl Erik

Andersen; Niels Andersen; Rod Anstee; Görgen Antonsson's marvellous website 'Prewar blues & gospel on microgroove'; John Baldwin; Sarah Banbury at Jane Balfour Films, London; Lars M. Banke; Stanley Bard; Derek and Tracy Barker at *Isis* fanzine; Clive Barrett; Frances Bartholomew; the late John Bauldie; Dylan Beattie; Viv Beeby at 'Poetry Please', BBC Bristol; Libby Bell; Martin Bell; Jan Bentley, Joe Donnelly and Alison, Jonathan Morrish and Trisha, Philip Saville and Elly Smith, all at one time at CBS Records (UK) and/or now at Sony Music Entertainment (London); Ed Bicknell; Wolf Biewald; Olof Björner; John Bodley at Faber and Faber, London; Stanley Booth; David Braun; Janis Bright; Jackum Brown; Sybie Brown; Richard Brunton; Diana Bryan; Evelyne and Paul Bubernak; Dave Budge; Don Burbage; Trevor Cajiao; Dave Callow; Andrew Capes; David Chance; the staff at the Center for the Study of Southern Culture at the University of Mississippi; Fiona M. Clark; C. F. M. Clarke; my grandmother the late Jessie M. Clarke; Larry Cohn; the late Ray Coleman; Maggie and Mel Collins; Ben Collis; Martin Colyer; Wendy Coslett; John Cowley; Phil Cox; Nadja Coyne at the *New Statesman*; James F. Cullinan at Finbarr International, Folkestone; Ted Cummings at MCA Records London; Karl Dallas; Andrew Darke; Dave's Disk Doctor Service Ltd.; Aidan Day; the late Michael Dempsey; Zachary M. Dillon; Dave Dingle; Pete Doggett and Mark Paytress at *Record Collector*; Mick and Nadine Douche; Eddie Ducati; Paul Duck, Alan Ward, Paul Wilson and especially Andy Linehan at the National Sound Archive (British Library); Glen Dundas and his book *Tangled up in Tapes*, especially editions 3 and 4; Madge Dundas; Larry Eden; Kay Ellis; Endcape Ltd. of Pickering; Tony Engle at Topic Records, London; William R. Ferris; Stephen Folkes; Dave Foster and Clio B at Hotshot Records/House of the Blues, Leeds; Roger Ford; Dr Greg Foster; Nigel Fountain; the late Edith Fowke; Raymonde Foye; Pete Frame's Family Trees; the excellent website of the Simon Fraser University Library, Vancouver; Tom Freeland; Greg French; Hans Fried; Jeff Friedmann; Larry Furlong; Peter Furtardo; Mel Gamble; Sandy Gant; John Garst; Simon Gee; Aimée L. German; Peter Gibbon; Sandy Gibson; the Gideons; Jackie Giff; Richard Gilbert; Charlie Gillett; Paul Gilroy; Jeff Gitter; Mr Glass at Ray's Jazz Shop, London; the late Ralph J. Gleason; Mick Gold; George Goldby; Bob Golden;

Gabrielle Goodchild; Chris Mitchell at Opportunities, Nawton; my parents Diana J. Gray and the late H. Mervyn Gray; my son Gabriel Gray; Judith A. Gray at the American Folklife Center at the Library of Congress, Washington, DC; my daughter Magdalena Gray; Arthur Green; Andy Greenaway; Dr Fred Grubb; Eileen Gunn; Phil Gunson; Urban Gwerder; Mark Harden's Artchive website; Peter Harrison; Paul and Anna Harvey; Jörg Hausmann; Seth Hayne; Michael Hayward; John and Henrietta Heawood; Agnes Hegel at CBS Disques, Paris; Manfred Helfert; Peter Hellens; Jim Heppell; Alex Hill (despite not needing him to know which way the wind blows); Rolande Hinton; Dave Hogg; Michael Horovitz; John Horsum; Duncan Hume; John Hume; Richard Hurley; Michele Hush; Ashley Hutchings; Ian Jack; Debra A. Jensen; Vivienne Jez; R. T. Jones; Norman Jopling; Janet Joyce at Cassell Academic; Kanawha County Library, West Virginia; Julie Kelly; Jean Kemble at the Eccles Centre for American Studies (British Library); Roberta Kent; Andrew Kershaw; Robert Koehler and friends in Austria; Dave Laing; Professor Robert Langbaum; Anne and Nancy Larson and family; Robin Leavis; C. P. Lee; Ada and Bonnie Leiberman; Paul and Gwynne Leng; John Lindley; Bob Linney; Sharon Linney; Grahame Lloyd; Guy Logsdon; my sister, Valerie Lowe; Rod MacBeath; Matt McConnell at Sony Music Nashville; Steve McDonogh; Roger McGuinn; Jean McKay; Iain McLay; 'David McLuhan'; Angela McRobbie; Marsha Maguire at the Experience Music Project, Seattle; Greil Marcus; Margo Margolis; Gaye and the late Oliver Mander; Paul Marsh; Diana Nicholas Marshall; Tomasz Masenski; Alison Menzies at Jonathan Cape, London; Linda Milner; Colin Moore; Andrew Morris; staff and contingent colleagues at Mount Pleasant, Reigate; Donald Muir, Penguin Books' Archive Department, Harmondsworth; Charles Shaar Murray; Derek Neil; Richard Neville; Cleophas Newhook; Rebecca Newhook; Andy Nieurzyla; Ben Nisbet; Rab Noakes; Kara Noble; the staff at North Yorkshire Public Libraries; the late Richard Oakley; Michael O'Connell and colleagues at Helter Skelter Books, London; Harold Ong; Iona Opie; the late Roy Orbison; Andrea Orlandi; Roger Osborne; 'Chrome Oxide'; Bill Pagel and his website BobLinks; Tom Paley; Jon Pankake; William Parr; Johnny Parth at Document Records, Vienna; Chris Payne and Stewart Gillies at the Newspaper Library (British Library); Dave Percival; Chris Perry; Dave Phillips; Serge Pieters; David Pirie; Jeff Place; Michel Pomarède; Carla Rafferty; Gerry Rafferty; Pete Reed; Denny Rice; Gillian Ridgley; Lesley Riley; Debbie Roberts; Wendy Robin; Jim Roemer's website; Jeff Rosen at Special Rider Music, New York; Neil Rosenberg; Mike Rowe; Richard Russell; Howard Rye; David Rymer; Naomi Saltzman; Burkhard 'Didi' Schleser; Fritz Schuler; Kenny and Donna Sclater; Andrew Scott; Marie Scott; Gavin Selerie; Adam Seiff at Tower Records, London; Christine Seville; the late Robert Shelton; Alyn Shipton at Bayou Press; Jeremy Silver; Camilla Simmons; Neil Slaven; Katherine Smalley at Henry Holt & Co.; Chris Smith; Ken Smith at Red Lick Records, Porthmadog, Wales; Simon Smith at the Poetry Library, London; Steve Smith; Jan Sobotka; the Society of Authors; Linda Solomon; Wes Stace; Pat Stead; Alison Steele at Narwood Productions, New York; Tommy Steele; Harriet Stein; C. Keith Stevens; Phil Stoker and Rob Hughes at Ace Records, London; Robert Strachan; Geoff Styche; Christer Svensson; the work of Michael Taft; Philip Tagg; Ray Templeton; Robert Tilling; Margaret Toivola; Kevin Tuohy; Amy Turner at Oxford University Press; Iain G. Tweeddale; Pat Tynan at Koch International; Sue Tyrrell; Phil Usher; Robin Valk;

Marion Venencia; Hein Versteegen; Rainer Vesely; Cathy Village; Gil Walker; Thora Wakeling at the Department of Continuing and Adult Education, University of Exeter; Michael Watts; John Way; Richard Weize, Hermann Knülle and Matthias Knischewski at Bear Family Records, Vollersode, Germany; Brian Wells; Dave Wheatley; Charles White; Cliff White; John White; Jennifer Farr Whittaker; John Widdowson at the Centre for English Language and Tradition, Sheffield University; the late David Widgery; Francis Wilford-Smith; Randy Edwards Williams at the Fife Folklore Archives at Utah State University; Paul S. Williams; Bob Willis; Margaret Willis; George Wilkinson; Val Wilmer; Arthur Nevill Wilson; Phil Wilson; Richard David Wissolik; Amy L. Witzel; Jan Mark Wolkin; Ian Woodward; Richard Wooton; John Wraith; Steve Wycherley; Larry Yudelson's website; and Matthew Zuckerman.

SPECIAL THANKS and much gratitude for crucial help with this edition to Wolfram Altenhövel, Alan Balfour, Sarah Beattie, Andy Benson, Nigel Hinton, Andy Muir, Peter Narváez, the Royal Literary Fund, Tony Russell, Linda Thomas and David H. Willis.

ACKNOWLEDGEMENTS

1986; **Brownsville Girl** (lyrics co-written with Sam Shepard), © 1986; **Had A Dream About You Baby**, © 1987; **Death Is Not The End**, © 1988; **Where Teardrops Fall**, © 1989; **Everything Is Broken**, © 1989; **The Man In The Long Black Coat**, © 1989; **Most Of The Time**, © 1989; **Ring Them Bells**, © 1989; **What Was It You Wanted?**, © 1989; **What Good Am I?**, © 1989; **Disease Of Conceit**, © 1989; **Shooting Star**, © 1989; **Dignity**, © 1989; **Series Of Dreams**, © 1989; **Wiggle Wiggle**, © 1990; **Under The Red Sky**, © 1990; **Unbelievable**, © 1990; **10,000 Men**, © 1990; **2 x 2**, © 1990; **Born In Time**, © 1990; **Handy Dandy**, © 1990; **Cat's In The Well**, © 1990; **God Knows**, © 1990; **TV Talkin' Song**, © 1990; **World Gone Wrong** sleeve notes, © 1993; **Love Sick**, © 1997; **Standing In The Doorway**, © 1997; **Million Miles**, © 1997; **Tryin' To Get To Heaven**, © 1997; **'Til I Fell In Love With You**, © 1997; **Not Dark Yet**, © 1997; **Cold Irons Bound**, © 1997; **Make You Feel My Love**, © 1997; **Can't Wait**, © 1997; **Highlands**, © 1997; **Under Your Spell** (co-written with Carol Bayer Sager), © 1986 Special Rider Music & Carol Bayer Sager Music.

The author is particularly grateful to Jeff Rosen at Special Rider Music for his unfailing cooperation, flexibility and patience over many years, and to Bob Dylan for consenting to my quoting so much from his extraordinary body of work.

The author and publishers also thank the undermentioned copyright owners for permission to quote from the following lyric material: from **Just A Dream (On My Mind)**, words and music by Big Bill Broonzy, © 1933 by kind permission of Universal/ MCA Music Ltd.; lyrics from **Time Is Drawing Near**, words and music by Sleepy John Estes, © by kind permission of Universal/MCA Music Ltd.; lyrics from **Maybellene, The Promised Land, Too Much Monkey Business** and **Nadine**, words and music by Chuck Berry, © ARC Music Corporation, by kind permission of Jewel Music Publishing Co. Ltd. and Tristan Music Ltd.; **Take Me As I Am (Or Let Me Go)**, words and music by Boudleaux Bryant, © 1954 Acuff Rose Publications Inc. and Acuff-Rose Music Ltd., by kind permission of House of Bryant and Music Sales Ltd., all rights reserved, international copyright secured; **What To Do**, words and music by Buddy Holly, © 1959 Peer International Corp., USA, Peermusic (UK) Ltd., used by permission; **One-Sided Love Affair**, words and music by Bill Campbell, © 1956 EMI Catalogue Partnership and EMI Unart Catalog Inc., USA, worldwide print rights controlled by Warner Bros. Publications Inc., USA/IMP Ltd., reproduction by permission of IMP Ltd.; **Jailhouse Rock**, words and music by Jerry Leiber and Mike Stoller, © 1957 by Elvis Presley Music Inc., all rights administered by Williamson Music, all rights reserved, lyric reproduced by kind permission of the Carlin Music Corp., London NW1 8BD; **It's Late**, words and music by Dorsey Burnette, © 1958 EMI Catalogue Partnership, EMI Unart Catalog Inc. and Matragun Music Inc. USA, print rights controlled by Warner Bros. Publications Inc., USA, Zomba Music Publishers and IMP Ltd., reproduced by permission of Zomba Music Publishers and IMP Ltd.; and **Tail Dragger**, written by Willie Dixon (as performed by Howlin' Wolf), © 1964, 1992 Hoochie Coochie Music, administered by Bug Music, London W14 0LJ, all rights reserved, used by permission.

We also wish to thank the following for permission to quote from copyright works: Thames & Hudson for permission to quote from *The Uses of Enchantment* by Bruno Bettelheim, © Bruno Bettelheim, 1976; HarperCollins Publishers Ltd. and Houghton Mifflin Company for permission to quote from *The Lord of the Rings* by

J. R. R. Tolkien, © 1954–55; Martin Bell, MP, and family for permission to quote from 'English Tradition and Idiom' by Adrian Bell, which originally appeared in Volume 2 of *Scrutiny*, Cambridge, 1933, and subsequently in *A Selection From Scrutiny, Volume II*; Macmillan & Co. for permission to quote from *Man and His Symbols*, edited by Carl Jung © 1964; *The Land Where the Blues Began* by Alan Lomax, © Alan Lomax, 1993, reprinted by permission of Pantheon Books, a division of Random House Inc. and Methuen Publishing Ltd.; for permission to quote from an interview with Bob Dylan by Jann Wenner in *Rolling Stone*, 29 November 1969, © by Straight Arrow Publishers Inc., 1969, all rights reserved, reprinted by permission; quotation from *The Oxford Dictionary of Nursery Rhymes*, by Iona and Peter Opie, 1951 revised edition, © Iona and Peter Opie, 1951, by permission of Oxford University Press; from '23rd Street Runs into Heaven' by Kenneth Patchen, from *The Collected Poems of Kenneth Patchen*, copyright © 1957 by New Directions Publishing Corp., reprinted by permission of New Directions Publishing Corp.; 'Bob Dylan: Genius or Commodity' by David Horowitz, © 1964, quoted by kind permission of *Peace News*, London; 'Sounds Authentic: Black Music, Ethnicity and the Challenge of a Changing Same' by Paul Gilroy, © 1991, quoted by kind permission of Paul Gilroy; 'From Refrain to Rave: the Decline of Figure and the Rise of Ground' by Philip Tagg © 1993, quoted by kind permission of Philip Tagg. We thank Andrew Darke, Nigel Hinton, Robert Strachan and Bob Willis for permission to quote from their un-published work. We also wish to thank Steven Goldberg for the use of quotation from his article 'Bob Dylan and the Poetry of Salvation' (© 1970 Saturday Review Inc.); every effort was made to trace this and other copyright holders.

Finally, the author wishes to thank those who commissioned articles from him from which small amounts of published and unpublished material have been revised within the present work, from fragments of an October 1967 article in *OZ* through to observations on Highway 61 made possible by the commissioning of the article on Bob Dylan's Duluth and Hibbing footsteps in the *Daily Telegraph*, November 1999. In between, the author thanks in particular commissioning editors at *Melody Maker* in the 1970s, the *Telegraph* fanzine and the *Independent* in the 1980s, *Homer, the slut* and *Isis* fanzines, *The Times* and *Daily Telegraph* and the part-work *The Blues Collection* in the 1990s, and by no means least Germinal Verlag, the publishers of the book *Bob Dylan: Fünfzig Jahre . . .*, 1993, in which early drafts of material now in Chapters 9 and 20 were first published, translated into German by Hein Versteegen.

Preface

In the late 1960s, until he began to de-construct himself with "Nashville Skyline", Bob Dylan was still the hippest person on the planet. In 1978, in the aftermath of the superlative "Blood On The Tracks" and the best-selling "Desire", Dylan toured Europe for the first time in twelve years, and was received rapturously by enormous audiences and by reviewers ('The Greatest Concert I Have Ever Seen,' declared Ray Connolly in the *Daily Mail*, 16/6/78, while Dylan's Top 10 hit single 'Baby, Stop Crying' (he's never had one since) was on juke-boxes everywhere.

Eleven years on, in 1989, Dylan finally managed a near-great album for the 1980s – "Oh Mercy" – once more returning himself to some level of critical and popular approbation, topped the following February by a triumphant, magical series of concerts at Hammersmith Odeon.

In between times, his public esteem had often been low. Throughout the early 1970s, after completing his self-dismantling with the widely despised "Self Portrait" album and releasing the underrated "New Morning", Dylan had wandered in the wilderness, backlashed by apostates, a pariah of the passé. At the beginning of the 1980s, the smart money was on post-punk youth and everyone over 30 was a boring old fart (specially the singer–songwriter). At the same time, the New Right's decade of greed was under way. In America the old New Left was reduced to shovelling cocaine up its nose just like the apoliticos of the entertainment industry; in Britain the old New Left was clinging to lefter-than-thou sects still convinced of the imminence of world socialism. Meanwhile Dylan's latest album was "Saved" and he was touring with ugly musicians around stadiums of the resentful damned. He was about as hip as General Franco.

Looming high and solid above Bob Dylan's alternating success and failure, and the times that were a-changin' all around us, there was a critical Hadrian's Wall constructed by the literati to keep out *all* the guitar-wielding barbarians. Elvis Presley, Bob Dylan, Johnny Rotten . . . they were all indistinguishable oiks howling on the borders of civilisation and threatening to destroy its culture. In America in the early 1960s, the literati considered Dylan a frightful oik even as an entertainer, let alone as an artist. John Updike reviewed concerts in Ipswich, Massachussetts, between 1961 and 1965. Of a Joan Baez concert of 1964, he wrote:

> [in] the unkindest cut of all, Miss Baez yielded the stage, with a delight all too evident, to a young man, Bob Dylan, in tattered jeans and a black jacket, three

months on the far side of a haircut, whose voice you could scour a skillet with. Miss Baez, this admirer was pained to observe, visibly lit up with love-light when he came onto the stage, and even tried to force her way, in duet, through some of the impenetrable lyrics that Dylan composes as abundantly as poison ivy puts forth leaves.

This (in contrast to Dylan's impenetrable lyrics) is the consummate word craft of America's great novelist, short story writer and poet, a Pulitzer prize-winner with a reputation as 'a keen observer of modern American life' in fiction 'assured, urbane and ironic' and 'as versatile as it is prolific'.[1]

Many of these people are still at it – but the wall does seem to be coming down. In Britain, right up till the mid-1990s, if you had forged a long-lost autobiographical novelette by Lytton Strachey's brother-in-law's third wife, you'd have secured its serialisation at the front of whichever 'quality press' review section you cared to sell it to. You'd have achieved reviews everywhere, whichever week suited you best, and TV producers would have vied to film a 'special' about it. In laughable contrast, if you were to discover a *Daughter of Tarantula* by Bob Dylan, you'd have been lucky to see it mentioned in the broadsheets at all.

As late as 1992 the 'radical' English playwright David Hare could imagine that he was summing up the battle-lines between civilised culture and its enemy, a cheap and destructive pop culture, in the phrase 'Keats versus Dylan'. Never mind that Bob Dylan had spent the previous three decades with his face set firmly against the vulgar and the cheap, or indeed that John Keats had been a cockney oik and upstart himself. Such was the climate of opinion still that Hare's comically inaccurate personifying of the divide caught on like a pop craze itself. Within minutes, that doyenne of the literary clerisy, A. S. Byatt, could go on BBC-2's all-purpose arts programme, *The Late Show*, and pronounce that the qualitative difference between Keats and Dylan is that with Keats, she could take you through one of his poems and reveal many layers . . .[2]

She couldn't take you through a Dylan lyric because she wouldn't know where to begin. What's disgraceful is not the preference for Keats, nor the ignorance about Dylan: it is the malappropriate self-confidence that has her thinking it reasonable to hand down these uninformed but lofty judgements. As if, indeed, her very unfamiliarity with Dylan's work affirms the loftiness that justifies dismissing it. Anyone not under the moonie spell of this clerisy might feel that if they were as uninformed about Keats as A. S. Byatt was about Dylan, they wouldn't rush onto TV to discuss his work.

Twenty years earlier, my book had suggested what huge numbers of people already knew by then: that Bob Dylan's work was worth some critical attention and

---

1.   John Updike, quoted in *Isis* magazine, no. 52, December 1993–January 1994, taken via the American magazine, *Rock and Rap Confidential* [no details given], from the anthology of Updike's concert reviews *Concerts at Castle Hill*, 1993. The quotes about Updike's literary reputation are taken from Ian Ousby's excellent *Cambridge Guide to Literature in English*, 1993 [corrected reprint 1995].

      Before Joan Baez started having Bob Dylan perform at her concerts (after his success at the Newport Folk Festival of 1963) she had given a similar guest slot to Flatt & Scruggs and to the Greenbriar Boys. How were their haircuts, John?

2.   *The Late Show*, BBC-2 TV, London, televised 25 February 1992.

could hold its own on its merits. I still owe a debt of gratitude to the late Michael Dempsey, the commissioning editor who first signed up *Song & Dance Man*, way back in 1971, in the face of the prevailing critical wind, and allowed me to argue a case for Dylan's being, if you must, on the same side as Keats.

While clearly failing to recommend itself to such important persons as David Hare or A. S. Byatt, nevertheless in the decades between first publication and now my book has continued to be cited in the burgeoning and wide-ranging literature about Bob Dylan, thanks partly to the happy accident of its historical position: it was the first full-length study of Dylan's work.

The second edition retained the structure of the first, while folding into it Dylan material from throughout the 1970s, up to and including the so-called Born Again Christian period that yielded the LPs "Slow Train Coming" and "Saved".[3] This third time, I have chosen a different approach: chosen not to try to re-thread the whole book in order to sew Dylan's recent work into it.

For one thing, if I wasn't careful I could spend my life re-working this book: always running in vain to keep up with Bob Dylan's ceaseless, prolific activity and having to try to re-shape a work that is essentially category-based rather than chronological, to accommodate it. For another, the known version of the book may retain some historical interest, has long been recommended to students – indeed I am told it still is – and yet has long been unobtainable. Perhaps this 'old' part of the book can still attract newcomers with an interest in Bob Dylan. The presence of the young in audiences at his concerts proves that many newcomers are drawn to him, in wave after generational wave, in spite of everything. Such people have in front of them the enviable pleasures of getting to know his vast back catalogue – and as it stands, without any updating, the 'old' part of this book is a guide to, and study of, that body of work, already covering all its major periods, including the 'Christian period'.

For these reasons, therefore, the present edition starts by republishing the core seven chapters of the 1981 text intact (except for the updating of its introduction, minor corrections of factual error and a small amount of pruning and changing of 'is' to 'was') but with substantial new annotations.

Then comes a series of new chapters on Dylan's work from the beginning of the 1980s up to the present day, taking in the albums from 1981's "Shot Of Love" to 1997's "Time Out Of Mind", plus the 1980s material offered by the retrospective box-set "Bootleg Series I–III", issued in 1991. There is, too, a critical look at the body of other people's work about Bob Dylan since 1980: a literature that has burgeoned. This leads into a discussion of post-structuralist ideas in relation to the whole of Dylan's work.

Included too is a substantial new study of how heavily and how creatively Dylan has drawn upon the blues through all four decades of his work. This is, for me, at the

---

3.   *Song & Dance Man: The Art of Bob Dylan*: Hart-Davis, MacGibbon, London, 1972; Abacus Books, London, 1973 [paperback]; E. P. Dutton & Co., New York, 1973; Shobun-Sha, Tokyo, 1973. *The Art of Bob Dylan: Song & Dance Man*: Hamlyn, London, 1981 [simultaneous hardback and paperback]; St Martin's Press, New York, 1982 [simultaneous hardback and paperback].

With the above exceptions, all books referred to in the present work are identified minimally in the footnotes and the text, and detailed fully in the Bibliography. All other works cited – songs, albums, articles, essays, magazines – are detailed in the footnotes at the time.

heart of the present edition; it seeks to understand Dylan's art from a perspective I wasn't qualified to write from in earlier decades. In total there are thirteen of these new chapters, amounting to some 75 per cent of the whole. To put it another way, the new edition is four times the size of the old.

At any rate, I have spent most of the now-disappearing present decade on this huge third and final edition. I hope the resultant book is a benign kind of labyrinth, or city-state. The workload, the surveying, tunnelling and pushing forward has been huge and much-planned. But by its nature it should be a living whole, with occupants who move around and change things and bring their own baggage along, or mislay it. As well as its main streets and major junctions, its arteries and veins, it should go into the narrow lanes and lumber-rooms and offer myriad byways and diversions: subterranean passages, you might say. Think of the longer annotations and footnotes not as irritating academese but as branch-lines, caves, lania, valves, optional scenic routes. You don't have to heed the tiny numbers that point to them – they can be ignored, like Public Footpath signs, or rabbit holes, or gates, that you may notice as you pass along the more straightforward route of the main narrative. Whether they distract or beckon is surely up to you.

While I have been working away, there has been the beginning of a change in the critical climate, as well as yet another change in the less rarified public mood. In 1997 Greil Marcus published a critical study centred upon one aspect of Bob Dylan's work, *Invisible Republic: Bob Dylan's Basement Tapes*, that was accorded a huge amount of reviewing attention in the press on both sides of the Atlantic, breaking down barriers thanks to Marcus' stature in cultural studies criticism; and in late 1998, a few months before being appointed the new Poet Laureate, Andrew Motion discussed the newly released 1966 concert recording from Manchester Free Trade Hall in terms of 'the tremendous beauty and subtlety of the songs and the matchless voice that sings them'.[4]

Meanwhile the public mood too seems unusually favourable towards someone who has always been an obdurate loner, and one so strongly associated with the 1960s that he always risks dismissal when people feel intolerant of the recent past in general and when that decade in particular is under attack, as it so often is.

Despite these perils, several things suggest at the present time that Bob Dylan is once again popular. There was an astonishing wave of warm re-appraisal for him when, in 1996, he was taken ill. Even newspaper reviewers, whose shared tenet for the previous twenty years had been that no one on the planet was more passé and to be sneered at, suddenly imagined his permanent absence and were surprised to find themselves feeling some regret over this. And then, in 1997, Dylan issued a new

---

4.   Andrew Motion, *Daily Telegraph*, 10/10/98.
Smaller holes had been made in the critical wall by those inside it a decade and more before Marcus and Motion. Christopher Ricks had written and spoken up for Dylan for many years, and in 1987 the rigorous *London Review of Books* published Danny Karlin's 'It ain't him, babe', 5/2/87, which included this fine rant: 'I have to confess to an unreasoning impatience with those who profess not to respect or understand Dylan's work. In 1600 the same people were going around saying that the drama was not a serious medium, that the theatre was frequented by riffraff and that guys like Shakespeare stole their plots and were only in it for the money . . . I know I ought to explain, patiently, that Dylan is the practioner of an original art . . . that his skills of composition and expression are indivisible, and provide him with a resource of extraordinary range, power and intensity; that he uses this resource to sing about things that matter . . . that, like all great artists, he tells some of the truth.'

album, "Time Out Of Mind", his first collection of new compositions in seven years, which reminded people of how striking and unique this artist was and is and always will be. He even picked up a set of Grammy Awards and a Kennedy Center Award, presented to him by President Clinton, who said of him: 'He probably had more impact on people of my generation than any other creative artist. His voice and lyrics haven't always been easy on the ears, but throughout his career, Bob Dylan has never aimed to please.'

Exactly. As we look back at the second half of the twentieth century from its closing moments, Bob Dylan still looks one of its dominant figures. But suppose that nobody likes the next albums (if there are any more albums of new compositions). Suppose that the newspapers revert to dismissing or reviling all his works. Suppose that endorsements by ex-President Clinton come to be an embarrassment, best forgotten (as of course they will be). None of that will make Bob Dylan any less interesting or important than in the past.

Michael Gray
Kirkbymoorside, North Yorkshire, 1999

Notes on the Recording and Release Information

Bob Dylan recordings

No discographical details are footnoted for officially released Bob Dylan recordings. This massive amount of detail would be a book in itself – and indeed is readily available in other books on Dylan, notably those by Glen Dundas and Michael Krogsgaard cited in the Bibliography. Nor are details of bootleg *releases* given here. But there is a general album-by-album profile in the Introduction, pages 1–16, and whenever *officially unreleased* Dylan material is discussed, place and date of *recording* are footnoted as precisely as possible.

Example: Bob Dylan: 'The Two Sisters (Bow And Balance)', St. Paul, Minnesota, May 1960. Bob Dylan: 'Weeping Willow', NYC, 17/11/93 (as here, all dates given in this book are set down in the order customary in Britain, i.e. day, month, year).

Rock'n'roll, R&B (rhythm'n'blues) and pop recordings

For records in these fluid categories, especially as in Chapter 3, with its enthusiastic lists of 1960–61 hit singles and its sideswipes at examples of contemporaneous crooner music, it would be near-impossible to document place and date of recording and full release details in every case. These records were, in the nature of things, recorded shortly before release; release on singles achieved wide dissemination on the radio and on juke-boxes at the time – a time when Bob Dylan was all ears – so that their subsequent reissue on LP is usually irrelevant. But for many records of particular appeal or significance in rock'n'roll history and/or that were a specific influence on Bob Dylan, this book aims to give the place and date of recording and the original 78 rpm and/or 45 rpm release details, and details of first vinyl issue in some cases. These may be supplemented by CD re-release details to help the reader interested in acquiring these tracks today. These guidelines tend to mean that good records get a discographical listing and bad ones don't.

Blues, gospel and hillbilly recordings

For blues, gospel and hillbilly recordings of the pre-war period (itself a term used oddly in musical circles: see below), as for folk recordings, stating the place and date of each recording means documenting details often lost in murk or myth but which, if pinned down, may be telling from many perspectives.

The special purpose of also noting when each recording first became available *on LP* is to establish when Bob Dylan first had ready opportunity to hear and absorb it.

Vinyl releases, LPs, form the main conduit through which the riches of pre-war blues, gospel and hillbilly recordings became known to the post-war world. Establishing when this work was first accessible to people is important for many purposes, including mine. When might Bob Dylan first have heard what? Answers are necessarily speculative. Dylan knew collectors of old 78 rpm records in both Minnesota and New York, and home-made compilations of such 78s circulated among those interested, on open-reel tapes. But since the main access to pre-war blues, gospel and hillbilly music was via albums, for Dylan as for most of us, it's at the heart of the matter to know what the original vinyl reissues of these old recordings were and when they were released.

It is a frustrating obstacle to research that so many of these albums bear no date. Time and again, those who compile these things tell you exactly what Tuesday afternoon in 1933 every track was recorded but then don't remember to put on their LP or CD even what year it is being released! You search the record label, sleeve and notes in vain for this basic information. The worst offenders in this respect include all the pre-1969 albums on Biograph (and some later ones), at least the first forty-odd Yazoo releases, and all Roots and Document/Wolf/RST Blues Documents releases.

At any rate, because of vinyl's importance, I avoid here any detailing of the extant 78 rpm shellac ('wax') releases. Unless otherwise stated, 'issued' here means 'issued on vinyl'. (In a small number of cases, first vinyl issue was in that alluring form, the EP, rather than the LP.) Second and third generation vinyl reissues are not listed, except where they have some historic significance of their own.

CD releases have the obvious virtue of enabling new listeners to acquire these recordings today and have replaced vinyl as the main way of passing on most old blues recordings. Indeed, the greening of the CD as a mass medium has prompted a huge increase in the availability of old music beyond golden-oldie pop. (It has also meant the careless slinging together of any old version of any old thing by any old blues singer in many cases. It is best to avoid – and to persuade your local record library to avoid – the many cheap CDs, often thrown together in Italy, with no information about where or when tracks were recorded. This is often because the recordings are inferior re-makes, in many cases taken from bored performances live in clubland.)

I have therefore listed good quality, conscientious CD releases in most applicable cases. There are, inevitably, exceptions. These are of two sorts. First, where recordings are cited with no suggestion that Bob Dylan's familiarity with them is relevant, the information given may be restricted to date and place of recording only. Second, now that the Austrian-based label Document Records has completed its extraordinary task of releasing almost *every extant pre-war blues and gospel recording* on CD, I have saved a great deal of space by not listing these, generally speaking. Sometimes a particular Document compilation is listed when this is clearly the best way to acquire a specific rarity.

The interested listener can obtain the Document Records catalogue by telephoning ++43-1-257-1377, and can assume in reading the listings in this book that whether or not a CD re-release from another company is given for a particular recording, there will be a Document CD available – that is, in all but a very few cases, usually where there has been no reason for companies owning the original recordings to allow the Document company to have them: for example Robert Johnson's work, owned by Columbia Records. In the vast majority of cases, there will be a perfectly adequate Document CD, with notes written by experts. However, it would be a dull record collection that consisted of shelf after shelf of identical-looking CDs from the same company, and there is no special advantage in spurning the wide range of alternatives. Nor will everyone feel like buying "Big Bill Broonzy Complete Recorded Works In Chronological Order, Volume 11 (1940–1942)" just to acquire 'Key To The Highway'.

These exceptions aside, the information footnoted on each blues, gospel or hillbilly recording cited is as follows (and in this order):

> name of the artist
> title of the recording, as on the original record label or company log
> place of recording
> date of recording
> title of the first vinyl issue of this recording
> record label
> catalogue-number
> place of issue (with large companies, their main city location)
> year of issue
> same details for CD reissues of the relevant recording, where applicable

Sometimes, for a specific reason, additional information is included in brackets. Example:

> Cannon's Jug Stompers:
> 'Minglewood Blues',
> Memphis,
> 30/1/28;
> "American Folk Music",
> Folkways Records
> FP 251–253,
> New York,
> 1952;
> CD-reissued "Cannon's Jug Stompers", Yazoo Records 1082/3, New York, c. 1991 [a CD reissue of a 1980s LP].

Items for which information could not be located at the time of going to press are identified as *nia* (no information available).

'Pre-war blues' meaning pre-Pearl Harbor or later

Throughout this book the term 'pre-war' in relation to American music (in practice usually the blues and hillbilly genres) refers to the period before the USA entered the Second World War in the aftermath of the Japanese bombing of Pearl Harbor at the end of 1941. Indeed the loosish term 'pre-war' extends later still, since the 'bible' of listings and discographies for the old blues, Dixon and Godrich's *Blues and Gospel Records 1902–1943* (superseded in 1997 by Dixon, Godrich and Rye's *Blues and Gospel Records 1890–1943*), chooses, as its title makes clear, a cut-off point of two years on from 1941, while the equivalent books listing 'post-war' blues recordings – by Leadbitter and Slaven and others – take their lead from Dixon and Godrich and begin with 1943, as do the 'post-war' gospel listings, Hayes and Laughton's 2-volume *Gospel Records 1943–1969: A Black Music Discography*.[1]

Music made as late as 1941 was, in white America at least, truly 'pre-war', in the sense not only of pre-dating the war but of being oblivious to it. While the black artist Ernest Blunt (The Florida Kid) had cut a 'Hitler Blues' in 1940, it was still possible in 1941, while cities all over Europe were being saturation-bombed, for an artist with the professional name of Adolf Hofner to enjoy widespread popularity in and around Texas. He and his band had a hit record, 'Cotton-Eyed Joe', that summer.[2]

A year later, recruits for the war included large numbers of blacks, many of them taken from the South, where they had no rights, and sent overseas to fight for 'their' country. In fact, some black Americans had been involved a lot earlier. Five hundred had volunteered to join the Ethiopian Army in 1935, when Hitler's ally Mussolini threatened to invade this never-colonised African country.

Bob Dylan, born in May 1941, was therefore a pre-war baby.

1.   Earlier editions of Dixon and Godrich had ended in 1942, recognising that such records ceased to be made after the Petrillo ban on recording on 1 August 1942. This ban was nothing to do with the rationing of shellac for the war effort, but was a total ban on new recordings imposed by the musicians' union, the American Federation of Musicians, and named after its leader, James Petrillo. The ban was, in Paul and Beth Garon's words, 'an attempt to stifle the competition that juke boxes represented for working musicians, and in order to collect royalties from the major labels'. As the Garons' book *Woman with Guitar: Memphis Minnie's Blues* (1992) explains, the Petrillo Ban had only modest success: 'In September, 1943, Decca agreed to the AFM's demand for royalties on new recordings . . . Capitol agreed in October . . . Victor and Columbia . . . held out until November 1944.' But this royalty-collection, of 1% of the retail price per record, was declared illegal, resulting in another, though less successful, ban from 1947 to 1948.

2.   The Florida Kid: 'Hitler Blues', Chicago, 7/11/40. Adolf Hofner & His San Antonians: 'Cotton-Eyed Joe', Dallas, 28/2/41, CD-reissued on "Retrospective 1925–1950", Columbia Legacy Roots N' Blues Series 47911, New York, 1992.

Introduction: An Album-by-Album Guide to Dylan's Work

I'm a poet, and I know it.
Hope I don't blow it.
Bob Dylan: 'I Shall Be Free No. 10'

This is not a biography of Bob Dylan but a critical study of his work. It doesn't look at what he eats for breakfast but at what he writes in his songs.

It is more about Dylan's words than his music, though it tries to take a proper account of both, because Dylan uses much *more* than language in his art. His words are presented not as poems but as parts of songs. His finished works of art are his *recordings*. Like his vocal performances and his music, his words are just ingredients.

This needs to be borne in mind when we analyse his lyrics – and this book makes no apology for doing that. Here at the beginning of the twenty-first century, those who want to understand the generations which grew up in the West in the 1960s to 1980s will find it vital to study Bob Dylan's art closely. There is a sense in which, more fully than F. Scott Fitzgerald, Dylan created a generation. The possibilities of our inner lives were expanded by the impingement of Dylan's art, by the impact of his consciousness on ours, and on so much that has followed.

Whenever an artist of such real power as Dylan emerges, there is a fatalistic desire, on the part of those who appreciate it, not to analyse but to submit. But there is a collaborative process involved in art's impingement: the artist's work must be receptively approached before it can function fully.

Dylan's work has hardly been ignored on every level of course, but much of the real impact of his art has still passed unnoticed while that other impact – that of the showbiz phenomenon – has been far from ignored. Dylan has been interviewed, his concerts written up, his records reviewed, with relish and persistence; but reviews and interviews are rarely designed for analysis so much as for a kind of flippant prying. The review is as far removed from real criticism as is the interview from real dialogue.

In Dylan's case there has been plenty of superficial message-hunting. It provokes, in the artist, an appropriate defensiveness:

Dylan: . . . I do know what my songs are about.
Playboy: And what's that?

Dylan: Oh, some are about four minutes, some are about five minutes, and some, believe it or not, are about eleven or twelve.[1]

What Dylan does not do is offer a sustained, cohesive philosophy of life, intellectually considered and checked for contradictions, though there is, in retrospect, a weighty consistency of purpose and stance in the work he has offered, even as it has embraced both the radical and the traditional. What he does offer is the artistic re-creation of the individual's struggle in our times, and therefore the imaginative re-creation of those times. His work is truly educative and thereby truly entertaining. Its virtue lies not in immediacy or pace, though it often has both, but in the perceptiveness of what it offers.

Dylan's work has that clear integrity capable of 'representing the age' and is competent, therefore, to go beyond it – to clarify by focusing, with a vital intelligence, on its special confusions and so to place it soberly inside the wider continuum.

At one time he wrote songs explicitly 'about' war, exploitation and suffering. That he no longer often does so is not a mark of any lack of concern or of any retreat from responsibility. An early Dylan song like 'A Hard Rain's A-Gonna Fall', with its clear didactic glimpses:

> I met one man who was wounded in love
> I met another man who was wounded in hatred

evinces the same kind of exploratory awareness that has matured, not disappeared, in Dylan's later work. He deals with the human world as it really is.

Dylan himself has described acutely what he believes his own contribution has been. Interviewed in 1985 for the the retrospective box-set "Biograph", summarised below, Dylan said that before he came along, rock'n'roll had never been enough:

> great catch-phrases and driving pulse rhythms and you could get high on the energy but they weren't serious or didn't reflect life in a realistic way. I knew that when I got into folk music . . . [Those] songs are filled with more despair, more sadness, more triumph, more faith in the supernatural, much deeper feelings . . . I needed that. Life is full of complexities and rock'n'roll didn't reflect that. It was just put on a happy face and ride, sally, ride, there was nothing even resembling 'Sixteen Snow White Horses' or 'See That My Grave Is Kept Clean' . . . If I did anything, I brought one to the other. There was nothing serious happening in music when I started.[2]

Dylan has not only used, within one of the most powerfully attractive forms of modern technology, the strengths of ancient balladry and of the earliest blues. He has also fused with the power of music the force of other kinds of poetry, creating work that is enriched by and builds upon the work of William Blake, Robert Browning, the French Symbolists, T. S. Eliot, the Beat Poets of the 1950s, and more. Yet in his use

---

1. 'The *Playboy* interview: a candid conversation with the iconoclastic idol of the folk-rock set', *Playboy*, March 1966. Actually this 'interview' was a substantial re-write by Dylan and the interviewer, jazz critic Nat Hentoff (who had written the sleeve notes to the 1963 "The Freewheelin' Bob Dylan"), based on an interview recorded NYC, October–November 1965.

2. Dylan, interviewed by Cameron Crowe, published within "Biograph", 1985.

of, and inspiration by, the poetry of folksong, at least one wheel has come full circle. In Dylan, as in John Bunyan before him, the subcultures surfaced.

In the 1960s Dylan's generation packed together its discoveries of innumerable subcultures and re-formed them into chaotic, kaleidoscopic but living experience. With a free intelligence, that generation derived a dynamic vision from rock music, folk poetry, cinematic experiment, comic books, communal living, philosophy, existential politics, drugs, and an early tacit recognition that the cultural mainstream had done little to combat the moral and imaginative imbecility of what was then called The Great Society.

Times have certainly changed. The genuine voice, if it survives at all, still speaks out. Bob Dylan's does.

Bob Dylan's first album came out in 1962, when even those now 40 years old had hardly been born. So what follows, to begin with, is a guide through all of Dylan's officially released albums – none of which (and this makes him unique) has been deleted. The dates given here are those of release, not recording.

1. Bob Dylan (1962). This features the 20-year-old Dylan, unique among the Greenwich Village folkies in being signed to the huge Columbia label, which had missed out on rock'n'roll altogether. But in staff producer John Hammond they had a man who'd been involved in Bessie Smith's recordings and those of many more great blues acts besides. He signed Dylan, spent less than 500 dollars in the studio and came out with an album few people liked and that didn't sell. The record company was all for dropping him.

This first album is, in retrospect, terrific. It has such a young Dylan on it that he sounds about 75. Only two of the songs are his own: one dedicated to his early idol Woody Guthrie ('Song To Woody') and the other owing its format and spirit to Guthrie's own work ('Talkin' New York').

The other songs are mainly traditional and/or old blues songs by men like Jesse Fuller, Bukka White and Blind Lemon Jefferson. Dylan comes across as obsessed with the romance of dying, but the speed, energy and attack in his guitar, harmonica and voice show how fresh and excellently 'unprofessional' he was.

2. The Freewheelin' Bob Dylan (1963). This was Dylan's first opportunity to show how fast he was to develop from one album to the next. All the songs were his own, though many were based on older folk melodies. He was better known in 1963 as a new songwriter of weird promise than as a performer, though this album not only brought together an impressive group of songs that have since become classics – 'Blowin' In The Wind', 'Girl Of The North Country', 'Masters Of War' and 'A Hard Rain's A-Gonna Fall' are all on one side, while the other includes 'Don't Think Twice, It's All Right' – but also gained him an unstoppable cult following among people who preferred the harshness of Dylan's performances to the string-soaked cover-versions other singers released.

3. The Times They Are A-Changin' (1964). Less of a leap forward, this was again a solo album mainly of stark 'protest' songs, all written by Dylan, though often with adapted folk melodies. Like his second album, it contained songs that have achieved classic status, particularly the title track and 'With God On Our Side'. It also includes the love song 'One Too Many Mornings', a song that should have served notice on Dylan's early cult followers (most of whom were students and liberals who considered themselves radicals, hated pop music and wore Dylan on their sleeves like a political armband) that Dylan was not just going to be a graphic protest singer. But no one seemed to notice, so that the next album came as a shock.

4. Another Side Of Bob Dylan (1964). Thousands screamed 'sell-out' – just as thousands more were to do later when he 'went electric', again when he 'went country' and yet again when he 'got religion'.

This album was much the same stark solo performance (though Dylan added piano and somehow more space and colour in the sound) but with the exception of the long 'Chimes Of Freedom' there wasn't a protest song or any overtly political theme anywhere on the record: and even 'Chimes Of Freedom' was, for many people, uncomfortably close to impressionism.

They were love songs – and many people felt betrayed. It must be hard now to understand how this album could so bitterly have angered so many; but it did. Yet it was clear to plenty of people at the time, and is all the more so looking back, that the love songs Dylan offered on this album were more true and more real – and ultimately more radical – than protest songs. 'All I Really Want To Do' and 'It Ain't Me, Babe' are historically important songs: they questioned the common assumptions of true love and the male-female relationship; they not only avoided possessiveness and macho strut but explained why as well. This was years before any of us understood that 'love' and politics weren't opposites – that there was such a thing as sexual politics.

This album also contained Dylan's specific recantation of the protest phase. 'My Back Pages' did this, and had the celebrated chorus line 'Ah but I was so much older then / I'm younger than that now'. And Dylan's voice sounds younger than on his earlier work: he has thrown off the mantle of the old bluesmen and assumed one of his own.

If I could have only about five Bob Dylan albums, this would be one of them. His writing and control of atmosphere on songs like 'To Ramona' and 'Spanish Harlem Incident' come across as early flashes of the creative explosion that he was to go through in 1965–66. A great album, and his last solo album until the 1990s.

5. Bringing It All Back Home (1965). Another breakthrough album and another sudden jump to new ground. One side of the record is solo and has four long tracks, each of which has become a classic – 'Mr. Tambourine Man', the visionary 'Gates Of Eden', 'It's Alright Ma (I'm Only Bleeding)' and the beautiful 'It's All Over Now, Baby Blue'.

This solo side of the album contained more than enough to justify Dylan's burgeoning popularity as a uniquely contemporary spokesman. But the other side was enough to gain him a new notoriety and to lose him even more devotees than his previous album had done. Unprecedentedly, here was this folk singer committing the ultimate sacrilege of singing rock'n'roll songs with electric guitars behind him. Students – serious-minded young people unaware of the social upheavals about to happen – were appalled that Dylan should resort to such triviality.

Mostly this side sounds pretty thin now, and a dress rehearsal/prototype for what was to come next. But it was undeniably innovative and gives us yet another collection of stand-out Dylan songs: 'Subterranean Homesick Blues', 'She Belongs To Me', 'Love Minus Zero/No limit' and 'Maggie's Farm' among them.

6. Highway 61 Revisited (1965). Dylan's first fully fledged eagle-flight into rock. Revolutionary and stunning, not just for its energy, freshness and panache but in its vision: fusing radical electric music – electric music as the embodiment of our whole out-of-control, nervous-energy-fuelled, chaotic civilization – with lyrics that were light years ahead of anyone else's, Dylan here unites the force of blues-based rock'n'roll with the power of poetry.

The whole rock culture, the whole post-Beatle pop-rock world – in an important sense the 1960s started here. It isn't only 'Like A Rolling Stone' and the unprecedentedly long Armageddon epic 'Desolation Row': it's every song. It's the carving out of a new emotional correspondence with a new chaos–reality. There it all was in one bombshell of an album, for a generation who only recognized what world they were living in when Dylan illuminated it so piercingly.

7. Blonde On Blonde (1966). To have followed up one masterpiece with another was Dylan's history-making achievement here. It aims, perhaps, at a more limited canvas than "Highway 61 Revisited" but evokes a much richer, more multi-layered, synapse-jumping consciousness. Where "Highway 61 Revisited" has Dylan exposing and confronting like a laser beam in surgery, descending from outside the sickness, "Blonde On Blonde" offers a persona awash inside the chaos and speaking to others who are acceptedly in the same boat – or rather, the same ocean. We're tossed from song to song, and they all move into each other. The feel and the music are on a grand scale, and the language and delivery are a unique mixture of the visionary and the colloquial, the warm and the alert. Dylan dances like his own 'Mr. Tambourine Man' through these songs, even though tossed and blown by disorientating, desperate forces. It seems against the spirit of the double-album's cumulative effect to single out particular songs, but they include 'Visions Of Johanna', 'Just Like A Woman', 'Memphis Blues Again' and 'Sad-Eyed Lady Of The Lowlands'.

8. Bob Dylan's Greatest Hits (1967). The title was offensive at the time; Dylan was no mere pop artist and his greatness had nothing to do with whether DJs loved his records or whether his singles ran up the charts. In fact never has so influential an artist had so few hit singles. More importantly, each of the previous albums had had its own unity. They'd never been collections of isolated tracks. So a 'greatest hits' collection made no sense at all, except in money terms.

The album was put out in what was considered the disastrously long silence from Dylan between "Blonde On Blonde" in 1966 and the next proper album in 1968. In those days, everyone made two albums a year and a long gap was supposed to be career death.

This was badly selected regurgitation and provides nothing new; nor does it give an accurate picture of his progress through the earlier recordings.

9. John Wesley Harding (1968). [Theoretically the US release-date was 27/12/67.] This quiet, authoritative masterpiece is not a rock album – it isn't categorizable at all. The back-up musicians are pared down to three: bass, drums, and, on two tracks only, pedal steel. Plus Dylan on guitar, harmonica and piano. Economy, in fact, is the key to this huge change of direction. There could be no greater contrast between consecutive albums than that between "Blonde On Blonde"'s richness and the taut asceticism of "John Wesley Harding". This album is no cheap thrill.

It is, though, a most serious, darkly visionary exploration of the myths and extinct strengths of America; its Calvinistic spirit gives it an eerie power in mixing the severely biblical with a surreal nineteenth century. American pioneer ethos. Dylan comes across like a man who has arisen from the final holocaust unscathed but sobered, to walk across an allegorical American landscape of small, poor communities working a dusty, fierce terrain.

The masterpieces within the masterpiece are 'I Dreamed I Saw St. Augustine', 'All Along The Watchtower' and 'I Pity The Poor Immigrant'. Then there are the last two tracks of the album: the à la Jerry Lee Lewis 'Down Along The Cove' and the brilliant country-pastiche song 'I'll Be Your Baby Tonight'. With these, Dylan was serving notice of the next sharp shift in direction that was to come from him.

"John Wesley Harding" was to be Dylan's last masterpiece of the 1960s – and in spirit it was most markedly not a part of the 1960s world at all.

10. Nashville Skyline (1969). Not Dylan's first Nashville album – much of "Blonde On Blonde" had, amazingly, been recorded there – but this was his first sustained leap into country music. Again a massive contrast to the previous album: down-home instead of visionary, warm instead of severely ascetic, optimistic instead of dark, and more under the influence of sunshine and the big sky than of catechism and nemesis. It also offered a complete change of language – away from the impressionistic and the allegorical; away from the distinctive complexity of his previous work.

Here Dylan suddenly embraces the simplicity and clichés that are the currency of ordinary Americans' speech. A new voice goes with it – gone is the husky, grating Dylan and on comes a light melodic, almost Orbisonian tenor.

A lovely album but not a heavyweight contender, though its effects were major ones. Country music was despised hick music when Dylan took it up. People were divided into the hip and the non-hip. The counter-culture was in full swing and riddled with its own self-importance and snobbery. "Nashville Skyline" was a hard pill to swallow: but it did 'em good.

11. Self Portrait (1970). A mistake. You could have got a good minor album out of it if you'd cut it down from the overblown double-album it is. There was no reason why Dylan shouldn't have made this new departure – largely into pop songs and Tin Pan Alley country material written by other people – but it just wasn't all that good. At the time it was again the cue for large numbers of Dylan's followers to give up on him. Best tracks are 'Days of '49', 'Early Morning Rain', 'Let It Be Me', 'Belle Isle', 'Copper Kettle' and 'Wigwam'.

12. New Morning (1970). This came a bit hastily after "Self Portrait", and seemed at the time a capitulation to the huge Dylan audience's demand that he return to the milieu of "Blonde On Blonde". Lines like 'The man standin' next to me / His head was explodin' / I was hopin' the pieces / Wouldn't fall on me' seemed a bit written-to-order. And Dylan, despite all the changes he'd gone through, had never done that before.

In retrospect, "New Morning" is a very individual album. A relative failure but a brave attempt to fuse the old surreal richness of feeling of the "Blonde On Blonde" era with a new desire to forge some stability out of rural-based concerns. This is all felt by Dylan in a diffident, pessimistic, confidence-lost way, and this comes out too in the strange hesitancy with which the album also attempts its musical fusion of a sort of grown-up acid-rock with both country picking and gospel. There is a considerable gospel feel throughout the album, created mainly by Dylan's own terrific untutored piano-work and by the use of an old church-type girl chorus.

This is a quirky album, from a Dylan not pointing a way for anyone, but still from a great artist remaining at his work knowingly in the face of not being creatively on top form in the phenomenal way he had been in the period 1964 to 1968. Warm and abiding, it sounds better and better as the years go by.

13. Bob Dylan's Greatest Hits Vol II [US title]/**More Bob Dylan Greatest Hits** [UK title] **(1971).** Again inevitably a collection that rides roughshod over both the real chronology of Dylan's career and the whole-album unities of most Dylan work. But at least here there are tracks not obtainable on other albums: the 1971 (hit) single 'Watching The River Flow', the 1965 masterpiece of put-down 'Positively 4th Street' and five previously unissued tracks. If it sounds odd to have previously unissued material on a 'greatest hits' collection, it wasn't so odd in the light of what songs they were. 'When I Paint My Masterpiece' (recorded 1971) was already well known from The Band's recording on their "Cahoots" album; 'Tomorrow Is A Long Time' (a nigh-perfect live performance from 1963) was a Dylan song that other people, including, to Dylan's delight, Elvis Presley, had recorded in the interim; 'I Shall Be Released', 'Down In The Flood' and, with playfully different lyrics, 'You Ain't Goin' Nowhere' were newly recorded (1971), outrageously loose versions of three songs that had long been popular from bootlegs of the famed 1967 Basement Tapes.

All this makes it an interesting album for collectors, although it would have been more valuable if it had rounded up his other previously only-on-singles tracks too. They could have had 'Mixed-Up Confusion' (1962), which had never had UK release; 'If You Gotta Go, Go Now' (1965), ditto; the live-in-Liverpool cut of 'Just Like Tom Thumb's Blues' (1966) issued only as the B-side of the 'I Want You' single; the 1971 B-side 'Spanish Is The Loving Tongue'; the 1965 A-side 'Can *You* Please Crawl Out Your Window?'; and the 1971 single 'George Jackson'. But record companies never do these things right.

[The American version of this double-LP has a slightly different track-list.]

14. Pat Garrett & Billy The Kid (1973). Dylan's first new album-proper since 1970 was 'only a film soundtrack'. It is a largely instrumental album, with all the characteristic roughness and lack of polish that has kept Bob Dylan less palatable to mass easy-listening taste than any of his infinitely less talented contemporaries such as Paul Simon or Paul McCartney.

Though a very minor collection in Dylan's catalogue, it is a finely atmospheric album, engaging in its own right and more effective as a part of the movie it was written for. It also includes the original of the perenially popular 'Knockin' On Heaven's Door'.

15. Dylan (1973). Essentially a malicious record company response to Dylan's signing with a new label, Asylum, in America, a deliberate release of the worst tracks they could find lying around in their vaults: Dylan warming up before recording other things; Dylan messing about; out-takes largely from the "New Morning" sessions; and all compounded by a mix that brought the back-up vocals up horrendously high.

Two ironies: despite all this malice aforethought, the album isn't nearly as bad as they meant it to be; and Dylan subsequently returned to Columbia/CBS because of Asylum's less effective sales distribution system, not because of this shoddy bully-boy tactic of an album. Best tracks: 'Can't Help Falling In Love', 'Mr. Bojangles' and 'A Fool Such As I'.

16. Planet Waves (1974). For the first ten minutes after this came out, it was hailed – as "New Morning" had been – as 'the best thing he's done since "Blonde On Blonde"'. Like "New Morning", it then suffered from a disappointment backlash from which it has never fully recovered. Put in the long back-projection of Dylan's recording career it now seems a potent, compelling album. Warm and emotionally rich, it points down no new road. Asserting the artist's right to prefer minor work on old canvases to doing no work at all, it is drawn from the inner resources of memory and a determination to record faithfully the artist's current state of mind in spite of tiredness, an unpopular grown-upness and some lack of self-confidence. Most of the songs recall, largely for the first time (except for 'Winterlude' and 'Went To See The Gypsy' on "New Morning") Dylan's Minnesota years. There is a strange tension created by the contrast between recollected childhood and adolescence and current father-figure weariness. The result is nostalgia-soaked but genuinely beautiful, with an eerie, compelling quality that marks this album as unique in Dylan's output. In this vein the stand-out tracks are 'Something There Is About You' and 'Never Say Goodbye'; there are also two versions of what became a perennial concert anthem, 'Forever Young'. And like "New Morning", the album sounds better now than then.

17. Before The Flood (1974). From Dylan's huge North American 'come-back tour' of 1974 with The Band, on which he revisited a large number of his old songs, this is a double-album of confident, brash rock'n'roll Dylan: a record of an artist exhilarated by being back on stage after a long absence and in the process largely ignoring the differences between one song and another. There is an over-speedy, breakneck quality here that does little justice to the lyrics and has Dylan mainly just throwing back his head and yelling. It has never been a favourite of anyone keen on Bob Dylan. Don't look to this album for any of the subtlety, nuance or understatement which have always been hallmarks of Dylan's genius.

18. Blood On The Tracks (1975). In stunning, total contrast, this album triumphantly shows more subtlety and nuance than anything he'd ever done, and as honed a use of understatement as on "John Wesley Harding". At the time this was the most unexpected leap of Dylan's career. After years of comparatively second-rate work and a considerable decline in his reputation, here was an album to stand with "Highway

61 Revisited" and "Blonde On Blonde": an album of genius; of powerful emotional complexity, unerring fresh insight and the kind of maturity (horrible word) that manifests itself not remotely as grown-up tiredness but as pure, strong intelligence. This was without doubt the best album of the 1970s.

19. The Basement Tapes (1975). This double-album marked the official release of a version of the world's most bootlegged bootleg: material cut by Dylan and The Crackers / The Band up near Woodstock in 1967 during the long silence between "Blonde On Blonde" (and Dylan's motorcycle crash) in 1966 and "John Wesley Harding" in 1968.

The core Dylan songs from these sessions actually do form a clear link between these two utterly different albums. They evince the same highly serious, precarious quest for a personal and universal salvation which marked out the "John Wesley Harding" collection – yet they are soaked in the same blocked confusion and turmoil as "Blonde On Blonde". 'Tears Of Rage', for example, is an exact halfway house between, say, 'One Of Us Must Know (Sooner Or Later)' and 'I Dreamed I Saw St. Augustine'. There is also a unique, radical corpus of spacey yet exuberant music as on 'Crash On The Levee (Down In The Flood)', 'Please Mrs. Henry' and 'Million Dollar Bash'.[3] Essential stuff, badly compiled. The interspersed tracks by The Band alone merely disrupt the unity of Dylan material, much more of which should have been here. Key items missing include 'I Shall Be Released' and 'This Wheel's On Fire'.

20. Desire (1976). The next newly recorded studio album after "Blood On The Tracks", it proved to be Dylan's biggest-ever seller, finding him a new following among teenagers who would hardly have been toddlers when the mid-1960s Dylan was so much in vogue.

After "Blood On The Tracks" it was bound to be a disappointment but it is an important album nonetheless – a work with its own distinctive unity yet with most of Dylan's traditional strengths too: not least wit, warmth, energy and a beautiful disregard for finishing things off with professional songwriter polish. It revealed too a Dylan still wanting to experiment and still refusing to stand in one place. The stand-out tracks are 'Isis', 'Romance In Durango' and 'Black Diamond Bay'.

21. Hard Rain (1976). A generally poor selection of tracks from two concerts that were far from being Dylan's best in the first place. After "Dylan" and the 1967 "Greatest Hits" collection, this was, at the time, Dylan's least essential album. Dylan's voice even sounded oddly anonymous at first.

Hindsight shows that this album heralds the ragged, postmodern Bob Dylan, right from the grungy instrumental ground-pawing ahead of the start of the first number. The running order now seems surprisingly well thought-out. It represents, too, the late phase of the historic Rolling Thunder Revue tour and captures the distinctive, bare-wired sound of Dylan's existential gypsy band. Stand-out track is

---

3.   The sessions had also included a wealth of traditional material revisited, the existence of which was far less known at the time of this release than became apparent in the 1990s, when it was widely circulated and was the main subject of Greil Marcus' book *Invisible Republic*, 1997.

'Idiot Wind', which, as Dylan grows ever more engaged, bursts open and pours out its brilliant venom.[4]

22. Masterpieces (1978). Japanese triple-LP set later released elsewhere. A lavish compilation, mostly of obvious selections from other albums but also collecting for the first time on album versions of 'Mixed-Up Confusion' (an alternative take from that on the 1962 single) and 'Can *You* Please Crawl Out Your Window?' (the single) from 1965; the live-in-Liverpool 1966 cut of 'Just Like Tom Thumb's Blues', the magnificent solo version of 'Spanish Is The Loving Tongue' and 'George Jackson (Big Band Version)' from 1971 (all previously only issued as B-sides of singles); plus an out-take from the "Desire" sessions, the inconsequential 'Rita May'. An expensive way of acquiring these.

23. Street Legal (1978). Released around the time of Dylan's first London concerts for twelve years, this is, after "Blood On The Tracks", arguably Dylan's best record of the 1970s: a crucial album documenting a crucial period in Dylan's own life. It is of astonishing complexity and confidence, delivered in Dylan's most authoritative voice and extremely badly produced. Remastering for CD reissue has failed to make sufficient aural amends.

24. Bob Dylan At Budokan (1978). This double-album was recorded live in concert in Japan, where Dylan began the tour with the band that appeared on the "Street Legal" album. A good recording that includes re-workings of myriad Dylan classics, it is a pity it caught Dylan and The Band before they reached the magical, incandescent form they hit later that year in Europe and North America. The tour was remarkable in re-asserting Dylan's power and relevance in an entirely different decade from the one he had first emerged to shape so significantly. The album is a pale souvenir of what went down but the freshness of focus Dylan brings to these songs is especially dramatic: 'I Want You', 'Ballad Of A Thin Man', 'Blowin' In The Wind', 'The Times They Are A-Changin'', 'Don't Think Twice, It's All Right' and 'All Along The Watchtower'.

25. Slow Train Coming (1979). Anyone else, riding as high as Dylan was in 1978, would have stuck with the same band and produced another "Street Legal"-type album. Dylan did no such thing. Converted to Born Again Christianity, he gathered different musicians around him and produced an album destined to be profoundly unpopular amongst almost everyone who'd ever valued him as a writer. It is not, however, an album that can be ignored and in some ways now seems a logical direction for him to have taken. Musically it's fine, and no one should have been surprised at Dylan choosing to add gospel to the many different modes of American popular music he has covered (and so well) on his artistic travels over the decades. Stand-out tracks are 'Gotta Serve Somebody', 'Precious Angel', 'Slow Train' and 'When He Returns'.

---

4.   The TV film *Hard Rain* (of which this album is not straightforwardly the soundtrack, though it includes some performances from the filmed concert) is a riveting, essential item and captures an extremely charismatic, energised Dylan, sounding harshly robust and looking uncannily like Jesus Christ – but more beautiful.

26. Saved (1980). The nearest thing to a follow-up album Dylan has ever made: a "Slow Train Coming II", and inferior. Stand-out tracks: 'Pressing On' and 'What Can I Do For You?'

27. Shot Of Love (1981). The first post-evangelizing album, a ramshackle collection of generally second-rate tracks with Dylan's voice often petulant and querulous, the music tired and the production thin. It excludes some of the best songs cut at the relevant sessions: a snatching of mediocrity from the jaws of distinction that Dylan was to manage again and again with his 1980s albums. Even the cover was careless and tawdry, whereas in the past a Dylan cover was rightly used to help define an album's distinctive character, to be devised with care and imaginative precision.

Time has not transformed this into a first-rate collection, but has made more engaging the interest in 1950s music on Dylan's part which suffuses its atmosphere. Best of the minor songs on the album is the Motownesque 'Watered-Down Love'. 'Lenny Bruce' is an endearing bad song. The stand-out track, and free of all these vocal, instrumental and production faults, is the defiantly classic 'Every Grain Of Sand'. Subsequent reissue of the album has added one of the good initial rejects, 'The Groom's Still Waiting At The Altar'.

28. Infidels (1983). Another ragbag collection of insipid material, hailed in America as a great return to form on Dylan's part. This is the sort of work that makes Dylan's earlier 'minor' albums sound like masterpieces. In depressing contrast to "Nashville Skyline", "New Morning", or "Planet Waves", there is on "Infidels" no warmth, no unity and no sense that real music is being created and played for pleasure by people who know what they want. There is instead the unwelcome return of the portentous quality of the evangelical albums of 1979–80, while the production is half-hearted and irresolute. It is Dylan beginning to say that he doesn't really want to write songs or make records any more, and to behave as if it hardly matters whether an album is any good or not. This is not a welcome stance from a great artist.

As with "Shot Of Love", it needn't have been this way: the sessions yielded important work excluded from the release, including Dylan's greatest single recording of the 1980s, the lapidary 'Blind Willie McTell'. Best of the released tracks: 'I And I' (though this admonishes you into feeling it's important, rather than claiming a place in your heart) and the album's one incontestable major success, 'Jokerman'.

29. Real Live (1984). How was it that such poor stuff could be chosen, time and again, from among such riches? You could easily compile a better live album from the Rolling Thunder Revue than "Hard Rain" and a much better one from the 1978 tour than "Budokan". You could hardly offer a worse live album from Dylan's 1984 tour of Europe than this. The choice of songs is hopeless, the choice of performances injudicious, the production inexcusably murky. How did the supposed ace producer Glyn Johns manage this? At the very least, Dylan's expensive, classy guitar should have a good sound. Dylan's major re-write of 'Tangled Up In Blue', featured prominently and exclusively on this tour, is included – but from a swaggering, mannered, unfelt performance. The album waywardly misrepresents this tour in particular and the whole glory of Bob Dylan in live performance generally.

30. Empire Burlesque (1985). Dylan was truly floundering in this period (it was the year of his appearance on "Live Aid", at which he finally blew his automatic right to headline any multi-artist event), and though this album has a cohesion lacking in those either side of it, it features undistinguished pop songs, most of which anyone could have written, and an overwrought production made worse by a horrible, supposedly modish remix.

Here is the shameful spectacle of a man whose early work avoids adroitly every pop dissimulation in work of unsurpassed, pioneering clarity of individual vision and vocal richness, now mewling his thin vocal way through a thick murk of formulaic riffs, licks and echo-laden AOR noises devised with a desperate eye on rock radio formats. Here is the artist whose mature intelligence revolutionised the love song in popular music, now reduced to lines like 'You to me were true / You to me were the best' and titles like 'Emotionally Yours'. Ugh. The album cover photograph signals how adrift is the artist of "Empire Burlesque": it shows Dylan the perplexed fashion victim in Bruce Willis jacket. Early Bob Dylan would have found the whole thing contemptible.

31. Biograph (1985). A 5-LP box-set retrospective of Dylan's work from 1962 to 1981, packaged with an unprecedented collection of personal and rare photographs and equally unprecedented interview comments by Dylan about the songs themselves, plus other interview material ranging over many topics in which Dylan, sometimes surly but more often open, remains unpredictable and spiky.

Though criticised by some collectors, it is a fine if quirky selection of previously issued album tracks plus a significant number of previously unreleased recordings: a different take of 'Mixed-Up Confusion' (1962); 'Baby, I'm In The Mood For You' (1962); the exquisitely performed 'protest' number 'Percy's Song' (1963); the incomparable 'Lay Down Your Weary Tune' (1963); by no means the best take of 'I'll Keep It With Mine' (1965); a fragment, previously unknown even to avid collectors, from the "Highway 61 Revisited" sessions, 'Jet Pilot' (1965); the wonderful 'I Wanna Be Your Lover' (1965); live cuts from the 1966 tour – the electric 'I Don't Believe You' and the acoustic solo 'Visions Of Johanna' and 'It's All Over Now, Baby Blue'; the belated release of the original Dylan & The Crackers 'Quinn The Eskimo (The Mighty Quinn)' (1967); a publisher's office demo solo of 'Forever Young' (1973); the original studio cut of 'You're A Big Girl Now' and the "Blood On The Tracks" out-take 'Up To Me' (1974); the lovely "Desire" out-take 'Abandoned Love' (1975); excellent live recordings of two other "Desire" songs, 'Isis' and 'Romance In Durango' from the first Rolling Thunder Revue (1975); a major song from the "Shot Of Love" sessions, 'Caribbean Wind' (1981); and a live 'Heart Of Mine' (1981). An affirmation of the astonishing variety as well as richness of Dylan's corpus, the collection was well received by the public and went some way to reviving that fickle thing, Dylan's critical reputation.

32. Knocked Out Loaded (1986). A title suggesting that its contents were thrown together when drunk bodes ill by its very defensiveness. Nevertheless, after the overblown robotic coldness of "Empire Burlesque", this third-rate assemblage of studio scrapings, taken from sessions in July 1984, December 1984–January 1985, November 1985 and May 1986, with vocals redone in May 1986, has a warmth and human frailty that at least lets you in. Tired R&B ('You Wanna Ramble') and rockism ('Got My Mind Made Up'); immaculately sung but shifty pop ('Under Your Spell'); a cover of Kris Kristofferson's wretched 'They Killed Him'; and Dylan's fine 'Maybe Someday' so badly produced that it is incomprehensible and could be sung by one of the Chipmunks. There's a tender rendition, well produced and refreshingly arranged, of the gospel standard 'Precious Memories'; a robust cut of a good minor Dylan song 'Drifting Too Far From Shore' (with mad drumming); and, hidden among the dross, 'Brownsville Girl', co-written with Sam Shepard: a wonderful and innovative major work, intelligent and subtle, from a Bob Dylan out from behind his 1980s wall of self-contempt and wholly in command of his incomparable vocal resources.

33. Down In The Groove (1988). Another title to undercut any idea that inspired work might lie within. After a silence of nearly two years, here was a further devaluing of the whole notion of a new Bob Dylan album as something significant and another refusal to offer new songs of his own.

If it had been better recorded and Dylan had brought some creative alertness to his vocals, instead of rasping through on automatic, this could have been a "Self Portrait II": there are interesting song selections here; but Dylan treats them maladroitly, fails to commend them as a purposive collection and throws in feeble makeweights – 'Had A Dream About You Baby', recycled from the soundtrack of the quaintly atrocious *Hearts of Fire* film of 1987; the risibly turgid 'Death Is Not The End', cut at the "Infidels" sessions and rightly rejected then; and two songs with lyrics by Robert Hunter rejected even by the Grateful Dead as under par – the tetchy, braggartly 'Silvio' and the shrivellingly dull-minded 'Ugliest Girl In The World'.

This quality of work is so far below that of Dylan's albums of the 1960s that it just depresses the hell out of you. Continued silence would have been more dignified than this.

34. Dylan & The Dead (1989). Live recordings from 1987 that you'd assume set out to humiliate Bob Dylan and prove how awful such joint concerts were: but in fact Dylan was given all the tapes and made these choices himself. He can't remember the words to any of the songs, the vocal sound is miserable and The Dead lumpenly uninspired. As ever with Dylan's live albums, it would have been possible to compile something distinctive and compelling instead, in this case from tapes that show Dylan and The Dead making sense as a unit blessed with the bounty of each partner's openness to the spontaneity of the moment. Richard Williams wrote of the 'wasted majesty' of this version of 'Queen Jane Approximately'; this was wishful thinking. Wasted, yes; majesty, no. Dylan's abject incompetence at groping for the words makes it rather a form of public self-abasement, excruciating and sad to witness.

35. Oh Mercy (1989). A confident staunching of the flow, with an album that is accessible, authoritative and substantial. Attentively written, vocally distinctive, musically warm and produced with uncompromising professionalism, this cohesive whole is the nearest thing there is to a great Bob Dylan album of the 1980s.

Daniel Lanois' determination to wrest such an album out of Dylan, and the plangent panache his production spreads across a variable collection of material made for something overrated at the time (understandably, after what had gone before); but it remains a singular, welcome item in Dylan's huge back catalogue. An honourable minor work, well received by the public and reviewers, and marred only by the feeling that Dylan has one eye on public approbation: that he is asking if this is the sort of album people want from him. Stand-out tracks: 'Where Teardrops Fall', 'Ring Them Bells', 'Most Of The Time', 'What Was It You Wanted?'

36. Under The Red Sky (1990). Dylan characteristically retreating from the mainstream production values of "Oh Mercy" and refusing to offer a follow-up. Nevertheless his penchant for a recently modish producer has him turn this time to Don and David Was of Was Not Was, who offer a rougher and less unified sound. It's a pity Dylan pads out the album with some substandard rockism ('Wiggle Wiggle' and 'Unbelievable') and the ill-fitting, foggy pop of 'Born In Time', because the core of the album is an adventure into the poetic possibilities of nursery rhyme that is alert, fresh and imaginative, and an achievement that has gone entirely unrecognized. Stand-outs: 'Under The Red Sky', 'Handy Dandy' and 'Cat's In The Well'.

37. Bootleg Series I–III (1991). A 3-CD (or 5-LP) box-set ranging over Dylan's career from 1961 to 1989, composed entirely of never-released material. Most artists couldn't muster a single out-take to hold alongside any of this; Dylan can provide fifty-eight recordings, almost every one of which is of numinous excellence, from the perfectly controlled solo performances of the infinitely variegated pre-electric period ('Kingsport Town', 'Worried Blues', 'Walls Of Red Wing', 'Moonshiner' and the unique 'Last Thoughts On Woody Guthrie'); the electric acid glory of the fast 'It Takes A Lot To Laugh, It Takes A Train To Cry' and of 'She's Your Lover Now', a gleeful masterpiece more redolent of its era than most things that came out at the time; on through incomparable studio performances of 'Tangled Up In Blue' and 'Idiot Wind' and other, more fragile, faltering works from the 1970s; riches from the 1980s which it was madness to have left unissued: 'Need A Woman', 'Angelina', 'Someone's Got A Hold Of My Heart', 'Lord Protect My Child', 'Foot Of Pride' and 'Blind Willie McTell'; and finishing with an out-take from "Oh Mercy" perhaps as strong as anything on the album, the compelling 'Series Of Dreams'.

This well-received collection could of itself establish Dylan's place as the pre-eminent songwriter and performer of the age and as one of the great artists of the twentieth century.

38. Good As I Been To You (1992). Dylan's return to a solo acoustic album, twenty-eight years after the last. Much maligned as being vocally impoverished and incompetently self-produced, and bemoaned for its lack of Dylan compositions, this endlessly rewarding demonstration of the strengths of traditional folksong and pre-war acoustic blues, the two forms used in flexible alternation, sets up all manner of resonance and dialogue, shifting and circling and forming a richly persuasive whole that works both as an impassioned treasury of folksong and an intimate revelation of how firmly some specifics of Dylan's own early styles and songs were founded upon this material.

There *is* a sad decline in Dylan's vocal range, including a dropping-away of his once unerring ability to place and control each syllable and each breath, each guitar note and each telling pause, with absolute precision and a maximised vividness of communication. Yet this album, imprecise, errant, at times blurred and furry, is a singular creation that gains as well as loses by Dylan's loss of the effortless certainty of youth. Dark, complex, surreal and fractured, it is like an inspired, lost work from some opium-thralled folk-archivist throwing his own torrid genius into celebrating the myriad strengths of anonymously created song: song from before there was a music industry to kill off its mystery and its purpose. Stand-out tracks: 'Hard Times', 'Arthur McBride', 'You're Gonna Quit Me', 'Diamond Joe' and 'Froggie Went A-Courtin''.

39. World Gone Wrong (1993). A follow-up of sorts: another solo acoustic album, though more focused, more clean-cut, less Gothic. Again the recordings are self-produced (and it does seem lamentable that when Dylan owns infinitely better acoustic guitars than ever he could have afforded when he first arrived in New York, and after thirty years of supposed progress in recording technology, he cannot produce a guitar sound as clear, vivid, biting, exuberant or controlled as he achieves on those earliest forays into the studio). Again, vocal decline is evident too.

Yet this is a fine album, at least as good as "Good As I Been To You" (most people prefer it), again asserting with inward intelligence and formidable interpretative skill the richly humane values and poetic power of communally created song, even as he commands this material so trenchantly that it can seem as if he had written it himself. With serious-mindedness and a strong sense of mystery, he insists on the continued relevance of these voices from the past, and takes us so deeply among them that he frees us from the tyranny of the present.

Stand-out tracks: 'World Gone Wrong', 'Love Henry', 'Ragged & Dirty', 'Delia', 'Two Soldiers', 'Lone Pilgrim'.

40. Greatest Hits Volume 3 (1995). Twenty-four years since the last 'greatest hits' package, and how remarkably seldom in this aeon has he had a hit of any sort. The last real hit Bob Dylan had in Britain was in 1978, with 'Baby, Stop Crying' – and that's not here. *Plus ça change.* Here instead is the previously unreleased track 'Dignity', an unfinished out-take from "Oh Mercy" put through the *in*dignity of a working-over by another modish-for-15-minutes hit-guru. 'Silvio' also seems to have been remixed, removing its posturing edge to re-present it as an amiable, light, poised little thing; it is still not worth including.

This is otherwise a well-planned selection, its non-chronological running-order creating some neat meeting-points: 'Ring Them Bells' (1989) is followed by 'Gotta Serve Somebody' from a decade earlier, emphasising similarities of theme and production; 'Series Of Dreams' gives way to 'Brownsville Girl'. The inclusion of 'Under The Red Sky' is right, and, admirably, the collection opens with a run of four long, demanding songs that stress, perhaps with some pride, Dylan's unrivalled weaponry of *words*: 'Tangled Up In Blue' (though this is the wrong choice from "Blood On The Tracks" – it has already been re-collected *and* an out-take issued, while the equally fine 'Simple Twist Of Fate' has never been re-collected), 'Changing Of The Guards' (a fine choice), 'The Groom's Still Waiting At The Altar' and 'Hurricane' (which comes out very strongly).

The studio albums issued since "Greatest Hits II" but unrepresented here are "Dylan", "The Basement Tapes", "Saved" and "Empire Burlesque".

41. MTV Unplugged™ (1995). The dreariest, most contemptible, phoney, tawdry piece of *product* ever issued by a great artist, which manages to omit the TV concert's one fresh and fine performance, 'I Want You', but is otherwise an accurate record of the awfulness of the concert itself, in which the performer who had been so numinously 'unplugged' in the first place ducked the opportunity to use television to perform solo the ballad and country blues material of his most recent studio albums. This is what happens when Bob Dylan capitulates and lets overpaid coke-head executives, lawyers and PRseholes from the Entertainment Industry tell him what to do.

42. The Best Of Bob Dylan (1997). An unnecessary compilation, especially so soon after "Greatest Hits Volume 3", contrived by the record company's TV-advertising division with no thought for how it cuts across Dylan's catalogue and certainly not for contributing usefully to it. Worse, for all this CD's claims of digital remastering and Super Bit Mapping™, the versions here of early material like 'Blowin' In The Wind' give an alarmingly poor idea of how these originally sounded: this represents a deeply disquieting form of re-writing audio history. It has one previously unreleased track, an unexceptional out-take of 'Shelter From The Storm'.

43. Time Out Of Mind (1997). The decade's most important collection of new Bob Dylan compositions (almost its only such collection): an unusually long album riddled with lazy writing and sludgy music bordering on the kind of night-club jazz that, almost four decades earlier, many of us had looked to Bob Dylan to vanquish ('Million Miles', ''Til I Fell In Love With You', 'Can't Wait'), plus the kind of rock that wins Grammies but makes you wish he'd stick to ballads ('Cold Irons Bound') and the kind of ballad that makes you wish he wouldn't ('Make You Feel My Love') . . . but also offering no less than four major songs: 'Standing In The Doorway', 'Tryin' To Get To Heaven', 'Not Dark Yet' and the especially magnificent 'Highlands', an audacious 16½ minutes long.

The album marks a return to the multi-layered production technique of Daniel Lanois, giving it a cohesive sound, disrupted only by the mediocre rockabilly of 'Dirt Road Blues', that complements Dylan's dour elegy, epitomised by 'Not Dark Yet'. What makes all this compelling is not its claims to shrivelled pessimism but its very human confessional quality and its intimate flashes of humour. The album is also experimental in its unprecedented use of lines from other songs. It ends with the inspired creative high-note of 'Highlands', an inventive mix of splendidly off-the-wall talking blues and visionary rhapsody.

44. Bob Dylan Live 1966: The Bootleg Series Vol. 4: The 'Royal Albert Hall' Concert (1998). (Snappy title.) The most enthralling, truthful, priceless concert performance ever issued by a great artist. Over thirty years afterwards, and in heart-stopping quality, here at last is the complete 'Albert Hall' concert of 1966 (actually from Manchester Free Trade Hall): the time-stopping, astonishing, riveting, synapse-crinkling acoustic solo half and, performed with the Hawks, the transcendent, revolutionary electric second half. This was what happened when Bob Dylan reached the absolute peak of divine inspiration and was utterly dismissive of the received wisdom of showbiz.

These, then, are the albums on which Dylan's reputation as an artist has been constructed. This book examines the work within them.

CHAPTER ONE

Dylan and the Folk Tradition

Strap yourself
To the tree with roots
You ain't goin nowhere.

Bob Dylan: 'You Ain't Goin Nowhere'

When Dylan first went East and arrived in New York, at the start of the 1960s, the repertoire and styles of delivery he brought with him provided a culture shock not only to Sinatra-tuned audiences but also to the patrons of the many small 'folk clubs' then in bloom around Greenwich Village. As he recalls the latter's reaction, it ran as follows:

You sound like a hillbilly:
We want folk-singers here . . .

The point, made here with a characteristic lightness of irony, is of course that Dylan *was* a folk singer; and to learn how his early work was received is to understand the various misconceptions that obtained in New York at that time and which, from New York, spread (though not back into the Appalachians) via college circuits and out across the Atlantic.

To sound like a 'folk singer' you were supposed to be smoothly ingenuous, Angry, and above all Sensitive. It is hard to pin down precise criteria but it's enough to say that Peter, Paul & Mary fitted the bill. With a name like that how could they fail? They were the Greenwich Village ideal – white, clean and middle-class to the point of cultivated preciousness. They had all the essentials required: coyness and a bourgeois gentility that functioned as marketable post-adolescent reproach.[1]

Young, white, middle-class Americans were thus provided with a handy collective psyche that was a palliative to all kinds of inadequacy. This was encouraged and strengthened by the arid folk preservation movement, which judged its music on 'purity of style', regardless of quality of content. A formidable alliance. If you could

---

1. Actually this describes only one of the several kinds of 'folk singer' around at the time. What wasn't permissible was to cross from one genre to another. As Dylan described it later: 'Folk music was a strict and rigid establishment. If you sang Southern Mountain Blues, you didn't sing Southern Mountain Ballads and you didn't sing City Blues. If you sang Texas cowboy songs, you didn't play English ballads. It was really pathetic.' [Bob Dylan: interview, "Biograph" box-set, 1985.]

only keep away the hillbillies, you could fill out life amiably enough with an indulgent, deadening orthodoxy.

This did not suit Dylan. His eponymous first album consisted mainly of his own impressionistic arrangements of traditional songs and songs like Blind Lemon Jefferson's 'See That My Grave Is Kept Clean',[2] performed without any gentility and with a voice that, far from suggesting a soul mate for Peter, Paul or Mary, suggested some black octogenarian singing personal blues at the back of his shack. The blurb that went out on the album could quite plausibly call Dylan the newest voice in country blues.

In fact Dylan's recordings of folk material are very much more extensive than those officially released suggest, but this first official album is a unit, a collection that stands up by itself.

There are tracks that ring a little false. On Dylan's rendition of 'Gospel Plow', for instance, the death wish of the young man (Dylan was 20) may be genuine but the evocation is not: wrongly, it relies on a pretence at the experience of age to 'justify' that death wish. So that what comes through is a clumsiness of understanding as to what the artist requires of himself.

Yet what comes through from the album as a whole is a remarkable skill and more than a hint of a highly distinctive vision. In the context of what was happening at the time – American folk culture all but obliterated and a stagnating 'folk' cult established as if in its place – Dylan's first album can hardly be faulted. It is a brilliant début, a performer's *tour de force*, and served as a fine corrective for Greenwich Village: it was the opposite of effete.

2.   Blind Lemon Jefferson, a great blues singer, also a guitarist and composer, born in the 1890s in Texas, and contemporary with Lonnie Johnson. He shaped the Texas blues and put it on record, though his recording career was, typically, very short (1926–1929). His records were a huge influence on hillbillies who heard them on the radio. He was the main blues influence on Leadbelly and, through Leadbelly, an important tutor to many, many others. He wrote the line 'I'm standin' here wonderin' will a matchbox hold my clothes', which crops up twenty-five years after Jefferson's death in Carl Perkins' 'Matchbox' and, around the same time as Dylan's first album release, in Sam Cooke's 'Somebody Have Mercy'. It's odd that Cooke should be wondering will a matchbox hold his clothes, because earlier in the same lyric he's standing at the bus-station with a suitcase in his hand . . .
    Blind Lemon Jefferson: 'See That My Grave's Kept Clean', Chicago, c. Oct. 1927; "Blind Lemon Jefferson Volume 2", Roots Records RL-306, Vienna, 1968. Blind Lemon Jefferson: 'See That My Grave Is Kept Clean', Chicago, c. Feb. 1928; "American Folk Music" [3 double-LPs], Folkways Records FP 251–253, New York, 1952; CD-reissued as "Anthology Of American Folk Music" [6-CDs box set with copious notes by many hands and including a CD-ROM of extras], Smithsonian Folkways Recordings SFW 40090, Washington DC, 1997 (compiled by Harry Smith, this crucial, pioneering compilation – and it was crucial to Bob Dylan from very early in his career – is detailed in Chapter 9); also CD-reissued on "King Of The Country Blues", Yazoo Records CD-1069, c. 1990.
    Blind Lemon Jefferson: 'Match Box Blues', Chicago, c. March 1927; "The Country Blues", RBF Records RF-1, New York, 1959. (After Smith's anthology, this compilation is the next crucial LP issue of previously hard-to-obtain pre-war blues material. It was compiled by Sam Charters and issued at the same time as his book *The Country Blues*, which was the main stimulus to the blues revival that hit Greenwich Village, Boston and elsewhere at the beginning of the 1960s. This LP too contained a number of recordings that plainly influenced Bob Dylan. The LP is discussed further in Chapter 9 and the book in Chapter 15.)
    Jefferson re-recorded 'Match Box Blues' twice, Chicago, c. April 1927; the first of these cuts issued on "The Immortal Blind Lemon Jefferson", Milestone Records MLP 2004, New York, 1967, and the second on "Blind Lemon Jefferson Volume 2". (The original recording is best: it was made for OKeh and exists in pretty good quality; the re-recordings were for Paramount, a label synonymous with cheap equipment and hence with atrocious sound quality. Unfortunately almost all Jefferson's sides were on Paramount.)
    Carl Perkins: 'Matchbox', Memphis, 30/1/57; Sun Records 261, Memphis, 1957. (An earlier cut, 'Matchbox', Memphis, 4/12/56, remained unissued until the box-set "Carl Perkins: The Sun Years", Charley Records, London, c. 1980.) Bob Dylan played around with a version of 'Matchbox' during his studio session with George Harrison, NYC, May 1970.
    Sam Cooke: 'Somebody Have Mercy', Hollywood, 15/2/62, RCA Victor Records, New York [and RCA Records RCA 1310, London], 1962.

The asset of irony appears again, and to greater effect, in the other self-composed song on the album, the reflective 'Song To Woody'. Here, the irony closes the lyric:

> *Here's to Cisco and Sonny and Leadbelly too*
> *And to all the good people that travelled with you*
> *Here's to the hearts and the hands of the men*
> *That come with the dust and are gone with the wind*
>
> *I'm a-leavin' tomorrow but I could leave today*
> *Somewhere down the road someday . . .*
> *But the very last thing that I'd want to do*
> *Is to say I bin hittin' some hard travellin' too.*[3]

Clearly, to say he'd been hitting some hard travelling too is not the last thing Dylan would like to be able to do.

It is with those final lines – which get their special strength not just from the understatement but from the carefully clipped reluctance of the cadence – that we get a fresh focus on the whole theme of the song. At the same time, we still hear the echoes of all those delicate rushes of confidentiality which, throughout the lyric, establish its tone.

Other aspects of the song also contribute to its appeal. There is the frank if implicit statement of what is, on Dylan's part, a plea for an innocent drop-out and the concern to find a new allegiance in the 'hard travelin'' ethos. Again there is a delicacy in handling this – a balance struck in perceiving both the harsh reality and the

---

3.   Guthrie travelled around with Leadbelly, Sonny Terry and Cisco Houston during the Second World War. Their recordings include a Leadbelly song, 'We Shall Be Free', on which Dylan based his own 'I Shall Be Free' and 'I Shall Be Free No. 10'. (The tune is the same in all three songs.) Part of the Leadbelly song runs: 'I was down in the henhouse on my knees / Thought I heard a chicken sneeze / It was only a rooster saying his prayers / Thanking his God for the pullets upstairs'. Dylan sings, among much else of precisely the same tone: 'Well I took me a woman late last night / I was three-fourths drunk, she looked alright / Till she started peelin' off her onion-gook / She took off her wig said how do I look? . . .'
Leadbelly: 'We Shall Be Free', NYC, May 1944 [with Woody Guthrie and Sonny Terry]; "Leadbelly Sings Folk Songs", Folkways Records FA 2488, New York, 1962, reissued as Folkways FTS 31006, New York, c. 1970, CD-reissued as FA 2488, 1995.
In fact this song goes back further, pre-dating the era of recordings: '. . . stanzas of 'You Shall Be Free' have been traced to the mid-nineteenth century,' writes John H. Cowley, in 'Don't leave me here: non-commercial Blues: the field trips, 1924–1960' in *Nothing But the Blues: The Music and the Musicians*, ed. Lawrence Cohn (1993). Splendid early versions on record are those by the Beale Street Sheiks, i.e. the great Memphis figure Frank Stokes plus Dan Sane: 'You Shall', Chicago, c. Aug. 1927; "Frank Stokes With Dan Sane And Will Batts (1927–1929)", Roots Records RL-308, 1968, and 'You Shall', Chicago, c. Sept. 1927; "Mississippi & Beale Street Sheiks, 1927–1932", Biograph Records BLP-12041, Canaan, New York, 1972.
Stanzas from 'You Shall' occur too in an early recording by Stokes' Memphis colleague Jim Jackson. His 1928 'What A Time' has verses close to Leadbelly–Guthrie–Terry's – and more to the point, rendered in what is ear-poppingly close to the style we think of as Dylan's on 'I Shall Be Free': not only vocal delivery and feel but the very same guitar-strumming too. You can't hear the Jim Jackson version without wondering whether Dylan knew it back then, though it had never been released on vinyl when Dylan cut 'I Shall Be Free' and 'I Shall Be Free No. 10'. [Jim Jackson: 'What A Time' (2 takes), Memphis, 28/8/28; "Kansas City Blues", Agram Records AB2004, Ter Aar, Holland, 1980 (take 2); "Jim Jackson . . . Vol. 2", Document Records DOCD-5115, Vienna, 1992 (take 1).]
There is further discussion of this song group in relation to children's song in Chapter 17.
Cisco Houston's album "I Ain't Got No Home" [NYC, early 1961, Vanguard Records VRS-9107, New York, 1962] includes two songs Dylan performs, Guthrie's 'I Ain't Got No Home' and the traditional 'Waggoner's Lad', and two traditional songs of tangential import for him in the 1980s, 'Danville Girl' (Dylan's early, unreleased version of 'Brownsville Girl' is called 'New Danville Girl') and 'Streets Of Laredo' (one of the 'Unfortunate Rake' cycle of songs discussed in relation to Dylan's 'Blind Willie McTell' in Chapter 15). Around the same time Houston recorded another version of 'Danville Girl', under its common alternative title, 'The Gambler' [NYC, c. 1961, "Railroad Songs", Folkways Records FA2013, New York, c. 1961].

romantic flavour of this ethos. The song not only reflects Guthrie faithfully but assesses his real but disappearing America from Dylan's, the young man's, perspective. We are offered a highly intelligent understanding of the subject.

This comes over, equally, in the rhythmic balance of the lyric – look at the third and fourth lines, the seventh and eighth, and so on; and likewise, the wind and the dust are there in the song's construction. Lines and syllables take the form of a list: the suggestion is one of restless movement within a pre-ordained pattern of repetition. The share-cropper's life rhythm.

In Guthrie's triumphant autobiography, *Bound for Glory*, we see him travelling around with the homeless families who are also the heroes of Steinbeck's *The Grapes of Wrath*; and while recalling one particular encounter, Guthrie quotes one of his own songs, 'Pastures Of Plenty'.[4] Dylan's tribute re-works this. One of Guthrie's verses runs:

> *I worked in your orchards of peaches and prunes;*
> *I slept on the ground in the light of your moon;*
> *On the edge of your city you'll see us and then*
> *We come with the dust and we go with the wind.*

Dylan's alteration of that last verb, from 'go' to 'are gone', shows his awareness that the era which produces such men is all but over.

Elsewhere, Dylan can use the tone of Guthrie's autobiographical writing unaltered, can capture it exactly, in song. The chaotic scurrying around of cram-jam-packed humanity, which Guthrie describes so well (particularly in the sequence on the box-car ride that opens and closes his book), is done precisely in this way:

> *Dogs a-barkin', cats a-meowin'*
> *Women screamin', fists a-flyin', babies cryin'*
> *Cops a-comin', me a-runnin'*
> *Maybe we just better call off the picnic.*

That is Woody Guthrie's voice. It's from Dylan's 1962 song 'Talking Bear Mountain Picnic Massacre Blues'.

Similarly, a line like

> *In the misty crystal glitter*

(from Guthrie's 'Grand Coulee Dam') clearly has its influence even on the Dylan of 'Chimes Of Freedom' – and you need only compare the writing and delivery of Guthrie's 'Talking About Songs' (1944) with particular passages of Dylan's 'Last Thoughts On Woody Guthrie' (recorded in live recitative performance in 1963 and finally released on the "Bootleg Series I–III" box-set, 1991) to hear yet another side of

---

4.   Woody Guthrie, *Bound for Glory* (1943); John Steinbeck, *The Grapes of Wrath* (1939).
   Woody Guthrie: 'Pastures Of Plenty', probably late 1947, "Ballads From The Dust Bowl", Asch Records 610, New York, 1947. While the words of Dylan's 'Song To Woody' refer back to those of 'Pastures Of Plenty', the tune is virtually identical to that of Guthrie's '1913 Massacre' [24/5/45, "Struggle", Asch Records 360, New York, 1946]. Surprisingly, no one has published a Guthrie sessionography and discography, and at present, basic recording details are hard to come by.
   (Dylan was taped performing 'Pastures Of Plenty' in St Paul, Minnesota, as early as May 1960, and he performed '1913 Massacre' at his Carnegie Chapter Hall recital, NYC, 4/11/61, sixteen days before recording 'Song To Woody'.)

Guthrie's voice: and it's surprising to find his influence still so strong at this point. Here's Woody Guthrie:

> I hate a song that makes you think that you're just
> born to lose – bound to lose – no good to nobody, no
> good fer nuthin' because yer either too old or too young
> or too fat or too slim or too ugly or too this or too that:
> songs that run you down or songs that poke fun at ya on
> account of yr bad luck or yer [pause] hard travelin' . . .
> I am out to sing songs that will prove to you that this is
> your *world*, that if it has hit you pretty hard and knocked
> you down for a dozen loops, no matter how hard it's run you
> down or rolled you over, no matter what color, what size
> y'are, how y're built . . .

and here's Bob Dylan's ambiguously titled 'Last Thoughts On Woody Guthrie':

> When yer head gets twisted and yer mind grows numb
> When you think you're too old, too young, too smart or too dumb . . .
> Why am I walking, where am I running
> What am I saying, what am I knowing
> On this guitar I'm playing, on this banjo I'm frailin'
> On this mandolin I'm strummin', in the song I'm singin'
> In the tune I'm hummin', in the words that I'm [pause] writin' . . .
> You need something to make it known
> That it's you and no one else that owns
> That spot that yer standing, that space that you're sitting
> That the world ain't got you beat
> That it ain't got you licked
> It can't get you crazy no matter how many
> Times you might get kicked . . .[5]

The great folklorist Alan Lomax wrote of Guthrie that 'he inherited the folk tradition of the last American frontier (western Oklahoma) and during his incessant wandering across the US he has recomposed this tradition into contemporary folky ballads about the lives of the American working class . . . No modern American poet or folk singer has made a more significant contribution to our culture.'[6]

5.   Woody Guthrie: 'Grand Coulee Dam', probably 1944, "Woody Guthrie" [set of three 78 rpms], Asch Records 347, New York, 1944. Woody Guthrie: 'Talking About Songs', WNEW Radio, NYC, 3/12/44. (The latter, broadcast during Guthrie's first show on WNEW, is quoted in Robert Shelton's *No Direction Home: The Life and Music of Bob Dylan* [1986] as being an extract from the Guthrie book *Born to Win*, a compilation of bits and pieces edited by Shelton [1965] [intended by the publishers, Macmillan, as a sort of follow-up to Guthrie's autobiography *Bound for Glory*].)
Bob Dylan: 'Last Thoughts On Woody Guthrie', live NYC, 12/4/63; on "Bootleg Series I–III", 1991.
6.   Alan Lomax, *The Penguin Book of American Folk Songs* (1964).
In *In the Deep South*, 1989, British journalist Roy Kerridge introduces himself like this: 'In between wanting to be a zoo keeper and an artist for the *Beano*, I yearned to be a collector of traditional songs, like Alan Lomax . . . My mother told me of brave Lomax's adventures in the Appalachians, where he was stabbed by the jealous hillbilly husband of an aged crone whose song he was recording: 'Oh Lovely Appearance Of Death'.'
(Brave Lomax is also the man who, with Pete Seeger, tried physically to pull the plug on Dylan's electric début at Newport, 25/7/65, wrestling on the ground with wicked manager Albert Grossman in the name of folk

If Dylan's debt to Guthrie is, as he admits, substantial it is not in essence just derivative. Few people can have gained so much from Guthrie's work even though that work is among the best of the American folk art accessible to us from the pre-1960s. When Dylan sings that 'I'm seein' y'r world of people and things' he is too modest: he has not so much seen as re-created.

Nevertheless, Guthrie's influence can be traced much further through Dylan's work than simply to tribute songs. Elsewhere on the latter's first album we recognise Guthrie's subject-matter – the hobo's America – and Guthrie's humour. In the famous Dylan 'protest songs' of his second and third LPs ('Blowin' In The Wind', 'Masters of War', 'The Times They Are A-Changin'', 'Oxford Town' and others) it is largely Guthrie's idealism. And it must have been Guthrie, rather than Dylan's 'first idol', Hank Williams, who impressed upon Dylan, by his example, the need of the artist to stand alone, true to his individual vision.[7]

Like his early 'hillbilly sound' this sense of responsibility to oneself and to one's art was not understood (it is not surprising) by the Greenwich Village/Newport Folk Festival devotees. Even when the protest phase was rampant, most of its fans preferred it with jam: preferred the sweeter versions of the 'Blowin' In The Wind' kind of song, by – the example is inevitable – Peter, Paul & Mary. There were, in fact, over sixty different recorded versions of that song, all performing the same function: anaesthetising the Dylan message. Columbia Records (CBS), being in it for the money, were caught both ways: on the one hand they forced the suppression of his 'Talkin' John Birch Paranoid Blues' and then they mounted a campaign with the somewhat mournful slogan 'Nobody Sings Dylan Like Dylan'.

In fact, of course, the 'protest' songs are rarely of outstanding quality: Dylan's performances of them can do little more than partly compensate, as it were, for the lack of anything in them *but* 'messages'. It is not just the clichés that mar these songs but – along with their obviousness – the assumption that cliché is necessary for emphasis: the assumption that the listener must be spoon-fed. Dylan the writer is giving us rhetoric, not art. In contrast, where societal comment is present in his later work – as for instance in 'Desolation Row' – Dylan's critique is always offered in a

---

purity. He also 'discovered' Muddy Waters, recording him on the plantation in late August 1941 and many months later condescending to mail him one copy of a couple of these sides. Still, Lomax, now 80 plus, has always been a busy man, toting barges and lifting bales in the fields of white and black folklore since he was a mere lad alongside his father, the equally distinguished John A. Lomax, and hoping in vain to earn this feisty old brute's love through emulation. For the Library of Congress the two scoured America, together and separately, starting in 1933, when Alan was 15, field-recording a rich array of people. His achievement in many areas has been enormous and incomparable.)

7.   The line 'An' my first idol was Hank Williams' is in Dylan's wonderful poem published as liner-notes to "Joan Baez In Concert, Part 2", Vanguard Records VRS-9113, New York, 1964 (on which Baez sings the traditional 'Jackaroe' with the same set of lyrics Dylan uses thirty years later for the version on "World Gone Wrong"). See also note 32.

Guthrie's impact on Dylan was not only direct – it also came via Ramblin' Jack Elliott, whom Dylan met and befriended early on in his time in New York City in the very early sixties. Ramblin' Jack Elliott was the singer–guitarist of whom Guthrie once remarked, 'He sounds more like me than I do.'

In 1975, Dylan popped up again with Elliott at a gig by the latter back at Greenwich Village's Other End Club – at which they duetted on Guthrie's 'Pretty Boy Floyd' and the old 'How Long?', and then Dylan débuted, solo, a brilliant new song, 'Abandoned Love', studio-recorded at the "Desire" sessions but not released until "Biograph", 1985.

Ramblin' Jack Elliott was subsequently one of Dylan's guests on the Rolling Thunder Revue tours and so can be seen in Dylan's 1977 film *Renaldo & Clara*, Circuit Films, US, directed Bob Dylan & Howard Alk, 1977.

form dictated by a most formidable art and not by an anxiety based on lack of trust in the listener.

We have already seen from 'Song To Woody' that the early Dylan was aware of such criteria; his early folk-protest-conservationist audiences were not. Here was a folk singer, by any sane definition of the term, who was first upbraided with the hillbilly tag and then, because he had written 'Blowin' In The Wind', told in effect to keep on writing that song, again and again, for the rest of his artistic life. When he broke away from this, the response was again an upbraiding: you sound like a pop star; we still want folk singers here.

The blankness of such a response was made clear at the 1965 Newport Folk Festival. For the first time, Dylan appeared with his electric guitar. The audience took this as a 'sellout' and shouted objections. After Dylan and his musicians walked off the stage he was, in the end, persuaded to return and reappeared, this time with his old acoustic guitar. The audience assumed that they had disciplined their idol into submission – and it condemns their intentions that this pleased them. Dylan sang the aptly titled 'It's All Over Now, Baby Blue'.

Such an explicit lesson should not have been necessary. The whole controversy about Dylan's songs and styles reveals a fundamental misunderstanding of his claim to be an artist and an almost total failure to appreciate the traditions of folk culture which Dylan's work has, with varying degrees of prominence, always displayed.

It isn't necessary to spend long on defining what American folk music is and is not. Traditionally, it has been that day-to-day music created by the people and for the people. It gives form to the democratic ideal. It moves below the mainstream of culture, the flow of which is sustained and altered by small élites.

In the present century, this music of the ordinary American people has become radically less regionalised. The Depression and dust-bowl times provided a focus on this inevitable shift. As the people moved from the farms and small communities, folk music moved to the media.

On the other hand, though the way of life from which folk music flowed naturally has essentially disappeared, the changes of environment forced upon millions of Americans by an ailing capitalist system have acted as stimuli to self-expression – however defensive that impulse must be – and so as a regenerative influence on the creativity of ordinary people. Urbanised life still provokes a means of invention of music and song undreamt of in the Cole Porter philosophy.

Alan Lomax wrote (in noting the effects of such environmental changes) that

> there are aesthetic needs that Hollywood and Tin Pan Alley do not yet know how to satisfy. Tomorrow the Holy Rollers, the hillbillies, the blues shouters, the gospel singers – the Leadbellies, the Guthries . . . who have formed our twentieth-century folk-music, will be replaced by other folk artists . . . [who] will give voice to the deep feelings and unspoken needs of their own time, as have all the folk-singers of the past.

Future or past, folk music must flow naturally from peoples' lives. When such lives were eked out traditionally in country communities, the primary material – to shelter in and to work with – was wood. This was the simple reason for the centrality of the acoustic guitar in folk music. Now that people buy their environments in units of electric technology, folk culture has new material to work with. Serious contemporary artists cannot ignore the technology that surrounds them and shapes their lifestyle; and they have every reason to utilise it not only for their art but also in the interests of the clear duty to reach an audience. The black folk artists of twentieth-century America have always understood this.

Disputing the validity of 'going electric' in folk music disregards the responsible resources of artistic work; and the attempts of the 'purists' to 'preserve' folk music from such moves can only, where successful, act to the detriment of folk music's potential for growth.

Two final observations here: firstly that to insist on all this is not to argue that the issue at stake is one of trendiness versus the old-fashioned; and secondly that other issues raised here – for instance, that of the borderline area between folk art and art proper (between the subculture and the mainstream) – are returned to at a later point. It seems more appropriate here and now to concentrate on the specific folk music roots, traditional and modern, in Dylan's work.

When American life was wholly localised and regional, there were four main types of American folk music (apart from the traditions preserved by those immigrants from non-English-speaking countries). These four were: Yankee, Southern Poor White, Cowboy and Black. All four figure strongly in Dylan's art, if in very different guises as that art has matured.

The Yankee, who first sang on packet ships and there revived the sea-shanties that had dropped out of circulation in the British Navy, adapted his songs to the newer environment when working in the forests that stretch from Maine to Dylan's home state of Minnesota. The nature of this life and work produced a tradition of song in which the workman was a hard and grimly realistic hero. A less 'reflective' Hemingway ideal.

The Yankee backwoodsman sang in a hard, monotonous, high-pitched, nasal voice; his songs used decorated melodies in gapped scale structures and words mattered more than tunes.[8] Those familiar with Dylan's early work will recognise aspects of it, both of style and content, in that description. Indeed, the close relation much of the early Dylan output keeps with this Yankee tradition is what makes that output difficult to attune to, not only for those trained to Gilbert and Sullivan (in which the words are nonsense and a-tune-you-can-hum is the main ingredient) but also for the pop-orientated.

There is perhaps little more in the Yankee tradition that claims Dylan as its modern voice. Although a song such as his magnificent 'Lonesome Death Of Hattie Carroll' turns an ordinary worker into a kind of heroine, Dylan makes this happen as a device, not an end in itself: a device for strengthening an essentially political and social polemic. He does the same with Medgar Evers and his killer in 'Only A Pawn In Their Game': the two men are just pawns in Dylan's 'game'.[9] On the other hand,

8.   Lasting, well-known traditional Yankee songs – many remaining quite close to their English antecedents – include 'The Erie Canal', 'The Bay Of Mexico', 'The Foggy Dew', 'Weary Of The Railway', 'Katy Cruel' and of course 'Yankee Doodle'.

9.   This song is discussed further later in the present chapter; details of the Medgar Evers murder case are given in note 22.

his tremendous 'North Country Blues' much more nearly exhibits a traditional Yankee perspective in that it deals very consciously with a working community's suffering, treated through the story of one family's misfortunes, and with that community's annihilation. The song provides a timely epitaph to the destruction of the folk culture such a community produced, while getting the dynamics of its construction from that kind of culture. When, on the much later album, "Self Portrait", Dylan returns to a Yankee song, 'Days of '49', he offers it quite rightly as a museum-piece even as he breathes new life into it.

Southern Poor White folk music, hillbilly mountain music, the music of the settlers, consisted of hybrids. Its songs fused Scots, Irish and English influences and yet expressed a new-world pioneer milieu. Songs like 'Come All You Virginia Girls', 'Old Blue', 'I Love My Love', 'Went Up On The Mountain' and 'Pretty Saro' reflected normal life all across the southern backwoods and testified to the cultural bonds between poor whites as far west as Texas and Oklahoma.

It was a tradition linked fundamentally to Calvinist precepts: to the passionate belief in sin, the concern for individual salvation and the surety of a God On Our Side. Uncle John, from Oklahoma, in *The Grapes of Wrath*, is in this sense the complete descendant of the pioneers who constructed the tradition.

With its vital mixing of ancient and fresh vocabulary and its truly pioneering grammatical freedom, this tradition offered what is the real core of folksong, a conserving process which is at the same time creative; and in his use today of that fundamental life-force, Dylan is the great white folk singer. He has drawn on this tradition in two ways: he has used its established characteristics for some of his song structures and he has used its very lively inventiveness as a source of strength for his own.

His adaptation of the traditional Scottish song 'Pretty Peggy-O', on his first album, gives a Texas accent a central rhythmic purpose. The guitar-work and melodic structuring on 'Ballad Of Hollis Brown' are straight from the Appalachians, where such forms and modes had evolved, in comparative isolation, over a period of almost two hundred years.[10] And a traditional song such as 'East Virginia' reflects the brooding about death which Dylan echoes throughout his first album (and sometimes in later work) and which is rooted as much in the orthodoxy of Calvinism as in black folk culture.

The Calvinist precepts are not, of course, taken up wholesale by Dylan: rather, he takes up the challenge, the encapsulating threat, of these ideas. In 'With God On Our Side', which appeared (on "The Times They Are A-Changin'") towards the end of his flirtation with the protest movement, it is the early part of the song, and not the later homilies on world wars and atom bombs, that is of real and lasting interest. It gives us Dylan assessing the inroads of pioneer religiosity on his own sensibility:

---

10. It is easy to oversimplify questions of cultural isolation in the Appalachian mountains. On the one hand we have clear evidence of its survival up to the First World War; on the other hand, there is this note by Paul Oliver, offered in his invaluable book *The Story of the Blues* (1969): 'Although the Appalachians divide North Carolina from Tennessee, the mountains provide no physical barrier and . . . numerous roads . . . break across them which . . . circulating singers used. Highway 70 was the most popular, linking the Atlantic coast by way of Raleigh, Ashville and Knoxville with Nashville and Memphis.' There is further discussion of this topic in Chapter 18.

> *O my name it means nothing*
> *My age it means less:*
> *The country I come from*
> *Is called the Mid-West.*
> *I was taught an' brought up there*
> *The laws to abide*
> *And that the land that I live in*
> *Has God On Its Side . . .*

There is an extraordinary sweep of implicit experience in those first four lines. The sense of the narrator's context – his sense of history and therefore of identity – makes itself felt quietly and yet has impact. The careful omission of any 'but' or 'yet' or 'and' between the second and third lines has a striking and forceful effect. This creation of effect by what is lacking, not by what is there, is characteristic of much Dylan material, and gets a fuller discussion later in this book.

The verse just quoted also provides an obvious dismantling of the Calvinist doctrine contained in the song's title, and it is a pity that as the later verses draw nearer and nearer to the 'protest' formula, this dismantling becomes correspondingly heavy-handed. In contrast, this first verse has a truly compelling delicacy. And it is able to give us very finely the narrator's sense of the intellectual and moral pressure of his upbringing in terms of 'folk education'. Clearly, those two lines do not provide a mechanically inserted or merely peripheral piece of information. Dylan is stating his awareness that the country he comes from has its claims upon him and upon his art, for both good and bad. (He nowhere draws more on his background familiarity with Calvinistic folk life than in his beautifully poised, pinched delivery on the early 'Quit Your Low-Down Ways' – a definitive cameo, as he does it – or the very much later 'Gotta Serve Somebody'.)

Dylan returns to Appalachian music on his 1970 double-album, "Self Portrait", to give us an odd but effectively atmospheric version of the traditional song 'Copper Kettle'. As with all the music he touches on this collection, he brings back to life the spirit of the age that the song is all about and does it immeasurably better than those purists to whom his version (it has violins and women on it) is anathema. And as if to emphasize further his ability to do this sort of thing, the same album offers 'Belle Isle', which reaches back even further into the traditional folk past, invoking those purely Celtic origins which are part of the founding ingredients of America's Southern Poor White music.[11]

The Cowboy music tradition was, like the Southern Poor White, a hybrid: it was basically an amalgam of Southern and Yankee brands of folk. In Lomax's phrase, 'the cowboy singer was a Yankee balladeer with a southern accent'.

---

11.   The origins of 'Belle Isle' are harder to establish than this suggests. (In previous editions of this book I laboured under the false impression that it was a parodic Dylan composition.) The song is further discussed in Chapter 5; but for a full discussion of its origins, see Michael Gray, 'Back to Belle Isle', *Telegraph*, no. 29, Spring 1988 and follow-up correspondence in subsequent issues, or Michael Gray, 'Grubbing for a moderate jewel: in search of the Blooming Bright Star of Belle Isle', *Canadian Folklore canadien* (Journal of the Folklore Studies Association of Canada), Vol. 8, 1–2 (one issue), 1986 (officially; in fact published 1989).

Dylan also returns to Appalachian folksong, as to the other forms of folk music under discussion, in his 1990s solo albums "Good As I Been To You" and "World Gone Wrong", discussed in Chapter 18.

As with the hillbilly genre, Dylan uses the cowboy tradition in two ways. He uses the structures and conventions, and he uses the atmospheric essence. This essence is the lyric magic that first takes its being from the 'noble' struggle of hard-living men in a hostile work environment (and later, much more famously, from the communion of the individual with his own loneliness in the environment of the great western plains). A traditional sample of the hard-struggle song is this:

> *Our hearts were made of iron, our souls were cased with steel,*
> *The hardships of that winter could never make us yield,*
> *Our food, the dogs would snarl at it, our beds were in the snow,*
> *We suffered worse than murderers up in Michigan-i-o.*

That recalls, in Dylan's output, more than his delighted use of that last rhyming device in his version of 'Pretty Peggy-O' ('He died somewheres in Loos-i-ana-o'). We can easily envisage Dylan singing – say, on "Self Portrait" – the lines just quoted.[12] Phrases like 'our food, the dogs would snarl at it' are well within what we've come to know as Dylan's scope. And to think back to 'Song To Woody' is to recognise a rhythmic effect similar to that achieved in the above, on phrases like 'Here's to the hearts and the hands of the men'.

This same flavour is prominent again in Dylan's 'Ballad of Hollis Brown' – even though there the sense of community is taken outside the song's characters and exists solely between the narrator and his subjects (and is only a one-way awareness, for the narrator's sympathy cannot reach them):

> *Way out in the wilderness a cold coyote calls*
> *Way out in the wilderness a cold coyote calls*
> *Your eyes fix on the shotgun that's hangin' on the wall.*

A very different song, from the same Dylan album, draws just as firmly on the idea of the hard struggle of good-hearted men to overcome adversity. The song is 'When The Ship Comes In', and it is a tribute to Dylan's intelligence and artistry that he can use the strengths of this theme from this tradition in the utterly different context in this song of a moral struggle, without any loss of poise. It is a much underrated song. Part of its appeal comes from its tune and from Dylan's performance. These two elements combine, and combine with the words, to sustain a maximum effect and energy (as, for instance, when we come to that simple word 'shout' in the last verse: the voice does indeed break into a shout, a celebratory exclamation, and hits the word as the tune hits the highest note in the verse).

Even as words-on-the-page, though, the song has a distinguished charm very much its own – like a glimpse into a world both real and unreal: morally mature (if severe) yet childlike in conception.

---

12. I cannot trace my source for the lines quoted but they are very close to verse 4 of 'Range Of The Buffalo' in Lomax's *Penguin Book of American Folk Songs* and very close to those of what is, according to Charles Darling's *The New American Songster: Traditional Ballads and Songs of North America* (1992), the progenitor of 'Buffalo Skinners'/'Range Of The Buffalo', i.e. 'Canaday-I-O', an 1854 re-working by Ephraim Braley of Maine of a British song 'Canada I.O'. The same genre gives us 'Diamond Joe', on Dylan's 1992 album "Good As I Been To You". That album's 'Canadee-i-o' is a quite different song.

The internal rhyming is so effective, driving the vision along in the rhythm of the oncoming ship as it meets, again and again, relentlessly, the swell of the sea:

> *And the song, will, lift, as the main, sail, shifts*
> *And the boat, drifts . . .*

Moreover, this internal rhyming collaborates perfectly with the alliterative effects (as well, of course, as with the tune):

> *Then the sands will roll out a carpet of gold*
> *For your weary toes to be a-touchin' . . .*

Never once does this immense charm come across as simplistic or faulty, and this is a more than merely technical achievement. The childlike allegory offered comes over as a quite unexceptionable moral cleanliness – a convincing wisdom.

This not only redresses anger; it yields a positive and spirited apprehension of the new age's possibilities:

> *Oh the fishes will laugh as they swim out of the path*
> *And the seagulls, they'll be smiling . . .*
> *And the sun will respect every face on the deck*
> *The hour when the ship comes in.*

Political yearnings do not sweep aside more ordinary joys: to talk of having sand between your toes, to feel glad of the imagined sympathy of fishes as well as of the overseeing of 'the ship's wise men', and to conceive, in the midst of creating a mood of general anticipation, such a particular image as that of a smiling seagull face – this is to encompass a wise and a salutary statement of hope.[13]

It accords with this achievement – this sustained control – that Dylan avoids painting 'the foes' as demons or fools. They are big enough to hold on to a certain dignity where the allegory goes biblical; and yet, beyond this, the apparently childlike vision applies to them too, humanising them even as it condemns:

> *Oh the foes will rise with the sleep still in their eyes*
> *And they'll jerk from their beds and think they're dreamin'*

13. Dylan may have been inspired in respect of the seagulls smilin' by the pseudo-folksong 'The Royal Canal', which, it has emerged, he and The Crackers/Band included among the rich assortment of material recorded on the Basement Tapes [Woodstock/West Saugerties, June–Oct. 1967]. In this, one verse runs: 'On a fine spring evening / The lag lay dreaming / The seagulls beaming / High above the wall'.

(It may also have influenced Dylan's 'I Shall Be Released', also on the Basement Tapes. In *Invisible Republic*, 1997, Greil Marcus calls 'The Royal Canal' . . . 'I Shall Be Released' without any hope for freedom'; and I note the particularity of Dylan's song repeating that phrase 'High above the wall' from within it.

It is possible too that Dylan's phrase 'the jingle-jangle morning', in 'Mr. Tambourine Man', was inspired by 'The Royal Canal', the chorus of which runs 'And that old triangle / Goes a jingle-jangle / All along the banks / Of the Royal Canal'. However, there are other possible sources for this. Tex Ritter's 'Jingle Jangle Jingle' [Hollywood, 11/6/42] is adjacent to his 'Blood On The Saddle' [Hollywood, 1/5/45], on the Ritter compilation "High Noon" [Bear Family Records BCD 15634, Vollersode, Germany, 1991]. 'Jingle Jangle' is also a record by the Penguins [Hollywood, 12/11/55; "Earth Angel", Bear Family BFX 15222, Vollersode, Germany, c. 1991].)

'The Royal Canal' [aka 'The Old Triangle'], by Brendan Behan, is a key element in his first play, *The Quare Fellow* [first produced Dublin, 1954, with Behan singing the song off-stage]. It was familiar repertoire in early 1960s Greenwich Village.

But they'll pinch themselves and squeal and they'll know that it's for real
The hour when the ship comes in.

As even this perfunctory glance shows, Dylan has taken us a long way, in 'When The Ship Comes In', beyond the cowboy tradition on which the song is based; and in any case, its basis is in the less recognisable of the two cowboy types. What needs to be considered now is Dylan's relation to the other type: that which corresponds to our image of the cowboy hero, that which is bathed in the romantic lyricism of saddle-sore silent men set against lonesome prairies and plains.

The traditional song 'I'm A-Ridin' Old Paint' well represents the genre:

Now when I die don't bury me at all
Just saddle my pony, lead him out of the stall
Tie my bones in the saddle, turn our faces to the west
And we'll ride the prairie that we love best.[14]

The cowboy nurtured an internal restlessness into something bigger than himself. His home became the Big Wide West – and he always felt compelled to be 'movin' on'. And how easy it was for this spirit to pass from the nineteenth-century cowboy to the twentieth-century professional hobo.

Dylan takes this up, sometimes comically, more often with a plausible earnestness. The comical example that springs to mind is from 'Country Pie', on "Nashville Skyline":

Saddle me up a big white goose!
Tie me on her and turn her loose!
Oh! me, oh! my
Love that Country Pie!

– a sympathetic send-up of the traditional song just quoted.

---

14.   This song was 'found' by Margaret Larkin, popularised by poet and folksong collector Carl Sandburg in his important anthology *The American Songbag* (1927), and republished by Alan Lomax, *Penguin Book of American Folk Songs*.

'Rake And Rambling Boy', a traditional ballad on the first Joan Baez LP ["Joan Baez", Vanguard VRS-9078, New York, 1960], has a final verse that shares the 'I'm Riding Old Paint' format: 'when I die, don't bury me at all / Place my bones in alcohol'. (Chapter 18 includes a note on Joan Baez's importance to Bob Dylan as a conduit of traditional material.)

'I'm Riding Old Paint' also shares common-stock ingredients with black song. An almost identical verse occurs in the middle of the splendid early 'blues' record by Papa Harvey Hull and Long Cleve Reed, 'Hey! Lawdy Mama – The France Blues' [Chicago, c. 8/4/27; "Really! The Country Blues", Origin Jazz Library OJL-2, New York, c. 1961]. This isn't really a blues at all, but an effervescent jostling of disparate verses from the rich memory banks of largely nineteenth-century repertoire by these songsters: men already of a certain age by the time they came to record. (Re the term 'songster', see Chapter 9.)

This might be the place to note something else about the West, cowboys and colour: 'Hollywood has left us with the impression that the West was peopled by little but cowboys. In fact, farmers outnumbered them by about a thousand to one. Even at their peak there were fewer than 10,000 working cowboys, at least a quarter of them black or Mexican . . .' (Bill Bryson, *Made in America*, 1994). And William Least Heat-Moon, driving toward the Hopi reservation across the Navajo territory that surrounds it, in Arizona, reports the modern scene thus:

In a classic scene, a boy on a pinto pony herded a flock of sheep and goats – descendants of the Spanish breed – across the highway. A few miles later, a man wearing a straw Stetson and pegleg Levis guided . . . a pair of horses tied together at the neck in the Indian manner. With the white man giving up on the economics of cowpunching, it looked as if the old categories of cowboys and Indians had merged; whoever the last true cowboy in America turns out to be, he's likely to be an Indian. (*Blue Highways*, 1983)

Dylan's expressions of this compulsion to move on, to not get entangled, are numerous. On "Self Portrait" he relaxes (as he does more conspicuously and perhaps less wholeheartedly on 'Country Pie') and handles Paul Clayton's famous 'Gotta Travel On' as the archetypal statement it is – in other words, he lets the words remain as simple as they are and puts the song across as music, and that music rides on beautifully. In contrast, he gives voice to the same roving compulsion in the disarming aphorism that brings his 'Ballad Of Frankie Lee And Judas Priest' to a close on "John Wesley Harding":

> *And don't go mistaking Paradise*
> *For that home across the road.*

In Dylan's more concentrated and sustained expressions of this same theme, of this negative-positive moral, their plausibility derives from their being always addressed to a particular woman or specific entanglements of which the narrator understands the full worth. It is never, in Dylan's hands, a merely boastful theme – never a Papa Hemingway conceit, an I'm-too-hot-to-hold bravado. The opposite impulse, the desire to stay and be entangled, is always felt to be present, though it cannot (until "Nashville Skyline") win.

Later still, on 'You're Gonna Make Me Lonesome When You Go', from the 1975 "Blood On The Tracks", things have progressed further – to the point where it is the woman who has the gotta-travel-on urge and the male narrator who must accept this philosophically.

Later still, on "Street Legal", the album that prepares us for the Born-Again Christian albums "Slow Train Coming" and "Saved", Dylan takes a further step – to the point where he again feels he has to move on and abandon love: but this time it is in order to embrace Jesus instead of 'the road'; to find a specific salvation rather than a nebulous, wandering 'freedom'.

We have one moving-on theme in 'Don't Think Twice, It's All Right', from the second Dylan album:

> *I'm a-thinkin' and a-wond'rin', all the way down the road,*
> *I once loved a woman – a child, I am told:*
> *I gave her my heart but she wanted my soul*
> *But don't think twice, it's all right.*

The same integrity of spirit underlies the 1964 song 'It Ain't Me, Babe':

> *You say you're looking for someone*
> *Who'll pick you up each time you fall,*
> *To gather flowers constantly*
> *An' to come each time you call:*
> *A lover for your life an' nothing more*
> *But it ain't me, babe.*

There are many more instances of Dylan using this 'gotta travel on' spirit. Perhaps his most directly autobiographical statement of it comes in the hastily composed yet excellent 'Restless Farewell', with which he closes his third album, "The Times They

Are A-Changin' ' ". Within the same collection, that word 'restless' is taken up again in a song Dylan has revisited often since, the lovely 'One Too Many Mornings':

> It's a restless, hungry feeling that don't mean no one no good[15]
> When ev'rything I'm sayin' you can say it just as good
> You're right from your side. I'm right from mine:
> We're both just one too many mornings
> An' a thousand miles
> Behind.

Often, then, this restlessness runs into what is for Dylan a search for the ideal, for nothing less than the perfect. It is only when we reach as far through his career as the "Nashville Skyline" album that we find this search largely discarded. Consciously, at last, an imperfect love can be accepted as salvation.

The last song on the album brings this out most explicitly: 'Tonight I'll Be Staying Here With You'. As its title suggests, it's a deliberate announcement of the fall from restlessness. The habit of always moving on has been kicked and the impulse to stay has at last succeeded:

> Throw my ticket out the window
> Throw my suitcase out there too
> Throw my troubles out the door
> I don't need them any more
> 'Cause tonight I'll be staying here with you
>
> I should have left this town this morning
> But it was more than I could do
> Oh your love comes on so strong
> And I've waited all day long
> For tonight, when I'll be staying here with you.

In the first of those verses, we get the direct announcement, and the first three lines give us the gestures that go with it. That 'should have left this town this morning', in the second verse, is a reference to the old travelling compunction now renounced, not to some particular journey's schedule. The point of the title line is that it isn't just tonight; the narrator has come to rest. Not even the train whistle heard in the distance can lure him back to homeless sojourns now.

When I first heard 'It Ain't Me, Babe' I specially liked that line 'A lover for your life an' nothing more', because in pop songs there never was anything more: to be 'a lover for your life' was the ultimate ideal. For me, then, 'It Ain't Me, Babe' was good in the context of this contrast and, five years of Dylan output later, 'Tonight I'll Be Staying Here With You' is good in that it can make use of its contrast to 'It Ain't Me, Babe'. It's not a step back, it's another step beyond (and it is in this same spirit of achievement that Dylan can reintroduce that 'I bless the day I found you' in 'Let It Be Me', so that despite its being an old pop song it too, under Dylan's auspices, shows the same progressive second step. It parallels 'Throw my ticket out the window').

---

15. A fine example, this, of the hillbilly traditions of grammar construction. Dylan's multiple negatives in this line are a direct inheritance from those traditions.

Love doesn't always come Dylan's way on "Nashville Skyline", but it does provide the focus of his desire. The second verse of the quiet 'I Threw It All Away' – the 'it' being love – echoes the cowboy ethos succinctly by using, as his image for the discarded love's value, the scenery the lonesome traveller has around him (though it acts also as sexual imagery):

> Once I had mountains in the palm of my hand
> And rivers that ran through every day –
> I must have been mad, I never knew what I had
> Until I threw it all away.

The emphasis there is on the problem of choice, but the choice propounded is again that between loving and moving on.

It may be said that there are much stronger influences in all this from modern country music ('Country & Western', as it was once called in England) than from the older traditional material. Let's not quibble too much about that: it is from the traditions that the modern amalgam derives, and in any case it is hardly possible to draw a line through some year in American history and say that behind the line stands virginal tradition and in front the whore of Nashville. There is more in Dylan's country pie than cowboy classics revisited (as we have seen) and more, equally, than the bland successors of Hank Williams can match.

At the same time, one of the many things that "Self Portrait" and the like can send us back to with a heightened appreciation is certainly Jerry Lee Lewis' old country B-side material – material like Hank Williams' 'Cold, Cold Heart', cut for the legendary Sun label in Memphis and issued as the 'flipside' (as we used to say) of 'It Won't Happen With Me' in 1961.[16]

As for the Dylan song that most clearly registers Hank Williams himself – 'One More Night', from "Nashville Skyline" – the tune of the verses is that of an old English popular song. Correspondingly, the lyric is not only consciously 'unoriginal' but actually recalls other lyrics:

> Oh it's shameful and it's sad
> I lost the only pal I had
> I just could not be what she wanted me to be
> I will turn my head up high
> To that dark an' rollin' sky
> For tonight no light will shine on me
> I was so mistaken when I thought that she'd be true
> I had no idea what a woman in love would do.

That couplet beginning 'I will turn my head up high' comes straight from the traditional cowboy song 'Lonesome Prairie'. There is a less exact, but none the less striking resemblance, between Dylan's last verse and a part of the famous oldie 'Blue Moon Of Kentucky' – and this is a resemblance that goes further than the lyric.

---

16. Jerry Lee Lewis: 'Cold, Cold Heart', Memphis, 9/2/61 c/w 'It Won't Happen With Me', Memphis, 12/6/61; Sun Records 364, Memphis [London American HLS 9414, London], 1961. (The latter features Wayne Moss on guitar; five years later Moss plays on "Blonde On Blonde".)

Dylan's use of the tune at this point, and the whole tone of his delivery, suggests the very early Elvis recording of it.[17]

Another aspect of the cowboy tradition is its special fondness for heroes, and Dylan comes to this on the "John Wesley Harding" album, as he reaches back into America's past for the secret strengths of her myths. The album is a 'retreat' – a turning away – from the chaos of the modern urban burden; yet clearly it is a regenerative spirit that drives Dylan to search back as he does. He engages, in this album, in a desperately serious struggle to free himself, and subsequently to free us, from the debilitating predicament our fragmented sensibility has placed us in: the predicament Dylan defined on his previous album, the druggy, urban, chaotic, compelling "Blonde On Blonde". There, 'Visions of Johanna' sums up this mess:

> *We sit here stranded*
> *Though we're all doin' our best*
> *To deny it.*

As Dylan comes, in "John Wesley Harding", to the myths and extinct strengths of America, he explores the world of the cowboy as well as the pioneer. The man in the title song is a cowboy and, indeed, a hero.

It is a modest exploration, in that the cowboy–outlaw is not an unusual subject for hero treatment; but what a delicate, subtle portrait the song offers. It is all so simple, so straightforward (like the system of values we have come to associate with the cowboy world): a ballad that tells the story of its hero's exploits. Yet at the end one still has no idea what actually happened, nor any clear indication of the narrator's attitude. We get clues but no bearings. It was never like this when Tennessee Ernie Ford sang 'The Ballad Of Davy Crockett'.[18]

The song's economy of organisation and language is noticeable at once. There is no use of simile and no reliance on images or symbolism. Following that, we notice a corresponding lack of what may be called 'moral centre'. Nine of the twelve lines provide what could be taken, at first glance, as testaments to the hero's worth and virtue: yet actually none is free from significant ambiguity – and these equivocations, collectively, have a piercing eloquence to offer.

> *John Wesley Harding was a friend to the poor*

In what way? To what extent? The claim has, deliberately, no core behind its apparent bluntness. It refrains from contradicting the suspicion that Harding's name could be added to a long list of men whose lives and interests are spent in opposition, effectively,

17. Elvis Presley: 'Blue Moon Of Kentucky', Memphis, 5–6/6/54; Sun Records 209, Memphis, 1954. The other side was 'That's All Right' (cut 5/6/54, the first day of Elvis' début commercial session). 'Blue Moon Of Kentucky' was composed by Bill Monroe in 1946.

(In the 1930s hillbilly mountain music continued in its old forms but also evolved into bluegrass. Prominent in this development were the Monroe Brothers. When they split up in 1938, Bill formed the Bluegrass Boys, got onto the Grand Ole Opry and in 1945 added Earl Scruggs on banjo. Their records 1945–48 are what all bluegrass is measured against.)

18. This was the title song from the 1954 US TV series and the 1955 Walt Disney film *Davy Crockett*, directed Norman Foster, which was made by re-editing the three 50-minute TV episodes. Words and music by Disney staff-writers Tom Blackburn and George Bruns. A hit for Fess Parker, who played Crockett, and for Bill Hayes and Tennessee Ernie Ford; for details see note 32 in Chapter 14.

to the lives and interests of the poor but to whom it is advantageous to seem to appeal. Plenty of hero reputations depend upon this pretence.

As for those two very reasonable questions raised by that first line of 'John Wesley Harding' – a friend in what way? and to what extent? – they are in no way answered by the rest of the song.

> *All along this countryside he opened many a door*

We could put similar questions in response to that and be met by a similar blank. The line opens no doors for us.

It works, as intended, by yielding an echo that lingers throughout the song: the echo of a second empty claim. To it must be added the corresponding echoes of the other claims that confront us. As we meet them, the next is this:

> *But he was never known to hurt an honest man.*

Dylan chooses the negative form of expression; the consciously reductive intention this reveals gets reinforcement from further negatives in the song, and it ends by giving us a pile-up of three of them:

> *But no charge held against him could they prove*
> *And there was no man around who could track or chain 'im down*
> *He was never known to make a foolish move.*

Not only is all this presented carefully in the negative, but it all serves to emphasise the deliberate vicariousness of the testimony we're given: 'He was never known to . . . He was never known to . . .'.

Back in the first verse again, the fourth line is linked to the third in such a way as to discredit any inference of virtue from either when they are considered together. He opened many a door but he was never known to hurt an honest man. That word 'but' gives the statements either side of it a cynical focus which the substitution of 'and' could have avoided had Dylan's intention been different (had Dylan's approach, for instance, been Hollywood's). The following lines add precisely nothing to our picture of the hero's character:

> *'Twas down in Chaynee County, the time they talk about . . .*
> *And soon the situation there was all but straightened out . . .*
> *All across the telegraph his name it did resound;*

and the inferences to be made do not concern his heroism, his virtue or his good deeds. They concern the far less earth-bound strengths of his fame and reputation. There is, again, a consciously reductive intention on Dylan's part: the intention of repeating, and giving a collective weight to, the idea that Harding had a reputation for . . . and then the vague list – lending help, opening doors, refraining from injuring the honest, almost straightening out some utterly unspecified 'situation', not getting tracked down, and, lastly, looking after himself cleverly.

Moreover, this repeated insistence on Harding's reputation casts a doubt on the veracity of what is being insisted upon. Thus Dylan trades on our methinks-he-doth-protest-too-much reaction, in order to increase further our sense of the empty centre of the story.

Two of the lines – but only two – work in a different way. 'With his lady by his side he took a stand' adds to those echoes of the unspecific in the way that other lines do, by that flamboyantly vague phrase 'he took a stand'; but it creates, with the other half of the line, an almost explicit condemnation. Within the cowboy ethic, the hero should neither have needed his lady by his side to give him his courage nor have placed her inside the danger zone.

The other line, 'He travelled with a gun in every hand', goes further. The wit of that phrase 'in every hand' serves quietly to highlight Harding's inadequacy. Such a reliance on his weapons suggests something discreditable. And in support of this, the phrase acts as a reference back to Dylan's earlier song 'With God On Our Side':

> *And the names of the heroes*
> *I's made to memorize*
> *With guns in their hands*
> *And God on their side.*

It is not, however, from these two lines of near-explicit criticism that 'John Wesley Harding' gets its power. This comes emphatically from Dylan's carefully constructed 'echoes of the unspecific', as I have called them – and these are indeed eloquent. In its three short verses, the song offers a keen critique of values pertinent not only to the nineteenth-century cowboy's world but to the heirs of that bygone civilisation in contemporary America. The clichés of thought exploded so precisely in the song are still in the way today; but Dylan has done battle with them. 'John Wesley Harding' joins with the rest of the album of that name to give us Dylan successfully engaged in the mature artistic attainment of reconstruction and revaluation: Dylan at his most seriously and intelligently creative.

Dylan's relation to the black folk music tradition is at least as strong and clear. Black folk music began by reflecting the basic dream of release – yet it first impinged upon white America as a novel, engaging entertainment (which is as telling an introduction to the history of race relations in the USA as the attempt to wipe out the Amerindian, the 'Red Indian', as we used to say). The distinctive, animated dancing of slaves won the attention and applause of their owners. Then enforced initiation into the prosaic mysteries of the Protestant tradition gave rise to spirituals which reflected a double burden: chains plus original sin.

These spirituals were first studied and collected by campaigners for the abolition of slavery, whose aim was to prove that the black man had a soul and should therefore be set free. Since then, the influence of white and black folk music on each other has been substantial. The black, although preserving African modes of tune and rhythm, has adopted many Celtic musical conventions even while retaining the habits of improvisation and adaptation, and the endless repetition of short, sharp phrases. Owing to African influence, correspondingly, white folk music has become increasingly more polyphonic and polyrhythmic.[19]

The blues, which emerged in the present century, relied on newly found African-

---

19.   This pre-blues period is discussed in rather more detail in Chapter 18, while the blues is examined in detail in relation to Bob Dylan's work in Chapter 9.

American dialects, 'spoken' through the guitar as well as the voice, latterly (but not always) in a 3-line, 12-bar verse pattern.

A song such as the old 'Blowin' Down The Road' illustrates the common ground that developed both musically and socially between blacks and poor whites. This was the seminal folksong of the Depression and of the New Deal. In form and origin a blues number, it became of expressive importance to millions of displaced whites. The *Grapes of Wrath* people understood the blues.

Woody Guthrie's autobiography certainly describes the experience of those times in a noticeably duo-racial way. The box-car ride of the opening and closing chapters is one in which blacks and whites are so jumbled together as to disarm any racial distinctions: they are all men who share the same nomadic discomforts; they are all looking unsuccessfully for a living; they are all outside the cop-protected communities:

> 'And remember-take an old 'bo's word for it, and stay th' hell out of the city limits of Tucson.' 'What kind of a damn town is this, anyhow?' 'Tucson – she's a rich man's bitch, that's what she is, and nothin' else but.'[20]

This same situation is handled again in the Guthrie song quoted earlier in this chapter. 'On the edge of your city, you'll see us and then / We come with the dust and we go with the wind'.

Both white and black are hungry, poor, 'a problem', the pawns of an economic game that demands unemployment for flexibility of labour – and therefore high profits – yet attacks, economically and socially, the people who have to provide its unemployment pool.

This kind of common ground reduces the difference between black and white perception. Guthrie's pen-and-ink sketches, included in his autobiography, feature people not easily classifiable by race – and indeed his sketches of himself make him look, if anything, more black than white. In the text he cites only one instance of racial prejudice amongst the hobo community.

Dylan, then, inherited black folk traditions not entirely from the outside – not as a separate form but as ever-present influences on other hybrid forms. This inheritance shows clearly right from the start. As Wilfrid Mellers expressed it: 'In the first phase of his career . . . [his] musical materials were primitive: modal white blues, hillbilly, Shaker songs and hymns, with an interfusion of (pentatonic) black holler, relating the young white outcast to the Negro's alienation.'[21]

Artistically Dylan, the middle-class white Minnesotan, also anticipated the (uneasy) attempts of the militant hippies to hold hands with Black Power at the start of the 1970s.

The strands for Dylan are pulled together by his 'Only A Pawn In Their Game', a song written after the murder of Medgar Evers.[22] The poor white is the pawn:

---

20. Woody Guthrie, *Bound for Glory*.

21. Wilfrid Mellers, 'Reactionary Progressives', *New Statesman*, 11/7/69.

22. Medgar W. Evers, prominent in the civil rights movement of the early 1960s and field secretary of the National Association for the Advancement of Colored People in Mississippi, was murdered in Jackson, 12 June 1963, causing a national outcry. Two rigged trials in the 1960s ended in deadlock. On 5 February 1994, in Jackson, Byron de la Beckwith, aged 73, was at last found guilty of Evers' murder and sentenced to life imprisonment. A statue of Evers

From the poverty shacks he looks
from the cracks to the tracks
and the hoofbeats pound in his brain
and he's taught how to walk in a pack, shoot in the back,
with his fist in a clinch,
to hang and to lynch, to hide 'neath a hood,
to kill with no pain;
like a dog on a chain, he ain't got no name,
but it ain't him to blame:
he's only a pawn in their game.

Dylan, however, comes closer to black culture than is suggested by this 'holding hands'; closer than he comes by singing to civil rights workers in Greenwood, Mississippi, at the start of his career.[23]

What the blues encompasses was summed up succinctly in Paul Oliver's book *Conversation with the Blues* (1965):

> The narrative and folk tales, the telling of 'lies' or competitive tall tales, the healthily obscene 'putting in the dozens', the long and witty 'toasts' and the epigrammatic rhyming couplets which enliven the conversation of folk negro and Harlem hipster alike, have their reflections in the blues. They are evident in the earthy vulgarity, the unexpected and paradoxical images, the appeal of unlikely metaphors, the endless story that makes all blues one.

For all this, Dylan's work shows an affinity that is often blatant and forceful. He has absorbed its characteristics into his thinking and thereby his vocabulary.

Another point made by Oliver is worth noting here too: that,

> . . . if the blues, like any folk art or indeed almost any art form, is illuminating in terms of a whole group it is still sung and played by individuals . . . the individual tends to become submerged . . . and even when the assessment of the major figures is made, the minor blues singer is forgotten.

To listen to much of Dylan's work – which at least between his break with 'protest' and his conversion to Christianity has in every sense put a consistent emphasis on the importance of the individual rather than the mass – is to feel that Dylan has not

---

stands outside the Medgar Evers Public Library on Medgar Evers Boulevard in today's Jackson.

    De la Beckwith was from Greenwood, Mississippi, the town where Robert Johnson was lethally poisoned in 1938. Greenwood had 11,000 people, half of them black, when Johnson played and died there. Byron de la Beckwith, one of the town's 5,500 whites, would have been a 17-year-old then.

    [1994 information: 'American Survey', *Economist*, 12/2/94. For a fuller account see Maryanne Vollers' book *Ghosts of Mississippi*, 1995.]

23.   Dylan came to Mississippi at the beginning of July 1963 with Theodore Bikel and Pete Seeger for a rally organised by the Student Nonviolent Coordinating Committee. On 6 July, three miles outside Greenwood, they and the Freedom Singers performed to around 250 black farm workers and 25 young whites and media people. Dylan, bravely, sang 'Only A Pawn In Their Game'. (A tantalising fragment is included in D. A. Pennebaker's film *Don't Look Back*, Leacock-Pennebaker, US, 1967.) The visit was reported in the small news item 'Northern Folk Singers Help Out At Negro Festival In Mississippi', *New York Times*, 7/7/63, in which 'Only A Pawn In Their Game' was singled out and cited for its theme, yet Dylan was identified as 'Bobby Dillon', a 'local singer'. The event is well documented in Robert Shelton's *No Direction Home*.

forgotten the minor blues singer at all. One guesses that he has listened to the minor figures wherever the somewhat random process of recording folk artists has allowed.[24]

He must have learnt and assimilated experience from the older songs and the older singers – singers who, in some cases, were 'discovered' or 're-discovered' in the 1960s. Mississippi John Hurt is one example, Mance Lipscomb another.

Lipscomb was 'discovered' in July 1960 by Mack McCormick and Chris Strachwitz and recorded – for the first time – a few weeks later in his two-room cabin. Dylan met Lipscomb at about this period, and we can get an idea of the aura of the man, and thus a hint of the insights he could have given Dylan, from the description of Lipscomb and a transcribed conversational fragment, in Paul Oliver's book. He was a 'Texas sharecropper and songster with a reputation that extends widely in Grimes, Washington and Brazos counties . . . A man of great dignity and natural culture . . . a veritable storehouse of blues, ballads and songs of more than half a century . . . He was born on 9 April 1895.'

This is Mance Lipscomb talking (the spelling is as in Oliver's transcript):

> I been playin' the git-tar now 'bout forty-nine years, and then I started out by myself, just heard it and learned it. Ear music . . . My pa was a fiddler; he was an old perfessional fiddler. All my people can play some kind of music. Well, my daddy . . . he played way back in olden days. You know, he played at breakdowns, waltzes, shottishes and all like that and music just come from me . . . Papa were playing for dances out, for white folks and coloured. He played Missouri Waltz, Casey Jones, just anything you name he played it like I'm playin'. He was just a self player until I was big enough to play behind him, then we played together . . . 'Sugar Babe' was the first piece I learned, when I was a li'l boy about thirteen years old. Reason I know this so good, I got a whippin' about it. Come out of the cotton-patch to get some water and I was up at the house playin' the git-tar and my mother came in; whopped me 'cause I didn't come back – I was playin' the git-tar:
>
> > Sugar babe I'm tired of you,
> > Ain't your honey but the way you do,
> > Sugar babe, it's all over now . . .[25]

Lipscomb must have been an invaluable contact for Dylan – the one a black Texan with a personal repertoire stretching back to 1908, the other a white Minnesotan would-be artist of the whole American people born in 1941. Not only could Dylan

---

24. Where Dylan heard what; the influence of 'minor figures' and unknown ones; the communal nature of much blues composition; and how this jells with post-structuralist ideas of the unfixed text and the death of the author – all these are central preoccupations of Chapter 9.

25. Paul Oliver, *Conversation with the Blues*.
   In Glen Alyn's *I Say Me for a Parable: The Oral Autobiography of Mance Lipscomb* (1993), Lipscomb (born Navasota, Texas 1895, died Navasota, Texas, 1976) talks of encountering Dylan (and of Ramblin' Jack Elliott first hearing of Lipscomb when Dylan played him a Lipscomb record) but specifies no dates. Lipscomb says Dylan followed him to 'Berkeley University' – 'And when I went off a duty he was settin round me, an hear what I was sayin, an pick up a lot of songs. He could imitate. But he wadna playin no gittah. Then. Takin you know, learnin from his head' – and 'from Berkeley to the UCLA'. On 18 May, 1963, Dylan appeared on the same bill as Lipscomb at the first Monterey Folk Festival. Specific songs that may have crossed from Lipscomb to Dylan are discussed in Chapter 9.

have gained a knowledge ready to work for him but also, in a specific and personalised testimony, a feeling for the intimacy of connection of words and music in the expression of a spirit and a theme.

> Song, speech and music are frequently one in the blues . . . the piano, guitar, even harmonica is a complement to the voice. Though he may play instrumental solos, the most characteristic blues artist sings through both voice and instrument(s).[26]

How striking is the pertinence of that passage to Dylan's work. Dylan plays piano, guitar and harmonica – three of the commonest blues instruments – plays instrumental solos on each and emphatically uses each as a complement to his voice. This is evident even in such a 'white' protest song as 'The Lonesome Death Of Hattie Carroll' (about a black woman), where, in the final refrain, the irregular strum of the guitar rises and falls, quickens and slows again, conveying the heartbeats of the narrator, while the harmonica phrases between the vocal lines act as graphs of his anger, shame and sympathy.

The huge instance in Dylan's work where this fusion shows vividly its creative force is in his wide-ranging, flexible, recurrent treatment of the classic Railroad Theme.

Just as the heroic-outlaw-of-the-West myth was, despite having European antecedents, significantly the product of the frontier social situation, so too the railroadman, the hobo and the railroad itself became folk heroes as a result of environmental circumstances. The railroad meant, or was at least seen to mean, freedom, opportunity, rebirth. It became, as in Guthrie's autobiography, a duo-racial symbol and experience. It is only natural and appropriate that a duo-racial consciousness is required to deal with such a theme in modern folk art. Dylan applies just such a consciousness to this focus.

It isn't altogether possible, however, to isolate or point to specific pieces of vocabulary or whatever and say there, precisely there, is the black ingredient; and that it is an ingredient subservient to the art as a whole argues against the value of any protected isolation of that sort. In his songs explicitly 'about' contemporary America – the protest songs, in the main – one of the aims is, as Mellers suggests, to express the relation of the spirit of the young white outcast to that of the alienated black. In Dylan's later work his encompassing of black traditions serves more subtly to enhance the expression of many different perceptions.

Musically, of course, this is often obvious. Beyond examples like that of 'Hattie Carroll' in which part of the impact comes from a blues-derived feeling for voice, words and instruments as complements, there are plenty of examples in Dylan's work of songs with the conventional 3-line, 12-bar verse structure, including, from his 1970s work, the outstanding 'Buckets Of Rain', 'Meet Me In The Morning', 'New Pony' and 'Gonna Change My Way Of Thinking'. Others use similar structures to similar effect.

One such song is the still-underrated 'Pledging My Time', from "Blonde On Blonde":

---

26. Paul Oliver, *Conversation with the Blues*.

Well they sent for the ambulance, and one was sent
Somebody got lucky, but it was an accident
Now I'm pledging my time to you
Hopin' you'll come through, too.

In that verse the black influence is especially strong. It goes beyond the music – the coiled insistence of guitar, harmonica, drums and voice – and beyond that character-istic bending of 'ambulance' in the pronunciation. There is also the curious ominous quality of those first two lines.[27]

They recall dramatically those stories of the legendary Beale Street in the Memphis of the 1930s, where Saturday night razor fights between blind-drunk blacks were so frequent that a fleet of ambulances waited like taxis at one end of the street. Killer ambulances, apparently, with drivers who made sure that if you weren't dead when they got to you, you were before they'd finished their night's work. (As these stories have blown up into myth, they provide a curious corollary to the stories about hospitals and doctors, and particularly surgeons, widely current in nineteenth-century England and passed into upper- and middle-class consciousness by terrifying children's nannies. The subject is aired in George Orwell's grim essay, 'How the poor die'.[28])

But it is Dylan's treatment of the railroad theme that merits a closer consideration. If it is a standard American symbol of freedom, the railroad also represents 'home' for the professional tramp of the dust-bowl years. The railroad symbolises other things too, from the real as well as from the dream world. The traditional black folksong which includes these lines:

When a woman blue, she hang her little head an' cry,
When a man get blue, he grab that train an' ride

makes the railroad a symbol of masculine social virility. Dylan, singing in the 1960s, emancipates contemporary woman. In 'It Takes A Lot To Laugh, It Takes A Train To Cry':

Don't the moon look good, mama, shinin' through the trees?
Don't the brakeman look good, mama, flagging down the double-E's!
Don't the sun look good goin' down over the sea
Don't my gal look fine when she's comin' after me! . . .

These lines are an adaptation of several things, including parts of Presley's version of 'Milkcow Blues Boogie' and from an older blues song that runs:

Don't the clouds look lonesome 'cross the deep blue sea
Don't the clouds look lonesome 'cross the deep blue sea
Don't my gal look good when she's comin' after me

27. The specifics of how Dylan has derived these lines from particular black recordings are discussed in Chapter 9.

28. George Orwell: 'How the poor die', *Now*, November 1946; collected in Orwell, *Shooting an Elephant and Other Essays* (1950); reissued in *Collected Essays, Journalism and Letters*, ed. Sonia Orwell and Ian Angus [4 volumes] (1968).

but the Dylan version in 'It Takes A Lot To Laugh, It Takes A Train To Cry' is also adapted from his own earlier song 'Rocks and Gravel' (unreleased):

> *Don't the clouds look lonesome shinin' across the sea*
> *Don't the clouds look lonesome shinin' across the sea*
> *Don't my gal look good when she's comin' after me.*[29]

Ten years after 'It Takes A Lot To Laugh', Dylan gives us another variant on those same lines, in 'Meet Me In The Morning', from "Blood On The Tracks":

> *Look at the sun, sinkin' like a ship*
> *Look at that sun, sinkin' like a ship*
> *Ain't that just like my heart babe, when you kiss my lips.*

(Dylan often does this: often preserves a phrase, a line or even a verse and, with perhaps some alteration, uses it again in a later song. The verse of 'Just Like Tom Thumb's Blues' that deals with 'my best friend my doctor' who 'won't even tell me what it is I got' is revisited in another song of the same time, 'Sitting On A Barbed-Wire Fence',

> *The Arabian doctor comes in 'n' gives me a shot*
> *But he wouldn't tell me what it was that I got,*

and the whole of the 'Outlaw Blues' verse beginning 'I got my dark sunglasses' is prefigured in an unreleased song of Dylan's called 'California'.[30] The plaintive line 'where are you tonight?' which gets the stress of repetition, with variants, all the way through 'Absolutely Sweet Marie' in 1966 is resuscitated twelve years later on 'Where Are You Tonight? (Journey Through Dark Heat)'. Again, fifteen years after the film *Don't Look Back*, Dylan quotes its title line in one of the best songs on "Saved", 'Pressing On':

> *Kick the dust off of your feet, don't look back.*

One of the very best instances of Dylan quoting himself occurs on the "Planet Waves" album, where, in 'Never Say Goodbye', he delivers a devastating punch by singing the line 'Ah! Baby, baby, baby blue!' in back-reference to his 1965 classic 'It's All Over Now, Baby Blue'. There is a noticeable parallel, too, between this joke from the 1970 'Day Of The Locusts':

---

29.   Elvis Presley: 'Milkcow Blues Boogie', Memphis, probably November 15 or December 20, 1954; Sun Records 215, Memphis, 1955 [1st issued UK on the EP "Good Rockin' Tonight", HMV Records 7EG8256, London, 1957]. I cannot identify the specific 'older blues song' quoted here; again, the common-stock nature of these lines, and Dylan's use of them, is a subject covered in Chapter 9. Bob Dylan: 'Rocks And Gravel (Solid Road)', Cynthia Gooding's apartment, NYC, probably March 1962. 'Rocks And Gravel (Solid Road)', Finjan Club, Montreal, 2/7/62. 'Rocks And Gravel (Solid Road)': NYC, 9/7/62 and 13/11/62 [out-takes from "The Freewheelin' Bob Dylan"]. 'Rocks And Gravel (Solid Road)': Gaslight Café, NYC, Oct. 1962. This is not in fact a Dylan composition but a traditional song.

30.   A version of 'Sitting On A Barbed-Wire Fence', NYC 15/6/65, was finally released on "Bootleg Series I–III", 1991. 'California', NYC, 13/1/65 [out-take from "Bringing It All Back Home"] is described in Bob Dylan: *Lyrics 1962–1985*, 1987, as an 'early version of 'Outlaw Blues''.

> The man standin' next to me
> His head was explodin'
> I was prayin' the pieces wouldn't fall on me

and this one from 'Isis' half a decade later:

> The wind it was howlin' and the snow was outrageous . . .
> When he died I was hopin' that it wasn't contagious . . .

while it is a striking feature of the "Slow Train Coming" album that 'Do Right To Me Baby (Do Unto Others)' is a re-write of 'All I Really Want To Do' from fifteen years and aeons earlier. Many other examples can be found in Dylan's large corpus.[31])

Back again on the railroad it is, paradoxically, the repetitive framework that helps a notable economy in the evocation of railroad feeling in those four lines from 'It Takes A Lot To Laugh, It Takes A Train To Cry'. In the music – of which the vocal tone and phrasing are parts – the drums and piano suggest not only the rattle of the train and, as such, a measure of its speed and mechanic vitality, but also the elation of the traveller who identifies with the locomotive's performance. The lyric's economy on adjectives and its emphasis on nouns – the moon, the sun, the brakeman, the trees, the sea, 'my gal' – makes for an exciting balance between the romantic and the concrete. Symbol and reality are fused.

This fusion, in context, recalls a passage from one of those autobiographical Dylan poems that got into print from time to time on the back of LP covers and in old underground magazines:

---

31. In this context it's funny that in the *Rolling Stone* interview with Dylan in 1969, editor-interviewer Jann Wenner uses the phrase 'unload my head' and Dylan, who has used that phrase in the 1965 'From A Buick 6', remarks on how good it sounds and says he'll have to write a song with that phrase in it (*Rolling Stone* no. 47, 29/11/69; collected in Craig MacGregor, *Bob Dylan: A Retrospective* [1972], reprinted as *Bob Dylan, the Early Years: A Retrospective*, 1990). This interview is greatly entertaining, with Dylan impersonating the amiable, unassuming solid citizen and prefacing his comments with 'Boy, . . .' and 'My gosh . . .' and 'Well, Jann, I'll tell ya . . .'

After *Song & Dance Man* came out in the USA in 1973, I was pleased to learn that only when Jann Wenner saw my comments on this interview of four years before did he realise Dylan had been 'putting him on'. *Rolling Stone* co-founder, the late Ralph J. Gleason, wrote: 'Wenner has only just found out that Bob put him on in that interview and somebody showed him Michael Gray's book.' (19/2/74, Berkeley, letter to Robert Shelton.) Gleason again: 'I told Wenner at the time that Dylan was putting him on . . . But it wasn't until you pointed out that bit about unloading his head and Dylan's reply that he ought to use that in a song, that Wenner caught on.' (14/3/74, Berkeley, letter to the author.)

It was the second time I'd displeased Wenner. The first had been with the report that the short-lived *Rolling Stone* London office commissioned from me on the second Isle of Wight Music Festival, at which Dylan appeared, in August 1969 ('That million dollar serenade', *Rolling Stone*, no. 42, London edn, 20/9/69). Wenner disliked this report so much that he didn't run it in the US edition, preferring the magazine to appear to have forgotten the entire event. ' "Wenner," recalls [London advertising manager Alan] Marcuson, "was fuming at the bit." ' Wenner hated the London office anyway, and the last proper British issue was 18/10/69 [source and quote, Nigel Fountain's *Underground: The London Alternative Press 1966–74*, 1988]; when Wenner's interview with Dylan appeared a month later, London retained only an 'Acting Manager' (Jon Ratner), though copies sold in Britain were still printed in England.

Gleason's letter to me added background information on Wenner and the workings of *Rolling Stone* at that time, i.e. when it was still San Francisco-based and (counter-)culturally important: 'Wenner . . . said he had to have the book's editor at arm's length to him. I never found out why, since he does not read books.' And: 'In order to understand Wenner's attitude towards Dylan, you first have to know that Wenner never saw him in the 12 or more concerts he gave in the San Francisco–Berkeley area over a three year period. Never once! . . . Wenner did not cop to any of this until after we got *Rolling Stone* started . . . Wenner['s] aim in those days was less to take over American publishing than to meet the Beatles.'

An' my first idol was Hank Williams
For he sang about the railroad lines
An' the iron bars an' rattlin' wheels
Left no doubt that they were real . . .
An' I'll walk my road somewhere between
The unseen green an' the jet black train[32]

Not only can Dylan give the railroad the importance a hard-travellin' hobo might give it, but can also use it as an axis round which to spin ideas of what is real and thus pursue his quest for the concrete.

The railroad appears in many other songs – 'Freight Train Blues' among them – and in several an essential ingredient is the railroad's importance where some fundamental choice is involved, related to the real or the true. In the poem just quoted from, the 'iron bars an' rattlin' wheels' provide a yardstick, albeit simplistic, of reality against which are contrasted smoother kinds of beauty – the nightingale sound of Joan Baez's voice is an instance he gives – and against which is balanced Dylan's consciousness of 'the unseen green'. In 'Tonight I'll Be Staying Here With You' (as already noted) the choice is between two lifestyles, with the railroad as the symbol of the one Dylan at last renounces. It calls to him on behalf of the 'keep travelling' spirit and it loses to new-found love:

I find it so difficult to leave
I can hear that whistle blowin'
I see that station-master too . . .
. . . tonight I'll be staying here with you.

He hears, but this time, at last, he doesn't follow.

In direct contrast, there is Dylan's first-album adaptation of the traditional 'Man Of Constant Sorrow', which equally relates to this particular choice. In this song, he wants the girl but cannot have her. He has travelled a long way to make the attempt to win her, and so the railroad becomes the symbol of a nomadic no-man's-land:

Through this open world I'm bound to ramble
Through ice and snow, sleet and rain
I'm bound to ride that mornin' railroad
P'raps I'll die on that train.

With this, of course, Dylan has come away from the concrete – despite the 'realism' of that wintry weather – and into the realms of romance. What could be more splendid, granted the imagined death-wish, than dying on that train? Even though 'Bob Dylan's Dream', with all its ponderous nostalgia, is launched with the lines

---

32. These lines are from Dylan's sleeve notes to "Joan Baez In Concert, Part 2" (see note 7). The poem appeared in *Circuit*, no. 6, c. 1967, one of the small arts journals inspired by Michael Horovitz's pioneering poetry magazine *New Departures*, founded summer 1959. With no other title than 'Joan Baez In Concert, Part 2', the poem was collected in Bob Dylan, *Writings and Drawings* (1972), and is in *Lyrics 1962–85* where, improbably, it is copyrighted 1973, almost a decade after its publication on the back of the Baez album.

> *While riding on a train goin' west*
> *I fell asleep for to take my rest*
> *I dreamed a dream . . .*

Dylan never quite returns to the dream mood given us by the 'Man Of Constant Sorrow' railroad.

There is a parallel of sorts on "Blonde On Blonde", in the surrealistic symbolism of 'Absolutely Sweet Marie', but the mood is very different. The solemnity is replaced by a good-natured if double-edged mockery:

> *Well your railroad gate, you know I just can't jump it*
> *Sometimes it gets so hard, you see*
> *I'm just sitting here beating on my trumpet*
> *With all these promises you left for me*
> *But where are you tonight, sweet Marie?*
>
> *. . . And now I stand here lookin' at your yellow railroad*
> *In the ruins of your balcony . . .*

but the symbol there, though used at both the beginning and the end of the song, is incidental. It is not a song that has much to do with trains.

The romance returns, but more respectably than in 'Bob Dylan's Dream', or even 'Man of Constant Sorrow', in another part of 'It Takes A Lot To Laugh, It Takes A Train To Cry', where the narrator grows lyrically expansive:

> *Well I ride on the mailtrain baby; can't buy a thrill*
> *Well I've been up all night, leanin' on the windowsill*
> *Well if I die on top of the hill*
> *Well if I don't make it, you know my baby will.*

That last line provides the ballast, taking the railroad romance away from narcissism and into a wider context, that of a more selfless and universal celebration of life. The goal here is to 'make it', to survive, not to die in glory on the train (although paradoxically, that conjectured dying 'on top of the hill' brings in by allusion a picture of history's most celebrated martyrdom, that of Christ on the cross on Calvary).[33]

Such celebration of life is, naturally, the business of any artist, but the use of the railroad theme, as of the highway theme, is the province very largely of the folk artist. Dylan is more than a folk artist – his social class, its literacy and education and his own creative insight and integrity all set him beyond that sphere – but his work has been gorged on the folk culture of America. It has provided a basis for his creativity, has literally been fundamental. In both senses, folk music is behind him.

---

33. Woody Guthrie's autobiography, *Bound for Glory*, takes its title from a song that uses this train-as-salvation symbol: the phrase 'Bound For Glory' comes from the song 'This Train', the chorus of which declares that 'This train is bound for glory, this train'. And of course it is precisely this use of the train symbol that Dylan finally comes to on the "Slow Train Coming" album, and in a couple of instances just prior to it – he sings Curtis Mayfield's 'People Get Ready' on the *Renaldo & Clara* soundtrack, and the glory train image runs through that, while the last track on the album leading up to "Slow Train Coming", "Street Legal", opens by forewarning us: 'There's a long-distance train rolling through the rain', and has Dylan riding that train to his new-found salvation. This theme is elaborated in Chapter 7.

CHAPTER TWO

Dylan and the Literary Tradition

> *. . . it's all bin done before,*
> *It's all been written in the book*
>
> Bob Dylan: 'Too Much Of Nothing'

> We talk nowadays as though the relationship between . . . [words and music] . . . constituted a problem; even as though there were a natural antipathy between them which composer and poet must overcome as best they may. Yet the separation of the two arts is comparatively recent, and the link between them would seem to be rooted deep in human nature.
>
> Wilfrid Mellers, professor of music and former *Scrutiny* literary critic.[1]

The folk tradition . . . the English literary tradition . . . it sounds like pigeon-holing but everything connects. A very intricate chain links the two and runs from pre-Aelfredian England through to contemporary America.

Because we have forgotten this, we find it hard to accept Dylan as a serious artist. He has chosen a medium we are unused to taking seriously: an inseparable mixture of music and words – and we grew up finding this a cheap and trivial formula. We should look back beyond the Elizabethan Age to the time when troubadours were an important part of our culture, when that culture was orally dominated and when sophisticated art was the same in kind as the heritage 'of the people'.

If Marshall McLuhan is right, if our electric technology is pushing us forward into another orally dominated age, then it shouldn't be surprising to find a serious artist once again at work in the medium Dylan has chosen.[2] Nor should it astonish us that such an artist can have reforged the links between folk and sophisticated culture.

---

1.   Source now unknown. Mellers' main work on Bob Dylan is the much later *A Darker Shade of Pale: A Backdrop to Bob Dylan* (1984).

2.   Marshall McLuhan, a Canadian academic, became a cultural guru of the 1960s and 1970s. He coined or made famous the phrases 'the medium is the message' and 'the global village'. His works include *The Gutenberg Galaxy: The Making of Typographic Man* (1962); *Understanding the Media* (1964); and *The Medium Is the Massage* [sic] (1967).

Dylan told Scott Cohen, *Spin*, Vol. 1, no. 8, Dec. 1985: 'I say, if you want to know about the '60s, read *Armies of the Night* by Norman Mailer, or read Marshall McLuhan . . . A lot of people have written about the '60s in an exciting way and have told the truth. The singers were just a part of it.'

Dylan's work needs this wide historical context. It is no good just looking at it against a background of Coca-Cola: no good making vague references to kids in the 1950s having increased spending power, or their cousins in the 1960s getting tired of the Stars and Stripes. To go back further, beyond Presley, Guthrie and Ginsberg, and see Dylan's art also in relation to the English literary tradition, makes more sense than simply to fool about with a few sociological guesses about what's made America tick for the last half-century. Those who feel, like Nik Cohn, that the significance of anyone with an electric guitar can be summed up as 'Awopbopaloobop Alopbamboom!' had better skip straight to Chapter 3.[3]

It is only comparatively recently, too, that folk and sophisticated culture have been separate. The gulf was not complete in England until the emergence of the Augustans, with their classicists and coffee-house smart sets, although it had started with Chaucer who brought to dominance an East Midlands dialect which became what we now call 'standard English'.

With only a few exceptions, pre-Elizabethan poetry was 'of the people'. Pre-Aelfredian poetry was all vernacular and all, in essence, orally disciplined, including 'Beowulf', the longest-surviving poem in Old English, written about a thousand years ago. It was sung, and its development was the responsibility of its singers; and so, roughly, things continued until the Norman Conquest. And in the long run, the English absorbed the Normans and the English language rose in importance.

The poetical literature that grew with it was again emphatically 'of the people' from Orm's 'Ormulum' (early thirteenth-century verse homilies by an Augustinian canon) to Langland's 'Vision of Piers Plowman' in 1362. 'Piers Plowman' might now be the province of university English departments, but in its own time it appealed to everyone. Written in the Old English manner in alliterative verse, it had an equal impact on those who wanted a reform of the Church and those labourers and serfs to whom Wat Tyler offered himself as a symbol of progress and hope.

Throughout the entire fifteenth century the divisive power of Chaucer's influence was fought by the ingredients of English life that worked towards keeping up the old cultural unity. In this transitional period, ballads, lays and so on blossomed alongside a renewed concern with classical literature. So the Elizabethan age that followed grew out of a cultural turmoil never equalled before or since, until our own times. Folk culture was intimately and creatively linked with literary culture in the age that has given us an unmatched richness of artistic achievement.

The links are clear enough in Shakespeare. He might have amused both the cockneys and the refined with his rustic caricatures – Bottom doing battle with Puck and the gentry – yet in his poetry he builds upon rural thought and metaphor, upon imagery springing naturally from a traditionally agricultural society. And so do the best of his contemporaries. As drama abandoned these folk foundations, and country communities went under to puritanism, so that drama declined.

All English literature lost out as a result, and the more recent onslaught of the Industrial Revolution made the loss irretrievable. As F. R. Leavis describes it, what was involved was '. . . not merely an idiomatic raciness of speech, expressing a strong

3.   Nik Cohn's *Awopbopaloobopalopbamboom: Pop from the Beginning* (1969) was a famous, successful book of its period, helping to create the Swinging London version of the New Journalism.

vitality, but an art of social living, with its mature habits of valuation. We must beware of idealizing, but the fact is plain. There would have been no Shakespeare . . . if . . . with all its disadvantages by present standards, there had not been, living in the daily life of the people, a positive culture which has disappeared.'[4]

At this stage in the narrative, enter John Bunyan, precursor in achievement of Bob Dylan. Although he was the worst, the least Miltonic, kind of puritan, epitomising narrow sectarianism, Bunyan restored the strengths of popular culture to mainstream literary culture after the two had gone their largely separate ways. He was thus Elizabethan in spirit, and he helped stave off the disappearance Leavis laments. Granted the new conditions, it is reasonable to say that what Bunyan did then, Dylan has done again: put the dynamics of folk culture back into sophisticated art, exalting the one to the level of the other's greatness.

The parallel between the two writers is worth pursuing: and to do so, it has to be said that *Pilgrim's Progress* is, in the best sense, a classic. Overriding its reductive intention – the disease of Calvinism trying to lacerate life with the stick of hell-fire – it offers an enriching humanitarianism.[5]

Its humanity comes across with that biblical dignity of expression which graces the language of all folk culture. Bunyan's work is a reminder of the powerful influence of the various English-language translations of the Bible, from Wyclif's version to the Authorized of 1611 – an influence that still operates powerfully on folk idiom both in England and America, as, indeed, Dylan's work testifies.[6] The Authorized version has been the most important: has been, for hundreds of years, the countryman's only book. In imagery and rhythm, it is popular, not classical; it harks back to and reflects the language of medieval England, while influencing seminally the language of twentieth-century America, especially black America.

Bunyan therefore harks back also to the language of medieval England – and so does Dylan. It is not mere coincidence – it is a question of common roots, shared cultural history. The Bible's linguistic influence is clear in all the kinds of American folk music dealt with in Chapter 1, all of which have affected Dylan's work.

As if to prove the point, Cecil Sharp discovered the popular culture Bunyan

4.   F. R. Leavis: 'Bunyan through Modern Eyes', in *The Common Pursuit* (1952) – though the topic of the old unity of folk and literary culture is aired more fully in another essay in the same collection, 'Literature and Society'.

5.   John Bunyan, *The Pilgrim's Progress: From This World to That Which Is to Come*, Part 1 published 1678, Part 2 in 1684. There is a brief discussion of Bunyan in relation to Dylan's 1983 song 'Jokerman' in Chapter 14, and in relation to 'Dignity' in Chapter 16.
      Bunyan's immense popularity and impact on mainstream literature won him few friends among the literary élite (sounds familiar?): '. . . Bunyan's *literary* reputation was almost non-existent before the Romantics, even among those who recommended *The Pilgrim's Progress* for religious instruction . . . Coleridge was one of the first literary voices raised in favour of Bunyan. Southey's 1830 edition of *The Pilgrim's Progress* . . . marked Bunyan's entry into the literary pantheon after a century and a half of well-bred put-downs.' So says Raphael Samuel, in his essay 'The discovery of Puritanism, 1820–1914', reprinted in his *Island Stories: Unravelling Britain – Theatres of Memory, Volume 2* (1998). This essay is a reminder of our shifting use and understanding of the term 'puritanism', and by extension of the unheeding way we bandy ideas in modish ways that we forget are merely modish, assuming them to have, instead, historical fixity.

6.   John Wyclif, c. 1320–1384. He and his followers translated the Bible into vernacular English for the first time, from St. Jerome's fourth-century Latin version (the Vulgate Bible), which had been used in English churches for a thousand years but understood only by the small, educated élite. (Wyclif translated the New Testament himself, though he didn't complete it.)

represented not fossilised but vitally alive in the remoter valleys of the Southern Appalachians during the First World War.[7]

Bunyan, then, is very much Dylan's forebear; and there are many and noticeable similarities of language in their work. It is from Bunyan, and certainly not from any rock'n'roll vocabulary, that Dylan gets this great and typical phrase from 'Joey' on the "Desire" album:

> . . . God's in heaven, overlooking His preserve.

And isn't this, for example, instantly recognisable as a line from the Dylan of the "John Wesley Harding" album?:

> Pray who are your kindred there, if a man may be so bold?

But it is not Bob Dylan, it is Christian in Pilgrim's Progress. And doesn't this comply almost exactly in rhythm and tone?:

> Oh what dear daughter beneath the sun could treat a father so:
> To wait upon him hand and foot and always answer no?

Thus Dylan's 'Tears Of Rage', which also illustrates, as do so many other Dylan songs, its creator's concern for salvation. In terms of the parallels with Bunyan, this is the nearest to a merely coincidental one, and yet even here coincidence is perhaps not the right word.

'Salvation' exposes universal predicaments which no serious writer ignores. Only the ideal behind the term has changed as succeeding philosophies have shifted it from generation to generation. Consequently, Dylan's idea of it was for a long time far from Bunyan's – though noticeably not very different from D. H. Lawrence's. When Bunyan was writing, of course, God existed. To his contemporary pamphleteers, salvation was a narrowly Christian matter (either you got there or you didn't) but it was a wider thing to Bunyan himself in spite of, not because of, his Calvinism. Since then God has been through many changes, all reducing his omnipotence. He has been through a career as Watchmaker Extraordinary in a Newtonian world – a career already made redundant by David Hume by the time Paley crystallised it – and on through Victorian loss of faith ('Oh God, if there is a God, Save my soul, if I have a soul!'), to twentieth-century oblivion and beyond.[8] The Dylan of the mid-1960s to

---

7.   Sharp raises this in Folk-Songs from the Southern Appalachians, ed. Maud Karpeles (1932) (from which F. R. Leavis quotes in 'Literature and Society', note 4).

Alan Lomax reminds us that 'these mountains were once the south-west frontier of the United States'. Those who arrived brought with them the banjo, dulcimer and fiddle, 'and they brought with them, as their invisible baggage, the great ballads of the past'. The Appalachians were 'Seventy thousand square miles of tangled green hills where British balladry could re-form itself while it was being cut to pieces by the Industrial Revolution back in England.' (Quoted from Lomax's TV documentary Appalachian Journey, Dibbs Productions for Channel 4 TV, London, 1990; video issued by Jane Balfour Films, London, 1990.)

(Karl Dallas reports: 'According to [A. L.] Lloyd [in Folk Song in England, 1957], legend has it that when Cecil Sharp was collecting in the Southern Appalachians . . . people sent messengers on ahead of him warning their friends to hide away their banjos and guitars, for Sharp's aversion to accompanied folksong became clear to them as soon as he started work. As a result, Sharp's treasured belief that the English – and Anglo-American – folksong tradition was largely an unaccompanied one was undisturbed.' [Karl Dallas: 'The Roots of Tradition' in The Electric Muse: The Story of Folk into Rock, by Dave Laing et al., 1975.])

8.   The 'prayer attributed to the Victorians', suggesting doubt rather than certainty as characteristic of the age, is cited in Walter E. Houghton's exemplary study The Victorian Frame of Mind (1957).

mid-1970s showed us our world too plagued and helpless easily to countenance that God was really dead. We identified with the tortured vision of the medieval Hieronymus Bosch. There was a serious anguish behind our trivia – hence the power of a book like Joseph Heller's *Catch-22*. With "Slow Train Coming" and "Saved", in 1979 and 1980, Dylan demands that we re-examine all this – and indeed that we re-examine Bunyan's vision and our notion of what our quest for salvation requires of us.[9]

What comes to mind on the impulse of Dylan's concern for salvation is a consciousness, modern yet universal, of how spiritual sickness damages the individual psyche. This is manifest in both Dylan's secular and religious work. It is a delicate thing, unspecific: a religious concern for life that need have nothing to do with theology. And in this sense, a Laurentian consciousness. Dylan points to this by projecting himself as spiritually healthy in a world that is patently not so; and confirming a sense of need, he attributes a similar quality to the women his songs celebrate:

> *My love she speaks like silence,*
> *Without ideals or violence,*
> *She doesn't have to say she's faithful*
> *Yet she's true like ice, like fire.*

There is more involved in that 'faithful' than a pop writer would be conscious of, and the clarifying 'like ice, like fire' suggests (with succinct understatement) just how much more. Again, the echo is of D. H. Lawrence: Lawrence deploring the merely lovable and trying to restore the elemental, asking us to go beyond a simplistic use of our senses, to be more real. Part of Lawrence's poem 'Elemental' runs:

> *Why don't people leave off being lovable*
> *or thinking they are lovable, or wanting to be lovable,*
> *and be a bit elemental instead? . . .*
>
> *I wish men would get back their balance among the elements*
> *and be a bit more fiery, as incapable of telling lies as fire is.*[10]

Dylan's 'she's true' plainly encompasses all this. Being true involves being true to yourself. True 'like ice, like fire'.

This sense of elemental tension comes up again and again in Dylan's work. In 'Gates Of Eden' we are given this image: 'With his candle lit into the sun / Though its glow is waxed and black' and in 'It's All Over Now, Baby Blue' there comes the expressive 'Crying like a fire in the sun'.

---

9.   The Dutchman Hieronymous Jerome Bosch (c. 1415–1516), whose painting foreshadowed surrealism and whose fantastical visions of hell's weird creatures and tormented souls (as in the *Garden of Earthly Delights*, c. 1505–10, now in the Prado Museum, Madrid), all making him highly popular in the twentieth century, was actually a well-to-do orthodox Catholic.

Joseph Heller, *Catch-22* (1961): an anti-war novel radical and individual in its hip black humour, which was widely loved and influential. One of those books that nudge the mood of the age along. In Britain it also occasioned the first use of the blurb line 'read it . . . and you'll never be quite the same again' (Corgi Books paperback, 5/-, 1964).

10.   D. H. Lawrence: 'Elemental', first published in *Pansies*, 1929.

At least as elemental, in 'Wedding Song', from the 1974 album "Planet Waves", is this:

> *Eye for eye and tooth for tooth*
> *Your love cuts like a knife*

where the Old Testament is invoked for its fierce, fundamental Jehovah power.[11] And again, from the same song:

> *What's lost is lost, we can't regain*
> *What went down in the flood . . .*
> *And I love you more than blood.*

Lawrence would have relished that one.

All this search for the quintessential man comes into an intelligent concern for salvation, a concern Dylan stands by in much of his work. It is there in 'Don't Think Twice, It's All Right' in the simple line (it is almost just a passing remark): 'Gave her my heart but she wanted my soul' and in his tender, appreciative 'To Ramona':

> *Your cracked country lips I still wish to kiss*
> *As to be by the strength of your skin,*
> *Your magnetic movements still capture the minutes I'm in.*

That 'strength' is felt by him, it implies a given moral strength, a Laurentian awareness of the real derived from an alertness of the physical senses.

Through the abrasive intelligence of work invested with such values, Dylan has changed a generation – has made it more sensitive to what is enhancing and what is impoverishing. It is as much as the artist can do.

It is to 'words' I now return. I have been tracing the historical links between, among other things, the language of folk culture and the language of literature. The creative links are worth examining too.

Why is it that there is such a marked similarity of impulse between idiom and poetic expression? How come the 'uneducated' countryman, whose life has been traditionally agricultural and whose vocabulary is limited, apparently carelessly produces those terse, ellipsed phrases that 'educated' people find unreachably admirable and evocative? Why is it that the unschooled Englishman or American with a rural background is closer to the poet than are most 'educated' men?

There are answers to these questions; and many a missing link thrown in as well, in an essay written by Adrian Bell and published over fifty years ago. It's an exciting essay (at least, it excited me). Bell argues:

> To understand how language is still reborn out of tradition in the unlettered mind
> . . . it is necessary to be immersed in the life until one thinks, as well as talks, in
> local usage. The countryman kindles as he speaks, assumes the authority of one
> rooted in his life, and that emotional quickening is the same in essence as the

11.   There is an exercise known as the Prisoner's Dilemma, which puts two people in a situation in which, locked into some form of mutual dependency, each must choose between cooperation or selfishness. It has been found that the best strategy is the simplest: tit for tat. (If the other cooperates, cooperate; if not, don't.) This is the new science of evolutionary psychology – but of course tit for tat is also the Old Testament received wisdom: an eye for an eye.

artist's – creative. In the glow of it he coins words. Linguistically, there is a kind of half-light in his brain, and on the impulse of an emotion, words get confused with one another and fused into something new – a new shade of meaning is expressed . . . [and the result is] not traditional words, but words born of momentary need out of tradition.

Bell concludes:

The countryman's speech is only roundabout to that superficial view which regards a poem as going a long way round to say what could be conveyed in a few words. Sustainedly, the emotional and muscular content of his idiom is almost equal to that of poetry for he possesses the same instinct by which the poet places words in striking propinquity: the urgency of his feeling causing his mind to leap intermediate associations, coining many a 'quaint' phrase, imaginatively just, though superficially bizarre.[12]

That phrase 'almost equal to poetry' stays in the mind – because isn't it exactly the half-praising, half-damning judgement that the work of a really good folk artist, a Woody Guthrie, inevitably receives? Thus such work is locked for ever within the labyrinth of its popular roots and fails to reach the notice of a literary public. Or much of a musical public, for that matter. Yet Bell's 'almost', coming after his other observations, shows again, I think, how natural and logical it is that a Dylan figure, like Bunyan before him, should have broken through the barriers to achieve recognised greatness by making the cultural mainstream from a folk source.

More than this, the section quoted above gives a striking insight, in effect, into the kind of poetry on the "Highway 61 Revisited" and "Blonde On Blonde" albums. It makes clear that the words on these albums do relate to what is normally agreed to be his folksong repertoire. It also gets us a lot further than most alternative accounts. It avoids (and exposes the emptiness of) the easy judgement of 'obscurity' – the judgement so often levelled at Dylan's mid-1960s work. It's ironic that while this 'obscurity' is so properly explained by attention to the creative impulse that makes for folk idiom, it should have been the folk purists who most vociferously condemned this section of Dylan's output.

There is another aspect of this general inquiry, which up to now has merely been stumbled against from time to time. That is: what has followed the 'positive culture' that Leavis says has disappeared? What has been the aftermath, for folk culture, of the twentieth-century acceleration in industrial technology? Are there any 'folk' left? What has happened to the countryman's life, daily and communal, now that the traditionally agricultural society is all but extinct in England and America?

Bell's essay deals with a part of this theme, though with fewer of the changes that have occurred this century, simply because he was writing in the early 1930s, and with a listing of the modern that has itself long since become poignantly quaint. That quaintness only makes his point the more tellingly, while his fundamental observations

---

12. Adrian Bell, 'English tradition and idiom', *Scrutiny*, Vol. 2, 1933; reprinted in *A Selection from Scrutiny, Volume II* (1968).

remain interesting and beautifully written. Tracing the decline of the 'uneducated' countryman in England, he writes of the young men:

> The first taste of education and standard English has had the effect of making them acutely self-conscious. They realise (and agricultural depression helps this) not that they stand supreme in a fundamental way of life but that they are the last left on a sinking ship. No-one decries civilization who has not experienced it ad nauseam. Modernity offers dim but infinite possibilities to the young countryman if only he can rid his boots of this impeding clay. Pylons, petrol pumps and other 'defacements' are to him symbols of a noble power. The motor-bus, motor-bicycle, wireless, are that power's beckonings. But he is late, he is held hapless in a ruining countryside, everyone else is laughing at him, he feels . . . The old men had their defence. They knew what they were. But he can't stay where they are. The contentment of it is gone.

And so Bell comes to argue that we

> must go to America for a modern counterpart of the old idiomatic vigour of common speech. American slang may be ugly and unpleasant, but it has the fascination of abounding vitality, hectic and spurious though that may be. It presupposes knowledge of a thousand sophistications, of intimacy with the life of a modern city, just as the traditional idiom presupposed a familiarity with nature and the processes of agriculture.

Bell underestimates the staying power of the old life, in England and America. In England many of the 'young countrymen' of 1933 held on in their agricultural villages and were still there in 'uneducated' old age – with their inventive idiom, despite their TV sets, by no means extinct. It is under pressure but it is not yet ruined. In America, agricultural living has hung on also, so that there is still no universal city idiom of the kind Bell plainly envisaged.[13]

Yet as early as 1925, Scott Fitzgerald was able to write to his publisher (from Paris, mind you) that 'the American peasant as "real" material scarcely exists. He is scarcely 10% of the population, isn't bound to the soil at all . . . and, if [he] has any sensitivity whatever (except a most sentimental conception of himself, which our writers persistently shut their eyes to), he is in the towns before he's twenty.'[14]

That too is oversimplified; but in Guthrie's *Bound for Glory*, and in the story of the blues – which is the story of an exodus from down-home to Chicago – we have the more complex truth: and it does not basically contradict Fitzgerald's view.

Dylan himself touches on this migration process in 'To Ramona':

> *I can see you are torn between staying and returning*
> *Back to the South . . .*

13. For a thorough and delightful confirmation that the ellipses of poetry are still thriving in the speech of rural and small-town Americans, you need only read William Least Heat-Moon's book *Blue Highways* (1983) in which he records the speech of dozens of such people encountered all along the backroads of the USA in 1978.

14. F. Scott Fitzgerald, letter to Maxwell Perkins, Paris, c. 1/6/25; in *The Letters of F. Scott Fitzgerald*, ed. Andrew Turnbull (1963). In the passage quoted, Fitzgerald is fulminating against the clichéd use of 'the American peasant' by contemporary novelists, and adds: '. . . using him as typical American material is simply *a stubborn seeking for the static in a world that for almost a hundred years had simply not been static*' [original emphasis].

and in effect again, on 'Slow Train':

> *I had a woman, down in Alabama*
> *She was a backwoods girl*
> *But she sure was realistic . . .*

As Thomas Wolfe said, you can't go home again.[15]

What remains, as much in England as in America, is an incredible hotch-potch of environmental influence. If it were otherwise, there would be no 'purist' folk movement, except in the museums and no problem in defining what today's folk music can be.

The hotch-potch echoes in the environment of countryman and city kid alike. McLuhan is right in the simple observation that you can't shut out sounds, ideas or people once they are globally broadcast. Not even the Southern Appalachian valley dweller can today have an insulated, self-expanding culture (if there ever was one). The language of even the oldest men and women must now be intruded by the language of American corporate television.

Everywhere in the West minority cultures are being tossed together and mixed with, on the one hand lumpen uniformity and on the other what passes as the *haute culture* of the age (and the process accelerates all the time), so that whatever our class or geographic centre, we have more in common with one another, more shared experience, than the men and women of any period since the heyday of the Elizabethan Age in England. Full circle. And this wheel's on fire – we are caught up in a kind of vulgar, neurotic renaissance. Hail the return, as McLuhan insists, to oral primacy.

Small wonder that Dylan should select, or rather, find himself at home in, an artistic medium not merely literary but involving a return to a medieval interdependence of words and music. 'Popular songs,' he said in 1965, 'are the only form that describes the temper of the times . . . That's where the people hang out. It's not in books; it's not on the stage; it's not in the galleries.'[16]

In the meantime, the uprooting confusion is in spate. The artist who doesn't try for 'originality' as something in limbo, but who uses re-creatively the heritage with his native air, must find himself today, not with a clearly defined background, but with a totally kaleidoscopic one ('collidescopic' is McLuhan's word).

Dylan's position inside the kaleidoscope is clear. A middle-class businessman's son, and Jewish, from small mid-western towns – Duluth and Hibbing, Minnesota – and then from the University of Minnesota, he had a perfectly natural exposure to innumerable winds of culture. The Mississippi River flows down from Minnesota through Iowa, Missouri, Arkansas and Louisiana – flows 1,700 miles to the Gulf of Mexico. For Dylan, Highway 61 leads to the dust-bowled 1930s, Kerouac and Kant, Chuck Berry's neon-California, the blues and Eliot's wasteland simultaneously.

---

15. *You Can't Go Home Again* is the title of a posthumously published (1940) novel by Thomas Wolfe (1900–1938). It may be, therefore, that Wolfe *didn't* say this at all; the novel was assembled, and possibly titled, by Edward C. Aswell.

16. Bob Dylan: re-quoted in 'The *Playboy* interview: Bob Dylan: a candid conversation with the iconoclastic idol of the folk-rock set', *Playboy*, March 1966.

If Dylan has grown in part from folk roots, so too literary culture has had its effect on his contribution. English and American literature is continued in Dylan's work: indeed is a wide-ranging presence within it.

First, it seems to me to contain many recollections of major English poets.[17] I have mentioned D. H. Lawrence already, if insufficiently; I have not yet dealt with others – with Donne, Blake, Browning and Eliot. (Eliot, of course, is American, not English, but I include him here because, like Henry James, he gave himself to Old World high culture.)

Dylan's work sometimes calls John Donne to mind, I think. Donne's modernity stems partly from the directness of statement so well represented in his famous opening lines: 'For Godsake hold your tongue, and let me love'; 'Now thou hast lov'd me one whole day'; 'Oh do not die, for I shall hate / All women so when thou art gone'.[18] One of Dylan's contributions has been to reintroduce such directness to white popular music.

(Black music, even in its pop-orientated forms, has always had a *double entendre* device so crude as to act as directness, effectively, as 1950s records like the Toppers' 'Let Me Bang Your Box' illustrate, though that is hardly metaphysical directness.)[19]

That Donne immediacy – directness balanced by intelligent discretion – is at work here:

> Go 'way from my window
> Leave at your own chosen speed

(the song is 'It Ain't Me, Babe'). And here:

> You got a lot o' nerve to say you are my friend

('Positively 4th Street'). And here:

> I hate myself for loving you

(the opening line of 'Dirge', from "Planet Waves").

These and others share with Donne more than plain directness – more than the conversational tone. More, even, than the measuredness both writers communicate, which takes its power from the sense that intellect is engaged in the communicating. Common to both is the bond between the passion and the rhythm.

---

17.   Not only major poets either. There is a widely reprinted poem Dylan seems to have come across 'from the fifteenth century', not in this case Italian but English, and anonymous, which has been given the title 'Western Wind' (though in its own day poems weren't titled). Dylan seems to have taken heed of this 'Western Wind' in his early song 'Tomorrow Is A Long Time'. Each of his three verses ends 'Only if she was lyin' by me / Would I lie in my bed once again'. The poem from five hundred years earlier, in its entirety, runs like this: 'Western wind, when wilt thou blow, / The small rain down can rain? / Christ, if my love were in my arms / And I in my bed again!'

The poem has been disseminated orally, like a folksong, for most of its history (in fact it's a fine example of the lack of separation between folk and literary culture), but it exists as a manuscript (British Museum MS. Royal Appendix 58) and has been collected repeatedly in twentieth-century anthologies, including both the Arthur Quiller-Couch *Oxford Book of English Verse* (1900–1930, 1939 and 1943, in which it has been titled 'The Lover in Winter Plaineth for the Spring') and the Helen Gardner *New Oxford Book of English Verse* (1972).

18.   John Donne (1572–1631). These opening lines are from 'The Canonization', 'Woman's Constancy' and 'A Feaver', all c. 1593–1601. Source: *John Donne: A Selection of His Poetry*, ed. John Hayward, 1950.

19.   The Toppers' 'Let Me Bang Your Box', NYC, 1954, Jubilee Records, 5136, New York, 1954.

It was another poet, Coleridge, who pointed this out in Donne's case. He wrote: 'To read Dryden, Pope, etc, you need only count syllables; but to read Donne you must measure Time, and discover the time of each word by the sense of Passion.'[20]

That must go down as an equally useful approach to Dylan's metre. Coleridge's point is proved by songs like 'The Lonesome Death Of Hattie Carroll' – or, come to that, 'Like A Rolling Stone'. The vibrant and intricate changes of rhythm in each occur through the investment of different words with differing degrees of feeling. In 'Hattie Carroll' the guitar-work enforces this relationship. It acts (as Chapter 1 also had occasion to note) as a musical graph of Dylan's heartbeats. The drumming on 'Like A Rolling Stone' does the same. (A much earlier example is the drumming on Presley's 'Hound Dog'.[21])

Another point in relation to Donne is this. Donne's tricksiness appeals to our habit of expending the intellect on trivia – and Dylan is not exempt from this, as songs from 'I Shall Be Free No. 10' through to 'Million Dollar Bash' transparently show. Donne in this sense suits our times very well. It takes a serious man to be funny; it takes a sizeable mind to write satisfying minor love songs. Donne would have made a great song writer for this reason. He could have done excellent, tricksy things for people like, say, Elvis Costello. A line from Donne's 'The Good-Morrow', for instance, would, adapted slightly, make a perfect Carole King title: 'You Make One Little Room An Everywhere'. And the phrase 'catch a falling star' originates with Donne, not Perry Como. The other John Donne opening that would work as intelligent, delicate, strong songwriting is that of his poem 'The Triple Foole':

> I am two fooles, I know,
> For loving, and for saying so
> In whining poetry . . .[22]

That shows perfectly the kind of conscious flirtation with ideas and nonsense that Dylan has exploited so well. The 1960s Dylan song most involved in this kind of tricksiness is perhaps '4th Time Around', from "Blonde On Blonde", with its stretched-out metaphors of sexual innuendo culminating in the rebounding pun on 'crutch' (dealt with in detail in Chapter 4), which Donne would have appreciated.

Finally, it is striking that Dylan finds it hard, just as Donne found, to subjugate his intensity and passion into an appropriate devotional stance in the later religious work. Both artists exhibit a constant difficulty with the war of the flesh and the spirit. Donne's secular love poetry gets to pointing towards Christ (notably in 'The

20. Coleridge, quoted from the Introduction in Hayward's book, *John Donne: A Selection of His Poetry*, which also quotes Coleridge's verse 'On Donne's Poetry', which begins with the splendid 'With Donne, whose muse on dromedary trots'. That last phrase, by chance, is paralleled (if parallels can be so bumpy) by Dylan's 'cemetery hips', from the opening song of the electric half of his 1966 concerts, 'Tell Me, Momma' (a parallel more pronounced when, on the bootleg that was for many years the only way to hear this, it sounded like 'cemetery kicks').

21. Elvis Presley: 'Hound Dog', NYC, 2/7/56; RCA Victor 47–6604, New York [HMV Records POP 249, London], 1956. The drummer is D. J. Fontana. On 'Like A Rolling Stone' the drummer is Bobby Gregg.

22. 'For love, all love of other sights controules, / And makes one little roome, an every where': 'The Good-Morrow'; 'Goe, and catche a falling starre' is the opening line of one of the two Donne poems titled 'Song'. These, plus the other 'Song' and 'The Triple Foole', quoted below in the main text, all belong to the period c. 1593–1601. Perry Como's record 'Catch A Falling Star' [NYC, 9/10/57] was, with 'Magic Moments' [NYC, 3/12/57], a double-sided hit in 1958 [RCA Records 20–7128, New York].

Canonization', where orgasm is likened to the death of Christ and the Resurrection) just as Dylan's does, on "Street Legal" and "Blood On the Tracks" in particular; and in the religious work of both men the passion they applied to lovers is no less lustily transferred to the Lord. At the same time, the religious work of both lacks general appeal, so that both artists end up with a substantial body of very popular secular work and a largely unheeded religious output.[23]

Going on to consider Bob Dylan in relation to William Blake, I turn first (taking the ridiculous before the sublime) to A. J. Weberman. Weberman called himself the world's only living Dylanologist, and gave up college to be so. He was sitting there in college and suddenly it came to him. 'Well fuck this shit, man,' he claims to have said to himself. 'Interpreting Dylan is a hundred times more interesting than going to school so I dropped out of school and became a Dylanologist full time . . . I really pushed my brain and I began to get some insight into Dylan.' Weberman played detective. He sniffed through files, kept an ear to the ground for useful rumours and combed Dylan's output for coded messages. Example: when Dylan uses the word 'lady' he means 'oligarchy'. So pushing our brains and letting insight dawn, we have 'Lay, Oligarchy, Lay', 'Sad-Eyed Oligarchy of the Lowlands' and so on.[24]

I bring this in here because there is an excellent reply to Weberman's position in an article by Greil Marcus and because the reply Marcus offers brings in, and usefully, William Blake.

Marcus explains the existence of Webermanesque interpretations by saying that people apparently have a need to know

> if Dylan is a transvestite or on heroin or stubbed his toe buying beer; and they want to convince themselves that Dylan is . . . wonderfully obscure and ambiguous, so that they won't have to feel insecure about listening to someone who did, after all, play all that really loud music that got in the way of the words. The game is still going on . . . 'As I Went Out One Morning', a song in which Tom Paine guest stars, is about a dinner Dylan attended years ago, at which he was presented with the Tom Paine Award by the Emergency Civil Liberties Committee. Dylan, during his acceptance speech, said something about how he might understand how Lee Harvey Oswald felt, and the audience booed. This interpretation makes Dylan a real interesting guy. He waits for years to get a chance to get back at an unfriendly audience, and all Tom Paine means to him is the bad memory of an award dinner. Poor Tom Paine. The fellow who came up with this job [Weberman] has said: 'I consider Bob Dylan America's greatest poet.' Well, naturally; why should such a mind waste his time on a lesser figure? It's not just

---

23.   John Hayward, in *John Donne: A Selection of His Poetry*, quotes a 'friend' of Donne making a comment that many will feel rings an approximate bell in Dylan's case: i.e. that Donne wrote 'all his best pieces ere he was twenty-five years old'. Hayward notes too that 'Donne did not suddenly sober down when he took Holy Orders at the age of forty-three.'

24.   I can't now locate the source of these quotations. Weberman's fame rested on his much-mooted but neverseen *Dylan Concordance*, his founding of the Dylan Liberation Front (he held a street party outside Dylan's Greenwich Village home on his 30th birthday), his taped phone-conversations with Dylan ('Dylan Meets Weberman', *East Village Other*, 19/1/71; *nia*) and his raids on Dylan's garbage can. This last, his real contribution, was an innovation in critical biography. Weberman's *My Life in Garbology* (1980) devotes its main chapter to Dylan and his dustbins. An affectionate account by John Bauldie of 'A meeting with Weberman, summer of '82', is in *All Across the Telegraph: A Bob Dylan Handbook*, ed. Michael Gray and John Bauldie (1987).

that such terms are pointless . . . but is this sort of thing – the Tom Paine Award Dinner Revenge – is this what makes a great poet?

Poetry, music, songs, stories, are all part of that realm of creation that deepens our lives and can endow our lives with a special kind of grace, tension, perhaps with beauty and splendor. Meaning has many levels – one might meet the artist himself on one of those levels, find friends on another, reach a fine solitude in the light of another man's creation on yet another level. That kind of power in art might be scary – it might be sure enough to survive interpretation and the enforcement of the particular . . . Take these lines from 'London' by William Blake:

> But most thro' midnight streets I hear
> How the youthful Harlot's curse
> Blasts the newborn infant's tear
> And blights with plagues the Marriage hearse.

Now what that 'means', it was once explained to me, is that a prostitute got syphilis, gave birth to a deformed child, the father of which also died of the disease . . . That can all be confirmed by balancing and referring the images in the verse – but is it necessary to grasp that . . . in order to feel the weight and power of Blake's vision of London? Blake's words transcend the situation about which he's writing.

Likewise, says Marcus, with Dylan: 'One will never "understand" 'Just Like A Woman' by proving, logically, that it is about transvestites or Britain (Queen Mary and the fog) even if, by some chance, the song really is "about" such things.'[25]

Dylan himself argues this case graphically at the end of 'Gates of Eden' where he commends his lover for valuing her dreams

> With no attempts to shovel the glimpse
> Into the ditch of what each one means.

(He won't like Chapter 7 of this book, which is, against my usual grain, biographically expositional.)

It isn't surprising that Marcus invokes Blake when alluding to the meaning of 'meaning' in poetry. This is partly because Blake's words are his own much more emphatically than with most poets. Blake fought off the vagueness and tiredness of meaning that common social usage imposes on words, by simply refusing to recognise that vagueness. His own thought didn't succumb to it, so his writing disregards it. He concentrated his thought. A great deal of intellect is telescoped (and used in the process of telescoping) into very few lines in his poetry.

---

25. Greil Marcus: 'Let the record play itself', *San Francisco Express-Times*, 11/2/69.

And compare those lines of Blake's on London with these of Dylan on New York; Blake's stark visionary influence is clear: 'I went out on Lower Broadway / And I felt that place within / That hollow place where martyrs weep / And angels play with sin'.

William Blake, 'London' [from *Songs of Experience* (1794), published together with *Songs of Innocence* (1789) as *Songs of Innocence and Songs of Experience: Shewing the Two Contrary States of the Human Soul* in 1794]. Bob Dylan: 'Dirge', 1974.

And yet, if Blake's words are in this way his own, don't his poems belong actually to the reader?

> *And did those feet in ancient time*
> *Walk upon England's mountains green?*
> *And was the holy Lamb of God*
> *On England's pleasant pastures seen?*
>
> *And did the Countenance Divine*
> *Shine forth upon our clouded hills?*
> *And was Jerusalem builded here*
> *Among these dark Satanic Mills?*
>
> *Bring me my Bow of burning gold:*
> *Bring me my Arrows of desire:*
> *Bring me my Spear: O clouds unfold!*
> *Bring me my Chariot of fire.*
>
> *I will not cease from Mental Fight,*
> *Nor shall my Sword sleep in my hand*
> *Till we have built Jerusalem*
> *In England's green and pleasant Land.*

That is a hymn, in England.[26] The scholarship of F. W. Bateson, on the other hand, emerged in 1950 with an interpretation so different as to be ironic. Blake wrote it, Bateson established, as an anti-ecclesiastical manifesto. The altars of Anglican churches were the 'dark Satanic Mills' that clouded men's vision of spiritual reality and polluted the sanctity of man's desires.[27]

But what about the hymn? What about the meaning almost everyone except Bateson and Blake himself has given that poem? We have had D. H. Lawrence's answer: never trust the artist, trust the tale.

The Blakeian influence on Dylan is apparent first as a question of 'thought': that is, in a labour of thought that achieves an economy of language by its concentration, and a tone almost of disinterestedness about what is actually experienced with intense emotion by the writer. In Blake we see this, for instance, in 'The Sick Rose'. In Dylan we see it in the make-up of the "John Wesley Harding" album (especially on 'I Dreamed I Saw St. Augustine') and in other individual songs throughout his repertoire. It is there, for example, in a song already looked at, 'Love Minus Zero/No Limit'.

26.   The hymn, with music by Hubert Parry, is known as 'Jerusalem', but the poem is part of Blake's preface to *Milton: A Poem in Two Books, To Justify the Ways of God to Men*, 1803–8. Blake's long poem *Jerusalem: The Emanation of the Giant Albion* (1804–20) is a wholly different work.

27.   F. W. Bateson: *English Poetry: A Critical Introduction* (1950).
    You don't have to go far through even the best known work of Blake to get at a clearer statement of his views on the debilitating effects of institutionalised religion. 'The Garden of Love' is representative: 'I went to the Garden of Love / And saw what I never had seen: / A Chapel was built in the midst, / Where I used to play on the green. / And the gates of this Chapel were shut, / And 'Thou Shalt Not' writ over the door; / So I turn'd to the Garden of Love / That so many sweet flowers bore; / And I saw it was filled with graves, / And tombstones where flowers should be; / And Priests in black gowns were walking their rounds / And binding with briars my joys and desires'. ('The Garden of Love' in *Songs of Experience*.)

That song, in fact, refers to the same theme as 'The Sick Rose': the theme of possessiveness destroying love.

Blake's short poem comes from *Songs of Experience* and runs as follows:

> *O Rose, thou art sick!*
> *The invisible worm*
> *That flies in the night,*
> *In the howling storm,*
> *Has found out thy bed*
> *Of crimson joy:*
> *And his dark secret love*
> *Does thy life destroy.*

Dylan deals with this same theme by positing an antithetical consciousness – an awareness of what a love that is not like a sick rose needs for survival:

> *My love she speaks like silence*
> *Without ideals or violence*
> *She doesn't have to say she's faithful*
> *Yet she's true like ice, like fire.*

The awareness I mention is conveyed by Dylan confronting the listener with a series of contrasts: the contrast between 'without ideals' and '[without] violence' – both of which colour that 'silence'; and the contrast (noted in an earlier context) between the tired, socially dulled 'faithful' and 'true' and the qualifying, regenerative 'like ice, like fire'.

As if thrown at these quick-firing contrasts, the listener is himself thrown into thought: he must flex his mental limbs or drown; and so, with the effort of swimming, he becomes conscious of the values Dylan conveys in the song, and aware that they are the values of health in love. Blakeian values, put across with Blakeian economy.

Very much like Blake's 'The Sick Rose', the brevity of 'Love Minus Zero/No Limit' belies its importance. It is light, delicate, poised; yet it handles intensely felt emotional experience, experience distilled by thought, so that what we are offered has neither an obtrusive atmosphere of intense feeling – none, as Leavis said of Blake, 'of the Shelleyan "I feel, I suffer, I yearn" ' – nor an obtrusive suggestion of how much intellect has gone into its making.[28]

One might apply that contrast of Blake and Shelley to one of the essential differences between Dylan and another poet–singer, Leonard Cohen. Cohen in any case often paddles in the maudlin, but an associated weakness in his work is exactly that Shelleyan quality of saying, as it were, 'Look at me: God! I'm sensitive!' A fundamental strength of Dylan's sensitivity is to avoid calling attention to itself.

---

28. The source of this Leavis quotation now eludes me, but its justification is to be found in the chapter on Shelley in Leavis' *Revaluation: Tradition and Development in English Poetry* (1936).

T. S. Eliot wrote that Blake had nothing to distract him from, or corrupt, his interests.[29] One thinks, in contrast, of the pressures on Dylan – the films *Don't Look Back*, *Eat the Document* and (even) *Renaldo & Clara* exposed their enormity – and yet how little he has allowed them to interfere with his preoccupations. 'I'm not interested in myself as a performer,' said Dylan in 1966.

> Performers are people who perform for other people. Unlike actors, I know what I'm saying. It's very simple in my mind. It doesn't matter what kind of audience reaction this whole thing gets. What happens on stage is straight. It doesn't expect any reward or fines from any kind of outside agitators . . . [It] would exist whether anybody was looking or not.[30]

And when Eliot tells us that Blake approached everything with a mind unclouded by current opinions, we can profitably reflect on how little of Dylan's variegated achievement has been shadowed by the clouds of other people's ideas. Dylan has had to reject other people's ideas of what singing should be, what song writing formulae dictate, what the pseudo-ethnic togetherness of his early Greenwich Village patrons demanded, and more besides. There is the additional testimony of his determined move over to what others labelled Folk-rock, then Acid-rock; his adroit retreat from all outside affairs from late 1966 until nearly two years later; his (infuriating to others) residence in New York State while an acid-rock/psychedelic scene he had played an unwitting part in founding played on into hopeless narcissistic decadence in California; and all his more recent pushes against the tide of the times.

Dylan and Blake share also the desire to fight off accusations of abnormality. Blake found it astonishing and perplexing that people should have considered him and his work deliberately puzzling and peculiar; Dylan told *Playboy*, in their mammoth interview with him in 1966 '. . . people actually have the gall to think that I have some kind of fantastic imagination. It gets very lonesome.'[31]

This commonly felt sense of isolation provokes stunningly similar face-pulling defiance in Blake and Dylan. Blake produced 'Island In The Moon' (written around 1784–85) and Dylan wrote waspish liner-notes on the "Highway 61 Revisited" album (1965). They share striking convergences of tone and technique. The following is from 'Island In The Moon':

> in a great hurry, Inflammable Gass the Wind-finder enter'd. They seem'd to rise & salute each other. Etruscan Column & Inflammable Gass fix'd their eyes on each other; their tongues went in question and answer, but their thoughts were otherwise employ'd. 'I don't like his eyes,' said Etruscan Column. 'He's a foolish puppy,' said Inflammable Gass, smiling on him. The 3 Philosophers – the Cynic smiling, the Epicurean seeming studying the flame of the candle, & the Pythagorean playing with the cat – listen'd with open mouths . . . Then Quid call'd upon

---

29.   T. S. Eliot, 'William Blake', 1920, in *Selected Essays 1917–1932* (1932). Eliot's assertion is not borne out by studies of Blake's life, however. It's very clear from Peter Ackroyd's *Blake* (1995) that recurrent penury very greatly 'distracted him from his interests'.
  Eliot's essay is further discussed in Chapter 12, note 14.

30.   'The *Playboy* interview': see note 16.

31.   'The *Playboy* interview'.

Obtuse Angle for a song, & he, wiping his face & looking on the corner of the
ceiling, sang: To be or not to be/Of great capacity/Like Sir Isaac Newton,/Or
Locke, or Doctor South . . .[32]

And from the sleeve of Dylan's "Highway 61 Revisited":

Savage Rose & Openly are bravely blowing kisses to the Jade Hexagram –
Carnaby Street & To all of the mysterious juveniles & the Cream Judge is writing
a book on the true meaning of a pear – last year, he wrote one on famous dogs of
the Civil War & now he has false teeth and no children . . . when the Cream met
Savage Rose & Openly, he was introduced to them by none other than Lifelessness
– Lifelessness is the Great Enemy & always wears a hipguard – he is very hipguard
. . . Lifelessness said when introducing everybody 'go save the world' & 'involvement! that's the issue' & things like that & Savage Rose winked at Openly & the
Cream went off with his arm in a sling singing 'so much for yesterday' . . . the
clown appears – puts a gag over Autumn's mouth & says 'there are two kinds of
people – simple people & normal people' this usually gets a big laugh from the
sandpit & White Heap sneezes – passes out & wakes up & rips open Autumn's
gag & says 'What do you mean you're Autumn and without you there'd be no
Spring! you fool! without Spring, there'd be no you! what do you think of that???'
then Savage Rose & Openly come by & kick him in the brains & colour him pink
for being a phony philosopher – then the clown comes by . . . & some college kid
who's read all about Nietzsche comes by & says 'Nietzsche never wore an
umpire's suit' & Paul says 'you wanna buy some clothes, kid?' & then Rose &
John come out of the bar & they're going up to Harlem . . .

When you consider in relation to Blake what is a difficult and central work of Dylan's,
you come inevitably to 'Gates of Eden'. The purposive force of what is palpably
Blakeian impinges in every verse. It is the major Dylan song prior to 'Every Grain Of
Sand' that is most like Blake, and like the most characteristic Blake at that. It begins
with this:

> *Of war and peace the truth just twists*
> *Its curfew gull just glides*
> *Upon four-legged forest clouds*
> *The cowboy angel rides*
> *With his candle lit into the sun*
> *Though its glow is waxed in black*
> *All except when 'neath the trees of Eden.*

And after seven others comes this concluding verse:

> *At dawn my lover comes to me*
> *And tells me of her dreams*

32. 'Island In The Moon' was left untitled and unpublished by Blake; first publication was in E. J. Ellis, *The Real
Blake* (1907). This work was a product of the co-editorship of Blake's work by Ellis and W. B. Yeats – 'Blake's
first proper editors', as Peter Ackroyd says in *Blake* (1995). Yeats' editorial work on Blake was done in 1893.
(There is a note in Chapter 7 on Dylan's possible use of Yeats' poem 'Vacillation'.)

With no attempts to shovel the glimpse
Into the ditch of what each one means;
At times I think there are no words
But these to tell what's true
And there are no truths outside the Gates of Eden.

In the whole, we have what Eliot, talking of Blake, calls naked vision.

The general themes of 'Gates of Eden' could not be more Blakeian and nor could their treatment. Dylan is treating of balances of opposites – of material wealth and spiritual; of earthly reality and the imaginatively real; of the body and soul; of false gods and true vision; of self-gratification and salvation; of mortal ambitions and the celestial city; of sins and forgiveness; of evil and good.

Not only are these Blake's themes, but they receive directly comparable handling. Both artists address themselves 'not to common sense, but to individual sense'. For Blake, as Max Plowman phrased it,

> all things existed in Eternity ... All things had external existence, and their manifestation in Time was a subjective sensory impression . . . and what he desired to do was to restore to the minds of men the continuous consciousness of infinity which he believed rationalism – or the tyranny of the reasoning over the poetic faculty – had largely obliterated ... He spoke of 'seeing the Eternal which is always present to the wise'; and said that 'if the doors of perception were cleansed, everything would appear to man as it is, infinite!'[33]

'Gates of Eden' is certainly an attempt to focus attention on that 'continuous consciousness of infinity', an attempt to point through the doors of perception; and Dylan's vision takes in our world, a world which largely fails to see 'the Eternal which is always present to the wise'.

Dylan tries to harmonise with (it is the Blakeian use of the phrase, meaning to come level with) songs the lonesome sparrow sings: the sparrow flying, humbly enough, between the earth and the heavens, passing between and observing equally the time-trapped foolish and the real, the infinite. The vision evokes this balance of flight, this tracking between opposites.

(Perhaps I'm appropriating the sparrow to an extent here. In the context, it must shoulder – if sparrows have shoulders – its biblical responsibilities. We meet these again in relation to 'Every Grain Of Sand', the subject of Chapter 12. Not a bird valued or admired by society, it is thereby more easily possible for the sparrow's sense of proportion to remain intact. Its salvation need not involve the difficulties of the proverbial camel negotiating the needle.)

This evocation of balance is very neatly enforced by the contrasts completed in every verse of the song

> *. . . he weeps to wicked birds of prey*
> *Who pick up on his breadcrumb sins.*
> *There are no sins inside the gates of Eden.*

33. Max Plowman, *An Introduction to the Study of Blake*, 2nd edn (1967). The Blake quotation about 'the doors of perception' is touched on further in Chapter 6.

and

> . . . *men wholly totally free*
> *To do anything they wish to do but die*

and

> . . . *the princess and the prince discuss*
> *What's real and what is not*

and many more. Friends and other strangers, the glimpse and the ditch, a savage soldier who merely complains, the candle cradled into the sun.

This elaborate establishing of opposite poles has its corollary in the frequent internal rhymes which lend weight to the underlying duality of everything presented. Waxed and black; all in all can only fall; Aladdin and his lamp; relationships of ownership; the foreign sun it squints upon; wholly totally free; no attempts to shovel the glimpse.

Not only do the contrasts referred to enforce a sense of the ever-present balance the song establishes: they also clarify its nature. The glimpse and the ditch focus the gulf between the perceptions of reason and of the poetic faculty; the incongruity of prince and princess discussing 'reality' makes vivid the same dichotomy.

I can't claim it's all crystal-clear. There is plenty that seems, to me at least, irrevocably obscure. The third verse, for instance, certainly evades me. It isn't that nothing of it impinges. There is a great deal of power in its last three lines, a power that has to do with the visual imagery at that point, with the dream picture:

> *Upon the beach where hound-dogs bay*
> *At ships with tattooed sails,*
> *Heading for the Gates of Eden.*

That word 'sails' impersonates the verb more than the noun, producing the movement of a huge black fleet sailing. Somehow there is a powerful accompanying sense of silence and finally a pure dramatic force given by the combination of that silence with the purposive, inevitable momentum of 'Heading, for, the Gates, of Eden'. This dramatic impact is electrified by the interplay of words and tune. With great sureness of touch, that 'Heading, for', introduced with a switch to a more economic rhythm, stays on the same musical note as 'sails' and so darkens the sense of purposiveness already noted.

Yet the rest of the verse fails to elicit much response beyond a sneaking desire to ask the kind of questions that Weberman might ask. Who is the deafened, shoeless hunter? Is it an event, or normality, for hounds to sit on beaches baying out to sea? Are the hounds coyotes and the sea therefore really a desert? Is the soldier Buffy Sainte-Marie's Universal Soldier, whose ostrich-act is to say, well, I'm just doing my job, and who is answerable to the politicians – shoeless hunters in that they do their fighting vicariously?[34] And if so, could the baying hounds be the Great Silent Majority

34. Buffy Sainte-Marie: 'The Universal Soldier', NYC, 1963–64, LP-issued "It's My Way!", Vanguard Records VRS 9142, New York, 1964. The lyric is published in *Poetry of Relevance 1*, ed. Homer Hogan (1970).

baying for the blood of those who frighten them, those with vision: pirates, ships with tattooed sails?

It's no good if you want to ask that sort of question: it's obscure because it only holds your interest on the surface. Its power is infirmly argumentative, not poetic, and so it doesn't convince. The poetic force lies in that part of the song that doesn't encourage questions but gives the imagination and the emotions palpable answers, yielding insights of poetic reality.

More than enough of 'Gates of Eden' does that. The song as a whole accommodates infinite replaying. It is effectively reminiscent of Blake, but it ranks as a major achievement and gets its Blakeian stature on its own merits. It has every distinction of great poetry, flawed but indestructible.[35]

'Gates of Eden' crops up again – to the extent that its form is the dramatic monologue – when we come down a little nearer to earth to consider Bob Dylan and Robert Browning together.

Notes Towards A Definition: the dramatic monologue differs from the soliloquy, to which it superficially approximates, in starting with an already established perspective, instead of searching for one as it runs its course. It looks outwards, so that self-revelation appears incidental. It takes the form of a one-sided conversation – half of a dialogue in which the imagined other participant gets only an implicit hearing. It is an open-ended excerpt from the mind of the speaker: it has, in Robert Langbaum's words, '. . . no necessary beginning and end but only arbitrary limits, limits which do not cut the action off from the events that precede and follow, but shade into those events, suggesting as much as possible of the speaker's whole life and experience'.[36] The unity of the form is its singleness of viewpoint: there is none of the inward search for such a viewpoint that characterises the soliloquy and gives that form its very different purpose and possibilities.

Browning mastered, as no one before him, this form – the dramatic monologue. Dylan has used it as no one else since.

Not that the similarity ends there. This is Browning (from 'Up at a Villa – Down in the City', published in *Men and Women*, 1855):

> Look, two and two go the priests, then the monks with cowls and sandals
> And the penitents dressed in white shirts, a-holding the yellow candles
> One, he carries a flag up straight, and another a cross with handles,
> And the Duke's guard brings up the rear, for the better prevention of scandals.

This is Dylan (from 'Subterranean Homesick Blues'):

> Better jump down a manhole
> Light y'self a candle,
> Don't wear sandals,
> Try to avoid the scandals

---

35.   As noted, Blake's influence on Dylan is discussed again, essentially in relation to Dylan's 'Every Grain Of Sand', in Chapter 12. The influence of that other great pre-Victorian poet, John Keats (1795–1821), is discussed, in relation especially to Dylan's 'Jokerman', in Chapter 14.

36.   Robert Langbaum, *The Poetry of Experience: The Dramatic Monologue in Modern Literary Tradition* (1957). Langbaum has written extensively on Robert Browning's work.

> *Don't wanna be a bum*
> *Y' better chew gum*
> *The pump don't work*
> *'Cause the vandals*
> *Took the handles.*

When Browning uses such rhyme schemes, G. K. Chesterton dismisses them as 'only mathematical triumphs, not triumphs of any kind of assonance'. When Dylan writes like that, Ewan MacColl pulls a face.[37] Both miss the point. The Browning piece works because the rhyme's preposterousness is consciously embraced as part of the irony. Dylan's works similarly. You can't make the effort of rhyming 'manhole' with 'candle' and then pile up sandals, scandals, vandals and handles in such proximity without being deliberate about it. In Dylan's music this purposiveness is complemented by the clipped concentration on four neighbouring notes – a concentrated musical 'monotony' that very neatly associates itself with the lyric idea of gum-chewing, so that the deadpan element of delivery is double-barrelled.

There is more in the comparison of those two passages than the startling parallel in rhyming words. If you read out the Browning verse in Bob Dylan's "Blonde On Blonde" voice (relishing Dylanesque words like 'penitents') you find them perfectly compatible. The brand of irony exhibited is common to both. Elsewhere, this shows up in equally dramatic similarities of technique. Part of Browning's 'Bishop Blougram's Apology' (also from *Men and Women*) runs as follows:

> *You Gigadibs, who, thirty years of age*
> *Write statedly for Blackwood's Magazine*
> *Believe you see two points in Hamlet's soul*
> *Unseized by the Germans yet . . .*

In 'Ballad Of A Thin Man' Dylan sings:

> *You've been with the professors and they've all liked your looks*
> *With great lawyers you have discussed lepers and crooks*
> *You've bin through all of F. Scott Fitzgerald's books*
> *You're very well read, it's well known;*
> *But something is happening here and you don't know what it is,*
> *Do you, Mr Jones?*

These two examples of mockery – adopting almost the same tone of voice, the difference being merely that the Bishop has to sound middle-aged and the Dylan persona sounds younger – become identical in tone when addressing their silent interlocutors. You, Gigadibs. Do you, Mr Jones?

Not only do the techniques resemble each other – and strongly enough to add to the impression that Dylan has looked acquisitively at Robert Browning's work. They are put to comparable uses. Both attack the complacency which makes men use their intellects as blindfolds. Norman Mailer says that people smoke cigarettes to distance

---

37.   G. K. Chesterton, *Robert Browning* (1903). Ewan MacColl was 'unable to see in [Dylan] anything other than a youth of mediocre talent': 'A symposium', *Sing Out!*, September 1965.

themselves from experience; Browning and Dylan maintain that burning up with the theoretical has the same effect. Bishop Blougram reproves Gigadibs for not being alive to the real world; Dylan posits the artificial safeness of vicarious living. And the same song extends his attack (and with mathematical rhymes again, too):

> You have many contacts
> Among the lumberjacks
> To get you facts
> When someone attacks
> Your imagination.

The same theme is echoed in Dylan's 'Tombstone Blues':

> Now I wish I could write you a melody so plain
> That could hold you, dear lady, from going insane
> That could ease you, and cool you, and cease the pain
> Of your useless and pointless knowledge

and perhaps also in 'Temporary Like Achilles':

> I'm trying to read your poetry
> But I'm helpless like a rich man's child . . .

and again, with a different focus, in 'Desolation Row':

> Her profession's her religion,
> Her sin is her lifelessness.

When the irony of Browning, as well as of Dylan, turns to this theme of life versus nullity of experience, the results are comparable more than once. Here is Browning again:

> Lord so-and-so – his coat bedropped with wax
> All Peter's chains about his waist, his back
> Brave with the needlework of Noodledom
> Believes!

Here is Dylan (again from 'Desolation Row'):

> And Ezra Pound and T. S. Eliot
> Fighting in the captain's tower,
> While calypso singers laugh at them
> And fishermen hold flowers
> Between the windows of the sea
> Where lovely mermaids flow
> And nobody has to think too much
> About Desolation Row

and Browning again:

> *you know physics, something of geology,*
> *Mathematics are your pastime; souls shall rise in their degree;*
> *Butterflies may dread extinction, – you'll not die, it cannot be!*

In Dylan's 'Desolation Row' we have a classic utilisation of the dramatic monologue form, with its exposition of how one mind sees the world around it, so that to listen to the song is like watching a film shot entirely from one camera angle, an angle that would not be one's own. But what may consequently appear fantastic is real. Implicitly throughout the song, and explicitly here at the end, Dylan argues the sanity of his 'perverse' perspective:

> *Right now I can't read too good*
> *Don't send me no more letters, no:*
> *Not unless you mail them from*
> *Desolation Row.*

In all this, Dylan's use of the dramatic conforms to Browning's use of it.

The differences are in the scope of the form in the hands of the two artists. Browning usually identifies the narrator and his environment explicitly; Dylan often fills in these details only implicitly – frequently using a belated introduction of his persona's position to achieve a particular effect. Thus in 'Desolation Row' it is only in the final verse that the persona dwells on his own position at all, and it is sprung on the listener that the whole song has been communicating on a person-to-person, and intensely personal, level:

> *When you asked me how I was doing*
> *Was that some kind of joke?*

And as we come upon this deliberately held-back switch from an apparently generally polemical dream to the personal pressing involvement of 'you', 'me' and 'I', the urgency and power of the vision Dylan offers is effectively magnified.

In 'Gates of Eden' the technique is the same. The last stanza so fixes the perspective that the rest of the song is thrown back upon us, with a demand for an immediate reassessment. The end of the song gives us the narrator's reflection that

> *At times I think there are no words*
> *But these to tell what's true*
> *And there are no truths outside the gates of Eden.*

and, quoting Steve MacDonogh, 'we are brought back to the starting-point of the monologue, where "The truth just twists / Its curfew gull just glides." . . . [and we] are made to examine what has gone before, the mention of the speaker's lover – providing the dramatic location of the song – bringing us back to a more concrete . . . level of understanding.'[38]

Another difference in the use to which Browning and Dylan put the dramatic monologue is that, whereas Browning projects varied fictional characters, Dylan, like

---

38. Steve MacDonogh co-founded, with the present writer, a small modern poetry magazine with a large title, *Cosmos*, in May 1969. Around then he wrote an essay (unpublished), 'Robert Browning and Bob Dylan: The dramatic monologue' (seventeen pages, undated) and generously allowed me to use it.

other modern poets, projects himself. This is one reason why (as, in fact, with F. Scott Fitzgerald, whose fictional heroes were largely himself from the unfortunate Anthony Patch to the unfortunate Mr Hobby) it is often exceptionally difficult to distinguish the created character from the man.[39]

There is a consequent further divergence between Browning's conventions and Dylan's. With Browning, the silent interlocutor is not merely silent but actually unnecessary. A mere tip of the hat to Victorian expectations. In contrast, Dylan's 'silent' interlocutor is not merely eloquent in helping to draw out the narrator's mood and predicament, but in many cases has a felt presence the exploration of which is central to the song's purpose.

In his songs to women, where they are the 'silent' ones, the portrayal of their characters is a main ingredient. On "Blonde On Blonde", for example, the image of a particular woman is deliberately established by the one-sided dialogue in 'Most Likely You Go Your Way (And I'll Go Mine)':

> You say my kisses are not like his
> But this time I'm not gonna tell you why that is
> I'm just gonna let you pass
> Yes and I'll go last . . .

By attributing to the woman the clichéd thought exposed in that first line, this 'exchange' shows itself as much concerned to colour in the woman as the narrator himself.

The same emphasis of purpose is apparent in many other songs – in '4th Time Around', where two women are portrayed in this extraordinarily implicatory way; in 'One Of Us Must Know (Sooner Or Later)'; 'Leopard-Skin Pill-Box Hat'; even in 'I'll Be Your Baby Tonight' to some extent; and perhaps most of all in 'Positively 4th Street':

> You see me on the street,
> You always act surprised;
> You say How Are You? – Good Luck!
> But you don't mean it
> When you know as well as me
> You'd rather see me paralysed:
> Why don't you just come out once and scream it?

The effect, in this passage, hardly depends at all on the 'How Are You?' and the 'Good Luck!' that the woman is permitted to actually say: the force of his portrayal comes from that masterfully irregular last line. Its length and pent-up cadence half-echo, half-mimic the scream she won't reveal: effectively, we see it in her eyes, hear it

39.   Anthony Patch is the hero of Fitzgerald's second novel, *The Beautiful and Damned* (1922) and, like Fitzgerald, an alcoholic; *The Pat Hobby Stories*, written in the last months of Fitzgerald's life and similarly autobiographical, were published posthumously in 1962.

in her head, and we can see her standing there. In all these songs, we see the women's faces, as we never do with Browning's Gigadibs.[40]

Abandoning the dramatic monologue at this suitable juncture, it has to be said that there are two other notable corridors between Dylan's work and Robert Browning's. The first is their equal relish for the blatantly grotesque.

Chesterton, thinking of Behemoth in the book of Job, wrote that 'the notion of the hippopotamus as a household pet is curiously in the spirit of the humour of Browning'.[41] It has the appeal of incongruity, and this scatters itself throughout Browning's work, in rhymes, names, ludicrous alliteration (that 'needlework of Noodledom') and in a Puckish garlanding together of temperamental incompatibles, as in 'The Cardinal and the Dog' (1890). In this short poem, the Cardinal lies on his death-bed at Verona and cries out aloud to try to stop 'a black Dog of vast bigness, eyes flaming' from jumping all over the sheets.

It is an area of humour Dylan enjoys as fully. His sense of the grotesque continually invades his visions both of carefree living ('Saddle me up a big white goose / Tie me on her and turn her loose') and of Apocalypse.

There is the common circus imagery – camels, clowns, freaks, masked faces, organ-grinders, dwarfs – and 'the phantom of the opera'; plus physically normal people with their trousers down, from the President of the United States to Dylan himself ('They asked me for some collateral an' I pulled down my pants').

This Browning-like celebration of the incongruous is everywhere in Dylan's mid-1960s work. 'Leopard-Skin Pill-Box Hat' devotes itself to this mood. It isn't only the panache of, say, 'you know it balances on your head just like a mattress balances on a bottle of wine' sung with appropriate top-heaviness (Chaplin on a tightrope) as just one line within a formal, 3-line, 12-bar framework. It's also the obvious pleasure taken in Dylan – prophet, visionary, seer – singing a whole song about someone's ridiculous hat. This same mood, Dylan as Puck, also figures beguilingly in songs like 'Million Dollar Bash' – where a Browning-like alliterative lunacy is much in evidence. The needlework of Noodledom lives:

> *Well that big dumb blonde*
> *With her wheel gorged*
> *And Turtle, that friend of theirs*
> *With his checks all forged*
> *And his cheeks in a chunk*
> *With his cheese in the cash*
> *They're all gonna meet*
> *At that Million Dollar Bash.*

---

40. It strikes me now that this is partly nonsense: I still assume that the 'me' in 'Positively 4th Street' is Bob Dylan, but since I no longer assume the 'you' to be a woman, I can't sustain the claim that we see her face. Yet to accept this shift of perspective is actually to strengthen the parallel with Browning. To hear the song as Dylan challenging the callow pigeon-holing and 'the dirt of gossip' (as he calls it elsewhere, in a phrase that might be Lawrence's) of those who see him on the street, is to place it closer to 'Bishop Blougram's Apology', in which the Bishop, falsely assumed to have grown worldly and corrupt, addresses 'an idealist . . . [T]he Bishop proceeds . . . to expose the young man's affected pose . . . and charges that in any age he would merely echo fashionable ideas.' (The précis is from Roma A. King, *The Bow and the Lyre: The Art of Robert Browning*, 1957.)

41. G. K. Chesterton, *Robert Browning*.

There is, finally, a more serious feature of most of Dylan's work that reaches back to Browning – to Browning the archetypal Victorian in experiencing (like Dorothea Brooke in George Eliot's *Middlemarch*) 'aspiration without an object'. Experiencing, that is, religious ardour without being able to focus it on traditional Christianity. Unable to worship God, George Eliot consecrated duty. Faced with the same predicament, Browning idealised love. So did Dylan.

As Walter E. Houghton explains it in *The Victorian Frame of Mind*: 'In an age of transition in which crucial problems, both practical and theoretical, exercised the thinking mind at the expense of the sensibility, and in which baffled thought so often issued in a feeling of impotence and a mood of despair, the thinker could find in love a resolution of psychological tensions, and a religion ... to take the place of Christianity.'

The first hint of this process at work in Dylan comes at the end of the "John Wesley Harding" album, where the agonised search for a more noble America ends in 'Close your eyes, close the door'.

"Nashville Skyline" admits the failure of John Wesley Harding's attempt to find psychic salvation in the myths of a bygone America, back in that continent's uncorrupted past. That quest has failed and the Dylan of "Nashville Skyline" has redirected his search towards fulfilment through love. As with the Victorians, that way lies salvation. 'Love is all there is.'

Correspondingly, when Dylan comes at the end of the 1970s to seek his salvation through Christ after all, he recognises that what remains constant is the aspiration, and that it is only the object of it that changes. This is stressed on 'Saving Grace':

> But to search for love, that ain't no more than vanity
> As I look around this world all that I'm finding
> Is the saving grace that's over me.

There is another Victorian whom Dylan's work occasionally recalls – Lewis Carroll. If, for instance, a substantial portion of Dylan's 'The Drifter's Escape' seems to remind one vaguely of the pack-of-cards trial scene in *Alice*, this is principally because it echoes the knowingly preposterous tone (and the metre) of many of the Lewis Carroll verses. The Dylan lines begin with this:

> Well the judge he cast his robe aside
> A tear came to his eye
> 'You'd fail to understand,' he said
> 'Why must you even try?'

and 'The Lobster-Quadrille' includes this:

> 'What matters it how far we go?' his scaly friend replied.
> 'There is another shore, you know, upon the other side ...'

which fits the Dylan tune as if purpose-built – as indeed it does the verses read as 'evidence' in the card-pack trial; and it's easy to imagine Dylan singing this one:

> He sent them word I had not gone
> (We know it to be true):

> *If she should push the matter on*
> *What would become of you?*

Resemblance extends also through much of the poem 'The Walrus and the Carpenter'; and while the song about Tweedledum and Tweedledee ends with these lines:

> *Just then flew down a monstrous crow*
> *As black as a tar-barrel*
> *Which frightened both the heroes so*
> *They quite forgot their quarrel*

the Dylan song ends like this:

> *Just then a bolt of lightning*
> *Struck the courthouse out of shape*
> *And while everybody knelt to pray*
> *The drifter did escape.*[42]

As, now, for affiliations with Eliot, well, the finely chiselled language of Dylan owes something emphatic to the tutoring of Eliot's early poetry; but the first thing to be said is this: folk-rock was Dylan's 'Prufrock'. With it, Dylan – like Eliot in 1917 – was alone in answering the demands of the times for a new poetry.[43]

'Prufrock' too is a dramatic monologue, but it is also a poem that threw away 'the canons of the poetical' and made nonsense of the distinction between 'seriousness' and 'levity' in art. It broke the rules laid down by tradition as to what the language of poetry should be. Folk-rock broke the rules again, and with similar results (even to the early hostility of academics to Eliot being echoed in the initial response to 'the electric Dylan').

Dylan used 'popular' as opposed to 'serious' music, and married it to fresh language, including much slang and entailing a full use of the double-meanings and double-imagery of cult terms – especially drug terms. The result was 'poetry that freely expresses a modern sensibility, the . . . modes of experience of one fully alive in his own age'. That description was written over sixty years ago, to cover Eliot's early work. It is every bit as accurate a comment on "Highway 61 Revisited" and "Blonde On Blonde".[44]

The other affiliations between Dylan and Eliot stem from this. There is the attempt

---

42.   Lewis Carroll (1832–1898), *Alice's Adventures in Wonderland* (1865; originally titled *Alice's Adventures Under Ground*) and *Through the Looking-Glass* (1871; full title *Through the Looking-Glass and What Alice Found There*). The trial scene and 'The Lobster-Quadrille' are from the former, 'The Walrus and the Carpenter' and 'Tweedledum and Tweedledee' from the latter.
    I note too that in 'The Mock Turtle's Story' (*Alice in Wonderland*) there is a line from the Duchess – she is herself quoting from a verse that must have been common in the period – that Dylan, as it happens, reproduces all but verbatim in 'I Threw It All Away', released the year after 'The Drifter's Escape': ' "'Tis so," said the Duchess: "and the moral of that is – 'Oh, 'tis love, 'tis love, that makes the world go round!' " '

43.   T. S. Eliot: 'The Love Song of J. Alfred Prufrock', *Poetry*, June 1915; reprinted in Eliot, *Prufrock and Other Observations* (1917).

44.   The quotation is from F. R. Leavis, *New Bearings in English Poetry* (1932). In 'Mr. Eliot And Milton' (*The Common Pursuit*, 1952) he describes Eliot as 'a poet confronted with the task of inventing the new ways of using words that were necessary if there was to be a contemporary poetry . . . when current poetic conventions and idioms afforded no starting point'.

to turn formlessness into form itself. 'The Waste Land' (1922) tries it openly; Dylan's attempts are usually checked by his allegiance to regular verses – a musical check on his lyrics. But though they may be regular, the verses of a song like 'Subterranean Homesick Blues' are hardly conventional – and the departure from convention reflects the attempt to interpret the formlessness of the age. 'I accept chaos,' Dylan wrote on the album cover of "Bringing It All Back Home", 'I am not sure whether it accepts me.'

Allied with the formlessness is the uprooting, urbanising process dealt with earlier in this chapter, and Dylan shares with Eliot the use of urban imagery and the expression of urban disillusion. Eliot first developed this in poems like 'Preludes' (from the *Prufrock* collection):

> The morning comes to consciousness
> Of faint stale smells of beer
> From the sawdust-trampled street
> With all its muddy feet that press
> To early coffee-stands

Dylan begins his 'Visions Of Johanna' with:

> Ain't it just like the night
> To play tricks when you're tryin' to be so quiet
> We sit here stranded
> Though we're all doin' our best to deny it . . .
> In this room the heat-pipes just cough
> The country music station plays soft
> But there's nothing
> Really nothing to turn off.

Yet only occasionally do you catch, in Eliot, the feeling of warmness towards language that is a Dylan trademark and which, in the context of urban disillusion, gives an added complexity and force to Dylan's work.

Not surprisingly, it is only in his early work that you come across a passage of Eliot's that Dylan might have written. An instance can be found in an early poem, 'Rhapsody on a Windy Night' (1917). Dylan could have written some of this:

> Along the reaches of the street . . .
> Every street lamp that I pass
> Beats like a fatalistic drum,
> And through the spaces of the dark
> Midnight shakes the memory
> As a madman shakes a dead geranium.

> . . . The street-lamp said, 'Regard that woman
> Who hesitates toward you in the light of the door
> Which opens on her like a grin.
> You see the border of her dress
> Is torn and stained with sand . . .'

That leaves no doubt about the influence of Eliot on Dylan. It's plainly a source of direct strength and carries the tutor's message: chisel your language. And Dylan has certainly done that:

> *Idiot wind*
> *Blowin' like a circle around my skull*
> *From the Grand Coulee Dam to the Capitol . . .*
>
> *. . . Down the road to ecstasy*
> *I followed you beneath the stars*
> *Hounded by your memory*
> *And all your ragin' glory*
> *. . . I kissed goodbye the howling beast*
> *On the borderline*
> *That separated you from me*

('Idiot Wind'). Again:

> *He sits in your room, his tomb*
> *With a fist full of tacks*
> *Preoccupied with his vengeance*
> *Cursing the dead that can't answer him back*
> *You know that he has no intentions*
> *Of looking your way*
> *Unless it's to say that he needs you*
> *To test his inventions*

('Can *You* Please Crawl Out Your Window?'). Or again – and here bringing in Eliot's use of allusion:

> *Yonder stands your orphan with his gun,*
> *Crying like a fire in the sun.*
> *Look out, the saints are coming through*
> *And it's all over now, Baby Blue.*
>
> *The highway is for gamblers, better use your sense.*
> *Take what you have gathered from coincidence.*
> *The vagabond who's rapping at your door*
> *Is standing in the clothes that you once wore:*
> *Strike another match, go start anew;*
> *And it's all over now, Baby Blue.*

That this influence has been direct is in any case confirmed by Dylan's allusions to Eliot's phrases. That oddly presented 'geranium' crops up again in 'Sad-Eyed Lady Of The Lowlands'; in 'Visions Of Johanna', there are echoes of 'The Waste Land' handful of dust: Louise holds a handful of rain.

> *In the room the women come and go*
> *Talking of Michelangelo*

writes Eliot; Dylan's 'All Along The Watchtower' changes the tense:

While all the women came and went.

This kind of obtuse allusion-making is a game that Eliot himself perfected. In the third section of 'The Waste Land', for instance, he writes:

> *To Carthage then I came*
> *Burning burning burning burning*

which, subtly enough for most of us, quotes from St Augustine's *Confessions*: 'To Carthage then I came, where a cauldron of unholy loves sang all about mine ears . . .' 'I Dreamed I Saw St. Augustine,' sings Dylan.[45]

The clearest of Dylan's cross-references occurs in the penultimate verse of 'Desolation Row' (a title, of course, not unlike 'The Waste Land') – the verse that does more than simply mention Eliot specifically:

> *And Ezra Pound and T. S. Eliot*
> *Fighting in the captain's tower . . .*
> *Between the windows of the sea*
> *Where lovely mermaids flow*
> *And nobody has to think too much about*
> *Desolation Row.*

This parallels the ending of 'The Love Song of J. Alfred Prufrock':

> *We have lingered in the chambers of the sea*
> *By sea-girls wreathed with seaweed red and brown*
> *Till human voices wake us, and we drown.*

Same imagery, same contrast, same argument.[46]

As for what Dylan has taken from the mainstream of American literature – well

---

45. St. Augustine of Hippo [now Annaba, Algeria], AD 354–430. He studied and lectured in Carthage before converting to Christianity c. 380. His *Confessions* is a spiritual autobiography. He died in Hippo in 430 as the Vandals were taking the handles.

Matthew Zuckerman (in 'If there's an original thought out there I could use it right now: the folk roots of Bob Dylan', *Isis*, no. 84, April–May 1999) points out an Eliot reference that comes between 'Visions Of Johanna' and 'I Dreamed I Saw St. Augustine', in the Basement Tapes song 'Too Much Of Nothing'. Zuckerman quotes the song's chorus – 'Say hello to Valerie, say hello to Vivien / Send them all my salary on the waters of oblivion' – and then comments: 'Vivien Haigh-Wood was the first wife of T. S. Eliot, who[m] he married in 1915. The couple formally separated in 1932 and he married Valerie Fletcher in 1947. Coincidence? Probably not . . . [and] "too much of nothing" is a fair précis of . . . [one theme of] 'The Wasteland''. He then offers these lines to illustrate the point: 'What is that noise now? What is the wind doing? / Nothing again nothing. / You know nothing? Do you see nothing? Do you remember / "Nothing"?'

46. 'Dylan in Ol' Possum's Diamond Mine' by Peter C. Montgomery, 1993, in *Bob Dylan's Words*, ed. R. D. Wissolik and S. McGrath (1994) is an interesting piece (it can't be called an essay: it's more a collection of notes) on Eliot's influence on Dylan. He suggests, as I have done, shared positions (questing poetry in the traditionally unpoetic; hence being drawn to 'images of darkness and decay in the modern city'); but he also finds concrete borrowings/parallels (e.g. from Eliot's 'Sweeney Agonistes' [1932]: 'I gotta use words when I talk to you / But if you understand or if you don't / That's nothing to me and nothing to you' cf. Dylan, from 'Some Other Kinds Of Songs': 'i hope you understand / but if you don't / it doesn't matter') and further deliberate allusions to Eliot's work within Dylan's (e.g. from 'Some Other Kinds Of Songs' again: 'holy hollowness . . . hollow holiness', an allusion to Eliot's title 'The Hollow Men' [1925]).

The same book offers some account of how Bob Dylan may have used Dylan Thomas' work: see Richard David Wissolik: 'Bob Dylan: or what's in a name?', 1993.

I find that I was wrong to have ignored, in this chapter, another American who was, like Eliot, unmistakably a British poet: W. H. Auden (1907–1973). Gavin Selerie has pointed out the strong particular similarities between

to deal with his relations to modern American poetry alone would take a whole book (so that what follows can only hope to provide some kind of eccentric, personalised outline), while there has also been a formidable amount of the kind of quick, urban prose that one side of Bob Dylan enjoys so much and has taken some strengths from – including Woody Guthrie's autobiography (dealt with elsewhere in this study), John Steinbeck, Nathanael West (to whom Dylan made acknowledgement by calling one of his "New Morning" songs 'Day Of The Locusts'), Raymond Chandler, Damon Runyan, John Dos Passos, F. Scott Fitzgerald, Norman Mailer, Arthur Miller, Jack Kerouac, William Burroughs; and so on and so on right through to Hunter S. Thompson. Too much to disentangle here.[47]

My outline restricts itself therefore to some elements of American poetry and their impingement on Dylan's songwriting scope.

There are two difficulties with this, in terms of pre-twentieth-century US poetry. The first is that so much of it echoes English literature anyway. Edward Taylor, often regarded as America's first great poet, was born in England. Emerson didn't begin writing poetry until after he had travelled abroad, touring Italy and meeting Coleridge, Carlyle and Wordsworth in England. Longfellow was a professor of modern languages and literature, spent a lot of time in foreign travel and pursuing an absorption with European literature, and as a poet offers obvious resemblances to Tennyson. Edgar Allan Poe went to school in England and worked outside the sphere of the reigning Boston–New York literati of his day. It was among British poets and critics that Whitman found his first admirers and, after the long period of disfavour into which his work fell after his death, it was in response to D. H. Lawrence's marvellous book *Studies in Classic American Literature* (1923) that Whitman was re-admitted to the American poetic pantheon of greats.

After Whitman, it is true, there is a large amount of truly American poetry, but then come Pound and Eliot and the Lost Generation, all trying to be un-American in Europe.

The other difficulty we come across, in measuring the influence on Bob Dylan's work of this pre-twentieth-century American poetry, is that the balladry of that poetry is so close to the traditions of folksong as to make it impossible to say whether Dylan derives some things from the one or from the other.

Let's begin where the echo is clearer – with Emerson. As an Englishman, I automatically link the pantheism of Dylan's 'Lay Down Your Weary Tune' with Wordsworth; but looking at the equivalent nineteenth-century poetry written by Americans and today learnt by American middle-class children in schools, it is the

---

Auden's poem/ballad 'Victor', 1937, and Dylan's 'Lily, Rosemary & The Jack Of Hearts', 1975. The Auden verses include, for example, 'Anna was sitting at table / Waiting for her husband to come back. / It wasn't the Jack of Diamonds / Nor the Joker she drew at first; / It wasn't the King or the Queen of Hearts / But the Ace of Spades reversed. / Victor stood in the doorway, / He didn't utter a word. / She said: "What's the matter, darling?" / He behaved as if he hadn't heard'. See Gavin Selerie, 'Tricks and training: some Dylan sources and analogues', *Telegraph*, no. 50, Winter 1994. [W. H. Auden, 'Victor', in *The English Auden*, ed. E. Mendelson, 1977.]

47. Nathanael West (1903–1940), *Day of the Locust* (1939), a novel. Jack Kerouac (1922–1969), so individual and influential a voice, is discussed further below, though he is primarily a novelist – albeit with a prose style that can rightly be called prose-poetry, as his masterpiece *On the Road* (1957) shows.

pantheism of Ralph Waldo Emerson (1803–1882) that shines out just as brightly – revealing at once a source of inspiration and tradition for that excellent Dylan song.

> *I inhaled the violet's breath,*
> *Around me stood the oaks and firs;*
> *Pine cones and acorns lay on the ground;*
> *Over me soared the eternal sky,*
> *Full of light and deity;*
> *Again I say, again I heard,*
> *The rolling river, the morning bird;*
> *Beauty through my senses stole;*
> *I yielded myself to the perfect whole.*

('Each and All', first published 1839.)

> *I stood unwound beneath the skies*
> *And clouds unbound by laws . . .*
> *I gazed into the river's mirror*
> *And watched its winding strum . . .*
> *The last of leaves fell from the trees*
> *And clung to a new love's breast*

('Lay Down Your Weary Tune', Dylan, 1963; discussed in some detail in Chapter 6.)

A keen correspondence occurs between Emerson's 'Goodbye', written in 1823 and published sixteen years later:

> *Goodbye to Flattery's fawning face . . .*
> *To crowded halls, to court and street*
> *To frozen hearts and hasting feet*

and Dylan's 'Wedding Song' of 1974:

> *I've said goodbye to haunted rooms*
> *And faces in the street*
> *To the courtyards of the Jester . . .*

Then there is Emerson's contemporary, Henry Wadsworth Longfellow (1807–1882), and his reputation's millstone, 'Hiawatha' (1855), which jingles in the memory as rhythm, the rhythm that is the basis of so much American song. It is a rhythm that suggests the music-and-words art; it does not stubbornly insist on its words-on-the-page lineage.

Not only 'Hiawatha'. Poems like 'Hymn to the Night', 'The Day Is Done', 'My Lost Youth', 'The Fire of Driftwood', 'The Bells of San Blas', 'The Arrow and the Song', 'The Ropewalk' – all have their primacy in jingling rhythms that wield assured, consistent drum-beats. Drummed into the memory from schooldays, this tradition of words as parts of song – of words as music – must act as a momentum of inspiration, however unconscious it may be, for Dylan. Longfellow's is the literary voice that murmurs underneath, just as, from the oral tradition, the old folksong patterns do.

It isn't odd, therefore, that specific snatches of Longfellow can be read in Dylan's voice, nor that it is less a matter of conscious technique that matches than a matter of ease of tone (derived from the rhythmic familiarity) and ease of vocabulary (derived from the familiarity of the voice that Longfellow gave to American writing). Here is such a snatch, from Longfellow's 'The Day Is Done' (collected 1906):

> *I see the lights of the village*
> *Gleam through the rain and the mist*
> *And a feeling of sadness comes o'er me*
> *That my soul cannot resist.*

The ease of tone and language there correspond so completely to the exhibition of the same qualities in Dylan's writing that no one would be surprised if Dylan had himself written exactly those lines anywhere on a 1970s album such as "New Morning" or "Planet Waves" or even "Blood On The Tracks", or on the 1989 album "Oh Mercy" or the 1997 "Time Out Of Mind".

And it is the same milieu entirely – the same operation of ease of tone and vocabulary upon the careful straightforwardness of what is being said – that Dylan gives us in the better parts of 'Sara', on "Desire":

> *Now the beach is deserted except for some kelp*
> *And the wreck of an old ship that lies on the shore*
> *You always responded when I needed your help*
> *You gave me a map and a key to your door.*

The rhythmic melody of that song, moreover, is itself an exact echo of Longfellow's 'Curfew' (1870):

> *No voice in the chambers*
> *No sound in the hall!*
> *Sleep and oblivion*
> *Reign over all!*
> *The book is completed*
> *And closed, like the day*
> *And the hand that has written it*
> *Lays it away.*

As for the mood and vocabulary of *that*, well what could be more quintessentially Dylanesque?

But it is the echo of Edgar Allan Poe (1809–1849) that hangs emphatically over some of Dylan's 1970s work, for good and ill. Poe's short poem 'To Helen', of which everyone knows two lines, usually without knowing where or whom they come from, removes the puzzle of all those embarrassingly florid pseudo-classical phrases of Dylan's that sit so uneasily in the choruses of 'Sara'. Where Helen is addressed in terms of

> *Thy hyacinth hair, thy classic face*
> *Thy Naiad airs . . . ,*

which Poe says have brought him home

> To the glory that was Greece
> And the grandeur that was Rome

(the lines everyone knows, of course), and adds:

> How statue-like I see thee stand . . .
> Ah, Psyche, from the regions which
> Are Holy Land!,

so 'Sara' is bombarded with:

> Sweet Virgin Angel . . .
> Radiant jewel, mystical wife

and

> Scorpio Sphinx in a calico dress

and

> Glamorous nymph with an arrow and bow.

Poe's influence has also been to the good – and very strong and direct it is too. It is the heart of Poe's stunning, direct confidence with rhymes, and particularly internal rhymes, that Dylan so positively inherits. The *tour de force* example of Dylan's 'No Time To Think' (1978):

> I've seen all these decoys through a set of deep turquoise
> Eyes and I feel so depressed . . .

> The bridge that you travel on goes to the Babylon
> Girl with the rose in her hair . . .

> Stripped of all virtue as you crawl through the dirt you
> Can give but you cannot receive . . .

is prefigured by that of Poe's scintillating 'The Raven' (1845):

> And the silken sad uncertain rustling of each purple curtain
> Thrilled me – filled me with fantastic terrors never felt before
> So that now, to still the beating of my heart, I stood repeating
> ' 'Tis some visitor entreating entrance at my chamber door'.

What of Walt Whitman (1819–1892)? His influence, after those unpromising first responses and that initial posthumous disfavour, now seems so deeply woven inside the body of modern American poetry as to be unmeasurable: it is his use of workaday experience and colloquial expression that represents the fundamental turning-point in American poetry from the drawing-room towards the street. And certainly it is Whitman's voice that makes possible Allen Ginsberg's *Howl*, itself a major influence on Dylan's mid-1960s work (as I suggest in more detail shortly) as on so much that came after it.

Perhaps Whitman's insistence on the interminable-list-as-poetry even made possible Dylan's 'A Hard Rain's A-Gonna Fall', 'Chimes of Freedom' and the whole idea of the 12-minute rock song, which seems suddenly to arise out of nowhere (or out of the longer old folk-ballads) from a context of 2½-minute pop songs. Alongside a conventional poem *Leaves of Grass* [a collection that grew and grew, from twelve poems in the self-published first edition of 1855 to 293 poems in the 1881 edition and more yet in the so-called 'Deathbed edition'] parallels 'Desolation Row' [or 'Highlands'] alongside a normal popular song.

After Whitman, there is a dramatic gap, except for one or two minor items that touch a little on Dylan's art. These aside, the gap seems to me to last through all of the American poetry that came between Whitman's death in 1892 and Kenneth Patchen's emergence in the mid-1930s.[48]

The minor items? Well, there's Edwin Arlington Robinson (1869–1935) – not a name bandied about much these days, but, like Poe and Whitman, a self-taught poet (and a Pulitzer prize-winning one at that), the bulk of whose work was achieved between 1910 and 1935, after an earlier career on the New York subways.

His poems forge the way, either directly or via his influence on modern ballads, for something in Dylan's early songwriting. Robinson's short, sharp, quirky poems like 'Richard Cory', 'Reuben Bright', 'Charles Carville's Eyes' – these contain those little detonations of observation that Dylan echoes in the better flashes of his hobo-hero, old-friend-hero songs.[49] This is from 'Richard Cory':

> *And he was always quietly arrayed*
> *And he was always human when he talked;*
> *But still he fluttered pulses when he said*
> *'Good morning', and he glittered when he walked.*

The echo of Robinson is perhaps not a point to insist upon. It is more in the nature of a hunch, a suggestion of a link there somehow, and offering it is simply to go along with F. R. Leavis' definition of the critic's task – that of saying/asking: 'This is so, isn't it?'[50]

The other minor correspondence I'd offer is that between e. e. cummings (1894–1962) and Dylan. There's the superficial correspondence of cummings' long

---

48. This account ignores the large impact of William Carlos Williams (1883–1963), who prefigures the Beats in his openness to the traditionally, mundanely 'unpoetic' and in his metric inventiveness. His impact, though, was long delayed: he was first published in 1909, but it was the post-war publication of *Paterson* Book I (1946), *The Collected Later Poems* (1950) and *The Collected Earlier Poems* (1951) which thrust him into prominence. (His novel *The Greater Trumps* [1932] inspired T. S. Eliot rather earlier, as noted in Chapter 14.)

49. 'Richard Cory', in *The Torrent and the Night Before* (1896), republished as *The Children of the Night* (1897). 'Reuben Bright' and 'Charles Carville's Eyes' ditto. Robinson's *Collected Poems* (1921, 1929, 1937).
   Hopelessly corrupted but recognisable by its title and crude narrative parallels, the poem re-emerges as a Paul Simon song (Simon & Garfunkel: 'Richard Cory', Nashville, 14/12/65; "The Sounds Of Silence", Columbia Records CS 9269, New York [CBS Records SBPG 62690, London], 1966). The LP-sleeve offers apologies to E. A. Robinson . . . rather than royalties. The poet died only in 1935; under European Community law, his copyright would have been protected until 75 years after his death; lucky for Paul Simon that US law requires active renewals every twenty-eight years to keep copyrights protected. He could therefore not only misrepresent and ruin the poem but take the proceeds too – including those from its recording by Van Morrison's early group Them: 'Richard Cory', London, April 1966; "The World Of Them", Decca (S)PA 86, London, 1970.

50. 'A judgment . . . aspires to be more than personal. Essentially it has the form: "This is so, is it not?" . . . a collaborative exchange.' F. R. Leavis, 'Mr. Pryce-Jones, the British Council and British culture', 1951, *Scrutiny*, vol. 18, 1951–52; collected in *A Selection from Scrutiny, Volume I*, 1968.

obtuse titles ('If Up's The Word; And A World Grows Greener', 1958) and Dylan's ('It Takes A Lot To Laugh, It Takes A Train To Cry', 1965) but cummings' are in each case titles that are the opening line of the poem in question; with Dylan, such titles are wilfully cryptic summaries of the mood contained in the song.[51]

But beyond that, I think it is a tone of pushy assertiveness that cummings often resorts to:

> his flesh was flesh his blood was blood;
> no hungry man but wished him food;
> no cripple wouldn't creep one mile
> uphill to only see him smile

(from 'My Father Moved Through Dooms Of Love', 1940) that Dylan debases further into those sentimentalised portraits of hobo-saints and friends in early songs (like 'Only A Hobo' and 'He Was A Friend Of Mine') and which he returns to, for instance, in 'Hurricane' and 'Joey' on the "Desire" album of 1976.[52]

When we come to Kenneth Patchen (1911–1972) we move, even more so than in alighting on e. e. cummings, from the kind of American poetry that is taught in schools (and comes from what can be called the academic mainstream) to the kind of poetry that you find for yourself after you've left school. Patchen's work was done in the 1930s–1950s and beyond, and he was, if such a thing is possible, typical of the jazz-influenced, jazz-culture-influenced generation of writers who ended up being called the Beat Generation.

Patchen, Jack Kerouac, Lawrence Ferlinghetti and Allen Ginsberg between them constructed an artistic milieu that Dylan, some years later, seemed so avant-garde in launching upon a mass market and a new generation. The Dylan of 1965–66 swims in a milieu taken from these men and their contemporaries. In a way all Dylan did with it was to put it up on stage with a guitar. His greatness lies in the way he did that, the cohesive, individual voice with which he re-presented it and the brilliance of his timing in doing so.

In Patchen's case, his influence on Dylan, whether direct or not, is first of all evident throughout Dylan's novel *Tarantula*. This, for example, from Patchen's 'I

---

51.   Actually Dylan's work acknowledges the notice he's taken of cummings' long titles. As noted in Wissolik and McGrath's *Bob Dylan's Words* (in the section '*Tarantula*: commentary and textual allusions': see note 52) a Dylan phrase very early on in *Tarantula*, i.e. 'a much of witchy', alludes to cummings' 'What If a Much of a Which of a Wind' [1944].

52.   There is more to cummings' impact than this. It's so obvious as to have remained unstated that Dylan's ostentatious refusal of capital letters all through '11 Outlined Epitaphs', 'Advice For Geraldine On Her Miscellaneous Birthday' (very much a modern poet's title), 'Some Other Kinds Of Songs', the "Bringing It All Back Home" and "Highway 61 Revisited" sleeve notes, 'Alternatives To College' and the "World Gone Wrong" sleeve notes, as well as in *Tarantula*, is all in the wake of e. e. cummings more than of any other individual.
Wissolik and McGrath in *Bob Dylan's Words* find three further tips of Dylan's hat to cummings' work in *Tarantula*: an allusion to his title 'Your Sweet Old Etcetera' [1925] and two direct quotes from the poem 'Buffalo Bill's' [1920]: 'Jesus he was a handsome man', and 'blue-eyed boy', both taken from the poem's final lines 'Jesus / he was a handsome man / and what i want to know is / how do you like your blue-eyed boy / Mister Death'. They note too that Dylan uses 'my blue-eyed son' recurrently in 'A Hard Rain's A-Gonna Fall'. I would add that the cummings passage is specifically echoed – the tone exactly seized and duplicated – in 'I Shall Be Free', where Dylan recites: 'What I want to know, Mr. Football Man, is / What do you do about Willy Mays . . .?' and then again (with T. S. Eliot thrown in too) in the 'Mouthful of Loving Choke' section of *Tarantula*: ' "& i think i'm gonna do april or so is a cruel month & how do you like your blue-eyed boy NOW mr octopus?" '.

Don't Want To Startle You' (1939), would fit well anywhere inside that excellent book:

> *I knew the General only by name of course.*
> *I said Wartface what have you done with her?*
> *I said You Dirtylouse tell me where is she now?*
> *His duck-eyes shifted to the guard. All right, Sam.*
> *. . . Who is that fat turd I said – he hit me with his jewelled fist.*
> *While his man held me he put a lighted cigarette on my eyelid.*
> *I smelt the burning flesh through his excellent perfume.*
> *On the wall it said 'Democracy must be saved at all costs.'*
> *The floor was littered with letters of endorsement from liberals.*

(There's even that direct cigarette–eyelid connection, which Dylan resuscitates in 'Memphis Blues Again' – just as a phrase of Patchen's, 'Cathedral evening' – which opens his 1950s poem 'Beautiful You Are', is used unaltered in Dylan's 'Chimes Of Freedom'.)

This, too, would pass for Dylan's work in *Tarantula*.

> *When they fitted the black cap over his head*
> *He knew that he'd never have another chance to be president.*

(It is from Patchen's 'All The Bright Foam Of Talk', 1939.)

Dylan inherits ideas from Patchen too, I think – or again, perhaps just from the milieu that Patchen was a creative part of. The poem 'The Rites Of Darkness' (1942) encompasses a lot of Dylan's Gemini-schizoid feelings about the glamour of urban wickedness and decadence, and at the same time the ever-visible presence of God, and about the nature of truth and beauty.

> *But no one sees the giant horse*
> *That climbs the steps which stretch forth*
> *Between the calling lights and that hill*
> *Straight up to the throne of God*

offers a notion that Dylan restates in the terrific 'Three Angels':

> *The angels play on their horns all day . . .*
> *But does anyone hear the music they play?*

while this, from Patchen's poem:

> *We can't believe in anything*
> *Because nothing is pure enough.*
> *Because nothing will ever happen*
> *To make us good in our own sight*

encapsulates succinctly attitudes Dylan has touched on many times, from the poem about Joan Baez through to 'Dirge' and 'Shelter From The Storm' where

> *Beauty walks a razor's edge*
> *Some day I'll make it mine*
> *If I could only turn back the clock . . .*

[right through to 'Highlands', in 1997, in which

> Well my heart's in the highlands:
> I'm gonna go there
> When I feel good enough to go].

I think, therefore, though I've never come across anyone who has said so except Gabrielle Goodchild in an essay on *Tarantula*, that Dylan has inherited something of both style and content from Patchen, and from that tradition of American poetry in which you let the poem write itself, as it were.[53]

And as it says on the dust-jacket of my copy of *The Selected Poems of Kenneth Patchen*, his work focuses on 'his direct and passionate concern with the most essential elements in the tragic, comic, blundering and at rare moments glorious world around us. He wrote about the things we can feel with our whole being – the senselessness of war, the need for love among men on earth, the presence of God in man, the love for a beloved woman, social injustice, and the continual resurgence of the beautiful in life.' Which is precisely what can reasonably be said (though one might not choose to express it quite like that) about the recurrent concerns in Dylan's work.[54]

Allen Ginsberg (1926–1997) too, more than Gregory Corso or Ferlinghetti, and as much as Patchen or Kerouac, opens for Dylan and for his whole generation the window on a bright, babbling, surreal, self-indulgent, sleazy, intensely alert world no predecessor had visited. *Howl* (1956) might not have been possible without

53.   Gabrielle Goodchild: '*Tarantula*: tangled up in a web', unpublished essay, 1979, now available for reference in the Robert Shelton Collection at the Experience Music Project archive, Seattle. An extract was published under the title (not the author's) '*Tarantula*: the web untangled', in *Conclusions on the Wall*, ed. Elizabeth M. Thomson (1980). Goodchild argues the relevance of Patchen's novel *The Journal of Albion Moonlight* (1941) (a title in turn acknowledging Blake). The essay was commissioned as background material for Robert Shelton's book *No Direction Home* (1986).

   I regret excluding *Tarantula* – a singular item in, but an honourable part of, Bob Dylan's work – from the present study. The novel is well attended to, though in note form, in '*Tarantula*: commentary and textual allusions', in *Bob Dylan's Words*, ed. Wissolik and McGrath (except that it is blind to the many blues references in the book, and you must put up with this sort of thing: 'complete appreciation of *Tarantula* and the rest of Dylan's work is not possible without knowledge of the "I Ching", Tarot symbolism and Robert Graves' *White Goddess*'). The book includes too Scott McGrath's essay 'Only a matter of time 'til night comes stepping in' (1993) which 'finds' in *Tarantula* a previously 'unknown poem', titled by McGrath 'To Maria'. That is: 'Seemingly incidental Spanish phrases are peppered throughout Dylan's novel . . . Put together and translated into English, the individual hidden phrases, all of which appear in chapters with the name "Maria" in the title, form the . . . poem.' This enterprising exercise seems justified by a plausible result.

54.   Kenneth Patchen, *Selected Poems*, 1957. Compare Patchen's title 'Nice Day for a Lynching', 1939, with Dylan's line from 'Talking World War III Blues': 'Good car to drive, after a war'. Perhaps Patchen's title 'Red Wine and Yellow Hair', 1949, resonates under Dylan's line from 'Angelina': 'Blood dryin' in my yellow hair . . .' while the poem '23rd Street Runs into Heaven', 1939, might offer the second brush of Patchen's wings that can be heard in Dylan's 'Three Angels', 1970. Patchen's lines include '. . . lights wink / On along the street. Somewhere a trolley, taking / Shop-girls and clerks home, clatters through / This before-supper Sabbath. An alley cat cries / To find the garbage cans sealed; newsboys / Begin . . .'.

   My suggestion of Patchen's poetry as an influence on Dylan's work was criticised as 'guesswork' in some Dylan fan circles, accompanied by the suggestion that only biographical 'fact' can establish these things; but in this case time and 'fact' have vindicated the Lit. Crit. method of deducing from the evidence of the work alone. Shelton's book, *No Direction Home*, first published five years after the American literature section of the present chapter, revealed that Patchen was a favourite writer of Tony Glover, Dylan's close and influential friend from the Dinkytown Minneapolis period (whose fine essay on Dylan's progress through to 1966 is published in the booklet of the 1998 official release "The Bootleg Series Vol. 4: Bob Dylan Live 1966"); then in Bob Spitz's *Bob Dylan: A Biography* (1989) Dylan's other intimate of the period, Dave Whittaker, states specifically that in the winter of 1960 he introduced Dylan to Kenneth Patchen's 'experimental verse'.

Whitman, but Dylan's debt to *Howl* is far more direct than Ginsberg's to *Leaves of Grass*.[55]

This is from *Howl*:

> *who jumped in limousines with the Chinaman of Oklahoma on the impulse of winter midnight streetlight smalltown rain,*
> *. . . who went out whoring through Colorado in myriad stolen nightcars . . .*
> *. . . who faded out in vast sordid movies, were shifted in dreams, woke on a sudden Manhattan, and picked themselves up out of basements hungover with heartless Tokay and horrors of Third Avenue iron dreams . . .*

There is not one line from this huge sprawling poem that cannot claim to be the deranged, inspired midwife of the Dylan of the mid-1960s, the Dylan of 'the motor cycle black madonna two-wheel gypsy queen' and the rest.[56] Dylan's achievement,

55. This account airily undervalues the impact of Corso and Ferlinghetti, and offers no evidence of the Kerouac connection. In minimal redress, therefore:

This passage from Corso's 'Marriage' (from *The Happy Birthday of Death*, 1960), chimes familiarly for followers of Dylan's 1960s work: 'So much to do! like sneaking into Mr Jones' house late at night / and cover his golf clubs with 1920 Norwegian books / Like hanging a picture of Rimbaud on the lawnmower'. Dylan himself cites Corso's earlier collection *Gasoline* (1958) as an influence: see note 56. In Corso's case it seems clear that Dylan has moved this work forward, making it more biting, multi-layered and consequential – less cautious, less anxious to please.

Lawrence Ferlinghetti is the Beat poet who most noticeably includes constant allusions to others' texts and titles, something we find in Dylan's 1960s poetry, in his songs and in *Tarantula*. Ferlinghetti's poem 'Autobiography' includes allusions to Eliot, Matthew Arnold, Thomas Wolfe, Allen Ginsberg, Woody Guthrie, Wordsworth, Thoreau and Melville. Specific passages also prefigure Dylan: e.g. 'I got caught stealing pencils / from the Five and Ten Cent Store / the same month I made Eagle Scout', cf. 'My Life In A Stolen Moment'. 'Junkman's Obbligato' [sic] chimes similarly, updating Eliot's glamorously sordid city in very much the Dylanesque way; e.g. 'Stagger befuddled into East River sunsets / Sleep in phone booths . . . / staggering blind after alleycats / under Brooklyn Bridge / blown statues in baggy pants / our tincan cries and garbage voices / trailing'. I couldn't read, in 'The Long Street', the unmemorable lines 'where everything happens / sooner or later / if it happens at all' without hearing Bob Dylan's voice reciting something with that same rhythm and that same last line on the unreleased early version of 'Brownsville Girl', 'New Danville Girl' [Hollywood, Dec. 1984]: 'Nothing happens on purpose / It's an accident / If it happens at all'. Another poem, 'Dog', with the recurrent line 'The dog trots freely in the street', might be the prompt for 'If Dogs Run Free'. (All these Ferlinghetti poems are from the group 'Oral Conversations' in *A Coney Island of the Mind*, 1958.) Dylan also alludes to Ferlinghetti's collection *Pictures from the Gone World* in his interesting sleeve note prose-poem for "Planet Waves": 'Yeah the ole days Are gone forever And the new ones Aint fAR behind, the Laughter is fAding away, echos of a staR, of Energy Vampires in the Gone World going Wild!' (For a note on the odd withdrawal of these notes, see Chapter 4, note 24.)

Kerouac's poetry book, *Mexico City Blues* (1959), Ginsberg told Wes Stace (Cambridge, 27/4/85), was a specific influence on Dylan: 'He read that in '58–9 . . . Somebody gave it him and . . . as he said . . . it [was] the first book of poetry which talked the American language to *him* . . .' [from 'Interviews and a poem: Allen Ginsberg, poet', in *All Across the Telegraph*, ed. M. Gray and J. Bauldie]. Dylan uses this title in 'Something's Burning, Baby' ('I got the Mexico City blues . . .'). While the impact of Kerouac's work has been unquantifiably wide (like Dylan's), Dylan often refers to Kerouac titles, commonly recycling them into his own. Thus *On the Road* (1957) – 'On The Road Again'; *The Subterraneans* (1958) – 'Subterranean Homesick Blues'; *Visions of Gerard* (1963) – 'Visions Of Johanna'; *Desolation Angels* (1965) – 'Desolation Row'. This last Dylan song also recycles a phrase direct from the Kerouac book: 'in the perfect image of a priest'; the same book also yields the phrase 'housing project hill', which Dylan throws into the same album's 'Just Like Tom Thumb's Blues'. (Kerouac's book was first published March 1965; the songs were recorded that August.)

56. And then with "Biograph"'s release in 1985 came a warm memorialising of all these influences by Bob Dylan himself:

Minneapolis . . . I came out of the wilderness and just naturally fell in with the beat scene, the Bohemian, BeBop crowd, it was all pretty much connected . . . people just passed through, really, carrying horns, guitars, suitcases, whatever, just like the stories you hear, free love, wine, poetry, nobody had any money anyway . . . there were a lot of house parties . . . There were always a lot of poems recited – 'Into the room people come and go talking of Michelangelo, measuring their lives in coffee spoons' . . . 'What I'd like to know is what do you think of your blue-eyed boy now, Mr. Death'. T. S. Eliot,

subsequently, of course, has included the remarkable fact of his being able to turn right round and become a major influence on Allen Ginsberg, as Ginsberg's liner-notes to Dylan's "Desire" album testify. As urged at the start of this chapter: literature, folksong, music – everything connects.

e. e. cummings. It was sort of like that and it woke me up . . . Jack Kerouac, Ginsberg, Corso and Ferlinghetti – 'Gasoline', 'Coney Island of the Mind', . . . oh man, it was wild – 'I saw the best minds of my generation destroyed by madness': that said more to me than any of the stuff I'd been raised on . . . what ever was happening of any real value was . . . sort of hidden from view and it would be years before the media would be able to recognize it and choke-hold it and reduce it to silliness. Anyway, I got in at the tail-end of that and it was magic . . . it had just as big an impact on me as Elvis Presley. Pound, Camus, T. S. Eliot, e. e. cummings, mostly expatriate Americans who were off in Paris and Tangiers. Burroughs, 'Nova Express', John Rechy, Gary Snyder, Ferlinghetti, 'Pictures From The Gone World', the newer poets and folk music, jazz, Monk, Coltrane, Sonny and Brownie, Big Bill Broonzy, Charlie Christian . . . it all left the rest of everything in the dust.

['I saw the best minds of my generation destroyed by madness' is the most frequently quoted line (it is the main part of the opening line) from Ginsberg's *Howl*; *Nova Express* is by William Burroughs (1964); *Pictures from the Gone World* (1955), referred to earlier, is Ferlinghetti's first book of poetry.]

Much earlier, Dylan had memorialised these influences, and the way that poetry and music, painting and film, American and European, had rubbed shoulders in the process, in a poem of his own – a section of the '11 Outlined Epitaphs' that made up Dylan's sleeve notes for his third album, "The Times They Are A-Changin' ", written 1963 and issued 1964:

with the sounds of Francois Villon / echoin' through my mad streets / as I stumble on lost cigars / of Bertolt Brecht / an' empty bottles / of Brendan Behan / the hypnotic words / of A. L. Lloyd / each one bendin' like its own song / an' the woven spell of Paul Clayton / entrancin' me like China's plague / unescapable / drownin' in the lungs of Edith Piaf / and in the mystery of Marlene Dietrich / the dead poems of Eddie Freeman / love songs of Allen Ginsberg / an' jail songs of Ray Bremser / the narrow tunes of Modigliani / an' the singin' plains of Harry Jackson / the cries of Charles Aznavour / with melodies of Yevtushenko / through the quiet fire of Miles Davis / above the bells of William Blake / an' beat visions of Johnny Cash / an' the saintliness of Pete Seeger.

François Villon, France's first great poet, 1431–c. 1465, became popular in the nineteenth century and again in the twentieth, not least when Ezra Pound translated some of his work. His 'Petit Testament', 1456, was followed by his 'Grand Testament', 1461, which includes his best-known work, 'Ballade des dames du temps jadis' – 'Ballad of the Ladies of Former Times' – containing the line 'Mais où sont les nièges d'antan?' – 'But where are the snows of yesteryear?', which Dylan consciously echoes earlier in '11 Outlined Epitaphs', beginning a section with 'ah where are those forces of yesteryear?'

Eddie Freeman I cannot trace. Poet Ray Bremser was an acquaintance of Corso and Ginsberg, and moved into Ginsberg's upstate New York farmhouse in 1970. Barry Miles, in his excellent *Ginsberg: A Biography* [1989] reports that when Ginsberg came to ask Dylan for $15,000 payment for his appearances in and work on *Renaldo & Clara*, he said he 'wanted a car and a stereo set and to give some money to Ray Bremser. The mention of Bremser, whom Dylan had heard read in New York in 1961, did the trick, and the money came through.' Bremser served prison terms between 1953 and 1965, when his *Poems of Madness* was published; in 1967 came the prose-poem *Angel*, with an introduction by Ferlinghetti, and in 1968 *Drive Suite*. Bremser's wife Bonnie published her *Troia: Mexican Memoirs*, 1969.

Allen Ginsberg died in his Lower East Side apartment at 2.39 a.m., on Saturday 5 April 1997, of a heart attack related to his terminal liver cancer, according to friend and archivist Bill Morgan. He was writing poems as late as the Thursday. On the evening after Ginsberg's death, Bob Dylan was playing in concert at Moncton, New Brunswick, and after performing 'Desolation Row' said it was Ginsberg's 'favourite song: that was for Allen'. [These details taken from *Isis*, no. 72, April 1997.]

CHAPTER THREE

Dylan and Rock Music

Bobby Vee to Bob Dylan who had, till that moment, been his pianist briefly: *'You might make it on your own but you don't make it with this band: you're fired.'* Or so the story goes.[1]

It Was Rock-A-Day Johnny Singin' Tell Your Ma, Tell Your Pa, Our Love's A-Gonna Grow Wah Wah . . .

Rock'n'roll happened as a strange, appealing mixture of 'race' and country music. Mix Fats Domino with Hank Williams and you get the beginning of rock'n'roll.[2] But rock took off *en masse* for whites because of Elvis Presley. Without Presley, Bill Haley would have been a nine-day blunder, like the Twist, and just as false; without Haley, Elvis would still have been a massive original talent. It simply wasn't Haley in 1955 that mattered, it was Presley in 1956, as even the *Billboard* charts bear out.

Haley's 'Rock Around The Clock' topped the US Hot 100 in 1955 only to be followed for the rest of that year by the appalling Mitch Miller, the Four Aces, the saccharine piano of Roger Williams and the saccharine gravel of Tennessee Ernie Ford. And 1956 began just as comfortably, with Dean Martin. Then – the false craze exposed – Kay Starr climbed up there with her peekaboo 'Rock And Roll Waltz', just as Frank Sinatra and Ella Fitzgerald were to yawn in on the Twist craze in 1962, crooning in the coffin-nails. After Kay Starr, it was naturally back to dinner-suits with the Nelson Riddle Orchestra and Les Baxter.

And that would have been that, but for 'Heartbreak Hotel', Presley's first nation-wide No. 1 hit record. It owed as much to Bill Haley as Dylan owes to Ringo Starr, and on its own it transformed the US charts and more besides. (The No. 1s that succeeded it that year were Cogi Grant's 'The Wayward Wind' and then 'Hound Dog' and 'Don't Be Cruel', both by Presley, the Platters' 'My Prayer' and back to Elvis for

---

1. It was true. See '1950s: did Bob Dylan really play piano for Bobby Vee?' in *All Across the Telegraph*, ed. Michael Gray and John Bauldie (1987).

2. In fact, this very combination eventually occurs. The song 'Jambalaya' uses creole language but was written by Hank Williams; Fats Domino's version is a classic.

   Fats Domino: 'Jambalaya (On The Bayou)', Philadelphia, 6/11/61; Imperial Records 5796, Los Angeles [London American Records HLP 9520], 1961.

'Love Me Tender'.) Popular music was forced to notice that the Second World War had come and gone. The give-me-the-moonlight regime was vanquished. Presley became the prototype: rock'n'roll was made in his image.[3]

In England, to begin with, Tommy Steele was supposed to be an Elvis, and in his attempts he focused on one of the changes that happened when popular music went pop. Before, you had to enunciate – every word had to be heard, though why that should have been is difficult to imagine, granted that the words so carefully delivered weren't generally worth any attention. With rock'n'roll the meaning of words, as a general rule, mattered less than their sounds, and the voice became an instrument. The grown-ups who laughed at Presley's 'mumbling' didn't understand. It was actually exciting to have part of the record where you didn't know what you were singing when you sang along with it. I still can't make out all the words on lots of 1950s records that I know, as records, very well. For instance, in 'Let's Jump The Broomstick' by Brenda Lee, there is what sounds to me like this:

> *Gonna Alabama*
> *Getcha-catcha-kamma*

Who needs to translate? – it's perfectly satisfying left like that.[4] (This revised usage of words was another Presley innovation: on Bill Haley's records, you *can* hear every word, from 'one o'clock' right through to 'twelve o'clock rock'.)

So there was Tommy Steele, back in England in 1956–57, trying to be Elvis Presley and therefore very consciously slurring the words. Only Tommy Steele did it, of course, like any cockney novice would, by leaving out all the consonants. It sounded, on his smash hit 'Singing The Blues', like this:

> *Weeeeeeeeeeeeeeeeeeeeellllll –*
> *I never felt more like a-singin' the blues*

3.   In *Billboard* (the Cincinatti-based weekly trade paper, rivalled by New York's *Cashbox*) the 1955 and 1956 Hot 100s had only ten No.1s during each year (by 1961 there were over twenty in the course of a year). 1955: Joan Weber, 'Let Me Go, Lover'; Fontaine Sisters, 'Hearts Of Stone'; McGuire Sisters, 'Sincerely'; Bill Hayes, 'Ballad Of Davy Crockett'; Perez Prado, 'Cherry Pink'; Bill Haley, 'Rock Around The Clock'; Mitch Miller, 'Yellow Rose Of Texas'; Four Aces, 'Love Is A Many Splendored Thing'; Roger Williams, 'Autumn Leaves' and Tennessee Ernie Ford, 'Sixteen Tons'. 1956: Dean Martin, 'Memories Are Made Of This'; Kay Starr, 'Rock And Roll Waltz'; Nelson Riddle, 'Lisbon Antigua'; Les Baxter, 'Poor People Of Paris'; plus the six just listed in the main text.

Re Bill Haley: in 1953 "Crazy, Man, Crazy' . . . by Bill Haley and His Comets became the first rock'n'roll song to make the best-selling lists . . . [their] 'Shake, Rattle and Roll' was in the top ten for twelve weeks from September 1954; 'Rock Around The Clock' was in the list for nineteen weeks, including eight at the top, from May, 1955.' (Charlie Gillett, *Sound of the City*, 1971.)

Re Presley: his professional recordings began 5–6 July 1954, for Sun Records, Memphis, including Arthur Crudup's 'That's All Right' and Bill Monroe's 'Blue Moon Of Kentucky', issued locally the same month (Sun 209). In the USA Sun released another single in 1954 and three more in 1955 (the last topped the national country chart) before selling Presley's contract to RCA Victor on 20 November. RCA reissued all five singles in December 1955, followed by eleven singles in 1956 – seven in August alone. Out of all this, the big nation-wide hits were 'Heartbreak Hotel' (No. 1), 'I Want You I Need You I Love You', 'Don't Be Cruel' c/w 'Hound Dog' (No. 1) and 'Love Me Tender' (No. 1). In Britain, first release was 'Heartbreak Hotel' in March 1956. In retrospect we can all prefer 'That's All Right' and the other Sun records, but at the time, except in Memphis and the South, Elvis arrived not in 1954 but 1956.

Elvis Presley: 'Heartbreak Hotel', Nashville, 10–11/1/56, RCA Victor 20–6420 & 47–6420 [78rpm & 45rpm], New York [HMV Records POP 182, London], 1956; 'I Want You I Need You I Love You', Nashville, 11/4/56, RCA Victor 20/47–6540 [HMV POP 235], 1956; 'Don't Be Cruel' c/w 'Hound Dog', NYC, 2/7/56, RCA Victor 20/47–6604 [HMV POP 249], 1956.

4.   Brenda Lee: 'Let's Jump The Broomstick', 1958, US Decca 30885, New York, 1959 [Brunswick 05823, London, 1961].

Cole'urorale'uoozz
Your love, dear.

This showed up the whole gigantic difference between American and British pop. The best of the American stars had music that grew out of their own local roots. They picked up genuine skills and techniques unselfconsciously. Their English equivalents always had to imitate. Tommy Steele was hardly from the same world as Elvis Presley: he was the archetypal cockney from a decent British slum, whose musical heritage was 'Knays Ap Muvvah Braan', and who sang with a guitar strictly for laughs (at first) when on leave from the Merchant Navy.[5]

Steele was superseded in Britain principally by Cliff Richard, as the BBC *6.5 Special* was superseded by the ITV *Oh Boy!* (The only way the latter stood out powerfully was that the studio was dark and trained a spotlight on the performer. Otherwise it was a copy. Lord Rockingham's XI, with their infuriating 'Hoots Mon', equalled asthmatic old Don Lang and his so-called Frantic Five.[6]) Cliff Richard was like Brigitte Bardot – or rather, like Bardot pretending to be Presley. He had a baby-doll face and pouted a lot. His hair was black, which made him sexier than Tommy Steele straight away, and he had long sideburns (or 'sideboards', as they were often called in England). He wore black shirts and white ties, giving a bit of teddy-boy toughness to his image. He wasn't very good.

The other male solo stars or would-be stars who emerged in Britain tended not only to imitate Presley but also to take on names designed to suggest his attributes: Marty Wilde, Billy Fury, Duffy Power, Vince Eager; and later, Robb Storme and, with more subtlety, Lance Fortune and Johnny Gentle. Yet no matter how hard they copied, they never learnt. As Nik Cohn said, the gulf between America and Britain showed at its widest when Elvis Presley became God and Tommy Steele made it to the London Palladium instead.[7]

In America, Ricky Nelson was pushed as a replacement Presley when Elvis went

---

5.   This may be slightly unfair to Steele. Born 1936, he was 'discovered' in London singing calypsos and Hank Williams material learnt while working on a cruise ship based in New York, but claims to have played back-up guitar for Josh White in the USA in 1955 (interview by the author, London, December 1974). His UK tour of November 1956 introduced the amplifier to the British stage. He made two good rock'n'roll records, both covers of US records (by Ritchie Valens and by Freddie Cannon): 'Come On Let's Go', London, Oct. 1958, Decca Records F 11072, London, 1958; and 'Tallahassee Lassie', London, July 1959, Decca F 11152, 1959.
    Guy Mitchell: 'Singing The Blues', NYC, 1956, Columbia Records 40769, New York [Philips PB 650, London], 1956 (the first US chart-topping single of 1957, and a British No. 1 too). Tommy Steele: 'Singing The Blues', London, 1956, Decca Records F 10849, 1956 (also a British No. 1).

6.   BBC Television's first youth show, *Teleclub* (1953), was taken off the air when rock'n'roll loomed in the USA (1955). BBC and ITV (launched 1955) ignored the new music till 1957 when the latter showed *Cool for Cats*, in which dancers, the Beat Generation, 'interpreted' new releases. Weeks later (16/2/57) the BBC launched *6.5 Special*, co-hosted by Jo Douglas and Pete Murray (6 pm to 7 pm had previously been blank). The historian Asa Briggs notes in Volume 5 of *The History of Broadcasting in the United Kingdom* (1996) that *6.5 Special* was striking in that 'The cameras played on the oddest and most incongruous of the dancers as well as the coolest and most adept' [quoted in 'The Voice of Britain' in Raphael Samuel's posthumously published *Island Stories: Unravelling Britain – Theatres of Memory, Volume 2*, 1998]. Both *6.5 Special* and its rival *Oh Boy!* (15/6/58) were devised by Jack Good. Don Lang had had a minor 1955 hit ('Cloudburst'); he and His Frantic Five, somehow getting the musical-anchor job on *6.5 Special*, had another small hit with 'School Day', 1957, and a No. 5 covering David Seville's US No. 1 'Witch Doctor', 1958. Lord Rockingham's XI, the *Oh Boy!* regulars, had a No. 1 later that year with the ridiculous 'Hoots Mon' (an instrumental interspersed with the cod-Scottishism 'there's a moose loose aboot this hoose') and a Top 20 follow-up in 1959, 'Wee Tom'.

7.   Nik Cohn, *Awopbopaloobopalopbamboom: Pop from the Beginning* (1969).

into the army. Gene Vincent tried it too; so did the very underrated Conway Twitty. Twitty must have been very badly managed, because after his first hit, the million-selling 'It's Only Make-Believe', he went into a rapid decline in popularity until his resuscitation in the US country market of the 1970s – and yet he cut many, many good records, from 'Is A Bluebird Blue?' through a great 'C'est Si Bon' to the masterly 'I Hope, I Think, I Wish'.[8]

So Presley was not a suffocating influence in America – he got a lot of people started on things that weren't just copies. Duane Eddy said that 'none of us would have got anywhere without Elvis', and Duane Eddy didn't sound at all like Elvis Presley.

The Americans not only had other things to offer; they were also very much smarter than the British and a lot more independent-minded. (Hard to credit today I know.) Partly, this was because they had vital popular music to draw on and partly it was because pop in America was never handled through one monopolistic institution. In America, local radio stations shaped the pop environment; in Britain, everything was obstructed, diluted, mishandled and misdispensed by BBC Radio, which had no idea what pop music was, didn't know how long it would last, didn't like or approve of it, and so hardly bothered to adapt to its demands. Radio Luxembourg, the only alternative lifeline, was little better. Reception was terrible, it was evenings only, and the DJs were mostly the same old men: Jack Jackson, Sam Costa, Pete Murray, plus younger, greasier people who tried to convert you to mainstream jazz. David Gell – a suitable name – had a show where either the title or the slogan was 'Music For Sophisticats'. Imagine what that was like.

In one way Luxembourg really was better than the BBC: it wasn't at the mercy of the infamous Musicians' Union. The BBC was the union's hapless lackey and fell in with its insistence that teenagers couldn't hear pop on the radio without listening at the same time to elderly orchestras and 'combos' politely said to perform 'live'. In any case, you have to single out the BBC, because of its hold over Britain's air waves, as the worst uniformity-machine of all in pop. And all this worked against the individual, the genuinely new, the imaginative and the delicate.

American radio, in contrast, was infinitely variegated. In any one town, DJs with gumption and enthusiasm could tap undiscovered markets, shape tastes – could play what they liked! – free from the dictates of playlists. Dewey Phillips in Memphis in the 1950s was one example out of many. It took a couple of decades before US radio completely ossified, becoming over-formularised through sheer greed.[9] Which goes to show that 'free enterprise' can stifle anything at least as fully as a nationalised industry if it tries. (A good British example is/was the British motorcycle industry, whose death was cheerfully presided over by its management in the teeth of

---

8.   Conway Twitty: 'It's Only Make-Believe', Nashville, 7/5/58, MGM Records E/SE 4217, Hollywood [MGM 992, London], 1958 (a No. 1 USA and UK). 'I Hope I Think I Wish', Nashville, 11/10/62, MGM Records SE 4709, Hollywood [MGM 1187, London], 1963. This last, a clever pop lyric with an innovative use of sub-text vividly evoking lovelorn gloom and wishful thinking, was given perfect performance by Twitty. The arrangement featured a distinctive piano part on very high notes which prefigures that on Dylan's 1989 recording 'What Good Am I?'
      Both Twitty tracks are on the 8-LP box-set "Conway Twitty – The Rock'N'Roll Years (1956–1963)", Bear Family BFX 15174 (9), Vollersode, Germany, 1985.

9.   The future loomed early: the first fixed playlist based on the national pop charts was introduced on Todd Storz's chain of Midwest stations in 1955.

impressive engineering and design teams that were unconsulted and eventually abandoned.)

Variety was also inbuilt for US pop and effectively excluded from its British equivalent because of the record company situation. In America, there were myriad small companies attuned to local communities and able to breathe because of local radio. By 1961, there were over 6,000 independent labels in America, and consequently hundreds of pop artists got auditioned, recorded, played and popularised who, regardless of their talent, would not have stood a chance in Britain. There, records were in the hands of the Big Four – Decca, EMI, Pye and Philips. It would be hard to say which was the most blinkered, slow-moving and unimaginative. They watched each other slavishly and so exacerbated the imitation process. To imitate was always safer than to innovate, and playing things safe was all they knew. Their reactions to the Beatles showed this. Decca rejected them because they didn't sound quite like anyone else around at the time. Eventually EMI risked them because, well, what can you lose when you don't have to pay an orchestra for the session? Then, bless my soul, people were buying their records! So all the recording managers rushed up to Liverpool (funny place, Liverpool: in the provinces, y'know) to sign up groups like the Beatles. And since they didn't really understand what the Beatles were like, they had to sign up more or less everybody.

Today, an even worse uniformity has crept across America too but in the 1950s and early 1960s, American pop was quite a contrast. Even at its most imitative, it had far more variety than British. After Presley, new artists sprang up all over the States, ready and able to revamp almost every form of popular music. Not just rockers trying for Presley's toughness and energy but also a good many truly individual voices who saw their chance and took it.[10] The best are legends: Little Richard, Chuck Berry and Jerry Lee Lewis. The many others included Buddy Knox, Lloyd Price and Ricky Nelson.

Nashville country music produced the great Everly Brothers, who first made it big back in 1957 and who still sound good today. Country pop also provided Don Gibson, John D. Loudermilk, Chet Atkins, Floyd Cramer, Patsy Cline and Skeeter Davis – as well as Johnny Cash and Marty Robbins. Also from the 1950s in America came Neil Sedaka, an ex-classical pianist with an exciting commercial teenybop sound. Brenda Lee was great too. Late 1950s USA also promoted a number of groups who found sounds of their own and developed them well and independently. The Platters

---

10. One of many good things offered by Peter Guralnick's *Last Train to Memphis: The Rise of Elvis Presley* (1994) is his re-creation of the way that, when Elvis went into the studio to make not only that first record but the ones that followed, no one knew what a record should be like. No formulae, no rules, no norms existed. They devised what sounded good out of nowhere. That anything might be possible and no one could know what – this was the essence of the moment, the fundamental artistic condition, and one that is today virtually inconceivable, let alone attainable. Elvis, the musicians, producer Sam Phillips: they didn't say 'Let's make a rockabilly record', or 'Let's aim for a crossover'. The categories were unformed. All they knew was that they were reaching for a new exciting noise to express the volatile moment.

Presley's very success created categories, including rockabilly, a genre that has enjoyed cult status ever since the early 1960s. Greil Marcus' *Mystery Train* (1971) is good on its essential mediocrity: 'most rockabilly singers weren't even imitating blacks, they were imitating 'All Shook Up'. Collectors call the likes of Alvis Wayne and Johnny Burnette geniuses, but their aggressive stance is never convincing and the flash is always forced.' The only snag with this existentially accurate analysis is that most 'authentic' rockabilly was recorded before the release of Presley's 'All Shook Up' [Hollywood, 12/1/57; RCA 20–6870 (78 rpm) and 47–6870 (45 rpm), New York, March 1957]. Any connoisseur will tell you that *if it's after 1957, it's suspect*. Bob Dylan's interest in rockabilly (unknown when this chapter was first written) is discussed elsewhere in the present work.

were first. Later came the Fleetwoods, Coasters, Teddy Bears, Danny & The Juniors, Dion & The Belmonts, and The Drifters. And finally, there were the odd individual voices with talents as original in their own ways as Presley's. Sam Cooke, who was very popular but never popular enough, especially in Britain; Ritchie Valens, who died; Chuck Berry, who was immensely clever; Duane Eddy, who couldn't last but who made hits that still sound good; and the very great Buddy Holly.[11]

Holly's voice, iridescing through 'It Doesn't Matter Anymore', lingered all through the summer of 1959.[12] It was the record that pinned down the year, just as "Blonde On Blonde" was to pin down 1966–67. And alongside it that autumn clustered the variegated sounds and images of the pop America that had flowered in the aftermath of Elvis' earlier impact. By March 1960, when Sergeant Presley was discharged from the army, there really was a whole scene going, and a scene of mixed-up confusion at that.

At this point, enter Bob Dylan. Some time the previous year he'd been playing harmonica in a Central City, Colorado strip-joint. In December 1960 he reached New York City, guitar at the ready and still listening to everything. By this time too he must have soaked up all the cumulative residue of skills – in lyric writing as well as in the music – of Presley, Chuck Berry and Fats Domino.[13]

The myth has been created that 1960 was an all-time low in pop, which would suggest that there was nothing much for Dylan to gather from it; would suggest that he'd have had to go back to the early rock giants for his pop education. But the myth is a lie: 1960 wasn't the best year ever but it introduced some beautiful sounds – a situation that held all through 1961–62 as well. The only thing missing was a genuine trend. All the good things were disconnected, separate end-products of the earlier rock

11. Most Sam Cooke work is of undimmed excellence: great records by a terrific songwriter and a masterful soul singer of panache, integrity and expressive generosity. In 1960–63 he was in his prime, not least in live performance (try "One Night Stand: Sam Cooke Live At The Harlem Square Club, 1963", NYC, 12–13/1/63, RCA Records PL85181, Rome, 1985). He died in 1964. Bob Dylan cut a version of Cooke's 'Cupid' with George Harrison, NYC, May 1970.

12. Buddy Holly: 'It Doesn't Matter Anymore' [written by Paul Anka: by far the noblest thing *he* ever did], NYC, 21/10/58, Coral Records C 62074, New York [Coral Records Q 72360, London], 1959.

13. To put these speculations in context: when this book was first written (1969–71) and published (1972), it was not stating the obvious to cite the impact on Dylan of Fats Domino, Chuck Berry, Buddy Holly, Jerry Lee Lewis, Ritchie Valens and the rest. All this stuff was regarded as laughably 'un-progressive' and irrelevant. It was felt that Dylan's writing '"Ambition": To Join Little Richard' in his Hibbing High School yearbook (1959) had been youthful misjudgement, pre-dating a damascene conversion to the integrity of folk music and then to the 1960s values of the new Dylanesque rock. Dylan himself deliberately made no further public acknowledgement of the pioneers of rock'n'roll or of the 2½-minute single until many years later, except by putting versions of the Everlys' 'Let It Be Me' and 'Take A Message To Mary' on "Self Portrait", 1970: something very badly received by a hip public. These debts should perhaps have been admitted readily by everyone: they were surely undeniable. No one was owning up to any of it back then. Similarly, no one talked about Elvis as a great artist except Greil Marcus in *Mystery Train*. The furtiveness about liking Elvis that was felt necessary among the hip was eventually confirmed by Dylan himself. He told Robert Shelton in retrospect: 'The thing Suze [Rotolo] could tell you . . . [is] that I played, back in 1961 and 1962, when nobody was around, all those old Elvis Presley records.' (*No Direction Home*, 1986.)

The cultural snobbery of the times was such too that not one music paper or magazine of the 1970s would publish such a thing as a Roy Orbison interview, despite the fact that, uniquely, he had worked both at the Sun studio in Memphis and at Norman Petty's in Clovis, New Mexico in the crucial mid-1950s. And despite the further credentials of his voice and those early 1960s singles, Orbison's mid-1970s live appearances were in cabaret. No one was listening or respectful of his artistry then. He was widely dismissed as a clapped-out, tawdry pop star, as *passé* as haircream and condoms. When he died (6/12/88), everyone said how they'd always loved him.

There *was* an oldies revivalism in the mid-1970s but with a reductive approach – kitsch (Sha Na Na), naff (Showaddywaddy), or at the low-cred end of the market (ELO's Top 10 'Roll Over Beethoven', 1973; Presley's Top 10 'The Promised Land', 1975).

years. This very disconnectedness made for unprecedented variety: so not only had Dylan grown up through the early years but he also had, at the start of his own career, a great deal happening in pop worth picking up on.

What were the things that invalidate the myth of pre-Beatles infertility?

The first thing to say is that this was actually a time when some rock came back. Gene Vincent with 'Pistol Packin' Mama', Eddie Cochran with 'Cut Across Shorty', and Brenda Lee with 'Sweet Nuthins'. Connie Francis tried it on 'Robot Man'; Ricky Nelson tried it, with blaring saxes, on 'I Got My Eyes On You (And I Like What I See)'. The Piltdown Men arrived; US Bonds came along with 'New Orleans' and 'Quarter To Three'; and Freddie Cannon did 'The Urge'. The Everly Brothers did 'Lucille'; Jerry Lee Lewis came back with a classic version of 'What'd I Say'; Presley himself made 'A Mess of Blues', 'I Feel So Bad' and 'Little Sister'. Del Shannon made a gallant attempt on his hit 'Hats Off To Larry', and they issued a great but doctored Buddy Holly rocker, 'Baby I Don't Care'.[14]

14.   Gene Vincent: 'Pistol Packin' Mama', London, 11/5/60, Capitol Records F4442, Los Angeles [Capitol CL 15136, London], 1960 (musical arrangement by Eddie Cochran). This reached the British Top 20 in June 1960. Cochran was killed, and Vincent hospitalised, in a car crash in England 17/4/60. They had just completed a tour headlined by Vincent. Eddie Cochran: 'Cut Across Shorty' [B-side of British Top 3 hit 'Three Steps To Heaven'], LA, Jan. 1960, Liberty Records 55242, Hollywood [London American Records HLG 9115, London], 1960.

In April 1987 Bob Dylan recorded two takes of Vincent's 'Important Words' during the "Down In The Groove" sessions, Los Angeles, though they remained unreleased. When Dylan recorded [at the same sessions as the "Good As I Been To You" tracks, Malibu, July-Aug. 1992] the old Jo Stafford hit 'You Belong To Me' [1952] for the soundtrack of Oliver Stone's *Natural Born Killers* film [UNV Interscope Records ITSC-92460, USA, 1994], Dylan's version was in clear remembrance of, though didn't copy, the version Gene Vincent includes on his best known album. (Gene Vincent: 'Important Words', Nashville, 18/10/56, Capitol 3617 [Capitol CL 14693, London], 1957; 'You Belong To Me', Hollywood, 10/12/57, "Gene Vincent Rocks! & The Blue Caps Roll", Capitol Records T970, LA [and London], 1958. ('You Belong To Me' was a US Top 20 hit in 1962 by The Duprees, NYC, *nia*, Coed Records 569, New York, 1962.)

Jerry Lee Lewis: 'What'd I Say', Nashville, 9/2/61; Sun Records 356, Memphis [London American Records HLS 9335, London], 1961. This was a British Top 10 hit in May 1961; the original version by its composer, Ray Charles ['What'd I Say (Part 1)' c/w 'What'd I Say (Part 2)', NYC, 18/2/59, Atlantic Records 2031, New York, 1959] was not released in the UK at the time. Jerry Lee Lewis also scored minor British Top 40 hits with rock'n'roll records in 1962 (an excellent version of Chuck Berry's 'Sweet Little Sixteen', Memphis, 5/6/62, Sun Records 379, Memphis [London American Records HLS 9584, London]) and 1963 (the Little Richard song 'Good Golly Miss Molly', Nashville, 11/9/62, Sun Records 382 [London American Records HLS 9688]). Bob Dylan performed 'What'd I Say' at Farm Aid rehearsals, LA, 19/9/85.

Elvis Presley: 'A Mess Of Blues', Nashville, 20–21/3/60, RCA Victor Records, New York, 1960; 'I Feel So Bad', Nashville, 12–13/3/61, RCA Victor Records, 1961; 'Little Sister', Nashville, 25–6/6/61, RCA Victor, 1961. ('I Feel So Bad' revived what had been a 1954 R&B hit for its composer, Chuck Willis ['I Feel So Bad', NYC, 17/9/53, OKeh Records 7029, New York]; other Willis hits included 'It's Too Late' [NYC, 13/4/56, Atlantic Records 1098, New York, 1956]: a song Bob Dylan might also have known from the recording of it by Buddy Holly [The Crickets: 'It's Too Late', Clovis, New Mexico, 1957, issued on their first LP, "The Chirping Crickets", Brunswick 54038, New York, 1957 (Coral LVA 9081, London, 1958)]. Bob Dylan performed 'It's Too Late' live in Buenos Aires, 10/8/91 and at the 'free rehearsal' given in Fort Lauderdale, 23/9/95.)

Del Shannon's 'Hats Off To Larry' was the follow-up to his striking hit single 'Runaway', 1960. The Traveling Wilburys, incl. Bob Dylan, recorded 'Runaway' (at the "Traveling Wilburys Vol. 3" sessions), Bel Air, April 1990; issued as a single, Warner Bros. Records W9523, Europe only, 1990.

Buddy Holly: '(You're So Square) Baby I Don't Care', Clovis, New Mexico, Dec. 1957, Coral Records Q 72432, London, 1961 [not issued as a USA single]. Holly had further British chart successes with rock'n'roll records in this period as follows: 'Midnight Shift', Nashville, 26/1/56 c/w 'Rock Around With Ollie Vee', Nashville, 22/7/56, Brunswick Records O 5800, London, 1959 (Top 30); 'Brown-Eyed Handsome Man' [a Chuck Berry song], Clovis, New Mexico, 1956 [overdubs by the Fireballs, Clovis, 1962], Coral Records C 62369, New York [Q 72459, London: different B-side], 1963 (Top 3); and 'Bo Diddley' [a Bo Diddley song], Clovis, New Mexico, 1956 [overdubs by the Fireballs, Clovis, 1962], Coral Records C 62352, New York [Coral Records Q 72463, London: different B-side], 1963 (Top 10).

Vincent, Cochran, Lewis and Holly enjoyed short-lived popularity in the USA but great longevity in Britain (though in the 1970s Lewis had some success in the USA as a country singer).

Apart from this unchristened rock revival, on came a superabundance of sounds that were newer, maybe cleverer, and which certainly stick in the mind. Blues singer Bobby Bland made it with 'Let The Little Girl Dance'. Floyd Cramer started something with 'On The Rebound' – something that came to final fruition on Dylan's "Nashville Skyline" track 'Tell Me That It Isn't True'. Clarence Frogman Henry was around, making delightful concert appearances as well as the records 'But I Do', 'You Always Hurt The One You Love', 'Ain't Got No Home', 'Lonely Street' and a great, great flop called 'A Little Too Much'.[15] Roy Orbison arrived, with grace, elegance of style and a voice that could not fail – the prototype voice for Dylan's 'Wild Mountain Thyme', 'I Forgot More' and part at least of 'Lay, Lady, Lay'. Ray Charles balanced nicely between soul and country. The Marcels did 'Blue Moon' and Ernie K. Doe did 'Mother-In-Law'. Dion found his 'Runaround Sue' sound and Neil Sedaka found 'Breakin' Up Is Hard To Do'. The Everly Brothers were better than ever, with 'Cathy's Clown', 'Nashville Blues', 'Stick With Me Baby' and 'Temptation'.[16]

Tamla-Motown was young enough to be refreshing, as on 'Please Mr. Postman' by the Marvelettes and 'Shop Around' by the Miracles. Phil Spector came along like Armageddon with the Crystals, Bob B. Soxx & The Blue Jeans and later the Ronettes. The Tokens did 'The Lion Sleeps Tonight', and 'B'Wa Nina' and Bruce Channel made 'Hey! Baby'. Presley made his beautiful 'Surrender' and Sam Cooke sang 'Nothing Can Change This Love'. There was 'Monster Mash' by Bobby Boris

15. After an early novelty hit 'Ain't Got No Home' (not the Woody Guthrie song) and renewed obscurity, Clarence Frogman Henry had a run of records with an unmistakable sound new to pop/rock'n'roll yet achieved with a dated but vivid charm: in fact a stripped-down New Orleans tromboney unit making snazzy, funny records to rival those of the more senior Fats Domino, beginning with the huge hit 'But I Do'. In 1962, Henry toured the UK on a package headlined by Bobby Vee and including Tony Orlando, then 16 years old; in 1964 he supported the Beatles and in 1965 the Rolling Stones. Most of his hits, including 'But I Do', were written or co-written by New Orleans artist Bobby Charles using the pseudonym Guidry. Charles wrote Bill Haley's hit 'See You Later, Alligator', which the Band and Bob Dylan transmuted into 'See Ya Later, Allen Ginsberg' during the Basement Tapes sessions [West Saugerties, June–Aug., 1967]. Charles was later a member of Paul Butterfield's Better Days and at "The Last Waltz", San Francisco, 25/11/76, a backing vocalist on Dylan & The Band's performance of 'I Shall Be Released'; Warner Brothers Records 3WS 3146, Los Angeles, 1978.
    Clarence Frogman Henry: 'Ain't Got No Home', New Orleans, Sept. 1956; Argo Records 5259, Chicago, 1956. 'But I Do' c/w 'Just My Baby And Me', New Orleans, c. Aug. 1960; Argo Records 5378 [Pye International Records 7N 25078, London], 1961. 'You Always Hurt The One You Love', New Orleans, c. March 1961; Argo 5388 [Pye Intnl 7N 25089], 1961. 'Lonely Street' c/w 'Why Can't You', New Orleans, c. March 1961; Argo 5395 [Pye Intnl 7N 25108], 1961. 'On Bended Knees' c/w 'Standing In The Need Of Love' (a secular re-write of gospel song 'Standing In The Need Of Prayer'), Memphis, c. July 1961; Argo 5401 [Pye Intnl 7N 25115], 1961. 'A Little Too Much' c/w 'I Wish I Could Say The Same', Memphis, c. July 1961; Argo 5408, [Pye Intnl 7N 25123], 1962. Excepting 'On Bended Knees' and 'I Wish I Could Say The Same', all these are on the CD "The Best Of Clarence Frogman Henry", MCA Records 19226, London, 1993 [unissued USA]. Beware cheap re-recordings on cheap re-releases.

16. The reference to Dylan's 'Wild Mountain Thyme' means the exquisite version of this traditional song that he sang at the second Isle of Wight Festival of Music, 31/8/69, which was officially recorded but never released; it has only ever circulated in particularly poor quality. Ditto for the comparable versions sung that night of 'To Ramona' and 'It Ain't Me, Babe'. All three were strongly redolent of Roy Orbison's distinctive vocals.
    It emerged later that even at the very height of Dylan's artistic genius and hipness, the tour of 1966, he could still (off-stage) bear in mind the Everly Brothers of exactly this sneered-at 1960–62 period: the film *Eat the Document* shows him performing their 1960 hit 'When Will I Be Loved?' in his Glasgow hotel room, 18–19/5/66. (*Eat the Document* was first screened in 1971 [twice] and remains, over 25 years later, rarely seen.)
    The Everly Brothers: 'Cathy's Clown', Nashville, 18/3/60, Warner Brothers Records 5151, New York [Warner Brothers Records WB 1, London], 1960. 'Temptation', Nashville, 1/11/60, c/w 'Stick With Me Baby', Nashville, 27/7/60, Warner Bros. 5220 [WB 42, London], 1961. 'When Will I Be Loved?', Nashville, 18/2/60, Cadence Records 1380, New York [London American Records HLA 9157, London], 1960. The Everly Brothers are discussed further in Chapter 5.

Pickett & The Crypt-Kickers. Add to all that the arrival of the Four Seasons, Jay & The Americans, the Shirelles' 'Will You Love Me Tomorrow' – a minor breakthrough – and 'Tell Him' by The Exciters. Then add 'I Sold My Heart To The Junkman' by the Blue-Belles, and 'I'm Blue' by the Ikettes. 'Letter Full Of Tears' by Gladys Knight & The Pips. 'Snap Your Fingers' by (the American) Joe Henderson. The Contours' 'Do You Love Me' and the Isleys' 'Twist And Shout'. Ketty Lester's 'Love Letters' and Claude King's wonderful 'Wolverton Mountain'. The devastating 'What's A Matter Baby?' by a resplendently vengeful Timi Yuro; and perhaps the very greatest of the lot, one minute twenty-eight seconds' worth of 'Stay', by Maurice Williams & The Zodiacs.[17]

Far from being bad years, plainly 1960–62 were very rich and very diversified. The dominant influence, if there was one, was the search for a new bi-racial R&B-type music. Lots of the vocal groups were looking for that, and in Britain at least it was accepted that these Americans had found it. So Billy Fury moved to phase three: not Presley, not Eddie Cochran, but by covering 'Letter Full Of Tears' he became a mixture of Gladys Knight & The Pips and processed cheese. A complex sound and, to go with it, rumours that he wrote strange and secret poetry no one was allowed to read. Decca were obviously quite proud of the new sound they'd given him – so Lyn Cornell, an ex-back-up singer from *Oh Boy!*, covered 'I Sold My Heart To The Junkman', and Liverpool's Beryl Marsden covered Barbara George's 'I Know'.

Underscoring developments at the time of this R&B quest there was, as usual, a corresponding country strength. It was there behind most of the rock revival records; it was there for Floyd Cramer; Ray Charles mixed it with his soul-singing. 'Blue Moon' and 'You Always Hurt The One You Love' are sort of country songs. The Everlys were from Country country and relied heavily on the songs of the Bryants – which included their 'Nashville Blues'. And Roy Orbison had emerged, like Presley and Johnny Cash before him, after a less successful start on the Memphis label, Sun. Long after the move to Monument Records and 'Only The Lonely' he was still singing pop-country songs on albums, including the much-recorded 'All I Have To Do Is Dream'.[18]

17. 'Shop Around' was written by, and the Miracles led by, Smokey Robinson, whom Dylan once declared 'America's greatest poet'. Bruce Channel [pronounced Chanel] topped the US charts and nearly did the same in Britain with 'Hey! Baby', Fort Worth, 1962, Smash Records SMA 1405, Chicago [Mercury Records AMT 1171, London], 1962. What made it was Channel's unusual voice combined with a distinctive featured harmonica, played by Delbert McClinton (though no one knew that sort of thing at the time). It influenced the Beatles' first record, 'Love Me Do', London, 11/9/62, Parlophone Records R 4949, 1962: a gloomy and insipid equivalent of Channel's vibrant classic.

18. The influence of Ray Charles' earlier R&B records on Dylan is discussed in Chapter 9. Charles' seminal crossover LP was "Modern Sounds In Country And Western", ABC Paramount Records 410, Hollywood [HMV Records CLP 1580 and CSD 1451, London], 1962. Regarded as a 'sell-out' by R&B purists, but widely welcomed as bringing fresh life into country and pop, it was influential and immensely successful, as were a number of hit singles taken from it – one of which was the lovely 'You Don't Know Me', Hollywood, 15/2/62, ABC-Paramount 10345, Hollywood [HMV POP 1064, London], 1962. Bob Dylan introduced this song into his concert repertoire (performing it with great affection) in Andrarum, Sweden, 27/5/89, and sang it at five further 1989 concerts and at five in 1991. 'You Don't Know Me' was written by Eddie Arnold and Cindy Walker. As with Dylan's contribution to the Willie Nelson–Bob Dylan song 'Heartland', it's alleged that Arnold wrote only the title of 'You Don't Know Me' and his co-writer all the rest. The Ray Charles version of 'That Lucky Old Sun' [Hollywood, 10/7/63, ABC-Paramount 10509, 1963] also seems the prompt for Bob Dylan's concert performances of this beguiling, neo-minstrel pop song (Farm Aid, Champaign, Illinois, 21/9/85; twenty-three concerts 1986; Madison, Wisconsin,

Altogether there was plenty happening for Dylan to notice, react to, pick up on: his pop education didn't need to have finished – couldn't have finished – in the 1950s.

Everything's Bin Returned Which Was Owed, Part I

What Dylan did gain from the years up to 1959 were lessons learnt from Fats Domino and Chuck Berry, Elvis Presley and Buddy Holly: relatively specific things from highly distinctive artists.

Fats Domino taught white pop fans about idiosyncratic flexibility in lyrics – particularly in rhymes – through odd emphasis (a Dylan trick) and odd pronunciation. In Domino's 'Good Hearted Man' he manages, by his accent and his disregard for consonants, to make the word 'man' rhyme with 'ashamed': no mean feat. He put out a record called 'Rockin' Bicycle' but he sang it 'Rockin' Bi-*sic*-l', and the words of that song are interesting too, in a simple but individualistic way.

There's plenty of evidence in Dylan's work of Domino's oddities of emphasis. For instance, in 'Absolutely Sweet Marie':

> Well I waited for you when I was a-half *sick*
> Yes I waited for you when you hated me
> Well I wai-ee-ted for you inside of the frozen traffic
> When ya knew I had some other place to be.

Domino also comes up, maybe accidentally, with the pathetic use of bathos, which again is something that Dylan has used. There is a Domino song that includes this amazing couplet:

> Her hands, were soft, as cotton
> Her face, could never, be forgotten.[19]

5/11/91; Hollywood, 19/5/92; and the 'free rehearsal', Fort Lauderdale, Florida, 23/9/95).

'Blue Moon' was a 1961 No.1 (USA and UK) by black vocal group The Marcels but in the late 1950s was associated in the rock'n'roll world with Presley. Dylan included a version on "Self Portrait", 1970. In 1993 it was found to have also been one of the four songs on the newly discovered first extant tape by Bob Dylan, made Hibbing, Minnesota, 1958. In 1994 'All I Have To Do Is Dream', an Everlys' US No. 1 in 1958 [Nashville, 6/3/58, Cadence Records 1348, New York (London American HLA 8618, London), 1958], was found to have been recorded by Dylan soon after "Self Portrait", i.e. with George Harrison, NYC, 1–2/5/70.

19. As it happens, the examples of Domino's work quoted here are from the beginning of the 1960s, but the same characteristics can be found in abundance in this great artist's earlier work too. Fats Domino: 'Let The Four Winds Blow' c/w 'Good Hearted Man', New Orleans, May, 1961; Imperial Records 5764, Los Angeles [London American Records, London], 1961. 'What A Party' c/w 'Rockin' Bicycle', New Orleans, Aug. 1961, Imperial 5779, [London American HLP 9456], 1961. The lines quoted are from 'Fell In Love On Monday', New Orleans, Dec. 1960, Imperial 5734, 1961. The Imperial sides are all CD-reissued on the £125 8-CD box-set "Out Of New Orleans", Bear Family BCD 15541, Vollersode, Germany, 1993. Beware cheap imitations. There is one fine post-Imperial Domino LP, the self-produced "Sleeping On The Job", New Orleans, 1978, Conmedia Records, Germany [Sonet Records SNTF 793, London], 1979.

In the classic photos, Fats Domino's head is a perfect cube, thanks in part to his trademark flat-top haircut. Unique to Domino in the 1950s, this became fashionable among young black males in the US and UK thirty years later.

Glen Dundas' *Tangled up in Tapes Revisited*, 1990, says Domino's 'Please Don't Leave Me' was among the songs Dylan rehearsed in Woodstock in September 1965. Decades later Dylan ventured a very Fats Dominoid live version of 'I'm In The Mood For Love' (Fats Domino: New Orleans, 3/1/57, B-side of 'I'm Walking', Imperial 5428, [London American HLP 8407], 1957; Bob Dylan: 'I'm In The Mood For Love', Hollywood, 3/8/88). It also emerged in the 1990s that Dylan sang the same song on the Basement Tapes [West Saugerties, June–Aug. 1967].

From Chuck Berry, Dylan learnt a lot more. Berry was ahead of his time, offering an urban slang-sophistication slicker than any city blues man before him. He offered a bold and captivating use of cars, planes, highways, refrigerators and skyscrapers, and also the accompanying details: seat-belts, bus conductors, ginger ale and terminal gates. And he brought all this into his love songs. He put love in an everyday metropolis, fast and cluttered, as no one had done before him. In Chuck Berry's cities, real people – individuals – struggled and fretted and gave vent to ironic perceptions. And it was all so controlled, so admirably neat. This is the first verse of his great song 'Nadine':

> As I got on a city bus and found a vacant seat
> I thought I saw my future bride walking up the street
> I shouted to the driver 'Hey Conductor! – you must
> Slow down! I think I see her, please let me off this bus.'

In 'Maybellene' he manages to cram three car names in as many lines:

> As I was motivatin' over the hill
> I saw Maybellene in a Coup de Ville
> A Cadillac a-rollin' on the open road
> Nothin' will outrun my V8 Ford

and in 'You Never Can Tell' every couplet has a special kind of wit and economy:

> They bought a souped-up jitney, 'was a cherry red '53,
> They drove it down to New Orleans to celebrate their anniversary . . .[20]

Chuck Berry also specialised in place names, as no one before or since has done. He releases the power of romance in each one, and thereby flies with relish through a part of the American dream. Place names are scattered around like syllables in songs like 'Back In The USA', 'Sweet Little Sixteen' and 'The Promised Land'.

The last of these is the story of the poor-boy from Virginia who makes it to success-land, California – although we never discover what he really finds there. The song mentions lots and lots of place names in passing, or rather, while the poor-boy's passing through, and several forms of transport. ('And that hound broke down an' left us all stranded in down-town Birmingham.') It ends like this:

---

20.   Chuck Berry: 'Nadine (Is That You?)', Chicago, 15/11/63, Chess Records 1883, Chicago [Pye International 7N 25236, London], 1964; 'Maybellene', Chicago, 21/5/55, Chess 1604, 1955; 'You Never Can Tell', Chicago, 15/11/63, Chess 1906 [Pye Intnl 7N 25257], 1964.

In both previous editions I rendered the quote from 'You Never Can Tell' as 'They bought a souped-up Jidney, 'was a cherry-red '53', quietly doubtful that there was any American car called a Jidney. No one ever commented. In 1995 I happened upon the explanation, in a passage from Bill Bryson's *Made in America* (1994): 'A notable absentee from the list of early American coins is *nickel*. There was a coin worth five cents but it was called a *half dime* or *jitney*, from the French *jeton*, signifying a small coin or a token. When early this century American cities began to fill with buses that charged a five-cent fare, *jitney* fell out of use for the coin and attached itself instead to the vehicles.' Chuck Berry's usage, then, is in the sense of 'they bought a souped-up old bus', where 'old bus' is in turn a term for 'unwieldy old car'.

Bob Dylan & Levon Helm performed 'Nadine' during Helm's Lone Star Café gig, NYC, 29/5/88, and Dylan sang it live in concert in Berry's home-town, St. Louis, 17/6/88. He played saxophone (!) while Larry Kegan sang Berry's 'No Money Down' live in Merrillville, Indiana 19/10/81 and Boston 21/10/81. Dylan also performed Berry's 'Around And Around' in concert in Leysin, Sweden, 10/7/92 (Chuck Berry: 'Around And Around', Chicago, 1958 [B-side of 'Johnny B. Goode', Chicago, 29/12/57], Chess 1691, 1958).

> *. . . come down easy,*
> *Taxi to the terminal-zone;*
> *Cut your engines an' cool your wings*
> *An' let me make it to the telephone:*
> *'Los Angeles, give me Norfolk, Virginia,*
> *Try Waterford 1009,*
> *Tell the folks back home this is the promised land calling*
> *An' the poor-boy's on the line!'*

Who else could take up two lines of a song in giving the operator the number? His much earlier classic 'Memphis (Tennessee)' takes this much further, the song's whole story being told to the telephone operator whose help he is requesting.[21]

He humanises these operators, of course, by explaining his situation to them. Dylan is probably conscious of turning this on its head when he uses the telephone to emphasise isolation in 'Talkin' World War III Blues':

> *So I called up the operator of time*
> *Just to hear a voice of some kind*
> *'When you hear the beep it will be three o'clock.'*
> *She said that for over an hour*
> *And I hung up.*

The urban slickness, precision and irony are there in many Dylan songs, including 'On The Road Again' – which could almost be 'You Never Can Tell' turning sour, with its wild domestic detail. And Dylan uses the same Berry qualities on 'Bob Dylan's 115th Dream', 'From A Buick 6', 'Highway 61 Revisited', 'Memphis Blues Again', 'Visions of Johanna' and so on.

Dylan also took over Berry's manipulation of objects and the details and ad-man phrases that surround them. There are plenty of equivalents of that 'cherry-red '53' in Dylan's rock songs.[22]

Dylan doesn't go in for the massed place names Berry parades so generously, although there is one song – less characteristic than just interesting – which crams in all the following names (it's the unreleased 'Wanted Man'): California, Buffalo, Kansas City, Ohio, Mississippi, Cheyenne, Colorado, 'Georgia by the sea', El Paso, Juarez, Shreveport, Abilene, Albuquerque, Syracuse, Tallahassee and Baton Rouge.

It's also true that Dylan could never have written a song like 'Tombstone Blues'

---

21.   Chuck Berry: 'Promised Land', Chicago, 25/2/64, Chess 1916, Chicago [Pye Intnl 7N 25285, London], 1964; 'Sweet Little Sixteen' (c/w 'Reelin' And Rockin'), Chicago, 29/12/57, Chess 1683 [London-American Records HLM 8585], 1958. ('Reelin' And Rockin'' was a UK top 20 hit fifteen years later, Chess Records 6145 020, London, 1973.)

   Chapter 9 notes that even so distinctive a lyricist as Chuck Berry has specific forebears from the pre-war blues world, with lyrics clearly up Berry's street. Within that same rich, under-familiar terrain are several records on which singers ask phone-operators to call their girlfriends, stating the numbers and sometimes the romantic purpose of their calls. Berry's 'Memphis (Tennessee)', Chicago, 7/6/58, c/w 'Back In The USA', Chicago, Feb. 1959, Chess 1729, 1959, also uses the operator as if she were a priest. (This was a belated UK Top 10 hit in 1963, c/w 'Let It Rock', Chicago, 29/7/59, Pye Intnl 7N 25218, London, 1963.)

22.   In this context these lines from Dylan's 1980s song 'Brownsville Girl' are interesting for yielding a car-ride and much detail: 'Till the sun peels the paint and the seat-covers fade / And the water-moccasin dies'. (The song is discussed in Chapter 16.)

without Chuck Berry; nor, especially, could 'Subterranean Homesick Blues' have come into being without him, either in its musical format or its words. It needed Berry's 'Too Much Monkey Business' first.[23]

The Berry song technique is to pile up, like a list, the pressures that are on the story's narrator, and to suggest their unreasonableness by their phrased sharpness and multiplicity. This is done fairly straightforwardly, but the simplicity adds to the effect. The last verse runs:

> *Workin' in the fillin' station*
> *Too many tasks*
> *Wipe the windows*
> *Check the tyres*
> *Check the oil*
> *Dollar gas?!*

Dylan, taking this up, makes it serve in a far more complex capacity. He widens the context and the predicament of the man under pressure. Chuck Berry might have a nasty job but Dylan has to fight off the whole of society:

> *Ah, get born, keep warm,*
> *Short pants, romance, learn to dance,*
> *Get dressed, get blessed,*
> *Try to be a success,*
> *Please her, please him, buy gifts,*
> *Don't steal, don't lift,*
> *Twenty years of schoolin' an' they put you on the day shift*
> *Look out kid . . .*

Chuck Berry – like Little Richard – also indulged a sort of consciously laughing and highly effective quirk that made for line-endings on little words that prose would never emphasise. They don't just work as fill-ins: they help define the mood and add to the individuality of the songs. There's a totally characteristic example, which could have come from either Little Richard or Chuck Berry, in the Credence Clearwater tribute song 'Travelin' Band' where the rhyming line after 'hotel' is 'oh well'. Dylan picks up on this too. He doesn't use it in quite the same way, ever, and the most interesting examples are where he modifies its function most, in two of his narrative funny-songs, 'Motorpsycho Nightmare' and 'The Ballad Of Frankie Lee And Judas Priest':

> *He said he's gonna kill* [pause]
> *Me if I don't get out the door in ten seconds flat*

and

> *For sixteen nights and days he raved*
> *But on the seventeenth he burst* [pause!]
> *Into the arms of Judas Priest . . .*

---

23. Chuck Berry: 'Too Much Monkey Business' c/w 'Brown-Eyed Handsome Man', Chicago, Feb. 1956, Chess Records 1635, Chicago, 1956.

But it's important to recall, I think, that Berry was pioneering all this at a time when most people were either saying 'Rock, baby, rock', or 'I love you when you do the —'.

His musical influence is widespread too. Chuck Berry's distinctive, driving cameos, tight-knit and self-sufficient, inspired most of the rock side of Dylan's "Bringing It All Back Home" and much of "Highway 61" and many other cuts, including, in slow motion, 'Sitting On A Barbed-Wire Fence'.

If Dylan learnt a lot from Chuck Berry, who stood out in splendid contrast to the sickly inanities of the worst of 1960s pop, he learnt a lot also from Elvis Presley. As everyone must know, Presley came from Tupelo, Mississippi, where he was born poor in the 1930s and moved to Memphis with his mother and unemployed father when he was 13; later he got a job driving a truck. (There's a very nice Dylan allusion to this, delivered in a tough, Presley voice, on the Basement Tapes song 'Lo And Behold': 'Goin' down t' Tennessee! get me a truck or somethin''.)

Very much a Southerner, Presley said 'Yes Ma'am, No Sir' to hostile press reporters, was inward with a simple gospelly religion (via the First Assembly Church of God) and loved the voice of Mahalia Jackson.

Presley had the formula for rock'n'roll within him: a natural upbringing on blues and country music in its living environment. His first record, issued by Sun for distribution only in the South, was Arthur Big Boy Crudup's blues 'That's All Right', sung with a kind of subdued freneticism that sounds hillbilly, amateurish and absolutely genuine. The change to 'Heartbreak Hotel' is a large but a logical one.

From 1956 to 1960, his music was fine. The poor southern white made good, the prophet of rock, the sexual threat to bourgeois virginity, the pop equivalent of Brando in *The Wild One*, the untouchable and inaccessible prototype superstar: all this was maintained by the records, not the reporters. And when he had gone plastic and the Beatles were screamed at instead, the failure, correspondingly, was in Presley's music, not in his image. Had his output 1962–64 been up to his pre-army standard, then the Beatles might have got no further than those wonderful 1961 American groups like Maurice Williams & The Zodiacs, Cathy Jean and The Room-Mates, Nino and The Ebb-Tides. The gap was open for Beatlemania not because of Presley's age or because kids were tired of solo stars but because something drastic had happened to his music.

What was it that had gone out of Presley's world? All the sex; all that curious amalgam of insinuation and bluntness that Presley had introduced and Jagger was picking up on; all the pregnant charisma that had, from the very beginning, more than compensated for the false posturing of everything in the pre-Dylan years; all the therapeutic, role-distancing humour; an impeccable control in a strong voice that understood (rare thing then) nuance; and an avowing, ever-present nobility.

When he started, the two most important things in his music were lack of inhibition and sex. Lack of inhibition is very important. Adolescents admired him because he could be socially unacceptable and get away with it, on stage and on record and in the mind, even if not more than once on the Ed Sullivan TV show. Sullivan was right, by his own lights, to take Presley's hips out of camera range: they were being rude. And certainly a lot of teen singers who came after him were to discover that getting up on stage and yelling WAAAAAHHHH!!! is like exposing yourself in public without being stigmatised.

Sexually, Presley offered a new world, at any rate to whites, and offered it with a blunt statement of interests. There was none of the sycophantic 'dating' appeal that was the context of most of the 1950s stars' recorded love affairs. 'At The Hop', 'Teenager In Love', 'Lonely Boy': these were the typical titles of the time – but not for Elvis. His titles suited the black labels that announced them (just as in England Cliff Richard suited the flat green of the old Columbia label).[24] Presley's titles were 'Trouble', 'I Got Stung', 'Jailhouse Rock', 'Paralyzed', 'King Creole' – these all fitted the various significant elements that made Presley a unique, thrusting and ominous force. He embodied an untapped violence (consider that prophetic, pre-Pete Townshend line 'He don't stop playin' till his guitar breaks') that a song like 'Trouble' made explicit and the kind of hard bravado that 'Jailhouse Rock' merged with ecstasy. 'Jailhouse Rock' is a direct descendant of 'Hound Dog', where the voice seems to rage like King Kong in chains.[25]

Of course, lots of rock stars tried to be aggressive and masculine. Lots, too, made love to the stage microphone – Gene Vincent most endearingly: but only Elvis Presley projected himself so well that he seemed often to be bearing down sexually on the listener.

This comes across best in the love songs. Here, he offered the constant implication of prior sexual experience and a corresponding cynicism others could never bring off.

> *Hey baby – I ain't askin' much o' you*
> *No n-no n-no n-no no baby – ain't askin' much o' you:*
> *Just a big-uh big-uh big-uh hunk of love will do.*[26]

That, for example, came across in 1959 as freshly candid, its message the forerunner of that line from Dylan's 'If You Gotta Go, Go Now': 'It's not that I'm askin' for anything you never gave before'. The two share the same ambiguity, the same ostensible politeness. Obviously, the mindless propagandist virginity-assumptions of others were as far away from late-1950s Elvis as from mid-1960s Dylan.

It was a unique stance at the time: unique, at least, in reaching the mass of white middle-class adolescents. Black pop naturally insinuated also, but more as a series of relaxed in-jokes than as a manifesto, let alone one for white libido. And even the likes of Chuck Berry, a black star with broad bi-racial appeal, cut innumerable maudlin

---

24. 'At The Hop' was a US No. 1 hit by Danny & The Juniors in early 1958 (knocked off No. 1 by Elvis Presley's 'Don't'); 'Teenager In Love' was a big 1959 hit for Dion & The Belmonts, covered in Britain by one of the better British pop stars, Marty Wilde (father of Kim), and by one of the most pathetic, Craig Douglas. 'Lonely Boy' was a US No. 1 for Paul Anka in 1959.

25. 'Trouble', Hollywood, 15/1/58, and 'King Creole', Hollywood, 23/1/58, were both written and recorded for the film *King Creole*, Paramount Studios, US, directed Michael Curtiz, 1958 (based on Harold Robbins' novel *A Stone for Danny Fisher*, 1952); "King Creole", RCA Victor LPM 1884, New York [RCA Victor RD 27088, London], 1958. 'I Got Stung', Nashville, 11/6/58, RCA Victor 47–7410, New York, 1958 [RCA 1100, London, 1959]. 'Jailhouse Rock', Hollywood, 30/4/57, title song from the MGM film, US, directed Richard Thorpe, 1957; RCA Victor 20/47–7035 [RCA 1028], 1957: a No. 1 hit single USA and UK, and also title track of a No. 1 EP, RCA Victor EPA 4114, 1957 [RCX 106, 1958]. 'Paralyzed', Hollywood, 2/9/56; on "Elvis", RCA Victor LPM 1382, 1956 and EP "Elvis Vol. 1", EPA 992, 1956 [UK single on HMV POP 378, London, 1957].

In 1980 Bob Dylan recorded a song of his own titled 'Trouble', issued on "Shot Of Love", 1981.

26. Elvis Presley: 'A Big Hunk O' Love', Nashville, 10/6/58, RCA Victor 47–7600, New York [RCA 1136, London], 1959.

slow-shuffles where all the words seemed to say, roughly, were 'Can I carry your books home from school, darlin' / Cos gee you're lookin' good'.

And think of the other white heart-throbs. Take Ricky Nelson's forte:

> *I hate to face your dad*
> *Too bad*
> *I know he's gonna be mad*
> *It's late . . .*
> *Hope this won't be our last date;*

or take the mournful, sexless world of Eddie Cochran (though admittedly these lines are classics, encapsulating most of pre-Dylan pop USA):

> *Six hot-dogs oughta be just right*
> *After such a wonderful night . . .*[27]

Presley, in contrast, got down to the eternal verities of passion underlying the middle-class Saturday night:

> *If you wanna be loved, baby you gotta love me too*
> *'Cos I ain't for no one-sided love affair:*
>
> *Well a fair exchange ain't no robbery*
> *An' the whole world knows that it's true . . .*

And Presley's cynicism had such pungency that it provided over the years a sharp, concerted attack on the two-faced conventions which were imposed on the children of the 1950s.

> *Why make me plead*
> *For something you need?*[28]

His delivery gave a stylishness and authority to these open, soliciting songs that was utterly lacking in the other rock artists. Not just by sneers but by his pent-up tremble in the bass notes, the sudden, full-throated rasps and the almost confessional mellow country moans. Presley was saying 'Let's fuck' a full six years before John and Paul were wanting to hold your hand. Millions of eager 17-year-olds, weary of the Fabian-style pudge-next-door could respond a good deal more honestly when Elvis sang 'Stuck On You', 'Treat Me Nice' and 'Baby Let's Play House'.[29]

Not surprisingly, considering the time span of Presley's ascendance, other songs, if quoted carefully, could give an opposite picture: a picture of Presley as effete and,

27.   Ricky Nelson: 'It's Late', Hollywood, 21/10/58, Imperial Records 5565, Los Angeles [London American HLP 8817, London], 1959. Eddie Cochran: 'Drive-In Show', Los Angeles, 1957, Liberty Records 55087, Hollywood, 1957.

28.   Elvis Presley: 'One Sided Love Affair', NYC, 30/1/56, issued "Elvis Presley", RCA Victor LPM 1254, New York ["Elvis Presley (Rock 'N' Roll)", HMV CLP 1093, London], 1956 (his first LP, & a US No. 1); and 'Give Me The Right', Nashville, 12–13/3/61, issued "Something For Everybody", RCA Victor LPM/LSP-2370, New York [RD-27224 / SF 5106, London], 1961.

29.   Elvis Presley: 'Stuck On You', Nashville, 20–21/3/60, RCA Victor, New York [RCA 1187, London] 1960; 'Treat Me Nice', Hollywood, 5/9/57, B-side of 'Jailhouse Rock', see note 25; 'Baby Let's Play House', Memphis, 5/2/55, Sun Records 217, Memphis, 1955 [HMV Records POP 305, London, 1957].

like all the Bobby Vees and Vintons, sycophantic. 'Girl Of My Best Friend' is a good example:

> *What if she got real mad and told him so?:*
> *I could never face either one again . . .*

But first, the delivery was never remotely effete, and even at his most melodic (which he was never afraid to be anyway and which he always carried off without false delicacy) there was a saving power. And second, such examples were simply untypical of what Presley stood for. In the same way, the sensitive unisex aura of Buddy Holly – who avoided plasticity in an opposite way to Presley – was sometimes absent from his world yet remained its distinctive feature. '(Annie's Bin A-Workin' On The) Midnight Shift' is in this respect an exception in the Holly repertoire, not an archetype.[30]

A final point on Presley's sexuality. It is true that the pre-rock chart-toppers and radio favourites, the night-club stars whose idea of perfection was a Cole Porter song and the Nelson Riddle Orchestra, dealt with sex too – but never, never with passion. Physical contact, desire, sexual aspiration always come across from Sinatra, Tormé, Fitzgerald, Tony Bennett and the rest as a kind of world-weary joke that goes with old age. The standard it's-one-in-the-morning-and-we're-pretty-smooth treatments of 'I've Got You Under My Skin', 'Night and Day', etc., could easily be addressed to a can of flat beer.

Against this lifeless background, Presley's initial impact coast-to-coast in America and in Britain was cataclysmic. Yet lack of inhibition, sex and the voice to carry it was not all that he offered. He also gave out a fair share of the vital humour that goes with the best hard-line rock and that Fats Domino, Chuck Berry and Little Richard all used very well.

This kind of humour shows itself aware of outside values and of the inextricable mixture of the important and the trivial, the real and the stylised, in the pop medium. And if you go back now to the original Presley recordings, the pungency and freshness of this humour still hit home. Think of the self-awareness of Elvis, polite Southern boy with grafted-on rebel image, pounding out this:

> *Ah sure would be delighted with your com-pan-y:*
> *Come on an' do the Jailhouse Rock with me . . .*

Or less subtle flashes such as this:

> *If you can't find a partner use a wooden chair*
> *Let's rock*

or

---

30.   Elvis Presley: 'Girl Of My Best Friend', Nashville, 3–4/4/60, issued "Elvis Is Back", RCA Victor LPM/LSP-2231, New York [RCA RD27171 (mono) / SF 5060 (stereo), London], 1960, and as UK single c/w 'A Mess Of Blues' [Nashville, 20–21/3/60], RCA 1194, London, 1960. Buddy Holly: 'Midnight Shift', see note 14.
In other respects, as Greil Marcus notes in a passage discussed in note 47, 'Midnight Shift' was archetypal Holly and prototypal Dylan.

> *She wore a clingin' dress that fit so tight*
> *She couldn't sit down so we danced all night*

or

> *Well there ain't nothin' wrong with the long-haired music*
> *Like Brahms, Beethoven and Bach,*
> *But I was raised with a guitar in ma hand*
> *An' I was born to rock. Well . . .*

or finally

> *Samson told Delilah, Delilah say Yeah?*
> *Keep your cotton-pickin' fingers out ma curly hair.*[31]

And yes, the deliberate yet essentially unselfconscious black reference in that last example indicates how inward, how fundamental a strength is Presley's understanding of the blues. Its idiom comes in naturally enough.

'A Mess Of Blues', 'One Night', 'That's All Right', 'Reconsider Baby' (the Lowell Fulson classic), 'Blueberry Hill', 'Anyplace Is Paradise', 'Lawdy Miss Clawdy', 'It Feels So Right', 'Heartbreak Hotel' – listen to any of these today and the claim that Presley is a great white blues singer (albeit a commercial one) is hard to deny.[32] And that he brought all this before a vast, non-specialist white audience in the drab Eisenhower era was a really explosive achievement.[33]

31.   The quotations are from, respectively: 'Jailhouse Rock' (see note 25) twice; 'Dixieland Rock', Hollywood, 16/1/58, issued "King Creole" soundtrack LP, see note 25 [in UK also as B-side of 'King Creole' single, RCA 1081, London, 1958]; 'C'Mon Everybody', Hollywood, 9–10/7/63, "Viva Las Vegas" soundtrack EP, RCA Victor, New York ["Love In Las Vegas", RCX 7141, London], 1964; and 'Hard Headed Woman', Hollywood, 15/1/58, issued "King Creole" LP, see note 25, and single RCA Victor 20/47–7280, New York [RCA 1070, London] 1958 (the last Presley single issued USA on 78 rpm).

32.   A Mess Of Blues', see note 30; 'One Night', Hollywood, 23/2/57, RCA Victor 47–7410, New York, 1958 [RCA 1100, London, 1959]; 'That's All Right', see note 3; 'Reconsider Baby', Nashville, 3–4/4/60, issued "Elvis Is Back", see note 30; 'Blueberry Hill', Hollywood, 19/1/57, issued "Just For You" (EP), RCA Victor EPA 4041, New York ["Elvis Presley", RCX 104, London], 1957; 'Anyplace Is Paradise', Hollywood, 2/9/56, issued "Elvis", RCA Victor LPM 1382, 1956 ["Elvis (Rock 'N' Roll no. 2)", HMV Records CLP 1105, London, 1957]; 'Lawdy Miss Clawdy', NYC, 3/2/56, RCA Victor 20/47–6642, 1956 [HMV POP 408, London, 1957: B-side of different single]; 'It Feels So Right', 20–21/3/60, issued "Elvis Is Back", see note 30; 'Heartbreak Hotel', see note 3.

Lowell Fulson (1921–1999): 'Reconsider Baby', Dallas, 27/9/54, Checker Records 804, Chicago, 1954 [LP-issued "Love Those Goodies", Checker LP 2973, Chicago, *nia*].

33.   I expressed this more concretely in an obituary of Elvis, *Temporary Hoardings* (Rock Against Racism youth newsletter), no. 3, September 1977: 'What Presley did in music was stunning. Everyone in Memphis – which was the heart of the new South – 50% black population – stayed on their own side of the tracks or across the air waves. Presley took the two and hurled them together. Black soul, hillbilly insistence. His fusion changed everything. It accelerated the Civil Rights movement. It jerked a dead generation alive. It changed the future. Sinatra symbolised a generation, Presley created one.' In Paul Gilroy's *There Ain't No Black in the Union Jack* (1987) this passage was quoted to back up Gilroy's point that 'the love of music' can be the 'organic counterpart' to the 'hatred of racism'.

Re Presley's early race-crossing, the book *Wheelin' on Beale* (1992) by Louis Cantor (author of a nondescript essay about Bob Dylan in *Conclusions on the Wall*, ed. Elizabeth M. Thomson, 1980) describes how popular Presley's early records were with black listeners in Memphis and how he was warmly received by black fans on a visit to/appearance at a black radio stars event in Memphis [the WDIA Goodwill Revue, 22/12/56]. But the same book makes clear that in this direction, i.e. from white singer to black audience, Presley was not first. 'Peace In The Valley', written by black singer, composer and music publisher Thomas Dorsey, was a hit by white artist Red Foley on black radio station WDIA in Memphis in 1951–52, years before Elvis recorded. And Tony Russell notes ('Clarksdale piccolo blues', *Jazz and Blues*, Nov. 1971) that in September 1941, Lewis Jones surveyed the juke-boxes in the black bars of Clarksdale, Mississippi, noting what was on them. There was a significant amount of

Some of these tracks remain undiminished in quality. 'Heartbreak Hotel' still sounds strangely ahead of its time, even now. 'Reconsider Baby', recognising the impossibility of copying Lowell Fulson's original, is a masterly creative alternative, its tribute to Fulson consisting in its very originality of treatment, using Nashville instead of city-blues musicians and drawing out of them a whole of celebratory oceanic power, drive and dignity.

Presley's voice had nobility – a clear, charismatic rarity to which a generation rallied and felt uplifted in hoping to protect: just as another generation intensely desired to protect the man whose voice lit up 'I Threw It All Away'.

There are many other links between the two. In the first place, Dylan would have heard at least part of his old blues material second-hand through Presley. Elvis' 'Milkcow Blues Boogie' (which Dylan uses in 'It Takes A Lot To Laugh, It Takes A Train To Cry') is from an old song by Kokomo Arnold – not a well-known name, I'd guess, up in Minnesota – who was born in Lovejoy, Georgia in 1901.[34]

Also, Dylan's lyric and tune on 'One More Night' are heavily reminiscent of Elvis' record of 'Blue Moon Of Kentucky'. 'That's All Right', Presley's first record, is down there in the Bob Dylan songbook. The clear allusion to Floyd Cramer's piano style on the end of 'Tell Me That It Isn't True' is an allusion to a style much associated with Elvis and his RCA Victor studios at Nashville.[35]

The opening lines of 'Lay, Lady, Lay' are doing what Presley has stood for all along. Dylan may be sexier (his sexuality somehow bringing in his intelligence) and therefore better at it, but it's the same kind of ennobled overture that comes across in a hundred Elvis songs:

Lay, lady, lay –
Lay across ma big brass bed

while altogether the immaculate soulfulness of 'I Threw It All Away' is like Presley's great 'Is It So Strange?'[36]

A smaller but none the less indicative parallel can be found between an Elvis

---

white music. Whites were less open about listening to black music, though of course they did, mostly in private until Elvis' generation. Presley was the first white to express his own sexuality through black musical potency.

34. Not an accurate guess in Dylan's case perhaps, though the main point remains true: that part of Dylan's familiarity with the blues must have come through to him via Elvis Presley.

We don't know when Dylan first heard Kokomo Arnold's own record of 'Milk Cow Blues', but we know that he knew it by July 1962, because on the tape of Dylan at the Finjan Club, Montreal, 2/7/62, he sings 'his' song 'Quit Your Low-Down Ways', which is blatantly built upon a verse from Arnold's song – a verse Presley doesn't sing. [Kokomo Arnold: 'Milk Cow Blues', Chicago, 10/9/34; "Peetie Wheatstraw and Kokomo Arnold", Blues Classics Records BC-4, Berkeley, 1960–61. Elvis Presley: 'Milkcow Blues Boogie', Memphis, probably November 15 or December 20, 1954; Sun Records 215, Memphis, 1955.]

Chapter 9 deals in some detail with the question of when Dylan first heard which pre-war blues records, and with the connections between 'Milkcow Blues Boogie', Arnold, Presley, Dylan and 'It Takes A Lot To Laugh, It Takes A Train To Cry'.

35. Floyd Cramer played on Presley's 10–11/6/58 session, the first post-Army sessions [March–April 1960] and much of Presley's post-1960 Nashville output. (Official logs notwithstanding, he was *not* on Presley's first RCA Victor session, 10–11/1/56, the one that included 'Heartbreak Hotel'. The never-credited pianist on this session was Marvin Hughes. (Source: Gordon Stoker of The Jordanaires, interviewed by Trevor Cajiao, Nashville, 1994, in *Elvis: The Man and His Music*, no. 25, December 1994.)

36. Elvis Presley: 'Is It So Strange?', Hollywood, 19/1/57, issued "Just For You" (EP). [Presley had earlier sung the song at the legendary 'million dollar quartet' jam-session at Sun Studios with Carl Perkins, Jerry Lee Lewis and, briefly, Johnny Cash: Memphis, 4 or 11/12/56.]

record already mentioned, 'Milkcow Blues Boogie', and Dylan's '115th Dream'. Both cuts begin and then stop and start again. Elvis says 'Hold it fellas!' and Dylan's producer echoes this with 'Hey, wait a minute fellas!' It may have been Dylan who, recognising the parallel, insisted on retaining it on the released version of the track. If so, it is not the only Dylan amendment of a Presley line. In the much later Elvis song 'Cotton Candy Land' there is this pre-packed line 'We'll ride upon a big white swan'; Dylan revisits it with suitable irreverence in his knowingly gauche 'Country Pie', as 'Saddle me up a big white goose!'[37]

There are many take-offs of Elvis slipped into Dylan's work – but it's significant of the considerable value of Presley's influence that they are never so much take-offs as tributes. Presley is melodramatic and Dylan mocks that, mocks the exaggeration; but always he does it with a smile that confesses he can't help falling for Presley, that he notices the good things just as keenly. These take-offs/tributes include the end, musically, of 'Peggy Day':

> ting, ting, ta-ba-ba *Love to*, ba ba-ba-ba ba,
> *Spend the night* ba-ba-ba-ba-ba-ba-bam,
> *With Peggy Da-ay!* ba-am, ba-am, ba-am, ba-am-ba-ba-am!

Elvis' songs often really do end like this, right from his very early 'I Got A Woman' through to 'Beach Boy Blues', 'Steppin' Out Of Line' and 'Rock-A-Hula Baby'.[38]

Dylan doesn't stop there. On the Basement Tapes version of 'Quinn The Eskimo (The Mighty Quinn)', which is very different from the "Self Portrait" one, the Dylan voice is deliberately near to the Presley voice of 'Trouble'. And two versions of 'Nothing Was Delivered' from those sessions evoke the Presley world. The one with the heavy piano-backing is a finely measured acknowledgement of Elvis' handling of Domino's 'Blueberry Hill'; the version with Dylan's monologue is a wide-open laugh at Presley's posturing monologues on 'That's When Your Heartaches Begin', 'I'm Yours', 'Are You Lonesome Tonight?' and, again, 'Trouble'. On the last of these especially, Elvis 'talks tough' like a kind of upstart Lee Marvin:

> *I don' look f' trouble but I*
> *Never ran.*
> *I don' take no orders from*
> *No kinda man*

and Dylan simply makes the hollowness transparent by using the same bravado on weaker lines. Elvis stands there as if all-powerful, delivering the goods; Dylan comes on like a swindled consumer to talk from positions of weakness in the same posturing voice:

37.   Elvis Presley: 'Cotton Candy Land', Hollywood, Aug. 1962, "It Happened At The World's Fair", RCA Victor LPM/LSP-2697, New York [RD/SF 7565, London], 1963.

38.   'I Got A Woman', Nashville, 10/1/56, "Elvis Presley", see note 28; 'Beach Boy Blues' and 'Rock-A-Hula Baby', Hollywood, 23/3/61, "Blue Hawaii", RCA Victor LPM/LSP-2426, New York [RCA RD 27238 / SF 5115, London], 1961 ['Rock-A-Hula Baby' was also a single]; 'Steppin' Out Of Line', Hollywood, 22/3/61, "Pot Luck", LPM/LSP-2523 [RD 27265 / SF 5135], 1962.

> *Now you must, you must provide some answers*
> *For what you sell has not bin received*
> *And the sooner you come up with those answers*
> *You know the sooner you can leave.*[39]

I had written that phrase about Presley's toughness – 'like a kind of upstart Lee Marvin' – long before Dylan made "Pat Garrett & Billy The Kid" with Marvin-surrogate James Coburn: but for the soundtrack album of that film, Dylan does three versions of a song called 'Billy', the last of which, 'Billy 7', is actually a beautiful imitation of how Coburn would sound if he were singing it. And the effect of this is, of course, to give us a Dylan parodying exactly the kind of toughness that belongs to Presley. He parallels the ethic of those lines just quoted from 'Trouble' unerringly, and sings with an astonishingly deep voice set against sleazy, smoky guitar-lines and even sound-effects of ominous thunder:

> *They say that Pat Garrett's got your number*
> *Sleep with one eye open when you slumber*
> *Every little sound just might be thunder*
> *Thunder from the barrel of his gun.*

Dylan also came clean, in the 1970s in acknowledging the special place Elvis Presley occupies in his canon of influences. The "New Morning" song, 'Went To See The Gypsy' seems to be about going to see Presley, and Dylan makes known his revering of Elvis not just by lines like

> *He can move you from the rear*
> *Drive you from your fear*
> *Bring you through the mirror*
> *He did it in Las Vegas and he can do it here*

but also by capturing the inevitable awkwardness of their meeting in these humorous lines:

> *I went to see the gypsy*
> *Staying in a big hotel*
> *He smiled when he saw me coming*
> *And he said 'Well, well, well!'*
> *His room was dark and crowded*
> *Lights were low and dim*
> *'How are you?' he said to me*
> *I said it back to him!* . . .

And when his record company issued their ragbag album of warm-ups and reject tracks, "Dylan" (1973), it contained Bob Dylan versions of two songs that were

39. Bob Dylan: 'Quinn The Eskimo (The Mighty Quinn)', West Saugerties, June–Aug. 1967; finally issued "Biograph", 1985. Elvis Presley: 'Trouble', see note 25. Bob Dylan: 'Nothing Was Delivered' [piano-prominent and monologue versions], West Saugerties, Sept.–Oct. 1967, unreleased. Elvis Presley: 'That's When Your Heartaches Begin', Hollywood, 13/1/57, B-side of 'All Shook Up' [see note 10]; 'I'm Yours', Nashville, 25–26/6/61, "Pot Luck", see note 38; 'Are You Lonesome Tonight?', Nashville, 3–4/4/60, RCA Victor 47–7810 (and "living stereo" version 61–7810), New York [RCA 1216, London], 1960.

Presley hits. Just as Elvis made versions of Dylan's 'Don't Think Twice, It's All Right' and 'Tomorrow Is A Long Time', so Dylan had done Elvis' 'A Fool Such As I' (a warm-up for the "Self Portrait" sessions) and an amazing version of 'Can't Help Falling In Love' (a warm-up for "New Morning").[40]

Years ago, when Dylan was held to be the absolute opposite, the antithesis, of Presley, it would have been, if not actually heretical, at least controversial to argue that Dylan could owe Elvis anything. Now, recognition has grown for what Presley has achieved. The clichés and artifice that are a discountable part of it to me must almost certainly be too obtrusive for new listeners except on a few classic tracks. But Dylan grew up with it too. There's more to appreciating what he derived from Elvis Presley than I have managed to convey. But it's there in the music.

For different reasons it's even harder to write anything useful about Buddy Holly. He had more personal talent, more charisma and more potential than anyone except Presley. Even on his very early recordings, where the studio sound, the arrangements and the type of song featured all drew heavily on Presley's earliest Sun cuts, you could not but be aware of a very different talent feeling its way and testing its strengths.[41] By the time he was having hits, he not only had a distinctive sound but also an integrity and an inquiring interest in country music and city blues. The famous Holly sound is on songs like 'That'll Be The Day' (Version 2: and it's instructive to compare it to the earlier, unstable version), 'Peggy Sue', 'Heartbeat', 'Every Day', 'Listen To Me', 'Tell Me How', and so on. Maybe his later ones are the best, with their slightly mellower sound – in particular, 'Peggy Sue Got Married', 'That's What They Say', 'What To Do', and the truly immortal record that was his latest release at the time of

40.   Elvis Presley: 'Don't Think Twice, It's All Right', Nashville, 16–17/5/71, "Elvis" [not same as 2nd LP, which had same title, 1956, see note 25], RCA Victor APL1–0283, New York [SF 8378, London], 1973; 'Tomorrow Is A Long Time', Nashville, 25–28/5/66 [the sessions include musicians Floyd Cramer, Pete Drake & Charlie McCoy], "Spinout", LPM/LSP-3702 ["California Holiday", RCA SF 7820, London], 1966.

In June 1969, *Rolling Stone* (no. 47, 29/11/69) asked Dylan whether there were any particular artists he liked to do versions of his songs; he replied (and was widely assumed to be joking at the time), 'Yeah, Elvis Presley. I liked Elvis Presley. Elvis Presley recorded a song of mine. That's the one recording I treasure the most . . . it was called 'Tomorrow Is A Long Time'. I wrote it but never recorded it.' Asked which Presley album this track was on, Dylan replied, ' "Kismet".' (This was existentially correct: Presley's 'Tomorrow Is A Long Time' was actually a 'bonus track' filling out the 'soundtrack album' for the awful mid-1960s film *Spinout* [MGM, US, directed Norman Taurog 1966], in Europe titled *California Holiday*; 'Kismet' was a song on the soundtrack LP of an even worse mid-1960s Presley film, MGM's 1965 "Harum Scarum" [Nashville, 24–25/2/65, RCA Victor LPM/LSP-3468, New York ("Harem Holiday", RCA RD/SF 7767, London], 1965]. The live recording of Dylan performing 'Tomorrow Is A Long Time', NYC, 12/4/63, was issued on "Bob Dylan's Greatest Hits Vol. II", 1971.)

In June 1972 Bob Dylan was 'spotted' attending one of Presley's four concerts at Madison Square Garden, NYC [9–11/6/72]. The idea, suggested by 'Went To See The Gypsy', that Dylan might have met Presley in Minnesota (a) when both were famous (b) after a Presley Las Vegas stint and (c) ahead of the "New Morning" songs being recorded ['Went To See The Gypsy', NYC, 3/3/70], is impossible, though they might have met elsewhere [Presley's first post-Army Las Vegas stints were July 31–August 28, 1969 and January 26–February 23, 1970; he then played six shows in Houston, Texas, February 27–March 1, 1970, staying at the Astroworld Hotel Feb. 25–March 2].

That Dylan might have seen Presley in concert in Minnesota is another matter: Presley first performed in Minnesota in St. Paul, 13/5/56; next, 15 years later, Minneapolis, 5/11/71; then St. Paul, 2&3/10/74; Duluth, 16/10/76; Minneapolis, 17/10/76; Duluth, 29/4/77; and lastly St. Paul, 30/4/77.

41.   Like Presley, Buddy Holly created some of the territory of rock'n'roll, virtually inventing the guitars–bass–drums beat group with composer–vocalist leader. His large body of timeless, unpretentious work, achieved in a very few years (cf. bluesmen such as Blind Lemon Jefferson and Robert Johnson) was given properly documented reissue by John Beecher & Malcolm Jones, with the 6-LP box-set "The Complete Buddy Holly", MCA Coral CDSP 807, London, 1979.

his death, Paul Anka's composition 'It Doesn't Matter Anymore' coupled with 'Raining In My Heart.'[42]

Holly's voice transcends the limits set by the words of his songs. 'What To Do', transcribed on to the printed page, may be fatuous and trite:

> The record-hops and all the
> Happy times we had;
> The soda-shops, the walks to school
> Now make me sad, oh!
>
> What to do
> I know my heartache's showin'
> Still not knowin'
> What to do

but on record Holly's voice moulds it, lights it up, so that it becomes a good deal more than trite – more, even, than acceptable sentimentality.

Holly died, if anyone doesn't know it, with Ritchie Valens in 1959, in a chartered single-engine plane that crashed in the snow in the early hours of 3 February, on its way to North Dakota.[43] The last things studio-recorded before his death were in some ways a little odd. The titles were 'True Love Ways' and 'Moondreams', and they were very mellow indeed. (One of them even used an aspidistra saxophone sound.) But if there's a hint that he might have been already slacking off into popular ballad land, the evidence of his musical interests belies it. He cut the only white commercial blues that could even touch Presley's best: 'Mailman, Bring Me No More Blues'. He could handle Bo Diddley and Chuck Berry too, not just competently but adding something

---

42.   Buddy Holly & The Three Tunes: 'That'll Be The Day' [1st version], Nashville, 22/7/56, US Decca Records 30434, New York, 1957. The Crickets: 'That'll Be The Day' [2nd, & hit, version], Clovis New Mexico, 25/2/57, Brunswick Records 55009, New York [Coral Q 72279, London], 1957. Buddy Holly: 'Peggy Sue', Clovis, 29/6–1/7/57, c/w 'Everyday', Clovis, 27/6/57, Coral Records 61885, New York [Coral Q 72293, London], 1957; 'Heartbeat', Clovis, June–Aug. 1958, Coral 62051 [Q 72346], 1958; 'Listen To Me', Clovis, 29/6–1/7/57, Coral 61947 [Q 72288], 1958. The Crickets: 'Tell Me How', Clovis, May–July 1957, B-side of 'Maybe Baby', Oklahoma City, 27–28/9/57, Brunswick 55053 [Coral Q 72307], 1958. Buddy Holly: 'Peggy Sue Got Married', NYC, Jan. 1959 [overdubs NYC, June 1959], Coral 62134 [Q 72376], 1959; 'That's What They Say' and 'What To Do', NYC, Jan. 1959 [overdubs NYC, Jan. 1960], "The Buddy Holly Story Volume 2", Coral LP 57326, New York [Coral LVA 9127, London], 1960 [and UK single Coral Q 72419, London, 1961]; 'It Doesn't Matter Any More' c/w 'Raining In My Heart', NYC, 21/10/58, Coral 62074 [Q 72360], 1959.
    The tracks recorded January 1959 were solo demos by Holly, made in his Greenwich Village apartment, after he had broken with both The Crickets and Norman Petty, with 1959–1960 overdubs by Jack Hansen, commissioned by Dick Jacobs (with whose 'Orchestra' Holly had recorded his last session, i.e. NYC, 21/10/58: the session that had yielded 'It Doesn't Matter Anymore' & 'Raining In My Heart' plus 'True Love Ways' and 'Moondreams', discussed in note 44). The January 1959 demo material was later re-acquired by Norman Petty, who made different overdubs, using The Fireballs, [Clovis, 1962–68] on this and other material. Through the 1960s and 1970s, therefore, with the US and UK companies issuing different releases, the two different sets of overdubbed tracks were issued more or less haphazardly. The box-set "The Complete Buddy Holly" (see note 41) contains both, plus Holly's undubbed original solo demo versions of *some* but not all these tracks. To the extent that some were not included – 'What To Do' and 'That's What They Say' among them – the box-set is mistitled.

43.   Bob Dylan saw Holly perform (at the Duluth Armory, 31/1/59) just days before the latter's plane crash death on 3/2/59. This was *the* rock star death of the 1950s, the first such death of huge significance to the rock'n'roll generation. The earlier death, by Russian roulette, of R&B artist Johnny Ace, backstage in Houston, Christmas Eve, 1954, is better known now than at the time, and Ace a lesser artist than Holly. (His 'Never Let Me Go' [Houston, 1954, Duke Records 132, Houston, 1954] was performed as a duet by Bob Dylan and Joan Baez at twenty-one of the 1975 Rolling Thunder Revue shows.)

of his own in a way that showed rare understanding. 'Bo Diddley' and 'Brown-Eyed Handsome Man' make the point with a kind of raw panache.[44]

As for the music on his own songs, it's riddled with the clichés of the time, but he handled these clichés with intelligence enough to show that had he lived he would have readily discarded them. People talk automatically about the Claptons of this world as 'the great guitarists'; I think there's a sense in which Holly was a great guitarist, boxed in by the restrictions of convention in his time. If he had lived . . . Greil Marcus said that Buddy Holly would have joined Dylan for a duet on, say, 'I Don't Believe You'. That sounds true to me, and true in part because of the similarities that exist in any case between the two singers.[45]

Control is a main point of resemblance. It was missing altogether from rock when the British beat group boom got going in 1964. One of the main things that marked out such groups from the solo stars they replaced was that a loose, ramshackle sound was considered good enough and a rather erratic vocal technique came into vogue. Suddenly, singers weren't sure where they were throwing their voices and didn't care which notes they were going to hit. Many of the solo stars had known exactly what their voices were doing – even when they were ripping it up. Little Richard was wild, but he was always in control. Presley always had this same sort of precision. So did the Everlys and Jackie Wilson, especially on his classic 'Reet Petite'. Buddy Holly had it too.[46]

Control in Holly was a special thing, tantamount to integrity – a precision demanded by artistic considerations, which was one of the things that made for his greatness. Dylan learnt a lot about such considerations, I would say, directly from Buddy Holly. There are times when both of them appear not to have this control, times when bits of phrasing sound at first hearing like bad mistakes, but they never

44. 'True Love Ways', 'Moondreams', 'Bo Diddley' and 'Brown-Eyed Handsome Man', for last two see note 14. The tenor saxophone on the beautiful 'True Love Ways' is by Sam 'The Man' Taylor. The pleasant surprise saxophone at the end of Dylan's "Oh Mercy" track 'Where Teardrops Fall' acts as a fond tribute to the Holly recording. This is discussed again in Chapter 16.
    'Mailman Bring Me No More Blues', Clovis, 8/4/57, Coral 61852, New York, 1957: B-side of 'Words Of Love', also Clovis, 8/4/57. 1st UK issue on "Buddy Holly" LP, Coral C 57210, London, 1958; not issued as a UK single until as B-side of 'Look At Me' [Clovis, May–July 1957], Coral 72445, 1961. 'Mailman', written for Holly, remains superb: one of those magic combinations of song, pace, conviction, sound, vocals, guitar-work (all Holly's) and mood. An undiminished, shimmering achievement.
    It was covered within weeks by country star Lefty Frizzell [Nashville, 10/5/57] but this cover remained unissued until the 12-CD box-set "Lefty Frizzell: Life's Like Poetry", Bear Family Records BCD 15550, Vollersode, Germany, 1992. (Frizzell, 1928–1975, was a highly influential honky-tonk singer of the 1950s, an idiosyncratic vocalist whose mark can be detected on the work of Merle Haggard and people like Randy Travis. He came out of the dance-halls of Texas, and 'If You've Got The Money I've Got The Time' made him a star in 1950s [the song was in Roy Orbison's early repertoire, across the other side of Texas from Buddy Holly's Lubbock homebase]. He had about thirty subsequent smaller hits. He was one of the first to record 'Long Black Veil', reaching No. 6 in the US country charts with it in 1959. He more or less drank himself to death at 47.)

45. Greil Marcus: 'Records', *Rolling Stone*, no. 35, 28/6/69.
    Dylan's 'Odds And Ends', on "The Basement Tapes", seems strikingly and wholly in the spirit of Buddy Holly & The Crickets records. (At the same time 'Odds And Ends', as Dylan will have been aware, is the title of a prominent Jimmy Reed record – prominent for featuring electric violin, played by the splendidly named Remo Biondi: Jimmy Reed: 'Odds & Ends', Chicago, 3/4/57, Vee Jay 298, Chicago, 1957. An 'Odds And Ends' was cut later by the rockabilly Warren Smith, Hollywood, 17/11/60, Liberty Records LRP 3199 / LST 7199 / LB 1181, Hollywood, 1961.)

46. Jackie Wilson: 'Reet Petite', NYC, July 1957, Brunswick Records 55024, New York [Coral Records Q 72290, London], 1957. This was a No. 6 UK hit in 1957 and a No.1 when reissued 29 years later [SMP Records SKM 3, UK, 1986].

are. The wild swoop-up/hiccup at the end of the title phrase in Holly's 'Tell Me How' is an example; Dylan provides others in 'The Times They Are A-Changin'' and, among others, 'Drifter's Escape'. The oddities are not mistakes, they're far more right than the expected alternatives that don't appear. A few more playings and they both prove their points. The control and precision were perfect after all and, when that realisation dawns, both artists have taught you something.

You can trace the effects of this teaching, as Holly gave it to Dylan, right down to similarities of timing, phrasing, emphasis, pronunciation. Greil Marcus, as usual, has dealt very well with this: 'Dylan and Holly', he wrote, 'share a clipped staccato delivery that communicates a sly sense of cool, almost teenage masculinity,' and he cites Buddy Holly's performance on 'Midnight Shift'. There, says Marcus, 'the phrasing is simply what we know as pure Dylan':

> *If she tells you she wants to use the caahhh!*
> *Never explains what she wants it faaahhh!*

Marcus goes on from there to make another but a connected point, in discussing some of the home-tape-recordings of Holly's voice that were released, after his death, with backing-tracks added:

> Sometimes, these ancient cuts provide a real sense of what rock'n'roll might have become had Holly lived. The same shock of recognition that knocked out the audiences at the Fillmore West when The Band . . . lit into Little Richard, takes place, with the same song, when the ghost of Buddy Holly is joined by the Fireballs for 'Slippin' And Slidin'' . . . An agile, humorous vocal is carried by a band that knows all the tricks. They break it open with the Everly Brothers' own seductive intro, constantly switching, musically, from song to song, while Holly ties it together. The guitarist actually sounds like Robbie Robertson, throwing in bright little patterns around the constant whoosh of the cymbals . . . it's certainly one of the best things Buddy Holly never did.[47]

There must be a good deal of similarity that is perhaps too intangible to document in order for that idea to strike home so sharply. Obviously, the 'Midnight Shift' resemblance is tangible enough, and we have it on innumerable Dylan tracks from 'I Want You' to 'On The Road Again' and from 'Absolutely Sweet Marie' back to 'When The Ship Comes In'. The last of these may seem a strange choice, but Buddy Holly could have sung 'When The Ship Comes In'. It has all the right tensions, all the polarities of high and low notes, rushes and lapses, that Holly alone among the pre-Dylan stars could easily control.

---

47.   Greil Marcus: 'Records', see note 45. The same 'shock of recognition' is there when Marcus first suggests the Holly–Dylan duet that would have happened had Holly lived. (The phrase 'shock of recognition', as applied to the blues-listening experience, is discussed in Chapter 9.)

  Buddy Holly: 'Tell Me How' [note 42], 'Midnight Shift' [note 14] and 'True Love Ways' [note 44]; 'Slippin' And Slidin'', NYC, Jan. 1959 [overdubs by the Fireballs, Clovis, 1962], US B-side of 'What To Do' [see note 42], Coral Records C 62448, New York, 1965 [UK B-side of 'Brown-Eyed Handsome Man' (see note 14), Coral Q 72459, 1963].

  Dylan acknowledged Holly's importance at his 1998 Grammy acceptance speech for Best Male Rock Vocal Performance and Best Contemporary Folk Album [New York City, 25/2/98], in which he also described having a sense of Holly's presence all through the recording of the "Time Out Of Mind" album, 1997 (almost forty years after Holly's death). He began performing Holly's great Bo Diddley-inspired song 'Not Fade Away' in concert, starting on the first night of the opening leg of the 1999 tour, Fort Myers, Florida, 26/1/99.

That brings home another fusion of delivery: an intangible additive in the voices. Both Dylan and Holly suggest a level of emotion at work below the words, way out beyond the scope of the lyric. Holly shows it incredibly well on, for example, 'True Love Ways', and Dylan uses it everywhere. In the end, perhaps the best way to encompass what Dylan has done via Holly is to say that Dylan really has replaced him.

You could say that Dylan has replaced Nashville too, that he has put almost all it stands for into a handful of songs there at the end of "John Wesley Harding" and on "Nashville Skyline".

I've been considering the major influences on Dylan's pop/rock music, and it's tempting to carry on through his countrified output, the material just mentioned, from exactly the same perspective. When you hear a song like his 'I'll Be Your Baby Tonight' it is easy to say, ah yes, Hank Williams – yet switch straight from the Dylan song to any Hank Williams album and the strong and derivative resemblance you imagined just vanishes. 'I'll Be Your Baby Tonight' isn't really like Hank Williams at all.

The answer is that the perspective is all wrong. Dylan owes a lot, not to Hank Williams (or anyone else) in particular, but simply to Nashville; it isn't 'influences' so much as stimulus.[48] Dylan hears Don Gibson bring something close to perfection, in

---

48.   Of course I'd now acknowledge Hank Williams as indeed a specific influence on Dylan, though a broad and founding one rather than one relied upon particularly for Dylan's 1968–1970 country music. As Dylan himself said all along: 'An' my first idol was Hank Williams / For he sang about the railroad lines / An' the iron bars an' rattlin' wheels / Left no doubt that they were real': 'Joan Baez In Concert, Part 2' sleeve note poem (published on Vanguard Records VRS-9113, New York, 1964).

Dylan has recorded and/or performed at least eleven Hank Williams songs, widely distributed through the decades of his career, as follows: 'Hey Good Lookin', live in Tuscaloosa, Alabama, 26/10/90. 'House Of Gold', live in Madrid, 15/6/89 and Athens, 28/6/89. '(I Heard That) Lonesome Whistle', at the home of Eve and Mac MacKenzie, NYC, 23/11/61; for WBAI Radio, NYC, c. 13/1/62 (probably broadcast 11/3/62); at the "Freewheelin' Bob Dylan" sessions, NYC, 24–25/4/62; live at Toad's Place, New Haven, Connecticut, 12/1/90; and live Penn State University, 14/1/90. 'Lost Highway' and 'I'm So Lonesome I Could Cry' backstage London, 3–4/5/65 (fragment included in the film *Don't Look Back*, Leacock-Pennebaker, US, auteured by D. A. Pennebaker, 1967). 'Kaw Liga', NYC, 28/10/75 for the soundtrack to the film *Renaldo & Clara* (extract used), Circuit Films, US, dir. Dylan and Howard Alk, 1977. 'Lost On The River', Malibu, probably March 1984, during rehearsal for *Late Night with David Letterman* NBC-TV appearance, NYC, 22/3/84. 'Weary Blues From Waitin'', live Lakeland, Florida, 18/4/76. 'You Win Again', West Saugerties, June–Aug. 1967 and in a drunken jam with Etta James and her band, Providence, Rhode Island, 9–10/7/86. 'Your Cheatin' Heart', live during guest performance at a Levon Helm & Rick Danko gig, NYC, 16/2/83. He performed 'Honky Tonk Blues' in concert in Tallahassee, 1/2/99 and on other similar dates.

Probably most of these were known to Dylan from the Hank Williams 78 rpm records he had back in Hibbing referred to several times, though not itemised, in Robert Shelton's *No Direction Home*, 1986. [Hank Williams: 'Hey, Good Lookin'', Nashville, 16/3/51, MGM 11000, 1951; 'A House Of Gold', *nia*, 1948–49, MGM 11707, 1954; '(I Heard That) Lonesome Whistle', Nashville, 25/7/51, MGM 11054, 1951; 'Lost Highway', Nashville 1/3/49, MGM 10506, 1949; 'I'm So Lonesome I Could Cry', Cincinnati, 30/8/49, MGM 10560, 1949; 'Lost On The River', Cincinnati, 22/12/48, MGM 10434, c. 1949; 'Weary Blues From Waitin'', *nia*, 1948–49, MGM 11574, 1953; 'You Win Again', Nashville, 11/7/52, MGM 11318, 1952; 'Your Cheatin' Heart' c/w 'Kaw-Liga', Nashville, 23/9/52, MGM 11416, 1952; 'Honky Tonk Blues', Nashville, 11/12/51, MGM 11160, 1952.]

Influence works in many ways. Chapter 2 noted how struck Dylan was by the particular mode of address e. e. cummings used in his poem 'Buffalo Bill': 'and what i want to know is / how do you like your blueeyed boy / Mister Death' – struck by its directness – and in the light of this, it interests me that two of Dylan's earliest songs, though three years apart and very different in style, share another particular mode of address: 'Hey, so-and-so . . .' The songs are 'Hey, Little Richard' (the very first known extant item on tape by Bob Dylan, recorded Hibbing, 1958) and 'Song To Woody', which begins its second verse 'Hey, hey, Woody Guthrie . . .' and its third 'Hey, Woody Guthrie . . .' Isn't it quite likely that Dylan was first struck by *this* mode of address in song when he heard it on Hank Williams' 'Hey, Good Lookin''?

its own small way, with 'Sea Of Heartbreak'; Dylan hears Jerry Lee Lewis break into extraordinary lyrical piano-work on beautifully poised performances of songs like 'Cold Cold Heart', 'Your Cheating Heart', 'Together Again' and 'How's My Ex Treating You?'; Dylan hears and befriends Johnny Cash; Dylan hears Flatt & Scruggs, Patsy Cline, Jack Scott, Marty Robbins and a hundred others, with and without international 'names' – all exploring different paths but from the same prolific headquarters.[49] So with "Nashville Skyline" Dylan decides to commit himself to a country music album and the result is stunning because he sees through to basics in whatever he tackles. He turns out an album unrivalled in country music, an album so precisely right, so faithfully lifelike and yet so alive, that it almost makes the rest of Nashville redundant.

In its own right, that's a major achievement – yet in the full context of what Dylan, as an artist, has done, it is only of minor importance. Country music just isn't that valuable. A one-man Nashville has so much less to offer than the Dylan of "Highway 61 Revisited" to "John Wesley Harding", or of "Blood On The Tracks".

But all the influences, including Nashville, have helped Dylan produce great work; and in turn Dylan made it possible for a revolution to take place in rock music.

49.   Don Gibson was one of Chet Atkins' protégés at RCA Victor in Nashville. A songwriter as well as a singer, his best known, most-covered song is 'I Can't Stop Loving You'. 'Sea Of Heartbreak' was among several countrified pop hits he had himself in the US and UK charts 1959–1963. Others included 'Lonesome Number One', 'Oh Lonesome Me' (revived by Neil Young), 'Sweet Dreams' (revived exquisitely by and on "Don Everly", Ode Records SP-77005, Los Angeles [A&M Records AMLS 2007, London], 1971: a brilliant LP), and 'Legend In My Time'. In 1989, Bob Dylan performed 'Legend In My Time' at three concerts.

Jerry Lee Lewis: 'Cold Cold Heart' [another Hank Williams song], details Chapter 1, footnote 16; 'How's My Ex Treating You?', Memphis, 14/6/62, Sun 379 [London American Records HLS 9584, London], 1962, the B-side of 'Sweet Little 16', see note 14. These were country B-sides to rock'n'roll A-sides; the others – 'Your Cheating Heart' and 'Together Again' – were country performances during two very different officially recorded live shows of the period, each excellent in its own way. 'Your Cheating Heart', Hamburg, 5/4/64, "Live At The Star Club, Hamburg", Philips 842 945, Germany [Philips BL 7646, London], 1964: a crude, exciting performance in a small, sweaty room, with the very British group the Nashville Teens as back-up band; very much the atmosphere and acoustics of early-1960s Liverpool beat-group venues. 'Together Again', Birmingham, Alabama, 1/7/64, "The Greatest Live Show On Earth", Smash/Mercury Records 67052, Chicago, 1964: a polished, crowd-manipulating performance, just as exciting as that in Hamburg, but with the sound and atmosphere of a huge stadium and a vast, fervent crowd, with proper American back-up musicians; messianic and majestic, the show also includes a sumptuous, exhilarating version of Tommy Tucker's 'Hi Heel Sneakers'.

Jack Scott was a rocker who found, after many a label switch, that the country-pop market was larger. His biggest success was the transatlantic hit 'What In The World's Come Over You', a hit in the UK alongside Jim Reeves' more lugubrious but comparable 'He'll Have To Go'. Bob Dylan performed Jack Scott's 'Let's Learn To Live & Love Again' at two concerts in 1990 (Berlin, 5/7/90 and Des Moines, Iowa, 26/8/90).

Lester Flatt and Earl Scruggs, bluegrassers, stand in a different relation to the Bob Dylan of "Nashville Skyline". Four months before Dylan recorded his album in February 1969, Flatt & Scruggs issued one called "Nashville Airplane", using the same musicians, on the same label (Columbia CS9741, New York [CBS 63570, London], 1968) and featuring countrified versions of 'Like A Rolling Stone' [Nashville, 18/7/68], 'Rainy Day Women Nos. 12 & 35' [Nashville, 9/9/68], 'I'll Be Your Baby Tonight' [9/9/68] and 'The Times They Are A-Changin'', [16/9/68], plus an instrumental, 'Freida Florentine' [17/9/68], in much the same vein as 'Nashville Skyline Rag' (which Scruggs and Dylan later re-recorded together [Carmel, New York, Dec. 1970] for the LP "Earl Scruggs: His Family And Friends", Columbia KC 30584, New York [CBS 64777, London], 1971). "Nashville Airplane" was a follow-up to Flatt & Scruggs' "Changin' Times" (Columbia, *nia*, New York [CBS 63251], 1967) which alongside 'Where Have All The Flowers Gone?' and 'Ode To Billie Jo' offered 'Down In The Flood', 'Mr. Tambourine Man', 'Don't Think Twice, It's All Right', 'It Ain't Me, Babe' and 'Blowin' In The Wind'. All these might be explained by the fact of Bob Johnston's becoming Flatt & Scruggs' producer as of September 1967 – except that their first recording of a Dylan song was in 1966: the rather good 'Mama You Been On My Mind', Nashville, 16/5/66, issued as a single (billed as by Lester Flatt, Earl Scruggs and the Foggy Mountain Boys), Columbia Records CO 43803, New York, 1966. All these covers of Dylan material are CD-reissued on "Flatt & Scruggs 1964–1969, Plus", Bear Family Records BCD 15879, Vollersode, Germany, 1995.

Who's Gonna Throw that Minstrel Boy a Coin?

There is another aspect of Dylan worth dealing with in the context of the old pop as much as the new rock: not Dylan the artist but Dylan the star. Dylan is the greatest rock'n'roll star in the world.[50]

Partly, of course, this is because he's the best rock writer and singer and performer there has ever been; but partly (and the two aren't by any means totally distinguishable) it's because he's become an idol, a superstar. In the summer of 1978 – a full twelve years after his 1960s cult zenith of popularity and at a time when punk was at its height – Bob Dylan pulled a quarter of a million people to Blackbushe for one concert. Special trains, RAC routes, the lot.

There are certain strategies which dictate impressively whether 'star material' makes it to legend status. One such successful strategy is to build up your rarity value. You reach a point when it is fatal to appear too often, when the occasional rumour is more effective than frequent hard news, when it's better only to release one record a year than to attempt a three-monthly assault on the charts, when it's best not to talk at all to the outside world, when it's necessary to shun the company of other celebrities, wise to turn down huge money offers, and above all essential to avoid TV.

This starts out as a simple showbiz rule, 'always leave the public shouting for more'; but it ends up vastly more complex and all-embracing in a pop world attended to by teeny-boppers and students, business executives and lefties – a world split between singles and albums, TV shows and weekend festivals, stage concerts, dance halls, discotheques and films – and under the constant if idle scrutiny of 'quality' newspapers, tabloids, weary Fleet Street music papers, and trendy paperbacks. You have to learn to dodge them all. Otherwise they burn you out before you're halfway there.

The star not only has that to deal with, but has to dodge every day a hundred other reductive approaches. In the early 1960s in England, there was a programme on BBC Radio (the Light Programme) called *Saturday Club*. This was a two-hour mixture of records and live appearances partly by pop artists and partly by played-out old dance bands, combos and foot-tappin' guitarists. Plainly a programme to avoid. No true star would have touched it with the wrong end of his chromium-plated microphone. Yet plenty of famous pop names agreed to perform on it not just as newcomers but long after they had become established. Bad strategy, bad management.

The man with the best manager was Presley. Once established, Presley withdrew

---

50. Time and changes in Dylan's own conduct have made this claim a relic of history rather than an ongoing truth, and much of the section built upon it now has an air of quaintness (nothing being more quaint than the recent past). I've left it intact as a record of how things once were, or at least of how they once seemed. Dylan's inept and inebriated appearance at *Live Aid*, Philadelphia, 13/7/85, put paid to his automatic right to headline any event, and since then his Never-Ending Tour, his increasing willingness to appear on TV, to be support-act to more or less anyone and to let even Bono of U2 climb on stage with him, his writer's block and his failure to sell records or get on the radio – all these developments have sabotaged the claims made in my text. Except that, despite it all, Bob Dylan still has 'legend status'. The part of my text that time has made most risible is the gushing about how Dylan is 'not just ten steps ahead of the media: he's three steps ahead of you too'. In most of the ways in which Dylan once appeared to know his way around better than the rest of us, he no longer does. And it's no longer still true that 'with every new album there's a progression' or that Dylan 'has always been ahead of his time'.

from all these lowly aspects of the pop scene, built up a reputation for declining huge appearance fees, stopped talking to newsmen, avoided television like the plague – and consequently emerged as the best-selling, highest-paid, most god-like and untouchable dream since Greta Garbo. Presley never came to Britain – turning down, among other things, an offer of $100,000 for one performance inside a magnifying bubble in the centre of a vast sports stadium. He couldn't, it was explained, afford to make the trip for 'that sort of figure'. It was 'not quite what we had in mind'.[51]

In contrast, Paul Anka performances were, in many parts of the world, two-a-penny. Result: Paul Anka became eminently touchable, the boy-next-door, one of myriad second-class stars. When you saw his name mentioned, momentary interest was engaged: you read the item. If he was coming to your home town, well, maybe you'd go and see his show if the supporting acts weren't too awful and if the price was right. But when you read the name Elvis Presley, lights flashed – and you knew you'd go anywhere, pay any price, to see him. His TV spectacular in 1968 (1969 in England: thanks again, BBC) was his first television appearance for over eight years.[52] And that's the way to do it.

That's how Dylan does it too. You wouldn't catch Dylan on *Top of the Pops*, or in bed for peace, or on the *Parkinson Show*. His scarcity value is enormous. Rumours about what he's doing are whispered around now and then; he limits himself, effectively, to albums, and never brings out more than one a year. When California was bursting with supposedly incredible rock groups and crowded out with every pace-setting Beautiful Person in the world, Dylan remained pointedly 3,000 miles away, in splendid isolation in New York State. 'Involvement is death,' he once wrote.

It sounds easy – refuse to appear for £50 and eventually someone will offer you £500. Do that once, throwing in a little controversy while you're at it – and then start refusing again. Easy or not, most people don't manage it: most people don't appear to even understand it. They're delighted with any rush of publicity, they pose for fifty photographers and comply with every tasteless idea these men come up with, they commit themselves to films that, if they're lucky, will never get a general release – and a year or two later they're astonished to find themselves rated about as exciting as Ray Conniff.

It's true that much of Dylan's uncooperativeness with the media is in response to their intrusions, their attempts to raise a man who is a great and a serious artist to their own level of vulgarity (on the journalistic Peter Principle); but it also comes from Dylan's shrewdness as an image-builder, a Garbo in rock music.

He plays with reporters brilliantly, showing up their bumbling, uncomprehending platitudes, keeping his distance, controlling them. A few examples. He allowed a film to be made, a semi-montage of parts of his 1965 tour of England – *Don't Look Back*. The reviews were a triumph for Dylan. The *Cleveland Plain Dealer* spluttered out this:

---

51.   The quotations here are taken from memory from newspaper accounts of the time. The assessment of Col. Tom Parker was revised a long time ago. For the counter-argument that in fact he was extremely bad at serving Presley, see Michael Gray: '25% of the King: Colonel Tom Parker obituary', *Guardian*, 23/1/97.

52.   *Elvis*, produced and directed by Steve Binder, video-recorded Burbank, California, 27–30/6/68, telecast NBC-TV, New York, 3/12/68; in UK televised as *The Fabulous Elvis*, BBC-2 TV, 31/12/69.

Should be buried . . . This is a cheap, in part, a dirty movie, if it is a movie at all . . . It is certainly not for moviegoers who bathe and/or shave. It is 'underground' and should be buried at once. Burn a rag, as was once said of filth. Phew!

It wouldn't have been very satisfactory if the *Cleveland Plain Dealer* had liked the film. Bad for the image. As for *Newsweek*, it really had to grovel – and in a way that must have amused Dylan greatly:

'Don't Look Back' is really about fame and how it menaces art, about the press and how it categorizes, bowdlerizes, sterilizes, universalizes or conventionalizes an original like Dylan into something it can dimly understand.

Dimly understand was right. The *New Yorker* informed its readership that parts of the film 'catch some moving essence of being young now'.[53]

Back in England four years later, for his one-hour appearance on the Isle of Wight, Dylan held a press conference. Not a convenient one in London, on his arrival at the airport, but one instead on the Isle of Wight itself. They all flew out there to ask him their questions, of course, and the questions were what you'd expect:

Reporter: A lot of the young people who admire you seem to be mixed up in a lot of drug-taking and so forth. What are your views on this problem?
Dylan: [assuming thick country accent]: Oh I don't have any of them views; I sure wish I did – I sure would like to share them with y'all.[54]

It isn't just funny answers, it's an ability to manipulate completely, to counteract instantaneously, the amorality of the media – and that seems to me a gigantic achievement. In our mass society, it is revolutionary warfare. Norman Mailer must be proud of him; no one else in the Western world has learnt to fight like this. The goat comes along, asks its questions, tries to have its customary shit – and Dylan, instead of evading like a politician, cuts through it all and so manages to speak directly to the people who are still 'out there' and who don't rely on *Reader's Digest* to give them their world-view.[55]

This triumph does more in the way of keeping Dylan a star than just maintaining his scarcity value. It also allows him to feed secrets to his fans, which in pop is very important. There you are at home reading a rumour in *Melody Maker*, August 1969. The rumour says that when Dylan comes to the Isle of Wight at the end of the month for his first appearance in Britain for over three years, he might finish his performance with a jam session with George Harrison, John Lennon, a couple of Rolling Stones, Eric Clapton and Ginger Baker, Humble Pie and the Bee Gees joining him on stage! And it's highly pleasurable to be in on a secret, to cut through this rubbish and know

---

53. W. Ward Marsh, 'Bob Dylan film "should be buried"', *Cleveland Plain Dealer*, 25/7/67; probably J. Morgenstern, 'A Face in the Crowd', *Newsweek*, 21/8/67; *New Yorker*, nia, 1967. The quotes from these reviews are among those reproduced (uncredited and undated) at the end of the book (of the film) *Don't Look Back*, D. A. Pennebaker (1967).

54. Dylan's press-conference: Seaview, Isle of Wight, 27/8/69. Dylan & The Band's performance: Ryde, Isle of Wight, 31/8/69.

55. The reference to Norman Mailer and goats takes up his own term for the press, used in those powerful docu-drama books of his like *Armies of the Night* (1970), which belong to and contributed to that radical period in US society discussed in Chapter 5.

the mind of this incredible man – because you know all the while that he's let the rumour grow by simply not denying it, that he's watched in amusement as the snowball machine rolls it out: and you know perfectly well that it won't happen. He'll no more appear on stage with those people than he'll enter the Eurovision Song Contest.

There are lots more peripheral pleasures involved in the star–fan system in pop, and Dylan doesn't miss a trick. He's not just ten steps ahead of the media: he's three steps ahead of you too – which enhances the fun of sharing secrets. It's fun hanging on to the coat-tails of his unfailing unpredictability.

You see him in concert in Liverpool in 1966. The board outside the theatre (which is really a huge, depressing cinema) says

2.45: THE SOUND OF MUSIC
7 PM: BOB DYLAN

and that's a joke the newsmen (and the cinema management too) wouldn't even notice. Anyway, you go in, you wait, and Dylan comes on for the solo half of his performance. He tunes up carefully before every number, he hardly glances at the audience, he wears a shabby, crumpled suit – and he doesn't speak. No 'Hi! It's wonderful to be here!', no 'Thank you very much, thank you', no 'I'd like to do a song now called . . .' The first time he speaks is in the second half, when the folkies are booing and heckling. Somebody shouts out, uncomprehendingly, 'Where's the poet gone?' and Dylan smiles, comes up to the microphone with a gentle corrective reproach: 'Not where's the poet, where's the saint gone?' And at the very end, no encore. Dylan almost runs off the stage at the end and is out of the theatre and away – with the audience still hoping against hope that he's still there really, that really he's just behind the curtain.[56]

Great! – the press don't understand it at all, but you do. You're in on the secrets and you've witnessed the agile rejection of all the showbiz charades.

And then you see him at the Isle of Wight and he twists it all around. 'Thank you, thank you – great to be here' he says, in the little shy voice of a moderate man, as if he's ever so surprised to find all those thousands of people turning up just to hear him. And he's dressed immaculately in white, just for the flashbulbs and spotlights. Fifty-five minutes later, he says 'We're gonna do one last song for ya now. It was a big hit for, I believe, Manfred Mann. Great group, great group.' He sings 'Quinn The Eskimo (The Mighty Quinn)' and walks off. The hoping against all hope begins – and back he comes, happy to please all the folks out there applauding. But the song he sings is yet another lampoon:

---

56.   Liverpool Odeon, 14/5/66; one song-performance from this concert, of 'Just Like Tom Thumb's Blues', was issued as B-side of 'I Want You' [the "Blonde On Blonde" version], Columbia Records 4–43683, New York [CBS 202258, London], 1966.

   The most dramatic moment of this spectacularly confrontational tour – aside from the high drama of the brave, numinous music itself – took place in nearby Manchester, where, at the Free Trade Hall, a voice from the crowd called out 'Judas!' and Bob Dylan responded, 'You're a liar!' This exchange was a curious re-enactment, though in circumstances less lethal, of that between the British public executioner and the Gunpowder Plot conspirator Sir Everard Digby three hundred and sixty years earlier. As Aubrey's seventeenth-century *Brief Lives* reports, 'When [Digby's] heart was pluct out by the Executioner (who . . . cryed, "Here is the heart of a Traytor!"), it is credibly reported, he replied, "Thou liest!"'

Who's gonna throw that minstrel boy a coin?
Who's gonna let it roll?

So where does that leave you, except still applauding twenty minutes after he has gone away? You stand there clapping not only the artist, but the idol as well.

Everything's Bin Returned Which Was Owed, Part II

Despite the influences of Holly, Presley, Berry and the rest, Dylan's work is far more original than derivative. He has been the big influence: he created the re-birth in rock.

Dylan goes beyond other people – with every new album there's a progression and this has happened so fast that in one sense Dylan has always been an outsider in pop – has always been ahead of his time.

The first time a lot of pop fans noticed him was when the 'The Times They Are A-Changin'' came out as a single in 1964. To pop-trained ears, it was a laughable record. The singer had a voice that made Johnny Duncan and The Blue Grass Boys sound in the same league as Mario Lanza – and plainly, the man hadn't even the most elementary sense of timing. He brought in the second syllable of that title word 'Changin'' far too soon – at a quite ridiculous point. What was the record company playing at? Just because Bob Dylan was the writer of an interesting song called 'Blowin' In The Wind' didn't mean he could expect to start singing all his other songs himself.

With that behind him Dylan invented a new form, folk-rock. "Another Side of Bob Dylan", his fourth album, is essentially rock music. The sound on the album is a rock sound, despite the fact that the backing is 'really' just Dylan with solo guitar and harmonica. The rock sound is evident everywhere on it, and Dylan doesn't achieve this by going mad on his guitar/harmonica/piano. He achieves it by implication.

'Motorpsycho Nightmare' is very much the same sort of song as 'Bob Dylan's 115th Dream', on the rock side of the fifth album; but 'Nightmare' doesn't differ from 'Dream' in being solo-work rather than rock – it differs in having a better and a heavier *implicit* rock sound behind it. And the whole of the fourth album has exactly that same superiority to the fifth. The explicit backings on the latter are often thin and clickety but the music the fourth album puts into your head – perhaps especially on 'Spanish Harlem Incident', 'I Don't Believe You' and 'Chimes Of Freedom' – is dazzling: strong and rich. It has the sort of richness Dylan achieved on "Blonde On Blonde" and in concert in 1966.

With "Another Side Of Bob Dylan", and more so with "Bringing It All Back Home", many of the folk fans flinched away, and the pop world didn't really catch on either till it was spoon-fed with the singles of 'Subterranean Homesick Blues' and 'Like A Rolling Stone'. Even with these, Bob Dylan was still clearly an outsider not just because such records were different, but also because they were peculiar. They lasted longer than two-and-a-half minutes: very odd.

But they made an impact, and again Dylan's originality as a rock artist was very clear. The folk fans who carried on listening called his new music 'folk-rock' because, well, he was a folk singer and yet there he was using electric guitars and things; and from the other side, the pop fans who began to listen also called it 'folk-rock' because, well, it was certainly rock and yet it was strange: it demanded intelligent attention.

Both groups of people were right. This was a new music, an original music. Dylan had made a profound connection between folk's articulacy and rock's virility. Here was rock music, part of the pop world, yet with it Bob Dylan was pumping out something with infinitely more dimensions than any one else had ever thought of in pop before. Pop had its isolationism torn away from it and was made to contemplate part of the real world too.

Perhaps it was just because Dylan was fully conscious of this achievement that he demanded such high standards from his rock musicians. Even for his first appearance in rock music, at the Newport Folk Festival in 1965 (a slice of which is included in the film *Festival*), he only enlisted the best – they were from the Paul Butterfield Blues Band. And as the words on Dylan's electric albums got more and more impressionistic, less and less specific, the music got ever more precisely 'right'.[57]

If the oddness of Dylan as a pop figure, with all his perplexing innovations, suggested that intelligence was assaulting the pop scene, that didn't mean that no clever people besides Bob Dylan had ever made their mark in pop. Among others Phil Spector, Mick Jagger, John Lennon, Joan Armatrading, Elvis Costello and David Bowie are all intelligent artists. Yet they haven't accomplished fundamental changes as Dylan has. They've come into rock music accepting it more or less as they've found it: all they've done is find themselves a corner each to sit in.

In contrast, Dylan has used his artistic intelligence to re-create the rock milieu. Far from accepting what he found and settling down in some lucrative little niche, he has burst the whole pop world wide open and built a new one (and with much more than the bricks of the old). Before Dylan you could have said that pop was like football. Millions of people liked it – millions of people like fish and chips – but it didn't matter. Dylan made it matter. He showed that a rock song could provide an appropriate form for universal statements. So the pop world split in two. Half was music that has rattled on regardless of change – regardless of Dylan. The other music, labelled 'progressive' when it began in the mid-1960s, couldn't have happened without Dylan.

You can't blame the Beatles for the 'improvements' in bubblegum, and you can't blame Dylan for all the cheap and nasty developments his work inspired before serious musicianship and artistry in rock music found itself.

First, predictably, in Dylan's wake came the Great Pop Protest Craze. It was, as Richard Mabey wrote,

> not a very long-lived fad, nor in statistical terms a very successful one. But it aroused a spirited controversy and left a faint but seemingly permanent impression . . . It had, in theory, every element that a truly popular form should have, and suffered, in practice, every injury that can befall such a form as it is shunted through our mass communications network.[58]

---

57. *Festival*, Patchke Productions, US, directed by Murray Lerner, 1967.
58. Richard Mabey, *The Pop Process* (1969).

The 'seemingly permanent impression' the protest craze left was, nevertheless, that people in pop felt obliged or permitted to engage with the outside world: to be seen to have outside interests, to think, to produce material that was less mass-minded. Dylan had already said it: the protest free-for-all just tarnished the Dylan legacy.

Some of what happened afterwards was pretty tarnished too. In England, Maureen Cleave could legitimately include the following in a glance back over 1966:

> pop singers in interviews said they were reading the works of Huxley, Sartre and Dr Timothy Leary. One even claimed to be reading *Ulysses* . . . But there were compensatory laughs . . . Andrew Oldham said Scott Engel of the Walker Brothers was the Joan Crawford of pop music, and Scott Walker said no he wasn't – he was the Greta Garbo . . . The *Sunday Telegraph* described Andrew Oldham as the Rolling Stones' 'creative manager' . . .
>
> Any pop singer, at a loss for something to say, said he was thinking of opening a boutique. (As Clement Freud so rightly pointed out, one feels such a fool without a boutique nowadays.) . . . Mick Jagger took to producing: 'Jagger,' said an admirer, 'who brought Nureyev to rock'n'roll is now the Zeffirelli of pop.' We saw the story of Donovan's life on television: 'My job,' he said, 'is writing beautiful things about beauty. You see, my life is beautiful.' . . .
>
> Nervous exhaustion was all the rage. Scott Engel was exhausted nervously; so was a Kink, a Yardbird and a Cream. Mick Jagger was reported to be nervously exhausted after buying furniture for his new flat . . . in the last few months even nervous exhaustion was on the decline.
>
> It was replaced by the conviction that everything was beautiful, groovy and gentle. Pop singers floated around loving people in a patronizing manner that was even more infuriating than their protest songs. 'When you are aware,' Donovan said, 'there are no such things as hate and envy: there is only love.'
>
> 'This industry of human happiness,' said Andrew Oldham crossly. Oh yes, there were laughs in plenty; but . . . it was the end of an era . . .
>
> The pop singers themselves have grown old; their faces on television look old, world-weary; bored faces that have seen it all. The future is bleak . . . but the present, while they sort themselves out, is pretty sordid. Nineteen sixty-six is the year the whole thing turned sour. Many found they hadn't made the money they ought to have made. The shock reduced them to complete inactivity . . . What, one wonders, will happen to them? They can't all be absorbed by boutiques.[59]

And yes, suddenly it was go to San Francisco with a flower in your hair, and after that Frank Zappa told the lefties at LSE that 'revolution is this year's Flower Power'.[60]

---

59. Maureen Cleave, *Evening Standard*, nia; taken from its reproduction in full in Mabey, *The Pop Process*. Interesting that 1966, now generally perceived as the middle of the Golden Age, could be dubbed at the time 'the year the whole thing turned sour'.

  (Maureen Cleave, a well-known 'straight' commentator on the London scene in the 1960s ['straight' then meaning the opposite of 'hip' and/or 'underground', rather than of 'gay'], had by this point published at least two pieces specifically on Dylan: 'If Bob Can't Sing It, It Must Be A Poem Or A Novel Or Something', *Evening Standard*, 16/5/64, and 'So Very, Very Bored . . . The Curious Mr. Dylan', *Evening Standard*, 27/4/65.)

60. Scott MacKenzie's '(If You're Going To) San Francisco (Be Sure To Wear Flowers In Your Hair)', Ode Records 103, New York [CBS 2816, London], a No. 1 transatlantic smash hit in the summer of 1967, was crass commercial opportunism but still represents a little corner of the 'summer of love'. Then came the student

You can't blame Dylan. He'd finished recording his 'protests' in 1963, and on his last solo album (the one with the rock sound) had issued his dismissive evaluation, 'My Back Pages'. By the time the protest craze was happening, it was one too many mornings and a thousand miles behind its founder.

With 'Mr. Tambourine Man', Dylan had started something else: the pop exploration of drugs. He carried it through – based, we all assume, on heavy personal use – and in the year that Maureen Cleave was characterising as 'sour', Dylan issued "Blonde On Blonde": acid-rock. It may not have been apparent at the time, but this was the great regenerative force. In terms of pop history, it was the single most important recording since Presley's 'Heartbreak Hotel'.

It was less the drugs than what Dylan had done with druggy music that caused the 'underground' explosion that followed "Blonde On Blonde" – an explosion of groups with (at first) strange names and genuine exploratory work. Dylan was father to all these groups: to Moby Grape, Big Brother & The Holding Company, The Doors, The Velvet Underground, Sopwith Camel, Country Joe & The Fish, Jefferson Airplane, The Byrds, Iron Butterfly, Procul Harum, etc., etc., etc. They were all descendants of Dylan, and so was "Sgt. Pepper's Lonely Hearts' Club Band".[61]

As his protest music had popularised and part-unified the anti-Establishment focus, so too his acid-rock/surrealist music made possible an alternative to that Establishment outside of tiny avant-garde minorities: he was catalyst in the mass adoption of the 'underground' that became what we now look back on as being representative 1960s culture. If the protest craze had shown that serious expression in pop music would have to steer clear, in future, of the Hit Parade and the leeches down Tin Pan Alley, then Dylan had shown that a viable alternative really was possible, given a certain singleness of purpose and a thing pop had never recognised before – integrity. Dylan's protest songs survived the craze, on the whole; Dylan carried on exploring without regard for trends, never a slave to pop's unwritten rules. And in this, to a greater or lesser extent, the underground groups were his offspring.

Not only that. The attempt to learn from drugs, the attempt to re-create drug experiences, the rejection of common-sense logic and the acceptance of mystery – Dylan accelerated the awakening to all this. His was the giant silhouette hovering above the crowds at the rock music festivals that characterised the era. And if such festivals confirmed that pop had changed and that the new music was 'concerned more with incantation than with communication' then Wilfrid Mellers was justified in introducing that phrase in the context of reviewing "Blonde On Blonde".[62]

Dylan himself, characteristically, always denied responsibility. No sooner had the Beautiful People scene, the all-you-need-is-love-and-a-rock-band scene, reached breakneck speed in San Francisco than Dylan was, well, breaking his neck, or claiming so, and staying away.

---

revolutions of 1968. On 27 May 1969, Frank Zappa, addressing students at the London School of Economics, made his famous remark 'Revolution is just this year's Flower Power.' Or that's how the remark has become in legend. It is believed that what he actually said, with less panache, was 'Demonstrations are just a fad.' [Michael Gray, *Mother! The Frank Zappa Story*, 1994.]

61. The Beatles: "Sergeant Pepper's Lonely Hearts' Club Band" LP, London, 1967, Parlophone Records PCS 7027 [PMC 7027 mono], London [Capitol Records SMAS 2653, Los Angeles], 1967.

62. Wilfrid Mellers, 'Sixties', *New Statesman*, London, 24/2/67.

After a near two-year silence, he issued "John Wesley Harding", which was a rejection of the new music, the love generation, drugs, revolution and almost every other focus of solidarity set up and encouraged by his earlier work. As Jon Landau wrote (many years before he became that 'new Dylan' Bruce Springsteen's producer):

"John Wesley Harding" is a profoundly egotistical album. For an album of this kind to be released amidst "Sgt. Pepper", "Their Satanic Majesties Request", "Strange Days" and "After Bathing At Baxter's", somebody must have had a lot of confidence in what he was doing . . . Dylan seems to feel no need to respond to the predominate trends in pop music at all. And he is the only major pop artist about whom this can be said. The Dylan of "John Wesley Harding" is a truly independent artist who doesn't feel responsible to anyone else, whether they be fans or his contemporaries.[63]

It wasn't really a rock album at all; it certainly hadn't got a rock sound, except for the country rock of the last two tracks – and they were less integral parts of the whole than signposts to yet another future. 'Down Along The Cove' and 'I'll Be Your Baby Tonight' foreshadowed "Nashville Skyline".

"John Wesley Harding" was out of even the new pop world (which was by then different enough from the old for the word 'pop' to seem embarrassing and inappropriate and the word 'rock' just had to replace it). But the new world rolled on, from the opportunity blueprints of "Blonde On Blonde", using the medium as an art form and producing, at its best, an abundance of creative, self-made music.

Even where the sources were musically/lyrically very different, it was still Dylan who had opened the door. Frank Zappa, for instance, didn't need "Blonde On Blonde" or "Highway 61 Revisited" musically but he needed Dylan to establish that 'pop' artists could claim and merit serious attention. And, like all the rest, he needed the example of Dylan's successfully ruthless focus on established values. Without him, the Mothers really would have been a freak show, largely unheeded and soon forgotten.

Bob Dylan, single-handedly, had created the sheer possibility of the situation Paul Williams was able to describe in the same issue of the same magazine as Jon Landau's review of "John Wesley Harding" above:

Rock groups who take themselves seriously are not always eager to cater to what they believe is the public taste – and of course their direct contact is not with the public but with the record companies and the radio stations, who have their own ideas as to what the public taste might be . . . The performer, then, is in a difficult position. Should he try to please the public, the record company or himself?[64]

Before Dylan, that question would never have got asked. Before Dylan, everyone put the public first. They all bowed to what they imagined were the common

63.   Jon Landau, 'John Wesley Harding', Crawdaddy, no. 15, May 1968, reprinted in Craig MacGregor, Bob Dylan: A Retrospective (1972). The florid albums referred to here are: The Beatles: "Sergeant Pepper's Lonely Hearts' Club Band", note 61; The Rolling Stones: "Their Satanic Majesties' Request", Decca Records TXS 103, London [London Records NPS 2, New York], 1967; The Doors: "Strange Days", Elektra Records 74014, Los Angeles [and London], 1967; and Jefferson Airplane: "After Bathing At Baxter's", RCA Victor LSP 4545, New York [RCA SF/RD 7926, London], 1968.

64.   Paul Williams: 'What goes on', Crawdaddy, no. 15, May 1968.

denominators of public taste. Dylan not only showed them all, or their successors, that you didn't have to go along with this: he also showed that when you didn't go along with it but offered honestly some personally satisfying alternative, you could release an undiscovered openness in the public. Bob Dylan unchained public taste. He did more than anybody else to develop in a mass audience the kind of receptiveness to things imaginative and non-trivial that was, before, the sole prerogative of élite minorities. His art has had that concrete an impact.

That's a sizeable claim, but it's well worth standing by it. Dylan himself, of course, wouldn't dream of standing by it. The interview he granted *Rolling Stone* in 1969 served to emphasise this:

> *RS:* Many people . . . all felt tremendously affected by your music and what you're saying in the lyrics.
>
> *BD:* Did they?
>
> *RS:* Sure. They felt it had a particular relevance to their lives . . . I mean, you must be aware of the way that people come on to you.
>
> *BD:* Not entirely. Why don't you explain it to me.
>
> *RS:* I guess if you reduce it to its simplest terms, the expectation of your audience – the portion of your audience that I'm familiar with – feels that you have the answer.
>
> *BD:* What answer?
>
> *RS:* Like from the film *Don't Look Back* – people asking you 'Why? What is it? Where is it?' . . . Do you feel responsible to those people?
>
> *BD:* I don't want to make anybody worry about it . . . if I could ease somebody's mind, I'd be the first to do it. I want to lighten every load. Straighten out every burden. I don't want anybody to be hung-up . . . (*laughs*) especially over me, or anything I do. That's not the point at all.
>
> *RS:* Let me put it another way – what I'm getting at is that you're an extremely important figure in music and an extremely important figure in the experience of growing up today. Whether you put yourself in that position or not, you're in that position. And you must have thought about it – and I'm curious to know what you think about that.
>
> *BD:* What would I think about it? What can I do?
>
> *RS:* You wonder if you're really that person.
>
> *BD:* What person?
>
> *RS:* A great 'youth leader' . . .
>
> *BD:* . . . there must be people trained to do this type of work. And I'm just one person doing what I do. Trying to get along – staying out of people's hair, that's all.
>
> *RS:* You've been a tremendous influence on a lot of musicians and writers. They're very obviously affected by your style, the way you do things.
>
> *BD:* Who?[65]

The answer to that question, of course, was everyone.

---

65. *Rolling Stone*, no. 47, 29/11/69. This is the interview described in Chapter 1, note 31.

CHAPTER FOUR

Dylan's Use of Language: Towards Complexity

Pourin' off of every page
Like it was written in my soul
From me to you
Tangled up in blue

Bob Dylan: 'Tangled Up In Blue'

Dylan's work through the 1960s shows a vivid growth in the complexity of his use of language. At the end of that decade, with few later exceptions, he begins to pare down and to opt for a new simplicity in his writing. This chapter and the next chart these two opposite progressions of his artistry.

Let's not make difficulties over defining 'imagery' and so on. As if to underline a disregard for unnecessary quibbles, I begin with part of a David Horowitz article that refers happily to Dylan's 'symbolic language' without saying what that means. Horowitz's term covers what, in dealing with the same song, I would mean by 'imagery'. The song is the early one 'A Hard Rain's A-Gonna Fall', and Horowitz writes:

> The artistic problems involved in treating such a subject (the threat of nuclear wipe-out – raised at the time of the song's composition by the 1962 Cuba Crisis) seriously (Dylan has given it a splendid satiric treatment in 'Talking World War III Blues') are seemingly insurmountable; but Dylan has done so in the only way possible: by employing an approach that is symbolic. Only a symbolic language could bear the strain of an event as absolute and apocalyptic as the total destruction of life on earth. Dylan's instinctive awareness of the capacities of symbolism is, in this song, turned to brilliant use. In 'Hard Rain', Dylan has adapted the melody and refrain of the traditional English song, 'Lord Randall', and by this very fact has set his own 'story' in a frame of concreteness;
>
> > *O where have you been, my blue-eyed son,*
> > *And where have you been, my darlin' young one?*
>
> But the actual tale which is told in answer to the traditional question takes place on an altogether different plane of reality from that of its source:

I've stumbled on the side of twelve misty mountains
I've walked an' I've crawled on six crooked highways
I've stepped in the middle of seven sad forests
I've bin out in front of a dozen dead oceans
I've bin ten thousand miles in the mouth of a graveyard
An' it's a hard, it's a hard, it's a hard, an' it's a hard,
It's a hard rain's a-gonna fall.

The cumulative effect of these images, an effect which is reinforced by the repeated rhythmic figure of the guitar accompaniment, is little short of overwhelming. We are besieged with images of dead and dying life, a kind of dynamic stasis, a perfect figurative medium for the vision at the brink:

I met a young child beside a dead pony
I met a white man who walked a black dog

I met a young woman whose body was burning
I met a young girl, she gave me a rainbow . . .

We have the start of many stories here, never to be finished, and in the very fact of this arrested promise an accurate rendering of the meaning of that awful apocalypse that may await us. Aptly, this style, which is so tuned to the reality, was actually dictated by it. For, as Dylan explains, 'Every line in it . . . is actually the start of a whole song. But when I wrote it, I thought I wouldn't have enough time alive to write all those songs, so I put all I could into this one.' Because of the precision of the tone and the adequacy of the vision, when it is over, and the respite won, the poet's resolve carries absolute conviction:

And I'll tell it and speak it and think it and breathe it
And reflect from the mountains so all souls can see it
And I'll stand on the ocean until I start sinkin'
And I'll know my song well before I start singin'
And it's a hard, it's a hard, it's a hard, and it's a hard,
It's a hard rain's a-gonna fall.[1]

I think the admirable David Horowitz accepts too readily that Dylan's articulacy is not so much individual as traditionally 'skilful'; it assumes that Dylan's early work compliantly fits in his non-literal language according to the long established literary rules.

This isn't the case. If you look *from the rules* to the work Dylan has produced, you get entangled in listing Dylan's 'failures', or, to put it another way, in emphasising Dylan's 'lack of sophistication' in handling language, or in defensively referring to his 'instinctive' talents. Such entanglement will reveal, in fact, not Dylan's faults but a

---

1.   David Horowitz: 'Bob Dylan: genius or commodity?', *Peace News*, 11/11/64, reprinted Richard Mabey's *The Pop Process* (1969). David Horowitz wrote, among much else, the excellent *From Yalta to Vietnam* (1967), a study of the Cold War and US imperialism. The prose quotation from Dylan in the last paragraph of the *Peace News* extract is taken from the sleeve of the "Freewheelin' Bob Dylan" LP, 1963. (*Peace News* was responsible, in the 1960s, for a mini-poster, handy for notice-boards and as a car-sticker, with the splendid motto 'Join the Army; travel to exotic, distant lands; meet exciting, unusual people and kill them.')

wrong perspective on the listener's or critic's part. Full as Dylan's work is of 'unsophisticated' imagery, the success – the eloquence and impact – of such language in Dylan's hands challenges any weighting of 'sophistication' as an evaluative term.

As for 'A Hard Rain's A-Gonna Fall', it is true that to a very large extent, Dylan's use of images is dictated by tradition; but it surely builds to a distinctive whole. Line upon line the pictures are piled up, some containing their own 'moral' via paradox:

> I saw a new-born babe with wild wolves all around it . . .
> I saw guns and sharp swords in the hands of young children . . .
> Heard one person starve, I heard many people laughin' . . .

and others with the same purpose but taking longer to say it:

> I met one man who was wounded in love,
> I met another man who was wounded with hatred . . .

and others which, citing two pictures, offer an analogy or parallel:

> Heard the song of a poet who died in the gutter,
> Heard the sound of a clown who cried in the alley . . .

Then again, there are images that stand alone, entirely detached, and do not apparently operate as direct moral diagrams:

> I saw a highway of diamonds with nobody on it . . .
> I saw a white ladder all covered with water
> I met a young girl, she gave me a rainbow . . .

The most interesting thing, perhaps, in terms of Dylan's achievement, is that although the fifth verse draws the morals almost specifically, and although the deliberate fragmentedness of the other verses does fit into a cohesive moral theme, the effectiveness of this theme still depends on the pictures rolling past, as if on and then off a screen, without opportunity of recall. In other words, there is a simple, strange sense in which for the song as a whole to succeed, each image within it asserts a segregated life of its own.

Even where Dylan does use traditional images (and there are many of them in his early work) he doesn't utilise them along traditional lines.

For example, think of the traditional rendering of someone's personality or spirit in terms of a 'light'. Referring to someone as giving out light is conventional, but the reference is normally indirect – as in this pastiche, constructed for the purpose of illustration:

> As Hartley's eyes swept the ballroom, his attention was called back, again and again, to the same animated face. Miss Satterthwaite (for indeed the face was hers) seemed to radiate an ethereal yet energetic light – and it was not long till Mr Hartley stood breathless in the glow of it.

The image of light is almost asleep: it is a traditional literary image traditionally used. Dylan, employing it more casually, rejuvenates it by his non-traditional, or at least non-literary usage. He takes it from the context of third person narration and plunges it into a direct conversation, so that it emerges with a refreshing bluntness:

> *It ain't no use in turnin' on your light, babe*
> *That light I never knowed*

and is given an effective extension:

> *An' it ain't no use in turnin' on your light, babe*
> *I'm on the dark side of the road . . .*[2]

The general point about Dylan's 'unsophisticated' imagery is that where it can be called unsophisticated, it usually carries corresponding strengths.

Often, for instance, with Dylan's least subtle imagery, he relies on a combination of simplicity and anger to yield a considerable effectiveness. This works well enough in 'Masters Of War':

> *But I see through your eyes and I see through your brain*
> *Like I see through the water that runs down my drain.*[3]

Consider too the simple effectiveness of the imagery in his 'Ballad Of Hollis Brown'. Here, the words are so riveting and so didactically visual that Dylan can even afford to echo the nursery rhyme about the crooked man without this distracting us:

> *You look for work and money*
> *And you walk a ragged mile*
> *You look for work and money*
> *And you walk a ragged mile . . .*

Neither are we distracted when we come to an apparently histrionic analogy like this:

> *Your wife's screams are stabbin'*
> *Like the dirty drivin' rain.*

The very lack of balance in the construction of that analogy enforces its realism. It is a way of the narrator saying 'I understand your desperation – your imbalance.'

This relationship between narrator and subject gives the song a strength that is more widely distributed than the isolated quotation above can indicate. We can turn back to David Horowitz's article for more on this point:

> Technically speaking, 'Hollis Brown' is a *tour de force*. For a ballad is normally a
> form which puts one at a distance from its tale. This ballad, however, is told in
> the second person, present tense, so that not only is a bond forged immediately

---

2.   Dylan's originality lies in that last line: in awakening the standard image of 'your light' (which may or may not have been novel in standing for 'your sexiness' and/or 'your full attention' rather than 'your character', as developed from biblical imagery into the blues) by taking it up and running with it, alerting us to it by seizing it only to twist it.

3.   'Masters Of War' also provides an example of Dylan's using an 'echo-image': that is, where the wording used to give one visual picture deliberately echoes other pictures, other moods – even another poet's voice: 'An' I hope that you die, and your death will come soon, / I will follow your casket on a pale afternoon'. The poet echoed in that second line is Eliot; and in recalling him, Dylan moderates his song's mood of anger with the Eliot tone of underlying sadness.

between the listener and the figure of the tale, but there is the ironic fact that the only ones who know of Hollis Brown's plight, the only ones who care, are the hearers who are helpless to help, cut off from him, even as we in a mass society are cut off from each other.

When even such an early song as 'The Ballad Of Hollis Brown' has such strengths, it is plainly useless to talk of his 'unsophisticated' approach.

Horowitz also points to the power of the blues in Dylan's hands; and here too it is fruitless to measure his worth by traditional literary criteria. Horowitz argues:

> Indeed, the blues perspective itself, uncompromising, isolated and sardonic, is superbly suited to express the squalid reality of contemporary America. And what a powerful expression it can be, once it has been liberated (as it has in Dylan's hands) from its egocentric bondage!
>
> A striking example of the tough, ironic insight one associates with the blues (and also of the power of understatement which Dylan has learnt from Guthrie) is to be found in the final lines of Hollis Brown:

> *There's seven people dead on a South Dakota farm,*
> *There's seven people dead on a South Dakota farm,*
> *Somewhere in the distance there's seven new people born.*

How much of the soul of contemporary American society and its statistical conscience is expressed in this sardonic image![4]

Dylan uses conventional figurative language to equal effect in one of the very earliest of his published compositions, 'Song To Woody', where he takes the obvious but worthwhile step of personifying the 'funny ol' world', which

> *Seems sick an' it's hungry, it's tired an' it's torn*
> *Looks like it's a-dyin' an' it's hardly bin born.*

That reliance on twisting the conventions of the figurative recurs in the obscure 'Train A-Travelin'', where we have an extended metaphor which uses a reality of pleasant associations to stand for an unpleasant ethos:

> *There's an iron train a-travelin' that's been a-rollin' through the years,*
> *With a firebox of hatred and a furnace full of fears . . .*
> *Did you ever see its passengers, its crazy, mixed-up souls?*[5]

The eloquence achieved by alliteration in that second line is typical of Dylan's 'unsophisticated' work. The use of the train metaphor is more complex: 'iron' is usually used in an approving way – as a coloured term indicating strength (as it is, for example, in Dylan's own much later 'Never Say Goodbye', 1974, where 'my dreams

---

4.   David Horowitz, note 1. I can't see what he means in writing of liberating the blues 'from its egocentric bondage' but this article was written very early in terms of the examining of blues lyric poetry and it is to its author's credit that he addressed the question of the differing claims of, and tensions between, the uses of symbolism as between 'high culture' and folk and blues art.

5.   Bob Dylan: 'Train A-Travelin'', NYC, March 1963, "Broadside Reunion", Folkways Records FR 5315, New York, 1972. The lyric is published in Bob Dylan, *Lyrics 1962–1985* (1986, UK 1987).

are made of iron and steel'). In 'Train A-Travelin'' it is associated with blindness, or stubbornness; it condemns a dogmatic quality (the direction of which is, of course, shown by that 'firebox of hatred').

This ultra-simplicity of imagery is partnered frequently by an opposite sort of quality to one of 'overriding anger' – partnered, that is, by an understatement. There is no anger here, and nothing complex either; but the effectiveness is undeniable:

> *Oh a false clock tries to tick out my time*
> *To disgrace, distract and bother me*
> *And the dirt of gossip blows in my face*
> *And the dust of rumours covers me*
> *But if the arrow is straight*
> *And the point is slick*
> *It can pierce through dust no matter how thick:*
> *So I'll make my stand*
> *And remain as I am*
> *And bid farewell and not give a damn.*

('Restless Farewell'.) None of those would be called complex images (or great ones) but in that an image's function is not to sit glistening for the critic's entertainment but rather to make more vivid the artist's idea, then they work perfectly. And they don't need the energy of a 'Masters Of War' anger-blast to help them. They are far from clichéd, and yet they are standard images. The element of surprise, which gives them their force, is the shift from the clock image as the centre to the dust image – and so from the sharpness of the ticking to the smothering softness of that 'dust'.

This early simplicity of language often works in a different general direction. Rather than just ignoring traditional literary rules, Dylan often deliberately breaks them – and the effects are not then so simple.

Consider, for instance, these two tiny lines from 'Eternal Circle':

> *Through a bullet of light*
> *Her face was reflectin'*

They don't provide the visual image one might expect – because visualisation is just about impossible. The picture given by 'bullet of light' is contradicted, and so cancelled out, by the 'reflectin'' face – for face challenges, by its very roundness of shape, any idea of light like a bullet, which is to say, like a fast straight line. Yet if there is no visualisation, there is still a response to that 'image' and still a purpose in its being there. It is a word–sound image; part of its strength is that its sounds are attractive – and they give the voice a kind of equivalent articulacy to the wiry strength of the accompanying guitar sounds.

By the time of the fourth album, "Another Side Of Bob Dylan", coming straight after 'Restless Farewell', one very characteristic type of image has emerged: images involving the elements. Dylan notices winds, rains, and so on keenly, using them dramatically in the action of his songs. His presentation of them is distinctive – so much so that anyone familiar with even a few Dylan songs would recognise all the following as being from his work:

> *The night comes in a-fallin'* . . .
> *The wind howls like a hammer* . . .
> *And the silent night will shatter* . . .
> *Through the mad mystic hammering of the wild ripping hail* . . .
> *The sky it is folding* . . .[6]

plus, to choose four lines together (from 'Walls Of Red Wing'):

> *As the night laid shadows*
> *Through the crossbar windows*
> *And the wind punched hard*
> *To make the wall siding sing*

or, to add a phrase that only strays slightly from an imagery of the elements:

> *. . . electric light still struck like arrows.*

That line is from the fourth album song 'Chimes Of Freedom', which is in one way the central song of the album. Ostensibly, the opposite is true: it is the last explicit 'protest song': the words have a message. Yet the message is not the important point – and it is as if Dylan uses this apparent message song to show his listeners that significance lies elsewhere. In doing that, the song offers the motto for the whole album. And indeed it has the album's 'sound', to note which brings us to what *is* the importance of 'Chimes Of Freedom': namely, that with this 'sound' – the echo, the voice, the chiselled word shapes, the sculptured, hard-grained phrasing – Dylan creates a world. It is in notable contrast that in the later, more 'out-of-this-world' Dylan work, its force is, paradoxically, an interpretative one, not a sculptural.

So far, I have focused on a general *simplicity* in Dylan's language; but Dylan is far more famous (albeit due to misconceptions, on the whole) for the antithesis of this – a complexity of language that runs over (so the charge goes) into the positively obscure. "Another Side Of Bob Dylan" begins the development of the new complexity.

The first hints of it come even earlier. The previous album, "The Times They Are A-Changin' ", offers an interesting example of poetic transference. On the beautiful 'One Too Many Mornings' the attributes of one thing are transferred onto another:

> *And the silent night will shatter*
> *From the sounds inside my mind* . . .

The prose equivalent, stripped of this transference, would be that the silence (of the night) will be shattered; as Dylan has it, the night will shatter. This transference succeeds: it comes across as forceful and unforced. It urges the inseparability of the night and the silence. It gives us creatively, and with a terse economy, the idea that if the night were no longer silent it would not be the same night.

A line in the unreleased 'Long Ago, Far Away' (1962) offers, in a sense, another

---

6.   'The wind howls like a hammer' is from 'Love Minus Zero/No Limit'; 'The night comes in a-fallin'' and 'And the silent night will shatter' are from 'One Too Many Mornings'; 'Through the mad mystic hammering of the wild ripping hail' is from 'Chimes Of Freedom'; 'The sky it is folding' is from 'Farewell Angelina'.

instance of transference – one involving slighter implications but an arresting visual picture:

> *People cheered with bloodshot grins.*[7]

From the fourth album, perhaps the most historically interesting song is 'Spanish Harlem Incident', which begins with this:

> *Gypsy Gal, the hands of Harlem*
> *Cannot hold you to its heat*

which, as far as his figurative language is concerned, is like a stylish and immediately impressive declaration of independence on Dylan's part. It's a pretty good image, and very individual.

Thus with 'Spanish Harlem Incident', and that fourth album, we find the really substantial beginnings of Dylan's famous complexity, the beginnings of what 1965 brought out with an explosion – the year that saw an amazing, breathtaking burst of prolific creativity, yielding a huge list of great Dylan songs and great Dylan recordings: the many major songs on "Bringing It All Back Home" and "Highway 61 Revisited" *and* 'Farewell Angelina', 'Positively 4th Street' and 'Can *You* Please Crawl Out Your Window?' – and what 1966 sustained on "Blonde On Blonde". 'Spanish Harlem Incident' is therefore especially interesting – historically interesting because of its pioneering slot in Dylan's output.

> *I am homeless, come and take me*
> *Into the reach of your rattling drums.*
> *Let me know, babe, all about my fortune*
> *Down along my restless palms.*

There, strikingly, is that individual style of impressionism that Dylan was to cultivate (and which attracted so many unfortunate imitations, including much from the Beatles, with their 'plasticine porters' and 'marmalade skies').[8] Dylan's impressionism works because in his imagery above, he begins simply enough with that non-literal, non-physical 'homeless'; and while he moves to that apparently vaguer 'rattling drums' yet the adjective there has a precision of its own: one is shown how appropriate the phrase is to the spirit of the girl as Dylan sees her. Next, there is a precise function in the uniting of two ideas in 'my restless palms' – the validity of the fortune-telling allusion being sympathetically strengthened by its connection to the singer's admitted desire for hand-in-hand contact. And the wish implicit there harks back to that 'come and take me' in the earlier line.

> *Gypsy Gal, you got me swallowed,*
> *I have fallen far beneath*

---

7.   Bob Dylan: 'Long Ago, Far Away', NYC, Nov. 1962 (songwriting demo for Witmark Music); it received limited release on the rare Warner Bros. 7 Arts Music Inc. demo LP XTV221567, USA, 1969. Like 'Train A-Travelin'', the lyric is published in Bob Dylan, *Lyrics 1962–1985*.

8.   These Beatles phrases are from 'Lucy In The Sky With Diamonds', London, 2/3/67, "Sergeant Pepper's Lonely Hearts' Club Band", Parlophone Records PCS 7027 [PMC 7027 mono], London [Capitol Records SMAS 2653, Los Angeles], 1967.

> *Your pearly eyes so fast an' slashin'*
> *And your flashin' diamond teeth.*

There is nothing contrived here, as the context and the recording yield up those lines. 'Swallowed' works neatly, and the unobtrusive reversal of the usual teeth and eyes metaphors again strikes the listener as unforced, evoking a real idea of the girl the song addresses. It is in terms of the girl that this near-Gothic effect works also:

> *The night is pitch black, come an' make my*
> *Pale face fit into place, ah! please!*

For such a girl, the night would make itself dramatic. Again, we feel that the girl's personality draws out this, in the final verse:

> *On the cliffs of your wildcat charms I'm riding,*
> *I know I'm round you but I don't know where.*

Dylan's language, throughout, is intent on eliciting a captivating vision of those 'wildcat charms'; and the singleness of purpose places his impressionistic imagery a long way from the random hit-and-miss impressionism of his imitators. Theirs is exhibited for its own sake and is its own reason for being; Dylan's is there to assist the communication of specific and personally realised themes.[9]

Correspondingly, it is only when he has no such theme – when he is expressing nothing more personally valid than a recognisable public feeling – that he succumbs to a vagueness and sloppiness of language that does resemble that of his imitators.

This happens in Dylan's archetypal protest song, 'The Times They Are A-Changin'', in which the aim was to ride on the unvoiced sentiment of a mass public – to ride, that is, as the spokesman for people who wanted to hear just such a 'fuck you of enraged self-assertion'.[10] As a result, the language is imprecisely directed and conceived too generally. It offers four extended metaphors and makes no more than an easy politician's use of any of them. The four are: change as a rising tide; change dependent on the wheel of fate; the Establishment as an edifice; and yesterday and tomorrow as roads to be opted for.

People enjoy the song in the sense that they approve of its theory; it is a less satisfying alternative to Country Joe & The Fish's 'Fish Cheer, Woodstock Version' –

---

9.   There is a further detailed critique of this song in Chapter 16.

10.   The phrase is Elia Katz's, from his article 'Dylan's unpublished novel', *Carolina Quarterly*, no. 21, Fall 1969; reprinted as '*Tarantula*: a perspective' in Stephen Pickering's self-published booklet *Praxis: One*, No Limit Publications, Santa Cruz, California, 1971. (This booklet, a follow-up to *Dylan: A Commemoration* (2nd edn July 1971), contains the best listing I know of articles about Dylan published 1961–71: though selective, it is extensive. Both booklets, though ill-written, offer a generous number of fine Dylan photographs, mostly donated from the collection of the Swiss underground figure Urban Gwerder, founder of the Frank Zappa fanzine *Hot Ratz Times* [11 issues, 1973–75].) An A4-sized reproduction of Pickering's *Dylan: A Commemoration* was published by Desolation Row Promotions, Welwyn Garden City (1995); ditto *Praxis: One* (1996).

which was the ultimate 'fuck you of self-assertion', and actually let a mass public in on the speaking.[11]

'The Times They Are A-Changin'' was certainly prophetic – but it has been outdated by the very changes the song itself threatened. Its message is politically out of date. On the one hand 'mothers and fathers throughout the land' are as ready as ever to criticise what they don't understand, but on the other hand the people who wanted change have rightly lost the optimism of expecting senators and congressmen to heed their political calls.

The Bob Dylan of the late 1970s fully acknowledged the way that the changing of the times had dated his song about them. When he sang it, for the first time in thirteen years, on his 1978 tour, he re-interpreted it as a sad, slow admission of his generation's failure. This version appears on the 'live' album "Bob Dylan At Budokan", where there is even the inspired touch of a Duane Eddy guitar sound to emphasise the anachrony of the song.[12]

'When The Ship Comes In' prophesies a socio-political ideal future too, and offers us Dylan singing of the coming change in terms of an arriving ship – which seems as unsurprising as the use of roads, tides and so on in 'The Times They Are A-Changin''. Yet 'When The Ship Comes In' has not been outdated by events. It survives because it is wisely unspecific – not out of vagueness, nor from an attempt to provide a common-to-everyone account. Necessarily and rightly, its references to coming changes are figurative to the point of allegory – because the important thing is (by contrast) the personal responses of the writer towards the anticipated future. The details, figurative, metaphorical, allegorical and symbolic as they are, define and illustrate these responses:

> *Oh the foes will rise with the sleep still in their eyes*
> *And they'll jerk from their beds and think they're dreamin'*
> *But they'll pinch themselves and squeal*
> *And they'll know that it's for real . . .*

11.   Country Joe & The Fish: 'The Fish Cheer', live, Woodstock, 16/8/69, "Woodstock", Atlantic Records SD 3–500, New York [Atlantic K26001, London], 1970. Here the Alternative Cheerleading, as it were, goes 'Gimme an F!' – 'F!' – 'Gimme a U!' – 'U!' – 'Gimme a C!' – 'C!' – 'Gimme a K!' – 'K!' – 'What's that spell??!!' – 'FUCK!'. The original version, within 'The Fish Cheer & I Feel Like I'm Fixin' To Die Rag', NYC, July–Sept. 1967, was issued on "I Feel Like I'm Fixin' To Die", the second Country Joe & The Fish LP, Vanguard Records VSD-79266, New York [Fontana Records TLF 6087, London], 1967, CD-reissued Vanguard VMD 79266–2, New York, c. 1990 [London, c. 1994]. Here the routine had involved the word 'fish' instead.
   (Their first album was the wonderful "Electric Music For The Mind & Body", Berkeley, Jan.–Feb. 1967, Vanguard Records SVRL 19026, New York, 1967 [Fontana Records TFL 6081, London, 1967], CD-reissued Vanguard Records VMD 79244–2, New York, c. 1990 [London, c. 1994]: the finest 'psychedelic' album ever made, still powerfully redolent of a vanished era in which the music genuinely seemed to be taking flight into unexplored skyways. It is utterly un-Dylanesque, yet Dylan manages to remind us of it by reproducing exactly its distinctive, 'dated' organ sound on his album "Time Out Of Mind" thirty years later.)

12.   Better still is the acoustic version performed on the 1981 tour, e.g. as heard on the widely-circulated bootleg "Hanging In The Balance", which captures the arresting performance Dylan gives in Bad Segeberg, West Germany, 14/7/81. Without altering a word but with a divergent set of chords, Dylan effectively reverses the song's meaning, making it a sad memorial to vanished hopes. Unfortunately he hasn't left it at that, but has performed it without end in the years since, and though occasional renditions have had their own minor attractions, the song has essentially become a meaningless Greatest Hit. Dropping it would show more integrity.

> *Oh the fishes will laugh as they swim out of the path*
> *And the seagulls, they'll be smilin'* . . .[13]

Where 'The Times They Are A-Changin'' gives us no sense of proximity to any individual's sensibility, 'When The Ship Comes In' plainly offers a sincere vision. It puts us in contact with a real and fine sensibility. It doesn't lean on mass sentiment at any point; mass sentiment can, if it likes, lean on it.[14]

Since 'Spanish Harlem Incident' (fourth album) has been so praised and 'The Times They Are A-Changin'' (third album) so disparaged, perhaps I have given the impression that by the time of that fourth album, Dylan had put bad writing behind him. This is not the case. 'Ballad In Plain D', also from the fourth album, is a very bad song, even though Dylan's performance goes a long way to minimising the faults. (With some lines, his voice can enhance sufficiently to give positive pleasure, as for instance at the very beginning:

> *I once loved a girl, her skin it was bronze . . .*)

The song is so bad partly because the words seem forced to fit the tune (and forced into rhymes also: 'Beneath a bare lightbulb / The plaster did pound / Her sister and I / In a screaming battleground / And she in between / The victim of sound . . .') and partly because words and tune so obviously don't fit. The lyric is full of Sensitive Teenage Hysteria; the tune is reflective.

The hysteria shows a more fundamental fault: the telling of what is a tale of adolescent-love-frustrated is done not from outside, not with a detachment capable of reassessing the significance of the things experienced, but from the inside, so that the assessment is as teeny and entangled as the experience. Dylan could only have made the song worth having if he had handled his theme 'afterwards': if he could have judged from a non-adolescent perspective. The song deals with a stage of immature development and yet Dylan refuses to see it as such. His allegiance is to the state of mind that experienced the story; his attitude towards his own immaturity is a long way from mature.

There is, throughout the song, a pretence at the quality of assessment that is so patently missing.

> *Myself for what I did, I cannot be excused*
> *The changes I was going through can't even be used,*

---

13.   It is partly the language of the Bible that propels this ship. Here is Matthew 24:29, in which Christ says he is quoting the prophet Daniel's prophecy of the last days (though in fact these words don't occur in Daniel): 'Immediately after the tribulation of those days shall the sun be darkened, and the moon shall not give her light, and the stars shall fall from heaven, *and the powers of the heavens shall be shaken*' [my emphasis]. This last sounds like a line of the song. (This part of the biblical text precedes a passage Dylan alludes to over 25 years later in 'Ring Them Bells': Matthew 24:31.)

14.   Another Dylan song that in this way resembles 'The Times They Are A-Changin'' and contrasts with 'When The Ship Comes In' is the much less well-known 'Paths Of Victory'. Its language is total platitude: not a single fresh analogy breaks up the flow of cliché: 'The trail is dusty/And my road it might be rough/But the better roads are waiting/And boys it ain't far off/Trails of troubles,/Roads of battles,/Paths of Victory/We shall walk'. An instantly forgettable and rather tiresome song – yet the theme is essentially the same as that of 'When The Ship Comes In'.

For the lies that I told her in hope not to lose
The could-be dream-lover of my lifetime.

It doesn't convince. By the time we've got past 'The changes I was going through' we are aware of a sort of self-idealisation on the narrator's part, enforced by that 'Myself' as it is cushioned and coddled by the tune, and emphasised also by that hint of deliberate mysteriousness. We don't get told about the changes, nor about the 'lies', but their existence (and apparent importance) is thrust at us with an exaggerated solemnity we are supposed to take at face value – to take with an equal solemnity.

The reliance on face value leads Dylan to some embarrassingly bad lines:

Of the two sisters I loved the young.
With sensitive instincts, she was the creative one.

Nothing in the song (and it has thirteen verses) shows us any of this: it is simply insisted upon.

There is one instance where the vagueness of imagery (which comes across, generally, as a kind of sulkiness) rolls back to give us an impressive glimpse of the boy–girl relationship gone wrong:

Till the tombstones of damage read no questions but Please,
What's Wrong? What's Exactly The Matter?

which is detached enough to see the two lovers from the outside and observe the way that those sad questions get asked, as they so often do when our relationships are crumbling. Through the rest of the song we have a dominant impression that despite that 'once' in the opening line, it all happened about two days before the song was set down, and that the motivation for the writing lay in the unsorted, ill-articulated aftermath of the experience. Only that motive could explain how such a bad song could have come from Dylan, especially at a time when so many good ones were emerging.

Perhaps, though, any transition period (as 1964 certainly was in Dylan's development) makes for vulnerability. At any rate, 1965 was far more hectic and found Dylan's use of language in a far greater state of flux. At one end we have 'It's Alright Ma (I'm Only Bleeding)', which is mainly a more circumspect re-working of, say, 'Only A Pawn In Their Game', yet merges this old approach to new language. Part of the song's impact is thereby its very patchiness – the way it keeps wowing from one sort of articulation to another. Thus Dylan makes even transitional experiment work for him not just as a way forward but as a procedure in its own right and for its own sake.

One minute the listener hears:

Advertising signs that con you
Into thinking you're the one
That can do what's never been done
That can win what's never been won
Meantime life outside goes on
All around you.

Very straightforward stuff. But then there's this:

> Temptation's page flies out the door
> You follow, find yourself at war,
> Watch waterfalls of pity roar . . .

The struggle towards a complex figurative language keeps bursting through in flashes like this. The image that takes us to the edge of the waterfall, to the juxtaposition of 'pity' and 'roar', is only one of many deepening-points in the song: it works and is abrasive in a more inward way than we would have expected from the earlier social commentary songs. It is more real than the mirror of his older 'realist' songs.

This veering away from mere external (political) generalisation goes hand in hand with a paradoxical change in external attitude. It appears (though not for the first time: 'North Country Blues', 'The Lonesome Death Of Hattie Carroll' and others all have their personalised moments) along with a more resigned, accepting posture:

> It's all right, Ma, I can make it . . .
> It's all right, Ma, it's life and life only

and along with a more savage and jaundiced vision of what he bitterly calls 'people's games':

> Disillusioned words like bullets bark
> As human gods aim for their mark,
> Make everything from toy guns that spark
> To flesh-colored Christs that glow in the dark
> It's easy to see without lookin' too far
> That not much
> Is really sacred.

All these changes seem to stem from Dylan discarding an anger that was the child of optimism – an indignation (as, for instance, in 'Masters of War') that could only be sustained so long as the belief in enlightened-congressmen-about-to-heed-the-call could itself be sustained. Dylan's graduation from the 'Masters of War' approach towards real poetry – the poetry of real experience – can in this way be seen as prompted not by a change in political *belief* nor by a *rejection* of politics (which is the same thing), but by a change in *assessment* of his political vision. To put it over-simply, Dylan became a more serious artist when profound political pessimism set in. The spectre of pessimism showed up pamphleteering songs as pitifully inadequate and rather silly. Dylan said so himself in 'My Back Pages' and again in the song we've just looked at:

> While one who sings with his tongue on fire
> Gargles in the rat race choir
> Bent out of shape by society's pliers . . .

'It's Alright Ma' is not the last of Dylan's protest songs, but it is the last in which the vestiges of the old attitude remain – the last of the type wherein anger (and anger of the kind that pleads for help from senators) replaces analysis with accusation, and, like 'My Back Pages', it specifically abdicates the protest function. The contemporaneous 'Gates Of Eden' (considered in Chapter 2) is very different in vision and organisation – and utterly different as an indicator of what Dylan had come to expect of himself as an artist.

This change seems complete by the time of 'Desolation Row' – a classic illustration of the distinction between accusation and analysis. 'Desolation Row' is a brilliant political analysis of American society and shows vividly the connection between its pessimism and a seriousness of intent.

Dylan chooses to offer his narration from inside Desolation Row itself, and so he can communicate one part of his gloom in a personalised way:

> *When you asked me how I was doing*
> *Was that some kind of joke?*

The intention of the whole, however, is not to repeat the theme of, say, 'North Country Blues', which was basically the chronicle of a community's suffering in the face of encroaching penury. In 'Desolation Row' Dylan is dealing with contemporary America in terms of its pollution of human values. He is no longer treating a particular side-effect of capitalism as a sort of overlying weight which affronts the dignity of golden-hearted miners and the conscience of liberals. Dylan is recognising a pervasive 'Amerika' (as it was called then), one that mutates all humanity and offers insinuatory as well as polarising challenges, challenges against which the old liberal blueprints are worse than useless. Dylan no longer expects solutions to arise out of reforms or legislation. Neither does he see any point in rallying around the home comforts of 'We Shall Overcome'. There is no broad solution. The most Dylan looks for is that we can each try to develop, individually, an unwarped perspective:

> *Right now I can't read too good*
> *Don't send me no more letters, no:*
> *Not unless you mail them*
> *From Desolation Row.*

Excepting its final verse, the song is Dylan's necessarily tentative expression of such a perspective for himself.

He comes back to essentially the same stance on the "Slow Train Coming" and "Saved" albums of 1979–80. His prepare-to-meet-thy-maker warnings are saying again that at most (but also at least) one has the fundamental duty to oneself of keeping a clear head above all the poisonous waters of chaos and corrosion in which our society makes us swim.

On 'Desolation Row', Dylan emphasises the complexity of the subject matter, in the first place by a sustained reversal of norms within the song: the beauty-parlour is filled with big hairy US Marines and it is the riot squad that needs putting down. Casanova, the sophisticate, is being spoon-fed; Romeo is moaning. The song is a striking and a sinister parade – and we come to see the chaos with clarity, come to see in the parade a barrage of folk heroes in careful disarray: participants, victims and agents of a disordered, sick society.

The other general characteristic of the song is associated with the sinister element: the song confronts us with recurring hints of imminent disaster. (Again, the similarities in "Slow Train Coming" and "Saved" are plain.)

For analysts of America committed to Big Bang Revolution, such hints are taken, of course, as signs of promise; but Dylan declines to go along with this approach (which, in order to simplify the 'solution', must warp the truth about the problems to be solved – must posit them as equally simple). In 'Desolation Row' the imminent disasters are past and present as well as future. The verses pile up and pile up, the sinister intimations pile up with them, and there is no suggestion (no 'hope', in other words) that the crescendo will ever be curtailed.

If it wasn't for the last verse, with its different function, the song could be circular: that verse re-asserts that the parade could pass not once, or even several times but endlessly, timelessly. The very lengthiness of the song enforces this impression, as it is meant to, and so does the long instrumental section between the penultimate verse and the last. This section takes the last verse away from the circular plane of the rest and sets it aside. Only on the page does it 'follow on' from the other verses; in reality it is off to one side, a satellite, alone but with a special focus that can be brought to bear on the rest at any point. When people consequently say that 'Desolation Row' has two endings, they could more usefully say instead that it doesn't have an ending at all.

But though the climactic catastrophe never quite comes, Dylan's intimations of disaster build up towards one. They come with ever-increasing intensity as well as to cumulative effect. At the beginning, the commissioner – who is blind – is tied by one hand to the tight-rope walker; the riot squad is bound to burst out somewhere; furtively, the ambulances move in and depart. Then we get these lines:

> Now the moon is almost hidden
> The stars are beginning to hide
> The fortune-telling lady
> Has even taken all her things inside . . .

Here Dylan carries us further into the darkness, linking the blanching of the moon and stars with the ominousness of the astrologer packing up and gravely going home after glimpsing the future. The neatness and power of these lines shows Dylan's success with a new economy of language.

What follows on has a neatness of not quite the same kind:

> All except for Cain and Abel
> An' the hunchback of Notre Dame
> Everybody is makin' love
> Or else expecting rain

and by this point in the song, we've had enough opportunity to note what a curious amalgam it is – part surrealism, part impressionistic metaphor, part allegory and part riddle: an anti-logic nightmare.

The most striking evocation of impending catastrophe is, however, achieved very simply – in the one arresting line

> The Titanic sails at dawn.

That summarises concisely the tone and colouring of the whole song. For all its simplicity (perhaps because of it) the analogy does not take away from the complexity of the overall vision. Dylan takes the *Titanic* to represent contemporary America, for the *Titanic* was the ship of the future, the 'proof' of man's civilisation and progress, the unsinkable ship which, on her maiden voyage, sank. And, according to the best stories (and Dylan relies on their currency: a neat case of poetic licence) when the ship began to sink the passengers refused to believe it was happening. The Palm Court orchestra kept playing and the people in the ballroom danced obliviously on.[15]

The different kinds of oblivion and denial in America – the various ways in which the dancing continues – are presented with an incisiveness maintained throughout the song. The focus on all this escalating malaise is kept strictly under control. The cumulative effect is, in this sense, fully allowed for. The swelling up of evil as we are given it never becomes histrionic: yet it operates powerfully as it grows through from the postcards of hangings, via the cyanide holes, and on past the factory

> *Where the heart-attack machine*
> *Is strapped across their shoulders*
> *And then the kerosene . . .*

The first two verses of the song are actually very general – introductory in a conventional way: 'Here is the parade'. It is when he gets to the third verse that Dylan begins to focus on specific components of the overall chaos and disease.

He fixes first on the modern liberal conscience:

> *The Good Samaritan he's dressing,*
> *He's getting ready for the show*
> *He's going to the carnival tonight*
> *On Desolation Row.*

By the time we meet this Good Samaritan the moon has already hidden and the stars are retreating. It is not the kind of darkness that should encourage dressing for dinner. Like everybody's making love, it is an inappropriate response. The wrong gesture at the wrong time. It is part of the lethal unawareness against which Dylan speaks out.

In their own ways, the other verses argue the same case, and the shift of

---

15.   Sailing from Southampton on 10 April 1912 (not at dawn), bound for New York on her maiden voyage, RMS *Titanic* sank after hitting an iceberg off Newfoundland on the night of the 14th to 15th, with the loss of probably 1,513 lives out of 2,207 (exact figures are still disputed). The 'orchestra' was in fact a quintet that played everything from Offenbach to ragtime; as the ship sank, it did not remain below but played up on deck. The last number was almost certainly not 'Nearer My God To Thee', as in myth, but the dance tune 'Songe d'Autumne', composed by Archibald Joyce. (Third-class passengers had to provide their own music and mustered an Irish piper and a fiddler.)

'God Himself could not sink this ship,' a woman passenger had been told. It took ten seconds' contact with the iceberg to start disproving this claim, but two hours and forty minutes to sink the ship. As Michael Davie notes (in *The Titanic: The Full Story of a Tragedy*, 1986), the tragedy 'was also man-made, the result of a state of mind – grandiose, avaricious and self-confident'. Tellingly, too, '34 per cent of male first-class passengers [were] saved . . . 8 per cent of second-class . . . 12 per cent in third . . . death and disaster were not such great levellers after all.' On the other hand, 354 crew survived and approximately 351 passengers.

The *Titanic*'s extra significance as expressed in a number of blues songs – blacks relished it as a symbol of whitey's come-uppance – is touched upon in Chapter 9.

The lines immediately following that 'Titanic' have their applicability too: 'Everybody is shouting/Which Side Are You On?' 'Which Side Are You On?' was an intensely political song composed by one Florence Reece (then aged 12), the daughter of a Kentucky miner. (The tune, incidentally, as Alan Lomax explains it, was a variant on the English 'Jack Munroe', the title phrase replacing 'lay the lily-o'.) It later became a national union song. It is cited also in Martin B. Duberman's political play *In White America* (1964). Dylan, interviewed in 1966 ('The *Playboy* interview: Bob Dylan: a candid conversation with the iconoclastic idol of the folk-rock set', *Playboy*, March 1966), made his attitude clear: 'Songs like "Which Side Are You On?" and "I Love You Porgy", they're not folk music songs: they're political songs. They're already dead.'

perspective in the final verse just emphasises and reiterates the point. It's a world of commissioners: we're all blind.

In the verse quoted just above, the argument applies – in so far as poetic language can be paraphrased down into particulars, which it mostly can't – in that the liberal conscience marries an indiscriminate humanitarianism to an equally effete set of fashionable reforming aims but never achieves sufficient vision to begin to transform society and thus gets nowhere. The Good Samaritan is blown from aim to aim and from idea to idea by the prevailing outrages and ailments of a society in flux. Dylan is urging instead the primary need to recognise and assert essential human values which must ultimately be re-established. The one place where the possession or rediscovery of the necessary detachment and honesty of response is possible, is, of course, on Desolation Row. It is worse than useless to go there in carnival mood.

Such blindness, manifest in other ways, comes under attack most urgently towards the end of the song, and in the eighth and ninth verses is given a kind of cause-and-effect examination. The seventh verse berates the bourgeoisie ('Across the street they've nailed the curtains'; 'They are spoonfeeding Casanova . . . poisoning him with words'); the eighth verse indicts the education system that the bourgeoisie has established. A system organised to enforce and perpetuate ignorance, Dylan paints it as a nightmarish machinery for bringing into line the potential enemies of the state (which is to say, of the status quo), the independent thinkers:

> Now at midnight all the agents
> And the superhuman crew
> Come out an' round up everyone
> That knows more than they do.

That is terrific. That 'crew' suggests, along with the opening phrase 'at midnight', the whole sinister morass of collective vandalism, political purges and press gangs.

Those lines insist, equally acutely, on an overriding presence of violence; it is conjured up in the first two lines of that verse, so that we are forewarned of the 'heart-attack machine' and the kerosene; and impressed upon us too is the near impossibility of escape. Dylan urges upon us anew a sense of the powerlessness of the individual

> . . . brought down from the castles
> By insurance men who go
> Check to see that nobody is escaping
> To Desolation Row.

The allusion, clinched by that 'castles', to Kafka's visions, makes this pessimism unequivocally clear.[16] Dylan has not merely argued, but has created for us, the

---

16. *The Castle* (1926), like *The Trial* (1925), is a posthumous novel by one of the founding figures of modern consciousness – the father, if you will, of alienation – the Czech writer Franz Kafka (1883–1924). Alan Bennett, in an excellent and modest essay on Kafka, makes the same allusion as Dylan (assuming, like Dylan, that the very word 'castle', in a certain context, connotes Kafka's work): 'His work has been garrisoned by armies of critics, with some fifteen thousand books about him at the last count. As there is a Fortress Freud so there is a Fortress Kafka, Kafka his own castle.' (From 'Kafka in Las Vegas', *London Review of Books*, no.14, 23/7/87; collected in Alan Bennett's *Writing Home*, 1994.)

Dylan's 'insurance men' may also allude to Kafka, since it was at the Workers Accident Insurance Institute that Kafka worked, and which formed for him a model 'kingdom of the absurd', in Bennett's phrase.

powerlessness just mentioned. It is not a polemic but a vision that he leaves us with, insisting that all any individual can do is hold to some integrity of personal perspective. And that, in the end, is exactly what 'Desolation Row' offers.

An earlier chapter argued that, like T. S. Eliot, Dylan has challenged the validity of traditional distinctions between poetic 'seriousness' and levity; it is equally true that Dylan has challenged, by his switching of modes of language within a single song, the traditional conceptions of 'serious' (which is to say scrupulous) technique.

Not only 'Desolation Row' offers this challenge: many of the songs that date from 1965 display a similar chaos of language, an amalgam to some degree of blues vernacular, impressionism, allegory and more.

'Like A Rolling Stone' is one such song. Its opening verse is straightforward, almost monosyllabic slang:

> *Once upon a time you dressed so fine*
> *Threw the bums a dime in your prime, didn' you?*
> *People'd call, say 'Beware, doll, you're bound t' fall'*
> *You thought they were all kiddin' you;*
> *You used to laugh about*
> *Ev'ybody that was hangin' out*
> *Now you don't talk so loud*
> *Now you don't seem so proud*
> *About havin' to' be scroungin' your next meal*
>
> *How does it feel?! Ah! How does it feel?! . . .*

The brevity and crispness of the language – city language, straight from the streets – combines with the pile-up effect of all those internal rhymes, fired past the listener as from a repeater-rifle, establishing at once the tone of bitter recrimination. The tone is modified as the language changes, as it accommodates a broader theme, a heightened appreciation on the narrator's part of Miss Lonely's fall to 'homelessness':

> *You said you'd never compromise*
> *With the mystery tramp, but now you realize*
> *He's not selling any alibis*
> *As you stare into the vacuum of his eyes*
> *And say, do you want to, make a deal?*
>
> *How does it feel?! Ah! How does it feel?!*

Here the words are longer, those '-ise' sounds slow-fading, the phrasing much less colloquial, the 'meaning', measured in prose terms, vaguer. This change of language keeps its momentum, and paradoxically, as the language gets 'vaguer' so the meeting of eyes between the narrator and Miss Lonely intensifies: they reach the point where understanding is searching and personal, and communication can be achieved at this pitch:

> *You never turned around to see the frowns on the jugglers an' the clowns*
> *When they all came down and did tricks for you . . .*
>
> *You used to ride the chrome horse with your diplomat . . .*

You used to be so amused
At Napoleon in rags and the language that he used
Go to him now, he calls you, you can't refuse . . .

This calculated lack of specificity becomes, in Dylan's hands, a positive entity grown out of and beyond the specific; and it opens up the way for the re-creation of many different universal relationships. As this use of language becomes a dominant characteristic of Dylan's writing (as it does in 1965) so he provides a whole series of songs which are scintillating studies of human relationships. The listener is no longer just a witness to incidents from Dylan's own life (as he was, say, with 'I Don't Believe You', 'Girl Of The North Country' and 'Boots Of Spanish Leather') nor a witness to incidents from other people's lives (as with 'North Country Blues', 'Hattie Carroll' and 'Hollis Brown'). Just as D. H. Lawrence moved from making art out of direct autobiographical experience to making much greater art out of universal experience, so the Dylan of the mid-1960s moved in a similar direction.

Perhaps the easiest song to clarify this is actually a later one, 'Dear Landlord': for the point of that song is that it doesn't matter 'who the landlord is' – it is simply 'Dear Someone'; the song captures the essence of a relationship we can recognise as possible between any two people. It no longer needs Dylan the man to take one of the parts.

But if this use of language (which is still in transition in 'Like A Rolling Stone') no longer offers us autobiography, its universal glimpses are, of course, rendered as through Dylan's eyes. And so, like any great artist, Dylan bequeaths us a part of reality we could not otherwise have received. To render things that are real in a genuinely new way (which takes more than an 'original style') is actually to have created something new and at the same time true.

'Like A Rolling Stone' is, naturally, not the only song from 1965 which is, in the sense discussed, transitional. 'It's All Over Now, Baby Blue', 'Positively 4th Street', 'On The Road Again' – all these are halfway-houses in the same sense. It is also true that many other Dylan songs from 1965 make no demands on the 'Napoleon in rags' type of language; in others that language is subjugated to themes still clustered around autobiography. Into these categories come, at a minimum, 'Bob Dylan's 115th Dream', 'Highway 61 Revisited', 'If You Gotta Go, Go Now' and 'Subterranean Homesick Blues'.

There are also songs full of the calculatedly unspecific that operate differently again: as, for instance, 'Ballad Of A Thin Man' and those two great songs 'Love Minus Zero/No Limit' and 'She Belongs To Me', along with others in which words function mainly by helping Dylan's voice to be the masterpiece of rock musicianship it had become by 1965, in particular, on 'From A Buick 6'. Nevertheless, there is a general direction to which songs like 'Like A Rolling Stone' are signposts.

The first one that truly marks the arrival of the new type was issued as a single (though with little commercial success): 'Can *You* Please Crawl Out Your Window?' In this song, the language flashes and sculpts, takes a hundred different photographs, captures a human possibility that comes across as always having been there, recurring and recurring, but never detected or seen in focus before. It needn't be a relationship we have been through for it to impress us as true – as accurately stated and real; and only the insensitive listener would feel a need to ask what the song 'means'.

It almost stands up just as words on the page; and while the recording is a fine thing (actually there are two fine recordings) the language of the song is at least as interesting as its music.[17]

Consider the phrase 'fist full of tacks'. Dylan uses that in at least three main ways. First, it gives us a visual image of sorts – it directs our awareness towards the man's hands: and these are kept before us implicitly when we come, later in the same verse, to his 'inventions' and again later when we come to 'hand him his chalk'. Second, 'fist full of tacks' gives us a vivid metaphor and at the same time yields a neat juxtaposition. The juxtaposition is of course that in the first half of the relevant line we get the man and the sweep of the room and are then zoomed down to the tiny contents of his closed hand.[18] The metaphor is characteristic of Dylan, and takes us all the way back to 'Talkin' New York', on his very first album, where he says

> A lot of people don't have much food on their table
> But they got a lot of forks 'n' knives
> And they gotta cut somethin'.

Those lines are explaining why his initial New York audiences were hostile: it is a figurative explanation. 'Fist full of tacks' operates similarly. It could be swapped, in a prose précis, with the word 'aggressively', and yet it does a lot more than the word 'aggressively' could do. The third way it works is in establishing a tone of verbal precision – it is an incisive, sharp phrase – which is important throughout the song. It influences the sound, later on in the song, of words like 'test' and 'inventions', 'righteous' and 'box', and links up, in effect, with that phrase 'little tin women' in the final verse.[19] 'Little tin women' is of exactly corresponding brittleness and precision. This impression is enforced in the music, too, by the guitar-work in particular and by various xylophonic effects in general.

Dylan provides a contrast to all this 'tin-tack' atmosphere: it is beautifully contradicted by that gangling (and warm) chorus line

> Use your arms and legs, it won't ruin you.

17.   The first single, NYC, 30/7/65, with Mike Bloomfield on guitar, Al Kooper on organ, an unidentified pianist, Harvey Goldstein (aka Harvey Brooks) on bass and Bobby Gregg on drums, was issued, mistitled 'Positively 4th Street', with the same catalogue number as that previous single [Columbia 4–43389, New York]. A second single, NYC, 30/11/65, with Robbie Robertson, Rick Danko, Richard Manuel, Garth Hudson and others, was correctly issued [Columbia 4–43477]; an out-take from the latter session has also circulated.

18.   The same happens in the comparable example of 'You walk into the room / With a pencil in your hand', from 'Ballad Of A Thin Man'. That too yields a visual incongruity by its juxtapositioning. It also uses the 'pencil' as a symbol – so that the two lines give us not only the man's entrance as others see it but also his own attitude (because, that is to say, to come in 'with a pencil in your hand' is plainly to be unreceptive to real life – to wish to be an observer and not a participant).

19.   In Bob Dylan, *Lyrics 1962–1985*, the phrase is given as 'little ten women', but this is surely a mishearing by the transcriber. An alternative mishearing, 'lilting women', is listed in 'Pardon, Monsieur, am I hearing you right?' in Gray and Bauldie, *All Across the Telegraph: A Bob Dylan Handbook* (1987). Neither so well suits – indeed the second contradicts – the chinking sharpness Dylan is chipping in with in the verses of the song. 'Little tin women' is surely right: Dylan had already used the phrase 'little tin men' in his poem 'jack o'diamonds', 1964, one of the poems forming 'Some Other Kinds Of Songs', published as sleeve notes to "Another Side Of Bob Dylan", 1964: 'jack o'diamonds / wrecked my hand / left me here t'stand / little tin men play / their drums now'. (Interesting that that 'left me here t'stand' is soon repeated also, becoming 'left me blindly here to stand' in 'Mr. Tambourine Man', a song he was singing at Ric von Schmidt's house in Sarasota, Florida, as early as May 1964, i.e. *before* he recorded the "Another Side Of Bob Dylan" LP (recorded NYC, 9/6/64, issued August 1964).

where the words enact the motion, where the listener is actually a part of the flailing limbs swimming out of the window – where, in other words, the sounds and impressions are rounded instead of thin, and soft rather than sharp. More generally, the whole of the chorus takes part in this exercise of contrast: the qualities of 'crawl', 'use', 'ruin', 'haunt', and Dylan's long-drawn-out 'want' are all antithetical to the qualities of that initial 'fist full of tacks'.

Another interesting ingredient in the same song is connected with the tremendous line

> *With his businesslike anger and his bloodhounds that kneel . . .*

because until we isolate that line, it doesn't occur to our visual response to have our murky, semi-existent bloodhounds actually *kneeling*. Dogs cannot easily kneel at all; yet in the sense that they are humble/faithful/servile, etc., they are kneeling, figuratively, while they stand. We meet the Dylan phrase accordingly: we visualise the atmosphere that corresponds to silent, standing bloodhounds ranged around the man – ranged, in fact, around his knee. By one of those Dylan tricks of transference, it is the man's knees that come into our picture, and not the dogs' knees at all.

There is, in this crucial mid-1960s period, one song that seems to stand altogether alone in Dylan's output and outside any pattern that can be devised for tracing the development of his art. That song is 'Farewell Angelina'. With no available recording of this by Dylan himself, the best known version of it is by Joan Baez. One tends, therefore, to think of the song as really a poem – as words-on-the-page.[20]

Doing so, it appears that the song does fit a pattern: it seems half-way from 'Can *You* Please Crawl Out Your Window?' to "Blonde On Blonde". Yet it isn't actually like that at all. 'Farewell Angelina' seems to introduce surrealistic language with a bang, in a new way for Dylan, while by the time of "Blonde On Blonde" he has adjusted that language almost out of recognition. It is in this sense that 'Farewell Angelina' stands alone. Where "Blonde On Blonde" works as a sort of contemporary technicolour surrealist movie, 'Farewell Angelina' seems like a black-and-white 1940s surrealist short (and 'Can *You* Please Crawl Out Your Window?' is not like a film at all).

> *Just a table standing empty by the edge of the sea . . .*

That is the line that encapsulates the song: its essential tone and its distinctive kind of image. A strange song: and the fact that there are still things in it that do seem characteristic of Dylan's other work does not make it, in overall effect, any the less strange – quite the opposite. The melody is typically Dylan: it has a similar expansive lightness and brightness to the near-contemporaneous 'Mr. Tambourine Man'. Some of the lines in the lyric add to this similarity:

20. Bob Dylan, it turned out, had indeed recorded it (NYC, 13/1/65, at the "Bringing It All Back Home" sessions). No tape ever circulated, however, until shortly before its sudden, surprise release on "Bootleg Series I–III", 1991. Joan Baez: 'Farewell Angelina', NYC, *nia*, issued "Farewell Angelina", Vanguard VRS-9200 (stereo VSD-79200), New York, 1965, CD-reissued Vanguard VRM 79200–2, New York and London, 1995. (The album contained three other Dylan songs, plus 'Will Ye Go, Laddie, Go' and 'Satisfied Mind'.) Baez's 'Farewell Angelina' was also a Top 40 hit in the UK [Fontana Records TF 639, London, 1965].

> *The triangle tingles and the trumpets play slow*
> *The sky is on fire, and I must go . . .*

and

> *. . . In the space where the deuce and the ace once ran wild*
> *Farewell Angelina, the sky is folding . . .*

But 'Farewell Angelina' is emphatically and fundamentally visual: a series of pictures, sometimes switching suddenly on and off, sometimes sliding into each other:

> *King Kong little elves*
> *On the rooftops they dance*
> *Valentino-type tangos*
> *While the make-up man's hands*
> *Shut the eyes of the dead,*
> *Not to embarrass anyone:*
> *Farewell Angelina,*
> *The sky is embarrassed,*
> *And I must be gone.*

Even that remarkable 'the sky is embarrassed' is an assertion we visualise; we picture the sky and picture it in relation to the song's other protagonists throughout the song. And this is all that is offered or required; if we receive all the visual glimpses, if we really can, instantly,

> *See the cross-eyed pirates*
> *Sitting perched in the sun*
> *Shooting tin cans*
> *With a sawn-off shot-gun*

then the song has worked.[21]

It is on the "Desire" album of eleven years later that Dylan returns to this photographic mode: on 'Sara', where we're offered snapshots again – of 'them playin' with their pails in the sand / They run to the water, their buckets to fill / . . . see the shells fallin' out of their hands / As they follow each other back up the hill' and 'Them playin' leapfrog and hearin' about Snow-White'.

When we come back to "Blonde On Blonde" and this mid-1960s progression, things are not so simple. We come to material where visual imagery is only one factor,

---

21.   The lyrics here are as performed by Joan Baez (note 20) and as given in Bob Dylan, *Lyrics 1962–1985*. The Dylan track released on "Bootleg Series I–III" (note 20) seems to capture an earlier draft (several of the respects in which it differs show a hesitancy about the words themselves and how to fit them into the melodic lines; and Dylan resorts to the same line twice in consecutive verses – 'The sky is flooding over'). We lose several of the passages I quote in the main text above: 'Just a table standing empty by the edge of the sea' is instead 'A table stands empty by the edge of the stream'; 'the music', rather than 'the trumpets', play slow; 'the night', rather than 'the sky', is on fire; the 'King Kong little elves' dance 'in' rather than 'on' the rooftops; we see the cross-eyed pirates 'sit' rather than 'sitting'; and 'the hero's clean hands', rather than the make-up man's, 'shut the eyes of the dead, not to embarrass anyone' – after which instead of the lovely Pathetic Fallacy of 'the sky is embarrassed', we get the first appearance of 'the sky is flooding over'. (There is also an extra verse, inserted between the published version's penultimate and last verses, and it is at the end of this extra verse that 'The sky is flooding over' again; by the time of the published version, this line has been dropped altogether.)

and one that fluctuates enormously in importance even within a single song – and we come to a surrealist language distinctly unlike the surrealism of Dali or Magritte. In one important sense, Dylan's vision throughout "Blonde On Blonde" much more closely resembles that of Bosch. There is no suggestion that the narrators in these 1966 songs stand, like Magritte, on the threshold of madness. On the contrary, they are sane men surrounded by the madness and chaos of other people and other things. The surrealistic pile-ups of imagery do not reflect the state of a narrator's (or Dylan's) psyche: they reflect the confusion which a calm and ordered mind observes around it.[22]

In this sense, the album is a whole and the individual songs are only parts; and it doesn't matter that sometimes the chaos seems to be America and sometimes seems to be the city life of particular sorts of people. It doesn't even contradict the spirit of the whole that a couple of the songs evoke a chaos that is inside the emotions of the narrator – the chaos of happy infatuation in 'I Want You', or of non-comprehension in 'Temporary Like Achilles'. 'I Want You' propounds a relationship between the lovers and the outside world that fits the general pattern of the album well, in that it lends itself, as a dichotomy, to a relation between internals and externals – between chaos and order:

> The cracked bells and washed out horns
> Blow into my face with scorn
> But it's not that way, I wasn't born
> To lose you . . .

> . . . She is good to me
> And there's nothing she doesn't see
> She knows where I'd like to be
> But it doesn't matter –

The chaos is there all right. And 'Temporary Like Achilles' bears some resemblance to this:

> Well I lean into your hallway
> Lean against your velvet door
> I watch upon your scorpion
> Who crawls across your circus floor.

That 'your hallway' suggests a place of potential refuge, and so raises again the fact of there being a gulf between narrator and outside world. The strength of the sense of refuge-seeking urged on us ('your hallway' is followed up by the repetition of the possessive adjective: 'your velvet door', 'your scorpion', 'your . . . floor') has been established earlier in the song by the eloquence of this:

> Kneeling 'neath your ceiling
> Yes I guess I'll be here for a while

---

22. Salvador Dali (1904–1989), the Spanish surrealist painter, however, said: 'There is only one difference between a madman and me. I am not mad.' (*The American*, 1956.) I am not sure that he need come into the Bob Dylan story at all. For notes on Magritte see Chapter 7, and on Bosch, Chapter 2.

> *I'm trying to read your portrait*
> *But I'm helpless, like a rich man's child.*

And when we say that those lines are so eloquent, we come to recognise them as having many of the characteristic strengths of Dylan's mid-1960s work, and having emphatically the strengths of the "Blonde On Blonde" collection.

In the first place, there is the refusal to incubate a 'serious' poetic language. How else could the slightly lugubrious voice relish its delivery of 'Kneeling 'neath your ceiling / Yes I guess I'? Thrown in for good measure, in the second place, is the sort of abrasive little generalisation that epitomises part of Dylan's intelligence: 'helpless, like a rich man's child'. This kind of side remark is always an odd mixture of humour and high seriousness. It is there to bring a smile but it has an open moral insistence behind it. However lightly introduced, the debilitating richness is cited with real severity. It is equally characteristic as a sample of "Blonde On Blonde" in the way that figurative language is the norm yet mixes easily with the literal.

It has also the vision of chaos and struggle that dominates the album – 'Kneeling . . . I'm trying . . . But I'm helpless' – and the richness of organisation (all that internal rhyming and odd, southern emphasis) and richness of sound. The words purr across to the listener: 'kneeling 'neath', 'ceiling', 'while', 'child', and 'portrait' so caressed that it sounds, literally, like 'poetry'.

But 'Temporary Like Achilles' is not the album's best song. A far better one – a truly superb song – is 'Absolutely Sweet Marie', in which the words are borne along on a sea of rich red music, bobbing with a stylish and highly distinctive rhythm. Dylan's voice is at its very best, handling the repeated line which caps each verse with as much alert variety in delivery as would be humanly yet still felicitously possible. Each time it arrives, the line is different: more insistent yet always spontaneously mooded. Dylan's harmonica also excels itself with an invincible, searing solo that bounces the boundaries of the blues.

The lyric overflows with all the qualities we specially associate with "Blonde On Blonde".

> *Well your railroad gate you know I just can't jump it*
> *Sometimes it gets so hard to see*
> *I'm just sitting here beating on my trumpet*
> *With all these promises you left for me*
> *But where are you tonight, Sweet Marie?*
>
> *Well I waited for you when I was halfsick*
> *Yes I waited for you when you hated me*
> *Well I waited for you inside of the frozen traffic*
> *When you knew I had some other place to be*
> *Now where are you tonight, Sweet Marie?*

The challenge to distinctions between 'serious' and 'light' poetic language is clear enough there, and so are the abrasive little philosophical points, flashed out with smiles.

> *Well anybody can be just like me, obviously*

is about as ambiguous as anything ever could be, and just as a joke pay-off line is clipped on to it, so later on in the song we come to this delightful alliance between sincere observation and jest:

> But to live outside the law you must be honest
> I know you always say that you agree . . .

Of course, to get the tone of that last line you need to go to the recording, as you do to get the full richness of sound that comes not only from the swirling, oceanic music but also from Dylan's bending of the words as he breathes memorable cascades of life into lines and phrases like these: 'with all these promises'; 'And now I stand here, looking at your yellow railroad/In the ruins of your balcony/Wondering where you are tonight, Sweet Marie'. Actually Dylan's handling of the single word 'balcony' shows how much and how appropriately he can reawaken tired old vocabulary and language.

'Absolutely Sweet Marie' also has its share of the glimpses of chaos, the effective communication of which depends on largely figurative expressions. It is easy to see how the metaphoric technique lights up the chaotic vision:

> . . . I just can't jump it
> Sometimes it gets so hard to see
> I'm just sitting here beating on my trumpet . . .
> But where are you . . .? . . .
>
> Well I don't know how it happened but the riverboat captain
> He knows my fate
> But ev'ybody else . . .
>
> You see, you forgot to leave me with the key.

The song also holds a characteristic richness of organisation: a well-integrated, almost self-perpetuating system of internal rhymes and subterranean rhythms, releasing Dylan's humour so well. It is there in his self-conscious – almost self-parodying – rhyming of 'halfsick' with 'traffic' and there in his mischievous matching of the ambiguous, ostensibly humble 'obviously' with that acidic fullstop on 'fortunately'. (And Elvis Costello, let it be said, could have learnt all he knows about agile, tricksy rhyming if this was the only record he'd ever heard.)

But Dylan's humour in this song is not achieved at the expense of seriousness. Throughout, we are conscious and appreciative that the narrator stands for self-honesty. His message is *be true to yourself*, and, as it is given in that epigrammatic 'to live outside the law you must be honest', its earnestness comes across.

It is also true that with each (freshly delivered) return to the 'But where are you . . .' line, we are returned to a mood appropriate to what is fundamentally an eloquent, outgoing love song. All of the imagery works at maintaining this. The frustration of 'I'm just sitting here' is ennobled, on the quiet, by that 'trumpet'; the 'promises' tumble from the tune with a reverential flutter and poignancy; and the reproaches all work, essentially, at widening our impression of the scope of the narrator's love – at saying here, look at what he has been through. Even 'the riverboat captain / He knows my fate' evokes, however illogically, visual images of romance:

glimpses of riverboat journeys on languid waters attended by weeping willows. The final verse perpetuates this romantic insistence, giving it Romeo's conclusive emphasis: 'In the ruins, of your, *bal*cony . . .'

To turn from the romantic associations of 'balcony' in 'Absolutely Sweet Marie' to the song that immediately follows it on the "Blonde On Blonde" collection is to be given quite a contrast.

'4th Time Around' is more than just a parody of the Beatles' 'Norwegian Wood'.[23] It begins as a cold, mocking put-down of a woman and a relationship untouched by love. For extra sarcasm's sake, it is set against a backing of fawning, schmaltzy guitar-work. But the drumming hints from the start at something more urgent and compelling than cold mockery, so that by the time the lyric switches attention to a second and love-tinged relationship, the tone of the song has been switched over too.

The contrast between the two women is plain enough:

> *She threw me outside* . . .
> *You took me in*

but the perspective is not that simple. The vast majority of it focuses on the 'she' part – suggesting the narrator's personal weakness and perhaps vulnerability; and in consequence this majority consists of language soaked in coarse sexual innuendo that brings out Dylan's skill in pursuing the suggestive.

(The songs on the Basement Tapes, recorded the year after "Blonde On Blonde", indulge in the suggestive to an unprecedented extent for Dylan, with lines like 'I bin hittin' it too hard / My stones won't take', 'that big dumb blonde with her wheel gorged', 'slap that drummer with a pipe that smells', and much of 'Please Mrs. Henry'. The 1974 "Planet Waves" returned more heavy-handedly and so less comfortably to this coarseness. It is there in the Dylan-written sleeve notes:

> Back to the starting point! . . . I dropped a double brandy and tried to recall the events . . . family outings with strangers – furious gals with garters and smeared lips on bar stools that stank from sweating pussy . . . space guys off duty with big dicks and duck tails all wired up and voting for Eisenhower . . .[24]

and it is there in the otherwise admirable 'Tough Mama', where Dylan lazily offers the awkward analogy 'Today on the countryside / It was hotter than a crotch'.)

Dylan's technique for delivering sexual innuendo is very interesting in '4th Time Around'. It is almost like a parody of a schoolboy reading Shakespeare aloud in class; instead of the frequently required line overflow, there is a pause – encouraged, but not

---

23. The Beatles: 'Norwegian Wood', London, 21/10/65, "Rubber Soul", Parlophone Records PCS 3075, London [Capitol ST 2442, Los Angeles], 1965 (the track on which George Harrison first plays the sitar). There is a strong parallel between the distinctive melody sung by John Lennon on 'Norwegian Wood' and the one Dylan uses for '4th Time Around'. It says something about how these two were perceived that Dylan was suspected (not least by Lennon) of parodying, rather than copying, the Beatles.

24. These "Planet Waves" sleeve notes by Dylan appeared on the back covers of the original issues of the LP [on Asylum Records S 7E 1003, Los Angeles, and on Island Records ILPS 9261, London, 1974] but not on the subsequent Columbia Records [and CBS] reissues. Nor are they collected in *Lyrics 1962–1985*. This is a pity, because despite my deploring their 'coarseness', they amount to an inspired evocation of the 1950s and how it felt to live through the Eisenhower years (General Dwight D. Eisenhower [1890–1969] was US President 1953–60).

exaggeratedly, by the tune – at the end of odd lines in the lyric. Into each pause comes all the innuendo and ambiguity that Dylan can muster:

> *I*
> *Stood there and hummed*
> *I tapped on her drum*
> *I asked her how come*
>
> *And she*
> *Buttoned her boot*
> *And straightened her suit*
> *Then she said Don't Get Cute.*
> *So I forced*
> *My hands in my pockets and felt with my thumbs . . .*
> *And after finding out I'd*
> *Forgotten my shirt*
> *I went back and knocked.*
> *I waited in the hallway, as she went to get it*
> *And I tried to make sense*
> *Out of that picture of you in your wheelchair*
> *That leaned up against*
>
> *Her*
> *Jamaican rum*
> *And when she did come*
> *I asked her for some.*

The pause Dylan creates at the end of 'And I tried to make sense' has a different purpose. (And after it, the lapse back for that pointed 'come' has an added force: it seems in every sense uncontrollable on the narrator's part.) With 'tried to make sense' the pause is to allow a change of mood to begin impinging. The tone is no longer jaundiced. From here on it is open and alert and more sensitive; for from the midst of the imagery appropriate to the narrator's sexual, loveless encounter, Dylan – and here is the touch of genius – produces a clear and striking counter-image:

> *. . . that picture of you in your wheelchair.*

With that, he establishes the hint that here, in the offing, is something with a warmer potential, something for which it is worth the narrator's while to salvage his own sensibility. Yet having produced this counter-image, Dylan allows it to recede and settle at the back of the listener's mind. Only at the very end is it reintroduced, to fuse into one clear perspective all the different threads of feeling and of imagery which run through the song. It ends:

> *And*
> *When I was through*
> *I filled up my shoe*
> *And brought it to you;*
> *And you,*

> *You took me in*
> *You loved me then*
> *You didn't waste time*
> *And I,*
> *I never took much*
> *I never asked for your crutch*
> *Now don't ask for mine.*

That 'crutch' has all the complex functioning a pun can ever have. As we are presented, triumphantly, with the mental cadence from 'wheelchair' down to that 'crutch' at the close, in the sweep of which the 'picture' is brought sharply to life, we have one of those fine, rare moments in poetry where although the technical device is seen functioning it does so with such supreme calculation and panache that its 'intrusion' actually enriches the finished work.

However good '4th Time Around' is (and however clever), it is, like 'Temporary Like Achilles', one of the minor works on "Blonde On Blonde". It is useful to look at others before coming to the major works on the album.

'Just Like A Woman', though it has become one of his best known works, is one of Dylan's uncomfortably sentimental songs. The chorus is trite and coy and the verses aren't strong enough to compensate.

> *. . . she aches just like a woman*
> *But she breaks just like a little girl.*

This is a non-statement. It doesn't describe an individual characteristic, it doesn't say anything fresh about a universal one, and yet it pretends to do both. What parades as reflective wisdom ('woman but . . . girl') is really maudlin platitude. It hasn't even engaged Dylan's skill in minimising the badness. It would, for example, be less bad if the 'But' of the pay-off line was an 'And' – for at least we would then be spared so blatantly lame and predictable a 'paradox'.[25]

On the other hand the part that we might as well call the 'middle eight' is beautifully done:

> *It was rainin' from the first an' I was*
> *Dying there of thirst an' so I*
> *Came in here*
> *An' your long time curse hurts but what's worse is this*
> *Pain in here,*
> *I can't stay in here,*
> *Ain't it clear that*
>
> *I just can't fit . . .*

Why that is so 'beautifully done' can be understood only from the recording. It is a question of delivery. Singing those words, those unit-construct lines, Dylan moulds

---

25. This is exactly the 'lameness' honed in on in Woody Allen's film *Annie Hall* [United Artists, US, 1977], in which a vacuous hippie character played by the wonderful Shelley Duvall recites the lines just quoted as if they're far-out and profound, and the character played by Allen (the usual character played by Allen) pulls a face that means he fails to see in them anything less empty-headed than their admirer.

and holds out to us a hand-made object with much tactile appeal. You need the recording for the indescribably plaintive resonance the voice yields up on those simple little words like 'rainin'', 'first', 'came' and even 'ain't'; and you need the recording above all because that long middle line demands Dylan's own pronunciation, by which 'curse hurts but what's worse' becomes five equal fur-mouthed jerks and 'what's' rhymes gleefully with 'hurts'. You have to hear Dylan doing it.

'Leopard-Skin Pill-Box Hat' is also a minor song. It's a good joke and a vehicle for showing Dylan's electric lead guitar-work, and that's really all.

Right from the opening line, Dylan's lyric takes advantage of the song's blues structure.[26] He uses the repetition of his first line in such a way as to make it a put-down, the repeated full description of the hat suggesting its owner's small mind under it:

> *I see you got your brand-new leopard-skin pill-box hat*
> *Yes, I see you got your brand-new leopard-skin pill-box hat.*

There are other smiles within the song – little flashes of malice and mockery – which don't depend on the blues structure but which ride along happily enough on its waves:

> *Well I asked the doctor if I could see you:*
> *It's bad for your health, he said . . .*

and

> *Well I saw him makin' love to you*
> *(You forgot to close the garage door)*
> *You might think he loves you for your money but*
> *I know what he really loves you for!:*
> *It's your brand-new leopard-skin pill-box hat.*

The best thing in 'Leopard-Skin Pill-Box Hat', though, utilises the blues structure devastatingly. It comes in the second verse, while Dylan is still disparaging the hat; he marries the long, downward trail of the standard blues third line to this:

> *You know it balances on your head just like a mattress balances on a bottle of*
>
> > *w*
> >
> > *i*
> >
> > *n*
> >
> > *e*
> >
> > *.*

It would be hard to find a better instance of words, tune and delivery working so entirely together. They mimic what they describe to (literally) giddy perfection.

(Another "Blonde On Blonde" song, 'Most Likely You Go Your Way (And I'll Go Mine)' treats lack of balance, too, in the middle-eight lines for which tune helps

---

26. In fact the song is founded upon a particular blues by Lightnin' Hopkins: 'Automobile (Blues)', Houston, 1949, Gold Star Records 666, Houston, 1949; LP-issued "Early Recordings", Arhoolie Records 2007, El Cerrito, California, 1965; CD-reissued on both "The Gold Star Sessions Vol.1", Arhoolie Records CD 330, El Cerrito, c. 1991, and "Vol. 2", Arhoolie CD 337, ditto. Hopkins re-recorded the song as 'Automobile Blues', NYC, 9/11/60, "The Blues Of Lightnin' Hopkins", Bluesville 1019, Bergenfield, New Jersey, c. 1960. Dylan's debt to Hopkins' song is discussed in Chapter 9.

words by seeming to falter and totter appropriately in the delivery of the lines, which include 'But he's badly built / An' he walks on stilts / Watch out he don't / Fall on you . . .')

The other song here that draws memorably on the blues – and rather more seriously so than does 'Leopard-Skin Pill-Box Hat' – is the superb 'Pledging My Time', superb precisely because of what it achieves as a blues (and which for this reason is dealt with not here but in Chapters 1 and 9).

Then there is 'Obviously 5 Believers', which sounds as if it belongs on the "Highway 61 Revisited" album rather than "Blonde On Blonde" (just as the thing aimed at in 'Outlaw Blues' was actually achieved on the later 'From A Buick 6') and is very much a blues-based rock song. It gives us a totally relaxed, in-command Dylan – so much so that he rightly hands over the harmonica part to Charlie McCoy, and the words don't matter one iota. The most that is really required of them is that they shouldn't interfere, and they don't. They even include lines already made familiar at the beginning of the album. The album starts with 'Rainy Day Women Nos. 12 & 35', with its simple punning chorus lines:

> But I would not feel so all alone:
> Everybody must get stoned

and the first finish of the album (since the final side is in essence separate from the rest), falling on 'Obviously 5 Believers', echoes that phrase explicitly:

> Guess I could make it without you honey if I
> Just did not feel so all alone.[27]

As for the major songs on "Blonde On Blonde", they strike me as being 'One Of Us Must Know (Sooner Or Later)', 'Memphis Blues Again', 'Visions Of Johanna' and 'Sad-Eyed Lady Of The Lowlands'.

The greatness of 'One Of Us Must Know' is to do with vague but dramatic impressions it carries in its music and its overall structure. It is manifestly, magnificently alive – like some once-in-a-lifetime party (and aptly the lyric impinges as if it is being delivered at a party, the voice rising and falling against a backdrop of bubbling noises and motion). The music flows over you in waves, so that the song suggests itself fleetingly as a rock equivalent of the party Scott Fitzgerald creates in *The Great Gatsby* (1925), where

> the orchestra is playing yellow cocktail music, and the opera of voices pitches a key higher. Laughter is easier minute by minute, spilled with prodigality, tipped out at a cheerful word. The groups change more swiftly, swell with new arrivals, dissolve and form in the same breath; already there are wanderers, confident girls who weave here and there among the stouter and more stable, become for a sharp, joyous moment the centre of a group, and then, excited with triumph, glide on through the sea-change of faces and voices and color under the constantly changing light.

27. This song too is further discussed, in relation to the blues, in Chapter 9, as are many "Blonde On Blonde" songs.

'One Of Us Must Know' is like that – not in its people or its social orientation but as regards its rhythms, its movement, its life. It breathes with a kind of majestic sexuality; it holds your attention with a symphonic warmth. The music never stops rising and falling and to complement this, ordinary little words, signifying little on their own, are caressed into a loving but subservient eloquence by Dylan's voice. Dylan singing the line

> *But you said you knew me an' I believed you did*

and words like '*pers-on-al*' and '*un*-der-*stood*' come across as merely part of the musical whole. A great song, and unlike Dylan's many beautiful songs celebrating the finding of a refuge, this one creates a relationship (sculpted by its narrator's implicit dialogue with the woman sharing it) but without putting the two lovers together against the world. The world whirls noisily around them, but is no threat. For once it does not howl like the wind: it jangles not intrusively but exactly like a party at which it feels OK to remain.

Beyond being an exciting rock music performance, 'Memphis Blues Again' is at least as great as 'One Of Us Must Know'. It shares with 'Visions Of Johanna' and 'Sad-Eyed Lady Of The Lowlands' a greater-than-average duration and a general high seriousness of intention. It also offers all those qualities noted earlier as being characteristic of the "Blonde On Blonde" songs, including a drugs imagery that gets no special stress. The narrator is someone just trying to get by in modern America: someone trying to get by, that is, without shutting off or closing up; someone who sees a lot happening around him but can't discern any pattern to it nor any constant but meaninglessness; someone who, in this situation, stays more outwardly vulnerable than he needs to because he retains a yearning, however vague, for some better kind of world.[28]

All this comes through to the listener from disconnected visual glimpses: that is how the imagery works. The song begins with this:

> *Oh the ragman draws circles*
> *Up an' down the block*
> *I'd ask him what the matter was*
> *But I know that he don't talk*

---

28. In this stance, in its sensibility, 'Memphis Blues Again' very much anticipates the influential Hunter S. Thompson book *Fear and Loathing in Las Vegas* (1972), which began life as a sprawling serialisation: 'Fear and loathing in Las Vegas', by 'Raoul Duke', *Rolling Stone*, nos. 95, 96, 11/11/71, 25/11/71. This formative and unequalled work of the New, or Gonzo, Journalism, takes exactly the position expressed so cogently in the Dylan song. His line 'And people just get uglier and I have no sense of time' especially prefigures the prose of Thompson's book – a book sub-titled *A Savage Journey to the Heart of the American Dream* – in which 'Every now and then when your life gets complicated and the weasels start closing in, the only real cure is to load up on heinous chemicals and then drive like a bastard from Hollywood to Las Vegas . . . not a good town for psychedelic drugs. Reality itself is too twisted . . . The TV news was about the Laos invasion . . . Pentagon generals babbling insane lies . . . The man was getting ugly, but suddenly his eyes switched away . . . The frog-eyed woman clawed feverishly at his belt . . . I turned away. It was too horrible.' Towards the end, Thompson acknowledges his debt: 'I listened for a moment, but my nerve ends were no longer receptive. The only song I might have been able to relate to, at that point, was "Mister Tambourine Man". Or maybe "Memphis Blues Again".' (The book is dedicated 'To Bob Geiger, for reasons that need not be explained here – and to Bob Dylan, for "Mister Tambourine Man" '.)

and the visual dominance is such that we get a picture to cover the third and fourth lines – they don't just pass over as abstract reflection. We see the singer standing disconsolate, aware that there is no point in trying to communicate.

The same applies throughout the song. The narrator is there in front of us, avoiding 'some French girl who says she knows me well', confronting Mona, believing the railroad men, thinking about Grandpa, hiding under the truck, winning his argument with the teen preacher, staggering around stoned and telling us that we just get uglier, smiling at black-haired Ruthie, and sitting patiently on Grand Street ('where the neon madmen climb'). It is only with the heartfelt cry of the chorus,

> *Oh! Mama! Can this really be the end?!*
> *To be stuck inside of Mobile with the Memphis Blues again!*

that the visual predominance dies away. We only picture Dylan saying 'Oh! Mama!' – we don't picture Memphis, Tennessee or Mobile, Alabama at all. They are not part of the visual language; they are symbols, words that stand for other things – hope and despondency, potential and restraint. They are abstract ideas.

This song is interesting too in the way that Dylan handles his moral point. He bestows an implicit blessing on some things and frowns on others. It is a question of drawing to the listener's attention that some things strike the artist as enhancing and others strike him as restrictive. The narrator himself is also made to represent certain values, certain virtues (and since we can associate the narrator directly with Dylan, this is easy enough, and a useful instance of how Dylan might use his personal legend to assist his art). These amount to a frank and sensitive openness to life, even at the expense of sophistication and propriety:

> *. . . An' I said Oh! I didn't know that! . . .*

> *. . . Ev'rybody still talks about*
> *How badly they were shocked;*
> *But me I expected it to happen,*
> *I knew he'd lost control! . . .*

which is contrasted with the machinations of the senator

> *Showing everyone his gun,*
> *Handing out free tickets*
> *To the wedding of his son*

and to the neon madmen of the modern city – the ones who have settled into it all – and to the claustrophobic ladies who 'furnish' him with tape, and so on.

The humour that breaks out beyond the histrionics of hamming up 'Oh! I didn't know that!' also aids the moral evaluation. The narrator only adds to our awareness of his virtue when he raps out

> *Y'see, you're just like me.*
> *I hope you're satisfied.*

Who wouldn't be?

Dylan ends the song with a disarming, memorable summary of the predicament he's been showing us that we are all in:

> And me I sit so patiently
> Waiting to find out what price
> Ya have to pay to get out of
> Going through all these things twice.

The language of 'Visions Of Johanna' has already been partly dealt with in Chapter 2, and any amount more could be said. The mixture of 'serious' and 'flippant' language; the mixture of delicacy and coarseness; the mixture of abstract neo-philosophy and figurative phraseology; the ambiguity that begins with the song's very title – because Johanna is not just a woman's name but also the Hebrew for Armageddon; the humour; the intensive build-up of the song's scope: all this is pressed into the service of a work of art at once indefinable and precise. It is, not for the first time, hard to say what the song is 'about' and yet it impresses as saying a good deal, and in doing so it engages a great many of Dylan's distinctive strengths.

The effects are precise in the sense that the glimpses we get (as Chapter 2 suggested with particular reference to the first verse of the song) are strikingly accurate recreations of experience.

The character sketches are very accurate too; for instance:

> . . . Little boy lost, he takes himself so seriously;
> He brags of his misery, he likes to live dangerously . . .
> He's sure gotta lotta gall
> To be so useless an' all
> Muttering small talk at the wall
> While I'm in the hall –

or

> In the empty lot where the ladies play blind man's bluff with the keychain
> An' the all-nite girls, they whisper of escapades out on the D-train
> We can hear the night-watchman click his flashlight,
> Ask himself if it's him or them that's insane . . .

Because the atmosphere there rebounds incisively off phrases like 'the empty lot', 'out on the D-train' and the 'all-nite girls', that night-watchman comes across as vividly as a character in Dickens. That 'click' that Dylan provides him with is precisely the kind of tiny detail that is a large part of Dickens' touch. Dylan gives us the same cartoon precision, deftly sketching in the night-watchman's mannered essentials. We don't need to know what clothes he wears, or the colour of his hair, or the shape of his nose. He is real and we have truly seen him, and *felt* him doubt his sanity.

But the idea of Johanna is what dominates the song. In putting this across, Dylan's weighting of language, his economical fusion of simple words and tune, is amazing:

> *And these visions, of Johanna,*
> *They've kept me up, past, the dawn . . .*

> *But these visions, of Johanna,*
> *They make it all, seem so, cruel . . .*

The broadness of the song's scope is clinched by this fixed focal point. In effect, it is because the narrator returns again and again to the single idea of his relationship with Johanna that he is able to be so receptive – to give an equal receptivity – to everything else he comes across. Thus (with an equal and splendid impersonality) the song can focus one minute on the coughing heat-pipes in Louise and her lover's room, where they are entwined and oblivious, and the next minute on casual speculation about museums. Since Johanna is so much the centre of everything, the outer circumferences are all equitably regarded and rendered: all seen dispassionately as equally significant and insignificant. 'Jelly-faced women', the secret of the Mona Lisa smile, the sounds of the night: they all flow with the same detachment through the narrator's mind, until

> *The harmonicas play the skeleton keys in the rain*

(a beautiful line: that connection between harmonica sounds and skeletons is a flash of real imaginative genius and fiery intuitive observation)

> *And these visions, of Johanna,*
> *Are now all that remain.*

To turn from 'Visions of Johanna' to 'Sad-Eyed Lady Of The Lowlands' is not only, as earlier implied, to turn from one major song on "Blonde On Blonde" to another; it is also to turn from a success to a failure – and a failure no more easily explicable than most things to do with Dylan's work.

It is unsuccessful, and rather grandly so, inasmuch as it is offered on the album as something of extra-special importance and doesn't live up to its billing. It takes up the whole of the fourth and final side of the double-LP, despite lasting only about one minute longer than 'Desolation Row', which slots in with three other songs on a single side of "Highway 61 Revisited". 'Sad-Eyed Lady Of The Lowlands' is not a more important song than 'Desolation Row'. It's long, it's attractive, it's puzzling and ambiguous, and Dylan's voice on it is very beautiful – but it isn't one of Dylan's great songs. All the same, the intention behind the song was clearly a major one and the recording is prominent enough to merit a special attention.

Let's begin by recognising a few ambiguities. The chorus of the song is full of them:

> *Sad-eyed lady of the lowlands,*
> *Where the sad-eyed prophets say that no man comes,*
> *My warehouse eyes, my Arabian drums –*
> *Should I leave them by your gate,*
> *Or, sad-eyed lady, should I wait?*

The 'warehouse eyes' juxtaposition is a fine enough encapsulation, perhaps, to compensate for the indolent vagueness of those 'drums' and the corresponding 'gate'.

Yet it is a little too encapsulated – like a diagram from which the listener has to fit the bits together: a sort of Poetic Language Kit that needs to be built at home. As for the rest of the chorus, the line preceding 'warehouse eyes' means absolutely nothing. It's just there for neatness' sake (which inevitably means that it is not artistically neat at all), for mood-setting repetition and rhyme. And the title line itself stands for – what?

It shouldn't matter. The lady's sad eyes are just as much warehouses as the narrator's; Dylan passes his myriad perspectives in front of those eyes, and what the song tries to communicate is the world which therein confronts them – the world that makes them sad. So 'she' is just a convention – a sort of camera. But in the vain hope of cutting down on our perplexity in response to the whole, we do find that the identity of the title person, or title symbol, matters to us.

The camera shots, the perspectives: do they create more than wistful but nebulous fragments? Do they add up to any kind of vision, as the whole presentation, duration and solemnity of the song imply that they should? No. Dylan is resting, and cooing nonsense in our ears (very beguilingly, of course).

The only thing that unites the fragments is the mechanical device of the return to the chorus and thus to the title; but because there is nothing to suggest a particular significance to that title (as, say, there is in 'Visions of Johanna' and 'Memphis Blues Again'), its intended function of holding things together virtually fails. It is, in the end, not a whole song at all but unconnected chippings, and only the poor cement of an empty chorus and a regularity of tune give the illusion that things are otherwise. The structure makes the song seem a complete entity; the sense of the song denies it.

All the same, these disunited parts are interesting and the spreadeagled "Blonde On Blonde" recording of it offers many of the features of Dylan's artistry.

Dylan delivers it like slow-motion waves, unfurling the phrases with a strung-out concentration that is at once committed, intense and yet mellow. He breathes out the lines – lines full of alliterative emphasis, melting and echoey atmosphere, and obscured, nebulous pictures:

> *The kings of Tyrus with their convict list*
> *Are waiting in line for their geranium kiss*
> *And you wouldn't know it would happen like this*
> *But who among them, really wants, just to kiss you?*
> *With your childhood flames on your midnight rug*
> *And your Spanish manners and your mother's drugs*
> *And your cowboy mouth and your curfew plugs*
> *Who among them do you think could resist you?*
> *Sad-eyed lady of the lowlands?*

The fourth line there offers a much cheaper cynicism than Dylan normally exhibits and the rhyming eighth line is unusually weak. The other six lines of that verse are more demanding. The opening couplet gets much of its force from its elaborate alliteration and internal rhymes: and how nicely the tune holds back fittingly on the word 'waiting' in line two. The power of the imagery, though, is fundamentally untraceable – for it is basically surrealistic and thus not susceptible to rationale or analysis. For me, 'the kings of Tyrus' is hardly visual at all; 'their convict list' is not really visual either – but it is distinctly atmospheric: it increases my sense of sadness, it suggests perhaps an irretrievable past. The 'waiting in line' gets disregarded almost entirely: it is just the outstretching hand that presents that marvellous 'geranium kiss'. Why try to explain the impact of that? And it is only natural, correspondingly, to give up on 'your cowboy mouth and your curfew plugs' – which yield perhaps less unadulterated impact but a great deal of unadulterated aesthetic pleasure. The singer's 'ru-u-u-ug' and 'dru-u-u-ugs' is perhaps a necessary device for lending the relevant couplet its impression of parallels, but beyond that, 'midnight rug' makes those 'flames' literal and visual, and is in itself evocative enough; and that sixth line:

> And your Spanish manners and your mother's drugs

brings in, with a skilful kind of equipoise, pleasantly conflicting ideas of elegance and tragedy, and lends both a harmony and counterpart to the misty moods of the whole verse.

Lines in other verses operate in much the same essentially surrealistic ways:

> With your mercury mouth in the Missionary Times . . .
> And your matchbox songs and your gypsy hymns . . .
> To show you where the dead angels are that they used to hide . . . ;

yet some operate less intensively. There are lines and lines of largely explicable simile, where the listener's problem is merely how to glean from them the moral slant. Is this sort of thing intended as praise or condemnation or neither (or indeed both)?:

> . . . your eyes like smoke and your prayers like rhymes
> And your silver cross and your voice like chimes . . .

They seem morally neutral because they are uninspiring; as the similes grow more distinctive (largely through becoming cliché, paradoxically enough) they lose their neutrality. By the time we have had 'your face like glass' (a classically back-handed compliment) and we reach 'your saint-like face and your ghost-like soul', we can't fail to be aware of Dylan's/the narrator's severity. His condemnation comes so powerfully through the line just quoted that the question which follows – ostensibly reverential rhetoric – comes across as a fairly heavy sneer:

> Who among them do you think could destroy you?

And yet – and yet – he seems to mean it all nicely – which means that at base, it is just badly written.

The concluding verse's second line, with its clever and derisive shorthand description of

> your magazine husband who one day just had to go

seems the only line that really isn't muzzy in its import.

In the end, whatever the song's attractions and clever touches, they have been bundled together, and perhaps a bit complacently, without the unity either of a clear and real theme or of cohesive artistic discipline.[29]

---

29. When I read this assessment now, I simply feel embarrassed at what a little snob I was when I wrote it. In contrast (and paradoxically), when I go back and listen, after a long gap, to Dylan's recording, every ardent, true

Dylan, later, seems to have been aware of this: seems to have abandoned the song – never singing it in concerts, and using the mention of it only as a calculatedly poignant tug in the much later, desperately special-pleading song 'Sara'.[30] It is also directly after 'Sad-Eyed Lady Of The Lowlands' in the chronology of his released recordings that Dylan draws back from this ever-thickening undergrowth of surreal, allusively complex language. After it, he begins, in general, the harder process of paring down towards a new simplicity.

feeling I ever had comes back to me. Decades of detritus drop away and I feel back in communion with my best self and my soul. Whatever the shortcomings of the lyric, the recording itself, capturing at its absolute peak Dylan's incomparable capacity for intensity of communication, is a masterpiece if ever there was one. It isn't like listening to a record: it *enfolds* you, to use a word from the song itself, in a whole universe.

30. 'Sara' includes 'Stayin' up for days in the Chelsea Hotel / Writin' 'Sad-Eyed Lady Of The Lowlands' for you'. The subject was memorably polemicised by Lester Bangs in a funny, wrong-headed froth of a review of the "Desire" album: 'if he really *did* spend days on end sitting up in the Chelsea sweating over lines like "your streetcar visions which you place on the grass", then he is stupider than we ever gave him credit for'. (Lester Bangs, 'Bob Dylan's dalliance with Mafia chic', *Creem*, no. 7, April 1976; republished in Thomson and Gutman, *The Dylan Companion*, 1990.) Bangs' phrase 'Mafia chic' picks up the coinage of Tom Wolfe in his book *Radical Chic and Mau-Mauing the Flak-Catchers* (1970) in which he excoriated New York socialites for their dalliance with Black Power, focusing on the appearance of prominent Black Panthers at a Leonard Bernstein party. Wolfe's later essay on the same period, 'Funky chic', is collected in *Mauve Gloves and Madmen, Clutter and Vine* (1976). An alleged meeting in 1970 between Bob Dylan and Black Panthers Huey Newton and David Hilliard is mooted in Anthony Scaduto's 'Won't you listen to the lambs, Bob Dylan?', *New York Times*, 28/11/71, and discussed in 'A profile of Howard Alk' by Clinton Heylin (with research assistance by George Webber) in Michael Gray and John Bauldie (eds), *All Across the Telegraph*.

CHAPTER FIVE

Dylan's Use of Language: Towards a New Simplicity

Love is so simple, to quote a phrase
You've known it all the time, I'm learnin' it these days

Bob Dylan, 'You're A Big Girl Now'

In contrast to "Blonde On Blonde", Dylan's surrealism is stripped down to a chilly minimum on "John Wesley Harding" – the most dramatic example being in that central song 'All Along The Watchtower'.

If 'Desolation Row' can be seen as a circular song, with its parade going on for ever, so too can 'All Along The Watchtower' – which is, among other things, a more economical, and far more chilling, restatement of the same theme. But how does it end, this song? There are two alternatives. Either it gets an added element of menace from the very endlessness of the nightmare vision offered as the song goes round and round, so that the helpless cry 'There must be some way out of here' *recurs after* 'The wind began to howl'. Or else, if it is not circular in that way, then it ends, as Richard Goldstein argued in a *Village Voice* review, on an emphatic full-stop – indeed, a terrifying full-stop. Just three clean, razor-sharp verses, with an end that signifies the end of *everything*:

> *Outside in the distance*
> *A wild cat did growl*
> *Two riders were approaching*
> *The wind began to howl.*

As Goldstein says, the suggestion of menace in those lines is far too ominous and powerful for them to be concluded with a series of dots.[1]

The general nature of the language in a song like this is impressionism revisited, no longer reflecting summer tension in the city, as did "Blonde On Blonde", but reflecting wintertime in the psyche instead.

By the time of the "Nashville Skyline" album, we find, not unexpectedly in view of its terrain, no trace of surrealistic imagery at all. The images on this album rest as firmly in logic and plain speaking as would be consistent with imaginative expression.

---

1.   Richard Goldstein: 'Pop Eye' column, *Village Voice*, probably 2/2/68.

They are founded in the logic of traditional rural life, dependent on that life's unvarying rhythms and verities – the seasons, the processes of agriculture, growth, replenishment and death:

> *Turned my skies from blue to grey . . .*
> *Tonight no light will shine on me . . .*
>
> *Once I had mountains in the palm of my hand*
> *And rivers that ran through every day . . .*

The impetus for lines like these is less a matter of image-coining than the use of idiom – idiom that is a natural product of rural culture. And those lines quoted above, if we regard them as holding images, comprise the sum total of imagery on the "Nashville Skyline" album – with four rather special exceptions.

First, that awkward, uncharacteristically saccharine pair of lines:

> *Whatever colours you have in your mind*
> *I'll show them to you and you'll see them shine*

which doesn't sound like Dylan writing and which stands out of the song in which it occurs ('Lay, Lady, Lay') – in the same way that the chorused phrase 'Take me down to California baby' stands out in the Basement Tapes song 'Yea! Heavy & A Bottle Of Bread'.

Second, that imagery which is integral to deliberately selected cliché, as with 'You can have your cake and eat it too' – again from 'Lay, Lady, Lay'.

Third, the images that are images only in the sense that they yield snapshots of the narrator predicament – as with, for instance, 'If there's a poor boy on the street' (from 'Tonight I'll Be Staying Here With You') or 'Shake me up that old peach tree' (from 'Country Pie').

The fourth and final exception is again from 'Lay, Lady, Lay' (an exceptional song!):

> *His clothes are dirty but his hands are clean*
> *And you're the best thing that he's ever seen . . .*

That reverses the expected moral weighting. The Noble Workman has honourably *dirty* hands, and in the West, clean hands belong only to the no-good gamblin' man. But this is not a double-edged commentary from Dylan, such as we had on the song 'John Wesley Harding': it is a plain statement of praise. What is surprising is that while you expect the image to work, as most of the album does, within the country music milieu, in fact 'clean hands' takes its ethic not from the mid-West but from the Bible, from Psalm 24, a Psalm of David:

> *Who shall ascend into the hill of the Lord?*
> *Or who shall stand in his holy place?*
> *He that hath clean hands, and a pure heart.*[2]

---

2.   From Psalm 24:2–3. In the take of the 1965 'Farewell Angelina', NYC, 13/1/65, that was finally released on "Bootleg Series I–III", 1991, Dylan sings of 'the hero's clean hands'.

That short catalogue above shows the exceptional – in the sense of uncharacteristic – moments on "Nashville Skyline": the broad mass of it is without surrealism, indeed without any imagery at all, and it uses a language of extreme simplicity.

, It was, after all, quite a shock, on a first play of "Nashville Skyline", back in 1969, to hear Dylan singing lines like

> *For your love comes on so strong . . .*

And when we come to the middle section of the same song ('Tonight I'll Be Staying Here With You') we find Dylan coming on even stronger with this 'new' language:

> *Is it really any wonder*
> *The love that a stranger might receive?*
> *You cast your spell and I went under*
> *I find it so difficult to leave . . .*

This compares closely with the middle section of the later song 'Hazel', from "Planet Waves":

> *Oh no I don't need any reminder*
> *To show how much I really care*
> *But it's just making me blinder and blinder . . .*

The joke-rhyming of 'wonder' and 'under', and even more so of 'reminder' and 'blinder and blinder', combined with the playful vacuousness of the melodies of both those sections, suggest the milieu of the Hollywood musical more than anything. They'd go comfortably inside 'On The Street Where You Live' from *My Fair Lady*. Not exactly Dylan terrain. So what is he playing at?

A useful comment was offered in a review of the "Self Portrait" album by Geoffrey Cannon, in the *Guardian* (26 June 1970). Cannon dealt with the 'You cast your spell and I went under' kind of language by saying that 'the coup of "Nashville Skyline" [was] to demonstrate that proverbs are aphorisms when used (as they always are, except in books) by a particular person to a particular person, in a place and a time. It's human context, not verbal dexterity, that lets words, especially words of love, work.' That account is a little dangerous, of course: we shouldn't be talked into gracing any old pop clichés with the accolade of being 'aphorisms'; nor should we forget that using clichés in a careless way trains people to *think*, as well as speak, in platitudes, and so trains people not to think at all. But Cannon's argument does apply to Dylan's work in the "Nashville Skyline" context.

When Dylan sings 'For your love comes on so strong', he is effectively saying that that phrase will do as well as any to cover the part of his feelings that can be put into words. And in saying that, he is rejecting a self-image of Dylan the brilliant poet in favour of a concept of himself as an ordinary man coping with love. That is how such phrases work. This is not Dylan patronising the ordinary mind; it is a confession, candid and accepting, that he is, in ways that it matters to be honest about, an ordinary man himself. And it is an off-loading of the Dylan Myth – which he was to do all over again from a different direction when he came to "Slow Train Coming" and "Saved" a decade later.

If "Nashville Skyline" began this off-loading process, and if its language was kept deliberately mundane, then the next album, "Self Portrait", pushed things very much further. Now, seen in the long back-projection of his work, it isn't gruellingly important that the album was so second-rate – but of course when it was new, in 1970, the adjustments necessary to come to terms with "Self Portrait" seemed enormous. Dylan was demanding more and giving less with this album.

At first hearing, much of the work was trite, rutted and simplistic, and that, in itself, had huge and perplexing impact. Here was an apparently second-rate collection of work from a man who, rightly or wrongly, had become accepted as the genius of our generation.

There were, of course, people who didn't face these difficulties – those who simply listened and enjoyed; and Dylan has always been on their side, against classification, with those who, in his view, know 'too much to argue or to judge'.

All the same, the question 'How should we respond to this album?' was a common one among those whose concern isn't disproportionately with Dylan's *music* at the expense of a concern with the words.

First, there is a blandness of defeat about it. It is there in the hoarse way he delivers that shouted, descending chorus line that breaks through at the end of the live 'Like A Rolling Stone' like a rattling of chains; and this spreads across everything on the album.

The sense of listless defeat comes across most clearly through Dylan's voice. It conveys, especially in the 'happy' songs, a sort of choking caution (just listen, for instance, to 'I Forgot More') – an impression that Dylan has walked, godlessly, close to the valley of the shadow of death and dare not now explore beyond the simplistic verities adhered to by Nashville, Tennessee. It is not so much mental plumpness as an exhaustion of courage – as if the Dylan of "Self Portrait" has placed himself under house arrest because the old Insanity Factory is too close to his gates. And while this kind of rest/retreat is understandable enough in the *man*, it doesn't do much for his art.

The parallel with the Born-Again Christian albums "Slow Train Coming" and "Saved" (especially "Saved") is very strong: on these, Dylan's panic at godlessness has him clinging, not to Nashville's country verities and simplicities, but to the gospel ones of the Bible Belt. The main virtue of 'Saving Grace' is that it confesses this need-to-cling, just as 'Watching The River Flow' was to do not long after "Self Portrait". Yet, on the positive side, just as "Slow Train Coming" and "Saved" are good enough to repay countless plays, so too "Self Portrait", albeit a very minor Dylan work, has its own riches; and now that the album is well into the past, it is easier to enjoy them.

First, the album does not lack warmth; and second, its self-deprecation can be seen as showing an egolessness which is, now and then, a welcome ingredient in Dylan's largely ego-emphatic output. As Bill Damon put it (*Rolling Stone*, 3 September 1970): 'With all of its unity and inclusiveness, "Self Portrait" is too complex to have a point of view . . . It is Eastern in its egolessness . . . Dylan does remind us on this album of all the ways we have known him . . . but Dylan's image serves only his music.'

Go on, admit it – even the cover painting has its virtues. It is enjoyable for its childlike technique and colouring, a relief from image-building ad-man photography, and interesting also because, like the painting Dylan did for The Band's "Music From

Big Pink" album,[3] it owes a lot to the pen-and-ink sketches of Woody Guthrie. (Dylan's debt in this respect became clear to anyone who has seen Guthrie's drawings when Dylan published *Writings and Drawings by Bob Dylan* in 1972).

Quite a throwback – and on one level, the whole album is a throwback. It is not, as Richard Williams maintained at the time, 'an attempt at the Great North American Album'[4] but it is a deliberate package of Golden Oldies, from folk to country to chart-climbing pop – and this in itself tells us something about how unprepared to be complex Dylan is in his use of language.

'I Forgot More' is a country classic, and Dylan sings it like Roy Orbison would.[5] 'In Search Of Little Sadie' and 'Little Sadie' are based on an older song, which Johnny Cash recorded as 'Transfusion Blues' when he was with the Tennessee Two on the Sun label and as 'Cocaine Blues' on later CBS recordings (one studio, one live with a prison audience). The storyline has remained much the same – it tells of an escape, an arrest, a trial and a jailing. But while Cash plods through a lifeless narrative, congealing in his artificial Manliness, Dylan ditches the worst platitudes and trans-forms others – by his timing – into wit and fills his narrative with creative idiosyncrasy. While Cash sings 'overtook me down in Juarez, Mexico' (a place already associated with Dylan in song, from 'Just Like Tom Thumb's Blues') Dylan has it 'They overtook me down in Jericho', which gives, as Geoffrey Cannon wrote, 'an echo of his persistent references to places of abstract myth. Cash places the arrest: Dylan puts it anywhere.'[6]

3. The Band: "Music From Big Pink", Capitol Records SKAO 2955, Los Angeles [Capitol ST 2955, London], 1968.

4. Richard Williams, 'New morning – and Bob starts all over again', *Melody Maker*, 24/10/70. Actually it's unclear whether Williams was endorsing this description. His piece (a review of "New Morning") begins: 'If "Self Portrait" was an attempt to record The Great North American Album, encompassing most of the musical forms and styles of that sub-continent . . .'

5. Johnny Cash had recorded 'I Forgot More Than You'll Ever Know', Nashville, 10/2/62, for the widely known LP "The Sound Of Johnny Cash", Columbia Records CS 8602, New York [CBS Records BPG 72073, London], 1962; but Dylan was almost certainly aware of the song much earlier. Dylan revisited it live in 1986, as a duet with Tom Petty, at 55 concerts. His introductory remarks about the song to the audience in Sydney, Australia, 24/2/86, perhaps reveal why he chose to include it on "Self Portrait". He said: 'Very seldom do you hear a real song anymore. But we were lucky enough to grow up when you could hear 'em all the time. All you had to do was just switch on your radio . . .' [Johnny Cash's 1962 recording was reissued, as it happens, the same year Dylan issued "Self Portrait", on the compilation "Country Gold, Volume 2", Harmony Records 30018, USA, 1970.]

6. In fact Cash was still billed with The Tennessee Two on his early Columbia sides, and 'Transfusion Blues' appears not to have been cut for Sun. Johnny Cash: 'Transfusion Blues', Nashville, 17/2/60; "Now There Was A Song", Columbia Records CS 8254, New York [CBS Records 62028, London], 1960. Columbia Records could not trace, in 1996, a second Cash studio recording pre-1970. 'Cocaine Blues', Sacramento, 13/1/68; "Johnny Cash At Folsom Prison", Columbia Records CS 9639, New York [CBS 63308, London], 1968 [Cash re-recorded it Nashville, 24/4/79; "Silver", Columbia 36086, New York (CBS 83757, London), 1979.].

  Dylan's version probably has nothing to do with Cash's. *Sing Out!*, Vol. 14, no. 6, January 1964, published 'Little Sadie' (along with 'Copper Kettle', which is also on "Self Portrait", and Dylan's own 'All I Really Want To Do') with this introduction:

  Woody Guthrie called it 'Bad Lee Brown' and others have titled it 'Sadie', 'Late One Night', 'Chain Gang Blues', 'Out Last Night' and 'Penitentiary Blues'. Clarence Ashley calls it 'Little Sadie', and it is his version we print here. According to D. K. Wilgus, the song seems to be an example of a 'blues ballad', which he describes as 'a loose, shifting, emotional narrative that celebrates and comments on an event instead of presenting a straightforward, detailed account.' 'Little Sadie', in all its various titles, has enjoyed wide currency among both Negro and white singers.

  Dylan was well aware of Ashley as a conduit of folksong: Ashley's pre-war recordings of 'The House Carpenter' and 'The Coo-Coo Bird' are on (and his 'Naomi Wise' and 'Dark Holler Blues' cited in) the 1952 Harry Smith 6-LP anthology "American Folk Music", which Dylan certainly knew by May 1961. Equally, Dylan was

Dylan's use of 'Jericho' makes allusion to something else from the Golden Oldie past, too. One of the little witticisms in the performance is the way Dylan's voice goes *up* as he sings the word *down*: and this is exactly what Elvis and the Jordanaires do with the same word in their classic version of 'Joshua Fit The Battle Of Jericho' on the "His Hand In Mine" album of 1960, of which I've no doubt that Dylan is extremely fond.[7]

The other oldies on "Self Portrait" are Gordon Lightfoot's 'Early Morning Rain', 'Like A Rolling Stone', 'Copper Kettle', 'Days Of '49', 'Alberta' (which Dylan, singing it twice, offers as 'Alberta No.1' and 'Alberta No.2'), 'Gotta Travel On', 'Blue Moon', Paul Simon's 'The Boxer', 'Quinn The Eskimo (The Mighty Quinn)', 'Take Me As I Am (Or Let Me Go)', 'She Belongs To Me' and two Everly Brothers hit songs, 'Take A Message To Mary' and 'Let It Be Me'.[8]

---

well aware of *Sing Out!* as a source of material. So one way or another it is probably no coincidence that Dylan's 'Little Sadie' on "Self Portrait" is nigh word for word the same as the lyric *Sing Out!* publishes as Ashley's.

Clarence Ashley: 'Little Sadie', Chicago, Feb. 1962; "Old-Time Music At Clarence Ashley's, Volume 2", Folkways Records FA 2359, New York, 1963. Clarence Ashley: 'The House Carpenter', Atlanta, 14/4/30, and 'The Coo-Coo Bird', Johnson City, Tennessee, 23/10/29; "American Folk Music", Folkways FP251–253, New York 1952; CD-reissued as "Anthology Of American Folk Music" [6-CD box-set] with copious notes by many hands and a CD-ROM of extras, Smithsonian Folkways Recordings SFW 40090, Washington, DC, 1997. Clarence Ashley: 'Naomi Wise' c/w 'Little Sadie', Johnson City, Tennessee, 23/10/29; 'Dark Holler Blues', Johnson City, Tennessee, 23/10/29 [originally on the other side of 'The Coo-Coo Bird'].

Dylan cut 'House Carpenter', NYC, 20/11/61, at his first LP sessions (it was finally issued 30 years later on "Bootleg Series I–III") and performed 'Naomi Wise' at Riverside Church 'Saturday Of Folk Music', NYC, 29/7/61 [broadcast WRVR-FM, NYC, 29/7/61]. Dylan put 'Naomi Wise' on tape again that December in Minneapolis, 22/12/61. ['Dark Holler Blues' is related to 'East Virginia Blues', which Dylan recorded in the "Self Portrait" period, i.e. with Earl Scruggs, Carmel, Dec. 1970, broadcast NET TV, US, Jan. 1971, and issued 'Festival Of Music' video, New Line Cinema 2015, New York.]

The retrospective LP "Getting Folk Out Of The Country", Bear Family Records BF 15008, Vollersode, Germany, 1975, by Bill Clifton and Hedy West also includes 'Little Sadie' [London, 1972] (and 'Mary Of The Wild Moor' [London, 1972], a traditional song Dylan performed in 16 concerts 1980–81).

7. Elvis Presley: 'Joshua Fit The Battle', Nashville, 30–31/10/60, issued "His Hand In Mine", RCA Victor Records LPM/LSP-2328, New York [RCA mono RD27211, stereo SF5094, London, 1961], 1960; CD-reissued "Amazing Grace: His Greatest Sacred Performances" [2-CD set], RCA Records 07863 66421 2, London, 1994.

8. 'Early Morning Rain' was barely an oldie: composer Gordon Lightfoot was 'discovered' by fellow-Canadian folkies Ian & Sylvia, who had a near-hit single, with the title track of their LP "Early Morning Rain", Vanguard Records VSD-79175, New York, 1965. (Dylan says on *Folksinger's Choice* [WBAI Radio, NYC, probably 13/1/62, probably broadcast 11/3/62] that he got 'Long Time Man Feel Bad', a song he performs on that show, from Ian & Sylvia. [It is on their first LP, "Ian & Sylvia", NYC, *nia*, Vanguard VRS-9109, Brooklyn, 1962, which also includes 'Rocks And Gravel' and 'Handsome Molly'.])

'Early Morning Rain' was then cut by Judy Collins, NYC, *nia*, for her "5th Album", Elektra Records EKS 7300, New York, 1965 (also including Dylan's song 'Tomorrow Is A Long Time', *nia*). Gordon Lightfoot signed to United Artists that year (his first US public appearance was at the 1965 Newport Folk Festival) and included 'Early Morning Rain', *nia*, on his LP "Lightfoot", United Artists, *nia*, Hollywood [UAS 6487, London], 1966. Beware Lightfoot's book *I Wish You Good Spaces* (1977) (a belated artefact of an earlier era, as its title hints), one of a series from Blue Mountain Arts of Boulder, Colorado, also offering the improbable *My Life and Love Are One* by Vincent van Gogh and *We Are All Children Searching for Love* by Leonard Nimoy.

Bob Dylan performed 'Early Morning Rain' at four concerts in 1989, two in 1990 and two in 1991, including a glorious version at South Bend, Indiana, 6/11/91, on which the band keeps up a distinctive circular rolling beat and Dylan marries its spiky, garage band compulsion to a delicately expressive vocal.

'Copper Kettle' is a traditional southern mountain song, much favoured around Greenwich Village in Dylan's time there. As mentioned earlier, it is on Joan Baez's third album ["Joan Baez In Concert", Vanguard VRS-9112, New York, 1962, CD-reissued Vanguard VDM 79112–2, New York and London, 1996], and was published in the same issue of *Sing Out!* as 'Little Sadie' [Vol. 14, no. 6, January 1964]. 'Days Of '49', as mentioned in Chapter 1, is a traditional Yankee song.

'Alberta' is a Doc Watson rag-doll of traditional black and white lyric off-cuts, pinned together and dressed up with a few arty chords, with Doc sounding not unlike Jim Reeves. It was issued on "Southbound", Vanguard Records VSD-79213 [Fontana TFL 6074, London], 1966, CD-reissued Vanguard VMD 79213–2, New York,

With 'The Boxer', Dylan's minimal re-write of the lyric is very telling – and typical of Dylan's ability to say more with less. He simply changes one word, from

And he carries a reminder
Of every glove that's laid him down

to

Of every blow that's laid him down.

That 'blow' means we actually see the boxer better: we comprehend that, outside the ring as well as inside it, his life is a series of defeats.[9]

The inclusion of two Everly Brothers songs was more striking at the time than it is now, since in recent years, through rock 'n' roll revivals galore, they have been acknowledged as crucial figures in the pre-Dylan era; but when "Self Portrait" came out, you weren't supposed to still like or even remember that old stuff – you were supposed to be Progressive and despise the 3-minute single.

People still take too much for granted the achievements the Everlys pulled off.

1988 [London, 1995]. (I had expected it to be on "Doc Watson", Vanguard VSD-79152, 1964, i.e. from when Bob and Joan Baez were an item and she was probably getting armfuls of free Vanguard records; but it isn't.) 'Alberta' was also reissued on "The Essential Doc Watson", *nia*, 1973 [Vanguard 45/46, London, 1976], CD-reissued "The Essential Doc Watson Vol.1", Vanguard VMCD 7308, 1987. Dylan scraps the arty chords and some of the words, and tacks in some others. The result, though casually reminiscent of 'Corrina, Corrina', 'Baby Let Me Follow You Down' and 'Girl Of The North Country', is dull, but not as dull as Doc's.

   'Gotta Travel On' is associated with a well-known figure in folk revivalist circles, songwriter and singer Paul Clayton. In the interview with Dylan by Cameron Crowe, published within "Biograph", 1985, Dylan says of him: 'Paul was just an incredible songwriter and singer. He must have known a thousand songs. I learned "Pay Day At Coal Creek" and a bunch of other songs from him.' As this implies, Clayton was a folksong collector as well as a composer, and while the "Self Portrait" record label credits Clayton as composer of 'Gotta Travel On' (and Glen Dundas' *Tangled up in Tapes*, 3rd edn, 1994, lists it as composed by Clayton, Lazar, Ehrlich and Six) in fact Dylan knew the song before he knew Clayton (which Robert Shelton's *No Direction Home* [1986] dates as in 1962): it is on the tape of Dylan made back in St. Paul, Minnesota, as early as May 1960 [unreleased]. Dylan later performs it at sixteen 1976 Rolling Thunder Revue concerts. Shelton says it was from Clayton's adaptation of the traditional 'Scarlet Ribbons For Her Hair' that Dylan took his 'Don't Think Twice, It's All Right' melody. Clayton, a companion on Dylan's 1964 car-ride through America, died in April 1967, electrocuted in his bath.

9.   The inspiration for Dylan's use of two different voices on 'The Boxer' may well be a pre-war gospel record, Blind Willie Johnson's marvellous 'Let Your Light Shine On Me', which in its chorus strongly prefigures that of Dylan's 'Precious Angel' and in using two voices on one track certainly shines a new light on 'The Boxer'. Johnson didn't have the technology to double-track his two voices, as Dylan does, but in switching suddenly from the one to the other (in mid-line, even, at the end) he makes the difference between them so stark that this becomes the central point of the recording, as with Dylan's double-tracking on 'The Boxer'. Dylan's familiarity with, and debt to, Blind Willie Johnson is discussed further in Chapter 9; suffice it to note here that Dylan would have encountered Johnson first on the 1952 Harry Smith anthology "American Folk Music" which included Johnson's 'John The Revelator', and he was able to attribute 'In My Time Of Dyin'' ('Jesus Make Up My Dying Bed') to Johnson by the time he cut it himself for the "Bob Dylan" album in 1961.

   [Blind Willie Johnson: 'Let Your Light Shine On Me', New Orleans, 10/12/29; "Blind Willie Johnson", RBF Records RF-10, NYC, 1965. 'John The Revelator', Atlanta, 20/4/30, "American Folk Music"; 'Jesus Make Up My Dying Bed', Dallas, 3/12/27; all CD-reissued "The Complete Blind Willie Johnson", Columbia Roots N' Blues Series COL 472190 2, New York, 1993.]

   Paul Simon's 'The Boxer', NYC and Nashville, 16/11/68, Columbia 44789, New York, 1969, is also on Simon & Garfunkel's "Bridge Over Troubled Water", Columbia Records KCS 9914, New York [CBS Records 63699, London], 1970. Until 1999 Dylan had not performed 'The Boxer' live but he had performed Simon's earlier songs 'Hazy Shade Of Winter' (two concerts, 1992) and 'Homeward Bound' (three concerts, 1991) and he contributed harmonica and back-up vocals behind the Grateful Dead on a rehearsal of Simon's later 'Boy In The Bubble', San Rafael, California, March–April 1987. In Spring 1999 it was announced that Dylan and Simon would tour together that June in North America. They débuted 'The Boxer' as a duet, West Palm Beach, 2/9/99, the first date on the tour's second leg.

They first topped the US charts in 1957 (with 'Wake Up, Little Susie') and from then till some time in the earlyish 1960s they were constantly in the charts, it seemed. They were very commercial and they were very good. At a time when most people 'found a sound' by accident, they developed one deliberately and intelligently, bridging what gap there was between pop and modern country music. And at a time when pop's understanding of music was near-retarded, the Everlys were consistently alert and curious. They handled their own arrangements and they had taste. By 1967 they were extremely passé.

At that point, Dylan wrote *them* a song, 'The Fugitive', which the Everlys never actually put out, though it turns up in Dylan's catalogue as 'Wanted Man'. His recording of their two hits on "Self Portrait" repeats his compliment to their deserved stature and to their undoubted influence. 'Let It Be Me' is a perfectionist's re-drafting of the Everlys' version, in effect; Dylan stays very faithful to their wistful and solid pop world. With 'Take A Message To Mary', Dylan returns the song (again, Bill Damon said it first) 'back to the Code of the West'.[10] It is a timely reminder that Dylan would not have been revisiting Nashville if the Everly Brothers had not brought it to all of us a decade earlier – long before either Dylan *or* Gram Parsons thought they were 'going country'.[11]

10. 'Wake Up, Little Susie' [Nashville, 1957, Cadence Records 1337, New York (London American Records HLA 8498, London), 1957] was their first US No.1 but their second huge hit, following 'Bye Bye, Love' [Nashville, April 1957, Cadence 1315, New York (London American HLA 8440, London), 1957].

The Everlys didn't record, let alone release, 'Wanted Man'; a rumour never quite stilled has it that they turned down 'Lay, Lady, Lay' too. (They did record the "Desire" sessions out-take song 'Abandoned Love' [London, 1984/5] for "Born Yesterday", Mercury Records CD 826 142–2/ LP MERH 80, Holland and London, 1985. They could have done this song justice, expansively and warmly, but a rigid rhythm and uncommitted vocals throw it away.)

The Everly Brothers: 'Let It Be Me', Nashville, 15/12/59, Cadence Records 1376, New York [London American Records HLA 9039, London], 1960; 'Take A Message To Mary', Nashville, 2/3/59 (c/w 'Poor Jenny', Nashville, *nia*), Cadence 1364 [London American HLA 8863], 1959; both LP-issued "The Fabulous Style Of The Everly Brothers", Cadence CLP 3040, New York, 1960.

Harking back not to the Everly Brothers' version but to the well-known later black cover by Jerry Butler and Betty Everett [Chicago, 1964; Vee-Jay Records 613, Chicago, 1964], Dylan re-recorded 'Let It Be Me' (with Clydie King as vocal duettist), Los Angeles, 1/5/81 (issued in Europe only, as B-side of 'Heart Of Mine', CBS A-1406, 1981); he also sang it in three 1981 concerts, contriving to imply that the 'you' the song addresses was Christ rather than woman. He has not revisited 'Take A Message To Mary'.

Bill Damon quoted, as earlier, from 'Herewith: a second look at "Self Portrait"', *Rolling Stone*, 3/9/70.

11. Not true. The young Dylan had taken an interest in country music on radio and on record in the late 1940s to early 1950s, pre-dating its re-energising by the Everlys and others of the rock'n'roll generation. This is evident not only from, for example, Dylan's 1986 comments on hearing songs like 'I Forgot More (Than You'll Ever Know)' on the radio when he was growing up (see note 5) and from the line 'An' my first idol was Hank Williams' in the sleeve-note poem for "Joan Baez In Concert, Part 2", Vanguard VRS-9113, New York, 1964, but from much other evidence. Robert Shelton's *No Direction Home* reports: 'I had always found Dylan more aware of the country currents than most other city folk singers . . . [around 1961] He often alluded to Hank Snow, Hank Thompson, Bill Andersen . . . He repeatedly told associates that he regarded country music as the coming thing, long before he cut "Nashville Skyline"'. And when Shelton, visiting Dylan's boyhood home in 1968, was shown the old records (78s and vinyl) left behind in his bedroom, he says they included 'a flood of Hank Williams's lonesome blues', some Webb Pierce and the LP "Hank Snow Sings Jimmie Rodgers."'

This last ["Hank Snow Sings Jimmie Rodgers' Songs", RCA Victor LSP/LPM-2043, New York, 1959] contains no material Dylan has yet utilised; but this was neither the first nor the last Snow LP of Rodgers material, nor the only evidence of Dylan's familiarity with Snow's work. In 1953 the 10-inch LP "Hank Snow Salutes Jimmie Rodgers" [RCA Victor Records LPM-3131, New York] had included 'My Blue-Eyed Jane' and 'Southern Cannonball' [both Nashville, 12/2/53]. Dylan recorded the former [Memphis, 9/5/94] for a Various Artists' Jimmie Rodgers 'tribute album', reportedly a project Dylan initiated [a tantalising snatch of Dylan's 'My Blue-Eyed Jane' is on the CD-ROM "Bob Dylan: Highway 61 Interactive", USA, 1994; a second Dylan version circulated on tape among collectors in 1997 and in late 1997 a third Dylan version supplanted both and saw release on the collection

The writers of so many of the Everlys' hits, Felice and Boudleaux Bryant, also wrote 'Take Me As I Am (Or Let Me Go)', which appears on "Self Portrait", and which has a title, though not a style, so appropriate to Dylan: it sounds like his motto from way-back-when.[12] Yet it redrafts the presentation of that motto, removing from it the big contradiction, the huge inconsistency, that used to apply. On the old tracks where Dylan was saying 'Accept What I Am, Tolerate', he said it without much tolerance at all, and delivered his message with a bitter impatience. (The only

---

"The Songs Of Jimmie Rodgers – A Tribute", Various Artists, Egyptian/Columbia Records 485189 2, New York: the first release on Dylan's own label Egyptian Records]; 33 years earlier Dylan was taped performing 'Southern Cannonball' at the Gleasons' home [East Orange, New Jersey, Feb./March 1961, unreleased]. "Hank Snow Sings In Memory Of Jimmie Rodgers (America's Blue Yodeler)", RCA Victor Records LSP/LPM-4306, New York, 1970, containing no material utilised by Dylan except 'Frankie And Johnny' [Nashville, 9/12/69], was followed by "The Jimmie Rodgers Story", RCA LSP-4708, New York, [RCA LSA 3107, London], 1972, on which Snow sings Rodgers' songs interspersed with narrations by one Albert Fullam. This too includes a Snow version of 'My Blue-Eyed Jane' [Nashville, 27/12/71], and on the sleeve notes Ernest Tubb remarks that 'Hank's special favorite in this collection is 'My Blue-Eyed Jane'.' [This LP was reissued as RCA Victor ANL1–2194, 1977, though without Tubb's sleeve notes.]

[Jimmie Rodgers: 'My Blue-Eyed Jane', Hollywood, 30/6/30, CD-reissued "Jimmie Rodgers: Riding High, 1929–1930", Rounder Records CD 1059, Cambridge, Massachusetts, 1991; 'Southern Cannonball', Louisville, Kentucky, 17/6/31, CD-reissued "Jimmie Rodgers: Down The Old Road, 1931–1932", Rounder CD 1061, Cambridge, 1991.]

Hank Snow, real name Clarence Eugene Snow, served more of a function for Dylan than as a purveyor of Jimmie Rodgers' repertoire. First, Dylan would certainly have heard him on the radio. (Snow worked at a radio station in Wheeling, West Virginia, in the mid-1940s but in 1945 moved to Hollywood and in 1949 appeared on the Grand Ole Opry, immediately becoming a regular.) Second, Snow wrote 'I'm Movin' On' (which Dylan performed at sixteen 1986 concerts, a 1988 soundcheck and three 1993 concerts) and he recorded, ahead of Presley '(Now And Then There's) A Fool Such As I', which Dylan performed on the Basement Tapes [Woodstock, June 1967], recorded at the "Self Portrait" sessions and saw released on the 1973 LP "Dylan". (Snow helped Presley's early career: star of the Opry when Elvis made his bottom-of-the-bill appearance on it, Nashville, 2/10/54, Snow soon had Presley on tour with him, and the first gigs booked by Col. Tom Parker were for Hank Snow Enterprises. It was also Snow who first told RCA Nashville, and his own music publishers, Hill & Range, about Presley. But when Hank Snow's 'I Don't Hurt Anymore' – another song Dylan cut on the Basement Tapes – was at No. 2 on the C&W charts for 18 August 1954, Presley's 'Blue Moon Of Kentucky' was at No. 3.) Snow also made the single 'Ninety Miles An Hour', which Dylan recorded on "Down In The Groove".

[Hank Snow: 'I'm Movin' On', Nashville, 28/3/50, 10-inch LP-issued "Country Classics", RCA Victor LPM-3026, New York, 1952 (reissued as 12-inch with extra tracks as LPM-1233, 1955), and on "The Best Of Hank Snow", RCA Victor LSP-3478, 1966. Hank Snow: '(Now And Then There's) A Fool Such As I', Nashville, 19/5/52, LP-issued "Country Classics", LPM-1233, 1955, and "The Best Of Hank Snow". Hank Snow: 'I Don't Hurt Anymore', Nashville, 1954, RCA Victor 5698, New York, 1954. Hank Snow: 'Ninety Miles An Hour (Down A Dead-End Street)', RCA Victor 8239, New York, 1963. Snow is billed as "The Singing Ranger" on two 4-CD sets of his RCA Victor work issued on Bear Family Records BCD 15426-DH and 15476-DH, Vollersode, Germany, 1988 and 1990, which include 'I'm Movin' On', '(Now And Then There's) A Fool Such As I', 'Singing The Blues', 'Poison Love', and as mentioned in Chapter 9, a song called 'I Just Telephone Upstairs'. The 1954–58 sides Snow recorded for radio play only are on a 5-CD set "The Thesaurus Transcriptions", Bear Family BCD 15488-EH, 1991, including another 'Frankie And Johnny'.]

But the most interesting instance of a direct influence of Hank Snow upon the young Bob Dylan came to light only in 1993, courtesy of the Dylan fanzine *Isis*. One issue had published the text of a 'poem', written in Bob Zimmerman's own hand, the original of which had been posted by an unnamed person to the fanzine's editor, Derek Barker. This 'poem' was a mournful tale narrated as if by a scared boy in hiding to avoid being beaten by his drunkard father. Five issues later, reader John Roberts wrote in to say that he had found an album on the cheap RCA Camden label, dated 1962, titled "The One And Only Hank Snow", and risked wasting his 75p on this unknown music because of its inclusion of a song, credited to Clarence E. Snow, titled 'The Drunkard's Son' and handily summarized in the sleeve notes as 'the mournful tale of a scared boy in hiding to avoid being beaten by his drunkard father'. Yes indeed. As Roberts nicely observes, if the 'Zimmerman Transcript' is authentic, which now seems established, it is a 'truly unique document – the first evidence we have of Bob's plagiarism!'

[*Isis*, no. 44, Aug–Sept 1992; no. 49, June–July 1993. Hank Snow: 'The Drunkard's Son', nia, first issue Canada 1942–9, nia; first US issue as a single, RCA 21–0303, New York, 1950; LP-issued on "The One And Only Hank Snow", Camden Records CAL-722, New York [RCA Camden CDN5102, London], 1962 (sleeve notes by Roy Horton).]

12. In fact 'Take Me As I Am (Or Let Me Go)' was composed solely by Boudleaux Bryant.

exception, I think, is 'All I Really Want To Do'). With 'Take Me As I Am' that paradox has gone. Gently, he re-states, having learnt to practise what he pleads for:

> *You're trying to re-shape me in a mould, love*
> *In the image of someone you used to know*
> *But I won't be a stand-in for an old love*
> *Take me as I am or let me go.*

For 'someone you used to know', read 'someone I used to be': the old love is the younger Dylan.

What of the handful of "Self Portrait" songs that Dylan wrote himself? How do they fit these messages of harking-back and of stressing simplicities?

'Living The Blues' is, in concept, a Golden Oldie in itself. It's less like the Guy Mitchell/Tommy Steele hit 'Singing The Blues' than people said at the time, but it's far from new. The structure is Tin Pan Alliance, and Dylan had débuted it earlier, on CBS-TV in 1969: a much faster version than the album one, drawing splendidly on Fats Domino-style piano-work. The album version draws correspondingly on the Jerry Lee Lewis not so much of 'High School Confidential' and 'Great Balls Of Fire' (though Dylan bows briefly to those on his earlier 'Down Along The Cove') as of his early 1960s country work: B-sides like 'Fools Like Me' and 'Cold, Cold Heart'.[13]

'Belle Isle' ('a model of non-linear narrative', Bill Damon called it) is effectively a Very Oldie too. It is deliberately unoriginal in story, language, structure and overall ethos – and is a terrific parody of the Celtic ballad. I think it still the highlight of the album.[14]

It can be seen as a link to the much earlier, beautiful 'Boots Of Spanish Leather'. They are both love *dialogues*, the latter ending with an estrangement and 'Belle Isle' ending as its sequel, with an imagined spiritual reconciliation, a neatening-up of existential history. Yet, granted its traditional Celtic model, 'Belle Isle' is also self-sufficient and self-contained. Like an island, in fact.

It's hard to avoid words like 'exquisite' in assessing the song, but it isn't that shallow. The tune flows out lightly and gracefully, like the gown billowing out around the maiden in the story; but the accompanying strings are sombre, more so than any appropriate Celtic mist would demand. Dylan treats the subject and the tradition it springs from with respect and a sympathetic mockery simultaneously; yet there is also

---

13.   In fact Dylan's 'Living The Blues' takes its tune, allegedly, from another, specific Jerry Lee Lewis record (composed by Claud Demetrius): 'I'm Feeling Sorry', Memphis, 10/9/57; "Jerry Lee Lewis – The Great Ball Of Fire" (EP), Sun Records EPA 107, Memphis, 1957 [in UK issued as B-side of 'You Win Again', London American Records HLS 8559, 1958].

   Guy Mitchell/Tommy Steele, 'Singing The Blues': for details see Chapter 3, note 5. Jerry Lee Lewis: 'Great Balls Of Fire', Memphis, 6–8/10/57, Sun Records 281, Memphis, 1957 [London American HLS 8529, London, 1958]; 'High School Confidential' c/w 'Fools Like Me', both Memphis, April 1958, Sun Records 296 [London American Records HLS 8780, London], 1958; 'Cold, Cold Heart', Memphis, 9/2/61, Sun Records 364, Memphis [London American HLS 9414, London], 1961.

14.   As confessed in an earlier chapter, 'Belle Isle' isn't 'a terrific parody of a Celtic ballad': it *is* a Celtic ballad, or at least a traditional one, its land of origin perhaps uncertain (see Chapter 1, note 11). You might think this makes the next few paragraphs less than sturdy, since they stand on the assumption that Dylan wrote the song. In truth, I find it makes surprisingly little difference to the validity of my text-and-performance analysis. As Christer Svensson pointed out in 'Stealin', stealin', pretty mama don't you tell on me', *Endless Road* fanzine no. 4, 1983, Dylan probably came across 'Belle Isle' in the *Sing Out!* booklet *Reprints from* Sing Out! *Volume 9* (1966); this also includes 'Copper Kettle', 'It Hurts Me Too' (here titled 'When Things Go Wrong With You') and 'Little Sadie'.

a tone in his voice that takes up that foreboding suggestion in the strings. There is a darker presence around the edges of this Romance.

This disperses for a little while near the end (before the strings impinge to bring it back again) when the full sunshine of Dylan's comedy bursts through:

> *Young maiden I wish not to banter,*
> *'Tis true I come here in disguise*
> *I came here to fulfil my last promise*
> *And hoped to give you a surprise!*
> *I own you're a maid I love dearly*
> *And you've bin in my heart all the while . . .*

That first line is joyously funny because through the archaism it is graceful, and the poise is kept so beautifully all the way to that 'banter': and Dylan singing these archaisms is the aural equivalent of A Sight To Be Seen. The second line, with its force falling so gleefully on 'disguise', makes it radiantly clear how far into the Celtic story-world Dylan is taking us, while the third line has a well-contrived calming influence – its words float down in a gentle spiral – so that the imminent absurdity of what follows doesn't overbalance and come too soon. The fourth line brings the fall – that ludicrously bad distribution of syllables, the awfulness of the rhyme and the bathos of the hope expressed (itself accentuated by the rush of syllables given over to its expression). It has all been perfectly timed. It is brilliant clowning, like that unbalanced line from 'Leopard-Skin Pill-Box Hat' on "Blonde On Blonde": 'You know it balances on your head just like a mattress balances on a bottle of wine'. Moreover, Dylan doesn't leave it there on 'Belle Isle', like some broken Humpty-Dumpty. With the lines that follow, all is restored. That 'I own' enacts the first flourish towards a restoration, as Dylan's voice gently hams up a bewildered search for the right note; the hush through 'you're a maid I' begins to get it back; the slowing-down on 'love' gives the necessary foothold; 'de-e-ear-ly' acts as one last wobble; 'And you've bin in my heart' is oh-so-nearly back in balance; and the eventual resolve of the voice's note with the music, at the end of 'all the while', announces the firm restoration of the balance. So then, as the emphasised beat comes down on the word 'me' in the line that follows:

> *For me there is no other damsel*

– where the voice and the music are precisely synchronised – Dylan re-sets the tone of the song, right there at the end. And in re-setting the tone there, and in the music that follows to close over the song, Dylan draws all its elements together: the sombre quality, the humour and the traditional Romance. The sum of these parts is, in 'Belle Isle', mystery. And mystery, as Dylan said in 1966,

> is a fact, a traditional fact . . . traditional music is too unreal to die. It doesn't need to be protected. Nobody's going to hurt it . . . All these songs about roses growing out of people's brains and lovers who are really geese and swans who turn into angels – they're not going to die.[15]

---

15. 'The *Playboy* interview: a candid conversation with the iconoclastic idol of the folk-rock set', *Playboy*, March 1966.

Likewise 'Belle Isle'. Its mystery, as much as its Celticness, is what makes it a traditional song and a brilliant achievement.

But there is something else to be said in relation to the kind of language Dylan deals in on "Self Portrait" (and "Nashville Skyline") – and it's a point that relates also to Dylan's consistent independence of rock modishness. "John Wesley Harding" is, as we noted earlier, a dramatic gesture of distancing; so too is "Self Portrait". It is very much out on its own, and one main way this is emphasised is in Dylan's rejection of the *language* of a modish rock culture here.

Before "John Wesley Harding", Dylan's language had been scattered with the old familiar phrases: 'hung up,' 'where it's at' and so on, along with much hip drugs terminology. With "John Wesley Harding" this disappears. "Nashville Skyline" shows a careful reliance on the language of 'ordinary men' and "Self Portrait" stays with this change of tack.

In 1966, Dylan said that he'd been unhappy with aspects of his use of language before 'Like A Rolling Stone' because

> I was singing words I didn't really want to sing. I don't mean words like 'God' and 'mother' and 'President' and 'suicide' and 'meat-cleaver'. I mean simple little words like 'if' and 'hope' and 'you'.[16]

With "Self Portrait", as with "Nashville Skyline", Dylan is reconciled to such words. Patrick Thomas, commenting on this shift (as evidenced on "Nashville Skyline"), wrote:

> the 'new' Bob Dylan lyrics, which wring out responses from words like 'suitcase' and 'rumours', are simply recognition of the fact that not all Americans feel the dead-weight of thrice-throttled, TV-choked English.

And he contrasts this 'new' Dylan language to the 'constant overstatement of urban vernacular'.[17]

On "Self Portrait", more than ever before, Dylan is using his 'ordinary language' with a dignity of expression which involves much of that weapon of the great artist, *understatement*.

The Dylan of the 1970s after "Self Portrait" returns overwhelmingly to singing his own, rather than other people's, material. From "New Morning" through "Blood On The Tracks", "Desire" and on through to "Saved", he shifts with fascinating agility through many modes of language, in all of which he develops his use of understatement, establishes his artistry and, with a wholly mature intelligence, frees himself from any obligation to cling on down any one linguistic track. His basic instinct, though, all through this second decade of his work, is towards a new simplicity of language.

"New Morning" arrived just a few months after "Self Portrait" and, while in singing style and timbre it shows something like a return toward "Blonde On Blonde" modes of expression, it signalled just the same that the new simplicity of language was not to be abandoned.

16.   See note 15.
17.   Patrick Thomas, 'Doug Kershaw' (interview), *Rolling Stone*, no. 39, 9/8/69.

Creatively, perhaps, beyond this chiselling of language, "New Morning" confirmed that, as he entered the 1970s, the rock poet genius of the 1960s was resting.

On it, Dylan has lost that amazing urgency of communication – that arresting quality, that abrasive presence – and has nothing much to say. Obviously the two things are connected, though one is a matter of delivery, of performance, while the other is a matter of vision. But the lack of one always betrays, in Dylan's art, the lack of the other.

Dylan sounds tired and abstracted and not really 'there' by his own standards. There is even a deterioration in his use of cliché – from, say, the obvious sharpness of "Blonde On Blonde"'s

> *You say you told me that you*
> *Wanna hold me but you*
> *Know you're not that strong . . .*

On the pleasant, slight 'If Not For You', the cliché is still knowingly offered – as if Dylan were back in 1966 – and carried to the point of self-ridicule:

> *Winter would have no Spring,*
> *Couldn't hear the robins sing*
> *I just wouldn't have a clue*
> *Anyway it wouldn't ring true*
> *If not for you*

yet the emptiness is as prominent as the confession of it.

When we come to 'The Man In Me' (not a Dylan song with much appeal to feminists, fairly enough), there is, because of this sort of emptiness, an added dimension of irony (which again, Dylan's own awareness of does not dissolve) in the lines

> *The man in me will hide sometimes*
> *To keep from being seen*
> *But that's just because he doesn't want to*
> *Turn into some machine . . .*

and it is reasonable to feel that the artist in Dylan, at least, ought not to be so much in hiding. The song has its own strengths, but it has no commitment. And really, it is a pretty pointless joke to have, in the middle section, Dylan pushing even closer to 'On The Street Where You Live' than he had done an album or two earlier, by almost quoting it exactly, in words and tune, here:

> *But oh! what a wonderful feelin'*
> *Just to know that you are near;*[18]

18. Cf. these lines from 'On The Street Where You Live', sung to Eliza Doolittle by the chinless wannabe boyfriend in Alan J. Lerner and Frederick Loewe's *My Fair Lady* – lines which, like Dylan's, are placed at the start of the 'bridge' or 'middle eight' of the song: 'And oh! the towering feeling / Just to know somehow you are near' (to which is paired 'The overpowering feeling / That any second you may suddenly appear').

[John Michael King sang 'On The Street Where You Live' on the Original Cast Recording LP "My Fair Lady", Philips RBL 1000, London, 1958; the show had premiered 4/2/56 in New Haven and opened 15/3/56 in NYC; the LP was issued to coincide with the show's London opening, 30/4/58. Both productions starred Rex

and similarly, when, in 'Winterlude', he strokes the listener with

Winterlude, this dude thinks you're fine

we're likely to feel that we've had enough songs now from 'this dude' and that we'd prefer to return to those of the genius whose best talents lurk somewhere under this blithe and stereotyped 'dude' personality.

The trouble is that Dylan loses control over this 'dude' persona, to the extent of letting two different selves get mixed up. This happens on 'Sign On The Window'. To rhyme

Build me a cabin in Utah

with

Have a bunch of kids who call me Pa

would be immaculate, with all that doubt about this formula-for-happiness shown up in Dylan's delivery, *if* when he came to the word 'Pa', the note was laid down firmly, like a trump card. That would be the real Dylan way – and however stylised, and therefore *personally* insincere, it would have flawless *artistic* sincerity. But Dylan quite simply delivers it wrongly (something I don't think he'd ever done before). He gives the word 'Pa' a wobble on the voice – a really awful tremolo-gentility. It's embarrassing, and it happens because Dylan mixes himself up with the dude.

Dylan's lack of anything much to say shows itself too, on "New Morning", in his conformity to what became a general trend in the pre-New Wave 1970s: the careful gathering up of whole clusters of ever-more-famous, ever-more-'professional' session musicians. No one could deny their abilities, but Dylan's earlier albums show how unnecessary these extra battalions are for him and his art.

This trend was being identified long before New Wave declared it lethal and destroyed it in 1977 (except in California, where they were too busy eating and dieting and eliminating thought from the shopping-list of things that interested them, and where, in consequence, the music has been unlistenably dull ever since).

Back in 1972, in the first edition of this book, I wrote that

the whole trend reveals, right across the scene, a huge disparity between the tiny amount the 1960s stars have left to communicate and the vastness of their access to the best studios and the very best supportive facilities, as a result of their previous (more primitively achieved) attainments. There they all are – George Harrison, Eric Clapton, Crosby, Stills, Nash, McCartney, Kantner, and more – all laying down increasingly trivial material, decorated and supported by increasingly exquisite, 'professional' accompaniments. And Dylan (on 'Self Portrait' and 'New Morning') is right there with them.

It becomes, before long, a spurious sort of panacea and, since it relies more

---

Harrison, Julie Andrews and Stanley Holloway. Most parents of people of Bob Dylan's generation owned either this album or the film soundtrack album; and in 1958 'On The Street Where You Live' was also a huge pop hit, not least a No. 1 in the UK, by crooner Vic Damone: Columbia Records 40654, New York (Philips Records PB 819, London), 1958.]

and more on the ordinary listener possessing extraordinarily good stereo (or, imminently, quadraphonic) equipment, it is debatable whether, under these conditions, technology is the servant or the master of the music.[19]

All this, of course, was punctured admirably by punk. It had got to the point where no one in Britain dared get on a stage, even in a pub, unless they had monstrous megawatt equipment and could play fifteen chords. The punk bands were important because they saw this for the nonsense it was, and did something about it – and the boom whereby hundreds of obscure singles of very primitive technical quality were issued on hundreds of tiny independent labels was a demonstration that, when you feel you do have something to say, the technology is not going to inhibit you.

Now Bob Dylan knew all this perfectly well all along, and most of his recordings, all through his career, have disregarded those debilitating 'standards' of technical production that came into vogue at the end of the 1960s: and that is why the way that these impinge on "New Morning" is especially irksome. And it does impinge: one's awareness of the technology – the ever-present sense that it is *there* – impinges on the music. This is, at the very least, ironic when, as happens on the title track of the album, it is used to extol the virtues of watching rabbits in the great outdoors.

Moreover, Dylan's specialising, at the start of the 1970s, in songs of rural simplicity – in which he comes on again and again in a Happy Family Man role as singer/narrator – confirms that he feels he has little to say.

Even in the album's rock song, 'One More Weekend', there is a facile combination of country-sounding slide guitar and noticeably cosy lyrics:

> *We'll go some place unknown*
> *Leave all the children home;*
> *Honey why not go alone*
> *Just you and me . . .*

This compares directly with the 1966 'Leopard-Skin Pill-Box Hat':

> *If you wanna see the sunrise*
> *Honey I know where*
> *We'll go out and see it sometime*
> *We'll both just sit there and stare*

and the change in the later song (which parallels the earlier one in structure and music too) to a married-couple situation is far from artless. Nor are the details of the

---

19.   The only name which, thirty-odd years on, needs any explaining, is Kantner. Paul Kantner (born 1941) was guitarist and vocalist in (and co-founder of) Jefferson Airplane, the only West Coast rival to the Grateful Dead as a fresh, inventive, ex-folkies-gone-underground-radical band. They offered sometimes hectoring lyrics but a powerful stance (including, from their inception as early as 1965, an enthusiastic avowal of drug-taking), and exploratory music that managed at once to sound thin yet warm. It is thoroughly dated, and splendidly of its time. By 1970 the group members seemed, like the Beatles, more interested in solo projects than in the band (though this staggered on, eventually turning into the altogether more music-industry-oriented Jefferson Starship). Jefferson Airplane was also the first big rock act on RCA Victor Records since Elvis Presley.

We must have come a long way downhill since "New Morning" sounded over-produced and too professional to me. Now it sounds almost recorded round the camp-fire in the woods, with smoky acoustic playing, ample space and a sense of music played from love, with much individual extemporising towards a collective whole, and with Dylan's lovely gospel piano as if miked up from inside some nearby clapboard church. It keeps on improving with the passing years.

realisation. While the vagueness of the exhortation in 'Leopard-Skin Pill-Box Hat' pithily evokes the narrator's deliberate callousness, the corresponding specificity of the plan suggested in 'One More Weekend' evokes only a timidity on Dylan's part; and while 'Honey' is used almost as belittling sarcasm on the 1966 song, the same word comes across very differently on the 1970 revisit. Here, used immediately after the situation reveals itself, it half suggests 'honeymoon', while the whole proposal urges what amounts to a second honeymoon. No wonder it's a slightly weary track and that its rock harshness does not convince.

Dylan's Happy Family Man role, irrespective of how it applied at the time to his private life, is unconvincing in his art. You don't render a vision of happiness by insisting that you're happy, or simply by using a bland voice.

This is what Dylan attempts, wrongly, on "Nashville Skyline" and "Self Portrait", and he does so again on "New Morning" – yet with a significant difference in how it comes out. Self-awareness of this fault shows through, on tracks like 'If Not For You'; the accompanying self-effacement, sometimes self-apology, makes for an odd contradictoriness not found in Dylan's other work.

First, Dylan slips into imitating himself – a trap many distinguished writers fall into, from Wordsworth to Mailer: trying to reach the floor and the door in 'If Not For You' just like in 'Temporary Like Achilles'; re-writing 'Leopard-Skin Pill-Box Hat' as 'One More Weekend'; roughing up his voice again so as to echo "Blonde On Blonde" rather clumsily; the 'old crossroad sign' in 'Winterlude' just like back in 'One Too Many Mornings'; the déja vu allusion to romantic, mid-1960s-style chaos in 'The Man In Me' where

> *The stormclouds are ragin'*
> *All around my door . . .*

and the blatant nostalgia of that line in the middle of the flawed but fabulous 'Sign On The Window': 'Sure gonna be wet tonight on Main Streeeeeet . . .'; plus, perhaps finally, what is in effect a reassurance that yes, after all, he still remembers Bob the young folkie rebel, when he ends 'Went To See The Gypsy' with this utter non sequitur:

> *So I watched the sun come risin'*
> *From the little Minnesota town*
> *From that little Minnesota town.*

On top of all this, there is a marked expression of explicit doubt about the family-man, countryman role. Thus the element of self-parody is far more apparent than on the two previous albums – to the extent, even, that birds become 'birdies' (echoing, in the process, Jerry Lee Lewis' 'Livin' Lovin' Wreck')[20] and the wife-and-children become merely a possible formula to try out:

20. Jerry Lee Lewis: 'Livin' Lovin' Wreck', Nashville, 9/2/61 (B-side of 'What'd I Say', Nashville, 9/2/61), Sun Records 356, Memphis [London American Records HLS 9335, London], 1961.

> *Build me a cabin in Utah*
> *Marry me a wife, catch rainbow trout*
> *Have a bunch of kids who call me Pa . . .*

And to clinch it, this is followed not only by a patently unconfident remark (made less positive still by its being repeated, as if for self-persuasion):

> *That must be what it's all about*
> *That must be what it's all about*

but also by the capping touch of genius – that intentionally ingenuous little 'Oh-oh-oh-oh!' which Dylan puts over the end of the riff that follows.

Throughout the album, also, there is a subtle but sustained falsification of the rural/patriarchal ideas: a persistent kind of Midas touch that deliberately makes the picture an idealised and therefore not a real one.

It shows in his going not to 'the hills' at the end of 'Day Of The Locusts' but to the American hills most artificialised by Tin Pan Alley, 'the black hills of Dakota'. It suggests Dylan rushing off to Doris Day; it makes his escape to the hills just a story, by making it just a joke – mere fictional allusion.[21]

Then, just as the next song, 'Time Passes Slowly', takes up the story in the hills, so also it takes up the unreality suggested in the earlier track:

> *Time passes slowly up here in the mountains*
> *We sit beside bridges and walk beside fountains*

warbles Dylan – and plainly, as he's testing whether we'll notice, there aren't any fountains up mountains. The very word suggests the Ideal, not the real. It offers a kind of exquisite, ethereal, pastoral conceit: a sort of Greek Mythology land, an Elysium. Something not there. Then, out of the disjointed but compulsive evocation of the strange and fragmentary 'Went To See The Gypsy', comes

> *Outside the lights were shining*
> *On the river of tears . . .*

which fits the rest of the song less than the album as a whole: its function is to ally and associate with the Elysian motif established in the earlier songs.

In 'Winterlude' the unreal becomes dominant and explicit. The title itself implies that the album is all a show, like, in this sense, *A Midsummer Night's Dream*. The

---

21.   Doris Day: 'The Black Hills Of Dakota', Hollywood, 16/7/53, Columbia Records 40095, New York [Philips Records PB 287, London], 1953. This was a Top 10 hit in Britain. The song, by Paul Francis Webster and Sammy Fain, comes from the soundtrack of the film *Calamity Jane*, Warner Brothers, US, directed David Butler, 1953. The soundtrack album (10-inch LP) is "Calamity Jane", Columbia Records CL6273, New York, 1953. (Dylan mentions Doris Day twice in *Tarantula*.)

At the same time, as the Doris Day record suggests and my text fails to acknowledge, the Black Hills of (South) Dakota are 'Indian country': in fact the state's best-known 'great men' include Crazy Horse and Sitting Bull and its major towns include Sioux Falls. Thus Dylan might be said, as so often on this album, to be invoking a two-headed image: one unreal and one real – in this case at once Hollywood/showbiz crooner terrain and a terrain associated with an ancient American culture (and one offering a starkly different milieu and set of values from those of the honorary-degree ceremony at Princeton from which Dylan is escaping at the end of 'Day Of The Locusts').

rhythm is waltz-time; the clichés focus on a dreamworld of romance – denying any corresponding 'real life' romance – the kind that sparkles through the Dixie Cups' record 'Chapel Of Love':[22]

> . . . *my little apple*
> *Winterlude let's go down to the chapel.*

And it's not only a waltz – it's a skating song. It's Dylan On Ice. This carries a further suggestion of the unreal: the ice-top as merely a precarious covering, a sheet hiding and transforming something else. Alongside this, the lyric reveals the snow on the sand – the shifting sand.

We can see this urged unreality through the rest of the album too: in 'New Morning' itself, with its intentional things-aren't-what-they-seem touch of

> *a country mile, or two . . .*

and in even the obvious theatrical mystique of the title of the next track, 'Sign On The Window', while 'The Man In Me' has as its theme the message keep-it-all-hid.

As for 'Three Angels', it impresses straight away as being not only surreal but as echoing that pop classic of *false* religiosity, Wink Martindale's 'Deck Of Cards'.[23] It also echoes closely a short, striking passage from Genet's *Our Lady of the Flowers*:

> But neither of the two seemed to care whether Divine was absent or present. They heard the morning angelus, the rattle of a milk can. Three workmen went by on bicycles along the boulevard, their lamps lit, though it was day. A policeman on his way home . . . passed without looking at them.[24]

As there, but more so, 'the real world' in Dylan's song passes like a pageant below the gaze of the narrator and his rather ungainly angels. Dylan's making them ungainly – keeping them perched up on poles wearing 'green robes, with wings that stick out' – is another wry confession of his intent.

The cumulative effect of all this carefully established unreality is to make "New

---

22. The Dixie Cups: 'Chapel Of Love', NYC, *nia*, the first release on the George Goldner–Jerry Leiber–Mike Stoller label Red Bird Records [Red Bird 10 001], New York [Pye International Records 7N 25245, London], 1964. It was a US No. 1. The Dixie Cups were a New Orleans act.

23. Wink Martindale: 'Deck Of Cards', *nia*, Dot Records 15968, Hollywood [London American Records HLD 8962, London], 1959. In the UK this was a recurrent hit: first charting in December 1959 (Top 20), re-charting in 1963 (Top 5) and, reissued on Dot Records DOT 109, re-charting again in 1973 (Top 30). This last time around, even more members of the British public bought the cover version by Max Bygraves [Pye Records 7N 45276].

It was on Wink Martindale's local TV show *Top Ten Dance Party* on WHBQ in the early months of 1957 that Elvis Presley first saw 19-year-old beauty-contest winner Anita Wood (he was watching the show, she was appearing on it), who would become his principal girlfriend 1957–60. Afterwards, Wood recorded 'I'll Wait Forever' [Memphis, 28/12/60, Sun Records 361, Memphis, 1961].

24. French playwright, novelist and poet Jean Genet (1910–1986), *Our Lady of the Flowers* (1944); original title *Notre Dame des Fleurs*.

Robert Shelton, *No Direction Home*, quotes Dylan (interviewed by Shelton on a plane between Lincoln, Nebraska, and Denver, Colorado, mid-March 1966): 'William Burroughs is a poet. I like all his old books and Jean Genet's old books.'

(In Wissolik and McGrath's *Bob Dylan's Words* [1994], Dylan's 'flowerlady' in *Tarantula* is cited as possibly alluding to Genet's *Our Lady of the Flowers*. You might add his 'all of the flower ladies' in 'Queen Jane Approximately'. A now-deleted section of the first edition of the present work suggested that 'Absolutely Sweet Marie' stresses the 'ruins of your balcony' in conscious reference to another Genet work, his play *Le Balcon/The Balcony*, 1956–57.)

Morning" very different in its vision from any other of Dylan's albums. It begins to express a new optimism-through-doubt. He may have little to say but he has the courage to know it – and to make, to pass his time, an intelligent critique of what he doesn't believe in anymore. 'New Morning' says for his country persona what 'My Back Pages' said about his protest persona.

What it says about his use of language is that as he steps out beyond the utter simplicity of "Nashville Skyline" and "Self Portrait" towards a new simplicity that can bear the demands of the creative artist Dylan cannot help but be, he is here already showing how the simple can encompass the subtle.

That Dylan could still be directly touched by something very much from the *urban* world was shown by the single that he issued at the end of 1971, 'George Jackson'.

Dylan starts the song very simply by declaring this response, and using the classic blues opening-line to say so:

> *I woke up this morning*

and then tightening up at once into the particular and the special – personalising it:

> *There were tears in my bed*
> *They killed a man I really loved*
> *Shot him through the head.*

It is exactly like the pre-1964 protest songs – even down to the formula of a guitar-backing till the end of the penultimate verse, then a harmonica solo laid on top, then guitar alone again through the last verse, then back with the harmonica for the fade-out.

What is *not* like the pre-1964 protest material is this:

> *They were frightened of his power*
> *They were scared of his love.*

That is the post-mystic Dylan – the post-acid Dylan; and in the light of Steven Goldberg arguing (see Chapter 6) that after "Nashville Skyline" Dylan's post-mystic politics would be reactionary, it is interesting to find those mystic traces in the middle of this committedly radical song.

It's also interesting to see the way the end of the song shows Dylan's most simple Blakeian language deliberately echoing one of George Jackson's most spirited (and un-Blakeian) remarks. Jackson says in one of his letters that, from now on, he's just going to divide people into the innocent and the guilty.[25] As Dylan re-states this, it is Us and Us, not Us and Them:

---

25. George Jackson, *Soledad Brother: The Prison Letters of George Jackson* (1970) (with a preface by our old friend Jean Genet).

   Eighteen-year-old Jackson was jailed for one-year-to-life in 1960 for driving the getaway car for a friend who stole $70 from a garage. The friend was released in 1963; Jackson stayed in San Quentin till 1969, when he was moved to Soledad. He joined the Black Panther Party (formed 1966) in 1969, and his book was based on letters to his family on the brutality and racism of the prison system. He spent long periods in solitary confinement. In January 1970, in a new bi-racial exercise yard, guards fired on fighting prisoners, killing three blacks; when a 'justifiable homicide' verdict was returned, a white guard was killed in the prison; Jackson and two others were arrested and moved back to San Quentin. On 17 August, when Jackson's trial was imminent, his brother Jonathan seized the judge and three jurors as hostages during another Black Panther trial; in the ensuing shoot-out, Jonathan

> *Sometimes I think this whole world*
> *Is one big prison yard*
> *Some of us are prisoners*
> *The rest of us are guards.*

Then, after a long gap, comes the magnificent "Planet Waves" album, which reveals a Dylan not so willing to have jumped back into a purely urban milieu.

It is demonstrably a Dylan album of the 1970s in managing to bind together elements of the city-surreal-intellectual world from which "Blonde on Blonde"'s language derived, with a new willingness to re-embrace older, folksier, rural strengths.

'Going, Going, Gone' shows this binding together admirably. Here is the city language:

> *I'm closin' the book*
> *On the pages and the text*
> *And I don't really care*
> *What happens next . . .*

Jackson, the judge and two others were killed. George Jackson's trial was postponed until August 1971; on 21 August, two days before it was due to begin, Jackson was shot dead by a San Quentin guard, allegedly while attacking guards during an attempted escape. (His two co-accused, John Cluchette and Fletta Drumgo, were later found not guilty of the murder of the guard.)

The history of radical political activity in the 1960s to 1970s in the USA (in 'Amerika', as we styled it then, taking the 'k' from the initials of the Ku Klux Klan, to suggest its political complexion) seems to have fallen from sight in the 1990s. When *Soledad Brother* was published, the *Sunday Times* called George Jackson 'one of the great voices of the American Left'. Now you look him up in vain in almost all the major encyclopaedia and in the reference works on who's who in recent political and public life. He's become an unperson. (The information on him given here is taken mostly from Edmund White's book *Jean Genet*, 1992.)

Yet at the time of Jackson's death, Amerika, waging war in Vietnam and Cambodia, was hugely in turmoil, and 'the left' was a real presence, with 'revolutionary action' called for among whites as well as within the Black Power movement. Malcolm X, the first modern black revolutionary leader, was assassinated 21/1/65; Martin Luther King was shot in Memphis, 4/4/68, provoking riots in 22 city ghettoes. The year 1968 also saw the Presidio Mutiny, San Francisco; a bloody conflict with students at Columbia University in April; and mayhem during the Democratic Party National Convention in Chicago (including a Yippie plot to dump LSD in a reservoir). One student was shot dead at 'People's Park', 20/5/69, as 2,000 National Guardsmen occupied the Berkeley campus, California, in order to regain an empty parking lot; protesters invaded Fort Dix, New Jersey, in October 1969; there was a student occupation of Harvard in 1969, and a strike at Berkeley in May 1970; four students were shot dead at Kent State University, Kent, Ohio, 4/5/70; the Santa Barbara branch of the Bank of America was fire-bombed by the Left in 1970; the Atlanta office of the South's biggest underground newspaper, *The Great Speckled Bird*, was fire-bombed by the Right in 1972. Governor Ronald Reagan of California was quoted as saying: 'If it takes a bloodbath, let's get it over with. No more appeasement.' Even rock concerts were considered to constitute political defiance in Amerika, as in the Soviet Bloc. Over 100 people were badly injured at the Rolling Stones' first Iron Curtain concert, 3/4/67, as police used tear-gas and batons against 2,000 fans storming the Warsaw Palace of Culture; likewise Jethro Tull and their audience were tear-gassed by police in Denver, Colorado, 10/6/71, putting 25 grown-ups and three babies into hospital.

(Sources: *Shots: Photographs from the Underground Press*, ed. David Fenton, 1971; Michael Horowitz [not the British poet] and Dana Reemes, 'Historic sites of psychedelic culture and research', 1977, in *High Times Encyclopedia of Recreational Drugs*, ed. Andrew Kowl, 1978; and Michael Gray: 'The Let It Rot calendar of death', *Let It Rock*, no. 28, April 1975 [re-published *Creem*, no.10, July 1976; *Record Mirror*, 29/10/77].)

A good contemporary account of this period is Roger Lewis' *Outlaws of America* (1972). The chapter 'Gimme some of that rock and roll music' includes what was at the time the best short summary of Bob Dylan's social significance in the 1960s. In 1975 another George Jackson book was published, *Blood in My Eye* (a manuscript completed 'just a few days before his death', said Penguin Books). This is cited in Chapter 18, re the blues song 'Blood In My Eyes'.

The story circulated in the music industry in the early 1970s that when Columbia Records in New York received a telephone enquiry as to whether a part of the royalties on Bob Dylan's record of 'George Jackson' would be going to the Soledad Brothers, the reply was: 'We don't think so. They're not on our label.'

I bin hangin' on threads
I bin playin' it straight . . .

I bin livin' on the edge . . .

and here is the urging of an older, simpler wisdom:

Grandma said 'Boy go follow your heart
I know you'll be fine at the end of the line
All that's gold doesn't shine
Don't you and your one true love ever part.'

Back on 'Memphis Blues Again' (on "Blonde on Blonde"), grandpa was just a joke; in 'Going, Going, Gone', grandma has insights to offer. She represents something stable and reliable (and, by the implication of her age, something resilient). And her old, simple wisdom is deftly stressed by Dylan having her speak that truism, that neat opposite of 'all that glisters is not gold'.[26]

Through the rest of the song Dylan presses on with this forging together of the two different worlds he'd previously walked through separately. He brings in an echo of his old folk-singer days with a near-quote from 'Don't Think Twice, It's All Right' – 'I bin walkin' the road' – and he binds a rural backwoods image and vaguer, mid-1960s-Dylan language together in the opening verse:

I've just reached a place
Where the willow don't bend . . .

It's the top of the end
I'm going, I'm going, I'm gone.

The whole album devotes itself to revisiting, as the adult with the mid-1960s surreal achievement behind him, the Minnesota landscapes and feelings from which he had emerged in the first place. 'Hazel' deals with a girlfriend he'd had long before he ever first set out for New York City and in 'Something There Is About You' he says it carefully and clearly:

Thought I'd shaken the wonder
And the phantoms of my youth
Rainy days on the Great Lakes
Walkin' the hills of old Duluth . . .

Somethin' there is about you
That brings back a long-forgotten truth . . .

---

26. 'All that glisters is not gold', often held to be from Shakespeare, in fact conflates two other formulations. The proverb, taken from the Latin, is 'All is not gold that glitters / All that glitters is not gold'; an allusion to this by the poet Thomas Gray (1716–1771) gives us the apparently more elevated but in fact merely archaic 'glisters', and not quite as expected: 'Not all that tempts your wand'ring eyes / And heedless hearts, is lawful prize; / Nor all, that glisters, gold.' This comes not from the one poem for which Gray is still remembered, 'Elegy Written in a Country Church-Yard' (published 1751), but from the odd source 'Ode on the Death of a Favourite Cat, Drowned in a Tub of Gold Fishes' (1747). And it wasn't his cat, it was Horace Walpole's.

> *I was in a whirlwind*
> *Now I'm in some better place.*

This same theme, of the inexorable tug of the past and the struggle to wed it to the present, runs through the album. It is there in 'Wedding Song', and, coming at the end of the album, these lines, with their chilling full-stop, emphasize the desperation the whole song examines:

> *I love you more than ever*
> *Now that the past is gone.*

An earlier image in the same song echoes across the years from the 1965 'Farewell Angelina':

> *I've said goodbye to haunted rooms*
> *And faces in the street*
> *To the courtyard of the jester*
> *Which is hidden from the sun . . .*

and 'Dirge' similarly says goodbye to old haunts – to the old folk days of Greenwich Village, such that the song acts as a re-write of 'Positively 4th Street':

> *Heard your songs of freedom*
> *And man forever stripped*
> *Acting out his folly*
> *While his back is being whipped . . .*
> *I can't recall a useful thing*
> *You ever did for me*
> *'Cept pat me on the back one time*
> *While I was on my knees . . .*
> *No use to apologize*
> *What difference would it make?*

So there is a lot of tension explored here, all stemming from the contradictory ways in which the past reacts upon the present. The chill desperation of 'Wedding Song' and the distanced vitriol of 'Dirge' show one side of the process; the enriching feelings of re-visiting on 'Something There Is About You' and 'Hazel' and 'Never Say Goodbye' show the other side. What all the songs reveal is this tension in the language: this struggle on Dylan's part to reconcile the city-surreal-intellectual approach to language with the newer, simpler approach.

As much as in 'Going, Going, Gone', for instance, you can trace the ebb and flow of these two previously separate modes of expression through a song like 'Tough Mama'. And it works well here: Dylan is beginning to succeed with his project of fusing the two:

> *Tough Mama*
> *Meat shakin' on your bones*
> *I'm gonna*
> *Go down to the river and get me some stones*
> *Sister's on the highway*

With that steel-drivin' crew
Papa's in the big house
His workin' days are through . . .

With "Planet Waves", without a doubt, Dylan has come a lot closer than he had on "New Morning" to forging his own new resources of language.

With "Blood On The Tracks" his progress suddenly shows through in a tremendous, unexpected leap forwards and upwards. This album is almost certainly his best and puts the constant struggle between "Blonde On Blonde" or "Highway 61 Revisited", and "Nashville Skyline" – the struggle enacted in "New Morning" and "Planet Waves" – dramatically behind him. There is no longer an ebb and flow between those two extreme modes of expression. There is, on a whole new plateau as it were, a successfully attained, fresh language that is the new simplicity – and in which, as ever in the best of Dylan's work, simplicity is deceptive, communicating more by being able confidently to say less.

"Blood On The Tracks" gives us, also, Dylan's scorching *urgency* at its very best, utterly free from the chains of the 1960s.

For this reason alone, its historical importance is immense. When it was first released, in 1975, its effect was colossal. An adjustment was needed, critically, to the fact that Dylan had so dramatically broken free of the decade with which he was so deeply associated by virtue of having so profoundly affected it. Some adjustment was necessary to the Dylan generation's consciousness, because with "Blood On The Tracks" it was Bob Dylan who had produced the most strikingly intelligent, apposite and entirely contemporary album of the 1970s.

Most people had assumed that, in effect, Dylan's decline at the end of the decade he had made his own, the 1960s, froze his seminal work – "Highway 61 Revisited", "Blonde On Blonde", the Basement Tapes, "John Wesley Harding" – into an historical religious object that one had to choose, by the mid-1970s, either to put away in the attic or else to revere perhaps at the expense of more contemporary artists. Instead, "Blood On The Tracks" legitimised Dylan's claim to a creative prowess – a power capable of being directed at us effectively for perhaps another thirty or forty years.

The common conception of how rock music moves forward needed to be adjusted too. That conception had always been that artists come and go in relatively short time spans, with careers peaking early. "Blood On The Tracks" challenged that idea. Here was a masterpiece fully ten years after Dylan's first major 'peak', "Highway 61 Revisited" – and one as different and as fresh as it possibly could have been. It addressed the post-1960s world, and our darkness within, with a whole arsenal of weapons.

Its creative genius is still very much an undiminished thing of the present. It has as much sheer freshness as Dylan's, or anyone else's, first album – as much genuine urge to communicate, as much zest. Yet it combines them all with a sharp wit and corrosive intelligence, and an impeccable judgement, so that the sum of these parts is a greater whole than any of Dylan's other achievements.

Like "Planet Waves", "Blood On The Tracks" deals, among much else, with the overlaying of the past upon the present – but gone, utterly, is any element of Dylan's myopic early-1970s insistence on eternal love and on its wholesome cocoon. In its place is a profoundly felt understanding of our fragile impermanence of control – so that in dealing with the overlay of past upon present, Dylan is dealing also (unlike "Planet Waves") with the inexorable disintegration of relationships and with the dignity of keeping on trying to reintegrate them against all odds.

'Tangled Up In Blue' deals with the way in which many forces – past upon present, public upon privacy, distance upon friendship, disintegration upon love – are further tangled and reprocessed by time. It's a scintillating account of a career and a love affair, and of how they intertwine. It becomes a viable history of fifteen years through one man's eyes, and in its realism and mental alertness it offers a vigorous challenge to all the poses of wasted decay that most 'intelligent' rock has been marketing since the fall from grace of the 1960s optimism.

As it would need to be, Dylan's writing here is chiselled by the full concentration of his artistry. He can coin a new mode of expression with an almost in-passing agility:

> Later on when the crowd thinned out
> I was about to do the same

– and there is the wit, tossed out as if it were easy, and there too is the bubbling spontaneity that Dylan achieves within the disciplined limits of a strikingly precise verse structure.[27]

He makes this work for him so well. There is, for instance, a rhyming spill-over towards the end of each verse, like this:

> I was standin' on the side of the road
> Rain fallin' on my shoes
> Headin' out for the east coast
> Lord knows I paid some dues
> Getting through –
> Tangled up in blue

It is there as that fourth line (rhyming with the second) spills over into the short fifth line (which rhymes with the sixth). As we listen to the song, these short spill-overs become more and more stabbing in their emotional effect as they become at the same time more and more agile and clever as rhymes. As here:

> She studied the lines of my face
> I must admit I felt a little uneasy
> When she bent down to tie the lace-
> -s of my shoe –
> Tangled up in blue

and finally, triumphantly, here in the last verse:

---

27.   The trick in Dylan's lines is also reminiscent of something that Colin Wilson, in *The Outsider* (1956), picks out of Jean-Paul Sartre's first novel *La Nausée* [*Nausea*] (1937), in which the narrator says of a café patron that 'When his place empties, his head empties also.'

But me I'm still on the road
Headin' for another joint
We always did feel the same
We just saw it from a different point
Of view –
Tangled up in blue.

Beyond that wonderful use of a formal, limiting shape and structure to yield scintillating leaps of feeling and expression, 'Tangled Up In Blue' contains a whole assortment of verbal spikes and explosions that all operate not as distractions from the main body of *feeling* in the song but as ways of evoking the emotional complexity and urgency of it all. That Dylan can make time, in the course of what is delivered as a fast, breathless narrative, for flashes like this:

I had a job in the Great North Woods . . .
But I never did like it all that much
And one day the axe just fell

shows an alertness and mental dexterity that augments the emotional seriousness and depth of the song. And there is an accompanying dexterity of sketching in, quick as a flash, a whole range of universally recognisable moments in fresh, intensely accurate strokes of language, from the evoked dialogue with inbuilt self-mockery here:

She lit a burner on the stove
And offered me a pipe
'I thought you'd never say hello,' she said
'You look like the silent type'

to the very funny sureness of touch in this summary of that common feeling of whatever-happened-to-*those* people:

Some are mathematicians
Some are carpenters' wives
Dunno how it all got started
I dunno what they're doin' with their lives

where that last line communicates the inevitable ambiguity of feeling – sadness at time's destruction of friendships and at the same time, truly, an indifference to where or what those people are now.

'Tangled Up In Blue', then, opens the album at a high level of intensity and brilliance. 'Simple Twist Of Fate' carves out its own indelible impression on the mind, and 'You're A Big Girl Now' presses on still further with the unsparing examination of whether a decaying relationship can withstand the strains of time and other lovers; and then with 'Idiot Wind' we return to these themes again but with a yet greater intensity.

Seen first as a sort of 'Positively 4th Street Revisited', it is not the album's most successful song. The too-personal bone-scraping jars:

Someone's got it in for me
They're planting stories in the press . . .

> *I haven't known peace and quiet*
> *For so long I can't remember what it's like . . .*
>
> *You'll find out when you reach the top*
> *You're on the bottom . . .*

It also produces, in Dylan, a need to step back from that extra-personal quality somehow: and he does so in the wrong way, by stylising his delivery of the anger so that his voice at those points comes across with a faked-sounding passion.

Yet this is a small element in the song. It deepens into one of infinitely greater emotional range than a 'Positively 4th Street'. The idiot wind that blows is the whole conglomeration of things that assail our integrity and of love that renders us hapless and out of control. The song locks us in a fight to the death, in a contemporary graveyard landscape of skulls and dust and changing seasons. Destruction and survival again.

The preoccupation with this just-possible survival one must fight for is urged most eloquently in this tremendous, evocative stanza:

> *There's a lone soldier on the cross*
> *Smoke pourin' out of a box-car door*
> *You didn't know it*
> *You didn't think it could be done:*
> *In the final end he won the war*
> *After losing every battle . . .*

That is matched, later in the song, by the extraordinary tugging wildness of this – a triumph of poetic strength:

> *The priest wore black on the seventh day*
> *And sat stone-faced while the building burned*
> *I waited for you on the runnin' boards*
> *'Neath the cypress tree while the springtime turned*
> *Slowly into autumn:*
> *Idiot wind*
> *Blowin' like a circle around my skull*
> *From the Grand Coulee Dam to the Capitol . . .*

(And what a rhyme!)

Then, in total contrast, we have the lightly sketched humane straightforwardness of 'You're Gonna Make Me Lonesome When You Go', which represents yet another fully-fledged success for Dylan's new simplicity of language. This is a conscious reversing of all those 1964-ish Dylan songs where he leaves his lover for the road. This time, she leaves him for the road. The strength of the song lies in its tone of lively philosophic acceptance: there is no self-absorption, much less self-pity. His love for her comes through from the way in which he accepts that she must go and so tells her his feelings unreprovingly:

> *I've seen love go by my door*
> *(Never bin this close before) . . .*

Much of the song is thus delivered – so lightly as to suggest that it's in brackets, with the same sparkling, generous humour. I think it astonishing that a man who, by the time he made this album, had been monstrously famous for over a decade and had been acclaimed as a genius before he was 25, could have the down-to-earth self-knowledge to throw out, in this song, so ordinarily humorous and puckish a phrase as the one that ends this stanza:

> *You're gonna make me wonder what I'm doin'*
> *Stayin' far behind without you*
> *You're gonna make me wonder what I'm sayin' –*
> *You're gonna make me give myself a good talkin' to.*

Again, as ever on this unsurpassed album, the simplicity of language represents the opposite of dullness of emotion. Throughout, from the deft movie script of 'Lily, Rosemary And The Jack Of Hearts' to the scrupulously checked-in intensity of 'If You See Her, Say Hello' (a marvellous re-write of 'Girl Of The North Country') and from the flawless blues of 'Meet Me In The Morning' to the barbed sanity of 'Buckets of Rain', "Blood On The Tracks" is the work of an artist who has never been of sharper intelligence nor more genuinely preoccupied with the inner struggles and complexities of human nature. Dylan's sensibility here is 100 per cent intact. He is also an artist who has lost, on "Blood On The Tracks", not one iota of his devotion to, nor expertise with, a wide range of American music.

   "Desire" (1976), the album that follows, inevitably has a narrower range, though Dylan's use of language on it – most of these songs were written, totally *uncharacteristically*, in collaboration, on the lyrics, with Jacques Levy – is another (and distinctive) success for the new chiselled simplicity.[28]

   The movie-spinning of 'Lily, Rosemary And The Jack of Hearts' is continued on 'Black Diamond Bay' and on 'Joey' – a song that works only if you take it as the classic American gangster movie in song, and not as a straight Dylan narrative twisted badly by phoney moral weighting. The featherweight pop song is back in Dylan's repertoire with 'Mozambique'. The protest song is back in 'Hurricane' (the weakness of which is shown by how much better the music is than the ideas behind the words; the hollowness of 'He could have bin the champion of the world' was assured, years and years earlier, by Dylan's own youthful 'Davey Moore'). And on the more substantial songs on "Desire" there is, regrettably, a distinct falling-away from the surgical incisiveness of the "Blood On The Tracks" collection by virtue of Dylan's shift of preoccupation, away from an engaged concentration on the corrosions of time

---

28. Levy had earlier co-written songs with Roger McGuinn for the Byrds, best-known of which (though it's hardly a recommendation) is 'Chestnut Mare'. A useful background article on Bob Dylan's work with Levy is John Bauldie's 'Jacques Levy and the "Desire" collaboration', *Telegraph*, no. 11, April 1983, collected in Gray and Bauldie (eds), *All Across the Telegraph* (1987). There is comment/speculation on Levy's contribution to the "Desire" song 'Romance In Durango' in note 30.
     [The Byrds: 'Chestnut Mare', Hollywood, early June, 1970, "Untitled", Columbia Records G 30127, New York (CBS Records 66253, London), 1970. The single, Columbia Records 2992, New York, 1970 (CBS Records 5322, London, 1971) was a hit only in the UK. Reissued on "Greatest Hits Vol. 2", Columbia KC 31795, New York, 1972, and on "History Of The Byrds", CBS Records 68242, London, 1973. 'Chestnut Mare' and "Untitled" came from the Byrds' seventh line-up, i.e. Roger McGuinn, Gene Parsons, Clarence White and Skip Battin.]

and failures of love, and towards a more mystical, religious focus. (As this applies in 'Isis', it is dealt with in Chapter 7.)

'Oh Sister' has this new emphasis:

> *We grew up together from the cradle to the grave*
> *We died and were reborn and then mysteriously saved*

and also stands as a pretty clumsy attempt at dialogue with the new 1970s generation of liberated women. It is clumsy not least in making bluntly clear, from lines like

> *And is our purpose not the same on this earth*
> *To love and follow His direction?*

that he has not been listening to a word they've been saying.

'Romance in Durango' is another pop song – but it is utterly marvellous, right from its flinty, glistening opening line:

> *Hot chili peppers in the blistering sun,*

which gets a supercharged impact from the minimal melody, the stabbed bunching of the syllables and the desert-burn of Dylan's voice. Pop song it may be – it is splendidly the heir of Marty Robbins' 'El Paso', and parodies that song's death-scene magnificently[29] – but it raises the pop song onto an undreamt-of high plane, through the compression of what is really skilful concentration in language. It has a strange dynamism, derived from interweaving long syllable-crammed lines –

> *We'll drink tequila where our grandfathers stayed*

– and sudden oases of more spacious lines in which, as often before, Dylan says more with less:

> *The dogs are barking and what's done is done.*[30]

---

29.   Marty Robbins: 'El Paso', Nashville, 7/4/59, Columbia Records 4–41511, New York [Fontana Records H 233, London], 1959.

30.   It's impossible to trace accurately those parts of the Bob Dylan–Jacques Levy lyrics which have been contributed by Levy. My own hunch is that, overall, Levy's input, like Sam Shepard's in the Dylan–Shepard lyric 'Brownsville Girl' in the mid-1980s, has been by way of additional *detailing*: that the co-writer encourages an attention to concrete objects and a tendency to insert or retain adjectives where Dylan's own bent is more for 'keeping things vague', as Joan Baez puts it in her own excellent song about Dylan, 'Diamonds And Rust'. Perhaps without Levy the opening line of 'Romance In Durango' would have been 'Chili peppers in the sun'. Or perhaps not.

There is, however, one specific touch in the same song which must surely have come from Levy – from his knowledge of psychotherapy, a subject in which Dylan has never expressed sympathetic interest (rather the opposite) but in which Levy trained. Levy would have known the subject matter described in this passage from Eric Berne's popularising book from the 1970s, *What Do You Say after You Say Hello?* (he may well have known the book and thus this passage itself):

> Amenhotep-haq-Uast's other name (besides Ikhnaton) was Nefer-kheperu-Ra-ua-en-Ra, whose hieroglyphs roughly translate as 'Take your lute and your scarab and enjoy the sun', while according to the Ikhnaton cartouche, he has traded this in for a cake and a feather ... This is like a modern, hippie script switch, either way: people with guitars get a yen for cake, or people with cake turn it in for a guitar.

In the Dylan–Levy song: 'Sold my guitar to the baker's son / For a few crumbs and a place to hide / But I can get another one ...' ('Romance In Durango', verse 2).

[Joan Baez: 'Diamonds And Rust', Los Angeles, 17–29/1/75, "Diamonds And Rust", A&M Records SP 3233, L.A. (AMLH 64527, London), 1975. Eric Berne, *What Do You Say after You Say Hello?* (c. 1972). Eric Berne's

All of this – the sternness towards a song like 'Oh Sister' and the near damning-with-faint-praise of a song like 'Black Diamond Bay' or 'Romance in Durango' – is to under-rate the "Desire" album in ways that are invited more by the fact of its coming after "Blood On The Tracks" than because of its own weaknesses. These, after all, are largely the result of its limitations of scope and intention.

More importantly, the album has exploratory strengths of its own that are easy to overlook and less easy to write about. Never before has Dylan so utterly made his word content the servant of his music. The precise, almost mathematical interlocking of the two is primarily what concerns him on this album. He is serving an apprentice-ship at something new. Who else would do that, after scoring so total a success as "Blood On The Tracks"?

I cannot indicate the nature of this apprenticeship – of honed communication of feeling, of emotion sparked off at the innate mystery of things and places and sounds – half so well as Allen Ginsberg does on his sleeve notes to the album. They merit several re-readings and they make a lot of un-pin-downable sense. In exactly the same way as the album itself, which is thus unique in Dylan's repertoire.

Being unique, and in the ways I'm suggesting, means that it lacks some of Dylan's use-of-language trademarks. One of these is his very special use of cliché, which is apparent throughout the rest of his work and to which we now turn.

'Dylan', wrote Richard Goldstein, 'approaches a cliché like a butcher eyes a chicken.'[31] It is a useful starting-point. There are indeed moments when, with a sudden flash, the knife comes down:

> *You say my kisses are not like his*
> *But this time I'm not gonna tell you why that is.*

But this setting-up of the tired old bird and then killing it in front of us is comparatively rare. Usually there is no explicit butchery. Dylan just *displays* the clichés, holding them up in relish of their absurdity and allowing them to fall over, squawking in the mud, of their own accord:

> *Well Frankie Lee he sat back down*
> *Feeling low and mean*
> *When just then a passing stranger*
> *Burst upon the scene*
> *Saying, 'Are you Frankie Lee, the gambler*
> *Whose father's deceased?*
> *Well if y'are there's a fella callin' ya down the road, an' they*
> *Say his name is priest.'*

---

most famous and successful book was the earlier *Games People Play* (1964), which injected copious amounts of psychobabble into everyday language and preceded the Joe South record of the same name, a hit in 1969.]

    (Ikhnaton is a variant spelling of Akhenaten/Akhenaton, the original name of Amenhotep IV, a king of the 18th Dynasty of Ancient Egypt, who died in 1358 BC.)

31.   Richard Goldstein, note 1.

Dylan also gives us many pictures where clichés help provide sympathetic sketches of human foibles, human weakness, people who wrap up warm in absurd but plausible self-deception.

These sketches flash past without warning in the most unexpected places, in the most unexpected songs. In 'Maggie's Farm', for instance (1965) – where suddenly, after three verses of bitter complaint explaining why the narrator 'ain't gonna work on Maggie's Farm no more', – the half-figurative language of the exposition gives way to this genuinely compassionate summary of Maggie's ma:

> *Well she talks to all the servants*
> *About Man and God and Law*
> *Everybody says she's the brains behind pa*
> *She's sixty-eight but she says she's fifty-four*
> *Ah! I ain't gonna work for Maggie's ma no more.*

So, as we see, she's an impossible, puffed-up old battle-axe rasping out dreadful philosophic homilies; and doubtless she takes advantage of her hick sons and workmen most unscrupulously (you can just see them all going about their labours muttering sullenly, and darkly telling this new hand, Dylan, that they reckon she's the brains behind pa). But all the same we smile for her on catching her at that little impotent touch of pretence, patting her hair into place and claiming to be 'only' fifty-four.[32]

Even in the love vision of 'Love Minus Zero/No Limit', in which Dylan exalts his raven-woman, he has time to infuse his observation of ordinary mortals with compassion as well as sharp observation:

> *In the dime stores and bus stations*
> *People talk of situations*
> *Read books, repeat quotations*
> *Draw conclusions on the wall . . .*

That finely set condemnation – using to the full the shoddy and sad associations yielded by 'dime' in that first line – is tempered by a corresponding sadness *for* them.

In other songs, Dylan uses the clichés for a more simple comic effect: they help to establish an image of Chaplinesque naïveté for the narrator – and since we see Dylan himself, tousle-headed and jerky, as the narrator, the clichés contribute to our seeing a Dylan of comic innocence:

> *Mona tried to tell me*
> *To stay away from the train-line*
> *She said that all the railroad men*
> *Just drink up your blood like wine*
> *An' I said Oh! I didn't* know *that! . . .*[33]

32. Unfortunately what Dylan actually sings is the less psychologically subtle 'sixty-eight but says she's *twenty-four*'.

33. The comic mock-innocence is multi-layered here. '*Oh!* I didn't *know* that!' comically has Dylan as narrator taking literally something that is both so lurid that it must obviously be figurative, and yet sounds so typical of the crazed, city-induced paranoias captured so perfectly all through "Blonde On Blonde", so that he portrays himself here as the innocent abroad, the country bumpkin in the city. But at the same time Dylan the writer also knows that he has taken Mona's lurid warning straight from a classic hillbilly singer–banjoist's record of the 1920s,

Later in the same song – 'Memphis Blues Again', from "Blonde On Blonde" – Dylan plays for a very similar effect, except that this time the contrast between the two levels of conversation glimpsed is not merely a contrast of figurative and literal language but also of the sophisticated and the hick:

> *When Ruthie says come see her*
> *In her honky-tonk lagoon*
> *Where I can watch her waltz for free*
> *'Neath her Panamanian moon*
> *An' I say Awh! C'mon now!*
> *Ya know ya know about my debutante . . .*

The figurative – which is to say, in this case, the surrealistic – language surrounding Ruthie suggests a sophisticated personal elegance in her. The words iridesce around her like a rich man's party – almost as if she had stepped, suitably unreal, out of a Leonard Cohen song. The very name 'Ruthie' fits perfectly the ethos of the lagoon, the fanciful moonlight waltzing and the necessarily sophisticated sensibility that would alight on 'Panamanian' (and it is *her* Panamanian moon). All this contrasts so beautifully with the inarticulate, ignorantly sceptical world of 'Awh! *C'mon* now!' – cliché as robust rejoinder, as deflator of pretence.

Dylan is equally capable of mocking *these* values, where he finds them over-simplified and tired: when, to return to the point about cliché, he finds them adhered to via automatic thought (i.e. non-thought). Hence, in 'Motorpsycho Nightmare' (1964), when the narrator comes to beg a sleeping-place for the night from a curt and intransigent boor of a farmer, we are shown the farmer eyeing him suspiciously, and then we get this:

> *Well by the dirt 'neath my nails I guess he knew I wouldn't lie*
> *He said 'I guess you're tired', (He said it kinda sly) . . .*

Oh that good old working-man's dirt beneath the nails![34]

As Dylan moves through the 1970s, he increases the versatility of his use of cliché.

Bascom Lamar Lunsford's 'I Wish I Was A Mole In The Ground' [Atlanta, 15/3/24, and Ashland, Kentucky, 6/2/28]. This song contains the line 'a railroad man, he'll kill you when he can and drink up your blood like wine', so that when Dylan has Mona re-purvey this, the comic innocence of '*Oh!* I didn't *know* that!' includes at least one layer of playful in-joking about what 'knowing that' involves knowing.

The 1924 recording was never LP-issued, but Dylan had long known Lunsford's 1928 recording because it was one of the tracks on the Harry Smith compilation "American Folk Music", mentioned in Chapter 1 and discussed in Chapters 9 and 18. And as Christer Svensson wrote in 'Stealin', stealin', pretty mama dontcha tell on me', *Endless Road* fanzine, no. 4, 1983, the same line 'later found its way into "Roll On Buddy" as recorded by Jack Elliott and Derroll Adams on a late 1950s 10-inch Topic album called "Rambling Boys"' (about which, as Svensson notes, Dylan tells Derroll Adams in *Don't Look Back*: 'I got a record of yours and Jack's . . . "The Rambling Boys"').

[Ramblin' Jack Elliott & Derroll Adams: 'Roll On Buddy', London, c. 1956, "Rambling Boys", Topic Records 10T14 (10-inch LP), London, 1957; reissued "Roll On Buddy", Topic Records 12T105 (12-inch LP), London, c. 1964; CD-reissued on "Ramblin' Jack", Topic Records TSCD477, London, 1996.]

Dylan later refers to 'Roll On Buddy' inside a song on his album "Time Out Of Mind", 1997 (see Chapter 19).

34.   Dylan shows a knowing alertness to a different kind of cliché, i.e. that acknowledged by movie convention, in the song's earlier sample of the farmer's paranoia, in which 'He cocked his rifle / And began to shout, / 'You're that travelin' salesman / That I have heard about.' Under the Hays Office Production Code, imposed on all Hollywood films made from 1930 to 1968, the phrase 'traveling salesman' could not be used 'in a context involving a farmer's daughter'. (Source: Bill Bryson's *Made in America*, 1994.)

"Planet Waves" gives us this robust bumping-together of two clichés, which wakes the sleeping meaning of each:

> You angel you
> You got me under your wing.

The much later 'We Better Talk This Over' works partly by a similar bumping together, unexpectedly, of two phrases of common currency:

> Oh child, why you wanna hurt me?
> I'm exiled, but you can't convert me

and it's generally true that the 'minor' songs from "Street Legal" – particularly 'We Better Talk This Over' and 'True Love Tends To Forget' – are dazzling successes at conveying much through saying little.

Perhaps the deftest of all his touches in cliché (and not being used by it), is the one Dylan brings off here (in 'True Love Tends to Forget'):

> You're a tear-jerker baby, but I'm under your spell
> You're a hard worker baby, but I know you well
> And this weekend in hell is makin' me sweat . . .

The first two lines lay the trap impeccably – they pile up the clichés so that the listener starts mentally snoozing. Dylan catches us off guard, and at that moment sets off the detonation of

> . . . this weekend in hell is makin' me sweat.

It is one of Dylan's best uses of cliché as drama, as subversion, as wit, and not least as understatement. His success at thus speaking volumes through saying little underlines just how well he brings this most individual use of cliché into the service of his fight, in the 1970s, for a new creative simplicity of language.[35]

Yet when Dylan experiments again with a *complexity* of language not unlike that of the 1965–66 songs, the one album he does it on is the one containing those two songs just quoted – the magnificent, much underrated "Street Legal" (1978).

This album has Dylan's best band, and its rich musical swirl is as unifying and affecting as that of "Blonde On Blonde" twelve years earlier. And while Dylan's delivery carries incomparably more authority, sureness and toughness on "Street Legal", his use of language is at times similarly dense and wild – packed tight with characters, incident, biblical allusion, surreal flights of fantasy and a restless emotional thrust.

The album establishes its own vocabulary, such that there is an identifiable wholeness here. It is one of the album's strengths.

Unlike "New Morning", the comparisons "Street Legal" prompts with "Blonde On Blonde" and the re-alighting on familiar techniques and preoccupations are not

---

35. The "Blood On The Tracks" out-take 'Up To Me' [NYC, 25/9/74], which saw the light of official day on the "Biograph" box-set in 1985, offers another great example of Dylan's alertness to cliché, his ability to let us see a tired phrase anew, ambushing it playfully: Dylan sings 'Well, I met somebody face to face – I had to remove my hat'.

the result of either tiredness or a suspect willingness to please. This is a major collection from a Dylan on top creative form. It is a Dylan, too, whose confidence is matched by his urgency. A kind of direct impatience burns through the whole work, from the harsh blues of 'New Pony' to the re-affirmation of youthful self-confidence that flashes through the middle of 'Is Your Love In Vain?':

> *I have dined with kings, I've been offered wings*
> *And I've never been too impressed . . .*

The same sureness of his own worth (an enjoyable quality when it is exhibited with panache) strikes us in the opening song, 'Changing of The Guards':

> *'Gentlemen', he said,*
> *'I don't need your organization*
> *I've shined your shoes*
> *I've moved your mountains and marked your cards . . .'*

and equally in the closing song, 'Where Are You Tonight? (Journey Through Dark Heat)'. Even on the James Dean level, this has as much flair as anything from "Blonde On Blonde":

> *If you don't believe there's a price for this sweet paradise*
> *Just remind me to show ya the scars;*

while these two extracts hold the authentic voice of the anarchic master-thief of the mid-1960s:

> *I'd have paid the traitor and killed him much later*
> *But that's just the way that I am*

and

> *It felt out of place, my foot in his face . . .*

Self-assurance also bristles through the audacious rhyming, in which Dylan often delights, but never more so than on this collection:

> *Señor, Señor*
> *Can ya tell me where we're headin'*
> *Is it Lincoln County Road or Armageddon*

and

> *I'm lost in the haze of your delicate ways*
> *With both eyes glazed*

and

> *She was torn between Jupiter and Apollo . . .*
> *And I couldn't help but follow*

and

> *I was lyin' down in the reeds without any oxygen*
> *I saw you in the wilderness among the men*

and most triumphantly and sustainedly in the breathtaking 'No Time To Think'. The song uses a profusion of slick, tricky internal rhyming – and its repetitious effect – to enforce the sense of a whirling merry-go-round created by the music's clockwork 6–8 rhythm:

> *I've seen all these decoys*
> *Through a set of deep turquoise*
> *Eyes and I feel so depressed:*
> *China doll, alcohol,*
> *Duality, mortality . . .*
>
> *The bridge that you travel on*
> *Goes to the Babylon*
> *Girl with the rose in her hair*
> *Starlight in the east, you're finally released*
> *Suspended with nothing to share.*

The album's rich swirl provides more of those classic epigrams – or mottoes/quotes that function as epigrams – such as were coming thick and fast from the mid-1960s Dylan: 'To live outside the law you must be honest', 'Don't follow leaders, watch your parking meters', etc., etc. This parade is joined on "Street Legal" by the hilarious, poky 'son this ain't a dream no more, it's The Real Thing!', and 'I don't have to be no doctor, babe / To see that you're madly in love'.

'Baby, Stop Crying' contains a couple of notable back-references too. The offer made to Queen Jane Approximately – 'when ya want somebody ya don't have to speak to, won't you come see me Queen Jane' becomes, in the newer song, reversed into the more conventional

> *Or if you just want a friend you can talk to*

– with Dylan deliberately exposing this conventionality as part of his evocation of a much more hapless narrator figure. 'Baby, Stop Crying' also uses exactly the same I know-and-you-know motif in its chorus as did the gloating, vicious 'Tell Me, Momma' of 1966 – again underlining in how different a relationship to the woman the song addresses its narrator now stands. He is no longer the hard, detached Brando figure of those days (the on-screen Brando who sneered at a pestering girlfriend 'Waddaya want me to do – send you some flowers?');[36] he is locked in helpless love this time around – coaxing, pleading, entirely entangled.

Finally there is, in 'Baby, Stop Crying', that magnificent sharp dart of humour, Dylan taking a moment out of the general bogged-downness of the song to flash us a little display of his deftness:

> *Go down to the river, babe,*
> *Honey, I will meet you there.*

36. *The Wild One*, Columbia, US, directed Laslo Benedek, 1954.

> *Go down to the river, babe,*
> *Honey, I will pay your fare*

– which parallels the same double-take of subject matter we find in the 1975 "Blood On The Tracks" song 'You're A Big Girl Now':

> *Bird on the horizon, sittin' on a fence*
> *He's singin' his song for me at his own expense . . .*

(and also, come to that, parallels what is at heart the same double-take process here, in the very much earlier 'Lay Down Your Weary Tune':

> *The cryin' rain like a trumpet sang*
> *And asked for no applause.)*

If, then, Dylan strays on "Street Legal" from his overall 1970s pursuit of a new simplicity of language, he does so only partially, and there is no disputing that he returns to it on "Slow Train Coming" and "Saved". These albums are examined in Chapter 7.

CHAPTER SIX

Lay Down Your Weary Tune: Drugs and Mysticism

Drugs and mysticism go together in the West because most of us are far from natural mystics. We need drugs to open Blake's doors of perception (as Huxley acknowledged).[1] The very word 'high' suggests the connection – to be high all the time would be to hold on always to a transcendent vision. It is being high, not the brute possession of drugs, which totalitarian law-and-order should make illegal, because, as it is, their Dream Police let the Blakes through the net.

Dylan is not a natural visionary in the sense that Blake is. Being an artist, he has vision, but that vision has not encompassed mysticism unaided. Everyday concerns abound in his work – his early self-immersion in the blues, his absorbed concern for music generally, and his songs of sociopolitical comment: songs full of the signs of competitive ego, surface ideology and Western logic, and infused with Old Testament concepts of vengeance. No way is Dylan's mind intrinsically Eastern. Dylan's mysticism must have come through drugs as well as literature.

It follows that, as with most of us, for Dylan 'the mystical experience' was surely sparked off by 'the acid experience'. The West has a million mystics now.[2]

---

1.   William Blake (1757–1827) wrote, famously: 'If the doors of perception were cleansed everything would appear to man as it is, infinite.' The passage continues: 'For man has closed himself up, till he sees all things thro' narrow chinks of his cavern' (from 'A memorable Fancy', in *The Marriage of Heaven and Hell*, c. 1790–93). Aldous Huxley (1894–1963) records his use of the psychedelic drug mescalin (obtained from the tops of the small cactus peyote, or *Lophophora williamsii*) to attain altered states of consciousness in *The Doors of Perception* (1954) and a sequel, *Heaven and Hell* (1956). (In the former, Huxley writes: 'This is how one ought to see, how things really are. And yet there were reservations. For if one always saw like this, one would never want to do anything else.') Blake's work is explored in relation to Dylan's in Chapter 12.

Between Blake and Huxley, of course, lie the English Romantics and French symbolists, poets who share with Bob Dylan and his contemporaries an eager use of drugs. The research on the nineteenth-century poets' use of their drug of choice, opium, was done by Alethea Hayter in her book *Opium and the Romantic Imagination* (1968). This was the basis for the speculative comparing of that period with the 1960s in the late Kenneth Allsop's sniffy essay 'The technicolor wasteland: on drugs and literature', *Encounter*, March 1969 (vol. 32, no. 3). Allsop's tirade against drugs appeared in *Encounter* soon after a scandal erupted over the discovery that the magazine had long been secretly funded by the CIA, a body that had also been secretly experimenting with LSD (see note 2).

2.   Acid = LSD. The initials are from the German *lyserg-saure-diathylamid*, because German chemist Albert Hofmann was the first to synthesise it, in Basle, 1943. The CIA started experimenting with it in 1947, often on people not told that they were guinea-pigs; psychiatric institutions did likewise in the 1950s (USA) and early 1960s (Britain). Non-addictive, non-toxic, this was the post-mescalin psychedelic drug of choice in the mid-1960s and a significant influence on the hippie counter-culture and thus the 1960s in general. It was made illegal in 1965 (USA) and 1966 (UK).

People's usage divided them into those who could use it as a cheap thrill – say, dropping it and going off to a stadium to see a rock concert – and those of us who couldn't: those for whom it was powerfully revelatory, if and

This sort of claim provokes a curious antagonism. We still like to believe in love at first sight; we find plausible the instant conversion of Paul on the road to Damascus; we trust photographs which snatch up scenes and situations in a fraction of a second; yet we use 'instant' as a derogatory term even where it misleads and over-simplifies to use it at all.

Acid only works 'instantly' in that it clarifies: what it clarifies is a wealth of experience and feeling acquired as slowly as life itself unfolds, assembled and blended gradually over the years.

Huxley's idea as to the way such a drug works seems very reasonable: that we operate 'normally' with a brain that filters the information we receive, obscuring much of the actual so that we glean only a narrow apparition of reality. The idea of the everyday filter is not, even in English literature, a twentieth-century idea.

George Eliot wrote in *Middlemarch* that most of us walk about necessarily well-wadded in stupidity because otherwise 'we should see the grass grow and hear the squirrel's heartbeat, and we should die of that roar which lies on the other side of silence'.[3] For Huxley, mescalin rolled back the filter. Acid appears to do the same. It is in this sense that it clarifies: it allows the receipt of perceptions and distillation of experience unwarped by the blinkers of the everyday brain.

From this acid starting-point, it makes sense to attribute 'the mystical experience' to Dylan, as Steven Goldberg does in a contentious 1970 article.[4] He doesn't mention drugs once, and wonders whether Dylan's young audience knows what Dylan is 'singing about', but he makes some good points anyway. He writes of Dylan's 'preparing to become an artist in the Zen sense' and explains:

> he was searching for the courage to release his grasp on all the layers of distinctions that give us meaning, but, by virtue of their inevitably setting us apart from the life-flow, preclude our salvation. All such distinctions, from petty jealousies and arbitrary cultural values to the massive, but ultimately irrelevant, confusions engendered by psychological problems, all the endless repetitions that those without faith grasp in order to avoid their own existence – all of these had to be released.

Acid releases. The barriers and masks we construct in 'coping' with our 'psychological problems' drop away. We release our grasp.

Goldberg's article continues:

> The strength, the faith, necessary for this release was . . . a major theme of Dylan's for . . . three years. In 'Mr. Tambourine Man', an invocation to his muse, he seeks the last bit of will necessary for such strength.

---

when used infrequently and in carefully chosen and controllable conditions. The Timothy Leary of the early 1990s was not a good advert for long-term heavy usage.

3.   George Eliot (1819–1880), *Middlemarch: A Study of Provincial Life*, her greatest novel (*the* greatest novel in the English language?), set in 1819–32, was published in parts, 1871–72.

4.   Steven Goldberg, 'Bob Dylan and the poetry of salvation', *Saturday Review*, no. 53, 30/5/70; collected in *Bob Dylan: A Retrospective*, ed. Craig McGregor (1972); reissued as *Bob Dylan, the Early Years: A Retrospective*, (1990).

That seems both pertinent and clumsy. Dylan is *not*, in 'Mr. Tambourine Man', asking for courage to give him 'the strength, the faith': he has the faith already. It shines through the song with a celebratory optimism directed at what he anticipates finding upon the 'magic swirling ship'. Yet the very next line of the song shows the pertinence of Goldberg's commentary, as Dylan sings 'my senses have been stripped'.

Goldberg goes on to explain how he sees Dylan striving toward a mystical vision from 1964 onwards – and, like all critics, Goldberg gets interesting only when he looks hard at specific work, as here:

> About the only redeeming virtue of Dylan's pre-visionary songs had been an attractive empathy towards the outsider. While Dylan was not to achieve the complete suffusion of vision with compassion until "John Wesley Harding", in "Highway 61 Revisited" he did begin to feel that the eternally incommunicable nature of the religious experience did not render human contact irrelevant. If his attentions were not loving, at least he was attempting to reconcile man's existence with his vision . . . 'Like A Rolling Stone', which is probably Dylan's finest song and most certainly his quintessential work, is addressed to a victim who has spent a lifetime being successfully seduced by the temptations that enable one to avoid facing his own existence.

Goldberg continues:

> Dylan's poetic talents are at their zenith in "Blonde On Blonde". Vision over-whelms him less than before, and he concentrates on finding peace through the kinds of women he has always loved: women of silent wisdom, women who are artists of life, women who neither argue nor judge but accept the flow of things . . . In "John Wesley Harding", Dylan reiterates his belief that compassion is the only secular manifestation of the religious experience; any code which demands more than pure compassion is generated in the imperfection of experience and does not flow only from a vision of God. Indeed, while change in Dylan's universe is the natural form of egotism, it is an individual's setting himself apart from the flow . . . "John Wesley Harding" is not a political philosophy and our attempting to view it as such is to drain it of the wisdom it has to offer. This album is Dylan's supreme work; it is his solution to the seeming contradiction of vision and life. His vision continues to preclude a political path to salvation, but finally overcomes the exclusion of humanity that had plagued his previous visionary songs . . . the creative manifestations of a life infused with God, gentleness and compassion replaces bitterness and cynicism. Where once there was confusion, now there is peace. Dylan has paid his dues. He has discovered that the realization that life is not in vain can be attained only by an act of faith . . . To the children of Pirandello,[5] drowning in their ennui and relativism, Dylan sings:

---

5.   Luigi Pirandello (1867–1936), Italian modernist playwright, novelist and short-story writer; his plays include *Right You Are (If You Think So)* (1917) and *Six Characters in Search of an Author* (1921) (titles which suggest their modernism: indeed the kind of modernism that doesn't seem easy to distinguish from postmodernism). His work prefigures that of Bertolt Brecht (Germany), Jean Anouilh and Jean Genet (France), and Eugene O'Neill (USA).

There must be some way out of here
Said the joker to the thief
There's too much confusion
I can't get no relief . . .

No reason to get excited
The thief he kindly spoke
There are many here among us
Who feel that life is but a joke

But you and I we've been through that
And this is not our fate
So let us not talk falsely now
The hour is getting late

The only way in which any of us can hope to play the thief, can ignite the faith of another and rob him of his confusion, is through love and compassion.

To me, however, the most interesting part of Goldberg's article is his citing of 'Lay Down Your Weary Tune' as a signal of Dylan's changing from politics to mysticism.[6] It isn't amazingly astute of Goldberg to point it out as signalling some change – a song more strikingly different from Dylan's earlier output would be impossible to imagine. All the same, it's a song that has received less attention than almost any other in the whole of Dylan's repertoire, so that it's of interest that Goldberg should focus on it at all. And no other song could enforce, for me, so strong a sense of the acid-mystic equation's validity. Goldberg cites it in terms of mysticism; I would cite it as Dylan's first acid song – the first concentrated attempt to give a hint of the unfiltered world and a supremely successful *creation*. Goldberg refers elsewhere in his article to Dylan's having 'heard the universal melody'. Nothing could better substantiate the spirit of such a claim than 'Lay Down Your Weary Tune' – one of the very greatest and most haunting creations in our language.

What strikes home immediately is its distance from what we know as acid-rock music. There is more here than the evocation of a feeling or mood: the song's chorus posits a philosophy through compassionate incantation, and the verses deal with an enchanted existence, wholly realised.

The tune, in A Major, runs through a simple 14-bar structure which, after its initial chorus statement, is repeated nine times – always with delicate variation.

By the device of having one self-renewing tune to serve both chorus and verses, Dylan doubles the sense of unity which covers the whole song and its images, as

---

6.   'Lay Down Your Weary Tune', NYC, 24/10/63, was an out-take from the sessions for Dylan's third LP, "The Times They Are A-Changin'" (and recorded the same day as its title track). Two days later he performed it, for the only known time, at his Carnegie Hall concert, NYC, 26/10/63, also recorded by Columbia for a planned but never issued album, "Bob Dylan In Concert".

The studio version, long thought to be an out-take from "Another Side Of Bob Dylan", 1964, remained unreleased not only at the time but for years, though the track could be found on the early bootlegs "Seems Like A Freeze-Out", "The Villager" and "A Rare Batch Of Little White Wonder Volume 3". It was at last officially released on the Bob Dylan box-set "Biograph", 1985. The wonderful live recording remains officially unreleased as of 1999.

Harunobu's umbrella shields his lovers in the snow.[7] We find an impression of perfect balance not only between verse and chorus but between the opposites focused by the words – between the night that has gone and the morning announced by its breeze; between the trees and the earth to which their leaves descend; between the ocean and the shore; between the rain that sings and the listening winds.

The melody seems to entwine itself around us, in allegiance to the associations of 'wove', 'strands', 'waves', 'unwound', 'unbound', and 'winding strum' in the lyric. And by its very impingement it urges the felicity of Dylan's analogies between nature's effects and the sounds of musical instruments. As it flows through each line, with a graceful and liquid precision, the melody nurtures and sustains in us an awareness of how involving and creative such analogies are made to be. The tune, in fact, offers itself as an embodiment of 'the river's mirror'; its water smooth does indeed run like a hymn.

In contrast, the solo guitar accompaniment involves itself less with the verses than with the chorus. Based on the three simple chords of A, D and E, it does offer a strength in its strings. Paradoxically, it achieves this strength through strumming: and this maintains a rhythm that is at once flexible – responsive to Dylan's voice – and insistent, almost marching (as on a pilgrimage) in its beat.

Dylan's voice on this track is as expressive as ever of distilled, unspecified experience and a fine sensibility, totally engaged. Handled by anyone else, it would not be the same song: which also means that the words of the song have a complexity that demands such a voice as Dylan's. For the whole song, words, music *and* performance are all central.

Bearing that in mind, as usual, we do need the whole lyric here in front of us to look at properly. The chorus comes first, and is repeated after each verse but the fourth:

> [chorus]
> *Lay down your weary tune, lay down,*
> *Lay down the song you strum,*
> *And rest yourself 'neath the strength of strings*
> *No voice can hope to hum.*
>
> *Struck by the sounds before the sun,*
> *I knew the night had gone.*
> *The morning breeze like a bugle blew*
> *Against the drums of dawn.*
>
> *The ocean wild like an organ played,*
> *The seaweed's wove its strands,*
> *The crashin' waves like cymbals clashed*
> *Against the rocks and sands.*

7.   The Japanese artist Suzuki Harunobu (1725–1770) was one of the most influential makers of prints (*ukiyo-e*) – the multi-colour print was invented five years before his death – and the originator of Nishiki-e brocade pictures. His depictions of dream-like figures were extremely popular in the Meiwa era (1764–1804) and fashionable for many decades afterwards.

I stood unwound beneath the skies
And clouds unbound by laws.
The cryin' rain like a trumpet sang
And asked for no applause.

The last of leaves fell from the trees
And clung to a new love's breast.
The branches bare like a banjo moaned
To the winds that listened the best.

I gazed down in the river's mirror
And watched its winding strum.
The water smooth ran like a hymn
And like a harp did hum.[8]

Never before or since has Dylan created a pantheistic vision – a vision of the world, that is, in which nature appears not as a manifestation of God but as containing God within its every aspect. (The nearest Dylan comes to such a view elsewhere – and it isn't really very close – is in 'When The Ship Comes In'. There, many aspects of nature are seen as indicators of a deity's feelings: the rocks, sun, sea-gulls and so forth function as signs that God is on Dylan's side.) In 'Lay Down Your Weary Tune', though, the pantheistic vision is complete.

Underlying an exhilaration so intense as to be saddening, there is a profound composure in the face of a world in which all elements of beauty are infused with the light of God. Rejecting, here, the Wordsworthian habit of mixing poetry with explicit

---

8.   It is not only the waters that run like a hymn. It is impossible not to hear Dylan's arresting opening lines when you hear the gospel song lines 'Lay down thy weary one lay down / Your head upon his breast' . . . and impossible for the Dylan who wrote the one not to have known the other: for, yes, it is one more presence on the Harry Smith anthology discussed in Chapter 5 ("American Folk Music", Folkways FP251–253, New York, 1952; CD-reissued "Anthology Of American Folk Music" [6-CD box-set] with copious notes by many hands and a CD-ROM of extras, Smithsonian Folkways Recordings SFW 40090, Washington, DC, 1997) – where the lines leap out at you, as presumably they did at Dylan, from the 'lining hymn' at the end of the sermon 'Oh Death, Where Is Thy Sting' by the Rev. J. M. Gates. In fact they come verbatim – except for that odd 'thy' – from the British hymn by Havergal and Bonar, 'I Heard The Voice Of Jesus Say'.

This begins 'I heard the voice of Jesus say / Come unto me and rest / Lay down thou weary one, lay down / Thy head upon his breast'. When we look at these four lines together, and then at the four lines of Dylan's chorus, we find much shared vocabulary as well as the close correspondence of Dylan's title line to the third line of the hymn-cum-gospel song. The Dylan song even alludes to the finding of a different restful breast, as it replaces Christian with pantheist worship; and that ''neath' in Dylan's chorus is common not to Dylan's characteristic vocabulary but to the world of hymns.

[Rev. J. M. Gates (with three singers): 'Oh Death, Where Is Thy Sting', Camden, NJ, 11/9/26, excerpted on "American Folk Music". 'I Heard The Voice Of Jesus Say', words Horatius Bonar (1808–1889), music Frances Ridley Havergal (1836–1879), collected in *Hymns Ancient & Modern Revised* (1972). Known throughout the English-speaking world, this is commonly described as 'the English hymn', but its words are by a Scotsman. The gospel version has been recorded by several outfits, including the Biddleville Quintette: 'I Heard The Voice Of Jesus Say Come Unto Me And Rest', Chicago, c. Oct. 1928, and 'I Heard The Voice Of Jesus Say', Long Island City, New York, c. April 1929; Norfolk Jubilee Quartette: 'I Heard The Voice Of Jesus Say', probably NYC, c. Feb. 1929; and during the Cottonwood Baptist Church (Rev. Samuel Davis) afternoon service at Garfield, Texas, 20/7/41, field-recorded for the Library of Congress. (There are many other Library of Congress field-recordings of the song but in these cases the repertoire choice was probably Alan Lomax's rather than the performers'. As noted elsewhere, 'I Heard The Voice Of Jesus Say' yielded another spin-off long before Dylan's 'Lay Down Your Weary Tune', namely Memphis early blues singer Jim Jackson's parody 'I Heard The Voice Of A Pork Chop', Memphis, 30/1/28. Dylan's is the sublime, Jackson's the pleasantly ridiculous.)]

philosophising, so that it is explained in a prose sense that the divine light shines through everything, Dylan registers the same conviction with true poetic genius – making that dissembled light a felt presence throughout the song.

The words not only work as images but also as symbols:

> Struck by the sounds before the sun
> I knew the night had gone.

The night, there, is both real and metaphorical, and so is the morning that follows. Dylan uses the same symbolism in 'When The Ship Comes In' (and that song calls to mind 'The Ancient Mariner' by the supreme English pantheist Coleridge),[9] which looks forward to the triumph of righteousness when

> . . . the mornin' will be a-breakin'.

This in turn relates closely to the chorus of 'I Shall Be Released':

> I see my life come shinin'
> From the west unto the east

(where morning breaks)

> Any day now, any day now
> I shall be released.[10]

It is, of course, a conventional metaphor, but a nonetheless effective one in the context of the song we're discussing, because its very conventionality prevents it from obtruding. The song would be much less powerful if the symbols were not contained within their corresponding realities – the symbolic within the real night, and so on.

The morning Dylan sings of in 'Lay Down Your Weary Tune' is heralded by a breeze: and again, Dylan accommodates the conventional associations – associations of freshness and change. The 'bugle' at once alters the complexion of the line. It places the morning more specifically – because the bugle is not commonly a secular instrument – within a context of salvation.

In the following verse, this religious complexion is supported by the 'organ', with its obvious associations with worship and later confirmed by the 'trumpet', by 'like a hymn' and 'like a harp'.

The pantheistic idea is also implicit in the rejection of all distinctions. Each part of nature focused upon is given equal weight: to no part is any directly qualitative adjective or adjectival phrase ascribed. The nearest Dylan comes to such ascription is with the 'clouds unbound by laws' and the rain that 'asked for no applause' – and these confirm the idea of God as an evenly distributed presence by suggesting a moral

9.   Samuel Taylor Coleridge (1772–1834): 'The Rime of the Ancient Mariner', his major contribution to Wordsworth and Coleridge's *Lyrical Ballads* (1798). This comprised 23 poems, without specifying who had written which; Coleridge had written four. 'The Rime of the Ancient Mariner' was placed first of the 23 in the first edition, but 23rd in the second edition, on which Wordsworth's name alone appeared. The collection was a seminal text of English Romanticism.

10.   There is a scriptural basis for this passage too: in Matthew 24:27, Christ quotes the Old Testament prophet Daniel, saying: 'For as the lightning cometh out of the east, and shineth even unto the west; so shall also the coming of the Son of man be.'

gulf between divinity in nature and the reductive inadequacy of man. The perception of this gulf is upheld by the last line of the chorus, which, were the implicit made explicit, would read 'No *human* voice can hope to hum'.

The song also rejects evaluative distinction between the various facets of nature by uniting them all in the central motif of the orchestra: each 'instrument' contributes towards an overall sound; each is concerned with the one divine melody.

This unity is substantiated by a wealth of onomatopoeic words within the song – strum, hum, bugle, drums, crashin', clashed, moaned and smooth. It is further developed, becomes multi-dimensional, because in response to this enchanted world the singer's senses (and therefore ours also) mix and mingle. An open acceptance of Baudelairean *correspondances* is involved.[11] There is a huge tracery of this sense-mingling in the song. What constitutes the strength of strings? Their sound? Their physical vibration? Their vertical parallel lines? Their tautness? Their recalling of classical Greece (the lute of Orpheus, the melodious divinity of Pan's music)?

The *emotion* experienced as dawn appears corresponds to the *sound* of drums,

---

11.   Charles Baudelaire (1821–1867), the first great poet of the modern city, spent his entire adult life in Paris on inherited money, and produced the enormously influential poetry collection *Les Fleurs du mal* (*Flowers of Evil*) (1857) plus other works including the novel *La Fanfarlo* (1847) and the poetry collection *Les Paradis artificiels* (1860). With the verse of Edgar Allen Poe (touched on in Chapter 2), Baudelaire's poetry, especially his sonnet 'Correspondances', was an important precursor of the symbolist movement (initiated by Verlaine and Mallarmé) which used symbols to explore and evoke cross-currents and 'illogical' affinities, especially between the senses.

Drugs commonly make this sense-mingling prevalent and vivid. As Kenneth Allsop noted in 'The technicolor wasteland' (note 1): 'Baudelaire . . . cherished a particular trick of hashish, familiar in mechanized form to the audiences of today's electronic acid rock: the infusion of the senses one with another.' He notes that 'Baudelaire started experimenting with opium while a Sorbonne student, emulating Poe's saturation of his work with the fumes and furies of opium – the *épouvantable mariage de l'homme avec lui-même* was a constant theme of Poe's which Baudelaire found enthralling.' cf. Bob Dylan, 1966: 'I wouldn't advise anyone to use drugs . . . But opium and hash and pot – now, those things aren't drugs; they just bend your mind a little. I think *everybody*'s mind should be bent once in a while.' Oddly, he went on to say this: 'Not by LSD, though. LSD is medicine – a different kind of medicine. It makes you aware of the universe so to speak; you realize how foolish *objects* are. But LSD is not for groovy people; it's for mad, hateful people who want revenge . . . They ought to use it at the Geneva Convention.' ['The *Playboy* interview: Bob Dylan: a candid conversation with the iconoclastic idol of the folk-rock set', *Playboy*, March 1966.]

Dylan's mention of Baudelaire on the terrific sleeve notes to "Planet Waves" implies that he was struck by the poet very early on: 'Duluth – where Baudelaire Lived & Goya cashed in his Chips, where Joshua brought the house down!'; cf. his saying, in the interviews for his "Biograph" box-set, that 'Suzie Rotolo, a girlfriend of mine in New York, later turned me on to all the French poets.'

Robert Shelton (in *No Direction Home*, 1986) quotes Dave Van Ronk on asking Dylan whether he was aware of the French symbolists:

> I did come on to Bob about François Villon. I also told him about Rimbaud and Apollinaire. I once asked Bobby: 'Have you ever heard about Rimbaud?' He said: 'Who?' I repeated: 'Rimbaud – R-I-M-B-A-U-D. He's a French poet. You really ought to read him,' I said . . . Much later, I was up at his place . . . On his shelf I discovered a book of translations of French symbolist poets that had obviously been thumbed through over a period of years! . . . I didn't mention Rimbaud to him again until I heard his 'A Hard Rain's A-Gonna Fall' . . . I said to Bob: 'You know, that song of yours is heavy in symbolism, don't you?' He said: 'Huh?'

Wissolik and McGrath's *Bob Dylan's Words* (1994) suggests a direct parallel between lines in 'Idiot Wind' – 'One day you'll be in the ditch, flies buzzin' around your eyes / Blood on your saddle . . . blowing through the flowers on your tomb' – and a passage from Baudelaire's *Les Fleurs du mal* poem 'The Carcass', in which two lovers see the rotting corpse of an animal in the road: 'The flies buzzed and hissed on these filthy guts . . . / And you, in your turn, will be rotten as this . . . / under the weeds / under blossoming grass'. Wissolik and McGrath suggest too a direct correspondence between lines from Dylan's '11 Outlined Epitaphs' – 'cats across the roof / mad in love / scream into the drainpipes' – and a passage from Baudelaire's 'Spleen LXXVII': 'My cat . . . wails in the rain-spouts like a swollen ghost.' (These translations may or may not be taken from *An Anthology of French Poetry from Nerval to Valéry*, ed. Angel Flores [1958] which Wissolik and McGrath suggest as the volume Dylan 'probably used in the early 1960s'.)

and mingling such as this helps give the verse its haunting pull on the listener – an effect far beyond the simple dynamics of alliteration in that

> . . . *breeze like a bugle blew*
> *Against the drums of dawn.*

'The ocean wild' produces an image of movement – a thing felt as well as seen (and the cadence of that phrase as carried by the melody emphasises the sensation) – and corresponds not only to the sound but also to the physical act of playing the organ. The correspondence between ocean and organ depends also for its total effect on the similarity of sound between the two words and on the striking antithesis between an ocean being clean and sharp and an organ seeming musty and somehow imprecise; yet at the same time the antithesis is resolved by the impression of depth (again, metaphorical as well as real) common to both.

Part of the sense-mingling achieved by 'the cryin' rain like a trumpet sang' is surrealistic. Fleetingly, we get a visual image of the rain becoming a trumpet. This belies the effect of that 'cryin'', because to transform itself (from silver-grey to gold) into a singing trumpet, the rain must pour out, if not upwards, then horizontally like musical notes on a sheet of manuscript. It is a tribute to Dylan's achievement that we can accept, in passing, this strangeness of effect without finding it a distraction.

Again, the cadence of the melody works perfectly: the notes that carry the words 'rain like a' ascend so that they enact the pressing down of consecutive trumpet stops. Not only that, but the 'a' is held, extended, so that the 'trumpet' emerges on resolving notes; and we accept the image readily because the music that presents it returns us to base. To produce the 'trumpet' image on homecoming notes lends it a certain familiarity. The image remains striking, but not incongruous.

The cadence is equally cooperative in the first line of that same verse, where again it enacts what the words describe: it allows a graceful unwinding of the voice from the cushioning effect of that 'unwound', where the second syllable lingers, in the air, and dissolves into the cascading fall of 'beneath the skies'.

In fact not one phrase in the lyric fails to gain an extra power from the cadence – which shows how delicate and responsive Dylan's variations are within his 'simple' and economical 14-bar melody.[12]

(None of these devices, of course, depends for its effectiveness on the kind of identification parade attempted above. Being poetic devices, they work inwardly and unseen. The song only needs its listener to have an open responsiveness to nuance.)

The song is enriched in another small way: it echoes the Elven songs that celebrate Lothlorien in Tolkien's *Lord of the Rings*.[13]

---

12. Joan Baez was a factor in Dylan's work on this melody, which he says comes from a (traditional) Scottish ballad. He says in the "Biograph" box-set interview: 'I wrote [that] on the West Coast, at Joan Baez's house. She had a place outside Big Sur. I had heard a Scottish ballad on an old 78 record that I was trying to really capture the feeling of, that was haunting me. I couldn't get it out of my head. There were no lyrics or anything, it was just a melody – had bagpipes and a lot of stuff in it. I wanted lyrics that would feel the same way. I don't remember what the original record was, but ['Lay Down Your Weary Tune'] was pretty similar to that – the melody anyway.'

13. J. R. R. Tolkien (1892–1973): *The Lord of the Rings*, first published in three volumes, 1954–55. Longer and more ambitious than *The Hobbit* (1937), *The Lord of the Rings* is a work of fantasy fiction, but grounded in Tolkien's huge knowledge of medieval languages, Anglo-Saxon literature and folklore. Its portrayal of an idealised rural England threatened with destruction by evil forces found favour in the 1960s among those who had grown

Like Dylan's world in 'Lay Down Your Weary Tune' Lothlorien is pastoral. ('Pastoral', of course, is most pointedly applicable to the Dylan song in that conceit which opens the fourth verse. The idea of leaves forsaking the branches – arms – of their first love for the welcoming breast of the earth is a surprising one for Dylan: surprisingly traditional. It seems to have escaped from a poem by, say, Wordsworth, or Thomas Hardy, or even Matthew Arnold.)

Like Dylan's world, too, Lothlorien is a paradise, spiritual because real. Colours and sounds are ennobled and enhanced, and that there is an ethereal quality which caresses everything is no denial of the intense reality. It is an extra quality, endowed by the light – which Dylan manages to suggest in his world also.

That 'Lay Down Your Weary Tune' does echo Tolkien is first apparent when Legolas sings 'a song of the maiden Nimrodel, who bore the same name as the stream beside which she lived long ago . . . In a soft voice hardly to be heard amid the rustle of the leaves above . . . he began:

> *An Elven-maid there was of old,*
> *A shining star by day:*
> *Her mantle white was hemmed with gold*
> *Her shoes of silver-grey.*
>
> *A star was bound upon her brows,*
> *A light was on her hair*
> *As sun upon the golden boughs*
> *In Lorien the fair.*
>
> *Her hair was long, her limbs were white,*
> *And fair she was and free;*
> *And in the wind she went as light*
> *As leaf of linden-tree.*
>
> *Beside the falls of Nimrodel,*
> *By water clear and cool*
> *Her voice as falling silver fell*
> *Into the shining pool.'*

You can at once hear Dylan's voice breathing the right kind of delicate life into those lines; that fourth verse, in particular, shows a similar (if much simpler) sort of writing, as regards mood and focus and technique – and beyond that, it's clear that the whole of the Legolas song fits Dylan's tune.

There are (less precise) connections too, between the Dylan song and this:

> *I sang of leaves, of leaves of gold, and leaves of gold there grew:*
> *Of wind I sang, a wind there came and in the branches blew.*
> *Beyond the Sun, beyond the Moon, the foam was on the Sea . . .*

---

up threatened by nuclear and environmental disaster. In consequence there has been in more recent years much modish derision (the easy sneer persists that it is hippie twaddle) of this vivid, absorbing work (one of those long books that you wish were longer still), which is of an imaginative quality far beyond the reach of most 'fantasy' novels.

(Again, the Dylan tune fits exactly.) That is a part of the song of 'Galadriel, tall and white; a circlet of golden flowers . . . in her hair, and in her hand . . . a harp'. And there we come across a similarity even between Dylan's song and Tolkien's prose.

Tolkien's prose is of interest – the prose that gives us the description of the land of Lorien, largely through Frodo's eyes – because it brings us back to Steven Goldberg's thesis and the mystic-acid equation. And just as Dylan's vision in 'Lay Down Your Weary Tune' corresponds to Frodo's perception of the land of Lorien, both correspond, in turn, to an aspect of what an LSD vision can offer, by transforming an ordinary world into an earthly paradise. Anyone who ever dropped acid will recognise this:

> Frodo stood awhile still lost in wonder. It seemed to him that he had stepped through a high window that looked on a vanished world. A light was upon it for which his language had no name . . . the shapes seemed at once clear cut, as if they had been first conceived and drawn at the uncovering of his eyes, and ancient as if they had endured for ever. He saw no colour but those he knew, gold and white and blue and green, but they were fresh and poignant, as if he had at that moment first perceived them and made for them names new and wonderful. In winter here no heart could mourn for summer or for spring. No blemish or sickness or deformity could be seen in anything that grew upon the earth. On the land of Lorien there was no stain. He turned and saw that Sam was now standing beside him, looking round with a puzzled expression . . . 'It's sunlight and bright day, right enough,' he said. 'I thought that Elves were all for moon and stars; but this is more Elvish than anything I ever hear tell of. I feel as if I was inside a song, if you take my meaning.'
> . . . Frodo felt that he was in a timeless land that did not fade or change or fall into forgetfulness . . . he laid his hand upon the tree beside the ladder; never before had he been so suddenly and so keenly aware of the feel and texture of a tree's skin and of the life within it. He felt . . . the delight of the living tree itself.
> . . . Frodo looked and saw, still at some distance, a hill of many mighty trees, or a city of green towers; which it was he could not tell. Out of it, it seemed to him that the power and light came that held all the land in sway. He longed suddenly to fly like a bird to rest in the green city.

Frodo, like Dylan, stood unwound beneath the skies and clouds unbound by laws: without confusion, in the discovery of release, attuned to the holy chord.

Steven Goldberg contends that Dylan returns to this position from "Nashville Skyline" onwards. Goldberg was writing before the release of any of the albums of the 1970s but his account includes predictions about the future, and no doubt he'd be happy for his remarks to extend at least to "Self Portrait" as much as to "Skyline". This is his concluding paragraph:

> It is only in the light of all that came before that . . . "Nashville Skyline" can be truly understood. Perhaps this is a failure of the work; certainly one would think so if he [sic] insists that any great work of art must stand alone. Alone, "Nashville Skyline" is a tightly written, cleverly executed series of clichés that would seem to be merely a collection of nice songs by a Dylan who has gotten a bit mentally

plump. As the final step in Dylan's search for God, however, it is a lovely paean. Dylan's acknowledgement of the joy of a life suffused with compassion and God. If this does not make the album particularly illuminating for the man who is unaware of Dylan's cosmology, to others it is evidence that he has finally been able to bring it all back home. He has heard the universal melody through the galaxies of chaos and has found that the galaxies were a part of the melody. The essence that Dylan has discovered and explored is a part of him at last. There will be no more bitterness, no more intellectualization, no more explanation. There will only be Dylan's existence and the joyous songs which flow naturally from it.

Predicting the future is hazardous and Goldberg might have known better than to do it in regard to Bob Dylan. No more bitterness, no more intellectualisation, no more explanation indeed. And "Nashville Skyline" as 'the final step in Dylan's search for God' – not quite.

CHAPTER SEVEN

The Coming of the Slow Train

Though thou loved her as thyself,
As a self of purer clay,
Though her parting dims the day,
Stealing grace from all alive;
Heartily know,
When half gods go,
The gods arrive.

Ralph Waldo Emerson, 'Give All to Love', 1847

Bob Dylan has always given us songs that burned with a moral sense. This was true in 1962 when he was transcribing the morality of Woody Guthrie:

Now a very great man once said
Some people rob you with a fountain pen
It don't take too long to find out
Just what he was talkin' about.
A lot of people don't have much food on their table
But they got a lot of forks 'n' knives
And they gotta cut somethin'

and it has remained crucial in Dylan's work ever since. He was happy to transcribe also an *Old* Testament vengefulness in the early gospel-influenced material:

Tell me what you gonna do
When death comes creepin' in your room?

(from the unreleased 'Whatcha Gonna Do') and, from 'Masters Of War':

Even Jesus will never forgive what you do

while 'Quit Your Low-Down Ways' includes this:

You can read out your Bible
You can fall down on your knees

Pretty mama and pray to the Lord
But it ain't gonna do no good ...[1]

The biblical quotations and allusions pour readily out of the early 'protest' songs such as 'The Times They Are A-Changin'', 'A Hard Rain's A-Gonna Fall' and 'When The Ship Comes In' too. But it is in the work that burgeoned in the mid-1960s that Dylan the moralist asserts himself forcefully with a new complexity which people have commonly mistaken for an amorality or a denial of moral judgement.

The songs that included 'she knows too much to argue or to judge', 'there are no sins inside the gates of Eden', 'to live outside the law you must be honest', 'don't follow leaders' and so on – that favourite side of Bob Dylan was never urging on us the unimportance of moral clarity. He was arguing that to achieve that clarity, the individual must shake off the hand-me-down conventional moral codes and the judgements we make thoughtlessly from them. He was pressing his generation to take the solo flight of responsibility for arriving at its own morality.

This is everywhere in Dylan's work from 1961 to 1978. When, in 1979, Dylan declared himself Born Again, the turnabout was in his acceptance, after all those years, of an outside, handed-down moral code – the Bible accepted as the authentic voice of God and Jesus embraced as the true son of God. It was a complete *volte face* from

live by no man's code

(on 'I Am A Lonesome Hobo', "John Wesley Harding", 1968) to

There's only one authority
That's the authority on high

---

1.   The first of these three quotations is from 'Talkin' New York', on Dylan's first album. I suspect that 'Whatcha Gonna Do?', copyrighted in 1963 and 1966 as a Bob Dylan song, rests heavily on an old black church song, variously titled, and recorded for instance in the 1930s as 'When Death Comes Creeping In Your Room' by the Golden Eagle Gospel Singers, Chicago, 11/5/37. I doubt that Dylan did more than tweak one or two lines, if that, of the lyric he publishes as his own in *Writings and Drawings* (1972) and *Lyrics 1962–1985* (1986). However, the line 'When death comes slippin' in your room' also occurs in the chorus of the otherwise dissimilar gospel song 'You're Gonna Need Somebody On Your Bond', recorded twice by the great Blind Willie Johnson ['You'll Need Somebody On Your Bond', New Orleans, 11/12/29, and the last side he ever recorded, the superior 'You're Gonna Need Somebody On Your Bond', Atlanta, 20/4/30; both reissued on the 2-CD set "The Complete Blind Willie Johnson", Columbia Legacy Records Roots N' Blues Series 472190 2, New York, 1993] and subsequently a standard repertoire item [often performed by Big Joe Williams as 'You're Gonna Need King Jesus' and by Sonny Terry and Brownie McGhee as 'I've Been 'Buked And I've Been Scorned'] and which moved across into the Folk Revivalist repertoire, not least because the superior take by Johnson was one of the tracks on "The Country Blues", RBF Records RF-1, New York, 1959: the compilation LP by Sam Charters that was the most important and influential early vinyl issue of old blues after Harry Smith's anthology of 1952 ["American Folk Music", set of 3 double-LPs (Vol. 1: Ballads; Vol. 2: Social Music; Vol. 3: Songs), Folkways Records FP251–253, NYC, 1952; CD-reissued as "Anthology Of American Folk Music" (6-CD box-set) with copious notes by many hands and a CD-ROM of extras, Smithsonian Folkways Recordings SFW 40090, Washington, DC, 1997].

Dylan cut two versions of 'Whatcha Gonna Do?', one at the "Freewheelin' Bob Dylan" sessions [NYC, 14/2/62] and another as a songwriter's demo (!) for Witmark [August 1963]. The latter is the version published in the lyric collections; the former I quote above.

'Quit Your Low-Down Ways', copyrighted in 1963 and 1964 as a Dylan song, may also derive ultimately from an old gospel song; certainly the verse I quote is lifted directly from the great Kokomo Arnold's own recording of his 'Milk Cow Blues' [Chicago, 10/9/34] (this is discussed in Chapter 9). As with 'Whatcha Gonna Do?', Dylan cut 'Quit Your Low-Down Ways' at the "Freewheelin'" sessions [NYC, 9/7/62] and as a Witmark demo [NYC, December 1962]. He also performed it – introducing it with 'Here's a funny one...' – at the Finjan Club, Montreal, 2/7/62. The "Freewheelin'" out-take was released on the "Bootleg Series I–III" box-set in 1991.

(on 'Gonna Change My Way Of Thinking', from "Slow Train Coming", 1979).

It was not, however, a sudden change from the hip amoralist to the priest: Dylan had seized on a new code, but remained utterly consistent in his preoccupation with struggling *for* a code.

Along with this unfailing sense of the need for moral clarity, Dylan's work has also been consistently characterised by a yearning for salvation. In fact the quest for salvation might well be called the central theme of Bob Dylan's entire output. To survive, you must attain that clarity of morality: you won't even get by without going that far, and then you must go beyond – get rescued from the chaos and purgatory and find some spiritual home.

This is the constant theme. It is as strong in the "Blonde On Blonde" period as in any other:

> *And me, I sit so patiently*
> *Waiting to find out what price*
> *You have to pay to get out of*
> *Going through all these things twice.*

That is how 'Memphis Blues Again' ends; and the chorus of that song emphasises this felt need to pass from one place to another – from one quality of life to another:

> *To be stuck inside of Mobile*
> *With the Memphis Blues Again!*

Twelve years later, he is waiting and yearning again:

> *This place don't make sense to me no more*
> *Can ya tell me what we're waiting for*
> *Señor?*

(from 'Señor (Tales Of Yankee Power)' on the 1978 "Street Legal" album) and in the interim we've had the same quest for salvation echoed again and again, from the 1967 'I Shall Be Released' to the 1974 "Planet Waves":

> *In this age of fiber-glass*
> *I'm searching for a gem*
> *The crystal ball upon the wall*
> *Hasn't shown me nothing yet*

('Dirge') and

> *My dreams are made of iron and steel*
> *With a big bouquet of roses hanging down*
> *From the heavens to the ground*

('Never Say Goodbye') and

> *I was in a whirlwind*
> *Now I'm in some better place*

('Something There Is About You').

The same quest for salvation permeates the whole of the "John Wesley Harding" album (1968) and "Blood On The Tracks" (1975) too.

It is the focus that shifts. Dylan's quest, as it is unfolded in the songs, has always been a struggle within him between the ideas of the flesh and the spirit, between love and a kind of religious asceticism, between woman as the saviour of his soul and woman's love seen as part of what must be discarded in the self-denial process necessary to his salvation.

In the early days, woman's love was not enough; all those gotta-move-on songs resulted. By the beginning of the 1970s, Dylan was focusing in the other direction, following the tenets of the "Nashville Skyline" album:

> *Love is all there is*
> *It makes the world go round*
> *Love and only love, it can't be denied*
> *No matter what you think about it*
> *You just won't be able to do without it*
> *Take a tip from one who's tried . . .*

('I Threw It All Away'). By the time of 'Wedding Song' on "Planet Waves", Dylan is even more specifically disavowing the asceticism of the "John Wesley Harding" collection, declaring that he chooses a woman's love rather than religion as his path to salvation:

> *What's lost is lost, we can't regain*
> *What went down in the flood*
> *But happiness to me is you*
> *And I love you more than blood.*

(More, that is, than the blood of the lamb on which later he is to become so keen.)

From "Blood on the Tracks" onwards, Dylan shifts from woman as saviour: and to trace this process is to hear his slow train in the distance – to find his quest for salvation refocusing itself into a quest for Christ.

On "Blood On The Tracks" and the next album, "Desire" (1976), Dylan is trying to do a balancing act – trying to fuse God and Woman:

> *In a little hilltop village*
> *They gambled for my clothes*
> *I bargained for salvation*
> *And they gimme a lethal dose*
> *I offered up my innocence*
> *Got repaid with scorn*
> *Come in she said I'll give ya*
> *Shelter from the storm . . .*

> *If I could only turn back the clock*
> *To when God and her were born*
> *Come in she said I'll give ya*
> *Shelter from the storm.*

The "Desire" album follows this through:

> Oh sister . . .
> . . . is our purpose not the same on this earth:
> To love and follow His direction
>
> We grew up together from the cradle to the grave
> We died and were reborn and then mysteriously saved.

What has to be said, drawing on the biographical evidence that's been available, is that the twists and turns between woman and God and trying to fuse the two – all these different focuses within Dylan's quest for salvation – are, from the mid-1970s onwards, crucially connected with Dylan's own separation from, reconciliation with and divorce from his wife Sara. She is the central figure around whom Dylan's struggle revolves – and Dylan himself made this clear and public, not only by that title 'Wedding Song' but yet more openly, on "Desire", with the naming of a song 'Sara'. Dylan's struggle to keep Sara ends up as his struggle to renounce her: his conversion to Born Again Christianity is the last step down a long road he's been travelling for years.[2]

The fact that it has been so personal a journey – not an objective narrator (The Artist) musing on Woman Versus God As Salvation in theoretical, philosophical terms – makes it more complex than the transitional songs that I've been quoting might suggest. The personal intensity adds other strands, which it is part of Dylan's struggle to try to interweave. Not only are we seeing Dylan-the-moralist move from the upholder of individual conscience to the priest passing on God's word; not only are we seeing a consistency in a Dylan whose songs have always been rich in biblical allusion and language; not only are we tracing Dylan's tussle between woman as sensual mystery and God; we are also seeing, as the albums of the 1970s unfold, Dylan's increased preoccupation with the idea of betrayal.

This strand begins to appear on "Planet Waves" – 'I ain't haulin' any of my lambs to the market-place anymore' – and it produces in Dylan's work something that at first comes across as an astonishing leap of arrogance: that is, that Dylan quite clearly starts to *identify* with Christ. He begins to do this not in the conventionally taught sense – that of Jesus is my friend, sent by God to be human just like me – but in the sense of confusing himself with Christ.

From "Blood On The Tracks" onwards, we are given parallel after parallel between Dylan and Christ: both charismatic leaders, both message-bringers to their people, both martyrs because both *get betrayed*.[3] In retrospect, it is as if Dylan

---

2.   I feel some unease about taking the biographical approach so baldly in this chapter – it had never been my chosen critical method before to 'interpret' the songs as if they were autobiographical statements, even though a general consciousness of the sort of person the artist was had inevitably been a part of what informed my writing about his work. The break-up of Dylan's marriage, though, and his conversion to Christ: these were subjects Dylan elected to tackle head-on in his work and it seemed valid to write about the pattern I saw as tracing through these changes in the albums released 1975–78. I still see these ingredients in the albums but feel some unease at having ascribed to the songs, crudely as it seems to me now, such direct bulletins on the state of the artist's marriage. See also note 8.

3.   It seems to me that in the period after his outburst of evangelism is over, in the early 1980s, he looks back at his Christ–Dylan parallels with an admirable rigour, a rigour which avoids simplistic revisionist declarations. In

eventually converts to Christianity because of the way he has identified with Christ and understood his struggles through his own.

Dylan had had one eye on Jesus ever since the motorcycle crash of 1966 (or ever since, as he confessed in 'Sara', he had 'taken the cure' the same year). The unreleased 'Sign On The Cross' from the 1967 Basement Tapes declared:

> *. . . I know in my head*
> *That we're all so misled*
> *And it's that old sign on the cross*
> *That worries me . . .*
> *You might think you're weak*
> *But I mean to say you're strong*
> *Yes you are*
> *If that sign on the cross*
> *If it begins to worry you;*

but it is from "Blood On The Tracks" onwards that Dylan's *identification* with Christ begins in earnest.

> *I came in from the wilderness . . .*
>
> *She walked up to me so gracefully*
> *And took my crown of thorns . . .*
>
> *In a little hilltop village*
> *They gambled for my clothes . . .*[4]

Those lines from 'Shelter From The Storm' are matched, in 'Idiot Wind', by:

> *There's a lone soldier on the cross*
> *Smoke pourin' out of a box-car door*
> *You didn't know it, you didn't think it could be done*
> *In the final end he won the war*

---

particular he looks at these issues in the great 1983 song 'Jokerman' on "Infidels", which is discussed in some detail in Chapter 14.

4.   The placing of a crown of thorns on Jesus' head is cited in only three of the four Apostles' accounts: Matthew 27:29, Mark 15:17, and John 19:2 – texts Dylan revisits in the evangelical period in 'In The Garden' on "Saved". The scriptural passage Dylan uses in 'Shelter From The Storm' for his wonderful couplet 'In a little hilltop village, they gambled for my clothes / I bargained for salvation an' they gimme a lethal dose' occurs in all four: mentioned fleetingly in Mark 15:24 ('And when they had crucified him, they parted his garments, casting lots upon them, what every man should take') and yet more fleetingly in Luke 23:34 ('Then said Jesus, Father, forgive them; for they know not what they do. And they parted his raiment, and cast lots'), it is explained a bit better in Matthew 27:35 and most fully in John 19:23–24: 'Then the soldiers, when they had crucified Jesus, took his garments, and made four parts, to every soldier a part; and also his coat: now the coat was without seam, woven from the top throughout. They said therefore among themselves, Let us not rend it, but cast lots for it, whose it shall be: that the scripture might be fulfilled, which saith, They parted my raiment among them, and for my vesture they did cast lots. These things therefore the soldiers did.' The mention that this happens 'that the scripture might be fulfilled' refers back to one of the Psalms of David, Psalm 22, which prophesies Christ and his suffering on the cross. It begins with a prefiguring of Christ's famous words 'My God, my God, why hast thou forsaken me?' (Psalm 22:1; later spoken by Christ as reported in Matthew 27:46 and Mark 25:34) and it includes this passage: '. . . the assembly of the wicked have inclosed me: they pierced my hands and my feet. I may tell all my bones: they look and stare upon me. They part my garments among them, and cast lots upon my vesture' (Psalm 22:16–18).

> *After losing every battle . . .*
> *I've been double-crossed now for the very last time*

(and the reference to that 'box-car door' not only reminds us of the image Dylan is to choose later of the 'slow train coming' but also reminds us that the links to his earliest influences are still there: Woody Guthrie's autobiography, *Bound for Glory*, is so titled because it is a quote from the old song 'This train is bound for glory/This train . . .' and part of the soundtrack from Dylan's film *Renaldo & Clara* consists of him singing a song popularised by those other early idols of his, the Staple Singers: 'People get ready/There's a train a-comin'' which uses the same train image to stand for the coming of the Lord.)[5]

There is another song, performed by Dylan at an impromptu guest appearance during a Jack Elliott set in New York in July 1975, that brings us back to Dylan's process of struggle for salvation in the terms we begin to see from "Blood On The Tracks" onwards.

Dylan starts to feel the slow train coming – starts to feel that, pushed on by what he sees as Sara's betrayal of him, he cannot continue to seek salvation through man–woman love. He is extremely reluctant to pull away from this direction, but he begins to recognise a compulsion within himself to seek salvation elsewhere.

The song he sang at the Jack Elliott gig includes this:

> *I didn't hear the turning of the key*
> *I've been deceived by the clown inside of me*
> *I thought that you was righteous but it's vain*
> *Somethin's tellin' me I wear a ball and chain . . .*

---

5.   Woody Guthrie: *Bound for Glory*, 1943.
'This Train' was in the black American gospel repertoire, indeed was a standard performance item for quartets, recorded by, among others, the catchily named Florida Normal & Industrial Institute Quartette [as 'Dis Train', NYC, early Sept. 1922], Bryants Jubilee Quartet [NYC, 20/3/31, as by The (Famous) Garland Jubilee Singers] and, prominently, Sister Rosetta Tharpe [originally NYC, 10/1/39], who re-cut it several times post-war. Her 1947 version [NYC, 1/7/47, Decca Records 48043 (78rpm), New York] was a hit on the 'race' charts. Post-war it has been recorded by everyone from Peter, Paul & Mary to Bunny Wailer. It is also one of the songs to which Bob Dylan refers so poignantly within his own lyrics on the 1997 "Time Out Of Mind". 'This Train' also became secularised into the Little Walter hit 'My Babe' [Chicago, 25/1/55, Checker Records 811, Chicago, 1955], 'written' by Willie Dixon.
The Staple Singers may have popularised 'People Get Ready' but I can find no evidence that they recorded it. However, Pops (Roebuck) Staples has recorded it, and a version of Dylan's 'Gotta Serve Somebody', Los Angeles, c. 1994, on "Father, Father", Point Blank Records VPBCD 19, Los Angeles [Point Blank 7243 8 39638, London], 1994. The song was first a hit by the Impressions, fronted by Curtis Mayfield, its composer: 'People Get Ready', Chicago, 26/10/64, ABC-Paramount Records 10622, Hollywood [HMV Records POP 1408, London], 1965. We know that Dylan was familiar with this more or less immediately after its release, for the Impressions album containing it ["The Big Sixteen", ABC-Paramount Records, Hollywood (HMV Records CLP 1935, London), 1965] is pictured on the cover of his own album "Bringing It All Back Home", issued March 1965. Mayfield re-recorded the song on "Curtis Live", NYC, 1970–71, for his own label, Curtom Records CRS 8008, Chicago, 1971.
Dylan was probably familiar, too, with the rough, bluesy version cut by the Chambers Brothers as title track of their début album: "People Get Ready", Los Angeles, 1966, Vault Records 9003, Los Angeles [Vocalion Records SVAL 8058, London], 1966. (They were a hit at 1965's Newport Folk Festival; Dylan brought them in on backing vocals on a rejected 'Tombstone Blues' take, 1965; and he praises them in the "Biograph" box-set interview, 1985.)
Dylan has recorded 'People Get Ready' three times, always obscurely: Woodstock, June 1967, unreleased; NYC, c. 28/10/75, not released officially but present on the *Renaldo & Clara* film soundtrack, 1978; and Bellmont/ New Bloomington, Indiana, 20/11/89, used on the soundtrack of the film *Flashback* [Paramount Studios, US, directed Franco Amurri, 1990], in which Dylan makes a brief appearance as a "chainsaw artist", issued on the soundtrack CD "Flashback", WTG Records 46042, US, 1990.

> *I march in the parade of liberty*
> *But as long as I love ya, I'm not free*
> *How long must I suffer such abuse?*
> *Won't you let me see ya smile before I cut ya loose . . .*

> *My head says that it's time to make a change*
> *But my heart is telling me*
> *I love you but you're strange . . .*

> *Let me feel your love one more time*
> *Before I abandon it.*[6]

This is the pivotal theme of all Dylan's major work of the 1970s. Dylan's journey is from Sara to Jesus.

The work this theme prompts is least interesting at either end – when the Dylan of the mid-1970s is simply pleading for Sara to stay with him and when the Dylan of 1980 is rather smugly declaring himself saved. The interesting work falls in the middle, when Dylan is in the thick of the dilemma just described:

> *My head says that it's time to make a change*
> *But my heart is telling me*
> *I love you . . .*

On the "Desire" album, in this respect, the crucial song is 'Isis':

> *Isis oh Isis oh mystical child*
> *What drives me to you is what drives me insane.*

The song is a long parable – thirteen verses – and Isis is the woman in his life, the Hebrew goddess who also stands for the sensual and material worlds. She is the woman who was the sad-eyed lady of the lowlands, the woman who offered shelter from the storm

> *With silver bracelets on her wrist*
> *And flowers in her hair;*

the woman whom, in 'Idiot Wind', he followed

> *Down the highway, down the tracks*
> *Down the road to ecstasy*
> *I followed you beneath the stars*
> *Hounded by your memory*
> *And all your ragin' glory.*

She is the woman in whom he has invested a spiritual significance which he knows, underneath, that he is beginning to doubt:

---

6.   This song turned out to be 'Abandoned Love', performed at the guest-appearance at Ramblin' Jack Elliott's gig at the Other End, Greenwich Village, NYC, 3/7/75, and recorded at the "Desire" sessions four weeks later. This version was issued on the "Biograph" box-set in 1985.

> *I married Isis on the fifth day of May*
> *But I could not hold onto her very long . . .*

The narrator in this parable goes off in search of something else – he does not know what – but he searches mistakenly in the same old material world:

> *I was thinkin' about turquoise*
> *I was thinkin' about gold*
> *I was thinkin' about diamonds*
> *And the world's biggest necklace*
> *As we rode through the canyons*
> *Through the devilish cold*
> *I was thinkin' about Isis . . .*

He goes with a grave-robber to plunder a tomb, still wrong-headedly concerned with the material world:

> *I broke into the tomb*
> *But the casket was empty*
> *There was no jewels, no nuthin'!*
> *I felt I'd bin had!*

He is tugged back to Isis, still hoping that salvation lies in her:

> *I came in from the east*
> *With the sun in my eyes . . .*

and then follows a marvellous verse in which we're invited to understand, as the narrator has yet to, that the return to Isis is not enough and can only be another temporary shelter before he sets off on the real, final quest. This is the undercurrent to the verse, but it works so well by evoking the re-embracing of Isis with magnificent tempting humanness. It also pins down in a few brief, deft strokes, a whole welter of comment on relationships in an age in which faithful monogamy is regarded as impossible – something one cannot maturely expect. 'This is a song about marriage,' said Dylan, introducing the live version in *Renaldo & Clara*:

> *She said 'Where you bin?'*
> *I said 'no place special'*
> *She said 'you look different'*
> *I said 'Well, I guess . . .'*
> *She said 'you bin gone'*
> *I said 'that's only natural'*
> *She said 'you gonna stay?'*
> *I said 'if you want me to, YES!'*

That is a truly great piece of writing.[7]

After 'Isis', after "Desire", we come to the really central album in the whole pattern of Dylan's journey from the

---

7.   Isis, *wife and sister* to the god Osiris, was the most important Egyptian goddess, but in later Greek mythology

Love is all there is

of "Nashville Skyline" to the

> *But to search for love – that ain't no more than vanity:*
> *As I look around this world, all that I'm finding*
> *Is the saving grace that's over me*

of "Saved".

The truly central album is "Street Legal" (1978) – on which every song deals with love's betrayal, deals with Dylan's being betrayed like Christ, and deals head-on with Dylan's need to abandon woman's love.

"Street Legal" is one of Dylan's most important, cohesive and complex albums – and it warns us, as pointedly as art ever should, of what is to come. It prepares us for Dylan's conversion to Christianity just as plainly as the end of "John Wesley Harding" prepares us for the country music of "Nashville Skyline", and just as plainly as "Bringing It All Back Home" signals what is just around the corner on "Highway 61 Revisited".

"Street Legal" brings it all together – Dylan the consistent moralist, Dylan the writer who draws heavily on the Bible, Dylan caught in the struggle between the flesh and the spirit, Dylan ending his relationship with Sara, Dylan the betrayed victim both of what he sees as Sara's love-in-vain and of all of us.

Consummately, Dylan pulls all these strands together on this album, both on its minor songs and its three outstanding major works, 'Changing Of The Guards', 'No Time To Think' and 'Where Are You Tonight? (Journey Through Dark Heat)'.

'New Pony', the first minor song, is a farewell to the world of sensual pleasures – a fond goodbye to the dirty blues ethic he is so good at and so fond of. It is the dark, deliberately nasty, revelling counterpart to that sad final blues from "Blood On The Tracks", 'Buckets Of Rain', in which, coming after the new-deal precariousness of a relationship in which he notes that

> *I know where I can find you*
> *Up in somebody's room*
> *That's the price I have to pay . . .*[8]

---

became a composite goddess, combining Ceres and Proserpina, Venus and Hecate – and therefore a moon goddess. (In 'Sara', on the same album, Dylan compares Sara to another moon goddess, by his allusion to the virgin huntress Diana: 'Sara, oh Sara / Sweet virgin angel . . . / Glamorous nymph with an arrow and bow'. As a deft allusion to the virgin huntress, this may have lightness of touch; unfortunately it has a heavy poesy – the sort of line you might like to imagine you'd find if Barbara Cartland wrote verse.) The Romans took to Isis too, the writer Lucius Apuleius (second century AD) depicting her as a polymorphous demon goddess (Magna Deorum Mater – great mother of the gods). Sylvia Plath had an enlarged print representing this Isis in her London sitting-room in 1960, and was entranced with the key story of the Egyptian Isis–Osiris myth – in which Isis searches for the dismembered body of Osiris and, finding the penis which has been caught by a crocodile, mates with it.

(Isis is mentioned again in Chapter 13, in relation to Dylan's 1980s song 'Angelina', which also alludes to Ancient Egypt.)

8.   Dylan complains in his comments on the song on "Biograph": ' "You're A Big Girl Now" well, I read that this was supposed to be about my wife. I wish somebody would ask me first before they go ahead and print stuff like that. I mean it couldn't be about anyone else but my wife, right? Stupid and misleading jerks sometimes these interpreters are.' I guess it must be down to me. In my defence, I say that I never mentioned Dylan's wife at all until after he chose to issue the explicitly autobiographical song 'Sara', on "Desire", and that if 'You're A Big Girl Now' isn't about his wife, it ought to be. Part of the song's sinewy strength is that it deals with an experience

('You're A Big Girl Now') he concludes that

> *I like the smile in your fingertips*
> *I like the way that you move your hips*
> *I like the cool way you look at me*
> *Everythin' about you is bringin' me misery.*

'New Pony' is the dark, spiteful corollary of that blues mood. It is there to remind us that Dylan is not quitting the world of sex and sin because he can't cope with it – 'New Pony' shows him on fine form – he is quitting because it isn't enough. As the gospel chant in the background repeats, over and over, his feeling underneath is

> *How much longer?*
> *How much longer?*

And of course that counterpointing of Dylan's sexy, sleazy blues voice by the gospel plea for deliverance is a brilliantly economic, forceful way of evoking the tussle between flesh and spirit that Dylan meets head-on throughout this album.

Then there is 'Señor (Tales of Yankee Power)', which on one level deals with something else entirely. Having an unusual narrator stance for Dylan, the voice here is post-Vietnam America, confusedly asking the Third World to reveal the way things really are. The white narrator seeks answers from the 'señor' – the Mexican/South American. The sub-title, 'Tales Of Yankee Power', is a nice irony.

> *Can you tell me where we're headin'*
> *Is it Lincoln County Road or Armageddon?* . . .
> *Will there be any comfort there, señor?* . . .
> *Can't stand the suspense any more:*
> *Can you tell me who to contact here, señor?* . . .
>
> *Let's overturn these tables*
> *Disconnect these cables*
> *This place don't make sense to me no more*
> *Can you tell me what we're waiting for, señor?*

But while it stands as a classic post-Vietnam song – expressing a very different American instinct for survival and progress from the desperate instinct that put Ronald Reagan in the White House – 'Señor' operates also on what Dylan elsewhere calls 'a whole other level'.

Like the rest of "Street Legal", it concerns Dylan's personal salvation quest as well as the one the USA ought to be embarking on. Here he seeks guidance in the attempt to make the leap from worldly meaninglessness to a new higher ground.

---

widespread among those of Dylan's generation, who found in the 1970s that much-vaunted theories of principled non-monogamy were a source of anxiety in practice, especially when feminism had emboldened all those ex-Hippie Chicks.

In the same interview passage, Dylan goes on to say: 'I don't write confessional songs . . . well, actually I did write one once and it wasn't very good – it was a mistake to record it and I regret it . . . back there somewhere on maybe my third or fourth album.' He means 'Ballad In Plain D', on "Another Side Of Bob Dylan" (the fourth album). We agree about this one; it is discussed in Chapter 4.

> *Let's overturn these tables*

is the Christ-gesture, a swift allusion to the routing of the money-lenders in the temple;[9] and nothing could be clearer than

> *This place don't make sense to me no more*

or the familiar theme of wishing he didn't have to wait any longer.

'Baby, Stop Crying' re-presents the themes of betrayal and salvation.

> *You bin down to the bottom with a bad man, babe*

is the dark, accusing opening line. The song goes on to try to reach the woman, despite the felt betrayal. It is urging her to join him down the new road to salvation, with Dylan still loath to walk that road alone without her:

> *Go down to the river babe*
> *Honey I will meet you there.*

This plea that she understand the need for a new baptism and the need to renounce – this plea that she accept his need for spiritual journeying, that she come along too – is developed in the album's major songs, to which we come later.

'Is Your Love In Vain?', a song that has Dylan asking a new suitor some plain, urgent, selfish questions, again evokes the struggler, the man unable to stop yearning for an earthly salvation, despite his rating earthly pleasures low:

> *Well I've been to the mountain and I've been in the wind*
> *I've been in and out of happiness*
> *I have dined with kings, I've been offered wings*
> *And I've never been too impressed.*

That also gives us another paralleling of Dylan with Jesus, by reminding us of Christ being tempted as he gazes down from the mountains with the devil as salesman at his side.[10]

The betrayal theme – and the spiritual restlessness – is continued in 'True Love Tends To Forget'. Love has failed in both ways, and this song attempts to bid failed love goodbye. But Dylan's resolve is not yet strong enough:

---

9.   Matthew 21:12: 'And Jesus went into the temple of God . . . and overthrew the tables of the moneychangers'; John 2:15: 'he drove them all out of the temple . . . and poured out the changers' money, and overthrew the tables.'

10.   Matthew 4:8–10: 'Again, the devil taketh him up into an exceeding high mountain, and sheweth him all the kingdoms of the world, and the glory of them; And saith unto him, All these things will I give thee, if thou wilt fall down and worship me. Then saith Jesus unto him, Get thee hence, Satan: for it is written, Thou shalt worship the Lord thy God, and him only shalt thou serve.'
    Luke 4:5–8: 'And the devil, taking him up into an high mountain, shewed unto him all the kingdoms of the world in a moment of time. And the devil said unto him, All this power will I give thee, and the glory of them: for that is delivered unto me; and to whomsoever I will I give it. If thou therefore wilt worship me, all shall be thine. And Jesus answered and said unto him, Get thee behind me, Satan: for it is written, Thou shalt worship the Lord thy God, and him only shalt thou serve.'
    Dylan refers to these passages again, indeed quotes verbatim from them, on his way out the other side of his evangelical period. 'Shot Of Love', 1981, includes 'I seen the kingdoms of the world and it's makin' me feel afraid.'

> *You told me that you'd be sincere*
> *But every day of the year's like playin' Russian roulette*
> *True love tends to forget.*

> *I was lying down in the reeds without any oxygen*
> *I saw you in the wilderness among the men . . .*

There is the betrayal – and, suggested by that 'wilderness', the love's failure in any case to provide a fulfilment of the spirit. True love is not going to offer him salvation; yet he still wants to try that route and cling for it:

> *You belong to me baby without a doubt*
> *Don't forsake me baby, don't sell me out*
> *Don't keep me knockin' about*
> *From Mexico to Tibet . . .*

It's possible that, aside from keeping up his tradition of using place names to distinctive effect, Dylan is here using the Mexico–Tibet see-saw to stand for two choices he can no longer accept: the warm, southern world of the sensuous and a cold, eastern, religious asceticism. Dylan knows he must reject, and soon, both his lover and the fashionable Zen-maintenance so popular as a refuge for displaced rich Americans, neither of which offers a way forward to the saving of his soul.

It is a typically audacious leap for Dylan that he can use Mexico as the symbol of earthly pleasures in this song while using it as an opposite symbol in 'Señor (Tales Of Yankee Power)'.

The song that follows 'True Love Tends To Forget' has Dylan a stage further on in his resolve. 'We Better Talk This Over' is an announcement, not to us but to his partner, that they must break up.

It dwells on the betrayal theme again, of course, but it shows Dylan mustering enough artistic detachment to evoke a truly credible narrative 'spontaneity', as if the lines of the song catch him veering between the planned we-must-split-up speech and unplanned, impulsive expressions of feeling. It is a great rendition, fired by a devastating straightforwardness. It begins:

> *I think*
> *We better talk this over*
> *Maybe*
> *When we both get sober . . .*

> *Let's call it a day*
> *Go our own different ways*
> *Before we decay*

and it's as clear from the tone of voice here as from the words themselves that this Dylan is indeed on the brink – and a great deal more in control of his destiny than he had been on the immediately previous studio album, "Desire", when he was singing that buffeted, desperate song 'Sara'.

'We Better Talk This Over' continues with this resolute yet untruthful bravado:

> *You don't have to be afraid of looking into my face*
> *We've done nothing to each other time will not erase.*

Plainly, that is expressing his consciousness of her *ineradicable* effect on him. The feeling of betrayal floods in again:

> *I feel displaced, I got a low-down feelin'*
> *You bin two-faced, you bin double-dealin'*

and prompts his re-affirmation that in pinning his faith on this world's love, he had been wrong:

> *I took a chance*
> *Got caught in the trance*
> *of a downhill dance . . .*
> *I'm lost in the haze*
> *Of your delicate ways*
> *With both eyes glazed.*

In the midst of those two clusters of rhyming lines, as the narrator's emotions urgently switch to and fro, we get this neat deftness of touch:

> *Oh child, why you wanna hurt me?*
> *I'm exiled, but you can't convert me*

And then, having voiced that conviction of the two lovers' separateness and estrangement, he switches again – to trying to reassure and to suggesting gently that she too should consider seeking salvation along lines other than man–woman love:

> *You don't have to yearn for love*
> *You don't have to be alone*
> *Somewheres in this universe*
> *There's a place that you can call home.*

Then comes the sad, small line

> *I guess I'll be leavin' tomorrow . . .*

This is very different in import and impetus, isn't it, from the declarations of leaving in the early 1960s songs? In those, the gotta-move-on instinct was to do with a restlessness that he wanted to indulge not resolve, and a markedly different awareness of the restrictiveness of a relationship.

Then the needle of betrayal injects itself back into the song:

> *The vows that we kept*
> *Are now broken and swept*
> *'Neath the bed where we slept*

and is only just withdrawn in time to end the song with warmer, more friendly resolutions of acceptance and departure:

> *Don't think of me and fantasize*
> *On what we've never had*

> *Be grateful for what we've shared*
> *Together and be glad . . .*

> *Time for a new transition*
> *I wish I was a magician.*
> *I would wave a wand*
> *And tie back the bond*
> *That we've both gone beyond.*

This whole fundamental struggle, and how Dylan begins to confess that it is Christianity that is beckoning (it being that to which his yearned-for 'new transition' points him), is developed and played out in the three major songs on the album: 'Changing Of The Guards', 'No Time To Think' and 'Where Are You Tonight? (Journey Through Dark Heat)'. They chart Dylan's voyage from Sara to Jesus very clearly indeed, in writing as absorbing, complex and vivid as anything Dylan has ever given us.

It is in these songs too that the writer's comparisons between himself and Christ come thick and fast as Dylan pulls all these themes and strands together and prepares the way unhesitatingly for the "Slow Train Coming" and "Saved" albums.

'Changing Of The Guards' is the first of these songs. It opens with Dylan reflecting on his own career, the time and energy spent; and at once we are back on the betrayal theme – but here it is betrayal by the world, not one woman.

> *Sixteen years*

is the opening line and is as economic a statement of Dylan's career-span, and the weariness felt, as it would be possible to make.

The second verse looks back to the beginning of that career:

> *Fortune calls*
> *I stepped from the shadows, to the market-place,*

and we know from that line that betrayal is being evoked. It deliberately echoes those other memorable lines on the same theme that 'Tough Mama' gave us on "Planet Waves" and that I have already quoted:

> *I ain't haulin'*
> *Any of my lambs to the market-place anymore.*

'Changing Of The Guards' develops this theme in several ways.

> *Renegade priests*
> *And treacherous young witches*
> *Were handing out the flowers*
> *That I'd given to you.*

Those lines, addressed to Sara, express the sadness felt at seeing his love songs misappropriated.

These lines, on one level, deal equally reprovingly with the record company – the people whose work puts Dylan in that market-place:

> *Gentlemen, he said,*
> *I don't need your organization*
> *I've shined your shoes, I've moved your mountains*
> *And marked your cards . . .*

But the betrayal, as in the other songs on this collection, is personal too. Beneath a 'cold-blooded moon'

> *The captain is down*
> *But still believing*
> *That his love will be repaid*

and Dylan, recognising with supreme regret that it will not be repaid, that it must be put in the past, recollects

> *The palace of mirrors*
> *Where dog soldiers are reflected;*
> *The endless road*
> *And the wailing of chimes*

(an allusion perhaps to his old 'Chimes Of Freedom' and as such, an echo of that passage in 'Abandoned Love' we looked at earlier: 'I march in the parade of liberty / But as long as I love ya, I'm not free / How long must I suffer such abuse?').

The recollecting continues:

> *The empty rooms*
> *Where her memory is protected,*
> *Where the angels' voices whisper*
> *To the souls of previous times.*

Her memory is all that can be held onto, in those empty rooms; she herself has been waylaid by the forces of worldliness:

> *They shaved her head*
> *She was torn between Jupiter and Apollo . . .*[11]
> *I seen her on the stairs*
> *And I could not help but follow*
> *Follow her down past the fountain*
> *Where they lifted her veil.*

And Dylan follows this immediately with a wild, potent evocation of feeling that shows him creatively in command of language and its freshness:

> *I struggled to my feet*
> *I rode past destruction in the ditches*

---

11. Like much in 'Changing Of The Guards', the intended meaning of this passage is opaque, except that the 'she' here is, like Dylan himself, torn between different gods or fundamental forces. Jupiter (Jove), the chief Roman god (borrowed from the Greek god Zeus), was god of the sky, hurler of lightning and thunderbolts, and the bestower of protection and victory in battle, reigning from Mount Olympus as lord of heaven. His son Apollo, in contrast, was the Greek and Roman god of the sun, music, prophecy and the pastoral life, and commanded the Muses.

> With the stitches still mending
> 'Neath a heart-shaped tattoo.

This imagery from what is the first song on the album is echoed brilliantly on its final song, where Dylan sings:

> If you don't believe there's a price for this sweet paradise
> Just remind me to show you the scars.

'Changing Of The Guards' involves too the Dylan–Christ parallel as he comes to deal with the present-into-future – his own rebirth:

> She wakes him up
> Forty-eight hours later
> The sun is breaking
> Near broken chains,
> Mountain laurel and rolling rocks.
> She's begging to know
> What measures he now will be taking.
> He's pulling her down and she's clutching
> Onto his long golden locks.

That 'what measures he now will be taking' is a marvellous flash of mischief: in the midst of repainting the resurrection, Dylan has the confidence and control to point up and laugh at the gulf between the power of biblical language and the cold jargon of contemporary life.

The song ends with a gentle attempt on Dylan's part to explain – and to urge Sara's acceptance of – what is to come from 'the new transition'. The times they are a-changing, he insists, in a radically different way from before.

To the world, to the 'gentlemen' of 'the organization', and to his lover too, he sings that the change must come now:

> But Eden is burning
> Either get ready for elimination
> Or else your hearts must have the courage
> For the changing of the guards.

It can be all right in the end:

> Peace will come
> With tranquillity and splendor
> On the wheels of fire

but there will be no worldly gain – no instant material dividend to be had from surrendering the old false life. It must be done anyway:

> Peace will come . . .
> But will offer no reward
> When her false idols fall
> And cruel death surrenders

> *With its pale ghost retreating*
> *Between the King and the Queen of Swords.*[12]

The embattled lovers must stop their self-destruction and accept the new regime in which truth of spirit is its own reward.

'No Time To Think' has Dylan still on the merry-go-round – the noisy, mechanical going-nowhere of 'real life'. The hypnotic yet ridiculous waltz rhythm underlines this, as do the incandescent jingle-jangles of internal rhyme:

> *Lovers obey you but they cannot sway you*

and so on.

So here we have Dylan back on the edge, knowing he must make the leap, resist old love and old earthly niggling, yet with the disputatious voices of love and money and public and pleasure and politics and philosophy all vying for his attention, leaving him no time to think.

It is an incredible song and certainly one of the most important he's ever written. Definitely up there with 'Desolation Row' and the other major epics. And in the context of the predicament Dylan ascribes to himself on "Street Legal", it is a brave, unequivocal song.

It opens with the clear statement of his conviction that without a re-birth, we are among the walking dead:

> *In death you face life with a child and a wife*
> *Who sleepwalks through your dreams into walls*

– and 'walls' suggests both the wraithlike quality involved in walking through them *and* the restrictiveness of their presence.

The voices call him back, with their bamboozling choices, their shallow temptations and abstractions:

> *Loneliness, tenderness,*
> *High society, notoriety*
> *You fight for the throne and you travel alone*
> *Unknown as you slowly sink*
> *And there's no time to think.*

There ends the first chorus. The second verse returns to the motif of the tarot, and the hint of the now-familiar betrayal theme:

---

12.   Dylan's 'Peace will come . . . On the wheels of fire' corresponds to the prophet Daniel's vision of the Day of Judgment: 'I beheld till the thrones were cast down, and the Ancient of days did sit, whose garment was white as snow, and the hair of his head was like the pure wool: his throne was like the fiery flame, and his wheels as burning fire' (Daniel 7:9). Soon afterwards: 'behold, one like the Son of man came with the clouds of heaven, and came to the Ancient of days, and they brought him near before him. And there was given him dominion, and glory, and a kingdom, that all peoples, all nations, and languages, should serve him: his dominion is an everlasting dominion, which shall not pass away, and his kingdom that which shall not be destroyed' (Daniel 7:13–14). Dylan's song ends, then, with his corresponding picture of the moment when 'cruel death surrenders / With its pale ghost retreating' – his allusion here being to the image in Revelation of the 'pale horse: and his name that sat on him was Death, and Hell followed with him' (6:8) and who in the end 'were cast into the lake of fire' (Revelation 20:15) – though Dylan here dare not assume attaining anything beyond the falling away of false idols.

> *In the Federal City you've been blown and shown pity*
> *One secret for pieces of change*
> *The Empress attracts you but oppression distracts you*

– the Empress standing, in the tarot pack, for an earthly wisdom, while that great phrase 'the Federal City' stands for the glittering, superficial world we all inhabit.[13]

The chorus that follows develops the betrayal theme, and this is where the Dylan-Christ duality comes in solidly and without compromise:

> *Memory, ecstasy,*
> *Tyranny, hypocrisy*
> *Betrayed by a kiss on a cool night of bliss*
> *In the valley of the missing link . . .*[14]

It is astonishing writing – tight, searing, and yet in full imaginative bloom in spite of the limits imposed by so strict and double-edged a rhyme-scheme.

The struggle out of the valley of the missing link is evoked again in the third verse:

> *I've seen all these decoys through a set of deep turquoise*
> *Eyes, and I feel so depressed*

and in its chorus:

> *China doll, alcohol,*
> *Duality, morality –*
> *Mercury rules you and destiny fools you*
> *Like the plague, with a dangerous wink . . .*

Then comes a reprise of the betrayal factor within Dylan's predicament:

13. The use of the tarot symbols in the work of Bob Dylan and others is touched upon in Chapter 14 in the discussion of the song 'Jokerman'.

14. As Dylan sang a hundred years earlier, in 'With God On Our Side': 'Through many a dark hour / I've been thinkin' about this / That Jesus Christ / Was betrayed by a kiss . . .'. Likewise, years later he sings on 'What Was It You Wanted?' (on "Oh Mercy", 1989): 'What was it you wanted / When you were kissin' my cheek?' The biblical texts include Matthew 17:22: 'And while they abode in Galilee, Jesus said unto them, The Son of man shall be betrayed into the hands of men'; Matthew 26:20–21: 'Now when the even was come, he sat down with the twelve. And as they did eat, he said, Verily I say unto you, that one of you shall betray me'; and Matthew 26:45–49: 'Then cometh he to his disciples, and saith unto them, Sleep on now, and take your rest: behold, the hour is at hand, and the Son of man is betrayed into the hands of sinners. Rise, let us be going: behold, he is at hand that doth betray me. And while he yet spake, lo, Judas, one of the twelve, came, and with him a great multitude with swords and staves, from the chief priests and elders of the people. Now he that betrayed him gave them a sign, saying, Whomsoever I shall kiss, that same is he: hold him fast. And forthwith he came to Jesus, and said, Hail, master; and kissed him.' There are equivalent passages in Mark 14:18, 41–45; Luke 22:14, 21–22, 47–48; and John 13:1–2, 21 and (without mention of the betrayal being 'by a kiss') John 18:3–9.

The earlier 'No Time To Think' line 'One secret for pieces of change' resonates with the same theme, like the more specific 'thirty pieces of silver' in the 1986 'Maybe Someday' (on "Knocked Out Loaded"). The biblical text here is Matthew 26:14–16: 'Judas Iscariot, went unto the chief priests, And said unto them, What will ye give me, and I will deliver him unto you? And they covenanted with him for thirty pieces of silver. And from that time he sought opportunity to betray him.' Equivalent texts, without specifying the amount of money, are in Mark 14:10–11 and Luke 22:3–6.

The 'thirty pieces of silver', many centuries on from the 'twenty pieces of silver' for which Joseph was sold into Egypt by his brothers (Genesis 37:28), suggests a remarkably low level of inflation. (More remarkably, the lords of the Philistines each paid Delilah 'eleven hundred pieces of silver' to betray Samson: to 'Entice him, and see wherein his great strength lieth, and by what means we may prevail against him' [from Judges 16:5].)

> *Your conscience betrayed you when some tyrant waylaid you*
> *Where the lion lies down with the lamb.*[15]
> *I'd have paid the traitor and killed him much later*
> *But that's just the way that I am.*

In the next chorus, the tarot motif itself contributes to the betrayal theme:

> *But the magician is quicker and his game is much thicker*
> *Than blood and blacker than ink*
> *And there's no time to think.*

The pressures are remorseless:

> *You glance through the mirror*
> *And there's eyes staring clear*
> *At the back of your head as you drink*
> *And there's no time to think.*

What a lot that conjures up. First, there is Dylan's perennial fascination with mirrors and the odd, playful way in which they call reality into question – as they have done

---

15. The lion lies down with the lamb in Isaiah – or rather, it doesn't quite: it lies down with the calf and the fatling; it's the wolf who lies down with the lamb (though possibly they're all cheek by jowl). In any case, the Christian understanding of this Old Testament passage is that it envisions Christ's peaceable kingdom-to-come: 'For unto us a child is born, unto us a son is given: and the government shall be upon his shoulder: and his name shall be called Wonderful, Counseller [*sic*], The mighty God, The everlasting Father, The Prince of Peace' (9:6); 'with righteousness shall he judge the poor, and reprove with equity for the meek of the earth: and he shall smite the earth with the rod of his mouth, and with the breath of his lips shall he slay the wicked. And righteousness shall be the girdle of his loins, and faithfulness the girdle of his reins. The wolf also shall dwell with the lamb, and the leopard shall lie down with the kid; and the calf and the young lion and the fatling together; and a little child shall lead them . . . They shall not hurt nor destroy in all my holy mountain: for the earth shall be full of the knowledge of the Lord, as the waters cover the sea' (11:1–6, 9). Dylan may have this passage in mind again in 'Lord Protect My Child', with its 'Till men lose their chains and righteousness reigns / Lord protect my child'.

The lion lies down with the lamb in William Blake, when he extemporises on the same biblical passage in the last of the *Songs of Innocence*, the exquisite 'Night', 1789, in which the rhythms of the rhyming and half-rhyming couplets forming each verse's second half (italicised here) are likely to remind us of those in 'No Time to Think': 'When wolves and tygers howl for prey, / They [i.e. angels] pitying stand and weep; / Seeking to drive their thirst away, / And keep them from the sheep. / *But if they rush dreadful, / The angels, most heedful, / Receive each mild spirit, / New worlds to inherit.* // And there the lion's ruddy eyes / Shall flow with tears of gold, / And pitying the tender cries, / And walking round the fold, / *Saying "Wrath, by his meekness, / And, by his health, sickness / Is driven away / From our immortal day.* // And now beside thee, bleating lamb, / I can lie down and sleep; / Or think on him who bore thy name, / Graze after thee and weep. / *For, wash'd in life's river, / My bright mane for ever / Shall shine like the gold / As I guard o'er the fold."* '

The same scriptural text is also the basis for one of the best-known paintings in all of Naïve Art, *The Peaceable Kingdom*, by Edward Hicks, who was born nine years before Blake's poem was first published. He Americanises the theme, including, in the background, Penn making his treaty with the Indians in 1681. What is great in Hicks' painting (as in Dylan's song) is the sense of inner warring required to attain, or even believe possible, the promised peaceable kingdom. The anguished eyes of the lion, glaring in mute appeal at the viewer, make the painting, once seen, unforgettable.

> Hicks painted no relaxed allegories in which wild animals find it easy to be tame. He shows, instead, 'man's cruel, selfish nature,' as symbolized in the carnivores, controlled by will rather than completely routed. The wolf, the leopard, and the lion do not, it is true, hurt the domestic animals, and those helpless creatures are not afraid of them, yet the great beasts, who were once infected with the lust for meat, are afraid of themselves. They stare . . . ahead with strained eyes that reflect inner conflict. The war against savagery has moved back into its primeval seat, the individual mind. It is never altogether won.
>
> (James Thomas Flexner, 'The Peaceable Kingdom' in *Man through His Art: War and Peace*, ed. de Silva and von Simson, 1963.)

in life and art over many centuries. Dylan shares with Alice the idea that you should be able to pass through mirrors to another reality on the other side. And here, not for the first time, he presents this notion as being of spiritual import. He did this on the "John Wesley Harding" album, at the end of 'I Dreamed I Saw St. Augustine', in which the 'I' figure, the narrator, sees himself as part of the world of blind cruelty victimising the saint. That song ends with Dylan therefore unable to pass through the mirror:

> *I put my fingers against the glass*
> *And bowed my head and cried.*

On the later album "New Morning" we're given this, in that odd little song 'Went To See The Gypsy':

> *He can drive you from your fear*
> *Bring you through the mirror*
> *He did it in Las Vegas*
> *An' he can do it here . . .*

There is more to the image in 'No Time To Think'. There is the vivid captured moment (of recognition) – of suddenly feeling someone malevolently watching you. Again, this brings an echo of an earlier song: 'I Wanna Be Your Lover' from 1965 (when Bob Dylan knew a great deal about malevolence), in which

> *Rasputin he's so dignified*
> *He touched the back of her head an' he died.*[16]

On top of that, there is another echo – and one that, when it strikes home, spectacularly turns around the whole way we visualise the image: the echo of that painting by Magritte where the man staring into the mirror sees the back of his own head.[17]

16. Bob Dylan: 'I Wanna Be Your Lover', several takes, was recorded with the Hawks, NYC, 5/10/65. It was not issued until the "Biograph" box-set in 1985, but a different take had circulated widely on early bootlegs, notably on "Seems Like A Freeze Out" and "40 Red White And Blue Shoestrings". The two takes have minor differences in the verses, in the use of words like 'and', 'but' and 'then', but the bootlegged version is the more assured in its vocal delivery. The lines I've quoted are from this version. The chorus, as Paul Cable notes in *Bob Dylan: His Unreleased Recordings* (1978) 'unashamedly rips off the Beatles' 'I Wanna Be Your Man' . . . But it works because, whereas the lyrics of the first three lines are identical to the Beatles' song, the last line veers off at a tangent.' The tangent has Dylan comically rhyming 'hers' with 'yours', as by an act of will, using his classic italicisation: 'I don't wanna be *hers*, I wanna be *yrrrs!*'

17. René Magritte, 1898–1967, the Belgian Surrealist (he worked in France only from 1927 to 1930), became in the 1960s one of the Western world's most popular and omnipresent artists. Many of his works have entered the public consciousness. Over many decades he pursued the same preoccupations, prominently challenging the relationship between reality and image, famously in *The Treason of Images / The Use of Words I*, 1928–29, in which a painting of a smoker's pipe is captioned 'Ceci n'est pas une pipe'. Likewise, many of his paintings include paintings that take up exactly the same space as the 'scenery' they both represent and block out (e.g. *The Human Condition I*, 1933), or depict broken windows on whose fragmented glass remains the 'scenery' from beyond the window (e.g. *The Key to the Fields*, 1933). Hence the comparable work mentioned in the text, with which Dylan's words resonate ('You glance through the mirror and there's eyes staring clear / At the back of your head as you drink'): this is *La Réproduction interdit / Reproduction Prohibited (Portrait of Mr James)*, 1937. (Edward James was an English art collector. On a bookshelf in the painting is a copy of Edgar Allan Poe's only novel, *The Narrative of Arthur Gordon Pym* [1838].)

(First to use the word 'surrealism' was the poet Guillaume Apollinaire, 1880–1918, in his text for the

Dylan is swift to summarise for himself the plain facts of the predicament he's been examining throughout the album:

> *You know you can't keep her and the water gets deeper*
> *It's leading you on to the brink . . .*

> *You've murdered your vanity burdened your sanity*
> *For pleasure you must now resist.*

On and on goes the struggle:

> *The bridge that you travel on goes to the Babylon*
> *Girl with the rose in her hair*

but in prospect at last there is

> *Starlight in the east, you're finally released*

the obvious echo there, of course, being of 'I see my life come shinin' / From the west unto the east / Any day now, any day now, I shall be released' plus, from 'Isis':

> *I came in from the east with the sun in my eyes*
> *I cursed her one time, then I rode on ahead . . .*

After that, we are back at once to the Christ–Dylan, and it is the Last Supper:

> *You turn around for one real last glimpse of the meal*
> *'Neath a moon shinin' bloody and pink.*[18]

The re-birth is coming closer, and the song ends on the theme of sacrifice and life-through-death:

> *Bullets can harm you and death can disarm you*
> *But no you will not be deceived*
> *Stripped of all virtue as you crawl through the dirt*
> *You can give but you cannot receive:*[19]

---

programme of *Parade*, Paris, May 1917, a major work of the avant-garde by Sergei Diaghilev's Ballets Russes with sets and costumes by Picasso, libretto by Jean Cocteau and music by Erik Satie.)

18.   As Peter reminds people in Acts 2:20, the Old Testament prophet Joel said that in the days before the New Jerusalem, 'The sun shall be turned into darkness, and the moon into blood'. In fact Joel was very clear on the point: 'The sun shall be turned into darkness, and the moon into blood, before the great and the terrible day of the Lord come. And it shall come to pass, that whosoever shall call on the name of the Lord shall be delivered' (Joel 2:31–32). And sure enough, in Revelation (6:12) we find that 'the sun became black as sackcloth of hair, and the moon became as blood'. This typifies the way the Bible deploys incantatory repetition, so that a phrase used in the Old Testament (once or many times) will recur (once or many times) in the New.

19.   This is a deft touch, punning as it does on two such different meanings of the word 'receive' – both in reference to biblical text. First, Dylan acknowledges Jesus' teaching, reported in Acts 20:35: 'remember the words of the Lord Jesus, how he said, It is more blessed to give than to receive'. Yet by singing the line the other way round, as if the giving were easy and the receiving more problematic – 'You can give but you cannot receive' – Dylan uses the allusion to lament his inability, at this point, to 'receive' Christ himself. And from this great line, the song swings into its final, and different, chorus. As noted elsewhere in the present work, this chorus is different precisely so as to signal that this is the end of the song (as well as of the world): a point elaborated in Christopher Ricks' essay 'Clichés that come to pass', collected in *All Across the Telegraph*, ed. Michael Gray and John Bauldie (1987). (First published in *Telegraph*, no.15, Spring 1984. A revised version of this essay was incorporated into Ricks' book *The Force of Poetry*, 1984.)

> *No time to choose when the truth must die*
> *No time to lose or say goodbye*
> *No time to prepare for the victim that's there*
> *No time to suffer or blink*
> *And no time to think.*

This final journey is the 'journey through dark heat' and out the other side that constitutes the album's final song, 'Where Are You Tonight?'

He has asked her to make the same pilgrimage alongside him; she has declined; he has gone alone.

As the song opens, Dylan is *on* the slow train:

> *There's a long-distance train rolling through the rain*
> *Tears on the letter I write*
> *There's a woman I long to touch and I'm missing her so much*
> *But she's drifting like a satellite.*

The second verse is a glancing reflection back to the old New York days. In 1965 we had that scathing song 'Positively 4th Street'; this time it is Greenwich Village's Elizabeth Street that is used to place that finished camaraderie – and thus to serve as a precursor for those lines on the "Slow Train Coming" album: 'My so-called friends have fallen under a spell'. Here, Dylan is anticipating the sneers of his New York world at the news of his desertion to Christ:

> *There's a neon light ablaze in a green smokey haze*
> *And laughter down on Elizabeth Street*

– followed at once by this terrific characterisation of New York City as the valley of death in whose shadow he and his lover have walked too long:

> *There's a lonesome bell tone in that valley of stone*
> *Where she bathed in a stream of pure heat*

– the effectiveness of which resides partly in the pure beauty of calling New York City a 'valley of stone' and partly in the strange double-take of juxtaposing cold stone and pure heat in one and the same place: conventional enough in linking death and hell, but unexpected in evoking the chill and the furnace at once.

Then Dylan's travelling reflections pause to dwell perhaps on the divorce, and the inexpressible gulf between the public story and the inner reality of what he feels went down:

> *. . . a woman in a rage . . .*
> *As she winds back the clock and she turns back the page*
> *Of a book that nobody can write . . .*
>
> *The truth was obscure, too profound and too pure*
> *To live it you had to explode.*

This leads directly to the recollected split-up and his new embarkation:

> *In that last hour of need, we entirely agreed*
> *Sacrifice was the code of the road*
> *I left town at dawn, with Marcel and St John*
> *Strong men belittled by doubt*[20]

(a great phrase, that) and then come these excellent lines admitting that while he could claim his own agony to be inexpressible, she could still pierce through any aggrandising mystification he might be putting up around himself:

> *I couldn't tell her what my private thoughts were*
> *But she had some way of finding them out.*

From there, the song shows Dylan's thoughts ranging through the whole spectrum of the leaving and its whys and wherefores. His irresolution is recollected here:

> *She could feel my despair as I climbed up her hair*

and, invoking the knowledge of his Gemini nature, again here:

> *I fought with my twin, that enemy within*
> *Till both of us fell by the way.*

Recollected too, and confessed, are the betrayals of each other:

> *The man you are lovin' could never get clean*
> *It felt out of place, my foot in his face*
> *But he should have stayed where his money was green*

and

> *I bit into the root of forbidden fruit*
> *With the juice runnin' down my leg.*

No wonder Eden is burning.[21]

In the penultimate verse we return to the idea of sacrifice: there is

---

20.   These are ideal companions – one emblematic of the past, the other of the future. The name Marcel is most readily associated with Proust (1871–1922), who is in turn associated with his ground-breaking novel sequence *À la recherche du temps perdu* (*Remembrance of Things Past*), published between 1913 and 1927, one of the masterworks of French literature and uniquely devoted to the exploration of the past and of the fragility of the routes through to it. 'The true paradises are the paradises we have lost', he wrote in one volume, *Le temps retrouvé*.

There are two St Johns: both, in context, the agents of future salvation. If Dylan means John the Baptist, then he is of course the harbinger of Christ; if St John the Divine, he is the conduit of Revelation. John the Baptist (c. 12 BC–c. 27 AD) was an itinerant preacher, the man who, prefiguring his cousin Jesus, came in from the wilderness, and baptised him in the River Jordan; St John the Divine is credited as author of the fourth gospel, three short epistles and the final book of the Bible, Revelation.

21.   The expression 'he should have stayed where his money was green' is not a common Americanism, but would have made sense to any pre-war bluesman. One of Furry Lewis' best records is 'I Will Turn Your Money Green' [Memphis, 28/8/28]. It means, in Dylan's line, he should have stayed where his money was good, or sizeable. All American banknotes are green, so the distinction being made is equivalent to the English 'the folding stuff' as opposed to the mere 'nickels and dimes' mentioned in Dylan's previous line.

'I bit into the root of forbidden fruit / With the juice runnin' down my leg' offers two levels of allusion. On the one, of course, it cites the Inciting Incident (as they say in film-making) when the serpent gets Eve to bite into the apple, the fruit of the tree of knowledge, and she gets Adam to do likewise (Genesis 3). At the same time, Dylan's lines echo knowingly a whole tranche of blues lyrics by many artists, Robert Johnson among them. (Dylan draws heavily on Johnson in the "Street Legal" period, but he draws on many less well-known artists too, as does Johnson. See Chapter 9.)

> *. . . a pathway that leads up to the stars;*
> *If you don't believe there's a price for this sweet paradise*
> *Just remind me to show you the scars.*

The last verse of the song – and of the album – announces Dylan's final arrival at re-birth. He has made it at last. Yet what is most striking here is the humanity, the generosity of feeling. There is no ending on any note of glee or superiority. There is only a gladness which Dylan admits to, while admitting also that it is lessened by the final loss of love:

> *There's a new day at dawn and I've finally arrived*
> *If I'm there in the morning baby, you'll know I've survived*
> *I can't believe it! I can't believe I'm alive!*
> *But without you it doesn't seem right –*
> *Oh! where are you tonight?!*

So there is "Street Legal" – indisputably a major album, and surely a charting of Dylan's move to embracing Christ.[22]

It is therefore only the *tone*, one of uncompromising certainty, that should surprise us on coming to "Slow Train Coming", after all the struggle between his twin selves so brilliantly documented by "Street Legal". The initial shock should properly be at the leap having *succeeded* – and so the tone of voice switching from the 'oh! but . . .' of "Street Legal" to the severe certainty of 'Precious Angel''s

> *You either got faith or you got unbelief*
> *And there ain't no neutral ground.*

The substance of what Dylan has to say on "Slow Train Coming" and "Saved", tone of voice aside, is not so very different from what he's been saying before. The import of that last verse of 'Where Are You Tonight?',

---

22.   Dylan also began to hint at his new faith halfway through the North American (last) leg of his 1978 world tour, when "Street Legal" was his current album. This section of the tour ran from 28 October (Carbondale, Illinois) through to 16 December (Hollywood, Florida). On 24 November (Fort Worth, Texas) he wore a metal cross around his neck, which had been thrown onto the stage for him from the audience in San Diego on the 17th. (For Dylan's own account of this, 27/11/79, see 'Bob Gets A Little Cross' in *All Across the Telegraph*, see note 19.) On the 26th (in Houston), he began to perform what became a series of re-writes of a passage in 'Tangled Up In Blue': instead of 'She opened up a book of poems and handed it to me / Written by an Italian poet from the thirteenth century', Dylan sang 'She opened up the Bible and started quotin' it to me / Gospel According To Matthew, verse 3, Chapter 33.' This was either a mistake or a tease: there is no Chapter 33. Nor does it work the other way round: there is no verse 33 in Chapter 3. But at the next concert, two nights later, Dylan cited a passage that made a most pertinent sense, singing 'She opened up the Bible, started quotin' it to me / Jeremiah Chapter 31, verses 9–33.' This passage states Jeremiah's prophecy of a new covenant. As Rod Anstee notes (letter to the present writer, Ottawa, 16/12/81): 'As a Jew, Dylan understood this to mean a remaking, a renewal of the old covenant of Moses. But in 1978, when he read or was shown this passage, his heart and mind were struck by the Christian interpretation of the passage, which is that it is a prophecy concerning the coming of Christ.' Its core is the verse Dylan would reproduce on the sleeve of his 1980 album "Saved": 'Behold, the days come, saith the Lord, that I will make a new covenant with the house of Israel, and with the house of Judah' (Jeremiah 31:31; this is repeated verbatim in the New Testament, in Paul's Epistle to the Hebrews, Hebrews 8:8). Dylan's tour continued. On 2 December in Nashville, he sang an early version of 'Slow Train' at the pre-concert soundcheck, and then during the final concert, he débuted another song later to appear on the "Slow Train Coming" album, 'Do Right To Me Baby (Do Unto Others)'.

. . . I've finally arrived . . .
I can't believe it! I can't believe I'm alive! ,

is restated on "Saved" in 'Saving Grace', which must stand as a direct, careful and courageous summary of his new position:

> *By this time*
> *I'd have thought that I would be sleeping*
> *In a pine box for all eternity:*
> *My faith keeps me alive.*

Dylan's brain, moreover, shows no sign of having been softened by his change of spiritual home.

There are some bad songs – songs where the lyrics are inadequate because they're content to parrot scripture or to insist upon, rather than creatively render, a point. But even some of these make terrific gospel music. In any case, there are good songs too – ones that seem to me to indicate a Dylan still alert and sharp.

The songs that stand out are 'Gotta Serve Somebody', 'Precious Angel', 'Slow Train', 'Man Gave Names To All The Animals' and 'When He Returns' (on "Slow Train Coming"); and 'Saving Grace', 'What Can I Do For You?' and 'Pressing On' (on "Saved"). There is also the excellent song released only as the B-side to the single of 'Precious Angel' but recorded during the "Slow Train Coming" sessions – the nuggety little 'Trouble In Mind', which alone would be sufficient to prove that Christian faith, despite one's fears to the contrary, did not dull Dylan's cutting edge.

It's a great little song – gospel with a real blues slouch to it – and the Dylan burn is here, delivered with as much italicised sarcasm as anything from the mid-1960s repertoire:

> *Well the deeds that you do*
> *Don't add up to zero*
> *It's what's inside that counts*
> *(Ask any war-hero)*
> *You think you can hide*
> *But you're never alone*
> *Ask Lot what*
> *He thought*
> *When his a-wife turned to stone*
>
> *Trouble in mind, Lord*
> *Trouble in mind!*[23]

23. 'Trouble In Mind' [Sheffield, Alabama, 30/4/79 + overdubs 5 and 6/5/79] was issued on the single Columbia Records 1–11072, New York [CBS Records S CBS 7828, London], 1979. The final verse of the recording is edited out of this release, but its lyric appears in Bob Dylan, *Lyrics 1962–1985*. The penultimate verse would have been the better omission, since, unlike the rest, the preaching is not sculpted by poetry and wit, but comes spluttering out in gobs of ugly prose ('They can't relate to the Lord's kingdom, they can't relate to the cross. / They self-inflict punishment on their own broken lives'). This track could usefully have been reissued on the "Biograph" box-set, 1985, but wasn't.

The mention of Lot's wife is a nicely achieved double-reference. Primarily, it refers to the story in Genesis in which God says he will spare Lot, his wife and two daughters when he destroys Sodom and Gomorrah with a hard rain of brimstone and fire. 'And it came to pass, when they [angels] had brought them forth abroad, that he said,

Dylan's humour is also a crucial ingredient in 'Man Gave Names To All The Animals', which works on several levels. It's a good children's song; it invites us to smile at the very idea of Bob Dylan writing one; and it's a gentle mocking of the more fundamentalist brethren the Born Again Dylan finds himself coming across in this period, as it tells the Garden of Eden story up to the Fall in ludicrously simplistic terms. It's interesting, too, that Dylan chooses to omit blaming Eve for the Fall, stopping the song on a beautifully hungover note at the arrival on the scene of the serpent.[24]

The repetitive structure and the outrageous casualness of the rhyming also add up to a joke we're invited to share. The representative tone and humour are here:

> *He saw an animal leavin' a muddy trail*
> *Real dirty face an' a curly tail*
> *He wasn't too small and he wasn't too big*
> *Mmm – think I'll call it a pig*

Escape for thy life; look not behind thee . . . lest thou be consumed' (Genesis 19:17); 'But his wife looked back from behind him, and she became a pillar of salt' (19:26). Yet when Dylan remembers Lot and his wife in 'Trouble In Mind', to illustrate the assertion 'You think you can hide / But you're never alone', he is also, consciously and with good humour, paralleling Luke, who famously exhorts us, and with memorable brevity (it's one of the Bible's shortest verses) to 'Remember Lot's wife' (Luke 17:32).

'Trouble In Mind' quotes much scripture verbatim too: in calling Satan 'prince of the power of the air', it quotes directly Ephesians 2:2; in singing that Satan will make you 'worship the work of your own hands' Dylan echoes one of God's frequent basic litanies against idolatry, expressed specifically in parallel in Isaiah 2:8: 'they worship the work of their own hands' and in Jeremiah 1:16: 'And I will utter my judgments against them . . . who have . . . worshipped the work of their own hands'.

In listing what else Satan will bring upon you, Dylan also has in mind a text (from Leviticus) that he uses, with contrasting calm and compassion, for 'I Pity The Poor Immigrant'. In 'Trouble In Mind' Dylan sings that Satan will condemn you to 'serving strangers in a strange and forsaken land'. Becoming an 'immigrant' like this is one of God's punishments for those who disregard his commandments: 'and I will make your heaven as iron, and your earth as brass . . . And your strength shall be spent in vain . . . and ye shall eat, and not be satisfied . . . And I will scatter you among the heathen . . . And ye shall perish among the heathen, and the land of your enemies shall eat you up' (Leviticus 26:19, 20, 26, 33, 38). There is a similar passage, though clearly it isn't the one Dylan parallels in 'I Pity The Poor Immigrant', in Deuteronomy: 'And thy heaven that is over thy head shall be brass, and the earth that is under thee shall be iron . . . The Lord shall smite thee with madness, blindness, and astonishment of heart . . . The Lord shall bring thee . . . unto a nation which neither thou nor thy fathers have known' (Deuteronomy 28:23, 28, 36). The phrase 'a stranger in a strange land' itself comes from Exodus 2:22. For God's recurrent exhortation to his people to treat such strangers with kindness, see note 35, re 'Covenant Woman'.

(There is a further discussion of Dylan's use of Leviticus and Deuteronomy in Chapter 14, in the assessment of his 1983 song 'Jokerman', which includes the lines 'Well the book of Leviticus, and Deuteronomy / The law of the jungle and the sea are your only teachers'.)

24. Dylan is, like the serpent, subtle: subtle about the serpent (the snake). He leaves its arrival clear yet unstated, evoked by the hissing sibilance at the ends of the first two lines ('glass . . . grass . . .') and then ending the song not with the verse's expected fourth line – there isn't one – but with a dot-dot-dot after the third ('He saw an animal as smooth as glass / Slithering his way through the grass / Saw him disappear by a tree near a lake . . .' In technical terms, Dylan employs two devices here: a form of your common (or garden) onomatopoeia – using words that sound like the thing they describe – and the less common device of aposiopesis: a 'significant breaking-off so that the hearer must supply the unsaid words,' as *Fowler's Modern English Usage* (2nd edn, rev. Gowers, 1965) puts it. Thus Dylan makes us supply the snake, and that is the end. As indeed it is, for humankind (and the serpent) in paradise.

In being subtle about the serpent, after being clumpily explicit about the other, clumpier animals, Dylan is again following scripture: Genesis 3, the account of the Fall, begins: 'Now the serpent was more subtil than any beast of the field which the Lord God had made'. (Dylan tracks this right through the scripture, too. It reappears when St Paul re-uses the passage in his second Epistle to the Corinthians: 'But I fear, lest . . . as the serpent beguiled Eve through his subtilty, so your minds should be corrupted from the simplicity that is in Christ' [2 Corinthians 11:3] and Dylan parallels him, again re-using the key word 'subtle', in a passage of 'Precious Angel': 'The enemy is subtle'.)

Man gave names to all the animals . . .

Dylan doesn't lose his sense of humour either when he comes to explaining how, after all that questing and yearning documented by "Street Legal", he was touched by a new woman's Christian faith. In fact there's an admirable comic self mockery about the way he tells it on the neo-title-track of the "Slow Train Coming" collection:

> *I had a woman*
> *Down in Alabama*
> *She was a backwoods girl but she sure was realistic*
> *She said 'Boy without a doubt*
> *You gotta stop your messin',*
> *Straighten out*
> *You could die down here, be just another accident statistic.'*

Neither is there anything brain-softened about the skilful way that Dylan treats the new woman/old lover themes. On 'Precious Angel' he can be speaking to *either* of them, depending how you care to take it, in the opening verse of what is a strongly confident song:

> *Precious Angel, under the sun*
> *How was I to know you'd be the one*
> *To show me I was blinded*
> *To show me I was gone*
> *How weak was the foundation*
> *I was standing upon . . .*[25]

25.   Angels, says the Bible, are sent from God to guide us and/or protect us (much like Good Fairies in fairy tales). Traditional Catholic belief is that every person has a guardian angel. Pope John Paul II re-asserted the existence of angels in 1986. They are defined attractively in Paul's Epistle to the Hebrews (in a passage that also yields the well-known phrase 'a little lower than the angels'): 'Are they not all ministering spirits, sent forth to minister for them who shall be heirs to salvation?' (Hebrews 1:14). Paul is saying that Christ, 'Being made so much better than the angels, as he hath by inheritance obtained a more excellent name than they' (1:4), has all the same been sent to earth in the form of a man, 'a little lower than the angels', for our sake: 'But we see Jesus, who was made a little lower than the angels for the suffering of death, crowned with glory and honour; that he by the grace of God should taste death for every man' (Hebrews 2:9). 'For verily he took not on him the nature of angels; but he took on him the seed of Abraham' (2:16). The word 'angel' comes from the Greek 'angelos', meaning messenger.

In the Christian hierarchy, nine orders of supernatural beings lie between God and people: seraphim, cherubim and thrones (contemplating God and reflecting his glory); dominations, virtues and powers (regulators of the universe); and principalities, archangels and angels (ministering to humanity). In a passage that transcends these risible delineations, Paul passionately lists some of these orders out of sheer exuberance: 'For I am persuaded, that neither death, nor life, nor angels, nor principalities, nor powers, nor things present, nor things to come, Nor height, nor depth, nor any other creature, shall be able to separate us from the love of God, which is in Christ Jesus our Lord' (Romans 8:38–39).

Angels in the Bible are always male: only in modern times have they become feminised and sexualised, by a process of colloquialisation, into women with 'heavenly bodies'. This transformation may have come in stages, via Florence Nightingale (1820–1910), who organised, for the first time, a nursing service, taking a team of nurses to tend the copious wounded of the Crimean War in 1854 (and reducing the war hospital death rate from 42 per cent to 2 per cent): these were readily thought 'ministering angels'.

Dylan, then, is punning on 'angel' in this song: i.e. calling the song's addressee an 'angel' because she has been sent by God to guide him to the Lord, and calling her 'angel' secularly because she has become his beloved sexual partner: she has to be a human creature for this union to be blessed, as the singer believes it is. Hence his line 'What God has given to us no man can take away.' This is taken straight from Matthew 19:5–6: 'they twain shall be one flesh . . . What therefore God hath joined together, let not man put asunder' (repeated verbatim in Mark 10:9) and echoes the equivalent verse in the Marriage Service in the Church of England *Book of Common Prayer*: 'Those whom God hath joined together let no man put asunder'. Dylan reconfirms that his 'precious angel'

On the other hand there is no mistaking the direct venom, despite his casual tone, on 'Slow Train', when he refers to the as-it-were secular lover of his past:

> Well my baby went to Illinois
> With some bad-talkin' boy she could destroy
> A real suicide case
> But there was nothin' I could do to stop it.

There is another, and much more obviously biographical, reference back to that past relationship, in 'Gotta Serve Somebody'. Those who remember pictures of the Dylans' white-elephant Malibu home, with its ostentatious dome of copper at the top, will get a flash of recognition here:

> You might be living in a mansion
> You might live in a dome . . .

It's a quietly slipped-in but honourable self-rebuke.

Underneath it, though, there remains plenty of smouldering rebuke for other people too, and as Dylan comes back, on these albums, to the "Street Legal" themes of wavering resolve and of betrayal, it rises to the surface.

> My so-called friends have fallen under a spell

begins one of 'Precious Angel''s verses – and he returns to this notion almost obsessively again and again:

> They show me to the door
> They say don't come back no more
> 'Cause I don't feel like they want me to . . .
> Oh! though the earth may shake me
> Oh! though my friends forsake me
> Oh! even that couldn't make me go back

(from 'I Believe In You') and from 'Slow Train':

> Sometimes I feel so low-down and disgusted
> Can't help but wonder what's happenin' to my companions

---

has this double function in the song's last verse, which begins: 'You're the queen of my flesh, girl . . . You're the lamp of my soul'.

As he puns on 'angel', so he does on 'sun' (making for a pun-packed opening phrase): 'Precious angel, under the sun'. It's part of Dylan's greatness that in the best of these Christian songs he can press into service so much scriptural moment, yet keep his lines sounding so casual, so conversational, so expressively relaxed. 'Under the sun', of course, has come into common currency, or at least been continually recirculated there, by its repeated incantation in memorably famous passages of the brief but hugely influential Ecclesiastes (upon which Dylan draws in many songs, from 'It's Alright Ma (I'm Only Bleeding)' to 'Pressing On' and from 'Jokerman' to 'Tell Me' – see Chapter 14): 'and there is no new thing under the sun' (Ecclesiastes 1:9); 'wise under the sun' (2:19); 'vanity under the sun' (4:7) etc. In this usage, 'under the sun' is conventional; yet Dylan's 'precious angel' is also 'under the sun' in the sense of being 'under the Son', a messenger of the Lord – and this is exactly how the pun is used in one of the very last verses of the Old Testament: 'But unto you that fear my name shall the Sun of righteousness arise with healing in his wings' (Malachi 4:2). We're likely to infer a further hint of angels flying around here too, by that 'healing in his wings', and to be reminded, in turn, that Dylan has visited this terrain, and wittily, before: 'You angel you, / You got me under your wing', as he sings in 'You Angel You' on "Planet Waves".

'Precious Angel' offers a wealth of further scriptural quotation and allusion, some of which is identified in the notes that follow.

and again (same song):

> *I don't care about economy, I don't care about astronomy*
> *But it sure do bother me to see my loved ones turning into puppets.*

But in his own wavering of resolve, he can turn for help both to his new 'covenant woman' and to Jesus:

> *You know I just can't make it by myself*
> *I'm a little too blind to see*[26]

('Precious Angel')

> *Don't let me drift too far,*
> *Keep me where you are*
> *Where I will always be renewed*

('I Believe In You') and

> *How long can I listen to the lies of prejudice?*
> *How long can I stay drunk on fear out in the wilderness?*

('When He Returns').

The same confessions of a faltering spiritual self-discipline are made, though without any of the personal touches of the above, in 'Solid Rock', where Dylan's language becomes at once generalised and scriptural:

> *It's the ways of the flesh to war against the spirit*
> *Twenty-four hours a day . . .*
> *And he never give up 'til the battle's lost or won.*

---

26.   The theme of blindness and light, here and in the song's chorus, comes from two specific passages of scripture: 2 Corinthians 4:3–4, 6: 'But if our gospel be hid, it is hid to them that are lost: In whom the god of this world hath blinded the minds of them which believe not, lest the light of the glorious gospel of Christ, who is the image of God, should shine unto them . . . For God, who commanded the light to shine out of darkness, hath shined in our hearts, to give the light of the knowledge of the glory of God in the face of Jesus Christ.' And 1 John 1:7 (a passage which unites two themes in Dylan's song, 'the light' and 'blood'): 'But if we walk in the light, as he is in the light, we have fellowship one with another, and the blood of Jesus Christ his Son cleanseth us from all sin.'

This last is picked up on in those great lines in which Dylan, the Jewish American descendant of Moses, and his 'precious angel', the black American descendant of slaves, are envisaged walking in fellowship: 'We are covered in blood, girl, you know our forefathers were slaves . . . But there's violence in the eyes, girl, so let us not be enticed / On our way out of Egypt, through Ethiopia, to the judgment hall of Christ'. Thus Dylan so wonderfully achieves a concentration of three meanings into that 'covered in blood': blood as in one's family and racial history (blood thicker than water); blood as in carrying the stain of people's inherent violence and sin; and blood as in 'the blood of Jesus Christ' which 'covers us' by cleansing us all from sin. He also manages, with these lines, to invoke the whole story of the exodus from Egypt under Moses (Exodus) and by taking that exodus 'through Ethiopia' he not only emphasises that his 'precious angel' is an African-American, but echoes the specific scriptural detail remembered not in Exodus itself but in the fourth book of Moses, Numbers (12:1): 'for he [Moses] had married an Ethiopian woman'.

The biographical parallel here is that it was black American actress Mary Alice Artes who helped bring Dylan to Christianity; she is 'first mentioned on 'Street Legal' LP cover . . . subject of 'Precious Angel' . . . Dylan reportedly bought her an engagement ring in early 1980; later that year he wrote relevant versions of 'The Groom's Still Waiting At The Altar' and 'Caribbean Wind'.' (John Bauldie, 'Four and twenty windows and a woman's face in every one: significant women in Bob Dylan's life and art', in *All Across the Telegraph*, see note 19.)

Even here, it's a typical Dylan flash to insert into this deadening scriptural fulmination that playfully modern phrase 'twenty-four hours a day'.[27]

Dylan resumes the personalised statement of this theme on 'Saving Grace' with the slightly mournful simplicity of

> *It gets discouraging at times, but I know I'll make it*
> *By the saving grace that's over me.*

It might be relevant to that wavering – or indeed to the idea of the intrusive pressures on Dylan from wayward friends and/or the world – that there is a marked decrease in the sort of Dylan–Christ identification that was so clear and prevalent on "Street Legal". The only example of it, really, on the Born Again albums is here from 'In The Garden':

> *The multitude wanted to make Him king, put a crown upon His head*
> *Why did He slip away to a quiet place instead?*

Plainly, Dylan is drawing a parallel here, and is acknowledging that he at least knows exactly why Jesus should have 'slipped away'.[28]

---

27. Dylan's text here is taken from Galatians 5:17: 'For the flesh lusteth against the Spirit, and the Spirit against the flesh: and these are contrary the one to the other'. But this theme doesn't have to be expressed with such dead preachiness. The Bible itself makes the same point elsewhere in far more human, attractive and poetic terms. In Romans, for example, Paul speaks, neatly, of those who 'served the creature more than the Creator' (1:25) and, not to exclude himself, admits that 'I see another law in my members, warring against the law of my mind' (7:23); while in his second Epistle to the Corinthians he says that 'while we are at home in the body, we are absent from the Lord' (5:6).
   The founding texts, as it were, behind the title and chorus of 'Solid Rock' (behind 'But I'm hangin' on to a solid rock / Made before the foundation of the world') are from John 10:4 ('and that Rock was Christ') and the verbatim 'before the foundation of the world' – one of those nondescript phrases which hook the attention by incantatory repetition throughout the New Testament. It is in John 17:24, Ephesians 1:4 and 1 Peter 1:20 (with the lesser 'from the foundation of the world' in Matthew 13:35, Luke 11:50 and Hebrews 4:3, and 'since the foundation of the world' in Hebrews 9:26). In the so-called *Good News Bible*, 1966–76, the full phrase has become so much *more* nondescript that the effect of repetition is nil, since it passes entirely unnoticed, being merely 'before the world was made'. This, of course, killing all figurative possibility, obviates the connection with 'solid rock'.) The full phrase, as Dylan uses it, allies most clearly with the idea of Christ as the Rock in 1 Peter 1:20, which describes him so: 'Who verily was fore-ordained before the foundation of the world, but was manifest in these last times for you'. In this way Christian orthodoxy solves the problem of how Christ can be such a latecomer yet can have been around all along: God, foreseeing the fall of humankind, pre-prepared the remedy that was to cure the disease. Even in Jewish orthodoxy, seven things existed before the creation of the world, and one was the Messiah.
   Introducing 'Solid Rock' in concert in Toronto, 20/4/80, Dylan plays the preacherman; as the music twitches restlessly behind him, ready to burst through, Dylan declaims from memory another text by Paul, from 1 Timothy 3:16: 'God was manifest in the flesh, justified in the Spirit, seen of angels, preached unto the Gentiles, believed on in the world, received up into glory'. Whether deliberate edits or faulty recollection prompts Dylan's changes, it works well enough: 'It [the solid rock] was manifest in the flesh! an' justified in the Spirit! an' seen by angels!, an' preached on in the world!' Had his audience been black church, you would have heard the 'Yes, Lord!'s and 'A-men!'s coming back at him between each ascending, clamourous phrase. As it was, his gospel-singer back-up vocalists supply these responses with mellifluous but authentic 'Oh yea-ea-eah!'s.
28. 'In The Garden' (the phrase itself is from John 19:41) actually centres upon two gardens, and two compelling sections of Christ's story: the part in which Judas betrays him to the armed gang of high priests and elders and their henchmen in the garden of Gethsemane and he is arrested (leading to his crucifixion); and the part in which, when he rises again from the sepulchre 'in the garden' at Calvary, Mary Magdalene and then the eleven remaining disciples meet him one more time in Galilee. Like the title phrase 'in the garden', Nicodemus, the named character in the song's second verse, serves to link the stories either side of the crucifixion, since he is there beforehand, asking Christ why a man must be born again (John 3:1–7) and he is there again afterwards, helping Joseph of Arimathaea to place Christ's body in the garden sepulchre (John 19:39). Dylan's first verse deals with his arrest, in the course of which Peter slices off a high priest's servant's ear and is all for further swashbuckling resistance. (He is over-keen to prove his ardour because Jesus has just told him he'll deny him three times before that rooster crows at the break of dawn.) Jesus now tells him to put his sword away: 'Put up again thy sword into his place: for all they that take the sword shall perish with the sword' (Matthew 26:52) or 'Peter, put up thy sword into the sheath:

Dylan's own need to seek the quiet place, the refuge, is a major theme of the "Saved" album. Not, as on "Street Legal", from the vantage point of standing on the edge, still seeking, but from the new 'saved' position of looking back. So it is a kind of fundamental gratitude for his salvation – for his very survival, in fact – that is being expressed.

We have it recurrently in many songs, from

> *You have given everything to me*
> *What can I do for You? . . .*
> *Pulled me out of bondage and You made me renewed inside*

and

> *Well I don't deserve it but I sure did make it through*

('What Can I Do For You?') to

> *I've been broken, shattered like an empty cup*
> *I'm just waiting on the Lord to rebuild and fill me up*

('Covenant Woman').[29]

Only occasionally does this get de-personalised and, as it were, philosophised into this sort of Bible-thumping creed:

> *I was blinded by the devil*
> *Born already ruined*
> *Stone cold dead*
> *As I stepped out of the womb*

('Saved').[30] That has a discomforting sense of insistence, whereas when he states it in personal terms, it is as plausible as it is plain:

> *I've escaped death so many times, I know I'm only living*
> *By the saving grace that's over me.*

---

the cup which my Father hath given me, shall I not drink it?' (from John 18:11). Dylan's next two verses follow and fuse texts from Mark 2:9 and John 5:1–30 and from Luke 19:37–38 and John 6:15. His last verse quotes from Christ's last words to the disciples after his resurrection: 'All power is given unto me in heaven and in earth. Go ye therefore, and teach all nations, baptizing them in the name of the Father, and of the Son, and of the Holy Ghost: Teaching them to observe all things whatsoever I have commanded you: and, lo, I am with you alway, even unto the end of the world. Amen.' (Matthew 28:18–20).

29. Dylan's lines here rest on a specific passage of scripture, from Isaiah 40:31: 'But they that wait upon the Lord shall renew their strength'.

30. These unpleasant opening lines are not only repellent poetry – stone-cold dead words – but advance a reasonable analysis repellently. Humankind's inherent evil – original sin, if you will – has been established beyond doubt in the twentieth century by the partnership of its discoveries about the inner psyche and its appalling external acts; yet Dylan's doctrinal rib-poking here makes for a particularly unattractive way of viewing a new-born baby. Even the particular Old Testament text he takes here sounds more humane than Dylan: 'Behold, I was shapen in iniquity; and in sin did my mother conceive me . . . Deliver me from bloodguiltiness, O God' (Psalm 51:5, 14). Elsewhere, the song touches partisanly on another doctrinal issue, i.e. whether it is faith, or works, or keeping to the law, which leads to individual salvation. This aspect of the song, and its scriptural basis, is given some attention in Chapter 14 (as indeed is original sin), in the course of discussing 'Jokerman'.

> By this time I'd-a thought I would be sleeping
> In a pine-box for all eternity
> My faith keeps me alive . . .

('Saving Grace').

Expressed that way, it's utterly convincing. The most casual reflection on how unimaginably great the pressure on him of *being* Bob Dylan must have been, argues for the truth of those lines. Just surviving the 1966 period was more than most of us could have managed, let alone the cumulative pressures of all the years since then. It isn't hard to see the appeal of a respite in Christ.

There is, too, a lot of intellectual and emotional honesty in these albums. First, there is the acknowledgement of that susceptibility towards religious belief inside all of us:

> . . . how be it we're deceived[31]
> When the truth's in our hearts and we still don't believe?

('Precious Angel'). There's also a sharp look at the way we rationalise away morality under the pressures of the modish and of peer group approval:

> You say everybody's doin' it, so I guess it can't be wrong.
> The truth is far from you, so you know you got to lie,
> Then you're all the time defending what you can never justify

('Trouble In Mind').

On the "Slow Train Coming" album there is also this admirable flash of cynicism:

> They talk about a life of brotherly love
> Show me someone who knows how to live it

and elsewhere Dylan's focus is equally unblurred. I think this line, from 'Saving Grace', is an astonishing piece of dark honesty, of which few of us would be capable:

> But to search for love – that ain't no more than vanity.

On the other hand, there can be no doubting Dylan's religious passion and his happiness to have it fixed so firmly in conventional, traditional Christianity. Nor can there be any disputing the fact that when he expresses this religious passion, he does so with huge power and skill. Listen to the *tour de force* performance on 'When He Returns', and to the vocal delivery, in 'Precious Angel', of the shuddering phrase 'to the judgment hall of *Ch-rist!!*'.

---

31. Dylan's use of the phrase 'How be it' here is a pleasing echo of the rich plain-speaking of the King James Bible, in which, especially in Paul's epistles, the phrase occurs with Zen-like, majestic, repetitive effect. Though Dylan's *Lyrics 1962–1985* gives it as a three-word phrase, the Bible has it as a single word, 'Howbeit'. A recent dictionary (Collins, 1994) says of this only that it is 'archaic' before mis-defining it as meaning either 'however' or 'although'. In fact, of course, it means exactly what it says, ellipsed from the longer 'How does it come to be that?' What we shorten to 'How come?', the King James Bible shortened to 'Howbeit?' It *is* archaic, meaning that it is language characteristic of an earlier period and not in common use. Yet its clarity and simplicity make it a model of effective rhetoric, and Dylan's use of it here – in exact accord with its use in the scriptures – sounds to have arisen naturally from his inevitably meeting the word within The Word. That's howbeit he's in tune with it.

The same skill and power is there, too, in this marvellous verse from what is the best song on "Saved" – namely, 'Pressing On', which builds triumphantly and shows as authoritative, agile and compelling a Bob Dylan as any other song you could pick from any year:[32]

> *Temptation's not an easy thing, Adam given the devil reign*
> *Because he sinned I got no choice, it run in my vein.*
>
> *Well I'm pressing on . . .*

The hit on that 'vein' is artistry of the highest sort, and the implicit analogy between the addiction to drugs and the grip of sin is a very fine touch, especially in the context of Dylan's own druggy history.

That is not the only instance, on the "Saved" album, of Dylan's using his old secular skills in a new devotional context. The other outstanding example comes in 'What Can I Do For You?'. That not only gives us, out of nowhere, the most eerie, magnificent harmonica-work Dylan has done since the stoned, majestic concerts of 1966 but also applies all Dylan's enviable seductive gifts. It is the same knowingly disarming tone of voice that yielded

> *Lay, lady, lay*
> *Lay across my big brass bed*

back in 1969 that is turned on, in 'What Can I Do For You?', to disarm Jesus. This is nothing less than devotional seduction – just listen to the voice:

> *I know all about poison, I know all about fiery darts*
> *I don't care how rough the road is, show me where it starts.*

The ability to pull off *that* audacity shows us as well, I think, that there has been, in the Born Again process, no drastic excision from Dylan's personality of the restless romantic fascinations he's always attested to in his work.[33]

---

32.   I should stress, not best *lyric* – for the words, aside from their appealing ardour, offer but small windows of opportunity (to appropriate a 1990s cliché) for letting in the listener's own imaginative daylight – but best *song*. 'Pressing On' seems an instant classic of a gospel song, one you can readily imagine being sung in black churches.

   And why not in white? Whatever Bob Dylan aficionados might feel about his Christian songs, the best of them surely comprise a body of work that brings to contemporary religious song something fresh yet well-grounded in traditional strengths, something passionate and full of an authentic saturation in biblical teaching. Anyone can hear that it wipes the floor with all that awful Pat Boonery, that horrid, pallid, acoustic-guitar-and-tambourine sing-song modernism and those gruesome Age of Aquarius lasers-and-love productions offered to white worshippers over the last thirty years. Dylan's religious work has gravitas.

33.   The seductive intimacy of the voice, as it handles these sumptuous, tactile syllables, is matched by the intimately personal, conversational nature of the lyric. It is a lyric given envigorating, cheering scrutiny, not least by exemplary, alert attention to detail, in Christopher Ricks' essay 'What he can do for you', originally written for *Telegraph*, no. 22, Winter 1985; collected in *All Across the Telegraph*, (note 19).

   The 'fiery darts' are taken from Ephesians 6:11–16, in which Paul exhorts us: 'Put on the whole armour of God . . . Above all, taking the shield of faith, wherewith ye shall be able to quench all the fiery darts of the wicked.' The central question asked in the song's title echoes the only question contained in the brief but lovely devotional Psalm 116:12: 'What shall I render unto the Lord for all his benefits toward me?' Dylan's song retains some of the tone and import of this Passover Psalm while taking nothing else specifically from it. This is shown beautifully by the way that while Dylan might be said to echo its 'thou hast loosed my bonds' (in verse 16) in his '[You] pulled me out of bondage', in fact Dylan's phrase more closely duplicates one found recurrently all through the Bible ('sold into bondage' and then brought 'out from bondage' are not only the core of the story of Exodus but by extension one of the central metaphors of Judaeo-Christian belief), such that we can recognise Psalm 116 as

"Slow Train Coming" shows this too. It takes the same Dylan who has always loved hoboes and the road to deliver these images:

> *You may be living in another country under another name*

('Gotta Serve Somebody') and

> *For like a thief in the night He'll replace wrong with right*
> *When He returns*

('When He Returns'). Jesus as thief-in-the-night is distinctly a Dylan idea.[34]
Similarly it takes the same artist who seizes name-sounds like 'Delacroix' (on

---

providing here inspiration rather than text.
    Another whisper of inspiration lurks behind this song too. The fifth and final verse of Christina Rossetti's lyric for the Christmas carol 'In The Bleak Mid-Winter' may have provided the prompt, for the distinctively intimate, nuzzling series of questions Dylan assembles in this song. The Rossetti verse is intrinsically less intimate, because it speaks of God in the third person rather than the second, and of that manifestation of God that was the baby Jesus, but it journeys ever nearer to intimacy as it proceeds, and it proceeds by means of posited questions, intoned in crucial humility, just as the Dylan song does: 'What can I give him, poor as I am? / If I were a shepherd I would bring a lamb; / If I were a wise man I would do my part; / Yet what I can I give him – give my heart.'
    [Christina Rossetti (1830–1894), 'Christmas Carol', aka 'In the Bleak Mid-Winter', first published in a periodical, then in the first collected edition of her work, *Goblin Market: The Prince's Progress and Other Poems*, 1875.]

34. The analogy is, of course, Christ's own idea. According to Matthew 24:42–44, Christ tells the disciples: 'Watch therefore: for ye know not what hour your Lord doth come. But know this, that if the goodman of the house had known in what watch the thief would come, he would have watched, and would not have suffered his house to be broken up. Therefore be ye also ready: for in such an hour as ye think not the Son of man cometh.' The same speech is reported also in Luke 12:39–40. This message is later relayed in two further passages. In Paul's First Epistle to the Thessalonians, he writes: 'For yourselves know perfectly that the day of the Lord so cometh as a thief in the night' (1 Thessalonians 5:2); and in the Second Epistle of Peter the Apostle, he too writes: 'But the day of the Lord will come as a thief in the night' (2 Peter 3:10). The pleasingly quirky oxymoron of 'day' and 'night' here naturally so worries the writers of the *Good News Bible* that they abolish it, so reducing the resonant poetry of 'like a thief in the night' to the dully unmemorable 'like a thief'. Bob Dylan, in creditable contrast, not only uses the whole line but, in making it 'Like a thief in the night / He'll replace wrong with right', offers a matching oxymoron, emphasising the odd ostensible contradiction at the heart of Christ's analogy, while accurately summarising the import of his message.
    'When He Returns' enfolds an extravagance of scriptural reference. Ahead of 'thief in the night', verse 1 alludes (by 'the iron rod') both to God's giving his rod to Moses – the rod by means of which Moses eventually effects the Israelites' escape from 'the iron hand' of the Egyptians – and to Isaiah's prophecy of Christ's coming, in which (in a passage immediately preceding the description of 'Christ's peaceable kingdom', discussed in note 15): 'there shall come forth a rod out of the stem of Jesse, and a Branch shall grow out of his roots: And the spirit of the Lord shall rest upon him . . . the spirit of the knowledge and the fear of the Lord . . . with righteousness shall he judge the poor, and reprove with equity for the meek of the earth: and he shall smite the earth with the rod of his mouth, and with the breath of his lips shall he slay the wicked' (Isaiah 11:1–2, 4). Aptly, Dylan's opening couplet matches 'the iron rod' with 'a mighty God' – aptly because this latter is not the anonymous phrase we might assume but is also drawn from, and so alludes to, a passage of Isaiah, the nearby 9:6 which again, as we saw earlier, envisages Christ's coming: 'For unto us a child is born . . . and his name shall be called . . . The mighty God.' Dylan's next line, 'For all those who have eyes and all those who have ears', uses a particular piece of rhetoric deployed time and again in the New Testament and founded upon a text from the Old Testament book of Ezekiel 12:1–2: 'The word of the Lord also came unto me, saying, Son of man, thou dwellest in the midst of a rebellious house, which have eyes to see, and see not; they have ears to hear, and hear not.' ('When He Returns' is not Dylan's first use of this: it's there as rhetoric in 'Blowin' In The Wind': 'Yes 'n' how many ears must one man have . . .?'; 'Yes 'n' how many times must a man turn his head / Pretending he just doesn't see?') In the New Testament we find the founding passage of 'Ezekiel' cited by Christ himself in Matthew 13:43 ('Who hath ears to hear, let him hear') and repeatedly by Christ and others in Mark and Revelation: 'And he said unto them, He that hath ears to hear, let him hear' (Mark 4:9); 'If any man have ears to hear, let him hear' (Mark 4:23); 'If any man have ears to hear, let him hear' (Mark 7:16); 'Having eyes, see ye not? and having ears, hear ye not?' (Mark 8:18); and 'He that hath an ear, let him hear' (Revelation 2:7, 11, 29; 3:6, 13 and 22).
    And all that's just in the first verse of 'When He Returns'. The second begins from the text of Matthew 7:14: 'Because strait is the gate, and narrow is the way, which leadeth unto life, and few there be that find it'. Dylan

"Blood On The Tracks") and 'Panamanian moon' (on "Blonde On Blonde") to alight with such relish and panache on 'Nicodemus' (on 'In The Garden'). And it evidences the Dylan of all those romance-of-the-road leaving songs of 1964, when we note the sheer lingering affection he bestows, in 1980, on the notion in this line:

You know that we are strangers in a land we're passing through

('Covenant Woman').[35]

Again, Dylan's capacity for aphorisms – like 'to live outside the law you must be honest' (1966) – is still alive and well on these religious albums. It would be hard to quarrel with the impact and panache of

---

echoes delicately the rhythms and the half-rhyming repetitions of this line, matching 'strait is the gate, and narrow is the way, which leadeth unto life' with his own 'Truth is an arrow, and the gate is narrow, that it passes through'. Indeed he uses this pattern for most lines in his song, including each verse's opening line: all three incorporate internally rhyming or half-rhyming pairings: 'The iron hand, it ain't no match, for the iron rod'; 'Truth is an arrow, and the gate is narrow, that it passes through'; 'Surrender your crown, on this blood-stained ground, take off your mask'. And this last, the opening line of Dylan's third and final verse, builds its balancing half-rhymes, whether by accident or design, from the balancing bookends of the Bible: 'Surrender your crown' cites Revelation 4:10, while 'this blood-stained ground' cites Genesis 4:10. The former describes the end days: 'The four and twenty elders fall down before him that sat on the throne, and worship him that liveth for ever and ever, and cast their crowns before the throne'; the passage from Genesis is in the account of the first murder after the Fall, when Cain has slain Abel and God asks: 'What hast thou done? the voice of thy brother's blood crieth unto me from the ground.' (Dylan uses this again in the fascinating unissued 1980 song 'Yonder Comes Sin', the subject matter of Chapter 11.) Finally, Dylan's 'He knows your needs even before you ask' is taken from the Sermon on the Mount: 'your Father knoweth what things ye have need of, before ye ask him.' (From Matthew 6:8, immediately before the passage we call the Lord's Prayer.) It's admirable that 'When He Returns' shoulders so much biblical text without ever groaning under its weight or losing its own strong identity.

35.   As trailered in note 23, here Dylan bends an ear to God's recurrent exhortation to his people to treat strangers with kindness. This is no mere Gentle Jesusism, but a command insisted upon time and again in the Old Testament. Essentially the point is marshalled to remind people of their own ancestral suffering as captive strangers in Egypt. Exodus 22:21: 'Thou shalt neither vex a stranger, nor oppress him: for ye were strangers in the land of Egypt'. Exodus 23:9: 'Also thou shalt not oppress a stranger: for ye know the heart of a stranger, seeing ye were strangers in the land of Egypt'. Leviticus 19:33–34: 'And if a stranger sojourn with thee in your land, ye shall not vex him. But the stranger that dwelleth with you shall be unto you as one born among you, and thou shalt love him as thyself; for ye were strangers in the land of Egypt'. Numbers 15:15–16: 'One ordinance shall be both for you of the congregation, and also for the stranger that sojourneth with you, an ordinance for ever in your generations: as ye are, so shall the stranger be before the Lord. One law and one manner shall be for you, and for the stranger that sojourneth with you'. Deuteronomy 10:19: 'Love ye therefore the stranger: for ye were strangers in the land of Egypt.' In the New Testament, this theme is linked to – returns us to – the question of angels. Hebrews 13:2: 'Be not forgetful to entertain strangers; for thereby some have entertained angels unawares'. This last is paralleled by, is perhaps the conscious inspiration for, part of the lyric of Woody Guthrie's 'Pretty Boy Floyd' (recorded by Dylan in 1987): 'And Pretty Boy found a welcome at every farmer's door. / Others tell you of a stranger that come to beg a meal / And underneath a napkin left a thousand-dollar bill'. (A few lines later, Guthrie adds a note 'from' Floyd, left with a gift of food: ' "You say that I'm an outlaw, you say that I'm a thief / Well here's a Christmas dinner for the families on relief." ' This dovetails into the argument of the song's most famous line: 'Some will rob you with a six-gun and some with a fountain-pen' – the line quoted by Dylan in his own early song 'Talkin' New York' – before the song ends with 'You won't never see an outlaw drive a family from their home.') The link between the biblical text and this quintessential Guthrie lyric tends to corroborate my notion that Dylan's lines from 'Covenant Woman', as delivered, still carry a residue of affection for those romance-of-the-road songs of an earlier era.

[Woody Guthrie: 'Pretty Boy Floyd', 26/4/39; reissued "Folkways: The Original Vision", Smithsonian Folkways Records SF400001, Washington, DC, 1988. Bob Dylan: 'Pretty Boy Floyd', Los Angeles, probably April 1987, "Folkways: A Vision Shared", Columbia Records OC 44034, New York [CBS 460905 1, London], 1988. Dylan's first known extant recording of this song (unissued) has him contributing back-up vocals, guitar and harmonica behind Ramblin' Jack Elliott, live NYC, 3/7/75 (his 1987 recording is modelled on Elliott's two classic recordings of the song ['Talking Miner's Blues' c/w 'Pretty Boy Floyd', London, c. 1956, 78 rpm Topic Records TRC98, London, c. 1956; and 'Pretty Boy Floyd', NYC, June 1960, issued "Jack Elliott Sings The Songs Of Woody Guthrie", Prestige Records PR13016, Bergenfield, New Jersey, 1960/61]). Dylan also performed the song live at the Bridge School Benefit Concert, Oakland, California, 4/12/88.]

Soon as a man is born, you know the sparks begin to fly

('What Can I Do For You?')[36] and hard not to remember that line after even one's first hearing of the "Saved" album. Similarly, it comes as a pleasurable surprise, on 'Pressing On', to find the Dylan of 1980 using in song a motto he had made his own as the title of a film about the Dylan of 1965:

Shake the dust off of your feet, don't look back

(my emphasis, although he gives it a hint of emphasis also).[37]

Yet another welcome element to be found in these albums is the attack Dylan

36.   In fact this is a wonderful example of a quite different one of Dylan's greatest strengths: his capacity for modernising and colloquialising an archaic and formal line or phrase – rescuing and re-charging it. Dylan does this all through his work, sometimes at the most unexpected yet felicitous moments, often playfully. (For instance: in 'Joey', from the 1976 album "Desire", Dylan's movie-like funeral scene has people weeping, immediately followed by Joey Gallo's old mafiosi friend Frankie muttering 'He ain't dead, he's just asleep' – plausibly colloquial yet an exact re-statement of Christ's words at the deathbed of a young girl he then brings back to life: 'He said unto them, Give place: for the maid is not dead but sleepeth' [Matthew 9:24]. And: 'Why make ye this ado, and weep? the damsel is not dead, but sleepeth' [Mark 5:39]. And: 'Weep not; she is not dead, but sleepeth' [Luke 8:52].)

This updating and re-charging, with a surge which both brings out the essentials of the old and adds new layers of meaning, is especially powerful and generous on the Born Again albums, since they offer such a concentration of biblical text and allusion. Here in 'What Can I Do For You?' Dylan gives this intelligent creative treatment to the words of Job 5:7: 'Yet man is born unto trouble, as the sparks fly upward.' His re-write, 'Soon as a man is born, you know the sparks begin to fly', gives it a sparky, edgy, threatening contemporaneity (which is the essence of contemporaneity), implying trouble without needing to keep the word 'trouble' in the line.

Christopher Ricks noted this (of this same example of Dylan's re-processing) back in 1981, saying in a radio interview [Cambridge, April 1981, in *1961 Revisited: Bob Dylan's Back Pages*, produced Grahame Lloyd, BBC Radio Wales, Cardiff, 1981, broadcast 24/5/81] that he loved 'the adaptation of biblical quotations and allusions so that they become at once entirely modern and straightforward and simple while nevertheless having a lot of ancient feeling in them. Now that feeling that sparks *can't* but fly up into the sky, and that's like our trouble . . . [he] turns that into a modern world of aggression and punch-up . . .'

The corollary Dylan argues for in his next line – that 'He gets wise in his own eyes' – takes its scriptural cue from the Old Testament book of (Solomon's) Proverbs: 'Be not wise in thine own eyes' (3:7), reiterated by the prophet Isaiah: 'Woe unto them that are wise in their own eyes, and prudent in their own sight!' (5:21). Again Dylan's re-processing involves a telling shift. As Ricks said in the same interview, 'to "get wise" is different . . . [again it's] . . . that rather ugly, threatening American idiom: "Don't you get wise with me." It's not the same as *being* wise . . . the lyrics are full of these very beautiful turns with old sayings.'

A final irony, as regards the trouble and the sparks, is that both arise only in the King James Bible translation – a case, as Jorge Luis Borges said of others' endeavours, where 'The original is unfaithful to the translation'. In the Greek and the Hebrew, 'trouble' is probably 'labour', and 'the sparks fly upward' is given as 'the sons of the coal lift up their flight' or 'dart upward', or in the Hebrew as 'the sons of the burning coal lift up to fly'. In the magnificent translation in Miles Coverdale's Cologne Bible of 1535, and for the Great Bible of 1539, edited by Coverdale (c.1488–1569), Job's words are different again: 'It is man that is borne unto mysery, like as the byrde for to fle.' This in turn rubs up against a well-known verse of the *Book of Common Prayer* (Coverdale once more), from the service for the burial of the dead: 'Man that is born of woman hath but a short time to live, and is full of misery.' If this plays subliminally behind Dylan's lines, it helps along his message: he not busy being re-born, is busy dying.

37.   'Shake the dust off of your feet' (half-echoing the song's earlier line 'Shake me up in my mind') is a quotation from Christ, transcribed in Matthew 10:14, Mark 6:11 and Luke 9:5: 'And whosoever shall not receive you, or hear your words, when ye depart out of that house or city, shake off the dust of your feet'; 'And whosoever shall not receive you, nor hear you, when ye depart thence, shake off the dust under your feet for a testimony against them'; 'And whosoever will not receive you, when ye go out of that city, shake off the very dust from your feet for a testimony against them'. The Jews considered themselves defiled by the dust of a heathen country (represented by the prophets as polluted land, e.g. Amos 7:7), so that to shake the dust of any city of Israel off your feet was a gesture, renouncing all further connection with it and placing it on a par with the cities of the heathen. Of course, the expression works without our knowing this, not least in the sense that standing still, failing to move forward, means gathering dust. Dylan deftly stresses the further sense, the you-won't-see-me-for-dust sense, by appending the motto 'Don't look back' (making it you-won't-see-me-and-I-won't-see-you). This is, in turn, a reminder of God's imprecation, discussed in note 23 re 'Trouble In Mind', that Lot and his family likewise should not look back at the wicked city. What's more, the phrase 'Don't look back', used in a 1980 Bob Dylan song and so

makes on what is essentially a Californian modishness. Dylan's America was always the Midwest and New York, and it always seemed wrong when he moved to California in the early 1970s. One remembered, at the time of his move, how it conflicted with the excellent sentiments he'd expressed on the unreleased mid-1960s song 'California':

> *San Francisco is fine.*
> *You sure get lots of sun.*
> *But I'm used to four seasons,*
> *California's got but one*

and when, around 1974–75, Dylan was starting to put himself back on the streets, it was only right and logical that it was the small clubs of New York City to which he returned for a series of unannounced guest appearances at gigs by Jack Elliott, John Prine, Muddy Waters and so on.[38] Just as he was never seduced by the hippy milieu of the late 1960s, so he proved himself unimpressed also by the Marin County-hunters. "Slow Train Coming" makes this crystal clear, from the somewhat obvious barbs of

> *Spiritual advisors and gurus to guide your every move*
> *Instant inner peace and every step you take has got to be approved*

('When You Gonna Wake Up?') to the beautifully trademarked Dylan bite of

> *Don't wanna amuse nobody, don't wanna be amused*

('Do Right To Me Baby (Do Unto Others)')[39] and

---

inevitably recalling a 1960s Bob Dylan film, is in this way a self-reflexive text, a self-contradictory one: that is, the very act of telling the listener 'don't look back' makes him or her look back. (As it happens, this contains a psychological truth: the one that leads you to feel that perhaps Lot's wife looked back precisely because she was told not to.)

[*Don't Look Back*, Leacock Pennebaker, US, directed D. A. Pennebaker, 1967, filmed on Bob Dylan's tour of England, April–May 1965.]

The inspiration for the title and chorus of 'Pressing On' is the text of Philippians 3:14: 'I press toward the mark for the prize of the high calling of God in Jesus Christ'.

Another scriptural précis in 'Pressing On' takes us back to the words of the preacher, Ecclesiastes: Dylan's 'What's to come has already been' restates Ecclesiastes 1:9: 'The things that hath been, it is that which shall be; and that which is done is that which shall be done' and 3:15: 'That which hath been is now; and that which is to be hath already been'.

38. Dylan appears to have moved to California in early 1973, after finishing the filming (in Mexico) of *Pat Garrett & Billy the Kid* [MGM, US, directed Sam Peckinpah, 1973]; but according to Robert Shelton's *No Direction Home* (1986) he didn't move into the house with the copper dome at Malibu till late 1976. The Greenwich Village gigs mentioned were: back-up harmonica-player for John Prine, Bitter End, September 1973; jamming with Muddy Waters' Band on the first night of their week-long residency at the Bottom Line, 30/6/75; at Ramblin' Jack Elliott's gig at the Other End, 3/7/75; and playing piano behind Bobby Neuwirth and Patti Smith at the Other End, 5/7/75. ['California', NYC, 13/1/65, an out-take from the "Bringing It All Back Home" sessions, is decribed in Dylan's *Lyrics 1962–1985* as an 'early version of "Outlaw Blues"' – but this was recorded all of two days later.]

39. The phrase behind the subtitle and chorus of this song is taken not from the passage in Deuteronomy 19:18–19, 20 that Dylan draws on in 'Wedding Song' and 'I And I': 'and, behold, if the witness be a false witness, and hath testified falsely against his brother; Then shall ye do unto him, as he had thought to have done unto his brother: so shalt thou put the evil away from among you . . . And thine eye shall not pity; but life shall go for life, eye for eye, tooth for tooth, hand for hand, foot for foot' (teaching drawn upon in the Old Testament story of Samson in Judges [15:10–11], in which the Philistines say to the men of Judah: 'To bind Samson are we come up, to do to him as he hath done to us', after which Samson tells them, similarly: 'As they did unto me, so have I done unto them'). Rather, Dylan is following Christ's reversal of the same passage of Deuteronomy in the Sermon on the Mount, in which he says: 'Therefore all things whatsoever ye would that men should do to you, do ye even so to

> *Well don't know which one is worse,*
> *Doing your own thing or just being cool*

('Gonna Change My Way of Thinking'). There is also that polite chastisement given in 'Precious Angel':

> *You were telling him about Buddha, you were telling him about Mohammed in*
> *   one breath*
> *You never mentioned one time the Man who came and died a criminal's death.*

And I suspect that it is as much California as anywhere that Dylan celebrates being spiritually rescued from on 'Saved':

> *Freed me from the pit*
> *Full of emptiness and wrath*
> *And the fire that burns in it.*[40]

Dylan's scorn of that West Coast milieu – where people cannot go any further west without falling into the ocean, and so pursue their eternal quest of the American dream through a cocooning consumerism, not just of things but of philosophies and people, and where they no longer have lives but only lifestyles – Dylan's contemptuous impatience is bound up with an essential seriousness of purpose that he has always

---

them: for this is the law and the prophets' (Matthew 7:12). This comes a few verses after his saying: 'Judge not, that ye be not judged' – which is the opening sentence of Matthew 7, and is echoed directly by the opening line of Dylan's song: 'Don't wanna judge nobody, don't wanna be judged'. (In Luke 6:37 Christ's words are given as 'Judge not, and ye shall not be judged'.)

A once-famous and still-interesting spin on this apparent clear choice between two contrasting ways of dealing with the world occurs in the children's book *The Water Babies* (1863), by Charles Kingsley (1819–1875), himself the embodiment of muscular Christianity and a leading figure in the so-called Christian Socialist movement. In *The Water Babies* the hero meets the fairy who punishes those who ill-treat others, Mrs Bedonebyasyoudid, and her sister, Mrs Doasyouwouldbedoneby. The first explains that she is 'the ugliest fairy in the world; and I shall be, till people behave themselves as they ought to do. And then I shall grow as handsome as my sister, who is the loveliest fairy . . . So she begins where I end, and I begin where she ends; and those who will not listen to her must listen to me.'

Christ's injunction 'all things whatsoever ye would that men should do to you, do ye even so to them' is rendered in modern Bibles as 'do unto others as you would have them do unto you', which Dylan uses directly as the final (and summarising) chorus-line of 'Do Right To Me Baby (Do Unto Others)'. He refers to it indirectly in the companion song 'Gonna Change My Way Of Thinking', for it is 'the golden rule' to which he refers. The idea of 'the golden rule' is common in moral philosophy; it 'designates a guide to conduct thought fundamental in most major religious and moral traditions . . . It has nothing to say about specific choices, nor does it endorse particular moral principles, virtues or ideals . . . [It] concerns, rather, a perspective thought necessary to the exercise of even the most rudimentary morality: that of trying to put oneself in the place of those affected by one's actions, so as to counter the natural tendency to moral myopia . . . Kant famously dismissed the rule as trivial and too limited to be a universal law . . . whereas John Stuart Mill claimed . . . that "In the golden rule of Jesus of Nazareth, we read the complete spirit of the ethics of utility."' (Sisela Bok, in *The Oxford Companion to Philosophy*, ed. Ted Honderich, 1995.) By extension 'the golden rule' refers to any important principle within any discipline or field of activity.

40.   The pit opens up in many parts of the Bible, but being saved from it is most insistently described in Job 33, in a cluster of near-adjacent verses (18, 23–24, and 28–30) that, though they talk of avoidance, make the fire and pit vividly present, in part by sheer repetition, as Dylan's lines do by sheer venomous relish: 'He keepeth back his soul from the pit, and his life from perishing by the sword'; 'If there be . . . one among a thousand, to shew unto man his uprightness: Then he is gracious unto him, and saith, Deliver him from going down to the pit: I have found a ransom'; 'He will deliver his soul from going into the pit, and his life shall see the light. Lo, all these things worketh God oftentimes with man, To bring back his soul from the pit, to be enlightened with the light of the living.' Dylan's lines also parallel a passage from the Psalms: 'He brought me up also out of an horrible pit, out of the miry clay, and set my feet upon a rock' (40:2).

evinced. In 1962 he was writing about the need to conduct one's life in the light of one's expecting death:

> *I will not go down under the ground*
> *'Cause somebody tells me that death's comin' round . . .*
> *Let me die in my footsteps*
> *Before I go down under the ground*

and even in the white heat of the mid-1960s he was saying that you have to decide how you behave in the face of the certainty that you will die.[41]

His conversion to Christianity prompted what is essentially a re-statement of that earlier agnostic seriousness, re-approached as 'Prepare To Meet Thy Maker'. It is one of the basic, major themes of "Slow Train Coming" and "Saved" – and it is a message Dylan urges on us regardless of our religious tenets. It is a message about not wasting our time in this world, regardless (effectively) of whether we believe there is another world to come.

For himself, in this period, he chooses to concentrate on this theme with a conventional Christian focus, but essentially it is a re-statement of the same conviction

---

41. Dylan's 'Let Me Die In My Footsteps', written to deride the craze for fall-out shelters (not the happiest solution to the threat of nuclear war, a threat often felt to be imminent in the 1950s-to-early-1960s, especially during the 'Cuba Crisis' of 1962), typifies Dylan's early ability to create songs of resonance and applicability beyond such particular prompts, though this one comes close to Pete Seegerish worthiness and soon bored its composer. (Its text is resurrected, surprisingly, to simple effect and without historical placement, in the film *Dangerous Minds*, Via Rosa/Buenavista/Simpson/Bruckheimer, US, directed John N. Smith, 1995.) But it shows that as early as 1962 Dylan was already confidently using biblical text without missing a beat. The second verse, which begins 'There's been rumors of war and wars that have been / The meaning of life has been lost in the wind', takes its text, without any nudging the listener towards noticing it, from the words of Christ given in Matthew 24:6 and Mark 13:7: 'And ye shall hear of wars and rumours of wars: see that ye be not troubled' and 'And when ye shall hear of wars and rumours of wars, be ye not troubled'. (This is cited again in Chapter 13.)

['Let Me Die In My Footsteps', NYC, 25/4/62, was issued on the almost immediately withdrawn first version of "The Freewheelin' Bob Dylan", 1963; with one verse excised it was finally issued on the "Bootleg Series I–III" box-set, 1991. Dylan played it privately to Izzy Young at the Folklife Center, 22/2/62, performed it in public in Montreal, 2/7/62, recorded it again as a Witmark song publishing demo, NYC, December 1962, and played guitar (under the name Blind Boy Grunt) behind Happy Traum on the latter's version cut NYC, 24/1/63; "Broadside Ballads", Broadside Records BR301, New York, 1963.]

Dylan's remark in the mid-1960s about behaviour in the face of the certainty of death comes in the course of the remarkable interview with Horace Judson from *Time* magazine, given at the Royal Albert Hall, London, 9/5/65, in which Dylan, wired up with youth's impatience (at least), and moving among lumpen dullards like some beautiful, ethereal alien from superior space, can say to the forty-something reporter: 'I'm saying that you're going to die, and you're gonna go off the earth, you're gonna be dead. Man, it could be, you know, twenty years, it could be tomorrow, any time. So am I. I mean, we're just gonna be gone. The world's going to go on without us. All right now. You do your job in the face of that and how seriously you take yourself, you decide for yourself.' (This is captured in the film *Don't Look Back*, see note 37, and transcribed in the book of the film, D. A. Pennebaker's *Bob Dylan: Don't Look Back*, 1968. Here the *Time* reporter is not identified, but he is named as Horace Judson in Peter Marshall's 'Hotel Blues', *Telegraph*, no. 54, Spring 1996.)

Although Dylan sounded prepared for death back on the 1962 'Let Me Die In My Footsteps', I wonder whether it wasn't reading Yeats in 1964 that gave him the conviction he expresses in the interview just quoted. Dylan's 'starry-eyed and laughing', from 'Chimes Of Freedom', echoes W. B. Yeats' phrase 'open-eyed and laughing', the one describing the stance of youth, the other the resolve of middle age. Yeats' line is from 'Vacillation': 'No longer in Lethean foliage caught / Begin the preparation for your death / And from the fortieth winter by that thought / Test every work of intellect or faith, / And everything that your own hands have wrought, / And call those works extravagance of breath / That are not suited for such men as come / Proud, open eyed and laughing to the tomb'. It is the precociously wise young Dylan of 1964–65 who seems to have taken this teaching to heart, as in his impassioned remarks to the man from *Time* magazine. So perhaps it was reading Yeats in 1964 that both fired up this resolve to do what you do in the knowledge that you're going to die *and* gave him the phrase he revises in 'Chimes Of Freedom'.

[W. B. Yeats (1865–1939): 'Vacillation', cited in *The New Natural Death Handbook*, ed. Albery *et al.*, 1997.]

as to the dignity of life and the individual's responsibility for controlling its quality and worthiness that he was expressing in the 1960s.

Dylan comes uncannily close to echoing William Blake here (and no one knocks *him* for believing in Christ). From a letter by Blake:

> Christ is very decided on this Point: 'He who is Not With Me is Against Me.' There is no Medium or Middle state.[42]

From Dylan's 'Precious Angel':

> *You either got faith or you got unbelief*
> *And there ain't no neutral ground.*

And from 'Gonna Change My Way Of Thinking':

> *Jesus said 'be ready*
> *For you know not the hour in which I come'*
> *He said 'who's not for me is against me'*
> *Just so's you all know where He's coming from*[43]

---

42.   I can't now trace my own source for this quotation but it should be found in *Blake: Complete Writings*, ed. Geoffrey Keynes (1969).

43.   Dylan combines two separate quotes from Jesus here by making that jokey link between when he's coming and 'where He's coming from'.

   As so often in these songs, layers of scripture are laid down in this one. Dylan's 'Jesus said "be ready / For you know not the hour in which I come" ' (like his "Saved" song 'Are You Ready?') is based on Matthew 24:42 and 25:13 and/or Mark 13:32, 35 and/or Luke 12:40: 'Watch therefore: for ye know not what hour your Lord doth come'; 'Watch therefore, for ye know neither the day nor the hour wherein the Son of man cometh'; 'But of that day and that hour knoweth no man'; 'Watch ye therefore: for ye know not when the master of the house cometh'; and 'Be ye therefore ready also: for the Son of man cometh at an hour when ye think not'. (This follows the thief-in-the-night analogy.)

   It's telling that Dylan chooses to sing 'He said "who's not for me is against me" ', the same uncompromising remark from Christ picked up on by Blake. It's to be found in Matthew 12:30 and Luke 11:23: 'He that is not with me is against me; and he that gathereth not with me scattereth abroad'; 'He that is not with me is against me: and he that gathereth not with me scattereth'. Yet had Blake and Dylan wished to emphasise tolerance rather than severity, had they wished to welcome rather than repel the widest possible constituency, they could have chosen a different set of texts, those in which Christ puts the argument the other, more liberal way round: 'For he that is not against us is on our part'; 'for he that is not against us is for us' (Mark 9:40 and Luke 9:50).

   The severer version Dylan opts for parallels two other pairs of absolute choices asserted in these songs – 'It might be the devil or it might be the Lord / But you gotta serve somebody' ('Gotta Serve Somebody'), and 'You either got faith or you got unbelief / And there ain't no neutral ground' ('Precious Angel'). The former has an Old as well as a New Testament basis. Joshua 24:15, in a passage dealing with the need to put away other idols and choose to serve God instead, begins: 'And if it seem evil unto you to serve the Lord, choose you this day whom ye will serve.' Like the chorus of Dylan's song, this urges that vacillation and moral shiftiness should be renounced in favour of clear-sightedness about an unavoidable clear choice. (As Deuteronomy 30:19 makes clear: 'I have set before you life and death, blessing and cursing: therefore choose life'.) This gotta-serve-somebody theme is taken up in Matthew 6:24: 'No man can serve two masters: for either he will hate the one, and love the other; or else he will hold to the one, and despise the other. Ye cannot serve God and mammon.'

   There is further lip-smacking relish of severity in 'Precious Angel'. 'Can you imagine the darkness that will fall from on high,' asks Dylan, clearly enjoying imagining it himself, especially the torture 'when men will pray God to kill them and they won't be able to die?' This dark scenario is laid out in the Old Testament and the New: Job 3:20–22 speaks of those 'bitter in soul; Which long for death, but it cometh not; and dig for it more than for hid treasures; Which rejoice exceedingly, and are glad, when they can find the grave'; and Revelation 9:6 looks forward (like Dylan) to a time of squirming: 'And in those days shall men seek death, and shall not find it; and shall desire to die, and death shall flee from them.' This is a prospect Dylan refers to a quarter-century beforehand, though with a healthy detachment on this earlier occasion, in 'Gates Of Eden': 'Leaving men wholly, totally free / To do anything they wish to do but die / And there are no trials inside the gates of Eden.'

and this clear call to self-examination is representative of the whole stance of these collections:

> *When you gonna wake up*
> *And strengthen the things that remain?*

('When You Gonna Wake Up?').[44] It recurs in the title of the "Saved" song 'Are You Ready?' and most pressingly – and when the song was new, a renewed Cold War made it seem as if it might be an urgent question, as it was in the era that had produced 'A Hard Rain's A-Gonna Fall' – here:

> *When destruction comes swiftly*
> *And there's no time to say fare thee well*
> *Have you decided whether you want to be*
> *In heaven or in hell?*
>
> *Are you ready? . . .*
> *Are you ready for Armageddon?*[45]

The trouble is, of course, that pressing and central as that theme might be, there is no disguising the fact that 'A Hard Rain's A-Gonna Fall' is an infinitely better song than 'Are You Ready?' – and that what makes these Born Again albums so flawed and shallow in the context of Bob Dylan's whole catalogue is that he has been satisfied, on these records, to assert and argue and declaim but he has hardly bothered anywhere on them to fulfil the more important tasks of the artist: he has not created worlds here, he has only argued about them.[46]

44.   Dylan's use of biblical language, and his use of modern American English, the one designed to last and the other designed not to, are, as noted earlier, admirably discussed in Christopher Ricks' essay 'Clichés that come to pass' (see note 19). Ricks starts by explaining the pros and cons of American English's transience, arguing that its 'distinctive poignancy . . . has much to do with its making its own transience an acknowledgement and not just an admission. The sense that some of the most vivid words in today's American language are – to take up the terms in which T. S. Eliot disparaged American slang – "inherently transitory", "certain to be superseded", "certain to pass away" and "cannot endure": this sense can then itself constitute some of the great effects of distinctively American writing.' Later in the essay Ricks includes a longer quote than I have given here from Dylan's 'When You Gonna Wake Up?': 'God don't make promises that He don't keep. / You got some big dreams, baby, but in order to dream you gotta still be asleep. / When you gonna wake up, when you gonna wake up, / When you gonna wake up and strengthen the things that remain?' Ricks then comments: 'There is the language to which [Dylan] means to awaken his audience is not American English, with its "big dreams", but the conservative interest and conserving force of the Revelation of the King James Bible: "Be watchful, and strengthen the things which remain, that are ready to die" [3:2]. The biblical line is itself one of the things which remains and it impinges newly within a sense of the language itself as elsewhere so "ready to die".'

45.   The 'renewed Cold War', in which Dylan's so-called Born Again albums were written, occurred in the period leading up to, and during, Ronald Reagan's presidency (1981–89). An ex-Governor of California, whose state régime had provoked recurrent, bloody battles against students, radicals and others, Reagan won the Republican Party nomination in 1980 on a sea of right-wing fundamentalist rhetoric. He defeated Democratic President Jimmy Carter in 1981, and thereafter, among much else, he invaded Grenada, blessed the CIA's creation and funding of the Contras (a terrorist army fighting the democratically elected Sandanista government of Nicaragua) and mined that country's harbours. He increased military spending massively, and chose 'Star Wars', i.e. the militarisation of space (announced 1983), rather than disarmament agreements with 'the evil empire', i.e. the USSR. You could say history proved him right in this last, much-scoffed-at characterisation. You could hardly say he made the American empire less lawless.

46.   As these (1990s) annotations suggest, I still feel that at worst Dylan's evangelical songs offer a dead language and a paucity of creative imagination, in contrast to so much of his earlier work: 'Are You Ready?' is much inferior to 'Three Angels', let alone to 'A Hard Rain's A-Gonna Fall'. It will be as clear, though, that elsewhere Dylan's sharp, deft attention to detail in his use of language, combined with a rich range of subject matter, yield songs that

In this sense, Dylan comes full circle, with "Slow Train Coming" and "Saved", back to the polemical, creatively sparse mode of writing that marked his early protest period. There is even the same radicalism – but of a sort that is, for rich Americans with no grasp of politics, an easier option than activism. Christianity allows you to be radical without arguing for any concrete, worldly attack on the status quo of the system. Thus Dylan can rail: 'You may own guns and you may own tanks' and 'You got gangsters in power and law-breakers makin' the rules' and 'But the enemy I see wears a cloak of decency' without any of the necessary corroborative political analysis. We are light years away, here, from the creativity and genius of "Highway 61 Revisited" or "Blood On The Tracks", "Street Legal" or "John Wesley Harding", or even from the more minor treasures of "Nashville Skyline", "Planet Waves" and "Desire".

Spiritually in this period, it may be that Bob Dylan had arrived. Artistically, he was coasting. And the history of Bob Dylan's output should have taught us that he not only doesn't stay in one place too long – he doesn't coast for long either. A creativity that had survived two decades was not going to disappear just because the 1980s had arrived.

---

can hold their own in any selection from his corpus. They offer a strange bonus, too, in their mesmerising special tension between text and recording. No other body of his work, I think, works so well 'on the page' (because so much of the lyric content hinges upon close attention to use of language itself as process, not least in Dylan's witty interaction with biblical text) and yet contains within it the writer's focusing of an intensely felt array of belief – the part of the whole brought alive so powerfully in some of Dylan's performances of these works, both in the studio and in such concert performances as in Toronto, 20/4/80.

CHAPTER EIGHT

Well I Investigated All the Books in the Library . . .

Despite the lit mob's traditional hostility to the idea of Bob Dylan as among the worthy, it is clear that while the 1980s and 1990s saw a slowing-down of output of new work by Dylan himself – they were his performance decades more than ones for new song collections – at the same time we saw the burgeoning of writing *about* him.

That much has been published about Dylan and his work in this period might seem to contradict the charge that he's been critically cold-shouldered almost entirely: but the detail of who has published what and when confirms it.

As noticeable as this boom itself has been its late arrival. When my own book was first published, Dylan had already been making records for over a decade: records that were immensely successful across age and class barriers, that were widely noted as having re-invented the limits of popular song; and that from 'A Hard Rain's A-Gonna Fall' through to "Highway 61 Revisited" and "Blonde On Blonde" had never shown any likelihood of suffering a revision downwards in esteem. By 1972 "Blonde On Blonde", Dylan's seventh album, was already six years old – yet despite not only those extraordinary songs and records but the unprecedented concerts of 1965 and 1966, the pioneering documentary film *Don't Look Back* and Dylan's unique iconic power within the most exciting decade since the 1920s – despite it all, we'd had just one critical book (by an outsider, me) one biography (by a workaday American journalist, Anthony Scaduto) and one spot-on article in *Esquire* magazine.

Frank Kermode's 'Bob Dylan: the metaphor at the end of the funnel' was a piece so out on its own when it was published, and so seldom followed-up since, that when the essence of what he was saying is quoted now in the 1990s, it seems astonishingly *modern*. Postmodern, in fact. Dylan, wrote Kermode,

> remains a poet, as he has remained a virtuoso of the voice – snarling, pushing words and tunes askew, endlessly inventive . . . His poems have to be open . . . inviting collusion. To write thus is to practice a very modern art, though, as Dylan is well aware, it is an art with a complicated past.[1]

That this perception of Dylan's postmodernism, so well understood in intuitive terms by so many of his listeners, has even now been so little taken up in the published commentaries, re-affirms the same thing as is clear from conceding just *how long ago*

1.   'Bob Dylan: the metaphor at the end of the funnel', Frank Kermode, *Esquire*, 77, 1972.

Dylan's first few albums were made: that the boom in books about Bob Dylan, having come only in the 1980s, has come very late indeed.

Even now, that boom is little thanks to the alertness of critics/reviewers as a clerisy or the perceptiveness of publishers. Almost the only books published by the mainstream have been the biographies – considered viable because they're likely to be about sex and drugs and fear and loathing and poetry, rather than just poetry. An honourable exception was the music critic Wilfrid Mellers' *A Darker Shade of Pale: A Backdrop to Bob Dylan*, awkwardly titled and more backdrop than Dylan, but published by Faber & Faber.

In 1986 Robert Shelton's *No Direction Home* finally came through from William Morrow (US) and New English Library (UK): but this was the long-awaited authoritative (even semi-authorised) biography from the ex-*New York Times* writer who had given Bob Dylan his first gig review and known him all through the careening early career years from before his first record till the post-acid-rock motorcycle crash of 1966. If anything on Dylan was going to get mainstream published, this was it.

Three years later McGraw-Hill (USA) and Michael Joseph (UK) published Bob Spitz's *Dylan: A Biography*, because it was in the spirit of Albert Goldman's bestsellers on Elvis Presley and John Lennon. Michael Joseph were so keen that they paid out for the British rights first and *then* consulted a 'Dylanologist' to find out what else about Bob Dylan was already on the market.[2]

Between then and 1997, only half a dozen books were published by mainstream imprints. Macmillan's *Dylan Companion* (1990), edited by Elizabeth Thomson (an editor on *Publishing News*) and David Gutman, was a follow-up to their *Lennon Companion*. Clinton Heylin's *Bob Dylan Behind the Shades* (1991), from Viking, was yet another biography. Richard Williams' *Dylan: A Man Called Alias* (1992) was a rather basic Dylan guidebook from Bloomsbury Press. Penguin published the paperback of *Wanted Man: In Search of Bob Dylan* (1992), edited by John Bauldie, only after this imprint had thrown away its long synonymity with quality and after rock books came to be among the things it flailed around signing up. It issued Bauldie's good book in this category in spite of itself, therefore, rather than from a commitment to critical commentary on the work of a major artist. Also in 1992, from Alfred Knopf, came *Hard Rain: A Dylan Commentary* by Tim Riley. In 1995 a listings book by Clinton Heylin, *Bob Dylan: The Complete Recording Sessions, 1960–1994* (a hardback), was published by the mainstream but small US imprint St Martin's Press, and in UK paperback by Penguin in 1996, slightly amended and under a different title, *Bob Dylan: Behind Closed Doors*.[3]

Excepting Bloomsbury Press, even these publishers were latecomers twice over: in each case, the editor–writers had to self-publish first. Elizabeth Thomson's first attempt at a collection of essays on Dylan, the 1980 *Conclusions on the Wall*, came from the so-called Thin Man Publishing of Prestwich. Clinton Heylin came to Viking's attention

---

2.   A US paperback edition came from Norton in 1993.

3.   An updated hardback edition of Heylin's early book *Stolen Moments* (re-titled *A Life in Stolen Moments: Bob Dylan Day by Day, 1941–95*) was published in the US in 1996 by the specialist imprint Schirmer . . . without a publisher's name on the title page at all. In the UK this is distributed by the music sales division of rock books specialist Omnibus Press. Schirmer has also published *The Bob Dylan Companion: Four Decades of Commentary*, ed. by Carl Benson, paperback, 1998.

because in 1988 he had first published (and successfully marketed, even on airport bookstalls) his Dylan book *Bob Dylan: Stolen Moments* via Wanted Man (no relation), which was in turn just the name John Bauldie used to suggest a publishing house when he started running the Bob Dylan fanzine the *Telegraph* from a room in his bungalow outside Bury, Lancashire in 1981. The John Bauldie book Penguin published twelve years later was a second collection of pieces from that fanzine, which had by then long been an admirable critical quarterly, no thanks to the lit mob.

Most work on Bob Dylan since the end of the 1970s has continued to come from fringe publishers and 'rock books' imprints. Jonathon Cott's *Dylan* came from the book division of *Rolling Stone* magazine; John Herdman's *Voice Without Restraint* needed Paul Harris Publishing of Edinburgh; the three books on Dylan's art as performance, by Betsy Bowden (one book) and Paul Williams (two), have come respectively from Indiana University Press and the esoteric Underwood-Miller of Novato, California. In Britain, Bowden's book hasn't been published at all; Williams' UK outlet is Xanadu for the hardbacks and rock-books-only imprint Omnibus for the paperbacks.

Similarly, Daniel Kramer's book of historic photos has been republished in large format by rock-books-only Plexus Publishing in the UK, and in the Citadel Press Underground Series in the US. The two best end-of-the-1980s studies of Dylan's work, Aidan Day's *Jokerman* and Stephen Scobie's *Alias Bob Dylan*, are from the academic publisher Blackwell (UK) and Red Deer College Press (Canada) respectively. The first collection of pieces from the *Telegraph* (*All Across the Telegraph: A Bob Dylan Handbook*, edited Gray and Bauldie) came from Sidgwick & Jackson, which sounds mainstream, belongs to Macmillan and is even located in Bloomsbury: but they issued it as a pop book alongside *Wham's Last Stand* (literally alongside it in their January–July 1987 catalogue), while Bauldie's *The Ghost of Electricity* (1989) was again self-published, and the hardback of the second *Telegraph* collection came from the obscure Black Spring Press, not so much a publishing house as a publishing cardboard box.

The crucial *Tangled up in Tapes Revisited* by Glen Dundas and the first two editions of an equivalent tome by Michael Krogsgaard, invaluable reference books collating exactly which Bob Dylan performances exist on tape, listing the repertoires of several hundred of his concerts and much more besides, have been self-published from Thunder Bay, Ontario and Copenhagen. Krogsgaard's third version, *Positively Bob Dylan*, finally gained him a publishing deal – with rock-listings specialists Popular Culture Ink of Ann Arbor, Michigan. Steve Michel's concordance of Dylan's lyrics (*The Bob Dylan Concordance*) did not find the support of an academic or mainstream publishing imprint; an approximate British equivalent, Dave Percival's more user-friendly but gruesomely titled *Love Plus Zero / With Limits*, is also self-published. So too is the extremely useful book of essays *Bob Dylan's Words: A Critical Dictionary and Commentary* (1994), edited by American academics Richard Wissolik and Scott McGrath.[4]

4.   In 1991 Richard Wissolik published a bibliographical listing (unfortunately a selection rather than an attempt to be inclusive) of work on Dylan, titled *Bob Dylan: American Poet and Singer: An Annotated Bibliography and Study Guide of Sources and Background Materials 1961–1991*. This too was self-published. Both were to be available on computer disk in 1996.

A sea-change seemed to occur only in 1997, when Greil Marcus' *Invisible Republic: Bob Dylan's Basement Tapes* was not only given mainstream publication, by Henry Holt in the US, but (as I mentioned in the Preface) also gained a vast amount of critical and reviewing attention in the press, really breaking through some form of barrier, thanks to Greil Marcus' stature in rock and cultural studies criticism.

Many of these books and other publications have added hugely to our knowledge of the background to Bob Dylan's work, the enormous extent of it and the ways in which it can be seen to be valuable. What follows, therefore, before the main business of looking at that work itself (from the post-evangelical period) is a survey of some of this burgeoning body of writing about Dylan's work, which is, of course, another way of looking at Dylan's work in any case.

To begin with the biographies is to begin with the salutary story of Robert Shelton's *No Direction Home*: a book that was, in essence, too long in the making for its own good. I must declare an interest here: in 1973 Shelton paid me to do some background work for it, including sketching out possible compilations of unreleased Dylan tracks. The information available back then, the tiny number of tapes that had percolated through, the discographies to draw on: these were worlds away from what was around by the time Shelton was finalising his manuscript some thirteen years later. Instead of scrapping, or asking me to update, these old lists, he published them unamended: exactly the sort of act Shelton was quick to see as cavalier in those who used his name on 'background work' down the years. I may have been the only person to feel discredited by default in this way (I don't know), but a certain carelessness and lopsidedness (as between its concentration on Dylan's early years and its all-too-perfunctory gloss over later periods) seemed basic to the book.

There were many reasons for this: Shelton was cruelly messed about by succeeding editors at his American publishing house, so that after originally planning for two volumes, the first up to 1966 and the second after, he was eventually denied this scope; after years of writing and re-writing some 300,000 words, he then had the dispiriting, time-demanding task of pruning 100,000 words out of it (with Dylan, of course, inconveniently active all across the interim).

All the while, since Shelton had chosen to move out of New York City to get the book written in the first place, and to move to a tiny cottage up a dirt track off Sydenham Hill in south-east London, he also found himself grappling with an isolation far worse than the interventions he foresaw himself suffering if he stayed in New York. There he'd been a medium-sized fish in a big pond. As folk music critic on the *New York Times*, fêted by the music industry as well as by agreeable sections of Greenwich Village, he was disdainful of the bribes constantly offered, yet resentful of others' profiting from the very integrity that kept him poor: ever bitter, for instance, that Dylan's manager Albert Grossman could use a Shelton review of a Janis Joplin gig to land her a huge Columbia Records contract (making Grossman mega-bucks overnight) precisely because Columbia knew Shelton's rave review could not have been bought.

So Shelton escaped from all that, and from the impossible pressures he felt would rain down on him from Dylan's office if he were in town trying to write what was agreed to be the big Dylan book . . . and landed up in a characteristically miserable, philistine part of south-east London where there was no music in the cafés at night (there were no cafés), no choice in the shops, it could take ninety minutes by wretched, filthy public transport to get in or out of the West End, there were no late-night buses, and certainly no equivalent to the cameraderie and sub-cultural street-life of the Greenwich Village in which Shelton had been a star. In Sydenham he was just a middle-aged American weirdo: a small fish in no pond at all but rather, out of water. And getting divorced.

Over and above that, he soon ran out of money and had to keep breaking off from the book to write bits of journalism – and as any freelance journalist knows, this means being underpaid, undervalued and badly treated as a matter of course.

His finances were under further pressure from paying storage on thousands of albums acquired from reviewing in New York (there's no such thing as a free platter). There was no room for them in the cottage, where the papers for the book alone took up a room full of filing cabinets. He generally wouldn't let people even peep into this room, though whether this was because the paperwork was a lot less, or a lot less ordered, than he wanted to maintain, or was just symptomatic of the paranoia he derided in Bob Dylan but came close to manifesting himself, I was in no position to decide. Either way, while he often surrounded himself with bright young things from *Let It Rock*, *Time Out* and the universities (one of whom was the aforementioned Elizabeth Thomson), essentially he worked alone: happy to draw out others on Dylan's work but reluctant with the quid pro quo of discussing his own ill-starred project.

Out of touch with any thriving arts scene of the kind he had helped to shape before his emigration, he was also out of touch with Dylan collectors. Wary because he had uncirculated tapes he feared having stolen, he was nonetheless given to tantalising others by describing some of these treasures – 'I've got a tape of Dylan teaching Robbie Robertson 'Sad-Eyed Lady of the Lowlands' in a hotel-room in March '66: I have it because I was in the room at the time', he once told me – and, more rarely, playing fragments of one or two of these things. The tantalising fragment I got was of a 1966 song, very 'She's Your Lover Now' / 'Sooner Or Later (One Of Us Must Know)', with the line 'So *strange* to *see* the chand*aliers* de*stroyed* . . .' At the same time he needed to keep all this stuff to himself to avoid dishonouring or losing Dylan's trust: a hard fear to live and work under since Dylan's trust was bound to be, in any circumstances, fitful.[5]

In the end, no wonder that despite its solidity, its wide-ranging interests and its many gems, the book is disappointing, tainted by a haste that usually betrays a too-quick project, not one nearly twenty years in the making. When it emerged at last, the reviews were mixed. The *London Review of Books* summed up one basic response of Dylan aficionados who had awaited it so long: 'It is not too harsh to accuse Shelton of squandering his opportunity . . . of unrivalled scope.'[6] It *was* too harsh,

---

5.   The tape in question subsequently passed from Shelton to John Bauldie and hence into general circulation among collectors.

6.   Danny Karlin, 'It ain't him, babe', *London Review of Books*, 5/2/87.

preposterously so; other mainstream reviews called it 'rather magnificent', 'brilliant', a 'triumph'. The truth, as Shelton himself conceded, lay somewhere in between. Perhaps its best accolade lies in its longevity. Time is on its side. Like many a Dylan album, initial anxious disappointment or dissatisfaction is replaced later by a fuller appreciation of its riches. Robert Shelton died, aged 69, in his adopted home town of Brighton, England, on 11 December 1995.

Next down the biographical unfairway came Bob Spitz, with *Dylan: A Biography*, a book which, in contrast, cost its author nothing in either time or pain. 'Spitz (by name and spits by nature)', as Andrew Ford noted, 'is the sort of writer who wants to grow up to be Albert Goldman . . . not much of an ambition.'[7]

And then there was Clinton Heylin, whose *Stolen Moments* set itself the blood-curdling task of documenting what Bob Dylan had done on every day of his life up till Heylin's completion date, and who followed up this triumph of train-spotting with *Behind the Shades*, which, unlike Shelton's book, pays Dylan's later years as much attention as the earlier ones, and attracted some good reviews. The ferocious denigration of Shelton's work, and its misrepresentation, were unnecessary weapons in Heylin's self-promotion, granted that his detailed spade-work was of such value.[8]

In 1997 and 1998, to bring the biographical round-up up to date, there came two biographies with a difference. Dave Engel's *Dylan in Minnesota: Just Like Bob Zimmerman's Blues* was self-published straight into paperback, with distribution by Amherst Press of Wisconsin, in the US, and not published at all in Britain. Uninvitingly laid-out, it is nonetheless a quite wonderful, in-depth, intelligent study of Dylan's family background, of Duluth and Hibbing and Dylan's growing up there, in the course of which Engel also offers an exceptional and well-researched local history of these places per se. This is a labour of love and hard work, crossing boundaries into genealogy and demanding of itself much rigour for detail. It deserves to have received far more attention than it has from either Minnesota Tourism or Bob Dylan aficionados. In 1998, also straight into paperback, published by a newcomer among rock book imprints, Helter Skelter of London, came C. P. Lee's *Like the Night: Bob Dylan and the Road to Manchester Free Trade Hall*, a most timely and readable account of that 'Judas!' moment and all that surrounded it.

There have also been one or two Dylan studies halfway between biography and critique, beginning with a section in that rave from the grave memoir *My Life in Garbology* by A. J. Weberman, which, remarkably, wasn't published until 1980. It describes this first so-called Dylanologist's application of his pioneering idea that the dustbins of creative artists would be revealing about their states of mind. This was a truly creative, anarchic breakthrough in the annals of criticism and biography, despite its being born of what might be looked back on as an especially ephemeral sixties speed-freak derangement. There was nothing deranged, or very interesting, about

---

7.   Andrew Ford, 'Wagner v. a man named Zimmerman', *Sydney Morning Herald*, 26/8/89.

8.   Robert Strachan, in 'The making of a rock biography: authority and critical space' (MA thesis in Popular Music Studies, University of Liverpool, 1997), notes in a scrupulously even-handed account that 'Heylin deliberately misrepresents *No Direction Home* in order to undermine Shelton's biographical authority at the same time as establishing his own.'

Jonathon Cott's halfway-house book *Dylan* (1985) but the photos were terrific. Gray and Bauldie's *All Across the Telegraph* (1987) and its follow-up (1990) also straddled the borders of biography and lit crit, as perhaps does the semi-biographical study from the fresh perspective of East German writer Gottfried Blumenstein, *Mr. Tambourine Man: Leben und Musik von Bob Dylan* (1991; published only in German and so a closed book to me) and, seven years later, English music journalist Andy Gill's indecisively titled *Don't Think Twice, It's All Right: Bob Dylan the Early Years, the Stories Behind Every Song* (US paperback from the obscure Thunders Mouth Press) or *Classic Bob Dylan 1962–69: My Back Pages, the Stories Behind Every Song* (UK hardback from the Carlton Seven Oaks imprint). This list is not exhaustive.

We are lucky to have the scrupulous reference books by Michael Krogsgaard and Glen Dundas, which help the rest of us out in many dozens of different ways, contributing to our understanding of, and the accuracy of, the data we lean on, which they make incomparably more accessible than it ever used to be. Unluckily for the tireless compilers of these works, however computer-assisted they may be, they face the recurrent task of having to update, and so re-order, this vast body of material. In November 1991, Dylan was handed a copy of Dundas' *Tangled up in Tapes Revisited* on his tour bus somewhere in the Midwest, and is reported to have handed it back remarking that it only showed where he'd been – and that he'd appreciate instead a book that showed him where he was going. I'm sure Glen Dundas understands that Dylan wasn't truly denigrating the book but simply giving a journalist a sound-bite that, as so many times before, sends out more complex resonances to those who know his work. Dylan well understands that past and future are not two separate books, and that, as he put it in 1981's self-searching 'Need A Woman', 'what's waiting for you in the future might be what you're runnin' from in the past'.

The fanzines too have been labours of love, more impressively in Britain than in America, which has produced only the long-defunct *Zimmerman Blues* and its spasmodic successor *Look Back*, a mix of goodish info and poorish articles that has already gone through three different managements, and the characterless 1990s newcomer *On the Tracks*. Until comparatively recently, Britain has supported three very different fanzines: the short-lived and splendidly named *Homer, the slut* (the reference is to a character in Dylan's novel *Tarantula*), the long-running, information-based *Isis* and, as cited above, the yet longer-running *Telegraph*.[9]

This last, founded and always edited by John Bauldie, was the best overall source of information and inquiry as regards the work of Bob Dylan through most of the 1980s and for more than half of the 1990s, right up to John Bauldie's untimely death.[10] Yet it was not immune from some of the same faults as any clique: often only

9.   *Homer, the slut* has since been closed down by its editor, Andrew Muir, and re-opened as a personal web-page. A new fanzine, *Dignity*, claiming to emphasise 'serious analysis', began as from November 1995, though in fact its editorial policy of not editing contributions has encouraged far too much of the what-I-thought-of-last-night's-concert school of 'criticism', while the protracted illness of editor John Baldwin has unfortunately meant much irregularity in the timing of its appearance. In Summer 1998 these fanzines were joined by *The Bridge*, visually an exact copy of what the defunct *Telegraph* had come to look like – same size, paper, typeface, use of colour photographs, and same mix of contents – intended as a tribute to Bauldie's vision while acknowledging the impossibility of duplicating his spirit.

10.   John Bauldie died, aged 47, in the crash of Chelsea Football Club Chairman and Dylan-fan Matthew Harding's helicopter, 22/10/96, less than a year after the death of Robert Shelton.

half-bothering to document information with proper detail, withholding information without saying so, maintaining an élite inner circle while using a populist tone, and often acquiring what reader Bob Jope called a 'back-slappingly jocular voice' that reminded him of 'the older generation of literary critics I struggled through at university and their over-familiarity with . . . "Jack" Donne, "Tom" Nashe, "Will" Shakespeare, or, perhaps ghastliest of all, "dear" Jane'.[11]

The witholding of information seemed to me the worst offence in a magazine coming from what called itself 'the Bob Dylan Information Office', and it may have arisen from its editor perhaps being less interested in informing the Bob Jopes than in collecting 'new' Dylan tapes, so that when a conflict occurred between these two activities – one requiring dissemination, the other secrecy – secrecy won out. In the *Telegraph*, no. 27 (1987), reader 'John Grundy, Cleethorpes' (a designation with uneasy undertones itself) wrote:

> One of the subjects I'd very much like to see covered . . . is the history of Dylan tapes and the consequent development of bootleg records . . . How did they become available? Why do some recordings remain unknown for fifteen years before mysteriously emerging? In short, what are the mechanics of this mysterious subculture from which we all benefit?[12]

Good, fundamental questions: and, perhaps more than any others, crucial equally to the two main (and often warring) factions of Dylan-listeners keen enough to subscribe to a specialist magazine, the lit crit types and the train-spotters. No answer was published.

Yet the explosion of material on Dylan and the documenting of his output that *has* appeared in the *Telegraph* – by a fine alliance of distinguished critics and so-called ordinary Dylan punters contributing (and free of charge) information, cuttings, obsessions, essays and all manner of feedback – add up to what its irreplaceable editor made into a greater body of scholarship and reliability of focus, serious and resourceful, than was ever available to us through the previous decades, and of a much higher standard than any approach to Dylan's work yet shown by any TV arts programme or 'quality press' arts section.

Additionally, an early offshoot, augmenting the work of the magazine itself, was its series of booklets in the *Wanted Man Study Series*, which included Aidan Day's 'Bob Dylan: Escaping on the run' (1984); Bert Cartwright's 'The Bible in the lyrics of Bob Dylan' (1985) and Nick de Somogyi's 'Jokermen & Thieves: Bob Dylan and the ballad tradition' (1986).

The critical *books* on Dylan's work in the last two decades begin with John Herdman's *Voice Without Restraint: Bob Dylan's Lyrics and Their Background* (1982), a modest and worthy contribution to close-to-the-text Dylan criticism, strong on ballad-tradition roots, though so avowedly influenced by my own book that it's hard for me to comment. Reading it gave me the eerie illusion of reading work of my own that I had no memory of ever having written.

Next comes Betsy Bowden's book *Performed Literature: Words and Music by*

11. *Telegraph*, no. 34, Winter 1989.
12. *Telegraph*, no. 27, Summer 1987.

Bob Dylan (also 1982), a pioneering attempt both to find an apt language for discussing in print the non-print parts of Dylan's art (whether the title augurs success at this task will strike readers differently) and, in the process, to look at the importance of performance for song as a whole. She is touching here on central concerns of present-day folklore studies, the drift of which throughout the 1980s has been away from 'text' and towards 'performance'.

The other books about Dylan as performer are by Paul Williams: *Performing Artist: The Music of Bob Dylan. Volume One, 1960–1973* (1990), *Performing Artist, the Middle Years: 1974–1986* (1992), and his anthology of articles and reviews, *Watching the River Flow: Observations on Bob Dylan's Art-in-Progress, 1966–1995* (1996). These books come with such lavish quotes of tribute from a bullyingly hip bunch of celebrities – including Sam Shepard – that it's hard to demur; but even before trying to read the first volume I felt like demurring, after emerging the other side of his 'review' of "Under the Red Sky" in the *Telegraph*, no. 37 (Winter 1990), the foamingly cutesy title of which warns of what is to come. It is called, with excruciating imagined Dylanesquerie, 'Those talking crazy, spilling my buttermilk, not one more kiss blues', and gushes with a folksy chumminess matched only by Senator Sam Irvine's single of 'Bridge Over Troubled Water'.

This is the opening tone he chooses: 'What do I think of "Under The Red Sky"? Is that what you wanna know, pal?' – at once prompting the answer: no, Paul. But of course he's not listening, he's bombasting: 'OK, I'll tell you. I fucking love it.' Despite what everyone else who's ever listened to Bob Dylan thinks, he claims that 'Wiggle Wiggle' gives the album 'a really wonderful beginning'. 'Unbelievable', he lies to himself, 'is just the sort of thing that could come over the airwaves and change the life of some kid who's never heard anything like this before.' Par for the coarse, then, that he should 'love' the engaging title track while noticing almost none of its particulars: 'Nice guitar playing, wow. And the vocal performance – 49 years old, singing with what's left of his voice, and he can come up with something like this! It's indescribable, it could drive you to drink. It could break your heart. Watch out. This is what we live for, isn't it? And this is why we read the *Telegraph* – in hopes of hearing someone else say that they felt it too?' No, Paul. In fact if this was what I lived for, I'd kill myself.

With special pleading like this 'febrile dithyramb', as George Beddow called it in a subsequent issue, who needs adverse criticism? As Beddow notes, 'The essence of Williams' unconvincing argument is that, while we should refrain from making too close an examination of what Dylan actually says, we should all nevertheless be profoundly grateful for the way in which he says it.'[13]

All this is singled out here because it summarises how a large, bellicose faction of Dylan 'fans' approach his work. It matters because the more we and Bob Dylan rub up against this airheaded apologism – which constantly seeks to blur critical perception or rubbish the attempt to apply any: it's how these people cope with finding much of Dylan's recent work less consequential, numinous and skilful than his earlier songs – the more it devalues his best work, old and new.

Beddow visits upon the same unfortunate album this vexed question of the downside of Dylan's recent work, citing the 'sterile familiarity of Dylan's thematic

13. *Telegraph*, no. 38, Spring 1991.

concerns . . . : a series of diluted, inert, far from startling vignettes of impending apocalypse; affairs of the heart in which women (still addressed by a near 50-year-old as "baby") insist upon distracting our oh-so-vulnerable . . . protagonist by means of their devious charms; and catchpenny sloganeering passing itself off as "social criticism".'

Such darkling doubts have had more soil to grow in in the 1980s and 1990s than ever before. Songs like 'Band Of The Hand' and 'Clean-Cut Kid' certainly sag under quantities of shallow, formulaic 'social criticism'. There are, distressingly, weary pop love songs that evoke no real people or feelings beyond an unstated weariness, and in which 'baby' is used with all the point and panache it would hold in a Neil Diamond song. And yes, contemporary Dylan often lets his obsession with imminent apocalypse run ahead of his creative authenticity in handling it: coming close to sounding like an old loony with a sandwich-board (with a message that rigid) whose attention is never responsively upon the real world, in which life goes on all around him. Proclaiming 'the end of the world is nigh' is not in itself profound; citing the awesomeness of Armageddon does not in itself make for an awesome citation. This syndrome produces, in Dylan's 1980s work, the over-declamatory 'When The Night Comes Falling From The Sky' and the specious coarseness of 'It's hell-time, man' and 'the last fire-truck, from hell'. Beddow is right to identify these negative developments. But with the exceptions of the 'catchpenny sloganeering' (a phrase guilty of its own charge, of course) of 'Unbelievable' and the dodgy pop-sponginess of 'Born In Time', the "Under The Red Sky" album is not the right target for these criticisms. "Empire Burlesque" is.

These and other topics to do with this 'downside of Dylan's recent work' get some scrutiny later.

If *Song & Dance Man* got there first (in the early 1970s) with Dylan's right to be in the canon – the High Culture Hall of Fame, to put it in terms the American music-biz might understand – and with a look at some of the work by others that might have inspired or coloured Dylan's own (though it looked as much at folksong, blues and rock'n'roll as at Blake, Browning and Eliot), so in the late 1980s came the first two books on Bob Dylan's work to deal in the parallel preoccupations of postmodernist, post-structuralist criticism – in which the canon has crumbled, the 'authority' of the author has gone and the most interesting source for the work is the work itself. This new criticism is especially alert to questions of identity, its fragmentedness and open-endedness.

In the case of Dylan, this means a stress on who-and-what Bob Dylan is, and what his 'text' is, and scrutiny of his 'self-referring' songs – for instance those products of the Muse which are *about* seeking, chasing and needing the Muse.

The books on Dylan in which such ideas have penetrated – ideas hovering in the outside critical-intellectual world since late-1960s/early-1970s work by Roland Barthes, Jacques Derrida and other cultural-studies guerrillas[14] – are Aidan Day's

---

14. This slow momentum of ideas really began far earlier, perhaps with a book of radical linguistics by Ferdinand de Saussure published in 1916, which leads into the post-Saussurean linguistics of the 1970s of Jacques Lacan, Louis Hjelmslev and others. There is also the German Rezeptionsästhetik developed from Hans Robert Jauss by Wolfgang Iser and others. Such slow dissemination of ideas is often simply because of language barriers. Cultural

Jokerman: Reading the Lyrics of Bob Dylan (1988)[15] and *Alias Bob Dylan* by Stephen Scobie (1991).

Scobie specifies some of these new critical notions: that 'the very idea of "canon" itself is now in question', that 'What dies in "the death of the Author" is . . . his authority: . . . the position of the author as the final criterion by which every reading of a work is to be measured and judged', and that rather than being 'concerned with Bob Dylan as biography', the aim is to deal 'with the alias Bob Dylan: "Bob Dylan" as text . . . multiple and shifting'.

This is why Day and Scobie both draw out the postmodernist significance of Dylan's 1965 sleeve note declaration about eyes and mouths: 'I cannot say the word eye any more . . . there is no eye – there is only a series of mouths – long live the mouths', with Scobie also noting Dylan's comments on 'Up To Me' in "Biograph": 'I don't think of myself as Bob Dylan. It's like Rimbaud said, "I is another".'

The writer Paul Auster explores these issues more or less contemporaneously with Scobie and Day, as in his novel *City of Glass* (1985), a detective story in which most of the mystery lies in the multi-layered sub-text, which, as Aidan Day says of Bob Dylan's work, is all about identity. Like the 'he' and 'you' and 'I' in a song like 'Tangled Up In Blue', the main characters here are always shifting. The supposed main character in Auster's novel is Quinn. Quinn writes mystery novels under a pseudonym, William Wilson. These novels have a hero called Work:

> Over the years, Work had become very close to Quinn. Whereas William Wilson remained an abstract figure for him, Work had increasingly come to life. In the triad of selves that Quinn had become, Wilson served as a kind of ventriloquist. Quinn himself was the dummy, and Work was the animated voice that gave purpose to the enterprise. If Wilson was an illusion, he nevertheless justified the lives of the other two. If Wilson did not exist, he nevertheless was the bridge that allowed Quinn to pass from himself into Work. And little by little, Work had become a presence in Quinn's life, his interior brother.

Then one day (and here, as Aidan Day might say, is the peculiarly postmodernist joke), Quinn answers the phone and the voice on the other end asks, ' "Is this Paul Auster?" ' . . . and the I and I and I and I curls around and around on itself. Or as Dylan has it in 'Brownsville Girl', 'the only thing we knew for sure about Henry Porter is that his name wasn't Henry Porter'.

The following passage too rubs shoulders with Dylan's own remarks on the relation between Bob Dylan and his creator, Robert Zimmerman:

> If he lived now in the world at all, it was only at one remove, through the imaginary person of Max Work. His detective necessarily had to be real . . . It was not precisely that Quinn wanted to be Work, or even to be like him, but it reassured him to pretend to be Work as he was writing his books, to know that he had it in him to be Work if he ever chose to be, if only in his mind.

---

studies hero Walter Benjamin was writing crucial essays in the 1930s that weren't translated into English for forty years.

15. With amendments, Day's book was republished in paperback in 1989; quotation in the present work is from this amended edition.

These are not the sole Dylan conjunctions you'll find in a reading of *City of Glass*. Here too is Paul Auster (the 'real' Paul Auster, the one who has written the 'real' book) on the I/eye pun:

> Private eye. The term held a triple meaning for Quinn. Not only was it the letter 'i', standing for 'investigator', it was 'I' in the upper case, the tiny life-bud buried in the body of the breathing self. At the same time, it was also the physical eye of the writer, the eye of the man who looks out from himself into the world and demands that the world reveal itself unto him. For five years now, Quinn had been living in the grip of this pun.

Scobie too leans heavily on the I/eye pun, often suggesting Dylan's use of it where no one else has suspected one. That's par for the critical course perhaps, and even more so on the post-structuralist course where the text is whatever you see in it: yet oddly he tends to lapse from this position to argue that Dylan's punning on I/eye is deliberate – which is actually to take the old-fashioned, pre-structuralist line that allows the author's surmised intention to 'authorise' the meaning being looked at.

Oddly too, Scobie doesn't mention one of the best instances, and one where Dylan incontrovertibly intends the pun, the point in 'Hurricane' at which Dylan sings:

> *And though this man could hardly see*
> *They told him he could i-dentify*
> *the guilty man,*

where Dylan's alert delivery lands on that i/eye, and at once re-emphasises it by the insistence of his internal rhyming at each end of the word ('i-denti*fy*'), to stress so deftly, and without a doubt, the sick(bed) injustice of framing (yes) the accused by getting a visual identification from someone who can hardly see.[16]

For Scobie, though, the point of Dylan's I/eye pun lies elsewhere than in its special felicity within particular songs: encapsulating the death-of-the-author theory's radical questioning of the way we view the individual and the self, it shows, as with his quoting of Rimbaud's 'I is another', that Dylan's own concerns embrace the modern critical issue of the overthrow of the (male) eye's authorial gaze upon the world. He points to the recurrent theme of the mask in Dylan's work, to the perpetual fluidity of Dylan's songs in performance and to his career-spanning series of different voices ('a series of mouths'). His argument is that 'the notion that we are not singular entities but variable and multiple personalities' is a major concern of Dylan's work itself, and that in this sense, 'far from being opposed to critical theory, Dylan's work thematises one of its central questions.'

The new criticism inspires Aidan Day's concentration too on areas of Bob Dylan's art that seem to reflect such ideas back at him – including those songs which, as he puts it so concisely, 'take as their immediate subject the creative processes by which they are themselves brought into being', his prime example being 'Mr. Tambourine Man'.[17]

16. This instance was pointed out by Danny Karlin, Department of English, University College London, in a review of Day's book in the *Telegraph*, no. 32, Spring 1989.

17. A version of Day's material on 'Mr. Tambourine Man' had been published the previous year in *All Across the Telegraph* (1987).

Likewise postmodern questions about how we see the individual and the self fire Day's interest in Dylan's 'non-linear narratives': songs like 'Tangled Up In Blue' that don't have a fixed or clearly identifiable voice telling a clear sequential story – songs which, he argues, reflect the non-linear (tangled up) way the human brain is currently thought to perceive and interpret the world in front of it and the past behind it. His concern here is for 'lyrics which open out into an exploration of the workings of the psyche as a whole': including 'Shelter From The Storm', 'Isis' and (via 'I Shall Be Released') 'Tangled Up In Blue'.

'Tangled Up In Blue', thanks especially to the re-confirmed open-endedness of its having had a spectacular lyric revision in 1984, is the crucial Dylan song for post-struckies. It takes them where they want to go. It excites them because, more than any other single Dylan song, it is not a single Dylan song. It is a living demonstration of how unfixed 'the text' is.

And that is by no means its only special value. It excites Neil Corcoran ('Going barefoot: thinking about Bob Dylan's lyrics')[18] because it goes a stage further, explicitly *declaring* its own open-endedness (making it too a self-referring text):

'Tangled Up In Blue' encodes an account of itself in its own variations; it becomes an allegory of its own procedures. Keeping on keeping on, getting on the train and riding, staying on the road and heading towards the sun become not only the activities recommended by the song, but what the song . . . does; it changes, it adapts, it refuses the consolations of the finished in favour of a poetics of process, of constant renewal, of performance rather than publication. Recommending the provisional as an ethic, it also embodies it as an aesthetic.

It excites Aidan Day also because of a fundamental effect that comes, he argues, from the way the lyric splits its 'I' into an 'I' and a 'he', and splits its 'she' into what may be a series of shes and into 'she' and 'you'. The effect is this:

Considerable inventive effort on the part of the reader is provoked whether the lyric is taken either as one story or as a series of stories. Co-operation in the making of the story may be demanded of the reader of any narrative. The specially modernist feature of 'Tangled Up In Blue' is that the fragmentation of linear structure, together with the indeterminacy generated by that fragmentation about whether we are in the presence of one or more stories, encourages specific awareness of the creative role of the audience in reading or hearing narrative.

That's at the heart of the new critical claim, and it's followed up by an eloquent, admirably confident passage of Barthesian generalisation about our deep psyches:

teasing us into generating story, 'Tangled Up In Blue' also explores the extent to which the mind is fundamentally disposed to think in terms of story or narrative. The conscious self is inseparable from the stories of its own life that it ceaselessly recites, however silently, to itself . . . in the same way cultures frame themselves through myths of origin, through histories and through fictions of the future . . . the subject of the lyric is in one sense the inescapability of the narrative impulse

18. *Telegraph*, no. 27, Summer 1987.

itself. But more than this, in its disturbance of narrative order the lyric simultaneously inquires into the possibility of something beyond such order.

Like Scobie, Day also looks at 'Brownsville Girl', but where Scobie concentrates
hugely on co-writer Sam Shepard and the putative Shepardisms of the lyric, Day just
remarks that the song was 'co-written by Dylan with playwright Sam Shepard'.
Likewise with 'Isis', he only mentions in a footnote that this too was co-written, with
Jacques Levy. Day has no interest in this aspect of either song's 'splitting of the "I" '.
Rather, he is concerned to note, as with 'Tangled Up In Blue', that in 'Brownsville
Girl' 'fixed points of view and clear narrative frames of reference are never resolved',
as 'scraps of memory and thought mix with other scraps in an unstable temporal
sequence'. The lyric 'plays with tenses and perspectives as it enacts the lack of
chronological structure in the inner life of the mind', and goes further than the earlier
song because throughtout it 'the mind's images and memories have only a questionably
"real" status', and in 'its exploration of memory, "Brownsville Girl" is preoccupied
with the question of whether it is ever possible to isolate a "true" or "real" self from
the cultural context within which that self takes shape'.[19]

Then Day slides back across the years to "Blonde On Blonde" and finds Dylan
(no, sorry, that's just what the post-structuralist mustn't say: finds Dylan's *lyric*) again
advancing a post-structuralist concern, by questioning the validity of 'the fixities of a
classical canon'. Day is very good here on what's very good about 'Mona Lisa musta
had the highway blues / You can tell by the way she smiles', noting that this frustration
with canonised fixity

> is pictured acutely and comically as being experienced from within the canon.
> *Established orders are not modified simply from without, but themselves contain*
> *the seeds of their own exhaustion* [my emphasis]. The colloquialism which here
> defines the Mona Lisa's unease – her boredom with her own status – itself
> constitutes an affront to and an erosion of the laws of approved respect that
> conventionally hem her in.

There could be no better fusion than this between the critic's clear statement of
his postmodernist idea (the sentence emphasised) and the equally clear summation of
how Dylan's intuitive lines evoke the truth of it. It's at such moments, and there are
many, that Day's seems a great book.

The resonance of those same Dylan lines is of course present for him and for us –
as a 'scrap of memory' – by the time Bob Dylan has become the canonised fixity and
we find him, on "Infidels", experiencing the Mona Lisa syndrome himself on 'Don't
Fall Apart on Me Tonight': 'It's like I'm stuck inside a painting / That's hanging in the
Louvre / My throat starts to tickle and my nose itches / But I know that I can't move'.
Yet as so often with the revisits in comparatively recent songs to ideas and images

---

19.   These ideas also correspond to contemporary science's notions about memory. For example, Gerald Edelman's
pioneering work on 'neural Darwinism' (the theory of neural group selection, which denies the 1980s notion that
the brain is like a super-computer and suggests instead that a rain-forest is a more pertinent model for its processes)
includes his assertion that 'to remember . . . is not so much a process of retrieving a fixed bit of coded information
as the generation of a new act of imaginative creation' (quoted in a UK Sunday newspaper magazine section, 1993).
The specialised version of his work is his book *The Remembered Present* (1989); the popularising version is his
book *Bright Air, Brilliant Fire* (1992).

from older ones, the newer version is less succinct, vivid and striking. 'Musta had the highway blues' is more audience-trusting, more humour-sharing, more quotable and far sharper than the expression of only some of what it contains in that clumsily catalogued, over-explained 'My throat starts to tickle and my nose itches / But I know that I can't move'. More is less.

The trouble with all thematic, or expressly ideological, approaches to Dylan's work is that just as they're too busy tracking down themes to care much for the distinctive effects of specific songs ('But what do all these effects actually *say?*' bewails Stephen Scobie, after "Under The Red Sky" has charmed him into loitering in the poetry and he cannot find his footing back to a nice thematic highway), so too they take no heed of differences in quality between one piece of work and another. David Pichaske writes[20] that while people have always stressed the changes in Dylan's work down the years, what strikes him is the similarities (on the face of it, an appealing line to take, until one sees which umbrella of similarity he's trying to hold over all that work): that all the songs are about the American dream; Aidan Day's essay 'Escaping on the Run'[21] says they're all about freedom; his book saying they're all about identity; and so on . . .

This approach works against noticing whether the newer songs are anything like as good as the older ones, or whether the newer songs are anything like as good as each other. 'When The Ship Comes In' is set alongside 'Clean-Cut Kid'; 'Man of Peace' alongside 'Jokerman'. Nick de Somogyi's essay 'Jokermen & Thieves' shows that it is possible to avoid this trap, for instance in bravely downgrading 'Love Minus Zero / No Limit' compared to later songs.[22]

The problem recurs with Stephen Scobie and his seeing archetypes everywhere: "Desire" is seen so much in terms of the father figure, the Osiris and Isis archetypes and the like, that he has no time to look at the dynamics of the songs and notice their different flavours or the different levels of successful creation achieved in them. You can get to the point where any Dylan song with a 'he' and a 'she' in it is discussed in terms of Oedipal signification. You so much lose touch with the particularities of the song that you don't bother about whether it's as alive as, say, 'Most Of The Time' or as dead as, say, 'Emotionally Yours'. (And come to that, you may as well be discussing a Scott MacKenzie song or a Stock–Aitken–Waterman song in the same terms.)

Dylan himself never seeks to hide within these fate-sealing archetypes, though he often brings them into play as one resonance among many in a particular song. While he writes mockingly in 1965 that 'Friends and other strangers from their fates try to resign / Leaving men wholly totally free to do anything they wish to do but die' – and follows this up years later with the more unpleasantly evangelical glee of invoking the time 'when men will pray God to kill them and they won't be able to die' – he also puts this terrific homage to energetic restlessness inside the 1984 rewrite of that great

20. 'Bob Dylan and the American dream: the prophet and the prisoner', David Pichaske (1986) (manuscript), a foreshortened version of which appeared in the *Telegraph*, no. 26, Spring 1987.

21. *Wanted Man Study Series*, no. 3, Wanted Man, Bury, Lancs., 1984.

22. 'Jokermen & Thieves: Bob Dylan and the Ballad Tradition', *Wanted Man Study Series*, no. 5, Wanted Man, Bury, Lancs., 1986.

song about energetic restlessness, 'Tangled Up In Blue': 'Got to find someone among the women and men / Whose destiny is unclear'.

When, therefore, the theme is the death-by-pedestal syndrome, we're lucky that Aidan Day doesn't offer us 'Visions Of Johanna' and 'Don't Fall Apart On Me Tonight' equally: lucky because what the thematic twinning of songs almost always ignores is that they're *not* equal in any of the ways that matter: the ways that attract people to some music more than some other, or to some writers more deeply than to most. Bob Dylan isn't important because he discusses 'the ossification of high cultural icons' or 'unemployment in relation to the new globalist capitalism' – there are plenty of people lecturing like that to very small audiences – but because Bob Dylan writes 'Visions of Johanna', 'North Country Blues' and 'Union Sundown', in which he renders such themes creatively – to value which is necessarily to care that some are more creatively alive than others.[23]

It seems a pity, therefore, that after many chapters admirably alert to language, and liberatingly adept at using it, Aidan Day ends up spending ten pages on the song his book is named after, 'Jokerman', as if it's a philosophy essay: you'd not think there was *poetry* there at all. Many lines of the poetry are quoted, but apart from the one phrase 'with fine ironic understatement' Day never says a word about how they work or what they achieve. They're just there on the page, shining out of prose like this: 'Recurrently imaged as occupying a position removed from ordinary reality he is at the same time never envisaged as fully transcending that reality . . . But, more complexly, across the lyric as a whole, the principle of the Jokerman resists containment within a constant dualistic frame of reference.'

It's all very well for a book like Catherine Belsey's *Critical Practice* (1991) (a handy introduction to the new criticism) to offer a defence of jargon: she makes a fair point that to deplore the denseness of jargon is usually to disguise being reactionary as 'using common sense', and that since the 'common sense view' is itself only another ideology it's a pity it wields what she gamely calls the 'tyranny of lucidity' – but Aidan Day wouldn't hone in on so brilliant a user of language as Bob Dylan at all if he didn't prefer language that's alive to language that isn't.

Stephen Scobie's *Alias Bob Dylan* is still more campaigningly post-structuralist (in fact it's so post-structuralist it doesn't have an index), though it begins boldly with a preface about Robert Zimmerman's childhood in the very odd milieu of Hibbing, Minnesota: an upbringing to give any artist-to-be a formative sense of the double, if not multiple, identity of everything. (I think of this when I hear Dylan's line 'Reality [h]as always had too many heads', on 1997's 'Cold Irons Bound'.) This first part of Scobie's book is inspired, well-written and a better slice of biography than we get in the biographies (not least for a wonderful description of why 'Every stage that Bob Dylan has played on for the last thirty years has been, after Hibbing High School Auditorium, an anticlimax': it's a pity the truth is not quite that neat or funny).

Indeed, despite his disclaimers, Scobie is actually very interested in Bob Dylan's biography. Aidan Day is such a clean-cut kid about his critico-ideological position

---

23.   For a discussion of 'North Country Blues' and 'Union Sundown' as companion pieces 'about' cheap labour and the new globalism, see 'Charity is supposed to cover up a multitude of sins' by Clive Wilshin in *All Across the Telegraph*.

that he *always* writes 'this lyric says': you won't catch him writing 'Dylan says', though the difference between text cleanliness and author heresy is only maintained by this fastidious insistence over which of these fundamentally interchangeable phrases he opts for. Scobie is not so scrupulous. Unlike Day, though he may stake out his claim to be poking at 'Bob Dylan' *as* text and not as authorial personal life, he still looks at length at which love songs might or might not be to and/or about Echo, Suze Rotolo, Joan Baez or Sara Dylan.

He goes on enormously, too, about Dylan's marriage, particularly in relation to Dylan's work since the mid-1970s, extrapolating from something close to prurient interest the ostensibly disinterested argument that the 'main theme' of "Desire" is 'the crisis of patriarchy', a theme he also insists on in relation to the "Street Legal" love songs and 'Brownsville Girl':

> Much of Dylan's later work is overshadowed by the figure of the failed, absent or dying father . . . In the unfolding drama of Dylan's lifework [he would put it that way, wouldn't he?: it still means 'in Dylan's personal life'] Christianity functions not only to replace the core of conviction in love, in himself as a father, which he lost in the breakup with Sara, but precisely to replace that image of the father with another that is simultaneously authoritative (the patriarchal God of the Old Testament, the lawgiver) and sacrificial ('the Man who came and died a criminal's death').

Actually, what cannot remain unnoticed here is that while this death-of-patriarchal-authority theme may or may not be important in the 'drama of Bob Dylan's lifework', it seems to be very important indeed to Stephen Scobie's. Indeed it seems *his* preoccupation when writing his book about Bob Dylan. This possible biographical baggage, left at the terminus where father figures lose their authority and their children, may explain why, when Scobie comes to look at "Under The Red Sky" (which he does with affection and articulate aplomb), he avoids acknowledging that these nursery rhymes and counting-songs are anything at all to do with children or evoke their presence and their domain. Back Alley Sally 'doing the American Jump' reminds him of the Basement Tapes but not that it's a game children play. When he's discussing, as he does at length, the key features of the 'play' Sam Shepard published in *Esquire* called 'True Dylan', he cites the eccentricities of the sound-track on the intermittently played cassette-machine, he details the noises-off and so on: but he doesn't mention that the talk going on between Dylan and Shepard, the talk that Scobie insists is grounded in the death-of-patriarchy, is repeatedly interrupted by Dylan going off to talk on the telephone *to his daughter*. Scobie writes again and again about the father figure but never mentions children. Such omission hints at a more self-absorbed interest in these matters than Dylan evinces, or than Dylan's songs propound.

This may jump off the page as intrusive speculation. Critics like me and Scobie, stepping into the arena by publishing books and promoting them, routinely make free with Dylan's biographical 'failings', obsessions and history – his marriage, its break-up and so on – yet shrink from the very same kind of extrapolation from critical writing of what may be even the most clamouringly relevant aspects of critics' own biographies.

However, challenging a double standard as between critics and creative writers is not my reason for this personal conjecture. What justifies it is tangled up in the (self-reflexive) provocations of the new criticism itself. It is the very post-structuralism Scobie champions which insists that the meaning of any text significantly includes the baggage of feelings and experience that its audience/listener/reader brings to it. Is this not a plausible instance of the theorist enacting his own theory?

Dylan's work itself recurrently looks to children as worth taking into account, or even as being morally clean, though he has long scorned the notion of childhood 'innocence' and insists instead on the idea of 'original sin', which is part and parcel (his baggage) of his post-'My Back Pages' insistence on the guilt within us all.

The importance of children is stressed as early as 'Masters Of War' with its 'You have hurled the worst fear that could ever be hurled / The fear to bring children into the world', while in the mid-1970s work 'Joey', Gallo changes his ways for the sake of the children, and the persona of 'Abandoned Love' avows that 'wherever the children go, I'll follow them'. In the 1980s Dylan prays 'Lord Protect My Child' and on 'Caribbean Wind' gives us one of the most observant, acutely simple lines ever written about the changed tuning brought about by parenthood: 'I hear a voice crying "Daddy," I always think it's for me.'

Regardless of what the critic, the reader or the creator brings to it, this crisis-of-patriarchy-is-the-key shoots its bolt (to quote a phrase) when it extends to saying, as Scobie does, that the chorus lyrics of 'Brownsville Girl' are deliberately bad, in cahoots with the line 'if there's an original thought out there I could use it right now', to fit the argument that 'the song is, at its center, concerned with the failure of creativity, linked to the death of the father in *The Gunfighter* and the death of patriarchal authority more generally'.[24]

This deliberate-bad-inclusion-by-Dylan theory was first advanced by John Hinchey, once an academic at Swarthmore College, in an essay on the 1981 "Shot Of Love" album.[25] It seems a tiresome road to go down, and likely to give the self-reflexive text a bad name. Would a Stephen Scobie student get far by offering 'It's hard to sort out my ideas on this one' as an essay on chaos theory?

Van Morrison asks for similar trouble with 'I'd Love To Write Another Song', from the 1989 "Avalon Sunset" album, a song which, far from offering insight into the elusiveness of the muse, is only a declaration of its absence, necessarily portentous and uninteresting. This particular cul-de-sac of postmodernism was possibly first explored by renowned avant-gardist Tommy Steele, with his early-1960s 'Hit Record', the lyric of which affects to put together a list of the ingredients you need to put together to have a hit record: thereby, and with cockney cheeriness too, taking as its immediate subject the commercial processes by which it is itself brought into being. Or not, since the record was a deserved flop.

This did not discourage others, and by 1974 we started to get knowing album

24. Neither Stephen Scobie nor Aidan Day mentions the comparable but valid self-reflexion of 'Watching The River Flow', which comes from 'those relatively barren years of the early 70s' in which, therefore, it seems 'appropriate that inactivity and lack of direction' is 'subject-matter in its own right', as John Lindley put it in 'Oh mercy', *Telegraph*, no. 34, Winter 1989. From the same short session, also addressing such themes, came 'When I Paint My Masterpiece'.

25. *Telegraph*, no. 22, 1985.

titles such as "I Thought Terry Dene Was Dead" (a compilation of Terry Dene tracks).[26] They have never been popular, partly because no one likes a smartypants and partly because titles that apologise for themselves come across not as winsome but as aggressive. Only this inbuilt lack of appeal explains why it took so very many years to make the short step from the 1974 "I Thought Terry Dene Was Dead" to the 1991 Patrick Humphries and John Bauldie book-title *I Can't Believe It's Not Butter*. Or was it *Oh No! Not Another Bob Dylan Book?*[27]

What follows is, in effect, another one.

26.   Van Morrison: 'I'd Love To Write Another Song', UK; probably late 1988; "Avalon Sunset", Polydor Records 839 262–4, London, 1989. Tommy Steele: 'Hit Record', London, 1962; "The Happy World Of Tommy Steele", Decca Records [S]PA 24, London, 1969. Terry Dene: "I Thought Terry Dene Was Dead", Decca Records SPA 368, London, 1974.

27.   Patrick Humphries and John Bauldie, *Oh No! Not Another Bob Dylan Book* (1991); in US published as *Absolutely Dylan: An Illustrated Biography* (1991).

One further book needs to be mentioned – one to which the reasonable response would be far from 'oh no! not another . . .'. Announced in 1998 for publication in February 1999 from Viking Books UK was Christopher Ricks' much-rumoured *Bob Dylan: A Critical Study* (a splendidly upright, plain-speaking title). It hasn't emerged and now a spokesperson says 'it won't happen'. If this is the case, I can't think of a greater prospective loss, either to Bob Dylan criticism or for the general reader.

CHAPTER NINE

Even Post-Structuralists Oughta Have the Pre-War Blues

Actually the first record I made was in 1935. John Hammond came and recorded me. Discovered me in 1935, sitting on a farm.

Bob Dylan, interviewed by Laurie Henshaw in 'Mr. Send-up', *Disc Weekly*, 22/5/65.

Dylan was the purest of the pure. He had to get the oldest record and, if possible, the Library of Congress record, or go find the original people who knew the original song.

Harvey Abrams, a student contemporary, on the 1960 Dylan, quoted in Robert Shelton's *No Direction Home*, 1986.

. . . he's a great authority on older rock'n'roll and blues forms. You can't stump him on a record . . . The most obscure Sun sides, the most obscure rockabilly stuff, the most obscure blues, he can sit down and play them and sing them for you. He really knows his stuff . . .

Don Was, interviewed by Reid Kopel, Los Angeles, 15/10/90, *Telegraph*, no. 37, Winter 1990.

The musical and poetic power, the recurrently affecting magic, of the pre-war blues is an astonishing joy to come upon, and to delve into, even as an outsider in time, space and race. It's like your early experience of rock'n'roll: it's as if you'd been born ready to hear it – even though you felt that it sounded like nothing on earth you'd heard before.

The British musician Brian Eno articulated something of how it was to hear the latter, to hear its strangeness and yet to feel at one with it, inwardly and at once, in ways that preceded and sidelined issues of racial ownership:

For years I just listened to this stuff like music from outer space – doo-wop and so on – and I never realised that these people were all black, that this was really modern black music; and here I was, a young white lad from Suffolk, who had a whole collection of it . . . Little Richard was probably my biggest influence when I was young . . . when I first saw a picture of him I thought, Oh, he's a black man, that's interesting; then gradually I realised that so were all the others . . . Of course

I didn't know any of the origins of it; I didn't know about gospel music or anything like that. But just the ways of singing, the uses of the voice, were so original and unrestrained.[1]

So it was – is – too with the astonishing diversity and richness of the pre-war blues. If you don't know this genre, you're lucky: there are thousands of these extraordinary recordings waiting to be heard – and more readily available, now that they're all on CD, than at any time in the past: certainly they're more widely available than ever they were to their original audiences.

Because it's so crackly on record, so lo-fi, so immured behind this white-noise wall, this black noise can seem inaccessible, unreachable. Don't be put off. You just sometimes have to play it terribly loud (and maybe go into the next room): then you'll hear all the joys and mysteries of esoteric vocals, guitar magic, sheer moody weirdnesses: all the synapse-crinkling giddy-hop that rock'n'roll gave you when you were thirteen.

Garfield Akers' 'Cottonfield Blues', especially the transcendent 'Part 2', comes across as the birth of rock'n'roll . . . from 1929! It's also as incantatory as Buddhist chanting or as Van Morrison's 'Madame George'. Or there's Blind Willie Johnson's 'Motherless Children Have A Hard Time' – a record from 1927. You hear it and you say of the guitar: if this was achieved then, how come it took thirty years to get to rock'n'roll (or forty years to get to Eric Clapton)?[2]

1.   Brian Eno 'at an informal workshop involving himself and about half-a-dozen hacks', Box, Wiltshire, 1993, as reported by Andy Gill, *Q* Magazine, no. 86, November 1993.

2.   Garfield Akers (c.1900-c.1960) recorded only four tracks: 'Cottonfield Blues – Part 1' and 'Cottonfield Blues – Part 2', Memphis, c. 23/9/29; issued "Really! The Country Blues", Origin Jazz Library OJL-2, New York, 1962; and 'Dough Roller Blues' and 'Jumpin' And Shoutin' Blues', Memphis, c. 21/2/30; issued respectively on "The Mississippi Blues No. 2", Origin OJL-11 and "Country Blues Encores", Origin OJL-8, both Berkeley, 1965; all CD-reissued on "Son House and the Great Delta Blues Singers (1928–1930)", Document Records DOCD-5002, Vienna, 1990.
     Van Morrison: 'Madame George', NYC, 1968, "Astral Weeks", Warner Brothers WS1768, US [K46024, London], 1968, CD-reissued 1990s.
     Blind Willie Johnson: 'Mother's [sic: a mistranscription] Children Have A Hard Time', Dallas, 3/12/27; "Blind Willie Johnson", RBF Records RF-10, NYC, 1965.
     Johnson (c. 1900–1940s) is discussed in Chapter 5, re his use of 'two voices'. Harry Smith's "American Folk Music" (see note 22) reissued Johnson's 'John The Revelator' [Atlanta, 20/4/30] in 1952; Sam Charters' 1959 reissue album "The Country Blues" (see note 24) included Johnson's 'You're Gonna Need Somebody On Your Bond' [Atlanta, 20/4/30]. His 'Jesus Make Up My Dying Bed' [Dallas, 3/12/27] became 'In My Time Of Dyin'' on Dylan's début album. All tracks now CD-reissued "The Complete Blind Willie Johnson", Columbia Legacy Roots N' Blues Series 472190 2, 1993.
     In fact 'Jesus Make Up My Dying Bed', often spelt as 'Dying-Bed' (a compound noun like 'praying-ground' and 'cooling-board'), is an old spiritual recorded by a large number of jubilee and gospel groups, sermons-with-singing preachers and many individual singers, among them Charley Patton ['Jesus Is A Dying-Bed Maker', Grafton Wisconsin, c. Oct. 1929], a figure as early and as eminent as Blind Willie Johnson, though not so early onto disc with the song.
     Johnson remains a mysterious figure, said to have been blinded deliberately by his step-mother when he was about 7 years old, according to Johnson's wife Angeline, interviewed by Sam Charters at her shack in Beaumont, Texas, 8/11/55; interview issued on "Blind Willie Johnson: His Story", Folkways FG3585, NYC, 1963, and transcribed in the notes to "The Complete Blind Willie Johnson". (The interview circumstances and the search for Johnson as the starting-point of Sam Charters' career as a blues-hunter are also described in these notes, thirty-eight years on.)
     Johnson recorded thirty sides between 1927 and 1930, some with Angeline, and then never recorded again. His death is a mystery still. His wife says in the same interview that he died of pneumonia in 1949; but Blind Willie McTell tells John and Ruby Lomax in November 1940 that he's had a recent letter from Johnson's wife informing him of her husband's death.
     1949 seems to have been right – yet the information McTell gives on other matters in the course of his afternoon with the Lomaxes is both prodigious and uncannily accurate. (See Chapter 15 for detail on *this*

Yet it isn't that the pre-war blues are proto-rock'n'roll that makes them so uplifting, exciting and vivid. The experience of the encounter is comparable; and the music may hold some of the main ingredients that rock'n'roll returned us to using – but the pre-war blues is a liberation and an enrichment because it's different, not merely more of the same. These old blues are at once thrillingly exotic and our common heritage.

Garfield Akers – a deeply obscure but compelling, intense and distinctive artist who reputedly played around Memphis in the 1920s to 1930s and again in the 1950s – should have been a tremendous star. His shockingly small number of recordings, or, say, Furry Lewis's 'I Will Turn Your Money Green', are whole new rich seams of their own, a fresh and revelatory 3-D world, as glorious to me now at fifty plus as ever Little Richard and Buddy Holly were to me forty years ago.[3] This blues world burns with its own heroic energy and vision, and across a musical spectrum of concentrated emotional expression from the utmost in delicacy and finesse to the most soaring invocations of cacophonous rapture and pain, while the language of the blues – blues lyric poetry – is one of the great streams of consciousness of twentieth-century America: a rich and alertly resourceful African-American fusion and reinvention of the language of the Bible and the dirt road, plantation and medicine-show, of the Deep South countryside and the city streets, of nineteenth-century children's games, folk tales and family lore and African folk memory: above all the language of the oppressed community and the individual human heart. For Bob Dylan then, as listener and as writer–composer, the specifics of an old record by Jim Jackson, Blind Blake or Memphis Minnie yield far richer pleasures than a Johnny Winters or an Eric Clapton concert.

This is not a matter of being politically correct about authenticity. The whole question of 'authenticity' in black music is highly complex and contentious, and involves matters far more consequential than whether Eric Clapton plays the blues. Paul Gilroy's riveting, if sometimes barely penetrable, essay 'Sounds authentic' cites a number of these issues, across which white-boy debates about authenticity in the blues are bound to stumble rather clumsily, and from which, as Gilroy writes, authenticity 'emerges as a highly charged and bitterly contested issue'.[4]

Primarily, there are the problems that arise for post-African, post-slavery blacks

---

interview.) Why doesn't Charters, writing the booklet for the Folkways LP in 1963 in the immediate aftermath of his most pivotal involvement in McTell's work, comment on this large discrepancy?

In late 1980, approaching Christian songs from a changed perspective, Dylan brought Maria Muldaur on-stage at one of his San Francisco concerts, to sing Johnson's 'It's Nobody's Fault But Mine'; in 1992 in the studios in Chicago, Dylan recorded it himself.

[Blind Willie Johnson: 'It's Nobody's Fault But Mine', Dallas, 3/12/27, "Blind Willie Johnson: His Story". Maria Muldaur: 'It's Nobody's Fault But Mine', live, San Francisco, 19/11/80. Bob Dylan: 'It's Nobody's Fault But Mine', Chicago, April 1992, unissued.]

3.   Furry Lewis: 'I Will Turn Your Money Green' [2 takes], Memphis, 28/8/28; take 1 issued "In His Prime 1927–1928", Yazoo Records L1050, New York, c. 1975; take 2 [the version originally issued on 78] issued "Frank Stokes' Dream . . . 1927–1931", Yazoo L1008, New York, 1968. Lewis is discussed further on in the present chapter.

4.   Paul Gilroy: 'Sounds authentic: black music, ethnicity and the challenge of a *changing* same'; London, unpublished, 1991. This work is now incorporated into Gilroy's book *The Black Atlantic* (1993). Gilroy is a pioneering black British writer in the field of cultural studies. The present work also draws upon Gilroy's in Chapter 18.

as to how their contemporary musics in different places around the world build on, or move away from, pre-diaspora black musics.

> The transnational structures which brought the black Atlantic world into being have themselves developed and now articulate its myriad cultural forms into a system of global communications. This fundamental dislocation of black cultural forms is especially important in the recent history of black musics which, produced out of the racial slavery which made modern western civilisation possible, now dominate its popular cultures.
>
> . . . If, for example, a style, genre or performance of music is identified as being expressive of the absolute essence of the group that produced it, what special analytical problems arise? What contradictions appear in the transmission and adaptation of this cultural expression by other diaspora populations . . . ? . . . Once the music is perceived as a world phenomenon, what value is placed upon its origins in opposition to its contingent loops and fractal trajectories?

Gilroy goes on to note that the problem

> of cultural origins and authenticity . . . assumed an enhanced significance as mass culture . . . acquired new technological bases and black music became a truly global phenomenon. It [took] on greater proportions as original, folk or local expressions of black culture were identified as authentic and positively evaluated for that reason, while hemispheric or global manifestations of the same cultural forms got dismissed as inauthentic and therefore lacking in cultural or aesthetic value precisely because of their distance (supposed or actual) from a readily identifiable point of origin.

For Gilroy, 'the unashamedly hybrid character of . . . black cultures continually confounds any simplistic . . . understanding of the relationship . . . between folk cultural authenticity and pop cultural betrayal'.

As he moves immediately to stress, 'Pop culture has, in any case, been prepared to endorse the premium on authenticity . . . The discourse on authenticity has been a notable presence in the mass marketing of successive black folk-cultural forms to white audiences. The distinction between rural and urban blues provides one good example of this.'[5]

Rather than argue, therefore, as to whether the blues can really be called the blues when purveyed by the Eric Claptons who speed 'black cultural creation on its passage into international pop commodification', I prefer to suggest, as I think Bob Dylan would, that *that* sort of blues is simply no longer interesting.

It can't be: it's no longer interest*ed* – in either the specifics of where it's come from or of what it's thrown away. Such is its shopping-mall forgetfulness that it makes you feel like agreeing, regardless of any other arguments pro or con, with the editorial stance of the American magazine *Living Blues* – a stance deplored in an interesting essay by the Mexican-American folklorist Peter Narváez – which is that the blues must

---

5.   And, Gilroy adds, 'it is not enough for critics to point out that representing authenticity always involves artifice. This may be true, but it is not helpful when trying to evaluate or compare cultural forms, let alone in trying to make sense of their mutation.'

be music by blacks, and that 'deprived of its historical base . . . the blues as purveyed by whites, is no longer the blues'.[6]

Yet Dylan stands in a different relation to 'black cultural creation'. In his relation to the blues, Dylan occupies a position as near to that of the poet or composer (even to the critic) as to the rock'n'roll performer. Indeed his work is a highly individual refutation of the *Living Blues* line.

If Dylan's stance is so different from that of the white frontmen of the transglobal blues industry, the difference arises from how he feels about the potency and the eloquence of the old blues records and the expressive vernacular of the world they inhabit. This is why what Dylan wants to do with this immense, rich body of work is experiment in how he might utilise its poetry, its codes and its integrity – to see how these may stand up as building blocks for new creative work – just as he (and just as the blues) uses the language and lore of the King James Bible. He is not concerned with translating a few lowest-common-denominator dynamics of the blues into some MTVable product.

First, he claims no blues singer specialism like a John Hammond Jr: it isn't, for him, his trademark. His stance does not downgrade blackness per se, and therefore does not carry the inherent sub-text that blues is essentially a matter of 'style'. It's interesting that when Dylan performed to specifically black audiences, as in Greenwood Mississippi in 1963 and at a women's penitentiary in New Jersey during the Rolling Thunder Revue of 1975, he didn't hesitate to sing about racial politics but chose to do so via his white 'protest' songs – 'Only A Pawn In Their Game' and 'Hurricane' respectively – rather than via blues songs. In contrast, witness the spectacle of John Hammond Jr imposing his fussy impersonation of an old blues-singer upon the embarrassed black occupants of a Mississippi bar-room for his TV documentary *In Search of Robert Johnson*.[7]

Second, Bob Dylan's interest and special dexterity is in exploring the innards of the blues, taking from the blues the strengths of its vernacular language (to some extent musically as well as lyrically) and building them into the core of his own work – into the machinery of his own creative intelligence. As I've suggested, he raids the Bible, he raids traditional white folksong, he raids nursery rhyme, he raids the poetry of the pre-war blues. To do this to such creative profit would be impossible without a mix of curiosity towards and respect for the original contexts from which these things are seized and reworked. This guarantees that, unlike many of those in the global blues industry, Dylan has no interest in seeing the blues 'deprived of its historical base'.[8]

---

6.   Paul Garon, 'Editorial', *Living Blues*, nia, quoted in Peter Narváez's essay '*Living Blues Journal*: the paradoxical aesthetics of the blues revival', collected in *Transforming Tradition: Folk Music Revivals Examined*, edited by Neil V. Rosenberg (1993).

7.   Bob Dylan: 'Only A Pawn In Their Game', Greenwood, Mississippi (civil rights rally), 6/7/63; and 'Hurricane', Clinton, New Jersey, 7/12/75. John Hammond Jr: *In Search of Robert Johnson*, Iambic Production for Channel 4 in association with La Sept; London, Channel 4 TV, 1991. Greenwood is where Robert Johnson played his last gig, and died.

8.   In this connection it's interesting that Narváez, concerned to argue against the *Living Blues* position, concludes his piece by citing two white blues artists whose working lives happen to have intersected with Bob Dylan's. He writes of finding it reprehensible when *Living Blues* fails to publish understanding appreciations of fallen blues artists such as Mike Bloomfield and Paul Butterfield [Bloomfield was in the Butterfield Band when

He also finds himself in fundamental sympathy with the idea of 'the blues-as-a-single-performance', to use Peter Narváez's phrase. Narváez reports that 'While historically many forms of downhome blues were played by soloists, and urban blues have always featured individual entertainers, [a] recent *Living Blues* survey indicates that blues fans today recognise blues as a collective activity, that is, a music played by groups who interact among themselves and with audiences'.

We can at once picture Bob Dylan's response. On the one hand, he too interacts with groups and with audiences. More so in recent years than ever before, in fact, live audiences seem indispensable to him. On the other hand, he has always believed in the power of the artist with the lone guitar and a point of view. As he said in 1985: 'I always like to think that there's a real person talking to me, just one voice you know, that's all I can handle – Cliff Carlisle . . . Robert Johnson. For me this is a deep reality: someone who's telling me where he's been that I haven't, and what it's like there – somebody whose life I can feel.'[9]

At the same time, he knows that the music and the poetry of the blues, its fundamental assumptions, are founded in an Africanness that is itself characterised by 'groups who interact among themselves and with audiences' (a theme that the great blues field-recordist and collector Alan Lomax, for instance, repeatedly stresses in his 1993 book *The Land Where the Blues Began*).[10]

In other words, the lone blues guitarist would have a different point of view, a wholly different way of expressing him or herself, if the culture from which the blues arose had not been a communal, democratically interactive one – one in which there is almost no hierarchical Artist Up Here and Audience Down There, but, rather, a collaborative performance in which the singer/musician takes cues moment by moment from the dancers/spectators and mingles physically among them, his or her repertoire as much a reaction as an imposition.

Dylan used him and others for the 1965 Newport Folk Festival gig; he also brought him in to play on 'Like A Rolling Stone']. Narváez elects to 'close by quoting from Mike Bloomfield's remarkably honest little book about his relationship with Big Joe Williams, "Big Joe & Me", for he articulates better than I ever could, the cross-cultural triumph of the blues tradition: "Joe's world wasn't my world, but his music was. It was my life; it would be my life. So playing on was all I could do, and I did it the best that I was able. And the music I played, I knew where it came from; and there was not any way I'd forget." '

Peter Narváez, '*Living Blues Journal*: The Paradoxical Aesthetics of the Blues Revival', see note 6.

Bloomfield's memoir, correct title *Me and Big Joe* (1980), describes not only Big Joe Williams himself but also going with Williams to visit Tampa Red, Sonny Boy Williamson, Tommy McClennan, Kokomo Arnold and others.

9.   Interview with Cameron Crowe for "Biograph", 1985.

10.   A description of such African song interaction can be found in Graham Greene's account of walking through the forests of Liberia, West Africa in the 1930s.

> I could hear [a] voice down the trail, proposing the line of an impromptu song which the carriers took up, repeated, carried on. These songs referred to their employers; their moods and their manners were held up to ridicule; a village when the carriers pressed through in full song would learn the whole story of their journey. Sometimes a villager would join in the chant, asking a question, and I could hear the question tossed along the line until it became part of the unending song and was answered.

[Graham Greene, *Journey Without Maps*, 1936.]

Liberia was an area of land (43,000 square miles) bought by the philanthropic (early nineteenth-century) American Colonization Society, which aimed to set up a settlement for liberated black slaves from the USA, the first arriving in 1822, i.e. many decades before the end of slavery. It became an independent country in 1847; its rulers were descended from black American settlers for almost 160 years. It was an inspiration to the back-to-Africa movement launched by the Jamaican Marcus Garvey (1887–1940), who in 1914 founded the influential, progressive Universal Negro Improvement Association in the USA, which did much to raise consciousness and improve conditions for blacks in the USA in the immediate pre-blues era.

This is a very different kind of participation from mass-marketed blues perform-ances in which big-name entertainers and high-energy tyro support groups please hyper crowds with the most easily magnified clichés of the genre transmitted through flashy guitar solos and greatest hits repertoire.[11]

Hence the complex reverberations Dylan deliberately installs inside the song title '[No-One Can Sing The Blues Like] Blind Willie McTell'. 'Discuss' is the implicit imperative lurking immediately beyond it. Yet despite everyone seeming to agree that this is one of Dylan's best creations, his own extraordinary deployment of the blues, and especially of blues lyric poetry, has still been very little discussed.

In a chapter called 'Under the re(a)d sky', in his 1991 book *Alias Bob Dylan*, Stephen Scobie mentions 'the blues' fondness for repeated lines'. This is a hair's breadth from writing of 'the sonnet's fondness for fourteen lines', and confesses an indifference to the blues that seems close to contempt. He's the loser by this, of course: not least because the world of blues lyrics has a great deal to say about the very areas – 'text' and identity – so central to post-structuralists like himself. We shall come to this large subject in due course.

First, though, let it be said that Scobie's passing over of the blues disadvantages him simply in terms of his missing or mis-explaining Dylan's creatively digested references to the blues milieu. For instance (a rather large instance), he puzzles about the use of the word 'lowlands' in Dylan's song 'Sad-Eyed Lady Of The Lowlands', conjecturing about the lowlands of Holland and having to argue their importance to European folk consciousness . . . but Dylan's metaphoric reference is more plausibly to the lowlands of the Mississippi Delta, the lowlands which imperilled people down in the floods, where all those crashes on the levee happened, and which have in turn flooded American folk consciousness. These are the lowlands that spread over the whole of the last side of "Blonde On Blonde", an album saturated in the blues.[12]

11.   I don't suggest that this is the sole relationship between white rock and the blues. There was conscientious, often creative *coverage* in several stages and places. Robert Gordon's fascinating *It Came from Memphis* (1995) argues that 'The rediscovery of the Delta blues artists began in the later 1950s' and that 'The first rock'n'roll audience was also the first blues renaissance audience' while D. Hatch and S. Millward in *From Blues to Rock: An Analytical History of Pop Music* (1987) say that 'awareness of Chicago blues, fostered . . . by visits to Britain by the originators and the recording of their compositions by groups such as the Rolling Stones, led inevitably to the discovery of the music's source, the blues of the Mississippi Delta,' while later, 'In America, it was the bands of the West Coast who used the blues most profitably during the mid-1960s, rather than the musicians from Chicago or the South.' Whatever the history, the repertoire that aspired to treat its blues material worthily included, among other things, much by Elvis (touched upon in the present chapter's main text) and his generation; plus: "The Rolling Stones No.2", Decca Records, London, 1964, which included Muddy Waters' 'I Can't Be Satisfied'; John Mayall and Eric Clapton's LP "Blues Breakers", 1966, which included Robert Johnson's 'Ramblin' On My Mind': 'an early (if not the first) attempt by a British band at music from this source,' say Hatch and Millward; Cream's début LP "Fresh Cream", Reaction Records, London, 1966, which included Hambone Willie Newbern / Muddy Waters' 'Rollin' And Tumblin'', Howlin' Wolf's version of Charley Patton's 'Spoonful', Skip James' 'I'm So Glad' and Robert Johnson's 'From Four Until Late'; and Led Zeppelin's début LP "Led Zeppelin", 1968, which included Willie Dixon's songs 'You Shook Me' and 'I Can't Quit You Babe'. From the West Coast, "The Doors", 1967, included Howlin' Wolf's 'Back Door Man', and the Doors' "LA Woman", 1971, included 'Crawling King Snake'. Jefferson Airplane put Memphis Minnie's 'Me And My Chauffeur' on their second LP "Surrealistic Pillow", 1967. Canned Heat covered 'On The Road Again' and 'Going Up The Country', 1968 (both trans-Atlantic hit singles), 'Dark Road' by Floyd Jones (itself based on Tommy Johnson's 'Big Road Blues' and other related songs) and Henry Thomas' 'Bull Doze Blues'. Their 1969 "Living The Blues" included Patton's 'Pony Blues'; their 1970 hit was with Wilbert Harrison's 'Let's Work Together'.

12.   The flooding of the Delta only became a problem when agriculture intensified, so that instead of the annual

Though the Delta flooded annually, 1927 brought a spectacular flood over an area the size of Scotland; workers were kept in camps at gunpoint to repair the levees; and blues singers were called in to help in the propaganda effort to get people to come to do flood relief work.[13]

As Big Bill Broonzy once explained to a European audience, 'They sent for a lot of musicians. They didn't have to send for me 'cos I was already there . . . and whoever wrote the best song got 500 dollars. So Bessie [Smith] got the 500 dollars, so we always played hers . . . "Back-Water Blues".'[14]

Dylan himself performed the song at New York City's Carnegie Chapter Hall in November 1961. It opens like this:

It rained five days and the clouds turned as dark as night
It rained five days and the clouds turned as dark as night
Lotta trouble takin' place, Lord, in the lowlands that night

which is interesting for its conventional prefiguring of Dylan's unconventional 'She can take the dark out of the nighttime and turn the daytime black' (a perfect blues line) and for that specific citing (and siting) of 'the lowlands'.[15]

Dylan himself talks about the crucialness of old blues couplets (though if he hadn't, we would know their importance to him from the vast extent to which he has drawn from their wells of material and added to them) in 1985: 'You can't say things

---

flooding replenishing the land naturally, it threatened the new inhabitants (imported Chinese as well as black labour) and the infrastructure. Levees had not been needed before this intensification. Indeed the *forests* of the delta were still being cleared in the years just before the 1920s. V. S. Naipaul (*A Turn in the South*, 1989) meets Louise, a woman of 80, in Jackson in 1987, who remembers the wilderness: 'The land hadn't been cleared and travel was hard . . . *And it was beautiful country* [her emphasis] . . . great oaks that had not been harvested. This was before the plantations . . . It was a land of flowers, all kinds of wild iris and wild violets, water lilies and alligators . . . I had malaria every summer when I was a child. It took a while to clear the Delta. It flooded every spring. When I was a little girl – say in 1915 – they were still clearing it. They would go and chop around these mighty oaks and they would let them die and then they would cut them . . . I took it for granted. I played in the woods . . . It was a privilege to live in the Delta. At night we would hear animals in the forest. A panther. It sounded like a woman crying.'

(Naipaul comments: 'There is no landscape like the landscape of our childhood. For Louise . . . the "big cotton patch" that the planters had created in the Delta was a disfiguring of the forest . . . [but] for Mary, born in the Delta forty years later, there would be no landscape like the flat, stripped land she had grown up in. She said: "I think there is nothing more beautiful than the flat, flat land and the big, big sky." ')

Alan Lomax's *The Land Where the Blues Began* (1993) has a good description of the clearing of the jungle to create the cotton wealth of the Delta, and argues that African agricultural know-how created the Delta farmland from the wilderness.

13. 'In 1927, when the Mississippi overflowed, it flooded an area the size of Scotland. That is a serious river.' [Bill Bryson, *The Lost Continent*, 1989.]

14. Big Bill Broonzy: [spoken intro to] 'Back-Water Blues', probably Paris 20/9/51, Big Bill Blues, Vogue Records LP 30037, Paris, *nia*. Bessie Smith: 'Back-Water Blues', NYC, 17/2/27; "Bessie Smith Volume 1" [10-inch LP], Jolly Roger 5002, New York, c. 1951. CD-reissued "New & The Blues: Telling It Like It Is", Columbia Roots N' Blues Series 467249–10, New York, c. 1991.

Lawrence Cohn writes in this CD's booklet that 'Bessie Smith's affecting 'Back Water Blues' [has] been included in the repertoires of large numbers of traditional performers since its initial appearance in 1927. It was the most successful, in terms of sales, of the almost two dozen blues that commented on the disastrous Mississippi river flooding of that year, an unprecedented calamity . . . Rather than offering a factual account of the tragedy, Smith's recording, through the accumulation of vivid, intimate details, and told from the perspective of one of its victims, presents an emotionally charged, deeply personal account of the flood that, as do all well-crafted blues, proved greatly moving to her listeners. The power and immediacy with which she addresses the subject is surely the reason hers eclipsed all other recordings dealing with this tragedy.'

Broonzy's own song on the subject is 'Lowland Blues' [by Big Bill], Chicago, 3/9/36.

Big Bill Broonzy was born at Scott, Mississippi, 26/6/1893 and died in Chicago, 14/8/58.

15. Bob Dylan: 'Backwater Blues', NYC, 4/11/61.

any better than that, really. You can say it in a different way, you can say it with more words, but you can't say anything better than what they said. And they covered everything.'[16]

Dylan's debt to the blues, and its revealing relationship to his own work, is a huge subject, so far largely unexplored. I hardly scratched the surface of the surface of it in the previous incarnations of this book, so I return to it here and now: especially since it has been possible to use, as an aid to exploring the pre-war blues, a pioneering book published in the 1980s, Michael Taft's wonderful *Blues Lyric Poetry: A Concordance*.

This work collates 'over two thousand commercially recorded blues lyrics of the "race records" era: that is, sung by African-Americans and produced in special series by the major recording companies in the United States between 1920 and 1942 . . . intended for the Afro-American record-buying public, rather than for the wider North American market.' This amounts to a transcribing of the lyrics of a good 20 per cent of the entire commercial output of pre-war blues recordings.

Essentially this work exists on computer at the Center for Computer Research in the Humanities at the University of Colorado. As such, of course, it can yield its information in many different ways. As an anthology of blues couplets listed by recording artist, it was first the basis of Taft's *Blues Lyric Poetry: An Anthology*, published 1983, and was then re-organised as *Blues Lyric Poetry: A Concordance* in 1984. In this form it is a general overviewing concordance (only one possible ordering of such a concordance): three huge hardback volumes, each of a thousand pages, plus Taft's eximious preface.

Augmenting one's own patchy familiarity with pre-war blues recordings themselves, it is possible to extrapolate enough detail from Taft's word-for-word transcription of blues lyrics to show how profoundly Dylan has absorbed the poetry of the blues, understands its power and offers it in his own work as 'a link in the chain'.[17]

One fundamental thing this concordance achieves is that by lining up alongside each other those words and phrases that recur in different songs by different artists, it reveals (in a way that only an encyclopaedic record collection and the disease of total recall would otherwise allow) which phrases and formulations are the common-stock of the genre and which are individual creations or individual applications. This is immensely helpful to an understanding of what Bob Dylan might be said to take from where.

For instance. Clinton Heylin writes that the song 'I Was Young When I Left Home' (on the December 1961 "Minnesota Hotel Tape"), though deriving its tune

16.   Dylan to Bill Flanagan for *Written in My Soul: Rock's Great Songwriters Talk about Creating Their Music* (1986).

17.   The phrase is taken from, though is, aptly, not original to, Dylan's summation, on tape, of how people pass on what has gone before to those who come after, in answer to questions about his perceptions of Woody Guthrie submitted to Dylan's office by BBC Radio Scotland producer Robert Noakes (aka Rab Noakes, 1970s singer–songwriter). Dylan's answers were despatched from his New York office 8/7/87, on a tape (9' 27"); part of the tape was used in programmes 1 to 3 of the 4-programme series *Woody Guthrie*, broadcast weekly from 30/9/87. Extracts were also used in the TV version of the 'Vision Shared' project (*A Vision Shared: A Tribute to Woody Guthrie and Leadbelly*, CBS-TV, New York, transmitted 17/6/87, later released as *Shared*, CBS Home Video, New York, 4/10/88), a version Dylan wisely avoided taking part in.

and some lyric phrases from the traditional '900 Miles', offers some 'aspects of the lyrics [that] seem wholly Dylanesque'.[18] He quotes these lines:

> Used to tell my ma sometimes
> When I'd see them ridin' blinds
> Gonna make me a home out in the wind

but then he backtracks that 'even here, the second line hints of [sic] Robert Johnson's 'Walkin' Blues': "Leavin' this morning, I have to ride the blinds"'.

The 'Dylanesque' lines are acutely chosen, but Heylin's conclusions mislead. First, the opening line, not derivative of any specific body of song, is the least individual of the three. Secondly, what makes the *last* line 'Dylanesque' – taking a common-stock phrase and tweaking it into something fresh: in this case taking the western folkloric 'gonna make me a home out in the west', and fusing it with the anonymous 'in the wind' – is also what's Dylanesque about the *middle* line.[19] We can recognise this by seeing that the point about that middle line is not that it echoes a Robert Johnson song but that it *doesn't*.

Johnson's song contains 'ride the blinds', but so do many, many other pre-war blues songs which, like Johnson's, were subsequently collected onto the reissue albums that largely determined which of the pre-war blues singers became known to the enthusiasts and revivalists Dylan moved among when he was young and after he left home. Indeed at least sixteen other such artists used 'Robert Johnson's' phrase on record before Johnson ever entered a studio. A 1929 harmonica instrumental record by Eddie Mapp, offering one of the all-time great virtuoso train-imitating harmonica performances, was *titled* 'Ridin' The Blinds'. The phrase was so widespread by 1935 (still before Robert Johnson recorded) that two singers could be found using it in different recordings cut in the same town on the same day (Chasey Collins and Otto Virgial in Chicago on Hallowe'en).[20]

18. Clinton Heylin: 'Them Ridin' Blinds', *Telegraph*, no. 27, Summer 1987.
     Bob Dylan: 'I Was Young When I Left Home', Minneapolis, 22/12/61.

19. The phrase 'out in the wind' recurs a year later in Dylan's version of the non-blues 'Kingsport Town' [NYC, 14/11/62], based via Guthrie's 'Who's Gonna Shoe Your Pretty Little Feet?' on an older ballad. Here, too, as John Bauldie notes in the "Bootleg Series I-III" booklet (Dylan's recording was finally issued officially on this 3-CD set), 'Dylan's distinctive turn of phrase can be heard amid otherwise formulaic lyrics . . . surely only Bob Dylan (and we can hear him come up with the alliteration even as he's performing the song) could have come up with "Who's gonna kiss your Memphis mouth when I'm out in the wind?"'

20. To indicate just how widely a 'common-stock phrase' spreads itself, this is a list (based on Taft's 20 per cent) of records on which the phrase 'ride the blinds' is used before Robert Johnson ever steps into a studio: Trixie Smith: 'Freight Train Blues', NYC, c. May 1924, "Trixie Smith: Masters of the Blues, Vol. 5", Collectors Classics Records CC-29, Copenhagen, c. 1971; Clara Smith: 'Freight Train Blues', NYC, 30/9/24, "Clara Smith: Volume Three", VJM Records VLP-17, London, 1969; Ed Bell: 'Mean Conductor Blues', Chicago, c. Sept. 1927, "Alabama Blues, 1927–1931", Yazoo Records L-1006, New York, 1968; Memphis Jug Band: 'Bob Lee Junior Blues', Atlanta, 19/10/27, "American Folk Music", Folkways Records FP 251–3, New York, 1952 (see footnote 22 below for more on this seminal compilation); Barbecue Bob: ''Fo' Day Creep', Atlanta, 10/11/27, "Barbecue Bob. Masters of the Blues, Vol. 10", Collectors Classics Records CC-36, Copenhagen, c. 1971; Tommy Johnson: 'Cool Drink Of Water Blues', Memphis, 3/2/28, "Country Blues Encores", Origin Jazz Library Records OJL-8, Berkeley, c. 1965; Sleepy John Estes: 'Broken-Hearted, Ragged And Dirty Too', Memphis, 26/9/29, "The Memphis Area, 1927–1932", Roots Records RL-307, Vienna, c. 1968; Blind Willie McTell: 'Travelin' Blues' and 'Come On Around To My House Mama', Atlanta, 30/10/29; James Boodle It Wiggins: 'Gotta Shave 'Em Dry', c. Oct. 1929, "Fillin' In Blues", Herwin Records H-205, Glen Cove, New York, 1973.; Barbecue Bob: 'Yo-Yo Blues no. 2', Atlanta, 17/4/30, "The Male Blues Singers, Vol. 1", Collectors Classics Records CC-3, c. 1965; Memphis Minnie: 'Chickasaw Train Blues': Chicago, 24/8/34, "Out Came The Blues", Coral Records CP-58, London, 1970; Leroy Carr: 'Big Four Blues':

Dylan, then, may or may not have first heard the phrase 'ride the blinds' from Robert Johnson. The strong likelihood is that he heard it elsewhere first. Either way, he had certainly heard enough pre-war blues by the end of 1961 to know that the phrase was recurrent. This chapter began with the testimony of Harvey Abrams, a student who knew the 1960 Dylan back in Minneapolis–St Paul (the Twin Cities), and who says that by that point Dylan was already one of those who 'had to get the oldest record and, if possible, the Library of Congress record, or go find the original people who knew the original song'. Even back in Hibbing, at the high school graduation party thrown by his parents, Bob had been given a number of Leadbelly 78s – and had found them revelatory. Shortly afterwards, in the Twin Cities, bohemian Dave Whittaker says he had a large collection of blues records that he and Dylan used to listen to all the time. We know too that in Minnesota Dylan did not have to rely upon LP reissues for hearing old blues: he had access to 78s owned by record-collectors like Jon Pankake, co-founder with Paul Nelson of the small but fierce *Little Sandy Review*.[21]

Dylan had *certainly* heard the phrase 'ride the blinds' on the Jenny Clayton & The Memphis Jug Band's 1927 track, 'Bob Lee Junior Blues' – because this was one of the tracks reissued by Folkways on an extraordinary 3-double-album set, the anthology "American Folk Music", which came out back in 1952, was the first collection to put black and white American folk musics together instead of keeping them separate, and was crucial source material for the whole revivalist scene that was to thrive in Greenwich Village and Boston by the end of that decade. Even if Dylan could be imagined putting himself in the position of remaining unfamiliar with this collection when those around him with similar aspirations were discovering it – Jon Pankake and his friends among them – what strongly suggests that Dylan already knew the collection by the time he wrote and put on tape 'I Was Young When I Left Home' is that the same tape, or earlier tapes by Dylan, contain his performances of

---

NYC, 14/12/34, "Blues Before Sunrise: Leroy Carr, Piano And Vocal", Columbia Records C-30496, New York, c. 1965; Big Joe Williams: 'Little Leg Woman', Chicago, 25/2/35, "Lonesome Road Blues: 15 Years in the Mississippi Delta", Yazoo Records L-1038, New York, 1973; Chasey Collins: 'Walking Blues', Chicago, 31/10/35, "The Country Fiddlers", Roots Records RL-316, Vienna, 1968; Otto Virgial: 'Little Girl In Rome', Chicago, 31/10/35, "Mississippi Bottom Blues", Mamlish Records S-3802, New York, c. 1973. Additionally, there is Eddie Mapp And His Harmonica: 'Riding The Blinds', Long Island City, NYC, c. May 1929.

Then comes Robert Johnson: 'Walking Blues', San Antonio, 27/11/36, "Robert Johnson: King of the Delta Blues Singers", Columbia Records CL-1654, New York, 1961. After him, among many others, come Tampa Red: 'Seminole Blues': Aurora, Illinois, 11/10/37, "Tampa Red: Bottleneck Guitar, 1928–1937", Yazoo Records L-1039, New York, 1973; Trixie Smith's remake of 'Freight Train Blues', NYC, 26/5/38, "Out Came The Blues", Coral Records CP-58, London, 1970; and Blind Boy Fuller: 'Step It Up And Go', NYC, 5/3/40, "Blind Boy Fuller with Sonny Terry and Bull City Red", Blues Classics Records BC-11, Berkeley, 1966. I note that the first three to record these hard travel blues were women.

21. For the Hibbing, Harvey Abrams and Jon Pankake information see Robert Shelton's *No Direction Home* (1986). For Dave Whittaker's testimony see Bob Spitz's schlock biography *Dylan: A Biography* (1989).

Jon Pankake was also involved with the Minneapolis Folk Society, the first organisation ever to issue a compilation LP of old 78 rpm folk material. The records he played Dylan from his collection included 'a Texas chain-gang song from an Alan Lomax album'. Asked, forty years later, which record this was, Pankake says: 'I no longer recall exactly . . . I strongly suspect that the album in question was Alan Lomax's "Texas Folk Songs" . . . It was a favourite of mine at the time and I would have been trying to introduce it to those who were interested in performing songs from the Library of Congress field-recordings . . . I thought then – and still do – that Lomax was one of the best interpreters of the music he collected.' (e-mail from Minneapolis to the present writer, 17/5/99.)

Dylan stole LPs from Pankake in 1959, as detailed later in the main text. But see also the penultimate paragraph of note 22.

versions of eight of the songs (not all blues) that are on the "American Folk Music" set.[22]

By then too – by the time of the December 1961 'session' that yields his 'ridin' blinds' – Dylan knew enough further blues and black gospel material already to have sung onto tape himself the traditional 'Delia' (a repertoire item of Blind Willie McTell to be revisited by Dylan over thirty years later on his 1993 folk and blues album "World Gone Wrong"), Big Bill Broonzy's 'This Train Is Bound For Glory', Gary Davis' 'Death Don't Have No Mercy' and 'Cocaine', Leadbelly's 'Aint No More Cane' and 'In The Pines', Bessie Smith's 'Back Water Blues', Muddy Waters' 'Still A Fool', Big Joe Williams' 'Baby Please Don't Go', Bukka White's 'Fixin' To Die', the Memphis Jug Band's 'Stealin', Stealin'' and Brownie McGhee's Leroy Carr-inspired 'In The Evening', plus the further blues on his own début album, recorded a month earlier – which includes Blind Lemon Jefferson's 'See That My Grave Is Kept Clean' and Curtis Jones' 'Highway 51 Blues' – plus the Jimmie Rodgers blues 'Blue Yodel No.8', aka 'Muleskinner Blues', and various unattributable 'blues standards' like 'Candy Man'.[23]

22.   "American Folk Music", set of 3 double-LPs (Vol. 1: Ballads; Vol. 2: Social Music; Vol. 3: Songs), Folkways Records FP251–253, NYC, 1952; CD-reissued as "Anthology Of American Folk Music" [6-CD box-set] with copious notes by many hands and a CD-ROM of extras, Smithsonian Folkways Recordings SFW 40090, Washington, DC, 1997.

   The anthology's deeply knowledgeable compiler, Harry Smith, was an eccentric character in bohemian New York, an avant-garde film-maker and a long-term resident of the Chelsea Hotel. He moved to Colorado in the 1970s but moved back to New York City to die, which he did six months later, in 1991. On a visit to New York in 1985 he was sleeping at Allen Ginsberg's apartment when Dylan called round to show Ginsberg the lyrics to "Empire Burlesque". Dylan was delighted that Smith was there, and wanted to meet him. Smith wouldn't get up. [Reported fully in 'The night Bob came round', by Raymond Foye, *Telegraph*, no. 36, Summer 1990.]

   His notes for the "American Folk Music" anthology are terrific, not least for their summarising the storylines of the songs almost in tabloid headline style: for instance, re 'Omie Wise': 'GREEDY GIRL GOES TO ADAM SPRINGS WITH LIAR: LIVES JUST LONG ENOUGH TO REGRET IT.'

   Of this set's 84 recordings, at least 30 have a Bob Dylan connection (detailed later). Those he had already taped performances of by the end of 1961 were 'The House Carpenter'; 'The Butcher's Boy (The Railroad Boy)'; 'The Wagoner's Lad'; 'Omie Wise'; 'John The Revelator'; 'The Coo Coo Bird'; 'East Virginia'; 'James Alley Blues'; 'K.C. Moan'; and 'See That My Grave Is Kept Clean'. He had also turned the collection's song 'Down On Penny's Farm' into his own song 'Hard Times In New York Town', and had turned 'A Lazy Farmer Boy', known also as 'The Young Man Who Wouldn't Hoe Corn', into his own 'Man On The Street'.

   The CD-reissue of "American Folk Music" includes Jon Pankake's essay 'The Brotherhood of the Anthology', detailing his own discovery of this music, and stating that he was introduced to, and epiphanously excited by, the anthology itself in 1959 by Paul Nelson, precisely when Dylan was around them. This is puzzling, though: Pankake's essay suggests that only after discovering Smith (staying up 'late that night listening with astonishment to [its] strange music . . . so utterly unlike the "folk-music" we had heard') did he begin journeying into this 'music emotionally shattering yet culturally incomprehensible'. By inference, this certainly downplays the Pankake–Nelson connection as a source for Dylan's pre-New York self-education in the blues.

   Before the flurry of commentary on the Smith anthology that came with, and was prompted by, its CD-reissue, a distinctive voice on the subject was Robert Cantwell's, in a sometimes mystical essay 'Smith's memory theater', *New England Review*, Spring/Summer 1991, republished as Chapter 6 of his book *When We Were Good: The Folk Revival* (1996).

23.   These are the earliest known recorded blues and gospel performances by Bob Dylan. Some songs in his very early repertoire are hard to categorize, but at the very least we can count the following:

   St. Paul, Minnesota, May 1960: 'Delia' and 'Blue Yodel No. 8 [Muleskinner Blues]'. Minneapolis, Autumn 1960: 'K.C. Moan'. Minneapolis, May 1961: 'Death Don't Have No Mercy', 'Still A Fool', 'James Alley Blues'. NYC [Gerde's Folk City], Sept. 1961: 'Ain't No More Cane'. NYC, 4/11/61: 'In The Pines', 'Gospel Plow', 'Backwater Blues', 'Fixin' To Die'. NYC, 20/11/61: 'Baby Let Me Follow You Down', 'In My Time Of Dyin''. NYC, 21/11/61: 'See That My Grave Is Kept Clean', 'Highway 51'. NYC, 23/11/61: 'Worried Blues'. Minneapolis, 22/12/61: 'Baby Please Don't Go', 'Candy Man', 'Stealin', 'Dink's Song', 'Wade In The Water', 'In The Evening' and 'Cocaine'.

   Linda Dahl, author of *Stormy Weather* (1984), a book of profiles of women (mostly jazz) singers, claims that Mary Williams Johnson, not husband Big Joe, wrote his classic 'Baby Please Don't Go'. Unfortunately Dahl's

Two of these songs Dylan had picked up from what was, after Harry Smith's anthology, the next crucial vinyl issue of previously hard-to-obtain pre-war blues material, the 1959 LP "The Country Blues", issued to accompany Sam Charters' pioneering book of the same name – the book that spurred so many people to go down south winkling out old blues singers from their anonymous penury and presenting them in northern coffee houses. The LP featured the Memphis Jug Band's 'Stealin', Stealin'', which Dylan sang onto the same 1961 tape as his own 'I Was Young When I Left home', and Bukka White's 'Fixin' To Die Blues', which Dylan put on his début album. The album also introduced most of its listeners to the work of Robert Johnson – it included his 'Preachin' Blues' – and to Blind Willie McTell's 'Statesboro Blues'.[24]

(Folklorists are often uneasy with the retrospective imposition on music and its practitioners of terms never used of that music or familiar to its practitioners at the time. Thus they no longer like the label 'songster', commonly used – as in this book – to denote those who had a repertoire far wider than, and often learnt before the development of, the blues, arguing that they never called themselves songsters and indeed had never heard the term. It is alleged that the equally broad term 'country blues' was invented by Sam Charters in the late 1950s, and had enjoyed no currency amongst pre-war blues musicians in the countryside or the town, nor among their audiences. One can see that there's a point at issue here. It's true that Muddy Waters' first song is called 'Country Blues', and he says he wrote it in 1938, but it may have

source is almost certainly careless assumption from the sleeve notes of a series of LPs on Rosetta, which were, like Dahl, trying to raise the profile of women's contributions to music. This admirable aim is not served by dodgy assertions. In any case, 'Baby Please Don't Go' is strongly based on the older common-stock number known as 'Don't You Leave Me Here'. At another point the same Mary Williams was the wife of Lonnie Johnson. Don't know if she wrote anything for him.

[Big Joe Williams: 'Baby Please Don't Go', Chicago, 31/10/35. 'Don't You Leave Me Here' was at least 30 years old by then. It was recorded in its traditional form by Papa Harvey Hull & Long Cleve Reed, as by Sunny Boy And His Pals, in Chicago, c. 8/4/27. (The same session yielded the wonderful 'Hey! Lawdy Mama – The France Blues'; "Really! The Country Blues", Origin Jazz Library OJL-2, New York, 1962, mentioned elsewhere in the present work.)]

Big Joe Williams, not to be confused with Joe Williams, singer with the Count Basie Band in the 1950s, was born in Crawford, Mississippi, in 1903; he died in Macon, Georgia, 17/12/82.

24. "The Country Blues", RBF Records RF-1, New York, 1959; Samuel B. Charters' book *The Country Blues* also 1959. Memphis Jug Band: 'Stealin', Stealin'', Memphis, 1928; Bukka White: 'Fixin' To Die Blues', Chicago, 8/3/40. Robert Johnson: 'Preaching Blues (Up Jumped The Devil)' [take 2], San Antonio, 27/11/36. Blind Willie McTell: 'Statesboro Blues', Atlanta, 17/10/28.

The rest of the LP comprised Blind Lemon Jefferson: 'Matchbox Blues'; Lonnie Johnson: 'Careless Love'; Cannon's Jug Stompers: 'Walk Right In'; Peg Leg Howell: 'Low Down Rounder's Blues'; Blind Willie Johnson: 'You're Gonna Need Somebody On Your Bond'; Leroy Carr: 'Alabama Woman Blues'; Sleepy John Estes: 'Special Agent (Railroad Police Blues)'; Big Bill Broonzy: 'Key To The Highway'; Tommy McClennan: 'I'm A Guitar King'; and Washboard Sam: 'I Been Treated Wrong'. Clearly a number of tracks here excited the young Bob Dylan's interest, and several are discussed further in the course of this chapter.

That Chuck Berry too knew his old country blues is suggested by how 'Berryesque' is the opening of another Peg Leg Howell song, 'Coal Man Blues' (though of course Berry may not know this particular recording): 'Woke up this morning about five o'clock / Get me some eggs and a nice pork chop / Cheap cigar and a magazine / Had to run through the street to catch the 5.15!' [Peg Leg Howell: 'Coal Man Blues', Atlanta, 8/11/26; "The Rural Blues", RBF Records RF-202, NYC, 1964]. Seventy years later, Dylan picks up this 'cheap cigar' and smokes it on the lovely "Time Out Of Mind" non-blues song 'Standing In The Doorway'.

Peg Leg Howell, real name Joshua Barnes Howell, was born in Georgia in 1888, so that he was one of those already almost 40 when he made his early recordings (he was Columbia's first field-recorded rural singer); he was also one of those 'rediscovered': he made one post-war LP, in 1963; this included a revisit to 'Coal Man Blues' (Peg Leg Howell: "The Legendary Peg Leg Howell", Atlanta, 11/3/63; Testament Records T-2204, Chicago, 1964). He died in Atlanta, 1966.

been titled by Alan Lomax; and Dock Boggs' 1927 'Country Blues', which is not a blues, and neither mentions the phrase nor describes a genre, seems arbitrarily titled.[25] Nevertheless, like 'songster', the term 'country blues' is useful shorthand, usually to signify southern blues played by people with guitars, rural or not. It would be especially hard to avoid it in the present study because so many of the blues reissue albums use the term.)

How Dylan came by Curtis Jones's 'Highway 51 Blues', used on his first album, is a useful illustrative puzzle. Jones (1906–1971), a blues pianist long resident in Chicago, recorded prolifically in the years 1937–41. His 'Lonesome Bedroom Blues' (which Dylan performed live in Japan in 1978) was recorded at his début session, and 'Highway 51 Blues' the following year at his third session. His first post-war (and only 1950s) recording was a brief one in 1953, but – 'discovered' in a fleabag Chicago hotel room in 1958 by three blues enthusiasts – he cut an album in New York City in 1960, performed at universities and clubs in Chicago in 1961–62 (including the Gate of Horn, a seminal place in Roger McGuinn's folk music education) and cut another album in 1962, "Lonesome Bedroom Blues". Both the title track and 'Highway 51' (and 'Stackolee') are on this album, but this was made *after* Bob Dylan recorded 'Highway 51' – yet 'Highway 51' was *not* included on the 1960 album, so Dylan couldn't have got it from that. The likelihood is, therefore, that he got it from Jones' original pre-war recording of the song on 78 rpm or from somebody's private tape of that record. There was no vinyl reissue of the track before Dylan made his own version in 1961.[26]

We know, though, from other examples that Dylan listened to the blues reissue albums emerging at the beginning of the 1960s more or less as soon as they were released. The crucial 1952 anthology includes two tracks by Henry Thomas but neither is 'Honey Just Allow Me One More Chance', which Dylan includes on "Freewheelin'" – 'first heard from a recording by a now-dead Texas blues singer', as Nat Hentoff's 1963 sleeve notes reported. That recording, made in Chicago in 1927, may have been heard by Dylan on the original 78 issued by Vocalion but the likelihood is that he heard it on "Henry Thomas Sings the Texas Blues", issued by the Origin Jazz Library, for a while the most important of the reissue labels, and active at the

25. Muddy Waters, conversation with Alan Lomax (in July 1942, according to Lomax's *The Land Where the Blues Began*, but in fact August 1941). Muddy Waters [McKinley Morganfield]: 'Country Blues', Stovall, Mississippi, c. 24–31/8/41 [field-recorded for the Library of Congress] vinyl-issued on the compilation "Afro-American Blues and Game Songs", AFS L-4, Washington, DC, 1962, and on "Muddy Waters: Blues Man", Polydor UK 236.574, London, 1969; the former CD-reissued Rounder Records CD 1513, Cambridge, Mass., 1999; also CD-reissued "The Complete Plantation Recordings: Muddy Waters: The Historic Library of Congress Recordings 1941–1942", MCA Records CHD 9344, London, 1993. Dixon and Godrich list two takes, but the latter CD's notes by Mary Katherine Aldin make clear that there only ever was one take. (A similar footnote appears elsewhere re Waters' 'I Be's Troubled'.)

Doc Boggs: 'Country Blues', NYC, 9/3/27, "American Folk Music", see note 22.

26. Curtis Jones: 'Lonesome Bedroom Blues', Chicago 28/9/37; 'Highway 51 Blues', Chicago 25/1/38. "Trouble Blues", NYC, 9/11/60, Bluesville 1022, New York, 1961. "Lonesome Bedroom Blues", Chicago 12, 27/1/62, Delmark DL606, USA, 1965. Bob Dylan: 'Lonesome Bedroom Blues', Tokyo, Feb. 20, 21, 23, 1978.

Jones was, in his low-key way, 'the bluesman's blues singer', in Paul Oliver's phrase. Other songs he wrote included 'Bull And Cow Blues', 'Alley Bound Blues', 'Morocco Blues', 'Skid Row', 'Suicide Blues' and 'Decoration Day Blues' (recorded by Jones but unissued, made a big hit by, and thereafter associated with, Sonny Boy Williamson I, and revived by Howlin' Wolf and Muddy Waters). His last recordings were for Blue Horizon in London in 1968. The last track he ever cut was 'Born In Naples Texas'. He died in Munich (11/9/71) and was buried in a pauper's grave.

beginning of the 1960s. This album was issued in 1961 (in a limited edition of 500 copies). Dylan was performing 'Honey Just Allow Me One More Chance' by April 1962.[27]

Dylan might have taken the commonly sung phrase 'ridin' the blinds' from virtually any of the many, many artists who used it – all of whom would soon have work put out on albums by the reissue companies like Yazoo and Folkways that were active in the period when Bob Dylan was discovering this wealth of music. And among those who had already put the expression on record before Robert Johnson were a number of other artists Dylan has cited or sung songs by (in one case even worked with) down the years: the Memphis Jug Band, Memphis Minnie, Blind Willie McTell, Big Joe Williams (with whom Dylan was to record three months later) and Tampa Red.[28]

It does not undervalue Robert Johnson's importance as a giant figure in the history of the blues, or as an influence on Dylan, to remember that he was still a boy when Charley Patton, Son House and their contemporaries first recorded – his own recordings were *all* made in three days in Antonio in November 1936 and in two days in Dallas in June 1937 – or to stress that the phrase being traced does not originate with that great originator. On the contrary, the danger is that since we've had Dylan's word, several times over, that Johnson was a such a key figure, we may see him in

27.   Henry Thomas: 'Honey, Won't You Allow Me Just One More Chance?' Chicago, 7/10/27; "Henry Thomas Sings The Texas Blues", Origin Jazz Library OJL-3, New York, 1961. Bob Dylan: 'Honey Just Allow Me One More Chance', NYC, April 1962 [LP version NYC, 9/7/62].

Henry Thomas' 'Fishing Blues' [Chicago, 13/6/28] is the last track on Smith's anthology. Paul Oliver, investigating the origins of both songs in *Songsters and Saints* (1984), reports that 'Honey' was field-collected for folksong collector Dorothy Scarborough by Mrs Tom Bartlett from Marlin, Texas, that her transcription 'corresponded closely' to the Henry Thomas version, that possibly Mrs Bartlett got it from Thomas himself, and that it was also recorded by (the far more obscure) Archie Lewis. Folk song collectors seem to have been on to Henry Thomas for 'Fishing Blues' too. Oliver writes: 'Another Texas collector, the historian Walter Prescott Webb, published a number of song fragments "obtained from a Gatesville negro named 'Rags'". They included a verse of 'If You Go Fishing' which was virtually identical to Henry Thomas's 'Fishing Blues'. Gatesville lies some fifty miles to the west of Marlin and it is tempting to think that "Rags" was none other than "Ragtime Texas" – Henry Thomas.'

(Oliver suggests that Thomas toned down the sexual suggestiveness of the lyric for his recording. Harry Smith, citing as an allied composition 'Fishing Blues' by Memphis Minnie, notes that 'references to fishing, other than as sexual symbolism, are rare in American folk music'. Bob Dylan says somewhere that 'Wiggle Wiggle' is 'a song about fishing'.)

A neat postscript to the matter of Dylan's knowledge of these songs emerged in 1994, with the first circulation of a fragment of studio-tape from NYC in 1970, soon after Dylan had been recording some of "Self Portrait". It's interesting because Dylan recalls *both* songs. A voice that sounds like producer Bob Johnson prompts Dylan, saying he wants to hear 'a song that had 'Mama' in it, or something, that you did' and Dylan starts singing, country style, 'I'm a-goin' fishin' all the time . . . I'm a-goin' fishin', you're a-goin' fishin', I'm a-goin' fishin' too'. The tune is so reminiscent of 'Honey' that at this point Johnson (if it's him) says 'No – "one kind of favour I'll ask a-you"!' and Dylan retorts 'Oh, yeah . . . Same guy!' And then sings a pleasant country version of 'Honey Just Allow Me One More Chance'.

Archie Lewis: 'Honey, 'Low Me One More Chance', Richmond, Indiana, 30/3/33. Memphis Minnie: 'Fishin' Blues', NYC, 3/2/32. Bob Dylan: 'Fishing Blues' [fragment] and 'Honey Just Allow Me One More Chance', NYC, May 1970, unreleased; tape circulated 1994.

28.   Like Dylan, these artists were also picking up on each other's songs at the time, and in several ways. Blind Willie McTell, for example, as elaborated in Chapter 15, had to hear records to learn successful songs, to be able to perform them at gigs. He also heard many performers, only some of whom recorded at all, through working alongside them, and it was the norm to take both stock and individually created phrases and use or adapt them in your work. McTell was a friend of Blind Willie Johnson (whose 'In My Time Of Dyin'' is on Dylan's first album) and he also knew Leadbelly, Tampa Red, Blind Blake and Blind Lemon Jefferson. He probably knew Barbecue Bob too: at least, both men often used the same accompanist, Curley Weaver. All these artists are discussed in due course in relation to Bob Dylan's use of the blues.

Dylan's work where he does not belong – which does no service to either artist, nor to understanding the blues.[29]

Dylan emphasises this himself in the 1963 poem 'My Life in a Stolen Moment': 'Woody Guthrie, sure / Big Joe Williams, yeah / It's easy to remember those names / . . . What about the records you hear but one time . . .?' (This is a core question, and we shall return to it.)

If we know, therefore, as Dylan knew, how *commonplace* a formulation is the phrase 'ride the blinds', we are then (only then) in a position to appreciate that what he does with it is the *most* original thing in the whole 3-line sequence quoted from 'I Was Young When I Left Home'.

The blinds were the spaces behind the tender and between baggage-cars on the train, where, if you could jump on undetected, you could travel free. Even if you evaded the railroadman's club, it was dangerous: even more so under the carriages where, in essence, if you rolled over you killed yourself. This is why, immediately after 'Leaving this morning, I have to ride the blinds', the other half of Robert Johnson's couplet is 'Babe I been mistreated, baby and I don't mind dying.'[30]

The very young Bob Dylan understood this, especially since the two themes in the blues that appealed to him most were death and travel, the two things that come together in 'riding the blinds'.[31]

29.   In any case, Robert Johnson's 'Walking Blues' recycles 'My Black Mama' by Son House, who was calling it 'Walking Blues' in the 1930s before Robert Johnson used the title for his own song (the title 'My Black Mama' was because the 'black mama' lyrics House took as his starting-point came from one of his mentors, James McCoy); House's 1942 field-recorded 'Walking Blues' re-emphasises this lineage. But see also note 220.

Muddy Waters' first recorded side, the August 1941 'Country Blues', is also founded upon House's 1930s 'Walking Blues'. The similarity between Waters' bottleneck playing on this and Robert Johnson's on *his* 'Walking Blues' has been widely noted but both are extremely similar to that on Son House's 'My Black Mama', and the field-recorded interviews with Muddy Waters make it clear that it was Son House who taught him bottleneck guitar.

(All this is detailed in 'Really the "Walking Blues": Son House, Muddy Waters, Robert Johnson and the development of a traditional blues', by John Cowley, in *Popular Music*, vol. 1, ed. Richard Middleton and David Horn, 1981.)

Robert Johnson: 'Walking Blues', detailed note 20. Son House: 'My Black Mama Part 1', 'My Black Mama Part 2', Grafton, Wisconsin, 28/5/30. Son House: 'Walking Blues', Robinsonville, Mississippi, 17/7/42, CD-reissued "Son House: The Complete Library of Congress Sessions 1941–1942", Travelin' Man Records TM CD 02, Crawley, UK, 1990. Muddy Waters: 'Country Blues', see note 25.

It should be remembered too, at least for interest's sake, that Robert Johnson's reputation is almost wholly retrospective: 'Between January and October of 1937 Johnson's commercial sponsors issued nine of his records, averaging one new release every month. Its first offering, 'Terraplane Blues' and 'Kind-Hearted Woman', proved to be his most successful work and probably served as the justification of his return session in Dallas seven months after the first. This time Johnson produced 13 sides in two days . . . The session produced no commercially successful sides, and when his ARC contract expired in June of 1938, he was not returned to the studio. At the age of 26, Johnson was a record industry has-been.' ('Robert Johnson' by Stephen Calt and Gayle Dean Wardlow, *78 Quarterly*, Vol. 1, no. 4, 1989.)

30.   Chapter 18 offers a brief consideration of the effect of the American railroads on the movement of people and song.

31.   In any case, some of this music was on the radio when Dylan was growing up, as was true for Elvis, who went into Sun Studios in 1954 already knowing *lots* of blues: 'We talked about the Crudup records I knew – 'Cool Disposition', 'Rock Me Mama', 'Hey Mama', 'Everything's All Right' and others, but settled for 'That's Alright', one of my top favourites', he said in a 1957 interview (quoted in *Sound of the City*, Charlie Gillett, 1971).

The teenage Bob Dylan was building himself a similar foundation re the blues and post-war R&B from the age of 13, according to Stan Lewis, the legendary Shreveport record store owner, plugger and radio show packager: 'Then I found DJs like Wolfman Jack who had shows on other independent stations willing to work R&B into their formats. One of those clear-channel stations had a 250,000-watt transmitter in Mexico. On certain nights its signal could be heard all over the country, even in Europe and South America. I couldn't believe some of the places

What's certain is that while the blues yields a score of 'riding the blinds', there is *no* occurrence of 'them ridin' blinds'. Dylan has invented this designation. It is not a small thing. His phrase compresses their lethal promise of opportunity and the desperation of those needing to travel in such a way. To refer to 'them ridin' blinds' is to express foreboding. And in being a different formulation, in standing out, it enacts the young man's confession of his later generation outsiderism (which Dylan makes explicit in the even earlier 'Song To Woody', with 'And the very last thing that I'd want to do / Is to say I been hittin' some hard-travelin' too'.) On 'I Was Young When I Left Home', that '*When I'd see* them' adds the confirming touch: he'd see them but he'd not say he'd 'ride the blinds' himself.

Yet when Bob Dylan revisited Minnesota briefly at Christmas 1961 and put that song on tape, he was returning from the New York City folk scene he had already entered with some success: he had made friends, found people to use, played on sessions for Harry Belafonte and Carolyn Hester, been written up in the *New York Times*, signed a record deal with a major label and been into the studios recording his first album.[32]

The Greenwich Village scene when Dylan was inveigling himself into it, and the live music he absorbed there, shouldn't be under-appreciated as a source of his education in the blues. Many links and connections come from this period, both from the older, black 'revived' singers and from among the young white revivalists. There was what Dave Laing called 'an urban school of musicians dedicated to re-creating the country blues: Dave Van Ronk, Spider John Koerner, Tony Glover' – around all of whom Bob Dylan came and went.[33] In fact Dylan had known Koerner and Glover back in 1959 in Minnesota but certainly in New York Dave Van Ronk would have been a valuable conduit for Dylan, not only from pieces of repertoire he performed – 'Van Ronk was a walking museum of the blues' whose 'impact on Dylan was enormous', according to Robert Shelton – but also because he was for a time roommates with our friend the blues researcher Sam Charters, perhaps giving Dylan access to Charters' invaluable record collection.

Dylan also got on well with Len Kunstadt, a major collector of 78s, whom Dylan knew through Victoria Spivey, whose record label Kunstadt helped manage. A sweetly youthful Dylan of this period is pictured with Spivey on the back cover of "New Morning" – the original art print photograph is owned by Kunstadt – and recalls the

---

I started getting orders from.' One place was Hibbing, Minnesota. Dylan was 'only 13 at the time. He used to call me at night, to order the records he'd just heard on the air. I thought to myself, Who is this rich kid, calling long-distance from the Midwest to order records? We'd chat and talk about the blues . . .' (From 'With the record man: a half century of Stan Lewis memories', Willard Manus, *Blues Access*, no. 26, Summer 1996.)

32.   Dylan played harmonica on Carolyn Hester's recordings of 'I'll Fly Away', 'Swing And Turn Jubilee' and 'Come Back Baby', NYC, 29/9/61, "Carolyn Hester", Columbia Records CL1796, New York, 1962 and on an out-take of 'I'll Fly Away' and 'Come Back Baby', both issued as 'bonus tracks' on the CD-reissue of the album, Columbia Legacy CK57310, 1994. The day these were recorded also saw publication of Robert Shelton's crucial review 'Bob Dylan: a distictive stylist' in the *New York Times* and while Dylan was at the Hester session he was offered the Columbia record deal by producer John Hammond. (Carolyn Hester was married to folk singer and avant-gardist Richard Farina, who later married Mimi Baez, Joan's sister.)

      Dylan plays harmonica on Harry Belafonte: 'Midnight Special', NYC, probably Dec. 1961, "Midnight Special", RCA Records LMP 2449, New York, 1962.

33.   From 'Troubadours & Stars', Dave Laing *et al.*, in *The Electric Muse: The Story of Folk into Rock* (1975). For more on Spider John Koerner and Tony (who is also Dave) Glover see Chapter 18.

sessions Dylan recorded with Spivey and with Big Joe Williams. Big Joe's three-week stint at Folk City in February 1962 was attended by Dylan most nights, while of Spivey herself Dylan has said: '. . . oh man, I loved her . . . I learned so much from her I could never put into words'.[34]

There was also the Reverend Gary Davis (aka Blind Gary Davis), recommended by Robert Shelton for a 'marvellously rough and penetrating voice' and for carrying on 'Blind Willie Johnson's tradition of "the holy blues" . . . Heartfelt blues vocal and guitar language, dressed up in religious togs by a curbstone preacher.' Bruce Bastin calls him 'superb' and 'a superlative guitarist'. Other blues connoisseurs are less keen.[35]

Born in South Carolina in 1896, his first recordings were made in New York City over three days in 1935. He next recorded in 1945 and frequently thereafter. He played Greenwich Village when Dylan was first exploring New York, and was on the folk festival and college circuits (appearing, for instance, at the Mariposa Festival of 1959 and Newport 1963). He died in New Jersey in 1972.

Davis was one of those with a wide well of repertoire drawn up from a long chain of blues history. Items in his sets that have a connection with Dylan's own include 'You're Goin' Quit Me Baby' [sic], 'Jesus Met The Woman At The Well', 'Motherless Children' and 'There Was A Time When I Was Blind'. Dylan was taped singing this last item and, as noted earlier, Davis' 'Death Don't Have No Mercy', in Minneapolis back in May 1961. (Aeons later, in the psychedelic Sixties, the Grateful Dead made a near-endless version of the latter one of their standards.[36]) And though on his first album Dylan credits 'Baby Let Me Follow You Down' as learnt from Ric von Schmidt 'in the green pastures of Harvard University', he was aware that it could be traced back to Davis' 'Baby, Let Me Lay It On You' and further back beyond that all the way to Memphis Minnie and her second husband, Joe McCoy. Davis finally

---

34. Robert Shelton, *No Direction Home*. British photographer Valerie Wilmer told the present writer [phone-conversation c. 1994] that Len Kunstadt owns the "New Morning" back-cover shot. Kunstadt was editor of *Record Research*, no. 67, April 1965, in which Spivey wrote a column, 'Blues Is My Business', describing Dylan at the time of the Big Joe Williams session. Bob Dylan recorded four songs with Big Joe Williams and Victoria Spivey, NYC, 2/3/62; two (harmonica and back-up vocals for Williams on 'Sittin' On Top Of The World' and 'Wichita') issued on "Three Kings & A Queen", Spivey Records LP 1004, New York, 1964, and two (harmonica for Spivey on 'It's Dangerous' and on the formless, retrospectively-titled 'Big Joe, Dylan & Victoria') on ditto Vol. 2, Spivey Records LP 1014, New York, 1972.

Dylan on Spivey, in interview by Cameron Crowe, "Biograph", see note 9.

Spivey, born Houston, Texas, 1906, died in Brooklyn in October 1976, as mentioned in the entertaining 'Billie and Bessie', in David Widgery's *Preserving Disorder* (1989).

(A book that should be illuminating on these matters – I haven't had access to it – is Robbie Woliver's *Bringing It All Back Home*, 1986, sub-titled *25 Years of American Music at Folk City* [i.e. Gerde's Folk City], which includes the chapter 'Bob Dylan: making the dream possible' and a performer roster from the club for 1960–85.)

35. Robert Shelton, *No Direction Home*. Bruce Bastin: *Crying for the Carolines*, 1971.

36. Davis' first recordings of these items were: Rev. Gary Davis: 'You're Goin' Quit Me Baby' [sic], NYC, 1963 or 1968; "Let Us Get Together", Kicking Mule SNKF 103, London, 1973. Blind Gary Davis [with Sonny Terry]: 'Jesus Met The Woman At The Well' and 'Motherless Children', NYC, April 1954; "Blind Gary Davis With Sonny Terry", Stinson SLP 56, New York, 1954. Blind Gary Davis: 'There Was A Time When I Was Blind', NYC, 29/1/56, "Rev. Gary Davis and Pink Anderson Gospel, Blues and Street Songs" Riverside LP 148, New York, probably 1961. Rev. Gary Davis: 'Death Don't Have No Mercy', Englewood Cliffs, NJ, 24/8/60; "Harlem Street Singer", Prestige/Bluesville BVLP 1015, Bergenfield, New Jersey, 1961. Bob Dylan: 'Death Don't Have No Mercy' and 'It's Hard To Be Blind', Minneapolis, May 1961. The Grateful Dead: 'Death Don't Have No Mercy', San Francisco, 2/3/69; "Live Dead" double-LP, Warner Brothers 2WS 1830, LA, 1969.

committed it to tape in 1968, his version predictably close to Blind Boy Fuller's, confirming that he had had it in his repertoire since the 1930s.[37]

Dylan recalls Davis in the Greenwich Village years as switching – oddly, for someone who was ashamed of his blues side and was supposed to have renounced it – between religious and devil's music: 'Strange, he used to sing 'Twelve Gates To The City', 'Yonder At The Cross' and then 'Baby, Let Me Lay It On You''. This typical piece of Dylan eloquence tells us with brevity something that's true in spirit and in its surprisingly specific detail too. The Davis discography confirms that Dylan's recollection is likely to be absolutely right. At a 1962 gig he sang 'Sally, Where You Get Your Liquor From' straight after 'If I Had My Way (I'd Tear The Building Down)', and when, later in the 1960s, he recorded at his music publisher's office, Davis followed 'Oh Glory, How Happy I Am' with 'Cocaine Blues'.[38]

Then there was John Lee Hooker. Dylan's friend Sybil Weinberger told the makers of BBC-TV's 1993 *Arena* Special 'Highway 61 Revisited' that in the early Village days, Dylan loved Hooker, and that whenever he was playing, Bob would be there. Nor was Hooker, for whom Dylan was also, famously, a support act (in April 1961), the only other black bluesman around.[39] Before Hooker, there had been Sonny Terry – a clear influence on Dylan's harp-playing, as Dylan told Cameron Crowe, for the

37.   Blind Gary Davis: 'Baby, Let Me Lay It On You', Ann Arbor, Michigan, 1968; "Lo' I Be With You Always", Kicking Mule LP 1, London, 1973.
      Memphis Minnie may have been the first to record this song, though her 1930 version is actually a vocal duet with Joe McCoy, with him doing the asking and her the spurning, so that the whole nature of the song is different. That is, before it becomes the familiar song of implicitly successful seduction, it is an inconsequential chat-up novelty item, a sort of early 'Come Outside'. The pattern of its early commital to record in its various guises seems to run like this:
      Memphis Minnie: 'Can I Do It For You – Part 1' and 'Can I Do It For You – Part 2', Memphis, 21/2/30; The State Street Boys [i.e. Big Bill Broonzy and others]: 'Don't Tear My Clothes', Chicago, 10/1/35; Walter Coleman: 'Mama Let Me Lay It On You', Chicago, 8/2/36, and Chicago, 3/6/36; Sheik Johnson: 'Baby Let Me Lay It On You', Chicago, 27/3/36; Blind Boy Fuller: 'Mama Let Me Lay It On You', NYC, 29/4/36; Georgia White: 'Daddy Let Me Lay It On You', Chicago, 11/5/36; Washboard Sam: 'Don't Tear My Clothes', Chicago, 26/6/36; Chicago Black Swans [i.e. again, Bill Broonzy and others]: 'Don't Tear My Clothes No. 2', Chicago, 26/1/37; State Street Swingers: 'Don't Tear My Clothes No. 2', also Chicago, 26/1/37.
      In the 1950s it became popular with New Orleans-based artists, including Professor Longhair, who recorded it in 1957, and Snooks Eaglin, who revived it in 1959 in its Big Bill Broonzy form as '(Mama) Don't You Tear My Clothes' – at which point its line 'You can rock me all night long . . . but don't you tear my clothes' is likely to have sounded as if it were pinching ideas from Carl Perkins' then recent 'Blue Suede Shoes'. [Professor Longhair, 'Baby Let Me Hold Your Hand', New Orleans, 1957; "Mardi Gras In New Orleans 1949–57", Nighthawk 108, *nia*. Snooks Eaglin: 'Don't You Tear My Clothes', New Orleans, 1959; "Snook Eaglin's New Orleans Blues", Heritage EP 301, *nia*. Re-recorded with 12-string guitar at same sessions as 'Mama Don't You Tear My Clothes', New Orleans, 1959; "That's All Right", Bluesville BV 1985 LP 1046, *nia*.]
      Two years after Snooks Eaglin, Dylan recorded it as 'Baby Let Me Follow You Down'.
38.   Bob Dylan to Cameron Crowe, "Biograph" interview.
      Davis first recorded his 'Twelve Gates To The City' as by Blind Gary, NYC, 26/7/35; "Rev. Gary Davis 1935–1949", Yazoo Records L-1023, New York, 1970. He never recorded the title 'Yonder At The Cross'. 'Baby, Let Me Lay It On You', *ibid*. Rev. Gary Davis: 'If I Had My Way' and 'Sally, Where You Get Your Liquor From', Paoli, Pennsylvania, 8/9/62; "Philadelphia Folk Festival Vol. 2", Prestige International PR13072, c. 1963. 'Oh Glory, How Happy I Am' and 'Cocaine Blues', NYC, mid-1960s; "Let Us Get Together", see note 36. For more on Davis see Robert Tilling's 1992 book *Oh! What a Beautiful City: A Tribute to Rev. Gary Davis 1896–1972*.
39.   Sybil Weinberger, interviewed on BBC2 TV's *Arena* profile 'Highway 61 Revisited', produced and directed by James Marsh, London, 1993.
      Hooker played at Gerde's on Hootenany Nite, 27/3/61 and then began several weeks' residency there, from 4 April onwards; Dylan certainly turned up to listen every night 4–10/4/61, ahead of his own fortnight as Hooker's support act, 11–24/4/61. Their only night off appears to have been 17/4/61.

"Biograph" notes in 1985: 'the harmonica part, well, I'd always liked Wayne Raney and Jimmy Reed, Sonny Terry . . . Lil Junior Parker'.[40]

Wayne Raney is the obscure name here (and the white man), and he was not a part of the folk revival scene. He and his co-harmonica-player Lonnie Glosson were hillbilly radio stars out of Arkansas – you could send off for their harmonicas by mail order. Raney–Glosson was the composing team behind Raney's hit 'Why Don't You Haul Off And Love Me', a song revived by Johnny Burnette (a post-rockabilly side: lots of strings, but real vocal energy). On Raney's version, he says he's '43'; Burnette amends this to '17'![41]

Most of Raney's songs, co-written with a number of different people, are demure love songs with an old-fashioned 'good-humoured' novelty element, in melody and lyrics (he has a penchant for terrible, occasionally repulsive, rhymes, such as 'sloggin'/ . . . on my noggin'); on his more guitar-based rockabilly items you can hear exactly why he influenced Johnny and Dorsey Burnette. 'Jack And Jill Boogie' is one of his best, and with a more prominent harmonica than usual, and 'Gone With The Wind This Morning' another Burnetteish track.[42]

Raney also played on post-war Delmore Brothers records (such as 'Blues Stay Away From Me', a song he co-wrote, which Dylan recorded with Doug Sahm and his band in 1972) and on various suitably obscure rockabilly sides. He also ran his own label, Rimshot Records, and is remembered for a dreadful record of his own called 'We Need A Whole Lot More Of Jesus And A Lot Less Rock 'n' Roll'. And while Sam Phillips is oft-quoted as having said of blues music 'This is where the soul of man never dies', it's less well-known that this poetic turn of phrase is itself a quote from a song title, 'Where The Soul Of Man Never Dies', recorded by Hank Williams . . . and composed by our Mr Raney.[43]

---

40.   Jimmy Reed (1925–1976) was hugely influential. His hits began in 1955 with 'You Don't Have To Go' and 'Ain't That Lovin' You Baby'; his many others include 'Baby What You Want Me To Do' [1960], 'Big Boss Man', 'Bright Lights, Big City' and his biggest US crossover (into pop) hit, 'Honest I Do' [1955], all made for Vee Jay Records, Chicago. His only scrape into the British charts was with 'Shame Shame Shame' [Stateside SS 330, London, 1964], which peaked at No. 45 in 1964. The Rolling Stones revived 'Honest I Do' [London, Feb. 1964] on their first album, "The Rolling Stones", Decca LK 4605, London [London Records PS 375, New York], 1964. A particular resemblance between Reed's harmonica-work and Dylan's is discussed later re 'Pledging My Time'.
      Sonny Terry (1911–1986), an exceptional harmonica player and a protégé of Blind Boy Fuller, was guitarist Brownie McGhee's long-term musical partner. They were especially popular with whites on the folk-blues scene.
      Little Junior Parker (1932–1971), harmonica player, band-leader and rather smoothie vocalist, wrote and first recorded Presley's 'Mystery Train'. Parker also cut 'You Wanna Ramble', which Dylan recorded in the 1980s (see Chapter 16). He is mentioned later in the present chapter in relation to Howlin' Wolf, in whose band he played. He also played behind Sonny Boy Williamson II.

41.   Wayne Raney: 'Why Don't You Haul Off And Love Me', Cincinnati, 6/5/49, King Records 791, Cincinnati, 1949. "Wayne Raney: Songs From The Hills", King Records LP 588, Cincinnati, reissued Dearborn, Michigan, 1987. Johnny Burnette: 'Why Don't You Haul Off And Love Me", *nia*, "Dreaming", Liberty Records 55258, LA, 1960; reissued on "Johnny Burnette Tenth Anniversary Album", United Artists UA 29643, London, 1974. (Lonnie Glosson, incidentally, recorded an 'Arkansas Hard Luck Blues' in about 1935: a record significant for its pre-Guthrie use of the talking blues style so widely thought of as deriving from Guthrie and in turn assumed to have been taken up from Guthrie by Bob Dylan.)

42.   Wayne Raney: 'sloggin . . . noggin' is on 'I Was There', Cincinnati, March–April 1955; 'Jack And Jill Boogie', prob. Cincinnati, prob. late 1948, King Records 732, Cincinnati, 1948, and 'Gone With The Wind This Morning', Cincinnati, March–April, 1955; all on "Songs From The Hills", *ibid*.

43.   Bob Dylan and others: 'Blues Stay Away From Me', NYC, Oct. 1972, on "Doug Sahm & Band", Atlantic SD-7254, New York, 1972. Delmore Brothers with Wayne Raney: 'Blues Stay Away From Me', Cincinnati, 6/5/49. (A selection of Delmore Brothers material, though excluding 'Blues Stay Away From Me', is CD-reissued on

The funny thing, though, about Dylan's citing of Raney as a harp-player who influenced him is that, at least on the Raney material I have heard, his harmonica-playing never really resembles Bob Dylan's at all.

Meanwhile, back in the Village, Dylan and Mark Spoelstra were 'The Dungarees' in 'Brother John & The Dungarees', playing back-up guitars and harmonicas behind the gospel and blues shouter Brother John Sellers at the Folk City hoot-nights.[44]

Lightnin' Hopkins, frequently playing the bigger venues, was a star in the Village at this time. So was Lonnie Johnson, of whom Dylan was to say, looking back in 1985: 'I was lucky to meet Lonnie Johnson at the same club I was working: and I must say he greatly influenced me . . . I mean, 'Corrina Corrina' – that's pretty much Lonnie Johnson. I used to watch him every chance I got, and sometimes he'd let me play with him . . . that's my favourite style of guitar-playing.'[45]

Mose Allison, also a popular Village performer, may have had a Radio-2-Jazz side to his style – such an unfortunate influence on Van Morrison (it's why *he* asks us to put up with Georgie Fame) – but Allison was from the Deep South and the downhome blues was his basic inspiration. His version of 'Baby Please Don't Go' was a fixture of Village musical life, and so was his uptown jazz re-interpretation of Bukka White's 'Parchman Farm', in which Allison paired the line 'Way down on Parchman Farm' with 'The place was loaded with rustic charm'. Though Bob Dylan would never have written such a pay-off line, the act of respecting source material and smiling at it at the same time is something we might recognise as Dylanesque.

There was another one-off performer whom Dylan had met, cross-examined and seen perform before he even reached the Village: this was the invaluable Jesse Fuller, who was temporarily on the Denver folk scene when Dylan dropped into it in 1959.

Fuller, best-known as a one-man band, inventor of the fotdella and composer of 'San Francisco Bay Blues', was born in Georgia in 1896 and endured a cruel childhood to become an eccentric, token-exotica figure in Hollywood who had a shoe-shine stand close to one of the film lots, got taken up by the stars and landed a small role in

---

Delmore Brothers & Wayne Raney: "When They Let The Hammer Down", Bear Family Records BFX 15167, Vollersode, Germany, c. 1990.) Wayne Raney: 'We Need A Whole Lot More Of Jesus (And A Lot Less Rock'n' Roll'), *nia*; "16 Radio Gospel Favorites", Starday SLP–124, Madison, Tennessee, 1961. Hank Williams: 'Where The Soul Of Man Never Dies', live at the Tulane Hotel, Nashville, Oct. 1949; "Hank Williams On Stage!", MGM Records MGM B3999, Los Angeles [MGM-C-893, London], 1962.

44.   Brother John Sellers, born Clarksdale, Mississippi, in 1924, was singing and dancing in gospel tent shows at 5, was abandoned by his parents, rescued from a bordello at the age of 10 by Mahalia Jackson (but what was she doing there?) and taken to live with her in Chicago, where he got to sing with Big Bill Broonzy and others. He was no great talent but he recorded from 1945, including while touring Europe with Broonzy in 1957. In the Village he was a Folk City regular, best on material like 'Wade In The Water'. Dylan played at his birthday party there in August 1961. Sellers appeared in the first Broadway production of the black playwright/poet/novelist Langston Hughes' *Tambourines to Glory*, 1963. (Hughes, 1902–1967, was a major young poet of the 1920s to 1940s Harlem Renaissance; *Tambourines to Glory* was first published as a novel in 1958.) Sellers died aged 74 in March 1999.

45.   Interview by Cameron Crowe, "Biograph". Lonnie Johnson (1894–1970), a great guitarist who influenced everyone, had a 'formidable technique', from whom Robert Johnson 'drew elements of his work', as Tony Russell summarises it in *Blacks, Whites and Blues*, 1970. He is one of the artists whose work was represented on Sam Charters' influential 1959 "Country Blues" LP, see note 24, though he was a city-dwelling, sophisticated man and artist who also swapped solos with Louis Armstrong on the latter's crucial 1927 jazz recordings ['Savoy Blues', I'm Not Rough' and 'Hotter Than That', "The Hot Fives & Hot Sevens, Vol. III", Columbia CK44422, New York, 1990] and featured on Duke Ellington's early classic 'The Mooche' [NYC, 1/10/28; "Jazz Series, Vol. 8; Big Bands (1924–1934)", Folkways FP 69 and FJ2808, New York, c. 1953]. He is mentioned in Chapter 18 in relation to his million-seller 'Tomorrow Night'.

the 1920s silent film *The Thief of Bagdad*.[46] He moved back to Georgia in the mid-1930s, and was an industrial worker for decades. He first tried to earn a living from music in 1950, moved back West and first recorded in about 1954, making a crucial slow-burner of an album, a 10-inch LP that was the first (possibly the only) release on the tiny Californian label World Song, issued in 1955. From it, Ramblin' Jack Elliott took, and was first to popularise in the folk-revival circles, 'San Francisco Bay Blues' itself; and though Dylan says he learnt 'Whoa Boys Can't You Line 'Em' from Spider John Koerner, Koerner is likely to have taken this song too from the Jesse Fuller album, on which it's titled 'Lining Up The Tracks'.

Two 1958 Fuller LPs won critical plaudits, and he performed successfully in Europe in 1960, but he was back in California picking cauliflowers for a living in 1961 while Bob Dylan was first recording 'San Francisco Bay Blues' in New Jersey and Minneapolis, and performing it at Gerde's Folk City in New York.

Fuller's own first East Coast appearances were in 1962 – by which time Dylan had put his song 'You're No Good' as the opening track on his début LP and Fuller had made four-and-a-half LPs of his own, though his very wide range of repertoire had him frowned on in some quarters during the strict revival period. The song notes to the album "Bob Dylan" say that 'You're No Good' was 'learned from Jesse Fuller', and indeed it must have been learned in person, back in Denver, since Fuller didn't record the song himself until 1963.

Twenty-odd years later, Bob Dylan says in the "Biograph" notes that 'Baby I'm In The Mood For You' (recorded in July 1962) was 'probably influenced by Jesse Fuller' too. In 1988, at the Bridge School Benefit Concert which took place in Fuller's adopted home town of Oakland California, Dylan opened his performance with 'San Francisco Bay Blues' (which he had earlier revived at Berkeley and in New York State during the first month of the Never-Ending Tour). In 1989, on stage at a Grateful Dead show in Los Angeles, Dylan played guitar on a performance of Jesse Fuller's 'The Monkey And The Engineer'. Fuller died in Oakland in January 1976.[47]

All those years earlier, in his pre-Village days, Dylan also got something very specific from the charmingly eccentric Fuller: it was from him, Robert Shelton says, that Dylan learnt how to use the harmonica-holder around his neck. (If this is true, it might be said to prove that Dylan didn't come across the crucial Harry Smith anthology "American Folk Music" until after his 1959 Denver visit – because there is a clear, if comical, drawing to show how to use a 'Dylan-style' harmonica-holder in the sleeve notes to the Harry Smith compilation.)

In Denver too, Dylan stole some records from black folk singer Walt Conley; God knows what these might have included. Earlier still, in Minneapolis, Dylan had

---

46. *The Thief of Bagdad*, Douglas Fairbanks, US, directed Raoul Walsh, 1924.

47. Jesse Fuller: 'San Francisco Bay Blues', El Cerrito, California, c. 1954; "Working On The Railroad", World Song Records LP 1, 1955 [issued on Topic, UK, 1957]. 'Lining Up The Tracks', issued ditto, re-recorded as 'Lining Track', San Francisco, 23/1/58, "Jazz, Folksongs, Spirituals & Blues", Good Time Jazz Records LP 12031, CD-reissued on Original Blues Classics OBCCD 564, USA, 1994. This album also includes what Ken Smith calls 'one of the best versions of 'Stagolee' you'll ever hear'. 'The Monkey & The Engineer', San Francisco, 12/4/58, "The Lone Cat", Good Time Jazz Records LP 12039, USA, 1958, CD-reissued Original Blues Classics OBCCD 526, US, c. 1992. 'You're No Good', San Francisco, 13/5/63, "San Francisco Bay Blues", Folk Lore LP 14006, *nia*. 'Lining Tracks' was also recorded by Leadbelly as 'Can't You Line 'Em' [NYC, 17/6/40; unissued] and as 'Line 'Em' [NYC, late 1943; issued Disc Records LP 660, *nia*.].

'borrowed' some records from Jon Pankake – among them the début album by Elizabeth Cotten, whose 'Oh Babe It Ain't No Lie' Dylan performed over thirty years later at his Toad's Place sets in New Haven, Connecticut. (More recently still, in some 1996 concerts Dylan included 'Sugaree', a Jerry Garcia/Grateful Dead reworking of a folksong much associated with Elizabeth Cotten in the early 1960s, 'Shake Sugaree': indeed it was the title of one of her Folkways albums; and on his first tour dates of 1997, in Japan, Dylan reintroduced 'Oh Babe It Ain't No Lie'.)

Born in North Carolina in 1892, Elizabeth Cotten had an unusual route into music and the folk revival movement: in 1943, at the age of 50, she moved to Washington, DC to work as housekeeper to ethnomusicologist Charles Seeger. Her début album, for Folkways in 1957, introduced 'Oh Babe It Ain't No Lie' and her most successful composition, 'Freight Train', which by April 1957 was a hit for others, including, in both America and skiffle-mad Britain, the Chas McDevitt Skiffle Group & Nancy Whiskey. ('Last Train To San Fernando' by Johnny Duncan & the Blue Grass Boys was to arrive just as Chas and Nancy were pulling out of the charts.)

Elizabeth Cotten performed at the Newport Folk Festival in 1964 (and is on the Vanguard release from that event, singing 'Oh Babe' and 'Freight Train' again), recorded another Folkways album in 1965–66 and played at the Mariposa Folk Festivals in 1970 and 1974. She performed at Carnegie Hall at the age of 76 and died at 95 in 1987.[48]

By the time Dylan was in New York City, there were also the Newport Folk Festivals out of town every summer, at which a number of 'rediscovered' blues artists appeared, hot from their decades of obscurity. Mississippi John Hurt was one of these. Discovered only in March 1961, he was on at Newport that July. Others touched by, and influential upon, the folk revival movement, included Big Joe Williams, Bukka White, Son House, Snooks Eaglin, Roosevelt Sykes, Sonny Terry & Brownie McGhee, Sleepy John Estes, Furry Lewis, Mance Lipscomb, Fred McDowell, Lightnin' Hopkins, Gus Cannon, Skip James and Tampa Red. Robert Shelton writes that the folk audience 'became highly knowledgeable about country blues'.

They knew something about a more urban kind of blues too. Eleven years on from his innovative (and electric-guitared) single 'I Can't Be Satisfied', Muddy Waters performed at Newport in 1960. It was, as the late Mike Leadbitter put it, 'Muddy's first real crack at the white market'. (Bob Dylan wasn't at Newport 1960 but a couple of years earlier, back in high school in Minnesota, he had already expressed admir-

48.   Elizabeth Cotten: "Negro Folk Songs And Tunes", Washington, DC, 1957, Folkways Records FG3526, New York, 1957. 'Freight Train' and 'Oh Babe It Aint No Lie', live, Newport, Rhode Island, 23–26/7/64, "Newport Folk Festival 1964 Blues II", Vanguard LP 9181, NYC, nia. 'Shake Sugaree', NYC?, February 1965, on "Shake Sugaree", Folkways 1003, New York, c. 1967. "Elizabeth Cotten Live!", nia Arhoolie LP 1089, El Cerrito, California, nia, also includes 'Freight Train' and 'Babe, It Ain't No Lie'.
     Jerry Garcia: 'Sugaree', San Francisco, 1971, "Garcia", Warner Brothers Records BS 2582, LA, 1972. It had become the Grateful Dead's 25th most performed song by the end of 1993, and appears officially as follows: 'Sugaree', San Francisco, 1974, "Steal Your Face", Grateful Dead Records GD LA620 J2GD 104, San Francisco, 1976; 'Sugaree', San Francisco 13/8/75, "One From The Vault", Grateful Dead Records GDCD40132, nia, 1991; and 'Sugaree', Pembroke Pines, Florida, 22/5/77, "Dick's Picks Volume 3" [2-CD set], Grateful Dead Records GDCD 4021, nia, c. 1994. The Grateful Dead also revived 'Oh Babe It Ain't No Lie', San Francisco or NYC, autumn 1980, "Dead Reckoning", Arista AL A2L 8604, USA, 1981.
     Bob Dylan: 'Oh Babe It Ain't No Lie', New Haven, 12/1/90, and as follows in Japan: Tokyo, 9–11/2/97; Kurashikim, 13/2/97; Fukuoka, 14/2/97; and Osaka 17–18/2/97. Bob Dylan: 'Sugaree', Berlin, 17/6/96; Utrecht, 20/6/96; Munster, Germany, 1/7/96; Pistoia, Italy, 7/7/96; Pori, Finland, 21/7/96 and Stockholm, 27/7/96.

ation for Waters and for Jimmy Reed.) Waters performed again (with his band) at the 1964 Newport Festival.[49]

That the young Bob Dylan could insinuate his creative imagination into the world of the older white and black folk artists to enrich even such very early songs of his own as 'I Was Young When I Left Home', with its lovely 'them ridin' blinds', therefore, is not in doubt. What interests me is to look far beyond his very early work to the period from 1964 onwards, when increasingly he freed himself from writing within borrowed folk formats: and to see the huge extent to which, having found the blues powerful and real, and having come to know it so intimately and inwardly, Dylan has drawn deeply from its poetry in creating his own. In the end, the main point isn't whether Bob Dylan discovered these people in or around Dinkytown or Greenwich Village, on the radio or via the incredible diverse riches of the blues records avalanching onto vinyl in the 1950s and 1960s. Engaging though it is to retrace his routes to these discoveries, in the end, the point is that he made them.

And he uses, *so singularly*, the huge amount he learnt in the construction of his own extraordinary work. No one else has used the blues in anything like the way Bob Dylan has.

Most people who are 'into' the blues take a few standard numbers and riffs from it and run with them in ever more amplified, clichéd, unrooted ways, or else, at the other extreme, bore us to death with their pedantic archival reproductions of obscurer-than-thou acoustic repertoire. The far smaller number of people whose work is genuinely enriched by the blues are usually musicians, rather than singer-songwriter musicians. Dylan takes myriad complex treasures from the pre-war country blues, both passionately and quietly, paying them at least as much loving attention as he pays to the vibrant strengths of those 1940s-to-1950s electric blues that made possible, more than we knew at the time, all the taken-as-givens of rock 'n' roll. And he draws all this cultural richness, the music and the lyric poetry of it, into the very core of his own work. Dylan has worked the blues so strongly and resourcefully that he has given it something back.

The nearest comparison might be Presley, if Elvis himself had written the great majority of the black songs he sang. For Dylan inhabits the blues as the best of the old bluesmen themselves did, fusing traditional and personal material into fresh, expressive work of their own, layered with the resonance of familiarity, the subconscious edits of memory and the pleasures of unexpected recognition, sharing the energy that flows between the old and the new, and between the individual and the common culture. He has used the blues with such insistent individuality, yet never in bad faith to the gravitas he found within it, or to the world in which its people had moved.

Interviewed in San Diego in autumn 1993, Dylan said:

---

49.   Sources: Robert Shelton: *No Direction Home* and 'Something happened in America', in *The Electric Muse*, Laing *et al.*, see note 33. Mike Leadbitter reviewing the LP "Muddy Waters At Newport", Checker Records 6467 416, London, 1973, in *Blues Unlimited*, no. 103, Aug./Sept. 1973.
     Val Wilmer's book *Mama Said There'd Be Days Like This* (1989) recalls that Muddy Waters caused 'controversy by playing the electric guitar in Britain' as early as 1958. In this respect, then – in producing an electric guitar in front of an audience expecting a 'folk' performance – the Bob Dylan of 1965 found himself re-enacting a scene already lived through by the great Mississippian bluesman.
     Chapter 1 describes Dylan meeting one of those on this list of the 'discovered', Mance Lipscomb, in 1960. He is further discussed in note 169 below.

The people who played that music were still around . . . [in the early 1960s], and so there was a bunch of us, me included, who got to see all these people close up – people like Son House, Reverend Gary Davis or Sleepy John Estes. Just to sit there and be up close and watch them play, you could study what they were doing, plus a bit of their lives rubbed off on you. Those vibes will carry into you forever, really, so it's like those people, they're still here to me. They're not ghosts of the past or anything, they're continually here.[50]

Indeed.

That the old blues have been seminal all through his career he has made plain in a series of clear signals, though we have not always paid attention. The early signals, already touched on, were that he was listening to Leadbelly and Odetta by 1959; he was performing blues songs as early as 1960; by June 1961 he was sufficiently confident of his blues harmonica playing to get himself taken on as session-player for Harry Belafonte's recording of 'Midnight Special', a traditional blues song that had been a key item in Blind Boy Fuller's repertoire; he was writing blues songs himself by January 1962; by March of that year he was proficient enough, and keen enough, to play harmonica on sessions with Big Joe Williams for Victoria Spivey; and that the original title planned for his second album was "Bob Dylan's Blues", reflecting the number of blues songs he recorded at the sessions for the album in April, July and October to December 1962. There is a telling out-take of 'Ballad of Hollis Brown' from 1962 (which despite its title is a blues-structured song) on which Dylan includes the stanza 'There's bedbugs on your baby's bed, there's chinches on your wife / Gangrene snuck in your side, it's cuttin' you like a knife'. I'd guess Dylan put in the bedbugs and chinches for extra 'realism', and was aware of them because they pop up commonly in the old blues. I'd guess that he dropped them again because he couldn't quite make them an authentic fit: not least because in the blues they are mostly objects of humorous exaggeration – as in 'I heard a moaning in the corner, Lord I tried so hard to see / It was a mother bedbug, Lord, praying for some more to eat', 'I had to get sinful with the bedbugs, to stop the chinches from taking my life', or 'Got myself a wishbone, bedbugs done got my goat' – not of solemn complaint such as Dylan is stuck with by the nature of his song.[51]

However, the signals kept on coming after that early period and have continued ever since. The 1965 album "Bringing It All Back Home" cites Sleepy John Estes in its sleeve notes and contains within its front-cover picture the front cover of the all-important first reissue album of Robert Johnson recordings, Columbia's "King of the Delta Blues Singers". For the making of the radical 3-minute-format-breaking rock

50. Bob Dylan, interviewed in a San Diego hotel, c. 3/10/93, by Gary Hill, for Reuters News Agency, wired to US newspapers 13/10/93.

51. Furry Lewis: 'Mean Old Bedbug Blues', probably New York, c. late October 1927; "Kings Of Memphis Town", Roots RL-333, Vienna, c. 1973. Blind Lemon Jefferson: 'Chinch Bug Blues', Chicago, c. October 1927; "Master Of The Blues: Blind Lemon Jefferson, Vol. 2", Biograph BLP-12015, New York, 1969. Bessie Smith: 'Mean Old Bedbug Blues', NYC, 27/9/27; "Jazz, Vol. 2: The Blues", Folkways FP55 and FJ-2802, New York, 1950. Other songs that couple bedbugs with chinches include Jefferson's 'That Black Snake Moan' [Chicago, c. Nov. 1926; "Black Snake Moan: Blind Lemon Jefferson", Milestone Records MLP-2013, New York, 1970] and 'Black Snake Moan' [Atlanta, 14/3/27; also "The Blues", Folkways FP55 and FJ-2802]; Leadbelly's 'New Black Snake Moan', [NYC, 23/1/35; "Leadbelly", Columbia C-30035, New York, c. 1970] and Washboard Sam's 'Jesse James Blues' [Chicago, 20/6/35; "Blues Classics by Washboard Sam", Blues Classics BC-10, Berkeley, 1966].

anthem 'Like A Rolling Stone' later the same year, Dylan flew in the blues guitarist Mike Bloomfield.[52]

Indeed the album title "Highway 61 Revisited" announces that we are in for a long revisit, since it is such a long, blues-travelled highway. Dylan could not have chosen a more apt and accurate route, a better song to allude to or a finer emblem for his own musical journey.

Consider the many bluesmen who had been there before him, all recording versions of a blues called 'Highway 61' – a blues in which, ironically, one of the things that varies, puzzlingly and fascinatingly, is the described route of the highway itself! It is, though, above all, a blues that exemplifies the shared, fluid, communal nature of blues composition: Roosevelt Sykes' unusually loose 'Highway 61 Blues' was recorded in 1932. The Sparks Brothers cut '61 Highway' the following year, in which Jack Kelly & His South Memphis Jug Band also cut 'Highway No. 61 Blues' and 'Highway No. 61 Blues No. 2', and, two days later, with violinist member Will Batts taking the vocal, another 'Highway No. 61 Blues'. Memphis Minnie's Joe McCoy (though he never recorded under this, his own name) cut 'Highway 61' in 1935.[53] The pre-war blues singer and pianist Jesse James' only session (in 1936) yielded four tracks, including the unissued 'Highway 61'. Then Charlie Pickett cut his brilliant 'Down The Highway' – a geographically inaccurate 'Highway 61 Blues' by another name – in 1937. And Sampson Pittman, a levee-camp worker and 'an excellent guitarist', field-recorded by Alan Lomax for the Library of Congress, cut 'Highway 61 Blues' in 1938.[54]

52. This predeliction for the blues was not indiscriminate: for 'Like A Rolling Stone' Dylan told Bloomfield he wanted 'none of that B. B. King shit', and however you feel about B. B. King, you know what Dylan means. [Mike Bloomfield, article in *Hit Parader*, June 1968; republished – but the quote given as 'none of that B. B. King stuff' – as 'Impressions of Bob Dylan', *On the Tracks*, no. 10, 1997.]

53. Roosevelt Sykes: 'Highway 61 Blues', Richmond, Indiana, 22/9/32; "Mr. Sykes Blues 1929–1932", Riverside RLP 8819, Holland, 1960s, and "Roosevelt Sykes The Country Blues Piano Ace (1929–1932)", Yazoo 1033, Newton, New Jersey, 1988. The Sparks Brothers: '61 Highway', Chicago, 2/8/33.

Jack Kelly and His South Memphis Jug Band: 'Highway No. 61 Blues' and 'Highway No. 61 Blues No. 2', NYC, 1/8/33 ["The Country Fiddlers", Roots RL-316, Vienna, 1968 and "Memphis Blues (1927–1939), Vol.2", Roots RL-329, Vienna, c. 1971 respectively] and, with Will Batts' vocal, 'Highway No. 61 Blues', NYC, 3/8/33; "Memphis Jamboree, 1927–1936", Yazoo L-1021, New York, 1970; all three CD-reissued "Jack Kelly & His South Memphis Jug Band Complete Recorded Works (1933–1939)", RST Blues Documents BDCD-6005, Vienna, c. 1991.

Joe McCoy [as Hallelujah Joe And Congregation]: 'Highway 61' Chicago, 15/5/35, CD-reissued on "Charlie & Joe McCoy Complete Recorded Works Volume 1 (1934–1936)", RST Blues Documents BDCD-6019, Vienna, 1992.

Wilber 'Joe' McCoy, an excellent guitarist, recorded 1929 to 1937, using names from Mississippi Mudder to Kansas Joe, joining the Harlem Hamfats in 1936 with his brother Charlie, both influenced by Tommy Johnson. Joe secured a reluctant Kokomo Arnold his record-deal, and wrote 'Oh Red', a big record for Blind Boy Fuller. In 1929 McCoy married Memphis Minnie, with whom he recorded many sides, with some great guitar duets, before they split up in 1935. McCoy was one of the earliest on record with the phrase 'shake, rattle and roll', which he built into his 'Shake Mattie': 'Shake shake Mattie, shake rattle 'n' roll / I can't get enough now, satisfy my soul.' [Chicago, c. February 1931; "Memphis Minnie Vol.2: With Kansas Joe, 1930–1931", Blues Classics BC-13, Berkeley, 1967].

54. Jesse James: 'Highway 61', Chicago, 3/6/36. (Re blues singers called Jesse James. In addition to the one just mentioned there are also two post-war blues/R&B singers called Jesse James: one, real name unknown, calls himself Sunny James on his Houston 1948 début session but Jesse James on his only subsequent session, in 1951; then there's the Jesse James whose real name is James McClelland; born in 1943, he first recorded in Oakland and LA in the early 1960s.)

Charlie Pickett: 'Down The Highway', NYC, 3/8/37; "The Rural Blues: A Study Of The Vocal and Instrumental Resources" (!), 2 LPs, RBF Records RF-202, New York, 1964 (RBF Records of New York were particularly active in blues reissues in the years 1959 to 1967, and their releases included country, Chicago, Atlanta and piano blues compilations. They were unusual in documenting not only what they reissued but their own release

It's odd that both the Will Batts and the Charlie Pickett accounts say that Highway 61 runs from Atlanta, Georgia to New Orleans, because it doesn't go anywhere near Georgia and runs several times as far as such a journey would be. Perhaps Batts never did get very far along it, and perhaps Pickett just copied Batts' stanza. Furry Lewis, performing the song in his twilight years, also has the route running from Atlanta, Georgia. Speckled Red (Rufus Perryman) cut a spirited post-war 'Highway 61 Blues' (with New York City at one end: which is especially surprising since he was a pianist who had hoboed, in Paul Oliver's phrase, 'from the Gulf to the Great Lakes').

At any rate this is also a song that carries on drawing people in the post-war period too, and does so both sides of, and heedless of, Dylan's own 1965 recordings. Fred McDowell cut '61 Highway Blues' in 1959 and Memphis Willie B cut 'Highway 61' in 1961, the same year that Smokey Babe cut 'I Went Down 61 Highway'. David Honeyboy Edwards cut 'Highway 61' in 1964, the same year that Fred McDowell revisited '61 Highway' in a version with an especially interesting lyric. It incorporates a stanza neatly fusing the highway with part of Patton's 'Pony Blues' – 'I'm gonna buy me a pony can pace, foxtrot and run / Lord when you see me comin' pretty mama I'll be on Highway 61' – and includes a verse that offers a perfect summary of Bob Dylan's mythic position in all this:

> I started school one Monday morning, I throwed my books away
> I wrote a note to my teacher: 'I'm gonna try 61 today!'[55]

Nathan Beauregard (born Ashland, Mississippi in about 1869; died Memphis, 1970) performed it, and spendidly, at the age of 99 at the 1968 Country Blues Festival in Memphis. His version of the 'longest highway I ever knowed' stanza has it running 'from New York City to the Gulf of Mexico'. James 'Son' Thomas was recorded singing 'Highway 61 Blues' on film in 1974. Sunnyland Slim cut a geographically correct version of the song (his expansive piano-work beautifully recorded) in 1983.[56]

dates. All too often, other labels supply copious notes about whether this track or that was recorded in the morning or afternoon of Tuesday 19 September 1933, plus the matrix numbers and much biographical information, but then forget to even state what *year* they're issuing their own reissue. Train-spotters . . .

Sampson Pittman: 'Highway 61 Blues', Detroit, 1/11/38; "I'm In The Highway Man", Flyright FLYLP542, Bexhill-on-Sea, 1980; CD-reissued on "The Devil Is Busy: Sampson Pittman", Laurie Records LCD 7002, Norwood, New Jersey, 1992. (The odd LP title "I'm In The Highway Man" perpetuates a mishearing by Alan Lomax from the 1930s of one of the other field-recorded items from the same trip, being the title he ascribed to a Frazier Family song performance fragment also issued on the LP.)

55. Furry Lewis: *nia*. Speckled Red (Rufus Perryman): 'Highway 61 Blues', *nia*. Fred McDowell: '61 Highway Blues', Como, Mississippi, summer 1959, Prestige 25010, c. 1961. Fred McDowell: '61 Highway', Como, 13/2/64; "Delta Blues", Arhoolie F1021, Berkeley, 1965, CD-reissued Arhoolie CD 304, El Cerrito, California, c. 1991. "Folk Blues USA", *nia*, CD-reissued on "Mississippi Delta Blues", Arhoolie CD 304, El Cerrito, California, c. 1991. (McDowell re-recorded the song again with white back-up musos in Jackson, Miss., September 1959; this version LP-issued on "I Do Not Play No Rock'n'Roll", Capitol ST409, New York, 1969.) Memphis Willie B: 'Highway 61', Memphis, 12/8/61; "Introducing Memphis Willie B.", Bluesville LP 1034, New Jersey, c. 1962. Smokey Babe: 'I Went Down 61 Highway', Scotlandville, Louisiana, 18/4/61; "The Country Blues", Denmark, c. 1962. David Honeyboy Edwards: 'Highway 61' Chicago, 17/3/64; "Ramblin' On My Mind: A Collection Of Train And Travel Blues", Milestone LP 3002, New York, 1968.

Charley Patton: 'Pony Blues', Richmond, Indiana, 14/6/29; "The Immortal Charlie Patton 1887–1934", Origin Jazz Library OJL-7, Berkeley, c. 1963.

56. Nathan Beauregard: 'Highway 61' live at the 1968 Country Blues Festival, Memphis, 20/7/68; "1968 Country Blues Festival", Sire SES 97003, New York [and Blue Horizon LP 7–63210, UK], *nia*. These late-1960s Memphis Blues Festivals are written about with much passion and splendid rhetoric by Stanley Booth: 'Even the birds were blue', in *The Rolling Stone Rock'n'Roll Reader*, ed. Ben Fong-Torres (1974): 'a moving, depressing account of

Of especial interest as well as brilliance is Charlie Pickett's 'Down The Highway'. It is brilliant for its torrential guitar-work, determinedly individual vocal delivery and its utterly successful, restless fusion of the two. This is a small masterpiece, from a man who made only four sides of his own in his life, this being the last of them, spread over two days in August 1937 (though as a musician he also enhanced sessions by Sleepy John Estes).

Dylan uses this title for a "Freewheelin'" song, a song that seems aware of Pickett's, but takes it no further than that, except that both use as an ingredient the format 'this highway runs from A to Z'. Charlie Pickett's runs 'from Atlanta in Georgie down to the Gulf of Mexico'; Dylan's has him 'a-walkin' down your highway ... From the Golden Gate Bridge / All the way to the Statue of Liberty'. And what's interesting about this early Dylan blues is that his awkwardness within the form is something he turns to advantage: he uses it, giving the song white layers, city-ironic layers, as well as black.

In fact the route he describes is a white one, but only because he's heading west-east in this instance. Dylan is describing here the route of the Lincoln Highway, the USA's first trans-continental highway, which opened in 1923 running between New York and San Francisco.[57] Heading east-west is often thought of as primarily a white route too – blues writer Bill Ferris, for instance, notes that Route 66 was the white escape route, while Highway 61, south-north, was the black escape route; and certainly Route 66 was the migration path for the displaced Okies of the dust bowl 1930s, as personified by the Joads, who take this highway in Steinbeck's *The Grapes of Wrath*: 'Route 66 is the path of a people in flight . . .' – but in *Nothing But the Blues*, Mark A. Humphrey writes that 'Industry was drawing blacks to the West Coast from the same Depression-ravaged states . . . that gave California its Okies. There were approximately seventy-five thousand black Los Angelenos in 1940 . . . By 1950 there were more than two hundred thousand.'[58]

There is no mistaking, however, the significant route in Dylan's musical life. Jack Kelly's 'Highway No. 61 Blues No. 2' includes the affecting 'I am in dear love with 61, I say it from my heart'; Arthur Crudup's 1941 story of 'Death Valley Blues' also takes place out on Highway 61, while for Roosevelt Sykes 'it breaks my heart, to sing

black bluesmen suffering the good intentions of their white admirers', as the book's blurb has it.

James 'Son' Thomas: 'Highway 61 Blues', Leland, Mississippi, summer 1974, filmed for *Give My Poor Heart Ease*, Yale Media Design Studio and The Centre for Southern Folklore, Memphis, directed Bill Ferris, 1975. An extract was shown on BBC2 TV's *Arena* profile 'Highway 61 Revisited', see note 39. (John Wesdon [*Living Blues* calls him Weston], a regionally known and younger Mississippi bluesman, also sang 'Highway 61 Blues' for the *Arena* cameras on location, 1993.)

Sunnyland Slim: 'Highway 61 Blues', Chicago, 26 or 29/1/83; "Sunnyland Train", Red Beans Records 002, 1983–4.

57. Later in the 1920s names were abandoned in favour of numbers. North-south highways were given odd numbers and east-west highways evens.

58. Bill Ferris, ex-Director of the Center for the Study of Southern Culture, University of Mississippi, Oxford, Mississippi, speaking to the BBC-2 *Arena* TV crew making 'Highway 61 Revisited', see note 39, as reported to the present writer by programme researcher Debbie Roberts. (In 1985, 'the federal highway department removed all the Route 66 shield signs along its 2,200 miles . . . Overnight this once great highway became a series of back highways and anonymous frontage roads,' Bill Bryson, *Made in America*, 1994.)

Mark A. Humphrey: 'Bright lights, big city: urban blues', in *Nothing But the Blues: The Music and the Musicians*, ed. Lawrence Cohn (1993).

about Highway 61 / I felt so blue when I was out on that lonely highway'.[59] But from among the many weary celebrations of this blues-soaked road two lines sum up its twin significance for Bob Dylan. On the one hand 'That 61 Highway', as Will Batts, among others, puts it, is the 'longest road I ever knowed'; and yet as Charlie Pickett sings, 'Now the 61 Highway, you know an' it runs right by my door'. Dylan's literal journey was, with a couple of diversions, east in stages to Greenwich Village. His existential journey was down Highway 61.

He saw it run right past his door in Duluth, Minnesota: and the further he moved along it, the deeper he went into the world of the blues.

As it runs past Duluth, it is on its way from right up at the Canadian border, and it goes on – nowadays almost deserted and reduced to the status of a county road for more than half this first portion of its route – down to St Paul, through Red Wing along the Minnesota side of the Mississippi River with Wisconsin on the other side. It drops down into Iowa, then into Missouri near Keokuk. Keeping south, always parallel to the Missisippi, Highway 61 passes St Louis and then, skirting the corner at which the south-eastern tip of Missouri meets corners of Kentucky and Tennessee, it plunges down into the north-east tip of Arkansas and goes on south till it meets the mythic city in the south-western toecap of Tennessee – Memphis – to reach which it finally has to cross the Mississippi River. In Memphis it almost meets its sister highway, Highway 51, which meets Beale Street and on which Graceland stands at No. 3764 in South Memphis. From there, while 51 runs due south, 61 veers south-south-west first, running down through the vast Mississippi Delta and eventually reaching Vicksburg, the first real town in 200 miles. Still running alongside the river, it crosses the state line into Louisiana south of Natchez, skirting round to the east of Baton Rouge and running on, past Lake Pontchartrain, into New Orleans and the Gulf of Mexico.

All through Dylan's white-heat hip period in the mid-1960s, when his creative greatness was in symbiosis with the foment of the times, he stayed rooted in the blues. He continued to put the word 'Blues' (like the word 'Ballad') into song-titles when no one else in rock did: indeed most people at the time thought Dylan's was deliberate ironic usage of a passé term. Even his constant use of the word 'mama' in the songs of this period is imported from the blues – in rock, few people used it (though one of Dylan's old favourites, Gene Vincent, commonly did), and in white folksong it really does mean 'mother': but in the blues, where it addresses a lover, or a prospective one, it occurs more frequently even than words like 'if' and 'when'.[60] In 1966 Dylan opened the electric-début second-half of each of his concerts with a bluesy, deranged rock song called 'Tell Me Mama'. Retrospectively his *Writings and Drawings* (1972), and the later *Lyrics 1962–1985*, spelling it 'Momma', have changed the lyric from one of Dylan's most cutting truth-attack put-downs to something blunted, smudged

59.   Arthur Crudup: 'Death Valley Blues', Chicago, 11/9/41, "Bluebird Blues", RCA Victor Records LPV-518, New York, 1965. (This is mentioned later, in relation to Dylan's song 'Dignity', and in Chapter 16 ditto.)

60.   In Taft, 'Mama' is the 29th most often-used word in the corpus: ahead of 'just', 'love', 'is', 'because', 'if' and 'when'. (The no.1 word, unsurprisingly, is 'I'; the rest of the top ten, in order, are 'you', 'to', 'the', 'my', 'and', 'me', 'a', 'in' and 'I'm'.)

and inaccessible; but the title is that of a song Robert Johnson wrote but didn't record.[61]

This is not the only blues title Dylan used directly in this period. While his 1965 song title 'On The Road Again' might be taken as a reference to Jack Kerouac's novel *On the Road*, it is also a well-known track by his old friends the Memphis Jug Band.[62] His Basement Tapes blues 'Long-Distance Operator' takes its title straight from a blues single, now rather scarce, by Little Milton, made in 1959, and his Basement Tapes rock song 'Odds And Ends' is the title of a prominent 1957 Jimmy Reed record – prominent for featuring electric violin, played by the splendidly named Remo Biondi. (It is an instrumental, and the relentless, pulsating, slow harmonica-work seems to me to be the model for Bob Dylan's on 'Pledging My Time'. Play the Reed track and then the opening of the Dylan one and you'll concede the strong resemblance.)[63]

And while the 1966 on-stage Dylan was using that Robert Johnson title 'Tell Me Mama', off-stage he could be found, as the fragmentary film of that tour, *Eat the Document*, revealed, playing a song that didn't sound like a blues at all from the delicate, faltering way that he explored it – but 'What Kind Of Friend Is This?' (copyrighted as Dylan's by Dwarf Music in 1978!) was what Robert Shelton called 'Apparently Dylan's adaptation of an old blues song' and was, specifically, a 1964 blues record by Koko Taylor, cut at her début session, called 'What Kind Of Man Is This?'[64]

---

61.   It was recorded by Johnny Shines, probably NYC, 1972; "Sitting On Top Of The World", Biograph 12044, Canaan, NY, 1972.

62.   Memphis Jug Band: 'On The Road Again', Memphis, 11/9/28; issued on a soon-withdrawn British EP, HMV 7EG8073, London, c. 1955, under the wrong title (i.e. as 'Overseas Stomp', another Memphis Jug Band track, itself more usually called 'Lindberg Hop', recorded the same day as 'On The Road Again'. [Memphis Jug Band: 'Lindberg Hop', 2 takes, take 1 issued Records LVA3009, New York, c. 1954.]) As it happens Dylan – as Blind Boy Grunt – contributed back-up vocals and harmonica to the version of 'Overseas Stomp' cut by Dick Farina and Eric Von Schmidt, London, 10–11/1/63, issued "Dick Farina & Eric Von Schmidt", Folklore F-LEUT-7, London, 1964.
     What made jug-bands unique is explained in an excellent short passage from Robert Gordon's *It Came from Memphis*:

> It creates a sound where there should be none, from instruments intended for other purposes . . . The handmade equipment – a guitar from a cigar-box, a harmonica from a corn-cob – conveyed an egalitarianism that reached into the guts of their audience . . . [while] the jug blowers made keeping the beat into a touch of God. Their *whoomp whoomp* filled with character, the musicians themselves responding to the audience's disbelief of their capabilities, pushing their talents to new heights while their heads floated off their shoulders from hyperventilating.

63.   Little Milton: 'Long Distance Operator', St. Louis, Missouri, 1959, Bobbin Records 103, St. Louis, 1960; LP-issued "Raise A Little Sand", Red Lightnin' Records RL0011, UK, 1975.
     Jimmy Reed: 'Odds And Ends', Chicago, 3/4/57, Vee Jay 298, Chicago, 1957. The figures Reed relies on more than Remo Biondi are his long-time guitarist partner Eddie Taylor, whose distinctive riffs 'make' Reed's records, and his wife, Mary Lee Mama Reed, who wrote much of his material. More re Reed appears in note 40 above.
     (An 'Odds And Ends' was also cut by rockabilly artist Warren Smith, Hollywood, 17/11/60, Liberty Records LRP 3199 / LST 7199 / LB 1181, Hollywood, 1961.)

64.   Bob Dylan: 'What Kind Of Friend Is This?', Glasgow hotel-room, 18–19/5/66; extracted in *Eat the Document*, New York, directed D. A. Pennebaker, edited Bob Dylan and Howard Alk, premiered New York, 9/2/71. Koko Taylor: 'What Kind Of Man Is This?', Chicago, 30/6/64, Checker 1092, Chicago, 1964.
     Glen Dundas' 1994 edition of *Tangled up in Tapes* credits Dylan's version 'Willie Dixon, adapted Bob Dylan'. Dixon's autobiography (*I Am the Blues: The Willie Dixon Story*, 1989) does not include it in the list of 500-plus songs he claims to have written, and Dylan sessionographer Michael Krogsgaard (*Twenty Years of Recording: The Bob Dylan Reference Book*, 1981) credits it to Koko Taylor herself. Whoever may claim the song,

At the end of the 1960s, when Dylan was said to be looking to found his own record label, its proposed name was 'Ashes and Sand': an ellipse of the blues expression 'ashes to ashes and sand to sand' (a far rarer cousin to the Bible's 'ashes to ashes and dust to dust'), which Blind Willie McTell sings in his 1931 song 'Southern Can Is Mine', and which Geeshie Wiley and Elvie Thomas had sung in their earlier 'Over To My House' ('I cried ashes to ashes, said sand to sand / Every married woman got a back-door man').[65]

Likewise, when Dylan named his own main music publishing outfit, he called it 'Special Rider Music', borrowing another piece of old country-blues idiom. 'Special rider' conventionally means favourite lover, which makes it a telling way for Dylan to choose to refer to his muse. He likes the poetry of the term, the elegance of which comes from an understatement achieved by everyday vocabulary (as with so much of the blues): a term that intimates affection and sex while also suggesting a magic journeying. Dylan finds it more sympathetic than the etiolated, twee ways the Muse is referred to (the word 'muse' itself sounds precious – very luvvie – and the worse for the capital M) in mainstream white Western culture, where its personification tends towards greco-roman lyre-playing women with wispy hair and long nylon dresses.

'Rider' itself is one of the 250 most frequently occurring words in the Taft concordance: so often used that it ranks ahead of 'feet', 'mother', 'help', 'stand', 'might', 'things', 'thinking', 'pay', 'jail', 'thought' and 'sleep'. But *Special* rider is more special: it seems to occur in only four pre-war songs and by implication – 'Ain't got no special, got no trifling kind' – in a fifth (though it may have occurred in some unrecorded songs and may occur more frequently in post-war blues). The four are: 'Special Rider Blues' by Skip James and by Son House, 'No Special Rider Blues' by Eurreal Little Brother Montgomery and 'Mean Old Frisco Blues' by Arthur Crudup; the implicit fifth is Ishman Bracey's 'Left Alone Blues'. How these relate to each other, and how Bob Dylan picked up on them, is scrutinised later.[66]

---

it is merely adapted from a gospel song, also called 'What Kind Of Man Is This?' (a title founded in turn upon a phrase in the biblical story of Christ calming the storm when he and the disciples are on the sea: 'What manner of man is this?' they ask themselves, as Christ commands the wind and waves: Matthew 8:27: 'But the men marvelled, saying, What manner of man is this, that even the winds and the sea obey him!'; Mark 4:41: 'And they feared exceedingly, and said one to another, What manner of man is this, that even the wind and the sea obey him?'; and Luke 8:25: 'And they being afraid wondered, saying one to another, What manner of man is this! for he commandeth even the winds and water, and they obey him.').

65.   Blind Willie McTell: 'Southern Can Is Mine', Atlanta, 23/10/31; "Blind Willie McTell: The Early Years (1927–1933)", Yazoo L-1005, New York, 1968. There's also the re-make 'Southern Can Mama', New York, 21/9/33; "Blind Willie McTell, 1927–1935", Yazoo L-1037, New York, 1973. Both CD-reissued "The Definitive Blind Willie McTell", Columbia Legacy Roots N' Blues Series C2K 53234, New York, 1994.
      Wiley and Thomas: 'Over To My House', Grafton, Wisconsin, c. March 1930; "Going Away Blues", Yazoo L-1018, New York, 1969. 'Geeshie' was a term still used by older southern blacks in the early decades of the century, to refer to the music of the Gullah people of the Georgia Sea Islands. Blind Blake says he's going to play a little geeshie (or Gheechee) music on his 'Southern Rag' [Chicago, c. Oct. 1927; "Blind Blake: Foremost Finger-picker", Yazoo L-1068, New York, 1984, now CD-reissued.].

66.   Skip James: 'Special Rider Blues', Grafton, Wisconsin, c. February, 1931; "Mississippi Blues 1927–1941", Yazoo L-1001, New York, 1968, and "Skip James: King of the Delta Blues Singers 1928–1964", Biograph BLP-12029, Canaan, NY, 1971. Son House: 'Special Rider Blues' [one fast and one slow take], Robinsonville, Mississippi, 17/7/42; "Negro Blues and Hollers", AFS Records L 59, Washington, DC, 1962 [CD-reissued Rounder Records CD1501, Cambridge, Mass., 1997]; CD-reissued "Son House: The Complete Library of Congress Sessions 1941–1942", Travelin' Man Records TM CD 02, Crawley, UK, 1990. Eurreal Little Brother Montgomery: 'No Special Rider Blues', Grafton, Wisconsin, c. Sept. 1930; "Piano Blues 1927–1933", Riverside RM8809, NYC, 1966. Arthur Crudup: 'Mean Old Frisco Blues', Chicago, 15/4/42; "The Rural Blues", RBF Records RF-202, New

Then when Dylan came to issue his first box-set retrospective collection, in 1985, he called it after one of the main blues reissue labels, "Biograph": a label that, as this chapter's notes have already indicated, specialised in the 1960s and 1970s in releasing work by Blind Lemon Jefferson, Ma Rainey, Blind Blake, Skip James, Leroy Carr, Papa Charlie Jackson, Memphis Minnie, Blind Willie McTell and other important figures.[67]

When Dylan published his selected *Writings and Drawings* in 1972, it was dedicated in part 'To the magnificent Woodie [sic] Guthrie and Robert Johnson who sparked it off'. *Playboy* asked Dylan in 1977 what music he listened to – by implication wanting to see whether he would confess to keeping an ear on what was contemporary and popular: Steely Dan, perhaps, or the Jacksons, or Bonnie Tyler. Dylan said: 'I listen to Memphis Minnie a lot.'[68]

The year that interview was published, 1978, is one during which Dylan draws especially deeply and recurrently from the waters of the blues. This is evident from that year's world tour – on which within 114 concerts he gave a total of 109 performances of six different blues songs by people from Tampa Red to Willie Dixon, as well as a remarkable Robert Johnsonised re-write of his own 'Going, Going, Gone' – and evident from that year's album "Street Legal", which is at least as soaked in the blues as any work of his before or since.

Even writing a song named after a disease or an illness, like Dylan's late-1970s song 'Legionnaire's Disease', is in a blues tradition. It joins a waiting-list that takes in Memphis Minnie's 'Meningitis Blues', TB songs by Leadbelly, Victoria Spivey and Sonny Boy Williamson I, Blind Lemon Jefferson's 'Pneumonia Blues', Blind Blake's 'Hookworm Blues' and 'Depression's Gone From Me Blues', Sylvester Weaver's 'Me And My Tapeworm', Bukka White's 'High Fever Blues', Vol Stevens' 'Baby Got The Rickets', Elder Curry's 'Memphis Flu', Champion Jack Dupree's 'Bad Health Blues', Josh White's 'Silicosis Is Killin' Me' and Buddy Moss's 'T.B.'s Killing Me', through Georgia Tom's 'Terrible Operation Blues' right on down to Blind Richard Yates' 'Sore Bunion Blues'.[69]

York, 1964. Ishman Bracey: 'Left Alone Blues', Memphis, 4/2/28; "The Famous 1928 Tommy Johnson – Ishman Bracey Session", Roots RL-330,Vienna, 1970.

67. Some of their releases have already been listed in the notes to this chapter; other Biographs included: "Mississippi John Hurt, 1928: His First Recordings" (BLP-C4, Canaan, NY, 1972); "Early Leadbelly, 1935–1940: Narrated By Woody Guthrie" (BLP-12013, New York, 1969); a volume of 1949 Blind Willie McTell recordings (BLP-12008, NYC, 1969) and a companion volume with McTell's rare 1949 recordings for the independent Regal label on one side and cuts from the same label's 1949 Chicago session by Memphis Minnie on the other ("Blind Willie McTell – Memphis Minnie, 1949 Love Changin' Blues", BLP-12035, Canaan, NY, c. 1972).

68. Interview by Ron Rosenbaum, Burbank, California, November 1977, published *Playboy*, March 1978.
    Memphis Minnie (1897–1973), real name Lizzie Douglas, is an important artist in the history of the blues: an assertive singer and able guitarist and the confident composer of several classics. Born in Louisiana, she moved to just south of Memphis as a child and was discovered on Beale Street in 1929. She and Joe McCoy moved to Chicago in 1930. 'Some accounts of her early life say she ran away from home and joined the circus for a stretch . . .', writes Linda Dahl in *Stormy Weather*; but when Dahl writes that 'she moved back down to Memphis in the mid-fifties in poor health. She spent the last years of her life in a nursing home and died in 1963' this date is wrong. In Paul Oliver's *The Story of the Blues* (1969), there is a photo of Minnie captioned 'at her Memphis home after a recent stroke'.

69. Memphis Minnie: 'Meningitis Blues', Memphis, 26/5/30; "Memphis Jug Band: Volume 2 (1924–1937)", Roots RL-337, Vienna, c. 1973. Leadbelly: 'TB Woman Blues', New York, 23/3/35; "Early Leadbelly, 1935–1940: Narrated by Woody Guthrie", Biograph BLP-12013, New York, 1969. Victoria Spivey: 'TB's Got Me Blues',

In 1983 Dylan wrote and recorded his own blues masterpiece 'Blind Willie McTell'. In 1986 when he titled his album "Knocked Out Loaded" he was quoting a phrase from a song on the album, 'Under Your Spell', co-written with the pop artist Carole Bayer Sager – but that Dylan lyric was itself quoting the phrase from 'Junko Partner', a 1940s semi-cajun blues that the deeply obscure New Orleans blues singer James Wayne recorded in Atlanta and which Dr John revived in the early 1970s.[70]

Those, then, are some of the external signals. It should therefore be no surprise to find that blues lyric poetry is everywhere in Dylan's work: in amongst the New York City hip culture of Dylan 1965 and the radical acid-rock of "Blonde On Blonde", in the evangelism at the start of the 1980s and work of more modest, mellowed knowingness such as Dylan gives us on the wonderful "Oh Mercy" song 'Dignity' (or doesn't, since in accord with his policy these days, he keeps this highlight-track off the album) right on through to the darkness of "Time Out Of Mind" towards the end of the 1990s.

In the course of that work he draws on blues lyric poetry in many ways, and moves through periods of greater and lesser exploratory debt to it. As is the process with that poetry itself, Dylan is sometimes leaning on a common cluster of song and sometimes on an individually created stanza – and sometimes taking a common cluster or individual stanza only to turn it inside out or to twist it round, to make of it something new.

It exemplifies his remarkable quiet ability to set himself unobtrusive creative goals and reach them – a side of his work inevitably overlooked inside a pop and media culture attuned only to notice and celebrate hugely dramatic artistic acts – that there is a pattern, though not a rigid one, to Dylan's uses of the blues. It is this: time and

---

Chicago, 7/7/36; "The Victoria Spivey Recorded Legacy of the Blues", Spivey LP-2001, Brooklyn, c. 1969. Sonny Boy Williamson I: 'TB Blues', Chicago, 21/7/39; "Blues Classics by Sonny Boy Williamson, Volume 2", Blues Classics BC-20, Berkeley, c. 1970. Blind Lemon Jefferson: 'Pneumonia Blues', Richmond, Indiana, 24/9/29; "Black Snake Moan": Blind Lemon Jefferson", Milestone MLP-2013, New York, 1970. Blind Blake: 'Hookworm Blues', Richmond, Indiana, 20/7/29; "No Dough Blues, Vol. 3: Blind Blake, 1926–1929", Biograph BLP-12031, Canaan, NY, 1972. Blind Blake: 'Depression's Gone From Me Blues', Grafton, Wisconsin, c. June 1932; "Down South Blues", Roots RL-313, Vienna, 1968.

Sylvester Weaver: 'Me And My Tapeworm', NYC, 27/11/27 (but, cut for OKeh but left unissued and untitled, the title was assigned to it only for its retrospective first issue; "Songs of Humour And Hilarity", Library of Congress Folk Music of America series LBC 11, Washington, DC, 1978).

Bukka White: 'High Fever Blues', Chicago, 8/3/40; "Bukka White", CBS 52629, London ["Bukka White: Parchman Farm", Columbia C-30036, NYC], 1969. Vol Stevens: 'Baby Got The Rickets', Atlanta 20/10/27; "More Of That Jug Band Sound, 1927–1939", Origin Jazz Library OJL-19, Berkeley, c. 1968. Elder Curry: 'Memphis Flu', Jackson, Mississippi, 16/12/30. Champion Jack Dupree: 'Bad Health Blues', Chicago, 23/1/41. Pinewood Tom (Josh White): 'Silicosis Is Killin' Me', NYC, 26/2/36. Buddy Moss: 'T.B.'s Killing Me', NYC, 18/1/33.

Georgia Tom and Hannah May: 'Terrible Operation Blues', New York, 17/9/30; "Big Bill Broonzy, 1928–1935: Do That Guitar Rag", Yazoo L-1035, New York, 1973. Georgia Tom and Jane Lucas: 'Terrible Operation Blues', Richmond, Indiana, 19/11/30; "Georgia Tom And Friends", Riverside Records Classic Jazz Masters series RM-8803, New York, 1966. Blind Richard Yates: 'Sore Bunion Blues', New York, c. 9/4/27; "Rare Blues of the Twenties, No. 1", Historical Records HLP-1, New York, 1966.

Some such titles use illness as a, yes you guessed it, sexual metaphor. 'Terrible Operation Blues' is one of these.

70.   James Wayne: 'Junko Partner', Atlanta, 1951; "Ray Charles In R&B Greats" [sic], Oriole Realm RM-101, UK 1963. Dr John: 'Junko Partner', New Orleans, 1972; "Gumbo", Atlantic Records [K40384 in UK]; reissued on "Let It Rock", Atlantic K40455, UK, 1973. A similar song, 'Junker Blues', had been recorded by Champion Jack Dupree (Chicago, 28/1/41), and this, cleaned up, became the far more competent and successful 'The Fat Man' by Fats Domino (New Orleans, 10/12/49, Imperial 5058, LA, 1950; CD-reissued "Fats Domino: The Early Imperial Singles 1950–1952", Ace Records CDCHD 597, London, 1996).

again when you come across these streams of blues consciousness in his work, the verbatim blues phrases (quoted either from the common-stock or from specific writers) are found inside his *non*-blues songs, while his blues songs offer the phrases innovatively tweaked. In this way blues lyric poetry runs into the mainstream of Dylan's work, while in the minority portion of that work that is itself structured as blues – and to which we turn first – Dylan makes a clear creative contribution to this major form of American music.

This can work in the least ostentatious of ways, on through to the inspired. At the least ostentatious end, there is, in 'Just Like Tom Thumb's Blues', the moment when Dylan sings the final, unremarkable 'I do believe I've had enough': which imports a non-blues phrase into the blues so aptly as to make it authentic. In Taft there are many dozens of 'I believe I' and 'I believe I'll'. Dylan's formulation 'I do believe I've' doesn't occur once. Likewise the corpus is full of 'what's the matter baby?', 'what's the matter now?' and 'what's the matter with you?' – but there isn't one 'What's the matter with me?', which Dylan uses to open the blues-structured 'Watching The River Flow'. Similarly, while there are many, many 'kill me dead's, and 'killing me dead's, only Dylan sings 'killing me alive'. (There is, in the blues, however, a halfway-house phrase, 'killing me on my feet', used in the title of a Sonny Boy Williamson II song – a record with an exquisite harmonica solo, one so physically direct yet of such delicate finesse that it could explain the soul of blues and R&B to Jane Austen. It was cut at the same session as 'Don't Start Me To Talkin'', the Williamson song Dylan performed on US TV in 1984.)[71]

Further along the spectrum of possibilities, the blues-structured 'Buckets Of Rain' gives us, with that dignified, humane concluding verse, effectively a re-write of an old blues couplet by Kid Wesley Wilson and Harry McDaniels (the words are probably Wilson's). Dylan's lines are

> All you can do is do what you must
> You do what you must do, and you do it well.

Wilson's are

> Whenever you do it, what ever you should
> Just do your best to do it good.[72]

Dylan's title 'Memphis Blues Again' manages to include implicit acknowledgement that there is another 'Memphis Blues' – indeed several. The classic W. C. Handy song 'Memphis Blues' (he wrote the melody, published in 1912; George A. Norton wrote the lyrics in 1913) was cut by Esther Bigeou at her début session as early as 1921. Ma Rainey sang 'Memphis Bound Blues' in 1925; Frank Stokes (with Will Batts on violin) cut a 'South Memphis Blues' in Memphis in 1929; Memphis Minnie's 'North Memphis Blues' was cut in Chicago in 1930.[73] Influence is often hard to trace. It just could be

---

71. Sonny Boy Williamson [II]: 'You Killing Me (On My Feet)', Chicago, 12/8/55; "Sonny Boy Williamson – One Way Out", Chess CHV 417, New York, 1975. All 'Don't Start Me To Talkin'' details note 195.

72. Kid Wesley Wilson and Harry McDaniels [as Pigmeat Pete and Catjuice Charlie]: 'Do It Right', New York, 5/9/29; "Rare Blues, 1927–1930", Historical Records HLP-5, Jersey City, New Jersey, c. 1967.

73. Esther Bigeou: 'Memphis Blues', NYC, c. 5/10/21. Ma Rainey: Chicago, c. Aug. 1925. Frank Stokes: 'South Memphis Blues', Memphis, 23/9/29. Memphis Minnie: 'North Memphis Blues', Chicago, 11/10/30.

that Dylan picked up his own song's Mobile–Memphis contrast from something he must have seen in print many times: Harry Smith's summary of the Uncle Dave Macon track 'Way Down The Old Plank Road'. While the recording itself would hardly suggest it, Smith's ellipse gives us 'WENT MOBILE, GET GRAVEL TRAIN, NEXT I KNEW: BALL AND CHAIN . . . NASHVILLE PRETTY, MEMPHIS BEAUTY.'[74]

As for the *format* 'stuck inside of Mobile with the Memphis Blues again', it parallels exactly that we associate with Bukka White's powerful 1940 track 'Aberdeen Mississippi Blues', with its simple

> *Sittin' down in Aberdeen with New Orleans on my mind.*[75]

Dylan's 'Obviously 5 Believers' and 'Leopard-Skin Pill-Box Hat', two of the other blues songs on 'Blonde On Blonde', are difficult to get a grip on in terms of how much creativity they exhibit. 'Obviously 5 Believers' is a filler track on the album, with a repetitive and undistinguished lyric; yet it stands in a distinguished tradition, its melody and structure taken wholesale from a classic song, 'Me And My Chauffeur Blues', by that great Dylan favourite Memphis Minnie: a song with a history that is complicated to unravel but serves as a fine indication of how communal composition can work inside the blues.

Memphis Minnie performed 'Me And My Chauffeur Blues' years before her 1941 recording. In 1933, Big Bill Broonzy lost a blues-playing contest to Memphis Minnie in a Chicago club, when he played 'Just A Dream' and she played 'Me And My Chauffeur Blues'. The judges were Sleepy John Estes, Tampa Red and the man who wrote the lovely 'classic' blues 'Trouble In Mind', Richard Jones. The prize was two bottles of whiskey. Broonzy, who must have had mixed feelings about losing to someone who might be called a protégé of his, says he lost the contest but ran off with the whiskey.[76]

Actually Broonzy's contest-loser, 'Just A Dream', is itself a terrific song with strong Dylanesque touches; you can hear him in your head singing this with relish and aplomb:

> *I dreamed that I got married,*
> *Raised up a family*
> *I dreamed I had ten children*
> *And they all looked just like me . . .*

---

74. Harry Smith, notes on Uncle Dave Macon: 'Way Down The Old Plank Road' [NYC, 14/4/26]; "American Folk Music", see note 22.

75. Bukka White: 'Aberdeen Mississippi Blues', Chicago, 8/3/40; "The Male Blues Singers", Collectors Classics CC-3, Copenhagen, c. 1965; CD-reissued "Parchman Farm Blues", Blues Collection CD 23 [magazine + CD], London, 1994.

76. Contest information from Big Bill Broonzy's book *Big Bill Blues* (1955), retold in Linda Dahl's *Stormy Weather* (1984), and discussed at length in the chapter 'Me and My Chauffeur' in Paul and Beth Garon's *Woman with Guitar: Memphis Minnie's Blues* (1992).
     Lawrence Cohn's notes to the Columbia Legacy Roots N' Blues series CD of Broonzy material ("Good Time Tonight", Columbia 467247–10, New York, 1990) describe Minnie as 'one of his many gifted protégés' but the track that most resembles Memphis Minnie's style, 'Come Home Early' (Chicago, 16/8/37), is strongly reminiscent of her mature work, suggesting another side to the question of who taught whom.

I dreamed I had a million dollars,
Had a mermaid for a wife
I dreamed I won the Brooklyn Bridge
On my knees shootin' dice.[77]

The story of the contest is especially interesting because if Broonzy is right about the date then Memphis Minnie was performing 'Me And My Chauffeur Blues' before Sonny Boy Williamson I put out his record of 'Good Morning, School Girl' and before competition judge Sleepy John Estes' 'Airplane Blues', though both are built on the same frame. Minnie's song even pre-dates the 1934 recording called 'Back And Side Blues' by Estes' pal from Brownsville, Tennessee, Son Bonds, cut at his début session, which 'Good Morning School Girl' also uncannily resembles. If Broonzy is *wrong* about the date of his story, then the contest probably took place in 1938 – still three years ahead of Minnie putting her song on record – in which case Son Bonds would seem to have been the first into the studio with a song using this strongly distinctive structure and tune. Either way, it doesn't seem to have been Sonny Boy Williamson's 'Good Morning, School Girl' that used this melody and structure first.

In 1938 the Estes song was mixed in with 'School Girl' by Williamson too (even using Estes' favourite accompanist, Yank Rachel, on mandolin), on his terrific 'You Can Lead Me'. Later that same year it was recycled by Blind Boy Fuller as 'Flyin' Airplane Blues'. As for 'Good Morning, School Girl' itself, this quintessential Sonny Boy Williamson I number, universally known as 'Good Morning, Little Schoolgirl', passed into the cor-blimey repertoire of every British beat group of the early 1960s.[78]

Memphis Minnie finally recorded 'Me And My Chauffeur Blues' in May 1941, and within a year the now-forgotten Mabel Robinson went into the studios in New York and cut that rare thing, a worthy jazz version: one that doesn't patronise or apologise for the blues simplicity of the song but seizes joyfully on its strengths and retails it again, in this case sizzling with panache from the trumpet, tenor sax, piano, guitar, bass and drums of Sam Price's Blusicians.[79]

---

77.   Big Bill: 'Just A Dream (On My Mind)', Chicago, 5/2/39. Big Bill: 'Just A Dream No. 2', Chicago, 14/9/39.

78.   Sonny Boy Williamson: 'Good Morning, School Girl', Aurora, Illinois, 5/5/37; "Sonny Boy Williamson", RCA [Treasury of Jazz no. 22] 75.722 [EP], Paris, 1963. Sleepy John Estes: 'Airplane Blues', NYC, 3/8/37; "The Blues Of Sleepy John Estes: Volume One, '934–1937", Swaggie Records S-1219, Australia, 1967. Son Bonds: 'Back And Side Blues', Chicago, 6/9/34. Sonny Boy Williamson: 'You Can Lead Me', Aurora, 13/3/38. Blind Boy Fuller: 'Flyin' Airplane Blues', Columbia, South Carolina, 29/10/38; "Blind Boy Fuller: Death Valley", Oldie Blues Records OL 2809, Holland, 1975].

79.   Memphis Minnie: 'Me And My Chauffeur Blues', Chicago, 21/5/41; issued on Paul Oliver's compilation "The Story Of The Blues", CBS [M] 66218, London, 1969; double-CD reissue of same, "The Story Of The Blues", Columbia 468992 2, NYC, 1991. Post-war Memphis Minnie did a four-song session for the Chess company's Checker label, re-recording 'Me And My Chauffeur' (with Little Walter on harmonica), Chicago, 11/7/52; "The Blues Volume 5", Cadet LP 4051, Chicago, 1966.
      Mabel Robinson: 'Me And My Chauffeur', NYC, 20/1/42. (Sam Price's Blusicians were more or less the US Decca house-band, and featured on very many sides of the period.) I mention its being 'that rare thing, a worthy jazz version: one that doesn't patronise or apologise for the blues', because so often jazz people regard the blues as beneath them and thereby disqualify themselves from performing it well. A splendid tirade from Big Bill Broonzy against these people is quoted in Lomax's *The Land Where the Blues Began*: 'Got they dark glasses on. Some of um wearin' their little bebop goatees.' Dylan came across them early in the shape of Herb Lovelle, who played drums on LaVern Baker's 'Tweedle Dee' and Dylan's 'Mixed-Up Confusion' and regarded both as slumming. Leonard Feather is another: look how awful a result he gets from Little Richard on his first sessions. Or look at how Ella Fitzgerald 'improves' Leroy Carr's 'When The Sun Goes Down' by changing 'and it sets up in the West'

In roaring contrast, in 1965, came a version by Big Mama Thornton which, more even than 'Ball And Chain', shows what a Thorntonnabe Janis Joplin was. Big Mama's 'Me And My Chauffeur' is not only uncannily Joplinesque, to put it the wrong way round, but offers the sort of grunge-rock that pterodactyls might have used as mating-calls. Less than a year later, Bob Dylan was disguising the song as 'Obviously 5 Believers'. (And as it happens, within weeks of Dylan's releasing this on "Blonde On Blonde", zydeco blues master Clifton Chenier was in the studios in Pasadena cutting his own version of 'Me And My Chauffeur Blues', titled 'Be My Chauffer' [sic]).[80]

George White's 1995 book *Bo Diddley: Living Legend* claims that the debt of Dylan's 'Obviously 5 Believers' is to a 1956 Diddley track, 'She's Fine, She's Mine', and you could make a case that the Dylan arrangement owes something to the shuffle-beat, maraccas and harmonica set-up Diddley creates, but White seems unaware of the earlier blues records upon which the Diddley record too is based. And if Dylan knew the Diddley track, he can only have come across it on either the original 1956 78 rpm record or by picking up the 1963 British EP "Chuck & Bo, Volume 2", because the former was its only US release and the latter its only vinyl release before Dylan recorded 'Obviously 5 Believers'.[81]

'Leopard-Skin Pill-Box Hat' is the more interesting Dylan song. In one way, it is utterly Dylanesque, and wholly redolent of that Warhol Factory New York City, so 1960s, so chic and fey, so knowing and druggy and poised, and engaging for its weird mix of energy and high comedy with its elaborate and ostentatious stance of ennui. Yet at the same time it is coachbuilt very closely upon the chassis of a Lightnin' Hopkins song from 1949, his 'Automobile (Blues)'. It is not just a melodic parallel. Hopkins begins:

> *I saw you ridin' round, you was ridin' in your brand-new automobile*
> *Yes, I saw you ridin' round, you was ridin' round in your brand-new automobile*
> *Yes, you was sittin' there happy with your handsome driver at the wheel*
> *In your brand-new automobile—*

and as Hopkins sings that extra last line, his voice takes that familiar downward curve and ends on that 'Dylanesque' long, sliding 'beeeel' that is a slippery mixture of a knowing sneer and some malicious envy. Dylan makes sly acknowledgement of his source in the last verse of his own song, with the in-joke admonition that 'you forgot to close the garage door'.[82]

---

to 'and it sets down in the West' – more correct but so much less poetic as to reduce the whole from the magical to the moronic. (For more on the Leroy Carr version, see note 195.)

80.   Big Mama Thornton: 'Me And My Chauffeur', Los Angeles, 1965, Kent Records 424, LA, 1965. Clifton Chenier: 'Be My Chauffer', Pasadena, late 1966; "Soul In The Beginning", Avco-Embassy Records LP 33006, 1970. He recorded it again as 'Me And My Chauffeur', Houston, 6/11/69, issued posthumously on "King of the Bayous", Arhoolie CD 339 (a re-release of the LP Arhoolie 339, *nia*, plus extra tracks, including this one), El Cerrito, California, c. 1992.

81.   Bo Diddley: 'She's Fine, She's Mine', Chicago, 10/5/55, Checker Records 819, Chicago, 1956; "Chuck & Bo, Volume 2", Pye International 44012, London, c. 1963. (Dylan recorded 'Obviously 5 Believers' in Nashville, 9/3/66.)

82.   Hopkins' first sessions, in Los Angeles in late 1946 and 1947, were for Aladdin, and yielded four singles. Immediately afterwards came his first Houston sessions, some for Gold Star and some for Aladdin again. The Gold Star sessions 1947–49, including 'Automobile (Blues)', are considered his best work.
      Lightnin' Hopkins': 'Automobile (Blues)', Houston, 1949; "Early Recordings", Arhoolie Records 2007, El

In taking from Lightnin' Hopkins, Dylan was driving down a very old road. Hopkins' label, Gold Star, was typical of the new wave of independent record labels being created in the early post-war period, after the ending of the Petrillo ban on recording but with shellac still hard to get hold of. As Paul and Beth Garon write in their excellent biography of Memphis Minnie, 'When shellac was scarce, record producers like Gold Star's Bill Quinn recycled thousands of old 78s (and no doubt many treasures among them) to provide the raw material for their new releases, giving a bizarre literalism to the notion of one style developing out of another. Many of Lightnin' Hopkins' early records were literally *made* out of melted down Minnie's and Big Bill's!'[83]

A country blues man with an electric guitar (born in 1912 and 'raised in the piney woods of East Texas', as Chris Strachwitz puts it), and a confident writer of autobiographical songs, Lightnin' Hopkins was influenced by Texas Alexander, Lonnie Johnson (who frequently accompanied Alexander on record) and Sleepy John Estes. The as-it-were oppositely named Lightnin' Hopkins is, in turn, a weighty influence. His in-your-face 1947 record '(Let Me) Play With Your Poodle' – one of those where the euphemism sounds at least as rude as the sexual term it replaces – is hardly original by most criteria: it's a Tampa Red number from 1942, and just a 'Step It Up & Go' kind of song in any case, but it's innovative because with Hopkins' electric guitar, piano by Thunder Smith and a drummer too, it sounds like rock'n'roll years ahead of its time. Hopkins, who continued to record prolifically, died in Houston in January 1982.[84]

Now to move from automobiles to buses. In performances of 'Let's Keep It Between Us', though not in the garbled and nondescript version of the lyric published in *Lyrics 1962–1985*, Dylan avows

> *Let's just move to the back of the back of the bus.*

This phrase is a classic Dylanism: it's like 'in the final end', in 'I Pity The Poor Immigrant', and is creative and interesting because it serves a similar purpose, which is partly to be emphatic but partly to acknowledge an existential or qualitative distinction between the ordinary and the emphasised meaning. 'Let's just move to the back of the back of the bus' stresses a solidarity with the oppressed – stresses that, as with Desolation Row, it is morally cleaner to be there – by drawing on the resonance the phrase 'the back of the bus' must have for anyone who grew up around or before

---

Cerrito, California, 1965 (the year before Dylan composed 'Leopard-Skin Pill-Box Hat') CD-reissued "The Gold Star Sessions Vol. 1", Arhoolie Records CD 330, El Cerrito, c. 1991, and "Vol. 2", Arhoolie CD 337, same details.

83. Paul and Beth Garon, see note 76.

84. Chris Strachwitz, notes to "Lightnin' Hopkins: Texas Blues", Arhoolie CD 302, 1989 (which mention Hopkins' original 'late 1940s' recordings for Gold Star though the album itself contains instead a 1967 re-recording). Lightnin' Hopkins' first sessions and subsequent Aladdin sessions – including '(Let Me) Play With Your Poodle'; LA, 15/8/47; LP-issued "Lightnin' Hopkins And The Blues", Imperial Records 9211, Hollywood, 1950s. – CD-reissued "The Complete Aladdin Recordings", Aladdin Records CDP 7968442, Holland, 1991. Re 'Step It Up & Go' songs, see Chapter 18. Tampa Red: 'Let Me Play With Your Poodle', Chicago 6/2/42.

As noted in Chapter 16, even with 'Brownsville Girl', Dylan rides a trail already explored by a blues singer. 'I Would If I Could', one of the best (which is to say, least self-indulgent) of Lightnin' Hopkins' 1960s sides, is a song about going to see a movie about Jesse James, in which the song's narrator drifts between 'real-life' and on-screen events awash with rumour and shooting. Lightnin' Hopkins: 'I Would If I Could', Houston, 18/12/67, is included on the Arhoolie CD with the Chris Strachwitz notes just cited.

the civil rights struggle in America. (The Freedom Singers, who appeared with Dylan at the 1963 Newport Folk Festival, used to feature a song called 'If You Miss Me At The Back Of The Bus'.)[85]

In fact Dylan's back-reference in 'Let's Keep It Between Us' to this example of racial inequality represents a return to the subject on his part. He refers to it first in one of the barbed jokes he puts into 'I Shall Be Free', originally recorded in December 1962 and issued on "The Freewheelin' Bob Dylan":

> . . . a can a black paint it fell on my head.
> I went down to scrub and rub
> But I had to sit in the back of the tub.

Choosing the back of the bus still involves taking a *stance*. It's where the surreptitious drinkers, the so-what youths sit, on the Greyhounds that cross the country. The contemporary back of the bus milieu is pinned down excellently in Irma Kurtz's book *The Great American Bus Ride* (1993).

'Let's Keep It Between Us' has a further black resonance: it is noticeably similar to Jimmy Witherspoon versions (and thence to Otis Spann's version) of 'Nobody's Business', a traditional song that goes back at least to the beginning of the century and has been recorded very many times. As sung by, for instance, Mississippi John Hurt or Frank Stokes (both of whom made Memphis versions in 1928), you wouldn't see any resemblance at all to the Dylan song – not even in theme, since what is nobody's business but the singer's includes killing his woman, so making it a me-against-everyone song rather than, as 'Let's Keep It Between Us' so eloquently is, an us-against-them song. But as Jimmy Witherspoon and Otis Spann perform it, as 'Ain't Nobody's Business' and ''Tain't Nobody's Biz-ness If I Do', the rich and stately musical progression, the mood and the theme are likely to strike you at once as the inspiration for Dylan's own rich and stately song. Witherspoon-Spann's friendlier version of the lyric says

> Me and my baby, you know we fuss and fight
> Just the next morning, baby we's all right
> Now ain't nobody's business, have mercy!, what I do:

from which you might say that Dylan has more or less reversed that 'fuss and fight' to put 'fuss' among his 'us' rhymes.[86]

---

85. Bob Dylan: 'Let's Keep It Between Us', e.g. live in Seattle, 30/11/80. The Freedom Singers' 'If You Miss Me At The Back Of The Bus' published in *Broadside*, no. 17, 1963.

86. Jimmy Witherspoon: 'Ain't Nobody's Business', Los Angeles, 20/11/47, issued Supreme 1506 then Swing-time 263, LA, prob. 1948; "Spoon Calls Hootie" (Polydor Jazz Masters Vol. 5), Polydor Special 545 105, London, 1966. Jimmy Witherspoon: 'Ain't Nobody's Business', Chicago, 15/8/56, unreleased till "Spoon So Easy", Chess MCA CH93003, USA, c. 1989. Otis Spann, with the Muddy Waters Band: ''Tain't Nobody's Biz-ness If I Do', Chicago, 30/8/66; "The Blues Is Where It's At", Bluesway Records 6003, New York, 1967.

An inspiringly good piece of black and white footage of Otis Spann performing this song at the piano (but without harmonica) was shown on an *Omnibus* programme on the blues made by Initial Productions, London, broadcast BBC2 TV, London, October 1993; this Spann footage was filmed in 1968 by the Canadian Broadcasting Corporation for the programme *Festival Presents the Blues*. (These details of where and when it was filmed were supplied by Jeff Rosen, who runs Bob Dylan's music publishing office.)

Mississippi John Hurt: 'Nobody's Dirty Business', Memphis, 14/2/28; "Mississippi John Hurt Complete 1928

The chorus of Dylan's blues-structured 'Gotta Serve Somebody' also reformulates a particular blues record, while also dealing with wider idiom and the older genre of the 'Negro Spiritual'. When, on the contemporaneous 'Precious Angel', he insists that 'there ain't no neutral ground', he is, as noted in Chapter 7, reiterating the words of the Bible as mediated through those of William Blake – 'Christ is very decided on this Point . . . There is no Medium or Middle state' – but when he re-presents this biblical insistence in 'Gotta Serve Somebody':

> Well it may be the devil or it may be the Lord
> But you're gonna have to serve somebody

it is as mediated through the form of blues lyric poetry. There is a formulation which, beginning with 'Ashes to ashes and dust to dust', then adds any one of a number of permutations of a clear-cut, no-middle-way choice, presented as 'if A don't get you then Z must': these include 'New York don't get me, Chicago must', 'The police don't get you, now the undertaker must'. One of these, from Joe Evans, prefigures Dylan's 'Gotta Serve Somebody' chorus thus:

> Ashes to ashes and dust to dust
> And if God don't have me you know the devil must.[87]

This is not the Dylan song's only debt. Both Memphis Slim's song 'Mother Earth' and Dylan's 'Gotta Serve Somebody' owe a modest indebtedness to the old 'Negro Spiritual' 'Ev'rybody Got To Die':

> Rich and poor, great and small
> Got to meet in Judgment Hall
> Ev'rybody who is living
> Ev'rybody got to die . . .
> Young and old, short and tall
> Got to meet in Judgment Hall
> Ev'rybody got to die[88]

but the debt of Dylan's song to Memphis Slim's is more than a modest one. This is from 'Mother Earth' (1961 version):

> You may own a half a city, even diamonds and pearls . . .
> You may play at race-horses, you may own a race-track
> You may have enough money baby to buy anything you like
>
> Don't care how great you are, don't care what you're worth
> When it all end up you got to go back to Mother Earth.

Recordings", Yazoo L-1065, Newton, NJ, 1988, CD-reissued Yazoo CD-1065, New York, nia. Frank Stokes: 'Ain't Nobody's Business If I Do Part 2', Memphis, 30/8/28; "Memphis Blues 1928–1930", RCA 2-LP NL89276, Paris, 1984.
    Like 'Dyin' Crapshooter's Blues' and other traditional songs, 'Nobody's Business If I Do' was copyrighted by the opportunistic studio musician-arranger Porter Grainger (and in this case Clarence Williams) in the 1920s.

87.   Joe Evans: 'New Huntsville Jail', New York, 20/5/31; "Early Country Music", Historical Records HLP-8002, Jersey City, NJ, late 1960s.

88.   'Ev'rybody Got To Die' reprinted (I have removed the minstrelisation of the text) from *The Treasury of Negro Spirituals*, ed. H. A. Chambers, 1964.

The core idea, the structure of the verses as you-may-be-rich-or-poor listings, the specific ways these are expressed – not just the 'you may own x or you may own y' and the occasional judicious use of that 'even z', but the effective device of quantum-leaping what 'rich' might mean, from 'you may play at race-horses' to 'you may own a race-track', which Dylan matches with his rather less neat 'you might be somebody's landlord, you might even own banks' – *and* the insistent 'ain't no escaping' that is the message of the chorus: all these, duplicated in Dylan's lyric, are there in Memphis Slim's.[89]

An echo of this same formulation lingers in secular form in another song, one the teenage Bob Dylan would have been familiar with, Elvis Presley's fourth single, 'Baby Let's Play House': 'You may go to college, you may go to school / You may drive a pink Cadillac but don't you be nobody's fool / . . . Come back baby, I wanna play house with you'. This was written by Arthur Gunter (his version an R&B hit earlier in 1955), though it was Elvis himself who threw in the line 'You may own a pink Cadillac': the one which, as it happens, best fits the pattern of the 'Mother Earth' / 'Gotta Serve Somebody' lyrics. And the line Elvis dropped to accommodate his Cadillac was 'You may have religion'. Dylan's core contribution is that he picks that religious ingredient up again and re-entwines it with the secular formulations of Memphis Slim.[90]

This may be the belated opportunity to venture a brief note about the relationship between the blues and spiritual/gospel music: as a generalisation about the song that arose from the slave labour of African-Americans, it seems broadly true that work songs give rise to the blues and relief-from-work songs give rise to spirituals and gospel music. Alan Lomax is excellent on the work song as the main source of the poetry of the blues, and might even interest those whose sole concern is Bob Dylan terrain when he happens to cite the work song version of 'Rocks and Gravel' (a song Dylan made early attempts at in 1962), which includes this:

> It takes a-rocks and gravel
> To make a solid road
> It takes a good-lookin' woman
> To make a good-lookin' whore.[91]

Karl Dallas points out that in Engels' essay 'The part played by labour in the transition from ape to man', it was conjectured that even the faculty of *speech* probably derived from communal labour: 'The development of labour,' Engels wrote, 'necessarily helped to bring the members of society closer together by increasing cases of mutual support and joint activity, and by making clear the advantages of this joint activity to each individual. In short, men in the making arrived at the point where

89. Memphis Slim: 'Mother Earth', Chicago, 1951; Premium Records 867, Chicago, 1951. Memphis Slim: 'Mother Earth', NYC 1961; "Memphis Slim: All Kinds Of Blues", Bluesville 1053, Bergenfield, NJ, c. 1961.

90. Arthur Gunter (1926–1976) cut 'Baby Let's Play House' at his first session, Nashville, 1954, Excello 2047, Nashville, 1955. Elvis Presley: 'Baby Let's Play House', Memphis, 5/2/55, Sun Records 217, Memphis, 1955 [HMV Records POP 305, London, 1957]. Actually Gunter didn't write it: he re-wrote it, taking it from Eddy Arnold's record 'I Wanna Play House With You'.

91. Alan Lomax, *The Land Where the Blues Began*. Bob Dylan: 'Rocks and Gravel (Solid Road)', NYC, March 1962 [unreleased]; ditto NYC, 25/4/62 [unreleased]; ditto NYC, 1/11/62; issued on the early, withdrawn "Freewheelin' Bob Dylan", 1963.

they had something to say to each other.' Dallas adds that contemporaneously, 'a nineteenth century sociologist, Bücher, expressed the view in his "Arbeit und Rhythmus" that speech originated in the act of labour itself, in the cho?used grunting necessary to co-ordinate efforts . . . it could be said that this primitive form of song actually pre-dates speech, and is the very first form of art.'

This contradicts the notion, advanced by Iona and Peter Opie and relayed in the later chapter on nursery rhyme, that the first form of song would naturally have been the lullaby. This is surely more likely, since birth – women's work, if you will – comes before communal work, and is just the sort of thing to have been disregarded by the nineteenth century's eminent dwems (dead white European males). Nonetheless, the work song must have come very early on. Perhaps these two conflicting claims can be united by our envisaging that first there would have been 'choused grunting to co-ordinate efforts' by gatherings of midwives assisting 'in the act of labour itself'.[92]

At the other end of the human story, the 'Ashes to ashes and dust to dust' expression discussed earlier sounds like the basis for the similar 'sugar for sugar and salt for salt'. I used to think this latter, used on Dylan's 'Down In The Flood', was Dylanesque playful weirdness, if not mysterious drug terminology, typical of the Basement Tapes sessions. Later I assumed instead that it was Dylan quoting one of these formulaic blues phrases, another common-stock motif. I'm now surprised to find that it seems an individually created variant, actually appearing on only one record: Rabbit Brown's 'James Alley Blues'. Dylan adapts this but slightly, shifting it from

> *I'll give you sugar for sugar, let you get salt for salt*
> *And if you can't get along with me well it's your own fault*

to include his own song-title within it:

> *Well it's sugar for sugar / And salt for salt*
> *If you go down in the flood / It's gonna be your fault.*

'James Alley Blues', one of only half a dozen sides Brown recorded – and, as we've noted, the one included on Harry Smith's 1952 anthology – has been hugely influential, not least on Dylan. It also includes 'I done seen better days but I'm putting up with these', which gets re-processed between two Dylan co-compositions. Mix together the Dylan–Shepard 'Brownsville Girl' line 'I feel pretty good but that ain't sayin' much / I could feel a whole lot better' and the Hunter–Dylan 'Silvio' line 'Seen better days but who has not?' and you're more or less back to Rabbit Brown's line. Brown's song *also* includes the more common-stock 'Sometime I think that you too sweet to die / Then another time I think you ought to be buried alive', variants of which can be traced in earlyish Dylan songs such as 'Black Crow Blues', with its 'Sometimes I'm thinkin' I'm / Too high to fall / Other times I'm thinkin' I'm / So low I don't know / If I can come up at all'.[93]

---

92. Engels, Dallas and Bücher quoted from *The Electric Muse*, by Laing *et al.*, see note 33.

93. Richard Rabbit Brown: 'James Alley Blues', New Orleans, 11/3/27; "American Folk Music", see note 22. Smith says Brown was one of the earliest musicians to learn the 12-bar 'blues' chord pattern, and the first and most important New Orleans folk singer to record; that he was famous for his dramatic guitar-playing which, on record, closely resembles that of Blind Willie Johnson; and that 'James Alley Blues' was recorded in a New Orleans garage on the same day as 'I'm Not Jealous', 'Never Let The Same Bee Sting You Twice', 'Mystery Of The Dunbar Child'

'Black Crow Blues' is itself terrific for the way that it tears into the blues structure with something so fresh, so invigoratingly off the wall, that it makes you laugh just to hear it. At the same time, and without sacrificing any of the hipness paraded by 'wasted and worn out' or 'My wrist was empty / But my nerves were kickin' / Tickin' like a clock', he nevertheless brings to it, particularly in the last verse, a special rural feel:

> *Black crows in the meadow*
> *Across the broad highway.*
> *It's funny, honey,*
> *I don't feel much like a*
> *Scarecrow today*

so that in the end it is a strange sort of *country* blues.

There's nothing 'country' about the following year's 'She Belongs To Me', but it is certainly a blues: a blues so fresh that when it came out, few people noticed its blues structure at all (something that was to be true, later, with a couple of Van Morrison's songs on "Astral Weeks"). As already noted, Dylan brings to 'She Belongs To Me' the wonderful line

> *She can take the dark out of the nighttime and paint the daytime black:*

a line that perfectly represents the spirit of blues lyric poetry, its particular form of expressive mind-set, while being wholly new.

Anyone who thinks it might be easy to construct a blues lyric – anyone who mistakes the haikuesque conciseness for simplicity – should try writing one. To try is to appreciate how much demanding craft, as well as creative instinct, is involved: and to appreciate something of Dylan's achievement. There are few finer examples than his immaculate blues of 1965, 'It Takes A Lot To Laugh, It Takes A Train To Cry', which among much else is an illustration of how he draws on the formulaic phrases of country blues and weaves them into the tapestry of his own work. He sings:

---

and 'Sinking Of The Titanic'. Sheldon Harris' *The Blues Who's Who*, 1979, also lists as his songs 'Gyp the Blood' and 'Downfall of the Lion'.

Brown was born in poverty in New Orleans about 1880 and died in poverty in New Orleans in 1937. Jane's [sic] Alley was a noted gang-fighting area of New Orleans, in which he was raised. (Louis Armstrong came from there too.) A street-singer, he often worked also as singing boatman on Lake Pontchartrain. He is mentioned as an influence on the sleeve notes to Dylan's first album, and Jaharana Romney (née Bonnie Beecher, an important pre-New York friend of Dylan's) says Dylan and Harvey Abrams (quoted earlier) sat around in the 10 O'Clock Scholar in Dinkytown mentioning obscure singers' names, and that she and Dylan met because she was able to join in. She'd go to Sam Goodys in New York to buy records, choosing 'any old record that looked like it had some kind of funky singer or blues singer . . . records by Cat Iron, Rabbit Brown – I've never heard of those guys since'. ['The Wanted Man interview: Jaharana Romney', by Markus Wittman, *Telegraph*, no. 36, Summer 1990.]

Cat-Iron, William Carradine, born Garden City, Louisiana, 1896, died in Natchez, Mississippi, 1958. The record mentioned can only have been a newish copy of his 1958 LP, recorded in Natchez the year he died there. "Cat-Iron Sings Blues & Hymns", Folkways LP2389, New York, was his only record, the fruit of his only recording-session. Tracks were traditional and gospel songs, including 'Poor Boy A Long, Long Way From Home' and 'Don't Your House Look Lonesome'. He had also been recorded on film in Natchez, 28/5/57, for a CBS-TV (USA) documentary called *Seven Lively Arts*, nia.

(It was with the then Bonnie Beecher, at her apartment in Minneapolis, 22/12/61, that Dylan put so many great performances on tape. The tape-deck, to which we owe so much, was her theatre arts teacher's reel-to-reel. Later, Dylan took Ms Beecher to see Woody Guthrie.)

> *Don't the moon look good, mama, shinin' through the trees?*
> *Don't the brakeman look good, mama, flagging down the 'Double E'?*
> *Don't the sun look good goin' down over the sea?*
> *Don't my gal look fine when she's comin' after me?*

The second line calls up a picture at once specific and resonant with the mythology of the train; the listener's 'camera angle' is that of the man or woman who, hidden in those trees, watches the brakeman so as to catch the moment, as the train slows, to board it unobserved. The language accords with the blues milieu, as its falling cadence enacts the slowing of the flagged-down train. Yet as evidenced by its three main ingredients, the line is pure Dylan. First, every glimpse of the 'brakeman' in the pre-war blues is in the context of a described conversation, not a visual picture: every one approximates to 'I asked the brakeman, please let me ride your blinds'. There is certainly no 'Don't the brakeman look good'! Yet slipped in here by Dylan as a sort of devil's advocate challenge to the logic of the repetitive formula he's working with, the remark has a humour and a humanity that is not disruptive of the formula but pushes out its boundaries. Second, there is the tiny evidence of idiom: while 'flag(ged) a/my train' is common, there is no 'flag/flagged/flagging *down*'. Third, 'Double E', 'double O' and the like occur frequently: but always in the wholly different sense meant in the formulaic 'Tennessee . . . double S, double E'.

So that second Dylan line is new and his own. The others are ancient and communal property. Old blues records are riddled with variants, like 'Don't the moon look pretty, shining down from that willow tree / I can see my baby and she can't see me', and 'Don't the moon look pretty shining through the trees'. The extent of Dylan's drawing on them (in this and a couple of earlier songs), can be seen from just one such old blues, Leroy Carr's 'Alabama Woman Blues'. The full lyric is:

> *Did you ever go down on the Mobile and K.C. Line*
> *I just want to ask you, did you ever see that girl of mine*
> *I rode the central and I hustled the L & N*
> *The Alabama women, they live like section men*
> *Don't cry baby, your papa will be home someday*
> *I've been away baby but I did not go to stay*
> *Don't the clouds look lonesome across the deep blue sea*
> *Don't my gal look good when she's coming after me.*[94]

Additionally, but by the nature of the process inseparably, Dylan's lines draw in the couplet Elvis Presley sings *so* beautifully in the cathartic, lulled middle of his stormy Sun recording of 'Milkcow Blues Boogie':

---

94. Respectively these are from: Bob Campbell: 'Shotgun Blues', New York, 30/7/34; "Country Blues Obscurities, Vol. 2 (1927–1936)", Roots RL-340, Vienna, c. 1972. Texas Bill Day: 'Billiken's Weary Blues', Dallas, 5/12/29; "Texas & Louisiana Country (1927–1932)", Roots RL-335, Vienna, c. 1971. Leroy Carr: 'Alabama Woman Blues', Chicago, 19/9/34; "The Country Blues", RBF Records RF-1, New York, 1959. Bob Campbell also recorded 'Dice's Blues' at the same session [now on the same album] which includes the stanza 'Jack of diamonds, jack of diamonds, will turn your money green / It's the luckiest card that a gambler have ever seen'. This too reverberates through the traditional blues and into Dylan's earlier work.

Don't that sun look good goin' down
Well don't that old moon look lonesome when your baby's not around?[95]

If I had to choose one revelatory musical moment to show how electrifyingly such stuff passes along, it would be this one. To hear Presley sing these lines is to hear it all: to hear the graceful, rueing heart of the old country blues – never better voiced than in the brilliant ellipse of the opening line of Blind Blake's 'One Time Blues' in 1927:

Ah the rising sun going down

yet to hear at the same moment the liberation of the soul that Elvis found in the blues almost thirty years later – a liberation he passed on to all of us whiteys when he first sang out – *and* in that same moment to hear too a sound that travels forward thirty-odd years to illuminate what Dylan has swirling around him when, on the 1990 '10,000 Men', he comes to sing its second line not as a full repeat of the first ('Ten thousand men on a hill', which might be thought abrupt and spare enough) but honed to the absolute minimalism of

Ten thousand men, hill,

so that Dylan, sounding old as the hills himself (and pronouncing 'he-yi-ull' exactly as Elvis always did), stands shoulder to shoulder across the sixty-year gap with Blind Blake. Sure has been a long hard climb; yet it has been a shared journey, and the terrain is constantly replenished.[96]

95.   Elvis Presley: 'Milkcow Blues Boogie', Memphis, probably November 15 or December 20, 1954; Sun Records 215, Memphis, 1955 [first issued UK on EP "Good Rockin' Tonight", HMV Records 7EG8256, London, 1957]. It's telling that, as Marcus points out, the composer credit on Presley's record is to Kokomo Arnold but the songs are almost wholly different. Perhaps Presley took the song from Johnny Lee Wills, whose 'Milk Cow Blues' was a big jukebox hit in 1941.
    When Dylan recorded 'Milk Cow Blues' [unreleased] in 1962, he used part of Kokomo Arnold's lyric, part of Presley's, part of Robert Johnson's 'Milkcow's Calf Blues' and part of Leadbelly's 'Good Morning Blues', shuffling these elements around in the course of two takes. [Kokomo Arnold: 'Milk Cow Blues', Chicago, 10/9/34; "Peetie Wheatstraw and Kokomo Arnold", Blues Classics Records BC-4, Berkeley, 1960. Robert Johnson: 'Milkcow's Calf Blues', Dallas, 20/6/37, 2 takes, one on "Bottleneck Guitar Classics, 1926–1937", Yazoo Records L-1026, New York, c. 1971; the other on "Robert Johnson: King Of The Delta Blues Singers", see note 20. Leadbelly: 'Good Morning Blues', NYC, 15/6/40, or NYC, Summer 1943. (Some of this as regards the Dylan versions is noted by Heylin, *Telegraph*, no. 27, Summer 1987, though he implies, mistakenly, that the Kokomo Arnold version and the Presley share the same lyric and he doesn't acknowledge that there are two takes of the Johnson song, with one or two variant lines themselves.)
96.   Another example of how timeless Elvis Presley's exciting new transmissions could be: 'That's alright, Mama, that's alright for you' figures in a much earlier blues classic than the Arthur Crudup song that Elvis turned into his revolutionary first record. It's a stanza from Blind Lemon Jefferson's seminal 'Black Snake Moan', cut in Chicago as 'That Black Snake Moan' in 1926 and re-cut in Atlanta as 'Black Snake Moan' in 1927. The lines 'Mama that's alright, sugar that's alright for you / That's alright mama, that's alright for you / . . . just the way you do' then recur the following year in one of the two takes of Ishman Bracey's terrific ''Fore Day Blues'. Then on the early Crudup side 'If I Get Lucky', in 1941, he not only tries out the lines 'That's alright mama, that's alright for you / Treat me low-down and dirty, any old way you do' for the first time but he has a way of hollering that admits a debt to Bracey as much as to Blind Lemon Jefferson. The connection makes perfect sense: we know that Crudup hung out in Jackson, Mississippi in the 1940s, when Ishman Bracey was the city's most popular and active musician. In turn, it was 150 miles up Highway 55, in Memphis, that Elvis saw Crudup perform. Somewhere there's an interview with Elvis in which he's asked, when he's the ultimate star, if he had imagined that kind of fame and success for himself when he started out. Elvis replies: 'No. When I started out I just wanted to be as good as Arthur Crudup was when I saw him live in '49.'
    [Blind Lemon Jefferson: 'That Black Snake Moan', Chicago, c. Nov. 1926; "Black Snake Moan: Blind Lemon Jefferson", Milestone Records MLP-2013, New York, 1970. 'Black Snake Moan', Atlanta, 14/3/27; "Jazz Vol. 2:

Dylan's 'It Takes A Lot To Laugh, It Takes A Train To Cry' makes other blues connections too. It opens with the lines

Well I ride on a mailtrain, baby,
Can't buy a thrill,

which manages to combine, as if it's the most natural thing in the world, one statement that seems clear and straightforward and one that seems opaque. No one ever says what this second line means. A possible explanation, in this song of self-imposed exile, is suggested in the lyrics of Bukka White's 'Black Train Blues':

I ride this train, keep the women from spendin' my change.[97]

Dylan's last verse begins 'Wintertime is coming'; on Robert Johnson's 'Come On In My Kitchen', the last verse begins 'Winter time's comin''. Dylan's last verse presses on with

I wanna be your lover baby
I don't wanna be your boss—

a neat formulation that is Dylan's own, and very much of its age – one of his lyric flashes that, like 'All I Really Want To Do', anticipates the stance of the women's movement of the later 1960s: yet for all its originality and topicality (and it takes nothing away from Dylan to note this) it is nonetheless prefigured by a similar formulation in the old pre-blues black song 'Salty Dog', a classic from the repertoire of all the old songsters and which the very young Bob Dylan referred to in his recorded 1961 performance of the parallel traditional song 'Candy Man'. As Blind Willie McTell recalls 'Salty Dog', on his 1956 'last session', he sings the relevant passage thus:

I don't wanna be your man at all
I just wanna be you' salty dog—.[98]

'Tombstone Blues' is the title of at least three blues recordings from the 1920s: all, as it happens, deeply obscure by virtue of having remained unissued. Lillian Miller

---

The Blues" Folkways FP55 and FJ-2802, New York, 1950. Ishman Bracey: 'The 'Fore Day Blues' (alternate take), Memphis, 31/8/28; "Jackson Blues 1928–1938", Yazoo L-1007, New York, c. 1968, CD-reissued YAZCD1007, New York, c. 1988. The lyric fragment quoted is not included on the better-known take, issued on "The Famous 1928 Tommy Johnson-Ishman Bracey Session", Roots RL-330, Vienna, 1970. Both takes are CD-reissued on "Ishman Bracey & Charley Taylor", Document Records DOCD-5049, Vienna, c. 1991. Arthur Crudup: 'If I Get Lucky', Chicago, 11/9/41; "Kings Of The Blues Vol. 3", [EP], RCA RCX204, London, 1962. Arthur Crudup: 'That's All Right', Chicago, 6/9/46, known by Elvis Presley from its issue on 78rpm on Victor 20–2205 (c/w 'Crudup's After Hours'), New York, 1946–7. Elvis Presley: 'That's All Right', Memphis, 5–6 July, 1954, Sun Records 209, Memphis, 1954.]

When I was at school, a boy with the splendid name of Dunsford Boyce, who later played drums in a Merseybeat group, had an early Presley EP and I had a Big Bill Broonzy EP. We swapped. Afterwards I felt I'd gone for shameful commerce and Boyce for honourable obscurity. Later I realised we'd both made decent decisions.

97. Bukka White: 'Black Train Blues' (a smouldering prototype for Elvis train songs, and White's first recording after getting out of Parchman Farm), Chicago, 7/3/40; "Mississippi Blues Vol. 1", Roots RL-302, 1968; CD-reissued "Parchman Farm Blues", Blues Collection CD 23, London, 1994.

98. Bob Dylan: 'Candy Man', Minneapolis, 22/12/61; unissued. Blind Willie McTell: 'Salty Dog', Atlanta, Sept. 1956; "Blind Willie McTell: Last Session", Prestige Bluesville 1040, Bergenfield, NJ, 1961 [Transatlantic Records, PR1040, London, 1966], CD-reissued Prestige Bluesville Original Blues Classics OBCCD-517-2 (BV-1040), Berkeley, CA, 1992.

and Lonnie Johnson both cut a 'Tombstone Blues' in 1927, and Bessie Smith cut one the following year. But the pattern of Dylan's chorus (Papa's doing this, Mama's doing that, some other relative's doing t'other) is older still, deriving from children's game-songs and imported unapologetically into black songs for grown-ups long before there was a form called the blues, and getting itself onto record in the 1920s. It's there, for instance, in the very title and sub-title of Vol Stevens' 1927 record 'Baby's Got The Rickets (Mama's Got The Mobile Blues)'.[99]

Nor would it be possible to read these four consecutive lines by Georgia Tom from 1928 without being put in mind of at least one other Dylan song of 1965 as well. Re-formulated, they infuse at least the chorus of 'Tombstone Blues', the opening of 'Subterranean Homesick Blues' and something of the spirit of both:

> *Daddy's got the washboard, mama's got the tub*
> *Sister's got the liquor and brother's got the jug*
> *My water-pipe's all rusted, water's running cold*
> *Someone's in the basement trying to find the hole.*

Only *something* of the spirit of the Dylan lines is there – the upbeat rhythmic facility – because the innovative transformation Dylan makes is via the context in which he places his own so-similar lines. The context removes the tone of jolly family just-folksiness, replacing it with an opposite consciousness: that of the alienated loner at odds with yet surrounded by people going obdurately about their incomprehensible business and, 'in the basement', communing with their own drug paranoia.[100]

Dylan can undertake the smallest tweaking of the smallest phrase from the blues and gain from it something memorable and expressive of his own mind-set. In that 1966 concert-opener 'Tell Me Momma' the couplet

> *You're just gonna make everybody jump and roar*
> *Now whaddaya wanna go and do that for?*

takes one of the commonest phrases in the blues – 'jump and shout' – and with minimal change refashions from it both a vivid evocation of the madness of the crowd

---

99. Lillian Miller: 'Tombstone Blues', Chicago, 27/10/27. Lonnie Johnson: 'Tombstone Blues', Chicago, 13/12/27. Bessie Smith: 'Tombstone Blues', NYC, 19/3/28. Vol Stevens: 'Baby's Got The Rickets (Mama's Got The Mobile Blues)', see note 69. [This last track is listed in Dixon & Godrich's *Blues Records 1902–1943* as having the subtitle, though this was not used on the original Victor 78 rpm label.]

100. Georgia Tom: 'Grievin' Me Blues', Chicago, c. 6/9/28; "Rare Blues of the Twenties, No. 1", Historical Records HLP-1, New York, 1966.

Georgia Tom was born in Villa Rica, Georgia, in 1899 and moved to Chicago in 1916. He was a backing musician for Ma Rainey 1924–28, played piano on Tampa Red's big hit 'It's Tight Like That' (1928) and in the 1930s worked with Memphis Minnie and novelty acts like the Famous Hokum Boys – in which Big Bill Broonzy was at one time lead-guitarist.

Dorsey wasn't really 'just-folksy' at all but a cool, sly, city dude. There's a wonderful photograph of him, republished in Paul Oliver's book *The Story of the Blues* (1969), in which, dressed sharper than we'll ever be, he's cupping his hands to light a cigarette. His eyes, feral and knowing, pierce the camera-lens: it's a shot the Hollywood of 1940s film noir would have killed for. Later, influenced by composer C. H. Tindley (who founded the Tindley Methodist Church, Philadelphia, where Bessie Smith is buried), he transformed himself into the gospel composer and publisher Thomas A. Dorsey, who wrote, among much else, 'Peace In The Valley' and 'Take My Hand, Precious Lord' (both recorded by Elvis in 1957; the former also a shimmering bravura cut by Little Richard in 1961, and performed *much* less satisfactorily by Bob Dylan in concert in 1989). Probably the last survivor of the key figures born around the turn of the century who were originally recording in the 1920s, Dorsey died in Chicago on 23 January, 1993. See also note 122.

he has conjured up to gawp at the 'momma' literally and mentally out on the edge *and* the comic expression of his own transparently feigned, callous incomprehension.[101]

There are times when Dylan makes no such innovative appropriation and is content merely to transmit, unrefreshed even by switched context, formulaic blues phrases inside blues songs, if not to lean on the unexceptional.

One example: I always thought that the weakest lines in that bluesy "Blonde On Blonde" song 'Temporary Like Achilles' were in the bridge section between the second and third verses, where he sings

> But is your heart made out of stone, or is it lime
> Or is it just solid rock?

The unrocklike limpness of that repetition, that tautology, seemed puzzlingly poor. It's just as poor, but no longer a puzzle, when we learn that Dylan has extrapolated it from Blind Lemon Jefferson's 'Lonesome House Blues', in which we get the more economical

> If your heart ain't rock, sugar it must be marble stone.[102]

To write a blues-structured song about 'Rita May' is to take an easy traditional road, down which Robert Johnson, Tommy McClennan, Tampa Red, Texas Alexander, Teddy Bunn and Fred McMullen have long since sent Katy Mae, Betty Mae, Betsy Mae, Jenny Mae, Ida Mae and Willie Mae. (Big Mama Thornton's name was also Willie Mae.) In the post-war period, one of Howlin' Wolf's first recordings was 'Dorothy Mae'. Chuck Berry's 'Maybellene' was, he said, originally to be 'a country number' called 'Ida May'.[103] And it isn't far from the opening line of Robert Johnson's 'Honeymoon Blues':

> Betty Mae, Betty Mae, you shall be my wife some day

---

101. The phrase 'jump and shout' is everywhere in the blues. One example out of dozens is Sleepy John Estes: 'Airplane Blues', see note 78.

102. Blind Lemon Jefferson: 'Lonesome House Blues', Chicago, c. Oct. 1927; "Black Snake Moan: Blind Lemon Jefferson", Milestone MLP-2013, New York, 1970.

103. Robert Johnson: 'Honeymoon Blues', Dallas, 20/6/37; "Robert Johnson: King Of The Delta Blues Singers, Volume 2", Columbia C-30034, NYC, 1970. Tommy McClennan: 'Katy Mae Blues', Chicago, 12/12/40; "'Cross Cut Saw Blues': Tommy McClennan (1939–1941)", Roots RL-305, Vienna, c. 1968. Tampa Red: 'No Matter How She Done It', NYC, 3/2/32; "Tampa Red: Bottleneck Guitar, 1928–1937", Yazoo L-1039, New York, 1973. Texas Alexander: 'Seen Better Days', San Antonio, 9/6/30; "The Country Fiddlers", Roots RL-316, Vienna, 1968. Fred McMullen: 'Wait and Listen', New York, 16/1/33; "The Georgia Blues", Yazoo L-1012, New York, c. 1968. Teddy Bunn: 'Pattin' Dat Cat', New York, 7/4/30; "Rare Blues, 1927–1930", Historical Records HLP-5, Jersey City, c. 1968. Howlin' Wolf: 'Dorothy Mae', Memphis, 17/4/52; "Legendary Sun Performers", Charly LP30134, London, 1977; alternate take issued on Delta Swing Records LP 379, *nia*, and on Blue Night LP 1667, *nia*. Robert Johnson also interjects 'hoo, Willie Mae' repeatedly towards the end of each extant take of 'Love In Vain', Dallas, 20/6/37; "Masters Of The Blues, 1928–1940", Historical Records HLP-31, Jersey City, NJ, 1969 and "Robert Johnson: King Of The Delta Blues Singers, Volume 2". Chuck Berry: 'Maybellene', Chicago, 21/5/55.

    There's also the real-life Jessie Mae Robinson, writer of 'In The Middle Of The Night' by Lucky Millinder, later covered by Little Richard; 'Black Night' by Arthur Alexander; 'Party' by Elvis and by Wanda Jackson; and 'The Other Woman' by Nina Simone and (again) by Arthur Alexander. Mae, though, is a southern, rather than a specifically black name. Elvis' granny, Vernon's ma, who accompanied Elvis to Germany after his mother's death, was called Minnie Mae. She had a daughter (Elvis' aunt) with the apt name Delta Mae, who died in 1993.

to Dylan's opening line:

> Rita May, Rita May
> You got your body in the way.

Nor is it far from Johnson's 'Little Queen Of Spades' line 'Everybody says she got a mojo' (I don't say the line is original to Johnson's song, but it's in there all the same) to Dylan's 'New Pony' line 'Everybody says you're using voodoo'.[104]

The only thing I like about the *Hearts of Fire* filler-song 'Had A Dream About You Baby' is the comic yet stylishly lazy

> Late last night you come rollin' across my mind.

I like the picture of someone feeling this image move across from one side of their head to the other: an image that recurs between the unmemorable verses, so that it enacts the in-between of 'in one ear and out the other' (it's a self-reflexive text, even). But I get at least as much pleasure from hearing the same main phrase in Skip James' '4 O'Clock Blues', thus:

> Brownskin girl, she rollin' across my mind

and in Hosea Woods' 'Prison Wall Blues', in which the rollin' is restless, as the recurrent thought is trapped inside the walls of the singer's head:

> The prison wall blues keep rollin' across my mind.[105]

And to go back to Betty Mae for a moment, that Robert Johnson song too offers almost this same phrase:

> Betty Mae . . .
> You rolls across my mind baby, each and every day.

In Dylan's rough-and-ready 'Chicago blues' number 'Enough Is Enough', performed only on the 1984 tour (so, naturally, not issued on its "Real Live" album), he bums the formulaic 'nickel is a nickel, a dime is a dime' from at least as far back as 1929 (year of the Wall Street crash, when suddenly a nickel wasn't quite a nickel any more), when it jingled in Walter Buddy Boy Hawkins' 'How Come Mama Blues', spreading quickly into a 1930 Birmingham Jug Band record, a King Solomon Hill record of 1932 and later records by Bill Wilber and Washboard Sam.[106]

The striking phrase 'nine below zero', embedded into Dylan's 1965 'Outlaw

104. Robert Johnson: 'Little Queen of Spades' [2 takes], Dallas, 20/6/37; one on "Masters Of The Blues, 1928–1940", Historical Records HLP-31, Jersey City, NJ, 1969, the other following year on Columbia C30034, *ibid*.

105. Skip James: '4 O'Clock Blues', Grafton, Wisconsin, c. Feb. 1931; "Skip James: The Complete 1931 Session", Yazoo 1072, Newton, NJ, 1988. Hosea Woods (with Gus Cannon): 'Prison Wall Blues', Memphis, 28/11/30; "More Of That Jug Band Sound, 1927–1939", Origin Jazz Library OJL-19, Berkeley, c. 1969.

106. Walter Buddy Boy Hawkins' 'How Come Mama Blues', Richmond, Indiana, 14/6/29; "Buddy Boy Hawkins & His Buddies", Yazoo L-1010, New York, 1968. Birmingham Jug Band: 'Giving It Away', Atlanta 11/12/30; Origin Jazz Library OJL-19, *ibid*. King Solomon Hill: 'Tell Me Baby', Grafton, Wisconsin, c. Jan. 1932; "Tex-Arkana – Louisiana Country, 1927–1932", Yazoo L-1004, New York, 1968. Bill Wilber: 'Greyhound Blues', Chicago, 22/7/35; "Country Blues Obscurities, Vol. 1 (1926–1936)", Roots RL-334, Vienna, c. 1971. Washboard Sam: 'I'm Not The Lad', Chicago, 26/6/41; "Feeling Lowdown: Washboard Sam", RCA Records LPV-577, New York, 1971.

Blues', is the title of one of Sonny Boy Williamson II's best-known harmonica-showcase songs,[107] while the Dylan song ends with 'She's a brown-skin woman but I / Love her just the same', which trusts the listener to know that he does not mean 'the same as if she were white' whether or not that listener knows that the line offers instead an allusion to a running debate on matters of colour that courses through the blues: a debate he touches on again in 1978 when, among the songs copyrighted as Bob Dylan–Helena Springs compositions is (along with another title with the word 'blues' in it, the nifty-sounding 'Romance Blues') a 'Brown Skin Girl', a title used on many pre-war blues records, such as the lovely, twinkling 1935 track 'Brown Skin Girls' by Cripple Clarence Lofton, and the earlier 'Brown-Skin Gal' by Barbecue Bob.[108]

These titles deal with the colour-coding of blacks by blacks into the basic categories 'high yellow, brown and black', usually accompanied in song by a statement of the singer's own sexual preferences. Blind Willie McTell, unhindered by his own blindness, is not averse to such discussion in his repertoire. This whole subject is readily understood to be confronted behind the title 'You Can't Tell The Difference After Dark', by Alberta Hunter.[109] The line 'the blacker the berry, the sweeter the juice/fruit' is widely advanced in blues lyric poetry. How these matters are touched upon by the Bob Dylan–Helena Springs song I don't know. (Talking of un-PC matters, there's a silly little joke decipherable on the tape of one of Dylan's 1978 Paris concerts when he introduces Helena Springs on-stage as 'a young lady who's also got a very bright future . . . and a great behind'.)

In Dylan's "Slow Train Coming" out-take 'Trouble In Mind', a 1979 neo-blues with a classic blues title, he sings 'When you're through with that Miss so-and-so . . .'. He may have taken that 'Miss So-and-So' directly from Robert Johnson's 'Ramblin' On My Mind', but she also occurs in two Roosevelt Sykes numbers, while 'Mrs. So-and-So' is (if the phrase has been heard aright) on Barrel House Buck McFarland's 'I Got To Go Blues', and there are many of those ancestors of Mr. Jones, the 'Mr. So-and-So's.[110] Sonny Boy Williamson I seems especially keen on him, putting him in at least seven different songs.

In the blues-structured 'Man of Peace' (1983), when Dylan comes in the seventh stanza to invoke images of imminent annihilation, he draws on the blues to do so for

---

107. Sonny Boy Williamson II: 'Nine Below Zero', Jackson, Mississippi, 4/12/51; "The Original Sonny Boy Williamson", Blues Classics BC-9, Berkeley, 1966. Re-made for Chess, 'Nine Below Zero' [3 takes], Chicago, September 1961; take 3 issued Checker 1003, Chicago, 1962, and LP-issued "More Real Folk Blues", Chess LP 1509, Chicago, 1964. So the re-make came out before the original: and a handy two or three years before Dylan was writing 'Outlaw Blues'.

108. The songs co-written with Helena Springs, at the time a Dylan back-up singer, are copyrighted to Dylan's Special Rider Music Company, 1978; no recordings have circulated.
 Cripple Clarence Lofton [with Big Bill Broonzy]: 'Brown Skin Girls', Chicago, 18/7/35. Barbecue Bob: 'Brown-Skin Gal', NYC, 15/6/27.
 'Brown Skin Gal', nia, is also a track by the Bahamian folk singer Joseph Spence, whose trademark dance-rhythm is used by Dylan on the fast studio version of 'Forever Young'. The Spence track is on "Bahamian Guitarist", Arhoolie CD 349, El Cerrito, California, c. 1991; another track is Spence's version of 'Mary Ann'.

109. Alberta Hunter: 'You Can't Tell The Difference After Dark', NYC, 20/3/35, "Classic Alberta Hunter: The Thirties", Stash Records LP ST115, Brooklyn, NY, 1978.

110. Robert Johnson: 'Ramblin' On My Mind', two takes, both San Antonio, 23/11/36; one Columbia CL-1654, the other C-30034. Barrel House Buck McFarland: 'I Got To Go Blues', Chicago, 20/8/34; "The Blues In St. Louis, 1929–1937", Origin Jazz Library OJL-20, Berkeley, c. 1969.

him. The opening line, 'Well, the howling wolf will howl tonight, the king snake will crawl', fuses two creatures long since appropriated into blues poetry: the howling wolf – which refers both to the mythic creature from the Georgia backwoods feared by rural blacks when darkness fell, and the fierce blues singer who took its name for his own, the great Howlin' Wolf himself – and the king snake that will crawl, which Dylan twists around but slightly out of Big Joe Williams' threatening 'Crawlin' King Snake', made in 1941. Or perhaps the snake too comes to Dylan via Howlin' Wolf, whose 'New Crawlin' King Snake' came out in 1966.[111]

That Dylan's images here might have come directly from the old rural blues songs – balancing the Big Joe Williams 'Crawlin' King Snake' there are two J.T. Funny Papa Smith cuts of 'Howlin' Wolf Blues' from 1930, one of which was a hit[112] – or via their more modern incarnations by the singer Howlin' Wolf, tells us something about the special value of the latter, and about the myth that there is a sharp divide between the acoustic rural blues and the electric city 'Chicago' blues.[113] This, then, seems the appropriate place to turn off down that dirt road for a Howlin' Wolf profile.

Though he was one of the four or five real giants of the tough, electric Chicago blues, and certainly the roughest and vocally most ferocious, he grew up in the pre-war country blues world and was a prime conduit through which much of this older blues music passed across into the new. While he was taught harmonica by Sonny Boy Williamson II – the one whose 'Don't Start Me To Talkin'' Bob Dylan performed a punk version of on the David Letterman TV Show in 1984, and who was in fact an older man than Sonny Boy Williamson I (who'd been murdered in 1948: he shares with Leon Trotsky the distinction of having being killed by an ice-pick) – Wolf learnt the guitar and much repertoire from one of the most influential figures in the history of the blues, Charley Patton, and even played some dates with Robert Johnson in 1930. His importance as a custodian, as much as a moderniser, of this pre-war material is in part explained by the fact that he didn't record at all until he was 41 years old. His early sides were made at Sun Records in Memphis, blues capital of the South, in which he had lived his whole life. Born near Aberdeen, in east Mississippi, in 1910, Chester Arthur Burnett moved west with his parents to the heart of the Delta when he was 13 and farmed on a plantation at Ruleville, close to Patton's homebase near Cleveland, Mississippi, on Highway 61, driving a plough pulled by mules. Except for a spell in the army, he continued to farm, while performing at fish fries and juke joints through the 1930s and early 1940s, turning professional only in the late 1940s. Most rural blacks who migrated north did so either in their teens or early twenties. It was exceptional that a man who had lived so long in the South should then move to

111. Big Joe Williams: 'Crawlin' King Snake', Chicago, 27/3/41; "Big Joe Williams: Crawlin' King Snake", RCA International INT-1087, London, 1970. Howlin' Wolf: 'New Crawlin' King Snake', Chicago, 11/4/66, "Change My Way", Chess LP CHV 418, Chicago, 1977.

112. J. T. Funny Papa Smith: 'Howlin' Wolf Blues No. 1' and 'Howlin' Wolf Blues No. 2', Chicago, 19/9/30; "'Funny Papa' Smith: The Original Howling Wolf", Yazoo L-1031, New York, 1972; there's also his 'Hungry Wolf', Chicago, c. April 1931 (cited again in note 137), same LP.

113. The sharpest divide between the acoustic rural blues and the electric city blues might be said to have been electricity itself, as Robert Gordon reminds us in *It Came from Memphis*. He says of the post-war South: 'The city had something that was less common in the country: electricity. And that made the city a louder place.'

Chicago, blues capital of the North, but Howlin' Wolf did so within two years of Sun Records' Sam Phillips leasing some of his first sides to Chess Records in Chicago. (Muddy Waters, his great rival, and five years his junior, was recorded as early as 1941, and moved to Chicago in the 1940s.) Accepting a cash advance from Chess Records, he *drove* to Chicago: 'the onliest one drove out of the South like a gentleman', he is quoted as saying.

A southern gentleman he remained. Wolf's 1952 'Saddle My Pony' is based in detail on Patton's 1929 'Pony Blues', and Wolf's 'Spoonful' on Patton's 'A Spoonful Blues'; the 1952 'Color And Kind', its remake 'Just My Kind' and the 1968 'Ain't Goin' Down That Dirt Road' all build on Patton's 1929 'Down The Dirt Road Blues'. Even Howlin' Wolf's biggest hit, the 1956 'Smokestack Lightnin'', was a remake of his own earlier 'Crying At Daybreak', which was in turn a restatement of Patton's 1930 'Moon Going Down'. A later 1956 session yielded 'I Asked For Water', based on Tommy Johnson's 1928 'Cool Drink Of Water Blues', and 'Natchez Burning', a remake of a song recorded earlier by Gene Gilmore and Baby Doo Caston about a dance-hall fire of 1940. Wolf's 1952 'Bluebird (Blues)', which he re-recorded in 1957 and re-fashioned two years later as 'Mr. Airplane Man', is a 1938 Sonny Boy Williamson I song (quite possibly via nearby Yazoo City singer Tommy McClennan: a singer whose vocal fierceness prefigured Wolf's and whose personal fierceness greatly exceeded it); 1952's 'Decoration Day (Blues)' is also from Sonny Boy Williamson I. In 1957 Wolf cut a splendid version of the old Walter Vincson & the Mississippi Sheiks 1930 standard 'Sittin' On Top Of The World', which Bob Dylan was to record first with Big Joe Williams; in 1966, the same year Wolf turned Big Joe's 'Crawlin' King Snake' into his own 'New Crawlin' King Snake', he also recorded 'Poor Wind (That Never Change)', which, to the tune of W. C. Handy's classic 'Careless Love', incorporated elements of Blind Lemon Jefferson's 1926 'See That My Grave Is Kept Clean', Papa Harvey Hull & Long Cleve Reed's 1927 'Hey! Lawdy Mama – The France Blues' and/or Fred McMullen's 1933 'Wait And Listen', and of the standard 'St. James Infirmary Blues', possibly via Blind Willie McTell's 'Dyin' Crapshooter's Blues' (discussed in a later chapter). The following year, Wolf cut 'Dust My Broom', which comes, via Elmore James or not, from Robert Johnson, who in turn had taken his title phrase from the lyric of Kokomo Arnold's 'I'll Be Up Someday'.

From 1959 or 1960 onwards, Chess was pressuring Wolf into recording not his own material but songs by the prolific Willie Dixon – but many of these, like the material Dixon had recorded as a member of The Big Three Trio in the 1940s, were strongly based on country blues songs from the 1920s and 1930s. While the label credits Dixon with having composed Wolf's 1961 hit 'The Red Rooster', Wolf himself said that the credit belonged to Patton, as had been true too with the 1960 'Spoonful'.

When Howlin' Wolf's career and influence was at it peak, therefore, which was from the mid-1950s till the mid-1960s, he was as synonymous with Chicago as Muddy Waters – and yet he never really sounded like the city. The world he invoked, in his uniquely spooky, surreal way, was in essence that of the back roads, the Mississippi swamplands made mythic and primeval, not far from Robert Johnson's crossroads, in the nighttime of the country soul. What he was bringing forward thunderously into the 1950s and 1960s, and making accessible to the likes of Elvis Presley on through to the Rolling Stones, and thus to the pop-buying public, was a rich meld of country blues lyric poetry. Wolf's 1954 side 'Evil' was transmuted into Elvis' 'Trouble' just four years later. In 1964, 'Smokestack Lightnin'', reissued in Britain, reached the charts, and Wolf appeared on *Ready Steady Go!* while in Europe as part of the American Folk Blues Festival. In 1965, as special guest of the Rolling Stones, who performed 'Little Red Rooster', Wolf performed his early-1950s 'How Many More Years' on the *Shindig* TV show in America.

By this time, Bob Dylan had already long been familiar with his work: which is why at times it is both impossible to tell, and perhaps unimportant to know, whether Dylan takes a line, or an image, or a flavour, from Howlin' Wolf himself or from somewhere in the earlier country blues as Wolf had done in turn. In March 1962, on the unedited tape made for a New York radio programme (it first emerged, on a bootleg CD, thirty years later), Dylan tells Cynthia Gooding – the Sarah Dunant of Greenwich Village – that he knows the work of both Muddy Waters and Howlin' Wolf: and goes on to perform a country blues version of 'Smokestack Lightnin'' that sounds closer in style to Charley Patton than Wolf's does. This says much for Dylan's recognition that Wolf was essentially a country wolf in city clothing. Four months later, at the Finjan Club in Montreal, Dylan performs the Memphis Jug Band's 'Stealin'', Robert Johnson's 'Ramblin' On My Mind' *and* Muddy Waters' 1950s number 'Still A Fool' (sometimes known as 'Two Trains Runnin', and possibly based on Tommy Johnson's 'Bye Bye Blues' of 1928).

If Dylan had gained nothing from Howlin' Wolf except an early piece of repertoire, there would be no reason here to give an account of Wolf at all. However, it seems as clear as such things ever can be that there is some direct inspiration. First, it's unlikely that Dylan's absorption of the Charley Patton legacy was never through Wolf, his last great pupil. Second, there must have been a time in Dylan's youth when, as for so many of us, the comprehensible beat, electricity and audible recording quality of Wolf and Waters made for a far easier way into much of the blues than the 'old-fashioned', gruesomely lo-fi recordings of the country blues.

So musically, as well as lyrically, Wolf was a conduit. His early band included Ike Turner and Junior Parker – whose elegant, cool 'Mystery Train' was to be transformed in the same Sun studio, via Elvis, into a founding classic for rock'n'roll – while the main guitarist Wolf used from 1954 onwards was the consummate Hubert Sumlin, whose best work is, for me at least, the finest electric guitar-playing in the universe. He plays solos of divine, deranged descending notes, tense as steel cable, grungy as hot-rod cars crashing, and as piercing as God cracking open the sky. Howlin' Wolf brought Sumlin up to Chicago from the south. He hailed from the Delta too: from Greenwood, Mississippi (where Robert Johnson was murdered in 1937 and where Bob Dylan commemorated the murder of Medgar Evers by singing 'Only A Pawn In Their Game' at a civil rights rally in 1963). Hubert Sumlin's influence is as plain as lightning on Mike Bloomfield – you can hear it on 'Maggie's Farm', Dylan's electric début performance at the Newport Folk Festival of 1965 – and on Robbie Robertson, as you can hear equally on the 1966 Dylan concert performances and on the LP "Planet Waves" from 1974.

There is another Wolf-Dylan conjunction on "Planet Waves" too, and it inhabits the boundary between the written word and pronunciation. Early on in his original sleeve notes to the album (long since vanished from the copies now available, and mysteriously absent too from Dylan's *Lyrics 1962–1985*), Dylan is recalling, with a careening and savage impressionism, what the 1950s had felt like; he writes of

> priests in overhauls, glassy eyed, Insomnia! Space guys off duty with big dicks & ducktails all wired up & voting for Eisenhower . . .

That pun on overhauls/overalls – clever because to perform the one you put on the other – may come directly from Howlin' Wolf. In his 'Sittin' On Top Of The World', instead of 'overalls', he sings the line that should include it as

> *Had to make Christmas in my overhauls.*

Of course it may not come directly from Wolf: as so often, Dylan could have picked it up from any one of a number of blues records or performances. Hear Tom Dickson's lovely 1928 recording 'Labor Blues', and singing out of it, as clear as a window, comes

> *Now I've got to take Christmas in my overhauls*

sung just like in Howlin' Wolf's 'Sittin' On Top Of The World' nearly thirty years later. Another twenty years on, Alan Lomax hears Napoleon Strickland sing the same verse, again in 'Sittin' On Top Of The World', and transcribes it like this:

> *Worked all the summer, part of the fall*
> *Took my Christmas in my overhalls*

while we can hear for ourselves, on Lomax's television programme about the Appalachians, that a Frank Proffitt song, 'Poor Man', sung for the camera by Frank Proffitt Jr (accompanying himself on a dulcimer, a string instrument like a lap-steel or an autoharp but straight from the middle ages), includes the stanza

> *Well I worked through the summertime*
> *And I worked through the fall*
> *Then I spent all my Christmas*
> *In a pair of overhauls*
> *There ain't a thing for a poor man in this world.*

Clearly then, this poetic ellipse has become common-stock among whites as well as blacks. It is not a universal Americanism, however. Just down the hills in Georgia, Blind Willie McTell, for instance, sings in his version of Blind Blake's 'That'll Never Happen No More':

> *Well it's Chicago women in the fall*
> *Got to make your days in your overalls*

and sings the word in the straight, unpunning, one might say middle-class, way.[114]

That freedom, that ability to pun, to make one word do two jobs – which need

---

114. Howlin' Wolf: 'Sittin' On Top Of The World', Chicago, Dec. 1957, Chess Records 1679, Chicago, 1958. Tom Dickson: 'Labor Blues', the last track cut at his only session, which was in Memphis, 27/2/28; "Frank Stokes' Dream . . . Memphis Blues 1927–1931", Yazoo L-1008, NYC, 1968, now CD-reissued. (Another instance is in

not be for a humorous purpose – is of course characteristic of Dylan, who usually exercises it (as Howlin' Wolf and the others do there) orally rather than on the page, but whose "Planet Waves" sleeve note shows that he can manage it on the page too.

The same was true for Shakespeare, as Christopher Ricks pointed out in a 1980 Australian radio broadcast about Bob Dylan. (Of course Shakespeare could do this orally as well as via flexible spelling, since most of his work was for the stage rather than the page.) Ricks gave an example taken from Dylan's 'Shelter From The Storm':

> He'll use his voice to get back some of the freedom which a poet used to have in the old days before spelling got finally fixed. I'm thinking of the way in which Shakespeare could spell the word 'travelled' so that it included 'travailed' . . . included worked as well as journeyed. So Dylan will sing 'moaning dove' and then print 'morning' . . .

This illustration is especially interesting to me because it too can be found in Howlin' Wolf's work. When Muddy Waters' 'Still A Fool' (which, as we've noted, Dylan knew) was issued by Chess, it was part of a triple-set that also included Howlin' Wolf's 'Moanin' At Midnight'. But this also ended up on the Chess rival label Modern, and was released by them under the odd title 'Morning At Midnight': a mistake of transcription that occurred because of Wolf's ambiguity with the very same words as Dylan. Just as Ricks picked up on it from 'Shelter From The Storm' simply because he liked it – as a pun it has, after all, no significant *meaning* in the Dylan song: it just sounds good – so too it's likely that Bob Dylan picked this up from Howlin' Wolf simply because he liked it. At least as likely as that he invented it à la Shakespeare.

A related feature of the blues (and one that Howlin' Wolf distils as well as anyone) is the warping of pronunciation to make a rhyme. In the earlier editions of this book I looked at this in some detail, suggesting Dylan's relish of it as prefigured by Fats Domino's ability to rhyme 'man' with 'ashamed' for instance; I wasn't to know that Dylan would surpass defiantly simple examples like rhyming 'hers' with 'yours' in the 1965 'I Wanna Be Your Lover' with the spectacular rhyming of 'January' and 'Buenos Aires' in 1981's great 'The Groom's Still Waiting At The Altar'. This is, of course, Dylan taking something widespread and running with it to score a previously undreamt-of goal. However, the pleasure of eccentric pronunciation in general and its use to make dodgy rhymes in particular is a fundamental delight rock'n'roll picked up from the blues. If Fats Domino was good at it, so was Howlin' Wolf. As with 'moaning/morning', he makes an attractive warped pronunciation rhyme in the 1959

Robert Johnson's 'From Four Till Late', where it occurs in the splendidly contentious verse 'A woman is like a dresser, some man always ramblin' through is drawers / It cause so many men wear an apron overhaul'. Robert Johnson: 'From Four Till Late', Dallas, 19/6/37; "King Of The Delta Blues Singers, Vol. 2", see note 103.)

Napoleon Strickland: 'Sittin' On Top Of The World', field-recorded Panola County, Mississippi, 1978(?); described by Alan Lomax in *The Land Where the Blues Began*.

Frank Proffitt Jr, field-recorded at his home in the Southern Appalachians, *nia*; telecast on *Appalachian Journey*, produced by Dibbs Directions for Channel 4 TV, 1990 (but also an episode in Alan Lomax's US-TV series *American Patchwork*, PBS, *nia*), issued on video by Pacific Arts Video and the Association for Cultural Equity, distributed in Europe by Jane Balfour Films Ltd, London.

Blind Willie McTell: 'That'll Never Happen No More', Atlanta, Sept. 1956; "Blind Willie McTell: Last Session", Prestige Bluesville 1040, see note 98.

'Howlin' For My Darlin'', making the verb and the noun of the title rhyme ('If you hear me howlin' / Callin' on my darlin'').

What this serves to remind us also is that Howlin' Wolf's records often built up the mythic, fairy tale beast connotations of the name itself. His song titles include 'Moaning At Midnight' and 'Crying At Daybreak', 'Howlin' For My Darlin'' (a remake of 'Howlin' For My Baby' from seven years previously), 'The Red Rooster', 'Tail Dragger', 'I'm The Wolf', 'Moanin' For My Baby'; 'Call Me The Wolf' and 'Howlin' Blues'. The last new album released in his lifetime was called "The Back Door Wolf".[115] He had been given the name at the age of three, by his grandfather:

'He just sit down and tell me tall stories about what the wolf would do, you know,' he told an interviewer in 1968. 'Cause I was a bad boy, you know, and I was always in devilment . . . So he told me the story 'bout how the wolf done the Little Red Rilin' [sic] Hood.' He goes on to recount a spendidly garbled version of the story, in which the fairy tale and the existential reality of his own childhood, the woods and the backwoods, are bound up together:

> the girl would ask him, 'Mr. Wolf, what make your teeth so big?' He said 'The better I can eat you, my dear'. Then said 'What make your eyes so red?' 'The better I can see you, my dear.' And so, you know, and then they finally killed the wolf and drove him up to the house, you know, and showed me the wolf. And I told him it was a dog. He said no, that's a wolf. I said well what do a wolf do? Say he howl: he say 'ooh-wyooooh!', you know, and so I got afraid of this wolf.

Granted Dylan's familiarity with Howlin' Wolf's records, and his own fusion of the singer's name with the beast-figure, already noted in 'Man Of Peace', it isn't surprising that there should be special conjunctions between the Wolf and the album by Bob Dylan that is itself a glorious fusion of fairy tale and nursery rhyme with the blues and the Bible, the 1990 "Under The Red Sky" (discussed far more thoroughly in its own later chapter).

Specifically, we can recognise flashes of Dylan's '2 x 2' and '10,000 Men' in the chorus of Wolf's 'I Ain't Superstitious':

> *Well I ain't superstitious, black cat just crossed my trail . . .*
> *Don't sweep me with no broom, I might just get put in jail*

while another line from '10,000 Men', Dylan's joke-exaggeration of multiple negatives, 'None of them doing nothing that your mama wouldn't disapprove', goes far enough to be impenetrable in meaning but barely goes further in construction than the last line of Wolf's 1954 song 'Baby How Long':

> *Ain't nobody never lived that didn't do somebody wrong.*

The Dylan song on "Under The Red Sky" that most successfully unifies children's song and folk tale, intimations of biblical retribution for our 'devilment' and the

---

115. "The Back Door Wolf", Chicago, 1973, Chess LP-50045, Chicago, 1973. NB: Most Wolf tracks are now available as follows in Britain: the Sun sessions on "Howlin' For My Baby", CD Charly 66, 1987, and "Howling Wolf Rides Again", Ace Records CDCHD 333, 1991; and the Chess recordings, including the interview-excerpt quoted, on the 3-CD "The Chess Box", MCA Records CHD3-9332, 1992.

country blues world is the sumptuously phantasmagoric 'Cat's In The Well'. This features the cat, the horse, the bull, the dogs and – dramatically, as the first omen that the innocent face imminent death – the wolf:

> *The cat's in the well, the wolf is looking down*
> *He got his big bushy tail dragging all over the ground.*

Dylan doesn't say why his tail drags on the ground, but this is elucidated in one of Howlin' Wolf's best records, 1962's shudderingly powerful 'Tail Dragger'. Its chorus runs:

> *I'm a tail dragger, I wipe out my tracks*
> *When I get what I want, I don't come sneakin' back*

and the first of its two irregular verses concludes with

> *The hunters they can't find him*
> *Stealin' chicks everywhere he go*
> *Then draggin' his tail behind him.*

The other verse calls up some more inhabitants of the animal kingdom, as Dylan's song does:

> *A cooder [?] drags his tail in the sand*
> *A fish wiggles his tail in the water*
> *When the mighty wolf come along, draggin' his tail*
> *He done stole somebody's dog.*[116]

So the wolf cannot be tracked, hunted down or stopped. The cat has no chance.

This is not the last of the lyric conjunctions between Dylan and Howlin' Wolf (others are cited later in other contexts) but it is the greatest, as one piece of barnyard apocalypse draws strength and meaning from another, from twenty-eight years earlier. And there's a general sense in which, because of Wolf's towering primitivism, the style he constructed, its psychic meld of electric power and old country darkness, if there had been no Howlin' Wolf, an album like "Under The Red Sky" would have been a different, thinner thing.

Noting, when I received the newly unearthed Cynthia Gooding radio show tape mentioned earlier, that the same year Wolf was recording his 'Tail Dragger', Bob Dylan was performing his 'Smokestack Lightnin'', I had to consider again a topic that arises in any case from the present chapter's scrutiny of what Dylan has taken from the blues. That is, the inequality of reward and credit as between the old black singer–songwriters and the newer white ones. Four years after 'Tail Dragger', and the beginning of Dylan's own recording career, Dylan, already a superstar, is visiting Tennessee, the state in which Memphis is located, to record the deeply blues-soaked album "Blonde On Blonde". In Memphis itself, Elvis Presley is residing in decadent luxury, resting on the laurels of a career launched from the Sun studios on a cover-version of an Arthur Crudup blues at a time when Arthur Crudup wouldn't even have

---

116. Howlin' Wolf: 'Tail Dragger', Chicago, 28/9/62; Chess 1890, Chicago, 1964, and "The Real Folk Blues", Chess LP-1502, Chicago, 1966, CD-reissued Chess MCA Records CHD 9273, USA, 1987.

been allowed to ride alongside Presley on a public bus. (Not that Crudup was in Memphis; he'd migrated to Chicago, where to begin with he'd lived in a wooden crate under the 'L' station.)

While Dylan is recording 'Pledging My Time', and Elvis is playing games at Graceland, forty miles south of Memphis on Highway 51, Mississippi Fred McDowell, the state's greatest living bluesman, is working in a gas station in Como, Mississippi.[117] As Stanley Booth notes in *Rythm Oil*, 'there is a telephone handy for when he gets calls to appear at places like the Newport Folk Festival'.

What can you say? Several things. Elvis had to live his whole adult life with the accusation that he'd somehow stolen this music, and had only succeeded at it because he was white. This is in every detail untrue. First, Elvis' early record producer, Sam Phillips, recorded Elvis singing blues because they both loved it; Phillips launched the careers of black artists (Howlin' Wolf included) as well as white, and willingly let each move on to bigger things than Sun could accommodate.

Against the wishes of the grotesque Colonel Parker, Elvis continued to record black material throughout his life, because his love for it remained undimmed when precious little else did. Rightly, he credited its composers on his records and paid them songwriting royalties. That his own music publishing outfits took hefty proportions was a corrupt practice endemic in the industry then and now, and certainly applied equally to the white songwriters who hit the theoretical jackpot of having Presley record their material. Low royalty rates, and royalties flowing into the wrong pockets, were aspects of the business that applied without regard to race, colour or creed. Roy Orbison told me in 1974 that he'd been signed to Sun Records for quite a while before he found out from an older songwriter that you were supposed to get paid when they played your songs on the radio; and when Orbison told Carl Perkins, it was news to him too.[118]

It's a myth too that Elvis stole 'Hound Dog' from Big Mama Thornton. White Jewish songwriters Leiber & Stoller wrote it, and offered it to Johnny Otis; he offered it to Thornton and stole the composer credit, which, as Greil Marcus wrote in his classic book *Mystery Train*, 'Leiber and Stoller had to fight to get back. Elvis heard the record, changed the song completely, from the tempo to the words, and cut Thornton's version to shreds.'[119]

Elvis made this material his own; he did something special with all of it. He couldn't have ignited a revolution through unfair good luck. That's the essence of it. And Dylan too, as the present chapter has been trying to show all along, takes from

---

117. Mississippi Fred McDowell, originally from Rossville, Tennessee (20 miles east of Memphis and 3 miles north of the Mississippi border), was never recorded in the pre-war period but, 'discovered' by Alan Lomax in 1959, his music was found to be unwearied by the passage of time and proved extremely influential. Ry Cooder would certainly credit him as a personal influence, and Bonnie Raitt virtually founded herself upon him. He died in July 1972.

118. And needless to say, when Wolf put out all those pre-Willie Dixon records of his, which he was happy to acknowledge were versions of songs by Patton, Tommy Johnson, Sonny Boy Williamson I and so on, the composer credit always went to Wolf. Similarly, Willie Dixon got later composer credits.

119. Greil Marcus, *Mystery Train* (1975). Marcus notes of the article 'How Elvis bleached the blues: black roots', by Clive Anderson, *Let It Rock*, Dec. 1973, that it is 'despite its title, a fine survey of the scores of black records Elvis has covered and changed in the last 20 years'.

the blues because he loves it, and then makes of it something his own. It's a creative process and creativity deserves success.

That success doesn't always come, that life is essentially unfair, is also true, but beyond the capacity of an Elvis Presley or a Bob Dylan to affect. Neither is its unfairness racially scrupulous. Consider the case of another old blues singer, Furry Lewis, about whom no black writer or singer has ever said a word, so far as I know, but of whom white Stanley Booth writes at length and about whom whiter Joni Mitchell sings briefly (in her horrible 'Furry Sings The Blues', the accident black-spot of her otherwise fine 1976 album "Hejira": she met Furry, in his capacity as a sort of Beale Street artefact; he didn't like her; er, that's it).[120] Like Hubert Sumlin, Furry Lewis came from Greenwood, Mississippi, but he moved to Memphis at the age of 6, in 1899. At 23, he lost a leg trying to catch a freight train outside Du Quoin, Illinois. A protégé of W. C. Handy, he recorded four sessions in the 1920s but the depression killed off his career and he didn't record again till 1959.[121] After the end of the 1920s he was never again a full-time pro.

He isn't even mentioned in Louis Cantor's history of Memphis-based WDIA, the first all-black radio station: 230 pages on how this wonderful station gave blacks their own voice, abolished Perry Como in favour of B. B. King, and put the blues on the air – but no change for a bluesman of Lewis' generation: he was still excluded.[122] So was

120. See Stanley Booth, *Rythm* [sic] *Oil* (1991). Booth's account of going with Furry Lewis to Mississippi John Hurt's funeral is discussed in Chapter 18.
   Joni Mitchell: 'Furry Sings The Blues', "Hejira", Hollywood, summer 1976, Asylum Records K53053, New York, 1976.
   In 1963, Dylan, using the pseudonym Blind Boy Grunt, contributed vocals and harmonica to Richard Farina and Eric Von Schmidt's recording of Furry Lewis' 'You Can Always Tell', London, 14–15/1/63; "Dick Farina & Eric Von Schmidt", Folklore F-LEUT-7, London, 1964. I don't know how much either Lewis or Dylan received from this; I don't imagine Farina and Von Schmidt received much either. The sleeve notes say of 'You Can Always Tell' that it is 'a tune based on Furry Lewis' 'Dry Land Blues' with additional verses'. [Furry Lewis: 'Dry Land Blues', Memphis, 28/8/28; "Kings Of The Blues", RCA 'X' LVA-3032 [10-inch LP], NYC, 1955.]
   Twenty-nine years later Dylan recorded Furry Lewis' version of 'Kassey Jones' ['Kassie Jones – Part 1' and 'Kassie Jones – Part 2', Memphis 28/8/28: yet another inclusion in Harry Smith's anthology "American Folk Music"] at the sessions co-produced by Dave Bromberg in Chicago, April 1992.

121. 'the old men whose music provided the foundation for it all were ignored. When they were not ignored, they were exploited; for example, Sam Charters made a Folkways album on Furry Lewis in 1959, for which Furry has received to date $75.' Stanley Booth: 'The 1969 Memphis Blues Shows', *Changes Magazine*, 1969. This article includes a good rant, of which this is a sample: 'Virtuosity in playing blues licks is like virtuosity in celebrating the Mass, it is empty, it means nothing . . . Johnny Winter can play rings around Furry Lewis; the comparison is ludicrous. But . . . Furry Lewis . . . was singing his *life* . . . Most of the young guitar virtuosos do not have lives; they have record collections.'

122. *Wheelin' On Beale*, Louis Cantor, 1992. On the other hand the blues singer turned pre-eminent gospel *song-writer* of Furry's generation, Georgia Tom Dorsey, was enjoying a hit on WDIA in the early 1950s courtesy of white artist, Red Foley, whose record of Dorsey's song 'Peace In The Valley' was a hit with black audiences – as was Elvis when he started out, as Louis Cantor notes. Dorsey's religious songs were not without controversy, though. Alan Lomax, in *The Land Where the Blues Began*, deplores these new me-me-me *gospel* songs of the 1940s as against the old *spirituals* of an earlier era, and deplores Dorsey's 'Take My Hand, Precious Lord' especially. He says the new songs elevated the preacher to a new primacy over the congregation that suppressed the previous democracy of worship. Yet it wasn't every church that had an all-participating congregation before the Dorsey generation came along.
   Elvis Presley made a classic soul-in-torment version of the song, as he did with 'Peace In The Valley'. Elvis' version recognises its genius, indeed makes it a work of darker genius, emphasising the intense, gothic spookiness of the lyrics – in which, for instance, 'the night is as black as the sea'. Its pinnacle is this re-statement of the biblical vision of the peaceable kingdom: 'Well the bear will be gentle and the wolves will be tame / And the lion shall lay down with the lamb / And the beasts from the wild shall be led by a child / And I'll be changed, changed from this creature that I am.' (Gordon Stoker of the Jordanaires recalls sending gospel records to Elvis when Elvis was in the US Army stationed in Germany. Stoker says: 'He loved black quartets, so I would send him those.' Source:

Frank Stokes, another giant of the early Memphis blues scene, who was still alive and living in neglect in Memphis when Elvis made his first records there. Stokes died, aged 67, in 1955. "Frank Stokes: Creator of the Memphis Blues", the reissue label Yazoo was calling him two decades later.[123]

Then there are the salutary cases of the innovative Noah Lewis and of Gus Cannon, another towering Memphis figure. When Bob Dylan chose to open his performance at the 1996 Aarhus Festival, Denmark, with an approximation of the Grateful Dead's 'New New Minglewood Blues', he's likely to have chosen it not because it's a Dead song but because it isn't: because, rather, it's based on 'New Minglewood Blues' by Noah Lewis's Jug Band from 1930, itself a re-modelling of 'Minglewood Blues' by Cannon's Jug Stompers (comprising, in this instance, Gus Cannon, Ashley Thompson and Noah Lewis) from 1928. The Dead's recording may well have reminded Dylan of the song, but there's no reason to suppose that he hadn't been familiar with the original Noah Lewis's Jug Band recording, since this had been vinyl-reissued in the early 1960s.[124] The key figure here, then, is the pioneering and splendid harmonica player Noah Lewis, whose work set new expressive standards in the pre-war period (and who is credited as the composer of 'Minglewood Blues' as well as of 'New Minglewood Blues': the two may share a tune but are otherwise

---

interview by Trevor Cajiao, Nashville, April 1994, *Elvis: The Man and His Music*, no. 25, December 1994.) See also note 100.

    [Elvis Presley: 'Take My Hand, Precious Lord' and '(There'll Be) Peace In The Valley (For Me)', Hollywood, 13/1/57; "Peace In The Valley" EP, RCA EPA-4054, New York, 1957, history's biggest-selling gospel EP.]

123. Frank Stokes (1888–1955) was, with Dan Sane, the Beale Street Sheiks, who recorded two dozen sides 1927–29, plus a further dozen solo sides. The Sheiks' début track, 'You Shall', prefiguring Dylan's 'I Shall Be Free' and 'I Shall Be Free No.10', is discussed in the notes to Chapter 1. "Frank Stokes: Creator of the Memphis Blues", Yazoo L-1056, New York, 1977; CD-reissued as Yazoo [CD] 1056, New York, 1990.

    Stokes' colleague Jim Jackson (whose 1928 'What A Time' *also* prefigures 'I Shall Be Free No.10', see Chapter 1) is another neglected figure in the same time and place. He was born in Hernando, Mississippi, in 1890 and died in the same tiny town 47 years later but lived, worked and recorded in Memphis in the 1920s and was famous for one of the biggest selling blues hits of the decade, 'Kansas City Blues', which sold almost a million. In 1950s and 1960s Memphis he wasn't remembered at all. Now he's remembered for a parody of the English hymn 'I Heard The Voice Of Jesus Say Come Unto Me And Rest', 'I Heard The Voice Of A Pork Chop'. (Chapter 6 notes the link between the hymn and Dylan's 'Lay Down Your Weary Tune'.)

    Jim Jackson: 'Jim Jackson's Kansas City Blues Part 1 & Part 2', Chicago, 10/10/27; "Kansas City Blues", Agram Records AB2004, Ter Aar, Holland, 1980. 'I Heard The Voice Of A Pork Chop' [2 takes], Memphis, 30/1/28; take 1 issued "Jim Jackson" (EP), RCA Victor Records RCX 7182, London, 1966: an 'early' vinyl release in a series from Victor's vaults devised by British blues baron Mike Vernon.

    This cheerily Dickensian song was covered, some months after the Jim Jackson session, by Blind Bogus Ben Covington: 'I Heard The Voice Of A Pork Chop', Chicago, c. Sept. 1928.

124. Bob Dylan: 'New New Minglewood Blues', Aarhus, Denmark, 15/6/96. Grateful Dead: 'New New Minglewood Blues', LA, Jan. 1967, "The Grateful Dead", Warner Brothers Records WS 1689, LA, 1967. (By the end of 1993 'All New Minglewood Blues' had become the Dead's 10th most performed song, and officially issued as follows: 'All New Minglewood Blues', San Rafael, California, 1978; "Shakedown Street", Arista Records AB 4198, New York, 1978; 'New Minglewood Blues', San Francisco, 1980; "Dead Set" [2 LPs], Arista Records A2L 8606, New York, 1981; 'New Minglewood Blues', Oakland, California, 26/12/79, "Dick's Picks Volume 5" [3-CD set], Grateful Dead Records GDCD 4024, California, 1998.)

    Noah Lewis' Jug Band: 'New Minglewood Blues', Memphis, 26/11/30; "The Great Jug Bands", Origin Jazz Library Records OJL-4, Berkeley, 1962; CD-reissued "Gus Cannon & Noah Lewis Volume 2 (1929–1930)", Document Records DOCD-5033, Vienna, c. 1991. Cannon's Jug Stompers: 'Minglewood Blues', Memphis, 30/1/28; "American Folk Music". CD-reissued "Complete Recordings: Cannon's Jug Stompers", Yazoo Records L-1082-1083, New York, 1990 [a CD reissue of a 1980s LP].

    Lewis' own records, all made in 1929 and 1930, usually feature his friend Sleepy John Estes on guitar. 'New Minglewood Blues' also includes Estes' great mandolin-playing sidekick Yank Rachel. (As for Minglewood itself, this was a sawmill and box factory, and by extension its immediate vicinity, north of Memphis, where Noah Lewis had once worked. The mill was pulled down in the 1950s.)

dissimilar songs – different in lyrics, pace and mood). Lewis was long thought to have been murdered in 1937, but Swedish researcher Bent Olsson discovered that in fact he had retired to Ripley, Tennessee in the 1930s, where in his old age he got frostbite, had both legs amputated and in the process got blood poisoning, from which he died in the winter of early 1961.

Cannon was by far the better-known figure by the time Bob Dylan reached Greenwich Village. As we've found, he was one of the featured artists on both Harry Smith's 1952 anthology "American Folk Music" *and* on the next crucial release of the period, Sam Charters' 1959 compilation "Country Blues". Cannon's track on the former, indeed, was 'Minglewood Blues' while on the latter was his 1929 cut 'Walk Right In', which was taken up by the Rooftop Singers, who topped the US charts with a single of the song, complete with beefy 12-string guitar sound, in 1963.[125]

Cannon's own career was first 'revived' in 1956 when he was recorded, for the first time since 1930, by Folkways. They let him cut two tracks. Then in 1963, in the wake of the Rooftop Singers' success, Cannon cut an album issued by Stax (!) which featured 'Walk Right In' plus standards like 'Salty Dog', 'Boll-Weevil' and 'Make Me A Pallet On Your Floor'. He also made appearances at the Newport Folk Festival. He survived to the age of 96, living long enough to still be around in Memphis at the time of Elvis Presley's funeral there in 1977.[126]

Despite his eminence and despite his 'rediscovery', Gus Cannon too suffered neglect, poverty and lack of respect. His situation is described eloquently by Jim Dickinson, the Memphis session-player who features on Dylan's "Time Out Of Mind" album twenty years after Cannon's death, and a friend of Stanley Booth:

> I knew these men were out there somewhere. Until the Samuel Charters book [*Country Blues*, 1959] there didn't seem any possibility of contacting them. In the summer of 1960, a friend and I followed the trail that Charters left to Gus Cannon . . . He was the yardman for an anthropology professor. Gus had told this family that he used to make records and he had been on RCA and they'd say, 'Yeah Gus, sure: cut the grass.' . . . He lived on the property, back over a garage, and he took us up into his room, and on the wall he had a certificate for sales from 'Walk Right In', for which of course he didn't get any money. And he had a

---

125. Cannon's Jug Stompers: 'Walk Right In', Memphis, 1/10/29; "The Country Blues", RBF Records RF-1, New York, 1959, CD-reissued DOCD-5033, *ibid*. The Rooftop Singers: 'Walk Right In', *nia*, 1962, Vanguard Records 35017, New York [Fontana TF 271700, London], 1962.

   Another Cannon record Dylan has performed is 'Viola Lee Blues', also attributed to the Grateful Dead or their influence, because they had covered it on their début LP thirty years earlier. Again, the Dead's version *may* have reminded Dylan of the song, but why should the posthumous sanctifying of Jerry Garcia suggest that Dylan wasn't as familiar with Cannon's record as with the Dead's, or that he didn't know Cannon's for nearly a decade before theirs surfaced? Even if Dylan never encountered the 78, Cannon's recording was on vinyl in 1962.

   [Bob Dylan: 'Viola Lee Blues', Sapporo, Japan, 24/2/97. Gus Cannon: 'Viola Lee Blues', Memphis, 20/9/28 [2 takes: after its initial release as a Victor 78, take 1 was issued on the cheaper Bluebird label paired with 'Minglewood Blues'; take 2, unissued at the time, achieved early vinyl issue on the EP "Alexis Korner Presents . . . Kings Of The Blues Volume 1: Cannon's Jug Stompers", RCA Victor Records RCX-202, London, 1962; both takes appeared on the double-LP "Cannon's Jug Stompers (1927–1930)", Herwin Records H208, New York, 1973.]

126. Gus Cannon: 'Old John Booker, You Call That Gone' and 'Kansas City Blues', Memphis, 5/12/56, "American Skiffle Bands", Folkways Records LP 2610, New York, 1957. Gus Cannon: "Walk Right In", Memphis, 10/6/63, Stax Records LP 702, Memphis, 1963 (only 100 copies were pressed of this consequently extremely rare LP).

copy of the record that Charters had made for Folkways, but he had no record-player. That was a real good introduction to the blues.[127]

Likewise right through to the 1970s Furry Lewis remained a street-sweeper in Memphis. Now and then in the mid-1960s he'd play a set between rock acts at the Bitter Lemon coffee-house in East Memphis.

Stanley Booth describes Lewis opening a Bitter Lemon set with 'a slow, sad blues, one that none of us had ever heard, a song without a name'; it opens, Booth reports, with

My mother's dead, my father's just as well to be.[128]

Next morning he's back sweeping the streets. At the crack of dawn, on his way to work, he passes the Club Handy. On the door is a handbill that reads BLUES SPECTACULAR, CITY AUDITORIUM: JIMMY REED, JOHN LEE HOOKER, HOWLIN' WOLF . . .

The very day after I was reading all this in Booth's book, I received a cassette of odds and ends by Wolf through the post, and as I sat reading some more Booth and playing the cassette, Wolf's massive voice started singing

Well, mama done died and left me,
Wooh, daddy done throwed me away . . .

It interests me that the *age* of the singer, in Wolf's case as in Furry Lewis', should be so utterly unimportant to them when it comes to the subject matter of their songs. They have no truck with our modern self-conscious ageism or apologism, and clearly when they sing about the lives of themselves and their peers, they experience those lives as unities. Furry Lewis as on old man, and Howlin' Wolf as a middle-aged one, still sing out about the childhood trauma of parental abandonment: they have no sense that they 'should have got over all that' in the contemporary way. At the same time they still sing too about romantic love: they have no modern sense of the shame of being politically incorrect 'dirty old men'. And they can sing out clear and free about imminent death: they have no sense that this is aerobically incorrect, or 'not nice'.[129]

In the 1961 'Goin' Down Slow', which features what may be Hubert Sumlin's all-time best guitar solo, Howlin' Wolf proves himself a *great* singer about imminent death, which will certainly have recommended him to Bob Dylan, to whose use of the blues we now more specifically return.[130]

*

127. Jim Dickinson, quoted in Chapter 6 of Robert Gordon's *It Came from Memphis*. (Gordon doesn't mention Frank Stokes either.)

128. Stanley Booth: *Rythm Oil*. Coincidentally, Booth also describes Lewis singing a blues about a Brownsville girl, with 'great long curly hair'. Most songs that name-check Brownsville are by Sleepy John Estes, and Lewis was probably remembering Estes' début single, 'The Girl I Love, She Got Long Curly Hair' [Memphis, 24/9/29]; these Estes songs, however, are about his hometown of Brownsville, Tennessee, not the Tex-Mex border town of the Dylan–Shepard 'Brownsville Girl'. Estes and his repertoire are discussed in some detail shortly.

129. Furry Lewis died, still poor, at the age of 88, in 1981.

130. Howlin' Wolf: 'Goin' Down Slow', Chicago, Dec. 1961, Chess Records 1813, Chicago, 1962 [c/w 'Smoke-stack Lightnin'', Pye International 7N 25244, London, 1964]. Wolf died at Veterans Administration Hospital,

Even when Dylan uses a straightforward blues phrase in a straightforward blues song, it can have an individual and specific function, as in the 1971 'George Jackson'. Dylan starts several songs with variants of that most familiar of traditional opening phrases 'I woke up this morning' – the blues equivalent perhaps of the narrative ballad's 'As I went out one morning'.[131] There is 'I woke in the morning, wand'rin',' in 1964's jumping 'Black Crow Blues', and 'Well I woke up in the morning there's frogs inside my socks' in the 1965 'On The Road Again'. But when Dylan comes to his lament 'George Jackson', his deliberate use of the plain, unvariant phrase to open the song is a way of quietly putting himself out of the picture to give Jackson all due prominence. The line may start with the word 'I' but the common-stock unobtrusiveness of 'I woke up this morning' acts in the opposite way to the standing out Dylan enacts with a 'them ridin' blinds': acts in this case to submerge what the post-structuralists would call 'the text of "Bob Dylan"', so as not to have it impede the text of 'George Jackson'.

When the 24-year-old Dylan referred to 'the ladies', in 'Memphis Blues Again' ('And the ladies treat me kindly / And furnish me with tape'), it seemed a very Dylanesque appellation – no one I knew under 50 used such a term, and in England it was imaginable only in the vicarage tea-party fake-gentility sense ('Would the ladies care for a peramulation of the shrubbery?'). I didn't know back then that he had borrowed it from the blues. It crops up in Blind Lemon Jefferson, Washboard Sam and Mississippi John Hurt songs: 'I'm always around the ladies' sings Jefferson; 'Now ask the ladies in your neighborhood' sings Washboard Sam; and Hurt sings a line that you could easily envisage Dylan delivering, say at the beginning of an out-take verse from 'Pledging My Time': 'It just gets better, so the ladies say' (a formulation, actually, that Dylan echoes with 'The best is always yet to come / That's what they explain to me' in 'If Dogs Run Free'). It may or may not be a foreshortening of the euphemism 'ladies of the night'. Either way, Dylan takes the term straight out of the blues and makes 'the ladies' sound a hip, quirky, druggy, caressive phrase. By context, he makes it new.

(When, however, Dylan shifts over from 'the ladies' to take the 'Saturday-night women' from Robert Johnson's 'Stop Breakin' Down Blues' – a phrase that uses 'Saturday night' as an adjective, meaning partying women, or 'loose women' – he does not use it verbatim but turns it into the parallel 'all-night girls' of 'Visions Of Johanna'.)[132]

We come across a rather different form of Dylan's having a special purpose in using old blues phrases in a blues song of his own in the case of his 1962 song 'Quit Your Low-Down Ways', finally issued on "Bootleg Series I-III" in 1991: and the

---

Hines, Illinois, 1/10/76 and is buried in Oakridge Cemetery, Hillside, a Chicago suburb. In a public park on the South Side there is now a lifesize statue of him. In 1991 he was inducted as a 'forefather' into the Rock and Roll Hall of Fame. Ugh.

131. Of the 2000 blues records concorded by Taft, 44 begin with '(Well / Say / Now / Mama / When / Oh / Lord) (I) Woke up this morning'; a further 68 include the phrase in mid-song.

132. Blind Lemon Jefferson: 'D B Blues', Chicago, c. Aug 1928; "Master Of The Blues: Blind Lemon Jefferson, Vol.2", Biograph BLP-12015, New York, 1969. Washboard Sam: 'Lover's Lane Blues', Chicago, 4/11/41; "Blues Classics by Washboard Sam", Blues Classics BC-10, Berkeley, 1966. Mississippi John Hurt: 'Candy Man Blues', New York, 28/12/28; "Mississippi John Hurt, 1928: His First Recordings", Biograph BLP-C4, Canaan, New York, 1972. Robert Johnson: 'Stop Breakin' Down Blues', 20/6/37, Columbia C-30034.

purpose seems to be that of constructing a whole song out of what seems thrown away precipitately in someone else's. The title verse, the chorus and thus the theme, plus that part of the structure where Dylan runs lines together in one unbroken filigree of lyrics, and even the gleeful falsetto – all this is taken directly from a verse of Kokomo Arnold's own brilliant recording of his 'Milkcow Blues': a verse neither Robert Johnson, nor the rockers, nor Bob Dylan, chose to include in *their* versions, yet which Dylan makes into 'his' separate song 'Quit Your Low-Down Ways'.[133]

The same material – 'You can read out your hymn book, you got your Bible too / Fall down on your knees' – *is* picked up and used in Big Joe Williams' 'Wild Cow Blues', recorded soon after Kokomo Arnold's track. In each case the style and spirit, the buzzing bee-sting joy of it, the salacious voyeurism, all come from the Kokomo Arnold treatment; but the contradictory religious anti-joy of the lyric gives away the fact that Arnold has snatched his material from an earlier gospel song, though it doesn't seem to have been a well-known one. Billy Mack And Mary Mack, an obscure vocal duo from New Orleans, cut 'You've Got To Quit Your Low Down Ways' for OKeh way back at the beginning of 1926, and re-cut it as 'You Gotta Quit Your Low Down Ways' for Bluebird ten years later.[134]

It may be that Kokomo Arnold was snatching at the song to parody the lip-smacking, flagellatory strut of the genre. Perhaps it was a gospel smash in the early 1930s, because its secular plunder seems to happen with a flurry around 1935. Kokomo Arnold's 'Milk Cow Blues' is 1934, Big Joe's 'Wild Cow Blues' is 1935, and so too is a record with the most scandalous secular re-use of the song's gospel rhetoric, 'Sissy Man Blues', again by Kokomo Arnold, which was immediately 'covered' by Josh White and the clumping pianist–singer George Noble. Kokomo Arnold gives it an attractively seething muscularity as a performance but as a song he makes it sound an undistinguished re-run of 'Milk Cow Blues'. Josh White is the one who establishes 'Sissy Man' as a distinctive song. His is also the most up-front performance, and the one closest in spirit to Dylan's 'Quit Your Low Down Ways'.[135]

It begins as if it's going to be 'Dust My Broom': 'I believe, I believe I'll go back home' is the opening line. Dancing lightly along, in the Kokomo Arnold way, its third verse begins as one of those splendid anti-preacher rants which Frank Stokes is so good at, in this case with 'Oh, church bell is tonin', one Sunday morn / I see some dirty deacon rung that bell, stole my good gal and gone' – and then slides into a familiar

133. Bob Dylan: 'Quit Your Low Down Ways', performed in Montreal, 2/7/62; recorded NYC, 9/7/62 and Dec. 1962. Kokomo Arnold: 'Milk Cow Blues', Chicago, 10/9/34; "Peetie Wheatstraw and Kokomo Arnold", Blues Classics BC-4, 1964.

134. Big Joe Williams: 'Wild Cow Blues', Chicago, 31/10/35; "Big Joe Williams: Crawlin' King Snake", RCA INT-1087, London, 1970. Billy Mack and Mary Mack: 'You've Got To Quit Your Low Down Ways', NYC, c. early January 1926. Mack and Mack: 'You Gotta Quit Your Low Down Ways', Chicago, 22/12/36.

135. Kokomo Arnold: 'Sissy Man Blues', Chicago, 15/1/35. Josh White [as Pinewood Tom]: 'Sissy Man', NYC, 18/3/35; CD-reissued on the 4-CD box-set "The Retrospective 1925–1950", Columbia Legacy Roots N' Blues 47911, New York, 1992. George Noble: 'Sissy Man Blues', Chicago, 5/3/35 and 20/3/35, the latter on "The Piano Blues Volume 9", Magpie Records PY 4409, UK, 1979. 'Sissy Man Blues' was also cut by Connie McLean's Rhythm Boys, NYC, 24/4/36.
    This last song has, in retrospect, another Dylan connection: like Dylan's version of 'Froggie Went A-Courtin'', it ends with this common-stock folksong component: 'I'm gonna sing these blues, I'm gonna lay 'em up on your shelf / You gonna hear these blues again baby, sure gonna sing 'em yourself.'

I says pleeeaaase, pleeeaaase [falsetto]
Send my good girl home
Cos I ain't had no lovin', Lord!
Since my gal's bin gone.

That 'Lord!', incidentally, is delivered with a sudden, well-aimed stab of in-your-face campness that is the *exact* prototype for the falsetto Mick Jagger has paraded as his own all these years. Then, bringing us to the title of his song, Josh White's fourth verse brings us also to the 'Quit Your Low-Down Ways' format, its words re-written with irreligious relish, after a quite splendid opening line:

I woke up this morning with my Polk County business in my hand
Lord if you can't send me no woman
pleeaa-heeaase, *send me some sissy man.*

(The vividness of that 'Polk' is optimised in the pronunciation, an excellent example of the oral pun, since it sounds at once like both 'pork' and 'poke'. Kokomo Arnold's version opts for the plainer 'woke up this morning with my pork-grinding business in my hand', which George Noble shortens to 'with my pork-grinder in my hand'.)[136]

Like Broonzy, Josh White suffers from having been popular as a songster–artist and familiar as a name, not only to baby boom rock fans but to their parents, long before the folk and blues revivals of the early 1960s canonised other, more excitingly unfamiliar figures. Broonzy and White (and to some extent even Leadbelly) are therefore eschewed as somehow a bit Uncle Tom. Yet 'Sissy Man' is a fine record, and its singer–guitarist clearly a most talented artist.

In any case, whatever the politics of their celebrity, these men have been, at the very least, invaluable conduits of antique repertoire. In their listings book *Blues & Gospel Records 1902–1943*, Dixon and Godrich note that after 1936 'Josh White's recordings become increasingly inclined to commercialism, and are only included for completeness.' Yet certainly Josh White influenced a generation of British seamen who discovered him, as the young Tommy Steele did, in New York City in the early 1950s, and who in turn brought home to ports like London and Liverpool treasure troves of otherwise-unobtainable blues and R&B records: heady exotica after the musical diet offered by British radio.

Where Dylan breaks with his pattern in the other direction, to deliver turned-inside-out or much-revised blues phrases inside non-blues songs, such references can sometimes appear oblique, especially to those temperamentally unsympathetic to the blues milieu and those deeply suspicious that such resonances and echoes, as with other kinds of resonance in Dylan's work, may be just something the critic has contrived to

136. A song called 'Baby Quit Your Low Down Ways' was recorded by our old friend Blind Boy Fuller in 1939, but it isn't the same song at all, and its title line is never exploited, indeed is never sung, except foreshortened to 'baby quit your ways'. I'm told that Odetta recorded such a title around the same period as Dylan did. Hers will be the least interesting variant. Blind Boy Fuller: 'Baby Quit Your Low Down Ways', Memphis, 12/7/39. Odetta: *nia.*

'read into' the work. Actually, the difficulty the critic faces in the rich terrain of Dylan's absorbtion of blues poetry is an opposite one: far from casting around for tenuous echoes and throwing in anything, however faint its echo may be, the problem is to stop the ears from hearing these echoes everywhere, as one allusion met down the highway of Bob Dylan's blues is so often at once surrounded by other echoes clamouring for space and attention.

Perhaps, for example, the reference to a 1931 blues by J. T. Funny Papa Smith that I hear twisted round in 'Heart Of Mine' *is* oblique but it echoes nonetheless: echoes in its marvellously 'Dylanesque' lines 'With blood in my eye, and malice in my heart / In places I used to go'. Likewise the following line from Leroy Carr's 1934 'Hard Hearted Papa' is so thoroughly of a piece with the style and spirit of Dylan's 'Shot Of Love' (1981) that it might be the opening line of a 'missing' stanza:

> *I don't even like what I drink, my food don't taste right at all.*[137]

The Leadbelly favourite 'Pig Meat Mama' offers a vivacious demonstration of something else we're likely to think Dylanesque. That is, given an ostentatious rhyme, he delivers it with a sly knowingness which, far from down-playing it, milks its comic extravagance to the full, by throwing in a pause just long enough to draw attention to itself immediately ahead of the clamorous rhyme. In this song from 1935, Leadbelly gives us

> *. . . Louisiana*
> *. . . Texacana*
> *. . . a girl named* [pause] *Silvana!*

This is a way of writing and delivering lines that we know well from many Dylan recordings, such as the 'Angelina' rhymes in the 1981 song of that name, the risky comedy of 'subpoena' being the one that pushes this furthest. It's the same glee that tops 'the castle honey' with 'El *[pause]* Paso honey' in 'She's Your Lover Now'.[138]

Other examples are more easily recognisable. The exchange between the hero and the judge in 'Joey' –

> *'What time is it?' said the judge*
> *To Joey when they met*
> *'Five to ten,' said Joey,*
> *Judge said 'That's exactly what you get'*

– is black humour in both senses: this specific variant of gallows humour, in recognition of the habitual gross injustice of the justice system, is yet another thing Dylan imports into his work from the blues. It picks up on a running joke that recurs throughout blues songs, as for instance in Lonnie Johnson's 'I Have To Do My Time' (1930), in which

---

137. J. T. Funny Papa Smith's 'Hungry Wolf', see note 112, and Leroy Carr: 'Hard Hearted Papa', New York, 14/12/34; "Leroy Carr: Singin' The Blues, 1934", Biograph BLP-C9, Canaan, NY, 1972.

138. Leadbelly: 'Pig Meat Mama', NYC, 25/3/35; CD-reissued "Leadbelly: King Of The Twelve-String Guitar", Columbia Roots N' Blues Series 467893 4, NYC, 1991. Actually, Silvana might not have struck Leadbelly as an especially attention-grabbing name: he had an adopted sister called [pause] Australia.

> *My baby said 'Mmm, judge, how much time did you give my man?*
> *Mmm, how much time did you give my man?'*
> *He says 'Only twenty-five years – I try to be light as I can.'*[139]

My next example is of something that also centres around accusation and injustice in the blues: something that Dylan picks up and uses in both a 1970s blues song and a 1960s non-blues item – one of his poems – but since the poem is the better piece of work, and reshapes the blues ingredient far more creatively, I offer it here, while we're examining his imaginative re-working of blues material inside non-blues work.

'Am I Your Stepchild?' may be an obcure item in Dylan's canon – it is omitted from *Lyrics 1962–1985* – but in 1978 he gave it the prominence of performing it fifty-three times in concert. It is what Stanley Booth calls 'a blues in the familiar accusation-lament pattern', and the song in the same pattern that he has in mind at the time, B. B. King's version of 'How Blue Can You Get?', shows what a pale companion the Dylan song is. As King performed this number (actually written either by jazz snob and critic Leonard Feather, or by his wife Jane Feather), at the Fillmore West in June 1968, the lyric built to this:

> *I gave you a brand-new Ford*
> *You said 'I want a Cadillac'*
> *I bought you a ten-dollar dinner*
> *You said 'thanks for the snack'*
> *I let you live in my penthouse*
> *You said it was just a shack*
> *I gave you seven children*
> *And now you want to give them back*[140]

which is not matched by even the best lines in the Dylan song. But the Feather song imitates more interesting and authentic (less 'clever') blues repertoire. The old song Alan Lomax calls 'Bad Luck Is Killing Me', which Joe Savage learnt as a young man in Parchman in the late 1940s, includes this:

> *Got me 'cused of thieving*
> *I can't see a thing*
> *They got my accused of forgery*
> *And I can't even write my name . . .*
> *They got me accused of taxes*
> *And I don't have a lousy dime*

139. Lonnie Johnson: 'I Have To Do My Time', NYC, 5/8/30, unissued until "Lonnie Johnson Complete Recorded Works Vol. 6", Document DOCD-5068, Vienna, 1991. CD-reissued [4-CD set] "Roots N' Blues Retrospective", Columbia Legacy Roots N' Blues 47911, New York, 1992.

140. B. B. King recorded 'How Blue Can You Get?' three times, according to Leonard Feather's notes to the compilation-LP "How Blue Can You Get? – Great Blues Vocals In The Jazz Tradition" (an ominous title), *nia*, CD-reissued RCA Bluebird ND8675B, which lists the song's writer as Jane Feather on the track-listing but in the notes has Leonard claiming that he wrote the song, 'in early 1949'. It was first recorded by Johnny Moore's Three Blazers (theirs is the version on the above compilation-album) and later by Louis Jordan, from whose recording B. B. King first heard it.
    Louis Jordan & Trio: 'How Blue Can You Get?', NYC, 5/6/51. B. B. King [& His Orchestra]: 'How Blue Can You Get?', NYC, 1963; Chicago, 21/1/64; and live at Cook County Jail, Chicago, 10/9/70.

> *They got me accused of children*
> *And ain't nar one of them mine.*[141]

This is all of a piece with songs such as Blind Willie McTell's 'Death Cell Blues', from the early 1930s:

> *They got me 'cused for murder, and I haven't harmed a man*
> *They got me charged for buglarin', I haven't even raised my hand . . .*
> *They got me 'cused for forging, and I can' even write my name . . .*

(in which the pathos is not reliant upon our knowing that the singer is blind) and, again, Lonnie Johnson's fastidiously mordant 'I Have To Do My Time', in which

> *The judge say I was guilty and he couldn't explain*
> *Charged me with forgery an' I cain't even sign my name.*[142]

But there is a piece of writing by Bob Dylan, much earlier and more successful than 'Am I Your Stepchild?', into which he imports an echo of these songs – and that is the poem 'My Life In A Stolen Moment': suggesting that even when his persecution was largely the fantasy stuff of the middle-class post-adolescent, his affinity for the blues world (and his familiarity with its poetry) ran deep:

> *Got jailed for suspicion of armed robbery*
> *Got held four hours on a murder rap*
> *Got busted for looking like I do*
> *An' I never done none a them things.*

Such alert writing. The blues echo is especially clear in that last line, with its perfectly mimicked appeasing cadence, which could come straight from Joe Savage's performance, while Dylan good-humouredly acknowledges his myth-making, his inexperience of such outward oppression, with a series of deft disclaimers. That 'four hours' makes something slighter and more acceptable of what would otherwise be the over-the-top, too easily refutable (and too self-aggrandising) claim 'Got held on a murder rap'. Then there's the double-joke of the last line itself: in the context of the previous line, it's a nifty audacity that he can claim never to have looked like he does; in the context of the whole fabricated autobiography the poem offers, it's funny that it ends with the laughing admission that it has *all* been made up.

Wonderful stuff. The self-deflation, though, is his only honourable course. As with 'Song To Woody' concluding with the tribute-confession that 'The very last thing that I'd want to do / Is to say I been hitting some hard traveling too', and the outsiderliness of 'them ridin' blinds', the poem must confess its writer's myth-making out of respect for the Joe Savages whose parallels of poetry have been born out of genuine jailings and busts and struggle.

---

141. Joe Savage: 'Bad Luck Is Killing Me', field-recorded by Alan Lomax in Mississippi in the 1970s, issued on video on *The Land Where the Blues Began*, Pacific Arts Home Video PBS 260, USA, 1981, and quoted in Lomax's book *The Land Where the Blues Began*.

142. Blind Willie McTell: 'Death Cell Blues', NYC, 19/9/33; "The Atlanta Blues", RBF Records RF15, New York, 1966; CD-reissued "The Definitive Blind Willie McTell", Columbia Legacy Roots N' Blues 53234, NYC, 1994.

The same inwardness with the world of the blues is modestly revealed in Dylan's enrolment of 'Jumpin' Judy' into 1965's 'I Wanna Be Your Lover' (released on "Biograph" twenty years later). She is not, contrary to most people's assumption, one of those 'made-up' quirky names, so many of which throng the populous world of mid-1960s Dylan songs. Jumpin' Judy was one of the heroines of the convict farms, where, amid the savagery of the regime, there was the allowing in of 'wives' at weekends:

> It's Jumpin' Jumpin' Judy
> She was a mighty fine girl
> Oh well she brought that jumpin'
> Baby to the whole round world.

Thus is she 'immortalized in song for her innovations', as Alan Lomax puts it. Or as Dylan puts it in 'I Wanna Be Your Lover', 'Jumpin' Judy can't go no higher'.

This line, so casual and unemphasised, thus playfully manages a three-layer pun on 'higher', acknowledging Jumpin' Judy as a figure who has achieved immortality in blues folklore, like Stagolee or John Henry, as well as punning on being stoned and on literal jumping.

There is a commercial recording, by Wiley and Wiley (Arnold and Irene), titled 'Jumpin' Judy Blues' from 1931; Allen Prothro's performance of 'Jumpin' Judy' was field-recorded by John and Alan Lomax for the Library of Congress at the Nashville State Penitentiary in 1933; an unidentified group of convicts was field-recorded singing the same song at the Shelby County Workhouse, Memphis, a couple of days earlier; and Kelly Pace's 'Jumpin' Judy' was field-recorded by John Lomax at Cumins State Farm, Gould, Arkansas in 1934. Another version, by prisoners known as Tangle Eye, Fuzzy Red, Hard Hair & group was field-recorded on Parchman Farm in the 1940s. The verse quoted above can be found incorporated into other songs too: for instance, as Dylan would have been aware, into Leadbelly's 1940 version of 'Midnight Special'. A version by Dick Farina and Ric von Schmidt (with lead vocal by von Schmidt) was recorded in London in 1963.[143]

When, in 'Don't Fall Apart On Me Tonight' (1983), Dylan sings 'But if I could I'd . . . build you a house made out of stainless steel', it is a 'found line' (in this case a fragment of conversation overheard in the street), as he mentions somewhere in the

---

143. Wiley and Wiley [Arnold and Irene]: 'Jumpin' Judy Blues', NYC, 23/7/31. Allen Prothro: 'Jumpin' Judy', Nashville State Penitentiary, c. 15/8/33; "Afro-American Spirituals, Worksongs & Ballads", Archive of Folk Song LP AFS L3, Washington, DC, 1956; CD-reissued Rounder Records CD1510, Cambridge, Mass., 1998. Kelly Pace: 'Jumpin' Judy', Gould, Arkansas, c. 5/10/34, also vinyl-issued AFS L3, detailed above, and extracted on "The Ballad Hunter: John A. Lomax Lectures on American Folk Music, Parts III and IV", Archive of Folk Song LP AFS L50, Washington, DC, c. mid-1950s. (This last LP also includes Pace's performance of 'It Makes A Long Time Man Feel Bad', a song perhaps picked up from this source by Ralph Rinzler, from whom Dylan had learnt it by March 1962: he says so while recording it for Cynthia Gooding's radio show, NYC, 11/3/62.) Tangle Eye, Fuzzy Red, Hard Hair & group [sic]: 'Jumpin' Judy', Parchman Farm, Miss., 1947(?); "Negro Prison Songs From The Mississippi Penitentiary", Tradition Records TLP 1020, Salem, Mass., c. 1959, CD-reissued as "Prison Songs V. 1: Murderous Home", Rounder Records ROUN1714, Cambridge, Mass., 1997.

Leadbelly: 'Midnight Special', NYC, 15/6/40; CD-reissued "Leadbelly: Midnight Special", The Blues Collection [magazine + CD] BLU NC 030, Editions Atlas, Paris, 1993 [Orbis, London, 1994].

Dick Farina & Eric von Schmidt: 'Jumpin' Judy', London, Jan./Feb. 1963; "Dick Farina & Eric von Schmidt", Folklore Records F-LEUT-7, London, 1964.

course of discussing songwriting, but it surely got itself 'found' by Dylan – it commended itself to his attention where very many others do not – because it had the resonance of echo. It echoes and contradicts his own earlier 'Build me a cabin in Utah', from 'Sign On The Window', which in turn echoes a common blues formula: the 'I'm-going-to-build-me-a' stanza. When you hear, as unavoidably happens, those two Dylan lines together, their place in the cumulative life of this stanza is hard to disavow. It is a stanza that takes in Memphis Minnie's 'I'm going to build me a bungalow, just for me and my bumble bee', Pearl Dickson's 'I'm going to build me a castle, out of ice and snow', Clifford Gibson's identical 'I'm going to build me a castle, out of ice and snow', Will Weldon's 'I'm going to build me a castle, fifteen storey high' and Willie Brown's 'I had a notion, Lord and I believe I will / I'm going to build me a mansion, out on Decatur Hill'. Clamouring for house-room here too are Joe McCoy's 'That Will Be Alright', which begins: 'I'm going to build me a house, out on the sea' (also echoed by Dylan's 'Well, meet me in the middle of the ocean' on his 1962 blues 'Down The Highway') and even Dylan's own 1990 third-person variant, 'He's got that fortress on the mountain / With no doors, no windows, so no thieves can break in' (from the magnificent 'Handy Dandy', on "Under The Red Sky"), which invokes a castle built out of ice and snow of the heart.[144]

When, on 1985's garrulous 'Seeing The Real You At Last', Dylan sings 'When I met you, baby, / You didn't show no visible scars', he is turning back to another blues formula. He does so in contradictory echo of Gus Cannon's 1928 line, 'When I first met you babe, you didn't have no hair at all', and at a discreet distance from Memphis Minnie's 'The first time I met you, you had the meat in your hand', but in more harmonious echo with Curley Weaver's 'When I met you baby, you didn't have no sometime ways', Blind Blake's 'When I first met you, you had your diamonds on', Blind Willie McTell's 'When I first met you mama, you were so nice and kind' and Henry Townsend's 'When I first seen you baby, you were so nice and kind to me' (itself receiving a re-echo in Dylan's blues song '10,000 Men', which ends with the enacted weakness – confessedly bathetic, confessedly tautological – of 'It's so sweet of you to be so nice to me').[145] The same song's 'Well I'm gonna quit this baby talk now' is a reference to a blues world expression too, often used in the imperative, as 'no more baby talk now!', which we find for instance in the sub-title of Roosevelt Sykes' 'The Train Is Coming (No More Baby Talk)'. The fact that it's felt to be useful to put

144. Memphis Minnie: 'Bumble Bee', Memphis, 20/2/30; "Rare Blues Of The Twenties" [sic], Historical Records HLP-2, Jersey City, NJ, c. 1967. Pearl Dickson: 'Twelve Pound Daddy', Memphis, 12/12/27; "Frank Stokes' Dream, 1927–1931 (The Memphis Blues)", Yazoo L-1008, New York, 1968. Clifford Gibson: 'Ice And Snow Blues', New York, 26/11/29; "Clifford Gibson: Beat You Doing It", Yazoo L-1027, New York, 1972. Will Weldon (with the Memphis Jug Band): 'Peaches In The Springtime', Memphis, 13/2/28; "Harmonicas, Washboards, Fiddles, Jugs", Roots RL-311, Vienna, 1968. Willie Brown: 'M and O Blues', Grafton, Wisconsin, 28/5/30; "The Mississippi Blues 1927–1940", Origin Jazz Library OJL-5, Berkeley, 1963. Joe McCoy: 'That Will Be Alright', New York, 18/6/29; "Memphis Jamboree, 1927–1936", Yazoo L-1021, New York, 1970.

145. Gus Cannon: 'Heart Breakin' Blues', Memphis, 9/9/28; "The Great Jug Bands", Origin Jazz Library OJL-4, Berkeley, 1962. Memphis Minnie: 'You Can't Give It Away', Chicago, 10/1/35; "The Early Recordings Of Memphis Minnie And Kansas Joe", Paltram Records PL-101, Vienna, 1971. Curley Weaver: 'Sometime Mama', Chicago 23/4/35; "Masters Of The Blues, 1928–1940", Historical Records HLP-31, Jersey City, NJ, 1969. Blind Willie McTell: 'Stomp Down Rider', Atlanta, 23/10/31; "Blind Willie McTell – The Early Years (1927–1933)", Yazoo L-1005, New York, 1968. Henry Townsend: 'Long Ago Blues', Chicago, 15/11/29; "St. Louis Town, 1929–1937", Yazoo L-1003, New York, 1968.

that sub-title there as a selling-point indicates its popularity as a phrase. Bill Gaither's song 'Babified Ways Girl' seems to address this theme too.[146]

One of Dylan's best-remembered lines of the 1960s is that snarl from 'It's Alright Ma (I'm Only Bleeding)', that

> *Money doesn't talk, it swears.*

But while this spin on the phrase 'money talks' is Dylan's, the notion of making such a spin comes down through the blues from even further back, in black-face vaudeville. A Victor catalogue of 'Darky ditties' from around 1903 contains, in the category 'Comic And Coon Songs by Arthur Collins', one called 'If Money Talks, It Ain't On Speaking Terms With Me'; years later the same idea had migrated into an early blues that begins

> *I can't make a nickel, I'm flat as I can be*
> *Some people say money is talking, but it won't say a word to me.*[147]

In 'Bob Dylan's 115th Dream', while 'I saw three ships a-sailin'' is, vernacular dropped 'g' apart, a verbatim quote from the Christmas carol, when you add in the line that Dylan adds, you find it is also a turnaround of a blues song's re-statement of the common folkloric commuter's lament about waiting for buses and trains and the wrong ones always turning up first. Dylan's

> *I saw three ships a-sailin'*
> *They were all heading my way*

neatly reverses a blues line from 1927:

> *They's two trains runnin', none of them going my way,*

from 'Frisco Whistle Blues' by Alabama's splendid blues artist Ed Bell (tagged in the Paramount catalogue as 'The Weird Guitar Player'), from his début session. Or, to approach the same putative traffic-jam from a later vantage-point, the line Dylan attaches to the carol's 'I saw three ships a-sailin'' makes a darting imaginative connexion with – perhaps deliberately echoes – the Muddy Waters song 'Still A Fool (Two Trains Runnin')', which Dylan himself performed a version of in Montreal in 1962. Thus you can say that Waters'

> *Well now two, there's two trains runnin'*
> *Well they aint never goin' my way*

becomes Dylan's

> *I saw three ships a-sailin'*
> *They were all headin' my way.*

The Muddy Waters song derives either from Robert Petway's pre-war classic 'Catfish Blues' or from his friend and performing partner Tommy McClennan's copy of it,

---

146. Roosevelt Sykes: 'The Train Is Coming (No More Baby Talk)', NYC, 31/3/38; "Roosevelt Sykes (1929–1942)", Best of Blues Records BoB3 [and CD15], Vienna, 1986. Bill Gaither: 'Babified Ways Girl', NYC, 23/6/38; "Bill Gaither . . . Vol. 3", Document DOCD-5253, Vienna, 1994.

147. Victor catalogue reproduced in Tony Russell, *Blacks, Whites and Blues*. Early blues song source unknown.

'Deep Blue Sea Blues', which both re-work a traditional Mississippi blues. Tommy Johnson's 1928 'Bye Bye Blues' has the similar line 'Well, two trains runnin', runnin' side by side' and the same tune as 'Still A Fool'. My guess is that Dylan got it from Muddy Waters and Waters primarily from McClennan.[148]

Nonetheless, of Muddy Waters' three verses, Dylan's version uses two and then adds two more, of which one shows a personalised contribution by Dylan himself and both show his familiarity with common-stock blues lyric poetry.

When Dylan sings 'Now it's all been done before, / It's all been written in the book' in 'Too Much Of Nothing', from the Basement Tapes, this is truly a self-reflexive text. His first line is more or less an explanation of what his second line means, and that second line eats up another slice of blues-world usage. The very phrase 'in the book' has indeed 'been done before', and written in the book of the blues. It is there in Leroy Carr's 'Papa Wants To Knock A Jug' from 1931 – 'What they was doing wasn't in the book' – and in Blind Lemon Jefferson's 1928 'Long Lastin' Lovin'', which ends with 'When she starts to loving, man it ain't in the book'. These may be said to use the expression rather more vividly than Dylan does, but what he does with it is to broaden its range, to apply it to life in general instead of merely to sexual athleticism.[149]

I hear in these lines from the 1983 'Union Sundown' a more individual, if a fainter, blues echo:

> *Well, you know, lots of people complainin' that there is no work.*
> *I say, 'Why you say that for*
> *When nothin' you got is US-made?'*
> *They don't make nothin' here no more.*

In its conversational cadence and its scathing grumpiness, as well as in its addressing of the overall issue of the state of the nation, this echoes a particular couplet by Lonnie Johnson from his 'Hard Times Ain't Gone No Where':

> *People raving about hard times – I don't know why they should*
> *If some people was like me, they didn't have no money when times was good*[150]

---

148. McClennan makes very similar vocal noises to Muddy Waters, though Waters must also have known the Petway and the Tommy Johnson records: Petway's was massively popular in the early 1940s, and Tommy Johnson, a huge influence on Howlin' Wolf, was a favourite of Waters' too. (Asked 'Did you ever know Tommy Johnson?', Waters replied: 'I didn't get to see Tommy . . . but he was my man after I heard him on record, man.' Interview by Jim and Amy O'Neal, 3/1/80 or 18/8/81, *Living Blues*, no. 64, March–April 1985.)
   Ed Bell: 'Frisco Whistle Blues', Chicago, c. September 1927; "Alabama Country, 1927–31", Origin Jazz Library OJL-14, Berkeley, 1967, and "Alabama Blues 1927–1931", Yazoo Records L-1006, New York, 1968. Muddy Waters: 'Still A Fool', Chicago, 1951. Bob Dylan: 'Still A Fool', Finjan Club, Montreal, 7/2/62, unissued. Robert Petway: 'Catfish Blues', Chicago, 28/3/41; "Robert Petway", French RCA Treasury of Jazz Series no. 51 EP, RCA 86–418, Paris, 1965. Tommy McClennan: 'Deep Blue Sea Blues', Chicago, 15/9/41; "Down South", Roots RL-313, Vienna, 1968. Tommy Johnson: 'Bye Bye Blues', Memphis, 4/2/28, "Jackson Blues", Yazoo Records L-1007, New York, 1968.

149. Leroy Carr: 'Papa Wants To Knock A Jug', Chicago, c. 20/1/31; "Leroy Carr & Scrapper Blackwell: Naptown Blues, 1929–1934", Yazoo L-1036, New York, 1973. Blind Lemon Jefferson: 'Long Lastin' Lovin'', Chicago, c. Feb 1928; "Black Snake Moan: Blind Lemon Jefferson", Milestone Records MLP-2013, New York, 1970.

150. Lonnie Johnson: 'Hard Times Ain't Gone No Where', Chicago, 8/11/37; "The Blues Of Lonnie Johnson", Swaggie Records [Jazz Makers series], S-1225, Victoria, Australia, 1969.

and, while I can't in logic quite justify it, I hear the same Dylan song, intertwined with that whole strand of his work that declares the end to be near, as harking back to Sleepy John Estes' acerbic, articulately doomy state-of-the-union summation in 'Time Is Drawing Near' (a Dylanesque sentiment these days). 'Union Sundown' notes:

> *They used to grow food in Kansas*
> *Now they want to grow it on the moon and eat it raw.*
> *I can see the day coming when even your home garden*
> *Is gonna be against the law.*[151]

Sleepy John Estes has this to say, and in the same tirading spirit:

> *Time, time is drawing near*
> *Now can't you see, more and more each year . . .*
> *Now my mother used to say, the sign will be*
> *We couldn't tell summer from winter no more by the birds of the tree*
> *Now it used to be the time, get a corn crop in March*
> *But now we can't get one in June 'n' neither July.*
> *Now you'd go to the church just to work for soul*
> *But now we go to buy one another's clothes.*

What an acute last couplet *that* is.[152]

Besides, there's nothing peripheral about what Dylan has taken and remodelled from Sleepy John Estes. Who does this sound like? An artist of great originality, whose work combines traditional and self-penned material, who went through a 'protest' phase, is '. . . not a particularly accomplished guitarist' and whose 'broken, fragmented song' is 'held in tension by the contrast between the tendency to disintegration and the rhythmic impetus of his strumming'. Well, yes, it is Sleepy John Estes but it might so easily be Touring Bob Dylan. (The quotes are from Paul Oliver's *The Story of the Blues*, 1969.)

To listen to a sweep of Estes' pre-war recordings is to have confirmed what Dylan himself hints at by his own prominent naming of Estes in his "Bringing It All Back Home" sleeve notes: namely that Estes is a *seminal* figure in Bob Dylan's blues education.[153] As so often, Dylan tells us something true but says it in so flip and casual

---

151. As David Pichaske has written (in his lengthy essay 'Bob Dylan and the American dream: the prophet and the prisoner', 1986, a foreshortened version of which appeared in the *Telegraph*, no. 26, Spring 1987), these lines are consistent with Dylan's career-long protestation at the corruption of nature. 'The dark songs of the middle sixties . . . are significantly without reference to the countryside . . . or, when nature does appear, it has been corrupted. The lagoon in Memphis has turned "honky-tonk"; the flowers in 'It's Alright Ma (I'm Only Bleeding)' are cultivated as "nothing more than something to invest in". One of the most devastating features of . . . 'Blind Willie McTell' is precisely the corruption of the natural landscape, which for Dylan was always a source of regeneration. The same fear is voiced in 'Last Thoughts On Woody Guthrie': "And yer sun-decked desert and evergreen valleys / Turn to broken down slums and trash-can alleys."' ('Isis' touches on the same theme too, with that quietly unpolemical line 'She was there in the meadow where the creek used to rise'.)

152. Or it would be if it were not only what Michael Taft transcribes but what Estes really sings. This is extremely doubtful. (Sleepy John Estes: 'Time Is Drawing Near', Chicago, 4/6/40; "The Blues Of Sleepy John Estes: Volume Two", Swaggie Records [Jazz Makers series], S-1220, Victoria, Australia, c. 1967; CD-reissued "Sleepy John Estes Complete Recorded Works Vol. 2 (1937–1941)", Document Records DOCD-5016, Vienna, 1990.)

153. Dylan mentions him again in the mid-1960s: to John Lennon in the taxi-ride filmed for, but not used in, *Eat the Document*. Transcribed by John Bauldie in *Mojo*, no. 1, 1993.

a way that we tend to disregard it. In this case, his notes to his first 'rock' album begin by declaring (quietly): 'i'm standing there watching the parade / feeling combination of sleepy john estes. jayne mansfield. humphrey bogart' – and sure enough, it transpires that those distinctively 'Dylanesque' clunking blues from 1965 owe much to Sleepy John Estes' pioneering work and very individual style, while the clear resemblance between Paul Oliver's description of Estes and our own picture of the older Bob Dylan's artistry suggests aspects of Sleepy John's influence beyond those Dylan displayed back in 1965 that have remained and grown within him. Dylan has said so himself, mentioning Estes again in that 1993 interview quoted earlier, replacing the trio Estes–Jayne Mansfield–Humphrey Bogart with Estes–Gary Davis–Son House.[154]

The evidence is everywhere. The very *title* of Estes' first hit, 'The Girl I Love, She Got Long Curly Hair' (1929), indicates by its distinctive jerky rhythmic strut, an Estes trademark, just how songs like 'California', 'Outlaw Blues', 'From A Buick 6' and 'Sitting On A Barbed-Wire Fence' are built to the Estes blueprint. You can hear it straight away in the special way the delivery of the line is chopped up to incorporate those odd, crucial pauses:

> *Now the, girl I love she got, long curly hair*

> *Well this, woman I got she's, killin' me alive.*

The half-correspondence of the words that begin those two lines merely adds to the certainty already felt that the one song has inspired the other.[155]

Nine months after cutting 'The Girl I Love', which was to prove Estes' most popular disc, he recorded a song he called 'Milk Cow Blues'. It bears no resemblance to anyone else's song of that name (and doesn't mention milk cows): but it bears a very striking resemblance to 'The Girl I Love, She Got Long Curly Hair'. It has the same knowing clunkiness, that hip manipulation of chunky pauses on the backbeat – a sort of sure-footed clog-dancing: and it is the clear model for 'From A Buick 6'. The special rhythm is the same. The tune is the same. Dylan's lyric even starts out in tribute to the Estes prototype. Where Dylan's 1965 song begins

> *I got this, graveyard woman you know she, keeps my kid*
> *But my soulful mama you know she, keeps me hid*

Estes opens this way:

---

154. Bob Dylan, San Diego hotel interview, see note 50.

155. A terrific selection of pre-war Estes material, including all the recordings mentioned in what follows except for 'Time Is Drawing Near', is available on CD on Sleepy John Estes: "I Ain't Gonna Be Worried No More: 1929–1941", Yazoo 2004, USA, 1992. The recordings discussed below are: 'The Girl I Love, She Got Long Curly Hair', Memphis, 24/9/29, and 'Milk Cow Blues', Memphis, 13/5/30; both on "Sleepy John Estes 1929–1940", RBF Records RF-8, New York, 1964; the latter track also on Sam Charters' 2-LP box-set "The Rural Blues", RBF Records RF-202, New York, 1964. 'Broken-Hearted, Ragged And Dirty Too', Memphis, 17/9/29; unissued. 'Broken-Hearted, Ragged And Dirty Too', Memphis, 26/9/29; RBF Records RF-8. 'Someday Baby Blues', Chicago, 9/7/35; "The Blues Of Sleepy John Estes: Vol. 1", Swaggie Records S-1219, Victoria, Australia, 1967. 'Who's Been Tellin' You Buddy Brown Blues', Chicago, 9/7/35; issued ditto. 'Drop Down Mama', Chicago, 17/7/35; issued ditto, and on "The Blues In Memphis, 1927–39", Origin Jazz Library OJL-21, Berkeley, c. 1969. 'Special Agent (Railroad Police Blues)', NYC, 22/4/38; "The Country Blues", RBF Records RF-1, New York, 1959. 'Little Laura Blues', Chicago, 24/9/41; "Treasury Of Jazz No. 30" [EP], RCA Victor 75.752, Paris, 1963. 'Time Is Drawing Near', Chicago, 4/6/40, see note 152.

Now, asked sweet mama let me, be her kid
She says I, might get 'bove you like to, keep it hid.

And the first vinyl release of this Estes recording was in 1964.

The same Estes song, as it happens, offers some common-stock blues lines that have Dylan connections from elsewhere in his repertoire. The line after the opening couplet just quoted is one we find Dylan singing in 'Blood In My Eyes': 'Well she looked at me, she begin to smile', and the line that ends the Estes 'Milk Cow Blues' is 'Now it's a, slow consumption an' it's, killin' you by degrees'. Dylan's matching line, with matching pauses, tune and strut, is 'Well if I, go down dyin' you know she, bound to put a blanket on my bed'.

The very first track Estes recorded was his own version of Blind Lemon Jefferson's 'Broke And Hungry', which he either misheard or re-wrote as 'broken-hearted', and which was given a characteristically lengthy Estes title, 'Broken-Hearted, Ragged And Dirty Too'. This début recording, made in Memphis in mid-September 1929, remained unissued; he had another go just nine days later, and this time achieved release. The version Dylan performs on "World Gone Wrong" is far more similar to the Sleepy John Estes than to the 1940s Willie Brown version cited in Dylan's sleeve notes.[156]

'Someday Baby Blues' is Sleepy John Estes' particularly heartfelt and individual variant of 'Sittin' On Top Of The World', which has in turn been revised and revisited in several guises. Chuck Berry's 'Worried Life Blues' uses the Estes chorus but thoroughly different verses; the Allman Brothers' version of the Muddy Waters version, 'Trouble No More', does the opposite, reinstating an approximation of Estes' verses while abandoning his chorus. When Bob Dylan sang it at Toads Place in 1990, it was recognised as the same song as Muddy Waters', and duly appears in the various listings of his performances as 'Trouble No More'; yet really Dylan brings it all home to Sleepy John Estes, reinstating his chorus and imbuing it with the customary Estesian pauses ('Someday baby, you ain't gonna worry, my mind, anymore'). The only vocal moment worth speaking of in Dylan's befogged performance is the fair imitation of Estes' voice he achieves on the penultimate delivery of that line.[157]

The Estes voice, on his slower numbers, also possesses a painful, crawling quality, always threatening to break down, always wavering between esoteric possibilities. He pulls himself along his vocal line like a snail over pebbles. On the slow songs, even the awkward lengthiness of his titles enacts this tortuous slow motion, matching the delivery, a fine example being 'Who's Been Tellin' You Buddy Brown Blues'. This is the very attenuation Dylan uses so effectively in the unreleased Basement Tapes song 'I'm Not There (1956)'.

Estes' 'Drop Down Mama', another 'From A Buick 6' prototype, has one of those 'It Ain't Me, Babe' openings: 'Go, 'way from my window quit scratchin', on my

---

156. A fuller discussion of this song is offered in Chapter 18. Blind Lemon Jefferson: 'Broke And Hungry', Chicago, c. November 1926; "Blind Lemon Jefferson, Volume Two", Milestone Records LP 2007, New York, 1968.

157. Chuck Berry: 'Worried Life Blues', Chicago, 12/2/60 (B-side of 'Bye Bye Johnny', same session), Chess Records 1754, Chicago, 1960. Allman Brothers: 'Trouble No More', NYC, Sept. 1969; "The Allman Brothers Band", Capricorn Records ATCO SD-33-308, New York, 1969. Muddy Waters: 'Trouble No More', Chicago, Oct. 1955, Chess Records 1612, Chicago, 1955. Bob Dylan: 'Trouble No More / Someday Baby Blues', live New Haven, Connecticut, 12/1/90.

screen' and a refrain which you have only to hear Estes deliver to connect with Dylan's jerky 1965 blues again. 'Now I may look like I'm crazy, poor John do know right from wrong' is clearly the eccentric piece of scaffolding on which Dylan builds 'Well I might, look like Robert Ford but I, feel just like a Jesse James'.

'Special Agent (Railroad Police Blues)' is another jerky blues, the vocal delivery an object lesson in the inspired eccentricity that sets the few aside from the many: the sort of vocal eccentricity that we may have found first in Fats Domino or Buddy Holly or Howlin' Wolf, in rock'n'roll or R&B, and which pulls us into this music when we're very young because it speaks to us from a strange, magic kingdom alluringly unlike school. Anyone who ever felt that way can recognise the authentic pull of Sleepy John Estes, as Bob Dylan must have done. He probably heard this Estes record before any other: it was included on Sam Charters' "The Country Blues" LP issued back in 1959.

This track also offers a salutary reminder that, as it were, there's nothing exclusively postmodern about the self-reflexive text. More than fifty years before Dylan played with 'I'll be back in a minute . . . You can tell me, I'm back' and 'now I'm back on the track' on his fine "Oh Mercy" recording 'What Was It You Wanted?', Estes was ending 'Special Agent (Railroad Police Blues)' with this devilishly clever pay-off line:

> Now special agent, special agent, put me off close to some town
> Special agent, special agent, put me off close to some town
> Now I got to do some recording: an' I oughta be recordin' right now![158]

It's been noted already how Dylan's 'Union Sundown' (1983) seems like a successor to Estes' 'Time Is Drawing Near' (1940), one of the 'protest' or social commentary songs that distinguishes the Estes repertoire; it could be added that the mild, unobtrusive element of social commentary implicit in Dylan's early blues 'Down The Highway' is less in the spirit of his own 'protest songs' than of Estes'. At any rate these are wholly Estesian lines:

> And your streets are gettin' empty
> And your highway's gettin' filled

and you have only to listen to four or five consecutive pre-war Estes recordings to hear how these apparently undistinguished phrases prove distinctively to belong to him.

Finally, there's Estes' 'Little Laura Blues', recorded in 1941. It is not an original tune – so that when Bob Dylan uses it on "Down In The Groove" for 'The Ugliest Girl In The World' (a lyric presented to him by Grateful Dead appendage Robert

---

158. There's a variegated list of postmodernist works that were created, like this Sleepy John Estes record, before the postmodernist era (and before the term was devised). A well-cited early example is *Tristram Shandy*, Laurence Sterne's eighteenth-century novel, which, as Ian Ousby's *The Cambridge Guide to Literature in English* (1995 edition) puts it, 'distributes its narrative content across a bafflingly idiosyncratic time-scheme interrupted by digressions, authorial comments and interferences with the printed fabric of the book' and 'stands in part against the idea of literature as finished product . . . With its black pages, wiggly lines, misplaced chapters and other surprises.' A smaller, less-discussed example is the notion of 'ghost words'. This is a term coined by William Walter Skeat (one of the nineteenth century's great editors of Old and Middle English) for 'coinages due to the blunders of printers or scribes, or to the perfervid imaginations of ignorant or blundering editors' – an idea whose time has finally come.

Hunter), you can't exactly say he's taking it from this Estes number; but you can say that other affinities exist between the two beyond their shared melody. Where Dylan's notional song-heroine is the ugliest, Estes' heroine is the most hopeless day-dreamer.

> *She's the dreamest gal, dreamest gal I ever seen*

is the chorus pay-off line (that neat compression 'dreamest' showing a lyric skill entirely absent from the Dylan–Hunter song), while in the verses Estes too offers a catalogue of a girl's ostensible failings, while the singer counteracts the little put-downs by declaring his own undeflected keenness. This is done with rather more subtlety and less self-congratulation by Estes than by Dylan–Hunter, but it ends up in the same place, which is to say in the approbationary bed, the crassness of 'But I love her' expressed this way instead:

> *Little Laura was a dreamer, most all her dreams come true*
> *She had a dream about lovin' and she knows just what to do.*

Another (in this case hillbilly) blues, 'Darn Good Girl' by the North Carolina white stringband team Buster Carter and Preston Young, occupied the same lyric territory as the Dylan–Hunter song fifty-five years beforehand (and a decade ahead of Sleepy John Estes), and with rather more expressive vigour:

> *. . . her legs are bowed*
> *All knock-kneed an' pigeon-toed*
> *A hump on 'er back and one false leg*
> *Wart on 'er neck as big as an egg*
> *Turned up nose and a [???] chin*
> *Darn good girl for the shape she's in.*[159]

The point here is not to load something as lightweight yet flaccid as 'The Ugliest Girl In The World' with any sort of analysis – it collapses soon enough subjected to a casual listen – but to understand it as another mode of Bob Dylan's interaction with the blues. We see that he would have been drawn to 'The Ugliest Girl In The World' precisely by his recognising it as a familiar creature from one of the minor byways of hillbilly music and the blues. In contrast, it's obvious that decades earlier Dylan recognised Sleepy John Estes as one of the big cats.

Another crucial and highly distinctive one is Skip James, the man who made the crucial recording of a 'Special Rider Blues', after which, as touched on earlier, Dylan named his primary music publishing company.[160]

---

159. Buster Carter and Preston Young [vocalist unknown], 'Darn Good Girl', NYC, 26/6/31; CD-reissued on the 4-CD box-set "The Retrospective 1925–1950", Columbia Legacy Roots N' Blues Series 47911, New York, 1992. Black examples of the same songtype may be Hazel Meyers' 'Plug Ugly (The Worst Lookin' Man In Town)', NYC, March 1924, and Bill Gaither's 'Orneriest Girl In Town', Chicago, 6/4/37, while Jazz Gillum's early track 'Sarah Jane', Chicago, 4/4/36, is a black performance of a hillbilly song that is certainly of the same genre as the Dylan–Hunter number.
  Stringbands were at their height around 1910. There were 15 in Mississippi's Coahoma County alone, playing to blacks and whites. (Lomax's *The Land Where the Blues Began* says that W. C. Handy wanted to write marches till he heard a stringband trio in a dancehall in Clarksdale – after which he wanted to write and collect blues instead.)

160. Peter Guralnick (*Feel Like Going Home*, revised edition 1992) says James took 'Special Rider' from Eurreal Little Brother Montgomery, adapting it for guitar: implying that James took it from Montgomery's 'No Special Rider Blues'; but Steve Calt's notes to the Yazoo compilation of James' 1931 sessions ["Skip James: The Complete

On Dylan's nigh-perfect "Blonde On Blonde" performance of 'Pledging My Time', the melody, the gulping movement of the melodic phrases *and* Dylan's mysteriously ominous line

Somebody got lucky, but it was an accident

all echo 'Come On In My Kitchen' by Robert Johnson, from thirty years earlier.[161] But while the restless melodic phrasing is Johnson's, the melody that inspires it is the same as 'Sittin' On Top Of The World', and the Johnson line that Dylan's echoes –

Some joker got lucky, stole her back again

– is itself an echo of a line from guitarist and pianist Skip James, the man who made 'Special Rider Blues' his own: it comes from James' brilliant 1931 début recording, 'Devil Got My Woman'.

This is not the whole story: Blind Willie McTell's 'Stole Rider Blues', recorded at *his* first session (1927) includes 'I stole my good gal from my bosom friend / That fool got lucky, he stole her back again', which anticipates Skip James' 1931 'Devil Got My Woman' *and* Robert Johnson's 1936 'Come On In My Kitchen', and it would be hard to say from whom Dylan picked up the line – as Dylan sings his matching line, his 'accident' rhymes neatly with the 'back again' offered by McTell, James *and* Johnson – except that James' line,

Somebody got lucky, stoled her back again,

is the closest to Bob Dylan's. And certainly Robert Johnson's line comes down from Skip James rather than from McTell. 'Devil Got My Woman' is also the *musical* basis of another Robert Johnson song, 'Hellhound On My Trail', while Johnson's '32–20' is an almost verbatim reworking of Skip James' '22–20 Blues'.[162]

1931 Session", Yazoo 1072, Newton, NJ, 1988] say it came from the other track from Montgomery's début session, 'Vicksburg Blues', Grafton, Wisconsin, c. Sept. 1930. For all other details see note 66.

161. 'Kitchen', here, writes Stephen Calt in 'Idioms of Robert Johnson', *78 Quarterly*, vol. 1, no. 4, 1989, 'is an obsolete slang term for vagina . . . indicating that the above couplet is sung from a feminine point of view.' cf. ' "Come in," she said, "I'll give ya / Shelter from the storm".' But Leroy Carr is surely using the same 'slang' (itself now surely well on its way to being 'an obsolete slang term') on two of his records, 'Papa Wants A Cookie' (indeed) from 1930 – 'But mama's got the lock on the kitchen door' – and the later (yet still pre-Robert Johnson) 'Bread Baker' from 1934 – 'Because in your kitchen baby, it's where the good stuff can be found'. By extension, of course, the use of kitchen goodies – food – to mean sex is one of the most widespread and least surprising in most cultures, certainly including the blues. Taft includes 68 uses of 'jellyroll', one of 'jellyroller' and 42 of 'jelly', for a start. Leroy Carr: 'Papa Wants A Cookie', Chicago, 2/1/30, and 'Bread Baker', NYC, 17/12/34; both reissued "Leroy Carr & Scrapper Blackwell: Naptown Blues, 1929–1934", Yazoo L-1036, New York, 1973.

162. Robert Johnson: 'Come On In My Kitchen' [2 takes], San Antonio, 23/11/36; one issued Columbia CL-1654. Skip James: 'Devil Got My Woman', 'Special Rider Blues' and '22–20', Grafton, Wisconsin, c. February 1931; "Skip James, King of the Delta Blues Singers 1928–1964", Biograph BLP-12029, Canaan, NY, 1970. James' only pre-war recordings were the ones done for Paramount c. Feb. 1931; the Biograph album boasts the dates "1928–1964" because it includes a 1928 Chicago test-pressing by someone else, wrongly attributed to James, and because it also draws on a session recorded at Falls Church, Virginia, 16/12/64, at which James cut 22 sides. BLP-12029 uses just two: 'I'm So Glad' and a revisit to 'Special Rider Blues'. 'Devil Got My Woman' was first vinyl-issued on "Really! The Country Blues", Origin OJL-2, USA, 1962.

Blind Willie McTell: 'Stole Rider Blues', Atlanta, 18/10/27; "Blind Willie McTell 1927–1935", Yazoo L-1037, NYC, 1973 (issued in stereo!). Robert Johnson: 'Hellhound On My Trail' [2 takes], Dallas, 20/6/37; one issued Columbia CL-1654. Robert Johnson: '32–20 Blues' [2 takes], San Antonio, 26/11/36; same issue details. [Another significant influence on Johnson, Kokomo Arnold, recorded 'Front Door Blues (32–20 Blues)', Chicago, 15/1/35.]

These songs came to Johnson via his Jackson, Mississippi contemporary Johnny Temple, an ex-protégé of Skip James, whereas for Dylan, James was accessible more or less directly; that is, he was both a figure of legend from the 1930s and one of the most important of the 'rediscovered' bluesmen in the couple of years immediately before "Blonde On Blonde" was recorded.

Another part of the same Skip James lyric becomes entwined in a different Dylan song, 'When I Paint My Masterpiece'. The 'wild geese' Dylan recalls himself following on a hilltop in 'When I Paint My Masterpiece' fly straight out of a number of old blues songs, in which they feature as a common-stock formulation. Whenever you hear the line

> *I lay down last night, tried to take my rest*

you can more or less bet that the next line will be

> *My mind got to ramblin' like the wild geese in the west.*

It occurs, for example, in Blind Boy Fuller's 'Weeping Willow', which Dylan performed at the Supper Club in New York in 1993 (discussed in Chapter 18).[163]

Sometimes the 'wild geese', with engaging grammatic licence, is singular ('my mind got to rambling like a wild geese in the west'). There are also several songs called 'Wild Geese Blues', as recorded for instance by Barbecue Bob, Alberta Jones and the theatrically masculine Gladys Bentley.[164] Yet because of Skip James' vocal intensity, and because of a tiny one-word change he makes to the couplet, these wild geese fly most vividly and particularly out of 'Devil Got My Woman', so that the image works as a most poignant lunge of the imagination suddenly arising out of his beautifully evoked restless yearning:

> *I lay down last night, tried to take my rest*
> *My mind got to ramblin' like the wild geese from the west.*

The more common 'in the west' is less moving, in both senses, than James' 'from the west': 'in the west' abolishes movement, leaving these birds, and the image, hanging motionless. Skip James' tiny change sets them flying across the sky, wild geese indeed, making the image one of visitational loveliness.

James was taught guitar by the unrecorded singer Henry Stuckey, born in the 1890s. James first saw him play in a Bentonia, Mississippi juke joint in about 1908, and learnt guitar from him after Stuckey's 1917 return from World War One, using pieces like 'Salty Dog' and 'Stack O'Lee'. James' own wonderful piano-accompanied

---

163. Blind Boy Fuller: 'Weeping Willow', NYC, 14/7/37; "Blind Boy Fuller On Down – Vol. 1", Saydisc Records SDR143, Badminton, UK, c. 1967. Bob Dylan: 'Weeping Willow', NYC, 17/11/93.

The Fuller version is memorialised post-war by Pink Anderson: 'Weeping Willow Blues', Spartanburg, South Carolina, 12/4/61; "Carolina Blues Man Volume 1", Prestige Bluesville 1038, New Jersey, 1962, CD-reissued Prestige Bluesville Original Blues Classics OBCCD-504-2, Berkeley, 1992. And 'Weeping Willow Blues', Spartanburg, July 1962; issued on the cleverly named "The Blues", Asch Records A101, 1967. On Anderson's version (which on "Carolina Blues Man Volume 1" gives composer credit to one Paul Carter, despite notes by Sam Charters stating that it was one of 'Fuller's pieces') the species of bird is the turtle dove.

Anderson, born in South Carolina in 1900, recorded in 1928, 1950, 1961, 1962 and 1970; he died in Spartanburg in 1974. He is the man who inspired the first half of the group name Pink Floyd, the other half deriving from another North Carolina blues artist, Floyd Council.

164. Barbecue Bob: 'Wild Geese Blues', Atlanta, 13/4/28. Alberta Jones: 'Wild Geese Blues', NYC, c. 28/9/28. Gladys Bentley: 'Wild Geese Blues', NYC, 2/11/28 and 15/11/28.

recording 'If You Haven't Any Hay Get On Down The Road' is based on a ragtime number Stuckey played on guitar as 'All Night Long', fused with the traditional 'Alabama Bound', learnt in James' youth from local fiddle-player Green McCloud. Stuckey, tracked down in 1965 by the blues collector and critic Gayle Wardlow, still refused to record, and died in 1966.[165]

Skip James concentrated primarily on his own compositions and continued to make many of them out of songs that were not really blues at all, but which he alchemised into blues by the sheer ingenuity of his wayward style. He also found his own eccentric, intelligent ways of enriching his guitar-work from his experience as a pianist, and vice versa. The brilliant, distinctive delivery James uses at the end of his vocal lines – an ostentatious yet felicitous filigreeing around the note – finds a pale echo in Bob Dylan's delivery on 'North Country Blues'. In full, skittering flight, as achieved by Skip James, it is, among other things, the key to Robin Williamson's Incredible String Band vocals.

James returned to Bentonia in the late 1940s, went on the road again with his wife in the early 1950s, but tired of travelling and retired. The drama of his recording career lies in the fact that he had only ever done one recording session, the substantial one from 1931 that had yielded so much. Then, thirty-three years later, 'rediscovered', he appeared like a ghost at the 1964 Newport Folk Festival, and was recorded there by Vanguard Records. The first of his four Newport songs was 'Devil Got My Woman' (and of the three others, two were also revisits to songs he had cut at his recording session of three decades earlier).

Peter Guralnick's book *Feel Like Going Home* (1971) is good on Skip James' 'rediscovery', and appears to give an eye-witness account of his triumphant perform- ance at Newport. It is also an account that recognises the agitation most of us can fall prey to in coping with the emergence of the much-loved, obscure artefact into clear accessibility:

> As the first notes floated across the field, as the voice soared over us, the piercing falsetto set against the harsh cross-tuning of the guitar, there was a note of almost breathless expectation in the air. It seemed inappropriate somehow that this strange haunting sound which had existed till now only as a barely audible dub from a scratched 78 should be reclaimed so casually on an overcast summer's day at Newport. As the song came to an end . . . the field exploded with cheers and whistles and some of the awful tension was dissipated.

Jon Pankake's colleague Paul Nelson, reviewing Skip James' performance as issued on one of the LPs of the festival, wrote that 'the rediscovered Skip James contributes four of the greatest blues performances . . . of recent years, his high, emotional falsetto singing and carefully considered guitar-playing setting a nearly impossible standard'.

James continued to record and perform after Newport – and not at all as a shadow of his former self, though it's expected that you should say so. To listen, for example, to his 1966 recordings for Vanguard's album "Skip James Today!" is to be

---

165. Gayle Dean Wardlow 'rediscovered' Ishman Bracey and mounted key research that led to the rediscovery of Skip James, Son House and Rube Lacey. In 1967 he was reportedly at work on a definitive history of the country blues. ('Who wasn't?' asks Tony Russell.) It has never surfaced.

astonished by the man's genius and chutzpah. He sounds like no one else on the planet; he sounds ageless and in his prime; his singing is still eerily beautiful and his acoustic guitar-work is inventive *and precise*. Play "Skip James Today!" up against Bob Dylan's 1993 album "World Gone Wrong" and much as I might love the latter, the former rebuffs with shining energy the notion that blurred guitar-work or last-gasp vocalising is all you can expect from the over-50s. (It is also, you won't be surprised to learn, immensely better recorded than the Dylan album.) Still, while one of these artists was recording "Skip James Today!", the other was recording "Blonde On Blonde". Can't complain. Further Skip James recording sessions followed in the 1960s. He died in Philadelphia in early October, 1969.[166]

We have looked, now, at several aspects of Dylan's extraordinary use of the country blues (and to some extent at how he has also drawn from its more modern counterparts). We've looked at his least remarkable usage – that is, when he deploys unmediated blues lines inside blues songs of his own – and at his least detectable usage, when he takes up blues lines that he twists or transforms and puts into his non-blues songs. More centrally, we have examined that clear pattern within his work wherein his own blues songs offer phrases and formulae from the great body of blues lyric poetry, but offer them creatively shifted, transformed and twisted. It remains now to see how richly and resourcefully he persists with the other side of that pattern: at how, throughout his *non*-blues songs, he insinuates blues lyric poetry more or less verbatim from that corpus.

We found, a little while back, that our friend Mr Estes hovers even among those who prefigure the opening of Dylan's 'It Ain't Me, Babe' – 'Go 'way from my window / Leave at your own chosen speed' being not so far from Estes' 'Go 'way from my window, quit scratchin' on my screen' – but he can be allowed to go away from our window now, because there are, behind this, phrases or fragments from a host of half-remembered as well as well-remembered songs, from the traditional 'Go 'Way From My Window', collected by folklorist John Jacob Niles and sung by Dylan on the May 1960 St Paul Minnesota tape, through to the cluster of songs behind Little Richard's 'Keep A-Knockin'' ('but you can't come in'). One prefiguration is the formulaic blues pattern, utilised not only by Estes but many others, that runs

> *Get away from my window, honey babe get away from my door . . .*
> *Say you get away from my window, don't knock at my door . . .*
> *Said get away from my window mama, don't knock at my back door . . .*
> *Get away from my window, stop knockin' on my door . . .*
> *Go away from my window, stop knocking at my door.*[167]

166. Skip James: 'Devil Got My Woman', 'Cherry Ball Blues', 'Sick Bed Blues' and 'Cypress Grove Blues', Newport, Rhode Island, 23–26/7/64; "The Blues At Newport 1964, Part Two", Vanguard Records VRS-9181 [mono] and VSD-79181, New York, 1965. Peter Guralnick: *Feel Like Going Home*. Paul Nelson quoted from *Sing Out!* magazine Vol. 15, no. 5, Nov. 1965. "Skip James Today!", NYC, Jan. 1966, Vanguard VLP 9219, New York, c. 1967.

There is just one occasion when the radiant wondrousness of Mr James crashes badly. His 1931 performance of '4 O'Clock Blues' holds a disquieting moment for those familiar with 1950s-to-1960s British culture. There you are, entranced by his precarious, eerie genius, when all at once the phrase his perilous falsetto offers is 'Goodbye my darling—', and he sounds exactly like Charlie Drake.

167. Respectively: Papa Charlie Jackson: 'Papa's Lawdy Lawdy Blues', Chicago, c. August 1924; "The Country

Not the sort of song you expect to find a blues line lurking inside, but there it is. Equally unexpected, perhaps, is to find one inside his "Nashville Skyline" country song 'To Be Alone With You' – but 'Night Time Is The Right Time' is described by Peter Narváez as a 'blues . . . love lyric', perhaps based upon a traditional or nineteenth-century song. At any rate, Roosevelt Sykes recorded it in 1937, and every verse ends with the refrain

> The night time is the right time
> To be with the one you love.

Sykes' record was sufficiently popular that both he and Broonzy recorded a 'Night Time Is The Right Time No. 2' in 1938, and the song surfaced again in the late 1950s when Ray Charles recorded it under the title 'The Right Time', including it on his influential album "Yes Indeed!", one of the LPs that every British rock'n'roll singer and then every beat group member seemed to possess. As British music-TV producer Jack Good recalled decades later, Britain's best, authentic, angst-ridden rocker, Billy Fury, used to open his live act 'with Ray Charles' 'The Night Time Is The Right Time' and oh gosh . . . You wouldn't be able to hear anything after that. The girls would be screaming and running down the aisles.'[168]

The song was being offered too in the abundant repertoire of the stylish and dapper Mance Lipscomb – who never recorded till 1960, by which time he was in his sixties (though still with a strikingly youthful way of moving around in performance) and had almost a thousand songs he could perform. His version includes

> Don't the moon look pretty, shinin' down through the tree
> I can see my woman but she can't see me
> Night time is the right time, be with the one you love.

The song was still sufficiently a blues-cred staple to be recorded by Eddie Boyd when he got together in London with John Mayall, Peter Green, John McVie and Aynsley Dunbar in the spring of 1967, and it has come around again since, titled 'To Be With The One You Love (Night Time Is The Right Time)' and recorded by Peppermint Harris, a 1950s staff songwriter for Modern Records who composed for Bobby Bland,

Blues: Volume Two", RBF Records RF-9, New York, 1964. Blind Boy Fuller: 'Stealing Bo-Hog', New York, 7/9/37; "Blind Boy Fuller with Sonny Terry and Bull City Red", Blues Classics BC-11, Berkeley, 1966. Will Weldon (with the Memphis Jug Band): 'Memphis Jug Blues', Memphis, 24/2/27; "Memphis Jug Band Volume 1: 1927–1929", Roots RL-322, Vienna, c. 1969. Anna Bell: 'Every Woman Blues', Long Island City, c. September 1928; "Anna Bell, Katherine Henderson, Laura Bryant. Acc. by Clarence Williams' Orchestra, 1928–1929", Historical Records ASC-21, New York, 1968. Noah Lewis (with Gus Cannon): 'Going To Germany', Chicago, 1/10/29; "The Great Jug Bands", Origin Jazz Library OJL-4, Berkeley, 1962.

168. Peter Narváez: 'Current blues recordings', *Journal of American Folklore*, no. 104, 1991. Roosevelt Sykes: 'Night Time Is The Right Time', Chicago, 29/4/37, and 'Night Time Is The Right Time, No.2', NYC, 31/3/38, both issued "The Honeydipper" on the mysterious White Label on Vinyl Records VLP9, Europe, mid-1960s. Big Bill [Broonzy]: 'Night Time Is The Right Time No.2', Chicago, 5/5/38; "Big Bill's Blues", Epic Records EE 22017, NYC, c. 1968.

Ray Charles: 'The Right Time', NYC, 28/10/58, Atlantic Records 2010, New York, 1958–9, and "Yes Indeed!", Atlantic LP 8025, New York [London Atlantic HA-E 2168, London], 1958; reissued on the 3-CD set "Ray Charles: The Birth Of Soul – The Complete Atlantic Rhythm & Blues Recordings, 1952–1959", Atlantic & Atco Remasters Series, Atlantic 82310–2, New York, 1991 [US only but available UK].

Jack Good's recollection of Billy Fury performing the song live is in Spencer Leigh and John Firminger's *Halfway to Paradise: Britpop, 1955–1962* (1996), and taken from Spencer Leigh's interview with Jack Good, Radio Merseyside, Liverpool, 28/9/91.

Junior Parker and Etta James.[169] So when Dylan's amiable country song has him singing

> They say the nighttime is the right time
> To be with the one you love

his casual presentation, as if of an anonymous off-the-cuff remark, actually delights in its absolute precision.

Another song the just-mentioned Mance Lipscomb offers in his repertoire is 'Jack O'Diamonds Is A Hard Card To Play' (in fact he is field-recorded performing it in his home town area of Navasota, Texas, in 1960, the first time he ever recorded), which is in turn another title phrase picked up wholesale and retailed by Bob Dylan inside a piece of his own work that is not a blues. It is, in fact, from one of those poems he calls 'Some Other Kinds Of Songs . . .', published as the sleeve notes on the back of the album "Another Side Of Bob Dylan". This long and generally inferior poem repeats several times, and then ends with,

> jack o' diamonds
> is a hard card t' play.

Sippie Wallace records a 'Jack Of Diamonds Blues' early in 1926, but this is not the same song Dylan quotes from. Dylan's stretches back to 'Jack O' Diamond Blues' by Blind Lemon Jefferson, recorded twice at the same session a couple of months later, in about May 1926. John and Alan Lomax field-record a performance of the song by convict Pete Harris, and one by James Iron Head Baker, both in Texas, in 1934; John Lomax and his wife Ruby field-record it again, this time by convict Casey Smith (aka Smith Casey!), in 1939. Three years later Alan Lomax also hears it as a fragment of song recalled in Mississippi by railroad worker Houston Bacon, born around 1900 and a gambler in his youth. It is recorded by a number of other black singers in the pre-war period. The repeated line 'Jack O' Diamonds is a hard card to play' also appears on Brother John Sellers' version, cut in 1954 and based closely on the Blind Lemon Jefferson record. Dylan implies that the version of the Jefferson song that he knows first is Odetta's – saying that by the time he appears in Dinkytown coffee-houses he is 'singing stuff like . . . "Jack O' Diamonds" by Odetta . . .'[170]

The interesting section of Dylan's poem lies at the beginning of its second stanza:

169. Mance Lipscomb: 'Night Time Is The Right Time', *nia*; "Mance Lipscomb Vol. 4", Arhoolie LP 1033, El Cerrito, California, *nia*, but still available 1992. Other songs Lipscomb recorded include 'Baby Please Don't Go', 'You Gonna Quit Me' (the Blind Blake song on Dylan's "Good As I Been To You"), 'Corrina Corrina', 'Mama, Let Me Lay It On You' and a song called 'When Death Comes Creeping In Your Room' – a title that strongly suggests it may prefigure Dylan's 'Whatcha Gonna Do'.
   Lipscomb's claim that Dylan took 'Baby Let Me Follow You Down' from 'his' 'Mama, Let Me Lay It On You' is in 'Playing For The White Folks', in *I Say Me for a Parable: The Oral Autobiography of Mance Lipscomb*, compiled and edited by Glen Alyn, 1993.
   Eddie Boyd: 'Night Time Is The Right Time', London, 14/3/67; "Eddie Boyd & His Blues Band", Decca SKL4872, London, 1967. Peppermint Harris: 'To Be With The One You Love (Night Time Is The Right Time)', *nia*, reissued Home Cooking LP HCS-116, US, c. 1990.

170. Mance Lipscomb: 'Jack O' Diamonds Is A Hard Card To Play', Navasota, 1960; "Mance Lipscomb Texas Sharecropper & Songster", Arhoolie LP 1001, *nia*. Sippie Wallace: 'Jack Of Diamonds Blues', Chicago, 1/3/26. Blind Lemon Jefferson: 'Jack O' Diamond Blues', Chicago, c. May 1926; vinyl-issued very early, on the 10″ Riverside LP Riverside 10–14, New York [London Records ALC 508, London], c. 1956–57. Pete Harris: 'Jack O' Diamonds', Richmond, Texas, May 1934; "Jack O' Diamonds", Flyright-Matchbox Records SDM265, Sussex,

jack o'diamonds
wrecked my hand
left me here t'stand
little tin men play
their drums now
upside my head.

This last line too is a blues phrase, which Dylan must have found on a record from the 1950s or early 1960s if he found it on a record at all. The phrase doesn't circulate on record before the 1950s. Prominently, it is used in the title of a Jimmy Reed record, 'I'm Going Upside Your Head', though Dylan couldn't have pulled it from this: Reed recorded it in August 1964, the same month Dylan's sleeve notes were published. The phrase is still in use among non-whites both in America and Britain. 1940s R&B star Johnny Otis wrote a book about the LA black music scene, published in 1993, called *Upside Your Head: R&B on Central Avenue.* This is not mere retro-referencing: the phrase re-surfaces in the mouth of a young British Asian, Chad, in Hanif Kureishi's novel *The Black Album*, set in London in 1989: 'I'll clip you upside your head.'[171]

According to Clarence Major's *Juba to Jive: A Dictionary of African–American Slang* (1994), the *meaning* of 'upside your head', disappointingly, is merely 'to land a fist-blow in the face, e.g. "Stay out of my way, man, or I'm gonna go upside your head."' But Dylan seizes it – perhaps knowing, perhaps not knowing its mundane meaning – and as his own use of it then shows, he finds within it a meaning altogether more alive: he hears it as a phrase surreal yet accurate, suggesting with all the ellipsed economy of poetry the presence of someone or something (a noise, as Dylan uses it) moving up the walls of the inside of your head.

This is great: but it touches on what should surely be one of the major questions about post-1950s appreciation of the blues, which until recently has largely been by whites. That is, is the meaning the white listener (in this case Dylan) assigns to 'upside your head' its inherent sub-text, or just a fortuitously positive by-product of cultural misunderstanding when whitey listens in on black talk?

Ray Charles also appears to be the more-or-less verbatim source for an earlier piece of work by Dylan than the 'Jack O' Diamonds' poem. The fragment of a song called 'Blackjack Blues', which the pre-Shelton biographer Anthony Scaduto says Dylan had told him was his 'first original folksong', is actually derived from Charles' 1955 R&B-charting single 'Blackjack'. The Dylan lyric fragment is:

Blackjack blues, yea yea yea
How unlucky can one man be?

UK, 1976. James Iron Head Baker: 'Jack O'Diamonds', Central State Farm, Sugarland, Texas, 21/5/34. Smith Casey: 'Jack O' Diamonds', Clemens State Farm, Brazoria, Texas, 16/4/39; "Two White Horses Standin' In A Line", Flyright-Matchbox SDM264, Sussex, UK, 1976. Houston Bacon: 'Jack O' Diamonds' [fragment during 'Interview'], Clarksdale, Mississippi, 8/8/42, in Alan Lomax: *The Land Where the Blues Began*. Brother John Sellers: 'Jack O'Diamonds', NYC, 10/3/54; "Jack O' Diamonds" [10″ LP], Vanguard Records VRS 7022, New York, c. 1954, reissued on "Brother John Sellers Sings Blues And Folk Songs", Vanguard Records VRS 9036, New York, c. 1962. Odetta: *nia*. Bob Dylan: interviewed by Cameron Crowe, "Biograph".

171. Jimmy Reed: 'I'm Going Upside Your Head', Chicago, Aug. 1964; VeeJay Records 622, Chicago, 1964. Hanif Kureishi: *The Black Album*, 1995.

> *Every quarter I make*
> *Old Blackjack takes away from me*

Ray Charles' first verse ends with this:

> *How unlucky can one man be?*
> *Well, every quarter I get*
> *Blackjack takes away from me*[172]

A later, unplagiaristic use of Ray Charles material by Dylan occurs in the mid-1960s. Robert Shelton says that Dylan and Phil Spector were in a Los Angeles coffee shop when they heard Ray Charles' 'Let's Go Get Stoned' (written by Ashford and Simpson) on the juke-box, and were struck by the openness, the upfrontery of the lyric. A few months later Dylan recorded 'Rainy Day Women Nos. 12 & 35', with its chorus of 'Everybody must get stoned'.[173]

There's a 1950s R&B single by Mickey & Sylvia called 'There Ought To Be A Law', which Bob Dylan owned back in Hibbing. Robert Shelton found it in a pile of old records in the corner of the basement at Bob's boyhood home. Shelton, examining this with his biographer's hat on in the late spring of 1968, can hardly have read the title of the Mickey & Sylvia record on the label without his brain adding '. . . against you comin' around'. Dylan's brain made the same connection when he was writing 'Ballad Of A Thin Man'.[174]

As for the idea of the full Dylan line itself, which somehow includes the speaker's defiant admission that it's inherently unreasonable, 'there oughta be a law against you comin' around' itself comes around thirty years after Robert Johnson's recording of 'I Believe I'll Dust My Broom' (1936), in which:

> *I don't want no woman wants any downtown man she meet*
> *She's a no-good donay, they shouldn't allow her on the street.*

This couplet – retained word for word by Elmore James in his 1950s hit versions of 'Dust My Broom' – is interesting for being at once very Johnsonian and Dylanesque. It begins with a back-echo of that line in Dylan's 'Need A Woman' about wanting a woman

> *. . . who don't make herself up to make every man her friend*

---

172. This Dylan appropriation was first pointed out by John White, an *Isis* subscriber, who notes that it is 'likely that Dylan heard the song on the brilliant "Yes Indeed!" album, released in 1958 . . . one of *the* albums to have at the time'. [John White, letter in *Isis*, no. 46, December 1992–January 1993.]
    Ray Charles: 'Blackjack', Atlanta, 18/11/54, Atlantic 1076, 1955; first LP-issued on "Yes Indeed!", see note 168. Ringo Starr was carrying a copy of the "Yes Indeed!" LP when he walked down the steps from the plane on the Beatles' first arrival in America (Kennedy Airport, New York, 7/2/64). The main soloist in the Ray Charles band of the 1950s to early 1960s was Dave 'Fathead' Newman; he and Bob Dylan play together behind Doug Sahm on 'Me & Paul', NYC, October 1972; "Doug Sahm & Band", Atlantic SD-7254, New York, 1972.
    Anthony Scaduto, *Bob Dylan: A Biography* (1972).

173. Ray Charles: 'Let's Go Get Stoned', Los Angeles, late 1965; ABC–Paramount TRC10808, Hollywood, 1966.

174. Mickey & Sylvia: 'There Ought To Be A Law'; NYC, 7/2/57; Vik Records 0267, New York, 1957/8. [Vik was a subsidiary of Victor, as was Groove, which also issued Mickey & Sylvia records.] Robert Shelton, *No Direction Home*.

(Johnson's doubling of 'want' replaced neatly by Dylan's doubling of 'make'), and ends with the comic 'they shouldn't allow her on the street': which, both as idea and cadence, Dylan might easily have used verbatim. You can hear him muttering that one very well, italicising 'street' as he goes.[175]

In the non-blues 'You're A Big Girl Now', Dylan juxtaposes the idea of 'a change in the weather . . .' with his own resolve that 'I can change, I swear' – exactly as Ethel Waters does in her early blues 'There'll Be Some Changes Made', which includes

> *Why there's a change in the weather, there's a change in the sea*
> *But from now on there'll be a change in me*[176]

In the Travelin' Wilburys' late-1980s Dylan song 'Tweeter And the Monkey Man', 'Tweeter' might be new but 'the monkey man' is straight from the blues world. One strategy for surviving the semi-itinerant life was for the male blues singer to attach himself to a sexy woman who could also cook and make money; in effect he would then rent her out to a 'monkey man' – a dupe who would give her money and gifts in the mistaken belief that he alone was her love-object: money that would end up in the

---

175. Robert Johnson: 'I Believe I'll Dust My Broom', San Antonio, 23/11/36; Columbia C-30034.
Stephen Calt writes of the term 'donay' that it is

> A black and Southern white variant of 'dona', a 19th century slang term for woman associated with Cockney and British circus slang . . . from respectful Italian, Spanish or Portuguese terms for 'lady'. [The standard English words 'dame' and 'prima donna' both derive from the same source.] . . . In Southern white song, it occurs as early as 1910, when 'Doney Gal' was collected by John Lomax [a song Bob Dylan was taped singing on the May 1960 St. Paul, Minnesota, tape]. It also occurred in a slave song, 'Off From Richmond', cited by [Thomas W.] Talley in [*Negro Folk Rhymes*, in] 1922 . . . Although Son House defined 'donie' as 'a no-good woman,' it had no pejorative implication.

[Stephen Calt: 'Idioms of Robert Johnson', 78 *Quarterly*, no. 4, 1989.]
Johnson's record was made on his first day in the studio (except for the 'vanity disc' or demo he made in Memphis in 1931–32, which is not thought extant) and it seems likely he picked his title-line up wholesale from a record released earlier that year, Kokomo Arnold's 'I'll Be Up Someday' [NYC, 18/2/36], in which is to be heard 'And I believe, I believe I'll dust my broom / So some of you low-down rounders, you can have my room'. This Arnold recording itself owes something to Arnold's own earlier 'Milk Cow Blues', as discussed elsewhere in the context of 'Dylan's' 'Quit Your Low-Down Ways'.
Pinning down the Elmore James 'Dust My Broom' details is not easy. Greil Marcus: 'As Peter Guralnick has written, Elmore James took Robert Johnson's 'Dust My Broom' and made a career out of it.' He recorded 'Dust My Broom' so many times that there's general confusion as to which is, as it were, *the* version. Charlie Gillett says perhaps the best is the 1953 'Dust My Blues' for Meteor: but the version called 'Dust My Blues' dates from 1955, not 1953. Marcus says James didn't record till 1953, while Mark Cooper, reviewing the "Immortal Elmore James" CD, 1992, says (presumably retailing the sleeve notes) 1952, and that he first cut 'Dust My Broom' then. Neither is right. James' début session, with Sonny Boy Williamson II on harmonica, began with *a* classic cut of 'Dust My Broom (I Believe My Time Ain't Long)', Jackson, Mississippi, Aug. 1951. This is the version that climbed the *Billboard* R&B charts and therefore most influenced the black community. This was on the small Trumpet label, after which the Bihari Brothers poached him and he made a version cut in Chicago c. Oct. 1952 for their Meteor label under the title 'I Believe' (as in 'I believe I'll dust my broom'). James re-recorded it as 'Dust My Broom' again in 1959 and again as 'I Believe' in New York City in 1962–63. [Elmore James: 'Dust My Broom (I Believe My Time Ain't Long)'; "Jewel Spotlights The Blues Vol. 1", Jewel Records LP 5015, 1973. 'I Believe'; "Underground Blues", 1969, Kent LP 535 / "The Legend of Elmore James", Kent LP 9001, *nia*. 'Dust My Blues', New Orleans, 1955; "20 Greatest Blues Hits", Kent LP 527, *nia*. 'Dust My Broom', Chicago, Nov. 1959; this may be Fire FLP-102, NYC, 1960. 'I Believe', NYC, 1962–3; "History of Elmore James Vol. 1", Trip Records TLX8007, Chicago, 1971. "The Immortal Elmore James", Music Club MC CD 083, *nia*, 1992 (taken from the 1959–63 period on Bobby Robinson's Fire label, with sax and rhythm-section). Greil Marcus, *Mystery Train* (1975); Charlie Gillett, *The Sound of the City* (1971); Mark Cooper, *Q* Magazine (1992).

176. Ethel Waters: 'There'll Be Some Changes Made', Chicago, c. Aug 1921; "'Oh Daddy!' Ethel Waters", Biograph BLP-12022, New York, 1970. Some of this – the idea of the sea-change but not the introductory 'change in the weather' – reappears in the Mexican duo Val & Pete's 'Yodel Blues Part 1', as 'There's a change in the ocean, in the deep blue sea . . . / That sweet mama don' come back, you'll see a change in me'. [San Antonio, 14/3/28; CD-reissued "White Country Blues (1926–1938)", Columbia Legacy Roots N' Blues 472886 2, New York, 1993.]

bluesman's pocket. The monkey man is thus a common character in blues songs, and a figure about whom these songs express mixed feelings, since he is at once both dupe and sexual rival. Son House said that the young Robert Johnson was a monkey man, though Johnson's own lyrics hardly suggest this. Skip James defined a monkey man as someone 'always grateful to touch the hem of a woman's garment'. He appears on record at least as early as 1924, in Ida Cox's wonderfully titled 'Wild Women Don't Have The Blues', and he makes a later appearance when Barbecue Bob says he's 'got what it takes to make a monkey-man leave his home' in the equally vividly titled 'Chocolate To The Bone' (the poetic force of which Dylan does his best to counteract on 'Yonder Comes Sin', with the surgical knife of 'her skin may be a different color than mine / but her blood is red and her bones are white').[177] We find the monkey man lurking too in the second couplet of Blind Lemon Jefferson's 'Teddy Bear Blues', with its 'I'm going to make my stop in Italy, where the monkey-man don't belong'; in Curley Weaver's 1950 'Trixie', his revisit to the whorehouse song 'Tricks Aint Walkin' No More', in which he invokes 'Two fat women laying in the shade / Waiting on the money the monkey-man made'; and in songs by Charley Patton, Charley Lincoln (Barbecue Bob's brother, though they had quite separate careers), Jake Jones, Blanche Calloway, Kid Bailey, Lonnie Coleman, Blind Boy Fuller, Papa Charlie Jackson, and Carl Martin.[178]

177. Ida Cox: 'Wild Women Don't Have The Blues', Chicago, c. Aug 1924; "Great Blues Singers", Joker Records SM-3098, Milan, 1978. Barbecue Bob: 'Chocolate To The Bone', Atlanta, 13/4/28; "Barbecue Bob. Masters Of The Blues, Vol. 10", Collector's Classics CC-36, Copenhagen, 1971.

Ida Cox (1896/1889–1967), one of F.S. Wolcott's Rabbit Foot minstrels, worked in such shows, including one of her own (the Raising' Cain Company), for more than half a century, and was one of the earliest recorded blues singers. She wrote many songs, including one about the graveyard with the wonderful title 'Bone Orchard Blues'. Indeed she seems to have been obsessed with the grave: her other recordings include 'Graveyard Dream Blues' (recorded at two sessions in 1923, the first several months ahead of its being recorded by Bessie Smith, after which it was covered by many a lesser female singer), 'Graveyard Bound Blues', 'Cold Black Ground Blues', 'Coffin Blues' and 'Marble Stone Blues'. Paul Oliver quotes a lyric of hers (without identifying its title), 'I'm goin' where the weather suits my clothes / Down where there ain't no snow and the chilly winds don't blow', which is, oddly, reminiscent of both Dinah Shore's 1949 hit 'Buttons & Bows' (the first line) and somehow of Bob Dylan's writing (the second). 'Buttons & Bows' [in UK Columbia Records DB 2446, London, 1949] includes 'I'm going where the climate suits my clothes . . . And I'm all yours in buttons and bows'. Cox continued to tour through the 1940s and into the 1950s but cut just one post-war session (NYC, April 1961), with Coleman Hawkins playing trumpet for her.

[Ida Cox: 'Bone Orchard Blues', Chicago, c. July 1928; 'Graveyard Dream Blues', Chicago, June 1923 and October 1923; 'Graveyard Bound Blues', NYC, late January 1925; 'Cold Black Ground Blues', Chicago, April 1925; 'Coffin Blues', Chicago, September 1925, and 'Marble Stone Blues', Chicago, c. August 1928. First vinyl issue was the 8-track LP "Ida Cox Sings The Blues", Riverside RLP 1019, New York [London Records AL 3517, London], 1953. The nine-song 'come-back' session, NYC, 11–12/4/61, issued "Blues For Rampart Street", Riverside RMP 374, New York, c. 1961. 'Graveyard Dream Blues' was also recorded by at least the following: Bessie Smith, NYC, 26/9/23; Mattie Hite (with Coleman Hawkins again), NYC, c. mid-Nov. 1923; Sara Martin, NYC, 11/10/23; Hazel Meyers, NYC, 1/10/23, and Josie Miles, NYC, 26/10/23.]

178. Blind Lemon Jefferson: 'Teddy Bear Blues', Chicago, c. June 1927; "Blind Lemon Jefferson, Volume Two", Milestone Records MLP-2007, New York, 1968. Curley Weaver: 'Trixie', Atlanta, 1950; "Blind Boy Fuller On Down – Vol.2", Saydisc SDR168, Badminton UK, c. 1970. Charley Patton: 'Love My Stuff', New York, 31/1/34; "Mississippi Bottom Blues", Mamlish S-3802, New York, probably 1973. Charley Lincoln: 'Hard Luck Blues', Atlanta, 4/11/27; "Rare Blues, 1927–1935", Historical Records HLP-4, Jersey City, NJ, c. 1967. Jake Jones: 'Monkeyin' Around', Dallas, c. Oct 1929; "Rare Blues Of The Twenties", Historical Records HLP-2, Jersey City, NJ, c. 1966. Blanche Calloway: 'Lazy Woman's Blues', Chicago, 9/11/25; "Louis Armstrong: The Blues Singers. Masters of the Blues, Vol. 8", Collector's Classics CC-32, Copenhagen, c. 1971. Kid Bailey: 'Rowdy Blues', Memphis, c. 25/9/29; "The Mississippi Blues 1927–1940", Origin Jazz Library OJL-5, Berkeley, c. 1967. Lonnie Coleman: 'Wild About My Loving', Atlanta, 12/4/29; "The East Coast States (Georgia-Carolinas-Virginia)", Roots RL-318, Vienna, c. 1968. Blind Boy Fuller: 'Pistol Snapper Blues', New York, 5/4/38; "Blind Boy Fuller with Sonny Terry and Bull City Red", Blues Classics BC-11, 1966. Papa Charlie Jackson: 'The Cat's Got The Measles', Chicago, c. Jan 1925; "Papa Charlie Jackson, 1925–1928", Biograph BLP-12042, Canaan, New York, 1972

The phrase is so widespread that many titles use it. Songs called 'Monkey Man Blues' have been recorded by Sara Martin, the Richmond Jazz Quartet, Peg Leg Howell, Minnie Hicks and Cripple Clarence Lofton, the more specific 'Chicago Monkey Man Blues' by Ida Cox and the still more explicit 'Get Yourself A Monkey Man, Make Him Strut His Stuff', cut by Butterbeans And Susie and by Viola McCoy. By extension, or by reversal, the woman who was spending her time and money on keeping a wandering man could call herself a 'monkey woman', as in Sara Martin's 1925 title 'What More Can A Monkey Woman Do?'.[179]

'Open the door, Richard', a line Bob Dylan uses repeatedly in his Basement Tapes song 'Open The Door, Homer', is taken straight from an R&B novelty item first recorded in the 1940s, revived in the 1950s by Ernie Barton & Billy Lee Riley (the latter one of Dylan's favourite rockabilly singers and the composer of some decent blues himself) and in the 1960s by Pigmeat Markham (1964) and Bill Doggett (1965). Hence Bob Dylan's chorus line, 'Open the door, Richard – I've heard it said before'.[180]

(Jackson was the first black folk artist to be recorded, and, like Gus Cannon, played the banjo, not the more flexible and thus blues-suited guitar). Carl Martin: 'Farewell To You Baby', Chicago, 8/1/35; "Guitar Wizards (1926–1935)",Yazoo L-1016, New York, 1969.

179. Sara Martin: 'Monkey Man Blues', NYC, c. 27/4/23. Richmond Jazz Quartet: 'Monkey Man Blues', Long Island, New York, c. Dec. 1928. Peg Leg Howell: 'Monkey Man Blues', Atlanta, 13/4/29. Minnie Hicks: 'Monkey Man Blues', Grafton, Wisconsin, c. Sept. 1930. Cripple Clarence Lofton: 'Monkey Man Blues', Chicago, 2/4/35; "Favourite Country Blues-Guitar Duets",Yazoo L-1015, New York, 1969; Ida Cox: 'Chicago Monkey Man Blues', Chicago, c. March 1924. Butterbeans And Susie: 'Get Yourself A Monkey Man, Make Him Strut His Stuff', NYC, c. 27/5/24, re-recorded as 'Get Yourself A Monkey Man (And Make Him Strutt His Stuff)' [sic], NYC, 21/2/29. Viola McCoy: 'Get Yourself A Monkey Man, Make Him Strut His Stuff', NYC, October 1924. Sara Martin: 'What More Can A Monkey Woman Do?', NYC, 23/11/25.

180. Ernie Barton with Billy Riley: 'Open The Door, Richard', Memphis, 25/2/59; Pigmeat Markham (*nia*, Chess 1891, Chicago, 1964); Bill Doggett (*nia*, 1965).
   Based on a Des Moines vaudeville act catchphrase by Dusty Fletcher (who took it from 1920s comic John 'Spider Bruce' Mason, Mason's lawsuit later claimed), it was written by Jack McVea, first recorded by Jack McVea & His All-Stars [Hollywood, September 1946, Black & White 792, Los Angeles, 1946] and became a huge R&B and pop charts hit of 1947, the catchphrase itself something of a national craze on the back of it. (The record also has a niche in popular music history in being the first with a fade-out ending in its own right.) The record was covered by, and a huge hit on the same two charts for, Count Basie [Los Angeles, 3/1/47; "Count Basie" [EP], RCA Victor EPS 5075, New York, c. 1959], black vocal group the Three Flames [NYC, c. February 1947, Columbia Records 37268, New York, 1947], Dusty Fletcher himself [NYC, 4/1/47, National Records 4012, 1947] and the influential Louis Jordan & His Tympany Five [Los Angeles, 23/1/47, US Decca 23841, New York, 1947], plus other pop chart hit versions, 'answer records' and more.
   [Detail on 'Open The Door, Richard' from *What Was the First Rock'N'Roll Record?* by Jim Dawson and Steve Propes, 1992 – but their source was 'Opening the door on Richard' by Tony Burke and Dave Penny, *Blues & Rhythm*, no. 17, March 1985.]
   Dylan sang Billy Lee Riley's 'Repossession Blues' in rehearsal for the 1978 tour in Santa Monica (1/2/78) and subsequently twice in concert (Osaka, 24/2/78, and Tokyo, 28/2/78), and performed Riley's 'Rock With Me Baby' at six US concerts in 1986. Riley, a country singer from Arkansas, wanted to be a blues singer but ended up in Memphis doing rockabilly for Sam Phillips at Sun. (He cut his blues sides, including 'Repossession Blues', under the pseudonym Lightnin' Leon.) He was a session-man and multi-instrumentalist (quite good on bluesy harmonica); Jerry Lee and Charlie Rich played piano on Riley's records, the best-known being his 1957 title (as by Billy Lee Riley and his Little Green Men) 'Flyin' Saucers Rock'n'Roll' (Memphis, 11/12/56 [with Jerry Lee], Sun Records 260, Memphis, January 1957; reissued "The Sun Story 1952–1968", Sun Records 6641 180, London, 1974).
   Riley is the man who had the gumption to turn on the tape-recorder when Sam Phillips and fundamentalist Bible-study boy Jerry Lee were discussing the evils of secular music at the session that later yielded 'Great Balls Of Fire' (issued "Good Rocking Tonight", Bopcat Records LP-100, Dutch bootleg, 1970s), and was a guest artist at Elvis and Priscilla Presley's New Year's Eve party at the Thunderbird Lounge, Memphis, 1968. Dylan brought Riley on as a guest at his concert in Riley's hometown of Little Rock, Arkansas, 8/9/92; he was introduced fulsomely by Dylan, who stayed on stage to play back-up guitar as Riley sang 'Red Hot'. Riley went on from this heartening evening's encounter to re-activate his own performing career.
   [The Billy Lee Riley 2-CD set "Classic Recordings 1956–1960, Including The Complete Sun Recordings", Bear Family BCD 15444-BH, Vollersode, Germany, c. 1990.]

Another catch-phrase, if you will – a phrase not limited to African–American song but found within it, at least in the worlds of jazz and R&B – is 'keep on keeping on', and Dylan does something particularly neat with it, while using it verbatim, inside 'Tangled Up In Blue'. Count Basie's motto was 'We gotta keep on keeping on'. Way back at Woodstock, in 1969, we hear the Band singing 'gonna keep on keeping on' inside 'Don't Do It (Don't You Break My Heart)'. But one of the memorable moments from 'Tangled Up In Blue' is deepened and enriched by the overlaying upon its inherent nobility, its dignified seriousness, of the bonus of a joke: a joke only possible because it rests on Dylan's alluding to another song from one of the genres that the blues spawned, soul music. Dylan's 'keep on keeping on' came pre-owned, to use a rag-trade phrase, from Junior Walker & The All-Stars' record 'Road Runner', written by Holland–Dozier–Holland:

> *I'm a road runner, baby*
> *Got to keep on keeping on.*

The deft if incidental joke of Dylan's re-write:

> *The only thing I knew how to do was keep on keeping on*
> *Like a bird that flew*
> *Tangled up in blue –*

is of course that the road runner, as immortalised in the cartoon series, *is* 'a bird that flew'. Indeed, he is celebrated as a hero for exactly that supernatural fleet-footedness so admired in the heroes of the black ballads.[181]

The same Dylan album draws on a sort of pre-soul record too. 'If You See Her, Say Hello' takes off from the starting-blocks of jazz singer Betty Carter who, with the Ray Bryant Orchestra, made the smouldering 'Tell Him I Said Hello', a record that would have been on the radio when Dylan was about 15 years old. Its lyric includes 'When you see him . . . tell him I said hello', 'Don't say yes or no' and 'things are slow', plus a phrase Dylan has thrown into live performances of his own song, 'come and go'. Indeed things do.[182]

There are tantalising cemetery-kicks of resonance swirling in the echoey sounds of 'Nobody 'Cept You' ("Bootleg Series I–III", 1991), where Dylan, as in 'Rank Strangers To Me', returns to a former home to find himself a stranger:

> *Used to play in the cemetery*
> *Dance and sing and run when I was a child*
> *And it never seemed strange*
> *But now I just pass mournfully by*
> *That place where the bones of life are piled . . .*
> *I'm a stranger here and no-one sees me.*

'I'm a stranger here' is a traditional song phrase, which in the blues occurs in many songs, including Blind Lemon Jefferson's 'Stocking Feet Blues', Willie Baker's 'No No

181. Count Basie: 'We gotta keep on keeping on', *nia*. The Band: Woodstock, 18/8/69: 'Don't Do It (Don't You Break My Heart)'. Junior Walker & The All-Stars: 'Road Runner', *nia*; Soul Records 35015, Detroit [Tamala Motown TMG559, London], 1966. The *Road Runner* cartoon series, Warner Bros., USA, devised by Chuck Jones, *nia*.

182. Betty Carter: 'Tell Him I Said Hello', USA, 13/5/55; "Social Call", Columbia JC 36425, New York, *nia*.

Blues' and Walter Vincson & The Mississippi Sheiks' 'Lonely One In This Town' ('Because I'm a stranger here, everybody turned their back on me').[183] In the later Dylan song 'Dignity' (from the "Oh Mercy" sessions, New Orleans, 1989), the narrator no longer gazes upon the friendly cemetery of childhood but upon the valley of death. The lovely line 'in the valley of dry-bone dreams' alludes to, and does not better, one wonderful sound-bumping line from that creative blues artist Arthur Crudup: 'I went down in Death Valley, among the tombstones and dry bones' – a line that Dylan might have written and been admired for; both return us to that 'place where the bones of life are piled'.[184]

Another "Planet Waves" non-blues song, 'Tough Mama', addresses its subject first by noting the 'meat shakin' on your bones': again not a quirky Dylanism but a verbatim quotation of blues idiom used widely – not least by Blind Lemon Jefferson in his 'Deceitful Brownskin Woman' ('Lord it's heavy-hipped mama and the meat shakes on the bone'), by Bo Chatman in 'Ants In My Pants' ('You're a red-hot mama, meat shakes on the bone') and by the great Tommy Johnson in his 'Big Fat Mama Blues'. Blind Boy Fuller has a song about *his* tough mama, and he calls her his 'Meat Shakin' Woman'.[185]

In 'Tough Mama' the narrator also asks if he can 'blow a little smoke on you?' This too borrows a phrase that recurs in blues songs, but transforms its meaning. In Dylan's line, it's the narrator who will blow a little dope-smoke on you; in the old blues songs it is the train that steals your lover away that will also blow its smoke on you, adding insult to injury: 'Take your last rider Lord, blow black smoke on you' (Ishman Bracey); 'done stole my man away, and blowed back dark smoke on me' (Memphis Minnie); 'It done taken your faro, blowed its smoke on you' (Tommy Johnson).[186]

On 'One Too Many Mornings', Dylan's distinctly delivered insistence that his restless hungry feeling 'don't mean no one no good' echoes Kokomo Arnold's 'Old Black Cat Blues' where 'this black cat blues mama, don't mean no one no good'. Another Kokomo Arnold song includes 'Now I could cut your throat mama, and drink your blood like wine'. This may be passing along another common-stock expression – when it is taken up in Dylan's 'Memphis Blues Again', where he shifts it

183. Blind Lemon Jefferson: 'Stocking Feet Blues', Chicago, c. October 1926; "Blind Lemon Jefferson: Black Snake Moan", Milestone MLP-2013, New York, 1970. Willie Baker: 'No No Blues', Richmond, Indiana, 9/1/29; "Country Blues Classics, Volume 1", Blues Classics BC-5, Berkeley, 1965. Walter Vincson & The Mississippi Sheiks: 'Lonely One In This Town', Shreveport, Louisiana, 17/2/30; "The Country Fiddlers", Roots RL-316, Vienna, 1968.

184. Arthur Crudup: 'Death Valley Blues', Chicago, 11/9/41, see note 59; two months later Washboard Sam recorded his 'Evil Blues' [Chicago, 4/11/41; "Feeling Lowdown: Washboard Sam", RCA LPV-577, New York, 1971], which uses some of the same lines but less poetically, ending with: 'Down in old Death Valley, tombstones and old dry bones / These old evil blues keep followin' me, Death Valley going to be my home'. (The Crudup 78 rpm record, which is further discussed in Chapter 16, was one of the few that Muddy Waters owned back in his shack on Stovall's Plantation when Alan Lomax visited him in the early 1940s, Lomax reports in *The Land Where the Blues Began*.)

185. Blind Lemon Jefferson: 'Deceitful Brownskin Woman', Chicago, c. October 1927; "Master Of The Blues: Blind Lemon Jefferson, Vol.2", Biograph BLP-12015, New York, 1969. Bo Chatman: 'Ants In My Pants', New York, 5/6/31; "Rare Blues, 1927–1930", Historical Records HLP-5, Jersey City, New Jersey, c. 1967. Tommy Johnson: 'Big Fat Mama Blues', Memphis, 31/8/28; "The Famous 1928 Tommy Johnson–Ishman Bracey Session", Roots RL-330, Vienna, 1970. Blind Boy Fuller: 'Meat Shakin' Woman', NYC, 6/4/38.

186. Ishman Bracey: 'Left Alone Blues', Memphis, 4/2/28; Roots RL-330, *ibid*. Memphis Minnie: 'Chickasaw Train Blues': Chicago, 24/8/34; "Out Came The Blues", Coral CP-58, London, 1970. Tommy Johnson: 'Cool Drink Of Water Blues', 3/2/28; "Country Blues Encores 1927–1935", OJL-8, Berkeley, c. 1963.

from an image of individual violence to one that sums up, with apt exaggeration, the menace the railroad men held in the communal imagination of the hobo poor ('She said that all the railroad men just drink up your blood like wine'), he hasn't had to shift it far. As noted in Chapter 5, Dylan has taken Mona's lurid warning straight from Bascom Lamar Lunsford's bluesy 'I Wish I Was A Mole In The Ground', a cavalcade of common-stock lines in which 'a railroad man, he'll kill you when he can and drink up your blood like wine'.[187]

When Dylan locates imagined future bleakness in the wind blowing through 'the piney wood', on 1985's sorry pop-song 'I'll Remember You', he is calling up a blues-world location. (In fact three of the echoes just looked at come together in another Blind Lemon Jefferson song, 'Piney Woods Money Mama', which in one couplet unites those 'piney woods', that 'don't mean no one no good' phrasing and the residue of that meat shaking on the bone:

> Lord heavy-hipped mama she done moved to the piney woods
> She's a high-stepping mama and she don't mean no man no good.)[188]

In 1981's 'Caribbean Wind' (issued on "Biograph", 1985), the auguries of 'the tearin' down of the walls' include Robert Johnson's 'hellhound' being loose, while, outside the narrator's window, the

> Street band playing 'Nearer My God To Thee'

is not only an allusion to the meaning-loaded *event* of the sinking of the *Titanic*, that historic frozen moment of disaster still vivid in the popular imagination, but to the group of blues songs that arose to express it decades before Dylan first uses its symbolic clout himself in the 1965 'Desolation Row' – a group of songs that includes Hi Henry Brown's 'Titanic Blues':

> Titanic sinking in the deep blue sea
> And the band all playing 'Nearer My God To Thee.'[189]

187. Kokomo Arnold: 'Old Black Cat Blues', Chicago, 15/1/35; "Kokomo Arnold. Masters Of The Blues, Vol. 4", Collector's Classics CC-25, c. 1970 and 'Slop Jar Blues', Chicago, 5/2/35; "Kokomo Arnold", Saydisc Matchbox Blues Series SDR-163, Badminton, UK, 1969.
   Bascom Lamar Lunsford: 'I Wish I Was A Mole In The Ground', Atlanta, 15/3/24, and Ashland, Kentucky, 6/2/28. The 1924 recording was never LP-issued, but the 1928 is one of the tracks on the Harry Smith compilation "American Folk Music". For details of the same line's reappearance on 'Roll On Buddy' by Jack Elliott and Derroll Adams, see Chapter 5, note 33.
188. Blind Lemon Jefferson: 'Piney Woods Money Mama', Chicago, c. March 1928; "The Immortal Blind Lemon Jefferson", Milestone MLP-2004, New York, 1967. On a later Jefferson song ['Bed Spring Blues', Richmond, Indiana, 24/9/29; "The Party Blues" (!) Melodeon Records MLP-7324, Washington, DC, 1966] the singer comes out explicitly with the switch that had always been hovering implicitly as to whose meat is shaking, the heavy-hipped tough mama's or the uneasy male narrator's: 'When she grabs you and turns you loose, makes the flesh tremble on your bones.'
189. Hi Henry Brown: 'Titanic Blues', New York, 14/3/32; "St. Louis Blues, 1929–1935: The Depression", Yazoo L-1030, New York, 1972. The clutch of such songs reflected African–American delight at the sinking of the *Titanic*, because it signified whitey's come-uppance, pride coming before a fall, and so on. This feeling, however, was not restricted to black Americans. The Russian symbolist poet Alexander Blok wrote: 'The sinking of the Titanic has made me indescribably happy; there is, after all, an ocean.' (Quoted in Peter Vansittart, *Voices 1870–1914* [1984].) Note 15 in Chapter 4 gives a summary of the facts of the sinking itself.
   The same Hi Henry Brown session also yielded his ferocious 'Preacher Blues' (same album), which demonstrates a rich strand of rural blues culture, the hostility to the local priest, who is seen as a parasite and predator, a sneak and a cheat. It is in many blues recordings, notably Madlyn Davis' 'Too Black Bad', Chicago,

Impending doom is also glimpsed for a moment in the generally optimistic 'God Knows', again called up by direct quotation, this time of a line from the traditional song 'Hold On', a blues version of which Dylan sang as 'Gospel Plow' on his first album. The line, which sums up the contrast spoken of in the Second Epistle General of Peter between the day of Creation and the coming day of Judgement, is 'No more water but fire next time'.[190]

On "Street Legal", within which Dylan seems to cut a wrist to mingle his own workblood with that of Robert Johnson – though in every case, as with 'them ridin' blinds', Johnson is not the only presence on this busy street – he tends again to put the direct blues phrases into his non-blues songs. A line from 'Changing Of The Guards' that arguably sums up that song is 'my last deal gone down'; this is an elision from Johnson's title 'Last Fair Deal Gone Down', itself a version of a much older song.[191] In 'Where Are You Tonight? (Journey Through Dark Heat)', 'horseplay and disease are killing me by degrees'; in Johnson's 'Preachin' Blues' it is *the blues itself* which is 'a low-down achin' heart disease / Like consumption, killing me by degrees', though this is but a variation on a widely mobilised pair of lines, on any of which Bob Dylan's might be drawing. The 'killing me by degrees' formulation occurs (and earlier) on Ishman Bracey's ''Fore Day Blues' (mislabelled as 'Four Day Blues' when first issued), recorded in 1928, on which

> . . . the blues ain't nothin' but a slow-killin' heart disease
> . . . sure kill you by degrees.

On Jimmie Rodgers' 'Blue Yodel No.12', recorded one week before his last session (which was thirty-six hours before his death from tuberculosis), he sings:

> Since my mama's gone I got that achin' heart disease
> It works just like a cancer, it's going to kill me by degrees;

while fractured into single lines the same formulation runs through work by Kokomo Arnold, Sleepy John Estes, Georgia White and Son House. 'Yes these blues, mama, ain't nothin' but a doggone heart disease', Kokomo Arnold sings on his 1935 record 'Old Black Cat Blues (Jinx Blues)'; 'The blues ain't nothin' but a lowdown heart disease' features prominently in Georgia White's 1938 'The Blues Ain't Nothin' But . . .'; the pay-off line in Sleepy John Estes' 'Milk Cow Blues' (a wholly different song, and recorded six and a half years before Robert Johnson's version of the

---

c. October 1928; "Tampa Red: Bottleneck Guitar, 1928–1937", Yazoo L-1039, New York, 1973, and the excellent 'You Shall [Be Free]' by Frank Stokes, Chicago, c. August 1927; "Frank Stokes With Dan Sane And Will Batts (1927–1929)", Roots RL-308, Vienna, 1968 (cut again the following month: the later take is on "Mississippi & Beale Street Sheiks, 1927–1932", Biograph BLP-12041, Canaan, NY, 1972): a song that clearly prefigures Dylan's 'I Shall Be Free'. There seem to be residues of this blues anti-clericalism in two 1983 Dylan songs: in 'Man of Peace', with its 'Could be the Führer / Could be the local priest', and in 'Jokerman''s 'rifleman's stalking the sick and the lame, / Preacherman seeks the same, who'll get there first is uncertain'.

190. Bert Cartwright ('The Bible in the lyrics of Bob Dylan 1985–1990', *Telegraph*, no. 38, Spring 1991) notes that this line paraphrases the words of 'a gospel song, 'The Rainbow Sign', sung by Dylan's female trio during his 1979 tour'.

191. 'The only one of Johnson's recordings that might have typified his early repertoire was 'Last Fair Deal Gone Down', a 16-bar 'rag' ditty Henry Thomas had recorded as 'Red River Blues''. ('Robert Johnson' by Stephen Calt and Gayle Dean Wardlow, *78 Quarterly*, no. 4, 1989.)
  Robert Johnson: 'Last Fair Deal Gone Down' [2 takes], San Antonio, 27/11/36; Columbia CL-1654.

standard song of that title) is 'Now it's a slow consumption, an' it's killin' you by degrees'; and 'The Jinx Blues Part One', one of Son House's 1941–42 Library of Congress tracks, rages like this against the dying of delight:

> *You know these blues ain't nothin but a low-down shakin', low-down shakin', achin' chill*
> *I said the blues is a low-down old achin' chill*
> *Well if you ain't had 'em honey I hope you never will*
>
> *Them blues, them blues is a worryin' heart, worryin' heart, heart disease*
> *Just like a woman you be lovin', man, it's so doggone hard to please.*[192]

(It's typical of Son House that he should expand the lyric with these long, erupting, erratic surges of repetition. It's one of the ways in which he and Robert Johnson are comparable stylists. In fact of all those, well-known and not, who had some influence upon Johnson, Son House looms largest and closest behind. Another vocal effect House employs time and again, yet always effectively and without ever quite losing its element of surprise, is in *not* repeating or approximating the whole of the first line of a verse as the second line, but instead beginning that second line with an 'mmm-mmm-mmm' and then repeating only the end portion of the first line, which often has a different resonance when divorced from its other half. Though he's by no means alone in doing it, this inspired, intelligent word-conjuring is one of the things that makes Son House great. He has a way, too, of using common-stock formulations yet always making his songs sound like works in progress, and he has a rare expressive intensity: he's one of the great originals, though behind him in turn looms the formidable shadow of Charley Patton, who also expands his lyrics with 'long, erupting, erratic surges of repetition'.)

The same non-blues Dylan song that gives us that 'disease . . . killing me by degrees' formulation also gives us 'he should have stayed where his money was green', a phrase he might well be picking up from, or at least have been reminded of its existence by, Johnson's song 'Little Queen of Spades', whose eighth line runs 'Let's put we/us heads together, ooh fair brown then we can make our money green'. But there is also, as noted elsewhere, 'jack of diamonds will turn your money green' on Bob Campbell's 1934 'Dice's Blues', and our 1928 Furry Lewis song (with a particularly attractive guitar part) 'I Will Turn Your Money Green'[193]

Another line in Dylan's 'journey through dark heat' is this:

192. 'Preachin' Blues' [2 takes], San Antonio, 27/11/36; one on "The Country Blues", RBF Records RF-1, New York, 1959. Ishman Bracey: 'Four Day Blues [sic]' [take 1], Memphis, 31/8/28; "The Famous 1928 Tommy Johnson–Ishman Bracey Session", Roots RL-330, Vienna, 1970. Jimmie Rodgers: 'Blue Yodel No. 12', NYC, 17/5/33; "Jimmie The Kid", RCA Victor Records LPM22123, New York, 1961. Kokomo Arnold: 'Old Black Cat Blues (Jinx Blues)', Chicago, 15/1/35; "Kokomo Arnold: Masters Of The Blues Vol. 4", Collector's Classics CC25, Copenhagen, c. 1970. Georgia White: 'The Blues Ain't Nothin' But . . .', Chicago, 21/10/38; "Out Came The Blues", Coral CP-58, London, 1970. Sleepy John Estes: 'Milk Cow Blues', Memphis, 13/5/30; "The Rural Blues", RBF Records RF-202, New York, 1964. Son House: 'The Jinx Blues Part 1', Robinson, Mississippi 17/7/42; CD-reissued on "Son House: The Complete Library Of Congress Sessions 1941–1942", Travelin' Man Records TM CD 02, Crawley, UK, 1990.

193. Robert Johnson: 'Little Queen of Spades' [2 takes], Dallas, 20/6/37; one on "Masters Of The Blues, 1928–1940", Historical Records HLP-31, Jersey City, NJ, 1969, the other the following year on Columbia C30034. Bob Campbell: 'Dice's Blues', New York, 30/7/34; "Country Blues Obscurities, Vol.2", Roots RL-340, Vienna, c. 1973. Furry Lewis: 'I Will Turn Your Money Green', Memphis, 28/8/28, "Frank Stokes' Dream . . . 1927–1931", Yazoo L-1008, New York, 1968.

I bit into the root of forbidden fruit with the juice running down my leg.

I always thought this was a more or less verbatim quotation from Robert Johnson too, but while it certainly makes sense, granted the context of other Johnson references, that Dylan should be quoting here from Johnson's 'Traveling Riverside Blues', this numinous evocation of sinful sex is built up from a common-stock base. At its plainest, it is here in (not Big) Joe Williams' bluntly titled 'I Want It Awful Bad' (which can be taken in two equally pertinent ways):

You squeezed my lemon, caused my juice to run

which gets developed in the direction of Dylan's line in Charlie Pickett's 'Let Me Squeeze Your Lemon':

Now let me squeeze your lemon baby until my love comes down

and is repeated without significant variation by Bo Chatman's 'Let Me Roll Your Lemon' and Sonny Boy Williamson I's 'Until My Love Comes Down'. Robert Johnson's lyric, almost alone in specifying the *leg*, offers this:

Now you can squeeze my lemon till the juice run down my leg.

The line that takes this theme and squeezes it with the most panache is in the musically agile Cripple Clarence Lofton's 'Monkey Man Blues':

. . . till it done give him the lemon leg.[194]

Another non-blues song on "Street Legal" is 'Is Your Love In Vain?', a title that enfolds within it Johnson's title 'Love In Vain'. But Dylan also seems to have one ear on Sonny Boy Williamson II in 1978. Does the Dylan title carry its echo of Robert Johnson direct, or by relay from Williamson's 'All My Love In Vain' (not the same song), which was cut at the same splendid session as the Williamson song Bob Dylan proved he knew by performing it with The Plugz on US TV in 1984, 'Don't Start Me (To) Talkin'', and which uses the same tune? It could be from either, and so could the echo in that other "Street Legal" title, 'Baby, Stop Crying'. Of course Dylan could have arrived at this without any back-echoes, as it were: it's no big deal as a phrase or as a notion. On the other hand you can't but notice that Robert Johnson's 'Stop Breakin' Down Blues' is a song with several Dylan connections, and that one is its baby-stop-crying imprecation, repeated many times: 'Stop breakin' down, please, stop breakin' down'. Nor can you deny that Sonny Boy Williamson's 'Stop Crying', recorded several times, presses the same plea: 'baby please, please stop crying'.[195]

194. Robert Johnson: 'Traveling Riverside Blues', Dallas, 20/6/37; Columbia CL-1654. Joe Williams: 'I Want It Awful Bad', Memphis, c. 24/9/29; "Great Harmonica Players (1927–1940): Volume 2", Roots RL-321, Vienna, c. 1969. Charlie Pickett: 'Let Me Squeeze Your Lemon', New York, 3/8/37; "The Country Blues: Volume Two", RBF Records RF-9, New York, 1964. Bo Chatman: 'Let Me Roll Your Lemon', New Orleans, 19/1/35; "Bo Carter – Twist It Babe" (1931–1940), Yazoo L-1034, New York, 1973. Sonny Boy Williamson I: 'Until My Love Comes Down', Aurora, Illinois, 13/3/38; "Blues Roots/Mississippi", RBF Records RF-14, New York, 1966. Cripple Clarence Lofton: 'Monkey Man Blues', detailed note 179.

195. Robert Johnson: 'Love In Vain' [2 takes], Dallas, 20/6/37; one on Columbia C30034. This offers one of his most biting, numinous lyrics, but it is grafted unashamedly onto the lovely melody of the prolific Leroy Carr's gorgeous classic 'When The Sun Goes Down' (cut the last day he was ever in a studio, just weeks before his death at 30 – though he sounds far older), a song already locally popular in the late 1920s. Leroy Carr: 'When The Sun

A very different Dylan creation that certainly hides a Robert Johnson line within it, and just where you wouldn't expect one, is in his 1963 'Last Thoughts On Woody Guthrie'. It's a poem almost as far from the blues as you can get; but when you've been listening to a lot of Robert Johnson, and then you hear Dylan reach for the conclusion of this lengthy poem with the simple and anonymous yet insistent, didactic line

And though it's only my opinion, I may be right or wrong

you're bound to hear behind it Johnson's

Baby it's your opinion, oh I may be right or wrong

and

It's your opinion, friend-girl, I may be right or wrong,

which come from the two recordings of Johnson's 'When You Got A Good Friend', one of which was issued on the seminal "Robert Johnson: King Of The Delta Blues Singers" two years before Dylan's performance of his poem.[196]

In 'Up To Me', an out-take from "Blood On The Tracks" released on "Biograph" in 1985, we hear this passage:

The old rounder in the iron mask, he slipped me the master key.
Somebody had to unlock your heart;
He said it was up to me.

Dylan's use of the quaint but useful hillbilly-cum-blues term 'rounder' in this polished, me-me-me singer-songwriterly work is another example of how his blues consciousness shines through in the most unlikely places. (It is typical of Dylan's eclecticism too that he should combine in the same line the blues-world reference to 'rounder' and the nineteenth-century French literary reference to Alexandre Dumas' novel *The Man in the Iron Mask*.)[197]

The 1983 'Sweetheart Like You' has those particularly horrible lines

Goes Down', Chicago, 25/2/35; "The Roots Of Robert Johnson", Yazoo L-1073, NYC, 1986.

Sonny Boy Williamson [II]: 'All My Love In Vain' and 'Don't Start Me To Talkin'', Chicago, 12/8/55; issued together as a 78rpm, Checker 824, Chicago, 1955, and on "Sonny Boy Williamson Sings Down And Out Blues", Chequer LP 1437, Chicago, 1960. Bob Dylan: 'Don't Start Me To Talkin'', NYC, 22/3/84, telecast NBC-TV *Late Night with David Letterman*, New York, 22/3/84.

Robert Johnson: 'Stop Breakin' Down Blues [2 takes], Dallas, 20/6/37; one issued Columbia C30034. Sonny Boy Williamson: 'Stop Crying', Jackson, Mississippi, 4/1/51 and again 10/7/51, both unissued; then Jackson 5/8/51, issued as a 78 rpm on Trumpet 140, Jackson, c. 1951; vinyl-issued "The Original Sonny Boy Williamson", Blues Classics BC-9, Berkeley, c. 1967. Re-recorded for Chess as 'Stop Cryin'', Chicago, 30/4/64; "This Is My Story", Chess 2CH-50027 [2 LPs], New York, 1972.

196. 'When You Got A Good Friend', San Antonio, 23/11/36 [2 takes]; one take issued Columbia CL-1654.

197. The related expression 'I'm on my last go-round' shows so well how style is inseparable from content that it is poetry in notion: its idea is expressed with such direct simplicity that it's very poignant, but far too robust to be sentimental. Like 'rounder', it belongs to the black and white folk culture of pre-war America (it's used in songs by, for instance, Jimmie Rodgers, Roosevelt Sykes and Bo Carter). There is no equivalent in 'literary' or mainstream culture, though God knows it's easy enough to identify with.

The Man in the Iron Mask was the fifth and final volume in Dumas père's series *The D'Artagnan Romances*, which had begun with *The Three Musketeers*. Dumas died at his son's house in 1870. Dumas fils survived into the age of the Paris avant-garde, and invented that apt term for one of its social groups, 'le demi-monde'.

You know, a woman like you should be at home
That's where you belong
Takin' care of somebody nice
Who don't know how to do you wrong,

the last line of which *Lyrics 1962–1985* amends slightly to

Who would never do you wrong.

If these lines had been written in the 1930s rather than the 1980s, they would be less combatively unpleasant. And actually they more or less were written in the 1930s, where they appear in a gem of pre-war white country blues, Carlisle & Ball's 'I Want A Good Woman', recorded in 1931. It opens:

I want a good woman to love me all day long . . .
One who will stay at home an' will never do me no wrong.[198]

On the ponderous, musically monotonous 'Something's Burning, Baby', a song that on the record and the page seems like Dylan on Mogadon, two of the more mysterious, compelling lines come right at the end: in fact in consecutive lines in the middle of the last verse, which runs:

Something is burning, baby, something's in flames
There's a man going 'round calling names
Ring down when you're ready, baby, I'm waiting for you
I believe in the impossible, you know that I do.

What do those middle lines mean? It might be that the blues milieu shines some light on them. What gives the 'man going 'round calling names' several layers of sinister resonance? First, it has behind it the not-quite-parallel invocation of a man going round *taking* names, which implies the figure of the company stoolie, and by extension any kind of thought-police. 'There's A Man Going Round Taking Names' is a song Paul Robeson and others sing.[199] The communal understanding, from childhood on up, is that you don't tell on people to the authorities: you don't name names. Within this understanding too is a recognition that discretion may be the better part of such valour: that it can be dangerous for the namer as well as for the named. And as Chinua Achebe writes in *Things Fall Apart*, his 1958 classic novel of Nigerian village life: 'Dangerous animals became even more sinister and uncanny in the dark. A snake was never called by its name at night, because it would hear. It was called a string.'

All this is given widespread expression in the blues using the very idiom Dylan employs. In speech it occurs as for example when Muddy Waters, in an interview, is

198. Carlisle & Ball [i.e. Cliff Carlisle and Wilbur Ball]: 'I Want A Good Woman', NYC, 27/10/31; CD-issued "White Country Blues 1926–1938, A Lighter Shade Of Blue", Columbia Legacy Roots N' Blues Series 472886 2, New York, 1993.

199. Paul Robeson: 'Dere's A Man Goin' Roun' Takin' Names', 1937, CD-issued "Paul Robeson Favourite Songs Vol. 1", Monitor Records MCD-61580, Mount Vernon, NY, 1993. Joshua White: 'There's A Man Goin' Around Taking Names', NYC, 13/11/33. Mary Ray: 'A Man Going Round Taking Names', Library of Congress field-recorded around Darien, Georgia, some time around 1926–28. Gertrude Smartts & Minnie Swearingen: 'There's A Man Goin' Round Takin' Names', LC field-recorded Washington, DC, 13/5/38.

reluctant to name someone who has done him down and says: 'I wouldn't call the name. I ain't gonna call the name.'[200]

In song, of course, calling a name can have several meanings, including the unsinister ('If you need me, call my name / I'll come a-runnin', like a choo-choo train', for instance, as Fats Domino has it); but included too is the meaning we're exploring. Furry Lewis sings 'I got a woman in Chicago, I'm scared to call her name'; Tommy McClennan sings 'Crazy about a married woman, afraid to call her name'; and Memphis Minnie sings 'That's the man, he's scared to call his name'. In Dylan's own song 'Outlaw Blues', from twenty years before 'Something's Burning, Baby', the narrator has 'a woman in Jackson / I ain't gonna say her name'.[201]

Second, the 'man going round calling names' calls up the clerk of the court calling up the accused to receive sentence, and the many other contexts in which when you're named – when your number's up – your time is up. This sense is yielded in the blues by Frank Edwards's 'Uncle Sam called the men down, name by name', and Robert Wilkins's 'Oh he's coming to call us boys, name by name'.[202]

Third, and related to all of this, stored in a deeper catacomb of memory, there is the old folk belief that the saying aloud of your name weakens you, or binds you, perhaps fatally. In the old ballads, when the hero is engaged in combat, it's when the woman calls out his name that he gets stabbed. As this nudges to the surface in Big Joe Williams' 'Please Don't Go' (not the same song as his earlier 'Baby Please Don't Go'), it comes up as 'Don't call my name, don't call my name, don't call my name / You got me way down here wearin' that ball and chain'.[203]

Then in Dylan's next line, where 'call' is transmuted to 'ring' (interchangeable words in the context of the telephone) what's compelling is the word '*down*': 'ring down' implies 'from up above', which is to say from heaven, yet 'baby' is too familiar a form of address to be directed at God, even for Dylan. Is the song addressing someone who has died? Was it a funeral pyre right in front of his eyes?

At any rate, 'ring down when you're ready, baby, I'm waiting for you', a line that is strange because of this telephone-from-heaven image, is made the more so by its being achieved so much by what's implied and not by what's stated. But the fact is that it is not a vague image alone in the world of song but one that echoes blues and gospel songs that have gone before it. In context, Dylan's line is not strange at all. In 1927, Papa Harvey Hull & Long Cleve Reed recorded 'Hey! Lawdy Mama – The France Blues', which assembled many traditional song fragments and collided them, several of which reappear in Bob Dylan's repertoire down the years – the song includes 'Have you ever took a trip, baby on the Mobile Line?', 'Well there's two black horses,

200. *Living Blues*, March–April 1984.

201. Fats Domino: 'If You Need Me', New Orleans, July 1953, Imperial Records EP 143, LA, 1956; CD-reissued "The Imperial Singles Vol. 2, 1953–1956", Ace Records CHD 649, London, 1997. Furry Lewis: 'Mistreatin' Mama', Memphis, 28/8/28; "Memphis Blues (1927–1939)", Roots RL-323, Vienna, c. 1969. Tommy McClennan: 'I'm A Guitar King', Chicago, 15/9/41; "The Country Blues", RBF Records RF-1, New York, 1959. Memphis Minnie: 'Squat It', Chicago, 10/9/34; "Memphis Blues (1927–1939), Vol.2", Roots RL-329, Vienna, c. 1970.

202. Frank Edwards: 'We Got To Get Together', Chicago, 28/5/41; "Country Blues Classics, Volume 2", Blues Classics BC-6, Berkeley, 1965. Robert Wilkins: 'Nashville Stonewall Blues', Memphis, February 1930; "The Memphis Area, 1927–1932", Roots RL-307, Vienna, 1968.

203. Big Joe Williams: 'Please Don't Go', Chicago, 12/12/41; "Big Joe Williams: Crawling King Snake", RCA International INT-1087, London, 1970.

standing on the burial ground', and this black variant of the traditional cowboy song 'I'm A-Ridin' Old Paint' (cited elsewhere in this book): 'Baby when I die, don't bury daddy at all / Well pickle daddy's bones, baby, in alcohol'. But it also includes this remarkable couplet:

> *Hello heaven, daddy want to give you a telephone*
> *So you can talk to your daddy any time when he's gone.*[204]

In gospel music, however, there's nothing so remarkable about this conceit at all. The same year that gave us 'The France Blues' also offered the Rev. Sister Mary Nelson's 'The Royal Telephone', recalled and recorded nearly forty years later for the Library of Congress by Mississippi John Hurt; in 1929 came Blind Roosevelt Graves' recording of 'Telephone To Glory'. (These telephone-to-heaven images were not restricted to black performance. In the early 1950s Hank Snow cut the religious song 'I Just Telephone Upstairs'.[205])

One of the most remarkable uses of this image occurs in a 'Negro Spiritual' text called 'Tone The Bell Easy', which is a version of one of the songs from Bob Dylan's first album, 'In My Time Of Dyin'', more usually called 'Jesus Make Up My Dyin' Bed' and associated with Charley Patton, Blind Willie Johnson and many gospel groups. The chorus of the 'Tone The Bell Easy' text runs 'Well well well / Tone the bell easy' (repeated twice) 'Jesus gonna make up my dyin' bed', the second verse brings in Mary and Martha (as 'Ring Them Bells' does, of course) and then, in amongst this timeless scene, verse eight picks up the telephone:

> *Ever since me and Jesus been married*
> *We haven't been a minute apart*
> *He put the receiver in my hand*
> *And the Holy Ghost in my heart*
> *Well well well, so I can call up Jesus . . .*

This is all part of what seems to me a rather naff kind of standard God-bothering rhetoric – part of the familiar recruiting ploy of 'it's-hip-to-be-Christian-cos-we're-jolly-modern'. 'Telephone To Glory', and the still more gruesome 'Ain't Gonna Lay My Receiver Down', are all of a piece with preposterous songs like 'Jesus Is My Air-O-Plane' by Mother McCollum (1930). Yet it isn't only Christians who go in for this sort of thing. In Martyrs Square, Damascus, a black bronze colonnade offers a massive and splendidly pompous commemoration of the opening of the Middle East's first telegraph link: a hot-line from Damascus to Medina, home of the one true God's prophet Mohammed. The colonnade rises twenty feet above its tall plinth, festooned in sculpted wires and loops of sculpted cable, topped by a model of a mosque. There

204. Papa Harvey Hull & Long Cleve Reed: 'Hey! Lawdy Mama – The France Blues', see note 23.

205. Rev. Sister Mary M. Nelson: 'The Royal Telephone', Chicago, 25/2/27 [and possibly NY, 21/4/27]; CD-reissued "Memphis Gospel: Complete Recorded Works (1927–1929)", Document Records DOCD-5072, Vienna, c. 1991. Mississippi John Hurt: 'Royal Telephone', Washington, DC, 23/7/63, unissued. Blind Roosevelt Graves and Brother [Uaroy Graves]: 'Telephone To Glory', Richmond, Indiana, 20/9/29. This song was also cut as 'I'm Going To Telephone To Glory' by, for example, The Heavenly Gospel Singers, Charlotte, North Carolina, 13/2/36.

   Hank Snow: 'I Just Telephone Upstairs', *nia*; CD-reissued "The Singing Ranger – I'm Movin' On'" [4-CD set], Bear Family BCD 15426-DH, Vollersode, Germany, c. 1990.

is, then, something about telegraphy that excites the religious imagination East and West alike.

In the end, its plausibility is all in the fine-tuning of words. There's nothing risible about 'People get ready, there's a train a-coming', or 'This Train Is Bound For Glory', or "Slow Train Coming", yet a title like 'Life's Railway To Heaven' invites immediate mockery. (This song was recorded in the 1920s by the extraordinarily named black artist Hermes Zimmerman.)[206]

The splendid 'big police', in the third verse of 'When I Paint My Masterpiece', comes from the blues too. We hear it in the third verse of Curley Weaver's 'Sweet Patunia', in which 'Early one morning about half past four / A big police was knockin' on my door', recorded in 1928; a year later the same couplet recurs on the Will Shade–Minnie Wallace song 'Dirty Butter' (Minnie Wallace's début recording).[207]

Another Dylanism that turns out not to be Dylan at all but Dylan directly quoting idiom used in the blues (in this case in songs by three different old country blues artists and at least two of the post-war Chicago bluesmen) is this, from 'Ballad Of Frankie Lee And Judas Priest':

> He began to make his midnight creep.

Blind Lemon Jefferson sings, in 1928, 'and he's always in his midnight creep'; Alice Moore sings, in 1929, 'I'm so black and evil that I might make a midnight creep'; and Lil Green sings, in 1940, of 'Watching my baby make that midnight creep'. The first verse of Howlin' Wolf's 1960 'Back Door Man' starts

> When ever'body's tryin' t' sleep
> I'm somewhere makin' my midnight creep

and the expression is reprised in, yes, 1962's 'Tail Dragger'.

> The mighty wolf makin' his midnight creep

---

206. 'Tone The Bell Easy' text taken (I have de-minstrelised it) from *The Treasury of Negro Spirituals*, ed. H. A. Chambers, 1964.

   Mitchell's Christian Singers: 'Ain't Gonna Lay My Receiver Down', NYC, 28/12/38. Mother McCollum: 'Jesus Is My Air-O-Plane', Chicago, c. mid-June 1930; CD-reissued "Guitar Evangelists: Complete Recorded Works (1928–1951)", Document Records DOCD-5101, Vienna, c. 1989. Hermes Zimmerman (no relation): 'Life's Railway To Heaven', probably NYC, c. April 1926; probably vinyl-unissued.

   Gospel songs, and records of hotshot preachers' sermons with accompaniments by their congregations, provide many entertaining titles, including these: 'Christ Was Born On Christmas Morn' (Cotton Top Mountain Sanctified Singers, Chicago, 29/8/29; 'Hell Is God's Chain Gang' (Deacon W. H. Gallamore, Atlanta, 11/4/29); 'Smoking Woman In The Street' (Rev. J. M. Gates, Atlanta, 23/8/39); 'The Black Camel Of Death' (Rev. J. M. Milton, Atlanta, 5/11/29); 'The Fat Life Will Bring You Down' (Rev. A.W. Nix, Chicago, mid-Jan. 1930); 'Straining At A Gnat And Swallowing A Camel' (Rev. J. M. Gates again, Atlanta, 18/3/29); 'Must I Be Carried To The Sky On Flowered Beds Of Ease' (Leadbelly, field-recorded for the Library of Congress in Washington, DC, 23/8/40); and, from the Rev. Emmett Dickinson And His Congregation, NYC, 10/10/31, 'He Came To Town Riding On His Ass'.

207. Curley Weaver: 'Sweet Patunia', Atlanta, 26/10/28; "I'm Wild About My Lovin', 1928–1930", Historical Records HLP-32, Jersey City, NJ, 1969. Minnie Wallace: 'Dirty Butter', Memphis, 23/9/29; "Memphis Blues 1928–1930" (double-LP), RCA/Ariola Jazz Tribune NL 89276, West Germany, 1984. (In the whole Taft corpus, all other 'Early one morning's continue with 'about the break of day': Curley Weaver's is the only one to vary this and be more specific. Dylan of course creates his own variant after the traditional 'Early one morning' that begins his 'Tangled Up In Blue'.)

is how the first verse opens. While Dylan's usage maximises the vividness of the phrase, Little Walter's tedious classic 'My Babe' as surely drains it away. I seem to have known this song all my life but had never heeded that it includes 'She don't stand none o' that midnight creepin''.[208]

Yet another such 'Dylanism' is his idiosyncratic use of 'positively' and 'absolutely', not in the flaccid, Kinnockian sense but as in 'Positively 4th Street' and 'Absolutely Sweet Marie'. The latter never held the sense of 'Marie-is-absolutely-sweet' as in 'Oh darling, it's absolutely spiffing' but instead worked the same way as '[you're so] Positively 4th Street' does, as '[she's so] absolutely sweet-Marie'.

I used to think these were Dylanesque inventions, at the very least his surreal extensions of a manner of speech appropriated by the camp – as in 'Oh yes, very Lana Turner' or 'very James Dean'. They seemed quintessentially Dylan in amphetamine-truth-attack mode. They turn out to be Dylan picking up, because delighting in, language from a very different genre, not young-hip-white-New-York-on-speed-circa-1965–66 but black New Orleans circa 1936, which is when Eurreal Little Brother Montgomery was singing, in 'Never Go Wrong Blues',

> *And she would be absolutely hospital bound*

– or even black New York circa 1928, which is when Victoria Spivey was singing, in 'My Handy Man', of being

> *Positively absolutely blind.*[209]

Sometimes even when the suggestion of a parallel turns out not to be one, it can at least illuminate the use of a metaphor. There may be nothing specific in 'Parchman Farm', or Son House's 'County Farm Blues', or 'Tim Moore's Farm' (an old field-hand's song Peter Narváez calls 'one of the few genuine protest-songs in the blues') that gives Dylan 'Maggie's Farm' on a plate, but just as it is a country-blues consciousness on Dylan's part that has him write the line 'When your rooster crows at the break of dawn' at the dawn of 'Don't Think Twice, It's All Right' – how many Suze Rotollos had roosters outside their New York City windows?: as Dylan says himself, in an LP liner-note poem, 'The rooster never crowed on MacDougal Street' – so too it is a country-blues consciousness more than an Orwellian one that has him,

208. Blind Lemon Jefferson: 'Competition Bed Blues', Chicago, c. July 1928; "Blind Lemon Jefferson: Volume 2", Roots RL-306, Vienna, 1968. Jefferson's 'Lock Step Blues' [Chicago, c. August 1928; "The Immortal Blind Lemon Jefferson", Milestone MLP-2004, New York, 1967] includes the less vivid 'I used to take my feet in a midnight tramp'.

Alice Moore: 'Black and Evil Blues', Richmond, Indiana, 16/8/29; "Gut Bucket Trombone: Ike Rodgers. Masters Of The Blues, Vol. 11", Collector's Classics CC-37, Copenhagen, 1971, and 'Black Evil Blues', Chicago, 18/8/34; "The Blues In St. Louis, 1929–1937", Origin Jazz Library OJL-20, Berkeley, c. 1968. Lil Green: 'Just Rockin'', Chicago, 9/5/40; "Lil Green: Romance In The Dark", RCA LPV-574, New York, 1971. Howlin' Wolf: 'Back Door Man', Chicago, June, 1960, "Howlin' Wolf", Chess LP-1469, Chicago, 1962, and 'Tail Dragger', Chicago, Sept. 1962, "Howlin' Wolf – The Real Folk Blues", Chess LP-1502, Chicago, 1966. Little Walter: 'My Babe', Chicago, 25/1/55, Checker Records 811, Chicago, 1955.

209. Eurreal Little Brother Montgomery: 'Never Go Wrong Blues', New Orleans, 16/10/36; "Little Brother Montgomery. Masters of the Blues, Vol. 9", Collector's Classics CC-35, Copenhagen, 1971. Victoria Spivey: 'My Handy Man', New York, 12/9/28; "Blues Singers: Jazz Sounds Of The 20's", Swaggie Records S-1240, Victoria, Australia, 1962.

in his city-hip period, alight on the symbol of the *farm* as a location of oppression. (County farms were prisons on which you served your sentence working the land.)[210] 'Shot Of Love' has a neighbouring blues-world touch about it too:

> *Don't need a shot of turpentine, only bring me to my knees.*

Who else in the 1980s would write of the once important but long-since redundant commodity 'turpentine' but Bob Dylan? It's another example of his carrying blues-world consciousness around with him so thoroughgoingly that it injects itself into his writing everywhere. Turpentine was a life-threatening drink of desperation during Prohibition, and its production one kind of industrial work among poor blacks in the 1920s and 1930s. Furry Lewis has a line in his 'Big Chief Blues', cut in 1927, that shows at once why the word makes it into the list of what Dylan doesn't need a shot of: Lewis sings of 'carbolic in my coffee, turpentine in my tea'. Eighteen-year-old Memphis Jug Band member Will Weldon's first solo track was 'Turpentine Blues', recorded within a fortnight of the Furry Lewis session, and it ends 'What you gonna do, boy, when your troubles get like mine? / Take you a mouthful of sugar and drink a bottle of turpentine'. Tampa Red recorded his own 'Turpentine Blues' four-and-a-half years later. Some of the Library of Congress field-recordings were made at a turpentine camp: in fact 'one of the Willie Browns', to quote a phrase, the male singer Willie Mae Brown, was field-recorded singing an unaccompanied 'Turpentine Blues' at the Aycock & Lindsey Turpentine Camp at Cross City, Florida in 1939, and so was another turps worker, David Wood. One James Byrd was recorded there too, as were the Dixie Harmony Four. A decade earlier, Pigmeat Pete and Catjuice Charlie (Wesley Wilson and Harry McDaniels) cut a side called 'On Our Turpentine Farm' on a visit to New York City in October 1929 (an interesting time to be there).[211]

Yet Dylan's analogy between the drug/alcohol 'shot' and 'a shot of love' is so concerned at the time to be the Christian equivalent of politically correct that he must

---

210. Son House: 'County Farm Blues', Robinsonville, Massachusetts, 17/7/42; "Son House And J. D. Short: Blues From The Mississippi Delta", Folkways FA2467, New York, 1960s. (This song adapts Blind Lemon Jefferson's 'See That My Grave Is Kept Clean', detailed note 228.) Lightnin' Hopkins: 'Tim Moore's Farm (Tom Moore Blues)', Houston, 1948; "Fast Life Woman", Dart LP 8000, Houston, early 1960s; CD-reissued "The Gold Star Sessions Vol. 1", Arhoolie Records CD 330, El Cerrito, California, c. 1991.

Peter Narváez: comment to the present writer, in St Johns, Newfoundland, autumn, 1985. Bob Dylan: sleeve note poem for Peter, Paul & Mary's LP "In The Wind", Warner Bros. Records WS1507, New York, 1963.

Surely the very term 'field-recording' locates the blues singer down on the farm – and the folklorist/collector too. Reviewed in the pages of *Sing Out!* in 1965 was Kenneth S. Goldstein's *A Guide for Fieldworkers in Folklore*. Ah, tote that barge, lift that bale . . . Another example, along similar lines, is John Lomax's more self-consciously titled 1947 book *Adventures of a Ballad Hunter*.

(Field-researchers were not of course restricted to those hunting for songs for the Library of Congress. Others were engaged, for example, on a project of the National Park Service, the Historic American Buildings Survey, which amassed over 500 photographs and over 100 scale drawings of slave dwellings and workplaces. These have been drawn on for, and some reproduced in, John Michael Vlach's *Back of the Big House: The Architecture of Plantation Slavery*, 1993.)

211. Furry Lewis: 'Big Chief Blues', Chicago, 9/10/27; "10 Years In Memphis: 1927–1937", Yazoo L-1002, NYC, 1968. Will Weldon: 'Turpentine Blues', Atlanta, 20/10/27; "Frank Stokes' Dream: Memphis Blues 1927–1931", Yazoo L-1008, NYC, 1968. Tampa Red: 'Turpentine Blues', Chicago, 7/5/32; CD-issued "Legends Of The Blues Vol. II", Columbia Roots N' Blues 468770 2/4, NYC, c. 1991.

Willie Mae Brown: 'Turpentine Blues', Cross City, Florida, 18/8/39. David Wood: 'Turpentine Blues' [and another song], Cross City, Florida, 19/8/39. James Byrd: 'Joe Maws, Witches And Haunts' [3 versions], Cross City, Florida, 19/8/39. Dixie Harmony Four: 'Poor Stranger Blues' [2 takes], same details. Pigmeat Pete and Catjuice Charlie: 'On Our Turpentine Farm': NYC, 7/10/29.

leave it bereft of both its sexual power and its druggy allure. In spectacular contrast, on both counts, is 'Think You Need A Shot' by Walter Davis, which, though his shyly countrified delivery undersells it, and his beautiful piano-work distracts, is one of the raunchiest lyrics in the language:

> You got bad blood mama: I believe you need a shot
> Now turn over here mama: let me see what else you got
>
> I doctors on women: I don't fool around with men
> Alright take it easy here mama while I stick my needle in
>
> Lord your ways is so loving and your skin is nice and soft
> Lord if you keep on drunk mama you going to make me break my needle off
>
> Lord my needle is in you baby and you seem to feel all right
> And when your medicine go to coming down: I want you to hug me tight
>
> Yeah your medicine come now baby: put your [foot, leg] up side the wall
> I don't want to waste none of it mama: I want you to have it all.[212]

Walter Davis might also be said to hover around Bob Dylan's consciousness in that he uses the phrase 'Don't The Clouds Look Lonesome?' as a song title, while another of his titles offers the beguiling 'I Like The Way You Spread Your Wings', encapsulating a pun along the same lines as Dylan's 'You angel you, you got me under your wing', though Davis' is erotic rather than cosy.[213]

And what else but deeply ingrained familiarity with the great body of blues lyric poetry on Dylan's part could explain the way that there is that occasional flashing moment in the old blues corpus where a line jumps out at the listener (or reader, as the eye drifts across the pages of Taft) which, though it may correspond to nothing Dylan has actually written or sung, strikes home nonetheless as *very Dylanesque stuff*? Here are just a few, starting with a couplet that, remarkably, combines two Dylan styles – its first line sounding like something from *Tarantula* and the second straight out of 'Brownsville Girl':

> . . . they call him spongy boy
> But that ain't his name, his name is plain Leroy.

Then there's

> I'm scared to bother round her house at night
> Got a police-dog, craving for a fight

---

212. Walter Davis: 'Think You Need A Shot', Chicago, 3/4/36; "Think You Need A Shot", RCA International INT-1085, London 1970. The song was covered by the lesser-known Jimmie Gordon, Chicago, 18/1/37, and re-recorded by Brownie McGhee as 'Bad Blood', NYC, 1952; "Home Town Blues", Mainstream Records LP 56049, USA, 1974.
   Davis was a vocalist/pianist from Grenada, Mississippi, who spent his life based in St Louis, though he travelled frequently. He made a huge number of recordings and worked with many other artists, including Big Joe Williams. He was *the* favourite singer of Muddy Waters, when the 29-year-old Waters was 'discovered', by Alan Lomax, still living 'in a brown four-room shack in the middle of a cotton field' on a Mississippi plantation in the summer of 1941. (Alan Lomax, *The Land Where the Blues Began*.)

213. Walter Davis: 'Don't The Clouds Look Lonesome?', Chicago, 31/10/35; 'I Like The Way You Spread Your Wings', Aurora, Illinois, 19/12/38. For a discussion of Walter Davis train songs in relation to Blind Willie McTell and Bob Dylan, see Chapter 18.

> *His name is Rambler, and when he gets a chance*
> *He leaves his mark on ev'ybody's pants*

and

> *My brain is cloudy, my soul is upside down*

while this is certainly attuned to Dylan in drug-vividly surreal, mid-1960s truth-attack mode:

> *. . . your hair is so short, swear to God I can smell your brain!*

and finally there's the one mention of mirrors in the entire corpus, which is contained in this very Dylanesque couplet:

> *There's a man in town who's called the ladies' lover now,*
> *Keeps his pockets full of mirrors . . .*[214]

It remains now to stress that this is dangerous territory to be too definite about. Not only is there a vast amount of this now-subterranean blues lyric poetry, too much for any one person to know, but as I hope to have shown, it is in the nature of this 'treasury of poetics', as Allen Ginsberg calls it, that communality and democracy of invention will tend to grow wider and richer than the inventions of the individual genius–poet.[215] Every time you hear something you think this lone person or that has imagined into being, beware: the likelihood is that it has been handed on down instead, like some strange mutating baton in a circuitous back-roads relay race.

And even when you think you know this, the task of relating this whole old blues world to the work of one 'individual genius–poet' is bound to trip you up. I found this out the hard way in the course of the study above. I was considering Dylan's 'New Pony', and it seemed to be going all right, and I finished my two pages or so of close-to-the-text comparative word scrutiny, and it went like this:

> Dylan's creative alertness in these matters is extraordinary: such fusion of heart
> and intellect, such artistic instinct. Consider the resourceful, informed brilliance of
> a small thing he brings off in the "Street Legal" blues 'New Pony'. This takes up
> an imagery that is saddled to a series of older songs:

---

214. Respectively these are taken from the following: Lil Green: 'My Mellow Man', Chicago, 21/1/41; "Lil Green: Romance In The Dark", RCA LPV-574, New York, 1971. Blind Blake: 'Police Dog Blues', Richmond, Indiana, 17/8/29; "The Georgia Blues", Yazoo L-1012, New York, 1968. Lonnie Johnson: 'Devil's Got The Blues', New York, 31/3/38; "The Blues Of Lonnie Johnson", Swaggie Records [Jazz Makers series], S-1225, Victoria, Australia, 1969. Kid Stormy Weather: 'Short Hair Blues', Jackson, Mississippi, 17/10/35; "Country Blues Classics, Volume 3", Blues Classics BC-7, Berkeley, 1966. Mamie Smith: 'Jenny's Ball', New York, 19/2/31; "Blues Singers: Jazz Sounds Of The 20's", Swaggie S-1240 [Jazz Masters series], Victoria, Australia, 1962.

215. 'I had some kind of American Blues in my heart without knowing it – I could sing but didn't reckon it important poetically, until I met Krishna & remembered Ezra Pound's ken that poetry & music, song & chant (and dance) went together before the invention of the printing press and long after – forgotten by the same academies that forgot that the genre of American Black Blues & rags was as great a treasury of poetics as Bishop Percy's "Reliques" & Scottish Border Ballads & Elizabethan song books & Tom O'Bedlam folk treasuries.' Allen Ginsberg: 'Explanation of first blues', *First Blues, Rags, Ballads and Harmonium Songs 1971–74* (1975).

> *I got a new pony, she knows how to fox-trot, lope and pace . . .*
> *She got great big hind legs*
> *And long black shaggy hair above her face.*

Arthur Crudup's 'Black Pony Blues' includes these:

> *I got a coal-black mare but Lord how that horse can run . . .*
> *Say she fox-trot and pace, and I rode that horse today . . .*
> *She's a coal-black mare, she's got long black curly mane*[216]

Actually there are two small creative touches by Dylan here. First, he takes what is the common-stock phrase '(you/she) got great big legs', which is used in direct reference to women (usually as a term of approbation) in blues by many, many people from Blind Boy Fuller ('Got great big legs and a little bitty feet') and Leroy Carr to Walter Roland and Charlie Bozo Nickerson – and he transfers it, uniquely, to the pony image.[217] He does something similar on his marvellous blues 'Cat's In The Well': 'bumpety-bump' may come from nursery rhyme and counting-song, but "Under The Red Sky" is founded as strongly in the blues world as in this child-centred folksong, and the blues corpus too offers 'bumpety-bump'. Dylan transfers it from man to horse. An Ed Bell blues of 1930 declares that 'A short stubble man go bumpety-bump / Because he ain't got the movements in his hump'.[218] In Dylan's song 'the horse is going bumpety-bump'.

Second – and this is the admirable, quiet achievement – while the pony image itself appears earlier than in the Crudup song – in Charley Patton's 'Pony Blues' and 'Stone Pony Blues' and in Big Joe Williams' 'My Grey Pony' – 'fox-trot' and 'pace' occur only in the Arthur Crudup variant and 'lope' occurs in none of these. *Its* deft insertion inside the Dylan lines reveals how alert he is to the fundamentals of blues topography. He hasn't plucked it out of nowhere, nor at random: for 'lope' is the very verb Blind Lemon Jefferson introduces to the blues when introducing the blues themselves, in the grandly leisured opening to his early 'Long Lonesome Blues' – and the sly simile he hitches to it shows how inspired is Dylan's appropriation:

> *Well the blues come to Texas loping like a mule.*[219]

216. Arthur Crudup: 'Black Pony Blues', Chicago, 11/9/41; "Bluebird Blues" RCA LPV-518 [Vintage Series], New York, 1965.

217. Blind Boy Fuller: 'Piccolo Rag', NYC, 5/4/38; "Blind Boy Fuller with Sonny Terry and Bull City Red", Blues Classics BC-11, Berkeley, 1966. Leroy Carr: 'Bo Bo Stomp', NYC, 16/8/34; "Blues Before Sunrise: Leroy Carr, Piano And Vocal", Columbia 30496, New York, c. 1965. Walter Roland: 'Big Mama', NYC, 2/8/34; "Piano Blues", RBF FR-12, New York, 1966. Charlie Bozo Nickerson (and the Memphis Jug Band): 'Got A Letter From My Darlin', Memphis, 26/11/30; "Memphis Jug Band: Volume 2 (1927–1934)", Roots RL-337, Vienna, c. 1973.

218. Ed Bell: 'Carry It Right Back Home', Atlanta, 4/12/30; "Alabama Country Blues (1924–1933)", Roots RL-325, Vienna, c. 1970.

219. Charley Patton: 'Pony Blues', Richmond, Indiana, 14/6/29, and 'Stone Pony Blues', NYC, 30/1/34, both on "Charley Patton: Founder Of The Delta Blues" [2-LPs], Yazoo L-1020, New York, 1970. Big Joe Williams: 'My Grey Pony', Chicago, 25/2/35; "Blues Roots / Mississippi", RBF Records RF-14, New York, 1966. Blind Lemon Jefferson: 'Long Lonesome Blues', Chicago, c. March 1926; "Blind Lemon Jefferson, 1926–1929", Biograph BLP-12000, New York, 1968. Blind Lemon Jefferson also uses the line "The blues came to [sic] Texas loping like a mule" in 'Got The Blues', Chicago, c. March 1926; "King Of The Country Blues", Yazoo Records L-1069 [double-LP], 1984.

The line 'The blues came from [sic] Texas loping like a mule' was also revived in the 1960s by Josh White,

That was it. The only trouble is, all that part about Dylan's brilliant insertion of 'lope' is completely wrong. I had it all written up and weaved into the rest of this text when I was looking back through very early issues of the *Telegraph* fanzine and suddenly found French correspondent Serge Mirronneau giving the following information apropos of Dylan's 'New Pony':

> Son House met Charley Patton in 1930. They played together and Patton recommended Son House to Paramount Records in the spring of 1930. Son House was rediscovered in the 1960s, and appeared at the Newport Folk Festival in 1964, where he performed [Patton's] 'Pony Blues' with new lyrics . . . One verse goes:
>
> > *Well the horse that I'm ridin', he can foxtrot,*
> > *He can lope and pace, lope and pace*[220] . . .

. . . And I'd just written *that* up when I played a newly acquired CD of the wonderful, powerful, moody Son House field-recordings of 1941–2, made between his early sides and the performances of the 'revival' years – and on 'The Pony Blues' this time around he's already singing '. . . he can fox-trot, lope and pace . . . he can fox-trot, lope and pace'.[221]

My mistakes in this matter are an object lesson: they serve to emphasise the communality, the open-endedness and the multi-layered nature of the blues – the very things Michael Taft is concerned to address in the preface to his concordance *Blues Lyric Poetry*.

---

with the asset of a fine performance by Sonny Boy Williamson II on harmonica, on the song 'The Blues Came From Texas', Chicago, 4/1/63; "In The Beginning", Mercury Records LP 20724, Chicago, 1963.

220. Serge Mirronneau, *Telegraph*, no. 7, August 1982. He is quoting Son House's version as it appears on the double-album "Great Bluesmen At Newport", Vanguard VSD 77–78, France, *nia* [in USA Vanguard 77/78, New York, 1976].

The label Paramount, mentioned by Mirroneau, was one of the earliest. The first to make records were furniture manufacturers: they made records to help sell record-players, which were pieces of furniture. Extraordinarily, in 1985 the collector Mike Kirsling found 42 Paramount test-pressings in the roof of a house in Illinois, and more left out in the snow. (As he took them home he prayed 'Please God don't let them be by white singers!': some were, some weren't.) Among them – it's almost too good to be true – was a Son House recording of 'Walking Blues' from 1930 – indeed, recorded the same day as his 'My Black Mama' – a record not known to have existed. This confirmed the song as an item in House's repertoire at least six years before Robert Johnson recorded it, though on this occasion he doesn't include the 'ride the blinds' couplet discussed in note 20. [Son House: 'Walking Blues', Grafton, Wisconsin, 28/5/30, unissued; first issued "Delta Blues 1929–1930", Document DLP 532, Vienna, 1988.]

For the discovery story see Bob Hilbert: 'Paramounts in the belfry', *78 Quarterly*, no. 4, 1989.

221. Son House: 'The Pony Blues', Robinsonville, Mississippi, 17/7/42; CD-reissued "Son House: The Complete Library of Congress Sessions 1941–1942", Travelin' Man Records TM CD 02, Crawley, UK, 1990.

"Son House: Father of the Delta Blues: The Complete 1965 Sessions", NYC, April 1965 (produced by John Hammond), Roots N' Blues Masters series, Columbia Legacy 4716622, New York, 1992 [2-CD set], has none of the power of his earlier work, but includes an exquisite, pathos-loaded rendition of House's 'Pearline' and is interesting for re-recordings of, among others, Blind Willie Johnson's 'John The Revelator' and, inevitably, Patton's 'Pony Blues'; this last, released for the first time, has House quite clearly singing the full line 'fox-trot, lope and pace'.

House owes more to Charley Patton than one song. His influence was crucial, and there are other specifics: not least that Patton's 'Screamin' And Hollerin' The Blues' [Richmond, Indiana, 14/6/29] is the influence behind House's 'The Jinx Blues' [Robinsonville, Mississippi, 17/7/42]. In turn, House was one of the great originators, and the looming influence on Robert Johnson and many others. He outlived almost all the rest, including many of his successors; he died in Detroit in 1988, aged 86.

First, he explains the special problems that arise in constructing a folkloric, rather than a literary, concordance: in having an *open-ended* and more or less infinite corpus of work to deal with, instead of a known, finite one – problems, in other words, to do with *defining the text*. These points are developed at some length, so that as the Dylan scholar reads through them, he or she is brought to the core of the divide between a literary and an oral culture and to Bob Dylan's pertinence to these matters as someone who straddles the oral folkloric cultures of the ballads and the blues *and* the literary culture, and who moves his own extraordinary fusion of it all forward into the *new* oral culture – the *non-linear, postmodernist* culture – of Marshall McLuhan's global village; in other words to Bob Dylan's pertinence as an artist who, almost at the very moment of 'going electric', proclaimed the death of the eye (book) and the re-emergence of the mouth (oral noise).

Here, as we touch on matters of concern to contemporary folklorists and issues raised by a book (or, more flexibly, a computer disk) concording *traditional* pre-Second World War songs, lo and behold: what should come hovering close at hand but the *postmodernist* concerns (and the very language) of post-structuralism. For what Neil Corcoran wrote of 'Tangled Up In Blue' is as true of the whole culture of the old blues: 'it refuses the consolations of the finished in favour of a poetics of process, of constant renewal, of performance rather than publication'.[222]

Michael Taft brings these post-structuralist concerns yet closer, as he goes on to stress one overriding point about the structure of blues lyrics and the functioning of the blues as a cultural (oral) form – and as, in making the point, he also explains the fundamental reason for having the concordance in the first place:

> the essence of the blues is the blues couplet. Indeed, the nature of this type of song is such that one might very well define the genre as one big blues composed of a large but finite number of couplets, lines and formulaic phrases; each individual text is but a sub-text of these couplets . . . the concordance reveals formulaic and linguistic repetitions in the corpus.[223]
>
> . . . I came to realize that the blues singers employed a type of formulaic structure in the composition of [the lyrics of] their songs . . . somewhat similar to that of epic singers far removed in space and time from these Afro-American artists . . . I had to re-order or 'deconstruct' lines and phrases . . . the purpose of a concordance is to re-order a text so that the analyst might visualize it in a new way.

From here Taft at once shows how the blues concordance and the concerns of current folklore studies yield special insights into the gist of lit crit post-structuralism

---

222. Neil Corcoran: 'Going barefoot: thinking about Bob Dylan's lyrics', *Telegraph*, no. 27, Summer 1987.

223. These, once revealed, can illuminate the world of which they are so expressive a part in many different ways. From Taft's *Blues Lyric Poetry: A Concordance*, I note the following, for instance: that after 'I', 'you', and the inevitable linking words like 'the', 'my', 'and' and 'a', the next most common word in the whole corpus is 'going'. 'Man' is more frequent than 'woman'; both are more frequent than 'Lord' (though the concordance doesn't include gospel songs). 'Train' is more frequent than 'river' and 'crying', 'night' more frequent than 'day'. 'Can' is more frequent than 'can't', 'good' more frequent than 'bad', but 'head' more frequent than 'heart'. 'Down' is more common than 'up', 'leave' more common than 'stay' but 'stay' more frequent than 'quit'. 'Drinking' and 'working' are equally common.

– so that indeed the blues bring us right back to the door of the apparently blues-indifferent Stephen Scobie, and right back to what interests Aidan Day.

Taft writes: 'in the case of folklore this jumbling of the text also reveals the way the singer and his audience *see* the text' [my emphasis].

This converges directly with what Day says about how we *see* altogether: how our minds give us 'this jumbling of the text' of our past. Taft goes on:

> Because of the formulaic nature of the blues, . . . when a singer sings a phrase or line, both he and his audience recognize that particular part of the song. Perhaps semi-consciously, they compare this specific singing of the phrase with other singings of that phrase and phrases similar to it. In an instant, the singer and his audience compare the way the sung phrase is juxtaposed with others, both in the song being sung and in other songs . . . Thus, every phrase in the blues has the potential of a literary richness far beyond its specific usage in one song.

Taft quotes Pete Welding as having been one of the few to discuss this property of the blues lyric:

> The blues is most accurately seen as a music of re-composition. That is, the creative bluesman is the one who imaginatively handles traditional elements and who, by his realignment of commonplace elements, shocks us with the familiar. He makes the old newly meaningful to us . . . providing the listener with what critic Edmund Wilson described as 'the shock of recognition', a pretty accurate description . . . of the process of re-shaping and re-focusing of traditional forms in which the blues artist engages.[224]

This 'process of re-shaping and re-focusing' was often a very deliberate one on the part of the individual creative bluesman. In *For What Time I Am in this World*, Colin Linden describes visiting Tampa Red in a nursing home on Chicago's South Side: 'He said . . . "When you make records, take some from me and some from everybody else to make it your own way".'[225] And Blind Willie McTell said that when writing 'The Dyin' Crapshooter's Blues' he 'had to steal music from every which way to get it – to get it to fit.'[226]

As Taft adds:

> If one were to illustrate how the audience undergoes this 'shock of recognition', how the mental processes of the listener bring about this shock, one would construct something like a concordance. Each word and each phrase would be lined up against all other words and phrases which are similar to it in all the songs in which the phrase occurred. By looking down a page in the concordance . . . one sees in an instant what must occur for the listener at the moment of 'shock'. Both

224. Pete Welding: 'Big Joe and Sonny Boy: The Shock of Recognition': record notes to "Big Joe Williams and Sonny Boy Williamson", Blues Classics BC-21, Berkeley, 1969.

225. *For What Time I Am in This World*, ed. Bill Usher, 1977.

226. Blind Willie McTell : spoken intro to 'The Dyin' Crapshooter's Blues', Atlanta, September 1956; "Blind Willie McTell: Last Session", Prestige Bluesville 1040, Bergenfield, New Jersey, 1961 [Transatlantic Records, PR1040, London, 1966], CD-reissued Prestige Bluesville Original Blues Classics OBCCD-517-2 (BV-1040), Berkeley, California, 1992.

the singer and his audience automatically re-order and deconstruct the text as it is being sung; that constitutes their method of appreciation and the basis of their understanding of the blues . . . The computer concordance is simply a concrete representation of this intuitive process.[227]

Brilliant stuff! And how well all this relates to Bob Dylan and his achievement – including Pete Welding's description of the creative bluesman's way of working, which so aptly applies to Dylan himself: 'the creative bluesman is the one who imaginatively handles traditional elements and who, by his realignment of commonplace elements, shocks us with the familiar. He makes the old newly meaningful to us.'

In one last illustration of this, consider Dylan's 1970s 'Call Letter Blues', recorded at the "Blood On The Tracks" sessions but left off the album and issued, in the end, on the "Bootleg Series I–III" in the 1990s.

This is the lyric:

> *Well I walked all night long, hearin' them church bells tone*
> *Yes I walked all night long, listenin' to them church bells tone*
> *Either someone needing mercy – might be somethin' I done wrong*
>
> *When your friends come by for you, I don't know what to say*
> *When your friends come by for you, I don't know what to say*
> *I guess I can't face to tell 'em, honey you just went away*
>
> *The children cry for mother, I tell 'em mother took a trip*
> *Well the children cry for mother, I tell 'em mother took a trip*
> *Well I walk on pins and needles – I hope my tongue don't slip*

---

227. Taft adds the observation that this is as relevant to literature as to folklore ('After all, Edmund Wilson was not referring to *folk* literature when he wrote of "shock"'): and goes on to mention 'Current theories of reader-response critics', which is to say one strand of the new criticism of the 1970s, propounded by the likes of Stanley E. Fish (thank God for that 'E.', or we'd mix him up with all those other Stanley Fish) in the nudge toward full-blown post-structuralism.

It may be no surprise that such a study of these 50- to 70-year-old blues as represented by a concordance had to wait until the 1980s, because it had to wait for 'the present state of computer hardware and software', as Taft commented at the time (his is in fact not only the first blues concordance but 'the first published concordance to a body of oral texts and thus the first truly folkloristic concordance'); but it may be a surprise that other, less high-tech studies of this wealth of material have only occurred almost equally recently. Despite the large number of individuals who had already devoted years of attention to the subject – Paul Oliver, Dixon and Godrich, David Evans, Bruce Bastin, Geoff Todd Titon, Peter Guralnick and many more – no academic folklore journal had ever devoted an issue to the blues till the *Southern Folklore Quarterly* (Vol. 42, no. 1) of *1978*! And, for example, no substantial biographical study of Blind Willie McTell was published until David Evans' in the large booklet accompanying the John Edwards Memorial Foundation's album "Atlanta Blues 1933" [JEMF-106, Folklore & Mythology Center, UCLA] in 1979.

Comparatively little such material was published in the 1960s when the reissue albums were first prevalent. And when Paul Oliver first published *The Story of the Blues*, for instance, in 1969, it was thought no photo of Robert Johnson existed. The excellent one – no mere snapshot either – now on the cover of the digitally remastered MC/CD double set "Robert Johnson: The Complete Recordings", Columbia Roots N' Blues series (467246 2.4) was 'discovered' but sat on by putative biographer Mack McCormick in 1971, then in 1973 was acquired and sat on instead (as was the other extant shot, reproduced in the booklet with the same record set) by Stephen C. LaVere, who has, at least for the time being, acquired the copyrights not only on these two photographs but also on Robert Johnson's songs – and by 1991 was already *hundreds of thousands* of dollars the richer as a result. The full scandal of this is examined in Robert Gordon's excellent piece 'The devil's work: the plundering of Robert Johnson' (with research assistance by Tara McAdams) in *LA Weekly*, 5–11 July 1991. Quite apart from the dodginess of LaVere's claim on Johnson's copyright, granted the communal nature of such songs in general, and the many clear specific debts owed by Johnson's songs to specific songs associated with other people, this situation seems laughably unjustifiable on every level from legal nicety to natural justice.

Well I gaze at passing strangers in case I might see you
Yes I gaze at passing strangers in case I might see you
But the sun goes around the heavens, and another day just drives on through

Way out in the distance, I know you're with some other man
Way out in the distance, I know you're with some other man
But that's alright, baby, you know I always understand

Call-girls in the doorway all givin' me the eye
Call-girls in the doorway all givin' me the eye
But my heart's just not in it – I might as well pass right on by

My ears are ringin', ringin' like empty shells
My ears are ringin', ringin' like empty shells
Well it can't be no guitar-player; it must be convent bells.

This is a blues of the highest order: carefully constructed, with real artistic detachment, to create what may be one of the most rawly autobiographical blues songs ever put on record. All through it, there is a tense and multi-layered struggle between a lashing out and a stepping back. It seethes with the vitriol of bitterness, the rage of betrayal, but in the midst of it, the singer fights for, and achieves, moments of wry equilibrium.

This warring of opposites is present everywhere. The neatly structured song may begin and end with bells, but there's slippage and disparity here, from the certainty of 'hearing them church bells' to the uneasy conjecture of 'it must be convent bells'. The song also begins and ends with an either-or. The opening verse's 'Either . . .' starts with the narrator's compassion for a vaguely envisaged 'someone needing', out there, before suddenly turning, with less compassion, on the self. The closing 'either-or' of the song makes strongly contrasting intuitive leaps between the secular, mobile, sexually active associations of that 'guitar-player' and the timeless austerity of those 'convent bells'.

In between, there's the beautiful simplicity of that line in which complete strangers might somehow include the intimately known 'you'. There's the quiet topsy-turvying joke of the narrator's not responding to the call-girls because his 'heart's just not in it' – the heart being, after all, exactly what *isn't* involved, on either side, in such exchanges. There are the conflicts between all these people in their different roles: the woman at the centre who is absent friend, absent mother, absent lover; the man who is the lover walking all night long, ears ringing 'like empty shells', the social diplomat handling the unknowingly intrusive enquiries of those 'friends', and the protective father.

Given this savage pull between the fury of betrayal and the galvanising of inner strength, it is a deft touch, psychologically right, that the song contains one of Dylan's characteristic bumpings together of two clichés, to produce out of the clash between them something new: furious duty walks a razor's edge on the surreally painful, black-humorously vivid 'I walk on pins and needles – I hope my tongue don't slip'. In the same verse, there is the equal deftness of that ambiguous 'I tell 'em mother took a trip', which lets us hear the attempted reassurance offered to the children that their mother is only temporarily absent, and at the same time gives us the very different message that he feels her 'trip' is into a kind of madness, of aberrational abandonment;

and Dylan's vocal delivery, unstoppering all the narrator's raw fury the first time he hits that word 'trip', vividly brings to life the bitter ambiguity of this pun. And then, topping this with a further truth, he uses the opportunity afforded by the song's blues structure to re-sing this same line as if in a wholly different mood, this time not in fury but resignedly, more mindful of the part of him that is the adult guardian than the part which is the spurned child–man.

It has always been a strength arising out of this 'limitation' of the form, in the hands of its best practitioners, to effect a change of feeling across the repeated line. When, here, Dylan traces this particular shift of feeling, he is also enacting precisely what the blues as a form can achieve at all times, since it is not a music for making people angry and miserable but for engendering resilience against anger and misery.

In achieving this complex surging of feeling, Dylan draws on the blues form itself yet more deeply. Its very familiarity, its commonality of language, woven in among those parts of the lyric that are Dylan's alone, allow him to allude to other blues, and other songs of his own, and so to bring into play other voices in the tumult, other reverberations. The upshot is that 'Call Letter Blues' demonstrates beautifully how 'the shocks of recognition', always within reach in the blues, can be activated – in this case many times over – not only as random soundings in the deep pool of the listener's subconscious but also consciously, to specific, pointed effect.

Consider how one or two of these work, starting with a case where the resonance from a familiarity in the lyric can only be *un*conscious. It is impossible, now, to hear that 'I gaze at passing strangers' followed by those 'call-girls in the doorway . . . I might as well pass right on by' without hearing the echo, from underneath, of lines Bob Dylan didn't write until six or seven years later: the lines from 'Every Grain Of Sand' in which, he sings, 'I gaze into the doorway of temptation's angry flame / And every time I pass that way I always hear my name'. This echo, unstriven for but par for the course, has the effect of emphasising as you listen to 'Call Letter Blues' that aspect of the narrator's plight common to both songs, which is the bleak gulf between him and the night world he finds himself wandering, and between the distraction of temptation and the real quest for passion lost or to be worked for.

The most striking echo from other work of Dylan's comes from that 'Way out in the distance', which jangles with the presence of 'Way out in the wilderness a cold coyote calls', from 'The Ballad Of Hollis Brown', and 'Outside in the distance a wildcat did growl', from 'All Along The Watchtower'. The effect is that behind the 'Call Letter Blues' line – 'Way out in the distance I know you're with some other man' – we feel that Hollis Brown bleakness, we feel that wind begin to howl, and the singer's attitude to that 'some other man' is coloured in for us by the parallel conjured out of the earlier songs – the parallel of the predator:

> *Way out in the wilderness a cold coyote calls*
> *Outside in the distance a wildcat did growl*
> *Way out in the distance I know you're with some other man.*

We set it down on paper one line after the other, but as the 'shock of recognition' works, it all comes through at once, the echoes of the older lines deepening the meaning and resonance of the line being sung.

Different echoes, that might arise consciously and unconsciously, are sounded at the start of the song. When Dylan sings in the opening line that he is 'hearin' them church bells tone', one of the things we might recognise him as hearing is the church bell tone that Blind Lemon Jefferson imitates on the guitar in his performance of 'See That My Grave Is Kept Clean', which the young Bob Dylan had certainly been listening to. And in writing 'Call Letter Blues' in 1974, Bob Dylan may or may not remember that the similar phrase he uses to end the second line, 'listenin' to them church bells tone', is the last line of a song he wrote himself many years earlier, in 1961–62, 'Ballad For A Friend'.[228] But whether he remembers this or not, it was already, back then, a line he knew he was picking up wholesale from the great common-stock storehouse of blues lyric poetry, and its chime, in every one of the old blues songs that shared it, is always the sound of death come around, or death nearby. By their very familiarity as a blues song image, those toning church bells at the beginning of 'Call Letter Blues' (a title that is itself an echo of the far more familiar 'Death Letter Blues') help signal the presence of the fear of loss. So it is that the familiar in the blues can inform and intensify the new.[229]

This, like Pete Welding's comment quoted just before we came to 'Call Letter Blues', also suggests how, in the process of recognising cross-currents in Dylan's own corpus, we deconstruct and re-order *his* 'text' in our minds. When Taft says that

> If one were to illustrate how the audience undergoes this 'shock of recognition', how the mental processes of the listener bring about this shock, one would construct something like a concordance. Each word and each phrase would be lined up against all other words and phrases which are similar to it in all the songs in which the phrase occurred. By looking down a page in the concordance . . . one sees in an instant what must occur for the listener at the moment of 'shock',

we can get a sense of the truth of his argument by looking at the index of titles, first lines and key lines at the end of Dylan's *Lyrics 1962–1985*. This acts like the fragments of a Dylan Concordance. Let your eye drift down these few pages and you'll get a few of these shocks of recognition yourself, and a sense of the process at work. How much more valuable a real Bob Dylan Concordance would be.[230]

228. Blind Lemon Jefferson: 'See That My Grave Is Kept Clean', Chicago, c. Feb. 1928; Harry Smith's "American Folk Music", 1952, note 22. Bob Dylan: 'Ballad For A Friend', NYC, Jan. 62, recorded as a music-publishing demo.

229. Various songs called 'Death Letter Blues' were recorded pre-war by, for instance, Ida Cox (Chicago, c. Aug. 1924), Clara Smith (NYC, 15/10/24), Leadbelly (Wilton, Connecticut, February 1935) and Jimmy Yancey (Chicago, 6/9/40); but the one widely familiar among those in Greenwich Village and other blues revival circles in the 1960s was the song recorded and performed widely by Son House. It was one of the first four tracks he recorded after his 'rediscovery': Rochester, New York, 1964; "Son House And Robert Pete Williams Live!", Roots SL501, Vienna, *nia*. He re-recorded it the following year as 'Death Letter' for Columbia: NYC, 12–14/4/65, "Father of Folk Blues", CS9217, New York, 1966; CD-reissued with previously-unissued alternate take, "Father Of The Delta Blues: The Complete 1965 Sessions", Columbia Legacy Roots N' Blues Series 47662 2, New York, 1992. He also performed it at the 1965 Newport Folk Festival, Newport, Rhode Island, 22/7/65; "The Newport Folk Festival 1965", Vanguard Records 9225, New York, *nia*.

230. There is a so-called *Bob Dylan Concordance*, by Steve Michel, but for several reasons this does not yield the revelations and riches that a full concordance of Dylan's lyrics would. First, it isn't laid out to allow it to reveal anything (Michel was unable to get the Dylan office's permission for a full setting-down of his lyrics). Second, it doesn't include Dylan's own variant versions – not even what he actually sings on the recordings, when this, as so often happens, differs from the sheet-music version. Third, Michel misunderstood the purpose or potential value of a concordance. The promotional blurb in his publisher's advance catalogue ('publisher' is a grand term here: Rolling Tomes essentially sells Dylan-connected artefacts by mail order) signalled a very un-Taftian approach: 'How many songs mention: Allen Ginsburg [sic]? . . . Hours of fun! Due in January, taking orders now!'

But with or without a concordance, the deepest pleasure yielded by those 'shocks of recognition' comes when they rise out of the music. The more you know of the blues corpus, the more you'll appreciate Bob Dylan's extraordinary regenerative use of it; and the better you know Dylan's output, the better placed you'll be to hear the blues coursing through it.

CHAPTER TEN

Closin' the Book on the Pages and the Text

As singer and composer, Bob Dylan has also wandered, perhaps as much as down the highways and byways of the blues, into the equally vast terrain of old white folksong's traditional balladry. I cannot deal here with this huge subject (I'm not qualified to do so), beyond making two or three basic observations about the ways that these ballads too raise postmodernist issues.

The 'disturbance of narrative order' discussed earlier, which Aidan Day says is the particularly modernist feature of 'Tangled Up In Blue', is surely the same 'disturbance of narrative order' achieved unselfconsciously by that unmodern form, the narrative ballad. Contrary to what may be our assumptions about them, the old ballads did not offer clear linear narratives either. They characteristically move forward by what modern consciousness can call 'jump-cuts'. In Betsy Bowden's book *Performed Literature* she comments on 'A Hard Rain's A-Gonna Fall' in apt terms: 'the line-by-line scene shifts . . . make it resemble a Child ballad being run through a projector too fast, for a Child ballad characteristically leaps – but stanza by stanza – from scene to scene of dramatic and emotional intensity.'

Ballads as widespread and tenaciously popular as 'Barbara Allen', 'The Unfortunate Rake' and those of the generic type to which 'Belle Isle' belongs are typical in inhabiting a world where people disappear and reappear unexpectedly, communication is rife with lethal error and people wear the masks of alias. They are typical too in switching, often without clarification, from one narrator's voice to another, from one situation and location to another and back again, and into the realm where 'I', 'she' and 'you' are well-nigh indecipherably split.

So these 'traditional' songs also give us clues to ways of seeing and patterns of mind in the pre-modern oral worlds that recounted them: and the evidence is that then too people acknowledged the random journeys of memory, the non-sequential nature of brooding and remembrance, and the human mind as an unknowable terrain of twists of fate and infinite possibility. Rigid, codifying, authoritarian ideas to the contrary were surely mere impositions from above by the eighteenth century – the Age of Reason – and from the subsequent proselytising awe of the ruling classes for frozen Greek and Roman cultures.

Nick de Somogyi's excellently alert 'Jokermen & Thieves: Bob Dylan and the ballad tradition' aims 'to demonstrate Bob Dylan's understanding of the "traditional song", and how the apparent anachronism of his indebtedness to it informs the body of his songs with an artistic concision, and mutual coherence, that yields true "greatness of

. . . thought".'[1] In parallel with what I hope to have shown vis à vis Dylan's debts to the blues, it is as much about how Dylan twists balladic forms as relies on them.[2]

Something that seems to me to arise from all the foregoing – something it seems crucial to say about Bob Dylan – is that, like Apollinaire, he is authentically both a radical *and* a conservative cultural figure.[3]

This surely corresponds not only to the truth about his achievement as regards the old oral culture and the new, but to almost any cultural object, any artist – indeed to the very way most people's minds work. Don't some people think you're a bit of a reactionary while others find you insufficiently respectful of prevailing orthodoxies? Don't you sometimes feel both? It's certainly possible to note both of, say, the whole process of *fashion* (not just fashion as an industry but as a sort of monitoring/impetus-giving machine ticking away within us) – or even of what the cultural studies writer Angela McRobbie refers to as 'the wish-images of consumer capitalism'. Of the latter she writes: 'Their dialectic character exists in the way they are on the one hand products of a class-divided society but on the other they also look forward to a more equal society free from scarcity and conflict.' Similarly, fashion is both 'a ritual of commodity worship' (a reactionary force) and yet is also 'progressive in its irreverent attitude towards tradition and in its vivid dramatization of change'.[4]

More widely yet more inwardly speaking, the socialist historian R. H. Tawney wrote eloquently that

> In every human soul there is a socialist and an individualist, an authoritarian and a fanatic for liberty, as in each there is a Catholic and a Protestant. The same is true of the mass movements in which men marshall themselves for common action. There was in Puritanism an element which was conservative and tradition-alist, and an element that was revolutionary . . . a sober prudence which would garner the fruits of the world, and a divine recklessness which would make all things anew.[5]

Isn't Catherine Belsey, in her combative 1990s guide to the New Criticism, *Critical Practice*, being rather authoritarian herself in going round like some Shining Path of academia, summarily dividing people and their ideas into what's authoritarian and what is not? She seethes with hate for the common sense (empiricist–idealist) ideology – and of course there's plenty in the 'common sense' view to seethe about, since so

1. *Wanted Man Study Series*, no. 5, Wanted Man, Bury, Lancashire, 1986. De Somogyi is also good here on 'Jokerman', and on the wind and the rain in old songs and newer.

2. John Herdman's book *Voice Without Restraint: Bob Dylan's Lyrics and Their Background* also deals well with ballad and narrative. A rather differently approached discussion of this large subject is contained in the essay 'Grubbing for a Moderate Jewel: In Search of the Blooming Bright Star of Belle Isle' by Michael Gray, *Canadian Folklore canadien*, Vol. 8, nos. 1–2, (1988).

3. Apollinaire 'desired to affirm both tradition and innovation as his true loyalties', as Roger Shattuck put it in *The Banquet Years* (1955).

4. Angela McRobbie, 'The Passagenwerk and the Place of Walter Benjamin in Cultural Studies: Benjamin, Cultural Studies, Marxist Theories of Art', *Popular Culture Journal*, Vol. 6, no. 2, 1992. Also published in McRobbie's *Postmodernism and Popular Culture* (1994).

5. R. H. Tawney (1880–1962), quoted without identification of where this passage comes from, in Raphael Samuel's essay 'Religion and Politics: The Legacy of R. H. Tawney' (1982) in Samuel's *Island Stories: Unravelling Britain – Theatres of Memory, Vol. 2* (1998).

often it is mere brutish anti-intellectualism – yet there's something a bit comical about her approbation of a series of supposed alternatives, each of which lasts less than a decade before disappearing, discredited, while the common sense ideology she keeps trying to hurl them at goes on having some validity for everyone all around her.

At the same time, it's an irony indeed that Comrade Belsey and Herr Doktor Leavis would actually find themselves in accord in taking the narrower 'common sense view', of literature or anything else, to be philistinism.

Accord between advocates of the New Criticism and the old critic they take to be anathema, F. R. Leavis, surely extends rather further than that. Stephen Scobie may go on (and on) about which love songs might address which of the women in Bob Dylan's personal life – but he finally has to admit, after eleven pages and eight footnotes on who might be whom, that 'The question is not so much how close Dylan is to the protagonist of these songs as how much distance he can achieve.' Quite. But this is in itself an example of us all agreeing, old Leavisites and politically correct new post-structuralists together, on a fundamental criterion of criticism. Scobie assumes here, exactly as F. R. Leavis did, that we all subscribe to objective-distance-mediation-of-art-is-good, subjective-personal-closeness-unmediated-by-art-is-bad. This is a wholly Leavisite position! Such accord, and in such territory, is exactly why T. S. Eliot called criticism 'the common pursuit of true judgment', and why Leavis so insistently endorsed it (not least in calling one of his books *The Common Pursuit*) that the phrase is often assumed to be his own.[6]

Nor are these the only conjunctions between the new criticism and its bête noire of the old. Leavis may have insisted on the canon but he also championed key ideas that prefigure post-structuralist positions. Leavis it was who, in the face of the contrary assumptions of his contemporaries, came up with his great dictum 'Form is inseparable from content': which is to say, he insisted that in text, 'style' is not something laid on top of its 'meaning', as if it were insignificant decoration, but is on the contrary inextricably a part of meaning: that 'style' itself carries meaning.

Moreover, when, on the title page of each edition of this book, I countered Bob Dylan's teasingly evasive remark 'I think of myself . . . as a song & dance man' with D. H. Lawrence's 'Never trust the artist. Trust the tale', it was from F. R. Leavis that I had learnt Lawrence's dictum.[7] Leavis promoted it, as Lawrence had proposed it, not in the orthodox, old-fashioned sense of what we were taught at school to call 'the intentional fallacy' – which simply seeks to separate the work from the known biography – but as a way of insisting that the author's judgment of his or her text is no more valid than anyone else's. This insistence is at least a step or two down the road towards Roland Barthes' contention in 'The Death Of The Author' that the author's 'reading' is only one reading. I wouldn't want to push a claim for Leavis' modernism further than that: though if the basis of Barthes' argument is that we none of us own the language we use, I'd have to suggest that this also is a tenet of Leavis'

6.   T. S. Eliot: 'The Function of Criticism', *Selected Essays: 1917–1932* (1932); F. R. Leavis, *The Common Pursuit* (1952).

7.   'Never trust the artist. Trust the tale. The proper function of a critic is to save the tale from the artist who created it.' D. H. Lawrence, *Studies in Classic American Literature* (1923); quoted in F. R. Leavis, *D. H. Lawrence: Novelist* (1955).

criticism – and one that (for instance in 'Literature and Society' and 'Sociology and Literature' in *The Common Pursuit*) he states explicitly.[8]

Now that we've returned explicitly to matters of text, and the problematic nature of it, we might turn to what, if text were not problematic, we could say was plainly the single most important book to do with Bob Dylan that was published in the 1980s: his own collected *Lyrics 1962–1985*, published in America by Alfred Knopf in 1986.

Of course it might be thought odd that the very work that all of us, from its author and his public to critics of every ideological hue, would agree is not meant to 'stand on the page' – the very work that has so insisted on the primacy of aural rather than literary experience – should be collected and published as a book at all.

There is an excellent and lucid discussion of this in Stephen Scobie's book, in which he notes that until 1985's "Empire Burlesque" (the Japanese-initiated "Budokan" album aside) 'Dylan . . . never printed the song lyrics on the album jacket or sleeve, as if he were insisting that the words should be heard, even misheard, rather than read', and that there are several ways in which *Lyrics 1962–1985* fails to be a definitive text – even in the ways that might have been possible. It 'is drastically incomplete'; it 'prints only one version of each song. Given Dylan's habit of extensive rewriting, this cannot help but produce an incomplete picture'. At the same time it is 'full of revisions [to the text of the original recordings], from the occasionally altered word to the completely rewritten song' and the 'order of songs is sometimes different from the order in which they appear on the albums; the "Basement Tapes" lyrics appear, illogically, neither at the date on which they were recorded nor at the date on which they were released. And so on.' In summary, Scobie says that the book 'bears many signs of carelessness and incompletion, as if Dylan lacked interest in publishing a complete, properly edited, and definitive text. Yet at the same time it shows such extensive revisions that one can only conclude that it was put together with a good deal of attention and care.'

Nor can the puzzle of this contradiction be resolved by speculation as to how much Dylan has been directly responsible for the end result. In the case of the text of 'Caribbean Wind', Clinton Heylin attributes changes for the worse from the recording to the page to errors of transcription,[9] as most people assume is the case with the apparently inevitable errors present when recording artists do put the lyrics on their album sleeves. Scobie seems to assume that a change for the worse to the lyric of 'Precious Angel' is Dylan's own revision; and certainly in the case of songs that have received extensive revision – 'Tell Me, Momma', 'I Shall Be Free', 'Goin' To Acapulco' and 'Need A Woman' among others – one must assume these to be Dylan's changes. Yet Dylan is of course at least as likely to be slipshod about all this as anyone working on his behalf. He is also likely, as he did publicly in the case of 1985's big aural package, the "Biograph" box-set, to deny having had much to do with its assemblage. You might think this a case of him wanting it both ways and in both senses: the

8.   Roland Barthes, 'The Death of the Author', in *Image, Music, Text* (1977). F. R. Leavis, *The Common Pursuit* (1952).

9.   Clinton Heylin: '*Lyrics 1962–1985*: a collection short of the definitive', rev. ed. *All Across the Telegraph: A Bob Dylan Handbook* (1987).

book's textual slipshoddiness, mixed with its curious, occasionally fastidious revision, is a statement by Bob Dylan or his office, which ought to come to the same thing.

This is not the case, however, in the sense most of us would understand by 'a statement by Bob Dylan'. The Bob Dylan we generally think of is the artist, the performer, the writer, the singer-songwriter, the public figure. Yet there is necessarily a world of business procedure out there which 'his office' oversees, and in some cases the eccentricities of *Lyrics 1962–1985* result from that overseeing.

For example, 'Let's Keep It Between Us' (another song with text revisions that make it inferior to the song as performed) is given in the book as belonging among the songs excluded from, or arising in the aftermath of, the 1981 "Shot Of Love" album, and it is copyrighted 1982. Yet Dylan was performing the song in concert in 1980 – and not once but nineteen nights running! Most of us would understand such public performance to be an act of publication, and so would a dictionary. The first meaning of 'publication' in the dictionary to hand as I write is 'the act of making publicly known'. Moreover, in Britain at least, if the song was deemed to be published by these performances, Dylan would have collected monies on them, via the Performing Right Society, as for every other published song performed in a public place. However, Bob Dylan's office recognises a nicety lost on the rest of us here, arguing that public performance is *not* in fact publication, and copyrighting 'Let's Keep It Between Us' only in 1982 when the singer Bonnie Raitt pressed her intention to record the song. (There is always an incentive to copyright a work as late as possible, because the later you copyright it, the later the copyright runs out.)

So there sits 'Let's Keep It Between Us', then, in *Lyrics 1962–1985*, alongside 'The Groom's Still Waiting At The Altar', copyrighted 1981 (because it was on the B-side of a Dylan single then), alongside 'Need A Woman', copyrighted 1982 (because that's when Ry Cooder put his inferior version of the song on record), and alongside 'Caribbean Wind', copyrighted 1985 (because only then did Dylan's version emerge, on "Biograph", though this song too was performed in concert in 1980). The last consideration in this sequencing of the songs in *Lyrics 1962–1985* is thus the one anyone outside 'the business', or anyone interested in scholarship, might assume would come first – a concern to order the songs to reflect accurately their order of composition.

In the case of trying to establish when 'Let's Keep It Between Us' might have been composed, there is an added puzzle. Even if you didn't know that it had been performed in 1980 – as one of the 'non-Christian' songs insinuated amongst the evangelical material that had alone comprised the previous tour's uncompromising repertoire – and if you didn't care to notice the tardy copyright date, it would still be likely to strike you as curious, coming upon it where it is in *Lyrics 1962–1985*, which is to say smothered by the press of religious songs that surrounds it, when it is itself so obdurately a secular song: a song which, if it is to have any meaning at all outside Bob Dylan's private codification, must surely be about trying to preserve a long-term human relationship that is in danger of falling apart.

This – to pay a moment's attention to its content – also makes it a most unusual, and valued, part of Dylan's work, so little of which addresses the realities of *maintaining* relationships, even though this is, for Dylan's contemporaries, an area of experience likely to be more pressing and central than the relatively easy romantic angst of regretting yet another break-up. Indeed the reason why so many people feel that while Dylan used to reveal the world to them, now he just plays concerts, is precisely because his main area of address (apart from a lonely obsession with the imminence of apocalypse) is splitting up and moving on, while they themselves are working through the harder, more complex business of sticking together, with or without raising children, at a time when shifting sexual roles continually affect how things are between individuals. They are, thereby, coping with a far more 'contemporary' life than the old one Dylan speaks to with all his stoic leaving-or-left-alone songs cocooned in romantic images of dusty roads and lonesome oceans.

Inasmuch as 'Let's Keep It Between Us' belongs neither with this oeuvre nor with the evangelical one in which it's located in *Lyrics 1962–1985*, where might it belong? When Dylan performed it in those 1980 concerts, its secular companions ranged from the 1962 'Blowin' In The Wind' to the 1978 'Señor'. No help there. It would have been highly unusual had Dylan been introducing a song written two or three years beforehand, yet the years preceding the 1979 "Slow Train Coming" do seem the most likely to have yielded such a lyric, while its music is especially lacking in clues, since it too is unusual in Dylan's repertoire for luxuriating in such a rich swathe of sumptuous chords (indeed it's exactly the kind of music most musicians will tell you Bob Dylan cannot write).

At any rate, what 'Let's Keep It Between Us' is doing kept between 'Every Grain Of Sand' and 'The Groom's Still Waiting At The Altar' in *Lyrics 1962–1985* is fulfilling some technical song-publishing logic; it cannot be assumed to be (and therefore isn't) illuminating the development of his work.

What no one seems to conjecture, in all this puzzlement as to who has made the book what it is, and what it isn't, is that this peculiar subversion of the idea of a definitive Collected Works might be anything to do with the book's publisher. Yet in Britain at least the publisher has certainly participated. Published by Jonathan Cape in London in 1987, *Lyrics 1962–1985* was issued in large-format paperback and, later, in pocketbook form by Grafton Books. Yet Cape also issued a limited edition hardback of 550 copies initiated at the behest of the specialist mail-order bookseller My Back Pages: itself a funny thing to do, on the face of it, with a work supposedly so far removed from the world of dusty gentility and literary antiquarianism, of slim and precious volumes, in which a limited edition of a few hundred copies might be felt to belong.

This British hardback, from which I have taken most quotations from Dylan lyrics used in this book, most definitely plays a part in subverting any such notions of an especially well crafted edition of a definitive text.

First, it offers a hideous front cover – a photograph of the lone sailor not strapped to the mast but becalmed in bad karma, neither credibly challenging our notions of how the bard should look nor conforming to them knowingly, as was achieved on the still witty cover of the "New Morning" album back in 1970, which offers a photo of Dylan that belongs with those of him accepting an honorary doctorate from Princeton: a close-up that gives its own sly critique of the conventional poet-intellectual book jacket shot. In lamentable contrast, the deeply mediocre picture on the cover of *Lyrics 1962–1985*, which has Dylan all open mouth and flared nostril, saturated in the colours of piss and sickly green, yields no message but old-lag-pub-rocker-in-eyes-shut-mid-song mode. Juxtaposed witlessly with the decades-sweeping import of the title and the declamatory big print of that ostentatiously singular word DYLAN, the whole suggests something that has overreached itself, something riding for a fall off its bardic pedestal – something of dubious value and no small pretension. The publishers could not have degraded so great a body of work, nor done its creator such disservice, if they had plotted to do so.

The inside flaps of the dust-jacket are left white, in candid confession of the sheer haste, and very possibly greed, with which this project was approached. Inside, two different coloured papers are thrown in together: most pages are hairy and dun, but the pages that sew up the lyrics of "Infidels" and "Empire Burlesque" are slippery and white. There is no mistaking who's been dun and who's been slippery.

There must be a sizeable proportion of the 550 people who bought this major British publisher's travesty of a limited edition hardback, and a lot more from among the wider readership of other editions of the book, who have found themselves much exercised by the sub-text of all this text. The incompleteness, the mix of inexplicable textual revision with apparent textual error, the inaccurate sequencing, the shoddiness of the physical artefact: anyone interested in Bob Dylan's work will have been struck by some of these ways in which the book fails to be the definitive text or the accurate retrospective collection.

The old orthodox response to this contrary sub-text is simply to regret the lack of care and attention to detail assumed to account for the shortcomings of the book. The postmodernist response is to welcome the contrary sub-text precisely because it does contradict and call attention to the gaps and shortcomings in the very idea of the definitive text and its corollary, the finished product.

Among the rest of these disturbances, Barthes would welcome the disruptive intrusion into *Lyrics 1962–1985* of the noises off, as it were, made by the song publishing / copyrighting / business side of it and of the sheer naffness of the UK hardback edition (which might be said to offer a critique of its own limitations). This is because both these kinds of disruption draw attention to, and thus fight against, the orthodox construct of the reader as passive consumer, and its consequent suppression of the process of production. Catherine Belsey's obliging précis of Barthes' position runs like this:

> books are literally commodities, of course, but the ideology of literary criticism places the reader more decisively in the position of consumer – consumer of a 'spiritual' value which constitutes a displacement of the idea of the value of a commodity . . . it was the Romantic movement, contemporary with the rise of industrial capitalism, which initiated the process of endowing certain texts with a worth which had little to do with mere enjoyment but depended instead on a magical and timeless value inherent only in great art.
>
> The distribution system . . . in capitalism has the effect of suppressing the process of production . . . Commodities are seen in their finished form among other commodities and not in the context of the factories in which they were made. Industrial areas of towns are located away from shopping areas. Even those advertisements which draw attention to the high technology or skill involved in the production process tend to do so by showing pictures of scientists in white

coats or craftsmen with chisels. They do not show workers and conveyor belts on the shop floor. The labour involved in production is suppressed . . .

A precisely similar suppression occurs in conventional literary criticism. The literary text is shown not as a construct, the result of a process, but as . . . the spontaneous expression of its author's subjectivity . . . The process of production is called creation, a mystical and mysterious occurrence conceived rather as a state of mind than as work. As a result, conventional criticism gazes in awe at the finished product whose value resides above all in its status as embodiment of the author's genius.

Whereas, Barthes says, 'the goal of literary work (of literature as work) is to make the reader no longer a consumer, but a producer of the text'.[10]

Belsey adds, apropos of the means-of-production argument, that the

author's name on the cover, known, established, famous, is the guarantee of access to his or her imagination, just as the brand name of the product guarantees the quality of the commodity. But the brand name on the product is the name of the employer or the company, not of the workers whose labour produced it. In a similar way, the author's name evokes given essences, qualities of insight and understanding, and not the labour of producing out of the available signifying systems of language and literature an intelligible fiction.

The reader must be his or her own producer of *this* text, or as the old-fashioned critic might put it, make of this what you will. For myself, I recognise that it represents the high moment of Marxist hegemony over literary studies, and that that moment has passed; that the shaky analogy between conveyor-belt and literary output is not, as Ms Belsey makes it sound, suggesting that writing is unskilled labour but rather, a form of unseen communal labour; and that the downplay of the role of 'labour' in production is bound up in the process under capitalism by which 'exchange-value replaces use-value': i.e. by which usefulness is secondary to profit. All the same, how is it suggested it would improve things if products *were* named after all the workers who produced them? Or if all the shops were in amongst the factories?

All this rests on the feeble contention that there is nothing 'mysterious' about stuff like poetry: nothing more to it than 'the labour of producing out of the available signifying systems of language and literature' (or *words*), 'an intelligible fiction'. Value vis à vis the creative imagination is fudged. Creativity is not redefined here, it's just denied. 'The process of production is called creation . . . rather . . . than . . . work.' Even in pedantic terms this seems insupportable. I don't know when I last saw *The Collected Creations Of* anyone.

I too recognise the foolishness of treating works of art as visitations from heaven into the mystical brain of the lone genius, and the unhelpful criticism that results and that may encourage the reader to be a passive consumer. Yet this is a wildly inaccurate parody of the positions most critics *and* most readers take, which, however much they vary, tend to be aware that literature is of its time and place, that reading is a

---

10. Catherine Belsey, *Critical Practice* (1991), and quoting from Roland Barthes, *S/Z*, translated by Richard Miller, published in Britain by Cape (like *Lyrics 1962–1985* itself), 1975.

collaborative, not a passive, process – and that a spirit of collaboration is not likely to be founded on the rubbishing of the specialness of creativity.

The analogy many old Marxists might prefer is between writer and weaver, which seems to take more account of the way in which the materials weaved are everyone's, in that the 'signifying systems' are not of the individual writer's invention but 'only' of his or her manipulation. Even so, there are many who weave competently, and then there are a few Rumpelstiltskins, able to weave gold out of straw.

In any case, proper scrutiny or demystification would recognise that alongside the writing itself, which surely *is* mysterious, and no more communally produced at the point where writer meets microchip or quill than a duck's egg is communally hatched, the writer's work is of many sorts – touting ideas around publishers, trying to find an agent, negotiating contracts, chasing overdue payments, buying printer ribbons, keeping accounts – none of which make his or her average day much like the factory worker's. More like the jobbing gardener's, who every day must go, cap in hand, hoping to get through to the back door up at the big house to see if there's any casual work available at whatever rate of pay the master cares to decide, to be paid at some unspecified time in the future.

Is the author co-worker with the secretary, assistant and editor, salesperson, typesetter and whoever else within the publishing and marketing industries? No. All these other people are on salaries or wages, get warm offices, paid holidays and sick leave, don't need to keep accounts, haven't had to buy the equipment they use, don't have to pay for their phone calls, and get enough money to live on, in most cases regardless of their competence. They might even get pensions. The writer is in no such position. Only for the very few are conditions significantly better than those decribed above, and for them too the work involves both their creativity and their taking care of business.

At any rate, to the extent that the intrusion of the 'taking care of business' upon otherwise contextless 'creating' is desirable demystification, the disruptions to Bob Dylan's collected works in *Lyrics 1962–1985* achieved by song-publishing/copyright logistics and hardback publisher incompetence are, for the Barthes of *S/Z*, to be understood as welcome ways in which the commodity refuses wholly to suppress the process of its production.

On the other hand for Stephen Scobie the subversion of the definitive text is Dylan-the-creator's own intended sub-text: 'Bob Dylan isn't interested in a definitive text', he urges, while Nick de Somogyi is interested by the extent to which, however short of the definitive it may be, the very fact of *Lyrics 1962–1985* rats on Dylan's aural-culture performerism. He writes of Dylan's career-long antipathy to the printed page, from his 1965 dropping as litter onto a London street the words to 'Subterranean Homesick Blues' (text carefully picked up again and printed on page 211) to the 'Don't . . . give me no book to read / It don't satisfy' of 1981's 'Shot Of Love' (text given on page 453).[11]

The essential unreasonableness of launching anti-book arguments in a book is of course widespread. The celebrated example is Marshall McLuhan's proclaiming the

11. Nick de Somogyi: 'Pretexts for Bob Dylan', *Telegraph*, no. 34, Winter 1989.

death of the book in a series of books.[12] A more recent extension of this self-contradiction is in the school of criticism exemplified by Simon Reynolds in his entertaining book *Blissed Out* (1988). This, as its title may suggest, looks to rock music for the drug-assisted rapture (I don't suggest there's anything wrong with that) of *now*, the enemy of which is held to be everybody else's discourse: everybody's except that of 'a renegade tradition' in which Reynolds and his colleagues,

> Instead of arbitration . . . opt for exaltation. Instead of interpretation and eluci-dation, they seek to amplify the chaos, opacity and indeterminacy of music. Instead of reading and writing, they prefer rending and writhing. Instead of legibility/legitimation, they prefer the illegible and illicit . . . the sheer waste of energy into the void . . . The renegades' fascination has been with what eludes content analysis. Its guiding conviction . . . is that the power of pop lies not in its meaning but its noise, not in its import but its force. And that rock, at its best, should be confused and confusing.

As you can tell at once, this position is arbitrated and elucidated with admirable skills of 'legibility' and analysis, with clear meaning banishing opacity, ordered by someone well versed in, and enjoying, the skills of reading and writing, in a demurely sequential flow of words on the unblissed-out page. And consider the sub-text of the brief 'biog' on the back cover. It says only this: 'Simon Reynolds was born in 1963 in London where he now lives. He is the co-founder of *Monitor*, a pop journal. Since 1986, he has written irregularly for the *New Statesman*, *The Guardian* and *The Observer*. He is a regular contributor to *Melody Maker*. *Blissed Out* is his first book.' No rending and writhing here, then: just writing, writing, writing . . .

All this anti-text also fits in with what has become the main cliché of Dylanology in the 1980s and 1990s: in which Dylan's constant 'reinterpretation' of his work in performance is insisted upon as showing – and actually as itself *arguing* – that there is no finished text of any individual song. I've always subscribed to the view that Dylan does indeed reinterpret his songs in performance – but in one important way I do demur from the notion that therefore there is no finished text. It seems rather too convenient for the Bob Dylan who has writer's block, or has lost his way.

How much nicer to go round saying that the song is a text in permanent revision, like Trotsky's revolution, than to say that yes, this important song was actually written in 1964 or 1965, and so was this one *and* this one *and* this one . . .

It's no small irony that while the never-ending-text theory is so radical and modern, it's also a great one to cling to for those who have lost the muse.

Yet while the Bob Dylan of the 1980s and 1990s is no longer, measured by his own earlier standards, prolific, and while he often loses sight of the meticulous standards he himself laid down as writer and performer, his heroic artistic struggle to survive and to be renewed has given us new work that, at its best, still offers unparalleled variety, an admirable insistence on exploration and a continued authentic uniqueness.

He might fail more often than he succeeds over these two decades, and he might

---

12. Marshall McLuhan, *The Gutenberg Galaxy* (1962); *Understanding Media* (1964), *The Medium Is the Massage* [sic] (1967) etc.

seem marooned inside an 'entertainment industry' that has lost, in this period, its last shreds of tolerance for unformatted openness – the very condition that once allowed such major creative leaps as Presley's fusion of hillbilly music with rhythm'n'blues or Dylan's own fusion of poetry with rock'n'roll. Yet he has continued the striving to explore and has mostly refused, to his great credit, the easier option of being Dylanesque.

As a result, the best of the new work he has offered over these last twenty years – songs devotional, dark, long, short, difficult, smooth, 'unfinished', tormented and funny – has taken us on routes that could never have been predicted. In the next few chapters, we examine them.

CHAPTER ELEVEN

Yonder Comes Sin: The Retreat from Evangelism

To look at Bob Dylan's work of the immediate post-"Saved" period is to begin with the unreleased song 'Yonder Comes Sin', which was recorded the month before the short 'Musical Retrospective' tour of November–December 1980. Exactly when 'Yonder Comes Sin' was *written* is impossible to say. A demo of 'Every Grain Of Sand' was made earlier than the recording of 'Yonder Comes Sin'; so it's entirely possible that 'Every Grain Of Sand' was written first. It doesn't feel like that, though. 'Every Grain Of Sand', re-recorded the following May and issued on the 1981 album "Shot Of Love", could not possibly have come from the "Saved" album. 'Yonder Comes Sin' sounds almost like an out-take from it.[1]

This most interesting song was taken by Dylan's music publisher for use as a song demo, but then kept back and subsequently said to be the one song of this period Dylan particularly wanted to keep unreleased and even unpublished. In common with the distinctive and near-contemporaneous 'Ain't Gonna Go To Hell For Anybody', it is omitted from *Lyrics 1962–1985*, unlike the unreleased 'Ain't No Man Righteous, No Not One'. Yet both of these 'Ain't' songs were at least performed in public – in fact the one left out of *Lyrics 1962–1985* was performed far more often than the other. 'Yonder Comes Sin' was never performed.

It is only known to exist, therefore, on that 1980 tape, on most circulating copies of which it terminates abruptly in mid-song. For most of us, therefore, it can only be said to half-exist. There were hopes of its emerging, complete, on the "Bootleg Series I–III" box-set and, had it joined those other previously unreleased 'religious songs' 'Ye Shall Be Changed' and 'You Changed My Life', it would have proved the strongest of the three – but these hopes were unfounded: a further indication, possibly, of Dylan's own retrospective hostility to the song.[2]

1.   Bob Dylan: 'Every Grain Of Sand', Santa Monica, 23/9/80, issued "Bootleg Series I–III", 1991; 'Yonder Comes Sin', Santa Monica, probably 23/10/80, certainly late Sept.–early Nov. 1980, unreleased.

2.   The title 'Ain't No Man Righteous, No Not One' is taken from the New Testament, in which Paul's Epistle to the Romans, chapter 3, verse 10, pithily summarises earlier scripture from an Old Testament Psalm of David (Psalms 14:2–3). Paul's summary declares: 'As it is written, There is none righteous, no, not one'. (Fuller details, including details of Dylan's performances of this song, are given in Chapter 14, note 19.)
      'Ye Shall Be Changed' is also based on a specific text from one of Paul's Epistles: in this case his First Epistle to the Corinthians, chapter 15, verses 51 and 52, provides Dylan's title and inspires the song's muscularly energetic chorus. Paul's words here are: 'we shall all be changed, In a moment, in the twinkling of an eye, at the last trump: for the trumpet shall sound, and the dead shall be raised incorruptible, and we shall be changed.' Dylan's chorus runs: 'In the twinkling of an eye / When the last trumpet blows / The dead will arise and burst out of your clothes / And ye shall be changed.'

This can be regretted for two reasons: its historical importance in Dylan's repertoire and its intrinsic worth. To recognise both involves recognising that along with the richness of the blues and the ballads, there is a third major source, over and above that of mainstream literary culture, for the poetic force of Bob Dylan's work – throughout Dylan's work, not just that of the so-called Born Again period – and that is the Bible: in which, of course, balladry and the blues are themselves already steeped, since the Bible is the one book that occupied a place in the homes of millions who could not read and has been a part of oral culture at least as much as of the literary one.

There is, as with the blues and balladry, a case to be made for the Bible's postmodernism. Claiming to be the ultimate definitive text, the unmitigated word of God, it emerges as a press of differing versions of the same stories, each tending to undermine the veracity of the other and much of the time proceeding by methods closer to collage than to conventional narrative sequencing, such that the fragmentary and prismatic nature of all testimony is the only unity averred. It also offers the simple a world in which people can live for several hundred years, dwell in the bellies of whales, cross divided seas and turn into pillars of salt, while offering the less simple the lesson that reading the text is a process of confronting questions of interpetation.

Bert Cartwright's 'The Bible in the Lyrics of Bob Dylan' divides Dylan's use of the Bible into five phases, the first three of which cover the 1960s and 1970s before the conversion to Christ. First is a pre-motor-cycle-crash phase, drawing on the Bible as 'part of the poor white and black cultures of America with which he sought to identify'; second is a Woodstock and "John Wesley Harding" phase, in which 'at times a biblical perspective is clearly assumed though not personally claimed'; third is the period from "Planet Waves" through till the late autumn of 1978, when the Bible is used 'as material for a sophisticated artist'.[3] Then comes the conversion. Cartwright quotes Dylan as telling Robert Hilburn, 'I had always read the Bible, but I only looked at it as literature. I was never really instructed in it in a way that was meaningful to me.'[4]

By Cartwright's analysis, therefore, when we reach the beginning of the 1980s, we are in the midst of the fourth phase of Dylan's use of the Bible, the phase that 'reveals his unabashed acceptance of Jesus Christ as Lord and his desire to express in life and song what his fresh study of the Bible as a believer was telling him'. Cartwright designates the fifth phase, 'in which biblical faith [has] been internalized sufficiently for it to serve subtly as Dylan's worldview', as being signalled by the 1983 release of the "Infidels" LP.

Yet a major change seems to me to occur *between* Cartwright's fourth and fifth phases. What we begin to see after the "Saved" album is Dylan's retreat from evangelism – not a recanting, but a move forward, away from the concern to preach to others (though as we've seen, the "Slow Train Coming" and "Saved" songs were

3.   *Wanted Man Study Series*, no. 4, 1985. When Cartwright, 'a Protestant minister with two theological degrees from Yale University', according to his booklet, deals with Dylan's first phase, he notes that Dylan was already familiar with the Bible in some detail. Cartwright includes interesting commentary on the Christ persona in songs from the second and third phases such as 'I Pity The Poor Immigrant' and 'Oh Sister'.

4.   *Los Angeles Times Calendar*, June 1980.

rarely as simplistic as that) and towards a more reflective interest in writing songs that examine the interplay in Dylan's own heart and mind between his Christian faith and other aspects of his life.

This is a specially interesting period: it finds Dylan moving beyond insistence on the tenets of faith toward the pain of recognising that faith gets tested, that 'sometimes . . . there's someone there, other times it's only me' and that it's altogether a more complex business than is suggested by 'You either got faith or you got unbelief'.

This shift is first signalled in concert on that November–December 1980 tour, on which the current 'religious' songs are for the first time entwined with songs by others, with the traditional ballad 'Mary From The Wild Moor' and with some of Dylan's own earlier work. On record, the same shift away from evangelism is signalled by the LP recorded in the spring of 1981, "Shot Of Love", and by the additional material recorded for that album but unreleased until later. Earliest of all these signals of change was 'Yonder Comes Sin' – a song that sounds, at first, thumpingly evangelical but isn't.

Modelled on the story of Jeremiah taking the word of God to his chosen people, who after their deliverance from Egypt have turned to the worship of false gods – a story summarised in the song's fourth and (as we have it on the incomplete tape) final verse – 'Yonder Comes Sin' sets up a series of dialogues, in parallel to the dialogues of the Book of Jeremiah as between God and the prophet and then between the prophet and the unheeding populace.

While the theme of both biblical book and song is backsliding from faith – 'Return, ye backsliding children, and I will heal your backslidings', as God tells Jeremiah to report him as having said (Jeremiah 3:22) – Dylan's remonstrance is directed mostly at himself.

Indeed he gives himself a hard time here not merely by invective, though that is present, but also by the disturbing recognition that backsliding is recurrent even among the most devoutly intentioned, and that this is so because other things besides the love of God hold authentic human attraction. Unlike the Book of Jeremiah, the song pitches against the evangelical voice affectionately rendered dialogues of enduring resonance from other kinds of life, and gives both the prophet and the secular voices a sympathetic ear, though the moral victory goes to the prophet.

The recognition that backsliding is not merely 'out there', contemptible evil to be railed against, distinguishes this song from 'Trouble In Mind', which also reports dialogues – between the protagonist and Satan and the protagonist and God – yet suggests a closed, cosy relationship between he who might be tempted and he who will always protect from temptation. In 'Trouble In Mind' the sub-text of the song is 'God and me, we're OK'; in 'Yonder Comes Sin' the sub-text is that evangelising is all well and good but that ordinary human life – enjoying old blues songs, flirtation, recollecting pre-conversion good times, present intimacy – is a valid arena too.[5]

This sub-text lies within the two middle verses of the song, between opening and

5.   Yet 'Trouble In Mind', of course, is *named* after a classic secular blues song, written by Richard Lewis in the 1920s and recorded and performed widely ever since. Dylan's own 'Trouble In Mind' was recorded at the "Slow Train Coming" sessions at Sheffield, Alabama, May 1979, and published in *Lyrics 1962–1985*. An edited-down version was issued as the B-side of a single, Columbia Records 1011072, New York, 1979.

closing verses of insistent preachifying. In the first, the narrator is addressing himself, and in much the same derisive terms as in the then-imminent "Shot Of Love" song 'Dead Man, Dead Man', the essence of his self-accusation being, as the third and fourth lines express it:

> You want the spirit to be speaking through
> But your lust for comfort get in the way.

The choruses, which build upon a call and response motif sung in part by Dylan and the gospel-singers behind him, and partly by these singers alone, are all lyrically different, but each one amplifies the self-criticism as it details the attributes of the singer's looming sinfulness. This choral catalogue begins:

> Yonder comes sin
> Walkin' like a man, talkin' like an angel.

The rhythm and music here define the embodied sin's mode of passage as essentially a strut – and one we're bound to respond to ambivalently, since it enacts empty vanity so well yet also has its own gospel music appeal – while in the words there's a neat allusion to another song here, and one of comic appropriateness. Elvis Presley's minor hit of 1963 '(You're The) Devil In Disguise' opens with a chorus of 'You look like an angel, walk like an angel, talk like an angel, but I got wise: you're the devil in disguise'.[6]

Dylan's line is followed by the less facile resonance of

> Proud like a peacock, swift like an eagle

which not only extends the menagerie of feathered creatures from angels to birds but returns us to Jeremiah, in whose Lamentations 'Our persecutors are swifter than the eagles of the heavens' (5:19). The implication, however, is that in the end, just as walking like an angel is hypocritical and being proud like a peacock mere vanity, so being swift like an eagle will not be swift enough to avoid the punishment of God.

There is a switch in the narrative voice at the start of the second verse, as it stops berating itself and addresses us. Here the sub-text gets some development. Like the musical strut of the chorus that has gone before it, the lyric now begins to give off strong whiffs of the allure of other calls on the singer's attention. In the opening four lines:

> See this woman standin' next to me
> She's foreign to your sight
> Well her eyes may be a different colour than mine
> But her blood is red and her bones are white

we are certainly asked to 'see' a flesh-and-bone woman, while we feel too the presence of an intimate, unknowable relationship. That splendid surgeon's view of matters of colour – 'her blood is red and her bones are white' – both cuts to the core and provides Dylan's gospel-song retort to the blues song designation 'chocolate to the

---

6.   Elvis Presley: '(You're The) Devil In Disguise', Nashville, 26/5/63, RCA Victor Records 47-8188, New York, 1963.

bone'.[7] In retorting to that, in paying it some attention, the song acknowledges the alluring secular world and invokes another dialogue: that between the two great traditionally opposing forms of black American music, gospel and blues (the devil's music). And where is that 'she's foreign to your sight' familiar from? Its deliberate awkwardness, a quaint declamatoriness, which exactly matches that of the title's construct 'yonder comes', is surely akin to the knowing archaisms Dylan uses for 'The Ballad Of Frankie Lee And Judas Priest', another song of dialogues that is to do with the conflicting claims of purity of heart and of pleasure, the rightness of belief and the foolishness of credulity.

The remaining lines of the second verse revert abruptly to the original narrative voice: Dylan is back to beating on his 'Dead Man, Dead Man''s chest. Prefiguring that song's impatient self-loathing:

> *The tuxedo that you're wearin', the flower in your lapel*
> *Ooh I can't stand it, I can't stand it*
> *You wanna take me down to hell,*

in 'Yonder Comes Sin' the derisive scolding is that

> *. . . your fifty-dollar smile confirms*
> *You're still tryin' to buy your way into the dreams of them*
> *Whose bodies will be food for worms.*

The song surges on, hurrying past the dodginess of this barb, straight into the second chorus. Here sin is not just yonder but lasciviously emboldened: it's

> *Standin' on the chair, standin' on the table,*

which again suggests something not altogether unattractive. Perhaps the song called to mind this time is Randy Newman's 'You Can Leave Your Hat On' (and perhaps there's a feather in it).

At any rate, the third verse opens not with further thunderous condemnation but with four lines that give us a new dialogue, in new tones of voice both secular and sexy. The narrator now seems to address a 'you' not previously encountered and

---

7.   An interesting expression, being apparently neither an individual's invention nor a well-known, widely used phrase. In raising, therefore, a puzzle about how such an expression might circulate, it touches on wider issues of dissemination and creativity in blues lyric poetry. The fact that so vivid an expression occurs only in a very small number of blues songs suggests that it was hardly a phrase on everybody's lips. Furry Lewis used it in the sixth line of his 'Good Looking Girl Blues', cut in 1927. Barbecue Bob made it a song title in 1928. It reappeared in the sixth line of Henry Thomas' great 'Don't Ease Me In', cut in Chicago only weeks after the Barbecue Bob session. The only other record I know of on which it recurs is by Frankie Half-Pint Jaxon (a sometime featured vocalist member of the Hokum Boys, aka Tampa Red's Hokum Jug Band), who also cut 'Chocolate To The Bone', in 1930. Yet while the well-travelled Jaxon probably picked up the song in the Barbecue Bob territory of Atlanta, where he spent some time, this doesn't explain the separate use of the phrase itself by Memphis-based Furry Lewis or Texas-based Henry Thomas. We know that Thomas – an old man by the time he came to record, which is partly what makes him especially valuable – was not by this time learning new songs, which suggests that the phrase must have enjoyed some degree of conversational circulation, or that it was simply a relatively unpopular line of common-stock blues lyric poetry. (Furry Lewis: 'Good Looking Girl Blues', Chicago, 9/10/27; "Memphis Blues (1927–1939), Vol. 2", Roots RL-329, Vienna, c. 1970. Barbecue Bob: 'Chocolate To The Bone', Atlanta, 13/4/28; "Barbecue Bob. Masters Of The Blues, Vol. 10", Collector's Classics CC-36, Copenhagen, 1971. Henry Thomas: 'Don't Ease Me In', Chicago, 13/6/28; "Henry Thomas Sings The Texas Blues", Origin Jazz Library OJL-3, New York, 1961. Frankie Half-Pint Jaxon: 'Chocolate To The Bone', Chicago, 28/10/30; CD-reissued "Frankie 'Half-Pint' Jaxon 1927–1940", RST Records Story of the Blues CD 3533–2, Vienna, 1989.)

presents the message that omens of death and retribution are at hand in wittily flirtatious terms, so that while we register that Dylan is reading these signs, what we hear is a chatting-up:

> *I say 'See them six white horses, honey?'*
> *You say 'I don't even see one.'*
> *You say 'Point them out to me, love,'*
> *I say 'Honey I gotta run . . .'*

It is a chatting-up we're meant to 'overhear', since it contains allusions to numinous moments from the singer's own romantic past: moments we're familiar with but which the current addressee may be imagined not to be. First there are the back-references to three different songs from Dylan's past, compressed into the single phrase 'six white horses' and what resonates off it. These glamorous coffin-pullers reappear here fresh from their cameo role in 'Absolutely Sweet Marie', a nimble song about lust and allure in which the narrator also declares himself to be on some kind of death row: the horses 'Were finally delivered down to the penitentiary', and this line, the one that follows the horses, is one we hear in our heads again as we hear the dialogue of 'Yonder Comes Sin'. At the same time, our immediate recognition that the horses do stand as coffin-bringers, and are thus by extension auguries of death, comes from the other song fragment we hear echo in our heads: that from Dylan's début LP version of Blind Lemon Jefferson's 'See That My Grave Is Kept Clean', in which

> *There's two white horses followin' me*
> *Waitin' on my buryin' ground.*

This in turn carries the echo of that line in another song from Dylan's first album, 'Fixin' To Die' (attributed to Bukka White), which brings us full circle to 'Yonder Comes Sin' by matching up that 'buryin' ground' with the archaism 'yonder' itself:

> *Look over yonder, to that buryin' ground.*

As far as I know, there is no blues reference to *six* white horses, and few other references to white horses at all, though an exception is Howlin' Wolf's lovely 'Poor Wind (That Never Change)', itself clearly based on the Blind Lemon Jefferson song, with which it shares the lovely common-stock line 'Can't you hear them church-bells tone?', as well as offering the slight variant of 'Tell 'em to dig my grave with a silver spade / Tell 'em to lay me down with a golden chain' and, yet more extravagantly than Dylan:

> *There's eight white horses in a line . . .*
> *They're gonna take me down to my buryin' ground.*

There are 'Two White Horses Standing In Line' in Smith Casey's field-recorded version, and a similar title was commercially recorded by The Two Poor Boys, but horses in the blues are more usually black, as in Jefferson's 'Black Horse Blues' and in Papa Harvey Hull and Long Cleve Reed's 'Hey! Lawdy Mama – The France Blues', in which

> *Well, there's two black horses, standing on the burying ground.*

Perhaps black horses were the Ford Executive Stretch Granadas, and white horses the Rollers, of their time and place.[8]

Actually, Bob Dylan has a bit of a thing about horses – even a way of pronouncing the very word that makes it evocatively Dylanesque. They make appearances throughout his song repertoire, as often as not conveying his sense of their quintessential absurdity or surrealism. '. . . I'm gonna ride into Omaha on a horse'; 'All the tired horses in the sun . . .': he often finds them innately comic like that. It is something to do with their blatant physicality, their potentially unmanageable size and sense of superiority, making them bizarrely unstable as creatures in service. Dylan relishes this – as we see in *Renaldo & Clara*, where one pale white horse (another symbol of death) breaks out of its small character role as the possession Joan Baez is swapped for, and, in a moment that catches it conscious of its own nosiness while splendidly unaware of the postmodernism of its action, snuffles its great long face and hot breath right into the camera. Even when Dylan tells Bill Flanagan that he can't set out to write a song 'about' something, he chooses 'horses' as his first example of things he can't write songs about.[9]

Those lines of 'Yonder Comes Sin' that invoke six of them, which is to say the flirtatious four lines of dialogue between the 'love' who sees the omens of death and the 'honey' who doesn't – and whose secular common sense is allowed to hold its own against his mystic premonitions, that retort 'I don't even see one' mocking the elaboration of his opening gambit question – also bring us more general, but unmistakable, echoes from Dylan's own mythic past. The sub-text of the woman's follow-up remark is 'Stay', which he counteracts unhesitatingly with his own 'Honey I gotta run' (the dialogue is, we note, structured so that he gets the first and last word), and this exchange sums up powerfully the one we find in almost all Dylan's love songs before 'Tonight I'll Be Staying Here With You'.

This is the foible in his work most often sneered at by women: that in Dylan songs women always did want him to stay and he always did have to be movin' on (except in 'Down The Highway', where they're both travellers, and 'Boots Of Spanish Leather', in which she has had the temerity to leave *him* behind). This archetypal exchange is all the more pungently rendered in 'Yonder Comes Sin' because the

8. Blind Lemon Jefferson: 'See That My Grave's Kept Clean', Chicago, c. Oct. 1927, and 'See That My Grave Is Kept Clean', Chicago, c. Feb. 1928. Bukka White: 'Fixin' To Die Blues', Chicago, 8/3/40. Howlin' Wolf: 'Poor Wind (That Never Change)', Chicago, 11/4/66; "From Early Till Late 1948–68", Blue Night LP 1667, *nia*. Smith Casey: 'Two White Horses Standing In Line', Brazoria, Texas, 16/4/39; "Afro-American Blues And Game Songs", [Library of Congress] Archive of Folk Song AFS L4, Washington, DC, 1956. The Two Poor Boys [Joe Evans & Arthur McClain]: 'Two White Horses In A Line', NYC, 20/5/31; "Early Country Music", Historical Records RC-8002, Jersey City, NJ, 1960s, CD-reissued "The Two Poor Boys", Document DOCD-5044, Vienna, c. 1990. Blind Lemon Jefferson: 'Black Horse Blues', Chicago, c. April 1926; Papa Harvey Hull and Long Cleve Reed: 'Hey! Lawdy Mama – The France Blues', Chicago, April 1927; "Really! The Country Blues", Origin Jazz Library OJL-2, New York, 1962.

I suspect that songs featuring white horses are more commonly by white performers. 'Six White Horses' itself is a bluesy song that entered the bluegrass repertoire via Bill Monroe & His Blue Grass Boys in 1940 [Atlanta, 7/10/40; "The Father Of Bluegrass Music", RCA Camden CAL719, New York, 1962] and thereafter proliferated: cut for instance by the Hodges Brothers [McComb, Mississippi, 1960–61; "Watermelon Hangin' On The Vine", Arhoolie Records 5001, Berkeley, c. 1971 reissue of the first country-series LP on the Arhoolie label, 1961, and still available in their 1992 catalogue] and by Flatt & Scruggs [Nashville, 27/1/57, CD-reissued on the 4-CD box-set "Lester Flatt & Earl Scruggs 1948–1959", Bear Family Records BCD 15472-DH, Vollersode Germany, 1991].

9. Bob Dylan: 'I Shall Be Free No. 10', 'All The Tired Horses' and interview quoted in Bill Flanagan, *Written in My Soul* (1986).

singer's 'Honey I gotta run', while playful and cheerily secular (that 'Honey' locates its tone), also expresses the higher urgency prompted by his glimpsing imminent retribution.

Dylan's wit is on good form here (to use an equine metaphor) and perhaps his scriptural correctness is too. Sin may be swift as an eagle, but God's wrath is swifter – and comes on horseback to punish those whose backsliding into sin has continued unabated even after the warnings of God's prophet Jeremiah: 'Behold, he shall come up as clouds, and his chariots shall be as a whirlwind: his horses are swifter than eagles' (4:13).[10]

Immediately after 'I gotta run', therefore, it is a prophet-like narrative voice from the present that cuts in for the rest of this third verse, tapping the preceding conversationalists on the shoulder and tugging us back from distractions, this time with a reworking of some of Paul the Apostle's words to the Corinthians (1 Corinthians 15:30–31): 'And why stand we in jeopardy every hour? I protest by your rejoicing which I have in Christ Jesus our Lord, I die daily'. In Dylan's song this becomes

> *I stand in jeopardy every hour*
> *Wondering what reason you have to rejoice.*

Then comes the reinforcing chorus, this time not only varying the lines that elaborate the title-statement but replacing the regular rhetorical question of the penultimate line, 'Can you take it on the chin?' (the slightly comic effect of which makes for another way that the song demurs from the earnestness of evangelising) with the clever 'Enough to put you in a tail-spin!'

What strikes first is the appropriately awkward fit of this line, emphasised by a delivery that enacts the confusion it is remarking upon – Dylan's timing here, resourceful as ever, first creates perplexed hesitation and then scurries along the line, to catch up, as it were, or regain the right road. What hits home later is that Dylan's half-rhyme for 'comes sin', 'tailspin', holds such a terrific pun, uniting modern language with scriptural import, as happens many times in Dylan's work of the 'Christian' period. Here Dylan appropriates the technological term, a figure of speech describing loss of control at the wheel of a machine, and applies it to define being caught by the devil himself: being sent spinning by ancient evil embodied with a tail. As a finishing touch, a flourish that expresses that 'being in a spin' while owning up to recollections of relishing it, we get perhaps the very best 'awwl-right!' he's ever done, mid-1960s notwithstanding.

The final verse of the song (as we have it) functions as if, like 'The Ballad Of Frankie Lee And Judas Priest', it starts with 'Well the moral of the story . . .', opening with straightforward summary:

> *Jeremiah preached repentance*
> *To those who would turn from hell*

---

10.   When vengeance came, it was by God's allowing the enemy to overcome his chosen people, ushering in the period of the Babylonian captivity. 'The snorting of his horses was heard . . . the whole land trembled at the sound of the neighing of his strong ones; for they are come, and have devoured the land, and all that is in it; the city, and those that dwell therein' (Jeremiah 8:16).

and moving at once to fuse the figure of the Old Testament prophet with the singer himself:

> *But the critics all gave him such bad reviews*
> *Put him down, at the bottom of a well.*
> *[He] kept on talking anyway*
> *As the people were put into chains*
> *Wasn't nobody there to say 'Bon Voyage!'*
> *Or shatter any bottles of champagne—*

and with those last two lines, companion lines to 'Lenny Bruce''s 'Never did get any Golden Globe award, never made it to Synanon', Dylan reaches his final chorus, and the end of a song that has proved alive and tough, witty and resourceful and full of reverberating awareness of life's conflicting positions.

CHAPTER TWELVE

Every Grain of Sand

'Every Grain Of Sand' deals very differently from 'Yonder Comes Sin' with what may be conflict just as fundamental, that between faith and doubt – though as we shall soon see, this interpretation of the song's theme seems open to doubt itself. What we come to first, in any case, long before we come to understand much of the lyric, is the music and the structure of the song.

I'm not sure why people like the demo-version issued on "Bootleg Series I–III": the music seems uncertain of itself – Fred Tackett's guitar-work and Dylan's keyboards make for a muted turbulence which fails to support the regularity of the song's construction – and this produces not an expressive tension between the two (as, say, between Robbie Robertson's guitar and Dylan's keyboards on 'Dirge') but an indeterminacy, while Dylan's voice strains unattractively in a key just out of reach. Far from carrying over into a suggestion of the hard struggle for faith, this merely sounds a failure of performance. And since Jennifer Warnes' singing is so low in the mix as to be unjudgeable, we might say that the best vocal on the track belongs to the dog that barks in the middle. Its voice, unlike Dylan's here, has a rounded, bell-like tone, harmonically rich and in every way expressive, while the timing of its entrance is startling but immaculate. It strongly recalls, in tone *and* timing, the imitations of the bells achieved to such beguiling effect by the back-up singers on that religious potboiler 'The Three Bells (The Jimmy Brown Song)' by Les Compagnons de la Chanson. (The back-up singers on Dylan's recording of 'Copper Kettle' do much the same job.[1])

The religious potboiler that bubbles in the background of *all* versions of 'Every Grain Of Sand', because it does touch on the words rather than the music, is 'I Believe', which Dylan will have known, if not from Frankie Laine, then certainly from Elvis Presley, whose 1957 recording was released on both "Elvis' Christmas Album" and alongside 'Peace In The Valley' (a song Dylan performed in concert in 1989) on the EP of that name. The short lyric of 'I Believe' (which in Britain we also had to put up with by David Whitfield *and* the Bachelors) lists things that seem ordered in the universe ('I believe for every drop of rain that falls, a flower grows') and in which the Master's hand can be discerned, including:

---

1.   Edith Piaf and les Compagnons de la Chanson: 'Les Trois Cloches', Paris, 1946; re-recorded without Piaf [Paris, 1948], it was issued as 'The Three Bells (The Jimmy Brown Song)', Columbia Records DB 2697 [78 rpm], DB 4358 [45 rpm], London, 1959, and covered (in English) by many artists, including the Browns: 'The three Bells', *nia*, RCA Victor Records 20-7555, New York [RCA 1140, London], 1959.

Every time I hear a new-born baby cry . . .

(where did these songwriters hang out: a maternity ward?)

. . . or touch a leaf, or see the sky
Then I know why, I, believe.[2]

The album version of 'Every Grain Of Sand', recorded April-to-May 1981, echoes another pop record also: it has the same intro as Roy Orbison's great single 'Crawling Back' (from his otherwise fallow period at MGM, after the run of Monument hits), with exactly the same stately arpeggios. Since this is an obscure echo, however, the predominant effect of the arpeggio'd intro is to establish, by the hint of formal *musique* it carries, the ordered nature of the whole song. Then Dylan's voice comes in: direct, serious and without melodrama. It is a broad, steadfast voice, not straining but submitting to the discipline of the formal, careful structure of the song, *its* orderliness an enactment of that claimed by the title. We are served notice that here is a submission to order on every level of the song's being.

There is no distracting small-talk. We are at once into the narrator's confession of feeling prompted to confession (to his crawling back), and then 'onward' into the 'journey' of following this through. There is no evocation of turmoil or chaos here: the experience of turmoil undergone is logged objectively. The recounting of the journey is unemphatic about the narrator's personal anguish; though the faith and possible doubt experienced is necessarily of a personal nature, the song is concerned to emphasise the stages of the journey rather than the declamatory 'me! me! me!' of it: so much so that the personal sojourn scrupulously follows scriptural signposts.

Consider how many of these occur in the first verse alone.[3] The opening line's 'confession' parallels that of Daniel (9:3–19) – and actually we too are following scriptural signposts here: 'Every Grain Of Sand' is an appropriate song to come to from 'Yonder Comes Sin' precisely because to do so means moving on from Jeremiah to Daniel – which is just what happens in the biblical narrative. It is when Daniel heeds the prophecies of Jeremiah that he makes his 'confession'. That is, he pours out his soul in fervent prayer to God, earnestly asking for pardon and restoration for his captive people.

This is why it is open to doubt as to whether Dylan's song is really about faith versus *doubt*. As with Daniel, when the song's 'voice' is 'reaching out somewhere', and when 'there's someone there' only sometimes, it may not be that he doubts God's existence, but that his knowledge of mankind's sins leads him to feel uncertain whether God is yet ready to answer his supplication. 'Oh Lord,' Daniel confesses, 'righteousness belongeth unto thee . . . to us belongeth confusion of face . . . because

2.   Frankie Laine: 'I Believe', *nia*, Columbia Records 39938, New York [Philips PB 117, London], 1953. Elvis Presley: 'I Believe', NYC, 12/1/57, issued "Peace In The Valley" EP, RCA Victor EPA 4054, New York [RCA Records RCX 101, London], 1957, and "Elvis' Christmas Album", RCA Victor LOC 1035 ['special de luxe edition', replaced by LPM 1951], New York, 1957 [RCA Records RD 27052, London, 1957]. David Whitfield: 'I Believe', *nia*, Decca Records F 11289, London, 1960. The Bachelors: 'I Believe', *nia*, Decca Records F 11857, 1964.

3.   *Lyrics 1962–1985* (1986, UK 1987), sets out the lyric in six 4-line stanzas but the more natural shape, hearing the song on the record, is as three verses each of eight lines and each ending with the title phrase. This is how it is described in what follows.

we have sinned against thee. To the Lord our God belong mercies and forgivenesses, though we have rebelled against him. Neither have we obeyed the voice of the Lord our God, to walk in his laws . . .' (9:7–10). So, as for Daniel, so for Dylan too it may not be a case of doubting God's existence but of doubting whether the time of confession will coincide with God's feeling it is time to show his mercy.

The perplexing 'pool of tears beneath my feet' in the second line of the song may be unperplexing if recognised as welling up in the spirit of the psalm supposedly written by Daniel, Psalm 119, verse 136 of which flows naturally on from his confession: 'Rivers of water run down mine eyes, because they keep not thy law'. The fifth line of the song can be understood to take as its text Luke 9:62, in which Christ says that once you are resolved to follow him, you should not delay or go back, even to tell your family you're leaving.[4] This accords with Christ's own childhood walk-out on Joseph and Mary (which always struck me as heartless). The trouble with taking the biblical text here to illuminate the line of the song is that it doesn't: it only narrows it down. 'Don't have the inclination to look back on any mistakes' holds a far wider psychological appeal, sets up a far deeper personal resonance and avows a far more attractive resoluteness than its biblical 'parallel'. The immaculately ordered yet blazingly inspired sixth line draws the explicit parallel 'Like Cain . . .'[5] The line that follows, 'In the fury of the moment I can see the Master's hand', may be said to allude to 'the cup of his fury', from the book that precedes Jeremiah, Isaiah (51:17), referred to again as 'the wine cup of this fury' in Jeremiah 25:15. If the allusion is deliberate, then here again Dylan is surely disavowing doubt: saying on the contrary that even during the 'moment' when God is withholding his mercy, he perceives his presence.

Those, then, are the scriptural signposts in the first verse. The second may have as many. Part of the point of the first two lines – in which the wrong sorts of metaphorical flora have 'choked the breath of conscience and good cheer' – is to take up the sustained metaphor in the parable of the sower, told by Christ and recounted by the apostle Mark ('as he sowed, some fell by the wayside . . . some fell on stony ground . . . And some fell among thorns, and the thorns grew up, and choked it, and it yielded no fruit. And other fell on good ground, and did yield fruit . . .': Mark 4:4–8).

It may be felt, on early hearings, that the connection between the lines of Dylan's song and this parable is tenuous, activated only by Dylan's direct importation of the word 'choked' – or at least that the usefulness of the parable to the song is small. In fact it goes deeper than that, and proves an example of how quietly and intelligently Dylan uses his biblical allusions to speak for him; to articulate his own position.

The point about this parable, as Christ explains to the apostles when they ask him, is that because of what it is about, it holds the key to *all* the parables. 'And he said unto them, Know ye not this parable? and how then will ye know all parables?' He explains it at once: 'The sower soweth the word' (Mark 4:13–14). So the parable

---

4.   Verses 61 and 62 read: 'And another also said, Lord, I will follow thee; but let me first go bid them farewell, which are at home at my house. And Jesus said unto him, No man, having put his hand to the plough, and looking back, is fit for the kingdom of God'. Which also prompts that other song-line, 'Keep your hand on that plow, hold on!', as sung on Dylan's début album, twenty years before 'Every Grain Of Sand'.

5.   In 'Yonder Comes Sin' too, Dylan has one of his narrative voices compare himself to Cain, though implicitly: in singing 'My brother's blood is crying from the grave', Dylan is echoing God's retort, after Abel's death, to Cain's famously callow impertinence 'Am I my brother's keeper?': 'And he [God] said, What hast thou done? the voice of thy brother's blood crieth unto me from the ground' (Genesis 4:9–10).

concerns how different sorts of people receive the word of God, and Christ goes on to delineate them.

Those who are by the wayside where the word is 'sown' are those who hear it but for whom 'Satan cometh immediately, and taketh away the word that was sown in their hearts'. Those who are the stony ground are those 'who, when they have heard the word, immediately receive it with gladness; And have no root in themselves, and so endure but for a time'.

Those who represent good ground, uncomplicatedly, are those 'such as hear the word, and receive it, and bring forth fruit' from then on, of varying richness: 'some thirtyfold, some sixty, and some an hundred'.

And then there is the other sort of person, among whom Dylan's narrator in 'Every Grain Of Sand' is making it clear that he counts himself one: 'And these are they which are sown among thorns; such as hear the word, And the cares of this world, and the deceitfulness of riches, and the lusts of other things entering in, choke the word, and it becometh unfruitful' (Mark 4:15–19).

Just as Christ designates as 'thorns' those things which crowd out the word of God, Dylan takes the metaphor *and* the piled-up poetic effect of Christ's own 'X of Y' construction – 'the cares of this world, and the deceitfulness of riches, and the lusts of other things' – and compresses these together into his own confession of such distractions: 'the flowers of indulgence and the weeds of yesteryear'. Meanwhile this sustained metaphor also cross-fertilises with the 'newborn seed' of the song's second line and with 'every leaf that trembles' in the eighth.

Likewise, on early hearings I wasn't convinced of the efficacy of 'conscience and good cheer'. In the context of the song alone, 'conscience' seemed one of those formal, dead words, like the earlier 'morals', while 'good cheer' carried such intrusive associations of hostelry-merriment that this dodgy antiquatedness choked the breath of any direct meaning the phrase might have carried. (You can imagine how the Bob Dylan of *Don't Look Back* would have taken to being exhorted to good cheer.) Yet in the context the song has itself established – the context of the return to God of the 'confession', the context of the parable of the sower – as a phrase for the word of God, Dylan's 'conscience and good cheer' is a deft, profound summation of what the word brings. It sketches in the stick and the carrot, as it were, involved in accepting God's law.

As for the phoney jollity of 'good cheer', perhaps this resonance is parochially English; in any case, for those who read the gospels, the phrase holds the stronger resonance of Christ's own usage, reported two chapters later by Mark, when the apostles see him walk on water: 'Be of good cheer: it is I; be not afraid' (6:50), which can itself be applied as a general exhortation, a motto that stresses the uplifting effect of the faith. Dylan's echo of the phrase here is thus entirely apt, and we come to understand just how much has been compressed into the two lines of the song which end with it.[6]

6.   The parable of the sower is also recounted in Matthew 13:3–8 and in Luke 8:5–8, with Christ's explications of it given in Matthew 13:19–23 and Luke 8:11–15. Unlike Mark's version, Matthew and Luke use the word 'seed', though only Luke quotes Christ as doing so to explain the parable ('Now the parable is this: the seed is the word of God'); and while Matthew quotes a shorter but otherwise near-identical version of Christ's poetic turn of phrase as regards the meaning of the choking by thorns – 'the care of this world, and the deceitfulness of riches,

It's possible, as Bert Cartwright's booklet 'The Bible in the Lyrics of Bob Dylan' suggests, that the next two lines in Dylan's song, 'The sun beat down upon the steps of time to light the way / To ease the pain of idleness and the memory of decay', refer back to the very end of the Old Testament, in the last chapter of the last book of which we find God telling Israel that 'unto you that fear my name shall the Sun of righteousness arise with healing in his wings; and ye shall go forth' (Malachi 4:2) and to a passage from Paul's Epistle to the Romans, as rendered in the Revised Standard Version of the New Testament, in which he looks forward to 'the Coming Glory', when 'the creation itself will be set free from its bondage to decay' ('shall be delivered from the bondage of corruption', as the Authorized Version has it, Romans 8:21).

That Dylan had been reading and reflecting on this Epistle is not in doubt: the passage just quoted is only three verses on from the one clearly used by Dylan as the basis of two lines from the contemporaneous 'In The Summertime'[7] – but the link between the lines of 'Every Grain Of Sand' and the biblical verses seem hardly to extend beyond their shared use of the words 'sun' and 'decay'.

Unlike the preceding lines of the song, which are illuminated by the passages of the gospels to which they refer, here neither the Malachi nor the Romans verse seems to open out or clarify what Dylan writes. Indeed in the case of the Malachi passage, it seems merely to confuse the issue, while limiting and weakening Dylan's range of meaning. The 'Sun of righteousness' is figurative, and is intended to mean the Son of God. Only by dint of forcing this passage to coexist with that from Romans, in which Paul talks of the Second Coming – the end of the world, and therefore of time, and therefore of decay – is it possible to speculate that Dylan's sun beating down 'upon the steps of time to light the way' and 'ease . . . the memory of decay' (a way of designating it as a thing of the past) refers to Christ providing guidance through to eternal salvation. At best, it's an awkward force-fit, it involves skipping over 'the pain of idleness' as if *it* has no function at all, and altogether it asks us to avoid the clearer and more simple idea that Dylan's reference to the 'sun' really is a reference to the sun, and not 'the Son'. As we shall note later, the idea of the sun guiding us through time seems a Blakeian one, and open to view from a number of angles. Insisting that Dylan intends a parallel to the verse of Malachi closes off all of these.

We are on surer ground in noting that the final line of Dylan's second verse returns us to the teaching of Christ as given in the gospel of Matthew, as does the final line of the whole song. Indeed Matthew 10:29–31, a passage that quotes Christ directly, is the founding text of the song's title theme: 'Are not two sparrows sold for a farthing? and one of them shall not fall on the ground without your Father. But the

choke the word' – Luke has Christ speaking less poetically but very clearly: 'And that which fell among thorns are they which, when they have heard, go forth, and are choked with cares and riches and pleasures of this life'. John's Gospel gives no account of the parable of the sower.

Christ's exhortation 'Be of good cheer: it is I; be not afraid' is also quoted, word for word, by Matthew (14:27), whereas the phrase 'Be of good cheer' is omitted from John's account (6:20) and Luke omits the whole story of Christ's walking on the water.

7.   '. . . the sufferings of this present time are not worthy to be compared with the glory that shall be revealed in us' (Romans 8:18, Authorized Version); '. . . the sufferings of this present time are not worth comparing with the glory that is to be revealed to us' (Revised Standard Version); 'but all that sufferin''s not to be compared / With the glory that is to be' (Dylan's 'In The Summertime'). Which argues, despite Cartwright's suggestion to the contrary, that Dylan's overwhelming preference – shared, you might presume, by anyone with a real feeling for language – is for the Authorized Version.

very hairs of your head are all numbered. Fear ye not therefore'. Or as Luke (12:6–7) reports it: 'Are not five sparrows sold for two farthings, and not one of them is forgotten before God? But even the very hairs of your head are all numbered. Fear ye not therefore'.

But what does this mean? And what does Dylan make it mean in his song? Christ's message here is not nearly so wide, liberal and all-inclusive as it sounds. What follows at once is: 'Fear ye not therefore, ye are of more value than many sparrows. Whosoever therefore shall confess me before men, him will I confess also before my Father which is in heaven. But whosoever shall deny me before men, him will I also deny before my Father which is in heaven. Think not that I am come to send peace on earth: I came not to send peace but a sword.' (Matthew 10:31–34; the equivalent passage of Luke, which omits the waving of the sword, is in 12:8–9).

Far from throwing God's infinite care over every tiny creature in his universe, as the early part of his speech might imply, it's a severe and conditional vision: it mentions the sparrows only to devalue them in the comparison with men and it excludes from God's care all but true Christian believers.

Christ's words 'the very hairs of your head are all numbered. Fear ye not therefore . . .' are re-worked in a later address to the disciples, reported by Luke: 'But there shall not an hair of your head perish' (21:18), and this reassurance too occurs in a specific and exclusive context: that of Christ warning his disciples of the future destruction of the temple, accompanied by 'great signs . . . from heaven' (21:11), and of Jerusalem, prior to the Second Coming of Christ. He is telling them that as long as they keep their wits about them, *they* will be all right: that every genuine Christian shall be protected when desolation falls upon the Jewish state and everybody else.

Clearly there are occasions when Dylan takes up this narrowed meaning: for instance he takes up the very prophecy of Christ which contains that 'there shall not an hair of your head perish', in the contemporaneous song 'Caribbean Wind' (discussed in Chapter 13):

> . . . there shall not be left one stone upon another, that shall not be thrown down . . . And great earthquakes shall be in divers places, and famines . . . But there shall not an hair of your head perish . . . And when ye shall see Jerusalem compassed with armies, then know that the desolation thereof is nigh.
>
> (Luke 21:6, 11, 18, 20)

> *Every new messenger brings evil report*
> *'Bout armies on the march and time that is short*
> *And famines and earthquakes and train wrecks and the tearin' down of the*
>   *walls.*
>
> ('Caribbean Wind')

That 'train wrecks' is one of Dylan's inspired modernising touches, serving to make the prophecy applicable to *our* near future; the rest of his list – though 'list' is a poor word to cover this marvellous, energetically chiselled writing – is as cited by Christ.[8]

---

8.   St Paul often echoes Christ's phrases also. On the disastrous sea-voyage described in Acts 27, he uses two

Moreover, though the context of the sparrows-and-numbered-hairs passage is not, like that of the later one, predicting the mass destruction of all but the chosen few at the end of the world, Christ's words in the later prophecy as reported by Luke make deliberate cross-reference to earlier rhetorics – that section of the parable of the sower, as given in Mark, on the distractions of 'the cares of this world, and the deceitfulness of riches', and the sparrows falling, as given in Matthew – thus binding the intent of the various passages firmly together. Telling the disciples that '. . . when ye see these things come to pass, know ye that the kingdom of God is nigh at hand', he cautions them: 'And take heed to yourselves, lest at any time your hearts be overcharged with surfeiting, and drunkenness, and *cares of this life* and so that day come upon you unawares. For *as a snare* shall it come on all them that dwell on the face of the whole earth. Watch ye therefore, and pray always, that ye may be accounted worthy to escape'[9] [my emphasis].

That, then, is the scriptural basis for the title theme of 'Every Grain Of Sand', in pursuit of which we have necessarily run on ahead to include the last line of the song. In following *all* its biblical signposts we had really reached only the end of the second verse. We need to go back to the start of the third to follow those that remain. That Christ's narrow meaning as regards the sparrows and the numbered hairs has sparked off innumerable other, broader ideas drawing on the same metaphors, some of which may reverberate through Dylan's song, I leave till a little later to consider.

Dylan begins his third and final verse with 'I have gone from rags to riches in the sorrow of the night'. While the phrase 'rags to riches' is a secular commonplace, used less often as a material boast than as a metaphor for the transforming value of love – as in the song 'Rags To Riches', by Adler and Ross, recorded originally by Tony Bennett in 1953, covered in the UK by David Whitfield, an R&B hit by Billy Ward & The Dominoes in 1954, revived by Sunny & The Sunglows (1963) and Lenny Welch

---

that we have come across in considering the biblical backdrop to 'Every Grain Of Sand' alone: 'And now I exhort you to be of good cheer . . . Wherefore, sirs, be of good cheer . . . for there shall not an hair fall from the head of any of you' (Acts 27:22, 25, 34). However, the latter phrase was a common expression, occurring in the Old Testament in both books of Samuel; in Chapter 14:45 of the first book, it is in this interesting configuration: 'Shall Jonathon die . . .? God forbid: as the Lord liveth, there shall not one hair of his head fall to the ground'.

9.   That the metaphor of the snare refers back to that of the sparrows is suggested by noting the context of Christ's words in Matthew, 'Are not two sparrows sold for a farthing? and one of them shall not fall on the ground without your Father'. The reference is to sparrows being *sold*. Birds were caught in snares like fishes in nets. According to Adam Clarke's *Commentary on the Bible* (1844 edition), the phrase 'on the ground' here may be a mistranslation from the Ancient Greek, in which 'to the earth' is almost identical to 'into a snare', which may have been intended. In any case, Clarke also notes that Christ seems to have borrowed his 'one of them shall not fall . . . without your Father' from the ancient Hebrew manuscript *Bereshith Rabba* (Section 79, Folio 77): 'sitting at the mouth of the cave, they observed a fowler stretching his nets to catch birds; and as often as the Bath Kol said, . . . escape! the bird escaped; but when it said, . . . a dart, the bird was taken. Then the Rabbin said, "Even a bird is not taken without Heaven. How much less the life of a man!"'

   I use Adam Clarke's *Commentary on the Bible* because it represents the informed but traditional thinking of believers, not academic outsiders. Clarke (1762–1832) was a polymath and, as it happens, a Methodist, and his *Commentary*, which was widely popular in its day, was informed by critical inquiry yet just pre-dates the influence of the German scholarship that drove a wedge between the intellectual theological élite and the 'punters' who attended church and accepted the Bible as the word of God. 'Adam Clarke's work is the first example of a Bible Commentary in Methodism which is not only scholarly in the sense of being erudite and learned, but is also beginning to be free to look critically at its subject.' (Stephen B. Dawes, *Adam Clarke: Methodism's First Old Testament Scholar*, Cornish Methodist Historical Association Occasional Publication no. 26, Redruth, Cornwall, 1994.)

(1966), and a minor hit for Elvis Presley in 1971[10] – and while the whole phrase is to be found nowhere in the Bible, nonetheless the Bible frequently applies the same metaphor to suggest the greater transforming power of God's love. Paul talks of 'the riches of his grace' in his Epistle to the Ephesians (1:7, compounded to 'the exceeding riches of his grace' a chapter later, [2:7]).

This is surely Dylan's meaning here, and to complete his fusion of secular phrase with religious meaning (something he so often does with quiet panache) he invokes a passage aptly located in the Book of Isaiah: aptly because it catches Isaiah making *his* confession, and citing those metaphoric 'rags' while supplicating for the riches of being returned to God's favour:

'But we are all as an unclean thing, and all our righteousnesses are as filthy rags; and we all do fade as a leaf: and our iniquities, like the wind, have taken us away' (Isaiah 64:6). Of course this also gives us the 'leaf' that Dylan uses earlier, and we remember that another of his songs, 'Ain't No Man Righteous, No Not One', gives a clear explanatory précis of this exact same biblical verse:

Put your goodness next to God's and it comes out like a filthy rag.[11]

Confirming the 'rags to riches' theme, and the context of confession in which it arises here, as in 'Every Grain Of Sand' – confession not to a God whose existence is doubted but one whose mercy has been withheld – the biblical verses that follow immediately are: '. . . thou hast hid thy face from us, and hast consumed us, because of our iniquities. But now, O Lord, thou art our Father . . . Be not wroth very sore, O Lord, neither remember iniquity for ever: behold, see, we beseech thee, we are all thy people' (Isaiah 64:7–10).

This passage comes almost at the end of the book of Isaiah, the prophet who comes immediately before Jeremiah, and who is giving here a confession on behalf of his people.[12] The confession relates to the period of the Babylonian captivity (which God had permitted the Jews to suffer to punish them for their great wickedness), as the prophecy of Jeremiah was to do also; and it was because of Jeremiah's prophecy as to when this should end that Daniel understood himself to be making *his* confession in the final days of that captivity. In the sequencing of this part of the Old Testament, the books run as follows: Isaiah, Jeremiah, [Jeremiah's] Lamentations, Ezekiel and Daniel. Ezekiel, interposed between Jeremiah and Daniel, lived under the Babylonian

---

10. Tony Bennett: 'Rags To Riches', NYC, 17/3/53, Columbia Records 4-40048, New York, 1953; David Whitfield: 'Rags To Riches', nia, Decca Records F 10207, London, 1953; Billy Ward & The Dominoes: 'Rags To Riches', nia, King 1280. Cincinnati, 1954; Lenny Welch: 'Rags To Riches', nia, Kapp 740, New York, 1966; Elvis Presley: 'Rags To Riches', RCA 47-9980, New York [RCA 2084, London], 1971.

11. Being appalling misogynists, what the ancients really mean by 'an unclean thing' and 'a filthy rag' is a cloth used to absorb menstrual blood. This was too much for the early Victorians. Clarke's *Commentary* (note 9) names the term only in Latin (*pannus menstruatus*) and adds: 'If preachers knew properly the meaning of this word, would they make such liberal use of it in their public ministry? . . . How many in the congregation blush for the incautious man and his "filthy rags!" ' The same passage of Isaiah is translated in an Old English manuscript bible as 'And we ben made as unclene alle we: and as the cloth of the woman rooten blode flowing, all our rigtwisnesses.' In contrast, I imagine the New English Janet Street-Porter version gives the passage as 'But we are all sort of at the wrong time of the month really, OK?'

12. Prophet, *nabi*, derives from *naba*, which means not only to foretell future events but also to pray and supplicate; and before they were termed prophets they were called seers, which was the translation of both *haroeh*, the seeing person, and *chozeh*, the person who has visions or supernatural revelations.

captivity too, and prophesied in Mesopotamia at the same time that Jeremiah prophesied in Jerusalem. Daniel prophesied in Babylon itself. Hence Dylan parallels his modern idiomatically casual usage of 'I got to confess' with its numinous scriptural meaning, re-inhabiting the person of Daniel, in the wonderful understatement of 'I been to Babylon, I got to confess' in 'Tight Connection To My Heart'.

To return to 'Every Grain Of Sand', it follows from the 'rags to riches' that with 'in the sorrow of the night' Dylan may have in mind Psalm 6:6, a most poetic Psalm of David and one which also shares the supplicatory intent of the passages alluded to earlier from Daniel and Isaiah: '. . . all the night make I my bed to swim; I water my couch with my tears'. The context is given in the first three verses of this psalm: 'O Lord, rebuke me not in thine anger, neither chasten me in thy hot displeasure. Have mercy upon me, O Lord; for I am weak: O Lord, heal me; for my bones are vexed. My soul is also sore vexed: but thou, O Lord, how long?'

It is hardly possible to read those lines without being conscious that they reverberate through many fragments of Dylan's work, even if we did not have Dylan's frequent expressions of admiration for 'some righteous king who wrote psalms beside moonlit streams' ('I And I', 1983). It seems to me too that the earlier 'fury of the moment', the present 'sorrow of the night' and the imminent 'violence of a summer's dream' are all stirred up by that marvellous 'in thy hot displeasure'.

When Dylan adds to this list that he has also 'gone from rags to riches in . . . the bitter dance of loneliness fading into space / In the broken mirror of innocence on each forgotten face' it may be, as Bert Cartwright suggests, that the 'mirror' alludes to the insistence of Genesis that 'God created man in his own image' (1:27) and that its 'innocence' being 'broken' alludes to the almost immediate eating from the tree of knowledge by Adam and our consequent banishment from the garden – but I'm bound to say that unlike the example of how 'in thy hot displeasure' at once leaps to illuminate the Dylan phrases which shift, hot and restless, around it, the possible scriptural signpost here does nothing to improve the poetry of Dylan's line, even if it offers to 'explain' its prosaic meaning. Similarly, though Cartwright suggests that in the next Dylan line, 'I hear the ancient footsteps like the motion of the sea', he is returning to Daniel, and to the text 'I saw in the night visions, and, behold, one like the Son of man came . . . to the Ancient of days' (Daniel 7:13) for myself I can't see that this assists the meaning of the Dylan line, nor that its poetry needs any help in this instance.

Likewise, there is surely no applicability, on any level, to Cartwright's suggestion that another phrase from Daniel – 'Thou art weighed in the balances, and art found wanting' (5:27) – is the scriptural basis for Dylan's 'I am hanging in the balance of [either] the reality of man [or] a perfect finished plan'. No coincidence of context or meaning exists here, and to urge it, purely on the basis that the phrase 'in the balance[s]' is in both, is to warp Dylan's intention. The Dylan line can carry a weight of meaning, and a breadth of implication, which is informed by the whole complexity of the title theme (this has been explored above and is explored further below) while the verse of Daniel means the narrow opposite of '*hanging* in the balance', and is the word of God to the sacrilegious and idolatrous King Belshazzar, as translated by Daniel at the king's request, from the writing that appears on the wall at his feast, and which is incomprehensible to everyone else who sees it. (The writing comprises the words ME-NE, ME-NE, TE-KEL, U-PHAR-SIN, and the quotation Cartwright refers to is Daniel's translation of the one word TE-KEL.)

On the whole, of course, Cartwright's listings of biblical 'annotations' are extremely useful and have provided many starting points for the scrutiny offered here; but I hope that this long interpretative exploration of scriptural signposts along the journey through 'Every Grain Of Sand' has suggested that there are more than enough genuine and usefully illuminating ones, without the Dylan reader/listener having to clutch at dubious and confusing extras to add to the pile.

All the same, I should like to add one dubious (though not confusing) extra myself, in reference to those terrific lines in Dylan's final verse

> *I hear the ancient footsteps like the motion of the sea*
> *Sometimes I turn, there's someone there, other times it's only me.*

There is a text, not from the Bible, but available on posters and cards at all religious bookshops, which, fairly repulsively, touches on Dylan's theme here, if we concede that in addition to the central question in 'Every Grain Of Sand' being 'Is God yet ready to show us his mercy?', as I have argued, it must also address, for most people who hear the song, the issue of doubt versus belief – and never so affectingly as in the lines just quoted. Coming in at a tangent to them, then, the religious homily I have in mind is one called 'Footprints In The Sand', by Anon:

> *I noticed that at times along the path of life there was only one set of footprints.*
> *I also noticed that it happened at the very lowest and saddest times of my life . . .*
> *and I questioned God about it.*
>
> *'God, You said that once I decided to follow You, You would walk with me*
> *all the way but . . . during the most troublesome time in my life there is only one*
> *set of footprints. I don't understand why in times when I needed You most, You*
> *would leave me.'*
>
> *God replied, 'My precious, precious child . . .'*

which doesn't sound much like God's mode of address, but let it pass:

> *'. . . I love you and I would never, never leave you during your times of trials and*
> *suffering. When you see only one set of footprints it was then that I carried you.'*

Quick thinking, Lord. Like Bob Dylan, we shall stick to the King James Version: in which there is, before we move away from this terrain, one last authentic scriptural quotation that holds to notions of God's guardianship over us and that might be said to hover over Dylan's lyric. This too comes from a Psalm of David:

'How precious also are thy thoughts unto me, O God! how great is the sum of them! If I should count them, they are more in number than the sand' (Psalm 139:17, 18), which occurs in the context of David's acknowledging that God is everywhere, and sees everything, and has guarded over him always, and that he is counted among the works of God, and that he cannot expect to understand all of his knowledge of God: '. . . the darkness and the light are both alike to thee. For thou hast possessed my reins: thou hast covered me in my mother's womb. I will praise thee; for I am fearfully and wonderfully made; and that my soul knoweth right well . . . Such knowledge is too wonderful for me; it is high, and I cannot attain unto it' (Psalm

139:12–14, 6). And that last is a conclusion which, as we shall soon see, Alexander Pope arrives at in his poem 'The Essay on Man', after *he* has been contemplating the falling sparrow and God's regard.

However narrowly Christ intended the significance of the Fatherly eye on the falling sparrow, a huge and broad sweep of ideas, including the liberal, the radical and the mystical, has been activated by the sheer poetry of possibility in Christ's *words*. Taken to embrace the idea that God cares for every sparrow, the implications are endless.

It has been possible to argue from this that the New Testament contradicts the speciesism of the Old, which appears to insist that the animal kingdom is ours to dispose of as we wish: 'dominion over the fish of the sea, and over the fowl of the air, and over the cattle, and over all the earth, and over every creeping thing that creepeth upon the earth' (Genesis 1:26) – though this too is open to debate as to the real implications of the word 'dominion', not to mention modern scepticism about the propriety of basing ideas about the relation of people to animals on those of a primitive farming community.

It was possible for the Victorians to take from Christ's remarks a means of reconciling Darwin's disturbing ideas of evolution, of natural selection, with that of God's providence. It was possible for Shakespeare to extrapolate from Christ's words a different set of considerations: to have Hamlet take from them, after the agonies of his inner struggles as depicted throughout the play (after 'toiling in the danger and in the morals of despair', in fact), something closer to a peaceful acceptance not only of the *idea* of death's inevitability but to the prospect that his own death might be imminent. It is at this juncture that Hamlet can say:

> ... There is special providence in the fall of a sparrow. If it be now, 'tis not to come; if it be not to come, it will be now; if it be not now, yet it will come. The readiness is all. Since no man of aught he leaves knows, what is't to leave betimes [i.e. early]? Let be.

'Hamlet is painfully aware of the baffling human predicament between the angels and the beasts, between the glory of having been made in God's image and the incrimination of being descended from Adam,' writes the critic Tillyard. Or, as Maynard Mack puts it:

> When we first see him ... he is clearly a very young man ... suffering the first shock of growing up. He has taken the garden at face value ... , supposing mankind to be only a little lower than the angels ... now he sees everywhere the general taint, taking from life its meaning ... Hamlet ... [has] felt the heavy and the weary weight of all this unintelligible world; and ... in his young man's egocentricity, he will set it right. Hence he misjudges Ophelia ... he misjudges himself ... he takes it upon himself to be his mother's conscience, though the ghost has warned ... 'Leave her to heaven ...' Even with the king, Hamlet has sought to play at God.

Later, Hamlet comes to understand that 'There is a divinity that shapes our ends / Rough hew them how we will'. Thus he comes round to feeling that 'Are You Ready?' is the question.

' "Readiness" here means both submitting to providence and being in a state of preparation. It is not that death does not matter . . . but [that] readiness matters more. Shakespeare's tragic heroes do not renounce the world. [For the] dying Hamlet . . . Such values are never denied, but at the end . . . they are no longer primary,' as Edward Hubler explains it. And the irresolvable questions remain: 'Are we to assume from Hamlet's references to heaven, divinity and providence that he is now convinced of the great moral design of creation? Or do we see a Hamlet bowing before a universe which defies man's intellectual attempts at comprehension?' (Robert Ornstein)[13]

This last question also seems to have preoccupied the exemplar of eighteenth-century man, Alexander Pope, though you would not know it by taking the relevant lines from his 1733–34 poem *The Essay on Man* out of context:

> [He] . . . *sees with equal eye, as God of all*
> *A hero perish, or a sparrow fall.*

For early Victorian believers, these lines were to suggest a shocking coldness of equality, an irreligious equalising of noble mankind and lowly sparrow: yet this is exactly what makes such a notion of God's guardianship over everything in the universe seem warm and benign to some more modern sensibilities. Pope's lines actually point up the contrast between the blindness of God's creatures ('Heaven from all creatures hides the book of fate . . . O blindness to the future! kindly giv'n') and the clarity of God's all-seeing vision, and his 'equal' may embrace the sense of the Latin word *aequus*: 'propitious' or 'benign'.

In any case, Pope is, as he says at the poem's beginning, simply rummaging around among these ideas himself:

> *Let us (since life can little more supply*
> *Than just to look about us and to die)*
> *Expatiate free o'er all this scene of man;*
> *A mighty maze! but not without a plan.*

Without suggesting that Bob Dylan has been trying to echo Pope (any more than that his song attempts to carry every other resonance or idea sparked off by Christ's words), I note that we can be reminded, by these last-quoted two lines, one after the other, of Dylan's two alternative endings for his song. In the album version and the version published in *Lyrics 1962–1985* this is

> *I am hanging in the balance of the reality of man*
> *Like every sparrow falling, like every grain of sand*

while in both the earlier demo version and the later concert version of 1984, it is

> *I am hanging in the balance of a perfect finished plan*
> *Like every sparrow falling, like every grain of sand.*

*

---

13.   All these quotations come from essays reprinted in the Signet Classic Shakespeare *Hamlet*, 1963, except the Tillyard quote, which is cited in the Maynard Mack essay without further attribution.

More certainly and thoroughgoingly, however, it is William Blake who, re-writing the Bible in his own unique way, hovers all around Bob Dylan's song in relation to its themes, its language and the rhythms of that language, though there is little conjunction of philosophy. Blake's philosophy, as Yeats claimed, brings him '. . . at last to forget good and evil in an absorbing vision of the happy and the unhappy'.[14] The ideas Dylan takes from the Judaeo-Christian religion are far more orthodox than Blake's. Yet Blake's interest in taking biblical text and flying it to mystical heights is evident everywhere in his work, as is Bob Dylan's interest in that work by his mystic predecessor; and never more so than around the texts behind 'Every Grain Of Sand'. (It's interesting that when Blake reaches his forties, he comes to accept, like Dylan, a degree of Christian orthodoxy previously refused: as pointed out in Peter Ackroyd's *Blake*, 1995, it is in 'Vala or the Four Zoas', the great epic poem of Blake's middle age, that he first uses the word 'saviour' and the phrase 'the Lamb of God'.)

Blake's poem 'On Another's Sorrow' (*Songs of Innocence*) urges:

> *Think not thou canst sigh a sigh*
> *And thy maker is not by;*
> *Think not thou canst weep a tear*
> *And thy maker is not near*

while in *Jerusalem* (1804–20) Blake writes that

> *. . . the Divine Lord & Saviour . . . suffers with those that suffer,*
> *For not one sparrow can suffer & the whole Universe not suffer also.*[15]

That mankind must love all things as he loves God is urged equally. In 'The Little Boy Lost' (*Songs of Experience*, 1789–94), the priest punishes the boy who, quite rightly by Blake's lights, tells God:

> *I love you like the little bird*
> *That picks up crumbs around the door.*

---

14. 'William Blake', republished in W. B. Yeats, *Essays* (1924). (Yeats' role as an early co-editor of Blake's work, with Edwin J. Ellis, is mentioned in Chapter 2 note 32, re Blake's 'Island in the Moon'.) T. S. Eliot too published a well-known essay on Blake, first published under the title 'The Naked Man' (*Atheneum*, 1920) and then revised and republished as 'William Blake' in *Selected Essays 1917–1932* (1932), in which he said that Blake 'has the unpleasantness of all great poetry'. Ignoring, or deploring others' ignoring of, the rigorous qualities of Blake that Eliot's remark (unlike Yeats') implies, twentieth-century social poets, such as Peter Porter, have recoiled from the beat/hippie revival of Blake, either disliking *per se* exactly those mystical qualities for which he is a New Age hero, or else objecting to his appropriation by hippies. 'William Blake, William / Blake, William Blake, William Blake, / say it and feel new!', sneers a verse of Porter's poem 'Japanese Jokes' (published in *Last of England*, 1970). Actually I prefer the poet and critic Fred Grubb's misremembrance of this salvo, as offered in the course of a book review ('Mountaineer', *London Magazine*, London, Dec. 1989–Jan. 1990): 'Blake! Blake! Blake! Say it and feel good'.

The greatest contemporary Blake scholar is perhaps the poet and critic Kathleen Raine, who has published a two-volume study, *Blake and Tradition* (1968), and an illustrated volume, *William Blake* (1970).

All my quotations from Blake are taken from *Blake: Complete Writings*, edited by Geoffrey Keynes, (1969), from the Dover Thrift Edition of *Songs of Innocence and Songs of Experience* (1992), and from Peter Ackroyd's *Blake* (1995).

15. *Jerusalem* is one of Blake's huge symbolic epics – in which the words, mostly in blank verse, are bound up with, indeed etched on copper plates as part of, his designs; Blake, who printed most of these works himself (his wife, Catherine, bound them), never intended words and pictures to be separated. The Blake poem/song we know as 'Jerusalem' ('And did those feet in ancient time . . .') is a quite separate work: it is actually part of the Preface to a different epic book by Blake, *Milton* (1804–08).

In the booklet of notes for the "Bootleg Series I–III" box-set, John Bauldie says that

> *. . . I can see the Master's hand*
> *In every leaf that trembles, in every grain of sand*

is 'echoing William Blake's 'Auguries of Innocence'', and that 'In the last verse . . . he turns, hearing those "ancient footsteps" which betray the presence of God (again the image is borrowed from Blake).'

To take the last first, I'm not sure what reference Bauldie has in mind here but perhaps he's thinking of this passage from the 'Introduction' to *Songs of Experience*:

> *Hear the voice of the Bard!*
> *. . . Whose ears have heard*
> *The Holy Word*
> *That walk'd among the ancient trees,*
> *Calling the lapsed Soul . . .*

which would be appropriate enough in the circumstances both of Dylan's 'religious position' at the time he was writing 'Every Grain Of Sand' and of his being one 'Bard' echoing the voice of another – though hearing the Holy Word that walked among the ancient trees does not present the same image as Dylan's hearing the ancient footsteps.

As for the echo from 'Auguries of Innocence', well, this is complicated. 'Auguries of Innocence' – which is a single, 133-line poem written in or shortly before 1803, and not part of the *Songs of Innocence* – begins with the well-known first stanza

> *To see a World in a Grain of Sand*
> *And a Heaven in a Wild Flower*
> *Hold Infinity in the palm of your hand*
> *And Eternity in an hour*[16]

but though the Dylan remark of 1976 quoted by Bauldie, 'I can see God in a daisy', directly parallels the *second* line of the Blake stanza here, and clearly this *is* re-echoed in Dylan's 'I can see the Master's hand / In every leaf that trembles, in every grain of sand', actually that 'sand' carries more complex connections between God, his creation, his love and human awareness of these things.

First, what Blake suggests by 'To see a World in a Grain of Sand' is something more complex than merely that the fact of the grain of sand reveals God's presence. Like his

> *How do you know but ev'ry Bird that cuts the airy way,*
> *Is an immense world of delight, clos'd by your senses five?*

---

16. The other 129 lines form the second stanza, and are a series of moral aphorisms of which the first is representative: 'A Robin Red breast in a Cage / Puts all Heaven in a Rage'. Another, of which we might be reminded by Dylan's allusion in 'Man In The Long Black Coat' to the beating of the dead horse, is: 'A Horse misus'd upon the Road / Calls to heaven for Human blood', while the *quid pro quo* of this interconnection is that 'The wild deer, wand'ring here & there, / Keeps the Human Soul from Care' and 'Every Wolf & Lion's howl / Raises from Hell a Human Soul'.

the lines of Blake referred to by Bauldie in fact press the idea that there is a world to be seen *within* a grain of sand, if our 'senses five' were not so closed – if our 'doors of perception' (this phrase too is Blake's) could be 'cleansed'.[17] That Blake intends this more visionary meaning is clear from a later working of the same theme, in *Jerusalem*, in which he writes:

> *. . . this Gate cannot be found*
> *By Satan's Watch-fiends, tho' they search numbering every grain*
> *Of sand on earth . . .*
>
> *There is a Grain of Sand . . . that Satan cannot find,*
> *Nor can his Watch Fiends find it; 'tis translucent & has many Angles,*
> *But he who finds it will find Oothoon's Palace; for within*
> *Opening into Beulah, every angle is a lovely heaven.*

Comparably, in *Vala*:

> *Then Eno, a daughter of Beulah, took a Moment of Time*
> *And drew it out to seven thousand years with much care & affliction*
> *And many tears, & in every year made windows into Eden.*
> *She also took an atom of space & opened its centre*
> *Into Infinitude . . .*

while Blake's *Milton* (1804–08) includes this:

> *Seest thou the little winged fly, smaller than a grain of sand?*
> *It has a heart like thee, a brain open to heaven & hell,*
> *Withinside wondrous & expansive,: its gates are not clos'd:*

and

> *For every Space larger than a red Globule of Man's blood*
> *Is visionary . . .*
> *And every Space smaller than a Globule of Man's blood opens*
> *Into Eternity of which this vegetable Earth is but a shadow.*[18]

Moreover, for Blake, this 'Eternity' is one in which everything that seems to pass away on the shadowy 'vegetable Earth' actually continues to be:

> *For every thing exists & not one sigh nor smile nor tear,*
> *One hair nor particle of dust, not one can pass away.*

17. Perhaps for Blake it becomes the same thing. What he writes here is: 'If the doors of perception were cleansed every thing would appear to man as it is, infinite. For man has closed himself up, till he sees all things thro' narrow chinks of his cavern' (from 'A Memorable Fancy' in *The Marriage of Heaven and Hell*, c. 1790–93); but in 'There Is No Natural Religion' [Second Series, c. 1788] he writes: 'He who sees the Infinite in all things, sees God. He who sees the Ratio [i.e. the rational] only, sees himself only. Therefore God becomes as we are, that we may be as he is'. Or perhaps as he puts it elsewhere 'A fool sees not the same tree as a wise man sees'.

18. This 'vegetable Earth' is echoed by that other modern poet who has brought William Blake into his own orb, Allen Ginsberg, in his memorable phrase 'the meat universe', by which he refers to the material world. See note 112 in *All Across the Telegraph: A Bob Dylan Handbook* (1987), for a brief elucidation by John Hinchey that links Ginsberg's applying the term in discussing Bob Dylan's film *Renaldo & Clara* [Circuit Films, US, directed Bob Dylan and Howard Alk, 1978] and in discussing the poems of William Blake.

From these wild visionary glimpses, it is almost mundane and prosaic to return to vegetable earth and find, in an untitled poem from Blake's notebook of 1800–1803, that

> . . . *every sand becomes a Gem*
> *Reflected in the beams divine.*

The sweep of Blake's vision surely embraces every possible sense in which every grain of sand is bound up with man's destiny and God's all-caring universe. It seems to me that the boundaries of Dylan's vision in his song are smaller and rather more modest, as is, always, his re-writing of the Bible.

However, that Dylan intends his embrace of Blake in 'Every Grain Of Sand' is indicated by his use of Blake's rhythms and Blake's language, as well as some commonality of theme. The rhythmic correspondence announces this embrace concisely and unmistakably. The whole song is built upon the heptameter, or septenarius, the 7-foot or 7-beat line, which is rare in English-language poetry but is one of Blake's principal trademarks, starting with 'Tiriel' (written about 1786), in which we find

> *A worm of sixty winters creeping on the dusky ground.*

This distinctive metre recurs throughout Blake's work, as here in *The Book of Thel*:

> *Why fade these children of the spring? born but to smile & fall*

and here (also from *Thel*):

> *Thou seest me the meanest thing, and so I am indeed;*
> *My bosom of itself is cold, and of itself is dark,*

and here (from *Jerusalem*):

> *Awake and overspread all Nations as in Ancient Time*
> *For lo: the Night of Death is past and the Eternal Day*
> *Appears . . .*

This 7-beat line is the distinctive foundation upon which Dylan builds the whole of 'Every Grain Of Sand'.

And Dylan's use of Blakeian language, and the commonality of theme? Beyond the echoes of Blake in Dylan's 'the ancient footsteps', and the half-echoes of Blake in Dylan's Bible-derived 'sparrow falling', the numbering of every hair and every grain of sand, there is that striking sun-steps-time combination in Dylan's majestic 7-beat line

> *The sun beat down upon the steps of time to light the way.*

The shining *idea* that line conveys – that the sun is there to light our way through time – is itself Blakeian, though Blake does not propose it; and so is the language in which it is propounded. The same sun-steps-time combination, though advancing a very different idea, is at the heart of 'Ah! Sun-Flower', from *Songs of Experience*:

> *Ah, Sun-flower, weary of time,*
> *Who countest the steps of the Sun,*

> *Seeking after that sweet golden clime*
> *Where the traveller's journey is done . . .*

The occurrence there of that one word 'journey' would not be enough to suggest, even after all these other echoes, that Dylan's use of the same word was Blakeian. However, granted that the other echoes keep sounding, it may not be unreasonable to hear in the whole phrase that offers it in Dylan's song, 'onward in my journey', an echo of Blake's line from *Milton*,

> *While he keeps onwards in his wondrous journey on the earth,*

and if so, then it's worth a moment's speculation as to whether Dylan bears in mind the visionary idea Blake propounds in his preceding lines: the idea that just as when you dream, you are unaware that your body is at rest, so too when you are journeying through your earthly life, your 'Immortal Self' is already reposing in Heaven.

However this may be, you cannot read Blake without noticing the particular words and constructions he likes a lot and returns to often – and some of these Blakeian words and word-patterns are taken up and resung in hugely varying works by Bob Dylan, as they have been by Allen Ginsberg.[19]

However, as the quotations from Blake already given here will have shown, there are, crudely, two Blake modes of poetic writing: the sublimely simple mode of *Songs of Innocence* and *Songs of Experience*, and the hyperactive complexity of the declamatory epic poems; and clearly, like Ginsberg, who can write carefully simple verse but also what he calls his 'long line' poetry (much influenced by Walt Whitman also), Dylan's work reflects both kinds of Blake – certainly more than I ever knew when I was writing earlier editions of this book. But in 'Every Grain Of Sand' Blake's presence is indicated by Dylan's use of specific Blakeian ingredients, rather than merely because in a general way Blake has been a major influence upon Dylan's work.

The recognition of the specific can best follow on, however, from the recognition of the general influence. Ginsberg may say he has to break his long line down to write like Bob Dylan (see his 1973 poem 'On Reading Dylan's Writings', *First Blues*, 1975) but in fact many of Dylan's most Blakeian lines are of the long visionary kind that Blake would punctuate with scattered capital letters and might end with an exclamation mark, as for instance like these disparate but equally Blakeian lines (respectively from 'Precious Angel', 1979, and 'Visions Of Johanna', 1966):

19.   Indeed the Blakeian influence on Ginsberg is so strong that in some cases what seems Blakeian in Dylan may actually have come *via* Ginsberg; for instance the line in Dylan's 'Ring Them Bells' that uses Christ's shepherd-and-his-sheep analogy – 'And the mountains are filled with lost sheep' – reminds me of the harmonium song Ginsberg sings in *Renaldo & Clara*, with its echoey last line 'And all the hills echoéd' – but this is Ginsberg directly quoting Blake: it is the echoey last line of 'Nurse's Song', from *Songs of Innocence* (1789). (Chapter 16 looks further at Dylan's use of this on "Oh Mercy".) Ginsberg has twice recorded this Blake poem, set to his own music, accompanied the second time around by Bob Dylan, whose gift of a Uher tape-recorder in 1965 encouraged Ginsberg to improvise one-chord music: 'I kept hearing musical fragments of Blake's "Grey Monk" moaning through my brain.' ("Songs Of Innocence And Of Experience Tuned By Allen Ginsberg", New York, 1968; Verve/Forecast FTS 3083, USA, 1969; reissued as "Allen Ginsberg", MGM Archetypes M3F-4951, USA, 1974. The later recordings of Ginsberg's Blake songs 'Nurses's Song', accompanied by Dylan, and 'The Tyger', New York, 17 or 20/11/71, have not been issued. The quotation from Ginsberg re fragments of Blake is taken from his 'Explanation Of First Blues' in *First Blues: Rags, Ballads and Harmonium Songs 1971–1974* [1975]. The introductory essay also talks of Ginsberg's singing the 'Grey Monk' in 'Lincoln Park, Chicago, at political convention time' in 1968, when 'Police state shock repair experienced after kidnapping by Secret Service & frustration of peace protest marches opened me to the immediate poignance of Blake's songs, their prophetic simplicity.')

> *On the way out of Egypt, thro' Ethiopia to the Judgment Hall of Christ*

and

> *The Ghost of Electricity howls in the Bones of her Face!*

In fact 'howl' is one of Blake's very favourite words (and the title of Ginsberg's first big Beat-founding poem, of course). He also likes 'Golden Loom' and 'the rolling thunder'. And, to bring us back directly to 'Every Grain Of Sand', if 'howl' is very Blakeian, so is that distinctive little word 'wintry', which Dylan chooses to use towards the end of the song.

Blake uses 'wintry' all the time, as in the final verse of an untitled poem from about 1793, found in his notebook, which has become titled after its first line, 'Let The Brothels Of Paris Be Opened':

> *O, who would smile on the wintry seas,*
> *& Pity the stormy roar?*
> *Or who will exchange his new born child*
> *For the dog at the wintry door?*

'The dog at the wintry door' is reused for Plate 25 of *The First Book of Urizen*, (1794) and again, almost identically, in *Vala* (1779) – 'It is an easy thing . . . To hear the dog howl at the wintry door' – a poem that also offers 'To listen to the hungry raven's cry in wintry season', 'then sleep the wintry days . . . & prepare for a wintry grave', 'rugged wintry rocks' and 'the wintry blast / . . . or the summer pestilence'.[20]

'Yellow as leaves of Autumn, the myriads of Angelic hosts / Fell thro' the wintry skies' comes from *Europe: a Prophecy* (1794); 'Thro' the wintry hail & rain' is a line from the 1800–1803 notebook – and in a poem etched on a cancelled plate for *America: a Prophecy* (1793) we get the exact prefiguring of Dylan's usage, in

> *. . . & his white garments cast a wintry light.*

The other specifically Blakeian thing about 'Every Grain Of Sand' is the formally ordered 'poetic' structural motif, insistently repeated throughout the song, that piles up 'the flowers of indulgence', 'the weeds of yesteryear', 'the breath of conscience', 'the broken mirror of innocence' and so on.

Dylan can't be said to use this construction as skilfully as Blake, whose best equivalents are far more vivid, fresh and original. These wipe the floor with Dylan's:

> *. . . in the dark delusions of repentance*

> *. . . shoes of indolence*

> *. . . Clouds of Learning*

---

20. Set to music by Mike Westbrook, Van Morrison performs Adrian Mitchell's arrangement of some Blake text (Mitchell calls it ' "Let The Slave", incorporating "The Price Of Experience" '), on "A Sense Of Wonder" (1984). The section Mitchell calls 'The Price Of Experience' is lines 397–418 of the Second Night portion of *Vala*. These lines include the first two of the poem's 'wintry' quotes given above. (The poetry called 'Let The Slave' on the Van Morrison album comprises lines 670–6 and 825–6 of the Ninth Night portion of *Vala*, one line I cannot locate ['For Empire is no more and now the Lion and Wolf shall cease'] and finally the first half of line 366 from the Second Night portion of *Vala*, which Morrison says four times over.)

and, famously,

> . . . *the horses of instruction*

as, come to that, does the King James Bible version of Psalm 40 (verse 3) with its 'thou hast made us drink the wine of astonishment'. Indeed to understand what is so good about those phrases is to appreciate why Dylan's, useful as they are in building up the orderliness of the song (an orderliness entirely necessary and right for its theme) are not without their problems.

The contrast in vividness as between Blake's and Dylan's phrases here is a matter of vigour of language and of meaning. That 'shoes of indolence' works not only by virtue of its soft-footed surrealism, its striking originality, the beguiling surprise of the image, but also because the image actively illuminates the idea it offers: there's a suggestion that indolence may or may not fit, that it can be stepped out of and discarded, that it isn't a part of the naked self – and so on, and so on. These hints about the nature of 'indolence' come directly from the imaginative choice of 'shoes'. The 'Clouds of Learning', more simply and obviously, suggests that 'Learning' may not clarify, may not illuminate at all (à la 'your useless and pointless knowledge', perhaps). It is different with the 'dark delusions of repentance'. This is a phrase that offers the oddity of neither quite yielding an image nor being quite matter-of-fact – an oddity that in itself makes for engaging complexity – so that the word-effect itself, the sheer physique of the cadence, predominates. It has a gorgeous hammering muscularity, a rhythm in which you can certainly hear a master's hand, and as it ends on that rat-tat and hiss, it recharges the word 'repentance', giving it an almost onomatopoeic eloquence. Blake does not make it 'poetic'; he makes it poetry.

In 'Every Grain Of Sand' Dylan's equivalents never quite keep the right side of the gap between the two. He manages it brilliantly in all manner of ways in all manner of songs throughout his repertoire, showing again and again the creative imagination *and* the judgement for equivalents of 'shoes of indolence' and for muscularity of writing that can stand alongside 'the dark delusions of repentance' – but he doesn't manage it via this particular form of construction here in this song.

His similarly structured image-carrying phrases are intermingled with echoing phrases that don't present images in the same way – the matter-of-fact ones like 'time of my confession', 'memory of decay' and 'pain of idleness' – so that there is variety in this usage coming and going throughout the song; yet he does not, in the end, quite carry it off. By the song's midway point, you feel that there have been too many of these phrases. Their vigour and illuminative power is not enough to stop the device itself obtruding. And once it obtrudes, you start to check on whether, individually, each of these constructions is really authentic.

That 'broken mirror of innocence', for instance: the 'broken mirror' image *may* inform innocence by means of some appeal to the intellect – you might be able to work out how this image is an apt one (or you might not: to begin with, is innocence the mirror or the broken mirror?) – but it certainly doesn't succeed by any direct, free appeal to the imagination, like the 'shoes of indolence'. It's too careful, too self-consciously writerly, too *constructed*.

Actually the very first of the song's such constructions seems uneasy. It is in the fourth line, and follows on from a sticking-point in the third. The lines are:

> *There's a dyin' voice within me reaching out somewhere,*
> *Toiling in the danger and in the morals of despair.*

The first problem here is: why is it a 'dyin'' voice? The thrust of the song is 'onwards' and, on the whole, upwards: at the very least, the 'voice'/persona is 'hanging in the balance'. It pulls against this to announce, so early on, the downward curve of 'dyin''. Unless we bring to our reading of the song the counterbalancing notion of becoming re-born, then 'dyin'' seems to preclude the possibilities that the song actually goes on to explore. We never catch the reversal of the downward curve. We get the 'dyin' voice . . . reaching out somewhere' – and we're never given the drama, the event, of its being found, of his being saved, of his recognising that when he reaches out 'somewhere' what he locates is the presence of God. All this is something we've missed, because when we find it happening, a few lines later, it is already in the continuous present:

> *In the fury of the moment I can see the Master's hand.*

We hear the words 'the moment' but we don't catch the moment: that 'can' puts it into the always of an ongoing process; what's missing is its being initiated by a rescuing *action*.

So 'dyin'' jars; and immediately after this uneasiness comes another, in the song's first 'X of Y' construction. There's nothing wrong with that 'Toiling in the danger', nor, in itself, with 'of despair': but 'Toiling . . . in the morals of despair' makes it go murky on us: makes it opaque and nebulous.

Then, after 'the fury of the moment', the third stanza begins with 'the flowers of indulgence and the weeds of yesteryear'. The first of these images works, but the crowding in of the second surely does it no favours. The doubling, as it were, draws our attention away from the specific felicity of 'the flowers of indulgence' and towards the device of the writing. Less would have been more: and better the flowers than 'the weeds of yesteryear'. The word 'yesteryear' is a self-reflexive text: it is itself a weed of yesteryear. I don't think it works, here. It doesn't carry any self-knowingness of usage, so that it tends to function by helping set a tone of official poesy which is exactly what makes for uneasiness about the 'X of Y' construction as it recurs.

The construction obtrudes here for another reason too. The flowers and the weeds are given no *immediate* verb – as in 'the flowers of indulgence and the weeds of yesteryear have choked the breath of conscience', which would advance the image by giving the direct follow-through of its analogy. Instead, introduced by the throat-clearing of 'Oh', and isolated from any verb, the flowers and weeds are left hanging there, thrust forward at us like a bunch of flowers, too obviously asking for a response:

> *Oh, the flowers of indulgence and the weeds of yesteryear,*

pause: so that we feel a 'yes, what about them?' before we reach

> *Like criminals, they have choked the breath of conscience and good cheer.*

The word 'they' shouldn't be needed, and proves that the flowers/weeds have been left to dangle at us, while the analogy-within-the-analogy of 'Like criminals' is a disaster. It disrupts the connection between the flowers/weeds and the choking, it offers no compensatory acuteness of its own, and would disrupt the line metrically as well if Dylan didn't squeeze it, in his delivery, into the unattractive compress of 'crim'nals'.

Three lines later comes another analogy-within-an-analogy; again it intrudes upon one of these recurrent 'X of Y' constructions, and again we're likely to suspect that if they were more *felt* and less writerly, such intrusions wouldn't happen. Nor, perhaps, would the construction itself happen so often as to become ponderous. At any rate, by the time we get to

> . . . *the doorway of temptation's angry flame*

it's too much. The doorway of a flame? Some mistake surely. Dylan many times takes two clichés, or two tired images, and by bumping them together revitalises them and makes something new; but this is not one of those times. The doorway of temptation, yes; temptation as fire, yes; but the doorway of its flame? This is image-overload: an image that merely makes a distracting nuisance of itself.

Yet nuisance, rather than disaster, is all it is. By the time we come to it, the orderly sweep of the song, and of its journey – set going despite the 'dyin'' by the surprising energy of resilience suddenly found for the start of the second stanza – has gained momentum, the lovely and strong-burning idea that the sun is there to guide us through time has been advanced, time's 'steps' have with Baudelaireian *correspon-dance* fused with the narrator's, the phrase 'light the way' has re-affirmed the presence of his progress – the combined press of which is shortly to be reinforced by 'every time I pass', 'onward in my journey' and the accompanying 'ancient footsteps' – so that despite the little local difficulty of the doorway's flame, we still picture vividly the narrator's walking past, and gazing into, the doorway of burning temptation.

It may not be the freshest of images but it's entirely appropriate to the song's concern with redemption, with the narrator's reconciliation with God. Its aptness is amplified by the resonance it carries from a fairy tale drawn from biblical terrain: a story which embraces both a doorway of temptation and a restored voice. In the Brothers Grimm's *Our Lady's Child*, after the dead heroine, unable to resist opening the one door forbidden to her in heaven, has lied to cover up her transgression, she is made mute and sent back to earth. Undergoing ordeals, she eventually finds herself about to be burnt at the stake. 'At this moment,' as Bruno Bettelheim summarises it, 'as she desires only to confess her misdeed, she regains her voice to do so . . . The lesson of the story is: a voice used to tell lies leads only to perdition . . . But a voice used to repent . . . and state the truth, redeems us.' Or in other words, like the narrator in Bob Dylan's song, she finds redemption at the time of her confession, in the hour of her deepest need.[21] *Our Lady's Child* also parallels the story of Daniel (10:12), who receives a vision from God, sent to tell him: 'Fear not, Daniel: for from the first day

21.   *The Uses of Enchantment*, Bruno Bettelheim (1976). (I draw on this book again in the chapter on "Under The Red Sky" and Dylan's use of nursery rhyme and fairy tale.) 'Like Biblical stories and myths,' Bettelheim writes, 'fairy tales were the literature that edified everybody – children and adults alike – for nearly all of man's existence.' J. C. Cooper (*Fairy Tales: Allegories of the Inner Life*, 1983) writes that stories 'revolving round a taboo and its contravention, such as opening a forbidden door . . . go back to the [ancient] Amor and Psyche myth.' The Brothers Grimm story *Our Lady's Child*, its biblical connection made clear by its title, parallels Psyche's descent into hell with its heroine's return to earth. Psyche is the Ancient Greek term for the soul.

that thou didst set thine heart to understand, and to chasten thyself before thy God, thy words were heard'.

More crucial are the internal aptnesses of Dylan's song. All his weeds of yesteryear and broken mirrors of innocence and memories of decay might offer uncomfortable poesy, as might the squashed-up 'crim'nals' (and as indeed might the awful phrase 'the balance of the reality of man' – a gawky X of Y of Z if ever there was one) but in the whole song – which, as he remarks to Bill Flanagan, is like no other[22] – there is more felicity than infelicity, more skill than discomfort, more poetry than poesy.

As already noted, order is the aim here, and it is manifest in every aspect of the song. It is not the quality one first looks to Bob Dylan to supply; traditionally, we are likely to value him more for his incomparable acid derangement, the universe of sizzling, surreal, chaotic wit that he creates in work like 'She's Your Lover Now' – a work in which an apt strength is his famous ability to fit into irregular lines however many syllables he likes, while another is his panache with madly dislocated rhymes ('sadness' with 'Charles Atlas', for instance) such that on every level he evokes a drug-soaked but keen alertness to a disorder he can relish: so much so that when the music and the vocal collapse before our ears, it is entirely in the spirit of the song.

With 'Every Grain Of Sand', where order is the appropriate order of the day, Dylan brings to this very different but demanding task a concentrated purposiveness that draws on another side of his multiform talent. Instead of dislocated rhymes, this song demands, and gets, exact ones, and in the most orderly pattern possible: which is, in a 4-line stanza, the AABB pattern rather than the easier and more common ABCB, or even ABAB. The reason why AABB is better at establishing orderliness is that in hearing the rhyme close on the heels of itself, we are made more aware of it, of its regularity: its mechanism constantly reaffirms that regularity. Yet it takes a skilful, judicious touch to achieve this effect without it toppling over into mechanistic intrusion – without our experiencing the rhyme as a clumping heaviness we await with fastidious dread, like corny rhymes that loom threateningly over the listener well in advance of their falling on the ears. It takes a restraint and a lightness of touch that involves resisting making any of those rhymes 'clever', to gain the effect required, so that each rhyme sounds to the listener as if it falls pleasingly into place. Dylan does this with such skill that the skill is inaudible. His AABB pattern never varies, and except for the last rhyme, at song's end, each rhyme is an exact one:

'need/seed', '-where/-pair', '-take/break', 'hand/sand', '-year/cheer', 'the way/decay', 'flame/name', '-stand/sand', 'night/light', 'space/face', 'sea/me'.

For the special occasion of the final, signing-off rhyme, there is special purpose in the last-minute variation, to the less precise pairing of 'man' with 'sand' (exactly paralleled in the alternative ending by 'plan' and 'sand'). This slight demurring from formal precision is the appropriate complement to the sense: the narrator does not quite achieve that all-ends-tied-up perfect neatness; he must sign off hanging in the balance, not neatly at rest.

The structural orderliness is present in many other ways. The three lines that

22.   Dylan, quoted in *Written in My Soul*, Bill Flanagan, on writing 'Every Grain Of Sand': ' "What's this like?" Well it's not like anything. "What does it represent?" Well, you don't even know . . . you try to hold onto the mood and finish. Or not even finish, but just get it to a place where you can let it go.'

contain the title of the song themselves make a pattern (like a sandwich), rather than offering a rigid repetition. That is, in the line at the centre of the song, we get the solo narrative journey of

> *That every hair is numbered like every grain of sand*

whereas with the first and last of the song's title lines, each offers a neatly balanced pairing, while at the same time the grammar of each pairing differs. The first is

> *In every leaf . . . in every grain . . .*

while the counterbalance in the last line is

> *Like every sparrow . . . like every grain . . .*

I don't mean to suggest that all this is overly neat. For the song to live and breathe, especially so that it can appeal to us in a postmodern and post-Christian age (which of course the song may or may not outlive), there has to be more to it than the classicism of order, however resourcefully the theme-serving structure achieves the detail of that order. The humane personal character that shines through the song, so that the individual's narrative superimposes itself upon both the scriptural blueprint and the formal construct – the living and breathing of the song – is achieved mostly on levels that fuse performance with poetry. Since it *is* a song, and not a poem, it may be fortuitous as to whether it works on the page too, though what I've been describing in the previous few paragraphs testifies as to how well much of the song does work on the page. There is one instance, as it happens, when Dylan's poetry, the expression of the individuality, works better on the page than on the recording.

> *The sun beat down upon the steps of time to light the way*

can be read, as it should be, as an uninterrupted line from start to finish: to do so is the most effective way to 'get' the idea the line proposes, and, as the long insistent burn of the uninterrupted line enacts its own meaning in its rhythm, to get too the sense of that sun's remorseless beating-down. This is how the line works best. In performance, this is interrupted by the pause after 'steps', which dislocates the phrase 'the steps of time', and in doing so makes less accessible the sense of the line and fails to let the rhythm of the line enact that sense. The sun doesn't beat down right across time here, it gets switched off halfway across.

Elsewhere in the song, though, such effects are perfectly achieved in the perform-ance. Look at the individual muscularity of what Dylan does with the sixth line in each of the three verses. These are, respectively

> *Like Cain, I now behold this chain of events that I must break.*

> *And every time I pass that way I always hear my name.*

and

> *Sometimes I turn, there's someone there, other times it's only me.*

Quite what the first-verse line means (what chain of events?) may be unclear, but the dexterity and confidence of control by which he achieves that brilliantly placed and far from facile internal rhyme – 'Cain' and 'chain' are marvellously held apart, held in a far more effective tension than any greater closeness would effect, by the equally emphasised 'behold', while the slight pause between 'chain' and 'of events' enacts the pulling effect required – make this one of the finest lines in the song. The shorter middle-verse line and the longer last-verse line each distribute their syllables quite differently, the one acting out the weary glide of guilty repetition and the other the fitful turning back and forth. Yet it is what Dylan does with the endings of these three lines that shows him, as poet-performer, so wholly on top of his material. As each line is delivered, particularity of form acts out perfectly his particularity of meaning. When he reaches 'I must break', word, delivery and music all make that break; when, called by temptation every time, he reaches 'hear my name', we get the opposite of a break: we get a lingering; and in the same place in the third verse, where there is neither the compunction of an 'I must', nor the clarity of an 'always', but only the shifting uncertainty of a 'sometimes . . . other times', what he manages at line-end this time, on that doubtful 'only me', is something halfway between a break and a lingering: it hangs in the balance, in fact.

Meanwhile, behind this living, necessarily irregular individuality, the imagery of the song, criticise it adversely as I might, none the less holds to its own systematic structure too. Not only are there the immediately adjacent matchings-up of, for example, 'rags to riches' and 'a summer's dream' to 'a wintry light', but more deep-seatedly we find such things as that the 'pool' of the first verse is matched by the 'sea' of the last, the 'reaching out somewhere' of the first matched by the 'hanging in the balance' of the last; 'newborn' discourses with both 'dyin'' and 'ancient'; 'footsteps' echo 'the steps of time'; and though the moon is never mentioned, perhaps its presence is implicit 'in the sorrow of the night . . . in the chill of a wintry light, / In the bitter dance of loneliness fading into space', so that as the cold moon fades into that 'space', this has its own pull upon 'the motion of the sea'. Since the broad theme of the song is the problematic one of understanding where we stand in creation, it is right that with the single, dodgy exception of the 'mirror', all its imagery is that of birth and death; the earth and the heavens; time and space; motion and fixity; humans and the animal kingdom; conscience, temptation and crime; the onward journey of consciousness; the ebb and flow of the elements.

Most broadly of all, these 'eternals' interact with the repeated auguries of impermanence that are placed throughout the song: an interaction focused so intensely by the title image of the grain of sand itself. This image, as we have seen Blake suggest, can be opened up from many angles. Crucially, the grain of sand is all that's left of solid rock, that classic symbol of dependable permanence, when the motions of the sea are through with it; the grain of sand is all that's left of nature's fecundity and 'the garden', when these have become desert wastes; and while Dylan sings of 'the steps of time', the phrase echoing softly behind that is 'the sands of time'. In all these ways, sand whispers of impermanence: its shifting quality is at odds with the clear fixity of 'a perfect finished plan'; it embodies 'the memory of decay'.

The grain of sand is also the poetic embodiment of the idea of the fundamental tiny particle of matter: and now we have quantum physics to tell us, by its tracking and tracing of the tiniest such particles, new things about our universe – crucially that there really *are* no absolutes. Quantum physics can detect, and even explain, things coming into existence out of nothing. This is the end for nature as Newtonian machine, in which every particle of matter is locked into a pattern that has forever been predetermined. It is the beginning of genuine indeterminism, in which it's possible to argue that not even God can know what is going to happen in the future. It is precisely the study of 'every grain of sand', in other words, that has killed off the credibility of any perfect finished plan. It's interesting that in revising the song, Dylan draws back from that 'perfect finished plan' to the more circumspect 'hanging in the balance of the reality of man' – and then sometimes in performance reverts once more to the earlier line: forever hanging in the balance of conflicting claims, because though the earlier line is too pat as philosophy, it's better poetry.

Of course, not even quantum physics can abolish God that easily: it's just that we do seem to have to keep changing our idea of what God is like. It's been said that 'anyone not shocked by quantum physics has not understood it'; and the new cosmology makes it imaginable that space and time may simply have flickered into existence by the laws of physics, not dependent upon a God to start it all off. Then again, God can still be thought of as out there, the great *auteur*-director, presiding (like Robert Altman) over the chaos of the set. You can argue, as Thomas Aquinas did, that it doesn't make any difference whether the universe began at a particular point or not: that at any moment, whatever *is* depends on God. Meanwhile the new cosmology also tends to re-offer us the old story. Coming after the traditional position, that God created the whole universe for the benefit of mankind, and after the scientific reductionism that followed – which held that nature, life and the human spirit were all created randomly by the blind, mechanical interactions of impersonal forces – now nature is looking like an elegant unity again, and one in which we (the very elements of our bodies fashioned in the stars) have an inescapable role. We're brought back, perhaps, to that part of the 'Desiderata' in which 'You are a child of the universe, as much as the trees and stars. You have a right to be here.' Seeing the Big Bang as the beginning of all space and time fits in with our old notions from the Book of Genesis: of 'Time moving in one direction, of a particular process unfolding,' as theologian Rowan Williams says, that has 'put back into our understanding of the universe elements of narrative . . . This is a story which moves forward, which accumulates.' It is possible, as for cosmologist Brian Swimme, to find in all this 'a God working with recalcitrant materials'. Sometimes I turn, there's someone there . . .[23]

All this, then, above and beyond the resonant effect of the line 'Sometimes I turn, there's someone there, other times it's only me', insinuates doubt into the claimed orderliness of the song, giving it a dynamic complexity that keeps it alive.

We find a sub-text of tension too in 'Every Grain Of Sand' from the very fact of Dylan's offering a song of submission to the authority of 'the Master's hand' to a

---

23. Quotations in this paragraph are taken from Part One of the TV series *Soul* by Anthony Clare, BBC-TV, London, 1992, and from the Max Ehrmann prose-poem 'Desiderata', much-derided for its hippiesque homilism though published in 1927 and widely loved and disseminated ever since. (The Latin-based seventeenth-century word 'desiderata' means things lacking and wanted.) It might be added that, as the theoretical physicist and theologian the Rev. Dr John Polkinghorne argues (a) the infant science of Complexity Theory offers a renewed unity-of-the-universe, and thus a re-revelation of the Master's hand, and (b) mathematicians see themselves as discovering what exists already – a world of absolute truths that are 'out there' and eternal – which is, in hippie parlance, God's bag. (Rev. Dr John Polkinghorne, Canon Theologian of Liverpool, on *In Our Time*, presented Melvyn Bragg, BBC Radio 4, 18/2/99.) Every hair is numbered . . . even Melvyn Bragg's.

secular, postmodernist, post-feminist audience. Yet the song and the performance are alive and open enough to have a wide appeal to non-believers. As Paul Nelson wrote, reluctantly, in a review of the "Shot Of Love" album, in this song 'he touches you, and the gates of heaven dissolve into a universality'.[24]

This universality is one of meaning and feeling. Essentially, to say that every hair is numbered, and that every sparrow falling counts, is simply to say that what we take to be innumerability does not make for valuelessness. The uncountable still count. This addresses the very heart of the problem we know that we have, for example, in responding to footage of those 'famines and earthquakes'; in responding humanly to any vast human disaster in some faraway place. The impersonality of the sheer numbers of the starving, the suffering, the wronged: we know how the mega-figures of death sever our sense of connection. Yet we know too that if any one of us matters, the only humane logic possible is that everyone – every one – matters also.

The universality of feeling that complements this simple humanitarianism at, as it were, the heart of the song, is finally given flight in Dylan's lovely, inspired, humane harmonica solos: using the soft, rounded, *different* harmonica that he introduced on the "Saved" LP, and which, typically, was widely resented at the time because it wasn't *the right one!* The first solo sketches out chunky, shuddering possibilities of frailty and resilience; the second, coming at the end of the song and fading into space, soars beyond it, spinning its disarming idiosyncracy around a beautiful melodic line and dancing with the freedom of acceptance, humility and grace.

Despite our preferring the modern intelligence and fractured sensibility – the non-submission to any traditional authority – of something like 'Visions Of Johanna', so well does 'Every Grain Of Sand' live and breathe that when, on "Biograph", the running-order gives us the full push-to-the-edge, follow-that! of a live 1966 'Visions Of Johanna', and then what has to follow it is the 1981 studio cut of 'Every Grain Of Sand', the stately 1980s song holds its own. That's some achievement.

24.   Paul Nelson: 'Shot Of Love', *Rolling Stone*, no. 354, 15/10/81.

CHAPTER THIRTEEN

Groom Still Waiting at the Altar?

With two exceptions, after his evangelical period Dylan's best songs of the early 1980s didn't appear on his albums at all. What "Shot Of Love" from 1981 and "Infidels" from 1983 have in common is that, except for 'Every Grain Of Sand' and 'Jokerman', they withhold the most interesting and substantial songs their recording sessions yielded in favour of inferior work. The major songs kept off these albums were: 'The Groom's Still Waiting At The Altar', 'Angelina' and 'Caribbean Wind' from the "Shot Of Love" sessions, and 'Foot Of Pride' and perhaps the best Bob Dylan song of the decade, 'Blind Willie McTell', from the "Infidels" sessions.

('The Groom's Still Waiting At The Altar' was issued as the B-side of a single and reissued on the "Biograph" collection of 1985; it has subsequently been built back into the "Shot Of Love" album itself – the first instance of such a revision in Dylan's canon. 'Angelina' remained unissued altogether until its appearance, a decade after its creation, on "Bootleg Series I–III" in 1991. 'Caribbean Wind', of which there are two vividly contrasting studio versions, remained unissued until one version appeared on "Biograph". At that time no other studio version was known to exist; nine years later, in 1994, collectors were surprised to find that an extraordinarily different second studio version suddenly slipped into circulation. This remains unissued. 'Blind Willie McTell', recorded in 1983, also remained unissued, despite much clamour for its release, until its inclusion on "Bootleg Series I–III". This song is examined and celebrated two chapters hence.)

There are other pleasant enough songs on "Shot Of Love" and on "Infidels", and others of comparable quality in among the out-takes: but essentially these omitted major songs are, along with 'Every Grain Of Sand' at one end and 'Jokerman' at the other, the real achievements of the period.

'The Groom's Still Waiting At The Altar' returns us towards the Dylanesque chaos of an earlier era, even though the fundamental structure of the song is a thoroughly conventional R&B/blues one, and even though the lyrics still keep the Bible close at hand.

Christ is the bridegroom and the bride for whom he waits is the Church, representing the Christian faithful. The analogy is drawn by John the Baptist, who says in John 3:28–29: 'I am not the Christ, but that I am sent before him. He that hath the bride is the bridegroom: but the friend of the bridegroom, which standeth and heareth him, rejoiceth greatly . . .' Yet what's appealing and interesting here is not the scriptural bewailing of people's fecklessness, nor the declamatory global sweep of

Dylan's customary 'look! the apocalypse is coming!', as given in the choruses of the song, but the chaotic absurdity both of the visions glimpsed and of the poetry that makes them, along with the directed energy of the performance – the pacing, shuddering expressiveness of the vocal, breathing in hot pursuit of the listener across the switchback longs and shorts of the verses and the punching ups and downs of the chorus melody.

The hooks on which are hung both the craziness of vision and the *tour de force* performance are the song's extremes of variation in line-length and its deranged, rule-breaking rhymes. Set against the conventional regularity of the music, these two delirious elasticities contract and expand the possibilities of structure like a mad concertina banging about inside an old, familiar cardboard box.

The only solidly inevitable rhyme is, aptly, that of 'altar' with 'Gibraltar'. All the others are unpredictable, switching between 'da *da* da' and '*da* da da' line-endings ('to want me' and 'snobbery', for instances), occasionally pushed to a '*da* da da da', as in 'obligated') and ranging restlessly between the orderliness of 'order' and 'border' and the purring blur of 'to haunt me' and 'to want me'; between ragged half-rhymes like 'humiliated' and 'obligated' – pushing snatched raggedness to the limit in putting 'cement' with 'innocent' and 'nauseated' with 'deteriorated' – and the jokingly precise and splendid 'temperature' and 'furniture'; and between the simplicity of 'to leap it' and 'to keep it', the tiny sneakiness of 'sent to me' and 'meant to be' and the take-a-bow outrageousness of the last verse's last rhyme – the incomparable pairing of 'January' and 'Buenos Aires'.

Matching these elastic contortions, the variations in line-length, over which Dylan's ever-resourceful delivery triumphs, careen between the *nine* syllables of one verse's and the *eighteen* syllables of another's.

These technical crimes and jokes of accomplishment fit the visions of the lyric. If the opening verse vividly evokes the bizarre grogginess of waking up, half-knowing where you are –

> *Prayed in the ghetto with my face in the cement*
> *Heard the last moan of a boxer, seen the massacre of the innocent*
> *Felt around for the light switch . . .*

– this surreal uncertainty, as to how things are and how they feel, is not dispelled but intensified by waking to daytime consciousness. 'Put your hand on my head, baby, do I have a temperature?' is such a great, funny line: itself enacting feverishness in its hypochondriacal fretting rhythm; expressing such distance from the person it addresses yet doing so with the intimacy of wholly conversational cadences – it is a masterly line of conversational speech, in which 'baby' is for once used inspiredly, clinching the tone of easy familiarity while suggesting that the speaker may not actually know who he's talking to – and playing to the hilt the absurdity of being so out of touch with how you feel that you need someone else to feel your head to tell you (an absurdity not reduced by our recognition that we have been there too). In doing all these things, the line also expresses the cry for help out of this chaos: a chaos of alienation that the speaker of the line knows he embodies as diseasedly as does the world around him.

It is, of course, a world of contradiction, polarity, violence and catastrophe, seething with nebulous omens and hopeless ambiguity. As so often, the modern locating detail is in bed with the timeless or ancient scene: in this case 'Cities on fire' (which might be of biblical antiquity) and 'phones out of order'. The same verse reverberates with the contemporary hell of South and Central American war zones in which the CIA funds the murder squads. As in Guatemala in June 1980 'They're killing nuns'. Yet any suggestion that this is a world rational enough to let us hope that socio-political protest might be effective is at once undercut by the adding of 'and soldiers', which topsy-turvies any inferred what-could-be-worse-than-killing-nuns? rhetoric. Meanwhile the timelessness of 'Cities on fire' also prises away from that 'killing nuns' any limiting contemporariness it may have, so that we find underneath its layer of modernity reminders of far older religious wars – indeed wars so old that they were inevitably religious ones.

Psychic doom and physical brutality collide into fused imperatives.

> *There's a wall between you and what you want and you got to leap it,*

Dylan sings, and as he sings it he puts up that wall between 'between you' and 'and what you want' with a pause, a vocal silence so solid you can hear that fevered head crash into it. The exhortation to act, ostensibly an affirmation of things decisive and positive, withers at once into the accompanying prediction of imminent failure. Even if you read the sign aright, and 'leap it' and 'take it', seizing the moment of 'tonight', what you gain still can't be held on to 'tomorrow'.

Under conditions like these, it comes as a surprise to the narrator – as something worth remarking on – when something works, when something happens as it could be expected to in an ordered world:

> *Got the message this morning, the one that was sent to me*

and Dylan follows this with the lovely lucidity of

> *About the madness of becomin' what one was never meant to be.*

It's typical of Dylan's intuitive intelligence that the song's only mention of 'madness' is here in its most rationally styled line.

Aside from the centrality of chaos, there is something else from a bygone Dylan era that reappears in 'The Groom's Still Waiting At The Altar', albeit briefly: a specific area of poetic focus that was at one time wonderfully prevalent in his work, and which, until it reappeared, I hadn't known I'd missed. It belonged, I suppose, to a particular period: that of his early post-hobo songs, as I was reminded by hearing again, at Radio City Music Hall in 1988, these lines from 'With God On Our Side':

> *The words fill my head*
> *And fall to the floor.*

The early New York City songs were full of things bouncing off the walls and floors and ceilings: full of walls and floors and ceilings bouncing with noises, and air and light bouncing and splitting and pounding like noise; air like walls and walls like air. It was a way of seeing – a recognisable suprarealism of his, and it yielded much evocative poetry:

'The night aimed shadows / Through the crossbar windows, / And the wind punched hard / To make the wall-siding sing' ('Walls of Red Wing'); 'When all at once the silent air / Split open from her soundin' voice' ('Joan Baez in Concert, Part 2'); 'And the silent night will shatter / From the sounds inside my mind' ('One Too Many Mornings'); 'The morning breeze like a bugle blew / Against the drums of dawn' ('Lay Down Your Weary Tune'); 'As her thoughts pounded hard / Like the pierce of an arrow' ('Eternal Circle'); 'midnight's broken toll' and 'while the walls were tightening' ('Chimes Of Freedom'); 'Crimson flames tied through my ears' ('My Back Pages'); 'Though the night ran swirling and whirling' ('I Don't Believe You'); 'the breeze yawns food' ('Some Other Kinds Of Songs'); 'the breath of its broken walls / being smothered' ('11 Outlined Epitaphs'); 'Beneath a bare lightbulb the plaster did pound' ('Ballad In Plain D'); and 'The wind howls like a hammer' ('Love Minus Zero / No Limit').[1]

I'd guess he doesn't usually stray this way any more because on the whole it's a very New York City apartment block feeling: it belongs in an environment no longer at the centre of Dylan's consciousness. It is a minor pleasure, therefore, to find a fair example of this specific poetic focus revisiting Dylan in the midst of 1985's 'When The Night Comes Falling From The Sky':

> *That icy wind that's howling in your eye*

and a greater pleasure to savour, in the version of 'The Groom's Still Waiting At The Altar' given in *Lyrics 1962–1985*, the marvellous

> *She was walking down the hallway while the walls deteriorated.*

This is so powerful because it has such, well, corrosive concreteness at the same time as such a strong nightmare mood. It's one of Dylan's most filmic lines – in fact it makes me remember Roman Polanski's film *Repulsion*, in which, in a scene that prefigures *Alien*, as the heroine–victim runs down a long passageway the plaster erupts out of shape: hands of plaster burst from the living walls, thrusting out to grab at her as she runs.[2]

Words like 'deteriorated' are notoriously hard to use without bathos: Dylan manages it perfectly here because he brings the word alive, allowing it to shake with its onomatopoeic aptness – the way it sounds so crumbly – by highlighting its sheer weirdness of meaning.

(Elsewhere he comes closer to the bathetic effect of lapsing into similarly formalised vocabulary. Perhaps *officialese* is a better way of describing what's wrong with this Joni Mitchell Syndrome. 'I just can't make it with you socially', she warbles somewhere, ruining an otherwise plausible song, and Dylan comes close now and then – as on 'Tell Me', one of the pleasant minor songs omitted from "Infidels" but issued on the "Bootleg Series I–III", in which we'd be better off without the Marin-

---

1.   By the time of this last example, framed as a simple simile, it is also a more consciously Baudelarian equivalent of earlier successes like 'your baby's eyes . . . are tuggin' at your sleeve' ('Ballad Of Hollis Brown') and that special Dylan vividness with images of people's mouths: 'people cheered with bloodshot grins' ('Long Ago, Far Away') and 'but you're smilin' inside out' ('Denise'). (Incidentally, how is it that one of the best lines from that song, as on the New York studio version, 9/6/64 – 'Are you for sale or just on the shelf?' – is omitted from *Lyrics 1962–1985*?)

2.   *Repulsion*, Compton/Tekli (Gene Gutowski), directed Roman Polanski, UK, 1965 (starring Catherine Deneuve as a maddened Belgian manicurist).

Countyism of 'what are you focussed upon?', especially since it jostles alongside the patronising awfulness and poker-up-arseness of 'Do you have any morals?')

Of the two relatively important differences between the text of 'The Groom's Still Waiting At The Altar' as given in *Lyrics 1962–1985* and as we hear it on the studio recording, the first is that on the record we lose the whole of that 'deteriorated' line, along with its less happy mate, 'Felt around for the lightswitch, became nauseated'.

We gain instead a couplet that starts with the improved line

> *Felt around for the lightswitch, felt around for her face*

(such plain-speaking, such tactile contrast, so strong an evocation of *groping*) but Dylan follows the extra vividness of that with the unduly lumbering

> *Been treated like a farm animal on a wild goose chase*

which, against all odds, is less of a line than the one we lose to it.

The other significant difference between the two versions of the song, and by far the more damaging, consists in what has happened to the words of the choruses as given in *Lyrics 1962–1985*, in which the performed version's consistent 'East of the Jordan, west of the rock of Gibraltar' is so tinkered about with that in five choruses the line is given in three ways: 'East of . . . hard as,' 'West of . . . east of', 'West of . . . west of', 'West of . . . east of' again, and 'West of . . . west of' again. The next line gets similarly silly revision, the consistent 'I see the turning of the page' of the recorded version replaced by 'I see the burning of the page', 'burning of the stage', 'burning of the cage', 'burning of the stage' again, and 'burning of the page' again. Even the 'Curtain risin' on a new age' is altered, in the third chorus, to 'Curtain risin' on a new stage'. Whatever switches between notions of text and performance ('page' and 'stage') may be embedded here, they remain fiddlesome alterations in which there's no pattern but only a mess, making clear how little any of them mean.[3]

After such wilful reductionism, it comes as a relief that the song's other changes are insignificant. One, indeed, is surely only an error of transcription: the text gives 'Mistake your shyness for aloofness, your shyness for snobbery' but should read 'Mistake your shyness for aloofness, your silence for snobbery'. This is mistaken shyness indeed. Meanwhile, if anything, the published text's 'I'd a-done anything for that woman if she didn't make me feel so obligated' seems truer than the studio version's 'I'd a-done anything for that woman if she'd only made me feel obligated': but not true enough to matter one way or the other to the success of this gloriously seething, restive song.

Dylan subjects the lines that suffer that transcription error to a more interesting shift elsewhere. He not only revises them but then imports them, in live performance, into an entirely different song, 'Watered-Down Love', that underrated minor item from "Shot Of Love". Performing 'Watered-Down Love' live in 1981, Dylan not only jumbles up the order of the verses as given on the studio recording (other, far slighter changes to the studio version are made for *Lyrics 1962–1985*) but he makes a new

---

3.   Nick de Somogyi certainly makes the most of them in his essay 'Pretexts for Bob Dylan (Part Two)', *Telegraph*, no. 35, Spring 1990.

fourth verse, the second half of which has a foreshortened limb from 'The Groom's Still Waiting At The Altar' grafted on to it:

> *I got to flee towards patience and meekness*
> *You miscalculate me, you mistake my kindness for weakness.*[4]

'Watered-Down Love' is underrated because neither critics nor radio, on which it would work well, have noticed that this is, aeons after his praising Smokey Robinson, Dylan's sketch for a Motown single; at the same time the lyric draws upon, and in a spirit of assiduous, humane inquiry, a well-known passage from Paul's First Epistle to the Corinthians.

For once, Dylan uses the text of the Revised Standard Version of this passage (from 1 Corinthians 13), rather than the King James. The latter is the source of phrases everybody knows – 'I am become as sounding brass', 'When I was a child I spake as a child . . . but when I became a man, I put away childish things' and the adjacent 'now we see through a glass darkly'; but the key word in the main body of the King James chapter is 'charity': hence its equally well-known concluding verse, 'And now abideth faith, hope, charity, these three; but the greatest of these is charity'. In the Revised Standard Version (and in Bible-U-Like) this key word is translated not as 'charity' but as 'love'. This is why Dylan goes with the Revised Standard Version in this instance.[5]

The bulk of the passage catalogues love's qualities – and 'Watered-Down Love' does the same. And says the same. This is the one:

> Love is patient and kind; love is not jealous or boastful; it is not arrogant or rude. Love does not insist on its own way; it is not irritable or resentful; it does not rejoice at wrong, but rejoices in the right. Love bears all things, believes all things, hopes all things, endures all things.

Dylan's lyric begins:

> *Love that's pure hopes all things,*
> *Believes all things . . .*

4.   Actually, on the early dates he takes the implicit repeated 'mistake' inherent in the 'Groom' line, importing it into 'Watered-Down Love' as 'You mistake me, mistake my kindness for weakness' (for instance in Oslo, 9/7/81, and Bad Segeberg, Germany, 14/7/81), but by the time of the North American dates, the line is as given in the main text above (as for example in New Orleans and Houston, 10/11/81 and 12/11/81 respectively), with 'miscalculate' brought into service to avoid the duplicating of 'mistake'.

5.   'I am become as sounding brass' comes from the first verse of the chapter, a verse Dylan also alludes to in the excellent "Oh Mercy" out-take song 'Dignity' (musically ruined and then issued on "Bob Dylan Greatest Hits Vol. 3"; live version issued on "Bob Dylan Unplugged", both released 1995). The full text of 1 Corinthians 13:1 (King James Version) reads: 'Though I speak with the tongues of men and of angels, and have not charity, I am become as sounding brass, or a tinkling cymbal'. In 'Dignity' Dylan sings: 'I heard the tongues of angels and the tongues of men: / Wasn't any difference to me'.

These powerful, memorable phrases in the King James Bible are, typically, watered down to nothing in the newer versions. For 'I am become as sounding brass' the Revised Standard offers 'I am a noisy gong'; the Good News Bible, blanching at even this bathetic directness, keeps the bathos and ducks the directness, making it 'my speech is no more than a noisy gong'. The Revised Standard Version almost accepts intact the Authorized opening words, 'Though I speak with the tongues of men and of angels', merely changing 'Though' to 'If'; the Good News Bible prefers the flaccid windbaggery of: 'I may be able to speak the languages of men and even of angels, but . . .' Verse 12, which in the King James begins 'For now we see through a glass, darkly', is changed in the Revised Standard to 'For now we see in a mirror dimly,' which the Good News Bible re-writes more wordily: 'What we see now is like a dim image in a mirror'. How true.

and goes on to interpret, embroider, develop, re-invent and extemporise on the passage in inspired, alert terms. Sometimes he street-talks it ('Believes all things' is followed by 'Won't pull no strings'); sometimes he expresses it in phrases more biblical than St Paul's ('Will not deceive you or lead you into transgression'); sometimes, as the song's opening shows, he sticks closely to the text. How easily and plausibly those lines about kindness and patience slip out of 'The Groom's Still Waiting At The Altar' and cross, in performance, into the lyric of 'Watered-Down Love'.

If 'Watered-Down Love' is based upon the gentle, almost Zen precepts of Chapter 13 of 1 Corinthians, 'Angelina' is romantically entangled in the visionary fever of Revelation – and of Ezekiel, the Old Testament book that the writer of Revelation seems to have had continually in mind. This is familiar territory in Dylan's work, a backdrop to songs from 'Blowin' In The Wind' to 'Dignity'. With 'Angelina' he is here again: and here as if for the first time, since the narrative seems that of someone wandering, lost, in a perilous landscape. The recording takes us on a long road, as through a trance or a dream, in which, as they are wont to do in dreams, time and place shift and a different logic prevails.

If this parallels perfectly the experience of reading the long, strange biblical passages to which it refers, it also makes 'Angelina' a difficult song to comprehend. In this respect it's like all the songs discussed here, though we might acknowledge that the least unclear song of the group, 'Blind Willie McTell', is also the most wholly successful.

'Angelina' is hard because of the disconnectedness, the impossible images, the general air of smudging that clings to it, and the collision of the narrative into different genres as it passes. You have to ask: what is he on about? You have to answer: I don't know. If the song works, this answer becomes: I don't know but it doesn't matter. As we've noted, the whole message of twentieth-century art has been the abolition of the clear narrative. The main question is not Am I sure I understand this? but, Do I like it? Does it stir me?

As ever, the way into the song is from the performance. It begins thrillingly, holding out infinite promise (which is of course impossible to deliver), shimmering into being like the gorgeous solo version of 'Spanish Is The Loving Tongue', with piano and voice: a warm, broad voice, though in this case with just a *little* too much nasal blockage in it. The first words are these:

> Well it's always been my nature to take chances
> My right hand drawin' back while my left hand advances.

This is doubly striking. First, the character of the opening line is surely unique in Dylan's work. Many Bob Dylan songs begin with that direct conversational tone but I can think of no other case in which its content appears candidly self-defining. Bob Dylan is not a man who writes 'I'm a man who . . .' It's never been his nature to define his nature.

On the heels of this novel opening gambit comes a second disarming reversal of our expectations. Logic must prompt our assumption (we needn't be aware we've made one until Dylan confounds it) that any enlargement upon the theme of this opening line must centre on that propensity 'always . . . to take chances'. We might expect that if a corollary capacity for caution is also to be acknowledged, it will be less emphasised than the declared taste for risk. Something along the lines of 'More leaping forward than backward glances'. We get the opposite. Dylan structures his second line to stress the 'drawing back' – the more so in that it's the preferred hand, the right hand, that is to be found 'drawing back' while the weaker, sinister hand 'advances'. In consequence this is a tantalising, provoking line, never quite satisfying but not dismissable as careless either. There's an ellipse in here: a stage in the logic of exposition has been squeezed unspoken into the crack between Dylan's first line and his second. The result is that the two lines themselves enact what they describe: Dylan has set up a tugging back and forth between them. It isn't comfortable but it is poetry.

Nor is there any carelessness in the structure of the song. Each verse is of eight lines, rhyming AAABCCCB, each last line being (with one deliberate exception, considered below) simply the title word 'Angelina'. After each verse comes a single line of refrain, acting as a simple echo ('Oh— Angelina! Oh— Angelina!'). There are no half-rhymes: the shape Dylan has chosen, with those clusters of three adjacent rhyming lines, only works if it delivers the pleasure of repetition, and it cannot deliver that if the rhymes are inexact. The 'echo' must be simple here too. Dylan knows not to settle for less.

If the AAA and CCC rhymes in the verses must be straight – no opportunity here for the twisted reach that gives 'The Groom's Still Waiting At The Altar' its rhyming of 'January' with 'Buenos Aires' – there is opportunity galore in the B rhymes, the 'Angelina' rhymes, for the flamboyant and extravagant. And Dylan seizes it. There are no half-rhymes here either: we meet them all head on. Nor are there any demure, quietening rhymes, rhymes designed to pass unnoticed: no Anglicist words like 'cleaner', no innocuous phrase – say, 'have you seen her?' Every one Dylan sings chimes its sing-song, ding-dong, two-tone bell, its Latin and Latin-American bell, as ostentatiously as possible: concertina, hyena, subpoena, Argentina, arena.

This engineering precision, the sturdy carriages of the five verses built to one blueprint, the ringing iron certainty of the rails of rhyme – these are sufficient to propel us through all the swirling mists and past all the looming, vague shapes of the song's narrative landscape.

The declaration that there is such a journey comes at the start of the second verse, with the deft line

Blood dryin' in my yellow hair as I go from shore to shore.

This sets the tone; it establishes the vague generality, the grand sweep, of the song's journey – and simultaneously supplies those specific details, the blood drying in the yellow hair: details that, far from clarifying, only serve to clinch how little we are to be left to feel we know. The 'yellow hair' tells us that the narrator's persona isn't Bob Dylan; the 'blood drying', while detailed, is wholly unexplained. The line that follows,

I know what it is that has drawn me to your door,

only serves to tell us that we *don't* know what it is, after which comes an immediate confession that much is unknown to the singer too:

But whatever could it be, makes you think you seen me before
Angelina?

We don't know, either, whether 'Angelina' is right or wrong in thinking this; we don't
even know if the singer knows whether she's right or wrong.

Yet 'Blood dryin' in my yellow hair as I go from shore to shore' yields more than
we've so far allowed. This blood flows from no ordinary wound: blood doesn't go on
drying all through the lengthy travail of going from shore to shore. Continual drying
suggests continual flow behind it. The aura here is of stigmata, of those favourite
phenomena of the Roman Catholic Church, statues that weep and effigies that bleed.
'Yellow' is less curious as a hair-colour on a plaster saint than a real person. At any
rate there's an atmosphere here that hints of those countries in which there are many
Angelinas and where the more lurid mysticisms of Catholic paraphernalia most nearly
make sense: the southern Mediterranean, Mexico, Central and South America. In
other words, this line suggests itself as the song's first tentative breath of the air of
magic realism.

'Argentina' is named, later in the song, inside a question as rhetorical as that just
quoted:

Tell me, tall man, where would you like to be overthrown:
In Jerusalem or Argentina?

Comically audacious rhetoric it is too, of course: no 'tall man' would like to be
overthrown anywhere. Singular or plural, dictator or junta, here Dylan adds in the
presence of political violence that permeates everyday life (the realism) and is as much
a part of the genre as the acceptance of the fantastical (the magic). What unites the
two is the feeling that anything can happen. For the ordinary peasant populace, no
outrage, no violent act, no bizarre rumour, no lurid superstition, no horror, no
miracle, can confidently be ruled beyond the realms of possibility. (When Dylan gave
concerts in South America in the early 1990s, he was described by a São Paolo
journalist in a phrase entirely characteristic of this sensibility: he called Dylan 'the
white monster of three decades'.)

In 'Angelina', the ingredient of menace has been located already, at the beginning
of the 'tall man' verse, in the deliciously sinister line

There's a black Mercedes rollin' through the combat zone.

In this part of the world the powerless see the Mercedes as the symbol of northern,
capitalist corruption. Dylan's line evokes the hushed purposiveness (that luxury auto's
self-confident 'rollin''), the invulnerability that comes from being the power behind
the fighting ('rollin' through the combat zone'), the cold unaccountability of the
sheltered occupant inside the cold, black machine. Its windows are surely as black as
its bodywork (we cannot see through this glass darkly), and its fat black tyres glide
over the dust. This is also the USA's territorial backyard: a place 'where the Stars and
Stripes explode' but the CIA determines 'the combat zone'. And in a compelling
double-image of soldiers in battle, suggestive both of pawns in the game and of hacked
up horror, we 'see pieces of men marching'. These elements of the song are companion-

pieces to that part of 'The Groom's Still Waiting At The Altar' in which 'They're killing nuns and soldiers / There's fighting on the border'.

There are many other vapours from this magic realist world in 'Angelina'. All these lines and phrases, these touches and details, accord with this Latin-American milieu: 'the monkey dances / To the tune of a concertina'; 'just step into the arena'; those 'spiral staircases'. This is also a land of blood feud and revenge, a culture in which it might be par for the course to find that 'She was stolen from her mother when she was three days old', and in which the inevitable follow-up report must be that 'Now her vengeance has been satisfied . . .' In the same climate, the overheated idolatry of a lurid Catholicism has people worshipping 'surrounded by God's angels', readily seeing or believing in a 'tree of smoke' and an 'angel with four faces', and 'Begging God for mercy and weeping in unholy places'. Oh Angelina, Oh Angelina . . . As the very noises of the recording whisper into the listener's mind, 'Spanish is the loving tongue'.

Dylan is drawn to this southern, Spanish door recurrently in his work, from romancing the breathy gypsy gal of 'Spanish Harlem Incident' to consulting the wise peasant Christ in 'Señor', and from the horse-ride across the Mexican desert with Magdalena in 'Romance In Durango' to the portrait of the peasant father in 'One More Cup Of Coffee'. There has even been an earlier Bob Dylan song with an Angelina in the title, 1965's 'Farewell Angelina'. And when Dylan sang about turning the other cheek before, in 'Queen Jane Approximately', the song's heroine was envisaged as turning that other cheek to 'bandits', who would then lay down their 'bandanas' (and complain).

Perhaps there is a precedent too for Dylan's being drawn to this world's magic realism. I've several times noted Dylan's remarks to Nat Hentoff in the 1966 *Playboy* interview that '. . . traditional music is too unreal to die', and so yields 'all these songs about roses growing out of people's brains and lovers who are really geese and swans who turn into angels'.[6] There may be compelling parallels between this 'unrealism' in the traditional folksong of neo-medieval rural Britain and Ireland and the 'magic realism' pinned down in the heavily folk-cultured fiction of modern South American writers like Gabriel Garcia Marquez. When, therefore, Bob Dylan experiments in 'Angelina' with the evocative poetic effects of this magic realism, it's likely that he finds these effects attractive in the same way as he finds attractive 'roses growing out of people's brains' and 'lovers who are really geese'. As I've had occasion to note elsewhere, Dylan's taste in narrative ballads has always been either for those of mystery or else for tales of horses and daughters and hangings, exile and injustice. In 'Angelina' he creates a narrative, though not a ballad, in which most of these elements coexist.

But 'Angelina' is a song that seems to pass through several different worlds. If the vaporous postmodernism of magic realism is one, Ancient Egypt, as filtered by Bob Dylan's imagination, seems to be another. Idolatry is heavily present in this world too. Egyptian gods appear predominantly in the form of animals. Horus is depicted as a sparrow-hawk, Khunm as a ram. Anubis has a hyena-like head, and so does Seth. The

6. 'The *Playboy* interview: Bob Dylan: a candid conversation with the iconoclastic idol of the folk-rock set', *Playboy*, March 1966.

god Thot is the dog-headed gatekeeper of the underworld. Depicted so superbly on the walls and in the tombs of an architecture that almost defies time, the idols of Ancient Egypt can readily be imagined to include, as Dylan's second verse has it,

> *. . . a god with the body of a woman well endowed*
> *And the head of a hyena.*

Equally, the vivid and tough first line of this verse, describing a man's face rather than a god's, does so in terms distinctively in tune with, even seeming to summarise, the Ancient Egyptian style, linear and clear:

> *His eyes were two slits, make any snake proud.*

In this context, several other lines and phrases take on a relevant resonance, including one or two that function quite differently in the song's other worlds. That phrase 'pieces of men marching' is one. Coexisting with its effectiveness in the Latin-American magic realist context it has another life in this one. Here we can make sense of it as describing how those rows of soldiers are rendered, parading everywhere that Ancient Egyptian carving and drawing survives: cartoon-like, each figure half-hidden by the next, each fitting into the next like jigsaw pieces. Those who are conquered enemies – and these are regularly depicted: the triumphalism of the conqueror demands it – become slaves, put to work building the architectural glories of kings who decree themselves gods and build as if to conquer eternity: in some cases building pyramids in the attempt both to pierce the sky and to decipher the stars. This is indeed

> *. . . trying to take heaven by force.*

This is a culture of ritual sacrifices and power-struggles, high priests and god-kings, incest and intrigue, in which it might well be part of the story that a daughter of the court could be 'stolen from her mother when she was three days old', and in which, by the time of the Ptolemaic dynasties, a young man might indeed have to 'just step into the arena'.

Dylan sets this world

> *In the valley of the giants where the stars and stripes explode.*

The 'Valley of the Giants' acts as his fictional addition to, or perhaps his summarising retitling of, the Valley of the Kings, the Valley of the Queens, the Valley of the Nobles and the Valley of the Workmen. This vast time and place, this trying to take heaven by force, is 'where the stars and stripes explode' in the sense that here one great, crumbled empire mocks the claims of another. As he sings in another song of the early 1980s, the fairly awful 'Neighborhood Bully',

> *Every empire . . . is gone*
> *Egypt and Rome, even the great Babylon.*

Two further wisps of Ancient Egyptian air thread their way around 'Angelina'. One, unsurprisingly, is evoked by the mention of 'milk and honey'; the other, very surprisingly, floats up from the phrase 'When you cease to exist.'

Both bring us to meeting points with the other world of the song, that of the Bible story. Merely by using the phrase 'milk and honey', Dylan reminds us that the children of Israel escaped from Ancient Egypt, embarking upon their own long journey and crossing the Red Sea from shore to shore to gain the promised land.[7]

The other point of contact lies in what the Ancient Egyptian and Judaeo-Christian belief-systems had in common. Here is a song about worshipping gods, a song in which, so far, all the stress has been on idolatry and the worship of many different figures. When we reach the terrain of apocalypse, we can expect a contrasting emphasis on the legitimacy of just one god, the God whose judgement day shall come and whose son Jesus Christ shall usher in a new heaven and a new earth: a new Jerusalem. Yet in fact the contrast between the multiple gods of the one and the monotheism of the other is not so certain or straightforward. The Ancient Egyptians too believed in monotheism: in one God of Gods, creator of all things, a God who, in the attractive phrase of the guidebook *Egypt*, edited by Giovanni Magi, 'is one and primordial'. In the holy books of the Ancient Egyptians too one finds the concepts of original sin and of redemption, the promise of a redeeming god and the resurrection of the flesh at the end of time. This God of Gods is Osiris, who 'married Isis', to quote another Bob Dylan song, and he, deified, ruled over the supreme court for the judgement of the souls of the dead.

Dylan seems aware of this belief-system – seems to allude to it within one of the song's sudden rhetorical questions. As with 'Tell me, tall man, where would you like to be overthrown . . .?', we suddenly come upon this in mid-song:

When you cease to exist, who will you blame?

This might seem a random interjection – yet it makes a specific sense in the context of Ancient Egyptian belief about the afterlife or lack of it: about what happens to those who beg God for mercy and are saved and what happens to those who beg God for mercy and are not saved. Magi summarises this belief as follows:

If the dead person had done more good than evil they became one of the 'true of voice' and thus a part of the mystical body of the god Osiris. If this was not so, the heart was eaten by an animal with the head of a crocodile and the body of a hippopotamus and *ceased to exist* in the other world. [my emphasis]

So Dylan's rhetoric translates, on this level, as 'When you are judged and not saved, who will you blame?': a meaning that sits happily with the implicit allusion to the devil, just two lines later, in the claim

Your best friend and my worst enemy is one and the same.

So we are back once again, whether we like it or not, to the question of ultimate salvation, of where we all end up at the end of the world. It's where we end up at the

---

7. Even today, Egyptians and Israelis share much in common, despite their clamorous divisions: they are both Semitic peoples, and they share the continuum of the desert as well as so much history. Dylan told an interviewer in 1983: 'My so-called Jewish roots are in Egypt.' (*Dallas Times-Herald*, 6/11/83.) Dylan, who is thought to have a flat in Tel Aviv, has crossed between Israel and Egypt more than once. A 1989 photograph in the booklet accompanying "Bootleg Series I–III", on which 'Angelina' is released, shows Dylan leaning on a sign, written in Arabic and English, that in English reads 'Don't Climb The Pyramids.' One of Dylan's favourite singers, Om Kalsoum, is Egyptian.

end of the song, guided by the Old Testament book of Ezekiel and the New Testament book of Revelation.

The long night's journey into day happens as follows: after 430 years under the Ancient Egyptians, the children of Israel escape, led by Moses, who brings them to the promised land (though Moses himself dies just before they reach it). They are not good children. Even before they arrive they give a lot of trouble, not least in their sneaking fondness for the old Egyptian idols. When they run amok at the very moment Moses is up on the mountain receiving the Ten Commandments, God wants to wipe out the lot of them then and there, and is only dissuaded by Moses. Spared, they gain the promised land and build Jerusalem. Life goes on and they relapse, the worship of false idols again a prominent part of their transgression.

God calls on a priest, Ezekiel, who is living in exile in Babylon, and commands him to take on the role of prophet, return to Jerusalem and warn the people that, as in Moses' time, next time they see him coming they'd better run: if they don't change their ways, he's going to kill them all.[8]

Ezekiel is guided by his visions, the first of which Dylan alludes to in 'Angelina''s magnificent and stately final verse, when he sings of journeying 'past the angel with four faces'.

Ezekiel Chapter 1, from verse 5 onwards, describes this vision of 'four living creatures' emerging from the midst of a fire:

> And every one had four faces . . . As for the likeness of their faces, they four had the face of a man, and the face of a lion, on the right side: and they four had the face of an ox on the left side; they four also had the face of an eagle.

Adam Clarke, writing about this in an interesting passage in his *Commentary on the Bible* that, for our purposes, links the angel with four faces to the 'god with a body of a woman well-endowed and the head of a hyena', notes that many such 'compound images appear in the Asiatic idols . . . some with the head and feet of a monkey, with the body, arms and legs of a man. Others with the head of the dog; body, arms and legs human . . . The head of a lion and the head of a cock, the whole body human, and the legs terminating in snakes.'[9] The irony here, then, is that the inspirational vision of Ezekiel calls up creatures reminiscent of the very idols his God deplores; it's a strength of Bob Dylan's song that, unfettered by editorialising, these resemblances can float through the lyric heeded or unheeded. As we noted earlier, this is a song about worshipping gods. You might say that 'Angelina' is a chimera about chimera.[10]

8.   In the Good News Bible, God's crossness is unintentionally funny. He comes across like a thwarted small-time hood: 'The Lord spoke to me. "Mortal man," he said, "this is what I, the Sovereign Lord, am saying to the land of Israel: This is the end for the whole land! Israel, the end has come . . . One disaster after another is coming on you. It's all over. This is the end. You are finished. The end is coming for you people"' (Ezekiel 7:1–7).

9.   Adam Clarke, *Commentary on the Bible* (1844 edition); for details on Clarke and his work see Chapter 12, note 9.

10.   'Chimera, or chimaera . . . : 1. Greek myth: a fire-breathing monster with the head of a lion, body of a goat and tail of a serpent. 2. a fabulous beast made up of parts taken from various animals. 3. a wild and unrealistic dream' (*Collins English Dictionary*, 1994).
    Reminding us that Dylan has been down this road before, Ezekiel is also where we find these angels' 'wheels on fire'. (The vision of the four-faced cherubim on the fiery wheels of the divine chariot revisits Ezekiel in Chapters 10 and 11.) The phrase 'fall by the sword', which Dylan uses so freshly in 'your fall-by-the-sword love affair with Errol Flynn' in 'Foot Of Pride', is part of God's admonition to Ezekiel in his vision ('and a third part shall fall by

Ezekiel tells God he can't do much because people always complain that he speaks in riddles. As in the past, God relents a little; but he remains so furious at his people's continued worship of false idols that he allows Jerusalem to fall to the Babylonians (in 586 BC). Ezekiel's last vision is an architecturally detailed one of how a new Jerusalem will be when the people restore themselves to righteousness.[11]

This vision of the twelve-gated city, and the earlier vision of the four angels with four faces riding around upon fiery wheels within wheels, are invoked more than half a millennium later in the Revelation Of St John The Divine and the Revelation To John: the revelation by Jesus Christ in heaven to his faithful, persecuted followers below that a day shall finally come when through him, God's enemies, including Satan, shall be defeated and the faithful shall be rewarded with a new heaven and a new earth: a new Jerusalem.

Revelation is no straightforward read, but memorably within its turbid prose arise the four horsemen of the apocalypse: 'And I saw, and behold a white horse; and he that sat upon him had a bow; and a crown was given unto him: and he went forth conquering; and to conquer'. This horseman is supposedly Christ, preaching the purity of the gospel and sending the darts of conviction into the hearts of sinners. Next 'there went out another horse that was red: and power was given to him that sat thereon to take peace from the earth . . . and there was given unto him a great sword.' The red horse's rider, then, is War. Next comes the black horse, Famine. '. . . And I looked, and behold, a pale horse; and his name that sat on him was Death, and Hell followed with him' (6:2–8).

In 'Angelina', then, when Dylan alludes to this passage, singing

I can see the unknown rider, I can see the pale white horse,

he fuses, with a quiet and clever touch, the 'pale horse' and the 'white horse'; and because he cannot say which he is seeing, he sees an 'unknown' rider. He is asking: is it Christ or is it Death that faces me? This is a question Bob Dylan often asks, and often urges us to ask ourselves.

As for 'the angel with four faces', this phrase is not only inspired by the biblical text but in detail – in its rhythm, shape, length and tone – it stays faithful to it,

---

the sword round about thee' (Ezekiel 5:12), with the phrase itself repeated in 6:11, 12, as well as elsewhere in the Bible). Another phrase from Ezekiel (31:16) is 'the trees of Eden', the phrase with which Dylan ends the first verse of 'The Gates Of Eden', while his lovely line 'in the valley of dry bone dreams', in 'Dignity', arises from the vision of the 'valley of dry bones' in Ezekiel 37.

11.   Ezekiel may have felt a failure at getting God's message across to his contemporaries, but his visions have had conspicuous success with twentieth-century songwriters. Before passages of Ezekiel were utilised in Bob Dylan songs, they inspired many gospel songs recorded by black groups and singers in the 1920s and 1930s. These include the Dixie Jubilee Singers: 'Ezekiel Saw The Wheel In The Middle Of The Air', NYC, 9/8/28; Warren Frazier: 'Zekiel [sic] Saw A Little White Stone', field-recorded for the Library of Congress in Darien, Georgia, c. 19/5/26; the Famous Myers Jubilee Singers: 'Ezekiel Prophesied To The Dry Bones', Chicago, c. May 1928; the Elkins-Payne Jubilee Singers: 'Ezekiel Saw De Wheel', NYC, 24/11/24; Bryant's Jubilee Quintet: 'Ezekiel Saw De Wheel', Richmond, Indiana, c. 24/4/28; Biddle University Quintet: 'Ezekiel Saw De Wheel', NYC, c. April 1920; Willie Lewis: 'Ezekiel', Paris, 23/4/35; Mitchell's Christian Singers: 'Come On Ezekiel Let's Go Around The Wall', NYC, 29/4/36; the Golden Gate Jubilee Quartet: 'Dese Bones Gonna Rise Again', Rock Hill, South Carolina, 2/2/39; and Blind Mamie Forehand: 'Wouldn't Mind Dying If Dying Was All', Memphis, 28/2/27. The vision of the valley of bones is also the textual basis for that ghastly song 'Dem Bones Dem Bones Dem Dry Bones', imposed on us by every ingratiating finger-snapper from, say, the Black & White Minstrels to Kenny Lynch.

echoing very precisely the Revelation phrase 'the sharp sword with two edges' (2:12).

The 'tree of smoke' is another quiet and clever poetic touch: it's a phrase Dylan invents to cover a great deal of spiritual territory. As so often, he seems to take the inherent poetry of the passage he's using and to set it free in his imagination. Chapters 8 and 9 of Revelation (both very short) go on to describe the destructions to be visited on those not saved – those without seals on their foreheads – and these visions encompass burning trees and several sorts of smoke: 'the smoke of the incense, which came with the prayers of the saints' and, in contrast, the smoke from the bottomless pit:

> And the fifth angel sounded, and I saw a star fall from heaven unto the earth: and to him was given the key of the bottomless pit. And he opened the bottomless pit; and there arose a smoke out of the pit, as the smoke of a great furnace; and the sun and the air were darkened by reason of the smoke of the pit. And there came out of the smoke locusts upon the earth . . .

(The locusts appear like horses with crowns like gold, faces of men, hair of women, heads and teeth of lions, tails like scorpions', and so on. Here yet again we contemplate images constructed as if by genetic pick'n'mixing.) Then comes a different army of horses, 'and out of their mouths issued fire and smoke and brimstone. By these three was the third part of men killed, by the fire, and by the smoke, and by the brimstone, which issued out of their mouths.'

There is lots more smoke later: 'And the smoke of their torment ascendeth up for ever and ever: and they have no rest day or night, who worship the beast'. This contrasts with 'And the temple was filled with smoke from the glory of God, and from his power'. When Babylon falls, we get yet another smoke – the smoke of her burning: 'And the kings of the earth, who have committed fornication and lived deliciously with her, shall bewail her, and lament for her, when they shall see the smoke of her burning' (the phrase 'the smoke of her burning' is repeated). Then in the next chapter we get 'And her smoke rose up for ever and ever' – which Dylan uses more directly in 'Ain't Gonna Go To Hell For Anybody', in which the melodically lovely bridge begins with

> *Smoke it rises for ever*
> *On a one-way ticket to burn*

(while, in "Saved", drawing on Revelation 12, the singer's saviour has

> *Freed me from the pit,*
> *Full of emptiness and wrath*
> *And the fire that burns in it*

> *I've been saved*
> *By the blood of the lamb*).

So the image Dylan invents in 'Angelina', 'the tree of smoke', seems entirely apt: a scripturally alert emblem, characterising the enormous sweep of turmoil that must unfold before the establishment of the new heaven and the new earth. A 'tree of smoke' seems especially apt since when the new Jerusalem is built, 'Blessed are they that do his commandments, that they may have right to the tree of life' (Revelation 22:14). This counterbalancing of the one tree and the other is given some emphasis in Dylan's work by his using that phrase 'the tree of life' in another song of the period, the lifeless 'Death Is Not The End':

> *Oh the tree of life is growing*
> *Where the spirit never dies*
> *And the bright light of salvation shines*
> *In dark and empty skies*
>
> *When the cities are on fire with the burning flesh of men*
> *Just remember that death is not the end.*[12]

It's not the least of Dylan's achievement with 'the tree of smoke' that while it sounds so *right* as a feature of the magic realist landscape – it could be drifting up from the pages of *One Hundred Years of Solitude* – it sounds just as accurately honed as a phrase compressing so much of Revelation.

The looser phrase 'surrounded by God's angels' enjoys a similar double-life. Encountered already as evoking a peasant culture's panting religiosity, now it re-imprints itself as part of a genuinely visionary picture: a brushstroke in Dylan's painting of the apocalypse. In this particular too we've shifted from Argentina to Jerusalem. Likewise

> *I see pieces of men marching, trying to take heaven by force*

acts now as another series of brushstrokes on this swirling canvas of an overcrowded sky thronging and exploding with fires and angels, armies and horsemen, the quick and the dead, the Lord and his heavenly hosts.[13] A renewal of meaning is given too to

---

12.   As with Ezekiel, Dylan draws on Revelation in many songs. 'Be watchful, and strengthen the things that remain, that are ready to die' (3:2) gives Dylan his stern refrain in 'When You Gonna Wake Up?': 'When you gonna wake up and strengthen the things that remain?' Close behind the four horsemen of the apocalypse (6:12), comes the line '. . . and the moon became as blood', which is likely to remind us of Dylan's 'Neath a moon shinin' bloody and pink' in 'No Time To Think'. (In Acts 2:12, 20, Peter reminds people that the Old Testament prophet Joel said that 'it shall come to pass in the last days, saith God . . . The sun shall be turned into darkness and the moon into blood'.) Revelation 11:18, 'And the nations were angry', and 13:8, 'the Lamb slain from the foundation of the world' (Christ crucified at the start of the Christian period), are called up in 'Solid Rock'. Then there is 'If any man have an ear, let him hear' (13:9). This phrase, or its near-exact equivalent, repeated a number of times throughout the course of the book, is a repetition of a passage from Ezekiel (12:1–2): 'The word of the Lord also came unto me, saying, Son of man, thou dwellest in the midst of a rebellious house, which have eyes to see, and see not; they have ears to hear, and hear not.' The same phrases recur as the words of Christ in the New Testament Gospels also (Matthew 13:43: 'Who hath ears to hear, let him hear'; Mark 4:9 and 4:23: 'He that hath ears to hear, let him hear'; Mark 7:16: 'If any man have ears to hear, let him hear'; Mark 8:18: 'Having eyes, see ye not? and having ears, hear ye not?'; Luke 14:35: 'He that hath ears to hear, let him hear'). cf. 'When He Returns': 'For all those who have eyes and all those who have ears' but also cf. 'Blowin' In The Wind': 'Yes, 'n' how many ears must one man have / Before he can hear people cry?' Dylan also uses Revelation 19:6, 'And in those days shall men seek death, and shall not find it; and shall desire to die, and death shall flee from them', fashioning from it this rumination in 'Precious Angel': 'Can they imagine the darkness that will fall from on high / When men will beg God to kill them and they won't be able to die?' Dylan draws upon a further passage of Revelation in the lyric of 'Foot Of Pride', considered below.

13.   John Milton's epic poem *Paradise Lost* (1667, revised edition 1674), which traces the fall of man and his disobedience towards God to Satan's expulsion from heaven, has much on Satan's legions trying to take heaven by force. The phrase echoes too the calmer prose of Matthew 11:12: 'And from the days of John the Baptist until now the kingdom of heaven suffereth violence, and the violent take it by force.'

that small phrase 'them spiral staircases': it becomes a figurative expression of the
circling motion of ascent as the beholder of such visions feels body and soul rise up,
up, up (like smoke) into that thrashing heaven. Beat a path of retreat from sin; choose
Christ not Death; choose between the part of oneself that draws back and the part
that advances; climb

> *. . . up them spiral staircases,*
> *Past the tree of smoke, past the angel with four faces,*
> *Begging God for mercy and weeping in unholy places,*
> *Angelina.*

Cutting across these general themes of worship and salvation, and recurring in
amongst these shifts from world to world, there is also present in 'Angelina' the more
personal cutting and shifting of a man–woman dialogue. Fragments of this dialogue
seem to fall within our hearing, like parts of a loudly whispered, fitful conversation
overheard on a moving train. The terrain outside the windows keeps changing; the
lovers' quarrel runs through the middle of it all, as a series of one-liners, occasionally
calmly resigned ('I've tried my best to love you but I cannot play this game') but
mostly seething with reproach and the malice of the hurt.

Yet these lines and phrases rarely turn out to be unconnected with the terrain
around them. We've seen how one line that sounds to be part of the lovers' quarrel,
the hissing 'When you cease to exist, who will you blame?', touches upon one of the
song's big themes, salvation, and has a special resonance of meaning in one of the
song's locations, the world of Ancient Egypt. Similarly, the memorable core of this
personal dialogue also leads a double life, its other one lived within the world of
contemporary political menace. These are the lines:

> *Do I need your permission to turn the other cheek?*
> *If you can read my mind why must I speak?*
> *No, I have heard nothing about the man that you seek . . .*

This is admirably captured quarrelsome rhetoric, authentic in its conversational tone,
in which belligerence is barely concealed beneath the sweetly reasonable, unanswerable
questions and hot jealousy hisses around the sides of an insistent disinterest. Attractively snappy, quotable stuff, this is clearly from the same pen, fifteen years on, as lines
like 'And you, you just sit around and ask for ashtrays: can't you reach?' (from the
quintessential 'She's Your Lover Now', 1966). But you can hear these same lines
altogether differently as well. It is a virtuoso display by Dylan to deliver gems of
heightened conversation that function simultaneously in a political (and as we shall
soon see, religious) context. These same lines are the voice of the tortured to the
torturer in the South American jail cell; they call out, at once hapless and defiant,
from those unholy places where anything can happen:

> *Do I need your permission to turn the other cheek?*
> *If you can read my mind why must I speak?*
> *No, I have heard nothing about the man that you seek . . .*

And there is a response, half a verse later: the voice of the other side, mouthing the
classic mitigating plea of the torturer and sadistic jailer everywhere:

I was only following instructions . . .

Less in extremis, this is the excuse of the jobsworth the world over too, the excuse of the minion who enjoys his little exercise of power on behalf of the authorities. In this instance

I was only following instructions when the judge sent me down the road
With your subpoena.

A lot of people have trouble with that 'subpoena'. They find it too ostentatious a rhyme. I find it untroublesome: it is offered with humour, acknowledging its own disruptive ostentation with a silent smile. Indeed Dylan maximises its impact by the deliberate abruptness of the line that disgorges it. Every other verse has a fourth line of eight, nine or ten syllables (not counting the extra syllables of filigree that Dylan's voice draws out of these '-ina' words). 'With your subpoena' is a brusquely foreshortened five-syllable line, and Dylan emphasises its brevity by his phrasing, so that 'subpoena' not only jumps out at us but jumps out early. And of course, to take the scene literally, it would 'jump out at you', would come as a nasty little shock, if the official at your door, or tapping you on the shoulder down the road, served you with a subpoena.[14]

There is one other juncture at which Dylan deliberately abandons the orderly pattern of his lines. Again, the effect is to surprise for a specific purpose. As I mentioned very early on, the last line of each verse is the one word 'Angelina', except in the penultimate verse. Instead of

. . . and she's wearin' a blindfold,
Angelina

we live vividly in the moment in the lovers' quarrel by hearing what is, in content, a blurted interjection ('But so are you') delivered as a blurted interjection in form too. Instead of what we expect, we get

. . . and she's wearin' a blindfold
But so are you, Angelina.

It is a clear, small illustration of a general truth often asserted in the arts: only those who have mastered the rules can break them successfully.

Not that 'Angelina' is wholly a success. Dylan's Cut-Up narrative, whereby phrase by phrase the flow of logic is defeated, and lines and half-lines fail to connect with those nearest them, but rather call out to others half the song away, while the 'me' and 'you' and 'she' and 'he' refuse identification: in the end, it fails to satisfy. We

---

14. Gavin Selerie points out an extraordinary possible source for this rhyme – indeed for the whole process of rhyming words with the name Angelina. His article 'Tricks and training: some Dylan sources and analogues' (*Telegraph*, no. 50, Winter 1994) reports: 'I don't think it has been noted before that Dylan's song echoes the opening chorus of Gilbert and Sullivan's *Trial by Jury*, which contains the lines: "For to-day in this arena / Summoned by a stern subpoena / Edwin, sued by Angelina, / Shortly will appear". Later in the operetta, Angelina is summoned . . . with the echoing recitative: "Oh, Angelina! Come thou into Court! Angelina! Angelina!"'

We know Dylan's sources are eclectic, but really: Gilbert and Sullivan!

Gavin Selerie adds that 'Gilbert derived the names of his principal characters from a ballad by Oliver Goldsmith, "The Hermit, Or Edwin And Angelina"' (written c. 1762, published 1766).

drink in the riches of ellipse and leaps of imagination, the compressed layering of meaning and powerful air of mystery that such a method achieves . . . and still we thirst for narrative clarity.

Yet what a compelling, grand failure 'Angelina' remains. Not mere smoke but a tree of smoke. This song about angels with many faces and gods made from more than one animal – it achieves the same multiplicity itself. Its lines and phrases often have two or three faces: they are frequently more than one kind of creature themselves. It may lack narrative clarity, but it has in abundance that other quality we demand of a complex work: it has unity.

This is partly achieved by its series of inner pairings, which extend far beyond the obvious – right hand, left hand; best friend, worst enemy; body of woman, head of hyena; Jerusalem or Argentina; vengeance satisfied, possessions sold; he's this and she's that; to love versus to play a game; rider and horse; tree and angel; the other cheek. As well as all these, which are all pairings placed in proximity, we can discern a further set more distantly placed: that 'right hand drawing back' at the beginning and that 'path of retreat' at the end; 'pieces of men' and body of this, head of that; the ambiguity of 'pieces of men marching' paralleled by that of 'Your servants are half dead'; 'tall man' and 'giants'; 'his eyes were two slits' and 'she's wearin' a blindfold'; the combat zone and the arena.

This satisfying inner cohesion, this sense of balance, is augmented by Dylan's reliance upon one Old and one New Testament book – especially since the New so attentively refers back to the Old. And since both look forward to the second coming of Christ, it is apt that Christ's first coming also has a presence in 'Angelina'.

This presence is evoked by another pairing: in this case a pair of allusions to Christ's words to the apostles from the Sermon on the Mount (Matthew, 5–8, and Luke 6, 11). For 'Do I need your permission to turn the other cheek?' not only operates as personal dialogue and political drama, as noted. It carries further resonance by alluding to Christ's dictum (Matthew 5:39): 'resist not evil: but whoever shall smite thee on thy right cheek, turn to him the other also'.[15]

To remember that this derives from the Sermon on the Mount is to hear as a back-echo something else in 'Angelina', from the very start of the song, that Dylan draws from the same well: that right hand drawing back while the left hand advances. We come to recognise that this notion of having our hands acting independently of each other is also from a dictum of Christ (Matthew 6:3): 'let not thy left hand know what thy right hand doeth'.

Here, then, another of the song's inner matches is made. Not only Ezekiel balanced by Revelation but Revelation balanced by the Gospels. Counterbalancing the boiling incomprehensibility of Christ's visionary Revelation from heaven to his apostle John, here is a glimpse of his calm, strong presence on earth, as he gives clear, kind guidance to all his apostles.[16]

---

15.   Christ's words are also given, if slightly differently, in Luke 6:29: 'And unto him that smiteth thee on the one cheek offer also the other . . .'

16.   If you go on to read Acts (i.e. the Acts of the Apostles, in which they in turn disseminate Christ's teaching) you find a context for another phrase from 'Angelina', 'her possessions have been sold': a context which contradicts our assumption that having your possessions sold is a bad thing. In the context of following Christ, it is what any new convert desirous of joining the apostles must do. Acts 2:44–45: 'And all that believed were together, and had

Dylan's performance, which is the other great strength of 'Angelina', enhances this sense of Christ's earthly presence. He sings the line

If you can read my mind, why must I speak?

with such quiet simplicity that you can hear it anew in this context, hearing not the lover's anger disguised by sweet reasonableness, nor the defiance of the political victim, but the mode of address we associate with Jesus when he's teaching: a mode of piercing but patient questioning.

The exquisite intelligence of Bob Dylan's performance throughout 'Angelina' is easy to disregard since it works with self-deprecating quietness; but all through the song his voice draws out its multiplicities of meaning and lights up its detail as no other artist could hope to do. And always it rises to the occasion: when the writing is at its best, the singing informs it with genius. On 'Angelina', these peaks of coordinated achievement arise on the second and the last verse.

Verse two begins with this compelling, audacious, witty, idiosyncratic, fresh, imaginative and playful line:

His eyes were two slits, make any snake proud

and Dylan sings 'twoooo slits' as two long, equal syllables. *Anyone* else would, less alertly, give an automatic greater length to 'slits' than to 'two', but Dylan gives them a poised, counterbalancing equality, sings them as if he has all the time in the world, and sings them not to achieve a belaboured hissing on 'slits', not to illustrate a sound at all, but to illustrate a picture: he draws out the 'two slits' as if he's actually drawing the two slits, or etching them with a knife.

He passes over the internal rhyme of 'make' and 'snake' without the slightest stress, and passes nonchalantly over the three internal chimes of the next line, in which 'face' is half-echoed by 'painter' and 'paint', knowing that the way 'face' is only half-echoed rescues the repetition of 'painter would paint' from its potential troublesomeness. In case this is still problematic on the ear, the next line is quick to yield its own contrasting internal rhyme, sounding a different vowel:

Worshipping a god with the body of a woman well endowed

and Dylan, fully alert to this, renders it perfectly, lingering on these syllables with measured sagacity. There is no excess of stress: he gives it just enough attention to

---

all things common; And sold their possessions and goods, and parted them to all men, as every man had need.' And Acts 4:34–35: 'for as many as were possessors of lands or houses sold them, and brought the prices of the things that were sold, And laid them down at the apostles' feet: and distribution was made unto every man according to his need.' Here is where Christianity and Marxism meet. (Karl Marx: 'From each according to his abilities, to each according to his need', from the essay 'Critique of the Gotha Programme', 1875 [currently available in English as a 1978 pamphlet published by Mezhgunarodnaya, USSR, still in stock 1995 at Central Books, London, and, with a Foreword by Frederick Engels, collected in *Marx and Engels: Selected Works Vol. 2*, 1962].)

This communism of the apostles goes back to the Sermon of the Mount ('Lay not up for yourselves treasures upon earth . . .' [Matthew 6:19; rediscussed in Luke 12]) and to Christ's telling the devout rich man that the one further thing he must do to enter the kingdom of heaven is to 'sell whatever thou hast, and give to the poor, and thou shalt have treasure in heaven' (Mark 10:21). Naturally the man balks at this, and he goes away saddened; the apostles balk at the idea too, prompting Christ to tell them 'It is easier for a camel to go through the eye of a needle, than for a rich man to enter into the kingdom of God' (Mark, 10:25.)

make it always pleasing to hear. Bound in with this come two instances of that other dangerous kind of chiming, so easy to overdo: alliteration.

> *Worshipping a god with the body of a woman well endowed*
> *And the head of a hyena.*

Such muscular writing; such impeccable execution. The 'woman well' can afford to toll emphatically because it precedes the third consecutive strong line-end rhyme, the third consecutive AAA rhyme, and since these have a cumulative effect upon the ear, the third one must sound so inevitable, necessary, firm and set that you can get away with more or less any degree of insistent alliteration on the way to it. As for 'And the head of a hyena', well, the small pause before 'hyena' and the sense of wariness achieved in that word's delivery (make any hyena proud), these are the brushstrokes of genius.

As John Bauldie puts it in the "Bootleg Series I–III" booklet, Dylan has a 'facility to make his voice reflect the meanings of the words he's singing'. He notes how in 'Someone's Got A Hold Of My Heart' Dylan's voice 'seems to wind around the words "wind around", or be as wide as "wide" or as easy as "easy".' In 'Angelina', comparably, Dylan sings 'Do I need your permission to turn the other cheek?' so that on the word 'turn' his voice enacts a turning: the sound pivots around inside his mouth. He gives us the full sense of the moment's drama – of the way that to turn the other cheek is actually to take strong, challenging, even aggressive, *action*.

This attention to detail, which always avoids reductive predictability in favour of intuitive flash, stays with us throughout the song's long journey. It gives us the extraordinary dying breath with which Dylan appears to expire on the long-drawn-out end of 'arena—' and then the final climb up the melodic steps which begins with 'up them spiral staircases' (no one else could sing that phrase at all, let alone with the sumptuous sadness and humane modesty Dylan brings to it) and which keeps ascending, words and melody perfectly at one, till the last cathartic incantation of the song title itself.

There is yet more unity achieved in 'Angelina' here: a link between some of Christ's teaching and, as it were, the song's Egyptian connection, and a link between that same teaching and a little of Dylan's own. In 1945, the Gnostic Gospels, known in Egypt as the Nag Hammadi Codices, were found near the town of Nag Hammadi, near Abydos, centre of the cult of Osiris and other death cults, and associated with Anubis, the jackal-headed god of embalming. These gospels are fourth-century Coptic translations of second-century Greek originals, except that the Gospel of Thomas might date from about AD 50, which would make it as old or older than the gospels of Matthew, Mark, Luke and John. The Gospel of Thomas contains 114 sayings of Christ, including some that inspired the early Greek mystics known as the Gnostics:

> If you bring forth what is within you, what you bring forth will save you. If you
> do not bring forth what is within you, what is within you will destroy you.[17]

---

17.   The Gnostics came to believe that the Old Testament's grumpy, vindictive old God was an evil being who had created the material world as a prison, and that Christ was a liberationist come to free humanity from Jehovah's dominion. They were declared heretics, and thus their Gospels were buried. Some of these can now be seen in the Coptic Museum in Cairo.

Bob Dylan is with the Gnostics here: these remarks have always made fundamental sense to him, and he restates them, or builds upon them, in at least two songs contemporaneous with 'Angelina'. He shares their assumptions in 'Need A Woman', when he observes that

> *Whatever's waiting in the future*
> *Could be what you're runnin' from in the past*

and he restates their message in that line from 'The Groom's Still Waiting At The Altar' in which he refers to

> *. . . the madness of becoming what one was never meant to be.*

You might also hear Christ's words as the impetus behind a compelling, quiet motto from 'Angelina' itself. There are lines of Dylan's that tiptoe into the brain without the warning that obvious brilliance signals: sayings that settle in unobtrusively and make themselves quietly useful about the place, until you find yourself calling on their services surprisingly often. The lovely last verse of 'Angelina' contains such a saying. To put it in context, you need this much of it:

> *In God's truth, tell me what you want and you'll have it of course*
> *Just step into the arena.*

This seems to me to express a great truth: that to get what you want, you must be prepared to put the whole of yourself into contesting for it: must fully enter the world in which lies the prize you seek, no matter how the odds are stacked, or how ugly the howling crowd . . . and that it must be a prize you truly want, your choice informed by some self-knowledge.

This is a truth Bob Dylan has expressed before – you might say his whole stance as an artist expresses it – but he has not put it in song before, as far as I know. Not that Dylan means the bit about achieving it 'of course': this is a sardonic touch, a flourish that belongs to the lovers' quarrel within the song. There is no 'of course' about it, as Dylan at once suggests by the almost strangled last gasp with which he finally lets go of the attentuated word 'arena'. The extrapolatable truth, then, is as compressed into that one pithy, adamant motto: 'Just step into the arena'. Before long you find you're saying it to yourself.

General books of quotations sometimes include one or two, rarely more, from Bob Dylan – and they're always 'The answer my friend is blowing in the wind' or 'The times they are a-changin''. They should of course have a plethora of quotes, from 'Are you for sale or just on the shelf?' to 'He bought the American dream but it was all wet' and from 'i accept chaos. i am not sure whether it accepts me' to 'What looks large from a distance, close up ain't never that big' – and they should certainly include 'Just step into the arena'. It may not be as catchy as 'To live outside the law you must be honest', but it holds as much truth, and one has more occasion to say it.

Dylan's own comments on 'Caribbean Wind', in the interview by Cameron Crowe for "Biograph", are interesting not only about this song but about his writing more generally:

I couldn't quite grasp what it was about after I finished it. Sometimes you'll write something to be very inspired, and you won't quite finish it for one reason or another. Then you'll go back and try and pick it up, and the inspiration is just gone. Either you get it all, and you can leave a few little pieces to fill in, or you're trying always to finish it off. Then it's a struggle. The inspiration's gone and you can't remember why you started it in the first place. Frustration sets in. I think there's four different sets of lyrics to this. Maybe I got it right, I don't know. I had to leave it. I just dropped it. Sometimes that happens. I started it in St. Vincent when I woke up from a strange dream in the hot sun. There was a bunch of women working in a tobacco field on a high rolling hill. A lot of them were smoking pipes. I was thinking about living with someone for all the wrong reasons.

I believe that once upon a time there may have been five versions rather than four. It was long rumoured that a version was taped during a get-together in Mark Knopfler's hotel room with various other musicians in late 1980, which has become referred to as 'the Knopfler Hotel Room Tape'. Dire Straits manager Ed Bicknell, no Dylan enthusiast, described this early version of 'Caribbean Wind' as 'one of the most beautiful songs I ever heard'. It was, says Bicknell, a solo guitar-and-vocals perform- ance by Dylan, and proved the only sustained performance of anything in the course of the usual jamming process of trying twelve bars of this, switching to something else, finding you don't know it and trying another doomed fragment of something else again. Unfortunately, Bicknell believes that no one present taped any of this material, and is surprised even to hear that its existence has been rumoured.[18]

Another version, details unknown, is believed to exist on tape and to be in the possession of mid-1970s Dylan sidekick Joel Bernstein: a version which, heard only by a few people (the present writer not among them), reportedly has different lyrics from the three versions that have circulated. These three are: the 'rattlesnake' version, a studio recording that emerged among tape collectors only in 1994 but that seems the earliest of the three; the version performed live at the Fox-Warfield in San Francisco on 12 November 1980, which certainly seems a halfway-house version so far as the lyric is concerned; and the studio version recorded on 7 April 1981 and released on the "Biograph" box-set in late 1985.

Since the Knopfler hotel room tape doesn't exist and I have not heard the Joel Bernstein tape the critique that follows naturally confines itself to the three other versions: the early studio version – the 'rattlesnake' version – which probably dates from October 1980 (Version 1); the one live performance Dylan gave the song, that November (Version 2); and the released version from April 1981 (Version 3). This certainly seems as if it is the last version Dylan offered before he 'just dropped it', and it is this version of the lyric that is so carelessly transcribed in the book *Lyrics 1962–1985*.

---

18.   Ed Bicknell in conversation with the present writer in c. April 1981 and again 31/8/95. Bicknell says the location was the Sunset Marquis hotel in Los Angeles, in c. September–October 1980, when Dire Straits were playing some dates at the Roxy just after the release of their album "Making Movies". Present were Bob Dylan, Tim Drummond, Mark Knopfler, two members of Bruce Springsteen's E-Street Band, Bicknell, two unidentified young women and music journalist Mike Oldfield. Other songs tried included, if memory serves, Buddy Holly items like 'That'll Be The Day'. The occasion is described in Oldfield's biography *Dire Straits* (1984).

I believe that even if there were no external evidence as to when these three versions were made, it would still be clear from the three sets of lyrics themselves that this was the order in which they were written.

Words given inside square brackets are far from certain:

Caribbean Wind Version 1 ('rattlesnake')
She was well rehearsed, fair brown and blonde
She had friends who were bus-boys and friends in the Pentagon
Playin' a show in Miami in the theatre of divine comedy
Talked me in the shadows where they talked in the rain
I could tell she was still feelin' the pain
Pain of rejection, pain of infidelity
Was she a child or a woman? I can't say which
From one to another she could easily switch
Couples were dancin' and I lost track of the hours
He was well prepared – I knew he was –
Paying attention like a rattlesnake does
When he's hearin' footsteps tramplin' over his flowers

The Caribbean winds still blow from Nassau to Mexico
From the circle of ice to the furnace of desire
And them distant ships of liberty on them iron waves so bold and free
Bringing everything that's near to me nearer to the fire.

She looked into my soul through the clothes that I wore
She said 'We got a mutual friend standin' at the door'
Yeah, y'know, he's got our best interests in mind.
He was well-connected but her heart was a snare
And she had left him to die in there
He had payments due and he was a little behind
But I slept in a hotel where flies buzzed my head
Ceiling fan was broken, there was heat in my bed
Street band playin' 'Nearer My God To Thee'.
We met in secret where we drank from a spring
She said 'I know what you're thinkin' but there ain't a thing
We can do about it so we might as well let it be.'

The Caribbean winds still blow from Nassau to Mexico
From the circle of ice to the furnace of desire
And them distant ships of liberty on them iron waves so bold and free
Bringing everything that's near to me nearer to the fire.

Atlantic City, two years to the day
I hear her voice cryin' 'Daddy!' and I look that way
But it's only the silence in the Buttermilk Hills that call.
Every new messenger bringin' evil report
'Bout rioting armies and time that is short
And earthquakes an' train-wrecks an' hate-words scribbled on walls.

Would I have married her? I dunno – I suppose:
She had bells in her braids and they hung to her toes
But I heard my name and destiny said to be moving on.
Then I felt it come over me, some kind of gloom
Gonna say 'Come on with me, girl, I got plenty a' room'
But I knew I'd be lyin'; and besides, she'd already gone

And them Caribbean winds still blow from Nassau to Mexico
From the circle of ice to the furnace of desire
And them distant ships of liberty on them iron waves so bold and free
Bringing everything that's near to me nearer to the fire.

Caribbean Wind Version 2 ('live')
She was from Haiti, bowed down at the table
[And then I took over the Lord]
At the show in Miami at the theatre of divine comedy.
[Told] about Jesus, [talked] about the rain,
She told me about the vision, told me about the pain
That had risen from the essence and the dividing of memory.
Was she a child or a woman? I really can't say
But somethin' about her said 'Trust me anyway'
As the years turned into minutes and the minutes turned back into hours.
[What about you,] played as a pawn?
It certainly was possible as the gay night wore on
But victory was mine and I held it with the help of God's power

And that Caribbean wind still blows from Trinidad to Mexico,
From the circle of light to the furnace of desire
And them distant ships of liberty on them iron waves so bold and free
Bringing everything that's near to me nearer to the fire.

Shadows moved closer as we touched on the floor,
Prodigal Son sitting next to the door,
Preaching resistance, waiting for the night to arrive.
He was well connected but his heart was a snare
'Cause she had left him to die in there
But I knew he could get out while he was still alive.
Flies on my balcony buzzin' my head,
Slayin' Bob Dylan [here] in my bed
Street band playin' 'Nearer My God To Thee'.
We met at the steeple where the mission bells ring
She said 'I know what you're thinkin' but there ain't a thing
You can do about it so you might as well agree to agree'

And them Caribbean wind blows hard from the Valley Coast into my back yard
[Doin' of] your love to the furnace of desire
And them distant ships of liberty on them iron waves so bold and free
Bringing everything that's near to me nearer to the fire.

Atlantic City by the cruel sea,
I hear a voice cryin' 'Daddy!' I always think it's for me
But it's only the silence in the Buttermilk Hills that's all
Every new messenger bringin' evil reports
Of rioting armies and time that is short
And earthquakes and train wrecks and death-threats written on walls
Would I have married her? I dunno – I suppose.
She had bells in her braids and they hung to her toes
But the curtain was risin' and, like they say, the ship will sail at dawn
And I felt it come over me, some kind of gloom
My voice said 'Come on with me girl, I got plenty of room'
But I know I'd be lyin', and besides, she had already gone

And that Caribbean wind still howls from Tokyo to the British Isles.
We never walked into that furnace of desire
And them distant ships of liberty on them iron waves so bold and free
Bringing everything that's near to me nearer to the fire.

Caribbean Wind Version 3 ("Biograph")
She was the rose of Sharon from paradise lost
From the city of seven hills near the place of the cross
I was playing a show in Miami in the theatre of divine comedy.
Told about Jesus, told about the rain,
She told me 'bout the jungle where her brothers were slain
By the man who invented iron and disappeared so mysteriously.
Was she a child or an angel? Did we go too far?
Were we sniper bait? Did we follow a star
Through a hole in the wall to where the long arm of the law cannot reach?
Could I-a been used and played as a pawn?
It certainly was possible as the gay night wore on
Where men bathed in perfume and practised the hoax of free speech

And them Caribbean winds still blow from Nassau to Mexico
Fanning the flames in the furnace of desire
And them distant ships of liberty on them iron waves so bold and free
Bringing everything that's near to me nearer to the fire.

Sea breeze blowin', there's a hellhound loose,
Redeemed men who have escaped from the noose
Preaching faith and salvation, waiting for the night to arrive
He was well-connected but her heart was a snare
And she had left him to die in there:
He was goin' down slow, just barely stayin' alive.
The cry a' the peacock, flies buzz in my head
Ceiling fan broken, there's a heat in my bed,
Street band playin' 'Nearer My God To Thee'.
We met at the station where the mission bells ring,

She said 'I know what you're thinkin' but there ain't a thing
You can do about it so let us just agree to agree,'

And them Caribbean winds still blow from Nassau to Mexico
Fanning the flames in the furnace of desire
And them distant ships of liberty on them iron waves so bold and free
Bringing everything that's near to me nearer to the fire.

Atlantic City by the cold grey sea.
I hear a voice cryin' 'Daddy!', I always think it's for me
But it's only the silence in the Buttermilk Hills that call.
Every new messenger bringin' evil report
'Bout armies on the march and time that is short
And famines and earthquakes and train wrecks and the tearin' down of the wall.
Did you ever have a dream that you couldn't explain?
Ever meet your accusers face to face in the rain?
She had chrome brown eyes that I won't forget as long as she's gone.
I see the screws breakin' loose, see the devil poundin' on tin,
See a house in the country bein' torn apart from within,
I hear my ancestors calling from the land far beyond

And them Caribbean winds still blow from Nassau to Mexico
Fanning the flames in the furnace of desire
And them distant ships of liberty on them iron waves so bold and free
Bringing everything that's near to me nearer to the fire.

The first promising thing about this song is its length. Dylan may have had trouble deciding which set of lyrics to offer, but each set is lengthy (three substantial verses of twelve lines each – most of them long enough that they could plausibly be rendered as two lines each – plus big incantatory choruses) and it is a fact that Dylan finds it hard to make trivial songs long songs. I know that by the Olympian standards demanded by the present writer when scrutinising Dylan's work at the beginning of the 1970s, even 'Sad-Eyed Lady Of The Lowlands' was found wanting (though this seemed, and still seems to me, a failure of his words to correspond to his intentions for them, rather than a failure to be consequential *per se*). More recent songs, such as 'Clean-Cut Kid' and 'When The Night Comes Falling From The Sky', do show that length is no guarantee of substance, but in the vast majority of cases, from 'North Country Blues' to 'Changing Of The Guards' and from 'Mr. Tambourine Man' to 'Jokerman', length in a Dylan song indicates time spent working on it, real interest in it by the writer himself, and thus real substance to it.

This is not at all to deny the importance of performance – indeed 'Caribbean Wind' shows the primacy of performance as well as anything in Dylan's canon. It's true that the lyrics of the 'rattlesnake' version and the "Biograph" version are substantially different (the live version is a halfway house, of interest only in showing how the earlier version turned into the later). The one is a dark, small-scale, close-up study of betrayal and insufficiency of trust and passion; the other is a sweeping celebration of being alive, and of love's integration of past, present and future. But the *dramatic* change is between the voices, noises, moods: the performances.

The way he sings the 'rattlesnake' version! He sort of moronises the tune – to thrilling effect. It is a very particular effect, too. There is no other Bob Dylan recording you can find the same voice on, and yet it is so entirely characteristic of what Bob Dylan's voice can do: it trusts the listener to enjoy the sly wit, free intelligence, relish of nuance and quick play that's pouring off the delivery of every phrase. All these flow through the performance, a torrent of fleeting joys that can't be put into words but which that voice, and the intimate attentiveness behind it, communicate at least as strongly as the meaning of words or the sound of music.

This is how Dylan so often used to be when it was hip to be hip and he was hipper by far than all the rest. There are few aural moments anywhere in Bob Dylan's work that give me more pleasure than the neo-moronic way he sings 'But it's only the silence in the Buttermilk Hills that call'. Indeed until, having been accurate and clear all the way through, he fluffs the words repeatedly on the final chorus, it's executed with faultless, yet experimental, footwork. The different exploratory way that he sings 'nearer to the fire' each time around on this recording will divide your friends into those with no patience for such amateur messing about and those who are intelligent, warm, generous and possessed of a sense of humour and an enquiring mind.

As for this version of the lyric, its special delights begin at the beginning, with the ambiguity of 'She was well rehearsed'. Formally it fits with her 'show in Miami' (this is the only version in which it is 'she', not the narrator, playing the show at the theatre of divine comedy) yet as the first thing said of someone it carries a nice asperity in suggesting a calculated quality. This is immediately refocused by saying that she was

> . . . *fair brown and blonde*
> *She had friends who were bus-boys and friends in the Pentagon.*

That long line is at once several things. It is equally pleasurable in its relish of the incongruity between 'bus-boys' and Pentagon heavies and its wholly Dylanesque relish of the words themselves. In this sense it might be a line from *Tarantula*. In fact his savouring of 'bus-boys' is like his savouring of the term 'sporting-house' when Dylan is himself the bus-boy in *Renaldo & Clara*. But the line also makes more complex the song's picture of the woman. Is her eclecticism in friends a mere part of her calculatedness, a discreditable tendency to appear all things to all men, or is it rather that she is, in Walt Whitman's words, 'large' and can 'contain multitudes'?[19]

The phrase 'fair brown and blonde' at first seems to hold a list of three alternative forms of appearance, so suggesting, like 'well rehearsed', a person of dissembling self-presentation. But Dylan is relishing words again here: he enjoys the way the phrase sounds like three incompatible things in one list while actually it speaks of only two things: 'fair brown' and 'blonde'. As noted elsewhere, 'fair brown' is an old black American term for a black American woman whose colour is neither as pale as 'high yellow' nor as dark as 'black'. In 'Three Women Blues', for example, Blind Willie McTell voices the common colour distinction of the day in boasting of having 'three

19. Walt Whitman, the father of the American poetic voice: 'Do I contradict myself? / Very well then I contradict myself / (I am large, I contain multitudes)'. From 'Song of Myself', one of the poems in his groundbreaking *Leaves of Grass* right from the first edition of 1855 (though 'Song of Myself', like the anthology, grew longer in later editions).

women: high yellow, fair brown and black'. (While received gentility had it that light skin was classiest, blues singers often expressed a preference for 'fair browns', declaring them to be warmer and sexier than aloof 'high yellows' while being less low-down than 'blacks'.[20])

The less than ideal lines

> *Was she a child or a woman? I can't say which*
> *From one to another she could easily switch*

reinforce the portait's ambiguity. They do so doubly, indeed, since the second of these lines is itself ambiguous. Is it mere plodding further explanation of the child–woman dichotomy (not a very interesting dichotomy, as the chorus of 'Just Like A Woman' has long since proved), offering us no clue as to whether such switching derives from her being manipulative or mercurial? Or, granted its context, might not the line be taken to mean that from one to another *person* she could easily switch her attention or her favours? – a meaning that chimes in with the whole song's atmosphere of shadowy infidelities. The line and this meaning are removed in Dylan's later versions of the lyric. In transition – on the live 1980 San Francisco version – the question becomes

> *Was she a child or a woman? I really can't say*

and the whole theme of her possible shiftiness is resolved at once by the line that follows, in which Dylan adds

> *But somethin' about her said 'Trust me anyway',*

and by the time we arrive at the issued version of the song, the "Biograph" version, the question has switched from 'Was she a child or a woman' to 'Was she a child or an angel?' and, attractively, the entire thrust of the question is transformed by being no longer something demanding debate in itself but just the first of a series of questions:

> *Was she a child or an angel? Did we go too far?*
> *Were we sniper bait? Did we follow a star*
> *Through a hole in the wall to where the long arm of the law cannot reach?*
> *Could I-a been used and played as a pawn?*

In the end the narrator arcs back to the theme of his fear of being manipulated again, but in this version the cavalcade of questions presses upon us with its own muscularity of rhythm and its own babbling diversity of kind, and with too much impatience to be moving on for any ponderous answers to come plodding along behind. The chopping between the associative sentimentality of 'a child or an angel' and 'follow a star' and the modern warfare-culture nastiness of wondering about being 'sniper bait' – what a great, great term – is inspired: psychologically truthful and a deft piece of writing that lifts the song way above the level of the earlier lyric. Keeping it up there is the similar surprise as Dylan, in classic fashion, takes two or three clichés and bumps them together to produce something new. Here they don't 'follow a star', full

---

20.   Blind Willie McTell: 'Three Women Blues', Atlanta, 17/10/28; "Blind Willie McTell: The Early Years (1927–1933)", Yazoo L-1005, NYC, 1968; CD-reissued Yazoo CD-1005, NYC 1990.

stop: they don't 'follow a star' up in the sky. They follow it through a hole in the wall – a neat rerouteing of one's expectation and a pleasing visual joke. And then comes 'the long arm of the law', following them following a star, and it too is visualised as reaching, comically and in vain, through the hole in the wall.

What we lose by Dylan's discarding of the 'rattlesnake' version includes the 'rattlesnake' itself, of course, though it seems to me that the great line

> *Paying attention like a rattlesnake does*

is sufficient unto itself and that the rest of the sentence tips it into bathos. I always re-listen in hope of hearing the line about the footsteps in the flowers without that discomforting, sinking feeling – but it can't be done, and it's tempting to guess that Dylan's own discomfort at the same point was what prompted his scrapping of the whole conceit. In the revisions, which all seem reasonable in the end, we also lose details like the attractive but dodgy 'She looked into my soul through the clothes that I wore' (a neat counterbalance to all the stress on *her* outward appearance) and the more general quality this early version possesses of sexual intrigue seen up close in the shadowy dance-hall in which much of the action takes place. It's always attractive when Dylan gets down to this kind of scrutiny: to a passage of songwriting in which (paying attention like a rattlesnake does) we hear what people whisper to each other, see their sidelong glances and feel, as it were, the breath of the protagonists close by. It is present in lines like

> *She said 'We got a mutual friend standin' at the door.'*
> *Yeah, y'know he's got our best interests in mind.*

This last is another ambiguous line: on the one hand you feel that she is describing Christ here – 'the servant is at the door', as Dylan puts it in 'Cat's In The Well' – but on the other hand in the context of this swirling scene of sexual jealousy and intrigue 'he' is someone else altogether and we feel a dark shadow fall in the gap between the lines: between her assertion and the narrator's suspicious response.

The same close-up scrutiny, the same small arena, is located in the good-natured self-mockery of the last half-verse:

> *Would I have married her? I dunno – I suppose:*
> *She had bells in her braids and they hung to her toes*
> *But I heard my name and destiny said to be moving on.*
> *Then I felt it come over me, some kind of gloom*
> *Gonna say 'Come on with me, girl, I got plenty a' room'*
> *But I knew I'd be lyin'; and besides, she'd already gone.*

This is funny, charming, alert and, as a laughing at himself (that high-flown 'destiny said to be moving on' deflated by the splendid 'I felt it come over me, some kind of gloom'), it is his warmest confession of the risibility of all those gotta-move-on Bob Dylan songs since 'Tonight I'll Be Staying Here With You'.

These losses of small-scale intimacy are compensated for by the lyric gains we make as we move across to the version released on "Biograph". We can hurry past the transitional version, because all its good points are there in at least one if not both the other versions, and it has only two or three moments at which it offers an improvement on both the earlier and the later drafts. One of these is at the start of the last verse. The 'rattlesnake' version has this:

> Atlantic City, two years to the day,
> I hear her voice cryin' 'Daddy!' and I look that way
> But it's only the silence in the Buttermilk Hills that call

which is attractive for that Dylanesque comic ambiguity – does 'and I look that way' mean looking to where the voice is heard, or does it mean 'and I can see that I look the way a "Daddy" looks'? – but which is clearly less real and true, and less moving and specific than the compelling final version:

> Atlantic City by the cold grey sea.
> I hear a voice cryin' 'Daddy!' I always think it's for me
> But it's only the silence in the Buttermilk Hills that call.

But though the 'Daddy' line is so much better here, it retains the irksome problem of the following line: that you can't say it's 'the silence . . . that *call*.' The hills can 'call' but it has to be 'the silence . . . that *calls*.' Every time you hear Dylan's line, it's the error of grammar that calls. Yet in the halfway-house version of the lyric, he solves this problem:

> Atlantic City by the cruel sea
> I hear a voice cryin' 'Daddy!' I always think it's for me
> But it's only the silence in the Buttermilk Hills, that's all.

That's better. (It might not be 'the Buttermilk Hills' but rather, as *Lyrics 1962–1985* has it, 'the buttermilk hills': a phrase of precise observation describing the colour cornfields can become just before harvest.)

As for the transitional version's other virtues, one derives from Dylan's putting his own name into the song (it makes more sense to discuss this a little later on) while the other is less certain. That is, you could argue a case, I suppose, that 'the cruel sea' would have been a nifty thing to have retained in the final version, since it throws a third book title into the mix, along with 'paradise lost' and 'the . . . divine comedy'. (*Paradise Lost*, John Milton; *The Divine Comedy*, Dante; *The Cruel Sea*, Nicholas Monsarrat.) But Monsarrat's 1951 novel of the Second World War, later made into a film starring Jack Hawkins, is the odd one out in this august company, so that it's a neater effect to omit it and leave in the other pair (both vast religious epic poems). Moreover, 'the cruel sea' sounds lazy shorthand here – very much akin to throwing 'a town without pity' into 1985's 'Tight Connection To My Heart' – and loses us the satisfying contrast achieved in the final version of the lyric between the more focused 'cold grey sea' and all those warm Caribbean waters elsewhere in the song.[21]

The final version pulls back from the dark intimacy of the first, propelling us for the most part up into the sunlight and the larger world. It seems like the song of a

---

21. *Paradise Lost*, John Milton, written 1658–63; first published 1667, revised edn 1674; *The Divine Comedy*, Dante Alighieri, written 1307–21; *The Cruel Sea*, Nicholas Monsarrat, 1951. *The Cruel Sea*, Ealing, UK, directed Charles Frend, written Eric Ambler, 1953. *Town Without Pity*, UA/Mirisch/Osweg/Gloria, US/Switzerland/Germany, directed Gottfried Reinhardt, 1961; title song a hit by Gene Pitney, 1962. See also Chapter 16 on Bob Dylan's use of this and many other films in his work.

man high up, looking out across a shining sea, feeling that warm Caribbean wind and glad to be alive: someone appreciatively recalling his encounter with the 'she' of the tale, now that it has settled into something like the right perspective in his mind.

In the first place, it makes such a pleasing noise, with its hissings like waves (most unusual for Dylan to include such a sound-effect on one of his records), its grand, singing melody, its visionary, passion-led chorus, and Dylan's light, fleet-footed vocal: it's a big record and it rocks along, yet it escapes the troubles big records tend towards. It has richness and depth. It's multi-layered. It gives off a feeling close to youthful rapture, yet it retains a touch of intimacy in its dancing parade of images, and there is no hint here of hectoring or bombast. The hissing surf running up the beach at us is a recurrent signalling of the record's acceptance of implacable forces, and of its creator's gladness of heart.

The images that wash over us most vividly are mainly the personal, affecting ones: that first verse description of falling for the black woman; the lying in bed hearing the band in the street outside his window; and the lovely aforementioned

I hear a voice cryin' 'Daddy!', I always think it's for me

as well as the compelling images of the chorus – attractive as word-sounds as well as pictures): 'them distant ships of liberty' and 'them iron waves'.

I can't justify it, but I want to say how remarkable it is that the singer's romance with the black woman is conveyed in a passage that begins by describing her as 'the rose of Sharon . . . / From the city of seven hills' – Jerusalem, rather than Rome or Sheffield. Perhaps it derives from the lines that follow, about 'the jungle where her brothers were slain' by the white man – nicely expressed as 'the man who invented iron and disappeared so mysteriously'. Perhaps he *doesn't* convey her blackness in this part of the writing at all: perhaps a hazy remembrance of biographical 'information' is what puts her into this picture. Or perhaps a hazy remembrance of biblical text is whispering a sub-text here. The second chapter of the Old Testament book the Song of Solomon begins with the Pharoah's daughter telling her new husband Solomon:

I am the rose of Sharon, and the lily of the valleys

after telling us in the first chapter that she is 'black, but comely'.[22]

In fact in this last version of 'Caribbean Wind', 'she' is more a composite figure,

---

22. The Song of Solomon 2:1 and 1:5. This short book, never referred to in the New Testament, can be considered 'the song of songs' either in the same sense as 'king of kings', i.e. meaning the best song of all, or in the sense of its being a song (not unlike some pre-war blues) assembled from many songs. Various characters speak in the song, yet who is speaking at any moment (who is 'I' and who is 'you') is never specified (not unlike some Bob Dylan songs). Making for an intriguing parallel with Dylan's situation at the time of writing 'Caribbean Wind' perhaps, The Song of Solomon is created when Solomon, years after his first marriage, chooses a black Egyptian girl (a Gentile) as his second bride. It is often argued in Bible commentaries that this is a metaphor for Christ's bringing the Gentiles to God as equals with the chosen people, but the intense sensuality of the song, plus the absence of its mention by Christ, his apostles or disciples, argues against this. Along with lingering, detailed contemplations of the lovers' mouths, breasts, feet and so on, the song details the ceremonial decoration of the new bride: 'Thy cheeks are comely with rows of jewels, thy neck with chains of gold. We will make thee borders of gold with studs of silver' (1:10–11). Perhaps Dylan's couplet 'Would I have married her? I dunno – I suppose: / She had bells in her braids and they hung to her toes' is his re-write of this.

Yet 'the Rose of Sharon' is also Christ himself, as we're reminded by the fine American poet Edna St Vincent Millay (1892–1950) in her spiky sonnet 'To Jesus on His Birthday' (in *The Buck in the Snow*, 1928, and then in

at least to begin with (and it is a real achievement of Dylan's lines that he can convincingly evoke affection for a composite figure). She is large – she contains multitudes. The lyric certainly begins by suggesting that she is from Israel, or, to those well-up on the Song of Solomon, that she might be the black and comely daughter of the Pharaoh, while the lines about the 'jungle' and 'the man who invented iron' switch us to a different historical meeting point: that between the Amerindians and the Spaniards who invaded those jungles well armed and on horseback. Like them, some of the images in 'Caribbean Wind' come and go so mysteriously, while others come out of the trees into momentary but memorable focus.

The vivid cameo, given in the second verse of every version, of the singer lying in bed and hearing the street band outside the window playing 'Nearer My God To Thee', is one of these. It also prefigures the opening scene of his 1983 song 'Man Of Peace', issued on "Infidels". Version 1 goes like this:

> But I slept in a hotel where flies buzzed my head
> Ceiling fan was broken, there was heat in my bed
> Street band playin' 'Nearer My God To Thee';

Version 3 goes like this:

> The cry a' the peacock, flies buzz in my head
> Ceiling fan broken, there's a heat in my bed,
> Street band playin' 'Nearer My God To Thee';

and 'Man Of Peace' begins like this:

> Look out your window baby, there's a scene you'd like to catch:
> The band is playing 'Dixie', a man got his hand outstretched.

In fact all these are prefigured by a verse in a 1929 song by Frank Hutchison, the brilliant white blues singer and slide guitarist whose version of 'Stackalee' Bob Dylan re-creates so lovingly and with such exuberant flair on "World Gone Wrong". In this case the Hutchison song is 'Cannon Ball Blues', and it includes

> I looked out the window far as I could see
> While the brass band are playing 'Nearer My God To Thee'[23]

which, it will readily be seen, acts like a retrospective ellipse of the 1980s Bob Dylan songs ('Man Of Peace' specifying looking out the window while the band is playing,

---

Collected Sonnets, 1941). This ends: 'Nobody listens. Less than the wind that blows / Are all your words to us you died to save. / O Prince of Peace! O Sharon's dewy Rose! / How mute you lie within your vaulted grave. / The stone the angel rolled away with tears / Is back upon your mouth these thousand years.'

(Tom Joad's little sister in John Steinbeck's *The Grapes of Wrath*, 1939, is also named Rose of Sharon, shortened to Rosasharn. She is married to Connie Rivers and pregnant at the start of the book. Her baby is born dead in the last few pages. In a corner of the barn a man of about 50 is dying of starvation. In the book's final paragraph she lies down beside him and breastfeeds him. The book's final sentence is: 'She looked up and across the barn, and her lips came together and *smiled mysteriously*.' [my emphasis, for what it's worth])

23.   Frank Hutchison: 'Cannon Ball Blues', NYC, 9/7/29; "Mountain Blues", County Records 511, New York, c. 1970; CD-issued on "White Country Blues (1926–38)", Columbia Legacy Roots N' Blues Series 472886 2, New York, 1993.

and 'Caribbean Wind' specifying being in a room hearing the 'Street band playing 'Nearer My God To Thee'').

The choice of songs overheard in the two Dylan songs may suggest the two contrasting sections of a funeral. 'Nearer, My God, To Thee' is an English hymn, written by Sarah Adams (1805–1848), whose father was a radical political journalist jailed for writing in defence of the French Revolution (and who might not have appreciated his daughter's hymn becoming the favourite of Queen Victoria); but in black America, 'Nearer My God To Thee', like 'Just A Closer Walk With Thee', is played dirge-like on the funeral march to the graveyard; coming back the music switches to the celebratory – to tunes like 'Dixie'.[24]

Which brings us to the question, postponed earlier on, of there being one other aspect of the transitional version which is bound to be interesting: that is, the postmodernist touch (if that's what it is) by which a Bob Dylan performance is of a song that mentions 'Bob Dylan' in the lyric (as Dylan says, 'As Rimbaud says, "I is another" ', and 'I'm only Bob Dylan when I want to be') but does so while describing his obliteration (implicitly by the narrator, the singer, who is of course Bob Dylan) . . .

> *Flies on my balcony buzzin' my head*
> *Slayin' Bob Dylan [here] in my bed*
> *Street band playin' 'Nearer My God To Thee'.*

This is terrific in triplicate: it's interesting as a device within a poem – you feel that Browning or Tennyson (or Walt Whitman) might have mentioned *their* own names with similar playful audacity (it is a very different usage, after all, from the simple egotism that prompts Bo Diddley and Jerry Lee Lewis to mention themselves as part of the intrinsic swagger of their look-at-me rock'n'roll songs); it is a dazzling post-structuralist joke to put old Roland Barthes' 'death of the author' so literally into the text (especially since at the same time he is actually *asserting* authorship more than usually by giving the author an unexpected, extra name-check inside the text itself); and it gives an extra comic touch to the 'Street band playin' 'Nearer My God To Thee'' line. As we know, these words are in every version of the song – and in every version they may be taken as an omen of imminent death – but only in the context of 'Slayin' Bob Dylan [here] in my bed' can they wittily give us the picture of a narrator lying there listening to his own funeral music.

(The very occurrence of the phrase 'Nearer My God To Thee' may be taken as an omen of imminent death in each version of the song because, as Dylan knows, it is a formulaic element in many old American songs [white ballads and black hero songs] that as their heroes lie dying, they mutter the phrase as their last words, signalling their brave acceptance that Death is about to take them. Bob Dylan heard an instance

24.   Val Wilmer has a nicely specific description of watching such a funeral in New Orleans in 1972: 'the people who followed the band, "Second Lining", strutted and waved their umbrellas aloft just like Ashanti dancers I'd seen in Ghana . . . With the Second Line made up of children and adults of all ages, I followed the hearse to the cemetery, the band playing funeral dirges such as 'Just A Closer Walk With Thee'. On the way back, their mood changed abruptly and they broke into a jubilant stomp, the Second Line strutting and posturing with hats and umbrellas. They played 'Rock Around The Clock' as well as 'The Saints'' (Val Wilmer, *Mama Said There'd Be Days Like This*, 1989, 1991). 'Nearer, My God, To Thee' collected in *Hymns Ancient and Modern Revised* (1972), and in *The Lion Book of Favourite Hymns*, compiled by Christopher Idle (1980), the latter offering the information on Sarah Adams.

of this device very early on in his musical education: for yet another track on the Harry Smith anthology of 1952 is the Carter Family's 'Engine One-Forty-Three', on which the very last words the Carters sing are 'And the very last words poor Georgie said were 'Nearer My God To Thee'.'[25])

There is a powerful charge of extra funereal electricity in the idea of the *band* playing 'Nearer My God To Thee' because, in popular mythology anyway, this is what the orchestra played on the *Titanic* as the ship was going down. This is a very popular event, and an iconic one, in pre-war black America. In fact this poignant moment is commemorated in another 1920s record, Richard Rabbit Brown's 'Sinking Of The Titanic', which shares with Frank Hutchison's and Bob Dylan's songs the citing of the hymn title within its own lyric:

> *The music played as they went down*
> *On that dark blue sea*
> *And you could hear the sound of that familiar hymn*
> *Singin' 'Nearer My God To Three'.*[26]

In 'Caribbean Wind' Version 2 the shadowy presence of the *Titanic* story is reconfirmed by the line

> *. . . and like they say, the ship will sail at dawn.*

This is so because not only do 'they say' so but because we've heard Bob Dylan say, in 'Desolation Row', that

> *The Titanic sails at dawn.*

The marine metaphor extends all through the song, of course. It is a lovely touch to describe the man 'just barely stayin' alive' in the well-known phrase that uses the analogy of dying man and sinking ship: 'goin' down slow'. Against this, of course, is set the conceit of the 'ships of liberty' and much else nautical: the 'iron waves so bold and free'; the warm winds of the Caribbean Sea; 'the Valley Coast'; another 'sea breeze blowin''; and, in contrast, the 'cold grey sea' or 'cruel sea' that reaches the oceanically named Atlantic City.

There is a further felicity to that phrase 'goin' down slow'. By its familiarity as the title of a classic blues record (written by Willie Dixon, spoken passages narrated by Willie Dixon, singing by Howlin' Wolf and with Hubert Sumlin's divine guitar solo) its deployment by Dylan here adds to the sense 'Caribbean Wind' gives us that it is

25.   The Carter Family: 'Engine 143', Camden, New Jersey, 15/2/29; issued [mistitled 'Engine One-Forty-Three' and incorrectly dated as 1927] on "American Folk Music", Folkways Records 251–253, New York, 1952, CD-reissued as "Anthology Of American Folk Music" [6-CDs box-set] with copious notes by many hands and including a CD-ROM of extras, Smithsonian Folkways Recordings SFW 40090, Washington, DC, 1997.

26.   Richard Rabbit Brown: 'Sinking Of The Titanic', New Orleans, 11/3/27; "Nearer My God To Thee", Roots Records RL-304, Vienna, 1968; CD-reissued "The Greatest Songsters: Complete Recorded Works (1927–29)", Document Records DOCD-5003, Vienna, 1990. In *The Lion Book of Favourite Hymns* (1980) Christopher Idle claims as fact that as the *Titanic* began to tilt, 'Baptist minister John Harper asked the band to play 'Nearer, My God, To Thee'. It was the last hymn in the lives of hundreds of people.' See also Chapter 4, note 15, and Chapter 9, note 189.

indeed about the singer's romance with a black woman. As we have seen, the further phrase 'she was fair brown', in the 'rattlesnake' version, functions in the same way.[27]

If the marine metaphor runs through the song, so does death. Matching that 'goin' down slow, just barely stayin' alive', 'her brothers were slain' and 'sniper bait', we have 'a hellhound loose', 'salvation', 'waiting for the night to arrive', 'her heart was a snare / And she had left him to die in there', 'the street band playin' 'Nearer My God To Thee', the 'ancestors calling from the land far beyond' and the cathartic 'Bringing everything that's near to me nearer to the fire' of the apocalypse.

We also have, as I noted in writing about 'Every Grain Of Sand' in the previous chapter, the lines

> *Every new messenger bringin' evil report*
> *'Bout armies on the march and time that is short*
> *And famines and earthquakes and train wrecks and the tearin' down of the walls*

in which Dylan again hints at the imminence of the apocalypse. He takes that little phrase 'evil report' from the Bible (it's in the Old Testament and the New: in Numbers 13:32 and 14:37, and in 2 Corinthians 6:8) and his famines-earthquakes-walls text from the Gospels. In that earlier chapter, that text was given as it appears in Luke (21:6, 11):

> there shall not be left one stone upon another, that shall not be thrown down . . .
> And great earthquakes shall be in divers places, and famines . . .

but in fact the parallel between the biblical text and Dylan's is more marked if we take Christ's words from the account in Matthew rather than from Luke. In Matthew Christ talks of what will happen in the last days, warns that there will be false Christs, and then adds, in language that precisely inspires not just the content but the very rhythm of Dylan's re-write:

> And ye shall hear of wars and rumours of wars . . . and there shall be famines,
> and pestilences, and earthquakes, in divers places . . . But he that shall endure
> unto the end, the same shall be saved

(Matthew 24:6–7, 13). I noted before that that 'train wrecks' is one of Dylan's inspired modernising touches, serving to make the prophecy applicable to *our* near future, while the rest of his list is as cited by Christ.

Moreover, we see at once that Dylan has trod this biblical path before: 'ye shall hear of wars and rumours of wars' is neatly reversed back in 1962 in Dylan's anti-nuclear-panic song 'Let Me Die In My Footsteps', in the line that begins the second verse (a verse altogether interesting for its comment on the biblical context):

> *There's been rumours of war and wars that have been*
> *The meaning of life has been lost in the wind*
> *And some people thinkin' that the end is close by*
> *'Stead of learning to live they are learning to die.*

---

27. Howlin' Wolf: 'Goin' Down Slow', Chicago, Dec. 1961 (B-side to 'You'll Be Mine', same session), Chess Records 1813, Chicago, 1962; in Britain 'Goin' Down Slow' was B-side to 'Smokestack Lightnin'' (Chicago, Jan. 1956), Pye International R&B Series 7N.25244, London, 1964.

> Let me die in my footsteps
> Before I go down under the ground.[28]

The most innocuous phrases, or even mere conjunctions of words, can turn out to be from the Bible. In Version 3 of 'Caribbean Wind' there is one within the line

> Ever meet your accusers face to face in the rain?

Acts 25:16, which is part of the account of Paul's being hounded by the Jews and taken into custody by the Romans, reports that 'It is not the manner of the Romans to deliver any man to die, before that he which is accused have the accusers face to face'. Here again, to know the biblical allusion's context is to register that the imminence of death hangs around Dylan's line.

There is also that metaphor of the heart as a 'snare', which is used in all versions of 'Caribbean Wind':

> He was well-connected but her heart was a snare
> And she had left him to die in there.[29]

'Snare' is a very biblical word: it is always being used, as Dylan well knows. The 'sparrows falling' in 'Every Grain Of Sand', as we noted, alludes to a passage of Christ's in which the sparrows fall into snares, and Paul employs the term frequently – for instance in the verse immediately preceding the famous quote 'the love of money is the root of all evil' (so often misquoted as 'money is the root of all evil', a different contention altogether): 'But they that will be rich fall into temptation and a snare . . .' (1 Timothy 6:9–10).[30] A 'snare' being a net to trap small birds (still used to catch songbirds along the Mediterranean coast), it is another small pleasure for the listener to 'Caribbean Wind' that when Dylan uses 'snare' as his metaphor, he prefaces it with 'He was well-connected'. Like a bird in a net (or a fly in a spider's web), he was in fact all too well connected when he was left to die in the snare of her heart.

It's evident, though, that these images of death which recur throughout the song never deaden it, nor give it 'some kind of gloom'. This is not one of Dylan's scowling, hand-wringing or triumphalist I'm-of-the-chosen-few songs. Rather it is a song in which humanity shines through: a song of light and colour and warm winds.

And resourceful writing. We've noted the pairing of 'paradise lost' and 'the . . . divine comedy', but we might note too the pairing of 'the place of the cross' and 'the station where the mission bells ring', of 'her brothers' and 'my ancestors', of 'the cry a' the peacock' and the cry of the child, and of the 'heat in my bed' and 'the furnace

---

28. The fourth line here, ''Stead of learning to live they are learning to die' has a different provenance. A translation into English of Leonardo da Vinci's *Notebooks* includes this: 'While I thought that I was learning how to live, I have been learning how to die.' (Found in *The Bloomsbury Book of Quotations*, 1994.) Of course Dylan returns to the topic with the aphorism 'He not busy being born is busy dying' in 1965's 'It's Alright Ma (I'm Only Bleeding)'.

29. In the live, transitional version this is given as 'but *his* heart was a snare [my emphasis] / Cause she had left him to die in there' but that 'his' is probably mere performance error.

30. Another verse later and we reach another text Dylan has drawn on: 'But thou, O man of God, flee these things; and follow after righteousness, godliness, faith, love, patience, meekness' (1 Timothy 6:11). Dylan turns this into 'I got to flee toward patience and meekness' in the live performances of 'Watered-Down Love' from autumn 1981, discussed earlier in the present chapter.

of desire'. Similarly, we've noted the juxtaposition of all these warm Caribbean waters and 'the cold grey' Atlantic, but the song holds other modest juxtapositions: of that 'furnace of desire' and 'the fire' of the apocalypse; of death-wielding 'iron' ('her brothers were slain / By the man who invented iron') and life-buoying iron ('distant ships of liberty on them iron waves'); of those iron waves and the devil's 'tin'; and of those 'distant ships of liberty' and 'the hoax of free speech'.

More overtly engaging is the gentle reversal of one cliché, as Dylan sings 'So let us just agree to agree', and his pleasurably arrogant refusal of another, as he avoids singing 'She had ... eyes that I won't forget as long as I live' in favour of the determinedly less fulsome 'I won't forget as long as she's gone'. (This is a determination to which he still holds in that beautifully sung but shifty "Knocked Out Loaded" song 'Under Your Spell', in which instead of the line anyone else would write, namely 'You'll never get rid of me as long as I'm alive', Dylan has it that 'You'll never get rid of me as long as you're alive.')

And what eyes she had! Sadly, it's typical of the carelessness with which *Lyrics 1962–1985* was compiled that it should offer as 'She had lone brown eyes' what is actually one of Dylan's very best descriptive phrases, the lovely

> *She had chrome brown eyes . . .,*

a quite wonderful way to place that unique, swimmingly liquid quality that young black people's eyes can have.

That acute, observant, fond phrase typifies the song. Warm yet sharp, intimate yet expansive, 'Caribbean Wind' is a complex and deeply affectionate work. And when it finishes, we can feel that, like life, the song is an ocean but it ends at the shore, with the sound of the hissing surf.

CHAPTER FOURTEEN

Jokerman

If the collection actually released on "Shot Of Love" missed out many of the sessions' best results, offering instead a bit of a pot-boiler of an album, at least it was a straightforward one, defiantly unpretentious about its limitations, its ragged and pinched sensibility. "Infidels", which came next, in 1983, was a pot-boiler pretending not to be. Granted that the sessions for it yielded such prolific and varied riches, this was a spectacular example of snatching defeat from the jaws of victory.

The French and the Americans hailed "Infidels" as a major return to form on Dylan's part. It wasn't. With the marvellous exception of 'Jokerman', it is so far short of representing on-form Bob Dylan that anyone who makes such claims for it has simply forgotten what thrilled them about him in the first place. It yields none of the heart-leap, delirium, amazement, laughter, joy-in-truth, turmoil or awe that can surge through you when you hear great Bob Dylan.

"Infidels" gives off very little feeling of anything. The upshot is that it has to pretend – to give off feigned emotion wrapped in a fog of mere professional competence. There's not only no sweat but no candour either. It might have been better to have no album at all than one on which he only *aims* to be Rockaday Johnny singing Tell Your Ma, Tell Your Pa ... Wah Wah – and then doesn't even have the courage of that conviction but instead, at the last moment, lays on this pretence of having something to tell.

This dissembling demeans him. Bob Dylan's real work, like Blake's, shouts Death! to such fakery and fudging. It's not that "Infidels" is a failure that matters, but that it is such a small, shifty failure. It doesn't fail bravely, having taken risks. By comparison, "Self Portrait" is an honourable, grand failure, and the much derided film *Renaldo & Clara* more so. By the standards Dylan so toweringly set over the years, "Infidels" is a real mudcake creature, failing in a small-minded, cheating way, so that to listen to that voice trying to do a salesman's job on it is distinctly discomforting. As I wrote in reviewing the album at the time, what comes across is a lack of self-regard on Dylan's part: as if he were beginning to piss away his stature as an artist.[1] In retrospect, it still seems true. Indeed, the overall graph of Dylan's behaviour in the 1980s can fairly be

---

1. 'Infidelity: time to put in the Plugz', *Telegraph*, no. 16, Summer 1984. This essay (on which the opening section of this chapter is built) also reviewed the appearance by Bob Dylan & The Plugz on the *Late Night with David Letterman* TV show, NBC-TV, New York, 22 March 1984, on which they performed, with some intensity, Sonny Boy Williamson II's 'Don't Start Me To Talkin'' plus two songs from the then recent "Infidels" album, 'License To Kill' and 'Jokerman'.

said to show just such a draining of his stature as an artist, and despite the huge amount of greased enthusiasm heaped upon it by American commentators, "Infidels" still seems to me to signal the beginning of this process in earnest. (This topic is enlarged upon in Chapter 20.)

Not for nothing had Dylan led us into forests of mystery and jungles of wonder all down the years, by truthful songs of infinite variety, from 'I'll Keep It With Mine' to 'Abandoned Love', from 'When The Ship Comes In' to 'Black Diamond Bay', from 'It Ain't Me, Babe' to 'Never Say Goodbye', from 'Visions Of Johanna' to 'Pressing On', from 'Sign On The Window' to 'Idiot Wind', from 'North Country Blues' to 'She's Your Lover Now'. So when we heard that "Infidels" was coming, and we held our breath, and then the bushes parted and this new creature hove into view, it was all too obvious, even in the murky dusk of 1984, that this wasn't a tyger at all. No fearful symmetry here, no burning bright, no fire in the eyes. This was the runt of some domesticated mongrel litter, by Hollywood out of Tin Pan Alley, set loose just for the tourists. A real Bob Dylan tyger wouldn't have looked at it twice.

The album's lack of conviction comes across in Dylan's sloppiness, his self-imitation and his recurrent reliance on counterfeit sentiment and rather reactionary non-ideas. The sloppiness has Dylan not bothering to finish things off or to find the apposite phrase where it's needed. Remember that foolish question asked aeons ago about Dylan's work by folk-snob Ewan MacColl?: 'What poetry? . . . the embarrassing fourth-grade schoolboy attempts . . .?'[2] That question is utterly dismissable as commentary on Dylan's characteristic work. How shaming, then, that it is spot-on as commentary on the ungainly and portentous lyric to 'License To Kill':

> For man has invented his doom
> First step was touching the moon.

Come on, Bob. If *you* were your English teacher you'd put your red pencil through this. Could do better. At best it reads like the kind of production-line folk-rock protest stuff that gave protest a bad name a couple of years after Dylan had left it behind. Remember laughing at Barry McGuire records? This reads exactly like one. Similarly

> And they set him on a path where he's bound to get ill.

Here the need to rhyme something with 'kill' demanded a poet's discretion and self-discipline. Instead of these taut qualities finding a taut and credible solution, the oh-that'll-do tiredness of Dylan's response, which actually confesses a self-contempt on his part, results in the embarrassing bathos of this risible but flaccid line.

The middle section of the song is just as feeble.

> Ya may be a noisemaker, spirit maker,
> Heartbreaker, backbreaker,
> Leave no stone unturned.
> May be an actor in a plot,
> That might be all that you got
> 'Til your error you clearly learn.

2.   Ewan MacColl: 'A Symposium', *Sing Out!*, September 1965.

Insofar as it is a list, it is a pallid, uninteresting one, engaging neither as images nor noises, thrown together without care or inspiration. Insofar as it goes through the motions of *saying* something, constipation intervenes – you could hardly pass a more ungainly line than ''Til your error you clearly learn': the schoolteachey tone and prosaic wording might be justified by clarity of meaning but here we cannot know, nor feel, nor be expected to care, what sort of 'error' this undefined narrator is waggling his finger about. And insofar as this section of the song marks a switch from 'Man . . . woman' / 'he . . . she' to suddenly addressing 'you', the switch is neither envigorating nor enlightening. The whole stanza is bluster, with a pontificating tone but without the energy or specificity to make for a decent harangue. He just couldn't be bothered to write anything better.

As a result, we lose our faith that there is any authenticity to the one interesting aspect of the song, the sexual politics implied in its juxtaposition of 'Man this, man that' with 'But there's a woman . . .', backed up by the title line's rhetoric, 'Who's gonna take away his license to kill?' Instead of earning our attention for this topic – the generally plausible one that men are bellicose and in thrall to machinery, while women are negotiators and in tune with nature's continuum – it is allowed to float out of focus by the feeble lack of disciplined craft and the lazy offering of so much bad writing all around it.

Another sloppiness in the album's crafting erupts as a rash of lumpen filler-words: '*sure* was', 'I *just* don't think that . . .' and '*kinda*' – all of which signal not an accurate creation of character, not the perceptive rendition of telling conversational idiosyncrasies in the 'voices' of individual narrators but a padding and waffling and bluffing through on Bob Dylan's part, instead of that opposite process, at which Dylan can be a master, of honing down and cutting through. Truth is an arrow. I just don't think that the truth sure is kinda an arrow, baby.

Dylan gives that 'kinda', on the horrible 'Sweetheart Like You', his patent Bob Dylan Gritty Croak, as if this bestows upon the performance an authenticating shyness. Well gee, ma'am, I er, I better twist my hat in my hands some. There is a tendency to resort to this rather dreadful John Wayne Sings Dylan hamminess all through the album. It is at its worst on the early part of 'Don't Fall Apart On Me Tonight' and throughout 'Sweetheart Like You' because that's where he needs great ladlefuls of it to try to disguise the void at the heart of the chatter. 'Don't Fall Apart On Me Tonight' is one of those songs that sounds best the first time you hear it and rapidly gets less impressive; the oleaginous artifice of Dylan's delivery and the flaccidity of the 'conversation' makes him sound, quite unintentionally, like some old roué trying to seduce little girls in the park.

What makes this excruciating is that Dylan clearly believes, as with 'Sweetheart Like You', that he's got away with it: that the old roué will be perceived as a genuinely sexy protagonist, giving voice to real desire, as on 'Lay, Lady, Lay', 'On A Night Like This' or any number of earlier songs. In fact the sham is so transparent that you feel the only reason for such songs existing at all is that Dylan has decided that each of his albums should have at least one of these charm-the-pants-off-'em Big Ballads, as part of a commercial formula. A revolting decision, a defeat of the integrity, from the artist who overturned all these awful formulae in the first place.

This phoney Crusty Charm derives not from observation of real feeling or real speech but straight from the ad-men. It is the same Hollywooden pretence that obliges brown bread ads to use folksy old-timers, after-shave ads to use voice-overs deeper than Jehovah's, and MTV fodder to feature the stifled-back-sob-and-pregnant-pause just before a whispered 'ah lurv ya', as if this makes for sincerity.

The real Bob Dylan has always spotted these mawkish lies a mile off and stood out against them with laughing, nimble instinct. That has always been part of his importance (as he knows perfectly well). The first time I heard 'The Times They Are A-Changin'' it was obvious immediately that here was someone who wasn't just pop-singing but truly communicating. You couldn't possibly feel that about 'Sweetheart Like You' or 'Don't Fall Apart On Me Tonight'.

Even Dylan's genius for fusing biblical text and contemporary American speech fails him here. The word 'vipers', in the first verse, is his import of biblical vocabulary:

> You know, the streets are filled with vipers
> Who've lost all ray of hope,
> You know, it ain't even safe no more
> In the palace of the Pope.

Used like this, 'vipers' passes by obliquely, with neither poetic bite nor any ring of conversational truth, but with just enough drawing of attention to itself for the listener to register where it's come from. Which is here: 'O generation of vipers, who hath warned you to flee from the wrath to come?' (both Matthew 3:7 and Luke 3:7): 'O generation of vipers, how can ye, being evil, speak good things?' (Matthew 12:34) and 'Ye serpents, ye generation of vipers, how can ye escape the damnation of hell?' (Matthew 23:33.)

It's a pity Dylan fails to pass off the biblical term as contemporary American speech – because if you take these lines in isolation, forgetting that their task in the song is to maintain the casually conversational tone, you can recognise that he succeeds with a secondary achievement (it's almost a private joke), punning on 'vipers' not as between the biblical and the contemporary but in melding the biblical with the jazz/blues patois of the 1920s to 1940s. A 'viper' seems to arise around 1925 as a street-term for a police informer (a spin on the phrase 'a snake in the grass', as is the modern term 'a grass' and the subsequent 'supergrass'); by the 1930s it is adopted, stigma-free, as a name for a dope-smoker or dealer. Hence the song 'If You'se [or You're] A Viper', recorded by many people from 1930s jazz violinist Stuff Smith to minor blues singers like Rosetta Howard and Lorraine Walton. These lines give the song's flavour: 'Dreamed about a reefer five foot long / The mighty mezz but not too strong / You'll be high but not for long / If you'se a viper'. There was another number called 'A Viper's Moan', there was Sidney Bechet's 'Viper Mad', and in *Really the Blues*, an unreliable but entertaining memoir by the indifferent jazz musician and consummate drug-dealer Mezz Mezzrow (a white man who lived as a black man), there is this splendid variation: 'Poppa, you never smacked your chops on anything sweeter in all your days of viping'.[3]

So Dylan's lines

3.   Stuff Smith: 'If You'se A Viper', NYC, 13/3/36. Lorraine Walton: 'If You're A Viper', Chicago, 9/2/29. Rosetta Howard [with the Harlem Hamfats]: 'If You're A Viper', NYC, 5/10/37. Sidney Bechet with Noble Sissle's

You know, the streets are full of vipers
Who've lost all ray of hope

work neatly enough in themselves on these two levels: as biblical and historical-streetwise allusion, as biblical and old doper talk. But by the time the next two lines have limped past us, we've lost more than we've gained. Dylan's 'vipers' get lost because the verse ends so bluntedly. The idea that 'the palace of the Pope' has traditionally been a 'safe' place seems exasperatingly dumb. It fits in with the kind of dumbness inherent in phrases like 'I just don't think that I could handle it', and indeed the phrase 'Don't Fall Apart On Me Tonight': both prime examples of nasty Californian therapyspeak.

And you'd have to go a long way to find a verse of such suffocating reactionary nonsense as this:

A woman like you should be at home
That's where you belong
Taking care of somebody nice
Who don't know how to do you wrong.

Each line provokes an 'ugh!' at the end of it; each line is a repressive lie. That the artist who sang of 'Chimes Of Freedom' can here sound so utterly dull-minded and anti-life, anti-truth, anti-openness . . . he sounds like the sort of parent who would have made the young Bob Dylan run away from home. It's hardly better when he moves on, later in the song, to the weary self-imitation of this:

Steal a little and they put you in jail
Steal a lot and they make you king.

This merely echoes 1963ish Bob Dylan echoing Woody Guthrieisms. It doesn't apply itself to any specific situation and it could have been chucked into any old Dylan song. What's worse, it's sung with a defeated pout where only the energy of real indignation could have redeemed it. On top of its being an idea he could have argued at any time, it's a commonplace. Here is the same idea, put into the mouth of the Belgrade revolutionary leader in Graham Greene's *Stamboul Train*, published in 1932 when Greene was 27: 'You put the small thief in prison, but the big thief lives in a palace.' And here it is, earlier still, in Eugene O'Neill's 1920 play *The Emperor Jones*: 'For de little stealin' dey gits you in jail soon or late. For de big stealin' dey makes you emperor.'[4]

In contrast, and far more interesting, is the political content of 'Union Sundown'. This is a genuine protest song in the Woody Guthrie tradition, and an honourable addition to it: a real 'state of the union' survey of *contemporary* American life; not an

---

Swingsters: 'Viper Mad', NYC, 10/2/38; issued "Sixteen Original Jazz Classics: Reefer Songs", Stash Records ST100, Tenafly, New Jersey, c. 1973. (This LP offers also offers Bob Howard & His Boys: 'If You're A Viper', *nia*, 7/2/38.) *Really the Blues*, by Mezz Mezzrow with Bernard Wolfe (1946, republished 1972); the quotations from this and from Stuff Smith's version of 'If You'se A Viper' appear in *The High Times Encyclopedia of Recreational Drugs*, ed. Andrew Kowl (1978).

4.   Graham Greene (1904–1991), *Stamboul Train* (1932). Eugene O'Neill (1888–1953), *The Emperor Jones*, first performed 1920, published 1921. The quote from the latter is taken from *Bob Dylan's Words*, ed. Wissolik and McGrath (1994). The use of 'Jones' here prefigures Dylan's in 'Ballad Of A Thin Man'.

unfocused third-hand generalisation but a specific analysis of a specific new development – something you couldn't have written about in the 1960s or the 1930s: the
huge-scale switching of traditional factory-work and manufacture away from the West
to the slave-labour markets of the Third World. 'Union Sundown' explores a real
theme here, and one that wasn't there to be explored in the decades when most of
Bob Dylan's political ideas were forged.[5]

Given that the song actually has something to say, and might have succeeded in
getting that across on radio, it was perverse that Dylan offered it as a recording that
may have its quirky charms for the ardent aficionado but which is wholly inaccessible
to the intelligent general public. Listen to it: the production is so *bad* – thin, cluttered,
tinny and above all mixed as if the vocal track was rather less important than the
snare-drum track – making it as difficult as possible to receive the words: not quite to
decipher them, but to be drawn in by them, since, with an absolute absence of melodic
appeal, they sound so heartlessly, querulously, haranguingly shouted (this humourless
hectoring is what poisons 'Neighborhood Bully' too) down some awful, distancing
megaphone. It sounds as if it's coming down a cheap transistor radio when it's coming
out of big speakers. This noise and this voice don't offer one-to-one communication;
they offer an alienating, attenuated petulance.

Why? So that the bleary, tired, slightly self-contemptuous Bob Dylan of the
1980s can complain about being misunderstood? It really is to be deplored that this
has become Dylan's stance. When he first arrived as a recording artist, he held his
head up, he addressed the whole general public with conviction and clarity, he trusted
their receptivity. Anyone could hear, and anyone could understand, exactly what
'Blowin' In The Wind' said. And 'The Times They Are A-Changin''. And 'When
The Ship Comes In'. If the meanings of the more experimental songs, 'A Hard
Rain's A-Gonna Fall' and 'Chimes Of Freedom', were, perhaps, not so clear,
Dylan's diction always was: the general listener could hear every carved-out word
and could feel that here was a singer communicating as directly as art would allow.
In contrast, 'Union Sundown' makes itself inaccessible to as many listeners as
possible, and comes through to the remaining few swathed in a maximum of audio-
obfuscation.

Even on the tracks where the production is competent, the music is so *boring*!
'Man Of Peace' is a good case in point. To make, now, a comment not made when
quoting it earlier in relation to 'Caribbean Wind', here is a lyric which, *on the page*,
begins strikingly with one of Dylan's great film cameos:

> *Look out your window, baby, there's a scene you'd like to catch*
> *Band is playin' 'Dixie', man got his hand outstretched.*

There is Dylan's marvellously economical scene-setting, which so immediately gives
you that specific vantage point, that director's choice of camera angle, and the detail
of the scene itself. And this is followed at once by the non-stop, alive humour of

---

5. There is some further discussion of the virtue of this song's modernity in Chapter 20. There is also a
discussion of the song's, and Dylan's, political ideas (and the suggestion that his 'North Country Blues' from twenty
years earlier might be considered a companion piece) in the essay 'Charity is supposed to cover up a multitude of
sins' by Clive Wilshin in *All Across the Telegraph*, ed. Michael Gray and John Bauldie (1987).

Could be the Führer, could be the local priest,

and with the exceptions of the slack third to fifth verses, which include the suspect Dylanesquerie of 'He can ride down Niagara Falls in the barrels of your skull', the lyric remains purposive, beguiling, alive and well crafted . . . yet as it comes through to the *listener*, that snappy beginning and the honed virtues of much of the rest of the song are lost in the musical tundra that must be traipsed across to reach them.[6]

This is made worse by Dylan's ill-judged remixing of the album in co-producer Mark Knopfler's absence – a remix which tends toward the lumpen and lacklustre. On the released version of 'License To Kill', for example, the riff in between the chorus lines is played only on the bass; on the unreleased alternative mix that was in circulation just ahead of the album's issue, the same riff is carried by a light, almost whimsical guitar, which lends it extra colour and, paradoxically, strength and a welcome optimism counterpointing the doomy prognostications of the lyric. Even 'Sweetheart Like You' sounds less stodgy and laboured on the early-circulated out-take than on the version Dylan chose for release. Even on 'Jokerman', discussed below, it is noticeable that the out-take, while offering lyrics which, where they differ, are on the whole inferior (lyrics Dylan was right to revise), offers a vocal performance and a musical backing more alive and lithe and open, and with a fuller exploration of melodic line.

The more unfortunate "Infidels" misjudgements, though, exactly as in the case of "Shot Of Love", concern which songs were included on, and which excluded from, the album. The sessions themselves revealed that Dylan was composing prolifically. He has enjoyed, so far as is known, no period like it since. There were at least seven fully realised songs recorded and rejected: 'Tell Me', 'Someone's Got A Hold Of My Heart', 'Death Is Not The End', 'Foot Of Pride', 'Julius & Ethel', 'Lord Protect My Child' and 'Blind Willie McTell'.

It would be hard not to concur with Dylan's rejection of the rather trivial 'Tell Me' (though similar misjudgement seemed to apply when this song gained later release on "Bootleg Series I–III": it was by general consensus the inferior of the two circulating versions, inferior musically and lyrically). Nor did the exclusion of 'Death Is Not The End' from "Infidels" impoverish the album. Yet in every other case, it would be ploughing a very lone furrow to suggest that here were recordings rightly rejected from the finished work. 'Julius & Ethel' is a minor work, but an incomparably more lively, refreshing and humane 'protest song' than 'Neighborhood Bully', while 'Someone's Got A Hold Of My Heart' (of which you might again say that the wrong take was chosen for "Bootleg Series I–III") is inarguably the superior contender to 'Don't Fall Apart On Me Tonight'. Then, in ascending order of importance, there is the admirable 'Lord Protect My Child', the very distinctive 'Foot Of Pride' and the incomparable 'Blind Willie McTell'.

'Lord Protect My Child' is admirable for its balance of the candidly personal and the usefully universal, and for its balance too between the expression of some of the fundamental feelings of the middle-aged adult for the growing-up, soon to be growing-

---

6.   Actually 'Tough Mama' prefigured 'Man Of Peace' in this respect: a record that should be pretty good but throws out a flatness that makes it one-dimensional and monotonous. 'Tough Mama' is a wonderful, skilful, crafted yet free-spirited lyric; as a production it's just dull.

away, child, and the coruscatingly angry analysis of the state of the outside world. It is one of the rare occasions when Bob Dylan 'comes clean' and deals concretely with plain questions about growing older, about parental responsibility and parental vulnerability, and about the impossibility of protecting your children or ensuring anything either side of your own demise:

> *For his age he is wise, and he's got his mother's eyes*
> *There's gladness in his heart, he's young and he's wild*
> *My only prayer is if I can't be there*
> *Lord, protect my child.*
>
> *As his youth now unfolds, he is centuries old*
> *To see him at play makes me smile*
> *No matter what happens to me, no matter what my destiny*
> *Lord, protect my child.*
>
> *When the whole earth is asleep you can look at him and weep.*
> *Few things you find are worthwhile*
> *And though I don't ask for much: no material things to touch*
> *Lord, protect my child.*
>
> *He's young and on fire, full of hope and desire*
> *In a world that's been raped – raped and defiled.*
> *If I fall along the way, and can't see another day*
> *Lord, protect my child.*
>
> *There'll be a time, I hear tell, when all will be well*
> *When God and man will be reconciled*
> *But until men lose their chains and righteousness reigns*
> *Lord, protect my child.*

Unlike a 'License To Kill' or a 'Union Sundown', in fact, 'Lord Protect My Child' is, in its candour and clarity, every bit as openly accessible to the general public as the songs that launched Bob Dylan's career. Holding back from "Infidels" his impeccable recording of it, with its assured, restrainedly ardent R&Bish vocal, was surely a major failure of nerve or of judgement.

One of the deftest touches in the song is Dylan's use of the language of Charles Wesley's great carol 'Hark! The Herald Angels Sing' – the point of which is to avow 'Glory to the new-born king'. Dylan, surveying the 'raped and defiled' world into which his own child has been born, looks forward to a time

> *When God and man will be reconciled.*

This echoes the fourth line of the carol, which looks for

> *Peace on earth and mercy mild*
> *God and sinners reconciled.*[7]

---

7.   The other Wesley carol which remains most popular, 'Gentle Jesus Meek And Mild', also corresponds to the essential sentiment of Dylan's song 'Lord Protect My Child': it begins 'Gentle Jesus, meek and mild / Look upon a little child'. Charles Wesley (1707–1788), a younger brother of John Wesley, the founder of Methodism, is reputed, scarcely credibly, to have written 6,500 hymns.

In spectacular contrast, spitting venom and excess, comes 'Foot Of Pride', surely one of Bob Dylan's most difficult songs of the 1980s or any other decade. There is nothing measured or fatherly or Wesleyan here.

To look at 'Foot Of Pride' demands one more look, with whatever reluctance, at the text of Revelation, as well as another look back to the Old Testament book of Daniel and to the New Testament gospels. This is the relevant passage from Revelation (17:3–5):

> and I saw a woman sit upon a scarlet-coloured beast, full of names of blasphemy, having seven heads and ten horns. And the woman was arrayed in purple and scarlet colour, and decked with gold and precious stones and pearls, having a golden cup full of abominations and filthiness of her fornication: And upon her forehead was a name written, MYSTERY, BABYLON THE GREAT, THE MOTHER OF ALL HARLOTS AND ABOMINATIONS OF THE EARTH.

Here then is the key to that very Dylanesque line in 'Foot Of Pride',

> They got MYSTERY *written all over their forehead* . . .

You might say it holds the key to the whole of Dylan's song. It's a song about today's iniquities – about contemporary Babylon.

That phrase 'BABYLON THE GREAT' is a reversed echo of one used in the previous chapter of Revelation (16:19), 'great Babylon'. The insistence on hanging the tribute-term 'great' around the neck of this evil empire achieves a specific effect: it implies *hollow* greatness. Already contained within the phrase is the implied inevitability of Babylon's destruction. Bob Dylan picks up on this very specifically in another 1983 song from the same sessions, 'Neighborhood Bully', a far lesser song but one that made it onto "Infidels":

> *Every empire that's enslaved him is gone,*
> *Egypt and Rome, even the great Babylon.*

This itself finds an echo in the unreleased rock'n'roll 'protest' song mentioned earlier, 'Julius & Ethel' [Rosenberg], victims of the American neighbourhood bully of McCarthyism – a song in which, with almost comic verve and simplicity, Dylan sings that

> *Every kingdom got to fall, even the Third Reich*
> *Man can do what he please, but not for as long as he likes.*[8]

And there is the core of the theme of 'Foot Of Pride'. Man can do what he please, but he is riding for a fall.

The biblical text which gives Dylan his precedent for envisaging God's intervention along these lines is in Daniel (and it is a text in which the phrase 'great Babylon' occurs again). Daniel is the book in which God's punitive foot comes down and splats Nebuchadnezzar, the Babylonian king (and in which the writing on the wall famously appears in the court of Nebuchadnezzar's son Belshazzar):

---

8.   Julius and Ethel Rosenberg (1918–1953; 1914–1953) were American citizens executed for passing nuclear weapons information to the Soviet Union.

The king spake, and said, Is not this great Babylon, that I have built for the house of the kingdom by the might of my power, and for the honour of my majesty?

While the word was in the king's mouth, there fell a voice from heaven, saying, O king Nebuchadnezzar, to thee it is spoken; The kingdom is departed from thee . . . The same hour was the thing fulfilled upon Nebuchadnezzar: and he was driven from men, and did eat grass as oxen . . .

And at the end of the days I Nebuchadnezzar lifted up mine eyes unto heaven, and mine understanding returned to me, and I blessed the most High, and I praised and honoured him that lasteth for ever, whose dominion is an everlasting dominion . . .

Now I Nebuchadnezzar praise and extol and honour the King of heaven, all whose works are truth, and his ways judgment: and those that walk in pride he is able to debase.

(4:30–31, 33–34, 37)

Here endeth the lesson. Man can do what he please, but only till that enormous Monty Pythonesque foot that monitors pride comes down from heaven and splats him.

Aptly, then, it is a very surreal Jehovah that hovers over us here in Dylan's contemporary Babylon: mankind is at his greediest and most California-callow, and Dylan at his most spiky and off-the-wall, in this eloquent, lengthy song. He seems to have enjoyed its composition hugely and he recites it with a snarling relish that's too nimble on the feet of its phrasing and timing to become bombastic or to overbear. It's a fine way, too, of side-stepping the attack on Christian humility (and the defence of pride) advanced so amusingly by that other master of the surreal, Max Ernst, who said: 'The virtue of pride, which was once the beauty of mankind, has given place to the fount of all ugliness, Christian humility.'[9]

It's a pity it's so hard to decipher Dylan's words: to hear their unfailingly entertaining farrago of vituperation, which must all the time be pulled out bodily from underneath the unremittingly dull rubble of the music. (Even putting the voice higher in the mix would help. The CD version is markedly clearer than the vinyl in this instance, though it still falls a long way short of the kind of audibility that would make listening to the record a pleasure rather than a chore.) It more or less defies the general, disinterested listener to take anything from it at all. As I can decipher it, the lyric is this:

> *Like the lion tears the flesh off of a man*
> *So can a woman who passes herself off as a male.*
> *They sang 'Danny Boy' at his funeral, and the Lord's Prayer*
> *Preacher talkin' 'bout Christ betrayed*
> *It was like the earth just opened and swallowed him up*
> *He reached too high and was thrown back to the ground.*
> *You know what they say about bein' nice to the right people on the way up?:*
> *Sooner or later you gonna meet them comin' down*

9.   Max Ernst (1891–1976), German Dadaist and surrealist; quoted (but without further identification of the source), in *The Hutchinson Encyclopedia* (1995).

Yet it ain't no goin' back
When that foot of pride come down
Ain't no goin' back

Hear ya got a brother named James, don't forget faces or names
Sunken cheeks and his blood is mixed;
He look straight into the sun and say 'Revenge is mine'
But he drinks, and drinks can be fixed.
Sing me one more song about your love-me-till-the-morning stranger
And your fall-by-the-sword love affair with Errol Flynn:
In these times of compassion, when conformity's in fashion
Say one more stupid thing to me before the final nail is driven in

Well there ain't no goin' back
When that foot of pride come down
Ain't no goin' back

There's a retired businessman named Red, cast down from heaven and he's out
        of his head,
He feeds off of everyone that-a he can touch.
He says he only deals in cash to sell tickets to a plane crash:
Not somebody that you play around with much.
Miss Delilah is his. A philistine is what she is.
She'll do wondrous works with your fate –
Feed you coconut bread, spiced buns in bed –
If you don't mind sleepin' with your head face down in the plate

Well there ain't no goin' back
When that foot of pride come down
Ain't no goin' back

Well they'll choose a man for you to meet tonight,
You'll play the fool and learn how to walk through doors.
How to enter into the gates of paradise? No!
How to carry a burden too heavy to be yours.
Yeah up on the stage they'll be tryin' to get water out of rocks,
A whore will pass the hat, collect a hundred grand and say 'Thanks,'
They like to take all this money from sin, build big universities to study in,
Sing 'Amazing Grace' all the way to the Swiss banks.

Well there ain't no goin' back
When that foot of pride come down
Ain't no goin' back

They got some beautiful people out there, man
They can be a terror to your mind and show you how to hold your tongue.
They got MYSTERY written all over their forehead,
They kill babies in the crib and say 'Only the good die young . . .'
They don't believe in mercy.

Judgment on them is somethin' that you'll never see.
They can exalt you up or bring you down bankrupt
Turn you into anything that they want you to be

Well there ain't no goin' back
When that foot of pride come down
Ain't no goin' back

Yes I guess I loved him too; I can still see him in my mind, climbin' that hill.
Did he make it to the top? Well he probably did and dropped:
Struck down by the strength of the will.
Ain't nuthin' left here, pardner:
Just the dust of a plague that has left this whole town afraid.
From now on this'll be where you're from,
Let the dead bury the dead, your time will come:
Feel that hot iron blow as you raise the shade!

Well there ain't no goin' back
When that foot of pride come down
Ain't no goin' back.

Ah yeah! Ah yeah!

What an explosion of words! What an unblocking of Swiftian vitriol!

And on the record, how surprisingly soon the vocal starts: as if Dylan can't be bothered with the music at all. Indeed there hardly is any: just a monotonous beat, with but a few words sung and the great majority recited – in a *tour de force* of Dylan's incomparable timing and phrasing. So much is the music the slave chained to the words that, as his verbal spleen intensifies, the music speeds up. (This isn't done for effect, and may not be noticeable as the record plays through, but if you replay it as soon as it's ended, you find that the pace at the start of the track is markedly slower.)

Nor is there any regularity to the rhyme scheme. Each 8-line verse works differently, as if driven entirely by need. The first verse, for instance, has not one internal rhyme; in the second verse the opening line resounds with one, and so does the seventh. The third verse does this too, except that this time the *same* sound that is used twice in the first line is used twice in the seventh also – and Dylan redoubles the amount of inner chiming by putting further internal rhymes inside lines three and five. In the next two verses, in strong contrast, we get no internal rhyming at all until the penultimate lines; and the last verse is different again, its comparable internal rhymes placed in lines two, five and six, and with a few extra ones packed together tightly at the beginnings of other lines ('Yes I guess I' is how the verse opens; 'Just the dust' marks the start of line five; 'Let the dead bury the dead' opens line seven, and the verse ends with Dylan making an emphasising, full-stopping neo-rhyme out of his final phrase 'raise the shade').

When we express it in symbols (ignoring, in the conventional way, incidental variant internals), we can see that the rhyme scheme of the verses of 'Foot Of Pride' is so irregular as to make the very term rhyme *scheme* an oxymoron:

> Verse 1: A,B,C,B,D,E,D,E.
> Verse 2: AA,B,C,B,D,E,FF,E.
> Verse 3: AA,B,CC,B,EE,F,AA,F.
> Verse 4: A,B,C,B,D,E,FF,E.
> Verse 5: A,B,C,B,D,D,EE,D.
> Verse 6: A,BB,A,C,DD,EE,E,D.

Yet such is Dylan's delivery, and the energetic, resourceful deployment of so much bouncing, resounding, tearaway rhetoric, so unstoppable is his firework display of ideas and images, so various and surprising are the objects and icons and bits of Bible he picks up and hurls as he fulminates his way through it all, that the disordered structuring of the verses is not merely not a weakness, but actually serves to unite, in spirit, the form and the content, as any art should. He makes himself sound impelled to disordered structure.

Non sequiturs add to this. The song begins with a most bizarre opening remark, and piles what appears to be a non sequitur straight on top of it:

> *Like the lion tears the flesh off of a man*
> *So can a woman who passes herself off as a male.*
> *They sang 'Danny Boy' at his funeral, and the Lord's Prayer.*

Whaaat? Whose funeral? Someone who had his flesh torn off by a sexual impostor? Is, then, the sexually identifying title 'Danny *Boy*' the song's first joke? Or is the picture of the man-eating lion a playful way of hinting that the song glances back to the book of Daniel (Daniel's survival in the lions' den being the one story about him that everybody knows)? This would still make 'They sang 'Danny Boy' at his funeral' the song's first joke.

Yet the song has its own ways of being accessible and consistent. Principal among them is its running joke, or rather, its climbing and falling joke. Dylan makes the lyric a series of jokes about going up to heaven and going down to hell, and they begin in this first verse, after what seems an odd remark to make about a funeral/burial:

> *It was like the earth just opened and swallowed him up.*

Well, yes. This is a very Dylanesque revitalising of a cliché. He makes us look at it anew, in this case by applying what is customarily a figurative expression in a literal situation. Dylan ends this life-restoring comment about death with one of his characteristic extra words: it wasn't like the earth just opened and swallowed him, it was like it just opened and swallowed him *up* – and in adding this word, Dylan achieves several things. First, he gives it emphasis (he repeats it, making it 'rhyme with itself' two lines later). Second, he makes a pun hover over it: in *fact* at a burial the earth is opened and swallows the body *down*, but Dylan uses '*up*' to lead straight into 'He reached too high'. This shadowy pun allows him, in turn, to usher in the first of his climbing and falling, up and down, to heaven and hell jokes:

> *It was like the earth just opened and swallowed him up*
> *He reached too high and was thrown back to the ground.*

(Actually, as so often, Dylan has a scriptural basis for his line here. When Moses tells his people to keep away from the wicked, he adds: 'If these men die the common death of all men ... then the Lord hath not sent me. But if the Lord make a new thing, and the earth open her mouth, and swallow them up, with all that appertain to them, and they go down quick into the pit; then ye shall understand that these men have provoked the Lord. And it came to pass, as he had made an end of speaking ... that the ground clave asunder that was under them: And the earth opened her mouth and swallowed them up' [Numbers 16:29–32]. And Deuteronomy 11:6 recalls 'how the earth opened her mouth and swallowed them up'.)

Strange stuff – which Dylan follows immediately by taking another cliché and making a joke from it. In any other context this, spread all across the two long last lines of the verse, would seem tired, slack writing, because it would be offering the cliché itself as the idea:

> *You know what they say about bein' nice to the right people on the way up?:*
> *Sooner or later you gonna meet them comin' down;*

but Dylan takes this hoary old showbiz maxim about career highs and lows, and turns it into a comment about going up to heaven and then being sent down again. Like *Paradise Lost*, this is a song about Satan's expulsion, about fallen angels. Its founding text is surely Isaiah 14:11–15:

> Thy pomp is brought down to the grave ... How art thou fallen from heaven, O Lucifer, son of the morning! how art thou cut down to the ground ... For thou hast said in thine heart, I will ascend into heaven, I will exalt my throne above the stars of God: I will sit also upon the mount of the congregation, in the sides of the north: I will ascend above the heights of the clouds; I will be like the most High. Yet thou shalt be brought down to hell, to the sides of the pit.

As 'Foot Of Pride' insists again and again, you can never assume that ascent means you've made it: you can be sent back down anytime.

The last four lines of the first verse end with 'up', 'ground', 'up', 'down', to be followed at once by the short chorus, with its insistence on 'back', 'down', 'back'. That's two ups and two downs in the space of seven consecutive line-endings.

The second verse takes a break from this theme, but Dylan reintroduces it dramatically at the beginning of verse three, as he conjures up this deft modern incarnation of Satan himself:

> *There's a retired businessman named Red, cast down from heaven and he's out*
>   *of his head.*

This is a terrific line: a retired, drunken businessman (hot, sweaty, greedy, unscrupulous, unfit) makes the perfect contemporary Satan. Naming him 'Red' straddles perfectly the modern world of American nicknames and the traditional depiction of the devil in hellfire colours, while 'cast down from heaven and he's out of his head' is a similarly neat pairing of two different kinds of being 'down and out'. Like the utterly amoral concert promoter in 'Highway 61 Revisited' who is happy to sell seats in the bleachers for people to watch a next world war, our man Red will 'sell tickets to a plane crash' (cash only) – and of course to cite a plane crash is to invoke another sort of down that should have stayed an up.

The next verse continues the theme, as we meet the 'beautiful people' with MYSTERY on their foreheads. When Dylan sings that

> *They can exalt you up or bring you down bankrupt*

not only is this another up/down, but it is another case, matching that in the first verse, where the 'up' itself is an extra word, so that in giving us an echo of his earlier usage, Dylan is again emphasising that small word. Swallowed him *up* . . . exalt you *up*. We register this 'up' as an extra word not only because it appears to create a tautology – the primary meaning of 'exalt' is to raise or elevate: it comes from the Latin *exaltare*, to raise, in turn derived from *altus*, meaning high – but also because here Dylan is, as so often, alluding in modern colloquial American English to another of his biblical texts, this time from the Gospels. Aptly, it is a text dealing with going to heaven or to hell. We find it in Matthew (11:20, 23):

> Then began he to upbraid the cities wherein most of his mighty works were done, because they repented not: . . . And thou, Capernaum, which are exalted unto heaven, shalt be brought down to hell.

In Luke 10:5, the corresponding passage (which follows shortly after 'let the dead bury their dead', which Dylan quotes almost verbatim a few lines later on in 'Foot Of Pride') gives Christ's words as follows: 'And thou, Capernaum, which art exalted to heaven, shalt be thrust down to hell'.

The ugliness of Dylan's colloquialising of this into 'exalt you up' makes it stand out, which adds to the emphasis given, as throughout the song, to that word 'up', and this emphasis is redoubled by Dylan's adding a matching extra word to the other half of the line too: instead of Christ's 'exalted . . . brought down' we have 'exalt you up' and 'bring you down bankrupt', while by making an internal rhyme of that 'up . . . bankrupt' Dylan gives it more emphasis still.

But is it a tautology? And, to ask a related question, doesn't that brutish-sounding 'exalt you up' remind us not only of 'swallowed him up' earlier in 'Foot Of Pride', but of some far older instance of Dylan's similar way with words? Actually, in my case I realised that I heard this older echo via someone else's tone of voice. It reminded me of Christopher Ricks discussing Bob Dylan, rather than Dylan directly: and I found the relevant passages (from Ricks and Dylan) in the critical essay 'Clichés that come to pass' and the song 'All I Really Want To Do':

> *I ain't lookin' to block you up,*
> *Shock or knock or lock you up.*

Ricks picks out that 'shock you up', where the norm would be just 'shock you', and suggests that here Dylan 'is giving a shake to the phrase "shake you up" '.[10]

Similarly, 'exalt you up' works as something other than tautology because adding 'up' changes the whole nature and tone of the process of 'exalting' someone. To exalt is to bestow something, to give graciously, to act benignly – to increase a person's

10. Christopher Ricks, 'Clichés that come to pass', in *All Across the Telegraph*, note 5.

dignity with dignity. 'They can exalt you up' suggests rough handling (shades of 'beat you up', 'fit you up', 'bang you up'): it suggests a violent kind of raising up, more an involuntary process so far as the recipient is concerned, an act that might be random and temporary, as by a tornado. And it suits Dylan's purpose because it implies, to use another cliché on the same subject, that what goes up must come down.

In the next (the final) verse, Dylan extends this theme further, with a pair of opening lines that offer yet another callous-sounding up-and-down joke – one last banana-skin scenario:

> . . . I can still see him in my mind, climbin' that hill.
> Did he make it to the top? Well he probably did and dropped.

Sod's law or God's law? Possibly both.

If that is the main thread running all through 'Foot Of Pride' there are other, less obtrusive connections too. The first verse's 'They sang 'Danny Boy' at his funeral' is balanced by the fourth verse's 'Sing 'Amazing Grace' all the way to the Swiss banks' (as it happens, a sort of re-angling of the well-known 'crying all the way to the bank'). The first verse's literalising of the normally figurative 'the earth just opened and swallowed him up' is enriched by more of the same in the second verse, with its 'before the final nail is driven in'. In contrast, the song begins with this funeral but ends by echoing Christ's exhortation to ignore one: 'Let the dead bury the dead'. (Dylan first alludes to this remark back in 'It's All Over Now, Baby Blue', with the line 'Forget the dead you've left, they will not follow you', and here it is again, almost verbatim, as indeed it is in another song of the 1980s, 'Under Your Spell'.) The biblical text is from Matthew 8:21–22 and Luke 9:60: 'And another of his disciples said unto him, Lord, suffer me first to go and bury my father. But Jesus said unto him, Follow me: and let the dead bury their dead' and/or 'Jesus said unto him, Let the dead bury their dead: but go thou and preach the kingdom of God'.

In describing the contemporary Babylon, in which people certainly are not preaching the kingdom of God or following Jesus, Dylan offers another apt pairing of allusions. In the second verse we find someone boasting that he can usurp one of the functions of God – 'He look straight into the sun and say "Revenge Is Mine"', whereas (as we know from Romans 12:19), 'Vengeance is mine: I will repay, saith the Lord'. Matching this, the snarling fourth verse of 'Foot Of Pride' predicts the spectacle of people trying to usurp another of God's prerogatives – 'up on the stage they'll be tryin' to get water out of rocks'.[11]

There is one more joke in 'Foot Of Pride' that, as it were, leaps out at you: the play on words in 'your fall-by-the-sword love affair with Errol Flynn'. As mentioned earlier, 'fall by the sword' is a phrase scattered through the Bible – one of the very many that give a unity of language to the Old Testament and the New, and to the

---

11. The quotation from Paul's Epistle to the Romans (12:19) is, more fully, '. . . for it is written, Vengeance is mine; I will repay, saith the Lord'. This makes it clear that Paul is restating an Old Testament text. In fact this is Deuteronomy 32:35. (Paul repeats it again in Hebrews 10:30.) The story of God making it possible for Moses to get water out of rock is given in Exodus 17:1–6, and summarised economically in Numbers 20:11: 'And Moses lifted up his hand, and with his rod he smote the rock twice: and the water came out abundantly, and the congregation drank, and their beasts also.'

words of the old prophets and of Christ and his apostles.[12] What is so bouncingly inspired about Dylan's using the phrase here is that he achieves a three-way pun on it. There's the biblical allusion and at the same moment the allusion to the twentieth century; and while Dylan uses God's phrase to sketch in the Hollywood hero's swashbuckling pose (his official trademark, as it were), he also allows it to act as a jokey sub-textual allusion to Flynn's famously enormous dick (his unofficial trademark). This is truly an off-the-wall fusion of the sacred and the profane, and entirely in the barking, biting spirit of what clamours to be recognised as Bob Dylan's most deranged song.

'Jokerman', alone among the released tracks from the "Infidels" sessions, is a song you can inhabit, as you can so much of Bob Dylan's earlier work. It isn't a sermon or a pop song but a real creation, a work you can wander inside, explore, breathe in, pass through, wrap around you. It looks different in different lights. It's always shifting, but this is because it's alive, not because it's nebulous (though it may be that too). Its complexity isn't off-putting, nor distancing. On the contrary, Dylan sings you through the complexity with almost as much generosity of expression, almost as much bestowing of concentrated warmth, as he gives out on, say, 'Sad-Eyed Lady Of The Lowlands', a nebulous and complicated song from another lifetime.

It is as much the warmth as the substance of 'Jokerman' that makes it such a welcome item in Dylan's corpus. The two qualities cohere in Dylan's openness toward the listener in confessing his fondness for the song itself, and in his palpably strong desire to communicate it (a desire often absent in 1980s Dylan).

I wouldn't have used the word 'substance' of 'Jokerman' when I first heard the recording. On the contrary I found it a curiously skeletal thing, as if it were the piece of paper with the dots on from which you might construct and colour in a Bob Dylan Song By Numbers. This effect was owing partly to the sparsity of its noises (an attractive sparsity, but an undeniable one: what you hear is the huge amount of empty space between the ultra-simple rhythm section, the minimal keyboards and guitar-playing and the strongly echo-chambered vocal line, making for a production as on no other record I know, by Dylan or anyone else) and partly to the way in which the song's title and the words of its chorus seem like pale, thin shadows of that great prototypical Dylan song, 'Mr. Tambourine Man':

> Jokerman dance to the nightingale tune,
> Bird fly high by the light of the moon,
> Oh— Jokerman.[13]

Not only does this remind us of 'Mr. Tambourine Man', but it reads more like somebody's notes, a hasty summary of a lyric heard fleetingly, than like a finished

---

12.   The phrase is used by the ungrateful Israelites, grumbling at Moses, and is then thrown back at them by Moses himself, in Numbers 14:14, 43. It is Isaiah's too, as he warns that 'Thy men shall fall by the sword, and thy mighty in the war' (Isaiah 3:25). Elsewhere the phrase belongs to God himself, for example in speaking to Ezekiel in a vision ('and a third part shall fall by the sword round about thee': Ezekiel 5:12.) The phrase recurs in Daniel (11:33), the book that immediately follows Ezekiel and on which, as we've seen, Dylan has already leant in constructing 'Foot Of Pride'.

13.   There is some discussion of the resemblances between these two songs and Edward Lear's 'The Owl and The Pussycat' in Chapter 17, note 67.

lyric. Strip it down by only two or three more words (the definite articles) and it could be one of Harry Smith's celebrated summaries – 'JOKERMAN DANCE TO NIGHT-INGALE TUNE. BIRD FLY HIGH BY LIGHT OF MOON. OH OH JOKERMAN' – directly comparable, for instance, to his summary of the song 'Present Joys': 'PRAISE LORD OF HEAVEN AND EARTH. PRESENT JOYS PASSING FAST. HEAVEN AT LAST'.[14]

The chorus of 'Jokerman' may be skeletal and derivative, fleshed out only by Dylan's extraordinary vocal resourcefulness (naturally he never sings it the same way twice), but the verses are richly textured and freely imaginative – carefully, densely structured yet rhapsodically fluent blocks of writing that glow with inspiration, recognisably of Bob Dylan's making without ever being 'Dylanesque'. There is many a lightly thrown out biblical allusion, but the lightness makes clear that these are valued more for their relishable poetics than for any sermonising usefulness. Starry-eyed and laughing with deft, acute touches only Bob Dylan could alchemise, in the writing and performance, 'Jokerman' is essentially a song like no other.

Sometimes Dylan seems to be singing about himself and sometimes about Jesus, but the whole is too fluid to need from the listener any analytic effort at separating out the one from the other. The intertwining of the two is, in any case, part of what the song evokes: one theme of 'Jokerman' is surely Dylan's mocking of the distance between his own fallibilities and the omnipotence of his Saviour, a recurring self-mockery that laughs at the superficial parallels between Dylan, mythic public figure and Artist-Creator, and Christ, mythic public figure and Son of The Creator. The post-Evangelical Period Dylan seems ruefully to acknowledge here that there had been foolish moments when he had taken such parallels solemnly. At the same time, Dylan also seems sceptical of the idea that Christ's powers are altogether a good thing – there's a hint that Christ too seems risible – and this in turn suggests both another rueful parallel (a real resemblance between two dodgy heroes) and one further opportunity to instance the singer's own failings – for to admit to such scepticism is to confess yet another failure: to confess that even in his much-vaunted embrace of Christ he is now faltering.

Thus the song begins with a nice mockery of superheroes and the singer's own mythic pretensions, in an opening verse that at once reveals that here is a work of a high order – chiselled, clever, complex, compressed and unapologetically articulate, yet carrying itself lightly, with likeable grace and poise, entirely free of solemnity or the didactic, and delivered with unguarded generosity of spirit:

> *Standing on the water casting your bread*
> *While the eyes of the idol with the iron head are glowing.*
> *Distant ships sailing in through the mist*

14. Harry Smith, notes re Alabama Sacred Harp Singers: 'Present Joys', Atlanta, 16/4/28 [misascribed to Birmingham, Alabama, by Smith], issued on Smith's compilation "American Folk Music", Folkways Records FP251–253, New York, 1952, CD-reissued as "Anthology Of American Folk Music" [6-CD box-set] with copious notes by many hands and including a CD-ROM of extras, Smithsonian Folkways Recordings SFW 40090, Washington, DC, 1997.

*You were born with a snake in both of your fists while a hurricane was
blowing.*[15]

There is so much here, and so adroitly put together. The opening line neatly combines
Christ's walking on the water, a New Testament story emphasising his godly power,
with the well-known proverb 'Cast your bread upon the waters: for thou shalt find it
after many days', an Old Testament injunction to humankind. This latter, from
Ecclesiastes, is the textual basis for the Jewish Passover ritual in which people take
bags of breadcrumbs and throw them into the river to symbolise the casting out of
their sins – hence Dylan's lovely 'breadcrumb sins' in 'The Gates Of Eden'.[16]

The combining of these two biblical moments in one modest line is one of Dylan's
skilful and intelligent achievements, quietly acerbic and inspired, like one of his
bumpings-together of two clichés. It makes for a splendid piece of self-mockery, since
it evokes so simply yet vividly the picture of the pretender, the 'Jokerman'. In the
incident being mimicked, Christ is not only godlike but, just as importantly, *purposive*:
He 'went unto them, walking on the sea'; but Dylan refuses '*Walking* on the water',
despite the tempting alliterative appeal of that phrase for use in a song sewn through
with alliteration and internal rhyming.

He chooses instead to show himself caught in a pose: in the comically functionless,
dithering position of 'Standing on the water'. The implication is of 'standing around'
and the further effect of this inaction is to stress the physical impossibility of the act.
You can almost credit that by dint of a swift and light enough stepping forward, a not
staying in one place long enough to put your weight on it, you might briefly walk
across water; you cannot but picture that standing still will make you sink. That the
self Dylan is addressing here is standing there casting his bread emphasises that his
real position, far from being godlike, is that of the humble sinner quite rightly in the
act of contrition. The contrast between that hopeless bravado and this humility makes
the situation still more comic.

The conjunction of the two biblical allusions in 'Jokerman''s opening line achieves
a further compression of meaning, deepening the import of the song. What Dylan
bumps together here are two texts that are associated with opposite notions. Christ's
walking on water may show him to be godlike, but also shows him urging upon his
followers one of his favourite messages: that anything can be achieved if you have
sufficient faith. Peter tries walking on the water immediately after Christ, and fails,
we're told, only through lack of wholehearted faith. Jesus catches him and asks (in
Matthew 14:31) rhetorically: 'O thou of little faith, wherefore didst thou doubt?' (As
we shall see, this insistence of Christ's on the power of faith – on its superhuman
physical power; power like a mythic hero's – is alluded to again in at least two other

---

15. *Lyrics 1962–1985* and the critics quoted below all have the distant ships sailing 'into' the mist (as if they are
disappearing). However, Dylan's studio recording definitely has 'in through' the mist (suggesting that they are
arriving).

16. Matthew 14:25: 'And in the fourth watch of the night Jesus went unto them, walking on the sea'. Mark 6:48:
'and about the fourth watch of the night he cometh unto them, walking upon the sea'. John 6:19: 'So when they
had rowed about five and twenty or thirty furlongs, they see [sic] Jesus walking on the sea'.
Ecclesiastes 11:1: 'Cast your bread upon the waters: for thou shalt find it after many days.' Ecclesiastes was
'the Preacher' ('the Philosopher,' in the *Good News Bible*), son of King David and himself a king of Israel (the
book is generally attributed to Solomon).

lines of 'Jokerman'.) Dylan bumps his allusion to this story about the power of faith into his allusion to a proverb from Ecclesiastes – famously the one book in the Bible which gives space and patience, a sympathetic airing, to doubt.

Ecclesiastes alone accommodates the idea of doubt not as a sin marking out the wicked and shameful but as a problem that is bound to visit, probably recurrently, those of goodwill and a reflective temperament. It offers a forum for our inevitable feelings about the brevity of human life, and about whether, being so brief, it isn't also meaningless. This is where 'vanity of vanities; all is vanity' comes from.[17] 'The Preacher' meditates aloud, as it were, about exactly the kinds of contradiction and injustice in life that cause us to doubt either God's existence or his kindliness, and to lose hope for the future. He admits that he cannot understand God.

Ecclesiastes clearly makes a unique contribution to the Bible. As the *Good News Bible* notes: 'Many of [its] thoughts appear negative and even depressing. But the fact that this book is in the Bible shows that biblical faith is broad enough to take into account such pessimism and doubt. Many have taken comfort in seeing themselves in the mirror of Ecclesiastes . . .'

Bob Dylan, then, opens 'Jokerman' with this fusing of allusions to a unique embodiment of the power of faith and a unique embodiment of the legitimacy of doubt. Thinking of Christ, he is also glancing into the mirror of Ecclesiastes.

Not for the first time. One of its themes is the difficult question of whether it is better to be alive, enduring and aware of the inevitable pain of the human lot, or to be dead and feeling nothing (the Preacher first looks at the question with pessimism, and later more hopefully). And Dylan addresses this dilemma, in the sleeve notes to 1965's "Bringing It All Back Home" and then with an explicit nod at the text of Ecclesiastes in a song contemporary with 'Jokerman', 1983's 'Tell Me'. In the first he writes that it is better to be a live nobody than a dead hero:

> . . . *i would not want*
> *t' be bach. mozart. tolstoy. joe hill. gertrude*
> *stein or james dean/they are all dead*

but in the second he simply poses the question to the song's addressee:

> *Which means more to you, a live dog or a dead lion?*

This is a direct allusion to Ecclesiastes 9:4, a part of the text in which optimism prevails and the Preacher decides the issue this way (the same way Dylan decided it back in 1965 when he wrote those sleeve notes): 'For to him that is joined to all the living there is hope: for a living dog is better than a dead lion'.

In the 1965 'It's Alright Ma (I'm Only Bleeding)' Dylan refers to two more of the main themes explored in Ecclesiastes – the hopeless limits of our understanding:

> *To understand you know too soon*
> *There is no sense in trying;*

---

17.   Ecclesiastes 1:2: 'Vanity of vanities, saith the Preacher, vanity of vanities; all is vanity'. This becomes the basis of what is almost an incantation, a repeated theme, as here (1:14): 'I have seen all the works that are done under the sun; and behold, all is vanity and vexation of spirit'.

and the always-unsatisfying way that the foolish and the wise so often get the same deal:

> *Although the masters make the rules*
> *For the wise men and the fools*
> *I got nothing, Ma, to live up to.*

This compares directly with Ecclesiastes 2:15–16:

> As it happeneth to the fool so it happeneth even to me; and why was I then more wise? Then I said in my heart, that this also is vanity. For there is no remembrance of the wise more than of the fool for ever; seeing that which now is in the days to come shall all be forgotten. And how dieth the wise man? as the fool.

In 1967's 'Tears Of Rage', Dylan echoes what is almost the very first preoccupation of Ecclesiastes, the shortness of the human lifespan and the impossibility of leaving anything that lasts (I don't suggest one *needs* Ecclesiastes to prompt this line of thought):

> *. . . you know we're so alone*
> *And life is brief*

while in the contemporaneous 'Too Much Of Nothing' (a title that in itself summarises the gloomy end of the Ecclesiastes meditative spectrum) he worrits away at other parts of the Preacher's text. The song's opaque second verse seems to follow a line of thought prompted by the beginning of Ecclesiastes Chapter 8, which advises people to be circumspect and at least appear obedient in front of a king, to be safe: and goes on immediately to the thought that no one knows anything about anything much, and certainly not about when they will die.

(Ecclesiastes 8:2, 5–9 [*Good News* version]: 'Do what the king says . . . As long as you obey his commands, you are safe, and a wise man knows how and when to do it. There is a right time and a right way to do everything, but we know so little! None of us knows what is going to happen, and there is no one to tell us. No one can keep himself from dying or put off the day of his death.')

Dylan's meditation boils this down to

> *Too much of nothing*
> *Can make a man abuse a king.*
> *He can walk the streets and boast like most*
> *But he wouldn't know a thing.*

('Curse not the king . . .', as Ecclesiastes says again in 10:20: the verse before 'Cast thy bread upon the waters') – after which Dylan adds at once, echoing Ecclesiastes far more plainly:

> *Now, it's all been done before,*
> *It's all been written in the book.*

This again is a main theme of Ecclesiastes, connecting with the idea of life's brevity and the impossibility of leaving anything behind. It's all been done before and it all disappears. Everything will be forgotten: so much so that we forget that everything in our own times has been around before, time and again. Ecclesiastes 1:11: 'There is no remembrance of former things; neither shall there be any remembrance of things that are to come with those that shall come after'.[18] And if the individual's life is so short, and what she or he tries to leave behind must sink without trace, then what can be the point? A key part of this is famously summarised in the first chapter (1:9):

> The thing that hath been, it is that which shall be; and that which is done is that which shall be done: and there is no new thing under the sun.

In his Christian evangelical period, Dylan returns to these themes, usually drawing on more positive ways of looking at them – as does Ecclesiastes, in spite of all the doubts, in the course of its meditation – or else with every appearance of relishing the gloom they might induce. Hence we find 'That which hath been is now; and that which is to be hath already been' (3:15) transferred almost verbatim into the second of these lines from 'Pressing On':

> *What kind of sign they need when it all come from within,*
> *When what's lost has been found, what's to come has already been?*

and in 'Ain't No Man Righteous, No Not One' the similarly near-verbatim

> *God got the power, man has got his vanity . . .*
> *Don't you know there's nothing new under the sun?*
> *Well, there ain't no man righteous, no not one*[19]

while another song contemporaneous with 'Jokerman' (and 'Tell Me'), the rather less approachable 'I And I', manages to snatch some kind of solace from the jaws of gloom with its use of yet another near-verbatim Ecclesiastes quotation. That song, looking frantically on the bright side, declares:

18. Dylan's lines just quoted ('Now, it's all been done before, / It's all been written in the book') are in one way an awkward fit here, I know, especially since there's a close parallel with what he offers immediately after '. . . i would not want / t' be bach. mozart. tolstoy. joe hill. gertrude / stein or james dean / they are all dead' in the "Bringing It All Back Home" sleeve notes, which is: 'the / Great books've been written. the Great sayings / have all been said'. The noticeable similarity of these passages suggests that 'It's all been written in the book' means that what has gone before gets preserved, of course, whereas the point argued in Ecclesiastes is that everything's been done before and never gets remembered. It's all been written in the book of human history but nobody reads the book; no one even remembers that if they did read the book they'd find that 'it's all been done before'.

19. The title line 'Ain't No Man Righteous, No Not One', paired here with the Ecclesiastes quotation, is a summarising by Paul, in his Epistle to the Romans (3:10) – 'As it is written, There is none righteous, no, not one' – of less memorably phrased words from an Old Testament Psalm of David (14:2–3): 'The Lord looked down from heaven upon the children of men, to see if there were any that did understand, and seek God. They are all gone aside, they are all together become filthy: there is none that doeth good, no, not one.' That is the Authorized Version; in the earlier version retained in the *Book of Common Prayer* (in which the Psalms are based partly on Middle English Psalters and partly on Miles Coverdale's translation in his Bible of 1535, itself based on William Tyndale's work) we find (14:1–4): 'The fool hath said in his heart: There is no God. They are corrupt, and become abominable in their doings: there is none that doeth good, no, not one. The Lord looked down from heaven upon the children of men: to see if there were any that would understand, and seek after God. But they are all gone out of the way, they are altogether become abominable: there is none that doeth good, no, not one.' Christ also uses this text, rebuking the man who calls him 'Good Master' with the words 'Why callest thou me good? there is none good but one, that is, God.'
     [Bob Dylan: 'Ain't No Man Righteous, No Not One', performed twice in concert: San Francisco, 16/11/79, and Hartford, Connecticut, 7/5/80; also performed with lead vocal by Regina Havis instead of Dylan on that tour's final night, Dayton, Ohio, 21/5/80. Though there is no known Bob Dylan studio recording, the lyric appears in *Lyrics 1962–85*, 1986, listed as a "Slow Train Coming" out-take. A reggaeish version was issued by Jah Malla: 'Ain't No Man Righteous', *nia*; "Jah Malla", Modern Records MR 38–135, New York, 1981.]

> *Took an untrodden path once, where the swift don't win the race.*
> *It goes to the worthy, who can divide the word of truth*

though in Ecclesiastes (9:11) the Preacher

> returned, and saw under the sun, that the race is not to the swift, nor the battle to
> the strong, neither yet bread to the wise, nor yet riches to men of understanding,
> nor yet favour to men of skill; but time and chance happeneth to them all.[20]

When Dylan cites Ecclesiastes in the opening line of 'Jokerman' (not by naming it but by quoting directly from it), he is not labouring its centrality to any understanding of what he's on about, but he is certainly returning to biblical territory he has drawn on many times, and if we know something of this book's special function as a forum for airing inherent problems to do with human purpose, we can hear more fully the song's greatness of resonance.

We can also recognise that the second verse of 'Jokerman' is, among other things, another venture among these themes of Ecclesiastes, a return to its notions of life's brevity:

> *How swiftly the sun sets in the sky;*

how we leave nothing behind:

> *You rise up and say goodbye to no one;*

how the master makes the rules for the wise men and the fools, and both face the same void:

> *Fools rush in where angels fear to tread*
> *Both of their futures so full of dread, you don't show one.*

A touch to make you smile here is how Dylan plays with the well-known 'fools rush in where angels fear to tread': it can't but cross your mind that one place it might be foolish to tread is 'on the water', and to picture even the angels being scared to try it is a neatly amusing way to suggest how much faith this might take.[21]

It's also noticeable that Dylan makes a series of steps out of taking steps here: first there's the standing on the water, then the fearing to tread, and immediately after this comes 'keeping one step ahead'. But this is rushing ahead: we must return almost to the start of the song in order to see how its ideas develop and its poetry works. So far we're really only at the end of the first line . . .

The second line of 'Jokerman', following up the self-mocking Christ-comparison

---

20.   The non-Ecclesiastes reference, 'It goes to the worthy, who can divide the word of truth', which Dylan pairs with the Ecclesiastes-based 'the swift don't win the race', derives from Paul's Second Epistle to Timothy: 'Study to shew thyself approved unto God, a workman that needeth not to be ashamed, rightly dividing the word of truth' (2 Timothy 2:15).

21.   Or as Bob sang once before (in the Peretti-Creatore-Weiss song 'Can't Help Falling in Love', primarily associated with Elvis Presley and featured in his 1961 movie *Blue Hawaii* [Paramount/Hal. B. Wallis, US, directed Norman Taurog] and recorded by Dylan in New York, August 1970): 'Wise men say only fools rush in'. The wise man in this case was Alexander Pope, who was 21 when he wrote 'For fools rush in where angels fear to tread' in *An Essay on Criticism* (1711). Another of its lines that has achieved the status of a proverb is 'A little learning is a dangerous thing'.

of the opening line, evokes the presence of some pagan idol, with iron head and glowing eyes – another fraudulent claimant to the godhead; but the pleasures the line yields are less in their moving forward the song's ideas or arguments than in their early revelation of what is to come in the gorgeous, sinuous intricacy of the writing itself: the compellingly attractive pattern of the lines. Hear how these first two work:

> *Standing on the water casting your* bread
> *While the eyes of the idol with the iron* head *are glowing.*

If the only rhyme you heard was this end-sound of the first line and its partner half-hidden three-quarters of the way along the next, the effect would be pleasurable. Unless it's too pat, or the text too facile, such that it sounds all form and no content, *any* such pairing will read as or sound attractive. Whatever it is in us that likes certain patterns will always like this one, will always enjoy the way the line runs on beyond the rhyme to finish on a different stressed sound altogether – one that promises, as 'glowing' does here, to be the first time around for another rhyme that will find its partner a little later (in this case with 'blowing'). Dylan, though, gives us the greater pleasure of hearing all these things, these rhymes resolved and promised, down lines festooned with the small and pleasing notes of other rhymes along the way:

> *Standing on the water casting your bread*
> *While the e̲y̲e̲s̲ of the i̲dol with the i̲ron head are glowing.*

It's noticeable that in performance Dylan's instinct is to avoid any danger of over-stressing these second-line chimes, so he under-represents their sameness. That is, while it might seem natural for us to read, say or sing it as 'while thee eyes of thee idol with thee iron head', maximising the rhyming sounds so that they are 'eye-thee-eye-thee-eye-thee-eye', Dylan instead sings it as 'while thee eyes of thuh idol with thuh iron head'. The subtle effect of this is not only to underplay these sounds, to restrain their bouncing soundalike exuberance, but at the same time to make sure that the half-buried rhyme of 'head', which must follow them, doesn't get buried altogether.

Dylan succeeds completely here, manipulating these technical effects of sound and rythmn in the best possible way, while satisfying the primary requirement of poetry or song: that the form must serve the content. Assuredly it does so here. The strong, quiet pulsing of the greater part of the line – 'While the eyes of the idol with the iron head' – and the drop down on to the quieter menace of 'are glowing': this evokes with great sensual accuracy the pulsing glow of the pagan idol's magic-power eyes, conveying both the spooky atmospherics and the hard physicality the pagan worshipper beholds.

It's pleasing to the ear, too, that the intricate rhyming pattern of the song's opening lines should be reinforced by some degree of repetition in the lines that follow, so that we can be sure we've 'got it' and can savour this pattern, for the rest of the song and for all replayings of it, without further struggle at pattern recognition. At the same time we don't want too rigid a repetition, which might make us hear the whole pattern as mechanical and therefore hollow. In 'Jokerman' the next two lines of the opening verse give just the right, fluid kind of reinforcement, confirming the pattern but modifying it:

> Dis*tant* ships *sailing* in *through the* mist
> *You were born with a snake in both of your* fists *while a hurricane was blowing.*

This time the extra internal rhymes are inside the first line of the couplet instead of the second, and work to emphasise the first end-rhyme and its half-submerged partner instead of playing against them, before delivering the promised resolving rhyme at the end ('blowing') for which our ears had been waiting since before these lines began.

The potential for struggle and difficulty, even anarchy and disorder, that it might seem this complex pattern could be courting, is banished reassuringly by the way that the verse comes to a close: those snakey four opening lines are held in check by the emphatic plainness (in form and apparently in content) of a straightforward rhyming couplet:

> *Freedom just around the corner for you*
> *But with truth so far off, what good would it do?*

Like the rhyming couplet at the end of a sonnet, the effect is calming, containing, neat. It shepherds the potentially unruly animals of the verse's four opening lines into the orderly confines of its pinfold.

It's a pinfold – a temporary resting-place, a holding-pen only – because while the structure of the *writing* has this calming, reining-in effect after the churning energies of each verse's first four lines – long lines that twist in upon each other – the structure of the *music* integral to it refuses to come to rest here, refuses to end the rhyming couplet on its resolved tonic note. Instead it holds itself over, as if unresolved, waiting for the driving chords that take over from the end of the singer's line (taking the music back up from doh to soh-fah) to usher the whole thing on into the chorus, which is its real resting-place.

As for the rest of the *content* of the first verse of 'Jokerman', this too is potentially unruly yet proves consistent. After comparing himself mockingly to Jesus, the god–man who walked on water, the singer comes to Hercules, another god–man famous for achieving the impossible. Before growing up to complete his epic labours, he is to be found as an infant strangling a snake in each fist.[22] Dylan cranks up the pretensions to superheroics neatly here, making the 'you' of the song '*born* with a snake in both of your fists' (a characteristic, imaginative twisting of the accepted image, this) and in the midst of a hurricane to boot. To greet such a superhuman figure adequately, the weather would have to be cataclysmic. To claim the same scale of import for your own arrival in the world is self-aggrandisement indeed. Moreover, as with the mock-parallel with Christ, Dylan tweaks the Hercules image so that instead of doing something useful, in this case strangling two serpents before they can attack those less strong than himself, Dylan's 'you' is in a useless and passive equivalent position: in this case just passively born holding snakes in his fists, to no clear purpose at all.

---

22.   He is commonly depicted this way in paintings and sculptures. (There is a commendably unflattering mosaic of a pasty baby Hercules clutching at serpents, in the astonishing collection of brilliantly imaginative Roman mosaics [AD 100–400] on the walls of the museum in Antakya [ancient Antioch], Eastern Turkey. David Swann's photo of a more idealised version (a sculpture), now in the Bibliotheque Nationale in Paris, is reproduced [but unidentified] in *Man and His Symbols*, ed. Carl Jung (1964, 1978), a book utilised below. Robert Graves too depicts him (*The Greek Myths*, 1955) as having 'proudly displayed the serpents, which he was in the act of strangling, one in either hand' while 'still unweaned'.)

The couplet that completes this opening verse offers a further quiet and rueful self-mockery, likeably modest in scale and applicable to anyone, so that it is presented untainted by any suggestion that the 'you' so mocked is in any way uniquely disadvantaged. But

> *Freedom just around the corner for you*
> *But with truth so far off, what good would it do?*

is also deft and attractive for being a quietly intelligent re-working, or exploring, of another small biblical text. Dylan's lines play with, appear to query, Christ's own maxim about freedom and truth (reported in John 8:32): 'And ye shall know the truth, and the truth shall make you free'.

It is only after this lovely opening verse that we come to the song's 'skeletal' chorus, and in context it becomes possible to hear the ellipsed simplicity of its words as a balm, a plunge into the unjudgmental natural world after the verse's crowding of ideas and doubt, perfectly matching the way that the musical tension resolves itself as *it* plunges from the end of the verse into the chorus. Let the mind rest. Let the body and the intuition dance. Give inspiration a chance:

> *Jokerman dance to the nightingale tune*
> *Bird fly high by the light of the moon*
> *Oh— Jokerman.*

This is not Bob Dylan's first use of the nightingale in his compositions, nor the first to encourage a sense of the presence of Keats behind the lines: a sense that Dylan is consciously reusing Keats' association of the nightingale with the muse, the inspirational power of nature and mystery. There is an early draft of 'Visions Of Johanna' – a song that details a particular kind of life in the contemporary city and speaks of the haunting visions that float above it – a draft which Dylan records on two occasions ahead of the main "Blonde On Blonde" sessions (yielding one uneasy, fast version and one sumptuous, slower one), in which he begins the final verse like this:

> *The peddler he [now] steps to the road*
> *Knowing everything's gone which was owed*
> *He examines the nightingale's code*
> *Still left on the fishtruck that loads.*
> *My conscience explodes.*[23]

Bill King, in 'The artist in the marketplace', hears this song as 'constantly [seeking] to transcend the physical world, to reach the ideal where the visions of Johanna become real. That can never be, and yet life without the quest is worthless: this is the paradox at the heart of 'Visions', the same paradox that Keats explored in his 'Ode on a Grecian Urn'.'[24]

That key phrase 'the nightingale's code', a lovely and wonderfully short encapsulation of the core idea of how unknowable is the mystery of nature's music, is founded

23. Bob Dylan: 'Visions Of Johanna', 30/11/65, Los Angeles [the fast one], and 21/1/66, NYC [the slow], unreleased. These early versions were long known as 'Seems Like A Freeze-Out' or 'Freeze-Out'.

24. Bill King: 'The artist in the marketplace', doctoral thesis (1975); quoted from Robert Shelton, *No Direction Home* (1986).

upon a familiarity with another of Keats' four great odes, the 'Ode to a Nightingale', a poem about both poetic inspiration and the fear of its loss.[25]

Dylan addresses this theme himself, of course, in 'Mr. Tambourine Man', and it is the correspondences between the Keats poem and 'Mr. Tambourine Man' that are drawn out as far as they will stretch in Nigel Brooks' essay 'The nightingale's code: the influence of John Keats on Bob Dylan', but Brooks also pays some attention to 'Jokerman' in this context. He writes:

> Here is a further song where Dylan is, at least on one level, addressing himself as artist in the guise of the jokerman, the trickster figure, the Fool . . . responding, in the chorus, to the music of nature as represented by the nightingale . . . In addition, the nightingale is associated with the moon, just as in Keats' 'Ode' where the poet declares of the bird:
>
> *Already with thee! tender is the night,*
> *And haply the Queen-Moon is on her throne.*[26]

The moon too is the muse, and always has been. Keats' long work 'Endymion', written shortly before the odes, is based on the legend of the Greek moon goddess; the heroine of Dylan's song 'Isis' is a moon goddess; and the main thrust of Robert Graves' book *The White Goddess* (the importance of which as an influence on Bob Dylan has been widely stressed), is that the moon goddess inspires poetry endowed with a magical quality.[27]

These lines from Keats' 'Ode' provide the title for the F. Scott Fitzgerald novel *Tender is the Night* and, as noted in an earlier chapter, this in turn seems a source of inspiration for Dylan's 'When I Paint My Masterpiece', another song about the elusiveness of the muse. But it might be that that song itself glances in Keats' direction too. Along with much else that has clinched his reputation, Keats had written 'Ode to a Nightingale', a poem about the fear of loss of inspiration, in an astonishing burst of inspired productivity in 1819. In the winter of 1820–21 Keats lay dying in Rome, in a house he'd rented at the foot of the Spanish Stairs. In 'When I Paint My Masterpiece', is Dylan thinking of Keats when he sings of 'a cold, dark night on the Spanish Stairs'?

While the chorus of 'Jokerman' surrenders to the intuition and the dance, invoking the muse of nightingale and moon, the very term 'Jokerman', which it introduces, perpetuates as well as summarises the song's arguments: it is a name that in itself mocks and deflates the idea of the 'superman'.[28]

25. John Keats: 'Ode on a Grecian Urn' and 'Ode to a Nightingale' written 1818–19 and published in *Lamia and Other Poems* (1820). The other two 'great odes' are 'To Psyche' and 'To Autumn', same details (*The Complete Poems*, ed. John Barnard, 1991). (Dylan once said: 'My favourite poets are Shelley and Keats', *Time* magazine, 25 Nov. 1985.)

26. Nigel Brooks: 'The nightingale's code: the influence of John Keats on Bob Dylan', 1993, in *Bob Dylan's Words*, ed. Wissolik and McGrath (1994).

27. John Keats: 'Endymion', 1818. Robert Graves, *The White Goddess: A Historical Grammar of Poetic Myth* (1948, rev. edn 1952). Graves' *The Greek Myths* might have served Dylan too. (There is a discussion of how the moon is viewed in traditional children's literature, especially nursery rhymes, and consequently of how Dylan uses it in "Under The Red Sky", in Chapter 17.)

28. As mentioned in a different context, 'Jokerman' has another precedent as a title: the blues record by Blind Willie McTell's friends the Georgia Browns (the vocal is by Buddy Moss): 'Joker Man Blues', NYC, 19/1/33;

In this respect Dylan's choice of Hercules is a good one. Seldom has a hero had so bad a time of it; both in his Roman form, and in his Greek, as Heracles, he is a dullard and a failure, with brute strength his only asset. Typically, of his twelve labours, the one most people remember is his having to clean out all the shit from the Augean stables. He was driven mad by his aunt-cum-adoptive mother, the goddess Juno (Hera to the Greeks); he killed his first wife and his own children and was poisoned by his second wife by mistake. In Roberto Calasso's distinguished and successful postmodern retelling of Greek myth, *The Marriage of Cadmus and Harmony*, he writes:

> As a hero, Heracles is a beast of burden . . . everything is obligation, right up to the atrocious burns that kill him. A pitiful seriousness weighs him down. All too rarely does he laugh. And sometimes he finds himself having to suffer the laughter of others . . . Even the people he thrashed didn't take him seriously . . . As a hero he is too human, blinded like everybody else. Catapulted into the heavens as a result of celestial exigencies, he is never to know what purpose his labors really served, and the pretext the events of his life offer him smacks of mockery.[29]

However, in 'Jokerman', as in life, the myth of the hero can be put to greater use than merely as a butt for mocking jokes and a device for self-mocking ones. Almost thirty years ago, the improbably but serendipitously named Canadian poet and critic Homer Hogan offered an interesting piece of work on the use of myth in a Bob Dylan song, in his essay 'Myth and the Ballad of Frankie Lee And Judas Priest', from which the following might serve as a useful briefing on the basics of the subject before we look specifically at the relevance of the hero myth to the preoccupations discernible in 'Jokerman':

> a fundamental paradox of human nature [is that] . . . consciousness grows along two conflicting lines. On the one hand, it requires a strengthening of one's unique powers and sensibilities, or what might be loosely called one's self or 'ego'. On the other hand, it calls upon him to multiply his thoughts and feelings by absorbing those of his fellow men . . . To live for and in others entails the destruction of the defensive, inward-pointing ego, and yet that ego is the core of consciousness; not to be part of the group consciousness, however, is also to court mental death since awareness that is not social is not human.
>
> . . . myth enters into this tension between ego-centred consciousness and social, or 'self-transcending', consciousness. But first we must see how ritual and art function in that connection. According to Carl Jung, Maude Bodkin and other philosophers and psychologists, man works out the tensions of the permanent conflicts in his inner life by means of ritual and, later, of ritual turned into art. Participating in ritual or contemplating art, man asserts his ego by identifying with such substitutes as animals, heroes, priests, and kings in whom the power of the gods has become manifest, and yet also experiences the loss of ego in group consciousness through imaginatively sharing in the suffering and sacrifice of these

"Georgia Blues", Travelin' Man Records TM 800, Crawley, 1983. (Here 'joker' is merely a term of disparagement about the singer's sexual rival.)

29. Roberto Calasso, *The Marriage of Cadmus and Harmony* (1988), translated from the Italian by Tim Parks (1993).

ego substitutes. Presumably this is what accounts for the universal, enduring appeal of tragedy; of fertility and winter solstice rites in which the death of a god or a god representative is necessary for life to be reborn in the land; and of initiation ceremonies in which the childish ego is symbolically killed through trial and ordeal so that the young boy can assume the spirit of a warrior.

...we might now describe 'myth' as a theme, story, or situation which is essential in a ritual working through an aspect of the self-contradictory career of consciousness.[30]

Jungians, then, see the hero myth as just such an aid to the individual's working out of who she/he really is, and which point along life's path to maturity she/he has reached – and this is clearly a main question Dylan is pursuing in 'Jokerman'. Dylan is no fan of psychoanalysis, but it is clear from his work that he is certainly interested in the significance of myth to the individual, and in 'Jokerman' his self-mockery exactly confesses that he has one eye on the gods while looking at himself. The Jungian approach is therefore telling.

Joseph L. Henderson[31] writes:

The myth of the hero is the most common and the best known myth in the world ... It also appears in our dreams. It has [a] ... profound psychological importance.

These hero myths ... [have] a universal pattern, even though they were developed by groups or individuals without any direct cultural contact ... Over and over again one hears a tale describing a hero's miraculous but humble birth, his early proof of superhuman strength, [[32]] his rapid rise to prominence or power, his triumphant struggle with the forces of evil, his fallibility to the sin of pride (*hybris*), and his fall through betrayal or a 'heroic' sacrifice that ends in his death.

... [The] essential function of the heroic myth is the development of the individual's ego-consciousness – his awareness of his own strengths and weaknesses – in a manner that will equip him for the arduous tasks with which life confronts him.

Henderson goes on to say that the first of 'four distinct cycles in the evolution of the hero myth' is 'the *Trickster* cycle'.[33] This 'corresponds to the earliest and least

30.   Homer Hogan, 'Myth and the Ballad of Frankie Lee And Judas Priest', in the anthology *Poetry of Relevance 1*, ed. Homer Hogan (1970).

31.   Joseph L. Henderson: 'Ancient Myths and Modern Man', in *Man and His Symbols*, ed. Carl Jung.

32.   Hence the infant Hercules strangling snakes and the toddler Superman in the 1980s movie *Superman* lifting up the back of a car unaided. And as we know from 'The Ballad Of Davy Crockett', Davy 'killed him a bear when he was only three'. (This title song from the 1954 US TV series and 1955 Walt Disney film was a hit for Fess Parker [Columbia Records, USA], Bill Hayes [London-American HLA 8220 in UK] and Tennessee Ernie Ford [Capitol CL 14506 in UK]. In Britain Max Bygraves felt himself a fit person to cover it. Crockett was played by Parker, prominently wearing a 'coon-skin cap', to which Dylan refers in both 'Subterranean Homesick Blues' and *Tarantula*. Aptly, John 'Sweetheart Like You' Wayne directed himself as Crockett in the 1960 film *The Alamo*.)

33.   As named by Dr Paul Radin in his pamphlet 'Winnebago Hero Cycles: A Study in Aboriginal Literature', Waverley Press, Baltimore, 1948 (part of the series *Indiana University Publications in Anthropology and Linguistics*). In Jung's *Man and His Symbols*, Radin's pamphlet is misnamed 'Hero Cycles Of The Winnebago'. Radin was *the* man in this field.

developed period of life. Trickster is a figure whose physical appetites dominate his behavior; he has the mentality of an infant', but ends up 'beginning to take on the physical likeness of a grown man'. (Hercules, for example.)

Later comes

the concept of the 'shadow' . . . Jung has pointed out that the shadow cast by the conscious mind of the individual contains the hidden, repressed, and unfavorable (or nefarious) aspects of the personality. But this darkness is not just the simple converse of the conscious ego. Just as the ego contains unfavorable and destructive attitudes, so the shadow has good qualities – normal instincts and creative impulses. Ego and shadow, indeed, although separate, are inextricably linked . . . The ego, nevertheless, is in conflict with the shadow . . . In the struggle of primitive man to achieve consciousness, this conflict is expressed by the contest between the archetypal hero and the cosmic powers of evil, personified by dragons and other monsters . . . Usually, in mythology, the hero wins his battle against the monster . . . But there are other hero myths in which the hero gives in to the monster . . . For most people the dark or negative side of the personality remains unconscious. The hero, on the contrary, must draw strength from it. He must come to terms with its destructive powers . . . i.e., before the ego can triumph, it must master and assimilate the shadow.

Another Jungian, M.-L. von Franz, develops this theme:

Whether the shadow becomes our friend or enemy depends largely upon ourselves . . . the shadow is not necessarily always an opponent. In fact, he is exactly like any human being with whom one has to get along, sometimes by giving in, sometimes by resisting, sometimes by giving love – whatever the situation requires.[34]

It will readily be seen by those familiar with Bob Dylan's work that these themes are raised in the second verse of 'Jokerman', in the couplet

> *Shedding off one more layer of skin,*
> *Keeping one step ahead of the persecutor within:*

a couplet which, it will also be recognised, re-expresses a theme Dylan has given voice to before, perhaps most clearly in that long line from 1978's 'Where Are You Tonight? (Journey Through Dark Heat)' – a song with a strikingly pertinent subtitle, from our present standpoint – which even includes the same rhyme:

> *I fought with my twin, that enemy within, 'til both of us fell by the way.*

We tend to relate these sentiments very directly to Bob Dylan the artist's career-long struggle to not ossify, and/or we hear them as parts of his dispatches from the front in the eternal struggle between the good and the evil. We tend to accept the assumption, therefore, that to be locked in this combat, fighting or trying to outrun 'the enemy within', 'the persecutor within', is to be properly, even nobly, engaged. So we hear, in 'Jokerman',

34. M.-L. von Franz: 'The Process of Individuation', in Jung's *Man and His Symbols*.

> *Shedding off one more layer of skin,*
> *Keeping one step ahead of the persecutor within*

and we think 'Yeah! Right on, Bob!' (even if we think it a bit less vulgarly than that). Yet Dylan may not view it this way at all, and may not feel for a moment that his writing leans this way.[35]

In the earlier of the two songs, after all, the upshot of fighting against 'my twin' was that 'both of us fell'; and certainly in 'Jokerman' the context in which Dylan places the couplet is one of great self-criticism. It seems truer to Dylan's understanding of things that he should be including in his catalogue of self-mockery the spectacle of himself haplessly and to no avail

> *Shedding off one more layer of skin,*
> *Keeping one step ahead of the persecutor within:*

a futile task, when in truth you need to 'assimilate the shadow', draw strength from its 'instincts and creative impulses' rather than seek to vanquish or escape it.

This is further suggested by the *detail* in the context in which the 'Jokerman' couplet occurs. Dylan informs the sense that self-mockery is at play here by the very contradictions he invites us to notice about the lines: the comic impossibilities of the visual images he makes mischief with here.

After the 'snakes' of the previous verse, 'Shedding off one more layer of skin' must make us think of snakes again – yet snakes don't 'keep one step ahead' of anything: they don't 'step' at all. What's more, shedding off layers of skin is a working from the outside towards the inside: to do that is to move *towards* the persecutor-or-whatever 'within', not to keep moving away from it. There are, then, booby-traps inbuilt into these lines: they're set up so that you're bound to see the foolish impossibility of the struggle to which they pretend to give a sympathetic hearing. Fools rush in where angels fear to tread. Or step. It is only the most primitive kind of hero, the Heracles, who tries to vanquish all the dragons: only the Trickster-level hero, the Jokerman. By addressing himself as such, and by comparing himself with Hercules, Dylan is expressing his feeling that he hasn't yet travelled much beyond this towards a mature self-realisation.

But he knows he's got somewhere. We're struck, as these themes float around the song, by the similarity between this Jungian idea of 'the shadow' and the Judeao-Christian idea of 'original sin' (as between 'the dragon' and 'the snake').

The two ideas diverge, they're not synonymous, but in crucial ways, as they touch upon the very stuff that 'Jokerman' is made of, they too seem like 'twins'. The core of both is to define the human being as containing within both the light and the dark: insisting that 'evil' is not 'out there', among 'the others', but is inside us all, and that all progress, individual and societal, must be built upon coming to terms with this

---

35.   Indeed in his tirade against 'interpreters', in the middle of comments about 'You're A Big Girl Now' published as part of the "Biograph" sleeve notes, 1985 (a tirade cited in an earlier chapter), Dylan makes several remarks that may or may not be relevant here: 'Stupid and misleading jerks sometimes these interpreters are – I mean I'm always trying to stay one step ahead of myself and keep changing with the times, right? Like that's my foolish mission. How many roles can I play? . . . contrary to what some so-called experts believe, I don't constantly "re-invent" myself . . . There's nothing in any of my songs to ever imply that I'm even halfway searching for some lost gold at the end of any great mysterious rainbow.'

literally inescapable, fundamental truth. The other way lies war and bloodshed, Hitler and fatwah, hatred and racism across the globe and a stunting immaturity in the heart. 'Jokerman', like so much of Bob Dylan's pre- and post-evangelical work, is written in acute awareness that we cannot just kill the dragons, and, as with most of the post-evangelical songs, sobered by his knowledge that in the evangelical period he did sometimes give way unwisely to that enemy within in the instant that he preached.

In 'Jokerman' it's fascinating how Dylan accommodates both the Jungian notion and the Judeao-Christian one, by using the superhero figure not only to measure his own fallibility and immaturity but to look, too, at whether he feels that Christ himself might not be a risible figure in the superhero mould while being the son of God and saviour of the world – himself a figure of fundamental duality.

This is an exploration to the edges of Dylan's faith: a meditation, much as is the book of Ecclesiastes, involving a hard look at the downside of his ultimate superhero. ('Over and over again one hears a tale describing a hero's miraculous but humble birth, his early proof of superhuman strength, his rapid rise to prominence or power, his triumphant struggle with the forces of evil . . . and his fall through betrayal or a "heroic" sacrifice that ends in his death.')

This is the mood of the lines that begin the next verse, if you take them as addressed to Christ – as you surely must, albeit not exclusively or unambiguously:

> *You're a man of the mountains, you can walk on the clouds,*
> *Manipulator of crowds, you're a dream twister.*

This is a strikingly acerbic lightning portrait, and in terms that maintain overtly the song's questioning of the superheroic. It expresses very mixed feelings about this Lord. In the first line there's an acknowledgement of grandeur but a mistrustful resentment of such power – and there's no mere acceptance-in-humility about 'Manipulator' and 'twister'.

This remains undeveloped in the rest of the verse. The problematic middle lines don't fit with the rest as descriptive of Christ at all, attractive and spirited though they are:

> *You're going to Sodom and Gomorrah but what do you care?*
> *Ain't nobody there would want to marry your sister.*

I can find no scriptural rationale for Dylan's envigoratingly deviant surprise ending to these lines. It's a twister (on the positive side). It's partly fresh because it throws in upon the song a different kind of humour. After all the self-mockery, here is a joke that may make room for self-mockery but that certainly does something else too: it laughs at – and twists round – those clichéd fears of the Upright and Respectable that the Wrong Sort might Move In Next Door and, horror, Marry Your Sister. Or Daughter. (Dylan did this once before, in another lifetime: 'But if you think that I'll let Barry Goldwater / Move in next door and marry my daughter / You must think I'm crazy! / I wouldn't let him do it for all the farms in Cuba', he sang in 'I Shall Be Free No. 10', giving the same paranoias a different shake-up.)

The remainder of the verse, its final couplet, which is

> *Friend to the martyr, a friend to the woman of shame*
> *You look into the fiery furnace, see the rich man without any name,*

seems to return to Jesus as the figure addressed – while, as always, leaving room for a parallel self-mockery, for Dylan still to be addressing himself in ruefully critical terms.

Yet as lines addressed to Christ, though they seem to allude to his inconsistency, they no longer carry the earlier acerbity. The biblical allusions here point the contrast between Christ's compassion for 'the woman of shame' and his stern parable about 'a certain rich man'. Prominently, Christ befriends Mary Magdalene, who in Christian tradition is usually taken to have been a reformed prostitute, and out of whom he expels 'seven devils' (Mark 16:9 and Luke 8:2). She plays a crucial role at the time of his crucifixion and resurrection, 'ministering unto him' (Matthew 27:56) and then being, with 'the other Mary', the guardian of his tomb whom the angel visits to show them he has risen, and the first to recognise him afterwards. There is additional material for Dylan to be alluding to here. Christ, 'a friend of publicans and sinners' (Matthew 11:19), tells the chief priests and elders in the temple: 'Verily I say unto you, That the publicans and the harlots go into the kingdom of God before you. For John [the martyr] came unto you in the way of righteousness, and ye believed him not: but the publicans and the harlots believed him' (Matthew 21:31–32).

In contrast is the parable of the 'certain rich man' (never named) who is in hell, 'tormented in this flame', and who begs mercy of Abraham, in whose bosom he sees Lazarus, the beggar he had always ignored at his gate. He begs mercy in vain, Christ notes approvingly (Luke 16:19–31).

Nevertheless, as at the very beginning of the song, it is the two-edged opening line of this verse – 'You're a man of the mountains, you can walk on the clouds' – that appeals to our imagination and that stands out, silhouetted against large ideas deriving from the meanings inherent in the biblical texts it alludes to. That 'you can walk on the clouds' (a sequel, in the song, to his walking on the water) refers to Christ's ascension into heaven, which is described in Acts 1:9: '. . . while they beheld, he was taken up; then a cloud received him out of their sight'. Dylan inspiredly describes this moment of transcendence in terms that conjure the superheroic – and this is compelling because transcendence is indeed crucial in the myth of the hero (and, to put it in Jungian terms, for achieving our own mature self-realisation for which the hero myths serve us as guides).[36]

So too the neat phrase 'man of the mountains' covers the several ways in which mountains matter in the story of Jesus. First, he is taken up into the mountains when

---

36. Joseph L. Henderson again, in Jung, *Man and His Symbols*:

 a sense of completeness is achieved through a union of the consciousness with the unconscious contents of the mind. Out of this union arises what Jung called 'the transcendent function of the psyche', by which a man can achieve his highest goal: the full realization of the potential of his individual Self.
  Thus, what we call 'symbols of transcendence' are the symbols that represent man's striving to attain this goal. They provide the means by which the contents of the unconsciousness can enter the conscious mind, and they also are themselves an active expression of those contents.
  . . . At the most archaic level of this symbolism we again meet the Trickster theme. But this time he no longer appears as a lawless would-be hero. He has become the shaman . . . whose magical practices and flights of intuition stamp him as a primitive master of initiation. His power resides in his supposed ability to leave his body and fly about the universe as a bird.

Bird fly high by the light of the moon . . .

he is tempted by Satan, who offers him all he surveys but fails to buy him off (Dylan uses this as the backdrop behind those lines from the 1978 'Is Your Love In Vain?': 'Well I've been to the mountain and I've been in the wind, / . . . I have dined with kings, I've been offered wings / And I've never been too impressed'). Second, just as God's law comes down from the mountain, via Moses, in the Old Testament, so Christ's equivalent is the Sermon on the Mount. And third, crucially, Christ repeatedly invokes the possibility of power over mountains to talk about the power of faith. As Matthew (21:21) reports it, Christ says: 'Verily I say unto you, If ye have faith, and doubt not . . . if ye shall say unto this mountain, Be thou removed, and be thou cast into the sea; it shall be done'. This is taken up and retailed later by Paul. His well-known address in 1 Corinthians, Chapter 13, to which we've many times referred, begins as follows:

> Though I speak with the tongues of men and of angels, and have not charity, I am become as sounding brass or a tinkling cymbal. And though I have the gift of prophecy, and understand all mysteries, and all knowledge, and *though I have all faith, so that I could remove mountains*, and have not charity, I am nothing. (1 Corinthians 13:1–2; my emphasis)

Paul is stressing that faith without love ('charity') is not sufficient, but in 'Jokerman' Dylan recognises a different internal biblical dialogue going on through the New Testament, and alludes to it, so suggesting for the second time a bumping-together of ideas that has Christ's insistence on faith's primacy in one corner and something else set against it. At the beginning of the song Christ's ardour for faith is bumped up against the sympathy for doubt allowed in Ecclesiastes. Now, Christ's insistence on the primacy of faith is in one corner, and the claims of God's *law* are in the other. For while verse three begins with

> *You're a man of the mountains . . .*

verse four begins with

> *Well, the Book of Leviticus and Deuteronomy,*
> *The law of the jungle and the sea are your only teachers:*

and the core of Leviticus and Deuteronomy is that they lay down the Hebrew *law*. The first catalogues the regulations for worship and all religious ceremonies, including the laws about offerings and sacrifices, ritual cleanliness and holiness in daily life and in worship; the second, a series of addresses by Moses, reviews the Ten Commandments and the laws that must govern Israel's life in the promised land: tithes, worship, ritual, civil justice, conduct in war, inheritance, sex, divorce and remarriage and more. The very word 'deuteronomy' means 'repeated law'.

Actually, Dylan achieves two things here, acknowledges two debates. Clearly the man-made, ordered specifications of law taught by 'the Book of Leviticus and Deuteronomy' are fundamental opposites to what you might learn from 'the law of the jungle and the sea': the 'strict codifications of moral order, on the one hand, and the amoral pulsions of nature, on the other', as Aidan Day puts it.[37] At the same time

37. Aidan Day, *Jokerman: Reading the Lyrics of Bob Dylan* (1988).

Dylan is acknowledging that, as if the difficulties of faith weren't enough, faith versus law is one of the great biblical debates.

It is the main thrust of the Epistle of Paul the Apostle to the Galatians, in which he insists that 'a man is not justified by the works of the law, but by the faith of Jesus Christ . . . for if righteousness come by the law, then Christ is dead in vain' (Galatians 2:16, 21). The primacy of faith is also the main thrust of Hebrews, Chapter 11, which begins: 'Now faith is the substance of things hoped for, the evidence of things not seen' (11:1) and goes on to begin almost every verse with the incantatory 'Through faith . . .', 'By faith . . .', 'But without faith . . .' as it recaps the whole Old Testament story: 'By faith Abel . . .', 'By faith Noah . . .' 'By faith Abraham . . .', 'Through faith also Sara . . .', 'By faith Isaac . . .', 'By faith Jacob . . .', 'By faith Moses . . .', and so on, until Paul can find himself 'Looking unto Jesus the author and finisher of our faith'. (Hebrews 11:3, 4, 5, 6, 7, 8, 11, 20, 21, 22, 23 and 12:2).

This debate goes on and on through the pages of the New Testament. James argues that 'Even so faith, if it hath not works, is dead, being alone' (James 2:17) and repeats for emphasis: 'But wilt thou know, O vain man, that faith without works is dead?' (2:20); but in Ephesians (2:8–9) comes the counter-argument from Paul: 'For by grace are ye saved through faith; and that not of yourselves: it is the gift of God: Not of works, lest any man should boast'. Dylan draws on this passage when, in his evangelical period, he joins in this debate explicitly in the title song of the album "Saved":

> *But by His mercy I've been spared.*
> *Not by works,*
> *But by faith in Him who called.*

(Incidentally it is from the same chapter of Ephesians that Dylan takes verbatim, for use in the "Shot Of Love" song 'Dead Man, Dead Man', the phrase 'prince of the power of the air': this is from Ephesians 2:2. The 'fiery darts' of the "Saved" album's 'What Can I Do For You?' are from Ephesians 6:16.)

In short, the point is that in 'Jokerman' when Dylan begins one verse with 'the man of the mountains' and the next with 'the Book of Leviticus and Deuteronomy / the law of the jungle and the sea' he is acknowledging both sides of the debate about faith versus law and a Christ who moves between the two. Except that it's more complicated than that, because so far the telling characteristics of 'the Book of Leviticus and Deuteronomy' have been over-simplified. Yes, they are the law books and they function by cataloguing and stressing the law – but they are also famously the sources for commandments which entreat us not to strict, cold or pernickety observance but to love and to compassion.

In other words these books of Old Testament Jehovah's Law contain within them the commandments which inspired Christ's later formulation of more loving rival commandments of his own. Deuteronomy is the source for what Christ calls the greatest of all commandments: 'And thou shalt love thy God with all thine heart, and with all thy soul, and with all thy might' (6:4), which is clearly as much a matter of faith as of law and which must echo ironically for listeners to the Bob Dylan of 'Jokerman', a song intent upon articulating the ultimate impossibility of such whole-heartedness and single-mindedness. Leviticus is the source for what Christ felt was the second greatest commandment: 'Thou shalt love thy neighbour as thyself' (19:18), and Deuteronomy (10:19) adds the corollary 'Love ye therefore the stranger: for ye were strangers in the land of Egypt'.[38] These commandments to love the stranger and thy neighbour as thyself, of course, are still in adamant opposition to 'the law of the jungle', but in a rather different opposition from that delineated earlier.

Christ, then, stands on all sides of the debate about faith versus law and on both sides of the law. As Nick de Somogyi puts it, in his always interesting and only occasionally impenetrable essay 'Jokermen and Thieves: Bob Dylan and the Ballad Tradition', the Jesus of 'Jokerman' is one who 'straddles both natural and theological planes, being both outlaw and lawmaker'. The song 'strongly identifies Christ with John Wesley Harding-type outlaws, and once again questions the possibility of viewing the complexities of faith in such terms'.[39]

De Somogyi takes the 'Jokerman' to be Christ almost exclusively and argues that Dylan uses the tarot pack as the basis for the name: 'The unnumbered Tarot card, the Fool . . . is the ancestor of the joker in latterday cards . . . As in 'All Along The Watchtower', the symbol of the "joker" can stand for Christ, deriving as it does from the Tarot fool.' He quotes a guidebook to the tarot as saying that the figure of the tarot fool derives originally from representations of Dionysus (in Greek mythology the god of wine and orgiastic excess) and that 'Like his successor Jesus, Dionysus was also an overturner of hidebound traditions and restrictive tyranny. He was the incarnate power of spiritual revolt and rebirth.'[40]

There's no denying Dylan's interest in the tarot: he parades it on the album-sleeve of "Desire". Robert Shelton notes that 'The Empress tarot card on the album jacket and two other cards displayed in the song folio, the Magician and Judgment, are from the so-called Rider pack of 1910, traditional emblems redesigned by A. E. Waite and drawn by Pamela Colman Smith.' Shelton adds that this Magician 'bears an uncanny resemblance to Dylan. The Magician card has also been called the Minstrel, the Conjuror, or the Cobbler. It once represented the travelling showman, a medicine man who told fortunes, sold quack remedies, and spread heretical ideas.'[41] Such a persona seems, in Dylan's work, interchangeable with the figure Nigel Brooks calls 'Dylan . . . addressing himself as artist in the guise of the jokerman, the trickster figure, the Fool.' This is the peddler/fiddler figure in 'Visions Of Johanna', the 'Minstrel Boy' of the Isle of Wight. As he sings in 'Memphis Blues Again'

> Well, Shakespeare he's in the alley
> With his pointed shoes and his bells . . .

Richard Wissolik and Scott McGrath, noting that the tarot pack is made up of twenty-two numbered major 'enigmas', the unnumbered fool (the joker) and fifty-six

---

38. Deuteronomy is also the source of a sound bite often assumed to originate with Christ: 'Man doth not live by bread alone, but by every word that proceedeth out of the mouth of the Lord doth man live' (8:3).

39. Nick de Somogyi: 'Jokermen and Thieves: Bob Dylan and the Ballad Tradition', *Wanted Man Study Series*, no. 5, 1986.

40. Paul Huson, *The Devil's Picturebook: The Complete Guide to Tarot Cards* (1972), quoted in *ibid*.

41. Robert Shelton, *No Direction Home*. A quotation from A. E. Waite's book *The Pictorial Key to the Tarot* (1971), is used apropos of 'Jokerman' in Aidan Day, 'Bob Dylan: Escaping on the Run', *Wanted Man Study Series*, no. 3 1984, referred to in note 44.

minor images, find an ingenious further root in the tarot, namely that 'the 22 major enigmas correspond to the letters of the Hebrew alphabet'. They also note – pertinently to our interest in 'Jokerman', in which dualism is so central – that 'Divided, 1–11, 12–22, the pack represents the binary of light/dark, active/passive, logical/intuitive . . .'[42]

The tarot further justifies its place in 'Jokerman' by the way that it appears to fit with the ideas of Jung and of the function of the hero myth that we have already found at the heart of the song. According to Wissolik and McGrath, 'The nature of the Tarot Pack . . . [is that] it parallels human struggle against self and others, and retells the story of the individual's path to *individuation* [Jung's term for the journey toward the higher Self].'[43]

Nick de Somogyi adds, apropos of the equating of Dionysus and Christ, that an earlier, unreleased version of 'Jokerman' includes the lines

> *So drunk, standing in the middle of the street*
> *Directing traffic, with a small dog at your feet*

and that a 'glance at the traditional design for the Tarot fool makes clear Dylan's image, modernised . . . perhaps a little blatantly, but still within the no-nonsense convention of religious balladry: a jealous Joseph [featured in the ballad 'The Cherry-Tree Carol'], a drunk Christ [in 'Jokerman']'.[44]

That the jokerman is the tarot fool, of course, puts a punning extra layer into the line 'Fools rush in where angels fear to tread', another commonplace reclaimed.

De Somogyi moves on to look at how all this relates to the song's chorus:

> In modern packs of cards the joker stands for anything, or (in our context) Everyman. 'Jokerman' is thus a richly ambivalent figure. The movement between earthly and transcendent symbolism is treated in the upward aspiration of the refrain, from earthbound dancer, to singing bird, itself singing by the light of an even higher moon – a process checked by the return to the central ambivalence and the ambiguity of the simple 'oh' . . . Part earthbound, and part God, the jokerman actualises the paradox of the Christian faith, the incarnation. The invocation can correspondingly be seen as either adoration or disappointment, of submission or accusation, and the song as a whole one of celebration or despair.

42. Wissolik and McGrath, *Bob Dylan's Words*.

43. *Ibid*.

44. 'The Cherry-Tree Carol' is Ballad no. 22 in F. J. Child's *The English and Scottish Popular Ballads*. As it happens it is also reproduced in Homer Hogan's *Poetry of Relevance 1* and features on Joan Baez's LP "Joan Baez: Volume 2", Vanguard Records VSD 2097, New York, 1961. (Note: de Somogyi mishears 'So drunk' as 'Stone drunk'; my quotation of his text incorporating the song lines corrects this.)

Aidan Day has also pointed out that the term 'Jokerman' may be based upon the tarot fool, 'whose number is nothing and who is represented as accompanied by a small dog' (Aidan Day, 'Escaping on the Run', 1984, see note 41): in fact, Day's observation to this effect pre-dates de Somogyi's. In contrast to de Somogyi, Day assumes that the Jokerman of the song's title refers predominantly to Dylan, not Christ. However, by the time of Day's book (*Jokerman: Reading the Lyrics of Bob Dylan*), (a) he has come to renounce the pre-post-structuralist position of his earlier essay and (b) he discusses 'the Christological stature' of the 'Jokerman'.

As with the title 'Jokerman', which it was noted is reminiscent of 'Joker Man Blues', there is also a blues world precedent for the clown/artist with the dog at his feet. The singer–guitarist Clifford Gibson (1901–1963) had a dog who performed tricks while Gibson played the blues. It was said that in his hometown of Louisville, Kentucky, the dog was the better remembered.

As I hope what I've already written suggests, I don't believe the song can be taken as an either/or. The whole point of the song seems to me rather to enact the need to grapple with the many-sided: to express in poetry rather than argument the uncomfortable truth that there *can* be no choosing anything as straightforward as one position or the other. There is no one or the other.

The song is fundamentally an expression of both celebration *and* something more negative: not, I think, despair but a rigorous scepticism. And as we've seen from the opening verses, the title 'Jokerman' refers not exclusively to this ambiguous Christ, towards whom Dylan feels a troubling ambivalence, but also, expressing his more habitual, inwardly directed ambivalence, to Dylan himself.[45]

We can hear many of the lines of the song's third and fourth verses with this more personal reverberation. Verse three begins with Dylan not only 'characterising himself as a joker, a minstrel entertainer', in de Somogyi's phrase – as a 'song and dance man' indeed – but deprecating more harshly, it seems to me, the superstar, rock hero figure that is his public self:

> *You're a man of the mountains, you can walk on the clouds,*
> *Manipulator of crowds, you're a dream-twister.*

He goes on to deplore his own capacity, especially in this role, for the sins of the flesh (or Dionysan 'orgiastic excess'):

> *You're going to Sodom and Gomorrah, but what do you care?*
> *Ain't nobody there would want to marry your sister*

and ends with a rock star's glimpse into the mirror of the dread-filled future:

> *You look into the fiery furnace, see the rich man without any name.*

Verse four begins by reflecting upon the contradictions in what the singer espouses, and there's an implicit deploring here of his tendency to extremes:

> *Well, the Book of Leviticus and Deuteronomy,*
> *The law of the jungle and the sea are your only teachers;*

but then comes a lovely passage in which Dylan good-humouredly uses the language we associate with yet another sort of dodgy hero, the outlaw hero of the traditional ballad (de Somogyi says the outlaw heroes of the ballads are depicted on milk-white steeds 'as a matter of course'), yet rushes on at once to up the superheroic stakes, switching from the milieu of popular oral culture to the milieu of Renaissance Art

---

45. *Fowler's Modern English Usage* (more properly H. W. Fowler's *A Dictionary of Modern English Usage*, 2nd edn, rev. by Gowers, 1965) has good, sharp comments on the use of the words 'ambivalent' and 'ambivalence', which has been rather frequent in recent paragraphs of my own as well as in Nick de Somogyi's texts:

> These terms were invented by psychoanalysts . . . to mean the coexistence in one person of opposing emotional attitudes towards the same object, or the simultaneous operation in the mind of two irreconcilable wishes. The words are new, but not the condition they describe: Catullus when he wrote 'odi et amo' . . . [was] suffering from ambivalence. The discovery of so imposing a word for so common a condition quickly led to its becoming a Popularized Technicality, with the usual consequence that it now has to do a great deal of work, of which some at least would be better done by other words . . . It will be a pity if the homely expression 'mixed feelings', which served us well and long, is wholly displaced by this usurper.

high culture, and presenting himself in grandiose terms via both, in the first line as ballad hero and in the second as sculpted 'rock hero':

> *In the smoke of the twilight on a milk-white steed*
> *Michelangelo indeed could've carved out your features.*

There is an extra playful resonance from Dylan's keeping up his self-mocking parallel with Christ here, since we know that Michelangelo – whose genius as a sculptor and painter towered over the High Renaissance, setting new standards in 'carving out the features' of the human body – focused mostly on subject-matter from the Bible: the Old Testament story on the Sistine Chapel ceiling, a huge Last Judgement on the altar wall, the twice-lifesize marble David, a huge Moses, and so on.

At the same time, there is a whiff of agreeable counterbalance to all the self-deprecation here. Bob Dylan's has always been a face of eminently carvable features, and he knows it. The listener who is intimate with Dylan's work will be struck by the parallel with that line from 'Angelina', in which a character has 'a face that any painter would paint'. Such a listener is also likely to recollect that when, in *Hard Rain*, the camera honed in commendably close on Dylan's face, it captured those features at once at their most carvable and at their most extraordinarily Christ-like. In any case, Dylan can feel positive that Michelangelo indeed could've carved out his features, and positive feeling helps keep the song warm and likeable and on the human side of sour.

Actually, both lines effect a similar sort of back-straightening affirmation. It may be that the singer mocks his grandiose pretensions with a smile that takes in the ballad cliché of the milk-white steed, framed as Hollywood might, or as in one of those old Samurai films that Hollywood has copied: the man on the big white horse appearing through a moody mist (just as those distant ships appeared through one at the song's beginning). It may be too that the Michelangelo connection is a boast or a vanity large enough to smile at. But the truth is that both lines also exercise a direct appeal to our imaginations. In both senses Dylan has had the face to engage Michelangelo's attention, while the milk-white steed has become a balladic cliché because it's such a powerfully evocative phrase. Nor, actually, is its use within those ballads so codified that it must always specify its rider to be the outlaw–hero, as Nick de Somogyi suggests. The rider can as well be unambiguous hero or villain, outlaw or landowner. In 'The Lass From The Low Country', which *Sing Out!* called 'one of the saddest and most beautiful of the old English ballads', the rider is a heartless 'Lord of high degree' but he still rides a milk-white steed:

> *One day when snow was on the mead*
> *He passed her by on a milk-white steed*
> *She spoke to him low but he paid no heed*

> *Oh sorrow, sing sorrow*
> *Now she sleeps in the valley where the wild flowers nod*

> *And no-one knows she loved him*
> *But herself and God.*

Similarly, in traditional versions of 'Gypsy Davey' – a song almost as old as Michelangelo's creations – it is the husband, not the gypsy, who says 'Go saddle up my milk-white steed'.[46]

What's more, in 'Jokerman' Dylan uses this 'cliché' to make such a robustly beautiful line of poetry, attention to the detail of which repays what little effort it demands – which isn't a lot, since part of its virtue is its appeal to the ear, on paper or on record. Indeed the whole fourth verse is a fine piece of writing, with some affinity for sculpture itself. It is full of variety, variety of word-sounds and rhythms and of imagery; it has a ceaselessly resourceful eloquence and energy; and it combines plain human warmth with great technical dexterity:

> *Well, the Book of Leviticus and Deuteronomy*
> *The law of the jungle and the sea are your only teachers.*
> *In the smoke of the twilight on a milk-white steed*
> *Michelangelo indeed could've carved out your features.*
> *Resting in the fields, far from the turbulent space,*
> *Half-asleep 'neath the stars with a small dog licking your face.*

There is one grammatical dent in this technical dexterity. Dylan gets his clauses jumbled so that he manages, but doesn't intend, to put Michelangelo on the milk-white steed. (It would surely have challenged even that maestro's genius if he had had to sculpt on horseback, especially in such bad light.) We unjumble as we listen, though: we know he means '*As you stand* in the smoke of the twilight on a milk-white steed', etc. and we indulge him willingly. Indeed the momentary comedy his mismatch creates adds to the verse's good humour and humanity. Errors aren't always endearing, but this one works that way.

This kink aside, it is all coach-built exquisitely. It is the best verse since the first in exploiting the flexible pleasures of the rhyme scheme and of the sense of movement that scheme encourages. In the first line, 'Leviticus' and 'Deuteronomy' is a simple pairing of biblical titles but a daring and successful pairing of *words*: a pairing because they're equally under-familiar and long, offering pleasurable passing challenges to the singer or the reader, yet they yield strongly contrasting noises, the Latinate nimble grittiness of the first yielding to the Gallic sonorous flow of the second. In turn these lengthy, eccentric words yield to the simple, familiar phrase 'the law of the jungle', from which flows the equally simple 'and the sea'. The whole movement to this point has been to take us to this sea, from the hissing foam of 'Leviticus', across the rocks of 'Deuteronomy', into the momentary upward pause of 'The law' and then tumbling through 'the jungle' and on to the swell of 'the sea'.

The control here delights. Again there's a matching and a contrasting of sounds and rhythms as much as of ideas going on along these lines: between 'the Book of

---

46. The quotations from and concerning 'The Lass From The Low Country', a title modernised by Dylan into 'Sad-Eyed Lady Of The Lowlands', are taken from *Sing Out!* Reprints, vol. 6, no. 3, Summer 1956. The line from a traditional version of 'Gypsy Davey', plus the dating of the song to 'about 1620', is taken from 'Michael Cooney And Sam Hinton Talk "Gypsy Davey"', transcribed in *For What Time I Am in This World*, ed. Bill Usher (1977). (In the same transcribed conversation, cf. de Somogyi saying that the milk-white steed line in 'Jokerman' 'strongly identifies Christ with John Wesley Harding-type outlaws', Hinton remarks, apropos of Woody Guthrie's version of 'Gypsy Davey' having 'truly Americanized' the song: 'You never hear American cowboys talking about milk-white steeds.') There is a more detailed scrutiny of versions of this song in Chapter 17.

Leviticus' and 'the law of the jungle', and between what's added on to each: 'and Deuteronomy', as against the three monosyllables of 'and the sea', its rhyming partner. Inside this, unobtrusively, lurks an even, 3-syllable match-up of rhyme itself between '-onomy' and 'an' the sea'. The second line ends by backing up this switch to the short and simple. You might wonder, at first hearing, what could possibly resolve, in any way which would make sense, a sentence which lashes together such disparate elements. It's like a competition tie-breaker – complete this sentence in not more than six syllables: 'Well, the Book of Leviticus and Deuteronomy, the law of the jungle and the sea are . . .'

The winning answer not merely makes sense but comes as blessedly, calmingly simple: '. . . your only teachers'. The word 'your' fits in at once, making an internal rhyme for 'law' and repeating the pause this sound lends to the line's rhythm, while the word 'only' even manages a subliminal whisper of reassuring simplicity as it passes by the ear. After the prominent multisyllabics of the first line, the whole of the long second line has only three words of more than one syllable and none exceeding two.

Dylan's controlling touch in the more compact third line is to keep to short words but change their nature altogether. Matching the complete switch of visual image and keeping the song vibrant, here the sound and character of the language is transformed. In place of the water-smoothed pebbles of line two, which sounds all burbling glugs and soft consonants, now we have chiselled, cutting 'k's, pressing 'm's, hissing 's's and a demanding series of internal rhymes and half-rhymes, forming words which are moody yet insistently precise – and which Dylan rescues from the edge of empurpled olde worlde-ness by the rigour with which he rubs them together.

This can be seen at work in detailed ways. Part of the appeal of 'twilight' is the way it rhymes within itself; its prettiness and, more dangerously, its aura of belonging to sentimental poesy, are held in check by its being rubbed up so interestingly against the half-rhyme 'milk-white' – an abrasion the more effective for both parties having olde worlde credentials. (Rubbing 'twilight' up against something of conspicuous modernity – say, 'megabyte' – would not neutralise the archaism; rather it would confirm it by stressing that the temporal factor imprisons both words.) Another purposive and pleasing half-rhyme is that between 'smoke . . . light' and 'milk-white', the near-echo of 'smoke' and 'milk' making taut and precise demands on the delivering voice, as does the whole phrase 'milk-white steed', which rewards with such savourable rhythmic pleasures.

Once 'steed' has enacted that head-held-high reining in, we're straight on into 'Michelangelo indeed'. 'Michelangelo' satisfies because here, after all these short words, is a name to match exactly, in syllable-count and tumbling, soft delivery, the prominent lengthiness of the earlier 'Deuteronomy', while 'indeed', so quick on the heels of 'steed', and after all the half-rhymes, begins to bring in the harvest of the verse's *full* internal rhymes, planted earlier:

> *Well, the Book of Leviticus and Deuteronomy*
> *The law of the jungle and the sea are your only teachers.*
> *In the smoke of the twilight on a milk-white steed*
> *Michelangelo indeed could've carved out your features.*

As before, the effect of the couplet at the end of each verse is to reaffirm this sense that a more reliable chiming of full rhymes is now in order, to steady things down before heading into the chorus. In this case, we get

> Resting in the fields, far from the turbulent space,
> Half-asleep 'neath the stars with a small dog licking your face.

This is a well-built 'steadying things down', too, since the words that provide the rhyme also describe the process: moving from the hugeness of 'space' down to the smallness of 'a small dog' and a 'face'. And rather as 'only' had the extra effect of suggesting simplicity when that was needed (because another meaning of only, i.e. 'nothing more to it than', bubbled under the express meaning 'sole'), so now the word 'Resting' lends its own steadying influence at just the point in the verse's structure when steadying is what's required. In fact the whole couplet contributes here, giving generously of the calm of its storyline so that this supports the song's structure as well as carrying its narrative. It does take us far from the turbulence. (This doesn't make it a self-reflexive text but a fine matching of form and content.) Within the narrative itself, what's more, to be 'half-asleep 'neath the stars' positions the Jokerman ideally for receiving the blessings of the chorus, the birdsong and flight, the moon and the muse.

Fittingly, there is in this passage something reminiscent of familiar parts of Keats' marvellous 'Ode': something more in the pastoral mood of it than in the lines themselves. Dylan's brief couplet captures something of this:

> I cannot see what flowers are at my feet
> Nor what soft incense hangs upon the boughs . . .

> Darkling I listen; and for many a time
> I have been half in love with easeful Death,
> Call'd him soft names in many a mused rhyme,
> To take into the air my quiet breath . . .

> Was it a vision, or a waking dream?
> Fled is that music:- Do I wake or sleep?

Dylan's 'Resting' might also be said to continue the list, formed gradually by the song, which begins with 'Standing' and then adds rushing, treading and stepping. The next verse, verse five, extends this list, beginning with 'stalking' and ending with the variant 'steppin' in'.

It forms another list too, though it turns out to be more the creating of a diversion than of a list. Quite unexpectedly, the fifth verse sounds as if it is proposing two new archetypes alongside 'Jokerman', who has been alone in his quirkily stylised name up till this point. 'The rifleman' creeps in, normalised by his definite article and his lack of a capital letter, but is soon found to be in direct competition with, and so offered as a direct parallel to, the more distinctive 'Preacherman'. Suddenly we meet Preacherman as well as Jokerman, and by implication Rifleman too.

It wouldn't be inappropriate, either, to come upon such muddied archetypes as these in a song named after an archetype and which takes us through a remapping of such John Bunyanesque terrain. That classic allegory *The Pilgrim's Progress*, subtitled

From This World to That Which Is to Come, famously uses unambiguous archetypes as its characters and places: the hero Christian (yes, another hero story that measures spiritual progress) has the companions Faithful and Hopeful, journeys through the Slough of Despond, meets Giant Despair, and so on. He also meets those who seem friendly but offer false advice, like Mr. Worldly Wise-man. Bunyan followed up the first volume of *The Pilgrim's Progress* with *The Life and Death of Mr. Badman*.[47]

In 'Jokerman', however, the parallels sound much more a matter of Dylan's opportunistically finding momentarily pleasing aural equivalents than of his advancing solid equivalent archetypes. We soon feel, rather, that 'Preacherman' is merely shorthand for your ordinary preacher in your typical American scene. He's prowling around out there just like your average psycho rifleman. (Bunyan's Mr. Badman has moved to America and become your ordinary badman too: in Britain he's the two-word 'bad man'; in the US, the single word 'badman' is common.) Despite the superficial parallel, then, we end up feeling that 'Jokerman' remains a singular nomenclative in Dylan's song: the only one styled more along the lines of Everyman than of 'the mailman', 'the binmen' or Jones The Fish.

All the same, while we're paying attention to the song's fifth verse – which is so different in character from the one before it, yet its equal as a concentrated, shining piece of writing – we register that the vivid term 'Preacherman' happily modernises, and/or Wild-Westernises, the title of the man whose voice dominates Ecclesiastes – The Preacher. And we register too that 'Preacherman' might work alongside 'Joker-man' as another name for Jesus, another name Dylan uses to express ambivalence about him. He may be the supreme Preacherman, the one who 'heals the blind and crippled' in 'In The Garden' and who is 'Friend to the martyr, a friend to the woman of shame' here, but now Dylan is looking askance at this relationship between the miracle-worker and the worked-upon. The effect of that brilliantly deployed phrase 'seeks the same' in these lines,

> Well, the rifleman's stalking the sick and the lame
> Preacherman seeks the same, who'll get there first is uncertain,

is to stop us seeing these two characters as simple opposites, one bad and one good, and to stop us assuming that they have healthily differentiated intentions toward the vulnerable. The rifleman is stalking victims, but 'Preacherman seeks the same' lets loose the thought that he too is preying on the sick and the lame, closing in on them for his own ends.

The intimations of menace erupt at once after these lines into the effulgent, cacophonous detail of firepower that paranoid America deploys:

> Nightsticks and water cannons, tear gas, padlocks,
> Molotov cocktails and rocks behind every curtain.

This splendid fusillade, with its internal full rhymes and half-rhymes, especially of 'sticks' and 'locks' and the whole spread of 'padlocks, / Molotov cocktails and rocks',

---

47. John Bunyan, *The Pilgrim's Progress: From This World to That Which Is to Come* (Part I, 1678, Part II, 1684); *The Life and Death of Mr. Badman* (1680).

is positively Miltonic. Its insistent listing may remind us of that moment in 'Caribbean Wind' when Dylan sings of

> *. . . armies on the march and time that is short*
> *And famines and earthquakes and train wrecks and the tearin' down of the wall*

(in which again there's the effective abrasion of an unemphasised half-rhyme, between 'earth*quakes*' and 'train *wrecks*'); but the more terse and plentiful catalogue hurled out – truly words as weapons – by

> *Nightsticks and water cannons, tear gas, padlocks,*
> *Molotov cocktails and rocks . . .*

has rather the crunching energy and belabouring detail, the remorseless assault, of Milton's great line from *Paradise Lost* Book II (line 621):

> *Rocks, caves, lakes, fens, bogs, dens and shades of death.*

The melodic pliability of 'Jokerman' proves glorious here. The lines that begin with 'Nightsticks' and run through to 'behind every curtain' are the third and fourth lines of the verse; they hold the same position as

> *Distant ships sailing in through the mist*
> *You were born with a snake in both of your fists while a hurricane was blowing*

and

> *Fools rush in where angels fear to tread*
> *Both of their futures so full of dread, you don't show one*

yet the melody Dylan uses to fire off verse five's armoury is quite different, and the rhythmic insistence of its repeated 2-note motif (*up*-down, *up*-down, *up*-down, *up*-down) perfectly suits the battering evoked by the words. This is fully on-form Bob Dylan, words inseparable from music and performance in work of great creative concentration, flexibility and imaginative precision.

Only as the verse ends do we come upon what might be a rare moment of inventive tiredness, as we hear of those 'false-hearted judges'. The listener is likely to feel that corrupt judges are stock characters, targets too frequent and too easy in Bob Dylan's corpus, unless they can be brought individually alive by narrative detail (as in 'Percy's Song', 'The Lonesome Death Of Hattie Carroll' and 'Seven Curses') or by comic absurdity ('The judge he holds a grudge / He's gonna call on you / But he's badly-built / And he walks on stilts: / Watch out he don't fall on you' in 'Most Likely You Go Your Way (And I'll Go Mine)'). They are more problematic here:

> *False-hearted judges dying in the webs that they spin,*

because though the listener is almost beguiled by the superficially attractive image of the judges as spiders, it isn't an image that holds up. You can't help objecting that if they're the spinners of the webs, why are they dying in them?: that's the fly's job, not the spider's. It's also a mistake to give them hearts, of whatever moral fibre, and then make them spiders. It may be anatomically true (or rather, half-true) but it doesn't ring poetically true here. Despite the lovely downward arc described by Dylan's delivery of that word 'dying', these judges start out altogether too big and red and meaty to be squeezed down into spiders – besides which, since the spider is tradition-ally a figure of duplicity in literature, the label 'false-hearted' is redundant as well as clumsy.

The song, though, hurries on past, giving them only a glance, not getting tangled up in them, and we are carried along to what Christopher Ricks calls 'one of the loveliest lines on "Infidels" ',[48]

> *Only a matter of time 'til night comes stepping in.*

Dylan finds here yet another pinfold: another way of using the words that precede the chorus to enact a readying for that chorus – in this case the words that close the verse evoke an act of closure. So naturally does this quietly emphatic line announce itself, a line so apparently simple and so loaded, that on first hearing you're almost certain to expect that this is to be one of Dylan's 'final end's: it sounds so apt as the last line of a last verse.

The finishing end proves not quite at hand. Not only does 'Jokerman' move on through another chorus and on into what really is the song's last verse, its sixth, but Dylan begins this with a line that manages to make that previous 'last line of a last verse' seem no finished thing at all: he makes it seem instead to have been only the first half of a rumination about omens in the sky, the second half of which now comes through to us:

> *It's a shadowy world, skies are slippery gray.*

The rest of this verse re-inhabits the song's biblical milieu, in a sequence that seems to offer more intimations of 'the end-days', as a new-born prince is dressed in scarlet and a future of corrupt and murderous deeds is predicted for him. This too is 'shadowy': is it worse to 'Take the motherless children off the street / And place them at the feet of a harlot' than to leave them motherless and homeless? But the compelling parts of the verse lie either side of this biblical allegory, beginning with that tremendous

> *It's a shadowy world, skies are slippery gray.*

It's admirable because Dylan isn't afraid here to open with the most basic of generalisations, one that summarises with the utmost simplicity the song's core argument and indeed what might be allowed as the core conclusion of human experience, the core truth about human nature, its inherent goodness and badness, the core truth as expressed in the Bible (sin and potential transcendence) and by psycho-analysis (the shadow and the transcendent self) and at the same time expressive of the modern sensibility, the Dylanesque insistence that unfixity is everywhere, that 'there are no truths outside the gates of Eden'.

Context is all, though. If we encountered 'Eh up, it's a shadowy world' in a song by the Housemartins, or 'It a shadowy world, mon' in a rap from Benjamin Zephaniah, we wouldn't seize on it as a numinous summary of the human predica-

---

48.   Christopher Ricks, 'Clichés that come to pass', in Michael Gray and John Bauldie, *All Across the Telegraph*.

ment. That it can register in this way in 'Jokerman' is because of what has gone before and what comes after.

The 'before' is five verses of a sustained work exploring these themes in poetry of focused imagination. The 'after' is the remainder of the line itself – and this gives us a phrase as quietly distinctive as the earlier one is quietly anonymous: 'skies are slippery gray'. That 'slippery' is itself slippery, almost by onomatopoeic enactment: the perfect word to fix the particular look of a certain sort of grey sky and to summarise the imperfect, ungraspable unfixity we live under.

At the end, this last verse prefigures the chorus – more precisely, the *end* of the verse prefigures the *end* of the chorus – in reiterating that rueful self-addressed remonstrance

> *Oh Jokerman . . .*
> *Oh Jokerman . . .*

and these lines end with something close to an explicit lamenting that the singer, most certainly the Jokerman of the title now, knows that wholehearted commitment to godliness is what Christ requires of each of us (is *all* Christ requires of each of us) yet cannot let go and give it. Rather he must respond in keeping with his troublesome vision of all-prevalent unfixity – in which even Christ is perceived ambiguously.

> *Oh Jokerman, you know what He wants.*
> *Oh Jokerman, you don't show any response.*

That is, he must respond with what seems no response at all, though the use of the word 'show' there, as of 'seek' earlier on, itself refuses any such neat simplicity. The whole weight of the song, as well as the remonstrative 'Oh Jokerman' in the line itself, presses us to feel here that while Jokerman doesn't 'show' any response, the turmoil within is strong and inescapable.

The importation of part of the *chorus*, that

> *Oh Jokerman . . .*
> *Oh Jokerman . . . ,*

into the *verse*, is also a technical indication that we are reaching the end of the song. It's exactly what Dylan does at the end of that neglected 1978 song 'No Time To Think', in which the title phrase occurs only in the chorus – until we reach the last verse, when the bulk of it takes over as the repeated opening phrase:

> *No time to . . .*
> *No time to . . .*
> *No time to . . .*
> *No time to . . .*

In both songs, repeating a key phrase from the chorus in a verse has the same function: it signals that the end is imminent. It does this by way of suggesting that a summing-up is being offered – and a summing-up is of course the beginning of the end.

'Jokerman' does indeed then end, with one last chorus: one last dropping of the argument in favour of the dance. Yet this cannot be fully entered into either: the finishing end is one last stepping back, one last compunction to qualify (one foot drawing back while the other advances), in the renewed self-deprecation of that very last

> *Oh— Jokerman!*

Nor is the invocation of the dance free of the process of argument: it is after all an assertion of the *idea* of renewal, of the *concept* of submission to the muse. And it insists, as the verses do, on the impossibility of unconditional surrender to any fixed position. Aidan Day writes: 'It's a dance invested with paradox in that it is both a dance of death and a dance of life: a dance simultaneously of matter and spirit.' He also describes it as 'at once a dance of death and a flight of the soul by a light that governs both creativity and waste'.[49] Day points out how trenchantly T. S. Eliot analyses such dance within the poem 'Burnt Norton', and quotes this Eliot passage:

> *Neither flesh nor fleshless;*
> *Neither from nor towards; at the still point, there the dance is,*
> *But neither arrest nor movement. And do not call it fixity . . .*[50]

Clearly this is argument as well as poetry. 'And do not call it fixity . . .' brings us full circle back to the central argument of the verses of 'Jokerman': that there can be no fixity. 'Neither flesh nor fleshless . . .': we're back in the unfixed terrain between the flesh and the spirit, between death and rebirth, between the Trickster and the transcendent self, and in the unfixed terrain that is unfixed because nothing, not even the figure of Christ, can be singularly anything.

Nor, in the end, can the song settle for, in Aidan Day's words,

> containment within [even] a dualistic frame of reference . . . even the usableness of the opposition between time and non-time, life and death, is called into question . . . Generating questions which it does not resolve, the lyric itself is presented to its audience in the form of a question or riddle. In its refusal to close lies its strength, its commitment to confront and challenge. And in that refusal it epitomizes the most distinctive perspective of Dylan's lyrical career: a continually renewed scepticism regarding the possibility of attaining absolutely final positions and a protest at the paralysing intolerance of such as settle for closed and fixed points of view. The work neither simply despairs nor simply celebrates. Recognising a 'hateful siege / Of contraries' it simultaneously exults in that siege.[51]

I quote this passage by Aidan Day at length as an admirable summary of *part* of what 'Jokerman' is all about, but it is Day's final point here that most needs stressing: that there is throughout the song not only an *acceptance* of unresolvability – not only

---

49.   The first quotation is from Day's essay 'Bob Dylan: Escaping on the Run' (see note 41); and the second from his book *Jokerman: Reading the Lyrics of Bob Dylan*.

50.   T. S. Eliot: 'Burnt Norton' (1935), collected in *The Four Quartets* (1943). The quotation is taken from Day's essay, in which he also relays a point made by Helen Gardner in her pioneering critical work *The Composition of 'Four Quartets'*, 1978: that Eliot's image of the dance around the 'still point' was suggested by his reading William Carlos Williams' novel *The Greater Trumps* [in UK, 1932], in which, as Day summarises it, 'in a magical model of the universe the figures of the Tarot pack dance around the Fool at the still centre'. (Dylan's awareness of T. S. Eliot's poetry is discussed in an earlier chapter.)

51.   Aidan Day, *Jokerman: Reading the Lyrics of Bob Dylan* (note 41). The 'hateful siege / Of contraries' is Milton again, *Paradise Lost*, Book 9.

some kind of resolute commitment to the notion that no position can command one's resolute commitment – but that there is exultation throughout the song too.

Part of this exultant spirit, the celebratory, dancing benificence that pours off the recording even more vividly and recurrently than off the page, seems to me to flow from the sense Dylan has, as it goes along, of what the song is achieving by its sheer concentratedness of application, its sheer wholeness and openness of engagement, its unguarded addressing of big themes resourcefully, maturely and anew.

As with 'Mr. Tambourine Man' there is a self-reflexive motor here. The song seems to celebrate inspiration by the sheer display of it. It enjoys itself. It is a pleasurable irony that, as with 'Mr. Tambourine Man', a song that is partly about standing in need of the muse succeeds in possessing it.

At the same time, another part of what 'Jokerman' enjoys about itself is a quite different quality from its handling of large themes. For all the attention given to these themes, the song tends to be at its best when dealing not with the cataclysmic and the significant but with the quiet and the everyday: the human in the tangible world.

Not that the one order of things doesn't invade the other. Many of the best lines in the song are, you might say, about the weather. Now that weather may be intended as more symbolic than real – it might be brought into play merely to augur this or that – yet somehow in 'Jokerman' real weather seeps in through the constructs of symbolism. Something happens that is in interesting opposition to what the critic John Carey claims when writing about Charles Dickens' use of the weather in his novels: that 'In Elizabethan drama the turmoil in the elements which accompanies human misdeeds like the murder of Duncan relates to a system of belief binding man to his universe. By the nineteenth century this kind of sympathetic weather has dwindled to a poetic convenience.'[52]

In 'Jokerman' what lingers, rather, is a sense of how interested in real weather the song is, and how interested in the human compunction to observe it *and* read auguries into it. The 'turmoil in the elements' which accompanies the Herculean birth claimed by the Jokerman,

> *... with a snake in both of your fists while a hurricane was blowing,*

is indeed mere 'poetic convenience', though as we noted earlier, that 'convenience' includes Dylan's mockery of exactly such conceits. But spread through the rest of the song is a series of notes about the weather in which Dylan is as focused upon the detail of reality, as intent upon accurate observation of the actual, as upon its correlative symbolic value. This comes through, as implied earlier, in the 'slippery' of

> *skies are slippery gray;*

in the 'smoke', which is another specifying of a kind of grey, in

> *In the smoke of the twilight ... ;*

and in the way that these skies are continually looked up at. The song is pervaded by the awareness that its events take place out in the elements all the time. Through the mist. Under slippery grey skies. In the smoke of the twilight. The sun sets in the sky.

---

52. John Carey, *The Violent Effigy: A Study of Dickens' Imagination* (1979).

Night comes stepping in. And we remain, even then, out under those skies: half-asleep 'neath the stars, and by the light of the moon.

Even the obvious symbolic 'meaning' of the near-detail-free line

So swiftly the sun sets in the sky

incorporates our mutual recognition (Dylan's and the listener's) that the analogy between the brevity of the day and of human life is not only enriched by being a part of the shared experience of all of humankind but by its being continually renewed with the days themselves.

The rhythm of ever-affecting poignancy is necessarily that of the ever-setting and returning sun itself. The recognition of the analogy, and of its poignancy, is itself part of the quiet, everyday reality of human life: you cannot pass a certain age without your every experience of an actual sunset incorporating, somewhere between the eye and the brain and the heart, its symbolic import also. What Dylan's line communicates, then, is as much humanity and reality as theory and debate. And what clinches this is that its rhythms are entirely devoted to expressing not force of argument but feeling: they give voice to exactly the simple human poignancy of observing the sun set and being touched anew by regret at life's brevity. The line's rhythms enact this brevity and regret.

So swiftly the sun sets in the sky

is the briefest opening line of any verse in 'Jokerman': nine syllables, delivered as two simple, falling phrases – the one following and repeating the path of the other, but yet more briefly, in a perfectly distilled replication of our experience – with the soft alliteration of its repeated 's' sounds acting as a sighing and a slippage.

(Dylan does something similar at the end of the later 'Shooting Star', on a final line that is again notably shorter than in the other verses, and again sighs with alliterative 's' sounds:

Saw a shooting star tonight, slip away.)

In 'Jokerman' Dylan's alertness in these matters has him switching at once from feelings and rhythms of quiet acceptance at the sun's setting to stubbornly resistant corollaries. The sun sets, but

You rise up and say goodbye to no one.

Against this, however, the elements must inevitably prevail. It's

Only a matter of time 'til night comes steppin' in:

another line in which the symbolic import is founded upon the common human feeling that enriches it and is disarmingly expressed. The song also has an eye on the weather and the elements when we arrive at one of the most attractive moments in all of 'Jokerman', the affectionately rendered and lovely scene in which the 'you' of the song is found

Resting in the fields, far from the turbulent space,
Half asleep 'neath the stars with a small dog licking your face.

These, of course, are the lines that have replaced those of the early draft version quoted earlier in which the 'you' of the song is instead

> *So drunk, standing in the middle of the street,*
> *Directing traffic with a small dog at your feet.*

The re-write is for the better, but what I like best is that Dylan makes such a change at all. He's often berated for withholding good work and offering less good, and for re-writing material that could profitably be left untouched. Here is a re-write that improves on every level a couplet that was 'good enough': an example of Dylan having sufficient incentive to say that 'good enough' wasn't good enough.

That early draft is in circulation among collectors in the form of an out-take from the "Infidels" sessions,[53] and though its overall similarity to the issued version suggests that Dylan made the changes, and the re-recording, in a matter of hours rather than weeks, the re-writes in the lyric are generally improvements. (Two lines differ completely in verse two; ditto in verse three. In the fourth verse one line differs completely, another by just one word and these are followed by the two lines just quoted above, in which the small dog is retained while all around him changes. Verses five and six change more substantially.) The exception seems to me to be in the second verse, in which

> *Friend to the martyr, a friend to the woman of shame,*
> *You look into the fiery furnace, see the rich man without any name*

replaces the less didactic and initially quirkier

> *Scratching the world with a fine-tooth comb*
> *You're a king among nations, you're a stranger at home.*

A curate's egg, this. We gain a weight of scriptural allusion by this exchange (and a deadweight, as a couplet of poetry) in place of the first draft's one such allusion, a much simpler and more familiar one to grasp. It is Christ who says of himself that 'A prophet is not without honour, save in his own country, and in his own house' (Matthew 13:57). This is extended in Mark (6:4) to 'A prophet is not without honour, but in his own country, and among his own kin, and in his own house', and abbreviated in Luke (4:24) to 'No prophet is accepted in his own country'. You might feel this is such a commonplace – recycled into 'no man is a hero to his valet' (French society hostess Anne-Marie Bigot de Cornuel, 1728) and into the proverbial 'familiarity breeds contempt' – that it is itself an example of the proverb's truth, so that Dylan's own restatement of it sounds mere cliché. You might feel further that his formulation is so uncompressed that it clumps along with ungainly laxity, and that this is aggravated by the way he echoes, loosely and less graphically, his earlier line 'You're a man of the mountains, you can walk on the clouds.' But it is surely no more leaden nor indifferently crafted than the replacement lines, while the other deletion,

> *Scratching the world with a fine-tooth comb,*

---

53. The dating is speculative. Glen Dundas' *Tangled up in Tapes*, 1994, places this out-take as recorded between 11 April and 8 May, 1983, NYC, and the issued version as 'early June–July 5' ditto, but then implies that this later date-band relates to vocal overdubs only. Dundas' 1999 edition narrows down the out-take date to either 13 or 14 April.

is fresh and distinctive. The more predictable formulation 'Searching the world with a fine-tooth comb' would have been transformed from the workaday by Dylan's use of this figure of speech to sum up Christ's fundamental *modus operandi*. To choose instead to place him as a prophet 'Scratching the world with a fine-tooth comb' is far fresher, more freewheeling and funny.

Elsewhere, though the changes to the lyric for 'Jokerman' are probably for the better, it seems reasonable to quote replaced passages where something in what is deleted illuminates what is retained. This applies to the more substantially altered last two verses of the song. What each change shows is how Dylan had to resist his tendency to see things from one viewpoint only – in essence to resist a didactic and evangelising stance – in favour of seeing the complexities beyond. So in the penultimate verse, in which he evokes the Preacherman who is no clear-cut opposite to the stalking rifleman, and inventively depicts American paranoia 'behind every curtain', we find that he has won through to these creations from an earlier draft that is far more black and white (in which the narrative voice is far more that of a preacher). Instead of

> *Well, the rifleman's stalking the sick and the lame,*
> *Preacherman seeks the same, who'll get there first is uncertain.*
> *Nightsticks and watercannons, tear gas, padlocks,*
> *Molotov cocktails and rocks behind every curtain,*

the earlier draft harangued us (not without brio) with

> *Well, a preacherman talkin' 'bout the deaf and the dumb*
> *And a world to come that's already been pre-determined*
> *Nightsticks and watercannons, tear gas and padlocks,*
> *Molotov cocktails and rocks can't drown out his sermon.*

Similarly where the issued version of the final verse offers the moral murk of

> *It's a shadowy world, skies are slippery gray,*
> *A woman just gave birth to a prince today and dressed him in scarlet.*
> *He'll put the priest in his pocket, put the blade to the heat,*
> *Take the motherless children off the street and place them at the feet of a harlot*

it is all much clearer in the earlier draft, wherein

> *A woman just give birth to a prince today and she's dressed in scarlet*
> *He'll turn priests into pimps and make old men bark,*
> *Take a woman of courage, a Joan of Arc, and turn her into a harlot.*

(I love the way that whereas any other white person singing 'scarlet' and then 'harlot' would maximise the rhyme by pronouncing each as '-arlut', Dylan sings 'scarlett' and then makes the full rhyme by singing 'harlett' to match! This is in the great tradition of idiosyncratic pronunciation exemplified in black song from Garfield Akers to Fats Domino and Howlin' Wolf.)

In the case of the rifleman and preacher, Dylan's re-write not only suits better his theme of how shadowy the world is, but also delivers better poetry. I'm not sure the latter is true of the final verse. The Joan of Arc line is tendentious but surely worth putting up with for the trenchant comic truth of that 'make old men bark'.

In fact the contrast between the two lines is instructive about what makes for creative expression and what makes for polemic. If Dylan had inveighed against an evil that threatened to 'Take old men and turn them into dogs' it would be hardly more enticing or nourishing to the imagination than 'Take a woman of courage, a Joan of Arc, and turn her into a harlot'. There's no room for imaginative interplay here. But to conjure an evil that threatens to 'make old men bark' is to take flight with words, not fancifully but acutely. It's acute as well as imaginative because behind it lies an amused but sympathetic perception of the real precariousness of the mind in old age, and so of the noises that might emerge from the mouth (there's some play on 'barking mad' here, of course, but no undue reliance on it). Elsewhere, it might be remembered, Dylan registers seeing

> *Old men with broken teeth, stranded without love.*

They are not stranded without the writer's love, and nor are those who might be made to bark under slippery skies.[54]

This rejected phrase is wholly in keeping with the spirit of the public, released version of the song. Both carry through them Dylan's consciousness that chaos is everywhere, that each of us comes close to barking. It's a compassionate song and a very open one, with Dylan not just mocking himself for the preaching phase but, far more courageously, examining how the things inside which drive us can drive us to the wrong places. This is strong, complex, intelligent writing – in some ways quite beyond what he could have handled in the 1960s. It comes from the Dylan who is unafraid to stand inside the chaos of passion and vulnerability, unafraid of risk and contradiction, prepared to acknowledge the fragility of each individual's hold on sanity and strength. It is, despite the difficult themes and the scriptural foundations, a fluid and imaginative, humane work.

Both studio performances (though more especially the unreleased take) are bathed with the radiance of the song's quintessential warmth, its generosity of heart and spontaneity of spirit. Dylan's voice is marvellously expressive and celebratory as he winds his ever-alert and flexible way through verses as richly baroque as any of his earlier work and a chorus as airy and light-footed as Fred Astaire.

'Jokerman' is always compelling, however its author treats it. Its melody, the long lines of writing, the bounty of its variety, its space – it's always attractive. After spacey studio performances, on which foreboding bass riffs brood behind vocals of shimmering reverie, there is the glorious amphetamine anarchy of the version performed with The Plugz on a New York TV show in March 1984, in which he and the punks behind him grunge out a 'Jokerman' that is an impassioned, howling anthem on the very edge of chaos yet as knowing and lithe, as snarlingly fey and postmodern, as Television's album "Marquee Moon", to which Dylan and The Plugz seem to pay tribute – and which is Tom Verlaine updating, via the Velvet Underground, the city-hipster-in-the-storm figure Dylan first invents for himself in 1966.[55]

54. The 'broken teeth' may carry a less charitable connotation, if Dylan is here alluding the psalm in which God 'hast broken the teeth of the ungodly' (Psalm 3:7).

55. Bob Dylan & The Plugz: 'Don't Start Me To Talkin'', 'License To Kill' and 'Jokerman', 22/3/84, NYC, telecast on *Late Night with David Letterman* NBC-TV, New York, 22/3/84. Television: "Marquee Moon", NYC, Autumn 1976; Elektra Records 7E-1098, LA, 1977.

When Dylan performs 'Jokerman' in concert in Europe that summer, it glowers along very differently, rising above the corporeal and musical torpor of that regrettably different guitarist Mick Taylor, impelled by a churning, magnificent grandeur. Even in Japan a decade later, when Dylan is taking the song fast again and it would demand much energy and precision to deliver the full lines and stay on top of them, and Dylan, regrettably, can't be bothered, choosing instead to dispense with the first 50 per cent of the long fourth lines of the verses (reducing that of the opening verse to 'Born with a snake in your fists, hurricane blowing', for example), even then, with him slurring the lines and hitting only their endings, the song still enriches every concert. Even though the same laziness has him prune it down from six verses to four (not always the same four) in *every* concert performance, 'Jokerman' is always welcome, always alive and benign, always rich and complex, always habitable, always ready to open up its labyrinthine possibilities.

Better even than 'Jokerman', perhaps – perhaps best of all Bob Dylan's work of the period – is 'Blind Willie McTell', an extraordinary song even for Bob Dylan to decline to release. This is surely the most significant known case of a great artist keeping back a great work since Coleridge withheld 'Kubla Khan' for almost twenty years nearly two hundred years ago. As I. G. Roberts comments, 'There can be very few instances in any field of the arts where such consensus gathers around a work rejected by its creator.'[56]

Dylan withheld 'Blind Willie McTell' for eight years, consenting in 1991 to the official release of the less transcendent of his two circulating recordings. He finally performed it in concert in 1997. The next chapter addresses itself to this, perhaps Bob Dylan's greatest work of the 1980s.

---

56. Samuel Taylor Coleridge (1772–1834) wrote 'Kubla Khan' on opium in 1797; it was finally published, in *Christabel and Other Poems*, at Byron's prompting, in 1816: *Complete Poems*, ed. William Keach. (Shortly after 'Kubla Khan', Coleridge wrote a series of 'conversation poems' addressed to friends. By chance one poem is called 'The Nightingale'.)

   I. G. Roberts quoted from 'Blind Willie McTell', *Homer, the slut*, no. 4, September 1991.

CHAPTER FIFTEEN

Bob Dylan, Blind Willie McTell and 'Blind Willie McTell'

Blind Willie McTell is no roaring primitive and no Robert Johnsonesque devil-dealing womaniser. He didn't lose his sight in a jook-joint brawl, or hopping a freight train. He didn't escape into music from behind a mule-plow in the Delta. He didn't die violently or young. Instead, blind from birth but never behaving as if this were a handicap, this intelligent, articulate man became an adept professional singer and 12-string guitar player who travelled widely and talked his way into an array of recording sessions.

He never achieved a hit record, but he became, as a live performer and a man, one of the most widely known and well-loved figures in and around Georgia. Working clubs and car-parks, playing to blacks and whites, tobacco workers and college kids, Blind Willie McTell – human juke-box and local hero – enjoyed a modest career and an independent life.

Since his death the re-emergence of his many recordings has shown that McTell was also one of the blues world's consummate artists. A well-kept secret among blues and folk fans in Britain and America since the 1950s, Blind Willie McTell is the last unrecognised superstar of the blues.

McTell recorded prolifically from the *early* days of blues recording and laid down a masterpiece the first day he ever set foot in a studio back in 1927. In the mid-1930s, as the Depression gripped, he dropped from sight. In 1940 a folklorist's wife found him playing at a drive-in barbecue, and he agreed to be recorded singing and talking for the Library of Congress. He was paid a dollar and his taxi-fare ('a dollar a day, it's worth . . .'), and dropped from sight once more: just another blind singer, and now in his early forties.

He survived, and managed a return to commercial recording in 1949–50, with sessions for a small indie label and for the bigger indie, Atlantic. But there was no market for his pre-war acoustic blues style by this time. Muddy Waters had already electrified Chicago. McTell disappeared once again. He was recorded, privately, one more time, in 1956 (by which time rock'n'roll was shaking up the blues in yet another way) and he died in obscurity in 1959 – the very year his great 'Statesboro Blues' became a major 'discovery' of the new folk and blues revival movement.

Many who kept up with Bob Dylan in the 1980s assumed for a long time that his song 'Blind Willie McTell' uses that particular singer's name almost at random, merely because Dylan likes the sound of it – or because it offers a far handier rhyme for other words (bell, well, yell, hotel, and so on) than the surnames of the blues greats Dylan was already known to admire. It's not irrelevant. Nothing unforced rhymes with Jefferson, Williams or Lipscomb, and there's something fatally plodding and obvious about 'Nobody can sing the blues like Robert Johnson.' It's quite likely too that Dylan, always alive to the multiple resonances words can emit, wanted to draw on the contrast, rather than the mere parallel, between the inarticulacy of his own early, flippant persona – Blind Boy *Grunt* – and the special aptness resonant in that of Blind Willie Mc*Tell*.[1]

People are mistaken to assume that the particulars of McTell's life and work offer no further illumination of Dylan's. So too are those who, having been inspired by Dylan's song to go off in search of McTell's records, have heard but a track or two and then turned away, disappointed to hear a smooth, almost mellow voice, more obviously eloquent of poise than suffering, rather than the rough, primeval tones of torment they had assumed McTell would offer.

There's a special irony here, for those who've long laughed at others whose fixed expectations about singing lead them to hear Dylan as someone who 'can't sing', in missing out on Blind Willie McTell's genius because his voice doesn't at once conform to another set of rules about what's real and what is not. There's even a faint career-spanning echo between that famous early ad campaign line from Columbia Records, 'No-one sings Dylan like Dylan', and 'No-one can sing the blues like Blind Willie McTell'. McTell may not roar and moan like a Howlin' Wolf or a Tommy McClennan – but to expect that he should is to hold to a caricatured, constricted view of what the blues singer ought to do for us that's dangerously like racism. The blues is multi-faceted, an outlet for expression across a huge emotional range. Blues singers don't have to be thrilling primitives.

No inferior shellac crackle dooms Blind Willie McTell to the ranks of the almost unlistenable, like Blind Lemon Jefferson and Charley Patton. His pre-war recordings, like his diction, can be as clear as a bell, aiding an immediacy and emotional directness that gives them both instant impact and lasting resonance. While playing the 12-string guitar better than Leadbelly, he has a voice as light and fluid as the young Elvis' – yet also, on his early blues sides, an intensity to match his vivid lyrics, the best of which show him to be an inspired individual composer within a milieu of shared, communal composition.

Even where his lyrics are commonplace, the voice on these early sides is quietly pained and strikingly intimate. That intimacy is partly a matter of trust: of assuming, as the young Bob Dylan also did, that complexity of feeling can be understood when expressed through intelligent restraint.

---

1.   In the present chapter, almost all the hard biographical information on McTell, and others' quoted speech, comes from the notes by David Evans and Bruce Bastin for an album featuring McTell, the Georgia Browns, Curley Weaver and Buddy Moss: "Atlanta Blues 1933", JEMF Records JEMF-106, issued by the John Edwards Memorial Foundation, Folklore & Mythology Center, UCLA, LA, California, 1979: the first time any substantial, accurate biography of McTell had been published – and only four years before Dylan wrote his song. The main section of the album notes, on McTell himself, is by David Evans based on original research by him and his parents from 1976; this remains, at the present time, *the* source for our knowledge of McTell's life.
    Interview material with McTell's wife Kate McTell comes, both via the above source and directly from David Evans' articles in *Blues Unlimited*, nos. 125–7, 1977; information on McTell's last session comes both from listening to it and from Samuel B. Charters' article 'Blind Willie McTell: A Last Session' in *Record Research*, no. 37, 1961.

This is very evident on 'Mama 'Tain't Long 'Fo Day', the gem among gems from McTell's début day in the studios, Tuesday, 18 October 1927. Early on, McTell tended to make songs more by putting together stock couplets from the great repository of blues lyric poetry than by conscious composition. Yet here, though the great opening lines of verses 1, 3 and 4 ('Wake up mama, don't you sleep so hard', 'Blues grabbed me at midnight, didn't turn me loose till day' and 'The big star falling, mama 'tain't long 'fore day') derive from early vaudeville women performers and Blind Lemon Jefferson, he re-works them into a song of real individuality, made unforgettable by his voice and playing. A universe of communication seems held in tension between the exquisite keening of his bottleneck guitar and the vulnerable, edgy hope ventured by the voice and the optimistic last line, the disarming 'Maybe the sunshine will drive these blues away'.

It's easy to hear too why the very different 'Statesboro Blues' became much loved: this 1928 recording is so rock'n'roll. The lyrics are full of tricksy, evocative expressions that baby-boomers like me recognise from Jerry Lee Lewis records and the like: 'Sister got 'em . . . brother got 'em . . .' and 'hand me my travelin' shoes'. In truth these come from old hokum songs and gospel, but McTell propels them forward with fresh exuberance in a song that also shivers with pain, firing a whole range of feeling very directly at the listener. The record's abrupt start signals its restlessness. It's as if McTell had begun before the machinery was ready and the first couple of notes of the tumbling opening phrase are missing. Sometimes the 12-string guitar sounds like people shuffling cardboard boxes, and this is one of those times.[2]

Woody Mann wrote of his idiosyncratic genius on this instrument: 'He treats each phrase of his music as a separate entity with its own rhythmical and melodic nuances . . . As McTell's musical stream-of-consciousness wanders, so do his bar structures; he may follow a verse of ten bars with another of fourteen.' As the British blues expert Simon Napier wrote in sleeve notes to an album of McTell's later work: 'He sounds like no other artist; nor does he apparently subscribe to the trends set by other artists . . .' and 'He has the compelling, dramatic voice of the best bluesmen coupled with the wit and imagery of the greatest folk-poet [sic].' All of which sounds sort of familiar.[3]

Blind Willie McTell, like Bob Dylan, is a complex, intelligent, articulate personality and artist, and behind Dylan's great song reverberates a thorough knowledge of McTell's exquisite work and, I think, Dylan's sense of a deep companionship of spirit between them. McTell's life is the stuff of exactly the sort of troubadour romance Bob Dylan fantasised for himself in his early years and has carried in his heart ever since. McTell is the blues singer Dylan would have been if he'd been 'born in time'.[4]

2.   Blind Willie McTell: 'Statesboro Blues', Atlanta, 17/10/28; "The Country Blues", RBF Records RF-1, NYC, 1959, issued alongside Sam Charters' pioneering book of that name; CD-reissued "Blind Willie McTell: The Early Years (1927–1933)", Yazoo CD-1005, NYC, 1990.

3.   Woody Mann, quoted from a then-unpublished guitar instruction book for Oak Press, New York, in sleeve notes by Stephen Calt and John Miller for "Blind Willie McTell 1927–1935", Yazoo L-1037, NYC, 1973. Simon Napier, sleeve notes, "Blind Willie McTell: Atlanta Twelve String", Atlantic Records SD 7224, NYC, 1972.

4.   Dylan's tribute to McTell is neither the first nor the most recent. The British folkish singer Ralph McTell's choice of professional name was itself a tribute, while five years after Dylan's song, the New England folkie Michael Hurley recorded a song about McTell and Ma Rainey meeting in a graveyard: 'Ma's Dream Blues', Burlington, Vermont, Autumn 1987; "Water Tower", Fundamental Records SAVE 051, USA and Leeds, 1988.

Very few documents exist about Blind Willie McTell except his recordings, and some of the documents we do have, such as his marriage and death certificates, contain, as David Evans and Bruce Bastin note, false or misleading information. As with Dylan, there's an elusive quality to McTell, something genuinely mercurial about his personality and the ceaseless movements of his life. Research has been hampered by the fact that he travelled widely throughout his career, and that he often went under a series of pseudonyms, in person and on recordings – and even, as we shall see, in death.

His very surname shifts and dissolves and re-forms as it is scrutinised. His father's name was McTear or McTier, and members of his family chose between these spellings. Willie's wife Kate claimed that the optional nature of the spelling was created so that one branch of the family could disassociate itself from another that was notorious for distilling whiskey. David Evans points out that there are 'many McTiers and McTears in this part of Georgia, both black and white' that 'Willie was the only one to spell his name McTell' but that the pronunciation remained the same, 'with an accent on the Mc and no distinction between a final r or l'.[5]

McTell's professional pseudonyms included Pig'n'Whistle Red, Hot Shot Willie, Georgia Bill, Barrelhouse Sammy and Blind Sammie (his real middle name *was* Samuel). Among his friends he seems to have been known as Willie in Atlanta, but in Thomson and Statesboro he was well known as Doog, Doogie and Dude, though some around Statesboro knew him as Willie and in one case as W. S.

The similarity of spirit between McTell and Dylan is present right from their adolescent years, though these are half a century apart. Here's what the black working-class McTell says about running away from home: 'I run away and went everywhere, everywhere I could go without any money. I followed shows all around till I begin to get grown . . . medicine shows, carnivals, and all different types of funny little shows.' And here's the white middle-class Bob Dylan: 'I ran away . . . when I was 10, 12, 13, 15, 15½, 17 an' 18 / I been caught an' brought back all but once' and 'I used to travel with the carnival . . . off and on six years . . . I was a clean-up boy; I used to be on the mainline on the ferris wheel; . . . all kinds of stuff like that. I didn't go to school a bunch of years.'[6]

David Evans could have written of the adult Dylan much the same as he wrote of McTell:

5.   David Evans, see note 1. Moreover, as someone attending the 1992 Bob Dylan Convention in Leicester pointed out to me, McTear/McTier comes from the familiar Scots name McIntyre.

6.   Blind Willie McTell, recorded at Ed Rhodes' record-shop, Atlanta, September 1956; "Blind Willie McTell: Last Session", Prestige Bluesville 1040, Bergenfield, New Jersey, 1961, reissued Prestige PR 7809, Bergenfield, New Jersey, 1966 [and in the UK for the first time then, as "Blind Willie McTell: Last Session", Transatlantic Records PR1040, London, 1966]; CD-reissued Prestige Bluesville Original Blues Classics OBCCD-517–2 (BV-1040), Berkeley, California, 1992. (This CD has been digitally remastered, and is astonishly 'clean' and crackle-free, which is especially useful when it comes to hearing McTell talking; yet the clean-up takes a slight edge, or bite, away from the singing voice. This CD-reissue is padded out with a couple of 'bonus tracks', as if it were an Elvis movie soundtrack album, which prove to be the two Atlantic 1949 tracks issued as a 78 rpm single in January 1950 ['Kill It Kid' c/w 'Broke Down Engine Blues' as by Barrelhouse Sammy, Atlantic 891, New York].

    Bob Dylan: 'My Life In A Stolen Moment' (1963) and from the interviews-and-songs session recorded for WBAI radio's *Folksinger's Choice* programme by Cynthia Gooding, NYC, probably 13/1/62, probably broadcast 11/3/62.

Even if we knew nothing about his life, we could tell from his recorded songs that he liked to travel. In them he mentions Atlanta, Statesboro, Macon, Savannah, Rome, Augusta and Americus in the state of Georgia, and at greater distance Baltimore, East St. Louis, Boston, Memphis, Birmingham, Newport News, Lookout Mountain, Niagara Falls, Alabama, Florida, New York, Virginia, Tennessee and Ohio . . . He had been to most or all of them.

This travelling was partly a seeking after work as a performer, but partly from restless inclination. He once told his wife Kate: 'Baby, I was born a rambler. I'm gonna ramble till I die.'

They share much else in common. Like Dylan, McTell tried other forms of creative art besides music. He could model in clay and once made Kate an ashtray in the shape of a human hand. Dylan too modelled in clay and once made a milk-jug, or 'cream pitcher', as photographer Elliott Landy put it, 'where the handle goes into the middle of the pitcher'.[7]

When a friend was murdered in Statesboro, McTell wrote a finger-pointing protest song, David Evans reports, 'in which he named the people who did the killing'. McTell also played other instruments besides guitar: the first thing he taught himself was harmonica and then accordion, and for many years after becoming a guitarist he often played harmonica on a rack fixed around his neck. Later he experimented with electric guitar and still owned one at the time of his death.

Like Dylan, Blind Willie McTell mastered a number of styles and he could adopt a different accent for a particular recording. When he cut 'Motherless Children Have A Hard Time' for Atlantic Records in 1949, he made it a memorial to his long-dead friend, the gospel singer and guitarist Blind Willie Johnson, by a sustained imitation of both Johnson's voice and the distinctive *atmosphere* of Johnson's recordings. When he cut 'Hillbilly Willie's Blues' in 1935 (which can segue straight into Dylan's 'Froggie Went A-Courtin''), he indulged his penchant for wry impersonations of the white hillbilly singers who lived up in the Appalachian hills above his native Georgia plains. This is a talent first glimpsed on a terrific, extremely quirky track from his début session in 1927, 'Stole Rider Blues': check out the 'white' opening, with its sedate pace and its 'ride the lonesome rail' (sung as if it's the cowboy song phrase 'ride the lonesome trail'), his delivery on 'ma good gal' and his accent on 'friend'. This is the finest record Jimmie Rodgers never made.[8]

McTell attended to white musicians as well as singers. His 'Warm It Up To Me', from September 1933, may have been a re-write of any one of a number of similar

---

7.   Elliott Landy, interviewed by Paul Williams, NYC, 3/11/87, published *Telegraph*, no. 30, Summer 1988.

8.   Blind Willie McTell: 'Motherless Children Have A Hard Time', Atlanta, October 1949; "Blind Willie McTell: Atlanta Twelve String", Atlantic Records SD 7224, NYC, 1972; CD-reissued Atlantic 7 82366–2, 1992. 'Hillbilly Willie's Blues', Chicago, 25/4/35; "The East Coast States Vol. 2", Roots RL-326, Vienna, 1969–70 [a Various Artists compilation].

     'Stole Rider Blues', Atlanta, 18/10/27; Yazoo L-1037, see note 3; CD-reissued (subtitled "Doing That Atlanta Strut") Yazoo CD-1037, NYC, 1991. This last is the track that, with its 'I stole my good gal from my bosom friend / That fool got lucky, he stole her back again', anticipates Skip James' 1931 'Devil Got My Woman' and Robert Johnson's 1936 'Come On In My Kitchen' (in turn echoed in Bob Dylan's weirdly brilliant 1966 blues 'Pledging My Time').

     The final example of McTell's hillbilly mimicry is on 'Wabash Cannonball' [Atlanta, Sept. 1956, "Blind Willie McTell: Last Session", see note 6].

songs, but it's noticeable that it resembles the white veteran guitarist Jimmie Tarlton's 'Ooze Up To Me', cut in McTell's home-base city, Atlanta, eighteen months earlier. (Tarlton, an early bottleneck player, is credited as composer of 'Columbus Stockade Blues', a song Bob Dylan already knew back in 1960 in Minnesota.)[9]

As noted in an earlier context, a list of the singers McTell knew personally reads like a list of the blues names that crop up in the Bob Dylan story. As well as being a great friend of Blind Willie Johnson (whose 'In My Time Of Dyin'' is on Dylan's first album), McTell knew Leadbelly, Blind Blake and Blind Lemon Jefferson. His great-uncle was the Rev. Thomas Dorsey, whose cool-dude son, the blues singer and pianist Georgia Tom, became Thomas Dorsey the pre-eminent gospel composer and publisher who wrote 'Peace In The Valley'. McTell knew both Georgia Tom and his sometime partner Tampa Red (whose 'It Hurts Me Too', 'Love With A Feeling', 'She's Love Crazy' and 'But I Forgive You' Dylan has covered).[10] Tampa Red and Georgia Tom had a big hit of 1928, 'It's Tight Like That', which McTell must have played live and which he certainly copied on record, with Curley Weaver, as 'It's A Good Little Thing'. In 1950 he and Weaver recorded 'You Can't Get Stuff No More', a Tampa Red–Georgia Tom hit from 1932, while one of their first two songs as The Hokum Boys, the 1928 'Beedle Um Bum', was remembered and recorded by McTell nearly thirty years later, at his 'last session' in 1956.[11]

Like Dylan, these blues artists were picking up on each other's songs all the time, and in several ways. For Dylan it is a matter of instinct and mystery as well as

9.   Blind Willie McTell: 'Warm It Up To Me', NYC, 14/9/33; "Blind Willie McTell: The Early Years (1927–1933)", Yazoo L-1005, NYC, 1968 (though the first six of this company's releases, among which was this McTell compilation, were on the Belzona label; this was then renamed Yazoo and the LPs swiftly reissued as such); CD-reissued Yazoo CD-1005, NYC, 1990. Jimmie Tarlton: 'Ooze Up To Me', Atlanta, 29/2/32; CD-reissued "The Complete Darby & Tarlton", Bear Family Records BCD 15764, Vollersode, Germany, 1994. Bob Dylan: 'Columbus Stockade Blues', St Paul, Minnesota, May 1960.

10.   ''It Hurts Me Too' is a 1940 Tampa Red song but . . . Elmore James . . . recorded a version of voice-cracking intensity in 1957,' as Giles Oakley notes in *The Devil's Music: A History of the Blues* (1976). (Tampa Red recut it himself post-war as 'When Things Go Wrong With You', with what became Elmore James' band.) 'Love With A Feeling' was a hit, covered by Tommy McClennan and others (and revived in the 1950s by Magic Sam). 'She's Love Crazy' is a more obscure item in Tampa Red's canon, and 'But I Forgive You' is from one of his last sessions, in the early 1950s. However, *all* the Tampa Red songs Dylan has covered, including 'It Hurts Me Too', were put out on one mid-1970s album.
        Tampa Red: 'Love With A Feeling', Aurora, Illinois, 16/6/38, 'It Hurts Me Too', Chicago, 10/5/40, 'She's Love Crazy', Chicago, 24/6/41, and 'But I Forgive You', Chicago, 21/4/52; all issued on "Tampa Red: The Guitar Wizard 1935–1953", Blues Classics BC-25, El Cerrito, California, 1974, apparently not CD-reissued. Tampa Red: 'When Things Go Wrong With You', Chicago, 24/3/49; "Tampa Red: Guitar Wizard", AXM2–5501, RCA, New York, 1975.
        Elmore James: 'It Hurts Me Too', Chicago, 1957, though issued as Chief single 7004, Chicago, wasn't issued on LP in the USA till "South Side Blues", Cobblestone LP 901, 1975, yet it was first LP-issued ten years earlier in the UK, on "Memorial Album", Sue Records ILP 927, London, 1965.
        Tommy McClennan: 'Love With A Feeling', Chicago, 12/12/40. Magic Sam: 'Love Me With A Feeling' [sic], Chicago, 1957, Cobra 5013, Chicago, 1957.

11.   Tampa Red and Georgia Tom: 'It's Tight Like That', Chicago, 24/10/28. Blind Willie McTell: 'It's A Good Little Thing', NYC, 14/9/33; issued, obscurely, as a bonus track on "Blind Willie Johnson His Story", Folkways FG3585, NYC, 1963; CD-reissued "The Definitive Blind Willie McTell", Columbia Legacy Roots N' Blues C2K 53234, New York, 1994. Blind Willie McTell: 'You Can't Get That Stuff No More', Atlanta, May, 1950; "Blind Willie McTell 1949: Trying To Get Home", Biograph BLP-12008, Brooklyn, New York, 1969; CD-reissued as "Blind Willie McTell: Pig 'n' Whistle Red", Biograph BCD126, USA, 1993.
        Tampa Red and Georgia Tom: 'You Can't Get That Stuff No More', NYC, 4/2/32. The Hokum Boys: 'Beedle Um Bum', Chicago, c. Dec. 1928. Blind Willie McTell: 'Beedle Um Bum', Atlanta, September 1956; "Blind Willie McTell: Last Session", see note 6.

deliberation: 'Yes, I am a thief of thoughts / not, I pray, a stealer of souls / I have built an' rebuilt / upon what is waitin' . . . a word, a tune, a story, a line / keys in the wind t'unlock my mind . . . I must react an' spit fast / with weapons of words / wrapped in tunes / that've rolled through the simple years / teasin' me t'treat them right . . . for all songs lead back t' the sea'.[12]

For McTell it was a matter of economic necessity to buy records and to learn successful songs, to be able to perform them at gigs; it was also a labour of love. McTell wasn't 'just' a bluesman, he was a 'songster': while it paid for him to have an adaptable repertoire, to be able to perform different sorts of material at different sorts of gigs,[13] it is clear from the way he talks about himself and his repertoire – on both the 1940 Library of Congress session and the "Last Session" in 1956 – that he took pride in being a 'songster', was acutely aware of the historic sequencing of his material and felt a deep affection for many kinds of song.[14] Equally, he felt entitled to reshape them.

He heard many performers through working alongside them, including very many who never recorded at all – among them the guitarist brothers Jonas and Hollis Brown from Atlanta. It was the democratic norm all through this world to take both stock phrases and individually created ones and use or adapt them in your own work. As McTell says during his "Last Session" of how he constructed 'The Dyin' Crapshooter's Blues', which in turn, as we shall see, becomes one of the building blocks for Bob Dylan's 'Blind Willie McTell': 'I had to steal music from every which way to get it – to get it to fit.' He also told Edward Rhodes, speaking of songs by other people that he performed, such as Blind Blake's 1927 'That Will Never Happen No More' (cut six

---

12.   Bob Dylan: '11 Outlined Epitaphs', sleeve notes to "The Times They Are A-Changin' ", 1964.

13.   In Atlanta, for instance, McTell (and Curley Weaver) played at the Pig 'n' Whistle on Ponce De Leon Avenue: a whites-only drive-in that became a regular nightly gig for McTell when he was in town. Weaver: 'It was a barbecue sandwich place, you know. We call it carhop. Different cars would call for him . . . And they'd say, "Well, I got him for an hour", or so long, you know. And they would just pay him for that length of time.' This was where Ruby T. Lomax, second wife of folklorist John A. Lomax, spotted him on the evening of 4 November 1940; they recorded the Library of Congress session of songs, interview and reminiscence in the Lomaxes' hotel-room next day; issued on "Blind Willie McTell: 1940", Melodeon MLP-7323, Washington, DC, 1966 [Storyville 670.186 and SLP186 in Europe]. I've heard it rumoured that this is now CD-issued by Biograph (Melodeon became a subsidiary of Biograph in 1972 or 1973) but I can't find anyone who has actually seen it. It certainly is on release as "Blind Willie McTell: Complete Library of Congress Recordings In Chronological Order (1940)", RST Blues Documents BDCD-6001, Vienna, 1990.
    In the 1930s and/or 1940s, McTell also played daytime concerts at the all-black Morris Brown College, and sometimes Monday nights at their Coliseum. At the 81 Theatre [sic] on Decatur Street, McTell played black dances, with his wife Kate dancing behind his guitar, 1934–5, and he worked Saturday nights here regularly long afterwards.
    In Statesboro, he played to tobacco workers while they ate at the Jaekel Hotel in 'tobacco season', July–August (he played this venue ten seasons running); at the Norris Hotel likewise; outside the tobacco warehouse on North College Street; and at Olliff Boyd's livery stable on Walnut Street. (Boyd was a white, still alive in 1976, who remembered McTell gathering a crowd here.) In Savannah he played in the railway station baggage-room and at the Silver Moon tavern, and in Augusta at Good Time Charlie's tavern. Not content with this busy round of state-wide travel, McTell regularly included Tennessee and the Carolinas in his work-scheme, and in winter moved down into Florida to play to tourists. These trips, like his recording sessions for numerous different labels, were planned: he made his own bookings, by phone; McTell was a full-time professional.

14.   Actually this is misleading. As noted in Chapter 9, in critical commentary this term 'songster' is used all the time, to define the old-timers whose repertoires stretch back to before the blues, yet it's unsatisfactory to use a term *now* that was unheard of *then* and thus completely unfamiliar to the very people we use it to describe. What is meant here of McTell, therefore, is not that he was proud of being a songster – he'd never come across the term – but that he was proud of his breadth of taste and repertoire.

months ahead of 'You Gonna Quit Me Blues'): 'I jump 'em from other writers but I arrange 'em my way.'

Dylan has certainly used McTell material his way. As mentioned in an earlier chapter, a very secular Blind Willie McTell line gets quoted in Dylan's 'Christian' song 'Gonna Change My Way Of Thinking'. The song is full of the one 'authority on high', waved over us in all his Jehovah-severity, and verse six opens with the narrator on his way to following what he's earlier called 'a different set of rules': he's now 'got a God-fearing woman'. Yet, concerned to insist that she's a multi-dimensional character, he effects the surprise of slipping in a bit of raunchy approbation – letting into his evangelical, flagellant mansion the fresh air of an outside world. He sings ambitiously of a woman who is both the queen of his flesh and the lamp of his soul: a woman so well balanced that

> She can do the Georgia crawl
> She can walk in the spirit of the Lord.

'Do the Georgia crawl' doesn't come straight from Blind Willie McTell, but it arises in Dylan's work because McTell used it. It's odds-on that Dylan himself knew the earlier song, Henry Williams' and Eddie Anthony's 1928 'Georgia Crawl' (in which the singer's 'Aunt Sally . . . Do the Georgia Crawl till she died away'). It was an influential recording in its own right, by a popular local string band, and McTell certainly knew it and took up its title phrase, making it his own by using it *often*, primarily on several versions of the song Bob Dylan finally puts on record himself on "World Gone Wrong" in 1993, 'Broke Down Engine [Blues]': a song Dylan suggests he came upon 'second-hand' yet which he calls 'a Blind Willie McTell masterpiece'.[15]

On McTell's first, and best, version of this song, 'Broke Down Engine Blues' from 1931, he sings

> What makes me love my woman:
> She can really do the Georgia crawl

which he repeats on a 1933 re-recording, 'Broke Down Engine'. He sings the variant line 'What make me love little Sara, she can do the Georgia crawl' (that 'Sara' an odd little coincidence) on the 1933 remake 'Broke Down Engine No. 2'. Three days later, McTell also puts a passing reference to 'that old Georgia crawl' into his version of 'East St. Louis Blues' – on which he also anticipates Bob Dylan by pulling in from elsewhere the folk refrain 'fare you well':

> Fare ye, honey, fare ye well.

15. Henry Williams and Eddie Anthony: 'Georgia Crawl', Atlanta, 19/4/28; reissued "The Country Fiddlers", Roots RL-316, Vienna, 1968, and on the 2-LP set "The Story Of The Blues" compiled by Paul Oliver, CBS Records (M)66218, London, 1969: now a 2-CD set, "The Story Of The Blues", Columbia 468992 2, New York, 1991. 'Georgia Crawl' was only one of a series of records named after such dances; there was the cash-in 'Georgia Stomp' [by Andrew & Jim Baxter, Atlanta, 16/10/28], and later the 'Georgia Grind' [by Blue Lu Barker, NYC, 20/4/39, and by at least two others], not to mention 'I Love To Georgia Brown So Slow' [by Wee Bea Booze, NYC, 19/3/42]. Blind Willie McTell himself recorded the 'Georgia Rag', Atlanta, 31/10/31; Yazoo L-1005, see note 9.

Bob Dylan quoted from a 1993 San Diego interview (see Chapter 9, note 50) and from his liner-notes to "World Gone Wrong", 1993. This album and liner-notes are further discussed in Chapter 18.

You can shake like a cannonball
Get out and learn that old Georgia Crawl.
Fare ye, honey, fare ye well.

. . . Fare ye, baby, fare ye well.
. . . Fare ye, honey, fare ye well.[16]

Bob Dylan recorded 'Fare Thee Well' in Minnesota back in May 1960, and then on another early, privately recorded performance, of the wonderful 'Dink's Song', he quotes roughly the same line from 'Fare Thee Well' that McTell quotes in 'East St. Louis Blues', using it, like McTell, as a repeated refrain: 'Fare thee well my honey, fare thee well.' He even throws in, right next to it, as McTell does, the phrase 'like a cannonball'.[17]

Just as Dylan puts that old Georgia Crawl to use in 1979 and 1993, so he uses other fragments from Blind Willie McTell recordings at different, widely spaced points in his work. McTell's 'Southern Can Is Mine', recorded the same day as his first 'Broke Down Engine Blues', includes these lines:

Ashes to ashes and sand to sand

and

You might wiggle like a tadpole, let it jump like a frog,[18]

which Dylan utilises on two occasions over twenty years apart. When it was announced that he would found his own record label in the late 1960s, it was to be called Ashes & Sand; in 1990, the other line from the same McTell song gets tweaked into service for the lyric (such as it is) of Dylan's 'Wiggle Wiggle'.

The lyric of 'Dignity', recorded 1989 and issued 1994, always puts me in mind of

16.   Blind Willie McTell: 'Broke Down Engine Blues', Atlanta, 23/10/31; Yazoo L-1005, see note 9. 'Broke Down Engine', NYC, 18/9/33; "The Atlanta Blues", RBF Records RF-15, NYC, 1966; 'Broke Down Engine No. 2', NYC, 18/9/33 and 'East St. Louis Blues (Fare You Well), NYC, 21/9/33; "Atlanta Blues 1933", JEMF-106, see note 1; all CD-reissued "The Definitive Blind Willie McTell", see note 11.
       As David Evans argues, since these recordings 'show significant textual and musical variation', they 'allow us an unusual view of the folk blues singer at work on a song over a period of years'. The same is true for many other pieces in Blind Willie McTell's repertoire. Among the songs McTell reinterpreted are: 'Delia' / 'Little Delia', 1940 and 1949; 'Death Cell Blues'/ 'Death Room Blues', 1929, 1933 and 1935; 'Your Time To Worry', 1933 and 1935 (with a different melody and only two similar stanzas out of seven); and 'Love Changin' Blues', 1929 and 1949. For the Bob Dylan listener, this too has a familiar ring (quite aside from considerations of the extended act of reinterpretation that has been his concert career). Among songs Dylan has reinterpreted in the studio (and/or put on tape in less formal circumstances) are 'Let It Be Me', 1969 and 1981, 'Girl of the North Country', 1962 and 1969, 'See That My Grave Is Kept Clean', 1961, 1967 and 1970, 'Song To Woody', 1961 and 1970, and 'New Danville Girl'/ 'Brownsville Girl', 1984 and 1986: plus back-to-back revisits such as 'In Search Of Little Sadie'/ 'Little Sadie', 1970; 'George Jackson' 1971; and 'Forever Young', 1973. And, like McTell, Dylan too has recorded 'Delia' twice: on the first extant tape we have of him performing solo, made at St Paul, Minnesota, in May 1960, and again thirty-three years later for the "World Gone Wrong" album of 1993.
17.   Bob Dylan: 'Fare Thee Well', St Paul, Minnesota, May 1960, and 'Dink's Song', Minneapolis, 22/12/61. The line 'And it's fare thee well my own true love', or perhaps 'And it's "Fare Thee Well My Own True Love"' is also used on Dylan's less engaging version of 'The Leaving Of Liverpool', which he calls 'Farewell', recorded as follows: on Studs Terkel's Wax Museum, WFMT Radio, Chicago, c. 26/4/62; on the so-called Banjo Tape (at either Gil Turner's or Gerde's Folk City), NYC, c. 8/2/63; at the Broadside Sessions, NYC, 19/1/63; and at the "Times They Are A-Changin'" sessions, NYC, August 1963.
18.   Blind Willie McTell: 'Southern Can Is Mine', Atlanta, 23/10/31; Yazoo L-1005, see note 9. A slower revisit to the same song, retitled 'Southern Can Mama', was recorded by McTell 21/9/33; Yazoo L-1037, see note 3.

the lovely McTell title 'Searching The Desert For The Blues', while 'Rough Alley Blues', sung by Ruth Willis but with McTell providing the guitar-work, chorus singing and spoken commentary, includes the line

Lay across my big brass bed.[19]

Then there is the talking blues 'Travelin' Blues', the stand-out track from McTell's session of autumn 1929. When we attribute Bob Dylan's talking blues style to Woody Guthrie, we forget that black artists also explored this form and that Guthrie himself listened attentively to black music.

Dylan started off by reminding us that Guthrie travelled with Cisco Houston, Sonny Terry and Leadbelly; on one of John A. Lomax's "Ballad Hunter" LPs there's an excerpt of a recording of 'A Discussion of Blues' by 'Woodrow Wilson (Woody) Guthrie'; and we noted in an earlier chapter how Dylan's 'I Shall Be Free' derived as clearly from the stupendous black Memphis artist Frank Stokes' 1927 'You Shall' as from the habitually suggested source, Guthrie's version of Leadbelly's 'We Shall Be Free'.[20]

Specifically, we forget that Blind Willie McTell's 'Travelin' Blues' is a renowned example of the genre. His artistry and quick intelligence combine here to produce a talking blues of great good humour and poise, deftly quoting snatches of older popular songs ('Poor Boy' and 'Red River Blues'), imitating train noises on the guitar, recounting a long dialogue between the speaker trying to bum a ride and the railroad man refusing and tormenting him, and sewing together all these elements and more into a quirky, playful, sardonic whole.

Passages of its lyric, as well as quirks of McTell's delivery, cannot but put us in mind of Bob Dylan. What could be more 'Dylanesque' than McTell's insouciant spoken opening?

19. Blind Willie McTell: 'Searching The Desert For The Blues', Atlanta, 22/2/32; "Bluebird Blues", RCA Vintage Series, LPV-518, NYC [RD7786, London], 1965 (this track might have been released first on the oddity "Country Blues & Gospel", Heritage Records H.302, Australia [?], 1964–5: a 6-track 33 rpm EP); CD-reissued "Blind Willie McTell: Statesboro Blues", BLU GNC 043, The Blues Collection/Orbis Publications, London [magazine + CD; notes by the present writer; German language edition April 1996]. Ruth Willis: 'Rough Alley Blues', Atlanta, 23/10/31, not vinyl-issued until 1974: and then only in Sweden ("Rough Alley Blues: Blues From Georgia 1924–1931", Magnolia Records 502, Stockholm, 1974). Had Dylan heard this rare 78 rpm in time to incorporate the line into the 1969 'Lay, Lady, Lay'? Perhaps there is another old blues record with the same line, but it certainly isn't a formulaic commonplace.

20. Frank Stokes: 'You Shall', Chicago, c. Aug. 1927 (his earliest); "Frank Stokes With Dan Sane And Will Batts (1927–1929)", Roots Records RL-308, 1968. 'You Shall', Chicago, c. Sept. 1927; "Mississippi & Beale Street Sheiks, 1927–1932", Biograph Records BLP-12041, Canaan, New York, 1972. Leadbelly: 'We Shall Be Free', NYC, May 1944 [with Woody Guthrie and Sonny Terry]; "Leadbelly Sings Folk Songs", Folkways Records FA 2488, New York, *nia*, reissued as Folkways FTS 31006, New York, c. 1970. In fact this song goes back further, pre-dating the era of recordings: '. . . stanzas of 'You Shall Be Free' have been traced to the mid-nineteenth century,' writes John H. Cowley, in 'Don't Leave Me Here: Non-Commercial Blues: The Field Trips, 1924–1960' in *Nothing But the Blues: The Music and the Musicians*, ed. Lawrence Cohn (1993).

Woody Guthrie: 'A Discussion of Blues' [excerpt]: Washington, DC, 1941, on "The Ballad Hunter, Parts I and II: John A. Lomax Lectures on American Folk Music with musical illustrations (1941)", AFS L49, Washington, DC, c. mid-1950s. This is excerpted from Guthrie's Library of Congress recordings. A 3-LP set of these was issued in 1966: "Woody Guthrie Library of Congress Recordings", Elektra Records EK-271/272/273, NYC, comprising '3 hours of songs and conversations'. This included twenty-two monologues, which, though unitemised, may include the 'Discussion of Blues', and/or more similar material. CD-reissued (oddly) as 3 CDs or 2 cassettes, "Woody Guthrie: The Library of Congress Recordings", Rounder Records Reissue Series 1041–1043, Cambridge, Massachusetts, 1993.

I was travelin' through South America
Walked up to a lady's house [pause]
Called her Grandma [pause]
Didn't know 'er name [pause]
She give me someth'n' to eat
Walked on down the road.

Strongly reminiscent of 'I Shall Be Free No. 10' and with something akin to the flavour of 'Motorpsycho Nightmare', the McTell song also anticipates not only Dylan's mood and delivery but even, with that 'Walked on down the road', a line of lyric, from 'Talking World War III Blues', while the memorable way Dylan mumble-jerks the line 'Well I asked for something to eat', on 1965's 'On The Road Again', is a direct echo of the way Blind Willie McTell delivers the same little phrase in 'Travelin' Blues'.[21]

For all his efforts, and the extraordinary quality of his talent, Blind Willie McTell's career was doomed. His return to recording in 1949 and 1950, for Atlantic and then for the small Regal label, were his first commercial sessions since his pre-war recording career had petered out with a short, unhappy session in 1936 from which nothing had been released (and from which nothing survives). These post-war recordings produced a last small set of 78 rpm releases, but no success or revival of his reputation as an artist. By this time he was fifty-something, and to the extent that he was known at all, it was as an old Atlanta street musician.

McTell does not seem to have become embittered, though he drank, at times heavily, and suffered health problems. Though he still had family and friends in the places he travelled between, many of his friends were dead. Perhaps everything seemed to have come to nothing.

This may explain why McTell, like Dylan, became in his middle years a convert to Christianity, at first so keenly that he experimented with the process of preaching (as Dylan did on-stage in the concerts of 1979–80). McTell gave a trial sermon at Mt. Zion Baptist Church on Piedmont Avenue in Atlanta, where he was a member and often played and sang on Sundays, and went so far as to get a licence to preach.

He was also a member of Tabernacle Baptist Church in Statesboro, performing here too – sometimes accompanying gospel quartets – and getting paid from the collection. At the radio station where he cut his 1949 sides for Atlantic Records, WGST in Atlanta, he sang spirituals on the air in the early 1950s, as he did for Radio WERD (then called WEAS) in the Decatur section of town.

His country gospel sides can delight: 'Pearly Gates' (Atlantic), 'Hide Me In Thy Bosom' and the second take of 'Sending Up My Timber' (Regal) make a thrilling trio. McTell was alive with conviction for these performances, whereas the blues sides he was obliged to give Atlantic, and those he threw in for Regal too, tend to be tired re-workings of his old material. Similarly, of course, Dylan's 'all-Christian' tour of 1979

---

21. Blind Willie McTell: 'Travelin' Blues', Atlanta, 30/10/29; Yazoo L-1005, see note 9.

showed him remarkably fired-up, while his new-found conviction inspired an explosion of songwriting more prolific than any since the mid-1960s.[22]

McTell's great 'Hide Me In Thy Bosom' sounds recorded behind fibreglass, yet at 52 he can still make you think of Presley's 'That All Right', his fluid vocal rides and swoops with such unloosed passion. There is also a particular, inspired piece of singing, early on in the track, that one can imagine Dylan coming up with. On repeats of the line later in the song McTell is content with the conventional 'feed me, feed me, feed me', which follows the rhythm and gets its excitement from sheer insistent repetition, but the first time around he hits instead a long, sustained, utterly unpredictable 'feeeeeeeeeeeeeeeed me', cutting across the rhythm and holding a note between the expected two. Dylan has done much the same in concert with the chorus of 'Knockin' On Heaven's Door', turning 'knock knock knocking' into 'kno—ckin'', and you can imagine him doing the same in the course of a live performance of something from "Slow Train Coming" or "Saved".

The themes they shared at this point in their lives are evangelically Christian. 'Sending Up My Timber' states the 'Are You Ready?' theme, performed with the same crusading spirit as the "Saved" sessions generally:

> It may be morn or night or noon
> But I do not know just how soon . . .

while McTell's Library of Congress session gives us a reminiscence about 'those old-fashioned hymns' his parents used to sing around the house before going out to work in the fields, one of which carried the same message:

> Are you just well to get ready? You got to die, you got to die
> Just well to get ready, you got to die
> It may be tomorrow, you can't tell the minute or the hour
> Just well to get ready, you got to die, you got to die.

Most interesting here is the switch from the righteous 'you' in 'Just As Well Get Ready, You Got To Die' to the affecting 'I', in 'I Got To Cross The River Jordan':

> I got to face my dear Saviour,
> I got to face Him for myself
> There's nobody here can face Him for me
> So I got to face Him
>
> And I got to work out my soul salvation . . .
> There's nobody here can work it out for me . . .
>
> I got to lie in some old lonesome graveyard
> I've got to lie there by myself

22.   Blind Willie McTell: 'Pearly Gates', Atlanta, October, 1949; "Blind Willie McTell: Atlanta Twelve String", see note 3. 'Hide Me In Thy Bosom' and 'Sending Up My Timber' [two takes], Atlanta, May 1950; "Blind Willie McTell 1949: Trying To Get Home", see note 11; CD-reissued "Blind Willie McTell & Curley Weaver: The Post-War Years 1949–1950", RST Blues Documents BDCD-6014, Vienna, 1991 [but incorrectly dates these tracks as from 1949].

There's nobody there can lie there for me
Lord, I got to lie there for myself.[23]

McTell sings this without melodrama, with great simplicity, such that we feel his faith to be a struggle: a summoning of courage a hair's breadth from the bereft. It clinches the case for Blind Willie McTell's ability to lament for us – to be the artist on to whose shoulders Bob Dylan can place the weight of his visionary requiem for America's past and everybody's future.

So does 'The Dyin' Crapshooter's Blues'. This is Blind Willie McTell's personalised version, one among a whole sequence of songs, based on the traditional English ballad 'The Unfortunate Rake' and which also becomes the black standard 'St. James Infirmary'. 'The Unfortunate Rake', 'St. James Infirmary' and 'The Dyin' Crapshooter's Blues' all end up wondrously transmuted into 'Blind Willie McTell'.

This is the nineteenth-century broadside version of 'The Unfortunate Rake', as sung by the distinguished British folk singer and folklorist A. L. Lloyd:

As I was a-walking down by St. James' Hospital
I was a-walking down by there one day
What should I spy but one of my comrades
All wrapped up in flannel though warm was the day

I asked him what ailed him, I asked him what failed him
I asked him the cause of all his complaint
'It's all on account of some handsome young woman
'Tis she that has caused me to weep and lament

'And had she but told me before she disordered me
Had she but told me of it in time
I might have got pills and salts of white mercury
But now I'm cut down in the height of my prime

'Get six young soldiers to carry my coffin
Six young girls to sing me a song
And each of them carry a bunch of green laurel
So they don't smell me as they bear me along . . .'

'Don't muffle your drums and play your fifes merrily
Play a quick march as you carry me along
And fire your bright muskets all over my coffin
Saying: "There goes an unfortunate lad to his home."'

The last verse becomes, in other versions, a chorus repeated between each verse, and its instructions about the fife, drum and march are more usually these, as in the version 'The Trooper Cut Down In His Prime' sung by Ewan MacColl:

Then beat the drum slowly and play your fife lowly
And sound the Dead March as you carry me along . . .

---

23.   Blind Willie McTell: 'Just As Well Get Ready, You Got To Die' and 'I Got To Cross The River Jordan', Atlanta, 5/11/40; "Blind Willie McTell: 1940", see note 13.

(Bob Dylan quotes from this in his "Oh Mercy" song 'Where Teardrops Fall':

> *We've banged the drum slowly and played the fife lowly*
> *You know the song in my heart*

so neatly suggesting that the song in his heart is the Dead March, and then, with a faith akin to McTell's in 'I Got To Cross The River Jordan', looking beyond death in hope of resurrection:

> *In the turning of twilight, in the shadows of moonlight*
> *You can show me a new place to start).*

The first extant text of 'The Unfortunate Rake' wasn't published until 1909, though it dates from 1848, when it was written down in County Cork from the performance of someone who'd learnt it in Dublin in 1790. That's one account, anyway; another says that 'The earliest text seems to be the eighteenth-century 'Buck's Elegy', set in Covent Garden.'[24] Either way, it was by oral transmission that this 200-plus-year-old song travelled around Britain and Ireland and to America, where it split into white versions and black.

The writer Karl Dallas uses its hydra-headedness to argue that the important things in folksong are often the incidentals:

> To ensure that we are understood, we surround the central message of what we are saying with all sorts of peripheral stuff . . . known to communications theorists as redundancy. These may be metaphors, expansions, all the colourful turns of phrase which make all the difference between true human speech and the bald deadpan statement of a telegram – which . . . is the easiest kind of message to misunderstand because it has zero redundancy . . .
>
> The story of 'The Unfortunate Rake' is interesting because . . . while the central message may change, so that the soldier dying of syphilis in eighteenth-century London crosses oceans, changes sex, becomes a cowboy dying of gunshot wounds on the streets of Laredo, coming to rest finally in New Orleans as the black hero of 'Gambler's Blues', more commonly known as 'St. James's Infirmary', one detail remains constant, a redundancy essential to convey the point of the changing story: the ceremonial funeral.

In fact all these versions share more than the centrality of burial: not only fragments of narrative – words and phrases that resettle themselves into the idiomatic language of different milieux – but in every case a structure built upon having two narrative voices, voices not in dialogue (as in, say, 'Boots Of Spanish Leather') but succeeding each other as monologues. We begin, invariably, with someone telling us how they come upon a dying person, and then the dying person takes over the tale briefly to explain why they're dying but mostly, as Dallas emphasises, to catalogue what they want by way of a funeral:

---

24.   From, respectively, the sleeve notes to the album "The Unfortunate Rake: A Study in the Evolution of a Ballad", various versions by various artists, compiled and edited by Kenneth Goldstein, Folkways Records FS3805, NYC, 1960; and from Roy Palmer's *The Oxford Book of Sea Songs* (1986).

Clearly the funeral is an essential part of the story . . . Though the identity of the hero and the cause of death changes, one thing remains – the triumphant laugh in the face of death . . . All the other details are varied to suit the singer and his community, to help him communicate this basic theme, that life is all there is, that man must die but death is not the end of the story (though there is no suggestion of life, punishment . . . or redemption after death; man has the last word, but on this earth).[25]

Actually 'the triumphant laugh in the face of death' is not always the evident approach. Some of these dying narrators depart this life with a strong sense of shame or regret. Each one, by wishing to extract the promise of a particular ritual of departure, aspires to securing a 'nothing in his life became him like the leaving of it' kind of final judgement from this world.[26] Perhaps this relates to Dylan's sense of Blind Willie McTell's special aptness as a creator of requiem, as evidenced by McTell's magnificent, personalised version of the song, his 1956 'The Dyin' Crapshooter's Blues', to which we soon attend.

The white variant that Ewan MacColl learnt from the Norfolk traditional singer Harry Cox, 'The Trooper Cut Down In His Prime', was sung by British soldiers in the Boer War, though his rendition is based on the First World War equivalent. This stresses that the burial involved is a military one (with its 'musket, fife and drum', as another old English song puts it)[27] while retaining the original hint that the soldier has died of syphilis. The flowers to mask the smell of death reflect the once common belief that the corpse of the syphilis victim decomposes quicker than others.

(Roy Palmer reports of the eighteenth-century 'Buck's Elegy' version that 'the onlooker's grief is compounded by the realization that he has contracted the same disease as his comrade, from the same woman . . .'; Palmer also publishes the text of a close relative of the MacColl version, the 'sea song' 'The Young Sailor Cut Down In His Prime'.)[28]

The version A. L. Lloyd has recorded, which is older, lightens up the funereal music instructions but locates the encounter around St. James' Hospital (a shift of just a mile or two from Covent Garden down to the far end of Piccadilly; St. James Hospital has since become St. James' Palace).[29]

25. Karl Dallas, 'The Roots of Tradition', in *The Electric Muse*, by Laing, Dallas, Denselow and Shelton, 1975.

26. The fuller passage (it is by Shakespeare, from a speech of Malcolm in *Macbeth*) is itself interesting here, in its recognition of a correspondence between dignity and grace, and an almost wanton lack of solemnity: 'Nothing in his life / Became him like the leaving of it / As one that had been studied in his death / To throw away the dearest thing he ow'd / As 'twere a careless trifle'. (Act I, Scene 4.)

27. The old English song invoking 'musket, fife and drum' in its chorus (for a marriage rather than a burial ceremony) is the traditional 'O Soldier, Soldier' in which a 'sweet maid' asks a soldier to marry her and he says he can't because he has 'no coat/hat/gloves/boots to put on', so that she gives him a pair 'of the very very best' of each from her 'grandfather's chest', only to find in the last verse that he still can't marry her 'For I have a wife of my own'. (The song was extremely popular in the first half of the century in England and has been widely collected, as for instance in 1920s books for schools like *Twice 44 Sociable Songs*, collected and arranged Geoffrey Shaw, 1927.)

28. Roy Palmer, *The Oxford Book of Sea Songs*.

29. Ewan MacColl: 'The Trooper Cut Down In His Prime', 1958; "Bless 'Em All", Riverside RLP 12–642, New York, 1958; collected on "The Unfortunate Rake", see note 24. A. L. Lloyd: 'The Unfortunate Rake'; "English Street Songs", Riverside RLP 12–614, New York, c. 1956; collected on "The Unfortunate Rake".

There are 'western' white-American versions, notably 'The Cowboy's Lament'. In this, the cause of death has been sanitised into a respectable fatal bullet wound, received in the card-house (a clean-up from 'whorehouse') and the flowers wanted on the coffin are no longer 'so they won't smell me as I pass along' but 'to deaden the clods as they fall' over the victim's grave. Harry Jackson heard a variant of this in Wyoming in the summer of 1938 that is 'The Streets Of Laredo'. Here, though the cause of death has still been sanitised into a nice manly shooting, vestiges of the original story are retained: the whorehouse (here called 'Maisie's') is preceded by 'the dram house', and the flowers are back to disguising the smell of the body on its way to burial. (Harry Jackson, who was also a painter, is the 'cowboy singer' quoted on the back of "Freewheelin'" as saying of Dylan: 'He's so goddamned real, it's unbelievable!')[30]

Other white versions include female ones, primarily 'The Bad Girl's Lament'. The man is 'unfortunate' but of course the woman is 'bad'. In her narrative she goes 'First to the ale house, then to the dance hall', while the girl in 'One Morning In May' goes 'Right out of the alehouse and into the jailhouse' – a construction Bob Dylan parallels in 'Walls Of Red Wing', inside which 'From the dirty old mess hall / You march to the brick wall'.[31]

(There's another pleasing construction, in the 'Rake' itself, that Dylan might once have been struck by: I guess that because it offers a phrase that strikes *me* as 'Dylanesque'. That phrase is

   . . . in the height of my prime.

This is a splendid prototype for what we think of as Dylan's patented doublings: doublings that at first sound like tautology but that prove to have perceptive meaning, like 'the finishing end' and 'let's move to the back of the back of the bus'.)

Doc Watson cut a version of the song using 'St. James Hospital' as the title, which he learnt from Alan Lomax, who learnt it, in turn, from James Iron Head Baker, who sang it for Lomax's Library of Congress archives in 1934 while an inmate of Central State Farm at Sugarland, Texas (which isn't in the centre of the state at all, but just a few miles outside Houston, in the south-east corner). This is a fascinating version for anyone wanting to contemplate the cross-currents between black and white, and between European and North American folksong – because while it is a black Texan version of the song, it seems a real halfway house between the old white 'Rake' and the later black 'St. James Infirmary'. Indeed it seems to meld elements of almost every possible variant: its title refers back to the English nineteenth-century broadside's

30. Harry Jackson, 'The Streets of Laredo', NYC, probably 1957; "The Cowboy: His Songs, Ballads And Brag Talk", Folkways FH 5723, New York, 1957; and collected on "The Unfortunate Rake", see note 24.

31. On "The Unfortunate Rake" (see note 24), 'The Bad Girl's Lament' is a Canadian variant sung by Wade Hemsworth, *nia*, taken from "Folk Songs Of The Canadian North Woods", Folkways FW 6821, NYC, *nia*. 'One Morning In May' is a Virginia variant sung by Hally Wood, *nia*, taken from "O' Lovely Appearance Of Death", Elektra EKL-10, *nia*, but learnt from the version collected by Alan and Elizabeth Lomax from Mrs Texas Gladden of Salem, Virginia, in 1941, issued "Anglo-American Ballads From The Archive of American Folk Song", AFS L1, Washington, DC, 1956. It was Hally Wood, also a song-collector, who collected the 'Worried Blues' that Bob Dylan picked up on, recorded so immaculately (NYC, 9/7/62) and finally released on "Bootleg Series I–III", 1991 – along with his own 'Walls Of Red Wing'.

location; its first narrator looks through the window, as Bob Dylan does in 'Blind Willie McTell'; it is set 'in the month of May'; the dying hero calls for his parents to come to his bedside, as in the 'Bad Girl's Lament', while he himself is a cowboy; his 'poor head is achin'' and his 'sad heart is breakin'', exactly as in 'One Morning In May' . . . and the singer who passes all this on into the world is a black prisoner serving time on a state 'farm'. The tune is also a striking mix, being, as Lomax notes, 'closer to the old folk settings than one usually finds in the west . . . [yet] . . . closely related to the later 'St. James Infirmary' . . . [It] provides the link between the folk ballad and the pop tune'.[32]

Then there is the truly marvellous, personalised requiem made from the same root-song by Blind Willie McTell, recorded as 'Dying Crapshooter's Blues' for John and Ruby Lomax in 1940, recorded again for Atlantic Records in 1949 – but recorded at its fullest and most realised at his almost unbearably poignant last session, made in the autumn of 1956.[33]

Earlier that year, a foreign student walked into a record shop in Atlanta and heard owner Ed Rhodes playing a Leadbelly track. 'D'you really like that old stuff?' 'I sure do.' 'Well there's an old guy just as good as that who sings in a night-club car-park down the street on weekends.' When Rhodes got round to checking this out, he found Blind Willie McTell in the parking lot of the Blue Lantern, performing hits of the day for nickels and dimes to dating white teenagers: a human car-park juke-box. McTell was reluctant to be recorded, but eventually came to Rhodes' shop, where Rhodes was finally able to record an hour of the 58-year-old McTell playing songs from across the whole range of his repertoire, and talking about his life.

There are several songs done at this last session that we also have on record from McTell's earliest times in the studios, and of course these make for compulsive comparison: the early exuberance and effortless, spot-on perfection, the later

32. Doc Watson: 'St. James Hospital', with the composer credit given to James Baker, *nia*, reissued on "The Essential Doc Watson Vol. 1", Vanguard 5308, New York, 1973, CD-reissued Vanguard VMCD 7308, New York, 1987. (This compilation also includes Watson's 'Alberta', his dreadful, cutesy version of 'Froggie Went A-Courtin'', and an excellent version [a re-recording: he had cut it first for Folkways, *nia*] of the early Frank Hutchison song 'The Train That Carried My Girl From Town', a song Watson made into a standard repertoire item. Bob Dylan refers to this Hutchison song obliquely in his notes to "World Gone Wrong", while writing of the 'McTell masterpiece' 'Broke Down Engine'.) James Iron Head Baker is also given the composer credit, at least in Glen Dundas' listing of songs Dylan has performed and recorded, *Tangled up in Tapes* [3rd edn], 1994, for the traditional song 'Ain't No More Cane On The Brazos (Go Down Old Hannah)'. Alan Lomax: 'St. James Hospital', *nia*, issued "Texas Folksongs", Tradition Records TLP 1029, *nia*, and collected on "The Unfortunate Rake", see note 24.

33. A (presumably Tin Pan Alley) version of 'Dyin' Crapshooter's Blues' was copyrighted in 1927 by pianist/arranger Porter Grainger, and four recordings made of it that year, all involving Grainger: Martha Copeland: 'Dyin' Crap-Shooter's Blues', NYC, 5/5/27; Mamie McKinney: 'Dyin' Crap Shooter's Blues', NYC, 24/6/27 (never issued); Viola [Violet] McCoy: 'Dyin' Crap Shooter's Blues', NYC, c. late Aug. 1927; and Rosa Henderson: 'Dyin' Crap-Shooter's Blues', NYC, c. late Sept. 1927. Grainger was pianist on the two earliest of these recordings. He was also pianist on Viola McCoy's first sides (1923), and though he was no longer her pianist by the time of her 'Dyin' Crap Shooter's Blues' session, they were still in contact. Grainger was also (briefly) a session pianist for Rosa Henderson, though again not on the session at which she cut the song. None seems to have been vinyl or CD-issued, and I've been unable to hear them, making comparison impossible between these, earlier folk versions of the song and the versions by Blind Willie McTell, i.e.: 'Dying Crapshooter's Blues', Atlanta, 5/11/40; 'The Dyin' Crapshooter's Blues', Atlanta, October 1949; and 'The Dyin' Crapshooter's Blues', Atlanta, September 1956; issued "Blind Willie McTell: 1940", see note 13, "Blind Willie McTell: Atlanta Twelve String", see note 8, and "Blind Willie McTell: Last Session", see note 6, respectively.

poignancy of comparative hesitation, faltering and loss (another familiar story); yet the 1956 recording also displays the same extraordinary memory for detail evident on the Lomax session of sixteen years before.

The special glory of the last session is, with its fabulous, lengthy spoken intro, 'The Dyin' Crapshooter's Blues', in which Blind Willie McTell transforms the format of the 'Rake' cycle of songs into the real-life story of the shooting by the police of a friend of his. Well worth quoting in its entirety, McTell's final-end version of 'The Dyin' Crapshooter's Blues' is a masterpiece, as great in its own way as anything he made, and certainly superior to his earlier recordings of the same song. Complete with the spoken introduction that clinches this, letting us into a much fuller understanding of the song, so that we can follow, and therefore value, its inspired mix of the personal and the archetypal, it runs like this:

[spoken:]
I started writin' the song in '29 – but I didn't finish it, I didn't finish it till 1932. Mr. Williams: his name is Jesse Williams. See, he got shot here, on Coda [?] Street. And after he gettin' shot, I taken him home. He was sick about three weeks after I taken home – sick from the shot.

And so he give me this request: and then, he wanted me to play this over his grave. That I did. See, I had to steal music from every which way to get it – to get it, to get it to fit. But I messed it up anyway, somehow or other, just to suit him.

I finally played what he wanted; but he got everything he wanted but the women from Atlanta. He didn't get the women from Atlanta, cos, see, it was too far for them to come. He was buried in New York. I taken him there in an ambulance. (Cost me two hundred – I think it was two hundred and eighty-two dollars, I think, and eighty-five cents I think a man charged me for takin' him home – but he was able.)

His father give him anything he wanted – give him everything he wanted but the women in Atlanta. He didn't have the sixteen women – the twenty-two women out the Hamilton Hotel: he didn't have that. We didn't have the twenty-nine out of North Atlanta – and he didn't have the twenty-six off of South Bell, that which might have – we called Hill Street. That's where he hung out at, y'know, durin' his – durin' his women-lovin' time, you know.

After gettin' shot, I carried him home. I sit by his bedside every day. And he would tell me what he wanted. I would tell his daddy. So after he died, daddy said, well, everything he wanted we're gonn' get. So he got everything 'bout it but the women from Atlanta.

So I had to play it: 'The Dyin' Crapshooter's Blues'. That's what I was s'posed to name it:

[sung:]
Little Jesse was a gambler night and day
He used crooked cards 'n' dice

Sinful guy, good-hearted but had no soul
Heart was hard and cold like ice

Jesse was a wild reckless gambler, wannaganga [wasn't gonna?] *change*
Ah [?] *many a gamblin' heart he led in vain*
Began to lose his money, began to be blue
Sattin' all alone, his heart had even turned to stone

What broke Jesse's heart while he was blue 'n' all alone
Sweet Lorrene had packed up and gone
Police walked up and shot my friend Jesse down
Boy they got 'im dead of day [?]

He had a gang of crapshooters and gamblers at his bedside
Here are the words he had to say
'Guess I ought to know
Exactly how I'd wanna go.'

How you wanna go, Jesse?

'Eight crapshooters to be my pallbearers
Let 'em be veiled down in black
I want nine men goin' to the graveyard, bubba
An' eight men comin' back

I wants a gang of gamblers gathered round my coffin-side
Crooked card printed on my hearse
Don't say the crapshooters [???] *life on me*
Life been a doggone curse

Send a poker-player to the graveyard
Dig my grave with the ace of spade
I want twelve polices in my funeral march
High Sheriff playin' Black Jack lead the parade

I want the judges 'n solicitor who jailed me fourteen times
Put a pair of dice in my shoes'

Then what?

'Let a deck of card be my tombstone
I got the dyin' crapshooter's blues.

Sixteen real good crapshooters
Sixteen bootleggers to sing a song
Sixteen racket-men gamblin'
Cover ten part [???] *while I'm rollin' along.'*

He wanted twenty-two womens out the Hamilton Hotel
Twenty-six off a South Bell
Twenty-nine women out of North Atlanta –
No, little Jesse didn't pass out so swell!

His head was achin', heart was thumpin'
Little Jesse went to hell bouncin' and jumpin'
Folks, don't be standin' round old Jesse cryin' –
He wants ev'ybody to do the Charleston whiles he's dyin':

One foot up, a toenail draggin'
Throw my buddy Jesse in the hoodoo waggon
Come here mama with that can of booze
The Dyin' Crapshooter's – leavin' the world –
The Dyin' Crapshooter's – goin' down slow –
With the Dyin' Crapshooter's Blues.

There are far more vestiges of our 'Unfortunate Rake' & Co. here than a first listen might suggest. The basic framework is of course the same: a first narrator comes upon, and tends, a dying second narrator, who then asks the first to sort out a particular set of funeral arrangements.

McTell's second narrator is not a soldier or sailor, buck or rake, bad girl or cowboy, but a gambler – not a sharpshooter but a cardsharp. He resembles these others. Like the cowboys, he is shot, and like the bad girls, he had it coming: he was leading a life of wasteful pleasure: 'I am a young maid and I know I've done wrong', runs 'The Bad Girl's Lament'; 'I used to seek pleasure . . . and Hell is my doom', runs 'One Morning In May'; 'Jesse was a wild reckless gambler . . . went to hell bouncin' and jumpin'', sings McTell; 'I first took to drinking and then to card-playing, / And then I got shot so I'm dying today', goes 'The Cowboy's Lament'.

McTell's crapshooter also has a father on hand to help oversee things while he's dying – so does the young Scotsman in the variant 'Noo I'm A Young Man Cut Down In My Prime', the girl in 'One Morning In May' and the cowboy in 'St. James Hospital' – and an absent, important lover. His 'sweet Lorrene' is matched by the Bad Girl's 'young man I first fell in love with' and the lamenting cowboy's 'another, more dear than a mother', met again in 'The Streets Of Laredo'.[34]

As in all the 'Rake' songs, McTell's crapshooter lays down exactly what he wants for his funeral: the specific numbers of pall-bearers and attendants, the pretty women, the music. Again, these echo down the years from old white Europe to black America: and they are present both as parallel ingredients and as surviving *words and phrases*. 'To sing [me] a song' is one. 'Six young girls to sing me a song', in 'The Unfortunate Rake' and 'Six pretty maidens to sing me a song', in 'The Bad Girl's Lament', becomes, in 'St. James Hospital'

I want sixteen young gamblers, papa, to carry my coffin
I want sixteen young whore gals for to sing me my song

and in McTell

Sixteen bootleggers to sing a song
Sixteen racket-men gamblin'.

---

34. 'Noo I'm A Young Man Cut Down In My Prime', Willie Mathieson, North-East Scotland, 1952, field-recorded by Hamish Henderson for the School of Scottish Studies; "The Unfortunate Rake", see note 24.

Like 'hell' and 'father', that 'sixteen' is a shared specific, found in 'The Streets Of Laredo' as well as 'St. James Hospital', and it comes echoing out of the 'six' found all across the cycle. This shows how things grow in the telling (and how America always likes things bigger): all the earlier, Old World variants expect more modest numbers. What they all do is specify *some* numbers. The young woman in 'One Morning In May' wants four young ladies, three young maidens, two parents, one doctor and one preacher; Jesse Williams wants seventy-seven women, various sixteens, possibly fourteen judges, twelve police, eight pallbearers, one solicitor and a poker-player.

In 'Rake' and 'The Streets Of Laredo' we get the phrase 'as they bear me along'; in 'Rake' and 'The Trooper' we get 'as you carry me along'; in 'The Cowboy's Lament' 'to carry me along'; in 'Bad Girl's Lament' 'as they carry me along'; in 'Bright Summer Morning' it is 'while passing along' – and McTell retains the phrase as 'while I'm rollin' along'.

Similarly with 'The Trooper''s 'His poor head was achin', his poor heart was breakin'', the Scottish 'My head is an-achin', my heart is a-breaking' and 'One Morning In May''s 'My poor head is aching, my sad heart is breaking' – this resilient element survives quite clearly in McTell's composition, in which

His head was achin', heart was thumpin' . . .

and while the question of the decomposition of the body is, not unnaturally, absent here, the references to 'this was during his women-loving time' and 'the women from the Hamilton Hotel' retain the old links with the whorehouse. The 'twenty-six women off of South Bell' would also have been 'Flash girls of the city', as the 'Trooper' variant has it: Bell Street Atlanta (now demolished, like almost every part of the city Blind Willie McTell ever knew) was a notorious avenue of vice and crime, celebrated – if that is the word, and it usually is in such songs, whatever their upstanding official theme – in a song McTell recorded in the 1930s, 'Bell Street Lightnin''.[35]

As for the music ingredient in 'The Dyin' Crapshooter's Blues', you might say that its military nature, the fifes and drums playing the Dead March, has disappeared in favour of 'the Charleston', and indeed of the blues song itself (McTell and Jesse Williams would no doubt be gratified to learn that their 'Dyin' Crapshooter's Blues' is a self-reflexive text). Yet the military ingredient still lingers, retained in the words 'march' and 'parade':

I want twelve polices in my funeral march
High Sheriff . . . lead the parade.

This has been retained, but also absorbed – absorbed into the dualistic black American burial rite, New Orleans style, in which the solemn march to the graveyard is followed by the life-affirming, celebratory dance back. Dead March and Charleston, as it were.

Another strand of still-surviving black culture absorbed the military fife and drum music as early as the seventeenth century. In the Deep South there are still fife and drum bands, borrowing their instrumentation from the War of Independence tradition

---

35. Blind Willie McTell: 'Bell Street Lightnin'', NYC, 21/9/33; JEMF-106, see note 1; CD-reissued "The Definitive Blind Willie McTell", see note 11. This song is a graphic re-working of Sloppy Henry's 'Canned Heat Blues', Atlanta, 13/8/28.

and using it for 'picnic music', historically when hired out for white social events and later to express their own rural spirit. Alan Lomax describes witnessing such music being played in 'the Hills' around Senatobia, Mississippi, in the 1940s by the Hemphill family – and describes it in terms that look back through the telescope of American history much as Bob Dylan does in 'Blind Willie McTell':

> the fife player, with the drums and guitars beating out a somber rhythm behind him, wailed and squeaked through a tune they called 'The Death March'. The country folk listened with stony faces . . . It was music harsh and crude and vital and rank as milkweed . . . a sound that Davy Crockett might have heard as he rode through these hills on his way to Texas . . . a music that suited the early days of this wild country when blacks and whites and Indians fished and hunted and swilled whiskey and ran from the great Mississippi in the shadowy edges of the American jungle.[36]

By the time Alan Lomax was listening to the Hemphills' fife and drum music in Mississippi, and Blind Willie McTell was singing an early version of 'The Dyin' Crapshooter's Blues' to Lomax's father in a hotel room in Georgia in 1940, 'St. James Infirmary' had become a standard of sorts, combining its own version of 'The Unfortunate Rake' and of that New Orleans post-funeral music. The classic dixieland version of the song is by Jack Teagarden, from 1941, but such renditions had been popular through most of the 1920s and 1930s: so much so that there was a long period during which, just as all early-1960s British beat-groups had to know 'Got My Mojo Working' (we all wondered what a mojo was, but didn't like to ask), so it was more or less obligatory for American jazz bands, black and white, to know 'St. James Infirmary'.[37]

Blind Willie McTell himself sings it, alongside 'The Dyin' Crapshooter's Blues', during his 1956 "Last Session". His performance languishes among the unissued items.

What all these songs do is allow some articulation of a fundamental human problem: how to face death. The use of two narrators allows an interplay, or balancing, between different strategies. In the early versions, the dying hero or heroine is often preoccupied with a sense of shame or unworthiness, while the person who comes upon them is confronting imminent loss, the impermanence of comradeship, the responsibility of bearing witness to death. The later versions mediate between these feelings of tenderness, sorrow and grief for another, and the dying person's own need to banish the fear of death by making light of it. This duality is especially heightened in Blind Willie McTell's 'The Dyin' Crapshooter's Blues', which begins with that long and attentive spoken account of caring for the dying friend, of the daily

---

36. Alan Lomax: *The Land Where the Blues Began* (1993). Lomax quotes our old friend David Evans: 'as early as the seventeenth century blacks may have "picked up" the skills of fife and drum playing from the militia units in New England and the Middle Colonies . . . During the eighteenth century there are numerous reports of black fifers and drummers.' (David Evans, 'Black fife and drum music in Mississippi', *Mississippi Folklore Register*, 6, no. 3, Fall 1972.) An example of a contemporary recording of such music is 'Alabama Bound' by Hezekiah & The House Rockers, *nia*, High Water Records LP 1011, USA, 1991, a label run by David Evans.

37. Jack Teagarden And His Orchestra: 'St. James Infirmary', Los Angeles, 26/5/41 (issued on a US Decca 78 rpm).

care over a period of weeks, the ambulance ride, the father on hand, the sorting out of practicalities – followed by the reductive mythologising of those practicalities by the careless victim ('Let a deck of card be my tombstone' . . . 'Life been a doggone curse'), and culminates in the first narrator's submission to the second's show of indifference:

> *Throw my buddy Jesse in the hoodoo wagon*
> *Come here mama with that can of booze . . .*
> *With the Dyin' Crapshooter's Blues.*

This is a very similar ending to the conventional one for 'St. James Infirmary':

> *Well now you've heard my story*
> *Have another shot of booze*
> *And if anyone should happen to ask you*
> *I got the St. James Infirmary Blues.*[38]

What makes 'St. James Infirmary' different is that it almost has three narrators. That is, the first narrator meets not a dying second narrator but a healthy one, who is in turn contemplating the death of a third character (his lover). Because death has already arrived in this construction, though only just, the lover doesn't get to speak, but its effect is to make the second narrator meditate upon his own mortality much like the dying second narrators of all the other songs.

The question of how many elements of the 'Rake' cycle Dylan imports into (it's tempting to say 'retains in') 'Blind Willie McTell' is only one of its aspects, but it's a starting point: it stresses their shared central purpose. Bob Dylan's rich and complex song, with a melody that winds across the path of the 'St. James Infirmary' tune, is also about the problem of how to face death, extended onto the grandest of scales. While implicitly it mourns the death of McTell, it struggles with the problem of how to face, to witness, to confront, the world's death rather than an individual one.

Like the 'Rake' songs, there are two narrators, and for the same reason, to summon more than one strategy in the face of death. In the Dylan song we find a first narrator who witnesses and a second who, says the first, could witness better.

> *Seen the arrow on the doorpost*
> *Sayin' this land is condemned*
> *All the way from New Orleans to Jerusalem*
>
> *I travelled through East Texas*
> *Where many martyrs fell*
> *An' I know no-one can sing the blues like Blind Willie McTell.*
>
> *I heard that hoot-owl singin'*
> *As they were takin' down the tents*
> *The stars above the barren trees was his only audience*

38. Taken from a short discussion at the Mariposa Folk Festival, Canada, 1972, and reproduced as 'Michael Cooney, Sam Hinton and Ken Goldstein talk "The Unfortunate Rake"' in *For What Time I Am in This World*, ed. Bill Usher (1977).

Them charcoal gypsy maidens
Can strut their feathers well
But nobody can sing the blues like Blind Willie McTell.

See them big plantations burnin'
Hear the crackin' of the whips
Smell that sweet magnolia bloom and see the ghosts of slavery ships

I can hear them tribes a-moanin'
Hear that undertaker's bell
Nobody can sing the blues like Blind Willie McTell.

There's a woman by the river
With some fine young handsome man
He's dressed up like a squire, bootleg whiskey in his hand

There's a chain-gang on the highway
I can hear them rebels yell
And I know no-one can sing the blues like Blind Willie McTell.

Well God is in His heaven
And we all want what's His
But power and greed and corruptible seed seem to be all that there is

I am gazing out the window
Of the St. James Hotel
And I know no-one can sing the blues like Blind Willie McTell.

What a song! And let me say at once that its opening verse parallels the beginning of the 'Rake' songs. Where they see a doomed comrade wrapped in white linen and cold as the clay, Dylan sees the same thing on the grand scale: he has

> *. . . seen the arrow on the doorpost*
> *Sayin' this land is condemned*
> *All the way from New Orleans to Jerusalem.*

In the next lines, he pluralises coming upon 'one of my comrades', remembering that 'many martyrs fell', and expressing a sympathy with other unwilling recruits whose presence is felt in this pageant of suffering and struggle: the tribes conscripted from Africa as slaves, the chain-gangs forced to build the highways, the rebels forced to fight. And between 'All the way from New Orleans to Jerusalem' and 'I travelled through East Texas' he sets up echoes of 'The Streets Of Laredo', in which the narrator 'born in South East Texas' says 'I've trailed from Canadee down to old Mexico'. Instead of a crowd round the bedside and people 'to sing a song',

> *I heard that hoot-owl singin'*
> *As they were takin' down the tents*
> *The stars above the barren trees was his only audience.*

In parallel with 'the women from Atlanta', 'them flash-girls', or 'pretty maidens',

Them charcoal gypsy maidens
Can strut their feathers well . . .

The flowers are here too. The 'Rake' songs have 'green laurel', 'white roses', 'red roses', 'wild roses', 'green roses' and 'those sweet-smellin' roses'; they also have, in 'The Streets Of Laredo', a southern setting in which 'the jimson weed and the lilac does bloom'. In 'Blind Willie McTell' we see a southern setting in which we 'smell that sweet magnolia bloom'.

Dylan's

With some fine young handsome man

matches 'St. James Hospital's 'with them handsome young ladies' and 'The Unfortunate Rake's 'some handsome young woman', and he unites the 'Hamilton Hotel' of McTell's narrative with the conventional 'St. James Infirmary' in his own, perfectly placed 'St. James Hotel'. Dylan also uses 'the window', from the James Baker/Doc Watson variant. This begins with the window:

It was early one morning I passed St. James Hospital
. . . I looked in the window . . .

and Dylan ends with it. I can't quite be certain, on either of the versions of 'Blind Willie McTell' that have circulated, that Dylan sings

I am gazin' out the window . . .,

which reverses the old Texan version and places Dylan as the dying inmate, quietly appropriate to the theme that we are all facing imminent death; it's always enticingly close to

I am gazin' at the window . . .,

which would leave it nicely ambivalent as to which side of the glass Dylan is on as he bows his head and cries, while staring at the bleakness of the futureless future.

Dylan can also use the same language as the 'Rake' cycle but undermine its meaning. That 'fine young handsome man',

He's dressed up like a squire . . .

which throws a shadow across his fine and handsome aspect: 'dressed up like' suggests both the counterfeit, weighted down by that 'bootleg whiskey in his hand', and the vain, fluffed up by the resonance of the earlier, matching 'strut'. Even the 'sweet magnolia' sounds quite unlike the 'sweet-smellin' roses' of the earlier songs. I don't know why, since Dylan adds nothing more beyond the phrase itself, yet we smell it as overripe and sickly. Where once the flowers were there to cover the smell of corruption, in Dylan's song they give off the smell of corruption themselves.

Falsity, vanity and corruption compound cruelty and pain. Everywhere people are fallen, in chains, under the whip in this maelstrom of history. I say 'maelstrom' because though it's been said that 'Blind Willie McTell' rolls backwards through America's past, in truth it offers no such consistent reverse chronology and its vision is not limited to American terrain, though it returns to it time and again, not least by the device of Blind Willie McTell's omnipresence.

This may disappoint the need for neatness but it is a strength of the song that most of its images evoke more than one era: more than one time *and* place, while pressing upon us, time and again, a running analogy between Old Testament and New World.

It begins at the beginning. The 'arrow on the doorpost / Sayin' this land is condemned' flickers with a picture of the marking out of Jewish houses in the pogroms of the 1930s and with the daubing of the doors of plague victims in medieval Europe, but it harks back, as both these later scenes must, to the first occasion to yield such an image: the time of the Passover, when the first-born in Egypt were slain in the night by God, after the people of Moses were instructed to mark a sign on their doorposts in lamb's blood so that death might pass over and spare their children: 'take of the blood, and strike it on the two side posts and on the upper door post of the houses', as God instructs Moses in Exodus 12:7.

What's so striking in Bob Dylan's lyric, what gives us the sense that poetry is at work, is that Dylan can use this as the opening of a song that holds out no hope that anyone shall be spared the destruction coming in *our* night. There may be a sign on the doorpost but whose first-born – whose future – is to be spared this time, now that the land has been

> . . . *condemned*
> *All the way from New Orleans to Jerusalem?*

We reach America explicitly enough, of course, when we get to 'East Texas, where many martyrs fell'. Across the border from New Orleans, Louisiana, it sticks in the memory as a stronghold of the Ku Klux Klan: a place where black victims were untold martyrs and where the same racist attitudes linger still. Yet 'martyrs' has other, primarily religious, connotations. The word is thrown in like a spanner, to wobble us off our course of easy assumption about the focus of the song. The word 'fell' has a distracting quality here too, somehow calling attention to itself by its declamatory vagueness.

'Takin' down the tents' gives us another glimmer of the Israelites, now on their way out of Egypt, but suggests too the medicine shows, the carnival tents that linger into the twentieth century from an older America. McTell and Bob Dylan both claim a bit of tent-cred in their early days – and for someone whose experience of it was mostly in the mind, Dylan wrote of it in thrillingly energetic detail in 'Dusty Old Fairgrounds', where we feel the pitching and dismantling of the tents as a routine, an activity, a part of life, all through the song. He claims a similar intimacy with this life when he discusses his own (now lost) poem 'Won't You Buy A Postcard?' in 1962.[39] The Hawks had medicine show experience; Elvis' manager, Colonel Parker, was an old carnie trooper. Even as recent a figure as the contemporary blues singer Robert Cray recalls that in the early days he and his musicians hit the road in an old truck and camped overnight in tents as they travelled (roaming the country like 'charcoal gypsy maidens'). But 'them charcoal gypsy maidens' also conjures up nubile black

---

39. *Folksinger's Choice*, WBAI Radio, NYC, probably recorded 13/1/62 and probably broadcast 11/3/62.

girls in 1920s cabaret routines, shimmying through the floorshows of smoky night-clubs in black and white movies: the sort in which the blues singers never get a look-in, because 'sophisticated' jazz combos deliver slicker, jollier routines more compatible with Hollywood sensibilities.

There is *almost* nothing ambiguous about time or place in the next section of the song, in which time is running backwards from *Gone with the Wind* to the roots of *Roots*: yet the word 'tribes' arrives strikingly here. It has a rigour that cuts across the assemblage of shorthand images of the Antebellum South. It dislocates the expected chain of words as 'martyrs' does earlier.

Aptly, 'them tribes' come pouring in across the very centre of the song: aptly because the analogy clutched in this double image, the analogy between the twelve tribes of Israel and the African tribes brought over on the slave ships, is the central analogy Dylan draws all through the song. It is, moreover, the classic analogy drawn by the oppressed American blacks themselves, all the way through till at least Blind Willie McTell's generation, as they compensated themselves for the miseries of this life by looking forward to justice in the next and reading the Bible's accounts of the struggles of the Israelites in order to voice their own aspirations. We shall overcome some day. That's why I'm sending up my timber. And I know no one can sing them hymns like Blind Willie McTell.

The 'woman by the river' might equally be biblical or Mississippian. She's timeless. The 'squire' suggests the seventeenth or eighteenth century, but 'dressed up like a squire' adds in all those nineteenth-century Southern landowners striding their estates in high boots and frilly shirts while the blacks, almost invisible, worked the land. The 'bootleg whiskey in his hand' can equally smell of the stills in the hills (where they ain't paid no whiskey tax since 1792) or of Prohibition Chicago, another milieu the old blues singers lived and worked in. The 'chain-gang on the highway' must keep us in that recent past but the 'rebels', whoever else they may be, insist on yelling to us from the American Civil War.

This multi-layering of the pageant takes its cue from the opening verse: crucially to our whole understanding of the song, 'All the way from New Orleans to Jerusalem' must be capable of pitching us both backwards and forwards – back from the New Orleans of now or of McTell's generation, the New Orleans where you might say black American music found its feet, to the Jerusalem of Bible days; and forward to the new Jerusalem dreamed of but now doomed not to be: dreamed of but 'condemned'.

One of Dylan's inspired touches here, in that nigh-perfect penultimate stanza, is to underscore his tolling of doomsday by alluding to, and then contorting, those well-known lines of optimism and hope,

> *God's in His heaven –*
> *All's right with the world.*

The twisting of this fresh-faced couplet into the brutish modernism of

> *Well God is in His heaven*
> *And we all want what's His*

could hardly be bettered: Dylan uses the mugging energy of the bare greed he describes to give his lines a slashing economy, hitting us with the switch from the lost innocence of the original.

Those lines are by Dylan's old friend Robert Browning – from the first section, 'Morning', of the dramatic poem 'Pippa Passes' – and Dylan's song takes from the poem more than just this one, expertly handled, crude allusion. To know the context is to see that Dylan snatches away not just the gentleness, nor even primarily the reassuring stasis or apparent permanence of those often-quoted lines, by replacing Browning's contentment with the bleakness of 'But power and greed and corruptible seed seem to be all that there is'. More especially Dylan contradicts Browning's vision of the world as fresh and pure because *young*, because purged by the coming of spring. This is the context:

> *The year's at the spring,*
> *And day's at the morn;*
> *Morning's at seven;*
> *The hill-side's dew-pearled;*
> *The lark's on the wing;*
> *The snail's on the thorn;*
> *God's in His heaven –*
> *All's right with the world.*[40]

(If Dylan's song has 'The Dyin' Crapshooter's Blues' and its predecessors as one broad model, Browning's lines come close to being a structural model too: to the extent that Dylan's verses can be said to set themselves out in reverse order, to roll backwards, so Browning sets out his scene 'backwards':

> *The year's at the spring,*
> *And day's at the morn;*
> *Morning's at seven . . .)*

Dylan's 'seed' deftly acknowledges this context, while shrivelling it away at once into the biblical rhetoric of 'corruptible seed' – a latency that promises only further decay in a world already old and exhausted. Dylan turns morning into mourning, replacing the lark on the wing with the hoot-owl in the barren trees.[41]

While Dylan sounds the undertaker's bell, the song itself never shrivels: it moves but it certainly doesn't depress. It examines the problem of how to face death but it tingles with life. The black girls, in that lovely, eccentric construction, strut their feathers. The song presses a sense of our senses upon us. *Blind* Willie McTell, his other senses heightened, is never far away. Yet true to McTell's uncanny visualising spirit, *seeing* is insisted upon. In one verse alone we see, hear, smell and see again. The first word of the song is 'seen'; the end of the song finds him 'gazing'. All through,

---

40. 'Pippa Passes' (Part 1, 'Morning'), which formed part of *Bells and Pomegranates* (a reference to Exodus 28:33–34), published in sections, London, 1841–1846.

41. The biblical text from which Dylan takes 'corruptible seed' is 1 Peter, 1:23–4: 'Being born again, not of corruptible seed, but of incorruptible, by the word of God, which liveth and abideth for ever. For all flesh is as grass, and all the glory of man as the flower of grass. The grass withereth, and the flower thereof falleth away.'

spooky as the plangent, coiling music, Dylan's sixth sense emits its vibrant, probing beam.[42]

Out of death, life arises. Out of bodily pain, the triumph of the spirit (pain sure brings out the best in people, doesn't it?). Out of singing the blues, compensation: even joy. Dylan celebrates, in this song – as Blind Willie McTell does in 'The Dyin' Crapshooter's Blues'. The work of art, as ever with Bob Dylan, is the recording, not the words on the page: but the words on the page demand from Dylan, and receive, two of his most focused performances: paying tribute to McTell's artistry, he rises to the occasion with the excellence of his own. What a song!, you say when you read the lyric. What a record!, you say when you hear the belatedly issued performance.

This is the spookiest important record since 'Heartbreak Hotel', and is built upon the perfect interweaving of guitar, piano, voice and silence – an interweaving that has space for the lovely clarity of single notes: a guitar-string stroking the air here, a piano-note pushing back the distance there. And if anything, the still-unreleased performance is even better, for its more original melody (less dependent upon the conventional 'St. James Infirmary' structure) and its incandescent vocal, which soars to possess the heights of reverie and inspiration. No one can sing the blues like Blind Willie McTell, but no one can write or sing a blues like 'Blind Willie McTell' like Bob Dylan.

Aptly, in view of their subject-matter, there is even a further correspondence between McTell's masterpiece 'The Dyin' Crapshooter's Blues' and Dylan's masterpiece 'Blind Willie McTell' – these two great songs about appropriate leave-taking – in the tiny detailing of how they take their leave of us. A *doubled rhyme* is one way to signal the end of a song, as Christopher Ricks points out apropos of 'Señor (Tales Of Yankee Power)', which ends with

> *Can you tell me what we're waiting fo*r, Señor?

Ricks calls this 'making a conclusive ending, that your conclusions can be more drastic,' adding that this is 'exactly what Andrew Marvell did in the greatest political poem in the English language: that is, the 'Horatian Ode''.[43]

Nowhere this side of Marvell will you find more effective use of such extra emphasis of rhyme as a signing-off device at song's end than when McTell ends 'The Dyin' Crapshooter's Blues'. He sings the final phrase as

> *It's the dyin' crap*-shoo-doo's blues:

putting equal and emphatic weight on each of these last sounds. As you might expect, Dylan finds a neatly equivalent little thing for the end of 'Blind Willie McTell'. In fact Christopher Ricks makes a generalisation in 1980 about Dylan's work which is prophetically accurate about this 1983 song: '. . . he's obsessed with two things. One

---

42. Spookily, too, perhaps, Dylan's recording of 'Blind Willie McTell' manages to commemorate not only the death of McTell but his birthday also. We know that McTell was born in 1899, and probably on 5 May. Either by eerie coincidence, or because Bob Dylan is a closet walking blues encyclopedia, when he came to record 'Blind Willie McTell' in 1983, he did so on 5 May. Note: 1901 is often given as McTell's birth year but there is no reason to accept this as truer than 1899.

43. Christopher Ricks, radio broadcast in Australia, *nia*, 1980. Andrew Marvell: 'An Horatian Ode upon Cromwell's Return from Ireland' (1650).

is human situations which you can't imagine ever really coming to an end, and the other is the simple technical question of how if you're singing a song you do something intuitive and imaginative to let people know that it really is the end.'[44]

In this case, paralleling 'The Dyin' Crapshooter's Blues', Dylan finds a solution to this 'simple technical question' that is an intuitive touch of tribute to McTell. Instead of a rhyme like those that conclude his other verses – 'bell/McTell', and so on – his last verse simply doubles that subliminal 'tell', pairing

> *I am gazing out the window of the St. James Hotel*

with

> *And I know no-one can sing the blues like Blind Willie McTell.*

The very phrase 'sing the blues' re-expresses in colloquial terms the ancient Hebrew custom of making *lamentations*, or mourning songs, 'upon the death of great men . . . and upon any occasion of public miseries and calamities'.[45] In the Old Testament book Lamentations (short for The Lamentations of Jeremiah), Jeremiah composes a lamentation on the death of Josiah the King, but also a lamentation upon the desolations of Jerusalem, which are visited on the Jews by God for their worship of false idols. In 'Blind Willie McTell' Dylan achieves a lamentation that serves to commemorate both public calamity *and* individual demise – to deal with the envisaged desolations to come – 'all the way from New Orleans to Jerusalem' – and the death of Blind Willie McTell.

In 1959, Sam Charters kicked off the blues revival in America with a book and record called "The Country Blues" – featuring McTell's 1920s classic 'Statesboro Blues'. Young urban whites started searching out old rural blacks. Charters, tipped off by someone from Atlanta, was told of the possible existence of the never-heard McTell "Last Session". By this time Ed Rhodes had sold his recording equipment and dumped all his tapes in the attic. By an extraordinary twist of fate, Blind Willie McTell's turned out to be the one undamaged tape in the pile. An album from the session was issued in 1961 and the search for McTell was rejoined.

All this came just too late. Blind Willie McTell had died the very year that, unbeknownst to him, he was at last receiving some acclaim as a great blues artist, for his recording of 'Statesboro Blues'.

Helen Edwards, with whom McTell had lived for fourteen years, died on Hallowe'en 1958; the following spring McTell, now 60, had a stroke, and moved back to Thomson to live with his cousin Eddie McTier. For a while his health improved and he even played guitar again out in the yard (and yet again people would pay to hear him). But suddenly in summer his health deteriorated again and he was admitted to Milledgeville State Hospital (actually a mental hospital), fifty miles from Thomson, on 12 August 1959. He died there one week later of 'cerebral hemorrhages'.

The body was taken to Haines and Peterson Mortuary in Warrenton. The funeral

---

44. Christopher Ricks, note 43.

45. Adam Clarke, *Clarke's Commentary on the Bible, Old Testament*, Vol. 4 (1844 edition).

was held at the cemetery of Jones Grove Baptist Church, five miles south of Thomson, off Happy Valley Road, in the midst of gently rolling open farmland. McTell had worshipped and sung here many times. Kate McTell learnt of the funeral only at the last minute, too late to fulfil *his* funeral request that one of his guitars be buried with him.

This was not the only slip-up. All through his professional life he had performed and recorded under pseudonyms. By mistake, because the man carving the stone mixed up the name of the person who'd commissioned it with that of the person it was intended to commemorate, Blind Willie McTell's gravestone offers us one last pseudonym. It reads

EDDIE McTIER 1898 – AUG 19 1959 AT REST

It puts him closer than Bob Dylan is likely to come to getting that wished-for 'unmarked grave'.

Postscript

But not close enough. Things have changed. The picturesque white clapboard church has now been rebuilt in concrete, which may or may not be sturdier. And in 1996 the freelance film-maker from Atlanta, David Fulmer, who managed to finance a 54-minute documentary film about McTell's life and work, *Blind Willie's Blues*,[46] paid for the replacement of McTell's gravestone with a new, far from anonymous one: a large new one with a large picture of a guitar on it, below the inscription

BLUES LEGEND 'BLIND WILLIE McTELL' BORN WILLIE SAMUEL McTIER
MAY 5, 1901 DIED AUGUST 19, 1959.

And the old, poetically appropriate, modest, pseudonymous gravestone? 'Well,' David Fulmer told me, 'they were just going to throw it away . . . so I put it on the back of my pick-up and now it's sitting here in my back yard in Atlanta.'[47]

Is this to be yet another phase in the ripping off of black Americans' heritage – a new wave of collector's item? Pay for a new headstone for your favourite dead blues hero and get yourself the unique souvenir item of the old one? David Fulmer can call his action upgrading or benificence or honouring Blind Willie McTell properly. I call it grave-robbing.

---

46. 'Blind Willie's Blues', Missing Lenk [sic] Video, Lawrenceville, Georgia 30244, USA.
47. David Fulmer, Atlanta, in phone call from the present writer, Athens, Georgia, 28/10/98.

CHAPTER SIXTEEN

Oh Mercy . . . the Second Half of the 1980s

> We try and we try and we try to be who we were . . . Sooner or later you come to the realisation that we're not who we were. So then what do we do?
>
> Bob Dylan, *Newsweek*, 6/10/97

Scattered around different parts of this book are sufficient sideswipes at the 1985 album "Empire Burlesque", starting with the summary offered in the Introduction, to indicate what I take to be its thin gruel of charms and its heavy weather.

When I first heard it, wanting to like it, I found things to like. 'Emotionally Yours' has a beautiful mix on its instrumental intro; 'Dark Eyes', the closing track, is welcome for its being a solo acoustic performance, in strong contrast not only to the rest of the album but to his entire released output of the previous five years; and, before this odd postscript of a track, there is too the welcome joyous affirmation with which the main body of the album closes, with 'Something's Burning, Baby', on the line 'I believe in the impossible, you know that I do'. This is a ringing re-statement of that consistent best-of-Dylan theme, which at the 1965 San Francisco press conference he expressed as 'All my songs end with "Good luck – I hope you make it".'[1]

The same song also holds one of those quietly successful metaphors for a recognisable state of mind, the simple and accurate 'You've been avoiding the main streets for a long, long while', and which is paired tidily some stanzas later with 'We've reached the edge of the road, baby, where the pasture begins'. The line that follows this:

Where charity is supposed to cover up a multitude of sins

achieves something else that Dylan is always good at: that transformation of a scriptural line into peculiarly tough, modern, colloquial speech, achieved with the fewest changes possible. In the First Epistle General of Peter (1 Peter), he warns the far-flung 'strangers' of Asia, Cappadocia and elsewhere that 'the end of all things is at hand: be ye therefore sober, and watch unto prayer. And above all things have fervent charity among yourselves: for charity shall cover the multitude of

---

1.   Bob Dylan, press conference, San Francisco, 3/12/65, telecast on KQED-TV, *nia*.

sins'.[2] Of course, the slight amendment from '*the* . . .' to '*a* multitude of sins' is long-established in common parlance. But Dylan, who knows perfectly well that the word 'charity' in the King James Bible means not a giving to good causes but *love* – as hinted by Peter's adjective here: his phrase is 'fervent charity' – seizes the contemporary meaning of 'charity' and seizes at the same time the opportunity to turn Peter's 'charity shall *cover* . . . sins' – meaning cancel them out – into the cynical, brusque modernism of 'cover up', meaning conceal by pretence. Thus he achieves a complete shift in meaning while changing the biblical text by hardly a word. It's a quiet, virtuous achievement.[3]

There were other straws to cling to. 'Tight Connection To My Heart (Has Anybody Seen My Love?)' could have been, despite its hopelessly unwieldy title, a hit single, certainly a radio hit, if Dylan's record company had done a decent promotional job on it – and when the album was new, there was something enlivening in the prospect of hearing Bob back on the radio, with his first hit since 'Baby, Stop Cryin'' seven years earlier. I used to walk around London's Clissold Park, playing the album on my Walkman and imagining this track insinuating itself into the heads of other people in the park – people outside the world of Dylan fandom. It didn't happen.

I liked some of the words. It may be slightly braggadocio but 'My hands are sweating / And we haven't even started yet' has an authentic, punchy cadence to it, while these lines, which come soon afterwards, conjure perfectly a conversational and a filmic moment: the figure in the doorway, turning and saying

> *I'm gonna get my coat,*
> *I feel the breath of a storm.*
> *There's something I gotta do tonight,*
> *You go inside and stay warm.*

At the end of the song, we reach, hot on each other's fleeing heels, two of Dylan's most memorable formulations: the inspired

> *What looks large from a distance*
> *Close up ain't never that big*

---

2.   1 Peter 4:7–8. When Peter counsels people 'above all things have . . . charity', he is joining in, as the phrase suggests, the discussion pursued throughout the New Testament on the relative merits, the relative saving grace and efficacy, of faith, hope, charity, works and the law. This gets some attention in Chapter 14.

The same song, 'Something's Burning, Baby', also rolls together with attractive economy two more scriptural references and a common-stock expression, in the couplet 'You can't live by bread alone, you won't be satisfied / You can't roll away the stone if your hands are tied'. The scriptural passages used here are from the Old and New testaments: from Deuteronomy 8:3: 'man doth not live by bread alone, but by every word that proceedeth out of the mouth of the Lord doth man live' and from the Gospels, from the account of Jesus having risen again from the sepulchre after his crucifixion. From Matthew 28:2 we get: 'the angel of the Lord descended from heaven, and came and rolled back the stone from the door' In Mark 16:3, Mary Magdalene and Mary the mother of James 'said among themselves, Who shall roll away the stone from the door of the sepulchre?' In Luke 24:2–3, 'they found the stone rolled away from the sepulchre. And they entered in, and found not the body of the Lord Jesus'. In John 10:1, 'The first day of the week cometh Mary Magdalene, when it was yet dark, unto the sepulchre, and seeth the stone taken away from the sepulchre'.

3.   For a discussion of Dylan's career-long hostility to 'charity organisations', see Clive Wilshin, 'Charity is supposed to cover up a multitude of sins', in *All Across the Telegraph*, ed. Michael Gray and John Bauldie (1987).

followed at once by a fusing of disavowal and longing that is both religious and secular, at once ideological and personal, and is achieved by a teasing scriptural reversal yet a real tenderness of tone:

> *Never could learn to drink that blood*
> *And call it wine*[4]
> *Never could learn to hold you, love*
> *And call you mine.*

In these ways, this, the album's opening track, serves notice that two of the collection's preoccupations will be the disparate ones of Hollywood movies and religion.

Filmic references are dotted throughout Dylan's writing. In the mocking 'Talkin' John Birch Paranoid Blues' he says of George Lincoln Rockwell 'I know for a fact he hates commies 'cus he picketed the movie *Exodus*.' 'She got movies inside her head,' he sings in 'Hero Blues' (in one variant 'nail-movies'), while 'Motorpsycho Nightmare' offers a playful focus on the Hitchcock film *Psycho* and mentions *La Dolce Vita*. I think he first specifies quoting from a film at the end of his unfailingly interesting '11 Outlined Epitaphs':

> *there's a movie called*
> *Shoot The Piano Player*
> *the last line proclaimin'*
> *'music, man, that's where it's at'*
> *it is a religious line . . .*

and we find unacknowledged fleeting quotation from film dialogue in his early work too. In the 1958 film of Tennessee Williams's play *Cat on a Hot Tin Roof*, Paul Newman says to Burl Ives: 'You don't know what love is. To you it's just another four-letter word.' 'Love Is Just A Four-Letter Word' is a pre-electric Dylan song. In Don Siegel's film of the same year, *The Lineup*, a drug trafficker says: 'When you live outside the law you have to eliminate dishonesty.' It's a very short step of elimination to Dylan's famous dictum from 'Absolutely Sweet Marie', 'To live outside the law you must be honest'. The "Self Portrait" instrumental track title 'Woogie Boogie' is also a quote from film dialogue. In the Marx Brothers' 1941 film *The Big Store*, Chico, a piano teacher, tells his pupils: 'Keep practising while I'm away – but remember: NO woogie boogie!'[5]

---

4.   There is, I suppose, an echo here of that line he uses twenty years earlier, in 'Memphis Blues Again': 'They say that all the railroad men just drink up your blood like wine'.

5.   *Exodus*, UA/Carlyle/Alpha, US, directed Otto Preminger, written Dalton Trumbo, starring Paul Newman, Eva Marie Saint, Ralph Richardson, Peter Lawford, Lee J. Cobb, Sal Mineo, Felix Aylmer, Uncle Tom Cobley and all, 1960. *Psycho*, Shamle/Alfred Hitchcock, US, directed Hitchcock and Saul Bass, written Joseph Stefano, starring Anthony Perkins and Janet Leigh, 1960. *La Dolce Vita*, Riama/Pathé, Italy/France, directed Federico Fellini, written Fellini, Tullio Pinelli, Ennio Flaiano and Brunello Rondi, starring Marcello Mastroianni, Anita Ekberg and Anouk Aimée, 1960.
      Tirez sur le pianiste, Films de la Pléiade, France, 1960; directed Francois Truffaut, written Marcel Moussy and Truffaut. (*Shoot the Piano Player*, Dylan calls it, but its English-language title is as often *Shoot the Pianist*.) Years later, Dylan recalls this film, when asking the playwright Sam Shepard if he had ever seen it. This is at their first meeting, prior to Shepard being subsumed into the Rolling Thunder Revue and the making of Dylan's own film *Renaldo & Clara* [Circuit Films, US, directed Bob Dylan and Howard Alk, 1977]. Shepard says yes he has

There is also the submerged presence of the singing cowboy movies in Bob Dylan's consciousness. These were both a successful Hollywood genre and a part of the early history of commercial country music. The stars were Gene Autry (whose *Tumbling Tumbleweeds*, 1935, was one of best of his 100-plus films and provided a title song that has proved recurrently popular), and then Roy Rogers. Though Tex Ritter was never that big, he made fifty-eight singing cowboy films and became a star in the 1950s with the theme tune to *High Noon*. One of his film-songs is 'Blood On The Saddle', a line Dylan alludes to ('blood on your saddle') in his 1970s song 'Idiot Wind', from "Blood On The Tracks".[6]

In the mid-1980s period covering the "Infidels", "Empire Burlesque" and "Knocked Out Loaded" albums, this linkage with Hollywood spreads like a craze for a new game in Dylan's work. The title "Empire Burlesque" itself, of course, flags this preoccupation. It doesn't merely present itself as offering a 'burlesque' of the Holly-wood 'empire', or allude to the chains of cinemas called Empires as does the glossy film magazine *Empire*, founded in 1989 – it's a more detailed reference than that. There were movie houses named Empire Burlesque.[7]

Inside the album, quotations come thick and fast, and almost entirely from distinctive films of the 1940s and 1950s, or from undistinguished vehicles for distinguished stars of the same period.

It's as easy to look at Dylan's use of movie dialogue film by film here as song by song. Certainly this approach worked well for John Lindley, whose 1986 article 'Movies inside his head: Empire Burlesque and *The Maltese Falcon*' first drew attention to this stealthy sewing-in of dialogue in the lyrics of this period, and led to a flurry of further discoveries by Dylan-following insomniacs watching old films on late-night television.[8]

As Lindley noted, *The Maltese Falcon* featured two of Dylan's Hollywood favourites (as well as Bogart in the role of the classic private eye Sam Spade) – Sidney Greenstreet and the great Peter Lorre[9] – and includes many fragments of dialogue magpied inside Dylan's songs:

seen *Shoot the Piano Player* and asks if that's the kind of movie Dylan wants to make. Dylan replies 'Something like that.' [Sam Shepard, *Rolling Thunder Logbook*, 1977.]

   Cat on a Hot Tin Roof, MGM/Avon, US, directed and written Richard Brooks, starring Elizabeth Taylor, 1958. *The Lineup*, Columbia, US, directed Don Siegel, written Stirling Silliphant, 1958. *The Big Store*, MGM, US, directed Charles Reisner, written Sid Kuller, Hal Fimberg and Ray Golden, 1941. [For this last connection, thanks to Christer Svensson, letter to the present writer, c. 1982, Molkom, Sweden.]

6.   Tex Ritter: 'Blood On The Saddle', Hollywood, 1/5/45; CD-reissued "High Noon", Bear Family Records BCD 15634, Vollersode, Germany, 1991, which also includes 'Jingle Jangle Jingle', 'Wichita', 'The Chisolm Trail' and 'Billy The Kid', all cut for Capitol Records 1942–57. Volume 4 of *Reprints From* Sing Out!, nia, also includes 'Blood On The Saddle'.

   A majestic, spacey, superb version of 'Tumbling Tumbleweeds' is the opening track of Don Everly's flawed masterpiece "Don Everly", Ode Records SP-77005, Los Angeles [A&M Records AMLS 2007, London], 1971.

7.   The Empire Burlesque in Newark, New Jersey, is mentioned in Philip Roth's *The Anatomy Lesson* (1983), notes David Hill in *Telegraph*, no. 29, Spring 1988. However, in 'The night Bob came round', by Raymond Foye, *Telegraph*, no. 36, Summer 1990: ' "What were you thinking of calling the album?" [Allen] Ginsberg asked at last. "Empire Burlesque", Dylan said . . . "That was the name of a burlesque club I used to go to when I first came to New York, down on Delancey Street," Dylan volunteered . . . How like him, I later thought, only volunteering information when it will mislead.'

8.   John Lindley: 'Movies inside his head: Empire Burlesque and *The Maltese Falcon*', *Telegraph*, no. 25, Autumn/Winter 1986. Readers' further sightings from other films were then published in *Telegraph*, nos. 26, 27, 28, 29 and spasmodically later.

9.   *The Maltese Falcon*, Warner, US, directed and written John Huston, also starring Mary Astor, 1941. Re these

I don't mind a reasonable amount of trouble

is a Sam Spade line and becomes, verbatim, a line in the "Empire Burlesque" song 'Seeing The Real You At Last'. Spade growls 'I'll have some rotten nights after I've sent you over – but that'll pass.' In the same Dylan song this becomes

> *Well I have had some rotten nights*
> *Didn't think that they would pass.*

Spade's partner says 'You don't have to look for me. I'll see you.' In 'When The Night Comes Falling From The Sky' Dylan sings

> *Don't look for me, I'll see you.*

The film gives us 'I don't care who loves who – maybe you love me and maybe I love you' and the song gives us

> *It won't matter who loves who*
> *You'll love me or I'll love you*
> *When the night comes falling from the sky.*

The film offers the exchange 'We wanna talk to you, Spade.' 'Well, go ahead and talk.' In 'Tight Connection To My Heart' Dylan offers

> *You want to talk to me,*
> *Go ahead and talk.*

Humphrey Bogart lines from several other films curl like his cigarette smoke into these Dylan lyrics too, though Dylan never attempts a Bogart delivery. It seeems to be that Bogart's style makes numinous to the movie viewer lines that would otherwise have no special ring to them – which is what one can so often say of Dylan's delivery also.

There are at least three snippets of Humphrey Bogart movie dialogue in 'Tight Connection To My Heart' alone: two from *Sirocco* (1951) and one from *Tokyo Joe* (1949).

The first of these comprises the line that Dylan uses as the starting-point of the song. Actress Marta Toren says 'I'm coming with you.' Bogart retorts: 'I've got to move fast: I can't with you around my neck.' Dylan sings

> *Well I had to move fast*
> *And I couldn't with you around my neck.*

Later in the same verse Dylan sings

---

favourites, Lindley quotes Dylan as saying: 'I can do a few other people's voices: Richard Widmark, Sidney Greenstreet, Peter Lorre. They really had distinctive voices in the early talkie films. Nowadays you go to a movie and you can't tell one voice from the other.' In the mid-1970s, during the making of Dylan's own film *Renaldo & Clara*, Sam Shepard reports that in a kitsch gun museum in Connecticut or Vermont, the crew were 'trying to film a scene . . . with Dylan and [Bob] Neuwirth. Some kind of *Maltese Falcon* take-off.' [Sam Shepard, *Rolling Thunder Logbook*.]

The film *The Maltese Falcon* is based upon the 1930 novel of the same name by Dashiell Hammett (1894–1961), the creator of private eye character Sam Spade.

I'll go along with the parade
Until I can think my way out.

This comes straight out of Bogart's mouth in *Tokyo Joe*. Further on in the lyric, we hear

But I can't figure out if I'm too good for you
Or if you're too good for me

while Bogart says to Marta Toren, back in *Sirocco*, that 'I don't know whether I'm too good for you or you're too good for me.'[10]

The song has another, more deeply buried filmic allusion. When Dylan sings

Well they're not showing any light tonight
And there's no moon
There's just a hot-blooded singer
Singing 'Memphis In June'

the figure who leaps to mind, not as hot-blooded singer but as composer of 'Memphis In June', is Hoagy Carmichael – and Carmichael launched the song in another movie, the 1945 George Raft film *Johnny Angel*.[11]

(Hoagy Carmichael is one of the many improbable people that Dylan has a bit of a thing about, possibly just to be perverse. Hoagy's photo is pinned up on the wall of the shack, with Bob and Sara loitering about, on the rejected prototype front-cover photograph for Dylan's novel *Tarantula*. Dylan's 'hot-blooded' is a neat small joke about Hoagy, whose many assets include a calculatedly lizard-like presence.)[12]

10.   *Sirocco*, Columbia/Santana, US, directed Curtis Bernhardt, written A. I. Bezzerides and Hans Jacoby, 1951. *Tokyo Joe*, Columbia/Santana, US, directed Stuart Heisler, written Cyril Hume and Bertram Millhauser, 1949. The lines from this latter film were recycled in the *Star Trek* episode 'The Squire Of Gothos', nia, in which (says Clinton Heylin, *Telegraph*, no. 29, Spring 1988) we get this exchange – *Sulu:* How far do we go along with this charade? *Kirk:* Until we can think our way out.

11.   *Johnny Angel*, RKO, US, directed Edwin L. Marin, written Steve Fisher, 1945.

12.   Carmichael was born and raised in Bloomington, Indiana, and when a retrospective 5-LP box-set of his work, "The Classic Hoagy Carmichael", was issued in 1988, with copious notes by John Edward Hasse, Curator of American Music at the Smithsonian Institution, it was published jointly by the Smithsonian and the Indiana Historical Society. (Americans always have a million places to go for funding. Imagine trying to get funding to research, compile, and write an accompanying book about Tommy Steele from the British Museum and the Bermondsey Historical Society.) Anyway, the box-set notes say this, among much else, and it might remind you of someone else (not Tommy Steele):

At first listeners may be distracted by the flatness in much of Carmichael's singing, and turned off especially by his uncertain intonation. The singer himself said, 'my native wood-note and often off-key voice is what I call "Flatsy through the nose" '. But . . . one becomes accustomed to these traits and grows to appreciate and admire other qualities of his vocal performances, specifically his phrasing . . . intimacy, inventiveness and sometimes even sheer audacity. Also, many . . . evidence spontaneous and extemporaneous qualities, two important ingredients in jazz.

'Memphis In June' was composed with lyrics by Johnny Mercer. In *Johnny Angel*, Carmichael played a singing, philosophical cab driver. ('After that I was mentioned for every picture in which a world-weary character in bad repair sat around and sang or leaned on a piano.') Subsequent film roles included being the pianist who sings 'Hong Kong Blues' in the Bogart–Bacall film *To Have and Have Not* – another Dylan hunting-ground for lyrics in the "Empire Burlesque" period: see below. The least hot-blooded version of 'Memphis' may be by Matt Monro, 1962; the best (and 'on a bandstand croonin' ') may be by Lucy Ann Polk, cut July 1957 in Hollywood. She'd sung in the bands of Bob Crosby, Kay Kyser ('she had an all-girl orchestra . . .' ?), Tommy Dorsey and Les Brown. Hoagy recorded the song in 1947 with Billy May & His Orchestra and again in 1956 with a jazz ensemble that included Art Pepper.

Carmichael played ranch hand Jonesey in the 1959–60 *Laramie* season. In 1972 he was given an honorary doctorate by Indiana University in Bloomington, where Betsy Bowden got *her* doctorate for a study of Bob Dylan's

In *The Big Sleep* (1946) Bogart mumbles that 'There's some people you don't forget, even if you've only seen them once.' Dylan sings this in the forgettable 'I'll Remember You' as

> *There's some people that*
> *You don't forget,*
> *Even though you've only seen 'em*
> *One time or two.*

The film's closing exchange, which is between Bogart and Lauren Bacall, goes like this:

> *Bogart:* What's wrong with you?
> *Bacall:* Nothing you can't fix.

Dylan intervenes more than usually with this one, making it, in 'Seeing The Real You At Last',

> *At one time there was nothing wrong with me*
> *That you could not fix.*[13]

In the same studio-producer-director-and-writing team's *To Have And Have Not*, the first film to pair Bogart with Bacall, he tells her to 'stop that baby talk'. In 'Seeing The Real You At Last' Dylan sings that he's

> *. . . gonna quit this baby talk now,*

while the same song's opening line comes straight from the lips of Bogart's co-star Edward G. Robinson in the 1948 *Key Largo*, another John Huston film and again pairing Bogart with Bacall. Robinson says: 'Think this rain would cool things off, but it don't.'[14] The Bob Dylan song begins with

> *Well I thought that the rain would cool things down*
> *But it looks like it don't.*

Indeed this song has so many film lines inside it that Dylan increases his hunting range into the 1960s – even into the 1980s – to find material. *The Hustler* (which the

---

performance art that became her book *Performed Literature* (1982). Carmichael died 27/12/81, and was buried back in Bloomington 4/1/82. His music remains viable, e.g. in the recordings of 'Stardust' (30–31/5/84) and 'New Orleans' (1986) by Wynton Marsalis.

    P.S. Hoagy Carmichael's first composition was called 'Freewheeling'.

    [Some of this information comes from the booklet published jointly by the Indiana Historical Society, Indianapolis, and the Smithsonian Collection of Recordings, Washington, DC, 1988, issued with the box-set "The Classic Hoagy Carmichael", compiled and written by John Edward Hasse, Curator of American Music at the Smithsonian Institution; issued in the UK as four LPs or three CDs on BBC Records BBC 4000 and BBC CD3007 respectively, London, 1988.]

13.   *The Big Sleep*, Warner, US, directed Howard Hawks, written William Faulkner, Leigh Brackett and Jules Furthman, starring Bogart and Bacall, 1946. Bogart is again a private eye, this time Philip Marlowe. Based on the novel *The Big Sleep* by Raymond Chandler (1939).

14.   *To Have and Have Not*, Warner, US, directed Howard Hawks, written Jules Furthman and William Faulkner, and also starring Walter Brennan and Hoagy Carmichael, 1945. Based on the novel of the same name by Ernest Hemingway, 1937, but just as obviously an imitation of the movie *Casablanca* [Warner, US, directed Michael Curtiz, 1942].

    Key Largo, Warner, US, directed John Huston, written Richard Brooks and John Huston, 1948.

Observer called 'The supreme classic of that great American genre, the low-life movie')[15] provides Dylan with these lines, almost verbatim:

> *I got troubles, I think maybe you got troubles*
> *I think we'd better leave each other alone,*

while the last two of the following four lines come out of the Clint Eastwood vehicle *Bronco Billy* (1980) and the first two, while they've not been identified, certainly sound as if we're back in one of Bogart's joints:

> *When I met you baby*
> *You didn't show no visible scars.*
> *You could ride like Annie Oakley*
> *You could shoot like Belle Starr.*

In *Bronco Billy*, Eastwood, in the title role, asked what kind of woman he's looking for, replies: 'I'm looking for a woman who can ride like Annie Oakley and shoot like Belle Starr.'[16]

It's small wonder that John Lindley was moved to write of 'Seeing The Real You At Last' (an ironic title, in this context) that so much appears to come from film dialogue that he 'would not be surprised to discover in time that the entire song . . . is constructed of lines from this medium'.[17]

---

15. *The Hustler*, 20th Century Fox/Robert Rossen, US, directed Robert Rossen, written Rossen and Sidney Carroll, starring Paul Newman, Jackie Gleason and George C. Scott, 1961. (The undated quotation from the *Observer*, London, is taken from *Halliwell's Film Guide*, ed. John Walker, 1995.)

16. *Bronco Billy*, Warner/Second Street, US, directed Eastwood, written Dennis Hackin, 1980. I forget who told me this, but the pithiness of the line is somewhat reduced if it is true that actually Belle Starr was a hopeless shot.
   The legendary outlaw is also the heroine of the rather dreadful film *Belle Starr* [20th Century Fox, US, directed Irving Cummings, 1941]. This in turn seems to have provoked a rather awful Woody Guthrie poem, 'Belle Starr', which Pete Seeger and Jack Elliott had no more sense than to put a tune to and record. The best verse, the rhymeless second, begins and ends with these sub-Dylanesque lines:
   > *Eight lovers they say combed your waving black hair . . .*
   > *Eight men heard the bark of the guns that you wore.*
   ['Belle Starr' by Woody Guthrie, published in Guthrie's *American Folksong* (1947); Pete Seeger & Ramblin' Jack Elliott: 'Belle Starr', *nia*, "The Badmen", Columbia Records L2L-1011, New York, *nia*, and published *Sing Out!*, Vol. 15, No. 5, November 1965.]
   In Clint Eastwood's case at least, the compliment of lifting dialogue has been repaid. In his later film *Pale Rider* [Warner/Malpaso, US, directed Eastwood, written Michael Butler and Dennis Shryack, 1985] one of the characters says 'Well, I wish there was something I could do or say, to try and make you change your mind and stay': verbatim lines, of course, from Bob Dylan's 1962 song 'Don't Think Twice, It's All Right'. (I have pointed out before that two 'key lines of film dialogue' in the film in which Dylan appeared as Alias (*Pat Garrett & Billy the Kid*, MGM, US, directed Sam Peckinpah, written Rudolph Wurlitzer, 1973) 'come straight out of two crucial songs from Dylan's own history. They are spoken by the film's two main characters even before the opening credits roll:
   > Billy: How does it feel?
   > Garrett: It feels like times have changed.'
   [first published in a footnote in *All Across the Telegraph*, ed. Michael Gray and John Bauldie, 1987].)

17. John Lindley, 'Movies inside his head', see note 8. However, not all the lines in 'Seeing The Real You At Last' derive from Hollywood. Dylan ends the song with a re-statement of the words of Jesus to Judas at the Last Supper (giving an extra frisson to the petulant and self-aggrandising bitterness of his stance throughout). 'Whatever you gonna do / Please do it fast' writes Dylan; 'Satan entered into him [Judas]. Then said Jesus unto him, That thou doest, do quickly' (John 13:27). It is a moment Dylan had used before, in 'The Groom's Still Waiting At The Altar' (1980) and 'Man Of Peace' (1983).

Nor have we finished yet with such sources for 'When The Night Comes Falling From The Sky'. Dylan sings within it the opaque

> *I saw thousands who could have overcome the darkness,*
> *For the love of a lousy buck, I've watched them die.*

Is it, as the grammar insists, *his* love of a lousy buck that makes him watch them die where he might have intervened, or is it, as plain sense might more readily suggest, *their* love of a lousy buck that dooms them, the singer being mere witness to all this greed and come-uppance? In any case, in *On the Waterfront* Karl Malden as the streetwise priest says far more straightforwardly that what oils the wheels of society is 'the love of a lousy buck'.[18] And while in *Twelve Angry Men*, one of the other jurors says to Henry Fonda, 'You thought you would gamble for support', in Dylan's song we get

> *But you were gambling for support.*[19]

Even that beautiful formulation of Dylan's in 'Tight Connection To My Heart', mentioned earlier, that

> *What looks large from a distance*
> *Close up ain't never that big*

turns out, although its pithiness and concentrated impact is Dylan's, to be inspired by a film line. At the end of the 1934 *Now and Forever*, Gary Cooper, about to be arrested, says of the cops: 'Close up they don't look as large as they do from a distance.'[20]

Inevitably, a line from one of Dylan's favourite films, the classic western *Shane*, also reappears on "Empire Burlesque". Shane says: 'I don't mind leaving, I'd just like it to be my idea.'[21] And here it is in 'Never Gonna Be The Same Again' (not a claim this line can make):

> *Don't worry, baby, I don't mind leaving*
> *I'd just like it to be my idea.*

In 'Clean-Cut Kid' – written for the "Infidels" album but re-recorded for and released on "Empire Burlesque" – the source for a fragment of the lyric seems to have been lifted fairly directly from a film of another Hollywood star whom Bob Dylan seems especially fond of, Elizabeth Taylor. In *The Sandpiper* headmaster Richard

---

18. *On the Waterfront*, Columbia/Sam Spiegel, US, directed Elia Kazan, written Budd Schulberg, starring Marlon Brando, Eva Marie Saint, Lee J. Cobb, Rod Steiger and Karl Malden, 1954. This is the film with the rather more widely quoted line 'I coulda bin a contender', which was perhaps in the back of Dylan's mind in 1975 when his lyrics for the chorus of 'Hurricane' include 'He coulda bin the champion of the world'.

19. *Twelve Angry Men*, Orion-Nova, US, directed Sidney Lumet, written Reginald Rose, also starring Lee J. Cobb and E. G. Marshall, 1957.

20. *Now and Forever*, Paramount, US, directed Henry Hathaway, written Vincent Lawrence, starring Gary Cooper, Carole Lombard and Shirley Temple, 1934.

21. *Shane*, Paramount, US, directed George Stevens, written A. B. Guthrie Jr, starring Alan Ladd, Jack Palance and Brandon de Wilde, 1953.

Burton says that the heroine's son should 'adjust' better. Mother Taylor snaps: 'Adjust to what?'[22] The song's opening rhetoric is

> *Everybody's askin' why he couldn't adjust –*
> *Adjust to what? A dream that bust?*

To stray, temporarily, from "Empire Burlesque", in order to tidy up those filmic references I know about from the surrounding albums, is to remember that a major song of the early 1980s, 'Caribbean Wind', deliberately alights in passing on another movie title, *The Cruel Sea*, and to look at another item that originated on the 1983 "Infidels". In 'Sweetheart Like You' Dylan asks ponderously

> *What's a sweetheart like you*
> *Doin' in a dump like this?*

You might think so undistinguished and recycled a line needs no hunting of its provenance, but it can't be helped: in *All Through the Night* (another Bogart film, and with Peter Lorre again too) he asks: 'What would a sweetheart like that Miss Hamilton dame be doing in a dump like this?'[23]

There is a further flurry of dialogue raids on the album that comes after "Empire Burlesque" too, Dylan's 1986 release "Knocked Out Loaded". In *Bend of the River* (1952) someone says to James Stewart: 'I figure we're even. Maybe I'm one up on ya.'[24] The opening verse of 'Driftin' Too Far From Shore' gives us

> *I didn't know that you'd be leavin'*
> *Or who you thought you were talkin' to.*
> *I figure maybe we're even*
> *Or maybe I'm one up on you.*

Later in the same song we reach the curiously period touch of

> *No gentleman likes makin' love to his servant*
> *Specially when he's in his father's house.*

This comes directly from yet another Bogart film, *Sabrina* (1954), in which actor Walter Hampden declares that 'No gentleman makes love to a servant in his mother's house.'[25]

Similarly there are brief quotations from two more films in another "Knocked Out Loaded" song, 'Maybe Someday'.

> *Forgive me baby, for what I didn't do*
> *For not breakin' down no bedroom door to get at you*

22. *The Sandpiper*, MGM/Filmways, US, directed Vincente Minelli, written Dalton Trumbo, 1965. Liz Taylor plays a bohemian artist living in a Monterey beach shack.

23. *The Cruel Sea*, Ealing, UK, directed Charles Frend, written Eric Ambler, starring Jack Hawkins, 1953, and based on the novel by Nicholas Monsarrat. *All Through the Night*, Warner, US, directed Vincent Sherman, written Leonard Spigelgass and Edwin Gilbert, 1942.

24. *Bend of the River* [in the UK *Where the River Bends*], U-I, US, directed Anthony Mann, written Borden Chase, starring James Stewart and Rock Hudson, 1952.

25. *Sabrina* [in the UK *Sabrina Fair*], Paramount, US, directed and written (and produced) Billy Wilder, starring Bogart, William Holden and Audrey Hepburn, 1954.

comes across from *Separate Tables* (1958), in which Burt Lancaster says to his ex-wife, talking of her new lover: 'He didn't break any bedroom door down to get to you.' And the splendid 'Dylanesque' put-down

> *I always liked San Francisco: I was there for a party once*

turns out, more's the pity, to come straight from *Out of the Past* (indeed), a 1947 film in which Kirk Douglas asks: 'Do you know San Francisco?' and Robert Mitchum mumbles back: 'I've been there to a party once.'[26]

On top of "Knocked Out Loaded" (or rather, quite a long way underneath it, which is saying something) 1986 gave us the single 'Band Of The Hand', recorded with Tom Petty & The Heartbreakers. This too looked back to Hollywood for a fragment of its lyric. In *I Wake Up Screaming* (1941) Laird Cregar says to the oleaginous Victor Mature: 'One day you'll be talking in your sleep, and when you do I wanna be around.' The song's last verse ends:

> *I know your story is too painful to share.*
> *One day, though, you'll be talkin' in your sleep*
> *And when you do I wanna be there.*[27]

And to move the process forward, briefly, further into the 1980s, we encounter at least another couple of these small raids on movies within Dylan's 1989 release "Oh Mercy". The title 'Man In The Long Black Coat' surely owes something to the Gregory Peck film title *The Man in the Gray Flannel Suit* (1956), while the song's lines

> *Somebody is out there*
> *Beating on a dead horse,*

if they do anything beyond making you wince, give a flashback to an equally momentary night-time scene in *Catch-22*, when the hero Yossarian glimpses someone literally flogging a dead horse, as he stumbles through the Italian urban nighttime seeing horror after phantasmagoric horror.[28]

In *The African Queen* – yet another 1950s Humphrey Bogart vehicle – there is the

26. *Separate Tables*, UA/Hecht-Hill-Lancaster, US, directed Delbert Mann, written Terence Rattigan, starring Burt Lancaster, Rita Hayworth, David Niven, Deborah Kerr, Wendy Hiller, Gladys Cooper, Felix Aylmer and Rod Taylor, 1958. *Out of the Past* [in the UK *Build My Gallows High*], RKO, US, directed Jacques Tourneur, written Geoffrey Homes, starring Mitchum, Douglas and Jane Greer, 1947.

27. *I Wake Up Screaming* [alternative and UK title, *Hot Spot*], 20th Century Fox, US, directed H. Bruce Humberstone, written Dwight Taylor, also starring Betty Grable, 1941.

It's a full circle of sorts that this wretchedly crude song (and performance) was itself specially provided by Dylan as the title song for a film. (His music has been used in many films but this was the first time he had specially recorded a song for a film in which he played no part himself.)

Band of the Hand, RCA/Columbia/Tri-Star, US, directed Paul Michael Glaser, 1986. Bob Dylan, with Tom Petty & The Heartbreakers: 'Band Of The Hand', Sydney, Australia, 8–9/2/86, issued on "Band Of The Hand" soundtrack LP, MCA-6167, USA, 1986, and on A-side of single MCA-52811, USA, 1986. Dylan, Petty & The Heartbreakers do not appear on any other track.

28. *The Man in the Gray Flannel Suit*, 20th Century Fox/Darryl F. Zanuck, US, directed and written Nunnally Johnson, 1956; based on the strange – half-literary, half-pulp – yet always beguiling novel of the same name by Sloan Wilson (1955). *Catch-22*, Paramount/Filmways, US, directed Mike Nichols, written Buck Henry, starring Alan Arkin, 1970; based on the novel of the same name by Joseph Heller (1961).

line 'Most of the time I know exactly what you're saying.' Dylan's song 'Most Of The Time' adapts this, with a series of lines saying mock-defiantly that he knows exactly what *he* is saying, including

> *Most of the time, I know exactly where it all went.*

And at the closing moment in the closing song of "Oh Mercy", in 'Shooting Star', what he chooses to say is

> *Saw a shooting star tonight*
> *Slip away*
> *Tomorrow will be another day . . .*

which neatly parallels the closing moment in *Gone with the Wind* – in which 'After all, tomorrow is another day' is both the heroine Scarlett O'Hara's last remark and, in the book on which the film is based, its final sentence.[29]

Actually it might be a revealing exercise, for someone with the time, to investigate how many of these reprocessed movie lines had already been reprocessed by the film scriptwriters, from the books on which many of the films were based. It might turn out that many of Dylan's film lines are actually from literary or theatrical works.

We know, after all, that *Cat on a Hot Tin Roof* reworks the Tennessee Williams play, that *The Maltese Falcon* began as Dashiell Hammett's novel, *The Big Sleep* as Raymond Chandler's and *To Have and Have Not* as Hemingway's – and in the case of the last two, the novelist William Faulkner worked on the filmscripts. *The African Queen* was scripted by the writer James Agee, *Separate Tables* by the distinguished but unfashionable British playwright Terence Rattigan, and was based upon his own play. *Sirocco* was adapted from *Coup de Grâce*, a novel by Joseph Kessel, and *The Cruel Sea*, scripted by the novelist Eric Ambler, from the novel by Nicholas Monsarrat. *Catch-22* is far more important as a novel than a movie, *The Man in the Gray Flannel Suit* more so too (though in this case its author, Sloan Wilson, confessed on his book-jacket that the book's title, which is what Dylan has echoed, was coined by his wife, Elise Pickhardt Wilson) and *Gone with the Wind* was a lengthily famous and best-selling novel before it was a mega-movie, though the movie has proved the more enduring. Given all this, surely at least some of those we recognise as movie lines in Dylan songs must actually have started their journey on the page, and could be found there, more or less verbatim.[30]

---

29.   *The African Queen*, IFD/Romulus-Horizon, UK, directed John Huston, written James Agee, starring Bogart and Katherine Hepburn, 1951. *Gone with the Wind*, MGM / Selznick International, US, directed Victor Fleming, George Cukor and Sam Wood, written Sidney Howard and others, starring Vivien Leigh, Clark Gable, Leslie Howard, 1939. Based on the novel of the same name by Margaret Mitchell, 1936.

30.   Tennessee Williams (1911–1983): *Cat on a Hot Tin Roof*, the play, 1955. Terence Rattigan (1911–1977): *Separate Tables*, the play, 1952. Joseph Kessel: *Coup de Grâce*, nia. Nicholas Monsarrat (1910–1979): *The Cruel Sea*, the novel, 1951. (For further discussion of Dylan's use of the title *The Cruel Sea* in 'Caribbean Wind', see Chapter 13.)

It's true that Truffaut's *Tirez sur le Pianiste* was based on a thriller by American writer David Coolis, *Down There*, but Coolis was primarily a screenplay writer. The same applies in other cases. *Out of the Past*, scripted by Geoffrey Homes, was based upon his novel of the same name but Homes (a pseudonym for Daniel Mainwaring) was mainly a screenwriter. *Key Largo* was based upon Maxwell Anderson's play, but he too primarily wrote for movies. *Shane* was built from the novel by Jack Shaefer, but the same is true of him and of Steve Fisher (*I Wake*

While this may be, it hardly alters the fact that the main and prominent conduit for these conversational titbits has been Hollywood, nor that it is the resonant, distinctive voices of movie stars who have set these phrases ringing in Bob Dylan's ears. Confirming this, it is one more noticeable feature of Dylan's mid-1980s songs that within them he mentions several stars by name.

In his early work, his approach is different. In 'Last Thoughts On Woody Guthrie' he says the hope that you need 'ain't made in no Hollywood wheat germ'. Hollywood luminaries are named inside his songs in the service of jokes – Brigitte Bardot, Anita Ekberg, Sophia Loren, Elizabeth Taylor and Richard Burton in 'I Shall Be Free', Tony Perkins in 'Motorpsycho Nightmare', Cecil B. de Mille in 'Tombstone Blues'.

Of the mid-1960s prose-poems, the "Bringing It All Back Home" liner-notes have throwaway mentions of 'jayne mansfield.humphrey bogart' sandwiched between 'sleepy john estes' and the wonderful invention 'mortimer snerd', and a list of people he doesn't want to be (because they are all dead) in which James Dean comes after 'bach. mozart. tolstoy. joe hill. gertrude stein'; 'Advice For Geraldine On Her Miscellaneous Birthday' cites no one; 'Off The Top Of My Head' and the "Highway 61 Revisited" liner-notes mention a plethora of names, not one of them a film star or director, and 'Alternatives To College' throws only Jerry Lewis into its huge babble of named characters. In '11 Outlined Epitaphs', in the rhapsodic list of people who are 'entrancin'' him, beginning with Francois Villon and ending seventeen names later, there is only one film star, Marlene Dietrich, her asset being her 'mystery'.

As shorthand descriptions, rather than as jokes, there are, I think, only two such names dropped into the first fifteen years' worth of his recordings – right up to and including the "Desire" album: 'Bette Davis style' in 'Desolation Row' (1965) and 'He looked like Jimmy Cagney' in 'Joey' (1975).

In the 1980s, this suddenly changes. We get more than that in 1983 alone. 'Up pops Errol Flynn', in John Lindley's happy phrase, in both the evangelical 'You Changed My Life' (1981) and in the extraordinary religious rant that is 'Foot Of Pride' (1983), followed by Clark Gable in 'Don't Fall Apart On Me Tonight' (1983), Peter O'Toole in 'Clean-Cut Kid' (1983 and 1985) and then Gregory Peck, the insistent hero of the unreleased 'New Danville Girl' (1984) and the "Knocked Out Loaded" magnum opus 'Brownsville Girl' (1986): a song that, among the many other things it does, also returns us full circle to the way Bob Dylan used *Shoot the Pianist* back in 1963. That is, it *tells* you about a film *and* then quotes from it:

> *Well there was this movie I seen one time*
> *About a man riding 'cross the desert and it starred Gregory Peck*
> *He was shot down by a hungry kid tryin' to make a name for himself . . .*
> *As the dying gunfighter lay in the sun and gasped for his last breath:*
> *'Turn him loose, let him go, let him say he outdrew me fair and square.*
> *I want him to feel what it's like to every moment face his death.'*

The film here is 1950's *The Gunfighter* – which Dylan manages to quote from in two songs running. The title of the song (co-written with Tom Petty) that follows

up Screaming began as his novel), Budd Schulberg (*On the Waterfront* was scripted by him from his own novel) and Reginald Rose (who scripted *Twelve Angry Men* from his own play).

'Brownsville Girl' on "Knocked Out Loaded" is 'Got My Mind Made Up'. This is a line of dialogue spoken four times in *The Gunfighter*.[31]

The same album quotes from another Gregory Peck Western, 1958's *The Big Country*. In its minor way, the insertion of dialogue from this film is remarkable: for what he inserts it into is a song that isn't even his own composition! The album's opening track, 'You Wanna Ramble', is a revival of an old R&B song by Junior Parker (the man who wrote and first recorded the Elvis Presley classic 'Mystery Train') – and in the middle of 'You Wanna Ramble', Dylan slips in his own addition

> *What happens tomorrow*
> *Is on your head, not mine . . .*

. . . except that it isn't his own addition, it's taken from *The Big Country*, in which Burl Ives warns: 'What happens here tomorrow is on your head not mine.'[32]

In all of this, what's likely to strike the reader is that these film script snatches, barely if at all modified by Dylan, are so unmemorable, so unarresting as content, yet in most cases so attractive, so tersely energetic and imitable, as conversational rhythms, as cadences of heightened moment: great movie lines, in fact, and understandably appealing to the contemporary American poet. In the other cases, Dylan's sub-editing, his tightening-up, gives them their radiance.

You might feel that they're easy building blocks for writer's-block sufferers, or for singer–songwriters with nothing special to say. Or you might feel that Dylan has, once again, made himself inward with, and then re-expressed creatively, yet another branch of American popular culture – one that may have been handed down from the on-highs of Hollywood but one that has without question inhabited the shared minds of millions of ordinary twentieth-century Americans.

While Dylan's writing so often brings together the worlds of modern American speech and of scripture – more calculatedly than merely via the echoes of the latter in the former[33] – in the mid-1980s one consequence of his continuing to be interested in scripture whilst at the same time pursuing this play with movie dialogue is that he takes the inevitable extra step of trying to fuse these two elements, elements described earlier as disparate: the language of Hollywood and of the Bible, the language of movies and of scripture. That is, we see in these songs several attempts to make a

31.   Bob Dylan: 'New Danville Girl', Los Angeles, December 1984.
      The Gunfighter, 20th Century Fox, US, directed Henry King, written William Bowers and William Sellers, 1950. [The detection of the recurring line 'Got my mind made up' in this film comes from Stephen Scobie's *Alias Bob Dylan*, 1991.]

32.   *The Big Country*, UA/Anthony/Worldwide, US, directed William Wyler, written James R. Webb, starring Peck, Jean Simmons, Charlton Heston, Carroll Baker, Burl Ives and Charles Bickford, 1958.
      Junior Parker: 'I Wanna Ramble' [sic], Houston, 10/6/54, Duke Records 137, Houston, 1954; Junior Parker: 'Mystery Train', Memphis, c. October 1953, Sun Records 192, Memphis, 1953–4; Elvis Presley: 'Mystery Train', Memphis, 11/7/55, Sun Records 223, Memphis, 1955.

33.   Dylan to Bill Flanagan, *Written in My Soul* (1986): 'Because the Bible runs through all U.S. life, whether people know it or not. It's the founding book . . . People can't get away from it. You can't get away from it wherever you go.'

particular phrase, taken from film, serve also as scriptural allusion and as part of his work's religious themes.

Actually Dylan's first name-check of Errol Flynn comes in an evangelical song, 'You Changed My Life' (1981) – in which Dylan makes this experiment with great audacity, choosing to sing, in the song's final verse, that he experienced his conversion to Christ not only as something sudden and something elemental, but also with the heightened dramatic impact of Hollywood. It certainly makes for a surprising effect, though it's doubtful how far this escapes bathos and a damaging undercutting of the gravitas he wishes to retain, despite its audacity:

> You came in like the wind,
> Like Errol Flynn:
> You changed my life.

It's also the case that Dylan's first co-option of dialogue from *The Maltese Falcon* is within an evangelical song. In this much-utilised film we get this:

> *Cop:* What is?
> *Sam:* [his last line of the film] The stuff that dreams are made of.

(The line is itelf a slight misquotation from Shakespeare's *The Tempest*.) In 'City of Gold', premièred in concert in San Francisco in 1980, Dylan makes this part of his armoury of preaching, as he sings

> There is a city of love
> Far from this world
> And the stuff dreams are made of.[34]

In 'Tight Connection To My Heart' this co-option may be apparent even in the reference to the singer being lulled to sleep

> In a town without pity
> Where the water runs deep.

Dylan is certainly mindful here of the film-title *Town Without Pity* (and no doubt remembers the horrible, overwrought title song that was a hit for the overwrought Gene Pitney)[35] – and the Protestant minister and commentator Bert Cartwright argues that this same passage is 'mindful of' Jeremiah 20:16 and Lamentations 2:17, which (though only in the Revised Standard Version) refer to 'the cities which the Lord overthrew without pity' and to the cities 'demolished without pity'.[36]

---

34. The line Sam Spade uses to bow out with, and Dylan in turn uses again, ends the speech with which Prospero, too, rounds things off in Shakespeare's last completed play, *The Tempest*, Act IV: 'We are such stuff / As dreams are made on; and our little life / Is rounded with a sleep'. Granted this context, Dylan may well be offering a spin on the Shakespeare as much as on the Spade, since the song's theme is, of course, that death is not the final curtain.
      Bob Dylan: 'City Of Gold', Fox Warfield, San Francisco, 10/11/80: a theatre that was itself a palace from the golden age of cinema.

35. *Town Without Pity*, UA/Mirisch/Osweg/Gloria, US/Switzerland/Germany, directed by Gottfried Reinhardt, starring Kirk Douglas; Gene Pitney: 'Town Without Pity', 1961, Musicor Records 1009, USA [HMV POP952, London], 1961. The film's theme has no relevance to Dylan's.

36. Bert Cartwright, 'The Bible in the lyrics of Bob Dylan: 1985–1990', *Telegraph*, no. 38, Spring 1991: a follow-up piece to his booklet 'The Bible in the Lyrics of Bob Dylan', *Wanted Man Study Series*, no. 4 (1985), cited in earlier chapters.

Similarly, when I recall the lines in 1986's 'Maybe Someday' that Dylan adapts from the Bogart film *Sabrina* – where the film's 'No gentleman makes love to a servant in his mother's house' becomes the song's 'No gentleman likes makin' love to his servant / Specially when he's in his father's house' – I recall Nigel Hinton's comments on this passage in an article on "Empire Burlesque" and "Knocked Out Loaded". He pointed out: 'Put a capital letter on "Father", of course, and there are all kinds of other resonances here . . . He makes his lines ring with mysterious possibilities: where one level works perfectly but where, if you care to switch contexts, the whole thing works on another level too. Thus 'Maybe Someday' is a warning farewell to a girl but . . . it needs only a slight sideways step to see that each line carries a moral/spiritual implication.'[37]

At any rate, the religious ramifications of the "Empire Burlesque" album's lyrics, too, are everywhere within it, and might be said to begin before the beginning, since 'Tight Connection To My Heart' is a revised version of 'Someone's Got A Hold Of My Heart', a song first recorded for the previous studio album, "Infidels", but left off that and reworked here. The lyrics of both songs (and there are several versions of the earlier one) overlap substantially. Between them, they seem to offer, among other things, a brief but conspicuous meditation on the meaning of the wilderness (the desert) for the Jewish writer and Christian believer. (One of the themes of modern Israeli writing, in poetry and novels, is the overwhelming importance of the wilderness outside.)

'Tight Connection' can be heard as addressed to Dylan's Jewish roots and to his friends of the old faith, concerning his being called to Christianity:

> *Well I had to move fast*
> *And I couldn't with you around my neck*

(again, film dialogue co-opted into a religious context)

> *I said I'd send for you and I did*
> *What did you expect?*

and as the singer depicts himself wandering around repeating the subtitle and chorus-line 'Has anybody seen my love?', he re-occupies the action at the start of the Song of Solomon ('the song of songs'), 3:2–3:

> I will rise now, and go about the city in the streets, and in the broad ways I will seek him whom my soul loveth: I sought him but I found him not. The watchmen that go about the city found me: to whom I said, Saw ye him whom my soul loveth?

Later in the song we reach the passage in which Dylan hears a lone voice, and says

> *Later he'll be shot for*
> *Resisting arrest*

---

37. Nigel Hinton, 'Into the future, knocked out and loaded', first published in *Telegraph*, no. 25, Autumn/Winter 1986, but quoted here from the version collected in *All Across the Telegraph*.

> *I can still hear his voice crying*
> *In the wilderness.*

Plainly this figure's fate parallels that of John the Baptist, whose wilderness cry prepares the way for the coming of Christ. This is recounted several times over in the Gospels, but with most emphasis and drama at the beginning of Mark (1:1–3), which declares itself as nothing less than

> The beginning of the gospel of Jesus Christ, the Son of God; As it is written in the prophets, Behold, I send my messenger before thy face, which shall prepare thy way before me. The voice of one crying in the wilderness, Prepare ye the way of the Lord, make his paths straight.[38]

The song's lines, though, need not act exclusively as a reference to John the Baptist. The wilderness is everywhere in the Bible and in the life of the tribes of Israel. We've already encountered text from the Song Of Solomon (Old Testament text) underlying part of this Song of Dylan, and surely the time of the Babylonian captivity seems hinted at everywhere within the song. In earlier drafts, when the song was still called 'Someone's Got A Hold Of My Heart' (itself a title with crucial non-secular meaning, in this context) a slightly variant version of these 'wilderness' lines,

> *I can still hear that voice*
> *Cryin' in the wilderness*

is immediately preceded by

> *I bin to Babylon,*
> *And I got to confess*

– with which Dylan both brings off once again his trick of refashioning biblical text into modern conversational idiom, and returns us to the terrain of the Old rather than the New Testament. As we noted while scrutinising 'Every Grain Of Sand', it was Daniel, living under the Babylonian captivity, who prophesied in Babylon itself, and understood himself to be making *his* confession in the final days of that captivity. Hence Dylan here calls up (for those interested) the person of Daniel as much as John the Baptist, in the wonderful, idiomatically casual understatement of 'I bin to Babylon, and I got to confess'.[39]

The New Testament is everywhere, however, and not merely to yield John the Baptist. In the particular early version of the same song that was eventually released, on 1991's "Bootleg Series Volumes I–III", Dylan chooses to begin with this:

---

38. Dylan certainly told his audiences in Israel about Christ. He performed two concerts there in 1987, remarkable in that each delivered a wholly different repertoire. The first concert included 'In The Garden', 'Dead Man' and 'Go Down Moses', plus the arguably 'Christian' 'Señor'; the second included 'Man Of Peace', 'Gotta Serve Somebody' and 'Slow Train'. Each concert also included one song from "Empire Burlesque". [5/9/87, Tel Aviv, and 7/9/87, Jerusalem.]

39. The function of the wilderness is fluid in the Bible as in Dylan's work. From Daniel's point of view, of course, Babylon *was* the wilderness. Then there's the interesting duality wherein it is repeatedly a sign of punishment by God that places are turned into desert wastes, as for instance when Jeremiah is told that Jerusalem will be a place of desolation for seventy years [Daniel 9], yet often the godly turn to the wilderness, prominent among them John the Baptist and Jesus, to seek a refuge from corruption. There is a parallel duality in the function of Dylan's aptly named 'Desolation Row'.

> *They say eat, drink and be merry*
> *Take the bull by the horns . . .*

and here, as he delights in the overkill of cliché rather than subtle understatement – piling on that 'take the bull by the horns' as a jokey spin on the 'eat, drink and be merry' line – he is once more inhabiting both contemporary idiom and the biblical text that he knows lies behind it. This time he brings us to Luke 12:16–20:

> And he spake a parable unto them, saying, The ground of a certain rich man brought forth plentifully . . . And he said . . . I will say to my soul, Soul, thou hast much goods laid up for many years: take thine ease, eat, drink and be merry.
>
>   But God said unto him, Thou fool, this night thy soul shall be required of thee . . .

so that the song begins, despite the playing with cliché, on this ominous note: hinting that 'this night' the most fundamental of things will get settled. ('There's something I gotta do tonight / You go inside and stay warm'.)

Dylan's next lines, in the early version,

> *I keep seeing visions of you,*
> *A lily among thorns,*

achieve again the paralleling of secular and devotional content, and the latter itself seems to work on several levels. It might be contemporary Israel that is the lily among the thorns of the desert, the wilderness; it might be the face of Christ, martyred 'among thorns'. At the end of *this* version of the song, instead of 'Never could learn to hold you, love, and call you mine' what we hear is

> *Never could learn to drink that blood*
> *And call it wine*
> *Never could learn to look at your face*
> *And call it mine.*

Instead of being a refutation of Christ, this is surely the singer's confession of doubt as to his own worthiness to look upon that face. As Paul was to stress to the Corinthians, recalling Christ's own words, you have to be worthy to drink that blood:

> After the same manner also He took the cup, when He had supped, saying: 'This cup is the new testament in my blood: this ye do, as oft as ye drink it, in remembrance of me. For as often as ye eat this bread, and drink this cup, ye shall shew the Lord's death till He come.'
>
>   Wherefore whosoever shall eat this bread, and drink this cup unworthily, shall be guilty of the body and blood of the Lord . . . For he that eateth and drinketh unworthily, eateth and drinketh damnation to himself, not discerning the Lord's body.   (1 Corinthians 11:25–29.)

At any rate, Dylan sets up chimes back and forth between various lines from the start and from the finish of the song, allowing one resonance to challenge or echo another. Thus too we get a teasing, beguiling dialogue between 'What looks large from a distance / Close up ain't never that big' at the end and, in this same early version, this touching but comic line in the opening verse:

> *Everything looks a little far away to me.*

This in itself is as fine an expression of beat disconnection as you'll find anywhere in Jack Kerouac or Bob Dylan – if only one could claim that, or anything remotely so rarified, for the whole of the "Empire Burlesque" album – but it also hangs in the air of the song, to meet up with that counterbalancing aphorism at the song's end.

Altogether, there is a difficult fretwork of these connections and correspondences – between 'Someone's Got A Hold Of My Heart' and 'Tight Connection To My Heart', between the writer's Jewish roots and Christian calling, between contemporary Israel and biblical days, between these and contemporary America, between the language of devotion and secular love and between the language of Hollywood and the Bible.

If it all hung together, and if attentive reflection upon these lyrics revealed its unity, the integration of all its elements, into a cohesive, explicable whole, however complex and however poetically ellipsed, then we should have a great song. Two great songs. Unfortunately, there is no such unity. The wholes are less than the sums of the parts. You know that the critic is struggling when he must resort, as I did earlier, to formulations like 'it might be . . . or it might be . . .'. He is on the perilous edge, at such moments, of the pit that commentators dig for themselves, in which there is a great partisan thrashing around in well-intended, ill-disciplined surmise – in surmise that dare not be rigorous – about works of art that refuse to offer either the clarity or the credible mystery of greatness.[40]

This credibility problem is inescapable throughout "Empire Burlesque". Everywhere you look, from the first moment you set eyes upon the album's cover, dodginess wheezes in your ear.

The lines of film dialogue are many, and a curiosity, and it may be fun to track and trace them: but what, in the end, do they achieve? They never stop being fragmented. The album never constructs itself into any sort of critique of Hollywood's 'golden age', as its title might seem to promise. (We must look forward to the remarkable 'Brownsville Girl', co-written with the playwright and film actor Sam Shepard, for something akin to that.) Nor do we ever escape the sense that while almost all these snatches of Bogart, Bacall and the rest speak from the films of Bob Dylan's formative youth – with their undeniable vividness, and their great dramas of lighting in black and white, films that must have flooded in upon him back in Hibbing, Minnesota – they end up woven into the opaque songs of "Empire Burlesque" because the bored, middle-aged Bob Dylan, to whom little seems vivid, has been watching them late at night in the pallid glow of the TV set, for lack of anything more purposive to do to fill up his time.

---

40. An artist as immoderately compelling as Bob Dylan is to those he gets his hook into inevitably attracts oceans of this specious amateurish commentary, as you will know if you have ever wandered through the websites and newsgroups devoted to him – the muddiest superhighway in the universe – or the deliberately unedited pages of the 'Dignity' fanzine.

In such ways, everything on the album that promises to be solid proves not to be. 'When The Night Comes Falling From The Sky' begins with one of those striking and attractive opening lines that have always been a mark of Bob Dylan's art:

> *Look out across the fields, see me returning.*

We do: we see our own version of the picture at once, and its appeal includes its timelessness. Those fields could be in Suffolk or the Gers, Idaho or the Peloponnese; they could be in the sixteenth century or any other time. There's a freedom here from 'the tyranny of the present'[41] (to quote somebody on the value of studying history), so that the space described – 'out across the fields' – is matched by the space the line allows you in the mind. The picture of the singer not as Bob Dylan Superstar but as whatever kind of peasant wanderer or exile springs to your mind – this too delights and leaves you free. (One way I experience this opening line is as the perfectly compressed beginning of a Thomas Hardy novel.)

At the same time I find it carries a very different resonance as a sort of negative flipside to some of the optimistic rhetoric of his dimly-remembered 'Paths Of Victory', in which the singer 'saw that silver linin' / That was hangin' in the sky . . . / My eyes they saw a better day / As I looked across the fields'. Now instead of silver hanging in the sky, the night is falling from it.[42]

Whatever picture we build up at the very start of the song, the space – how far we look out across those fields – is soon further defined as we feel the bite and the sheer force of compression of the opening line of the second verse:

> *Well I've walked two hundred miles, now look me over.*

There is immediate drama, too, in the way the song's narrator claims to be able to 'look out across' and see right through things. The tantalising way that as he's coming in at journey's end across those last fields, he can somehow *see* that smoke is in her eye, and knows that she's burning his letters in the fireplace – this mystic, piercing intuition is brought alive to us in the opening moments, in the first three lines of the song, so that when he restates this claim to special powers later, its effect is harmfully didactic: 'I can see through your walls and I know you're hurting', the second verse begins; 'I can hear your trembling heart beat like a river', begins the third. We don't need to be *told* he can see through walls: we've registered it via poetic truth already.

What drags it all down, though, is nothing so refined as mere slippage into prosaic restatement. Rather, it is the overkill of the performance – everyone's performance, from Dylan's inaccurately self-imitative, strained vocal, which chooses pop radio's drama-queening gulp where once he had the intuitive sense and integrity to choose understatement, to the by-the-yard rockism of the music, into which the temporarily sought-after producer Arthur Baker can no more inject real life than could Frankenstein into his dead metal monster. Bombast is not life. The numbing drumbeat and

---

41. I cannot trace the originator of this phrase.

42. There is, if you wish, an undertow of biblical text here too. Dylan's 'Look out across the fields, see me returning' echoes Christ's words reported in John 4:35: 'behold, I say unto you, Lift up your eyes and look on the fields; for they are white already to harvest'.

tintinnabular echo, far from being vibrant, let alone heartfelt, are merely wearing – and so, in the end, is the 'apocalyptic retread', as Terry Kelly called it, of the lyric, with its portentous title and clamorous proclamations of imminent doom.[43] It isn't the sky we experience falling: we're never made to believe in that at all. The falling sensation we're aware of is of the whole song rushing downhill all the way.

This histrionic clamour leaves no corner of the album untouched. It conspires with the contagion of 'baby's that spatters the lyrics, to make for an album that seems to go out of its way to be cheap pop music, the very thing Bob Dylan had spent a lifetime setting himself against (and getting the credit for so doing). It seemed a shaming irony, when the album was new, to see Dylan posing and pouting in that gruesome 1980s music-biz suit, surrounded by the sort of any-old-pop-splodge-will-do hep-artwork that was equivalent to putting a silver Afro wig on Debbie Reynolds as her image makeover for the end of the 1960s: a tacky, implausible add-on doomed to humiliate rather than rejuvenate.[44]

It seemed a sadder irony that for the first time in his twenty-three years' worth of releases, Dylan had chosen to have the album's lyrics printed on the inner sleeve just when he had a set of lyrics less worth printing than ever before. I suppose it makes it easier to count all those vacuous 'baby's: six of them in the short lyric of 'Never Gonna Be The Same Again'; eleven of them of in 'Emotionally Yours'; fifteen in 'Something's Burning, Baby', often dribbled out in clusters of three within a 4-line stanza.

Nigel Hinton, in the essay already quoted from, confronts what's absent at the heart of the work Bob Dylan offers on this album:

> Images such as 'Madame Butterfly, she lulled me to sleep' are mere words – nothing about the picture is really *known*. The same sense of words arbitrarily brought together is found throughout the 'love' songs:
>
>> *I'll remember you*
>> *When I've forgotten all the rest.*
>> *You to me were true*
>> *You to me were the best.*
>
> There's nothing living in such lines; they don't ring with truth . . . Instead, there is a feeling of formula about the writing. A girl is a 'living dream' and the songs are full of vague statements, some of which seem to be there merely to fit the rhyme:
>
>> *I could be unraveling wherever I'm traveling . . .*[45]

43.   Terry Kelly, 'Bob Dylan and the art of forgery', *Bridge*, no. 2, Winter 1998: an interesting essay that I find myself more often disagreeing than agreeing with, its title explained early on by his noting that 'W. H. Auden once defined poems which were merely imitative of a writer's early work or style as "forgeries".' Summarising "Empire Burlesque" he also writes that it offers 'Dylan forgeries: unconvincing snatches of contrived local detail in otherwise unremarkable tracks ('Tight Connection To My Heart . . .'); personal bitterness masquerading as verbal incisiveness ('Seeing The Real You At Last'); clumsy social epigrams ('Clean-Cut Kid'); . . . and that ultimate populist Dylan forgery, 'Dark Eyes', its very wordiness and stilted literariness being in inverse proportion to its actual eloquence.'

44.   In Bob Dylan's case, this was achieved by one Nick Egan, who 'designed' the album cover; no one is credited for the horrible Pop Spiv casual jacket Bob is morosely posed in. In Debbie Reynolds' case, regardless of who was responsible for it, the silver Afro wig is 'placed' in a coruscating aside by Hunter S. Thompson in *Fear and Loathing in Las Vegas*, 1972.

45.   Nigel Hinton, 'Into the future, knocked out and loaded', see note 37.

He picks clear examples here. That bothersome 'unraveling' bothers me not on quite the same ground as Hinton's. Whether something sounds to be there simply to achieve a rhyme is not such a simple issue. In the lines above, we're only tempted to assume that he 'needed' that 'unraveling' if we accept that he needed the 'traveling'. Plainly, though, he could have thrown out the pair and turned to something less obtrusive, had he been bothered. In a song where he's happy with an internal 'rhyme' like

> *I could be dreaming but I keep believing*

there is clearly no compunction to be immaculate in these matters. Nor to say anything in particular. Therefore there's nothing about that 'traveling' that urges the necessity of its retention. It would just as well serve the song had he written

> *I could be mooing whenever I'm chewing . . .*

Conspicuous rhyme, as many another Bob Dylan song illustrates to many a differing effect, is not bad by definition. There's nothing wrong with 'jeez I can't find my knees' or 'your long-time curse hurts but whut's worse'.

One of the times conspicuous rhyme is a failure – sticking out like a sore thumb – is when a verb our ears are accustomed to hearing as transitive is used as an intransitive one, and sounds awkward in consequence. This is surely the first problem with 'unraveling', to English ears like Nigel Hinton's, just as it is awkward on anybody's ears to hear 'to slide' used without a preposition after it, as in that other "Empire Burlesque" song, 'Dark Eyes', where

> *. . . the midnight moon is on the riverside*
> *. . . and it is time for me to slide.*

In such a context – and it is always context that decides these things – you don't slide, you slide *into* something or *out of* somewhere or *down* something, or whatever it may be. So 'slide' as the end of the sentence there shouts its discomfort, and this is what makes it sound inserted 'merely to fit the rhyme'.

Similarly, in English English, you unravel *something* – your knitting, a mystery, or a forkful of spaghetti – you don't just *unravel*. Yet to write that is to recognise at once that this formulation of American English makes perfect sense: its psychological truth and aptness is immediately apparent. In any case, you might well hear 'he unravelled', the intransitive verb option, simply as shorthand for the English English, transitive version.

As it happens this is handily illustrated in a spoken narrative by Bruce Phillips (Utah Phillips: a sort of authentic version of Ramblin' Jack Elliott, very knowledgeable about unions and radical groups like the Wobblies, a union songs jukebox and a great raconteur; Dylan did his song 'Rock Salt And Nails' during the Basement Tape sessions in Woodstock in 1967, and he performed at the 1973 Mariposa Folk Festival, which Dylan attended). In the narrative I have in mind, Phillips talks wonderfully about bums and tramps and moving around, and in the midst of it he says this: 'It would be too pat to say that a lot of people are out bumming, riding trains, or doing day labour from one skid to the next because of economic circumstances . . . Something broke inside their head and a number of things got unravelled and never got ravelled back together. It just became so aggravating that the person ran away from it.'[46]

We can see here that the formulation 'inside their head . . . a number of things got unravelled' is merely 'they just unravelled' before its ellipse by the instinctive poetic process of conversational usage. So if it isn't *that* that's wrong with Dylan's

> *I could be unraveling, wherever I'm traveling . . .*

and it isn't the mere fact of a conspicuous rhyme per se, then what is it? Why is it bothersome? The answer, as so frequently, is context. It's what happens either side of it that either validates it or cannot. If the part of the song before this line had seemed impelled to communicate anything specific or graspable, particularly anything about a realised individual's real state of mind – inner or outer turmoil, to take the plain example – then we could arrive at 'I could be unraveling, wherever I'm traveling' and find it the plausible confession of a plausible predicament. Arriving at it from a series of nebulous, careless, unassembled building-blocks of doggerel, we cannot but find it suspect. The further context of what comes next merely ensures that our suspicion is well-founded. When Dylan adds on that

> *. . . even to foreign shores,*

especially delivered, as this is, down the pompously moronic slow fall of the tune, the unthinking vacuousness of the sentiment must confirm it as phoney. That 'even . . .' – what does it pretend to mean? That under normal circumstances he's only likely to start unravelling in the good ole USA? It's just specious nonsense. It holds none of the psychological truth that it must hold to hold water. It unravels itself: it is its own undoing – and that's why it sounds stuck in 'merely to fit the rhyme'.

There is another pertinent example in Dylan's work of the second half of the 1980s, in 'Man In The Long Black Coat' on "Oh Mercy" (a work more properly discussed later in this chapter), which seems worth mentioning here. This example has been widely held up to ridicule for a lyric sore thumb sticking out 'merely to fit the rhyme'. It is the word 'float' in the formulation

> *People don't live or die, people just float*
> *She went with the man in the long black coat.*

Again, the point is that context decides these things. In fact here you might reasonably argue that it is not the word 'float' that offends per se, but the formulation 'People don't live or die, people__', which sets it up for a fall. If you're going to go for such a grandiose pitch at declaiming a secret of the universe, you have to offer something that will float rather better than 'just float'. That's asking for an attentiveness you can't satisfy. But if, instead, Dylan had gone in for something rather more modest – something along the lines of, say

---

46.   Bruce Utah Phillips, transcribed in *For What Time I Am in This World*, ed. Bill Usher (1977). Phillips' work includes the LP "Good Though!", Philo Records PHIL1004, North Ferrisburg, Vermont, 1973, CD-reissued Philo/Rounder 01167 1100425, Cambridge, Massachusetts, 1996, and the book *Starlight on the Rails and Other Songs* (1973). I believe he is also featured in the video 'The Wobblies: History and Song', Broadside TV, 204 East Watauge, Johnson City, Tennessee 37601, *nia*. 'Rock Salt And Nails', often associated with Ian Tyson (of Ian & Sylvia), was first recorded, along with other Utah Phillips compositions, on a Flatt & Scruggs album from the mid-1960s (*nia*).

> *Some people sink or swim, some people float*
> *She went with the man in the long black coat*

or, still less obtrusively ambitious, something like

> *People just drift along, people just float*
> *She went with the man in the long black coat*

then no one would have singled out 'float' for ridicule or squeamish disapprobation. Context is all.

At least all these songs illustrate an issue worth discussing. 'I'll Remember You',

> *When I've forgotten all the rest.*
> *You to me were true,*
> *You to me were the best,*

lacking any such point of interest, is just perversely impoverished doggerel. It's unassessible: it never touches your critical apparatus. No matter how low you set your standards, a verse like this just limbos underneath that line. There isn't a child in England or North America who couldn't write a verse less empty and clumsy than that. Yet these are a Bob Dylan song's opening lines!

This isn't even mediocre pop music. Pop doesn't have to equal empty. One of pop's virtues can be an economical directness, which has yielded strong opening lines from many unpretentious artisans down the years. And of course it is Bob Dylan who has proved and re-proved himself the master of the Donne-like, Marvell-ous *start*, combining with éclat a conversationally authentic directness with a compelling beckon into the song for which it speaks. It is a world away from 'You to me were true / You to me were the best'. He to himself is untrue, he to himself should give a rest.

To gauge how severe is this decline in standards, simply take a minor old song and a minor "Empire Burlesque" song and compare them: say, 'Spanish Harlem Incident' and 'Emotionally Yours'. The differences in vocal performances on such early and such later recordings is discussed in this book's final chapter. Here, consider the songs themselves.

Whatever aspect of the two you choose, there's simply no contest.

Compare the titles. 'Spanish Harlem Incident' has a deft particularity, even after all these years: in its cultural allusiveness – the playfully used mock movie title or mock headline it conjures – it carries the spark of an alert mind, not taking itself too seriously but on the ball, while as a comment on its contents – a making light of the feelings expressed with such energy in the song – it contributes to the expression of those feelings, signalling the singer's wistful regret that such affairs must pass. What does the title 'Emotionally Yours' signify? Bullshit and sludge. There's nothing alert, sparky or culturally allusive here; no deft particularity – no particularity at all. It makes no comment, other than by default, since anyone alert to language themselves will be warned off by the clumsy untruth at its core.

Compare the repeating line that ends the verses – the device that is as near to having a chorus as either song comes. In 'Spanish Harlem Incident' we get

> *I got to know babe . . .*

(yes, there's one 'babe' in each of the three verses)

> *Let me know babe, all about my fortune*
> *All along my restless palms*

and then

> *Let me know, babe – I'm nearly drowning –*
> *If it's you my lifelines trace*

and then

> *I got to know babe, will you surround me*
> *So I can know if I am really real.*[47]

What we have here, then, is a sustained conceit, that of 'gypsy gal' = fortune-teller, deftly used, to say that in the *moment* evoked in the song, the singer feels that his future is in her hands. This is sustained for the conclusions of the first two verses – and without a pop cliché in sight – not with 'your heart is in my hands', but rather in language new to popular song, and with a particularity that convinces you there's a specific person envisaged here, and a particular moment experienced: these are 'restless palms'. This also allows the verse's end to balance its beginning, in which

> *. . . the hands of Harlem*
> *Cannot hold you to its heat.*

This conceit, this calculation and planning, if you will, in the composing of the lyric, far from having the effect of making it seem a construct of artifice, enables the song's authenticity to flow. Its last verse ends with just the necessary minimal difference to signal that it *is* the song's end, and to finish with a renewal of ardour and urgency, acting as a protestation at coming to the end of the affair it describes. Where the other verses both end with 'Let me know', in the last this becomes 'I got to know'. What of the repeated line at each verse end in 'Emotionally Yours'?

> *And I will always be emotionally yours.*
> *And I will always be emotionally yours.*
> *But I will always be emotionally yours.*

The 'And' becomes 'But' to signal song's end. Nothing else moves, in any sense.

Compare strikingness of openings. 'Spanish Harlem Incident' opens vividly, with a clear-sighted placement of person and cityscape that yet leaves the listener to fill that picture in – trusts the listener to do so – while beginning as it means to go on, with a poetic conceit, and one that coheres with what will follow:

> *Gypsy gal, the hands of Harlem*
> *Cannot hold you to its heat.*

'Emotionally Yours' also begins as it means to go on:

---

47.   These lines, and more, have been subjected to stupid twiddles of alteration in the version of the song published in *Lyrics 1962–1985* (1986).

Come baby, find me, come baby remind me, of where I once begun.
Come baby, show me, show me you know me, tell me you're the one.

On this evidence the writer is sorely in need of reminding of where he once begun.

Further, the one song has vivid imagery, the other virtually none. Does 'come baby, lock me into the shadows of your heart' do anything but palely loiter in the shadows of 'come and take me / Into the reach of your rattling drums'? Something is *happening* in the specific moment, something is being visualised in the Harlem night, when the Dylan of 1964 sings

> *The night is pitch black, come an' make my*
> *Pale face fit into place, ah please!*

not least because something is happening to *enact* it in the dynamics of the line itself. Dylan expresses his awkward fit with the marvellous awkward fit of the word distribution and the inspired onomatopoeic stuttering of those alliterative ps and fs along that insistent, urging second line. Nothing is happening when the Dylan of 1985 sings

> *Come baby, shake me, come baby, take me, I would be satisfied.*
> *Come baby, hold me, come baby, enfold me, my arms are open wide.*

The verbs of imprecation hold no urgency here: they're there because they rhyme; there's no enactment of any of the demanded shaking or taking – and nothing for the visual imagination to get a grip on, except for the stiff cliché of 'my arms are open wide'. Where the earlier minor song is personal and fresh and fired by particularity, the later one is tired before it starts, and its only stuffing is the dullest of pop cotton-wool.

You'd think it should be the other way around. In 1964 Bob Dylan had good reason to be drawn to pop. Pop was exciting right at that point, not least to Dylan. This was the era when he was freeing himself from the constraints of 'folk', taking his car-trip around America and hearing, inevitably, the Beatles on the radio all the time. The 1960s was really beginning. Yet the young Bob Dylan, absorbing all this, was nevertheless writing songs that benefited from his saturation in all the richness of folksong.

By 1985 what had been fresh was stale, what had been youthfully alive was encrusted in crap, what was underground and radical had become corporate mega-product, with rock music no more culturally separate from Reaganism than the Pentagon. Weird time for Bob Dylan to join the party, and for his writing to benefit only from saturation in the shallow histrionics of corporate rock.

The worst crime is not hooking into something cheap and gross but hooking in badly and missing its point. You'll fall down. This surely happened when Bob Dylan latched onto Arthur Baker, the remix guru who was invited to go through these recordings discoing them up. Or down. The vapid, inhuman drumbeat that Arthur Baker imposes, and the concrete stadium acoustics he throws over everything, were picking up on the most reactionary kind of disco music, the kind most cynically mass-produced from above – just at the moment when a significant part of youth's masses appeared to be creating, with rave music, a genuine alternative on the dance-floor: one that was, at least potentially, anti-reactionary, anti-Reaganite, communally created and democratic.

Different musical structures reflect different societal structures. In 1993 Philip Tagg delivered at a cultural studies conference a most interesting paper on, among other things, the possible big significance of the difference between rock and rave.[48] In it, Tagg asks:

> What sort of socialisation strategy is encoded in . . . rock? It seems to me that we are hearing individuals who beat the fascinating but overbearing system by screaming louder than it, by roaring or chain-sawing their way through it . . . Hence the heavy-metal audience's arm raised in a collective V-sign as the singer or lead guitarist rides away into another heroic urban sunset. Unfortunately, the emancipatory potential of this . . . strategy can degenerate into the vulgar entre-preneurial egoism of the Thatcher and Reagan era and into its musical equivalent – hyper-melodic pomp and its elevation to a hegemonic position . . . we have witnessed the obvious promotion of the corporeal from Youth Subcultural Division Four to the premier league of capitalist culture. Young US-Americans are not recruited into the marines by Sousa marches but by Van Halen . . . Vauxhalls are sold to the tune of 'Layla', Fords to the ex-Queen guitarist Brian May's 'Driven By You.'

In contrast, these 'monocentric types of socialisation strategy are clearly less popular with today's ravers because . . . they do not go much for cohesive melodic statements and seem to eschew, both musically and socially, big figures'. Rave, he argues,

> is something you immerse yourself into together with other people. There is no guitar hero or rock star or corresponding musical-structural figures to identify with; you just 'shake your bum off' from inside the music . . . The music is definitely neither melody nor melody plus accompaniment. Nor is it just accompaniment any more than West African polyrhythm . . . Polarising the issue, you could say that perhaps techno-rave puts an end to nearly four hundred years of the great European bourgeois individual in music . . . does rave music say 'up yours' to 'performance', 'achievement', 'competition', 'enterprise' and all those other nauseous thatcheritic buzzwords?[49]

---

48.   Philip Tagg, 'From refrain to rave: the decline of figure and the rise of ground'; paper delivered at the Convegno sulle culture del rock, Istituto Gramsci/La Repubblica, Bologna, Italy, May 1993; edited version published in *Popular Music*, vol. 13, no. 2, 1994.

49.   Tagg's elucidation of these points runs like this:

> Particularly remarkable is rave music's penchant for the Phrygian, a mode virtually unused previously in any form of internationally well-known music apart from what came out of Spain in the form of malguenas, farrucas, fandangos and flamenco music. From a Eurocentric viewpoint, this is the mode of Spain, gypsies, Balkans, Turks and Arabs . . . Why Phrygian? Have British rave musicians taken a stand for the new-age traveller and gypsies? Have European and North American bedroom boffins started to support the pan-Islamic movement or is the Phrygian thing a musical 'up yours' . . .? Or has everyone been listening to rai music? Or is the Phrygian mode just new and different? If so, why that particular difference and not another? . . .
>
>   Why the breakneck tempo? Why the explicit metronomic pulse on the kick-drum? Why the constantly dense but distinct acoustic set-up? Why no prominent bass-line? Why so many effects of the film soundtrack type? Why do tracks last five minutes and not three? Why so few sung male vocals?

I transmit these points not to suggest that Bob Dylan should have been subsumed by rave – I'm not as unhappy as Philip Tagg with the notion of the great individual in music – but to stress that dragging the likes of Arthur Baker into his arena in order to tart up "Empire Burlesque" delivered Dylan into the worst of both worlds: it convinced neither the market that turns corporate rock product into platinum nor those whose ear and mind is on the lookout for an alternative to this mainstream. If you use your position in the evil empire of the music business to send someone out to buy you some disco clothes, you'll end up in the clothes of the emperor. Shopping for modishness is still just shopping.

It's certainly no substitute for the desire to communicate. With "Empire Burlesque" there's no sense that any of these songs – is there a single verse? – needed to be written. He's doodling, and sometimes he's very good at it, but it's a poor substitute for feeling impelled to communicate and to look you in the eye. This is not what can be said of 'Idiot Wind' or 'Boots Of Spanish Leather', 'She's Your Lover Now' or 'Love Henry'. To hear, or even to read on the page, a song as humane, shining, sharp, impeccable, considered, conscientiously built and wholeheartedly offered as, say, 'When The Ship Comes In' (to take, like 'Spanish Harlem Incident', another song normally described as 'minor' in Dylan's work), and then to hear, or read, something like 'Never Gonna Be The Same Again' or, yes, 'Emotionally Yours', is to feel it as plainly shameful that the artist capable of the one can be reduced to offering the other. It's as if you revisited the Sistine Chapel and found Michelangelo airbrushing Ronald McDonald on the ceiling.

Occasionally – not often – Dylan can lift some of this wretched material in live performance: he can so misuse his best expressive skills as a singer that, pressing them into the service of a song as empty and inauthentic as 'I'll Remember You' or as suspect as 'Dark Eyes', he can convince you that there really is something tangible inside them after all.

It was Dylan's concert in South Bend, Indiana, in November 1991 that raised 'I'll Remember You' above that limbo line. That one night, it was, through Dylan's focus and inspirational vocal performance, far better than it ought to have been. He shared with his audience a lovely unrestrained vocal searching; it was mannered but exploratory, his quick-witted good taste and instinct always in evidence. It soared, despite itself.[50]

In the case of 'Dark Eyes' – of which Nigel Hinton said 'I'm slightly suspicious of people who declare that they "... live in another world / Where life and death are memorised"' – it was without question live performance that brought it alive, and the performance was the series of duets of the song that he sang with New York new

Why so many women singing short phrases in quite a high register with so much reverb? What does this male-female division of vocal 'labour' signify in terms of gender role ideals? ... why is there so little tune and so much accompaniment? I cannot answer any of these questions satisfactorily here. What I hope to do, however, is ... [take] account of radically new musical and social conditions influencing the production and use of rave music. (Philip Tagg, note 48)

50. Bob Dylan: 'I'll Remember You', South Bend, Indiana, 6/11/91: an exceptional concert even within the 'good patch' he went through that November, after a year better known for the general awfulness of his performances. That night there was also a fine 'Watching The River Flow', with a lovely quiet vocal set against terrific grunge-band guitars, and a wondrous run of consecutive inspired performances, on 'Shelter From The Storm', 'Early Morning Rain', 'Gotta Serve Somebody' and 'You Don't Know Me' (this last managing to be both the ultimate prom band moment and an affecting tribute to Ray Charles).

wave artist Patti Smith in the 1990s. Here, in the tingling electricity between them as they traded verses and duetted on the choruses, the song was the conduit of a beauty and excitement it had never possessed.[51]

Some tracks done at the album's recording sessions also promised a little more when they started out than after Arthur Baker had got hold of them. 'Tight Connection To My Heart', in this manifestation, has a sexy, Marvin Gaye type of a shuffle beat and comes across as a convincing attempt at a soul single with a Bob Dylan vocal: it hits, as they say, a nice groove and justifies itself on these musical terms such that you don't need to start scrutinising its lyric, any more than you would want to with a Doris Troy record, or one by Mary Wells. This version begs to be on radio. It got lost by being Bakered. Serve 'em right.[52]

Some of these "Empire Burlesque" out-takes were of songs that never did emerge officially, and there are small morsels of merit in one or two of these too. There's the kernel of an atmospheric, savage, inner-city album lurking somewhere inside a track called 'Waiting To Get Beat': it holds a genuine menace and in two or three strong lines conjures a vivid picture of a narrator who knows he's going to be murdered, by organised crime, in revenge and as a lesson to others. This song inhabits a recognisably more contemporary urban hellscape than any created in Dylan's earlier work, and to hear it gives a hint of what a 1985 album might have been: of a distinctive identity it might have had, fired by a speeding, youthful-voiced Bob Dylan, if whatever mood and flash of vision had inspired this track had been maintained instead of smothered by weary striving and music-biz cheap shots.

There was another rejected song, 'Straight A's In Love', which, like several others such as 'Who Loves You More (Baby I Do)' and the truly dire 'Go 'Way Little Boy', seemed determined to wish themselves back into the world of 1950s minor rock'n'roll – a form of infantilism, and horrible to hear – yet 'Straight A's In Love', splendidly un-PC in its 1950s take on the dumb blonde (or brunette), includes in its detailing of how thick the 'you' in the song is, the triumphantly funny one-liner 'You could

51.   Nigel Hinton, see note 37. (This seems the nearest to the right place to mention – so I do – that 'Dark Eyes' too has its founding biblical text. 'All I see are dark eyes' Dylan complains; the text that fills this in is from Christ's Sermon on the Mount. It is transcribed in Matthew 6:22–3: 'The light of the body is the eye: if therefore thine eye be single, thy whole body shall be full of light. But if thine eye be evil, thy whole body shall be full of darkness'. In Luke 11:34, this is given as 'The light of the body is the eye: therefore when thine eye is single, thy whole body is also full of light; but when thine eye is evil, thy body also is full of darkness'. It seems to me an irksome labelling, though, that goes against the grain of so much else. What of those beautifully described 'chrome brown eyes' in 'Caribbean Wind'? A very large proportion of the world's human beings, and the overwhelming majority of its noble animals, have 'dark eyes'.)
    Bob Dylan & Patti Smith: 'Dark Eyes', 10/12/95, Boston; 11, 14/12/95, NYC; 13/12/95, Bethlehem, Pennsylvania; 15–17/12/95, Philadelphia. Many Dylan followers suspect that he felt challenged by Patti Smith's still possessing a fierce anti-showbiz, anti-bullshit credibility that had in his own case been compromised by that point: that she therefore kept him on his toes as no performance with his own band alone would have done. As it was, he rose higher than his toes. (And his whole body was full of light.)

52.   Within days of writing this passage I was delighted to find, in an advance copy of the new 4th edition of Glen Dundas' book *Tangled up in Tapes* (1999), that Dylan had recorded a version of a classic that each of these women artists had contributed to the music: an instrumental version of the Doris Troy hit 'Just One Look' and a vocal version, with Clydie King, of Mary Wells' 'My Guy', at his home studio in Malibu in March 1984. Less than a year later he recorded the un-Bakered version of 'Tight Connection To My Heart' that seems inspired by exactly that kind of nicely pre-funk soul music.
    Doris Troy: 'Just One Look', NYC, 5/3/63, Atlantic Records 2188, New York [London-American HLK 9749, London], 1963; Mary Wells: 'My Guy', Detroit, 2/3/64, Motown 1056, Detroit [Stateside SS288, London], 1964.

confuse Geronimo with Johnny Appleseed!' Unlike so much else here, it took Bob Dylan to devise that.[53]

None of which redeems the album that did emerge, leaving "Empire Burlesque" a strong contender for the ill distinction of being Bob Dylan's least admirable album.

The following year's release, "Knocked Out Loaded", 1986, is an altogether less cohesive but warmer collection of work, containing within it a few more small morsels of merit – a few *amuse-gueules* (though they tend to amuse the boys more) – and one banquet: the lavishly compelling, fresh 'Brownsville Girl', a genuine achievement both in the cooking up and in Dylan's bravura presentation of its narrative.

The small likeable things are very small, when you remember what an overwhelming amount of major work almost any one of Bob Dylan's albums of the 1960s had offered. With the whole of "Knocked Out Loaded" except for 'Brownsville Girl', you're reduced to noting things such as that on his cover-version of the awful Kris Kristofferson song 'They Killed Him' there's a terrific bass-guitar part, some lovely singing and the extraordinary nerve of, or joke of, the children's vocal chorus; that 'Driftin' Too Far From Shore' has some quietly pleasurable lyrics and ends wittily, as Nigel Hinton remarked at the time, with a fade that has 'you' drifting away and the singer avowing that he 'can finish this alone, honey'; that his cover of 'Precious Memories' combines, oddly but refreshingly, a kind of steel-band sound with the hillbilly hymn music of the 1940s[54]; that 'Got My Mind Made Up' has a not unpleasant riff, a Duane Eddy guitar part, a decent country guitar part, the welcome freshness of the line 'I'm going off to Libya!' (especially since Dylan has lost none of his winning way with a place-name's pronunciation) and some endearingly fey,

---

53.　Bob Dylan: [the unreleased] 'Tight Connection To My Heart', 'Waiting To Get Beat' and 'Straight A's In Love', NYC, Feb. 1985; 'Who Loves You More (Baby I Do)' and 'Go 'Way Little Boy', NYC, July 1984. ('Who Loves You More' *begins* with a lovely, snakey, youthful voice that becomes emptily mannered as utter lack of lyric content, completely derivative melody and rockist genre drain the lifeblood from his vocal performance. His chutzpah shrivels before our ears. After the stimulus of the surprisingly good guitar solo it's noticeable that Dylan returns to the vocal fray with a new banana's worth of energy.)

'Straight A's In Love' is the name of an old record by Johnny Cash, Memphis, *nia*, Sun Records 334, Memphis [London-American HCSD 9070, London], 1960.

Geronimo (1829–1909) was the chief of the Chiricahua Apache Indians and a war leader who led campaigns in the Southwest against white settlers and US federal troops until his final capture in 1886. He became a farmer in Oklahoma and dictated his book *Geronimo's Story of His Life* (1906) three years before his death.

Johnny Appleseed (1774–1845), real name John Chapman, born Massachusetts, journeyed west in c. 1797, moving ahead of the pioneers, planting apple orchards throughout the Midwest using apple seeds from cider mills and also spreading religion. A follower of Emanuel Swedenborg, he was a self-appointed Church of the New Jerusalem missionary and a peacemaker between native American Indians and settlers. He died in Indiana after over fifty years' travel. He is a key mythic figure in mainstream US history: very wholesome, very white. He is also the alter ego chosen by wholesome and white Pete Seeger for the regular column he has contributed for hundreds of years to the American folk magazine *Sing Out!*, of which he is an associate editor.

54.　'Precious Memories' is a popular gospel song, covered for instance by the Edwin Hawkins Singers and Aretha Franklin, and popular too among white gospel groups like The Blackwood Brothers Quartet, a prominent influence on Elvis Presley. Indeed Dylan may have known that, at Elvis' request, the Blackwoods sang 'Precious Memories' at the climax of Gladys Presley's funeral. They were her favourite quartet, and this her favourite hymn.

[Edwin Hawkins Singers: 'Precious Memories', *nia*, reissued on "The Best Of The Edwin Hawkins Singers", Sequel NEM 636, *nia*. Aretha Franklin: 'Precious Memories', *nia*, "Amazing Grace" LP, Atlantic Records, NYC, 1972, CD-reissued on Atlantic 260 023, NYC, 1993. The Blackwood Brothers Quartet: 'Precious Memories', Gladys Presley's funeral, Memphis, 15/8/58. (A plane crash in Clanton, Alabama, killed original Blackwoods members Bill Lyles and R. W. Blackwood, c. 28/6/54, after which younger brother Cecil Blackwood and J. D. Sumner joined the group. The latter features prominently on Elvis Presley's 1970s recordings and concerts.)]

youthful singing on lines such as 'I ain't your dog . . .'; and that 'Under Your Spell', so long as you're not expecting a song of weight, is immaculate pop, immaculately sung, with one delightfully arrogant Dylanesque touch in its lyric – where, while anyone else would have written

> *You'll never get rid of me as long as I'm alive*

here the line becomes

> *You'll never get rid of me as long as you're alive –*

and with some particularly fine vocal 'ooh's.

Then there's 'Maybe Someday', the best of the album's minor songs, which also has some fine 'ooh-ooh's and 'ah-hah's, a guitar solo so crudely expressive that it sounds as if Dylan contributed it himself, something about it reminiscent of Elvis Presley's version of 'A Fool Such As I', and some adroit lines that Buddy Holly might have written if he'd been more daring in his lyrics (and it's a very Buddy Hollyish title, of course). In other words, one way and another it has a healthy feeling of being in the spirit of rock'n'roll. Dylan's audacity is alight here, as he delivers flamboyant cascades of words that may be rather well sung, down lines of infinitely variable syllabic length while always managing to fit them into the tight regularity of the musical structure. I say 'may be rather well sung' because the recording is subject to a spectacularly poor production – by the artist himself, if we're to believe the sleeve credits – so that the aural quality of the voice as it comes through is, as we critics say, piss-poor.[55]

There are, too, the usual biblical reference-points. In an old issue of the *Telegraph* fanzine, there is a passage dealing with 'Maybe Someday' on the letters-to-the-editor page, that says this (though it is unclear from the layout whether its concluding sentence is reader Graham Ashton of Brownhills' contribution or editor John Bauldie of Romford's):

> had you noticed that 'Maybe Someday' quotes from T. S. Eliot? In 'Journey Of The Magi' Eliot has 'And the cities hostile and the towns unfriendly'. Later in the same poem there's mention too of 'pieces of silver'. So in Dylan's [two] lines
>
> > *Through hostile cities and unfriendly towns,*
> > *Thirty pieces of silver, no money down*
>
> he gets in allusions to Eliot, the Bible and Chuck Berry![56]

It's interesting that Dylan's lines should use Eliot's – and they do: I suspected that the hostile cities and unfriendly towns were no more Eliot's than Dylan's but were a biblical allusion, but this doesn't seem to be so. But in the simpler matter of the 'thirty pieces of silver', what's neat is that while everybody knows and uses that bit, Dylan's addendum of 'no money down' (a Chuck Berry song title) explains not just the

---

55. For an elaboration, see Chapter 20's discussion of the decline and fall in production values on Bob Dylan recordings.

56. *Telegraph*, no. 28, Winter 1987.

payment but the terms of the payment – that there was to be no money paid up front to Judas – and does so with wit and economy.[57]

'Brownsville Girl', its lyric composed jointly by Dylan and Sam Shepard, is of a different order. Stephen Scobie believes it to be 'a masterpiece, a song that must rank among the five or six best songs Dylan has ever written'. Nigel Hinton writes that 'When Dylan is working at this level of creativity – a level that puts him head and shoulders above everyone else – there's a magic evocativeness about everything he writes that gives the words enormous possibilities.'[58]

Many of them are, however, the words of Hollywood cliché. The best scrutiny of the song I've encountered is by Aidan Day in his book *Jokerman: Reading the Lyrics of Bob Dylan*, in which he gives it eight pages of commentary – and without ever saying whether he thinks it's any good or not![59]

Agreeing in effect with Stephen Scobie's explanation of the song's structural complexity – that it 'never develops a single, coherent narrative: rather it presents the fragments of several possible narratives, sometimes evoked and discarded within a line, whose relationship to each other remains unspecified' but that these fragments are 'thematically congruent' – Aidan Day offers two main reasons why the song has been structured in this way, such that, as he puts it, 'scraps of memory and thought mix with other scraps in an unstable temporal sequence'.

The first purpose of such a structure – a structure that would once have been in danger of being thought no structure at all but is now in danger of being thought Standard Postmodernist – is that the lyric 'plays with tenses and perspectives as it enacts the lack of chronological structure in the inner life of the mind'.

But – and this is Day's main theme – it is 'not only the fluidity of memory or mind which the lyric dips into. It is that throughout 'Brownsville Girl' the mind's images and memories have only a questionably "real" status.' For this, he suggests, is a song about how cliché invades the memory and mind. He says that the opening two verses of this 17-verse song describe memories held by the narrator that are composed of 'the stock diction and conventions of a Western':

> *He was shot down by a hungry kid tryin' to make a name for himself.*
> *The townspeople wanted to crush that kid down and string him up by the neck.*
> *Well the marshal, now he beat that kid to a bloody pulp.*
> *As the dying gunfighter lay in the sun and gasped for his last breath:*
> *'Turn him loose, let him go, let him say he outdrew me fair and square.*
> *I want him to feel what it's like to every moment face his death.'*

Well, yes, these are memories composed of 'the stock diction and conventions of a Western', in that, as we've seen, they are a description of what is remembered as

---

57. T. S. Eliot: 'The Journey of the Magi', 1927, in *Collected Poems 1909–1935* (1936). Chuck Berry: 'No Money Down', Chicago, December 1955, Chess Records 1615, Chicago, 1955.
    'And they covenanted with him for thirty pieces of silver' – i.e. no advance payment: 'no money down'. (Matthew 26:15).

58. Stephen Scobie, *Alias Bob Dylan* (1991); Nigel Hinton, see note 37.

59. All references to Aidan Day's work refer to the chapter 'That enemy within' in the 1989 paperback edition of his book *Jokerman* (1988).

important from a particular film, *The Gunfighter*. But as Aidan Day suggests, they are also stock Western ingredients. There's nothing described here that *sounds* unique to the particular film the song's narrator is describing. The opening moment is 'a man riding 'cross the desert'; the storyline of the renowned gunfighter always being challenged by some 'hungry kid tryin' to make a name for himself' and the dialogue quoted – all these are familiar commonplaces of the cowboy film as a genre: you could say that it's their grinding familiarity on the screen that accounts for the death of the genre at the box-office in modern times.

Aidan Day argues that this cheap cliché is being emphasised, exposed, pointed out, by Dylan, and with regret and even disdain. After all, this is the song that has him exclaim 'Oh! if there's an original thought out there I could use it right now!': a line that, says Day, 'reflects upon one of the fundamental preoccupations of the lyric'.

Tracking this theme through the song, Day quotes, as I have just done, those opening two verses and then says: 'It is when this crescendo of cliché has been reached in the last line of the second verse . . . that the recollections momentarily break and the speaker expresses his disdain for the formulae purveyed by the film. But disdain is accompanied by a recognition that such formulae are, inescapably, a part of the raw material of memory and mind.' And to illustrate this sense of what's being communicated by the song's narrator, Day quotes its next two lines, which are:

> Well I keep seeing this stuff and it just comes a-rolling in
> And you know it blows right through me like a ball and chain.

It's true that these lines suggest rueful acknowledgment that something of no special value, 'this stuff', continually invades the mind unbidden. This is brought acutely to life at the end. From similes of what's in the air, and therefore unavoidable – it comes 'a-rolling in' like the tide, it 'blows right through me' like the wind – Dylan makes the inspired switch, and we find that it blows right through him with far greater invasive violence: 'like a ball and chain', like the very fabric of your house being demolished. And the sudden surprise of the switch to this image enacts the effect it describes.

At the same time, 'like a ball and chain' carries its other meaning into the song: the 'ball and chain' that ties the prisoner down, the effect of which is to underline that the narrator cannot escape 'this stuff' rolling in. The brilliant touch on Dylan's part here – the first of so many in this song – is that while 'ball and chain' is itself a cliché, the effect Dylan puts it to is anything but tired.

But is Dylan's main emphasis really on the exhausted unoriginality of these Hollywood scenes? Just as people so often parody the things they are most fond of, so Dylan's feeling for Hollywood images and filmgoer's memories here is surely 90 per cent affection and only 10 per cent challenge and demurral.

Several things inside and outside the song itself suggest this.

To work from within, firstly the words are not wholly weighted as Day suggests. The summary Dylan offers of the film's key points, which takes up those entire first two verses, reveals a noticeably straightforward desire to communicate what's up on the screen in the film's dramatic action. In the earlier version, 'New Danville Girl', Dylan's equivalent passage is also scrupulous in saying at the outset that he remembers little about the film, yet that which is remembered is given clearly and in some detail.

For a narrative so 'unstable', 'fragmented' and 'indeterminate', it starts out with an almost urgently expressed clarity.

Nor are words the sole evidence here. There is also the way Dylan says them. There is no demurral in his voice, no sneer at or apology for the clichéd nature of the scenes he describes in these first two verses, and when he steps back, to give us the lines about how he keeps seeing 'this stuff', the change of expression in his voice, far from adding distance, is surely from engaged summarising to a confessed warmth, to ruefully acknowledged fondness.

It's the same all through the song. Great affection, enthusiasm and yearning are expressed for the very scenes from 'his own life' that are described as if they too are scenes from movies: 'Ah but you were right: it was perfect as I got in behind the wheel'; 'Well we're drivin' this car and the sun is coming up over the Rockies'; 'It was the best acting I saw anybody do'.

There is a mass of external evidence, too, that while Dylan is indeed examining here the way that film and artifice entangles itself inside us, colouring some of our most personal inner chambers with cheap public art, he puts little stress on deploring it.

He told Bill Flanagan that 'Brownsville Girl' was written partly in response to a song by Lou Reed, called 'Doin' The Thing That We Want To', which starts by referring to going to see a play (the Sam Shepard play *Fool for Love*, in fact) and describing what struck the singer about it. This is done in the most vague and lackadaisical terms, and the song is of no great complexity or depth. 'Brownsville Girl' owes it nothing at all in structure, complexity of concept or use of language. But Reed's song advances a simple message: that certain films and plays are 'very inspirational'.[60]

Now, of course, Dylan's 'response' to this song might have been to want to say the opposite, but granted that he chose the most prominently featured of Lou's very inspirational people to help him write the song, and granted the long history of his own fond references to films, outlined earlier in this chapter, I don't think so.

Moreover, the narrative Dylan so carefully gives us at the beginning of 'Brownsville Girl' is the perfect articulation, within the genre of the western, of Dylan's most perturbed feelings about his own dilemma as a celebrity. He identifies readily and completely with the gunfighter who can't go anywhere without being stared at, measured up and challenged, perhaps lethally and by the very people who admire the skills on which that celebrity is based. Even the death that the gunfighter feels 'every moment' might indeed be hovering for Dylan in real life. Every 'star' has felt this since death came up on John Lennon from a 'fan'. Dylan speaks about this in the interview

---

60.   Lou Reed: 'Doin' The Thing That We Want To', *nia*, "New Sensations", RCA Records PL84998, New York, 1984. Referred to by Dylan in his March 1985 interview for Bill Flanagan's book *Written in My Soul* (1986). Sam Shepard, *Fool for Love*, the play, premiered San Francisco, 8/2/83, directed Shepard; then New York City, May 1983, again directed Shepard. (The film *Fool for Love*, Cannon/Golan-Globus, US, directed Robert Altman, written Shepard, starred Shepard, Kim Basinger, Randy Quaid and Harry Dean Stanton, 1985.)
      Here, however, Dylan rides a trail already explored in song, by a blues singer–songwriter long before Lou Reed. 'I Would If I Could', one of the best of Lightnin' Hopkins' 1960s sides, is a song about going to see a movie about Jesse James, in which the song's narrator drifts between 'real-life' and on-screen events awash with rumour and shooting. [Lightnin' Hopkins: 'I Would If I Could': Houston, 18/12/67; "The Texas Blue Man", Arhoolie F1034, Berkeley, c. 1967; CD-reissued "Lightnin' Hopkins: Texas Blues", Arhoolie CD 302, El Cerrito, California, 1989.]

with Cameron Crowe for the "Biograph" sleeve notes. *The Gunfighter* is a film about fame and how lethal it can be, and this is intensely interesting to Bob Dylan. When he hears 'this stuff' about wanting the hungry kid to feel what it's like for the weary hero, he doesn't hear stock convention and cliché: he identifies with it through and through. (Ostensibly contradicting this, near the end, comes one of the song's moments of suspect bravado – one at which Dylan himself seems to burst out of the narrator's clothes and, as it were, expose himself, to say with a swagger, as if the demands of celebrity don't intimidate him at all, 'They can talk about me plenty when I'm gone'.)

Given all this, it's a central irony that the narrator in Dylan's song is himself a fan, of the Hollywood star Gregory Peck. The film was 'about a man riding 'cross the desert and it starred Gregory Peck' he says without a pause, the lack of pause suggesting unrestrained keenness, right there in the song's second line; 'All I remember about it was it's Gregory Peck' he says later; then he's 'standin' in line in the rain to see a movie starring Gregory Peck . . . I'll see him in anything'; later still, thinking of the first movie again, he says, like a shy fan confessing fan behaviour, 'I think I sat through it twice'.

Having set this up, one of the best touches, a touch that stops the narrator's fandom seeming too off-kilter, too mad, is that despite all this Peckery, he can still say of the 'you' who rescues him in court that *this* was 'the best acting I saw anybody do'. Then, rounding things off neatly at the end by returning to the beginning, he says two 'fanlike' things in the two final lines, punning on 'stars' in the second:

> All I remember about it was it starred Gregory Peck . . .
> Seems like a long time ago, long before the stars were torn down.

This irony is energised when we know that Bob Dylan really does consider himself a fan of Gregory Peck. In 1971, the *Jerusalem Post* reported Dylan thus, when they asked how he'd spent his 30th birthday: ' "We went to see a Gregory Peck movie – I'm quite a fan of his," he said with a laugh.'[61]

Here is one corridor in the song, then, down which Dylan offers us a look back and forth between what is real and what is not. Meanwhile his admiration for Gregory Peck is another reason for disputing Aidan Day's claim that 'Brownsville Girl' sets out to deplore the invasion of the memory and mind by Hollywood cliché and falsity.

In any case, the very point about *The Gunfighter* upon which critics and viewers are agreed is that it stood out from the run of the genre: that it avoided the stock conventions and cliché and went to some trouble in the pursuit of authenticity of look

61. Catherine Rosenheimer, *Jerusalem Post Magazine*, 4/6/71.
    There is a particular line in the 'New Danville Girl' lyric, too, that I think reveals that Dylan has indeed paid an authentic attention to Peck's career. It's in other ways a throwaway line – and he does throw it away before recording 'Brownsville Girl' – but it touches upon a particular moment of difficulty for Peck fans, which you would surely only know about if you were one. The line is 'He's got a new one out now – you know he just don't look the same', which is amended to 'He's got a new one out now – I don't even know what it's about'. The amendment could apply to any film, but the complaint that 'he just don't look the same' was one I remember my mother making when Peck suddenly stepped out of his romantic lead persona – although at 62 he was by this time far too old to maintain it – and, with heavy make-up transforming his face to give him, oddly, an almost Japanese look, played evil Nazi Dr Josef Mengele in *The Boys from Brazil* [ITC/Producer Circle, US/UK, directed Franklin J. Schaffner, written Ira Levin and Heywood Gould, 1978]. I note too that Dylan mentions 'Mengele's bones' in the "Biograph" interview of 1985. (Peck had also stepped outside his matinee idol persona to play Captain Ahab in *Moby Dick*, Warner/Moulin, UK, directed John Huston, 1956.)

and feel. Robert Warshow, writing in *The Immediate Experience*, even admires the way that the film is shot 'in cold, quiet tones of gray, and every object in it – faces, clothing, a table, the hero's heavy moustache – is given an air of uncompromising authenticity.'[62]

It's striking too that although Dylan peers in and out of 'what's real and what is not', he as often emphasises the distinction as plays with the slippage between them. The very first thing he says about the film emphasises that it *is* just a film: as soon as he's mentioned a character, he jumps outside it to say, without a break in the sentence, that the film is a Hollywood star vehicle:

> *Well there was this movie I seen one time*
> *About a man riding 'cross the desert and it starred Gregory Peck.*

Equally, when the song's narrator describes episodes or fragments from his own 'real life' as if they were from movies, he makes it perfectly clear from his delivery – the tone is of wry self-amusement, of awareness of his own immaturely self-conscious way of seeing these things.

One of the light touches with which he achieves this is that while on screen 'a man [is] riding 'cross the desert', in the narrator's 'own' life, he says that 'you' came to him 'on the Painted Desert'. As Aidan Day noted, this 'apparent reference to the Painted Desert of Arizona bears an ironic connotation of artifice, a hint of the state of a film set: "the *painted* desert".'[63] This is matched, right at the end of the song, when the idea of the set, the artificial backdrop, is suggested again with that final phrase 'the stars were torn down'.

It's an irony, then, that while the film goes all out for outer realism, Dylan's narrative both does the opposite and doesn't. On the one hand the song is *more* realistic than the film, because the film straightforwardly counterfeits authenticity whereas the song keeps its eye on the difficult matter of what's real and what isn't, and on the invisible passageways that slip us between the real and the fictional, all the time. At the same time the song refuses the realistic style of the film's narrative, as, in Aidan Day's phrase, it 'plays with tenses and perspectives as it enacts the lack of chronological structure in the inner life of the mind'.

Yet the parallels present themselves insistently. The film's hero is no hero at all, but a man who lives by the gun and dies by it. He is a failure as an integrated human being: isolated, incapable of mercy with or protecting his family, roaming without purpose and without the nourishment of any sort of intimacy. In the song, the narrative and chronology may be unclear but it is made apparent over and over again that here too the narrator's memories are of failed relationships, failed connections and failure to protect either himself or those he loves. Unlike the stock Western hero, the song's narrator abandons women, or is abandoned by them, or both:

---

62. Robert Warshow, *The Immediate Experience*, 1964, quoted in Halliwell, see note 15.

63. This works exactly, it seems to me, as I suggested Dylan's use of another geographical feature worked in 'Day Of The Locusts' on the "New Morning" album of sixteen years earlier. There 'the Black Hills of Dakota' are real but also resonate with the voice of Doris Day singing a 1950s pop song of immense unrealism set in the most Hollywooden Old West you could devise, while the title 'Day Of The Locusts' is itself another item inspired by Hollywood resonance (being taken, as noted in Chapter 2, from Nathaniel West's novel about Hollywood, *Day of the Locust*, 1939).

Way down in Mexico you went out to find a doctor and you never came back.
I would have gone after you but I didn't feel like letting my head get blown off

(this cowardice re-emphasised later on when

> *. . . shots rang out.*
> *I didn't know whether to duck or to run. So I ran)*

or else he needs to be rescued by women instead of the other way round:

> *Well you saw my picture in the Corpus Christi Tribune. Underneath it it said 'a*
>   *man with no alibi'*
> *You went out on a limb to testify for me. You said I was with you.*

It heightens the contrast between the heroic cowboy archetype and the song's less-than-reliable narrator that the song sets his nebulous exploits in western terrain also. Stephen Scobie notes that the title of the early version, 'New Danville Girl', 'perhaps evokes the "Danville train" robbed by Jesse James and ridden by Virgil Cain', while 'Brownsville seems intended to unify the geographical references – San Anton[e], the Alamo, Amarillo, Corpus Christi – along the border area between Texas and Mexico that has fascinated Dylan from 'Just Like Tom Thumb's Blues' . . . As a border town it stands between the various realms of history, fiction and myth . . .'[64]

Border towns are where people cross from one kind of place to another, yet where the conjunction of the two makes for an ill-defined, nebulous entity. I've been prompted to write of corridors and invisible passageways already, and the prompt has been that uncertain crossings of one sort or another are a recurrent motif in 'Brownsville Girl'.

The first thing we see is a man crossing the desert – always a risky business, a place in which to lose your way. When the narrator steps into the action himself, he soon says, in some agitation, that he's 'too over the edge'. Then he and whoever is with him cross 'the panhandle'. This is a term for a narrow strip of land in one state that projects into another (in this case the Texas Panhandle): another place of nebulous boundaries. But there's also a frisson here of crossing a moral boundary: a stain that seeps in here from the word's other meaning. To panhandle is to accost people and beg from them – in Greyhound bus stations in the US today you still see notices

---

64.   Stephen Scobie, *Alias Bob Dylan*. His reference to the 'Danville train' and to 'Virgil Cain' is a reference to the song by The Band 'The Night They Drove Old Dixie Down', *nia*, "The Band", Capitol Records STAO-132, Hollywood, 1969.
    If that explains 'Danville' – which, aptly, is also, if I remember it aright, a train junction in the middle of nowhere – it doesn't explain why this is *'New*' Danville'. What does is the fact that there is a traditional song called 'Danville Girl'. I noted in Chapter 1 that Cisco Houston's album "I Ain't Got No Home" [NYC, early 1961, Vanguard Records VRS-9107, New York, 1962] includes a version, and that around the same time Houston recorded another version under its common alternative title, 'The Gambler' [NYC, c. 1961, "Railroad Songs", Folkways Records FA2013, New York, c. 1961]. There's also Pete Seeger's 'Danville Girl', *nia*, on "Darling Corey", Folkways Records FA2003, New York, c. 1960.
    'Danville Girl' bears no relation to 'New Danville Girl' beyond its being about drifting around the country, occasionally thinking about a woman.
    To switch to yet another level of reality, Brownsville is distinctive in being one of the most polluted places in the Western world. Between the raw sewage and the chemicals dumped in the river by American factories built on the Mexican side of the river to exploit Mexico's lax pollution laws (and its cheap labour), infant mortality levels in Brownsville are horrendous and by the end of the 1980s the chemical cocktail (high levels of benzene and mercury, 53 times the US permitted level of xylene and more) had resulted in over one hundred babies being born without any brains. Mexican babies, of course.

declaring 'Absolutely No Loitering, Profanity, Panhandling' – so that what we take at this point in the song is a fleeting sense of a further moral instability here, a further crossing of boundaries. When they arrive 'where Henry Porter used to live', Ruby tells them they've crossed another invisible borderline: 'She said "Welcome to the land of the living dead".' Next thing we know, with another switch of scene, the narrator feels vulnerable – violent danger seems to loom – even in the act of the smallest crossing: 'I was crossin' the street,' he says, 'when shots rang out.' Then, matching the earlier phrase 'too over the edge', the woman who saves him with an alibi is said to have gone 'out on a limb' in doing so. There is also 'somethin' about you baby' that belongs in another world, while the narrator has left a part of himself behind in another place of uncertain territorial identity and, these days, uncertain authenticity too, 'the French Quarter', way down yonder in New Orleans. The theme is stated most directly and concentratedly in the narrator's protestation that he's 'always been the kind of person that doesn't like to trespass, but sometimes you just find yourself over the line'. Finally, crossing is not only a recurrent theme in the song: the song itself eschews linear narrative the better to stand by its core: a series of memories and recollections crossing and re-crossing the narrator's mind.

This tracking and tracing, in 'Brownsville Girl', of notions of how these realms blend or fuse or confuse with reality, can only communicate, in the end, one aspect of what's absorbing in the song and why it's so pleasurable and rich an item in Bob Dylan's body of work.

There is also the joy of his matchless delivery, timing and phrasing, the humour that runs through the song, and the skill in its language: a skill I touched on – seems like a long time ago – when reflecting on the unexpected brilliance of that 'ball and chain' in the third stanza.

There are a few features of the early version, 'New Danville Girl', both in the writing and in the performing, which it's a pity we have to lose in the transfer to 'Brownsville Girl': but not many, and it's easy to see why they are discarded. This is an unusually clear example of the recording chosen for release being superior to the unreleased, and there is no doubting that from a comparative look at the lyrics alone we could tell which was the tentative early attempt and which the later, more fully realised success. We could tell the same from Dylan's delivery too: there are hesitant, uncertain moments all through 'New Danville Girl' – they're easily allowed for, granted how beautifully he leads us through so much of it, but they're detectable falterings, while 'Brownsville Girl' has none.

In stanza five, after the second line's 'We slept near the Alamo', we lose the long-delayed first moment of singing on 'New Danville Girl', which comes on the lost half-line 'and fell out under the stars'; and then two lines later, after 'you' go out for the doctor and never come back, we lose the lovely rhyme for those 'stars', with 'I stayed there a while till the whole place, it started feelin' like Mars'. This is a fine piece of Dylanesque observation, suggesting the weird bleakness of aloneness 'under the stars' in huge space, and he sings it with a gorgeously youthful expressiveness – but it has to go, because it zooms us too far out from the cowboy genre and the western. So too we lose 'like when she sings "baby let the good times roll"' because that too is too specific a reference to something from a competing genre. The world of Shirley & Lee and their sexy soul music's vivid bounciness, this too is an incautious distraction from the border town world of Danville and its realms of history, fiction and western myth. The Bob Dylan who knows and loves old records like Shirley & Lee's 'Let The Good Times Roll' is not the one that he has in mind for this song's narrative.[65] Likewise we lose the attractive line 'Sounded to me like I was bein' chased by the midnight choir' – a phrase that could surely have stayed but which isn't crucial and was probably deleted because it carries overtones of the supernatural, and therefore also threatens to jump the genre barrier.

A kind of music is abandoned directly, as well as by allusion, when we move from the earlier to the later recording. In the earlier, there is an instrumental break after the first chorus, in which the lead instrument is an almost comically plaintive and wonky harmonica from Dylan, making strangely half-indecipherable noises akin to those on 'Jokerman'; and after the third chorus comes a caressingly expressive electric guitar solo, at once soaring and dignified, impassioned and restrained, simple and imaginative, grungy and refined. I can think of no better electric solo on any studio recording in Bob Dylan's work – and it has to go, because again, this song must single-mindedly occupy the cowboy and western genre, not criss-cross in and out of rock music signifiers.[66] When it comes to 'Brownsville Girl', these pauses after the choruses are mostly abolished, and we are propelled right out of the Hollywood-epic whoosh of the overblown, declamatory chorus music straight back into the narrative, with its more urgent, greater articulation of detail and its far longer lines that must be spoken fast to fit the musical frame. Thus we lose too the simpler, more appealing music on the choruses themselves, where you can hear the rock musicians playing and the vocal lines are sung with a sort of matching pop normalcy; instead we get an epic blare that might be from a full orchestra playing a movie score, with trumpet and sax, women singers and echo, and with the trumpet blurting out high above the rest with a distressingly stiff riff, a stentorian, martial oscillation between two uninteresting notes.

(The chorus is the one element that doesn't seem to me to be improved in the re-make. I think its Hollywood heaviness just makes the excessively clichéd lines themselves more ponderous and less admissable. Nor does the change from 'take me all around the world' to 'show me all around the world' seem any improvement.)

We also lose some of the greatest 'oohs' and 'ah's in Bob Dylan's entire repertoire, and there seems no good reason for this, beyond the fact that they do seem impelled by the need to fill in spaces, whereas in 'Brownsville Girl' it is words and more words that fill them in. The 'awh' that he has Ruby say in 'New Danville Girl', in the line 'awh, you know some babies never learn', is many-splendoured, and after the lost line 'And everything he did in it reminded me of me' comes an 'ah-ah-ah!' of sublime seductive grace. At the end of the last verse – which offers the unquestionably inferior 'But that was a long time ago, and it was made in the shade' (much inferior, that is, to 'Seems like a long time ago, long before the stars were torn down') Dylan releases us by releasing a most exquisite, yearning 'Yeah—'. And after the last chorus, Dylan returns to give us one more benediction of really lovely long 'oh's and 'ah's that linger for us at the song's final end.

---

65. Shirley & Lee: 'Let The Good Times Roll', New Orleans, May 1956, Aladdin 45–3325, Los Angeles, 1956.
66. The guitar solo is by Ira Ingber.

However, these consummately enunciated pseudo-words of exclamation, these most articulate of grunts, are dissipated by fill-ins. Time and again – which is too many times – we get the sort of 'yes you are' or 'yes you do' that garrulous soul-singers cannot resist sticking in like punctuation-marks at their line ends. Thus we get, in the court-room moment, 'You went out on a limb to testify, and you said I was with you, *ah yes you did*' – and it's filler. It distracts. Then just six lines later we get 'Yeah I feel pretty good but you know I could feel a whole lot better, *ah yes I could*' – and it too is filler and too close to the other one not to obtrude. Its effect in weakening the line is demonstrable. It is the tightened-up 'Brownsville Girl' version that sticks in the mind, even though in fact it's only one word shorter. It's more focused, and its rhythm propels it more purposively along: 'You know I feel pretty good but that ain't sayin' much – I could feel a whole lot better'. That *is* a whole lot better. Nor does 'New Danville Girl' conquer this verbal tic at that point. The very line after that 'ah yes I could' ends with an 'oh yes I am' tagged onto it. And because it's so palpably meaningless, it's delivered without anything by way of rigour or persuasive grace.

There seems a similar failure of nerve, an implicit confession of the weakness of what's being said, in the two consecutive verses that are transformed much more thoroughly than most when it comes to the re-write. These:

> *You know it's funny how people just want to believe what's convenient –*
> *Nothin' happens on purpose – it's an accident – if it happens at all*
> *And everything that's happening to us seems like it's happening without our*
>   *consent*
> *But we're busy talking back and forth to our shadows on an old stone wall*
>
> *Oh you got to talk to me now baby, tell me 'bout the man that you used to love*
> *Tell me about your dreams just before the time you passed out,*
> *Ah yeah, tell me about the time that our engine broke down and it was the worst*
>   *of times*
> *Tell me about all the things I couldn't do nothin' about*

become these:

> *You know it's funny how things never turn out the way you had 'em planned.*
> *The only thing we knew for sure about Henry Porter is that his name wasn't*
>   *Henry Porter*[67]
> *And you know there was somethin' about you baby I liked that was always too*
>   *good for this world*
> *Just like you always said there was somethin' about me you liked that I left in the*
>   *French Quarter.*
>
> *Strange how people who suffer together have stronger connections than people*
>   *who are most content.*

---

67. There is a faint, insignificant echo here – I mention it only because the one always reminds me of the other – of Nat Hentoff's remark in the notes on the back of "The Freewheelin' Bob Dylan", discussing the fact that Dylan adapted 'Honey Just Allow Me One More Chance' from an old 78 rpm record by Henry Thomas (detailed in Chapter 9). Hentoff writes: 'Dylan can only remember that his first name was Henry.'

I don't have any regrets. People can talk about me plenty when I'm gone.
You always said people don't do what they believe in, they just do what's most
    convenient, then they repent
And I always said 'Hang onto me baby and let's hope that the roof stays on!'

In the earlier draft, the first three lines in this passage are distractingly 'philosophical', and of uncertain rhythm and tone, while it's as he delivers the fourth – a line too crummily opaque even for Bob Dylan to get away with – that his conviction falters in front of our ears. The lines after that also begin without quite expressing any particular mood you can get a grip on, and when the tone and import do emerge, on the ratty last line – 'Tell me about all the things I couldn't do nothin' about' – they emerge as an unwelcome petulance, a lurch back into some private quarrel that seems to exclude us. We often don't know what's going on in this song, but only here are we made to feel excluded.

The 'Brownsville Girl' version solves all these problems, and provides some of the most likeable, intelligent touches in the whole song. The narrator who needs rescuing by women, who doesn't go after them to protect them because he's afraid for his own skin, and who runs away when he hears gunshots, the narrator who at the same time empathises with the gunfighter up on the screen, the narrator who is no Gregory Peck – in the re-write of the song he is also, unstained by petulance or cod-philosophising, a keenly realised individual, a wittily self-deprecating hopeless romantic who likes women and has heart.

He's generous-minded. The exchanges between him and 'you' in these eight lines have a radiant charm that exudes the narrator's awareness of how different the two of them are – how hopelessly boyish he is, and how maturely rooted she is. He delights in the way that what they say to each other comes in from such different starting-points of personality, as if the two glance off each other in passing. When, much earlier in the song, he exclaims 'You know I can't believe we've lived so long and are still so far apart', the tone is partly of genuine surprise (a tone echoed twice in the passage under discussion here, as he exclaims 'Strange how people who suffer together have stronger connections than people who are most content!' and 'You know it's funny how things never turn out the way you had 'em planned') – but 'I can't believe we've lived so long and are still so far apart' also carries in its tone not rebuke or complaint but actually a relishing of difference. He appreciates their difference. Thus here he says the unanalytical 'there was somethin' about you baby I liked that was always too good for this world' – which confesses his male vagueness of sentiment, and his transparent hint of a macho chat-up line there that he knows he can't sustain and doesn't fool her for a minute – and this is matched by the mismatch of 'Just like you always said there was somethin' about me you liked that I left in the French Quarter' – which is comically so much more specific, even though we as listeners don't expect to know what it might be, and they might not either. It contains, but isn't limited to, the joke of describing a quality someone used to have but has lost as if it were an object like your watch or your hat that you might leave behind by accident at the airport or wherever.

Then in parallel to this we get the energised, good-natured exchange of the final two lines above, in which he is tolerant of her potentially sour cynicism, or, if you will, her potentially cold analytic turn of mind as he reminds her of her saying that 'people don't do what they believe in, they just do what's most convenient, then they repent' before recalling that he would counter this sort of approach with wildly unanalytical, worlds-away stuff like 'Hang onto me baby and let's hope that the roof stays on!'

Again, the gulf between the two approaches is comically presented, and without presenting her universe reductively, he makes it clear that his own, while riddled with impracticality and shameless bravado, nevertheless has virtues of its own: indomitable energy, cheeriness, spontaneity, inclusivity. He may be a sucker for the grand gestures of romanticism – he admits that both this 'you' and also Ruby with her 'some babies never learn' have a healthy scepticism towards the way that he flops about in the world – but the self-deprecation and warm susceptibility that shine through him have their validity too. And really, what's the point of living in this terrain, this border territory of history, fiction and myth, where every place name is soaked in romantic resonance – the Alamo, Amarillo, the Painted Desert, San Antone – if you're not a romantic?

Ruby's cynicism hasn't got her anywhere. She feels this literally, and is 'thinkin' of bummin' a ride back to from where she started'. So much for how strongly *her* suffering has forged connections with the man whose washing she is hanging on the line. And so much for her stoicism. This is shown to be flimsy, in any case: although she changes the subject every time money comes up, she initiates the topic of 'how times were tough'. She's thinking of bumming a ride back to where she came from, yet when she asks how far the narrator and his companion(s) are going, she is good-naturedly sceptical that they will really get anywhere.

Her sense of feeling stuck may discolour her view of everything, or may be unsullied realism. We can hear her observation that 'even the swap meets around here are getting pretty corrupt' either way. No-one has any monopoly on what's real or true in this song, any more than they can stake any claim to heroic qualities.

This balance is so beautifully maintained. Look at the highly comic way that the narrator's boyish declamatory flamboyance with grand gestures is undercut by the detail. 'We're goin' all the way' he tells Ruby,

> *till the sun peels the paint, and the seat-covers fade, and the water-moccasin dies . . .*

Till the *seat-covers fade*? Man! This guy's so wild he doesn't even care about the state of his car's seat-covers!

Meanwhile, of course, the exchanges we've been discussing, between the narrator and the 'you' towards the end of the song resemble nothing so much as great fragments of movie dialogue. They could belong to Bogart and Bacall.

The whole song, come to that, offers the extra irony of being in itself like a half-remembered movie with its episodes and flashbacks and cuts, its panning camera-eye and its widescreen pageant that Dylan projects up there for us so hypnotically.

A very vivid one it is too. How is it, for instance, that we see Ruby so clearly out there in the dusty yard, hanging out that washing in the dry western air, where your eyes can follow the flat land way off in the distance? How is it that we feel the complexity of her character from the very few lines of dialogue we hear her speak? What a creation she is. Can anyone else create so much in so few frames?

Hidden inside this rhetorical question is the particular question, Can Sam Shepard? Of the two co-lyricists of this song, Shepard is the one who writes screenplays; but in the end this is a song, not a screenplay, and Bob Dylan is the one who writes songs. To put this question another way: in 'New Danville Girl' and 'Brownsville Girl', who wrote what?

The comic interplay between the narrator's voice and the Greek-chorus grunts of the female backing-singers, which tiptoe in in the song's eleventh verse, seems an innovation: something new to Dylan's oeuvre, and therefore quite likely to be a dramatic element imported by Sam Shepard – it's plays that have Greek choruses, after all – but this is a guess, and you might say that Dylan seems very comfortable with the innovation, and embraces its comic potential with flair yet with restraint, never allowing it to dominate or grow tiresome.

That eleventh verse begins with Dylan's voice saying 'Well they were lookin' for someone with a pompadour'. Then he says 'I was crossin' the street when shots rang out' – but halfway through this, after he's said 'I was crossin' the street', the women say 'oh!', emphatically yet in the quiet of the deep background, and the effect is of them interrupting him to say 'oh you were in that scene too, were you?' At the end of his sentence, after 'when shots rang out', they say it again, this time as if saying 'What were *you* doing there?' Then he says 'I didn't know whether to duck or to run. So I ran,' and the women say 'ooh!' And they repeat that 'ooh!' at the end of the next line, which is ' "We got him cornered in the churchyard!", I heard somebody shout'. So by the time we reach the next line, the one about seeing his picture in the *Corpus Christi Tribune*, there's a half-subliminal flirtation going on between them, to heighten the comic effect.

Later this flirtation comes to a head – almost a head-on collision – when his 'I don't have any regrets. They can talk about me plenty when I'm gone' is followed by a loud, long-drawn-out *'Oh yeah?'* and then when he delivers his final Big Gesture line – 'I always said "Hang onto me, baby, and let's hope that the roof stays on!" ' the Greek chorus women gasp out a sort of miaow without the 'm' – the sort of complex vowel-sound exclamation you might think they needed to listen to Bob Dylan to be able to achieve. It's an almost slapstick moment, more Buster Keaton than *Bonnie and Clyde*, giving us the fleeting picture of the narrator and his 'baby' roaring off hanging onto each other only to crash a short way down the dusty road, and of the Greek-chorus women emitting the comic 'eeaaoww!' of envisaged pain as he gets this come-uppance.

It's guesswork, and I'm biased – but it seems to me that 'New Danville Girl' has a lot of short lines that seem to resemble the terse minimalism of Shepard's dialogue in, say, *Paris, Texas*, in which the monosyllable rules, and Dylan sounds as if he finds some of this inadequate and awkward to deliver, whereas 'Brownsville Girl' is delivered by someone so wholly in command of his material that perhaps it *is* rather more his material. On the other hand, as I suggested when facing the same problem about joint authorship between Dylan and Jacques Levy on some of the "Desire" songs, there are certain orders of detail that Dylan's own songs never show much interest in but that are prominently featured in some of the co-written ones, which argues that they are the co-writer's babies.[68] In the case of the Dylan–Shepard collaboration, the sort of detail that seems to me unDylanesque includes 'your platform heels', 'her red hair tied back' and possibly 'the swap meets' and 'the water-moccasin'. I could be wrong.

All I think can be said with any certainty is that while 'Brownsville Girl' is a unique item in Bob Dylan's work, there are a large number of unique items in his work, part of his greatness being his extraordinary range, and there is nothing about 'Brownsville Girl' to make you feel that Bob Dylan couldn't have written it. Its themes and preoccupations are wholly in keeping with those he offers all through his writing; its fictional characters stand in line jostling without any incongruity among the many others he's created down the years; the interest in the silver screen has been evinced throughout his songwriting life, and never more so than in the mid-1980s; the 'unstable temporal sequence' of its narrative structure, and the shifting between 'you's and other 'you's and between 'you's and 'she's, are all features we're familiar with from other, earlier Bob Dylan songs; the wit and sense of humour are Dylan's; the very idea that a song can be that long is Dylan's.

Finally, when we come to the released version, 'Brownsville Girl', the absolutely masterly delivery by Dylan makes it his, whoever contributed what in the drafting of it. No one in the world can deliver a talking song or a half-talking song as Bob Dylan can. It's a facet of his genius that he has remained in full control of, apparently from the first day he opened his mouth, and until now. This mastery, and his audible joy in it – a generous, sharing joy – is there right back at the beginning of the 1960s when he records 'Talkin' New York' on his first LP, and when he produces the perfect mimicry of the voices on 'Black Cross'; it's there in the faultless dumb-hick impersonation he gives us in 'Clothes Line' on the Basement Tapes sessions of 1967; it's there when he preaches during the evangelical concerts of 1979; and it's there undiminished at the end of the 1990s on the final track on "Time Out Of Mind", the exalted 'Highlands'.[69]

The same genius is in command of every breath and pause, every unseen tilt of the head, every sung and every spoken syllable, every long line and every switch of mood, in 'Brownsville Girl'. It's a long *tour de force* not a moment too long, and the Bob Dylan who incandesces through it is the full Bob Dylan, the Bob Dylan of genius and generous intelligence, fully engaged.

One of the marks of its excellence as a performance, and a particularly important one granted the actorish subject-matter of the song, is that there is never an adumbration of luvvieness in it. He sounds so fully open to spontaneity of expression and unrehearsed conversational flow that he makes it sound easy *for him*. Yet to hold the printed-out lyric in your hand while playing the recording through headphones, and

---

68. The relevant passage re Levy's contribution to 'Romance In Durango' is in Chapter 5, note 30.

69. Bob Dylan: 'Black Cross', privately recorded Minneapolis, 22/12/61. This was a piece performed by Lord Buckley [LA, 12/2/59; "Way Out Humour", World Pacific WP–1279, LA, 1959], whose LP "The Best Of Lord Buckley" [Crestview Records CRU–801 and CRU7–801,1963] stands on the mantelpiece on the front-cover photograph of Dylan's "Bringing It All Back Home". Buckley's recording of the Robert Service poem 'The Shooting of Dan McGrew', under the title 'The Ballad Of Dan McGroo', [LA, 12/2/59, "Lord Buckley Blowing His Mind (And Yours Too)", World Pacific WP–1849, LA, 1966; or Oakland, early 1960, "Bad-Rapping The Marquis de Sade", World Pacific WPS-21889, 1969], has been suggested as an influence on Dylan's 'Lily, Rosemary and The Jack Of Hearts'.
'Clothes Line', West Saugerties, September–October 1967.

to mark which passages are spoken and which sung as it unfolds: this alone is enough to show you what unmitigated genius he brings to it.

There are whole passages where he alternates a spoken with a sung line, one-two one-two one-two, without this ever once striking you as a rigid pattern, or a technique, or something calculated; others where speech holds for several lines and then soars into singing in mid-line, again without ever sounding like set policy – without style ever seeming to take its leave of content; and others – for example 'dyin' gunfighter lay in the sun and gasped for his last breath' – where breath is so special that it is impossible to say if this is sung or not. There are lines that no one else would decide to sing rather than speak; yet Dylan sings them as if to do so is the most natural thing in the world. In 'New Danville Girl' for instance he *sings* 'Way down in Mexico you went out to see a doctor and you never came back'. In 'Brownsville Girl', after the first chorus, there is a passage of ten consecutive spoken lines, and when the line after that breaks into song, the flow from one to the other is at once immersingly beautiful and quite unobtrusive. The least high-flown lines are sung with an exquisite, yearning caress that never comes anywhere near to the overwrought MTV sob but animates the desire and sense of loss behind the prosaic. Listen to this detailing in the superb way he sings lingeringly of 'your busted down Ford and your platform heels'. The word 'heels' has never been stroked so expressively in its life. (In 'New Danville Girl' he doesn't sing this line at all.)

Nor does Dylan overdo it when it comes to the more obviously strokeable. When we lose 'New Danville Girl''s 'fell out under the stars' to 'Brownsville Girl''s 'your skin was so tender and soft' the gain is in the sublimity of delivery rather than in the words. Dylan's voice enacts these words. There is nothing pejoratively soft, or easy, about the tenderly careful touch of his voice on the several syllables he carries us through on 'soft'. His comic timing on bits like 'I didn't know whether to duck or to run. So I ran' is faultless, as is the sexy grace he brings to pronouncing place-names.

The *combination* of sexy grace and comic timing inside the same phrase is an achievement unique to him. It's there all through this song. Listen to it on a line that would be flat in anyone else's narration: 'Well, you saw my picture in the *Corpus Christi Tribune*.' His delivery carries an intimate comic openness that trusts the listener to hear his silent relishing of the statement's comic incongruity, as the picture of that picture in that paper pops into our minds with the suddenness of the flashbulb we see his face caught in.

Altogether, the delivery is astonishing. Not a false moment, not a foot wrong. Keeping up a curious tension between the very measured, slightly *too slow* musical accompaniment and the urgency of his voice, he gives a faultless performance, infinitely fluid and expressive, from beginning to end a plausible, intelligent and immensely humane persona and narrator, and alert to the turbulent complexities of every moment.

After that came the ragbag of badly recorded mediocrities called "Down In The Groove", for which even the album cover seemed determined to prove that this must be the poorest record Bob Dylan had ever offered the public. For years we referred to it as "Flared Trousers" in our house, but this analogy proved ill-judged. Flared trousers had, after all, once been fashionable, and in the late 1990s loomed surprisingly close to being fashionable again. "Down In The Groove" was never, nor could it be, relevant in our times. Being unfashionable is no sin, of course; putting out a frowsy collection of stained, ill-assorted old trousers in the name of a great artist, and so devaluing the very act of issuing a Bob Dylan album – something which had for very many years been an *event* – this was the miserable sin of it.[70]

In the nick of time, at the last possible moment, Bob Dylan made a fine album in the second half of the 1980s. To apply the crucial psychological fit of the old LP technology (a pattern brusquely abolished by the CD), it is an album that stays on the turntable, one side's end ushering in the other's beginning, over and over again. 1989's "Oh Mercy" is a cohesive, sustained, many-layered work, full of openness, new writing, dignity and resonance, offering unexpected pleasures. Such is its cohesion that whatever theme within it, or aspect of it, you discuss, you find yourself drawing on key words, phrases or lines that match each other directly yet come from inside many different songs. Quoting from one, you reach readily for matching, supportive quotations from at least a couple of others too.

From the uncertain tone of voice with which its title challenges and greets us, to the ambiguous goodbyes of its final track, "Oh Mercy" uses an intelligent poetry and a rich swathe of sound to draw the listener in on beguiling, fundamental debates. Within ten short and 'simple' songs a vast amount happens. Dylan the consummate vocalist finds a voice to carry equal parts doom, optimism, passion, instruction and humility: a voice as old and solid as rock, yet playing fleeting host to many of its creator's younger voices. Dylan the Christian achieves a renewed symbiosis between his religious and secular selves. Dylan the street-poet reasserts his talent for pressing cheap talk and careless idiom into scalpel-language that explores both the world and words themselves.

Within the compelling dialogue of its own constituent parts, many other dialogues rise and fall: between the characters he has invented; himself and other people; the artist and the audience; certainty and doubt; God and man; old and new.

Of the unpromising opener, 'Political World', the best you can say is that Dylan here serves notice that he has regained his alert interest in being precise about the lengths of his lines. The one line here that seems to uncoil further than the rest is 'You've always got more than enough rope'. In 'What Was It You Wanted?', it's the extreme and abnormal brevity of this second line –

> *Was it something important?*
> *Maybe not*

– that makes it so dismissive. In the last song, the three-verse 'Shooting Star', the first two verses offer a last line of five leisurely syllables, which stretch out the reflectiveness of what's being said:

> *Saw a shooting star tonight*
> *And I thought of you—*

---

70.   What a pleasure it is for this critic to have actually spent less time writing about these songs than Bob Dylan took writing them. (He wrote only 'Death Is Not The End' and co-wrote 'Silvio' and 'The Ugliest Girl In The World'.)

and

> *Saw a shooting star tonight*
> *And I thought of me—*

but for the song's final end we get instead the brevity of three fleeting syllables, allowing this line too to act out its meaning:

> *Saw a shooting star tonight*
> *Slip away.*

'Everything Is Broken', with its benign light touch on the delivery of the title line refrain, turns into as insistent a list-making song as 1979's 'Gotta Serve Somebody', ending, accompanied by a fine, slashing harmonica, as the list proclaims Dylan's unique blend of blues and armageddon poetry:

> *Hound dog howlin'*
> *Bullfrog croakin'*
> *Everything is broken.*

Dylan believes in this blend, of course: it was the theme of one of his greatest songs of the same decade, 'Blind Willie McTell'. And indeed "Oh Mercy" draws on the blues almost as much as "Blonde On Blonde" does, and on two or three tracks offers wonderful parallels of that album's mix of throat-red vocals and soft rock music with a blues harmonica and blues lyrics.

There are lists everywhere too. Echoing 'Chimes Of Freedom' from a quarter of a century earlier there is the list of those for whom we should 'Ring Them Bells', the lovely resonances of which include an echo of the 'iron hand' from 'When He Returns' in the neat sense-mixing achievement of 'Ring them bells with an iron hand'.

In 'Everything Is Broken' there is such a long enumeration of broken things that you start to hear the song as pressing a case that everything is in some sense contaminated with brokenness: that there's some ontological flaw in the fabric of being. Such a notion might run parallel to that of original sin, but this song's itemising approach doesn't make it seem quite the same thing.[71]

Of course, the trouble with list songs is that they have to be very good to escape the charge of being so easy to write that they're hardly songs at all. This suspicion lurks with 'Everything is Broken': you could say it's an easy list song that anyone could write, and as sung in concert, Dylan suggests this worthlessness himself. He never bothers to learn his own lyric, and clearly thinks that he can sling any old things together on the spur of the moment. If he could do that with inspired imaginative commitment, it would be exciting improvisation. But when it's merely a

---

71.   I am grateful to Colin Low, creator of the Kaballah Frequently Asked Questions website, for the meat of this paragraph and for the following comments in response to my asking how 'Everything Is Broken' might fit with Kabbalistic beliefs: 'The idea that the creation is in a fallen state is still central to many orthodox Chassidic traditions . . . One of the primary objectives of rabbinic Kabbalah (i.e. the sort still hidden within Chassidism) is yichudim, or 'unifications', putting together that which has become separate. The power that separates . . . is called Din, or judgement. Although Din is a necessary adjunct to physical existence [it is] believe[d] that the power of Din is unbalanced, and human conduct makes it more so . . . With this background, the song makes a kind of sense. One could say that Dylan had a vision of Din, and translated that into an ontological brokenness.' (e-mail, 22/3/99.)

lazy routine of mumbled monosyllabic line endings, and when he fails even to come up with matching rhymes for half of these, and resorts instead to the deliberate slurring of non-words – of feigning words – what we get is unexciting and (which is why I mention such song performances here) in effect a damning critique of his own song.

This is not a suspicion one harbours in the case of 'Most Of The Time', other than in the general and perpetual sense with almost all songs or poems, whoever the writer, that we are aware, somewhere underneath our other responses, that some sections have been needed to make the work long enough to be a whole work – that some lines or verses are as much there to make up a quota as to press their own intrinsic urgency upon us.

'Most Of The Time' escapes the suspicion that anyone might have written it even though it can be regarded almost entirely as a songwriting exercise, a run for its own sake along an extremely well-worn path. We recognise at once as familiar to us from Tin Pan Alley the basic *device* of the lyric, which is to keep denying 'she' matters to him, so as to make it clear that she does. We find it in dozens of songs from the country standard 'She Thinks I Still Care' to the popular standard 'I Get Along Without You Very Well' and 10cc's 1975 hit single 'I'm Not In Love'. Yet when the device is honourably handled, it does correspond to a human truth we recognise, and 'Most Of The Time' is, in this respect, well-tailored. Besides, there is more to it than that. Beguiling for its 'If You See Her, Say Hello' heartache, it is more engaging still for its explicit sub-text, the probing and interesting list of what the artist feels it takes to keep going and keep sane:

> *I don't cheat on myself . . .*
> *I don't compromise . . .*
> *I'm strong enough not to hate . . .*
> *I'm halfway content . . .*
> *I'm clear focussed all around . . .*
> *I can keep both feet on the ground . . .*
> *I can hold my own . . .*
> *Stay right with it when the road unwinds . . .*
> *I ain't afraid of confusion, no matter how thick . . .*

It may seem a rather general assemblage at first, but actually it has an imaginative particularity. For example, it's by no means received wisdom that refusing to compromise is a good survival strategy. Nor does it say 'I keep' but 'I *can* keep both feet on the ground', suggesting the belief that this form of 'realism' is better as an option than a rigid stance. Again, most people (most of the time) talk of where the road winds – which is why the Beatles sing of a long and winding road; it's a nicely Dylan touch that he sings of a long and *un*winding road. Again, being unafraid of confusion is a very Bob Dylan position, all of a piece with his 1965 sleeve note prose poem for the "Bringing It All Back Home" LP, in which he says 'I accept chaos'. At any rate, this other agenda, this interest in what it takes to keep on keeping on, is what sets the song apart, raising it above Tin Pan Alley and Nashville.

Perhaps it is also why, despite its conventional songwriterliness, it is impossible to listen to 'Most Of The Time' without assuming autobiographical content. That list of what resilience or coping consists in is essentially characteristic of Dylan himself – with perhaps one or two claims that strike a discordantly less plausible note.

The one we balk at is the claim that 'Most of the time my head is on straight' – this from the artist whose 1966 tour alone did more than anyone to justify the compatibility of mind-altering substances and sublime creativity, and whose live performances two decades later were so often transparently marred by the befuddlements of alcohol. So instinctively do we demur, therefore, at the claim 'Most of the time my head is on straight' that when Dylan came to sing this song in concert in the early 1990s, it provided a moment of rare spontaneous banter *about* a piece of lyric – about this very line – between this performer and his audience. Dylan, in San José, California, one night in 1992, sings this autobiographically contentious opening line to the song's second verse:

> Most of the time, my head is on straight

and a faction in the crowd guffaws, demurs, says 'Oh yeah?' and Dylan, fast, builds the response 'Oh, *yeah*—' straight into the performance, as a quick prefix to the next line's

> Most of the time . . .[72]

The rest of the song's careful and considered list, though, clearly describes a person exactly like Bob Dylan – and accepting *this* personal correspondence carries us inevitably into speculation about the autobiographical content of the other part of the song: that is, about how far Dylan has his ex-wife Sara in mind here. It gives the song a touching, deeper resonance that its writer may not welcome but that he does nothing to avoid or preclude. Not least is this pressed in upon us because one of the things the song keeps stressing is how far back in time the relationship was. A song like Willie Nelson's 'Funny How Time Slips Away' obviously goes through the motions of discussing this passing of time between the romance and the re-meeting of ex-lovers, yet it does nothing inward to really suggest that the time gap amounts to more than a year or two – a time span that would only seem lengthy to someone a great deal younger than Willie Nelson. In 'Most Of The Time' we feel that the time span has been substantial even through the most well-seasoned adult's eyes:

> I wouldn't know her if I saw her, she's that far behind.

The song also has time enough and space to let in comedy – comedy of the gentlest kind, as in the squeakier-voiced 'she aint even in my mind!' which not only has fun with the methinks-he-doth-protest-too-much syndrome but delivers this in a bridge section that mischievously imitates that Dylan-imitator Mark Knopfler – and comedy of the darker kind. When his catalogue of successes at coping with the vagaries and grind of life includes this:

---

72. Bob Dylan: 'Most Of The Time', San José, 9/5/92. Dylan builds his 'Oh, yeah!' retort into the song as surely as he builds 'You're a liar!', his response to the audience cry of 'Judas!', into the fabric of 'Like A Rolling Stone' in Manchester, 17/5/66. That's my interpretation, anyway: but it may be – I can't quite be sure from the San José tape – that Dylan actually *anticipates* rather than hears a sceptical response, and puts in his 'retort' to forestall it. Either way, it's clear that *he* is aware of the autobiographical credibility gap.

I can smile in the face [pause] . . .

you anticipate that the line will conclude with 'of danger', 'difficulty' or 'trouble' – something to that effect. Instead it's

. . . of mankind

delivered with a beautifully understated gallows smile, the more powerfully to express that this is the most difficult thing of all to endure.

The song accommodates this range of mood and weight while balancing its two main parallel strands, lost love and retained sanity. And how far the song pursues the latter!

Rigour of pursuit is also the virtue of 'What Good Am I?' – for along with the lists on "Oh Mercy" comes a capacity for probing insistence, on asking more and more questions. This song of Christian humility, with its awful Anthony Newleyan title, may not be what people want Bob Dylan for, and if viewed as plain autobiography, it too may be less than convincing: but having raised it, who else could press the question so far?

'Disease Of Conceit' (which sets out, yes, more lists – a list of the consequences of having the 'disease' and another of how it creeps up on you) appears at first to be about to go into the business of berating, somewhat in the style so widely disliked on "Saved". It is, if you will, a sermon. Yet here the singer does not exclude himself – sings, in fact, with the voice of experience. He begins with an assertion of how widespread is the contagion he sees:

There's a whole lot of people sufferin' tonight from the disease of conceit.

What might be righteous gloating turns out to be the implicit compassion of someone who is saying that they've been in the same condition. The middle portion of each verse delineates from the inside, from implied personal experience, how 'the disease of conceit' invades 'your body and your mind', 'eats into your soul' and, just as important in terms of how hard it is to guard against its invasion, 'comes out of nowhere'.

The recording's grand sound on this song is saved from the grandiose by the counter-pull of an eccentric, disaster-courting bathos that Dylan just succeeds in juggling. And though ponderousness threatens, it is avoided by two lithe strengths. One is the audible grinning humour: the deft conjuring up of those hearts 'shaking' instead of aching; the similar slight sideways step he takes with the rhyme in the same place in the first verse, which has him offer us 'struggling' as a struggling rhyme for 'suffering'; and the comic imaginative precision with which he chews that 'piece of meat'. You hear the laugh in mid-delivery at these moments.

If this is preaching, it seems far closer to black church than white. Yet it has little of the evangelising of the early 1980s Christian albums, indulging just two unmistakeable ingredients of a preachy agenda. First there is the conventional religious rap of the song's bridge section:

Conceit is a disease that the doctors got no cure

(though here I always want to shout 'for! . . . got no cure *for!*')

They've done a lot of research on it but what it is they're still not sure.

This takes the standard religious position that science doesn't hold the key, and plays it very nicely with the high comedy of that second line, with its ludicrous picture of white-coated men and women in laboratories holding up test-tubes and scrutinising slides in the quest for a cure for conceit. The mock-seriousness of the line itself, its *People's Friend* tone of voice, incorporates the comic playing dumb that Dylan does so well elsewhere (for instance in 'Memphis Blues Again', when the narrator is told that 'all the railroad men just drink up your blood like wine' and he says 'And I said "*Oh*, I didn't *know* that . . ."') but which is riskier here, because in a song that puts all its eggs in one thematic basket, it is bound to seem so much closer to *really* sounding dumb: especially when delivered along a sumptuously rich musical line and without any vocal emphasis on comic expression – without any Dylanesque exaggerated italic inflection.

The second preachy touch is offered where it gains the extra emphasis of its placement at the end of the song. The list of dire symptoms – 'rips into your senses', 'Turn you into a piece of meat' – concludes with this overtly religious tut-tut-tut: that the disease of conceit will

> *Give you the idea that you're too good to die.*

With that idea, you're not ready to die, whereas it is a fundamental part of the Judaeo-Christian message – and one that has always appealed to Bob Dylan – that you must be ready. This concluding part of the song is the nearest he comes to the message of "Saved" – to its preacherous 'Are you ready? I hope you're ready'. This time, however, the line is slipped in with a take-it-or-leave-it disinterest that is far less likely to offend.

The other lithe strength of the song is the simple, dramatic immediacy of effect – it is a technique of the sermon: a rhetoric of repetition – achieved by every verse's 'tonight':

> *There's a whole lotta people sufferin' tonight . . .*
> *There's a whole lotta people in trouble tonight . . .*
> *There's a whole lot of people dying tonight . . .*

'Tonight' is the apposite moment, too, in the closing 'Shooting Star', and these urgent 'tonights' combine with the many threatening skies and imminent darknesses that hang over the entire album:

> *Far away in the stormy night . . .*
> *. . . in the flickering light . . .*
> *In the turning of twilight, in the shadows of moonlight . . .*
> *. . . a hurricane breeze . . .*

and

> *If I turn a deaf ear to the thunder in the sky*
> *What good am I?*

Time is pressing – running out so fast that it's 'beginning to crawl', as in the folk-legendary moment before death when time is supposed to slow so much that your whole life can pass before you.

And the world's on its side
And time is runnin' backwards.

Elsewhere on the collection he asks

Is the whole thing goin' backwards? . . .

Of course, proclaiming that the end of the world is nigh does not give automatic access to armageddon's seriousness; nor does mentioning the Sermon on the Mount mean that you take on its profundity. Dylan misjudges this badly in the middle section of 'Shooting Star', a horrible embarrassment for its vulgarity of tone and delivery – it counterfeits passion by means of a rasping coarseness. Trying to snatch for that armageddon gravitas, it brings nothing to it but crude over-reaching – no imagination, no pity, no personal human feeling until too late:

Listen to the engine, listen to the bell
As the last fire truck from hell goes rolling by
All good people are praying
It's the last temptation, the last account,
The last time you might hear the sermon on the mount
The last radio is playing.

By the time we reach that little wisp of human feeling, that wistful regret in the last line, it's already been too grating and declamatory to be credible.The rasping delivery of that phoney 'last firetruck [pause] from hell' is its clinching coup de gracelessness. This is so exasperating, too, because the simple, pared-down dignity of the song's verses offers something qualitatively different: a quiet work, in effect a sad and properly serious leave-taking, fit for any final occasion.

Time was, in any case, when things that are normally said to run forwards could run backwards in Bob Dylan's work without it having to signal the imminent end of the world. In '11 Outlined Epitaphs' the night ran backwards, and this suggested freshness of vision, rather than the world's exhaustion:

Al's wife claimed I can't be happy
as the New Jersey night ran backwards
an' vanished behind our rollin' ear . . .
'I'm happy enough now'
'why?'
'cause I'm calmly lookin' outside an' watchin'
the night unwind'
'what'd yuh mean "unwind"?'
'I mean somethin' like there's no end t' it
an' it's so big
that every time I see it it's like seein'
for the first time'
'so what? . . . what about the songs you sing on stage?'
'they're nothin' but the unwindin' of
my happiness'

(Ah, Bob: what a long time it is since your singing your songs on stage was the unwinding of your happiness!)

Other things too have shifted their loaded meanings in "Oh Mercy" – things that Dylan is more likely to recall his earlier usages of than perhaps he is with that night that 'ran backwards'. On 'All Along The Watchtower' the ploughmen were no better than the businessmen: none of them along the line knew what any of it was worth. On 'Ring Them Bells', in which the singer laments (and so beautifully – words and delivery make it so) that

> Oh it's rush hour now
> On the wheel and the plow,

the plough is a symbol of old sureties and old solid values, of immemorial human activity, and of a fundamental innocent hope, when human inventions were benign and benefited all. The inspired use of the 'rush hour' analogy right there – a simple way of reiterating that this is the end of the day – compresses into these two irreproachably short, modest lines (lines made entirely of monosyllabic words) the heightened contrast between the benign and timeless 'wheel and . . . plow' and the fume-choked destructiveness of contemporary inventions.

There is an extra and affecting delicacy of feeling, too, in the way that Dylan's line

> On the wheel and the plow

echoes a plaintive blues line by our old favourite Blind Blake from seventy years before. It is not merely the 'plow' that runs a parallel furrow but the shape and the rhythm of the line – five or six rising and tumbling one-syllable words in each, resolving on a poignant falling cadence – and its import too: the shared pining for vanished rural simplicities. 'I got the Georgia blues' sings Blind Blake, stuck in the cold modern city,

> For the plow and hoe.[73]

Dylan offers another lament for this passing away in 'Everything Is Broken', with its

> Broken hands on broken plows.

This too, appropriately to such a looking-back, looks back to older songs: songs that in turn look back to the solid verities of scripture. On Dylan's first album he sang 'Gospel Plow' (a variant of the traditional song more commonly known as 'Hold

---

73. Blind Blake: 'Georgia Bound', Richmond, Indiana, 17/8/29; "Blind Blake: Blues In Chicago", Riverside Records RLP8804, Holland, 1960s. The melody is exactly that used later by Robert Johnson for 'From Four Till Late' [Dallas, 19/6/37; "King Of The Delta Blues Singers, Vol. 2", Columbia Records C30034, 1973; CD-reissued "The Complete Robert Johnson", Columbia, 1990s], one of the songs used by Bob Dylan in the 1978 concert versions of his "Planet Waves" song 'Going, Going, Gone'.

When I first encountered the Blind Blake song, as a lyric transcribed by Michael Taft in his *Blues Lyric Poetry* (1983), the line in question paralleled Dylan's line in 'Ring Them Bells' even more completely than on the recording, for Taft had inserted a second 'the' into Blake's line, so that it read 'For the plow and the hoe', exactly matching 'On the wheel and the plow'.

On'), the repeated insistence in which is that you should 'keep your hand on that plow, hold on'.[74]

With such shifts of attached meaning in Bob Dylan's work – this shift of the import of 'the plow' from being the symbol of unheeding exploitation on "John Wesley Harding" – the "Oh Mercy" album puts itself, as Dylan albums often do, in dialogue with the artist's other works, just as the commonalities of phrase and theme set up dialogues within the album between one song and another (of which again our 'plow' is an example).

Sometimes these correspondences are so elusive one hardly dares suggest them – yet if they strike the same echo time after time, regardless of their slimness of resemblance, then so be it: they do. One such occurs early on in the album's second song, 'Where Teardrops Fall'. In general this would seem to be modelled as a late-1950s quality pop song, something of the order of Ricky Nelson's 'Lonesome Town' perhaps, or Buddy Holly's 'Moondreams' and 'True Love Ways', which it particularly resembles by means of the immensely welcome soft saxophone (a pool of aural colouring encountered nowhere else on the album) brought in for its instrumental close-out. But in the second verse of the song, to hear

> *Far away and over the wall*

is to be transported back to Dylan's own 'Walls Of Red Wing', a very different species of song, yet one that deals with the same era that Ricky Nelson and Buddy Holly bestrode, and comes from the consciousness of the same Bob Dylan: the one who was Robert Zimmerman, and heard records rather than making them, and watched Buddy Holly from the Duluth audience, and empathised with the young offenders inside the nearby (and locally famous) walls of Red Wing Minnesota's reformatory. Far away indeed from the Bob Dylan of "Oh Mercy" in New Orleans at the end of the 1980s.[75]

He's mentioned walls in any number of songs in the decades between these two, without ever triggering the same retrospective link in the mind: but that

> *Far away and over the wall,*

sung so yearningly, simply does. It's a line that distils the yearning of those 'inmates' he 'remembers quite clearly'. The voice here creates such a firm imaginative moment, too: calling up at this very point not only an enacting rise and fall – an up and over – but a kind of soft furriness in the singing so that as his voice travels 'over the wall' he creates the tactile experience of it, the scraping of his clothes against it as he goes.

---

74. The biblical basis for this is Christ's unkindly insistence that applicants to discipleship must not delay, even to bid farewell to their families, before pressing on. In Luke 9:59–62 this is given as follows: 'And he said unto another, Follow me. But he said, Lord, suffer me first to go and bury my father. Jesus said unto him, Let the dead bury their dead: but go thou and preach the kingdom of God. And another also said, Lord, I will follow thee; but let me first go bid them farewell, which are at home at my house. And Jesus said unto him, No man, having put his hand to the plough, and looking back, is fit for the kingdom of God.'

75. Ricky Nelson: 'Lonesome Town', Imperial 5548, Los Angeles, 1958. Buddy Holly: 'True Love Ways' and 'Moondreams', NYC, 21/10/58. Bob Dylan: 'Walls Of Red Wing', an out-take from the "Freewheelin'" album, eventually released officially on "Bootleg Series I–III", 1991. Dylan performed 'Lonesome Town' many times on his 1986 tour of the US. As noted in Chapter 3, he saw Holly perform at the Duluth Armory, 31/1/59, just days before the latter's death in a plane crash on 3/2/59. In his speech accepting Grammy awards for Best Male Rock Vocal Performance and Best Contemporary Folk Album [New York City, 25/2/98] he referred to this experience, saying that he had felt Holly's presence while recording "Time Out Of Mind" almost forty years later.

There's a similar – and incontestable – correspondence down the more than quarter-century from 1963's 'Restless Farewell' to 1989's 'Most Of The Time', from

> . . . the dust of rumors covers me
> But if the arrow is straight
> And the point is slick
> It can pierce through dust no matter how thick

to

> I don't build up illusion till it makes me sick
> I ain't afraid of confusion no matter how thick.

There's a parallel too between the lyrics in the bridge sections of 'Everything Is Broken' and those in the equivalent portions of that other simple blues-patterned song from almost two decades earlier, 'Watching The River Flow'. There

> Why only yesterday I saw somebody on the street
> Who just couldn't help but cry

and

> Why only yesterday I saw somebody on the street
> That was really shook

while on 'Everything Is Broken', expressing the greater desperation of twenty years down the line, this is ellipsed to

> Seems like every time you turn around
> Someone else just hit the ground.

A similar hardening of gloom comes elsewhere in the same song, when a vision we encountered in the magnificent 1978 "Street Legal" song 'No Time To Think', in which the singer can feel in his mind

> . . . the breaking of jaws
> And the sound of the keys as they clink,

is pared down on 'Everything Is Broken' to the brutalised minimalist asperity of

> Broken bodies, broken bones.

There is also a passage in the course of "Oh Mercy" that takes up again a matter he looked at in 'New Danville Girl' yet gave up on trying to get right by the time it came to 'Brownsville Girl'. Back on his agenda here, it is the Buddhist idea that everything is pre-ordained.[76] When Dylan chivvies away at it in 'New Danville Girl' he fails to find a way to handle it with the noncommital and diffident scepticism he seems to wish to bring to it. In that earlier song he lunges at it like this:

---

76.   I take the briefest possible summary of how Buddhism comes into it from, as it happens, the novel *Snow Falling on Cedars* by David Guterson (1994): 'He was a Buddhist and believed in the laws of karma . . . everything comes back to you, nothing is accidental.'

You know, it's funny how people just want to believe what's convenient:
Nothin' happens on purpose – it's an accident – if it happens at all
And everything that's happening to us seems like it's happening without our
    consent
But we're busy talking back and forth to our shadows on an old stone wall.

This is presented in long conversational lines, and the writer's hesitant scepticism is expressed not exactly between the lines but between the phrases in the lines – in the way, especially, that he delivers the constituent parts of that second long line as a series of afterthoughts or hasty qualifications, hasty embellishments of the argument, one after the other, in imitation of the diffidence of someone who knows they're not being very persuasive but cannot but keep adding more, in little appeasing flurries, instead of being quiet.

He drops this altogether from 'Brownsville Girl', leaving only a reshaped version of the first of those four lines, put into someone else's mouth and sounding, in its reworked context, more as if it questions the Catholic practice of confession than any Buddhist tenet (though it need not be heard as so specific, presenting its speaker as touting a theological line). Yet he returns to the latter fray with a markedly re-structured version of the 'New Danville Girl' approach in these distinctive lines from 'Man In The Long Black Coat' – lines that are pared down, precise, formal and deftly economic where his previous attempt was cluttered and chatty:

There are no mistakes in life
Some people say
And it's true sometimes
You can see it that way.

It's a brilliant formulation, with that hugely important pause after the third line, followed up by the deliberate playful ambiguity of the way the third and fourth work together. The effect is that at first when you hear it, he makes it sound as if he's agreeing, with some qualification, to the proposition advanced first:

There are no mistakes in life
Some people say

to which he seems to add at once

And it's true sometimes.

The pause there is long enough to imply that full stop, before he undercuts it with

You can see it that way.

It's a splendid moment, confidently achieved with a minimum of wordage: and as such, an unusually successful revisit to earlier terrain.

The other preoccupation of 'New Danville Girl' and 'Brownsville Girl' carried over on the "Oh Mercy" breeze is the central one of the crossing of lines. In the second verse of 'Shooting Star', the singer wonders whether his relationship with the addressee foundered because of his crossing, unknowingly, of some personal panhandle; whether, despite being, like the persona in 'Brownsville Girl', 'the kind of person that doesn't like to trespass', she found that he had crossed 'over the line'. Thus in 'Shooting Star' he asks

> *Did I miss the mark or*
> *Over-step the line*
> *That only you could see?*

There's one other echo from 'New Danville Girl' carried forward into 'Shooting Star': not, this time, a thematic matter so much as a small, endearing human touch. In 'New Danville Girl' the narrator says of Gregory Peck in one of the films he keeps 'trying to remember' that

> *. . . everything he did in it reminded me of me.*

The 'Shooting Star' lines that top and tail verse two (and follow immediately after the lines just quoted) carry the very same tiny twist:

> *Saw a shooting star tonight*
> *And I thought of me.*

In 'Disease Of Conceit' there's an example of what I take to be a different order of resemblance. It isn't only artists who find certain things re-engaging their attention, sometimes after lengthy intervals but decade after decade, without there being anything to explain their presence. Nor are these fleeting recurrent visitors necessarily anything as conceptual as themes or as concrete even as pictures in the mind, sounds, smells, word formations. They can be as small as a mental house mouse and glimpsed so fast that you're not sure they were there at all: certain cadences, mental doodles, inflections into which perhaps the same one or two syllables or noises insist on forming themselves in the head, a certain anxiety long absent but felt again when you find yourself standing in a space that feels smaller than it ought, a certain table or slab of wood that seems to make you drum your fingers the same way on it every time.

They are patterns, anyway, of one kind or another, and you may or may not recognise them as you revisit them, or are revisited by them. They recur involuntarily, and aren't necessarily perceived as recurrent. I believe that this, rather than either deliberate self-imitation or a reliance on old inspiration, accounts for why a songwriter or poet might build these repeat patterns into their work. At any rate, "Oh Mercy" evidences one or two of these Bob Dylan house mice. I think one is nesting inside the 'Man In The Long Black Coat'. There is no intentional resemblance between this song and 'Sara', recorded nearly fifteen years earlier, but the pattern of syllable clusters and spaces in this – especially as exaggerated by Dylan's live performances of it:

> *Now the beach, is deserted, except for, some kelp*
> *And a piece, of an old ship, that lies – on the shore*
> *You always, responded, when I needed your help –*
> *You gimme, a map, and a key to your door*

is reproduced so closely as to be almost a cloning here (again, especially as exaggerated by Dylan's live performances of it):

There's smoke, on the water, it's bin there, since June
Tree trunks, uprooted, neath the high— crescent moon
Feel the pulse, and vibration, of the rumbling force
Someone, is out there, beating on a dead horse.[77]

Likewise, the cadence of 'step into your room' and the pause and fall to the rest of the
line after it, as well as the phrase itself, is repeated between 1981's 'Watered-Down
Love', with its

Won't step into your room, tall dark and handsome,

and 1989's 'Disease Of Conceit', with its

Steps into your room, eats into your soul.

Perhaps the same phenomenon of casual habituality explains too another kind of
revisiting that we pick up on in "Oh Mercy". Being an excellent mimic, Bob Dylan
has used many different accents, and therefore many different pronunciations of the
same word, in the course of his recording life – consider the general change for the
worse, the shift away from real life towards MTV half-life, in his handling of the word
'love', which ends up in the uPVC of "Time Out Of Mind"'s 'Make You Feel My
Lurve'; or the extremity of contrast between his way with the word 'square' 1961's
'The Girl I Left Behind' and in 1997's 'Standing In The Doorway'.[78] Yet the years
disappear uncannily as we hear, on 'Disease Of Conceit', how he renders the word
'bury' – approximately as 'barry' – in 'Then they bury you from your head to your
feet' (a wacky way to put it). This is a distinctive and beguiling noise, as Dylan
produces it (possessing, that is, an aural charm the name Barry doesn't necessarily
enjoy by rights) – and absolutely classic Dylan, one wants to say: it is identical to the
same noise as made by the Bob Dylan of decades earlier. Likewise in 'Where Teardrops
Fall' it's a noticeably youthful Dylan who lands on the phrase 'if we meet' and a very
Dylanesque landing indeed on 'fireball *heat*'.

Yet "Oh Mercy" offers, as I suggested earlier and as it's worth re-emphasising
here, freshness as well as all these revisits to and dialogues with past work.

As with the handling, in 'Man In The Long Black Coat', of the Buddhist notion
that nothing is an accident, there is another fine achievement in the same song. It
offers no playful ambiguity in this case, but there is certainly a comparable tautness of
compressed expression plus a brutal, energetic plainness, deployed to communicate
with preacherly impact, using a formality of structure – a rigour, if you will – not
often associated with Bob Dylan's work. He places it in the mouth of the preacher,
saying that

. . . there's a sermon he gave,
He said every man's conscience is vile and depraved.

---

77.   As I noted in Chapter 2, this is (consciously or unconsciously picked up) the rhythm of Longfellow's 'Curfew',
1870.

78.   Bob Dylan: 'The Girl I Left Behind', NYC, 29/10/61, broadcast live on *Oscar Brand's Folk Song Festival*,
WNYC Radio.

> *You cannot depend on it to be your guide*
> *When it's you who must keep it satisfied.*

With those last two lines sounding more George Eliot than Bob Dylan, it is a sharply astringent rebuke to irreligious, liberal humanism, secure in its confident drawing upon a phrase of St Paul to Titus (who says that, except in the irreproachably pure, 'conscience is defiled'[79]) and bristling with an acid vigour achieved through pre-planned terseness and tough-mindedness.

There is another formally precise, expressively adept, rectilinear couplet, this time with the added neatness of emphatic internal rhymes and better temper, contributing to the probing questions in 'What Good Am I?':

> *If my hands are tied, must I not wonder within*
> *Who tied them and why, and where must I have bin?*

It's a joy to hear it for its sly economy and for the fact that work and clarity of thought have gone into its expression and come out toughly as unshowy self-criticism, with the inspired ambiguity of 'where must I have been' meaning both what sins must he have been living around and why wasn't he paying attention.

Both of these themes are clearly preoccupied with religious matters, and the album spends a good deal more time in this terrain than we have so far covered.

'Where Teardrops Fall' – to begin in this peculiarly apparitional and vaguely mapped corner of the terrain – might as easily be taken as addressed to the Lord as a lover. Bert Cartwright writes that 'Far from being a love ballad, this song delves the depths of sorrow and contrition' – the *depths*?: they find no concrete imaginative expression; they touch on, rather than get to the bottom of, sorrow and contrition, but yes, that fourth stanza 'sounds more like a confession to God than a fond remembrance of lost love':[80]

> *I've torn my clothes and I've drained the cup*
> *Strippin' away at it all,*
> *Thinkin' o' you when the sun comes up*
> *Where teardrops fall.*

Cartwright goes on to note that 'I've torn my clothes' is a common Hebrew expression of deep grief, and illustrates it from 2 Samuel 3:31, which describes the response to a killing: 'And David said to Joab [the killer] and to all the people that were with him, Rend your clothes, and gird you with sackcloth, and mourn'.

You could say that the title, too, fits this notion of mourning and sorrow. Where *do* teardrops fall? In penitence, secular or religious, one weeps in any dark or private place – making, in Bob Dylan's case, 'the pool of tears beneath my feet' or 'tears in my bed', as he puts it in 'Every Grain Of Sand' and 'George Jackson'.

With 'Where Teardrops Fall', the song's sense of offering a sad farewell is deepened by the wonderful way that the final verse presses cliché into service. Deep world-weariness is rendered so vividly by the inspired stroke of reciting

---

79. From Titus 1:15.
80. Bert Cartwright, 'The Bible in the lyrics of Bob Dylan: 1985–1990', see note 36.

Roses are red, violets are blue

as if to say that everything learnt, everything heard, everything seen, has come to ashes, while Dylan's usage is validated by his transformation of the two-parter cliché into a three-item list by the adding of a surprising further statement that echoes the others but shifts the ground away from their visual simplicity and 'plain truth' into metaphysical realms:

Roses are red, violets are blue,
Time is beginning to crawl . . .

It's as fine an example as anywhere in Bob Dylan's work of the cliché being rescued from cliché by context.[81]

Bert Cartwright finds a scriptural text, too, to support the theme of 'Everything Is Broken', that vision of brokenness discussed earlier: 'The earth is utterly broken, the earth is rent asunder, the earth is violently shaken,' reads the Revised Standard Version of Isaiah 24:19; in a rare instance of the King James Version reading less poetically, it has 'The earth is utterly broken down, the earth is clean dissolved, the earth is moved exceedingly'. But the context, yielding a fuller meaning of what Dylan might be envisioning, comes in the preceding verse, for which the King James poetry is just fine: 'for the windows from on high are open, and the foundations of the earth do shake'. The chapter and this vision end soon afterwards, on a climax: 'Then the moon shall be confounded, and the sun ashamed, when the Lord of hosts shall reign in mount Zion, and in Jerusalem, and before his ancients glorious'.[82]

The song on "Oh Mercy" that expresses Dylan's seeking of this apocalyptic moment most eloquently is 'Ring Them Bells'. Bert Cartwright, quoting Sean Hagan's view that it is 'perhaps the most powerfully biblical song since 'Every Grain Of Sand'', concludes that here Dylan sets forth his core dilemma and explains, in effect, why 'cynical melancholy' undercuts any solace he might have been expected to derive from religious faith.[83] Cartwright states:

On the one hand [Dylan] sees the world reverting to chaos as 'they're breaking down the distance between right and wrong' – the pessimistic note on which the song ends . . . Dylan . . . sees Christ triumphantly bringing the present world to an end and with vengeance dealing out retribution to make things even. And he expects to share with Christ and his saints in handing out that retribution. Yet on the other hand Dylan desperately wants this world to be better. He thirsts for justice and compassion here and now.

So 'Ring Them Bells' expresses a painfully pessimistic view of a run-down

---

81. Indeed at the 'Days Of '49' Dylan Convention in Manchester in May 1990, during the panel discussion of "Oh Mercy" by Aidan Day, Stephen Scobie and myself, 25/5/90, Scobie suggested, only half in jest, that *in context* 'Roses are red, violets are blue' is the best line on the album. It was clear what he meant.

82. Isaiah 24:23. You cannot but be reminded, by that 'sun ashamed', of Dylan's 'the sky is embarrassed' in the 1965 'Farewell Angelina' [a take of which, NYC, 13/1/65, was finally released on "Bootleg Series I–III", 1991 – a take that manages to duck out of this lovely line].

83. Sean O'Hagan, 'The overdue resurrection of Saint Bob', source and date unknown, quoted in Cartwright, see note 36, first item.

world with a wistful yearning that its peoples would care 'for the poor man's son' . . . 'for the blind and the deaf'; for 'the child that cries / When innocence dies'.

It may be that the average listener has trouble accepting such a thirsting 'for justice and compassion here and now' from someone whose song begins with the combative, divisive and excluding peel

> *Ring them bells ye heathen . . .*

though the phrase that follows offers what is surely an indulgent as well as a lovely description of the present day world as

> *. . . from the city that dreams.*

Yet those who, not unreasonably, regret the approach that sings of 'ye heathen' and, later,

> *. . . the chosen few*
> *Who will judge the many*
> *When the game is through*

might still be able to appreciate the construct of the song, as argument and poetry, and perhaps even be able to applaud, for example, the timing of the thrust of this unpalatable message within the song's structure.[84]

The whole first verse is a beautifully wrought statement of the world's pre-apocalyptic moment, evoking at once a visionary picture of a world looked at from high up. One of the central ironies through which Dylan expresses contradictory feelings – the desire for the imminent end yet a passion and compassion for our own world – is by the sense he communicates of sunlight and rapture seen from some mountainous vantage point, of a love of nature and the resplendent scenery of the natural world which spreads out beneath the singer and the listener and especially beneath the reach of the bells that ring out over it all. In the course of the song, the rapturous yearning for a new world spills its light too onto a shouting celebratory list of these earthly glories, beginning in the first verse with deep valleys and streams, and flying on over the four strong winds, the weeping willows, the sheep on the mountains and 'the lilies that bloom'.[85] The world may be 'on its side' – like a dying animal, says Bert Cartwright – the willows weeping and the sheep lost, but they glow in the consciousness of the singer of this song. When the envisioned bells ring out

> *. . . from the sanctuaries*
> *'cross the valleys and streams*

---

84.   Matthew 22:14: 'For many are called, but few are chosen.'

85.   On the other hand while Dylan's 'where the four winds blow', in the second verse, makes an inevitable contribution to this evocation of the rapturously wild natural world, it also has its import in the scriptural scheme of things, in the unprepossessing rap about 'ye heathen' and 'the chosen few'; it alludes, in this context, to the envisaging of Christ's second coming, as given in Matthew 24:31: 'And he shall send his angels with a great sound of a trumpet, and they shall gather together his elect from the four winds, from one end of heaven to the other'. I doubt that Fats Domino had this in mind when he made his congenial single 'Let The Four Winds Blow' [New Orleans, May 1961; Imperial Records 5764, Los Angeles (London-American Records HLP 9415, London), 1961] but I don't doubt that the latter crossed Bob Dylan's mind in the course of either writing or recording (or both) that line from 'Ring Them Bells'.

it is an ordered world seen in the mind's eye, the world of medieval godly men like the monks at Rievaulx Abbey building 'sanctuaries' and 'the fortress' of the believer in clean green landscapes.

The contribution of the lost sheep on the mountains to these pastoral scenes is redoubled by the echoes they bring us of Allen Ginsberg and his use of Blake, as well as directly from the Bible. Dylan's

> *Oh the shepherd is asleep*
> *Where the willows weep*
> *And the mountains are filled with lost sheep*

harks back to Ginsberg, in Dylan's film *Renaldo & Clara*, playing the shoe-box harmonium and singing 'And All The Hills Echoéd', with its

> *And the hills are all covered in sheep.*

But this is taken directly from 'Nurse's Song' in the *Songs of Innocence* by William Blake, the ideal mentor for such a song as 'Ring Them Bells', given that his visionary humanity is the other side of the song from its 'ye heathen' severity. The context in which the sheep arise in Blake's song seems pertinent too. The nurse's voice is followed by that of the children, each with their opposite perspective. In Dylan's song, the core contradiction we've noted means that he takes up both positions, speaks with both voices:

> 'Then *come home, my children, the sun is gone down*
> *And the dews of night arise*
> *Come, come, leave off play, and let us away*
> *Till the morning appears in the skies.'*

> '*No, no, let us play, for it is yet day,*
> *And we cannot go to sleep;*
> *Besides, in the sky the little birds fly,*
> *And the hills are all cover'd with sheep.'*[86]

The biblical basis for these 'lost sheep' is in both Old and New Testaments. In Ezekiel 34:6, 'My sheep wandered through all the mountains, and upon every high hill . . . and none did search or seek after them'. In Matthew 10:6–7, Christ exhorts the apostles to 'go rather to the lost sheep of the house of Israel. And as ye go, preach, saying, The kingdom of heaven is at hand'. Yet if Christ himself is the shepherd, is it impatience for his second coming that has Dylan exhort us to the ringing of bells while 'the shepherd is asleep'?

His invocation of the saints, meanwhile, one in each of three verses, deepens and confirms the physical picture of the tangible world below that the song gives us, with its sense of convent bells and priory fortress, of holy intermediaries to whom the

---

86. Allen Ginsberg, 'And All The Hills Echoéd' [?], performed during the Rolling Thunder Revue and filmed for and included in Dylan's film *Renaldo & Clara*. For more detail see Chapter 12, note 19. William Blake's title 'Nurse's Song' is used for a poem in each half of *Songs of Innocence and Songs of Experience*; the one quoted is from the former, and quoted from the 1794 edition. Dylan's song, by chance or no, mentions both 'the child' and 'innocence'.

chosen pray from within the cloisters of calm-centred, ordered lives, and with the natural world still glorious outside the gates, however doomed and time-pressed it may be – the natural and human world to whom the saints are exhorted to reach out. We have

> *Ring them bells Saint Peter where the four winds blow . . .*
> *Ring them bells Sweet Martha for the poor man's son . . .*

and in the final verse the intriguing

> *Ring them bells Saint Catherine from the top of the room . . .*[87]

which manages to make us sit up and take renewed notice. Does it suggest the top of the world? It's so oddly specific yet so unexplained. It worries the listener, yet it succeeds by its wayward and obtuse specificity in keeping the song imaginatively alive. It forestalls any sense we might otherwise have by this point that Dylan is dozing through his format, and that the physical and tangible is – in a phrase of John Carey's on Dickens – 'being allowed to float out of focus in the interests of religion'.[88]

Appropriately, the song has yet another text behind it: an old 'Negro Spiritual' called 'O Peter Go Ring-a Dem Bells'. There is no resemblance beyond what's clear from the title, however: this song is celebratory, and its lyric has no words beyond these:

> *O Peter go ring-a dem bells*
> *I heard from heav'n today*
> *I thank God, and I thank you too*
> *I heard from heav'n today.*[89]

Dylan's infinitely darker and more complex song ends with a Dylan theme: that of 'breaking down the distance between right and wrong'. Another missing of the mark,

---

87.   Saint Peter, who died in about AD 64, was leader of the apostles and always listed first. Dylan's song bows to this convention. Christ appeared to Peter first after the Resurrection. Told he would be the rock on which the church would be built and that he would be given the keys of the kingdom of heaven, he was given the mission of feeding the lambs and sheep of Christ's fold. The most notable miracle-worker among the apostles, he has been invoked as a saint since very early times and is held to be both highly powerful and very accessible.

Saint Martha ('Sweet Martha') was also Christ's contemporary, the sister of Mary and Lazarus. Receiving Jesus in their house at Bethany, Martha was reproved for complaining that Mary hadn't helped much with the washing-up, supposedly showing Christ's placing of the contemplative life's virtues above those of the active life. Yet in John (11:1–46), Martha's faith in Christ's divine power during the raising of Lazarus prompts his soundbite 'I am the resurrection and the life'. The patron saint of housewives, no pre-medieval legend surrounds her death. Aptly, then, Dylan invokes her name for both practical aid ('for the poor man's son') and for her faith ('so the world will know that God is one').

Saint Catherine of Alexandria, supposedly fourth century AD, was persecuted for her Christianity and broken on the wheel. This itself broke, however, and she was beheaded. Milk, not blood, flowed from her head. Her body transported by angels or monks to Mount Sinai ('the top of the room'), her cult began in the ninth century, flourishing in medieval times. Her intercessionary value is threefold: as a bride of Christ (she had refused to marry the Emperor), as the epitome of the skilled advocate (she had disputed successfully with fifty philosophers), and as the protectress of the dying.

[This information comes from David Hugh Farmer's *Oxford Dictionary of Saints*, 1987.]

88.   John Carey, *The Violent Effigy: A Study of Dickens' Imagination*, 1979.

89.   Found in, and taken from, H. A. Chambers' *The Treasury of Negro Spirituals*, 1964. Because I take it directly from this source I have retained its minstrelised title and spelling.

another overstepping of the line, another in the series of crossings that has interested him throughout the work of this period – and, of course, another brokenness.

The biblical allusion in 'What Was It You Wanted?' has the virtues of being an obvious one, one Dylan uses only as a piece of shorthand familiar to everyone, and one more likely to remind us of earlier songs in which Dylan has used it than to tax our secular patience. The song is another list, if you will – a list of distancing questions Dylan fires at someone who seems to be encroaching on his space. It might be a woman, an ex-lover, but the song works savagely well as an address to Dylan's insatiable audience (or indeed his critics). One of the questions, early on in this bombardment, is the allusive

> *What was it you wanted*
> *When you were kissin' my cheek?*

Dylan has placed this reference in his own song from the early 1960s, 'With God On Our Side', which reminds us bluntly that 'Jesus Christ was betrayed by a kiss'. There is a touch of this too, later that same decade, in the magnificent 'She's Your Lover Now', in which he says with wondrous sneer

> *I see you kiss her on the cheek*
> *Every time she gives a speech.*[90]

'What Was It You Wanted?' also carries a pretty good sneer, although as with 'Everything Is Broken' the song so squeezes out anything but its remorseless listing that its singularity of purpose precludes the free flow of human tumult that is part of the glory of a 'She's Your Lover Now' or even a 'Subterranean Homesick Blues' (to remember a very superior list song).

Nevertheless, singularity of purpose gives 'What Was It You Wanted' the virtue of probing insistence, as we noted earlier of 'What Good Am I?', but this time in opposite mode: not with the humility of 'What Good Am I?' but with the biting standoffishness Dylan has always been superbly good at. The venomous energy of 1966 has gone, no longer fuelling his animus, but in its place is a withering coldness that he turns on and off and on again as the song proceeds.

When it begins, of course, the listener is not to know that he or she might be the addressee, and that the song will build so vituperative a pyramid of stony rebuffs, from the polite opening skirmish of

> *What was it you wanted?*
> *Tell me again so I'll know.*

The sole miscommunication here might be through the narrator's not having quite heard one remark; the conversational tone implies, so readily that we don't even register it, that these two people know each other. The next lines take one gentle step backwards from this implied level of mutual understanding, as he asks – but so that it might be gentle coaxing – what is going on inside the other person's head at this point,

---

90. The text is in the gospels, as in Luke 22:48: 'But Jesus said unto him, Judas, betrayest thou the Son of man with a kiss?'

and expressing this commonplace question in a gently comic phrase of great quotability, as Dylan so often does:

> *What's happening in there*
> *What's going on in your show?*

Yet there is the hint in that turn of phrase of the narrator's gaze being on something less personal. It's another small step back from intimacy.

Then comes the postmodernist joke, the self-reflexive text joke discussed in Chapter 9 about being 'back in a minute' as his voice gives way to an instrumental break before returning with

> *What was it you wanted?*
> *You can tell me, I'm back*

and the immediate further egging of this postmodernist pudding with

> *We can start it all over*
> *Get it back on the track.*

This 'we' is still implying some shared purpose, some connection between the speaker and the spoken-to. It is undercut at once by the abruptness of the next lines, culminating in that shorthand charge of betrayal:

> *You got my attention:*
> *Go ahead, speak*
> *What was it you wanted*
> *When you were kissin' my cheek?*

Even here, though, as the voice halts and the harmonica takes its place, the tone that Dylan uses on harmonica pulls us some way back from this attacking harshness – it is a harp of gentle reproach. What uncertain place does the addressee stand in now?

When Dylan's voice returns, it is with a verse that colours in *his* incomprehension of that other person, by stressing his puzzlement at what is being asked of him – building to the splendidly groggy

> *What was it you wanted?*
> *Do I have it here in my hand?*

After that the singer moves to an almost exaggerated politeness, with

> *Would you remind me again*
> *If you'd be so kind?*

before moving on into deeper and deeper levels of failure to grasp 'what's going on in your show'. The questions that rebuff come thick and fast now, like the fog they suggest is descending. This is indeed an atmosphere in which nothing is clear except the narrator's denial of any relationship at all, let alone shared intimacy:

> *I ain't keepin' score:*
> *Are you the same person*
> *That was here before?*

and then the wary

> *Did somebody tell you*
> *That you could get it from me?*

followed up with the impatient directness of this second question, fired off immediately after the first:

> *Why do you want it?*
> *Who are you anyway?*

Then comes a simple metaphor for questioning the reality of the addressee, while reprising the conceit of 'your show' introduced earlier:

> *Is the scenery changing?*
> *Am I getting it wrong?*

This is inspired, though, for the other effect it achieves. That is, it makes a renewed and sly contribution to the self-reflexive backbone of the song, for the question 'Is the scenery changing?' asks too whether the singer's song is shifting its ground – to which the answer is of course 'Yes', since the whole song leads us through these shifts of position and perspective all the time. The irony is that while his questions become more and more of a freeze-out of the person depicted as standing there wanting something, in self-reflexive mode the very same questions are genially good-humoured, and share the joke with us. This running gag concludes with the next question, which asks

> *Is the whole thing goin' backwards?*

Again, the answer of course is 'Yes': the whole song has been depicting a running backwards from any notion of intimacy: that exactly describes the arc it is concerned to draw.

This is topped by the lethal high comedy of the next line, an inspired moment of venom wholly worthy of 1966, as he drops the self-reflexive cleverness to bring in a quite different kind of playing with the playing of songs in a song, suddenly asking

> *Are they playing our song?*

If there's a more savage comic rebuff than that anywhere, I don't know it.

I think the song's extraordinary command of its measured manipulations slips a fraction after that, as Dylan reaches the last four lines – because he goes into them sounding, for the only time in the song, merely tetchy, demanding

> *Where were you when it started*
> *That you want it for free?*

This is a slip of his lip into rhetoric that sounds opaque yet from a too-specific agenda – as if he's reduced the possibilities to the bathos of mere complaint about his own career. He loses us here, but pulls us back for the song's final dénouement, for a final line that pulls off yet another unexpectedly distancing question that we might have seen coming but that we don't:

What was it you wanted?
Are you talking to me?

The song's distinction, as *we* move back from *it*, is that so fine an exposition of non-communication is created entirely from conversational remarks. It flows with the casual and natural cadences of informal speech, through changes of mood expressed in fluidly handled changes of line length and with a suggested give and take that gives the illusion that this monologue is dialogue.

The other great fluidity of "Oh Mercy" as a whole lies in its music: in the noises it makes. Daniel Lanois' production is a multi-layered, echo-laden, plangent concoction not to everybody's taste. Yet in service to the cohesion of Dylan's words, the album achieves too a musical cohesion, spun from this production, from Lanois' tapestry of misty threads. Curls of aural smoke drift across the speakers like wraiths in moonlight. Keyboard figures prink in and move away with puzzled hesitation, as if going back for something they've forgotten. An accordion murmurs. Chirping crickets squat in the long grass under the verandah. The four winds blow softly; electric twilight sighs. Dylan's voice looms out of nowhere as from the bottom of a well, or rolls in like boulders over the brows of dusty hills. The slide of a guitarist's thumb along a string sounds as clearly as the note it plays. An omnichord shimmers. Red-throated guitars coil and burn and snake away. Percussion totters.

Nebulous noises emit from instruments that usually make other sounds. Things listed as keyboards howl in the middle ground like old refrigerator motors. The thundercloud bass on the luxuriantly unhurried intro to 'Man In The Long Black Coat' is not played on a bass guitar at all. Three of the tracks have no drums. 'Most Of The Time' begins like deep, leisurely waters of guitar to which the dark contemplative bass comes to drink, its melodic tongue dipping into this water. Dobros reverberate. Bass riffs thrum and pass like ghost ships in the night.

This is not to deride its mistiness. It's sheer foundation is that things come and go. Things weave. It isn't, like fog, a suffocating blank. It's not foggy at all. It often has a limpid clarity. And only on 'Man In The Long Black Coat' does the album swirl into the gothic. When it does, it is Dylan's lyric that puts it there, while the restraint of the music – inside which something unlisted in the credits but sounding like a cello buzzes a small mournful melody underneath the gossiping of guitars and the absence of drums – holds it inside the lambent, unlurid whole.

This is ensemble playing rather than background support for a series of solos. Even the occasional slicing through by Dylan's fine harmonica-playing evidences ensemble responsibility. He has submitted himself to the rules of the house. Lanois has insisted that Dylan do much of the guitar-playing himself and that this playing come up to standard. Under these conditions, Dylan's harmonica-playing also rises to the occasion – he plays it better than he had in years. When the music is wholly cooperative, it isn't the occasional solo *per se* that clashes – but playing decent harmonica solos is an obligatory part of not standing out from the rest; playing incompetent solos would have been the route to being too obtrusive. We get, therefore, a highly competent bluesy harmonica on 'Everything Is Broken', a beautifully forlorn harp phrasing early on in 'What Was It You Wanted?', becoming almost tenderly reproachful next time in and then growing out into an extended solo of fine playing ahead of the last four stanzas – a solo with a terrific patent Bob Dylan harmonica howl – and returning at the end of the song with a further burst of excellent, felt, incisive blowing. At album's end, on the song that bids any number of farewells, we get at song's end a most beautifully sad farewell on harmonica: one last piece of playing here that you could reasonably be allowed to call classic Bob Dylan harp.

Dylan's piano-playing is in here too, but that is always up to standard. It is the one instrument he has played with consistency all down the years. You'd recognise his playing anywhere – it is of course more technically limited, more personal and refreshing than that of any pianist he might hire instead – and I always wish there were more of it; but unlike his guitar-playing or his harp-work, his piano has remained unfalteringly true: chunky, inventive and heartfelt always, a joy to listen to on anything from a live 1966 'Ballad Of A Thin Man' to the studio performances of 'Spanish Is The Loving Tongue' and, here, 'Ring Them Bells' and 'Disease Of Conceit' – and when he sat down and played this last number live on his last night in London in 1990, he diluted the rare, pure rapture of the audience only by his chronic inability to get the words right, not by any diminution in the distinctive skill or thrilling spirit of his piano-playing.

Actually, on the album it might not be recognisable on 'What Good Am I?'. Here it is unusual for being played not in Dylan's own inimitable style but very high up on the keyboard in the exact style of a whole cluster of 'pop ballad' records made in the very early 1960s: records like Sam Cooke's B-sides 'Love Will Find A Way' and 'Nothing Can Change This Love'.[91]

On 'What Good Am I?' this tinkling yet ruminative piano makes a very specific contribution: while the lyric is persistent in its questioning, the music pursues the questions still further. Through the track, the piano acts as an echo of these questions, re-asking them in its modest, quiet phrases; at the end this process becomes emphatic, the whole ensemble taking up where the piano leaves off, so that the track ends with the music in effect re-stating and re-stating the title question, coming back and coming back, after the long pause that pretends to be the ending.

The musical intro to 'Where Teardrops Fall' is unusual for Dylan too: that is, if you heard it on the radio and didn't know it, you would never guess that it was a Bob Dylan record until his voice comes in. It sounds like garage band Nashville, with its echo-cranked snare drum knock at the entrance, sounding more like a little drummer-boy automaton, an amplified parade-of-the-toy-soldiers drum, followed in above the stiff rhythm by an almost ludicrously 'straight', unsubtle lap-steel plang-planging along on the melody line like a child at the Christmas panto.

Nor is it always plangent miasma elsewhere on the album. There is, as suggested earlier, the bloodline of the blues running through it, and there is its cracker cousin, rockabilly, too. The bass riff used in 'Everything Is Broken', and relied upon far more heavily in live performance of the same song, is taken from Weldon Rogers. Rogers is an impressively obscure rockabilly (or wannabille) artiste who wrote the song Dylan often used, perversely, to *greet* his 1986 US tour audiences: 'So Long, Good Luck & Goodbye'. Rogers cut his own record of it at Norman Petty's legendary custom studio

---

91. Sam Cooke: 'Love Will Find A Way' (c/w 'Bring It On Home To Me'), RCA 47–8036, New York, 1962, and 'Nothing Can Change This Love' (c/w 'Somebody Have Mercy'), RCA 47–8088, New York [RCA 1310, London], 1962.

in Clovis, New Mexico some time in that marvellous music year, 1957. The bass riff is re-used thirty years on, here on "Oh Mercy". Not everything is broken.[92]

There is also, from this era, a subdued Duane Eddy guitar under the second verse of 'Shooting Star', underpinning the generous stretch of the album's musical sourcing. And there are many other lovely touches within the Lanois weave. 'Most Of The Time' ends with an exquisite layered fade-out, its audio creatures retreating satisfied and quiet to their lairs.

And then there's the voice, the only one heard on "Oh Mercy". Surprisingly, there are no back-up vocalists of any sex or colour. Only Dylan. As I argued a good few pages ago, he finds a voice to carry equal parts doom, optimism, passion, instruction and humility. He sounds as old as the hills, yet we hear some of his younger voices breaking in. It is a voice for any adult with rock'n'roll in their veins.

In terms of that claim, it's a pity that the album opens with as weak an upbeat track as 'Political World'. Despite the multi-layering of the three guitars and dobro, and the double drumming (there are conga drums in there, credited as 'percussion'), and despite one or two isolated flashes of cutting edge, this is exactly the kind of rockin' number that shouldn't have made it onto the album. There's no wildness, no clear sense of what he's on about and no heart in it, and therefore it's impossible to warm to. It's a bore, as so many of these things are.

This is especially unfortunate since one of the tracks recorded at the "Oh Mercy" sessions but then left off the album positively cries out to be its opening track. At least as upbeat and rockin' as 'Political World' but an infinitely better piece of writing, with a far more appealing melody and a great deal of generous energy and good humour, that great song 'Dignity' would also have begun the album with an effective statement heralding of one of its core assets. The search for dignity is writ large all over "Oh Mercy"; the song 'Dignity', which describes the heartfelt yearning for a more dignified world, would have been its ideal opening track, and one that scorches along musically, declaring its allegiance to the timeless appeal of the blues while sounding, above all things, fresh. Its lyric, meanwhile, though 'Dylanesque' in that it sounds like no one else's work and sounds like a restrained, mature revisit to a mode of writing that you might otherwise call mid-1960s Dylan, is fully alert and freshly itself, admits of no leaning on laurels, and has the great virtue that while not every line can claim the workaday clarity of instructional prose, the song is accessible to anyone who cares to listen and offers a clear theme, beautifully explored, with which anyone can readily identify.

Mel Gamble writes:

> It fits in with 'Oh Mercy', an album which seems . . . to be based on self-examination . . . [and] the attempt to separate the important from the distractions and irrelevancies that clog up day to day life . . . the song is sung from the perspective of a fifty-year-old man, one who has been many places, done many things, yet isn't clear what is of real worth . . . The song looks at old men, wise

92. Bob Dylan: 'So Long, Good Luck & Goodbye', débuted as his set-opener San Diego, 9/6/86, and used as such at 17 further 1986 concerts. Weldon Rogers: 'So Long, Good Luck & Goodbye', *nia*, 1957. The same riff is also the basis of 'Melo Melo' (1978), written by Serge Gainsbourg, on the LP "Ex-Fan des Sixties – Baby Alone In Babylone [sic]" by Jane Birkin (CD-reissued Phonogram 514124–2, 1992).

men, drinking men, sick men, all of them searching for something within. Dylan has been all these people and more.

Gamble also says of 'Dignity' that it is both one of those songs that 'you know [is] going to be special' when you first hear the opening bars, and one of those where 'you never want the song to end'.[93] For others, it is one of those like 'A Hard Rain's A-Gonna Fall', where every line might be the beginning of a separate song.

That would be a lot of separate songs – 'Dignity' has sixteen verses of four lines each. Recurrently the singer describes a lengthy search for dignity in the turmoil of a fragmented world in which people jostle and hustle among themselves but show no sign of genuine community, and in which places are also described as lost, inhospitable and bleak. All this is achieved, however, at a rollicking pace and with dancing deftness and indomitable humour, so that the mood of the song is the opposite of bleak.

The verses divide between two different rhyme schemes. The predominant one uses the attractive AAAB pattern, with the 'B' the same in every verse of this construction, because each one ends on the title word 'dignity' – and how he loves to land on it! He rolls it around in his mouth, slowing it down, feeling its contours – 'dig-ni-teeee!' – as if in the very act of saying it he can be exploring its elusive qualities. This core construction, and many of its lyric ground rules, are established in the opening verse:

> *Fat man lookin' in a blade of steel*
> *Thin man lookin' at his last meal*
> *Hollow man lookin' in a cottonfield*
> *For dignity.*

The singer, then, is not alone in searching for dignity. Some of the song's characters are bumming and hustling, watching their backs or chancing their arm but many are, though living in what seems to be insoluble isolation, united with the narrator in a common yearning for the dignity that seems to be missing in contemporary life. No moral superiority is being claimed here by the writer. This is the ballad of a thin man, fat man, hollow man, wise man, young man, poor man, blind man, drinkin' man, sick man and Englishman. Plus a couple of somebodies, the cops, Mary-Lou, the maid, Prince Philip, the sons of darkness and the sons of light, another somebody and a someone, plus the tongues of angels and tongues of men in general.

There are eleven more verses of this construction, plus four that are built differently, in an AABC pattern, where the B and C may or may not half-rhyme. The first time around, they do (this is the third verse):

> *Somebody got murdered on New Year's Eve*
> *Somebody said Dignity was the first to leave*
> *I went into the city, went into the town*
> *Went into the land of the midnight sun*

93. Mel Gamble: 'Dignity', *Homer, the slut*, no. 5, January 1992.

in which there is a half-rhyme between 'sun' and 'town'. The next time around, in verse seven, there is a sort of semi-rhyming, if you will, between 'men' and 'me':

> *I went down where the vultures feed*
> *I would have gone deeper but there wasn't any need*
> *I heard the tongues of angels and the tongues of men*
> *And there wasn't any difference to me.*

(That second line is a fine example of the song's freshness, with its apparent spontaneity of direct address – its undercutting of the declamatory by the unexpected straightforwardness of its informal conversationality, its clipped modernity of tone.) But in the two verses of this pattern later in the song – verses eleven and fifteen – there is no such half-rhyming, and the unusual AABC pattern is strictly observed. The effect is not at all that you notice, in listening, an absence of resolving rhyme, but that combined with the unresolved fifth note of the scale on which the final word of each verse lands, your ear waits for what is to come: tells you that there *is* more to come, that the search for dignity is itself not resolved. Thus form becomes realised as content.

The difference of shape between the two kinds of verse is matched by quiet distinctions in their subject matter. The format of 'Fat man . . . Thin man . . . Englishman . . .' never occurs in the AABC verses, which tend to focus on places the narrator goes – great, sweeping places – rather than on characters:

> *I went into the city, went into the town,*
> *Went into the land of the midnight sun . . .*
> *I went down where the vultures feed . . .*
> *In the bordertowns of despair . . .*
> *Into the valley of dry-bone dreams . . .*

When he does encounter people in these sections of the song, they too are presented in vague or sweeping generalised terms:

> *Footsteps runnin' cross the silver sand . . .*
> *Somebody got murdered . . .*
> *Somebody said . . .*
> *Someone showed me . . .*
> *I heard the tongues of angels and the tongues of men . . .*
> *I met the sons of darkness and the sons of light . . .*

However, these distinctions between the two sorts of verses are never stressed, and the entire song is repeatedly interwoven with threads of correspondence, sometimes of the most delicate and subtle kind and sometimes with robust, abrasive mock correspondences that keep you stimulated and guessing all through the song. Thus there are phrases that echo each other in form but depart in content, for example as when that 'went into the city, went into the town' is slyly mismatched later by 'went into the red, went into the black', or when different kinds of metaphor are bumped together as if they are of the same order, or even as if they are not metaphors at all but actual physical actions, as with the splendid

> *He bites the bullet and he looks within,*

where there is the added surreal implication that the one 'action' is consequent upon the other: that he bites the bullet and then looks within to see what damage the bullet has caused, or where it's landed, and whether he's still alive.

There are many such games played here, and played lightning-fast, in passing. Since Dignity is spoken of throughout as a missing character, as in detective fiction (as in a film), might not 'Somebody' be a character too – such that when Dylan sings that

> *Somebody got murdered on New Year's Eve*
> *Somebody said Dignity was the first to leave*

this not only has the odd effect of making Dignity the prime suspect (rather than simply a Good Guy) but also makes it possible to see at this murder scene that it is Somebody's own dying testimony that fingers Dignity. The opening couplet alone has weird comic resonances.

> *Fat man lookin' in a blade of steel*
> *Thin man lookin' at his last meal,*

which draws on the two meanings of 'his last meal', certainly achieves by doing so a bizarre fleeting doubt as to whether the fat man isn't wielding either a carving-knife or an executioner's blade – either way putting him into an unsettling and uneasy relationship with the thin man. At the very least, you wonder whether the thin man is looking at his own last meal or at the fat man's stomach, into which what should have been his own meal has just disappeared. Then there is this quiet implied pun on thinning hair, almost at the end of the song (balancing the thin man at its beginning):

> *Combin' his hair back, his future looks thin.*

My favourite comic moment occurs in this surreal 1-line scene:

> *Met Prince Philip at the home of the blues*

though it is then very pleasingly augmented like this:

> *He said he'd give me information if his name wasn't used*
> *He wanted money up front, said he was abused*
> *By Dignity.*

It would be high comedy merely for a Bob Dylan song to mention Prince Philip, but to place him in so unlikely a milieu as anywhere that might call itself 'the home of the blues' creates a glorious incongruity. It also creates a sort of namesake version of Prince Philip in the mind, because by putting him together with the idea of the blues, it conjures up a figure in that other destination point of the black diaspora, the Caribbean, in which there are plenty of flamboyant singers and musicians calling themselves names like Prince Buster.[94] Making you hear Prince Philip as a name of this sort is a fine bonus comic pay-off. As the lines pile up, of course, so does the

---

94. Prince Buster, a Kingston-born (1939) but London-based Jamaican, enjoyed the longest-lasting popularity of those on the Bluebeat label whose music, which became known as 'bluebeat' to white Britons (he was a mod hero c. 1964) but was called 'blues' by its originators, combined ska, gospel, R&B and the New Orleans second-line jump. Later called rock-steady, Buster's work (not always on Bluebeat, which closed in 1967) includes the famous 'Judge Dread' plus 'Ghost Dance', 'The Lion Roars' and 'Tongue Will Tell'.

preposterousness of the Prince Philip idea. Hence no sooner have we savoured the picture of this meeting, and its meeting-place, than we relish the notion of him acting like a cheap con artist, offering to sell suspect information right there on the street and then throwing in a hard-luck story for good measure – or else we picture him now as being someone else, someone who *is* a con artist, with Dylan throwing in the extra joke that while this person is claiming to be an extravagantly high-profile, and indeed notoriously indiscreet, figure, at the same time he is trying to do a deal that hinges upon protecting his anonymity. And at the end of the verse, if we take it that this is Prince Philip, there is the wonderful way that Dylan's 'said he was abused / by Dignity' works as a compressed summation of how it might feel to be trapped inside the machinery of the Royal Family. To characterise a lifetime of dressing-up and parading about in risible ritual and ceremonial show as 'abused by Dignity' is confident cutting to the bone indeed. And to put this complaint into the mouth of someone as brutishly insensitive and graceless as Prince Philip, whose name is a byword for the unthinking verbal abuse of others, is delicious. To achieve all this in thirty words is, well, Dylanesque.

The song also offers Dylanesque moments at which you cannot tell whether it is the narrator or someone else in the picture, and indeed this is one of them:

> *Someone showed me a picture and I just laughed*
> *Dignity never been photographed.*

Without making a conscious decision, you might find that you always imagine that photograph to be of Bob Dylan. Similarly, when we come to those

> *Footsteps runnin' 'cross the silver sand*
> *Steps goin' down into Tattoo Land*

you can picture this as the singer's footsteps – he went here, he went there, he goes somewhere else, and now he's running across the sand and then taking the flight of steps down; or you can see it as the singer following, like the detective on the case, the fleeing suspect's footsteps and chasing the echoing sound of those steps running down. Is it him or it is another? Either way, it supports the sustained conceit of the song, in which Dignity is cast as being on the run, and the strange inbuilt tension that provokes.

The detail of the song is always careful; everything dovetails; everything is balanced; and where there is doubt, ambiguity or contradiction, it is intended. The list of who is looking where, for example, shows evidence of the kind of care that seems absent in the listings in 'Everything Is Broken'. The young man looks 'in the shadows that pass' – a poetic ellipse of the idea that the young, impatient of history and precedent, are entranced by the illusions of the moment, believing that 'now' is the only worthwhile moment, while his opposite – not the old man but the wise man (the old not necessarily being wise at all) – looks 'in a blade of grass': that is, in something that sounds just as fragile and temporary as a passing shadow but is strong enough to hold several connotations. We might take it that, like every grain of sand, it is in such things as the blade of grass that the believer 'can see the Master's hand'; or, like Blake, we might take it that in looking in the blade of grass, again as into a grain of sand, he is seeking a vision of the world. Perhaps, unlike the young man in thrall to the temporarily fashionable, the wise man understands that the natural world is all that really matters. Yet again, by its very temporariness, the blade of grass tells the essential truth that 'everything passes' – that everything 'comes to pass', to quote from Bob Dylan and to remember a fragment of a different poet's work (John Crowe Ransom's 'Spectral Lovers') quoted by Christopher Ricks in the essay on Dylan's use of American English and English English, 'Clichés that come to pass':

> . . . *swishing the jubilant grass*
> *Beheading some field-flowers that had come to pass.*[95]

At times, too, 'Dignity' offers unlooked-for extra tidiness, as when that 'blade of grass' in verse two echoes the 'blade of steel' in verse one, or when, in that first verse, there is the neat gradation in lines one-two-three of men who run fat-thin-hollow, while all through the song small surprises act as cumulative energy, a recurrent renewal of stimulus, as when we expect, after 'searching high, searching low' that 'searching everywhere I' will be completed by 'go' and isn't: it's 'searching everywhere I know' instead. In the twelfth verse, out of nowhere, and to most pleasing effect, we suddenly get, for the first and only time, an extra rhyme, by means of an internal rhyme, on one of the AAA lines:

> . . . *got no coat*
> . . . *in a jerkin' boat*
> *Tryin' to read a note somebody wrote*
> *About dignity.*

This both disrupts the pattern we've grown to know and at the same time, of course, is there not for mere surprise for it's own sake but because it also makes the line enact the 'jerkin'' motion he's ascribing to the boat. (Regrettably, he has always revised this line in concert to eliminate the internal rhyme, altering it to the inferior 'Tryin' to read a letter somebody wrote'.)

In offering these little twists away from what you'd anticipate in the lyric, Dylan mimics the providing of little twists in the storyline, which is what you'd expect from the detective fiction genre.

What is so liberating and invigorating about 'Dignity' is that while it is free-spirited and ineffably relaxed, fluid as mercury and malleable as clay on the wheel, it is at the same time meticulously assembled, as beautifully thought-out and thrillingly well-crafted as a major tap-es-treee.

Nigel Hinton declares it to be his favourite of all the 'big' songs of the last twenty years: more loved than 'Brownsville Girl', 'Angelina' or even 'Blind Willie McTell'. He writes:

> What I particularly like about it is the consistency of its conceit: Bob Dylan as Sam Spade, or any one of those hard-bitten, cynical LA-based private dicks, conducting his B-movie, film noir hunt through the corrupt world in search of the missing character, Dignity. I like the array of characters – all those sons of

---

95. John Crowe Ransom, 'Spectral Lovers', *nia*, quoted in Christopher Ricks, 'Clichés that come to pass', *All Across the Telegraph*, ed. Michael Gray and John Bauldie.

darkness and sons of light – typical of the wonderful supporting actors who people those films (Sidney Greenstreet as the Fat Man, Elisha Cook Jnr. as the Blind Man, and Thelma Ritter as the maid, perhaps?).

And I love the little familiar scenes from those movies – the murder at the New Year's Eve party, the wedding of Mary Lou who, frightened and nervously looking over the singer's shoulder at the other guests, whispers that she could get killed if she told him what she knew (played by the young Lauren Bacall?), and the continual echo of films – the drinking man in a crowded room full of covered up mirrors could come straight from *Citizen Kane* (played by Joseph Cotten – drink, instead of cigarettes). The images come straight from a medley of dimly-remembered movies: the chilly winds blowing the palms; the house on fire; looking out of a window from behind billowing net curtains while asking the maid for some hot poop on the case; the border towns of despair (Mexico, of course – perhaps *A Touch of Evil*, Orson Welles' Tijuana masterpiece); the blackheart wind sending those tumbleweeds rolling down the dusty street while the English-man (Leslie Howard) stands there so incongruously, combing his hair back; the sick bed of the man who lovingly fingers his books while praying for a cure; and the con artist pretending he's Prince Philip and trying to bum some money in exchange for dodgy information – 'abused by dignity', him: ha!

Dignity is also so perfectly what the Sam Spade persona would be looking for. Truth, Fame, Fortune, Hope, Faith and all the other rewards offered by the world or the illusions offered by the purveyors of the spiritual world have been seen through by this guy – he's heard the tongues of angels and the tongues of men and he can't see any difference. The most he can hope for is to live with dignity: but in this corrupt and deluded age, where and what is it? And in this topsy-turvy place the most you get by way of help is a note that somebody wrote – but of course you're trying to read it on a rolling river in a jerking boat: a wonderful metaphor for the struggle of trying to make sense of things. Such an alive and direct picture of us all, without comfort (no coat) and with nowhere to hide (fade), in our little craft being swept headlong towards the rapids, trying to find out why.

And the language is so Chandleresque: 'the valley of dry-bone dreams', 'bites the bullet', wind 'sharp as a razor blade'. The song even ends in the kind of despairing, enigmatic way that the best films noirs do – standing at the edge of the lake, knowing that everywhere leads to dead ends and that the case won't get solved. It's a black and white masterpiece.[96]

I find this exposition almost as cheery and compellingly lively as the song itself, though I had never once 'seen' the song as a movie myself, and certainly don't see it in black and white (for me it unfolds, like the whole sound of the "Oh Mercy"

96. Nigel Hinton: e-mails to the present writer, 30 & 31/3/99, reprinted with permission. The two films he cites are: *Citizen Kane*, RKO, US, directed Orson Welles, written Herman J. Mankiewicz and Welles, starring Welles, Joseph Cotton, 1941: in which when the Randolph Hearst-type newspaper mogul dies, 'a magazine reporter interviews his friends in an effort to discover the meaning of his last words' [*Halliwell's Film Guide*]; and *A Touch of Evil*, U-I, US, directed and written Orson Welles, starring Welles, Charlton Heston, Janet Leigh and Marlene Dietrich, 1958: in which a 'Mexican narcotics investigator honeymooning in a border town clashes with the local police-chief over a murder' [*Halliwell's Film Guide*].

sessions, and like "Blonde On Blonde", in red and gold). But as with so much of Dylan's finest writing, its credible possibilities are open and the opposite of limiting.

'Dignity' makes perfect sense in that film noir context – it holds its own, as Hinton says, as that sustained conceit. Yet the song's fundamental quest for something both precious and elusive through a world of travail holds to a far more ancient archetype, and as such resonates on other levels. The archetype of this quest is also contained, for instance, in the search for the Holy Grail (medieval legend having it that the bowl used by Christ at the Last Supper was brought to Britain by Joseph of Arimathea, so that in the time of knights in silver armour, seeking its whereabouts was a physical and spiritual quest). It is there too in the 'Pilgrim's Progress' of John Bunyan's hero, Christian (of which more shortly).[97] While Bob Dylan summarises such questing in a single line of his 1970s song 'Dirge' –

> *In this age of fiberglass, I'm searching for a gem –*

'Dignity' devotes itself to envisaging such a quest.

It succeeds at doing so in the genre of Hollywood film noir, but there's also more than a hint here of the ordeals of Job, when God has afflicted him and he wanders, seeking recognition and the restoration of dignity, and asking 'How long will ye vex my soul, and break me in pieces with words?' As he wanders, he asks the servant for recognition – in effect, have you not seen *me*?, just as Dylan's narrator asks the maid has she not seen Dignity. As we know, Job's faith triumphs and he finds acceptance in the end, but not before being in the position Dylan parallels at the inconclusive end of 'Dignity', where there are

> *So many dead ends, so much at stake.*

In Job's case he cries out that God 'hath fenced up my way that I cannot pass, and he hath set darkness in my paths'.[98] As with Job, there is a strong mood of 'How long, Lord?' (or as Dylan expresses it elsewhere, 'How much longer? How much longer?') about the wanderings here in search of 'Dignity', which ends on

> *Sometimes I wonder what it's gonna take*
> *To find dignity.*

As Dylan does so magnificently well elsewhere, here too we have a case where he rides the parallel lines between biblical language and modern American speech. Nigel Hinton hears 'the valley of dry-bone dreams' as 'so Chandleresque' – yet, as noted in Chapter 9, this lovely phrase draws upon, but does not better, one wonderful sound-bumping line from blues artist Arthur Crudup, 'I went down in Death Valley, among the tombstones and dry bones': a line that Dylan might have written and been admired for.[99] In turn, as Crudup's mention of 'Death Valley' hints, this is poetic compression

---

97. John Bunyan, *The Pilgrim's Progress: From This World to That Which Is to Come*, Part I published 1678, Part II 1684.

98. The passage quoted is at the start of Job 9 [actually verse 2], and continues through the dead-end dark paths [verse 11] and asking the servant's recognition [verse 16] through to the terrific 'and I am escaped with the skin of my teeth' [verse 20].

99. Arthur Crudup: 'Death Valley Blues', Chicago, 11/9/41, "Bluebird Blues", RCA Victor Records LPV-518, New York, 1965.

of biblical text. The 'valley of the shadow of death' resides in the Old Testament book that follows Job, Psalm 23, verse 4 – through which *its* narrator, David, walks fearing no evil, knowing that God is with him. Many gospel lyrics have been founded upon this text: the splendid 1930 Lonnie Johnson title 'Death Valley Is Just Half Way To My Home' may hover in the back of Arthur Crudup's and Bob Dylan's mind. There's also 'You've Got To Walk That Lonesome Valley', a 'sermon with singing' by Rev. F. W. McGee.[100]

Among the hundred and twenty-three other verses of the King James Bible that contain a 'valley', many others involve travail experienced as rather more arduous than David's, and these include 'the valley of slaughter' and 'the valley of the dead bodies' in Jeremiah, and in Ezekiel 'the valley which was full of bones'.

The phrase 'dry bones' comes only from Ezekiel (37:3–4), in which the prophet, set down in a valley of human bones, is asked by God, 'Son of man, can these bones live?' to which Ezekiel replies 'O Lord God, thou knowest'. So God says 'say unto them, O ye dry bones, hear the word of the Lord'. Through Ezekiel's unlimited faith and willingness, and God's power, the whole valleyful of bones becomes fleshed out, and the people of Israel come alive again. This is not, in the end, the same place as Death Valley, and it is *this* vision that is the stimulus for further gospel songs called 'Dry Bones In The Valley' and even 'In The Valley Of Dry Bones'. In turn, Dylan's 'In the valley of dry-bone dreams' draws upon these phrases.[101]

The song holds other moments and phrases where Dylan bestrides such parallel lines. Nigel Hinton's 'Sam Spade persona' can quite well be described as having 'heard the tongues of angels and the tongues of men' and seen through both. You can hear the phrase on the tongue of Dylan's old favourite, Humphrey Bogart; yet as Dylan and Nigel Hinton both know, the phrase rearranges that in St Paul's address to the Corinthians: 'Though I speak with the tongues of men and of angels, and have not charity, I am become as sounding brass, or a tinkling cymbal'. (1 Corinthians 13:1.)

Dylan swaps this around doubly. First, either for the sake of cadence or the more neatly to make his point that there 'wasn't any difference' between them, he puts his angels before his men. Second, where Paul's illustration has him speaking with the two kinds of tongue, Dylan has his narrator listening to them instead. And in saying that there 'wasn't any difference', Dylan manages to emphasise the part of Paul's text that he doesn't actually cite at all: that those he hears speaking are all 'as sounding brass, or a tinkling cymbal'.

There is one other extraordinary parallel that Dylan achieves inside his song. While Nigel Hinton hears the lines

---

100. Lonnie Johnson: 'Death Valley Is Half Way To My Home', NYC, 23/1/30. Rev. F. W. McGee: 'You've Got To Walk That Lonesome Valley', Chicago, 7/6/27, CD-reissued on "Rev. F. W. McGee Complete Recorded Works Volume 1 (1927–1929)", RST Blues Documents BDCD-6031, Vienna, *nia.*

The fusion of biblical with modern American speech is contained in the very name Death Valley, a US National Monument in California–Nevada (serendipitously just west of Las Vegas and almost immediately south-west of Skull Mountain and the Nellis Air Force nuclear testing site).

101. Jeremiah 7:32 and 21:13 contain 'the valley of slaughter'; Jeremiah 21:40 'the valley of the dead bodies'; and Ezekiel 37:1 'the valley which was full of bones'.

[The Jubilee Gospel Team: 'Dry Bones In The Valley', Long Island, New York, c. Sept. 1928. Joe McCoy: 'Dry Bones In The Valley', Chicago, 15/5/35. Rev. R. McFryar: 'In The Valley Of Dry Bones', NYC, 29/8/28.]

> *Drinkin' man listens to the voice he hears*
> *In a crowded room full of covered-up mirrors*

as part of 'the continual echo of films', in this case calling to mind Joseph Cotten in *Citizen Kane*, the same lines also depict a scene from Jewish religious ritual. To observe the practice of shiva, during the period of mourning after a funeral, the committed mourners must gather together in one of their houses and remain there a week. Inside the house, no music can be played and every mirror must be covered.[102]

Far more thoroughgoingly, however, 'Dignity' parallels Christian's journey of quest for the Celestial City in *Pilgrim's Progress* (a quest presented as a dream in Bunyan's book). Christian too has to pass through the Valley of the Shadow of Death, as well as a river (the River of the Water of Life), somewhere on fire (the Burning Mount) and despair (the Giant Despair). Dylan's long geographical cataloguing of his wide-ranging journey ('searching high, searching low'), including travelling into the city, into the town, into the land of the midnight sun, down where the vultures feed, across the silver sand, down into (in a beautifully Dylanesque flash of existential truth) 'Tattoo Land', as well as along so many roads and up against so many dead ends, is the equivalent of the geographical catalogue in *Pilgrim's Progress*, which takes in the Hill Difficulty, the Valley of Humiliation, By-path Meadow, Doubting Castle and, most famously, the Slough of Despond.

And just as Dylan's song presents the quality of Dignity as a character, so Bunyan gives us characters called Ignorance, Much-afraid and, yes, Mercy. The Dylan song is sly, quick-witted, darkly modern and full of Americana where Bunyan's work was pious, plodding and bursting with seventeenth-century England, but Bunyan's work was written as an allegory of the Christian life and 'Dignity' too can withstand being seen, and even intended, as just such an allegory.

Nigel Hinton sees his movie ending 'at the edge of the lake, knowing that everywhere leads to dead ends and that the case won't get solved'; but does the song end so darkly? The last word is not of dead ends but with the 'How long, Lord?' question, the keep-on-keeping-on faith that adheres underneath all trials and tribulations, implying that the quest will be pursued and that eventual success is anticipated. It is only in the meantime, and sometimes, that resolve flags:

> *Sometimes I wonder what it's gonna take*
> *To find Dignity.*

'How long will ye vex my soul, and break me in pieces?', as Job puts it when times are tough in different times – and the point about Ezekiel's valley of dry-bone dreams is that in the end, through faith, new life is given.

Dylan's song, suiting our times, is quick-on-the-ear, in effect quick-on-the-eye, and as implied already, dancingly alert. It rollicks along, as 'on a rolling river', not cheap rockism 'n' roaring but real lithe Bob Dylan, and its detail committedly well-chosen.

---

102. I'm grateful to the article 'The importance of "Señor (Tales Of Yankee Power)" when considering Dylan's conversion to Christianity (I'm exiled. You can't convert me)' by Kevin Lawler and Steve Watson in the fanzine *Dignity*, no. 16, June 1998, for the observation that 'room full of covered-up mirrors' offers a correspondence to the practice of Shiva.

'Dignity', then, would have made a terrific opening track on "Oh Mercy". Or rather, it would if they'd left it alone. When the unfinished out-take circulated among collectors, it sounded *great*. You could play it not only to non-Dylan fans but even to people who thought they actively disliked him and *they'd* say it was great, and how come Dylan didn't release it, it would be a hit, you could just hear it on the radio . . . and you'd say, well, it's par for the course.

All it needed was an instrumental solo in the middle. It had an emphatic, compulsive rhythm that everybody loved, Dylan's vocals were strong and high in the mix, and his piano was Dylanesquely spiffing. One solo was *all* it needed . . . So instead Dylan left it off the album and took it away from Daniel Lanois and then gave it to one of these this-month's-gurus, Brendan O'Brien, producer of Pearl Jam, and the first thing Brendan did was abolish its stand-out rhythm. Then he put all these silly 'modern' noises on. Then he pushed Dylan down in the mix so you hardly notice any keyboards at all and so that this long, immensely entertaining lyric, delivered with great panache by a Bob Dylan firing on something like all cylinders, is no longer accessible or ready to jump straight out of the radio at you but instead needs painful attending to. Sometimes I wonder what it's gonna take . . .

That wasn't the last of it, either. Once they'd made sure it couldn't possibly be a hit, they released it on "Greatest Hits Volume 3", in 1995 – immediately before putting out another version, the limp live version on the "MTV Unplugged™" album, also in 1995. There, with Brendan Bloody O'Brien playing an organ that wouldn't have worked at all if it *had* been 'unplugged', *and* getting 'very special thanks' on the sleeve notes, the song emerges a little better than the ruined studio version, largely because it had novelty value in amongst all these weary, gruesomely dreadful re-treads of 'Rainy Day Women Nos. 12 & 35' and the rest. It has never yet become a song he cares to perform often in concert, and when he does he's perfectly capable of turning it into dreary jobsworthiness, like any other 'fast' song that he doesn't bother to know his own lyrics for. Yet when he performs it feeling fully alive and happy with it as a vehicle of wide-ranging expressiveness, as he did in London in 1995, then it comes into its own again, poor thing, leaving Brendan O'Brien light years behind and re-attaining accessible eloquence, excitement and, yes, dignity.[103]

The other important song left off "Oh Mercy", presumably through Dylan's usual latter-day lack of instinct in these matters, is the extraordinary 'Series Of Dreams'. It might seem harder to accommodate on the album, because it has a 'bigger sound' than the rest: still multi-layered and echo-laden (still Lanoiserie, in fact) but distinctive. Yet try putting it at the beginning of Side Two. It works there. It's always heartening to put on an album side and have something special, something of strong and unusual impact, something *major*, hit you straight off. And after it, with the rest of the side the same, the very differently contemplative 'Most Of The Time' would slip in nicely; or swap round 'Most Of The Time' and 'What Good Am I?' so that the expansive quiet of the latter would come in as a sea-change after 'Series Of Dreams', and would place 'Most Of The Time' as neighbour to 'Disease Of Conceit', with the final two tracks unchanged, still ending on 'What Was It You Wanted?' and the exquisite leave-taking of 'Shooting Star'.

103. 'Dignity', Brixton, London, 29/3/95.

At any rate, 'Series Of Dreams' is a tantalising recording, and with a lyric of provocative opacity which, in standard postmodernist style, takes such opacity as its theme. It is a song that discusses itself, perhaps. There is also, we note, a strong correspondence between a lyric that drifts in and out of recollections of a series of dreams and Lanois' "Oh Mercy" production, which offers precisely such an effect. Things come and go. Things weave. All the more reason for its inclusion on the album. Odd, then, that for 'Series Of Dreams' we get a different sound: an ostentatiously Big sound. Yet while it comes across as in the spirit of Phil Spector's Wall Of Sound, it is actually just Lanois Plus, now with extra guitars and drums. The entwining is thicker, the layering deeper, as befits a song about dreams. And as I. G. Roberts put it, 'the urgent throbbing of bass and drums . . . evokes the quickened heartbeat and rapid eye movement of dreamsleep'.[104]

Various versions are in circulation among collectors, and with minor variations in parts of the lyric, but it seems reasonable to focus on the composite edited take officially released, not, alas, on "Oh Mercy" in 1989 but two years later as the final track on "Bootleg Series I–III". Here, with 1991 overdubs to thicken the mix and deepen those layers still further (yet with sole producer credit still given rightly to Daniel Lanois) the recording has five guitars, including a 12-string, two drummers plus percussion, keyboards and two bass guitars.[105]

This is a mix out of which Bob Dylan's voice indeed comes to the surface as out of a dream, and does so thick with weariness and age – a deeper voice than he's used on anything since the jokey 'Billy 7', which has always seemed to me a comic impersonation of James Coburn's Pat Garrett, from the *Pat Garrett & Billy the Kid* soundtrack album of fifteen years beforehand.

'Series Of Dreams' is a far more substantial song than 'Billy'. And like so many of the Bob Dylan songs in which, to use Joan Baez's splendid formulation, he is 'so good with words, and at keeping things vague', the lyric nevertheless has enough gravitas to be interesting and to enfold diverse possibilities. Is it about dreams or about inspiration – the muse, the processes of creative imagination?

If a theme of the song is indeed inspiration, then it is surely a meditation both upon the lack of it and upon the essential inexplicability of its presence. Regarding the lack of it, he states right at the beginning that he is thinking of journeys to a place

> *Where nothing comes up to the top*
> *Everything stays down where it's wounded*
> *And comes to a permanent stop.*

He is stuck

> *Where the time and the tempo drag*
> *And there's no exit in any direction . . .*
> *And the cards are no good that you're holdin' . . .*

104. I. G. Roberts: 'Series Of Dreams', part of 'The Box Set Part II' by various authors, *Homer, the slut*, no. 4, September 1991.

105. One of the things added on this version is a riff a hair's breadth from the memorable one on a particular Phil Spector 'wall of sound' record, the Crystals' 'Then He Kissed Me', *nia* (London-American Records HLU 9773, London), 1963. The 'Series Of Dreams' version of this catchy riff is hinted at right from the start but comes in decisively from the beginning of the third verse onwards.

(an ugly way round to put that last clause, though) and where perhaps inspiration is envisaged as entirely belonging to the past. As he puts it in the song's repeated final two lines

> *I'd already gone the distance*
> *Just thinkin' of a series of dreams.*

In one of the unreleased versions of the song there is, too, the lovely

> *And you're walkin' out of the darkness*
> *And into the shadows of doubt.*[106]

As to the matter of the muse's intrinsic unknowability, perhaps the song goes back to what Dylan said he used to feel about his songwriting, which was that songs came to him unbidden, in the air – or unconsciously, which is to say like dreams – and he just wrote them down. 'Series Of Dreams' is scrupulously a song that talks not only of dreams but of lack of striving – in fact perhaps more of a conscious policy of refusing conscious effort:

> *Wasn't thinkin' of anything specific . . .*
> *Nothin' too very scientific . . .*

(a gruesome phrase, that 'too very': altogether too very ungainly)

> *Wasn't making any great connection*
> *Wasn't fallin' for any intricate schemes . . .*
> *Wasn't lookin' for any special assistance*

while in one unreleased version of the song that has an extra verse after the first one, there is, additionally,

> *Wasn't goin' to any great trouble . . .*
> *Nothin too heavy, to burst a bubble.*[107]

All this rejoins themes he pursued all those years ago in the poetry of '11 Outlined Epitaphs' – 'if it comes, it comes / if it won't, it won't', and of 'Joan Baez In Concert, Part 2' – 'An' I'll sing my song like a rebel wild . . . / But at least I'll know now . . . / Not t' push / Not t' ache / An' God knows . . . not t' try—'.

I. G. Roberts touches on this aspect of the song too, saying that he has 'come to see in the song an insight of [sic] the creative process. Dylan is not the first artist to say, when asked where the inspiration comes from, that he doesn't always know.' Roberts then quotes an apt remark by Paul Williams, who writes (of "Highway 61 Revisited"): 'The creative artist is an explorer who penetrates an unknown realm, and brings back more than . . . he knew he was looking for.'[108]

Rumination both upon the nature of dreams and upon what constitutes authenticity of imagination would be brave, heavyweight subjects to tackle – but Dylan also

---

106. Bob Dylan: 'Series Of Dreams', out-take, New Orleans, March–April 1989.

107. ibid.

108. I. G. Roberts, see note 104. Paul Williams: *Performing Artist: The Music of Bob Dylan, Volume One, 1960–1973* (1990).

rebuffs by the series of denials he plants inside it any promises or expectations set up in the song itself. 'Wasn't thinking of anything specific,' he insists.

Yet just as Dylan swims into these ruminative waters in spite of his disclaimers, so too does he risk one or two modest dream-sequence moments: a small series of dreams. At the outset –

I was thinkin' of a series of dreams
Where nothing comes up to the top –

the analogy in that second line is so general as hardly to parade itself as analogy at all, as it holds to the conventional notion of coming to consciousness as a coming to the surface either in deep water or from under the ground, and correspondingly of dreaming as a form of journeying below the surface of the workaday world. Yet no sooner has that burbled over us than we hear the unexpected switch, from 'nothing comes up to the top' to

Everything stays down where it's wounded.

By this sudden, unpredicted switch to an analogy of the dream idea or dream picture being like a wild animal, Dylan in effect wakes the listener from his or her own dozing journey of join-the-dots assumptions. As befits a dream sequence, we move on at once from this surprising line – in which the surprise is actually the writing, the way he puts it, rather than the idea. The likening of the dreaming mind to a wild animal in itself conforms readily enough to the ideas of this last century, the century of psychoanalysis: it suggests that we are in the realm of instinct and sexuality, and outside the realms of self-conscious mediation, free from the intellect's restraints. Dylan's plunge straight to the volatile heart of it, in that short, eccentric deployment, is where its strangeness lies.

Suggesting strangeness, of course, is part of the duty of evoking the sphere of dreams. That vivid third line achieves this visually, too. Out of the throbbing swirls of the track's initial monochrome waters, suddenly we're in jungle undergrowth, not drowning but waving at Henri Rousseau. Just as suddenly, we're moved on again, with

And comes to a permanent stop.

That, however vaguely put, suggests not an animal but a mechanistic analogy, and the swift switch is conveyed by that 'And', where an 'Or' would have played safer but made for a distancing break between the two analogies.[109]

In the next verse we're clearly inside a dream when, without knowing where we are, we find that 'there's no exit in any direction' except for 'the one that you can't see with your eyes'. In the bridge section, after that second verse, we are similarly stuck without the customary supports. In waking life you might find yourself stuck in a card game in which 'the cards are no good that you're holding' but they would not

109. Henri Rousseau, 1844–1910, French self-taught naïve painter, eventually associated with Picasso and the poet Apollinaire, but a unique figure, his 'junglescapes' offer an unforgettable mix of fantasy-exotic subject matter and precise clarity of depiction. See for example *Surprised! Tropical Storm with Tiger* (1891), in the National Gallery, London; the superb *Repast of the Lion* (1907), in the Metropolitan Museum of Art, New York City; and *The Dream* (1910), in the Museum of Modern Art, New York City.

be cards so strange that you would wonder if perhaps they were 'from another world' (and in which they might make a fine hand, if only you could comprehend what any of them meant or what the game was).

Emboldened, Dylan offers a third verse in which he more willingly specifies some particulars, perhaps even the core components, of 'a series of dreams', beginning with clear narrative statements about these essentially unclear, mysterious realms:

> *In one, the surface was frozen*

(we're back to the waters or the ground of the song's first lines)

> *In another I witnessed a crime*
> *In one I was runnin', and in another*
> *All I seemed to be doin' was climb.*

(Climb*ing*, Bob: 'all I seemed to be doin' was climbing', or 'all I seemed to do was climb' but *not* 'all I seemed to be doin' was climb'. That's three grammatical mangles in one song: most uncharacteristic.)

With this last, Dylan seems so emboldened, so willing to risk specificity, that we are even invited to register the fact that we have entered classic Freudian dream territory. Freud saw dreams of climbing as representing the sexual act. In *The Interpretation of Dreams* (1900) he writes: 'It is not hard to discover the basis of the comparison: we come to the top in a series of rhythmical movements and with increasing breathlessness and then with a few rapid leaps, we can get to the bottom again.'[110] (You'll find out when you reach the top, you're on the bottom, as Bob was to say three-quarters of a century later.)

For me, though, the most dream-like image the song offers is in the bridge section, in which we hear of

> *Dreams where the umbrella is folding*
> *And into the path you are hurled.*

(That 'hurled' is delicious: it keeps the umbrella in sight because it puts the rhyming word 'unfurled' into the mind: the one makes you anticipate the other, though it never arrives.)

The umbrella is one of those physical objects that we see differently because of art and ideas. In Dickens' England, they look merely vulgar. 'Elaborately undignified,' as John Carey explains, 'they immediately locate their owner in the lower class.'[111] In traditional (which is to say turn-of-the-century style) New Orleans, the umbrella is part of the ritual paraphernalia of the funeral procession and party. Once surrealism comes along – that great mind-changing movement that was all of a piece with psychoanalysis and the revelatory new importance it attached to dreams – the umbrella is never the same again. It's as if it has been invented for surrealism to focus on.

---

110. I am grateful to J. R. Stokes for this quotation apropos of 'Series Of Dreams'. It is contained in his long and perfectly dreadful article 'Facing fifty with a folded umbrella', in *Homer, the slut*, no. 5, January 1992, in which he floats a ludicrously reductive theory that 'Series Of Dreams' is Dylan bemoaning and detailing his sexual impotence, in code.

111. John Carey, *The Violent Effigy*, see note 88.

'Elaborately undignified' still, but freed to be ostentatiously absurd, the umbrella has become Magritte's just as surely as Monet owns the water-lily. And once it is Magritte's, it belongs to the sphere of dreams. We see it as both essentially absurdist and dream-like. Watch, in Africa, a lone figure walking with trance-like grace and unhurried dignity across the horizon of bush, umbrella's silhouette held up against the sun: this is an inherently dream-like picture, almost a Jungian archetype. Umbrellas rarely make it into songs; they make it into this one because it is a song about dreams.[112]

Alan Lomax wrote that 'Singing and making music are a kind of dreaming out loud, pulling the listener into the dream and thus taking care of his deep needs and feelings.'[113] Let that be a last word on the matter.

Even without 'Dignity' and 'Series Of Dreams', "Oh Mercy" is an album of considerable dignity and maturity; yet Dylan is talking to the young as well as his own generation – and getting listened to. When the album was new it was easy to find people who had never heard his early work yet, hearing this, were brought up short by its directness.

Sometimes those of us who have been listening to Bob Dylan's records since before he ever 'went electric' are the most disadvantaged when it comes to hearing such directness on an album like "Oh Mercy". An 'Everything Is Broken' is never going to stand up against a 'Lonesome Death Of Hattie Carroll', nor a 'Ring Them Bells' against a 'Lay Down Your Weary Tune', but certainly it all stands up against the unlistenable prefabricated awfulness of corporate rock.

The very title "Oh Mercy" may well be at least partly a semi-private exclamatory acknowledgement that the latter gap is a wide one. In the interview for 1985's "Biograph", Dylan says of contemporary music 'Oh mercy! Spare me please! These things are just hooks, fish hooks in the back of your neck . . . nothing means anything, people just showing off, dancing to a pack of lies'. Dylan will also be aware, however, that 'mercy' is a recurrent key word in the scriptures, and his album title may have any number of such placings in mind. Proverbs 16:6, for instance, offers a statement that may be apt to Dylan's purpose, as he offers an album rooted in Judaeo-Christian belief and serious-mindedness: 'By mercy and truth iniquity is purged: and by fear of the Lord men depart from evil'.

At any rate, the decent, virtuous meaning of that horrible word 'maturity' hangs about the album on every level. It's striking that the earlier era of popular music to which "Oh Mercy" harks back time and again is a specific one, distinguished by records in which the stars of rock'n'roll's first wave were themselves offering more 'mature' work: not neccessarily better than their wilder, earlier recordings but recognisably solid, rich and four-square. Just as 'Shooting Star' has the whisper of a 1960 Duane Eddy guitar in it and 'What Good Am I?' has the tinkling piano of mature Sam

---

112. For more on René Magritte, 1898–1967, see Chapter 7, note 17. Fats Domino's 'My Girl Josephine', *nia*, Imperial 5704, Los Angeles [London-American HLP 9244, London], 1960, is one song that does mention umbrellas (New Orleans again, like 'Series Of Dreams'): and again, like Fats' 'Let The Four Winds Blow' (see note 85), it's a record from that period to which "Oh Mercy" so often harks back. In Domino's case both come in his golden period between the early high-voiced, big-band blues records and the loss of interest in composing that followed, or coincided with, his move away from Imperial Records.

113. Alan Lomax, *The Land Where the Blues Began* (1993).

Cooke ballads, and of Brenda Lee records not like 'Let's Jump The Broomstick' but like the slow, sumptuous 'I'm Sorry'; just as 'Ring Them Bells' alludes to the 1961 Fats Domino single 'Let The Four Winds Blow'; just as 'Series Of Dreams' is a production that tips its hat to the genius of Phil Spector – and sounds inspired also by one of the only decent records Paul Anka ever made, the turbulent 'Love Me Warm And Tender' (again an early 1960s 'mature' record, in the period between Anka the precocious teenager and Anka the hoary lyricist of 'My Way' and '(You're) Having My Baby'); just as 'Dignity' gives a name-check to 'Mary Lou', which is to recall Ricky Nelson's exquisite 'Hello Mary Lou' (his last hit as 'Ricky' before 'maturing' his name to Rick); and just as 'Where Teardrops Fall' is reminiscent of Nelson's poised and pensive 'Lonesome Town', and has that Buddy Holly sax – not, that is, the sound of early Holly, or even of "The Chirping Crickets" – but of the Last Sessions Holly of October 1958 – so too "Oh Mercy" has a vivid, warm chunkiness, and a balance between its noticeable music and its very upfront vocals, that hark back in general and in spirit to the records of that same era: not youthful, early rock'n'roll but the good solid stuff of 1958 to 1961. The lead vocals were always upfront then, the drums were way down at the back, and – again as on "Oh Mercy" – if there were solos at all they were extremely foreshortened.[114]

This explains why (though instinctive connection is made first and explanation later) "Oh Mercy" makes me think of records like Conway Twitty's majestic trans-atlantic hit single of 1959, 'It's Only Make-Believe': the deep voice, the vividly chunky music, the mix of restraint and intensity. It holds something too of that very short but particular period in Elvis Presley's recording career, when he first came out of the army in 1960. 'Where Teardrops Fall' and 'Shooting Star' have the feel of the Elvis of 'Fame And Fortune' – an Elvis who sounds more of a grown-up but hasn't yet lost his power or authority. Likewise, 'Dignity' could no more be attributed to the Dylan of 1965 than the Presley of 'A Mess Of Blues' could be mistaken for that of 'Anyplace Is Paradise', let alone the Presley of the Sun sides. Yet as with 'A Mess Of Blues', 'Dignity' comes very close to holding its own; the loss of youthful blitz is almost compensated for by the mature fluidity. Almost.[115]

114. Sam Cooke, see note 91. Brenda Lee: 'Let's Jump The Broomstick', nia, 1958, US Decca 30885, New York, 1959 [Brunswick 05823, London, 1961]; Brenda Lee: 'I'm Sorry', nia, US Decca 31093, New York, 1960.
      Paul Anka: 'Love Me Warm And Tender', nia, RCA Victor Records 7977, New York [RCA1276, London], 1962. Paul Anka: '(You're) Having My Baby' (ugh!), United Artists Records UA454, Los Angeles [United Artists Records UP 35713, London], 1974.
      Ricky Nelson: 'Hello Mary Lou', nia, Imperial Records 5741, Hollywood [London–American Records HLP 9347, London], 1961. Ricky Nelson: 'Lonesome Town', see note 75.
      Buddy Holly & The Crickets: "The Chirping Crickets", Clovis, New Mexico, May–July 1957, Brunswick Records 54038, New York, 1957 [Coral LVA 9081, London, 1958].
      (Not every old record from this approximate period mentioned on "Oh Mercy" is worthy in its own right. Bobby Vinton's 'Roses Are Red', nia [Columbia Records DB 4878, London], 1962, exemplified the kind of flaccid, clean-cut goo that pop was becoming: the very stuff that prompted the young Bob Dylan to take the 'folk' route instead.)

115. Conway Twitty: 'It's Only Make-Believe', Nashville, 7/5/58, MGM Records E/SE 4217, Hollywood [MGM 992, London], 1958 (a No. 1 USA and UK). Elvis Presley: 'Fame And Fortune', Nashville, 20/3/60; Elvis Presley: 'A Mess Of Blues', Nashville, 20–21/3/60, RCA Victor Records, New York, 1960; Elvis Presley: 'Anyplace Is Paradise', Hollywood, 2/9/56, issued "Elvis", RCA Victor LPM 1382, 1956 ["Elvis (Rock 'N' Roll no. 2)", HMV Records CLP 1105, London, 1957]; Elvis Presley's Sun sides, Memphis, 1954–55.

When I first heard it, and had to rush-review it, I thought "Oh Mercy" was a *great* album, and I began with this hasty claim: 'In the nick of time, at the last possible moment, Bob Dylan has made a great album in the 1980s.'[116] At the beginning of its discussion in the present chapter, I dilute this to 'a fine album'. A *great* album would mean it was up there with "Blonde On Blonde" or "Blood On The Tracks". It isn't. But it is a fine album. If you're attempting to put things in order, you might feel that it sits somewhere not far below "New Morning" and "Planet Waves" . . . and a high crescent moon or two above the Hollywood Hills of "Empire Burlesque".

116. 'The great crusader: Dylan's "Oh Mercy" ', *Daily Telegraph*, 30/9/89.

CHAPTER SEVENTEEN

Nursery Rhyme, Fairy Tale and "Under The Red Sky"

Having offered an album as polished, careful and well-produced as "Oh Mercy", and having enjoyed a renewal of critical and some commercial success with it, needless to say what Bob Dylan offers next, "Under The Red Sky", is an album raw enough to put off immediately anyone who turns to it for more of "Oh Mercy"'s plangent restraint. Not only is it raw, but, paradoxically, it is riddled with nursery rhyme and to a lesser extent fairy tale.

No one writing this century seems to link nursery rhyme and fairy tale, nor even mention the one while discursing upon the other. Iona and Peter Opie's massive standard work, *The Oxford Dictionary of Nursery Rhymes*, published in 1945, ignores fairy tales, though the Opies later published *The Classic Fairy Tales*. Bruno Bettelheim's landmark study of fairy tales, *The Uses of Enchantment*, ignores nursery rhymes. Vance Randolph, perhaps America's last great southern folksong collector, has written on and collected both fairy tales and children's songs, yet separates the one wholly from the other. He collected folktales in the Ozarks, Arkansas, publishing them in *The Devil's Daughter and Other Folk Tales* in 1955; much information on the songs and nursery rhymes behind 'Froggie Went A-Courtin'' was included in his *Ozark Folk Songs Vol. 1: British Ballads and Songs*, first published in 1946.[1]

This rigid division does not obtain, of course, so far as the stories offered by fairy tales and nursery rhymes themselves are concerned, nor in the minds of the children they appeal to, nor in earlier collections. Wedderburn's sixteenth-century *The Complaynt of Scotland* includes fairy tales and songs, and so do Halliwell-Phillips'

---

1. My main sources for the present chapter are: Bruno Bettelheim's *The Uses of Enchantment* (1976); Iona and Peter Opie's *Oxford Dictionary of Nursery Rhymes* (1945, revised and reprinted 1951); and Iona and Peter Opie's *The Singing Game* (1985). (Peter Opie died in 1982, after which Iona completed *The Singing Game*, a companion volume to their *Children's Games in Street and Playground*, 1969.) I have also drawn on the Opies' *The Oxford Nursery Rhyme Book* (1955) and on Jean Harrowven's *Origins of Rhymes, Songs and Sayings* (1977), as well as the other sources listed in the Bibliography.

The main early collections used by the Opies and mentioned in what follows are *Gammer Gurton's Garland or The Nursery Parnassus*, ed. Joseph Ritson (1784); *The Nursery Rhymes of England*, James Orchard Halliwell-Phillips (1842[–c. 1860]); *Popular Rhymes and Nursery Tales*, James Orchard Halliwell-Phillips (1849); and *The Traditional Games of England, Scotland and Ireland*, Alice Bertha Gomme, 2 vols. (1894–8). The Opies' other sources include the *Gesta Romanorum* (a book of stories, plus attached moralisations, thought to have been compiled in England in the late thirteenth century, printed in Latin), and *The Complaynt of Scotland*, Wedderburn (1549?), plus the usual folksong source materials such as the works of F. J. Child.

Since this chapter centres far more around nursery rhyme than fairy tale, Bruno Bettelheim's main sources require no listing or summarising here, though I note that he too cites one of the early collections of children's material, Halliwell-Phillips' *Popular Rhymes and Nursery Tales*.

nineteenth-century collections. Nor is there any rigid separation of the two forms in the work of Bob Dylan that draws upon them.

It may even be that each has its roots in an internationally common form, the canto-fable: that is, a work that switches back and forth between verse and prose. The late nineteenth-century collector Joseph Jacobs wrote in 1898 that in addition to the well-known canto-fables of France, the same form can be detected in the Arabian Nights' tales, in the folk tales of Zanzibar and in parts of the Old Testament (as in the stories of Lamech and Balaam), and that among folk tales everywhere there remain many traces of the canto-fable. Jacobs concludes that 'there seems to be a great probability that originally all folk-tales . . . were interspersed with rhyme and took therefore the form of the canto-fable', though such highly conjectural theorising is a much discredited approach among the current generation of folklorists, who mistrust speculation about the ancient past.[2]

Even so, the distinction between adult song, nursery rhyme and fairy tale is not clear-cut, as at least three conjunctions on Dylan's album "Good As I Been To You" make clear. 'Yes kind sir I sit and spin', sings Miss Mousie in 'Froggie Went A-Courtin'', describing just what princesses locked in the towers of fairy tales must do. In the traditional 'adult' song that bears his name, Arthur McBride is told that he'll 'sup on thin gruel in the morning', a phrase offering the language and food of fairy tales. 'Like a diamond in the sky' sings the hardbitten narrator of 'Little Maggie', describing her eyes in the language of 'Twinkle Twinkle Little Star'.

'Little Maggie', despite her adult drinking problems, carries echoes of another child-centred song too, the so-called 'witch-dance' song known as 'Round Apples'. (Witch-dances are those where children hold hands to dance in a circle but with their backs to the centre of the ring. They may merge with adult dance and ritual as they disappear into the mists of time all over Europe.) 'Round Apples' is interesting not only in resembling 'Little Maggie' but for an authentic mystery and a vividness of language that much adult song might envy. Its full lyric is this:

> Round apples, round apples,
> By night and by day,
> There stands a valley
> In yonder haze.
> There stands Moira Rogers
> With a knife in her hand.
> You dare not touch her
> Or else she'll be hanged.
>
> Her cheeks were like roses
> But now they're like snow.
> Poor Moira, poor Moira,
> She's dying I know.
> We'll wash her with milk

2. *English Fairy Tales*, Joseph Jacobs (republished 1968). Jacobs notes that in the Grimms' collection, verses occur in nos 1, 5, 11, 12, 13, 15, 19, 21, 24, 28, 30, 36, 38, 39, 40, 45, 46, 47: i.e. in a large number of the first fifty tales.

> *And dress her in silk*
> *And write down her name*
> *With a gold pen and ink.*[3]

As the Opies note, none 'of the recordings of this Scots ring game ... has a long history, yet some of the texts are as compelling as traditional ballads, in the way they reach out to uncontrollable, foredoomed tragedy'. F. J. Child writes that children's game songs are 'the last stage of many old ballads', and for Robert Graves 'The best of the older ones are nearer to poetry than the greater part of the *Oxford Book of English Verse.*'

A specific example to back up such a claim is reiterated by the drama critic Ivor Brown: 'G. K. Chesterton observed that so simple a line from the nursery as "Over the hills and far away" is one of the most beautiful in all English poetry'.[4] (Bob Dylan finally uses this very line – and so knowingly yet so delicately – in his wonderful song of 1997, 'Highlands'.)

The Opies emphasise that the adult–child distinction is not a clear one when they add that

> Chesterton would have been more exact if he had said 'preserved by the nursery' rather than coming 'from the nursery' ... the farther one goes back into the history of the rhymes, the farther one finds oneself being led from the cot-side ... the overwhelming majority ... were not in the first place composed for children ... They are fragments of ballads or of folksongs ... remnants of ancient custom and ritual ... and may hold the last echoes of long-forgotten evil ... Some are memories of street cry and mummers' play ... Others are based on proverbs ... They have come out of taverns ... They are the legacy of war and rebellion ... They have poked fun at religious practices ... and laughed at the rulers of the day ... They were the diversions of the scholarly, the erudite, and the wits.

(Riddles had their adult heyday in the Elizabethan age. They must have appealed to the Jeremy Beadles and crossword-puzzle fans of the period.)[5]

The age of the extant nursery rhyme varies enormously: many are ancient, but many others arise in the nineteenth century. 'We can say almost without hesitation that, of those pieces which date from before 1800, the only true nursery rhymes (that is, rhymes composed especially for the nursery) are the rhyming alphabets, the infant amusements (verses which accompany a game), and the lullabies.'

Yet 'At least a quarter, and very likely over half of the rhymes are more than 200 years old ... nearly one in four of all the rhymes are believed to have been known while Shakespeare was still a young man.' Lullabies and the counting-out rhymes are millennia old, and the 'infant amusements' can be ancient too. These include, as we

---

3.   Quoted in *The Singing Game*, Iona and Peter Opie, from a 1912 publication.

4.   Cecil Sharp, rigid old-school folklorist that he was, nonetheless recognised the validity of nursery rhymes as a branch of folksong, collecting nursery rhyme material for his book *Nursery Songs from the Appalachian Mountains* (1923). Incidentally, the Opies notice that 'most English nursery rhymes are better known in the States, and in the case of the older ones, often known in versions nearer the original, than they are in their home country'.

5.   In a later period, the limerick form was lifted from a nursery rhyme, 'There Was A Sick Man Of Tobago'.

shall see, 'How Many Miles To Babylon?' and 'Handy Dandy', both of which Dylan draws upon in "Under The Red Sky".

It is also in the nature of children to join in oral tradition very strongly, which makes them useful curators of folksong. So much so that there are instances of verses that make one chance written appearance and then no other till they reappear intact six or more generations later. A classic example relates to Dylan's work. Of the ballad 'Lord Randal', on which Dylan imposed his brilliant, visionary 'A Hard Rain's A-Gonna Fall', there is a nursery rhyme version with as many variants as the adult ballad, the best-known in England being 'Where have you been today, Billy, my son?' The Opies report that Robert Jamieson wrote in *Illustrations of the Northern Antiquities* in 1814 that 'Lord Randal' 'has had the good fortune in every country to get possession of the nursery, a circumstance which, from the enthusiasm and curiosity of young imaginations, and the communicative volubility of little tongues, has insured its preservation'.

Another reason why there has been an unclear distinction between child and adult song is that in many periods there has been an unclear distinction between child and adult altogether. As the Opies note, 'in the seventeenth and eighteenth centuries children were treated as "grown-ups in miniature" . . . Many parents saw nothing unusual in their children hearing strong language or savouring strong drink. And behaviour was not as abashed as it is today.' Or rather, yesterday. Yet the Opies note too that 'The nursery . . . upholds the fact . . . that English folk-songs treat more with maids and courting than with hounds and the chase . . . Folk-songs, in and out of the nursery, most often describe homely and everyday events.'

An example of a nursery rhyme that does something akin to 'poking fun at religious practices' – but which may be said to be valuable despite its deflationary intent because it nonetheless keeps the images in oral circulation and hands them down to the young: passing on shadows of the older poetic imagination in spite of themselves, as it were – is 'If all the world were paper / And all the sea were ink / If all the seas were bread and cheese / What should we have to drink?' This, the Opies point out, is a parody of the extravagant devotional language

> in ancient Jewish and Medieval Adoration. The translation, by Rabbi Mayir ben Isaac (. . . eleventh–twelfth centuries), of a Chaldee ode sung in synagogues during the first day of the Feast of Pentacost goes, in part, 'Could we with ink the ocean fill . . . / And were the skies of parchment made . . . / To tell the love of God alone / Would drain the ocean dry . . .' . . . Sayings intended to illustrate the inexhaustible fullness of the Law appear in the Talmud: 'If all seas were ink and all rushes pens / and the whole Heaven parchment, and all sons / of men writers, they would not be enough / to describe the depth of the Mind of the Lord.' . . . The Koran contains passages using the same imagery.

A similar idea is expressed in the last verse of John's gospel, the very last verse of the Gospels altogether: 'And there are also many other things which Jesus did, the which, if they should be written every one, I suppose that even the world itself could not contain the books that should be written. Amen.' (21:25). Whether such hyperbolic poetic language is risible or not – begs to be parodied or not – is today a matter of individual taste, where once it was not. Adam Clarke's *Commentary*, defending this kind of hyperbole against Victorian scriptural sceptics, also quotes similar 'sea-ink, heavens-paper, trees-pens' examples from ancient Jewish texts, argues that everyone for whom they were written understood that a reasonable, narrow meaning was to be ascribed to them anyway, says that the convention of hyperbole was understood as such, and gives a modern equivalent:

> the common French expression *tout le monde*, which literally means *the whole world*, is used in a million of instances to signify the people present at one meeting, or the majority of them, and often the members of one particular family. And yet no man who understands the language ever imagines that any besides the congregation in the one case, or the family in the other, is intended.

Anyway, it is the nursery rhyme parody, rather than the Chaldee ode, that puts the images of seas of ink and worlds of paper into childhood consciousness (though the appealing image this parody loses – trees as pens, writing on the sky – is retained in the Koran), as does European folklore.

A nursery rhyme that, without parody, preserves in simple, direct and evocative form the ancient and more complicated prayers of adults is one (of two) called 'Matthew Mark Luke and John':

> *Matthew Mark Luke and John*
> *Bless this bed that I lie on*
> *Four corners to my bed*
> *Four angels round my head*
> *One to watch and one to pray*
> *And two to bear my soul away.*

This preserves the prayer known as 'The White Paternoster' (a witch, featured in a 1685 non-fiction study by George Sinclair, incanted a 'black' one), mentioned by Chaucer in 1387, but stretching much further back through Celtic pre-Christian 'charms' to Jewish cabbalistic prayers ('at my right Michael, at my left Gabriel, before me Uriel, behind me Raphael') and right back to ancient Babylonian incantations ('Shamash before me, behind me Sin, Nergal at my right, Ninib at my left').[6] Dylan, as we have seen earlier, touches on this notion of four guardian angels, one at each corner, in the form in which it arises in Ezekiel, as 'the angel with four faces' in 1981's 'Angelina'. Other nursery rhymes that bring before everyone images and symbols from less accessible strands of myth and from the Bible are those that tell of the man in the moon (as discussed later).

However, a residue of 'adult' ingredient is far from being what we need to find in order to imbue the nursery rhyme with value or interest. In fact a consideration of the triviality or worth of nursery rhymes must begin by dispelling such assumptions.

The first point to accept is that we were misled in being taught that the characters

---

6.   The source for this information is the paper 'Animula Vagula Blandula', by A. A. Barb, read to the English Folklore Society 16/11/49, cited by the Opies. An interesting pre-war gospel song, in relation to this topic, is 'I Want Jesus To Walk Around My Bedside', recorded for example by the Selah Jubilee Singers: NYC, 28/4/39; "Jubilee To Gospel: A Selection of Commercially-Recorded Black Religious Music 1921–1953", JEMF J108, Los Angeles, 1980.

who populate the nursery rhyme world are all specific historical figures who are being attacked, lampooned or celebrated in verse – that Little Jack Horner is 'really' the Pope, or King James I, or whoever. This is a widely held belief, to hold which we often experience as a sign of our sophistication in early adolescence. It is quite unfounded and arises from a clutch of wholly fraudulent nineteenth-century books written by self-deluded train-spotters. There have been times when it has proved happily apt to mock kings and queens and politicians by comparing them to nursery rhyme characters; this continues to be apt, on occasion. But in almost every case ever cited, the nursery rhyme character arises before the real life satire–victim is even born. This conjunction of 'meaning' is temporary.

Similarly, Iona and Peter do well to write of the Europe-wide ring-game song 'Ring a Ring o' Roses' in these robust terms:

> in satisfaction of the adult requirement that anything seemingly innocent should have a hidden meaning of exceptional unpleasantness, the game has been tainted by the legend that the song is a relic of the Great Plague of 1665; that the ring of roses was the purpuric sore that betokened the plague, that the posies were the herbs carried as protection against infection, that sneezing . . . was the final fatal symptom of the disease, and that 'all fall down' was precisely what happened. This story has obtained such circulation in recent years it can itself be said to be epidemic . . . Those infected with the belief seem unperturbed that no reference to 'Ring a Ring o' Roses' appears in Pepys' careful record of hearsay during the long months of the Plague, nor that Defoe's 'Journal of the Plague Year' indicates no contemporary concern with either sneezing or redness of spots; nor by the fact that the song can be found, unassociated with sneezing and falling down, in America and all over Europe; nor by the fact that the linking of the song and the plague seems not to pre-date World War II.[7]

The real value of nursery rhymes lies not in all this dodgy historical de-coding but in their poetry, their vivacity, their energy of character, story and language, and in the democratic, communal process (the oral tradition, to put it in folklore or lit crit terms) that invents them and keeps them alive. As the Opies note, 'these trivial verses have endured where newer and more ambitious compositions have become dated and forgotten'.

As mentioned in passing in the much earlier discussion of the "Under The Red Sky" song 'Cat's In The Well' in relation to Howlin' Wolf's blues, nursery rhyme has its value as a venerable yet living, expressive form of folklore – one with its own internal logic and integrity, celebrating the vibrancy of direct yet magical language. When Dylan comes to use it so thoroughgoingly on "Under The Red Sky" he is exploring one more form of Anglo-American folk culture and another part of his roots.

As the power and popularity of fairy tales also attest, children are often more in touch with their deepest psychic geography than we grown-ups are. The child's verse

---

7.   This myth is kept in circulation in *Bob Dylan's Words: A Critical Dictionary and Commentary*, edited by the American academics Wissolik and McGrath (1994), in a reference to Dylan's using the phrase 'ring around the rosey' in his novel *Tarantula*.

is father to the man's poetry and it is a superficial mind that automatically dismisses it. Indeed I don't understand how anyone who much appreciates Bob Dylan's genius can rubbish a song as reverberative, warm and true as 'Under The Red Sky' because it is 'kiddie-stuff' any more than you can validate a song as dead and untrue as 'Trust Yourself' or 'Never Gonna Be The Same Again' on grounds of its supposed 'grown-upness'.

Dylan, you may remember, chose for the inner sleeve to "Shot Of Love" this well-known passage from the gospel of Matthew (11:25): 'I thank thee, O Father, Lord of heaven and earth, because thou hast hidden these things from the wise and prudent, and hast revealed them unto babes.' And even if you're so hip and intellectual and so divorced from the world of children that you're intolerant of the nursery rhyme's 'simplicity', then perhaps in responding to "Under The Red Sky" from 1990 you could heed part of the hip young Dylan's 'Advice For Geraldine On Her Miscellaneous Birthday' from 1964:

> *. . . if his terms*
> *are old-fashioned an' you've*
> *passed that stage all the more easier*
> *t'get back there.*

The proper dividing line between adult stories and fairy tales is at least as blurred as that between grown-up song and nursery rhyme. Bruno Bettelheim finds this unsurprising:

Like Biblical stories and myths, fairy tales were the literature that edified every-body – children and adults alike – for nearly all of man's existence.

. . . nothing can be as enriching and satisfying to child and adult alike as the folk fairy tale . . . Through the centuries (if not millennia) . . . they came to convey at the same time overt and covert meanings – came to speak simultaneously to all levels of the human personality, communicating in a manner which reaches the uneducated mind of the child as well as that of the sophisticated adult. Applying the psychoanalytic model of the human personality, fairy tales carry important messages to the conscious, the preconscious, and the unconscious mind, on whatever level each is functioning at the time.

. . . When the unconscious is repressed and its content denied entrance into awareness, then eventually the person's conscious mind will be overwhelmed by derivatives of these unconscious elements, or else he is forced to keep such rigid, compulsive control over them that his personality may become severely crippled.

. . . However, the prevalent parental belief is that a child must be diverted from what troubles him most . . . There is a widespread refusal to let children know that the source of what goes wrong in life is due to our own natures . . . Instead, we want our children to believe that, inherently, all men are good. But children know that *they* are not always good; and often, even when they are, they would prefer not to be. This contradicts what they are told by their parents, and therefore makes the child a monster in his own eyes . . . The fairy tale . . . confronts the child squarely with the basic human predicaments . . . evil is as omnipresent as virtue.

(All this, of course, is very recognisable as Bob Dylan thematic territory.[8])

Bettelheim finds it natural, therefore, that 'our common cultural heritage finds expression in fairy tales, [which] . . . also abound in religious motifs; many Biblical stories are of the same nature as fairy tales. Most . . . originated in periods when religion was a most important part of life; thus, they deal, directly or by inference, with religious themes.'[9]

We have already noted the way that Dylan's 'Every Grain Of Sand' shares a fundamental theme with the Grimms' story 'Our Lady's Child', in which, after the heroine, unable to resist opening the door forbidden to her, has lied to cover up her transgression, she is made mute and sent back to earth. Undergoing ordeals, she is to be burnt at the stake. 'At this moment, as she desires only to confess her misdeed, she regains her voice to do so . . . The lesson of the story is: a voice used to tell lies leads only to perdition . . . But a voice used to repent . . . and state the truth, redeems us.'

Bettelheim doesn't always find that biblical story and fairy tale have equally effective psychological sub-texts. From his viewpoint, fairy tales are healthier and thereby more humane. 'Hansel and Gretel', despite the power struggles between brother and sister, in the end offers reassurance concerning deep anxieties, 'even in their most exaggerated form – anxieties about being devoured' (a theme Dylan also brings into his abandoned-brother-and-sister story, 'Under The Red Sky'); on the other hand, notes Bettelheim, 'As the story of Cain and Abel shows, there is no sympathy in the Bible for the agonies of sibling rivalry – only a warning that acting upon it has devastating consequences.' Fairy tales are psychologically preferable.

However, Bettelheim does not lose sight of the fact that the fairy tale 'could not have its psychological impact on the child were it not first and foremost a work of art'. It is, in the end, as works of art and imagination that fairy tales and nursery rhymes survive and hold their interest. Nothing could show this more clearly than the way a creative artist as resourceful as Bob Dylan has used them in his own vast body of work.

Bob Dylan's use of nursery rhymes prior to "Under The Red Sky"

Dylan has alluded to nursery rhymes and children's song, and used nursery rhyme formulae, all through his career. This includes performing, and referring to, songs by others either specifically written for children or where it is the child's penchant for oral repetition that has preserved parts of ancient folksongs as songs we've come to

---

8. Bettelheim adds that 'since polarization dominates the child's mind, it also dominates fairy tales. A person is either good or bad, nothing in between.' At the same time, Bettelheim also perceives that 'The question for the child is not "Do I want to be good?" but "Who do I want to be like?"'

9. The same connection is made by a different route in Roger Shattuck's description of the 1880s adolescent Erik Satie: 'at about the age of sixteen he . . . [became] deeply drawn to the mystic doctrine and ritual of the Catholic faith. In literature he turned to Flaubert and Hans Christian Andersen, an unusual combination of tastes which suggests that he discerned in both writers their veiled yet deep-seated religious preoccupation. It is what makes Flaubert at his most earnest often read like an author of fairy tales, and Andersen like an author of stories not at all for children but for unbelieving adults.' (Roger Shattuck, *The Banquet Years: The Origins of the Avant-Garde in France 1885 to World War I*, 1968.)

call 'nursery rhymes'. (Indeed this division into child and adult repertoire is itself comparatively recent. Before 1824 'nursery rhymes' were simply called songs.)

As it happens, even the coffee-house in which Dylan made his début, the 10 O'Clock Scholar in Dinkytown, was named after an ancient nursery rhyme (one in print as early as 1784):

> A diller, a dollar
> A ten o'clock scholar
> What makes you come so soon?
> You used to come at ten o'clock
> But now you come at noon.

Since 'diller' and 'dollar' are thought to be dialect terms for 'dullard' (the Opies say 'diller' is a Yorkshire word for a schoolboy dull at learning) this suggests that coffee-house owner David Lee held sardonic views about the students who spent their time on his premises instead of studying. It gives an extra fillip of sub-text, too, to Dylan's position as a university drop-out and his launching of a career ever since replete with disparagement of academia.

A traditional ballad Dylan performed at the start of his career, 'Barbara Allen', is linked to one of his recent recordings, 'Froggie Went A-Courtin'', by the halfway house of a children's circle-game song, 'Old Roger', which begins:

> Old Roger is dead and laid in his grave . . .
> They planted an apple-tree over his head . . .
>
> The apples grew ripe and ready to fall . . .
> There came an old woman a-picking them all . . .
>
> Old Roger got up and he gave her a knock . . .
> Which made the old woman go hippety hop . . .

and ends with

> The bride and the saddle they lie on the shelf,
> If you want any more you must sing it yourself.

In the game, one child plays dead in the middle of the circle until the time comes to jump up and counter-attack the apple-stealer. That it may have been a song before it turned into an acted-out game is suggested by the ancientness of the opening line and the common use of the closing lines at the end of folksongs. As song or drama, what it shares with 'Barbara Allen', of course, is its expression of the ancient belief that the soul can pass into a plant or tree, and that the plant or tree can then embody the person. A parallel children's game is called 'Dead Man Arise'. In many versions of Cinderella, including the Grimms', the lonely heroine is looked after by a tree that grows out of her mother's grave. In Greek mythology, when Adonis is killed by a wild boar, an anemone grows from his heart. This shared belief is one of the examples of the unkillable 'mystery' of traditional song that Dylan mentions specifically in the 1966 *Playboy* interview, when, giving it his inimitable twist, he refers to 'all these songs about roses growing out of people's brains'. It is a strong enough idea that it appeals equally to adults as the resolution of the tragedy of the 'Barbara Allen' story, in which the plants grow from the lovers' breasts and intertwine above their graves, and to children who love the drama of the dead person becoming the tree that can arise and hit back.[10]

The nursery rhyme 'The Cuckoo Is A Merry Bird' was said in 1796 to have already appeared in a children's book that had been published for years, if not for generations. Dylan was performing it, as 'The Cuckoo Is A Pretty Bird' (the title of the four-verse version published by Cecil Sharp in *Folk-Songs from Somerset* in 1906), at the Gaslight in October 1962.[11] If you look at the track list of Dylan's very earliest tapes, several songs seem equally user-friendly to children: 'Go Tell It On The Mountain', 'Red Rosey Bush' and 'Who's Gonna Shoe Your Pretty Little Feet?' You can hear the lullaby that croons through this last song – the gentle one-two rockabye-baby motion and a lyric that consistently addresses the departed lover as if she were a child (who will hold your hand? who will put your shoes on?) – even on the adult version Dylan recorded as 'Kingsport Town' in late 1962.

'The Bells of Rhymney', an Idris Davies poem set to music by Pete Seeger, is another song Dylan knew and performed early on: he was taped playing it on guitar back in 1961 and then singing it with the Crackers on the Basement Tapes in 1967 (by this time in a lovely version that seems to suggest Dylan's familiarity with the version the Byrds put on their first album, 1965's "Mr. Tambourine Man"). A protest song about industrial misery and exploitation in Wales, its majestic poignancy is achieved by its open re-writing of the children's game-song 'Oranges And Lemons':

> *'Oh what will you give me?'*
> *Say the sad bells of Rhymney*
> *'Is there hope for the future?'*
> *Say the brown bells of Mythr*

rising to the audacious

> *'Even God is uneasy'*
> *Say the moist bells of Swansea.*

(This compelling couplet is omitted by The Byrds.) It is a use of children's song that Dylan mirrored exactly in his own work when he used 'Who Killed Cock Robin?' to build 'Who Killed Davey Moore?', mentioned again below. Dylan himself mirrored 'Oranges And Lemons' in mirroring 'The Bells of Rhymney' in a short section of his fourth LP's sleeve note poetry '11 Outlined Epitaphs':

> *the underground's gone deeper*
> *says the old chimney sweeper*

10. 'Old Roger' was field-recorded in Glasgow in 1961, at about the same time Dylan was learning 'Barbara Allen'. (The first extant tape of Dylan performing 'Barbara Allen' is NYC, October 1962.) 'The *Playboy* interview: Bob Dylan: a candid conversation with the iconoclastic idol of the folk-rock set', *Playboy*, March 1966.

11. Uncle Dave Macon, a white born in 1870 who sang and played banjo, has two recordings on the Harry Smith anthology "American Folk Music" (Folkways Records FP-251 to 253, New York, 1952, CD-reissued as "Anthology Of American Folk Music" [6-CD box-set] with copious notes by many hands and including a CD-ROM of extras, Smithsonian Folkways Recordings SFW 40090, Washington, DC, 1997), one of which, 'Way Down The Old Plank Road' (1926), includes both a verse from Clarence Ashley's version of the 'Coo Coo Bird' and a verse based on the nursery rhyme 'Solomon Grundy' (which goes 'Solomon Grundy / Born on a Monday / Christened on Tuesday / Married on Wednesday / Took ill on Thursday / Worse on Friday / Died on Saturday / Buried on Sunday / This is the end / Of Solomon Grundy'). Bob Dylan: 'The Cuckoo Is A Pretty Bird', same gig as 'Barbara Allen', detailed note 10.

> *the underground's outa work*
> *sing the bells of New York*
> *the underground's more dangerous*
> *ring the bells of Los Angeles*
> *the underground's gone*
> *cry the bells of San Juan*
> *but where has it gone to*
> *ring the bells of Toronto.*[12]

Dylan was also recorded performing some of Woody Guthrie's children's songs in early 1961, and he kept them in his repertoire while he was conquering New York. These included 'Car Car' (East Orange, New Jersey, February–March 1961, Bonnie Beecher's apartment that May, and in performance at the Gaslight in September 1961) and 'Howdido' (Beecher's, May 1961).[13] Almost twenty years later, in a speech on stage at the Fox-Warfield Theatre in San Francisco in 1980, Dylan talks of Leadbelly switching from prison songs to children's songs, using this as a parable about his own switch from street-legal to Christian songs.[14]

---

12.   Idris Davies' poem 'The Bells of Rhymney', collected in *So Early One Morning*, a selection of Welsh poetry (in English) compiled and edited by Dylan Thomas (1954). (This is where Pete Seeger found the poem.) Idris Davies was born in Rhymney, Monmouthshire, in 1905, went down the mines at 14 and died of cancer in 1953, the same year Dylan Thomas died of alcoholic poisoning.

Bob Dylan: 'The Bells Of Rhymney', 2nd MacKenzies Tape, recorded at the home of Eve and Mac MacKenzie, NYC, c. 4/12/61, unissued, and with the Crackers, West Saugerties/Woodstock, NY, June–Aug. 1967, unissued. The song's first recorded appearance by Seeger seems to have been in 1958, when he performed it at Carnegie Hall, and its second in 1959, when he performed it at the Newport Folk Festival (along with a song called 'One Grain Of Sand'). Pete Seeger: 'The Bells Of Rhymney', NYC, 27/12/57, issued "Pete Seeger & Sonny Terry at Carnegie Hall", Folkways FA 2412, New York, 1958; and 'The Bells Of Rhymney', Newport, Rhode Island, July 1959; issued "Folk Festival At Newport (Vol. 1)", Vanguard Records VRS-9062 and VSD-2053, New York, 1960. The song was published in *Sing Out!* Vol. 8, no. 2, 1958 (and included in 'Reprints From *Sing Out!* Vol. 3', c. 1962).

The Byrds: 'The Bells Of Rhymney', Hollywood, 14/4/65, issued "Mr. Tambourine Man", Columbia Records, New York [CBS Records 62571, London], 1965. This LP includes not only 'Mr. Tambourine Man' but also 'Spanish Harlem Incident', 'All I Really Want To Do' and 'Chimes Of Freedom'. The sleeve notes, by Billy James, a very minor figure in the Los Angeles rock scene, are a fine sample of mid-1960s cool gibberish.

Re the comparison with 'Who Killed Davey Moore', I note that *Broadside* magazine, No. 22, 1963, published a song credited to Norman Rosten & Peter [sic] Seeger, titled 'Who Killed Norma Jean' (and that *Broadside*, No. 25, 1963, included a song by Phil Ochs titled 'Davey Moore').

13.   Not that I've ever met a child (or adult) who liked to listen to Woody Guthrie singing his awful, dreary children's songs, with their plodding, morose jollity. Since Guthrie spent as little of his time as possible with his own children, it's no wonder he misjudged his audience. (I'm told Arlo and some other relatives have 'revived' them on a spooky 1990s album that mixes old Woody Guthrie vocal tracks with new recordings; nia.)

There was a bout of interest in children's songs among the folk revival crowd in the early 1960s. A round-up of available LPs published in *Sing Out!* Vol. 13, no. 3, summer 1963, included the following: "Rhythms Of Childhood With Ella Jenkins", *nia*, Folkways FC 7653, New York, *nia*; Jean Ritchie: "Children's Songs And Games From The Southern Mountains", *nia*, Folkways FC 754, New York, *nia*; Pete Seeger: "Children's Concert at Town Hall", NYC, *nia*, Columbia CS 8747 [mono CL 1947], New York, *nia*; Pete Seeger: "American Game And Activity Songs For Children", *nia*, Folkways FC 7003 [10-inch LP], New York, *nia*; and the Leadbelly album detailed in the next footnote. The same issue of *Sing Out!* also publishes the song 'Sweet Potatoes', which it says is available on another Pete Seeger album of children's songs "Song And Play-Time", *nia*, Folkways FC 7526, New York, *nia*.

14.   Bob Dylan, San Francisco, 12/11/80: 'He made lots of records there [in New York]. At first he was just doing prison songs, and stuff like that . . . He'd been out of prison for some time when he decided to do children's songs. And people said "Oh my! Did Leadbelly change?" . . . But he didn't change. He was the same man.' Quoted from 'Bob Dylan's Leadbelly Parable', *All Across the Telegraph*, ed. Gray and Bauldie, 1987. Leadbelly's album "Negro Folk Songs For Young People", Folkways FC 7533, New York, c. 1962, was reviewed in *Sing Out!* Vol. 13, no. 3, NYC, Summer 1963; the review concluded: 'It's the same Leadbelly full of power, love of life and deep sense of humanity.'

It's interesting here that Dylan stresses the contrast between one repertoire and another yet insists on the indivisibility of the artistry that straddles them. He's right to do so. There may be a clear distinction between 'prison songs' and 'children's songs' but on the whole the child–adult distinction can be as unclear in the blues as in white folk tradition. It makes perfect sense that the album on which Dylan specifically explores the poetry of nursery rhyme, "Under The Red Sky", is a very bluesy album: there is plenty of street-game, counting-song and nursery rhyme usage in the blues (including blues recordings with a Bob Dylan connection).

This would be unsurprising, even ignoring the presence of such material in adult oral culture generally, if blues critic Stephen Calt is right in asserting (he offers no evidence) that more or less all early blues lyrics come from what people were taught in elementary school, and that this was mostly 'old saws' and the Bible. Never mind that Calt's intention is dismissive of blues lyrics, 'old saws' and the Bible. A study of what some of the country blues artists of the 1920s had been taught at school (if they'd had a school to attend) might indeed be revealing as to how these rich sources of orally expressive language related to their blues lyrics. One of the earliest *white* folk recordings after discs replaced cylinders was 'A Day In A Country School', made in 1899, which, as Harry Smith notes, includes 'a unique recording of chanted mathematical problems'. There may be no equivalent black folk recording but there must be written accounts by ex-teachers from black schools of the period. There is also a large number of field recordings of teacher-and-pupil groups made later, in the 1930s and 1940s, for the Library of Congress. Most of them languish unheard in Washington.[15]

As it happens, an early Bob Dylan composition acts as a demonstration of how closely blues lyric poetry can stick to the cadences and phrasing of the King James Bible. There is, in the blues (and in hillbilly music), a common-stock formulation that runs like this: 'Well I ain't no fireman an' I ain't no fireman's son / But I can stoke your boiler till the fireman come', with a large array of variations in the occupation denied and the service offered. I used to think it typical of Dylan's witty usage of the blues that the unique variant he initiates in 'Long Time Gone' twists the formula away from its normal sexual innuendoing and into a different realm, *and* typical that he elects to use it in a song that isn't a blues at all:

> *If I can't help somebody*
> *With a word or a song.*
> *If I can't show somebody*
> *That they are travelin' wrong.*
> *But I know I ain't no prophet*
> *An' I ain't no prophet's son.*
> *I'm just a long time a-comin'*
> *An' I'll be a long time gone.*

15.   Stephen Calt, foreword to Stefan Grossman's guitar tutor book *Country Blues Guitar* (c. 1970–73). Probably because Calt makes his point in such an obscure place, it has remained 'unanswered' by other commentators. 'A Day In A Country School', New York, 15/11/1899, made by George Graham (issue details unknown): cited by Harry Smith in the sleeve notes to his 3 double-LPs compilation "American Folk Music", see note 11. Recordings by teacher-and-pupil groups made for the Library of Congress are itemised in Dixon and Godrich's *Blues and Gospel Records 1902–1943*, 1982. Some, relating to what follows, are specified in note 17.

That still *is* an alertly used and unique variant on the blues format: but it also shows him, back in 1962, confidently at ease with his biblical texts, for Dylan has taken almost verbatim the words of Amos in Amos 7:14:

> *I was no prophet, neither was I a prophet's son.*[16]

For present purposes the point we are guided towards by the young Bob Dylan is that while it's true that his variant rests on the blues formulation, it's clear that the whole blues formulation itself rests on the Bible. It's just one instance, but it is telling precisely because it is far from obvious, and hence suggests compellingly that in blues lyric poetry far more than we assume may indeed have come straight from the Bible via the conduit of the local church or classroom.

At least as important is the material that came from the playground: the ring-games, chants and rhymes that children learnt from each other. There's a very interesting section on black children's game-songs in Alan Lomax's book *The Land Where the Blues Began* which reminds us that, as in an older England, the distinction between children's and grown-ups' song is blurred partly because the distinction between children and grown-ups is blurred, and partly because the function of chants and game-songs in the Mississippi Delta (he is writing of the late 1930s to early 1940s) was to give an apprenticeship in sexual competence:

> Willowy girls, just moving into womanhood and as graceful as gazelles, usually led the games. The younger ones from ten down through six followed them . . . Littler ones, down to three, stumbled along, doing the best they could – everybody helped, nobody tried to exclude the small fry . . . The games allowed the girls to be very bold, and to try out all sorts of ploys in the safety of the dancing ring . . . The perennial favourite, 'Sally Water', has the girl kneeling in the middle of the ring. As her friends sing, she mimes their words, then shakes her little backside round the ring till she gets to the one 'she loves the best'. There she must be kissed.
>
> . . . *Shake it to the east, Sally, shake it to the west, Sally,*
> *Shake it to the very one that you love the best, Sally.*

This is immediately recognisable as the lyric behind one of Little Richard's anthems of sexual innuendo, 'Tutti Frutti', but innumerable older blues songs use the same couplet, showing how easily these childhood verses slide straight into the sandpit of adult imagination.

Lomax adds:

> Not long ago these games were played by mixed groups and the erotic feelings were strong . . . Everyone learned about choosing and being chosen. That was the theme of game after game – the rapid choice of lovers. Turn taking, sharing, but above all choosing, swiftly and boldly, then pleasuring the one chosen, and on to

---

16. Bob Dylan's 'Long Time Gone', stated in *Lyrics 1962–85* to be copyrighted 1963, is known to have been recorded at the home of Dave Whitaker, Minneapolis, 11/8/62 (and subsequently as a Witmark demo, NYC, March 1963, and at the home of Eve and Mac MacKenzie, NYC, 12/4/63). Amos 7:14 quoted from 'The Bible in the lyrics of Bob Dylan', Bert Cartwright, *Wanted Man Study Series*, no. 4, 1985.

the next – they called this 'stealing partners'. Sexually active at ten or eleven, with marriage maybe only a couple of years off, a Delta country girl needed to know how to sort through the males, and how to move between marriage partners. Indeed, the most popular of the stealing-partner games was one with the refrain 'satisfied'.

It takes a rockin chair to rock.	SATISFIED!
It takes a soft ball to roll	SATISFIED!
It takes a song like this	SATISFIED!
To satisfy my soul.	SATISFIED!
I ain't never been	SATISFIED!
I ain't never been	SATISFIED!

This is another recognisable blues refrain: you can hear it everywhere; it's a particular favourite of Big Joe Williams, for example, and it comes smoking down the track at the end of Kokomo Arnold's magnificent 'Milk Cow Blues', though it is a verse Bob Dylan omits when he covers the song:

Takes a rockin' chair to rock, mama, a rubber ball to roll
Takes a li'l teasin' brown, pretty mama, just to pacify my soul
Lord I don't feel welcome – Wheee! – no place I go.[17]

Small wonder, then, that much usage of nursery rhyme itself in blues lyric poetry is as simple sexual metaphor. Jane Lucas and Big Bill Broonzy's 1930 'Pussy Cat Blues', begins with Ms Lucas singing the immortal 'You can play with my pussy but please don't dog it around / If you going to mistreat it no pussy will be found', to which Big Bill, wittily bringing in the nursery rhyme, ripostes: 'Pussy cat, pussy cat: where have you been so long?' (combining nursery rhyme question with 'Corrina Corrina' format), before adding the less clear, if attractive 'Lord the mouse done been here, packed his grip and gone.' The near-identical 'Oh pussy cat, pussy cat, where you been so long?' is also the opening on Bo Chatman's 'Pussy Cat Blues', and a similarly sexually-laden variant is Memphis Minnie's 'Bumblebee, bumblebee, where

---

17.   Alan Lomax quoted, with his lyric transcriptions from his and Lewis Jones's Library of Congress field recordings of 'Little Sally Water' and 'Satisfied', from *The Land Where the Blues Began*, 1993.
    Library of Congress field recordings of 'Satisfied' include versions by: children at Drew, Mississippi, 24/10/40; children from Mount Powell School, York, Alabama, 30/10/40; Leora Anderson 'with five others', near Edwards, Mississippi 27/5/39; a 'Satisfy' by Dixon and Godrich's lights but 'Satisfied' by the Archive of Folk Songs, by Anne Williams and group, Moorhead Plantation, Lula, Mississippi, 12/8/42, issued "Play & Dance Songs and Tunes", AFS Records L9, Washington, DC, nia.; and a 'Satisfy' by Mable [or Mary] Lou Brewer and 'group' at Coahoma County School, Coahoma, Mississippi, 10/8/42.
    As for Little Sally, Lomax's book unfailingly calls her Water yet the Library of Congress field recordings listed in Dixon and Godrich always title this song 'Little Sally Walker', which seems more likely. These recordings include versions by: 'Eight Girls' at Kirby Industrial School, Atmore, Alabama, c. Oct. 1934; 'Four Little Girls' at a 'Negro Church, Tupelo, Mississippi', 8/5/39; Wilford Jerome Fisher and Ruthie May Farr at Merryvale, Louisiana, 15/5/39; Eva Grace Boone with children, Brandon, Mississippi, 25/5/39, issued AFS L9, detailed above; Susie Miller with a group of five children at Vicksburg Baptist Academy, Vicksburg, Mississippi, 29/5/39; Hettie Godfrey, Livingston, Alabama, c. 1/11/40; Emma Jane Davis with group at someone's house in Friar's Point, Mississippi, 26/7/42. The only listing I can find of both songs by the same performers is by Mrs Laura and Ruby Clifton (not children), Tupelo, Mississippi, 10/5/39. I cannot trace any recording of both songs by children made in Coahoma County, as Lomax suggests is the location.
    Little Richard: 'Tutti Frutti', New Orleans, Sept. 1955, Specialty Records 561, Hollywood, 1955. Kokomo Arnold: 'Milk Cow Blues', Chicago, 10/9/34; "Blues Classics By Kokomo Arnold And Peetie Wheatstraw", Blues Classics BC–14, Berkeley, 1964.

is you been so long?' In Sleepy John Estes' 'Jack and Jill Blues' 'Now it was late last night when everything was still / Now me and my baby was playing old Jack and Jill.' And granted that the nursery rhyme line 'Mary had a little lamb' has always invited a smirk, it's positively refreshing to find it gambol across the lyric of Winston Holmes' and Charlie Turner's 1929 'Skinner' as brightly as this (with a neat pun on 'fleas' and 'fleece'):

> *Mary had a little lamb with fleas as black as jet*
> *I went home with Mary last night an' I ain't stopped scratchin' yet.*[18]

Yet, as you would also expect, there is a rich variety of other usage of nursery rhyme, counting-songs, street-games and fairy tale in the blues. Blind Willie McTell's 1930 'Talkin' To Myself', his 1933 'Lord, Send Me An Angel' and his colleague Curley Weaver's 1950 'Ticket Agent' all recall being 'a boy playing mumble-peg'. The skipping rhyme 'Cat's Got The Measles' ('Cat's got the measles, the dog's got the 'flu, the chicken's got the chicken-pox and out goes you!', in a common, still-contemporary English primary-school playground version) becomes the blues record 'The Cat's Got The Measles' ('Now the cat's got the measles, dog's got the whooping-cough') by Papa Charlie Jackson in 1925. And as confirmed by the lyric of Jesse James' 1936 'Southern Casey Jones', a common 1920s and 1930s term for a nightgown was a 'mother hubbard':

> *Slipping and a sliding all across the streets*
> *With their loose mother hubbard and their stocking feet.*[19]

18.   Jane Lucas & Big Bill Broonzy: 'Pussy Cat Blues', New York, 15/9/30; "Big Bill Broonzy 1928–1935: Do That Guitar Rag", Yazoo L-1035, New York, 1973. (In Dixon and Godrich's *Blues and Gospel Records 1902–1943*, the track is listed as 'Pussy Cat, Pussy Cat'.)
      Bo Chatman: 'Pussy Cat Blues', New Orleans, 15/10/36; "Bo Carter, 1931–1940", Yazoo L-1034, New York, 1973. (Bo Carter was the pseudonym on OKeh and Bluebird for Bo Chatman; he also recorded with the Mississippi Jug Band. His brother Lonnie Chatman is credited in Glen Dundas' *Tangled up in Tapes*, 1994, as composer of the Mississippi Sheiks songs covered by Dylan on "World Gone Wrong", the title track ['The World Is Going Wrong' as the Sheiks have it] and 'Blood In My Eyes' ['I've Got Blood In My Eyes For You']. Walter Jacobs and Lonnie Chatman are similarly credited by Dundas for 'Sitting On Top Of The World', recorded by Dylan in 1962 [with Big Joe Williams] and 1992 [on "Good As I Been To You"]. For recording details of these see Chapter 18.) Bo Chatman first recorded a 'Pussy Cat Blues', NYC, 4/6/31: a session at which he also cut, among others, 'My Pencil Won't Write No More', 'Pin In Your Cushion', 'Ram Rod Daddy' and 'Banana In Your Fruit-Basket', all CD-reissued on "Bo Carter Complete Recorded Works Volume 1 (1928–1931)", Document Records DOCD-5079, Vienna, 1991. ('Banana In The Fruit-Basket' [sic], and 'Pin In Your Cushion' were re-cut San Antonio, Texas, 26/3/34.)
      Memphis Minnie: 'Bumble Bee', Memphis, 20/2/30; "Rare Blues of the Twenties No. 2", Historical Records HLP-2/ASC-2, Jersey City, NJ, 1966; similar lyrics may be found also in her 'Bumble Bee Blues', recorded with the Memphis Jug Band, Memphis, 26/5/30; "Country Blues Classics, Volume 3", Blues Classics BC-7, Berkeley, 1966; and her 'New Bumble Bee', Chicago, 1/7/30; "Memphis Minnie, Vol 2: With Kansas Joe, 1930–31", Blues Classics BC-13, Berkeley, 1967.
      Sleepy John Estes: 'Jack and Jill Blues', NYC, 3/8/35; "Sleepy John Estes 1929–1940", RBF Records RF-8, New York, 1964 – and of course the only other famous 'Sleepy' is a dwarf in the Disneyised *Snow White*.
      Winston Holmes and Charlie Turner: 'Skinner', Richmond, Indiana, 21/6/29; "Early Folk Blues Vol. 2: Hometown Skiffle", Saydisc SDR 206, Badminton, Gloucestershire, c. 1969; CD-reissued "Kansas City Blues", Document Records DOCD-5152, Vienna, 1993.

19.   Blind Willie McTell: 'Talkin To Myself', Atlanta, 17/4/30; "Blind Willie McTell: The Early Years (1927–1933)", Yazoo L-1005, New York, 1968. 'Lord, Send Me An Angel', New York, 19/9/33; "Atlanta Blues 1933", JEMF Records JEMF-106, LA, 1979. Curley Weaver: 'Ticket Agent', 1950, issued Sittin' In With Records 547, New York. 'Cat's got the measles, the dog's got the 'flu [etc]' heard in the playground at Thornton-le-Dale Primary School, North Yorkshire, 1994. Papa Charlie Jackson: 'The Cat's Got The Measles', Chicago, c. January

As such lines also suggest, the language and rhythms and some of the assumptions and conventions of nursery rhyme and fairy tale – such as that animals speak, or that you can use a magic potion – run so deeply through the blues, and form so fundamental a characteristic of the humour of the blues, that it may be impossible to separate many of the common-stock formulations of the one from the other. For example, this sort of structure, which is everywhere in blues lyric poetry:

> *Preacher in his pulpit, bible in his hand*
> *Sister in the corner crying there's my man*

(and which shares a lot with a formulation Dylan used in 'Get Your Rocks Off' but is here quoted from a blues song:

> *Now two old womens are running hand in hand*
> *One found out the other one had a man)*

is clearly based on children's game-chants and nursery rhymes like 'Old Willie Winkie, Running Through The Town'.[20]

When I first heard Dylan's 1990 song 'Cat's In The Well', I misheard the line 'Back alley Sally is doing the American Jump' and thought Dylan had combined two Little Richard song references here, putting 'Good Golly Miss Molly' and 'Long Tall Sally' together to make 'By golly Sally is doing the American Jump'. 'Long Tall Sally', with its flashing *Beano* cartoon scenes – 'saw Aunt Mary coming and 'e got back in the alley' – is a reminder that The Aunt is a figure of nursery rhyme or pantomime dimensions in the blues, as in other folksong. Perhaps mythologising your own family, or the neighbours, accounts for some of the 'Old Mother Hubbard' rhymes we have. At any rate 'Aunt Louise she bought blue goose cheese' in Teddy Bunn's 'Pattin Dat Cat', quoted again below, belongs in a pantomime cast with Will Shade's 'Old Aunt Anna, long and tall / Her feet's in the kitchen, her head's in the hall' (not unlike Alice in *Alice in Wonderland*), not forgetting that 'There's Old Aunt Sally, old and grey / Do the Georgia crawl till she died away'.[21] They could be joined by many other aunts, and uncles too.

How clear is the connection – or rather how unclear the division – between adult and nursery rhyme mode, is shown by halfway house lyrics like this:

> *Martha's sitting up on that fence*
> *Yowling like she didn't have no sense*
> *Blackbird cheeping in a tree*
> *Said to the redbird skeedle-um-skee.*

1925; "Papa Charlie Jackson 1925–1928", Biograph BLP-12042, Canaan, NY, 1972. Jesse James: 'Southern Casey Jones', Chicago, 3/6/36; "Out Came The Blues Vol. 2", Ace of Hearts AH-158, London, 1967.

20. Hi Henry Brown: 'Preacher Blues', NYC, 14/3/32; "St. Louis Blues, 1929–35: The Depression", Yazoo L-1030, New York, 1972. Washboard Sam: 'My Feet Jumped Salty', Chicago, 26/6/41; "Feeling Lowdown: Washboard Sam", RCA Vintage Series LPV-577, New York, 1971.

21. Little Richard: 'Long Tall Sally': New Orleans, 7/2/56, Speciality Records 572, Hollywood, 1956. Teddy Bunn: 'Pattin Dat Cat', NYC, 7/4/30; "Rare Blues, 1927–1930", Historical Records HLP-5, Jersey City, c. 1967–8. Will Shade, with the Memphis Jug Band: 'Take Your Fingers Off It', Chicago, 7/11/34; "The Jug Bands: Memphis Jug Band 1929–1934", Joker SM-3104, Milan, 1971. Henry Williams & Eddie Anthony: 'Georgia Crawl', Atlanta, 19/4/28; "The Country Fiddlers", Roots RL-316, Vienna, 1968.

Or consider this, from one of Frank Stokes' wonderful anti-preacher tirades:

> *Oh well you see the preacher lay behind the log*
> *A hand on the trigger, got his eye on the hog*
> *The hog said hmmm, the gun said zip*
> *Jumped on the hog with all of his grip.*

This song even turns the Lord's Prayer (which is itself, of course, primarily a children's prayer) into the pattern of a counting-song. It begins:

> *Well it's Our Father who art in heaven*
> *The preacher owed me ten dollars he paid me seven.*

Stokes' 'You Shall', as mentioned elsewhere, is the basis, whether via Woody Guthrie and Leadbelly's 'You Shall Be Free' or not, of Dylan's 'I Shall Be Free', and illustrates the free way in which talking chickens and roosters are par for the course in adult as well as children's songs.[22]

The magic potion from the fairy tale world that is also employed in the blues is called variously 'goofer dust', 'goomer dust' or 'goo-goo dust'. In the American story 'Aunt Kate's Goomer Dust', for example, this magic potion, sprinkled into the father's pants, makes him fart, discombobulating him so that he can be tricked into letting his daughter marry the lad of her choice. In Cripple Clarence Lofton's 'I Don't Know' (repeating almost verbatim lines from fellow pianist Romeo Nelson's 'Gettin Dirty Just Shakin' That Thing') he sings that

> *. . . I'm going to poison you*
> *Sprinkle goofer-dust around your bed*
> *Wake up some morning, find your own self dead.*

The same year Romeo Nelson recorded his number, Will Ezell cut the delightful piano solo 'Heifer Dust', about which the sleeve notes on the occasion of its reissue simply comment: ''Heifer Dust' (a magic powder), a graceful and mannered composition . . .' – as if reference to a magic powder were the most natural thing to find in the smoky bars and city ghettoes of 1920s America.[23]

The affable familiarity blues artists show towards toads and frogs suggests yet another entanglement in the fairy tale and nursery rhyme world. The handiness of frogs and toads as creatures of metaphor may arise from their omnipresence in the rural backwoods America inhabited by the country blues musicians, but the equal handiness of frogs and toads as creatures of myth and magic, of sexuality and transformation, can never have been deleted from the minds of those employing them

22. Teddy Bunn: 'Pattin Dat Cat', see note 21. The Beale Street Sheiks [Frank Stokes & Dan Sane]: 'You Shall', Chicago, c. August 1927; "Frank Stokes With Dan Sane And Will Batts (1927–1929)", Roots RL-308, Vienna, 1968. A variant performance was recorded within a month (Frank Stokes: 'You Shall', Chicago, c. Sept. 1927; "Mississippi & Beale Street Sheiks, 1927–1932", Biograph BLP-12041, Canaan, NY, 1972).

23. 'Aunt Kate's Goomer Dust', in *The Devil's Daughter and Other Folk Tales* by Vance Randolph, and republished in the *Virago Book of Fairy Tales*, ed. Angela Carter (1990). Romeo Nelson: 'Gettin' Dirty Just Shakin' That Thing', Chicago, 9/10/29; "Rugged Piano Classics, 1927–1939", Origin Jazz Library OJL-15, Berkeley, c. 1967. 'I Don't Know', Cripple Clarence Lofton, recorded privately, probably Chicago, c. 1938–9; issued Swaggie Records S-1235, Victoria, Australia, late 1960s, and on "Cripple Clarence Lofton & Walter Davis", Yazoo L-1025, New York, 1971. Will Ezell: 'Heifer Dust', Chicago, c. Feb. 1929; "Chicago Piano", Chicago Piano Records 12–002, UK, 1973; CD-reissued c. 1990. Ezell was one of the most celebrated pianists of the late 1920s; his entire output for Paramount in Chicago 1927–29 is on this compilation.

in song. Even if you could have written a song about being a poor little toad without being aware of the import of the toad as a sexual symbol in the unconscious mind, you couldn't write a song about someone being as ugly as a toad without being aware of the classic kiss-a-frog-to-find-a-prince theme. That 'Hoppin' Toad Frog', by our old friend J. T. Funny Papa Smith, can be read as a typical slice of blatant sexual innuendo does nothing to stop us recognising that it can also stand as the song of the frog in the fairy tale 'The Frog King':

> *Mom would you let a poor little old toad frog hop down in your water pond*
> *I'd dive down and come right out, and I won't stay in your water long.*
> *But I know for myself and your front yard is where I get my load*
> *Way you talk you like my hopping: why don't you keep me for your little toad?*[24]

The Man In The Moon is another nursery rhyme character represented in the blues, in one lovely couplet that prefigures Bob Dylan's song 'Under The Red Sky':

> *The wolves howled at midnight, wild ox moaned till day*
> *The man in the moon looked down on us but had nothing to say*

and ends Whistlin' Alex Moore's 1929 'West Texas Woman'.[25]

Robert Johnson wrote a song called 'Little Boy Blues', which he didn't record, though Robert Junior Lockwood did. It begins:

> *Little Boy Blues, please come blow your horn*
> *My baby she gone and left me, she left me all alone*
> *Now the sheep is in the meadow and the cows is in the corn*
> *I've got a girl in Chicago, she loves to hear me blow my lonesome horn.*

A 'Little Boy Blue' was also recorded by Scrapper Blackwell (twice) in his all-too-brief 'rediscovery' period, while in an early phase of Sonny Boy Williamson II's career Williamson was billed as Little Boy Blue. (A promotional photograph of him as Little Boy Blue is reproduced in the notes to "The Complete Robert Johnson" 2-CD set.)[26]

In fact the entwining of nursery rhyme and fairy tale into such music extends right

---

24. J. T. Funny Papa Smith: 'Hoppin' Toad Frog', Chicago, c. April 1931; "Funny Papa Smith: The Original Howling Wolf, 1930–1931", Yazoo L-1031, New York, 1972. (There is some discussion of the sexual import of frogs in fairy tales a little later.)

25. Whistlin' Alex Moore': 'West Texas Woman', Dallas, 5/12/29; "I'm Wild About My Lovin', 1928–1930", Historical Records HLP-32, Jersey City, NJ, 1969.

26. 'Little Boy Blues', Robert Lockwood, Chicago, 30/7/41; "Country Blues Classics Vol. 3", Blues Classics BC-7, Berkeley, 1966; CD-reissued on "Mississippi Blues (1935–1951)", Various Artists, Wolf Records WBCD-005, Vienna, *nia*. He re-recorded the song over forty years later on "Contrasts", Trix Records 3307, 1973, now CD-reissued Trix Records CD 3307, 1991. (As a child, Robert Junior Lockwood intended to become a pianist but Robert Johnson, who lived with Lockwood's mother and acted as his step-father for a period in Helena, Arkansas, inspired him to take up guitar instead. 'He took time with me and showed me things, and he didn't do *that* with *nobody*,' Stephen C. LaVere quotes him as saying.) Robert Johnson: "The Complete Recordings", Columbia Legacy Roots N' Blues Series, CBS 467246, New York/London, 1992. Stephen C. LaVere, notes to ditto.

Scrapper Blackwell: 'Little Boy Blue', Indianapolis, 4/6/58; "Indianapolis Jump", Flyright LP 523, Weybridge, Surrey, 1976. Scrapper Blackwell: 'Little Boy Blue', Indianapolis, July 1961; "Mr. Scrapper's Blues", Prestige Bluesville LP 1047, 1961–2.

(Blackwell's début recording was 'Kokomo Blues', Indianapolis, 16/6/28; "Scrapper Blackwell (1928–1934)", Yazoo L-1019, New York, 1970. This is a less than distinctive lyric, and Blackwell's dexterity as a player is not here put into the service of a catchy, cohesive whole – but it is recognisably the number Robert Johnson re-makes into his classic, 'Sweet Home Chicago'. Having survived almost three decades beyond his partner Leroy Carr, who drank himself to death in the mid-1930s, Blackwell recorded again after a 23-year gap in 1958, 1959, 1960 and 1961 but then died when he was shot in Indianapolis in October 1962.)

through to Chuck Berry's incorporating 'hey diddle diddle' into 'Roll Over Beethoven', all those 'My mommy told me that she would buy me a rubber dolly' songs becoming R&B hits for Shirley Ellis ('The Name Game' and 'The Clapping Song' were both hits made from children's playground chants of some antiquity), and Thomas Higginbotham, the singer–composer of 'Hi Heel Sneakers', choosing to call himself Tommy Tucker. 'Nursery Rhyme' is on a 1960 Bo Diddley album, 'Babes In The Woods' and 'Hey, Red Riding Hood' on others; 'Nursery Rhyme Rock' is one side of a 1956 single cut by the gospel/R&B singer Wynona Carr at her first secular session; 'Nursery Rhyme Blues' is a track by Merrill Moore. 'Hickory Dickory Dock' is a 1950s recording by Etta James, and that nursery rhyme's title phrase is also thrown into the lyric of Buddy Holly's 'Rock Me My Baby'. Lloyd Price reached No. 15 in the American R&B charts in 1959 with 'Three Little Pigs'; Arthur Alexander's 1966 single 'Baby For You' (his début single for Monument Records, after escaping from Dot) incorporates the title line and the next line from the children's rhyming prayer 'Now I lay me down to sleep', which first appeared in print in Thomas Fleet's *The New-England Primer* in 1737. Two hundred and thirty years later, Buddy Guy recorded 'Mary Had A Little Lamb', with a lyric that was the nursery rhyme almost verbatim.

And, completing a circle, the boy who was taught guitar (and 'Little Boy Blues') by Robert Johnson, Robert Junior Lockwood, became the old man who taught Lonnie Pitchford, a young blues singer from Bentonia, Mississippi, who was filmed in 1991 (by blues documentarist Robert Palmer) performing the traditional blues-style nursery rhyme 'Johnny Stole An Apple' on a home-made one-stringed instrument.[27]

In his own work, Dylan is just as unapologetic about resting on nursery rhyme material. The 1961 'Man On The Street' shares its opening line, 'I'll sing you a song, ain't very long', with the nursery rhyme that runs 'I'll sing you a song / Though not very long / Yet I think it's as pretty as any / Put your hand in your purse / You'll never be worse / And give the poor singer a penny' (the second half of which is likely to

27.   Chuck Berry: 'Roll Over Beethoven', Chicago, Feb. 1956, Chess Records 1626, Chicago, 1956. Shirley Ellis: 'The Name Game', Congress Records 230, New York [London-American HLR 9946, London], 1965; and 'The Clapping Song', Congress 234, New York, c. 1965. Tommy Tucker: 'Hi Heel Sneakers', NYC, 27/11/63, Checker 1067, 1964. Bo Diddley: 'Nursery Rhyme', Chicago, Spring 1959; "Have Guitar – Will Travel", Checker Records 2974, Chicago, 1960 (first UK-issued "Bo Diddley Rides Again", Pye International NPL 28029, London, 1963); 'Babes In The Woods', Chicago, July 1962, "Bo Diddley", Checker Records LP 2984, Chicago, 1962 ["Bo Diddley", Pye International NPL 28026, London, 1963]; 'Hey, Red Riding Hood', Chicago, 25/7/65, "500% More Man", Checker Records LP(S) 2996, Chicago, 1965. Wynona Carr (with the Bumps Blackwell Band): 'Nursery Rhyme Rock', Los Angeles, 1956; "Jump Jack Jump!", Specialty SP2157, Hollywood, c. 1973; an alternate take is on "The Specialty Story Volume 1", Ace Records CH134, UK, c. 1983. Merrill Moore: 'Nursery Rhyme Blues', Hollywood, 18/2/57, Capitol F-3788, Hollywood, 1957, CD-issued "Boogie My Blues Away", Bear Family Records BCD 15505-BH, Vollersode, Germany, c. 1990. Etta James: 'Hickory Dickory Dock', probably LA, probably 1958; "Twist With Etta James", Crown CLP 5250, Culver City, 1961, and "Best Of Etta James", United LP 7727, LA, 1963. Buddy Holly: 'Rock Me My Baby', Oklahoma City, 27–28/9/57; reissued "The Complete Buddy Holly" 6-LP box-set, MCA Coral (given as cat. no. CDSP 807 on the box but listed as CDLM 807 in the discography inside), London, March 1979. Lloyd Price: 'Three Little Pigs', NYC, 1959, ABC-Paramount single 10032, NYC, 1959. Arthur Alexander: 'Baby For You', 1966, Monument Records, Nashville, 1966. Buddy Guy: 'Mary Had A Little Lamb', Chicago, 18/9/67, Vanguard single 35060 and "A Man And The Blues", Vanguard Records LP 79272, New York, c. 1967. Lonnie Pitchford: 'Johnny Stole An Apple', Bentonia, Mississippi, 1991; included in Robert Palmer's *Deep Blues*, 1991, a film based on his book of the same name, shown UK TV 1993.

remind us of Dylan's later song 'Minstrel Boy').[28] The 1962 'Rambling Gambling Willie' is prefigured by Scotland's 'Rattlin Roarin Willie', and both 1962's 'A Hard Rain's A-Gonna Fall' and the following year's 'Girl Of The North Country' have significant nursery rhyme connections. As already noted, the folksong on which the former is based, 'Lord Randal', was one of those preserved in oral tradition by its nursery rhyme version. Not only does Dylan's version still have room for nursery rhyme topography like the 'six crooked highways', rebuilt in the footsteps of the crooked man who walked a crooked mile – which Dylan echoes more audibly still in 'Ballad Of Hollis Brown', with its 'walked a rugged mile' – but the apocalyptic heart of Dylan's version may itself have been midwifed into existence in some chamber of his imagination by a tradition of ostensibly visionary nursery rhymes. They include this one, which, widely known in the mid-seventeenth century and still popular with London schoolchildren two hundred years later, has been preserved in American nursery rhyme collections – and which can certainly be called Dylanesque:

> *I saw a peacock with a fiery tail*
> *I saw a blazing comet drop down hail*
> *I saw a cloud with ivy circled round*
> *I saw a sturdy oak creep on the ground*
> *I saw a pismire swallow up a whale*
> *I saw a raging sea . . .*

I say 'ostensibly' visionary, because, like 'Every Lady In The Land' and 'I Saw A Man With No Eyes' – cited later – this one belongs to a corpus of riddle or trick nursery rhymes which rely for their effects on layout and punctuation, the re-ordering of which reduces them to the mundane. As Walter de la Mare commented on the one just quoted, 'So may the omission of a few commas effect a wonder of the imagination.'[29]

The entanglement of 'Girl Of The North Country' in traditional childlore is of a different order, and brings together both nursery rhyme and fairy tale. Dylan's song is clearly based upon one or more versions of the traditional or broadside song 'Scarborough Fair' – which does not necessarily include the repeated line 'Parsley sage rosemary and thyme' taken up by Paul Simon.

> *Is any of you going to Scarborough Fair?*
> *Remember me to the lad as lives there*
> *For once he was a true lover of mine*

---

28. For a more detailed discussion of Bob Dylan songs that begin with this kind of market-stall sales pitch, see my 'Grubbing for a Moderate Jewel: In Search of the Blooming Bright Star of Belle Isle', *Canadian Folklore canadien*, *Journal of the Folklore Studies Association of Canada*, Vol. 8, 1–2, St John's, Newfoundland, officially 1986 but in fact published 1988. An earlier version of this essay, 'Back to Belle Isle', appeared in the *Telegraph*, no. 29, Spring 1988.

29. *Come Hither*, Walter de la Mare (1923); quoted by the Opies. De la Mare may have put it in that reductive way as a backlash against what was, at the time, a device of modernist experiment. Gertrude Stein: 'A comma by helping you along holding your coat for you and putting on your shoes keeps you from living your life as actively as you should lead it.' Apollinaire had published a number of unpunctuated poems in 1912, contemporaneously with Marinetti. In critic Roger Shattuck's words 'Lack of punctuation alone modifies their line, for it removes the conventional signs of logical development and opens each poem to new sequences and interpretations.' (Stein and Shattuck quoted in Roger Shattuck's *The Banquet Years: The Origins of the Avant-Garde in France 1885 to World War I.*)

is a version collected in the 1890s, while a variant that uses 'time' in place of 'thyme' was collected by F. J. Child from an 1827 manuscript:

> *Did ye ever travel twixt Berwick and Lyne?*
> *Sober and grave grows merry in time*
> *There ye'll meet wi a handsome young dame*
> *Ance she was a true love of mine*

which, if located on a different 'borderline' (Berwick is the last English town on the east coast, before you reach Scotland), is very close to Dylan's lyric. His goes on to hope his ex is wrapped up warm against the howling wind; the Scottish borders version also moves on to questions of clothing:

> *Tell her to sew me a holland sark*
> *And sew it all without needle wark*
> *And syne we'll be true lovers again.*

But the clothing factor here is far more important than it is for Dylan's narrator. Here the protagonist is sticking close to the key part of a far older story – one that is the basis for both a fairy tale set down by the Grimms and the nursery rhyme which (published at least as early as 1784) preserves in its most common and accessible form the folksong cycle that lies behind both Dylan's and Paul Simon's recordings.

The nursery rhyme, echoed by the lines above, is 'Can You Make Me A Cambric Shirt?', which, like so many folksongs, has two narrators and comprises their dialogue. It starts with the male narrator asking:

> *Can you make me a cambric shirt*
> *Parsley, sage, rosemary and thyme*
> *Without any seam or needlework?*
> *And you shall be a true lover of mine.*

The second and third verses place two further seemingly impossible demands (about washing and drying the shirt) upon the female being courted, and she then counters with three impossible demands of her own, which she says the man must sort out first ('Can you find me an acre of land / Between the salt water and the sea sand? / Can you plough it with a ram's horn / And sow it all over with one peppercorn?' and 'Can you reap it with a sickle of leather / And bind it up with a peacock's feather?'). The song ends, therefore, with the rather modern belligerence of the woman's summing up retort:

> *When you have done and finished your work,*
> *Parsley, sage, rosemary and thyme,*
> *Then come to me for your cambric shirt,*
> *And you shall be a true lover of mine.*

The fairy tale version of this story (included in the Grimms' *Fairy Tales* and in the *Gesta Romanorum* of about 1300, and possibly linked with similar oriental stories of even greater age) concerns a king so rich that he was more interested in a wise than a wealthy wife, and therefore tested the maid chosen for him by his friends by sending her a three-inch-square piece of linen and asking her to make him a full-sized shirt from it. 'The girl,' note the Opies, 'replied that if the king would send her an implement in which she could work the shirt, she would make it for him. So the king sent her "Vas debitum et precosium", the shirt was made, and the king married her.' No one now knows quite what that Latin phrase meant, or what trick it encompassed, but we get the gist of it. The point is that the core of the story is so strong that in every extant version, in prose and verse, one of the tasks set is always the making of a shirt. This, as F. J. Child writes, is because 'A man asking a maid to sew him a shirt is equivalent to asking for her love, and her consent to sew the shirt is equivalent to an acceptance of the suitor.'

Thus the nursery rhyme and the fairy tale carry the deepest reverberations of the narrative that Dylan's song picks up on – and they predate the folksong variants in which it is an old love who is challenged or, as in 'Girl Of The North Country', merely remembered. All the same, Dylan's 1960s song still holds in its invoking of the coat the vestigial traces of the pre-medieval tale, and it is the surviving nursery rhyme that shows the links between the two.[30]

The 1963 'Percy's Song' (issued on "Biograph", 1985) begins and ends in the shadows of nursery rhyme. It opens with

> *Bad news, bad news,*
> *Came to me where I sleep*

in which the repetition, for dramatic emphasis' sake, of the words 'bad news', echoes the 1690s broadside ballad 'The Unconstant Maiden':

> *Bad news is come to town*
> *Bad news is carried*
> *Bad news is come to town*
> *My love is marry'd,*

which is itself in parodic echo of the nursery rhyme

> *Brave news is come to town*
> *Brave news is carried*
> *Brave news is come to town*
> *Jemmy Dawson's married,*

while the ending of the Dylan song, the lovely but formulaic

> *And the only tune*
> *My guitar could play*
> *Was, 'Oh the Cruel Rain*
> *And the Wind'*

leans on a construct from the nursery rhyme 'Tom He Was A Piper's Son', with its repeated

---

30. The repeated 'Parsley, sage, rosemary and thyme', however, may be a survival from a far older incantation listing plants believed to have magic properties: 'parsley, sage, rosemary, thyme, juniper, gentle, holly, ivy and broom', according to the Opies.

> *And all the tune that he could play*
> *Was 'Over the hills and far away'.*

As mentioned already (in a comparison with songs based on the nursery rhyme 'Oranges And Lemons'), Dylan uses with deliberate transparency the format of 'Who Killed Cock Robin?' in 1963 for the 'serious' protest material of

> *Who killed Davey Moore? . . .*
> *Not I said . . .* [etc].

(He was not the first to do so: Byron, writing on the death of Keats in 1821, wrote the lines 'Who killed John Keats? / "I" says the Quarterly / So savage and Tartarly / "'Twas one of my feats"'.)

The immediate echo behind the opening of 'With God On Our Side',

> *Oh my name it ain't nothin*
> *My age it means less,*

may (as once discussed at length in the *Guardian* letters page) derive from a Dominic Behan song, but behind that reverberate the many echoes of a children's game-song variously called 'Queen Mary', 'Sweet Dolly' and 'Sweet Mary', and having many a relation with no name at all.[31] The game, dating back centuries, is an Ur ring game – a simple, fast dancing game with one child in the middle of a ring – and the common factor in the lyric is that the song always starts, as Dylan's does, with the formula 'My name is X, my age is Y'. Hence

> *My name is Queen Mary, my age is sixteen,*
> *My father's a farmer on yonder green*

or

> *My name it is Jean, and my age is fifteen;*
> *My father's a farmer, he lives on the plain*

or

> *My name is sweet Dolly, my age twenty-three,*
> *My father's a farmer over the Red Sea.*

---

31.   The great irony of the Behanites grumbling about Bob Dylan 'stealing' these opening lines is of course that the lines themselves are a succinct statement of the folksinger's essential position. Karl Dallas says as much when he quotes 'the old cowboy song' (he doesn't identify it further) as having 'the role of the songmaker down to a T': *'My name is nothing extry / So that I will not tell.'* Dallas is arguing that 'in a situation where all things are in common, communal ownership and, in the sense that as each man changes what he hands on he puts his own individual stamp upon it, communal authorship may make anonymity the very essence.' He stresses that in a folk culture,

> there should be a continuous process of re-creation in which the forces of tradition, variation and selection interplay dynamically; consequently, authorship should be increasingly difficult to establish and each member of [the community] . . . should regard the culture as personally his; the composer and/ or performer will be regarded as comparatively insignificant, more as the servant of his community than its leader; the distinctions between audiences and artists will tend to blur or break down.

Karl Dallas, 'The Roots of Tradition', *The Electric Muse*, by Laing *et al.*, 1975.

The Dylan song not only twists the formula of the opening line but shares with these far-flung children's versions the same rhyming pattern – each verse rhymes lines one with two and lines three with four – and shares the time signature of the tune, which is in 6/8.[32]

Boots of Spanish leather were celebrated in song as the finest – as objects of desire – in nursery rhyme and singing-game in the nineteenth century. In *Sons and Lovers*, published in 1913 and set in Nottinghamshire, D. H. Lawrence has Mrs Morel hearing children sing this in the street as the day is getting dark:

> *My shoes are made of Spanish leather*
> *My socks are made of silk*
> *I wear a ring on every finger*
> *I wash myself in milk*

and variants collected earlier include 'Our boots are made of Spanish leather' and 'My boots are made of Spanish leather'.

That so much meaning is encapsulated, as Dylan settles for these expensive boots at the end of the dialogue with his departed lover, is proof that this is one of the most deft, economical lines of writing in his whole repertoire. Yet it carries more than the young man's hiss of embittered rebuke. Underneath this literal pay-off, other reverberations rumble. If, like Mrs Morel, we can hear the children singing the same words in the background, this adds an extra poignancy to the way the hurt scorn of Dylan's title line both confesses the 'rejected' lover's immaturity and tacitly acknowledges that the other has grown away from him. It's a further irony that the lines the children sing express aspiration towards such a grandiose, unreal idea of adulthood.

That there has not been, traditionally, any clear distinction between the two states is made very clear by the other song invoked in the background by Dylan's title 'Boots Of Spanish Leather' – the omni-present 'Gypsy Davey' or 'Blackjack Davey', in which many versions bring us either boots or gloves of Spanish leather. Both, of course, carry similar strong sexual import, as is emphasised in almost every variant of the narrative. As Dylan himself performs the song on "Good As I Been To You", the shoes and the gloves are the objects around which the whole struggle for possession of the heroine is fought. First the gypsy insists:

> *'Pull off, pull off them high heeled shoes*
> *All made of Spanish leather*
> *Git behind me on my horse*
> *And we'll ride off together*
> *We'll both go off together.'*

It is charged with significance, therefore, as we learn that

---

32.   An Ur ring game-song is quoted in Wolfgang Schmeltzel's 'Quodlibet', 1544. 'Queen Mary' published in the *Journal of the English Folk Dance and Song Society*, June 1915 (but a variant still heard in Harrogate in 1959); 'Sweet Dolly' heard in the streets of Soho in 1907; the unnamed third song quoted above collected (by T. G. Stevenson) in *Scottish Ballads and Songs* (1859), but these lines and six others from the same song also collected from a Newfoundland fisherman in 1929, published in *Ballads and Sea Songs of Newfoundland*, Elisabeth Greenleaf and Grace Mansfield (1933, reprinted 1968).

> *Well she pulled off them high heeled shoes*
> *Made of Spanish leather . . .*

The shoes here represent the life of money, the official life, the regime of the husband; the gypsy's command that she discard them is a demand for an outward show of her rejection of all this and of her submission to him instead. Her compliance is inevitably an act of undress. Later in the song, the boss–husband tries for the same enacted surrender. He tries to make the heroine's removal of the gloves the signal of her submission to him, only to find that she makes their discarding the brazen signal of her refusal:

> *'Pull off, pull off them long blue gloves*
> *All made of the finest leather*
> *And give to me your lily-white hand*
> *And we'll go home together*
> *We'll both go home together.'*

> *Well she pulled off them long blue gloves*
> *All made of the finest leather*
> *Gave to him her lily-white hand*
> *And said goodbye forever . . .*

In Woody Guthrie's version of 'Gypsy Davey', which the young Bob Dylan who was writing 'Boots Of Spanish Leather' knew like the back of his lily-white hand, the heroine is commanded

> *'Take off, take off your buckskin gloves,*
> *Shoes of Spanish leather,*
> *And gimme the touch of your lily-white hand,*
> *We'll go back home together'*

and her defiance, indicated differently, is just as uncompromising:

> *'I'll not take off my buckskin gloves,*
> *Shoes of Spanish leather . . .'*

The ballad's heroine, at the same time as dealing in this symbolism of sex and power – and in doing so accepting responsibility for the momentous decision to abandon her baby – is a girl of only fifteen herself. Yet fifteen was the optimum age for a girl to marry in the Middle Ages, which is the period to which this traditional ballad harks back. It is the marriageable age in fairy tales too, including 'Cinderella', in which the shoe holds an equally strong sex-symbol role as the object of desire around which true love is measured by testing who fits, physically.[33]

In his inimitable, gently off-kilter way, Bob Dylan sets 'Cinderella' humming in the background of another song of his a couple of years later, as he finishes '4th Time Around' (another love triangle song) with these confusing signals of sexual symbolism:

---

33. Here lies another example of fairy tale and nursery rhyme coinciding – in the shared sexual significance of the shoe in 'Cinderella' and in the rhyme 'Cock A Doodle Do!': 'Cock a doodle do! / My dame has lost her shoe; / My master's lost his fiddle stick / And they don't know what to do!'

> *And when I was through*

(which is to say, through with *her*, the other woman)

> *I filled up my shoe*
> *And brought it to you.*
> *And you, you took me in . . .*
> *And I, I never took much,*
> *I never asked for your crutch,*
> *Now don't ask for mine.*

Similarly, 'Boots Of Spanish Leather', especially the loaded potency of its ending, would be less complex if it did not offer all these reverberations from children's song, fairy tale and an ancient ballad with a child–woman heroine.[34]

The 1963 'Seven Curses', as its title implies and its denouement makes clear, deals in spell-like invocations of numbers in a way that is modelled on the stuff of fairy tales, while in 'Motorpsycho Nightmare' when the psychotic farmer asks 'What do doctors / Know about farms, pray tell?' the narrator's enigmatic response picks up on the fairy tale milieu underlying that 'pray tell' and he answers 'I was born / At the bottom of a wishing well.'

Dylan playfully parodies children's counting-songs in 1964's 'I Shall Be Free No. 10', which is structured as a concrete protest against those who bow to an orderly counting up or down, such that the vowel sounds of the rhymes are predetermined. Dylan parades instead a comic use of any run of numbers that ends on the vowel sound he wants (and throws in an early allusion to the fairy tale 'Jack And The Beanstalk' in passing):

> *I said 'Fee, fie, fo, fum, Cassius Clay, here I come*
> *26, 27, 28, 29, I'm gonna make your face look just like mine*
> *Five, four, three, two, one, Cassius Clay you'd better run*
> *99, 100, 101, 102, your ma won't even recognise you'*
> *14, 15, 16, 17, 18, 19, gonna knock him clean right out of his spleen.*

Of course in that last line, it doesn't matter which 'teen' number he alights on for the rhyme with 'spleen', yet the gangling repeats set up a comic mantra of their own, capped by Dylan's bonus internal rhyme – 'clean' as well as 'spleen'. This stanza contains a further play with numbers, since their recitation all through the narrator's fantasy boxing-match makes them sound like a surreal version of another sort of counting, the referee's.

The last verse of 1964's 'Ballad In Plain D'

---

34. It may be that D. H. Lawrence was aware of the echoing of lines from 'Gypsy Davey / Blackjack Davey' in the children's street song/game he has Mrs Morel overhear in *Sons and Lovers*, since the theme of the ballad is one he seems especially drawn to. He explores it in his novella *The Virgin and the Gypsy* (1930).

In the collection *For What Time I Am in This World*, ed. Bill Usher (1977), there is a short section called 'Michael Cooney and Sam Hinton Talk 'Gypsy Davey'', in which Sam Hinton remarks at the end: 'One fascinating thing about folk music is that sometimes you find reference to old, old customs. In this song it's 'take off your shoes of Spanish leather' . . . if you look at the shoe as a symbol, it has strong sexual connotations. Not only that, but it's mentioned in the Old Testament. At one point Ruth and Naomi swear to the permanence of a bond by giving a shoe in exchange.'

Ah, my friends from the prison, they ask unto me
'How good, how good does it feel to be free?'
And I answer them most mysteriously
'Are birds free from the chains of the skyway?'

echoes the nursery rhyme 'The Man In The Wilderness' plainly and simply (sufficiently
that you can sing this nursery rhyme verse to his tune):

The man in the wilderness askéd of me
How many strawberries grew in the sea?
I answered him, as I thought good,
'As many red herrings as grow in the wood'

and in 'Restless Farewell', the regular way that each verse begins – 'Oh all the money
that in my whole life I did spend'; 'Oh ev'ry girl that ever I've touched', 'Oh ev'ry foe
that ever I faced' and so on – is modelled so closely upon a nursery rhyme (one
collected by Halliwell-Phillips in 1844, and which preserves the opening lines of a far
older song) that as with the example above, you can envisage Dylan singing the
nursery rhyme lines to his 'Restless Farewell' melody:

Of all the gay birds that e'er I did see
The owl is the fairest by far to me
For all day long she sits on a tree
And when the night comes, away flies she.

Dylan didn't appear to know, when asked to supply a rhyme for the word 'orange'
at a 1965 press conference, that the question was based on a nursery rhyme that
expresses (and answers) much the same challenge:

What is the rhyme for porringer?
The king he had a daughter fair
And he gave the prince of Orange her[35]

but he was alive to much of the nursery rhyme and fairy tale world at that time: alive
to its innate surreality and its capacity for holding fundamental truths, as well as being
quick to revivify its characters and bend them to his own requirements.

'Desolation Row' creates a world of mermaids and poisoning and of reciting the
alphabet, of figures from the circus and from melodramas of fairy tale proportions
(doesn't 'The Phantom of the Opera' rewrite 'Beauty and the Beast'?) and children's
folk heroes (Einstein wants to be Robin Hood). Cinderella is the cool, knowing star
of a whole verse: a heroine identified with the narrator, one of the sane figures in the
song's phantasmagoric pageant, one of those who has a hold on reality, because she
lives *on* Desolation Row. In the prose poem 'Alternatives To College' (1965) Dylan
mentions, or rather tags other people as, 'little bo peep' and 'simple simon' and refers

---

35.   Bob Dylan, press conference, San Francisco, 3/12/65, telecast on KQED-TV, *nia*. Either because he's 'a poet'
or because his press conference answers invite his being seen as a smartypants, he's suddenly challenged to offer a
rhyme for the word 'orange'. He's momentarily interested but offers no retort. That this orange is an old chestnut,
and Dylan only one more tricksy wordsmith to have it thrown at him, is clear not only from the nursery rhyme
just quoted, but from the fact that, as the Opies report, 'Money has been won and lost by those who, boasting of
their rhyming abilities, have been challenged with this word.'

twice to 'crippled mermaid', likely to be an allusion to the Hans Christian Andersen fairy tale 'The Little Mermaid', in which the heroine's fishtail is swapped, on account of love for a prince, for legs too painful to walk on.[36] In *Tarantula*, written 1965–66, Dylan alludes to the nursery rhymes 'Jack and Jill went up the hill' (with 'would you like to buy a pail? jack,'), 'Ring A Ring O'Roses' ('ring around the rosey') and 'The butcher, the baker, the candle-stick maker' (the unaltered 'candle-stick maker').

Even one of the great anthemic truths of Dylan's quintessential 1965 song 'Like A Rolling Stone' –

> *When you ain't got nothing, you got nothing to lose*

– had been said before, in the same direct way, in pre-nineteenth-century nursery rhyme:

> *There was an old woman*
> *And nothing she had*
> *And so this old woman*
> *Was said to be mad*
> *She'd nothing to eat*
> *She'd nothing to fear*
> *She'd nothing to lose . . .*

It's also so obvious that we're likely to miss it that Dylan's 'Like A Rolling Stone' is the only classic rock music record whose opening words are those of every classic fairy tale: 'Once upon a time . . .'

In 'Visions Of Johanna' the ladies play a version of the children's game Blind Man's Buff (nicely punned into 'blind man's bluff') and we meet Little Boy Blue's cousin 'little boy lost', while another of Dylan's white-heat hip period songs is of course called 'Just Like Tom Thumb's Blues' (in the eighteenth century nursery rhymes were sometimes called 'Tommy Thumb's songs'). The 1969 'Country Pie' parallels this identification of song narrator with nursery rhyme hero in the line 'Little Jack Horner's got nothing on me',[37] and the same song's 'Saddle me up a big white goose / Tie me on 'er and turn her loose' is in effect the song of Old Mother Goose, because

> *Old Mother Goose*
> *When she wanted to wander*

---

36.   This typical slice of mid-1960s Dylan prose-poetry is copyrighted 1985, upon its first inclusion in an official collection of his work (*Lyrics 1962–1985*) but even here, in this sloppy, history-rewriting assemblage, which places the Basement Tapes songs as if they are 1970s compositions, 'Alternatives To College' is admitted to belong between "Highway 61 Revisited" and "Blonde On Blonde". An additional Dylan reference to a nursery rhyme character has been inserted into the lyric of 'I Shall Be Free' as it appears in *Lyrics 1962–1985*: appended to the lines 'I chased me a woman up the hill / Right in the middle of an air-raid drill' is 'It was Little Bo Peep!' Perhaps there is an out-take version of the song on which this line occurs, from the "Freewheelin' Bob Dylan" sessions (many versions were recorded, 6/12/62), the *Broadside* sessions (he's known to have cut a version in March 1963) or as a Witmark demo (ditto April 1963); more likely is that the extra line was added in 1985 for the song's re-publication in *Lyrics 1962–1985*.

37.   Swift and Byron also made use of the figure of Little Jack Horner, and Thomas Love Peacock (in 'Melincourt', 1817) said the nursery rhyme provided 'one of the most splendid examples on record of the admirable practical doctrine of "taking care of number one"'. There is further comment re Little Jack Horner later, in relation to the subject of *pies*.

> *Would ride through the air*
> *On a very fine gander.*[38]

(Nursery rhymes are still called 'Mother Goose songs' in the USA.)

In the nursery rhyme 'There Was A Little Woman', the woman falls asleep, a pedlar cuts off most of her petticoats, and when she wakes she doesn't recognise herself:

> *She began to shiver*
> *And she began to shake;*
> *She began to shake*
> *And she began to cry*
> *'Lawk-a-mercy on me,*
> *This is none of I!'*

Then she decides that if it is her, her dog at home will wag his tail, and if it isn't her, he'll bark:

> *Home went the woman*
> *All in the dark*
> *Up got the little dog*
> *And he began to bark;*
> *He began to bark*
> *And she began to cry*
> *'Lawk-a-mercy on me,*
> *This is none of I!'*

Not only is the theme of being so disoriented that you can't even recognise yourself entirely Dylanesque, but the rhythms of these lines are born to rock'n'roll – just deliver them as Dylan might, with the syncopated strut that suggests itself – and in very specific ways they're reminiscent of both 'Down Along The Cove' (the last two lines of the nursery rhyme paralleled by its verse ending

> *She said 'Lord have mercy, honey*
> *I'm so glad you're my boy!')*

and, more thoroughly, the rattling comic narrative of the earlier 'Bob Dylan's New Orleans Rag'.

The name of the music publishing company Dylan formed in the early 1970s, Ram's Horn Music, recalls at least two different nursery rhymes: 'Can You Make Me A Cambric Shirt?', discussed above, and another quite separate nursery rhyme with many local British and American place-name variants, of which this is one example:

> *Little lad, little lad, where were you born?*
> *Far off in Lancashire under a thorn*
> *Where they sup buttermilk with a ram's horn.*

---

38. After the goose has laid the golden egg and this has been lost and recovered, the rhyme ends: 'And Old Mother Goose / The goose saddled soon / And mounting its back / Flew up to the moon.'

We shall have more buttermilk later. (I don't suggest that these nursery rhymes are the primary associations with the name 'Ram's Horn' for Dylan. It has its religious significance too. The Shofah, or Shophar, is the name of the ceremonial ram's horn sounded daily in the synagogue during the month of Elul and repeatedly on Rosh Hoshanah. It was used by the ancient Israelites as a warning or summons. When Joshua fit the battle of Jericho and the walls come tumbling down, the trumpets were, as the song says, rams' horns. Then of course there's the Memphis Minnie song that's a special favourite of Bob Dylan's, the well-known 'Me And My Shofar' . . .)

The centre of that tantalising 1973 song 'Nobody 'Cept You' (released for the first time on "Bootleg Series I–III" in 1991) concerns childhood play and dance and song:

> Used to play in the cemetery
> Dance and sing and run when I was a child

and in adding that

> . . . it never seemed strange

to be playing, singing and dancing in

> That place where the bones of life are piled

Dylan is speaking for all children here, not making himself out to be individually interesting or quirky. Graveyard play among children and young adults is so ancient a custom as to merge back into the ring-dances of antiquity. Heraklion Museum in Crete has a depiction of a ring-dance made in pottery in about 1350 BC; in the apocryphal 'Acts of St John' (written in the mid-second century AD) Christ takes the centre while the apostles dance round him. Such dancing and singing – called 'caroling', and not necessarily in a circle, but as likely by the early Middle Ages to be in a sort of wild, snaking procession (we also see a sort of caroling, with Dylan holding a trumpet, in *Renaldo & Clara*) – grew to be both a main activity on feast days and the bane of the church authorities. The church always opposed secular dancing – the ecclesiastical councils tried for over a thousand years to ban it – not only because such dancing was pagan and sexy (like the ring-games of the black children in 1930s and 1940s Mississippi described earlier) but because of the wide-spread habit of using graveyards to dance in. Etienne de Bourbon, made Inquisitor in about 1235, fulminated against 'those most sacrilegious persons who tread down the bodies of holy Christian folk in the churchyards'.

The ghostly presence hovers here of the ancient legend of 'The Devil At The Dance', in which a young girl disobeys her parents by attending such a graveyard dance. The Devil makes off with her. In one version they fly off leaving hoofprints on the rocks by the sea; in another version, to which Bob Dylan might be referring in 'Idiot Wind', they take off through the roof of a burning church.

> The priest wore black on the seventh day
> And sat stone-faced while the building burned.

When nursery rhyme meets the blues meets Dylan usage, the common-stock phrases can be hard to align. In a genre so riddled with sexual innuendo and double entendre as the blues, for example, it's sometimes hard to know whether a phrase or a line belongs in the nursery or the porn shop. Take 'Little Red Wagon'. One long-term Dylan collector tells me he was told years ago that this was a blues term for anal sex – which certainly puts a different perspective on Dylan's 'Buckets Of Rain' lyric

> *Little red wagon*
> *Little red bike*
> *I ain't no monkey but I know what I like*
> *I like the way you love me strong and slow . . .*

Actually, it is *not* a common blues term – there isn't a single 'little red wagon' in Michael Taft's blues lyrics concordance. 'Little Red Wagon' is, however, a recording by the supermodel-faced blues artist Georgia White, and by a happy coincidence the very next track she laid down at the same session is called 'Dan The Back Door Man'. On the other hand 'Won't You Ride In My Little Red Wagon?' by Hank Penny & His Radio Cowboys (featuring a young Boudleaux Bryant) was a western swing recording from 1939, and songs about anal intercourse didn't usually make it onto radio shows. That wasn't the meaning of the term 'western swing'.

'Little Red Wagon' is in any case the title of a Woody Guthrie song (in the 1987 'radio' interview on Guthrie's impact, cited earlier, Dylan mentions it as one he knew early on) and a well-known traditional phrase in children's song. It's here, for example, in an Indiana counting-and-rhyming version of the 'Skip To M'Lou' game where someone keeps dropping out of the circle:

> *Pig's in the parlor what'll I do? . . .*
> *Mice in the buttermilk two by two . . .*
> *Little red wagon painted blue*
> *Skip to m'lou my darling.*[39]

On the 1976 album "Desire", 'Sara' has Dylan recollecting wistfully a time when his own children were playing such a game and being told one of the Grimms' fairy tales: 'playin' leapfrog and hearin' about Snow White'.

You could add that in the line 'I left town at dawn, with Marcel and St. John . . .' on 1978's 'Where Are You Tonight? (Journey Through Dark Heat)' there lingers vestigially the idea of setting out on one's journey protected by the apostles, which is articulated in one of the two main nursery rhymes called 'Matthew Mark Luke and John' (the lovely Scottish version of which then runs 'Hau the horse till I loup on / Hau it fast an hau it sure / Till I get owre the misty muir'). You might feel too that the chorus of the 1984–86 'Brownsville Girl', rhyming 'Brownsville girl' with 'Browns-ville curl', is asking to be a reminder of the nursery rhyme attributed to Longfellow –

39. Georgia White: 'Little Red Wagon', Chicago, 7/12/36, "Georgia White", Jazz Society Records L-P19, Stockholm, 1966, and 'Dan The Back Door Man', Chicago, 7/12/36, not issued till "Georgia White: Complete Recordings . . . Vol. 2", Document DOCD-5302, Vienna, 1994. Hank Penny & His Radio Cowboys: 'Won't You Ride In My Little Red Wagon', Memphis, 4/7/39; "Tobacco State Swing", Rambler Records R 103, El Cerrito, California, 1980. The Georgia White song would suggest that the phrase 'that's your (little) red wagon' means 'that's your preoccupation, not mine', or, to use a more familiar and comparable expression, its metaphor also taken from the nursery, 'your hobby-horse'. This meaning is confirmed by the recording by Arthur Crudup: 'That's Your Red Wagon', Chicago, 22/10/45, not issued on LP until "Give Me A 32–20", Crown Prince Records IG-403, Stockholm, 1983.

'There was a little girl and she had a little curl / Right in the middle of her forehead' –
and that in the mid-1980s song 'When The Night Comes Falling From The Sky',
Dylan's line 'For the love of a lousy buck I've watched them die' offers an inflation-
linked twist on the nursery rhyme confession 'I love sixpence better than my life.' At
any rate there is nothing tenuous about the (mis)quoting of the nursery rhyme 'The
rose is red, the violet blue' in the dark last verse of 'Where Teardrops Fall' on 1989's
"Oh Mercy".

And then there are the Basement Tapes, flashes of which cannot but visit the
listener to "Under The Red Sky", and which often hover knowingly around the
nursery (Dylan says so explicitly of 'Quinn The Eskimo', telling interviewer Cameron
Crowe that 'I guess it was some kind of a nursery rhyme'), while 'See Ya Later
Alligator' mutating into 'See Ya Later Allen Ginsberg' is a vigorous example, caught
on tape, of the spontaneous wordplay process common to the playground. Likewise
Roy Kelly writes (in a long, excellent essay 'Bunch of Basement Noise', 1992) that
'Apple Suckling Tree' is 'nonsense lyrically . . . What, after all, is an apple suckling
tree?' and that the song seems 'like a twisted kind of nursery rhyme with a floppy rock
beat, a children's chant with a knowing, surrealist nod' – perhaps forgetting that
plenty of nursery rhymes are of 'a twisted kind' anyway, and often have knowing,
'surreal' qualities of their own.[40]

Kelly's main point is that 'musically it sounds . . . like Bob and The Band were
plugging into some subterranean source, a common flow of American music.' This is
close to reiterating what Greil Marcus wrote in the sleeve notes to the teasing sampler
of the same 1967 material issued as "The Basement Tapes" in 1975:

> they seem to leap out of a kaleidoscope of American music no less immediate for
> its venerability. Just below the surface . . . are the strange adventures and poker-
> face insanities chronicled in such standards as 'Froggy Went A Courtin'' . . . 'Cock
> Robin' . . . or a song called 'I Wish I Was A Mole In The Ground' . . . one side of
> 'The Basement Tapes' casts the shadow of such things and in turn is shadowed by
> them.

In other words, not only can Dylan's work give off the shadows of nursery rhyme
but the obverse can apply too. Consider the several 'Dylanesque' (and 'Blakeian')
shadows in this nursery rhyme:

> *There was a man of double deed*
> *Sowed his garden full of seed*
> *When the seed began to grow*
> *'Twas like a garden full of snow*
> *When the snow began to melt*
> *'Twas like a ship without a belt*
> *When the ship began to sail*
> *'Twas like a bird without a tail*
> *When the bird began to fly*
> *'Twas like an eagle in the sky*

40. Bob Dylan: interview published with "Biograph", 1985. Roy Kelly: 'Bunch of Basement Noise', *Telegraph*,
no. 43, Autumn 1992.

> *When the sky began to roar*
> *'Twas like a lion at the door*
> *When the door began to crack*
> *'Twas like a stick across my back*
> *When my back began to smart*
> *'Twas like a penknife in my heart*
> *When my heart began to bleed*
> *'Twas death, and death, and death indeed.*

The Opies comment on its being a 'rhyme of strange fascination; many people have recalled the awe-inspiring effect it had on them when children, and yet how they continued to want it repeated to them'. At any rate, it has the sort of poetic muscularity often found in pre-1980s Dylan, and to read it through is surely to be reminded of fragments of, at the very least, 'Farewell Angelina' and 'You're A Big Girl Now', as well as to savour an ending that seems to belong with 'Love Henry', a traditional song that seethes with adult themes of murder, betrayal and damnation, and that Dylan re-invests with all its latent intensity on 1993's "World Gone Wrong".

"Under The Red Sky"

It is unsurprising that in middle age, and with his own children grown, Bob Dylan should revisit the arena of the nursery rhyme and the fairy tale. Like me, he is the sort of age at which re-examinations of the central self, impelled by what is not called 'mid-life crisis' for nothing, become unavoidable and important. The song of the middle-aged adult is in the lines he addresses to himself in 1981's 'Need A Woman':

> *Searching for the truth the way God designed it*
> *When the real truth is that I may be afraid to find it*
>
> *. . . Whatever's waiting in the future*
> *Could be what you're running from in the past*[41]

The need to face this explains why so many people who in their twenties and thirties seem unfettered by their own childhoods have recourse to psychotherapy in their forties. To sort out – to understand, and so achieve harmony with – the inner being of the adult, you must return to the fundamental psychic haunts of the child.

This doesn't interest young adults – they are still fired up by the post-pubertal world in which it is glorious and empowering to be free of the parental bonds and actively engaged with the outside world in a time zone of infinite future. This is why young adults so often feel greater hostility to the middle-aged, who still appear to be cluttering up what the young see as their own rightful arena, than to the very old, who are both off on the sidelines and, commonly, altogether more serene, playful and candid than the grumpy and disappointed middle-aged. The song of the young adult is summed up by the I'm-not-even-twenty-five Bob Dylan of 'Positively 4th Street':

---

41.   These lines do not appear in the trivialised version of the lyric published in *Lyrics 1962–1985* but they are sung by Dylan on the excellent take issued belatedly on the "Bootleg Series I–III" box-set, 1991.

And though I know you're dissatisfied
With your position and your place
Don't you understand
It's not my problem . . .

It is the middle-aged adult, for whom much post-pubertal projection has come to nothing, who sees that many assumptions long clung to have been delusions and that many struggles ostensibly with the outside world are in truth unresolved ones within, and who feels that time is suddenly short. This is the person for whom it makes deep, imperative sense – the child being father to the man – to rewalk the hallways of one's earliest years, in which inner strengths and fears first took shape.

It is these that fairy tales address and nursery rhymes re-echo, as is confirmed by the wealth of material on fairy tale published in the field of psychology. Hence, too, the special emphasis on the sexual psychology of the fairy tale in the American poet Anne Sexton's book *Transformations*, which rewrites some of the Brothers Grimm stories in poetry, including 'Snow White' – in which she stresses the phallic significance of the dwarves, calling them 'those little hot dogs' – and 'The Frog Prince' (a re-telling of the Grimms' 'The Frog King'), in which she writes that

At the feel of the frog
the touch-me-nots explode
like electric slugs . . .
Frog is my father's genitals.[42]

To each his own: what Bob Dylan the man and Bob Dylan the artist choose to make of the fairy tale and nursery rhyme literature may well be two different things, and it's no part of my purpose to speculate on the former. It's enough to say that it is right and unsurprising that it's the middle-aged Dylan who creates an album like "Under The Red Sky", which steps so merrily and resourcefully into the fairy tale and nursery rhyme arena: unafraid to use its 'simple' language straightfowardly but far more often imbuing it with – releasing it into – new shapes and scenes and resonances from his own intelligent imagination.

How much he uses! How much he knows! This isn't a case of throwing in a few obvious references to, and quotes from, nursery rhymes as well and widely known as 'Mary Had A Little Lamb' and 'Sing A Song Of Sixpence', as he does when he gives 'Jack Frost' a co-producer's credit for the album. Bob Dylan is either inwardly familiar with, or has researched energetically into, a huge number of nursery rhymes and children's game-songs. (He has certainly obliged me to do likewise to run along behind

---

42. *Transformations*, Anne Sexton, 1971. The title of her first book of poetry, *To Bedlam and Part Way Back* (1960), echoes the nursery rhyme 'How Many Miles To Babylon?', as Dylan echoes it in 'God Knows' on "Under The Red Sky" (discussed below). Sexton, born in 1928, was part of a Boston literary scene in the late 1950s that included Robert Lowell, Sylvia Plath, Archibald MacLeish and Robert Frost. She was sometimes a patient at the same hospital to which Robert Lowell went periodically when he was manic and in which Sylvia Plath spent four months in the late 1950s. Both women were pupils of Lowell and met occasionally (as 'suicides sometimes meet', in Sexton's phrase), to drink triple martinis. Poet and Plath biographer Anne Stevenson suggests that Sexton's success in writing confessional poetry may have prompted Plath's own use of private material in her work. Both did commit suicide, Plath in 1963 and Sexton in 1977. She has been at the centre of a recent controversy because tapes made by her psychotherapist have been made available to a biographer: not a form of bootlegging to which Bob Dylan has been subject, though perhaps only because he avoids psychotherapy.

him.) He seems to have poked into as many corner cupboards of the genre as he has in the pre-war acoustic blues. The evidence is scattered like a paperchase all across the lyrics of "Under The Red Sky".

Time and again, the most innocuous and the most striking phrases Bob Dylan sings here, the most modestly slipped-in and the most 'Dylanesque', prove verbatim quotations from nursery rhymes and game-songs most of us don't know. These run from 'there was a man who had no eyes' to 'thank you for my tea' and from 'a stick in his hand' to 'eat off his head'. Other allusions prove non-verbatim only because Dylan has deftly reversed them, as with 'that soft silky skin' and 'the barn is full of the bull'.

This would be all well and good, but not especially valuable, if it were no more than a game, though the element of play involved – even the suspicion that it might have started out as a game on Dylan's part – is attractive, and of course accords with the spirit of the genre itself. What makes "Under The Red Sky" more satisfying than that is that Dylan goes beyond *knowing* a great deal of nursery rhyme. He respects its capacity to be numinous and he gives the poet within him free rein to explore it.

As we saw in the case of 'I Saw A Peacock With A Fiery Tail', the power and poetry of nursery rhyme language is often put to the service of trickery, the solving of which has a strongly bathetic effect as the poetic evaporates into the mundane. One of the things Dylan does so marvellously on this album is to reoccupy the innate poetry, freeing it from its servitude to cheap trickery, letting it fly off as it might in directions suggested by Dylan's own feeling for it.

This is evident, for example, in 'Handy Dandy', one of the album's best songs, where he takes some of the inherently magical language deployed in a nursery rhyme riddle, to which the solution is merely 'an egg', and allows it freer rein on its mystical level. The riddle goes like this:

> *In marble walls as white as milk*
> *Lined with a skin as soft as silk*
> *Within a fountain crystal clear*
> *A golden apple doth appear.*
> *No doors there are to this stronghold,*
> *Yet thieves break in and steal the gold.*

Reoccupied by the lyric of 'Handy Dandy', the numinous charge of this language is retained and extended in Dylan's

> *He got that clear crystal fountain*
> *He got that soft silky skin*
> *He got that fortress on the mountain*
> *With no doors, no windows so no thieves can break in.*

I love what he does here. It's the same side to Dylan's genius that we encounter when, time and again, he takes a phrase from the Bible, cuts to its core and colloquialises it.[43] Here, paring the nursey rhyme down from six lines to four, he strips away the old

---

43.   In fact there is a biblical connection here: the nursery rhyme itself echoes a passage from Christ's Sermon on the Mount, as Dylan will certainly know. In Matthew 6:19–22, Christ's words are given as: 'Lay not up for

Classical Greekery – the marble walls, the golden apple – and transforms what's left from florid or portentous Victorian formalism into a poetry that combines mystic potency with the rhythms and cadence of street-talk. So the vicarishly nineteenth-century versifying tone of

> *Within a fountain crystal clear*

is turned around (literally, with the last three words) into the street-smart, pretend inarticulacy of

> *He got that clear crystal fountain;*

the purring poesy of

> *Lined with a skin as soft as silk*

is clipped to the conversational

> *He got that soft silky skin;*

and the conclusion

> *No doors there are to this stronghold,*
> *Yet thieves break in and steal the gold*

with its oversupervising 'Yet' and its earthbound explanation for the break-in, is doubly transformed by Dylan. The stronghold/fortress soars into the mountains, magnifying the scale of the scenario and intensifying our sense of the isolation of this unspecified 'He'. At the same time – by abolishing the 'gold', by making the break-in feared instead of fact, by increasing the check-list of security provisions and by the effect of that nervy rhythm in describing them

> *(he got that . . . he got that . . . he got that . . . ,*

which had been street-easy before, now echoes as nervily as

> *no doors, no windows . . . no thieves)*

– by all these touches, Dylan gives *his* conclusion a modern sensibility, evoking the paranoia at the heart of the re-written scenario, and without one supervisory word pointing up its lonely madness:

> *He got that clear crystal fountain*
> *He got that soft silky skin*
> *He got that fortress on the mountain*
> *With no doors, no windows so no thieves can break in.*

While dismantling the riddle of the rhyme, Dylan has given it the mystery of art.

In the same song, he picks up 'a basket of flowers' from a nursery rhyme (cited in discussing the album's title-song, 'Under The Red Sky', below) and he snatches a stick

---

yourselves treasures on earth, where moth and rust doth corrupt, and where thieves break through and steal: But lay up for yourselves treasures in heaven, where neither moth nor rust doth corrupt, and where thieves do not break through and steal: For where your treasure is, there will your heart be also.' (This is reiterated more briefly in Luke 12.)

from another riddle, one of the nursery rhyme riddles beginning 'Riddle me riddle me ree':

> *Riddle me, riddle me ree*
> *A little man in a tree*
> *A stick in his hand*
> *A stone in his throat*
> *(If you read me this riddle*
> *I'll give you a groat).*

The Opies say that a number of riddles have been based on the imagery of 'a stick in his hand, a stone in his throat', the solution being either a cherry (as here) or the hawthorn berry. Bob Dylan drops this in in passing, as the marvellously dodgy hero 'Handy Dandy' is chatting someone up with

> *. . . a stick in his hand and a pocket full of money.*

It's one of those admirable, quiet, intelligent achievements of Dylan's: he slips in this obscure, innocuous quotation; he re-writes it in such a way as to satisfy us by its twisted echo of the original – both catalogue 'a stick in his hand' and a something else, and both mention money; and he puts his quotation and his re-write in the service of inventive depiction. Handy Dandy, an utterly authentic Dylan character, as *Paris, Texas* as the narrator of 'Clothes Line', as laconic as Hoagy Carmichael, strolls through this wonderful, good-natured song enigmatically yet as recognisable as any Hollywooden hero. As he finishes his drink, gets up from the table and says 'OK boys I'll see you tomorrow', we realise that there's a final parallel between the riddle-me-ree verse and what Dylan has done with it: the central figure in each demands to be explained. Dylan's is the better riddle.

The listener's 'Who *is* this?' is unanswered, but dissatisfaction at the lack of a clear answer is counter-balanced by the sheer pleasure offered by this pay-off line – a fourfold pleasure, coming from savouring the image evoked, the words chosen, the demands these make so gleefully upon the singer's skill in timing their delivery *and* Dylan's absolute success in meeting these demands. All these points, about the pictures you get from the song and about the pleasures of the words and of their high-wire delivery, are met also in this single confidently invented, supremely free-form line:

> *Sitting with a girl named Nancy in a garden feelin' kind of lazy.*

For all this audacity, all its refreshing sunlit glimpses – for all its authenticity as a Bob Dylan song – it's one people don't altogether embrace. The chorus is to blame. No one likes a line such as 'Handy Dandy, just like sugar and candy' (it's the tautology I dislike most). It's there because it's part of the song's traditional baggage, and Dylan leaves it in because he's feelin' kind of lazy.

'Handy Dandy' is a game and a rhyme. The rhyme is one of those which, like 'Humpty Dumpty', has a Scandinavian equivalent and is of a type that has close equivalents all over northern Europe. In some cases what seems a nonsense rhyme in one language ('Jeck og Jill' in Danish) makes sense in another. Some may result from long oral traditions, others from direct translations. The game is one in which a small object is juggled from hand to hand and then the rhyme is said as you're challenged to guess which hand it's in.

This is so old that it was already known before the creator of *Piers Plowman*, William Langland, wrote of 'his handidandi' in 1362. Variants include

> *Handy dandy, riddledy ro*
> *Which hand will you have, high or low?*

and

> *Handy pandy, Sugary candy*
> *Which will you have?*

and

> *Handy-dandy, Jack-a-dandy*
> *Which good hand will you have?*[44]

(I picture Bob Dylan here, his right hand drawin' back, while his left hand advances.) The same rhyme was quoted by George Chapman in his play *The Blinde Begger of Alexandria* in 1598:

> *handy dandy prickly prandy, which hand will you haue?*[45]

and referred to in this crucial speech in *King Lear*:

> Lear: *Handy dandy, prickly prandy . . . What, art mad? A man may see how this world goes without eyes.*

(Or, as someone once put it, 'you don't need a weatherman to know which way the wind blows'.)

> *Look with thine ears: see how yond justice rails upon yond simple thief. Hark, in thine ear: change places, and, handy-dandy, which is the justice, which is the thief?*

(Another 'Dylanesque' question, this.)

As Andrew Muir noted, Lear's speech here is part of the scene described by Hugh Haunton in *The Chatto Book of Nonsense Poetry* as having

> as vivid a place in the history of nonsense as in that of madness. The dialogue is shot through with queer, garbled, oracular language, and shifts back and forth between reason and madness, pathos and absurdity. It's not only the most vivid representation of the fool in literature, but in its vision of violent social upheaval

---

44.   There is also a rhyme, not associated with the game, that Pope and Carey alluded to when attacking the syrupy poetry of their contemporary Ambrose Philips: 'Handy spandy, Jack-a-Dandy / Loves plum cake and sugar candy / He bought some at a grocer's shop / And out he came, hop, hop, hop, hop.' A variant begins 'Namby pamby Jack-a-Dandy'. 'Namby pamby' was Pope and Carey's nickname for Philips, and at the top of their own poem of that name they quoted another nursery rhyme as follows: 'Nauty pauty, Jack-a-Dandy / Stole a piece of Sugar-Candy / From the Grocer's Shoppy-shop / And away did Hoppy-hop.' Not that these antecedents improve Dylan's chorus one jot, jot, jot.

45.   Chapman, a dramatist and translator, and contemporary of Shakespeare, is now best known for his great translation of Homer.

and broken authority suggests that through the language of madness and adopted madness the characters make touch with truths and feelings outside the pale of their normal language. What they say in their terrible crisis makes sense . . . but it takes a route that zigzags giddily across the border with nonsense.[46]

Stripped of that pain, more Edward Lear than King, Dylan's 'Handy Dandy' also gives us broken soundbites that make no sense yet make perfect sense, and glimpses of characters who challenge each other with crazy truths, as it takes us on a route that zigzags giddily across the border with nonsense.

Would that all the songs on the album worked this well. The mere inclusion of 'Born In Time' disrupts. It belongs to another album. "Empire Burlesque", perhaps. Being charitable, "Knocked Out Loaded". At any rate it has nothing to do with the use of nursery rhyme or fairy tale, and little to do with anything beyond the marketing notion that there ought to be a Seductive Big Ballad on each Bob Dylan album. It has two wonderful lines – 'you're comin' through to me in black and white', 'you're blowin' down a shaky street' – but in the end its opaqueness exasperates and smacks of pretension: not only does the title provoke the question 'Born in time for what?' and then fail to answer it, but it leaves you feeling that Bob Dylan doesn't know what he means either. The fairy tale that comes to mind here is 'The Emperor's New Clothes'. Pity that little boy wasn't in the studio to tell Bob to come off it. Instead we have the betraying declamatory tone that is never necessary when a Dylan song is real. 'Born In Time' is a slippery 'I'll Remember You'.

'TV Talkin' Song' is also a misfit here, except in the sense that it tells a silly story, and refers to a medium that has to some extent replaced the storybook for today's children.[47] The ending, as a 'twist', is both bathetic and unoriginal. We've heard it before, and even if we hadn't we could still see it coming. One of the times it's been done before is in 'Black Diamond Bay': but whereas the switch from real life to 'seeing it on TV' in that song gives a jolt of perspective and shows (not asserts, but shows) how badly, how inhumanely TV distances us from reality, in 'TV Talkin' Song' no shift of perspective is achieved, and the theme that TV absorbs all into its maw, even an anti-TV tirade, is half-heartedly put forward. It also prompts the question: Isn't Dylan disqualified from making this complaint by his own declining capacity for resisting TV's pressures? You can quite see him making 'TV Talkin' Song' a single and watching the video of it on MTV. This would make it a self-reflexive text, of course, but he would also be having his cake and eating it too.

'2 x 2', with its refreshingly unDylanish, post-Beatleish instrumental intro, is perfectly at home on "Under The Red Sky": it is a simple counting-song (of the sort

---

46.   Andrew Muir, *Homer, the slut*, no. 2, January 1991, quoting from *The Chatto Book of Nonsense Poetry*, ed. Hugh Haunton (1988).

47.   Except that the earlier Dylan song that 'TV Talkin' Song' reminds us of, aside from the infinitely superior 'Subterranean Homesick Blues' (and, insofar as they also deal with the theme of television, 'Talking John Birch Society Blues' and 'I Shall Be Free'), is 'The Drifter's Escape': and, as an earlier chapter argued, 'The Drifter's Escape' is itself reminiscent of a particular scene in that supreme classic of children's story *Alice Through the Looking-Glass* (in which, to quote Hugh Haunton again, 'dialogue is shot through with queer, garbled, oracular language, and shifts back and forth between reason and madness, pathos and absurdity'). 'TV Talkin' Song' and 'The Drifter's Escape' resemble each other in that one has 'this is ten times worse . . . attendant and the nurse' while the other has 'situation's worse . . . send for the nurse'; and one has 'Outside the crowd was stirring' where the other has 'you could feel it in the crowd'.

Dylan parodies in 'I Shall Be Free No. 10'), requiring for that very reason little comment. Its very title is a clear echo of the well-known children's song 'The Animals Went In Two By Two,' which is in turn the story of Noah's ark, told in Genesis 6:19–7:9, a connection Dylan re-articulates in the darker couplet 'Two by two they step into the ark / Two by two they step in the dark'. Most flaccid line in the song is 'Six by six, they were playing for tricks'; best line is the funny, truthful 'Nine by nine they drank the wine / Ten by ten, they drank it again'. The song is inevitably reminiscent, too, of the nursery rhyme counting-song 'This Old Man', which Dylan went on to record the year after "Under The Red Sky" for an album in support of the Pediatric AIDS Foundation.[48]

'Wiggle Wiggle', 'Unbelievable' and 'God Knows', the bleary mediocrities of the "Under The Red Sky" collection, nonetheless entwine themselves in the nursery rhyme corpus enough to invite a little exegesis.

'Unbelievable', like 'Handy Dandy', raids two different tricksy nursery rhymes, one a riddle and the other a hand-game (like handy dandy). Again, Dylan jettisons the 'puzzles' but retains the characters. Unlike with 'Handy Dandy', he does very little with them beyond this momentary recycling: certainly not enough to make 'Unbelievable' a good song or compensate in lyric interest for its musical tedium. The riddle is 'There Was A Man Who Had No Eyes':

> *There was a man who had no eyes*
> *He went abroad to view the skies*
> *He saw a tree with apples on it*
> *He took no apples off, yet left no apples on it*

(the solution is that he has one eye, the tree has two apples and he takes one off) while 'Lady, Lady in the Land' is 'an infant amusement' or playground game, one of an almost infinite number of variants stretching back probably for millennia and listed in print at least as early as 1534 (by Rabelais), the object of which is explained by the rhyme itself:

> *Lady, Lady in the land*
> *Can you bear a tickly hand?*
> *If you laugh or if you smile*
> *You'll ne'er be lady in the land.*

Dylan marries these two up, so that

> *Once there was a man who had no eyes*
> *Every lady in the land told him lies,*

a combination that might also be said to refer back to Lear's speech incorporating the man without eyes quoted earlier. Dylan's lines are an exaggeration of Lear's position: it was not every lady who told him lies, the point about Cordelia being that she couldn't tell the lies demanded of her by Lear himself. The best small thing Dylan does here is to take the second line from the riddle about the man with no eyes:

48. Bob Dylan: 'This Old Man', Malibu, California, early 1991; "Disney For Children", Disney Records 60616–2, Los Angeles, 1991.

He went abroad to view the skies

(as the writer of the album's title track does) and rewrites it. As we know, the man in the riddle actually has one eye, so he can go out and 'view the skies'. The man in Dylan's song really has no eyes, and Dylan evokes his greater helplessness in the re-write, in which

He stood beneath the silver skies,

to which Dylan adds a rewritten fragment from yet another nursery rhyme, changing Little Bo Peep's empathetic pain felt for her regained but wounded sheep –

She found them indeed but it made her heart bleed
For they'd left their tails behind them –

into the pain the man with no eyes feels for his wounded self:

He stood beneath the silver skies
And his heart began to bleed.

Dylan's

You go north and you go south
Just like bait in the fish's mouth,

from earlier in the song, is a twisted twisting of another game, 'King William', a kissing-game in which the person who is 'it' must

Choose to the east and choose to the west
Choose the one that you love best.[49]

This is strikingly similar to 'Little Sally Walker', the game played by the black girls in the Mississippi Delta and witnessed by Alan Lomax in the 1940s.

'Wiggle Wiggle', a title about as alluring as 'Woogie Boogie' or 'Emotionally Yours', incorporates fleeting moments from several different variants of a similar singing-game called 'Kentucky' that, while retaining some mention of the early 1920s dance, the Shimmy, inexplicably 'swept the country [Britain] with the speed of a pop song in the mid-1960s', and enjoyed similar transatlantic success, according to the Opies. This, stripped down melodically almost to a one-note chant, includes the lines

Rumble to the bottom, rumble to the top . . .
Twisty twisty twisty, twisty all around . . .
Oh shake it, baby shake it, shake it if you can

followed by the splendid

Shake it like a milkshake and drink it like a man.

This might indicate that the Sam Cooke song 'Shake', from which 'Wiggle Wiggle' has taken the line 'Shakin' like a bowl of soup', itself owes something to this piece of

---

49.   These lines are followed immediately by 'If she's not here to take her part / Choose another with all your heart': sentiments echoed in the 1970s by Stephen Stills' refrain 'If you can't be with the one you love, love the one you're with.' (Stephen Stills: 'Love The One You're With', *nia*, 1970, Atlantic Records 2778, New York [2091046, London], 1971.)

communal juvenilia. Then there's a Hank Ballard & The Midnighters single from 1954, 'Sexy Ways', that seems to embrace the singing-game song and prefigure 'Wiggle Wiggle' rather more:

> *Wiggle wiggle wiggle wiggle*
> *I just love your sexy ways*
> *Upside down, all around*
> *Any old way, just pound pound pound.*[50]

These resemblances don't stop 'Wiggle Wiggle' being, like 'Unbelievable', a slice of off-the-shelf rockism, compared to which Sam Cooke's record is philosophy in motion and Hank Ballard's a fresh and vibrant masterpiece. "Under The Red Sky" co-producer Don Was claimed in an interview that 'Wiggle Wiggle' is Dylan writing 'Tutti Frutti'.[51] This is stoned dithyrambling. The Dylan song is retro, stale, guarded *and* uninventive, where Little Richard invented something exciting that was radical, fresh and open. 'Wiggle Wiggle' is to 'Tutti Frutti' as Kenny Ball is to Louis Armstrong.

Nor is 'Wiggle Wiggle' much improved by its nod towards one of several nursery rhymes called 'Little Robin Redbreast':

> *Little Robin Redbreast*
> *Sat upon a rail*
> *Niddle noddle went his head*
> *Wiggle waggle went his tail,*

which survives from older, ruder versions.

Dylan also gives a nod to his own earlier 'children's song', 'Man Gave Names To All The Animals'. Where that song ends by forbearing to name the last animal as the snake, 'Wiggle Wiggle', having a snake at the end too, hisses the word out loud, its final line being

> *Wiggle like a big fat sssnake.*[52]

---

50. Sam Cooke: 'Shake', *nia*, RCA Victor 47–8486, New York [RCA 1436, London], 1965. Hank Ballard & The Midnighters: 'Sexy Ways', Cincinnati, 24/4/54, Federal Records 12185, Cincinnati, 1954.
   Dylan's exact title first belonged to an obscure 'commercial' pop-rock single by unfamous vocal group the Accents, dating from 1958, itself a tired and nondescript copy of the pop classic 'Little Bitty Pretty One' and stressing the primacy of womanly wiggling over beauty and fine clothes ('so wiggle wiggle wiggle for me'). Written by group member Robert Draper Jr, the record scraped up to no. 51 in the US Hot 100. (The Accents: 'Wiggle Wiggle', NYC, 1958, Brunswick Records 55100, New York [Coral Records Q 72351, London], 1958; CD-reissued "The Golden Age Of American Rock'n'Roll Volume 5", Ace Records CDCHD 600, London, 1995.)

51. Don Was, Los Angeles, 15/10/90; interview in *Telegraph*, no. 37, Winter 1990.

52. While 'The Drifter's Escape' is reminiscent of the poem about Tweedledum and Tweedledee in *Alice Through the Looking-Glass*, so in forbearing to name the snake at the end, 'Man Gave Names To All The Animals' is reminiscent of a poem in *Alice's Adventures in Wonderland*, ''Tis The Voice Of The Lobster' (a parody of Isaac Watts' ''Tis The Voice of a Sluggard'). In Carroll's first edition this was only six lines but in later editions came the longer version, which ends:

> *. . . the Owl and the Panther were sharing a pie.*
> *The Panther took pie-crust, and gravy, and meat,*
> *While the Owl had the dish as its share of the treat.*
> *When the pie was all finished, the Owl, as a boon,*
> *Was kindly permitted to pocket the spoon;*
> *While the Panther received knife and fork with a growl,*
> *And concluded the banquet –*

Where the unnamed snake of 'Man Gave Names To All The Animals' functions as religious symbol, here it is sexual symbolism that rears up, making the naming seem emphatic.

This phallic import needn't be exclusive. There's also something Beatrix Potter-like about 'wiggle like a big fat snake', and perhaps a propensity for sudden paw-swipes of black humour is common to both the Potter stories and this song. But in the end, the song and its recording are failures: a lyric anyone could write (the problem would be wanting to) and the sort of weary rockism you might hope to avoid in the back room of your local pub.

'God Knows' is weary too. Even the pun of its title is taken off the peg from Joseph Heller's 1984 novel, *God Knows*. The song's folksy, Jesse Fullerish moments of savoured gauche buoyancy are weighed down by the harsh sound and declamatory tone of the rest, and trivialised by Dylan's decision to take the easy option and make it yet another list-song. God knows this, God knows that, God knows the other, God knows it's a struggle to fill out an album these days. It isn't a song that needed to be written, nor has it any authentic inconsequential flash. It's one of those the aficionado tries to like, over and over again, but cannot. Consider what happens during Dylan's 1994 Woodstock II performance: from the opening, which is 'Jokerman', right through till the end of 'It's All Over Now, Baby Blue' this is magnificent, fully engaged Dylan. He starts into 'God Knows' – and we all lose interest, starting with the composer. It's a song without resonance, without heart or soul, a professional songwriter's filler. Not even what the Opies call the 'inherent mystery of the lines' that are warped and weaved in from the nursery rhyme 'How Many Miles To Babylon?', one of the most popular lullabies of the past four hundred years, can give it allure.

The rhyme itself, which once had a game attached to it, goes:

> *How many miles to Babylon?*
> *Three score miles and ten.*
> *Can I get there by candle-light?*
> *Yes, and back again.*
> *If your heels are nimble and light,*
> *You may get there by candle-light.*[53]

(A longer Scottish version includes a couplet that will appeal to the Dylan of 'Romance In Durango', 'Spanish Is The Loving Tongue' and 'Seven Curses':

> *Will I get there by candle-light?*
> *If your horse be good and your spurs be bright.*)

---

53.   The Opies write: 'Babylon, it has been suggested, is a corruption of Babyland. More probably it is the far-away luxurious city of early seventeenth-century usage. [Have these people never heard of the biblical Babylon?] "Can I get there by candle-light" was a saying common in Elizabethan times . . . Sir Huon of Bordeaux, Puck explains to Dan, succeeded King Oberon, but he was lost on the road to Babylon.

> *'Have you ever heard, "How many miles to Babylon"?'*
> *'Of course,' says Dan flushing.*
> *'Well, Sir Huon was young when that song was new.''*

(The Opies quoting from Shakespeare's *A Midsummer Night's Dream*.) There is another nursery rhyme beginning 'There was a man of Babylon', though this is a variant of 'There was a man of Thessaly', a nonsense rhyme, and may be confused with the ballad 'The godly and constante wyse Susanna', printed 1562–63, which begins with the similar 'There dwelt a man in Babylon', a line quoted in *Twelfth Night*.

Dylan's song fades out on this:

> *God knows there's a heaven,*
> *God knows it's out of sight*
> *God knows we can get all the way from here to there*
> *If we have to walk a million miles by candle-light*
> *God knows there's an answer . . .*

Another nursery rhyme dances on its heels in the background of the lullaby: 'Jack be nimble, Jack be quick / Jack jump over a candle-stick'. Alongside all this elderly language Dylan deliberately offers the risible modernism of 'out of sight', not merely as crude pun but to suggest its aptness to the question of what we know of what God knows; yet the effect is strained, drawing attention to itself as conscious effort out of proportion to any achievement in meaning. Dylan has done this before, and managed it better, in his conjunction of Christ and 'where He's coming from' on 1979's 'Gonna Change My Way Of Thinking' (another song hard to warm to).

The nursery rhyme's opening lines,

> *How many miles to Babylon?*
> *Three score miles and ten.*

suggest that the question is 'How long is a life?', with Babylon standing for death. In 'God Knows' matters of life and death are raised more insistently yet so shabbily as to be discountable. It's one of those songs where Dylan resorts to fulminating about the apocalypse without drawing you in to any sense of real life first, so that there's no aura of impending anything: nothing alive in the beginning in the world of this song, no one for this sword of Damocles to fall on. There's just bitter, dusty old Preacher Bob grinding his teeth and posturing. Even the one glimmer of living observation in the song turns out to be posited the less satisfying way round.

> *God knows the secrets of your heart*
> *He'll tell them to you when you're asleep,*

the one moment that gives the listener a picture, is a disappointment after the superior mishearing of one's first encounter with the song:

> *God knows the secrets of your heart*
> *You tell them to Him when you're asleep.*

(The first line here is a re-write of Psalms 44:21, in which God 'knoweth the secrets of the heart'.)

There's no further glimmer of life anywhere in the song. Dylan grunts out the formulaic dark mutterings – 'God knows there's gonna be no more water / But fire next time' – and is content to match that quotation with more prosaic cliché. 'God knows you ain't gonna be taking / Nothing with you when you go.' God knows this is wretched non-writing, even if Bob Dylan doesn't.

A much better, if patchy, song is '10,000 Men', discussed as a blues in an earlier chapter. It contains two lines taken straight from the poetry of nursery rhyme, the one as quiet and nondescript as the other is, in the context Dylan gives it, grotesque and bizarre.

The quiet-as-anonymous 'thank you for my tea' at the end of the song,

> *Baby, thank you for my tea*
> *It's really so sweet of you to be so nice to me,*

may not be much of a line in itself but it's a quietly clever fusion of blues and nursery rhyme worlds. There's a common-stock blues couplet, found for instance in Dylan's old friend Henry Thomas' beautiful, affecting 'Don't Ease Me In' (recorded at the same session as his 'Fishing Blues'), in which

> *She brings me coffee and she brings me tea*
> *She brings me everything but the jailhouse key*[54]

so that for the blues aficionado 'Thank you for my tea' is a recognisably apt remark to hear addressed to the visitor in a blues song (especially one about ten thousand men who are 'just out of jail', sung by a narrator who has women standing at his window and sweeping his room) while in a 'Little Robin Redbreast' nursery rhyme that is apparently quite separate from the one that Dylan almost quotes from in 'Wiggle Wiggle', we find another visitor and the 'Dylan line' verbatim:

> *Little Robin Redbreast*
> *Came to visit me*
> *This is what he whistled*
> *'Thank you for my tea.'*

In strong contrast, Dylan imports into an earlier part of his song a phrase that is also straight from a nursery rhyme but which, while it is explicable, mild and unexceptional in context, becomes, plucked out of context and released like a wild card into the realms of free play, so bizarre that people commenting on the album tend to pick it out as one of Bob Dylan's truly weirdest moments. The phrase is 'eat off his head', and here it is in its nursery rhyme context:

> *A long-tail'd pig*
> *Or a short-tail'd pig*
> *Or a pig without any tail*
> *A boar-pig or a sow-pig*
> *Or a pig with a curly tail*
> *Take hold of the tail and eat off his head*
> *And then you'll be sure the pig hog is dead.*

This nursery rhyme is actually a street-vendor's cry from the eighteenth century, when sellers with trays of little sweetmeat pigs were common. When Tom Tom the piper's son stole a pig and away he run, it was this sort of pig he stole, not a real one. The clinching salesman's couplet at the end is designed to charm, not frighten, the children.

54. Henry Thomas: 'Don't Ease Me In', Chicago, 13/6/28; "Really! The Country Blues", Origin Jazz Library OJL-2, New York, c. 1961. The same first line and an almost identical matching line can also be found for example on Sam Collins: 'The Jail House Blues', Richmond, Indiana, or Chicago, c. 23/4/27, issued same LP.

Dylan's is a terrific stealing of this pig. He takes it and runs it right inside the madness of a luridly jealous mind:

> *Hey! Who could your lover be?*
> *Let me eat off his head so you can really see.*

It's a reversal as neat as it is bizarre to shift eating off his head so you can 'be sure the pig hog is dead' to eating off his head 'so you can really see' who he is underneath, which, as it were, turns on its head the most basic notion of how to tell one person from another. (In fact Dylan makes a different reversal from the same nursery rhyme decades earlier, in *Tarantula*, in which 'the pig jumps on him [the good Samaritan] & starts eating his face'.)

Why someone with ten thousand women in his room should be jealous of his visitor's lover is as unexplained as everything else in this disjunctive narrative. Inasmuch as the women are

> *Spilling my buttermilk, sweeping it up with a broom*

they are also brushing the nursery rhyme world, in which

> *Milkman, milkman, where have you been?*
> *In Buttermilk Channel up to my chin*
> *I spilt my milk and I spoilt my clothes.*

That last line is almost replicated, in its phrasing and its rhythmic thrust, by one in the "Oh Mercy" song 'Where Teardrops Fall':

> *I've torn my clothes and I've drained the cup,*

while that 'Buttermilk Channel' might remind us too of a feature in an earlier 1980s Dylan song, 'the Buttermilk Hills', whose silence sounds like 'a voice cryin' "Daddy"'.[55] A woman sweeping a room with a broom also occurs in the long nursery rhyme 'Two Little Kittens', in which

> *The old woman seized her sweeping broom*
> *And swept the two kittens right out of the room.*

And so to 'Cat's In The Well', already discussed as a song of barnyard apocalypse (alongside Howlin' Wolf's 'Tail Dragger') in an earlier chapter:

---

55. 'Buttermilk Hill' is also a traditional Irish song, believed to have the same origin as 'Johnny I Hardly Knew Ye', according to the Canadian group the Travellers, label-mates of Dylan in 1962, who were recorded performing the song in the Soviet Union that year. The Travellers: 'Buttermilk Hill', USSR, 1962; "The Travellers On Tour", Columbia Records of Canada FL 299, *nia*. In 1965 a version by Julie Felix was included on an album alongside 'Masters Of War', 'Don't Think Twice It's All Right' and 'Pastures of Plenty'. Julie Felix: 'Buttermilk Hill', *nia*; "Julie Felix", London Records LL 3395 [mono] / PS395 [stereo], London, 1965.

Dylan can be presumed to know also 'Ole Buttermilk Sky' by Hoagy Carmichael (one of his 1940s hits). Hoagy Carmichael: 'Ole Buttermilk Sky', *nia*; "Hoagy Carmichael Sings Hoagy Carmichael", MCA Records MCL 1620, London, 1974 (indeed it is the song immediately after 'Memphis In June' on this compilation). Dylan is probably familiar too with a harmonica-solo blues record by Ellis Williams: 'Buttermilk Blues', Johnson City, Tennessee, 24/10/29; CD-issued "Great Harp Players (1927–1936)", Document Records DOCD-5100, Vienna, c. 1991.

. . . The cat's in the well, the wolf is looking down
He got his big bushy tail dragging all over the ground.

. . . Cat's in the well, the gentle lady is asleep.
She ain't hearing a thing: silence is a-stickin' her deep.

The cat's in the well and grief is showing its face
The world's being slaughtered and it's such a bloody disgrace

. . . The cat's in the well and the horse is going bumpety-bump
Back Alley Sally is doing the American Jump.

The cat's in the well and Papa is reading the news
His hair's falling out and all of his daughters need shoes

. . . The cat's in the well and the barn is full o' the bull
The night is so long and the table is oh so full

The cat's in the well and the servant is at the door
The drinks are ready and the dogs are going to war

. . . The cat's in the well, leaves are starting to fall:
Goodnight my love, may the Lord have mercy on us all.

More substantially than '10,000 Men', and in amongst its end-of-the-world material, this eloquent song uses nursery rhyme aplenty, and a little fairy tale too, starting with the obvious founding of Dylan's title upon the well-known 'Ding dong bell, pussy's in the well' and/or on a more obscure nursery rhyme featuring a more exactly equivalent feline:

Dingle dingle doosey
The cat's in the well
The dog's away to Bellingen
To buy the bairn a bell.

Wells themselves, of course, for the modern western urban listener, are objects of another age. 'Jesus Met The Woman At The Well' evokes one of the ages they represent; in the blues, they are resonant of a life of hand-drawn water in pre-war rural backwoods USA; and they evoke equally the life of medieval Europe in folksong and the magic wishing-well that is an essential prop in fairy tale.

This is not the only moment in 'Cat's In The Well' where nursery rhyme and blues lyric poetry fuse into one. 'Bumpity Bump' is the title of a Joe Turner-style early record by Smiley Lewis, a vaguely farmyardish piece of nonsense in which instead of cat and wolf 'the dog jumped the rabbit' (the chant 'hop, skip and jump' exactly replaces Turner's own 'Flip, Flop and Fly' on the song of that name) and as for the dog, 'his heart went bumpity bump'.[56] But Dylan's horse going bumpety-bump has a much earlier and more direct ancestry, and one in which, as in the Dylan song, there

---

56. Smiley Lewis [with the Dave Bartholomew band]: 'Bumpity Bump', New Orleans, March 1955, Imperial Records 5356, Los Angeles, 1955.

is father–daughter difficulty, a wild creature invading the domestic scene and much falling down. This is the nursery rhyme 'A Farmer Went Trotting':

> *A farmer went trotting upon his grey mare*
> *Bumpety bumpety bump*
> *With his daughter behind him so rosy and fair*
> *Lumpety lumpety lump*
>
> *A raven cried 'Croak!' and they all tumbled down*
> *Bumpety bumpety bump*
> *The mare broke her knees and the farmer his crown*
> *Lumpety lumpety lump.*

Meanwhile Back Alley Sally is doing the 'American Jump' – yet another game with a rhyme to go with it, and one in which the theme of falling down recurs:

> *American jump, American jump*
> *One – two – three!*
> *Under the water, under the sea*
> *Catching fishes for my tea*
> *Dead or alive?*

The game, like the farmer's grey mare, holds together child and grown-up. The grown-up holds the child's hands and jumps him or her up and down till the word 'three', at which there's an extra big jump so that the child's legs twist around the grown-up's waist. While saying 'under the water' the child is held but falls slowly backwards; when asked 'Dead or alive?' if the child answers 'alive' it's pulled up again, if 'dead' it's allowed to fall down, and if 'around the world', the child is whirled round and round. This is, then, an appealing fantasy version of how we face life, death and the world around us: a version in which, improbably, we choose our own fate and determine our own future. It's an ironic reference on Dylan's part, in a song which, like so much of his recent work, seems preoccupied with less rosy views of how we face life, death and the world around us. It's a further irony that his Back Alley Sally – an appellation that could equally be the tag for a child or an adult – appears to be playing this game by herself.

Like 'Cat's In The Well', many nursery rhymes are set around farmyards, and it is no surprise that a number of their dramas take place in barns. There's the English 'There was a little boy went into a barn' and the American 'Jemmy Jed went into a shed', and there's the muted drama of this better-known nursery rhyme, in which well-being within the ordered domain of the farmyard is threatened not by the unpredictable swooping down of wolf or raven but by that regular enemy, winter, against which the barn offers some (limited) protection:

> *The north wind shall blow*
> *And we shall have snow*
> *And what will poor robin do then, poor thing?*
> *He'll sit in a barn*
> *And keep himself warm*
> *And hide his head under his wing, poor thing.*

Before winter comes, the typical 'picture book farm' scene, which Dylan's song parallels, is laid out for us in this nursery rhyme:

> *The cock's on the woodpile a-blowing his horn*
> *The bull's in the barn a-threshing of corn*
> *The maids in the meadows are making of hay*
> *The ducks in the river are swimming away.*

(Is the widespread popularity of such formulaic verses perhaps the explanation for the term 'a cock and bull story'? Were these verses in such common currency that their opening lines recognisably ushered in a particular kind of fiction: that is, a children's story in which things are idealised and simplistic?) In any case, Dylan parallels the nursery rhyme's 'a-blowing' and 'a-threshing' with his own 'a-sticking' as well as assembling his parallel menagerie, with cat, wolf, lady, horse, bull, servant and dogs in place of cock, bull, maids and ducks.

The line about the bull in the barn has proved popular: it is retained in a 1740 manuscript from Wiltshire published in the British journal *Folk-lore* in 1901, while a chant collected by Gomme is even called 'The Bull's In The Barn'. Dylan's expressing this in reverse, in that lovely line 'The barn is full o' the bull', is one of his funny, graphic touches, not only punning playfully – his reversal of words letting the contemporary Americanism of 'you're so full of bull[shit]' chime alongside the old nursery rhyme language – but more arrestingly conjuring up such a swift comic picture, yet one that draws on our sense of the bull's fundamental character: its bulging muscularity, its hugeness, its bull-at-a-gate, bull-in-a-china-shop unwillingness to be contained (its *bullishness*), and the equally vivid picture of the storybook or comic-strip barn's propensity to be so full that it strains and creaks and bulges.

Dylan is not finished with nursery rhyme and story there. The 'Dylanesque'

> *The cat's in the well and Papa is reading the news*
> *His hair's falling out and all of his daughters need shoes*

brings together a handful of such antecedents. It is a North African belief that ancient stories – myths and fairy tales – that revolve around the breaking of a taboo (such as the opening of a forbidden door) should never be told out loud in the daytime. To do so (to be heard 'reading the news') is to risk having your hair fall out. 'The Shoes That Were Danced To Pieces', sometimes called 'The Twelve Dancing Princesses', is a Brothers Grimm fairy tale in which the king is tearing his hair out because despite locking them up in their room every night, every morning all of his daughters need new shoes, having danced the old ones to pieces. The pairing of 'news' and 'shoes' occurs in a rhyme for the paring of fingernails:

> *Cut them on Wednesday, you cut them for news*
> *Cut them on Thursday, a new pair of shoes*

while one of the (eleven) verses of 'Old Mother Hubbard' goes

> *She went to the cobbler's to buy him some shoes*
> *But when she came back he was reading the news.*

Shoes and alleys figure too in the album's purposive, dignified and beautifully performed title song. With great originality it pleaches the poetry of nursery rhyme and folklore, fairy tale and the Bible into a 'simple', memorable whole. It is the song that sets the tone and establishes the territory for the better-intentioned, which is to say serious-minded, parts of the album:

> *There was a little boy and there was a little girl*
> *And they lived in an alley under the red sky*
> *There was a little boy and there was a little girl*
> *And they lived in an alley under the red sky*
>
> *There was an old man and he lived in the moon*
> *One summer's day he came passing by*
> *There was an old man and he lived in the moon*
> *And one day he came passing by*
>
> *Someday little girl everything for you is gonna be new*
> *Someday little girl you'll have a diamond as big as your shoe*
>
> *Let the wind blow low, let the wind blow high*
> *One day the little boy and the little girl were both baked in a pie*
> *Let the wind blow low and the wind blow high*
> *One day the little boy and little girl were baked in a pie*
>
> *This is the key to the kingdom and this is the town*
> *This is the blind horse that leads you around*
>
> *Let the bird sing, let the bird fly*
> *One day the man in the moon went home and the river went dry*
> *Let the bird sing, let the bird fly*
> *Man in the moon went home and the river went dry.*

'There was a little this and there was / he had a little that' is a common formula. Nursery rhymes that begin with it include

> 'There was a little boy and a little girl'
> 'There was a little girl, and she had a little curl'
> 'There was a little hare, and he ate his pasture bare'
> 'There was a little man, and he had a little gun'
> 'There was a little man, and he wooed a little maid'
> 'There was a little maid, and she was afraid'

plus the comparable 'Shoe a little horse, shoe a little mare', 'There was a crooked man, and he walked a crooked mile', 'There was an old woman who had a little pig', 'There was a king met a king' and 'There was a mad man and he had a mad wife'.

'There was a little boy and a little girl', collected in 1810, is the one that resonates most clearly through 'Under The Red Sky':

> *There was a little boy and a little girl*
> *Lived in an alley.*

> *Says the little boy to the little girl*
> *Shall I, oh shall I?*
>
> *Says the little girl to the little boy*
> *What shall we do?*
> *Says the little boy to the little girl*
> *I will kiss you!*

In the nursery rhyme, there is time enough for playful romance. Not so today, Dylan seems to suggest, living 'Under The Red Sky': the alley is a narrower, darker place, nearer to the oppressive, narrow habitat of the old American underclass widely described in the blues – from Rabbit Brown's 'James Alley Blues' onwards – than the airy playground of the children's clapping song 'Here Comes Sally Down The Alley'. (The temptation to rhyme 'Sally' with 'alley' is an old one: the English poet Henry Carey, c. 1693–1743, is best-known as the inventor of the term 'Namby Pamby', disputed author of 'God Save The King' and undisputed author of the poem 'Sally in Our Alley'.) In the blues the alley is even more lowdown than the street, with 'doin' the alley boogie' a Lucille 'Shave 'Em Dry' Bogan speciality. She also sings that

> *They call me Pig Iron Sally because I live in Slag Iron Alley:*
> *And I'm evil and mean as I can be.*

No place for children. Yet of course children also play here, and it's an environment in which boys and girls grow up fast, one kind of game quickly becoming another, as in the fluid Blind Willie McTell song 'Georgia Rag':

> *Down in Atlanta, on Harris Street*
> *That's where the boys and gals do meet*
> *Out in the alley, out in the street*
> *Every little kid that you meet*
> *Buzz all around like a bee*
> *Shake it like a ship on the sea.*[57]

In 'Under The Red Sky' we are never invited to consider the question of romance between the little boy and the little girl: we are concerned with their very survival – and by extension, our own. All through the song survival is in doubt, with Dylan carefully handing us symbols that may or may not bode ill. As we've seen, even the alley is of ambiguous import; as we shall see, even being baked in a pie may not be fatal.

The red sky is the principal sign of possible ill-omen, and one invoked by Christ in addressing people's minds to his Resurrection, that most pivotal matter of life and death. It is a sign Bob Dylan has used before. On the version of 'Someone's Got A Hold Of My Heart' belatedly released on "Bootleg Series I–III" but recorded at the "Infidels" sessions of 1983, he sings:

> *Well I just got back from the city of red skies.*

57.   Lucille Bogan [as Bessie Jackson]: 'Down In Boogie Alley', NYC, 1/8/34, and 'Pig Iron Sally', NYC, 31/7/34, both issued "Lucille Bogan & Walter Roland (1930–1935)", Roots RL-317, Vienna, 1968. Blind Willie McTell, 'Georgia Rag', Atlanta, Hallowe'en 1931; "Blind Willie McTell: The Early Years (1927–1933)", Yazoo L-1005, New York, 1968.

This city is Babylon, bastion of worldly corruption (and symbol of death in the nursery rhyme 'How Many Miles To Babylon?'), to which he has 'got to confess' he's been. Christ himself, as reported in Matthew 16:2–4, invokes the dual symbolism of the red sky when he's berating the corrupt sects of his day, and telling them that the only 'sign' they can expect is the Resurrection:

> When it is evening, ye say, It will be fair weather: for the sky is red. And in the morning, It will be foul weather today: for the sky is red and lowring. O ye hypocrites, ye can discern the face of the sky; but can ye not discern the signs of the times?

This might be said to be the key text, and a markedly 'Dylanesque' one, that Dylan is seeking to press home on 'Under The Red Sky' the song and "Under The Red Sky" the album. Christ's speech continues:

> A wicked and adulterous generation seeketh after a sign; and there shall no sign be given unto it, but the sign of the prophet Jonas.[58]

Nursery rhyme, being sometimes more rational than we credit, takes the practical experience related here and boils it down to

> *Red sky at night, shepherd's delight*
> *Red sky at morning, shepherd's warning.*

A peculiarly apt Indian equivalent is reported by Alexander Frater in his book *Chasing the Monsoon*. He reports that in the British Empire period officials published a collection of almost 2000 peasants' proverbs (about 25 per cent were monsoon proverbs). Frater meets an antiquarian bookseller who knows this rare book and who tells him that 'the one that best sums it up is, "If the sky fails, the earth will surely fail too".' Bob Dylan's sentiments exactly.

Then there's the moon, and the old man in it. Is he a malign visitor, an incidental player, or the keeper of a benevolent eye upon the little boy and the little girl? The Steven Scobie argument, in *Alias Bob Dylan*, that the moon symbolises some kind of evil intent, seems almost wholly unsupported. From the earliest times the moon was beneficial – it was what we measured time by (the Sanskrit root *me-*, to measure, is at the back of the word for moon in all the Teutonic languages). In classical mythology the moon is several different heroines, all of them romantic: Hecate before she has risen and after setting; Astarte when crescent; Diana, or Cynthia, she who 'hunts the clouds', when in the open vault of heaven (alluded to by Dylan in 'Sara': 'Glamorous

---

58. Christ is here responding not to his own followers but to the Pharisees and the Sadducees, who try to get him to show them a sign from heaven to prove himself, as if they're wanting to join him. This speech is his retort. Note that 'adulterous' here is not meant in the secular sense but leans on the image in the Sacred Writings of the Jewish people as 'married' to God but become unfaithful. The Pharisees had begun as a purist sect: the name comes from 'parash', to separate; they had formed in order to separate themselves from the national corruption about two hundred years before Christ. There is some excellent invective against them by Jesus (and against lawyers, while he's at it) in the account given in Luke 11:39–52, though the parallel account of the remarks about reading the weather is less vivid, omitting the red sky altogether (Luke 12:54–55), and is separated from the remarks about it being an evil generation seeking a sign (Luke 11:29). The section referring to the sign of Jonas (Jonah) is saying that the only 'sign', or miracle, that is still to come shall be that of his resurrection from the dead, a miracle typified by the case of Jonah. This is spelt out more clearly in Luke's account, according to which Jesus adds that 'For as Jonas was a sign unto the Ninevites, so shall also the Son of man be to this generation' (Luke 11:30).

nymph with an arrow and bow'); Phoebe the sister of the sun; and Selene, or Luna, lover of the sleeping Endymion, when seen as moonlight on the fields.

In the villages of West Africa, as Chinua Achebe's pioneering 1958 novel *Things Fall Apart* reports, instead of the silence imposed by fear on a dark night, 'a moonlight night ... would be different. The happy voices of children playing in open fields would then be heard'.

In nursery rhyme too, the moon is contemplated with perfect equanimity, the classics of the genre being

> *Boys and girls come out to play*
> *The moon doth shine as bright as day*

and

> *I see the moon and the moon sees me*
> *God bless the moon and God bless me.*

Far from being sinister, or even cold, the moon is a companion for the child. Variants include the British 'I see the moon and the moon sees me / God bless the sailors on the sea', said like a prayer when moonlight shines in through the child's bedroom window, and the American all's-well avowal of 'I see the moon, the moon sees me / The moon sees somebody I want to see.' Bob Dylan throws his own allusion to this into 'Wiggle Wiggle': its opening verse ends with 'Wiggle till the moon sees you.' The moon is a friend and a familiar. The expression 'to cry for the moon' began as an allusion not to unreasonable ambition or greed but to children's wanting the moon as a plaything. The French equivalent translates as 'He wants to take the moon between his teeth.' The moon is also benign in the legend that everything was saved and treasured there that was wasted and squandered on earth: misspent time, broken vows, unanswered prayers, fruitless tears, unfulfilled desires.

As for the man in the moon, he may have an ignominious biblical history but today we might consider him more sinned against than sinning. He's discernible when the moon is eight days old: a figure leaning on a fork, on which he carries a bundle of sticks gathered, sacriligiously, on a sabbath. Some people also discern a small dog at his feet (which is why, in *A Midsummer Night's Dream*, 'This man, with lantern, dog and bush of thorn, / Presenteth moonshine'). Another tradition says the man is Cain, his dog and bush being respectively the 'foul fiend' and the thorns and briars of the Fall. Later legend claims that he was banished to the moon for trying to stop people attending mass by throwing his sticks across their path.

He comes from the Old Testament book of Numbers 15:32–36:

> And while the children of Israel were in the wilderness, they found a man that gathered sticks upon the sabbath day. And they ... brought him unto Moses and Aaron, and unto all the congregation. And they put him in ward, because it was not declared what should be done to him. And the Lord said unto Moses, The man shall be surely put to death; all the congregation shall stone him ...

And they did.[59]

In nursery rhyme, the man in the moon's past is not held against him and at worst he takes on the moon's 'lunatic' influence, becoming an inspired simpleton, as in the English folksong (printed 1660 and reprinted as a broadside soon after) of which the nursery rhyme 'The man in the moon drinks claret' is the first few lines.

In other nursery rhymes, when he is not receiving food, as in 'As I Went Up The Apple Tree'

> *All the apples fell on me*
> *Bake a pudding, bake a pie*
> *Send it up to John MacKay*
> *John MacKay is not in*
>
> *Send it up to the man in the moon*[60]

he is providing it, as in 'There was a man lived in the moon', the chorus of which Dylan comes pretty close to quoting – his

> *There was an old man and he lived in the moon . . .*
> *There was an old man and he lived in the moon*

being prefigured by its

> *There was a man lived in the moon, lived in the moon, lived in the moon*
> *There was a man lived in the moon*
> *And his name was Aiken Drum.*

Here the man in the moon is a figure of bounty, clothed in provisions, satisfying primitive needs: 'he played upon a ladle . . . his hat was made of good cream cheese . . . his coat was made of good roast beef . . . And his name,' far from being Cain, was the nonsensically jolly 'Aiken Drum'. Most of his clothes get eaten by Willy Wood, who then chokes to death on Drum's haggis breeches. This man in the moon then, a mugger's victim, is hero not villain of his story.

So might it be with the old man who lives in the moon in Dylan's song. You might conclude, granted that it's when he goes home that the river runs dry, that it's not his visit that parches it – that his 'summer's day' visit has no discernible effect for good or ill: that at worst the man in the moon is being neutral, as in that exquisite blues couplet quoted earlier, in which

59. Moses did not relish God's inclination towards such severity, and eventually did something about it. As Michael Haag writes in his guidebook *Egypt* (1993):

> What might come to mind as you watch the dawn up here [on Gebel Musa, claimed as the Mount Sinai of the Bible] is . . . the extraordinary exchange between God and Moses . . . (Exodus 32) . . . 'Go, get thee down,' God says to Moses, 'for thy people have corrupted themselves. Let me alone, that my wrath may wax hot against them, and that I may consume them.' To which Moses replies: '. . . Turn from thy fierce wrath, and repent of this evil against thy people.' Considering that God had already once drowned the world and had promised the fire next time, you have to admire Moses' audacious attempt to shame God into forgiveness. And it worked, for 'the Lord repented of the evil which he thought to do unto his people'. It is the great theme that develops through the Bible, this covenant, this civilising relationship, between God and man, and between man and man, and it is on the mount that it takes its first step forward.

60. Reprinted in *Homer, the slut*, no. 2, January 1991, from *The Mother Goose Golden Treasury*, edited by Raymond Briggs (1966).

> *The wolves howled at midnight, wild ox moaned till day*
> *The man in the moon looked down on us but had nothing to say.*[61]

And yet . . . Dylan makes you work through conflicting implications here. Just as in that Whistlin' Alex Moore verse, you're left feeling that this 'neutrality' means an unwillingness to be helpful or protective. There's a leaving-them-to-their-fate coldness at the end of both songs. Even on his first appearance in 'Under The Red Sky' he comes 'passing by'. If he passes right on by, he doesn't really visit the little girl and the little boy at all. On the other hand, the very same phrase might equally well mean that he arrives on the scene, bestows his presence, makes his presence felt, becomes a figure in the action. Isn't it also implied that the man in the moon is the speaker of the soothing and benign lines that follow directly upon his 'passing by'?:

> *Someday little girl everything for you is gonna be new*
> *Someday little girl you'll have a diamond as big as your shoe.*

So we are left, as by every other image in the song, with some dynamic tension as to whether the man in the moon is a force for good or ill. This is, of course, as we noted earlier, the arena in which fairy tales take place, since their fundamental message to the child is that good and ill are both within.

Dylan has taken

> *Someday little girl you'll have a diamond as big as your shoe*

from the nursery rhyme

> *Little girl, little girl, where have you been?*
> *Gathering roses to give to the queen.*
> *Little girl, little girl, what gave she you?*
> *She gave me a diamond as big as a shoe*[62]

and he strays from the strictly verbatim only in order to improve the slightly vague 'big as a shoe' to the more specific, and so more vivid, 'big as your shoe'.

Next comes

> *Let the wind blow low, let the wind blow high.*

Inevitably this reminds us of lullabies ('When the wind blows, the cradle will rock'), if not also of the nursery rhyme quoted earlier in which when the wind blows the robin

---

61.   Whistlin' Alex Moore: 'West Texas Woman', see note 25. This lovely song has been tiresomely re-recorded by Dave Alvin as 'East Texas Blues', Los Angeles, Jan. 1994; "King Of California", Hightone Records HCD 8054, Oakland, California, 1994.
      Although this couplet offers the only reference to the man in the moon in Taft, blues lyric poetry includes a number of striking titles incorporating the moon itself and offering some degree of convergence with the final line of 'Under The Red Sky': not least 'When The Moon Run Down The Valley In The Stream' (recorded by various people, including Miss Louise Collins, Smyrna, Delaware, 5/6/41); 'When The Moon Goes Down In The Valley Of Time' (by the Alphabetical Four, NYC, 16/8/38); 'When The Moon Goes Down In Blood' (by Augustus Track Horse Haggerty and Jesse Bradley, Huntsville, Texas, 22/11/34) and 'The Moon Went Down And Vanished Away' (by various, including the Pilgrim Brother Quartet of the Friendly Will Baptist Church, Austin, Texas, 6/7/41).
      In line with the other cultures cited in the main text a few paragraphs earlier, the moon is regarded positively in the blues world. 'Don't the moon look pretty' is recurrent, while in Taft there isn't a single instance of the moon auguring bad news or evil.
62.   Quoted in Muir, *Homer, the slut*, no. 2, January 1991, from *The Helen Oxenbury Nursery Rhyme Book*, 1986.

must shelter in the barn. But there is also a children's singing game, collected by the Opies, called 'The Wind Blows High'. Like so many others, it has numerous British and American variants. Each opening couplet is a variant of this one, to which Dylan's song alludes. It was collected in Washington, DC, in 1886:

> *The wind blows low, the wind blows high*
> *The stars are dropping from the sky.*[63]

English versions tend to offer a lesser opening line but a lovely second one:

> *The wind, the wind, the wind blows high*
> *The rain comes scattering down the sky.*

Both these variants fit neatly 'Under The Red Sky' in pointing to the sky as an imminent source of bad tidings.

On the face of it, what happens next is bad news indeed for our protagonists:

> *One day the little boy and the little girl were both baked in a pie.*

Pies are of course quintessential prized objects in the nursery rhyme world: things to savour and gobble, things to conceal other things, things to threaten to put people in, things to put people in. They occur everywhere: in 'Simple Simon', 'Georgie Porgie', 'Round about, round about, Maggotty pie / My father loves good ale and so do I'; 'Dame Get Up And Bake Your Pies'; 'There was an old woman / Sold puddings and pies'; 'Sing A Song Of Sixpence'; 'Punch and Judy / Fought for a pie / Punch gave Judy / A knock in the eye'; 'Little Jack Horner' and many more. The man in the moon's waistcoat is made of pie crust.

Yet as already conceded, the same worlds that savour all these pies allow their inhabitants to survive being baked in them. Bettelheim writes that 'one of the most widely spread mythical incidents in the world [is] the reappearance of living people out of the monster that has devoured them.' We saw earlier that when Christ cites the red sky he proceeds to allude to Jonah's survival in, and escape from, the belly of the whale as a prefiguring of his own Resurrection. In nursery rhyme this is a reassuring sub-text in 'Sing A Song Of Sixpence' – the rhyme we all recognise as Dylan's source for the exact phrase 'baked in a pie' – in which

> *When the pie was opened*
> *The birds began to sing*

('let the bird sing . . .'), and it is openly the cheery theme of another nursery rhyme, less familiar but also giving us the phrase 'baked in a pie', first published in 1843 (and which Bob Dylan seems to have known in an earlier age, when he borrowed its 'Baby and I' to make his 'Lady and I' in 'Desolation Row'):

---

63. Each version proceeds to cite a local geography, as here: 'He is happy, he is pretty / He is the boy of Washington City' – a format recurrent in black and white song. In the 1980s it popped up in the Top 50 hit single 'The Bell Of St. Marks' by Sheila E and in Lick The Tins' recording of the traditional 'Belle Of Belfast City' ('She is handsome, she is pretty / She is the Belle of Belfast City'). Sheila E: 'The Bell Of St. Marks', *nia*, USA, c. 1984. Lick The Tins: 'Belle Of Belfast City', *nia*; "Blind Man On A Flying Horse", Sedition Records ZCSED 9001, UK, 1986.

> *Baby and I*
> *Were baked in a pie*
> *The gravy was wonderful hot*
> *We had nothing to pay*
> *To the baker that day*
> *And so we crept out of the pot.*

One way and another, then, you can find implicit reason to hope that in 'Under The Red Sky' the hero and heroine do not perish when baked.

With or without them, the song continues, extending its extraordinary tapestry of nursery rhyme, fairy tale and biblical threads.

> *This is the key to the kingdom*
> *And this is the town*
> *This is the blind horse*
> *That leads you around . . .*

It is just fourteen verses after his red sky speech, in the same chapter of Matthew, that Christ tells Peter he is the rock upon which 'I will build my church; and the gates of hell shall not prevail against it. And I will give unto thee the keys of the king-dom of heaven.' (This is taken to bestow not the means of entering but the power to admit or not admit others. Simultaneously, the keys are the true knowledge of the doctrine of the kingdom of heaven. The word 'church' here means assembly or congregation; it does not mean an institution. This text, including the passage that follows it immediately, is understood very differently by Protestants and by Catholics.) The words that follow directly on from 'the keys of the kingdom of heaven' are 'and whatsoever thou shalt bind on earth, shall be bound in heaven, and whatsoever thou shalt loose on earth shall be loosed in heaven' (repeated in 18:18, and, in different words, in John 20:23), part of the meaning of which refers back to the belief held by the Jews that everything that was done on earth according to the order of God was at the same time done in heaven. Adam Clarke, in his *Commentary on the Bible*, says that, for instance, 'when the priest, on the day of atonement, offered the two goats upon earth, the same were offered in heaven. As one goat therefore is permitted to escape on earth, one is permitted to escape in heaven.' This compares nicely with the pagan belief, mentioned above, that everything wasted on earth is saved and cherished on the moon.

The phrase 'key to the kingdom' occurs first in Dylan's work on the Basement Tapes song 'Sign On The Cross':

> *Well, it's that old sign on the cross*
> *Well, it's that old key to the kingdom,*
> *Well, it's that old sign on the cross . . .*
> *That worries me*

and as the context here makes unsurprising, 'Key To The Kingdom' is an old gospel song. It has a plain-speaking chorus that makes it clear that to be given the key to the kingdom is no small thing – and is just the sort of special power which protects many a fairy tale hero/ine:

I got the key to the kingdom
And my enemies can't do me no harm.[64]

However, the phrase is the title-line of a palindromic nursery rhyme too:

This is the key of the kingdom:
In that kingdom there is a city.
In that city there is a town.
In that town there is a street.
In that street there is a lane.
In that lane there is a yard.
In that yard there is a house.
In that house there is a room.
In that room there is a bed.
On that bed there is a basket.
In that basket there are some flowers.

Flowers in the basket.
Basket in the bed.
Bed in the room.
Room in the house.
House in the yard.
Yard in the lane.
Lane in the street.
Street in the town.
Town in the city.
City in the kingdom.
Of the kingdom this is the key.[65]

The item around which this jingle pivots with two faces, the basket of flowers, is one that Dylan uses in 'Handy Dandy', in which the line 'he got a stick in his hand and a pocket full of money' is balanced in the last verse by 'he got a basket of flowers and a bag full of sorrow'.

As Dylan uses the nursery rhyme's 'This is the key of the kingdom' for the second bridge of 'Under The Red Sky', he makes it sound like a song to accompany a winding-through-the-streets game (a 'Chains and Captives' game, to use the Gomme classification), like 'Thread The Needle', 'How Many Miles To Babylon?', 'The Big Ship Sails' and 'Oranges and Lemons':

This is the key to the kingdom
And this is the town

---

64.   It was recorded, for example, in 1929 by both Bessie Johnson & Her Sanctified Singers and by the wonderful Washington Phillips (who sang and accompanied himself on something called a dulceola). Bessie Johnson & Her Sanctified Singers: 'Key To The Kingdom', Atlanta, 21/3/29; CD-reissued "Memphis Gospel", Document Records DOCD-5072, Vienna, 1991. Washington Phillips: 'I've Got The Key To The Kingdom', Dallas, Texas, 2/12/29; CD-reissued "Storefront & Streetcorner Gospel (1927–1929)", Document Records DOCD-5054, Vienna, *nia*. (Bessie Johnson is the splendid uncredited singer on track 48 on the Harry Smith anthology [see note 11], the very lovely 'He Got Better Things For You', Memphis Sanctified Singers, Memphis, 3/10/29.)

65.   Taken from *Traditional Nursery Rhymes and Children's Verse*, Michael Foss (1976).

> *This is the blind horse*
> *That leads you around.*

It is easy to hear these lines that way, since they end by nominating (almost self-reflexively) something that 'leads you around', but by this point we've already picked up some sense of a game being chanted, thanks to its back-echoes of old familiars like the finger-rhyme 'Here's the church and here's the steeple / Open the doors and here's all the people'.

Like all the rest, the blind horse is, as it were, a symbol that looks both ways. The blind leading the blind is Not Good; why should the blind leading the baked be any better? On the other hand, the blind horse suggests itself as Falada, a sort of equine fairy godmother, the benign guardian to the little girl in the fairy tale 'The Goose Girl'. Falada may be a 'blind' horse (in fact decapitated rather than blinded) but it holds the key to the regaining of her rightful kingdom, and guides the little girl towards it not by explicit instruction but by the enigmatic hints of a repeated spoken rhyme, to prompt the heroine towards worthier, more mature action. Here is a rare and relishable instance of fairy tale and adult folksong coming together: for the rhyme spoken by the horse in the story is echoed by the words of the folksong 'Pretty Peggy-O' as sung by Dylan in recent years (for instance at Hammersmith, February 1990):

> *If this your mother knew*
> *Her heart would break in two.*

In the fairy tale the repeated rhyme eventually nudges the Goose Girl, who is really a dispossessed princess, into breaking out of the Goose Girl role in which a servant's duplicity has trapped her. Let the bird sing, let the bird fly.

There is, moreover, a nursery rhyme dealing with a directly comparable theme: the eventual compunction not to stay safely in a role someone else has assigned you but to break out to chase fulfilment, and possible danger, in a wider world. And it is a nursery rhyme in which a blind horse is the agent for the plunge into the unknown. We all know its beginning –

> *My mother said I never should*
> *Play with the gypsies in the wood.*

It ends:

> *The wood was dark, the grass was green*
> *Up comes Sally with a tambourine*
> *. . . I went to the river, no ship to get across*
> *I paid ten shillings for an old blind horse*
> *I up on his back and off in a crack*
> *Sally tell my mother I shall never come back.*

Like 'the key to the kingdom', then, the blind horse can be a means to salvation, making Dylan's stanza, against all initial expectation, positive from start to finish.

This theme, that breaking free of one's inner constraints is an imperative, tallies with something the "Under The Red Sky" album's co-producer, Don Was, told an interviewer that Dylan had said of its title-track: 'It's actually about people who got

trapped in his hometown. I think it's about Hibbing and about people who never left
. . . He said, "It's about my hometown." '[66]

It is almost unprecedented for Dylan to let out this kind of explanation as to what
a song is 'about'. This doesn't mean he didn't say it, any more than it means he's right,
or that he'd have offered the same 'explanation' twenty-four hours later: but it sits well
enough alongside the song as I've tried to describe and discuss it. There is even a
precedent for this sort of scenario in nursery rhyme. Instead of it being the little girl and
little boy trapped in the alley under the red sky who eventually get baked in a pie (fatally
or not), there is 'A little cock sparrow', who only avoids ending up in a pie by fleeing:

> *A little cock sparrow sat on a tree*
> *Looking as happy as happy can be*
> *Till a boy came by with his bow and arrow*
> *Says he, 'I will shoot the little cock sparrow*
>
> *His body will make me a nice little stew*
> *His giblets will make me a little pie too.'*
> *Says the cock sparrow, 'I'll be shot if I stay'*
> *So he clapped his wings and flew away.*

Let the bird sing, let the bird fly.

There is one other kind of rubbing-together between nursery rhyme and this album:
when a Dylan line recalls a nursery rhyme verse which in turn recalls another nursery
rhyme which in turn prefigures another Dylan line. For instance, where Dylan's 'horse
is going bumpety-bump' recalls 'A Farmer Went A-Trotting', *its* 'tumbled down' and
'broke . . . his crown' is something already familiar to us from 'Jack And Jill', and
recalling this reminds us that they were the little boy and the little girl who 'went up
the hill' just like the '10,000 Men' of 'The Grand Old Duke of York'.[67]

---

66.   Don Was, Los Angeles, 15/10/90; interview in *Telegraph*, no. 37, Winter 1990.

67.   A more tendentious connection of this sort can be made as follows, beginning not with a line but with an image:
the promotional video made for 'Unbelievable' includes a pig with a ring in his nose. We already know a pig with a
ring in his nose from one of the best-known poems by the father of nonsense verse, Edward Lear, 'The Owl and the
Pussy Cat'. The relevant section is this: 'They sailed away for a year and a day / To the land where the Bong tree
grows / And there in a wood a Piggy-wig stood / With a ring at the end of his nose . . .' But consider how the poem
proceeds from there: "Dear Pig, are you willing to sell for one shilling / Your ring?' Said the Piggy, 'I will.' / So they
took it away, and were married next day / By the Turkey who lives on the hill. / They dined on mince, and slices of
quince / Which they ate with a runcible spoon / And hand in hand, on the edge of the sand / They danced by the light
of the moon . . .' Thus the image leads us to the children's poem, and in turn the children's poem ends by bringing us
back to Dylan, since the Turkey is to be found, like Dylan's '10,000 Men', 'on the hill', while the owl and the pussycat dance, like the 'Jokerman' to the nightingale's tune, as the bird flies high 'by the light of the moon'. Moreover, at
the end of the poem the Owl and the Pussy Cat also dance 'hand in hand, on the edge of the sand'; similarly the
end of 'Mr. Tambourine Man' finds Dylan on 'the windy beach' wanting 'to dance . . . with one hand waving free'
while in '2 x 2' the unspecified 'they' also 'danced on the shore' (Lear, quoted in *The Big Golden Book of Poetry*,
1965. His *Book of Nonsense*, including 'The Owl and the Pussy Cat', was first published in 1846 and pioneered the
abandonment of severe moralising as the principal ingredient then fashionable in children's literature.)

   NB. In the Wissolik and McGrath collection *Bob Dylan's Words* (1994), the interesting short essay 'The
Nightingale's Code: The Influence of John Keats on Bob Dylan', by Nigel Brooks, connects 'Mr. Tambourine Man'
and the 'Ode to a Nightingale', particularly re their endings.

   NB2. Edward Lear may have based his poem's title on that of the medieval English poem 'The Owl and the
Nightingale'.

   You might also pick that video piggy up as a biblical reference on Dylan's part: to Proverbs 11:22 (they are
the proverbs of Solomon, son of King David, and are addressed to his own son, fatherly advice to a child), in

The soundings of such rhymes half-submerged beneath the songs on the album give it some of the interplay between songs that we're aware of but feel no need to pin down: some of the cross-referencing between one song and another of which it's sufficient to say that it helps our sense of the album's unity.

There is explicit cross-referencing in spades. The first track on Side 1 has you 'dressed in green'; the first track on Side 2 has women 'dressed in white' and men 'dressed in Oxford blue'. (These also echo nursery rhyme: 'dressed all in green', for instance, occurs in two related playground songs: 'Hector Protector' and the lurid, untitled rhyme that goes 'Jumbo had a baby all dressed in green / Jumbo didn't like it, sent it to the queen / The queen did not like it because it was so fat / Cut it up in slices and gave it to the cat'. In turn they are also reminders of old blues and gospel songs Dylan recorded decades earlier: the Rev. Gary Davis' 'Cocaine', for example, has 'yonder come my baby all dressed in blue/purple/white' etc. as its running format; in the traditional 'Wade In The Water', yonder come the children 'all dressed in red'. The 'Handy Dandy' line 'He got an all-girl orchestra and when he says "Strike up the band!" they hit it' also refers us to an earlier Dylan performance of a song he didn't compose himself: 'Strike Up The Band!' is the name of the musical that contained the relatively obscure Gershwin song 'Soon', the one which, to general puzzlement in Easy Listening circles, Bob Dylan chose to perform at the Gershwin Gala in 1987.[68]) The drink and the table at the end of 'Handy Dandy' are echoed by the table and the drinks in 'Cat's In The Well'. From '2 x 2', 'Three by three they're turning the key / Four by four they turn it some more' is matched by the mild joke, mentioned earlier, from the same song, 'Nine by nine they drank the wine / Ten by ten they drank it again', which in turn is echoed in 'Wiggle Wiggle' by 'Wiggle till you're high, wiggle till you're higher'. The 'ton of lead' in 'Wiggle Wiggle' weighs in with the 'lead balloon' that's 'Unbelievable'. In the title song, the children live under the ominous red sky; in 'Unbelievable' the blind man stands beneath 'the silver skies', while we 'must be living in the shadow of some kind of evil star'. The 'land of money' in 'Unbelievable' is matched by people 'digging for silver and gold' in '10,000 Men'. The allusion to traditional folk territory in '2 x 2', 'the foggy dew', is matched by 'the gentle lady' in 'Cat's In The Well'. I have no particular song in mind as regards the

---

which, cataloguing things to go for and things to avoid in order to live a righteous life, Solomon warns that 'a fair woman which is without discretion' is like 'a jewel of gold in a swine's snout', a handy tip for those steering their way through the music business. This is not Dylan's first snuffle through this particular scriptural terrain. Fifty-five verses later we begin to find passages Dylan built upon for the 1981 'In The Summertime': 'Poverty and shame shall be to him that refuseth instruction' (13:18), which reiterates a main tenet of the whole book of Proverbs (it is insisted upon many times, and returned to in the very direct words of 20:6: 'Train up a child in the way he should go: and when he is old, he will not depart from it.'), and then 'Fools make a mock at sin' (14:9) and 'a stranger doth not intermeddle' (14:10). Further on in the same book, we return to the silver and gold and apples of 'Unbelievable' and the nursery rhyme riddle behind it about the man with no eyes. Proverbs 26:11 tells us: 'A word fitly spoken is like apples of gold in pictures of silver.' In the next chapter, and all of a piece with the fair woman without discretion being like the gold ring in the pig's nose, we have the nearest thing to an 'explanation' for Dylan's 1966 song title 'Rainy Day Women Nos. 12 & 35': 'A continual dropping in a very rainy day and a contentious woman are alike' (Proverbs 27:15). This connection is suggested in Wissolik and McGrath's *Bob Dylan's Words* (1994).

68. Bob Dylan: 'Cocaine', Minneapolis, 22/12/61, unissued; live at the Gaslight Café, NYC, Oct. 1962, unissued; and back-up vocals and harmonica on the version by Dick Farina & Eric von Schmidt, London, 10–11/1/63, "Dick Farina & Eric von Schmidt", Folklore Records F-LEUT-7, London, 1964. Bob Dylan: 'Wade In The Water', Minneapolis, 22/12/61, unissued. Bob Dylan: 'Soon', Brooklyn, NYC, 11/3/87, unissued.

latter phrase: it simply sounds an archaism from the olde Englishe ballade worlde; but 'the foggy dew' is a direct reference to the title of one of the hoariest of traditional folksongs, 'The Foggy Foggy Dew'. Dylan's use of the phrase is another example of his liberating the inherent poetry from the inconsequential. He lets it invoke a scene of atmospheric tenderness:

> *Two by two to their lovers they flew*
> *Two by two into the foggy dew.*

In contrast, 'The Foggy Foggy Dew' itself is a nudge-nudge song, almost a rugby song, in which the running joke is that the singer repeatedly justifies having sex with 'a fair young maid' by claiming he was merely sheltering her 'from the foggy foggy dew'. Bob Dylan has used this song before, though very differently. Its

> *When I was a bachelor I lived all alone*
> *I worked at the weaver's trade*
> *And the only only thing that I did that was wrong*
> *Was to woo a fair young maid*
> *... Was to keep her from the foggy foggy dew*[69]

is recognisable, not least in its rhythms and cadence, yet utterly transformed, lurking behind this verse from Dylan's 'Up To Me', a "Blood On The Tracks" out-take released on the 1985 "Biograph" box-set:

> *Oh the only decent thing I did when I worked as a postal clerk*
> *Was to haul your picture down off the wall near the cage where I used to work.*

To continue tracking the album's cross-references: in 'God Knows', 'God knows you ain't pretty' echoes 'you were plain' in 'Born In Time'. The sudden vocal mimicry on the fade-out of '2 x 2' – the distinctive comic voice he pulls out of the air for 'Don' tread on-a m-m-me-ee' – is matched by his sudden vocal mimicry of that girl called Nancy in the middle of 'Handy Dandy', where

> *He says 'Ya wanna gun? I'll give ya one' ...*

and as she replies, Dylan, with a touch of inspired, freewheeling lunacy, ventriloquises her voice so that she speaks in a perfect imitation of the lame, idiot-savant sidekick Chester in the iconic 1950s TV cowboy series, the aptly titled 'Gunsmoke':

> *... she says 'B-boy, you t-talkin' crazy!'*

(The main character in 'Gunsmoke' was Matt Dillon, who has sometimes been suggested as the source for Robert Zimmerman's name change to Bob Dylan.)

Comfort food is everywhere, but almost nowhere is it real: 'like sugar and candy' in 'Handy Dandy'; 'like a bowl of soup' and 'like a pail of milk' in 'Wiggle Wiggle'; figurative 'milk and honey' in 'Unbelievable'; 'buttermilk' and 'tea' in '10,000 Men'; 'that vine' to smoke in 'Unbelievable'; 'a pie' in 'Under The Red Sky'; figurative

---

69. Quotation from 'The Foggy Foggy Dew' from the recording by Burl Ives, *nia*, "Burl Ives Volume 3", Decca Records DL 5093 [10-inch LP], New York, 1949.

'forbidden fruits' in 'TV Talkin' Song'; a full table and ready drinks in 'Cat's In The Well'; more wine in '2 x 2'; 'another brandy' in 'Handy Dandy'.

Sometimes the half-submerged things float back to other works of Dylan's. It's impossible, for instance, in the context of this nursery rhyme album, not to think of 'Cat's In The Well' as a sort of follow-up to 'Ring Them Bells', thanks to the involuntary adhesive of 'Ding dong bell / Pussy's in the well'.

Layered in amongst all this are the unsubmerged cross-references to earlier work from Dylan's repertoire. Perhaps it would be less indulgent of the artist to call most of these mere repetition. The very opening line of the album,

> *Wiggle wiggle wiggle like a gypsy queen*

is the third appearance of gypsy queens in Dylan's corpus, and, as happens tellingly often when Dylan repeats himself, the reintroduction is a lesser thing than its forbears. 'The motorcycle black madonna two-wheel gypsy queen' in 'The Gates Of Eden' is first and most memorable; 'Billy 7' giving us 'Gypsy queens will play your grand finale' is second, and second-best. These exotic creatures are on a falling curve, their appearance on 'Wiggle Wiggle' a throwaway. Unsurprisingly, the same song's 'you got nothing to lose' is a lot less striking as the pay-off to 'Wiggle wiggle wiggle' than to 'when you ain't got nothin'' on 'Like A Rolling Stone'. We noted earlier the way that the restive crowd and the available nurse in 'TV Talkin' Song' hark back to 'The Drifter's Escape', and that there's a superficial resemblance too between 'TV Talkin' Song' and 'Subterranean Homesick Blues': it is just as plain that those earlier songs, and song performances, are better – more purposive, witty, spiky and fresh.

As many people have noticed, the spirit of the Basement Tapes that is present on "Under The Red Sky" reveals itself most explicitly in that fourth stanza of 'Unbelievable', where the exhortation to

> *Kill that beast and feed that swine*
> *Scale that wall and smoke that vine*
> *Beat that horse and saddle up that drum*

seems merely to extend a list begun on 'Lo and Behold' with

> *Round that horn and ride that herd*

and continued with more engagingly wayward panache on 'Tiny Montgomery''s

> *Scratch your dad*
> *Do that bird*
> *Suck that pig*
> *And bring it on home*
> *. . . Now grease that pig . . .*
> *And gas that dog . . .*
> *Play it low*
> *And pick it up.*

Even when an "Under The Red Sky" re-run of some earlier Dylan writing is not in itself inferior, it necessarily seems inferior because it is a re-run. This is unfair on the contemporary artist, but perhaps it's an unfairness that time sorts out, when the work has all become so old that, seen down posterity's wrong-way-round telescope, the time-gap from 1967 to 1990 disappears. Either way, an example seems to me to occur in '2 x 2', where Dylan makes one of his lovely embraces of the modern and the ancient together, comparing the mad polluting technology we trust in now with the blind superstition we've always bowed to, in his rhetorical questions

> *How much poison did they inhale?*
> *How many black cats crossed their trail?*

This suffers from coming twelve years later than the same embrace of the now and the timeless on

> *. . . let's disconnect these cables*
> *Overturn these tables*

in 'Señor (Tales Of Yankee Power)' on "Street Legal". Similarly, while 'Born In Time' offers a lovely off-kiltering of the standard poetic 'You are the sun and the moon' that concertinas nicely the ambivalence between the elemental/eternal, in

> *You were snow, you were rain*

and the quite literally material

> *You were striped, you were plain,*

this is diminished by his having been down this way before, in 1981's 'Lenny Bruce', in which

> *They stamped him and they labelled him like they do with pants and shirts.*

All that said, there is, quite in addition to its unique and creative use of nursery rhyme, some fine, fresh writing and some sumptuous vocal performance on the album: an album that offers three wholly worthy additions to Bob Dylan's body of work in 'Under The Red Sky', 'Handy Dandy' and 'Cat's In The Well'. This last, on top of its many already-catalogued virtues, contains one of the best lines of writing on the album – the deft, sharp stab of the second line of this couplet:

> *. . . the gentle lady is asleep*
> *. . . silence is a-stickin' her deep.*

This image, vivid and surprising, sudden and steely, in which silence is evoked as a pinioning visitation, a compressive staunch, seems to draw the blade of intensity from traditional ballads like 'Love Henry' without losing the good-humoured patoiserie of contemporary American street-talk.

'Handy Dandy', the discomforting banality of its chorus aside, is a sustained, successful work in which well-hewn writing interlocks with a bravura vocal performance, making for a warm, humorous, often black-humorous, hymn of celebration to human quirkiness and flexibility. Its rhythms writhe so enjoyably: the overall framework proceeds at so stately a pace, made the more ocean-linerish by the richness of sound of Dylan's voice and Al Kooper's organwork; yet within this Dylan moves so restlessly, so variegatedly, as he surveys his chameleonic dodgy hero – one who seems a different person in every brief encounter, so that 'he' 'you' 'she' and 'Nancy' seem to multiply, giving us refracted passing glimpses of people and conversation, all sunlit for a moment and then gone again, all with their own daubs of obdurate disorder, vulnerability, darkness and hope.

Each fragment possesses a different rhythm of speech to which Dylan's singing is superbly alert. Ray Davies or the John Sebastian of Lovin' Spoonful might have devised the line lauded earlier, the luxuriantly unfurling 'Handy Dandy, sitting with a girl named Nancy in a garden feeling kind of lazy' (either might be the unconscious influence behind it). No one but Bob Dylan could paint this onto the same canvas as so many other cadences and contrasting modes of speech. There's the intimate, inquisitorial brevity of the conversation which begins with the nursery rhyme about what little boys and little girls are made of (slugs and snails and puppy-dog tails . . . sugar and spice and all things nice . . .), adultising it into darker colloquialisms about inner being:

> You'll say 'What are you made of?'
> He'll say 'Can you repeat what you say?'
> You'll say 'What are you afraid of?'
> He'll say 'Nuthin: neither 'live nor dead.'

As we 'overhear' this, drifting across to us on beguiling waves of music, we are not so charmed that we don't pick up the prevarication and bragging on our hero's part. It is, furthermore, a moment at which Dylan uses a nursery rhyme from within a fairy tale, and uses it brilliantly, to paint in the right psychic backdrop against which to pick out that hollow bragging. The rhyme, the one that begins 'Fee, fie, fo, fum / I smell the blood of an Englishman', is spoken by the giant in the fairy tale 'Jack And The Beanstalk'. The next line is the one Dylan so niftily puts into the mouth of Handy Dandy: the giant boasts that

> Be he 'live or be he dead
> I'll grind his bones to make my bread.

It too proves a hollow boast, of course: the giant loses in the fight with brave little everyman Jack. Dylan echoes that 'Be he 'live or be he dead' so closely in Handy Dandy's 'Nuthin': neither 'live nor dead' that he repeats the slight awkwardness of diction noticeable in the giant's remark, such that in each case you can't quite decide whether it's an overtly foreshortened ''live' or a more slippery half-swallowed 'alive'.

There is a further strength and harmony in Dylan's use of 'Jack And The Beanstalk', a tale Dylan alluded to in such a different way in 1964's 'I Shall Be Free No. 10' (and again, in passing, in the phrase 'swap that cow' in *Tarantula*). It contributes to a main theme of the album in being another powerful parable about the need to journey towards maturity, like the fairy tale 'The Goose Girl' and the nursery rhyme 'My Mother Said', which (as we've seen) Dylan draws on in his 'blind horse' image. Like them, 'Jack and The Beanstalk' deals with the child's dilemma caught between its early need for parental love and guidance ('instruction', in the terminology of the book of Proverbs) and the eventual desirability of trusting oneself and moving towards independence. Jack plays his hunch, charged with the task of taking his cow to market to get a good price; his mother ridicules his folly in swapping the cow for a supposedly magical bean; Jack faces the consequences and in the end beats the giant. What looks large from a distance . . . Jack proves wiser than his mother, arguably through faith, centred upon faith in himself. It's a fairy tale Bettelheim scrutinises in detail along these lines in *The Uses of Enchantment*, and a classic example of the humane inner importance of the genre.

To return to Dylan's distinctive dexterity with rhythms and modes of speech, there's the switch from the calm and patience with which he spreads the child's comfort food over the eleven syllables of 'Handy Dandy, just like, sugar and candy' to the apparent clipped brevity of the line that follows – apparent because this line too is eleven syllables – in which the grown-up's comfort food is cynically provided instead: 'Handy Dandy: pour 'im another brandy'. And there's the joyous, acrobatic horde of syllables that comes streaming past us at some point in every verse. As well as lazing around with Nancy (a 24-syllable line, since Dylan makes the word 'la-zy' into a lazy 'la-za-a-ay'), there's also the technical wizardry of the line in which we get a quick-fire narrative list of what the hero does, ending with the slow drawl of his remark: 'He finishes his drink, he gets up from the table, he says "OK boys, I'll see ya tamarro-o-ow"' (twenty-six syllables as Dylan delivers it, since again the last word is given extra syllables). Best of all, there is the playful self-reflexive joke of the singer having to hurry to fit in, to not run out of time on, the preposterously long

> He'll say 'Darlin' tell me the truth: how much time I got?' She'll say 'You got all the time in the world, honey.'

Imagine anyone but Bob Dylan achieving the necessary timing and phrasing here. Not possible.

Any listener ever exhilarated by what Philip Larkin called that 'cawing, derisive voice' and Bruce Springsteen called 'the toughest voice I had ever heard . . . somehow simultaneously young and adult', and drawn into the churning worlds Dylan has evoked – any such listener to "Under The Red Sky" is going to hear, within its nursery rhymes and fairy tale landscapes, many echoing shouts of joy and rejuvenation all the way from "Highway 61" and The Basement.[70] The distinctive achievement of this album and no other is the tugging dynamics that come from combining *this* voice with *that* sensibility. It has the extraordinary, ancient, bio-degradable voice of Dylan in concert these days – so gorgeously capable of guard-down reverie and so shaky it can enmesh the irritatingly simplistic phrase 'Handy Dandy' in about eighteen vowel sounds – and yet its sensibility embraces that quirky, youthful, mischievous, restless surrealism of his mid-60s electric blitzkrieg. 'The cat's in the well and the barn is full o' the bull' . . . There's no arguing here, you either smile in the face of this winking, open audacity or you 'don't get it', which is to say it doesn't get you. The same applies to the matchless comic timing and mock derangement, the blazing, eye-rolling, *Alien*- and *Invasion of the Bodysnatchers*-recalling, alert paranoia – potent for all its comedy – of the pay-off line in this couplet:

---

70. Philip Larkin: in 'Jazz Review', *Daily Telegraph*, London, 10/11/65, quoted in Thomson and Gutman's *The Dylan Companion* (1990). Bruce Springsteen: speech on the occasion of Dylan's being inducted into the so-called Rock And Roll Hall Of Fame [yuk!], NYC, 20/1/88.

Your mind is your temple, keep it beautiful and free
Don't let an egg get laid in there by somethin' you can't see.

This is also terrific for the way that while the first line is founded upon biblical text –
Paul's 'Know ye not that ye are the temple of God, and that the spirit of God dwelleth
in you?' (1 Corinthians 3:16) – Dylan's inspired, paranoid second line pushes things
one step beyond Tom Paine's stirring retort to the same passage. In his post-French
Revolutionary work *The Age of Reason* (1794–96), Paine wrote: 'I do not believe in
the creed professed by the Jewish church, by the Roman church, by the Greek church,
by the Turkish church, by the Protestant church, nor by any church that I know of.
My mind is my own church.' Dylan moves the analogy on, so that it has shifted from
God's orderly domain to revolutionary, innocent, late eighteenth-century autonomy to
dark late twentieth-century fear of undetectable alien invasion. That he can do this
without getting bogged down in religious dispute himself is to his credit. Equally so is
his readiness not merely to sympathise with but to identify with those on their
soapboxes at Speakers' Corner (at whom most merely sneer): to offer a narrative that
describes their irrationality, their unconnectedness with others so clear-sightedly, in
that quirky line 'To anyone passing by, that's who they're talking to', and yet goes on
to listen to and then recount so compellingly the anti-TV speech heard there. Would
any other great artist so cheerfully identify himself with the famously unheeded ranters
of Hyde Park?

One of the many ways in which Bob Dylan is so unlike other performers in
popular music is that whereas most compose their faces one way for a love song and
another for a shake-your-ass song (for 'Wiggle Wiggle', in fact) – the equivalent of
people who come at you saying 'but seriously, though' and expect reverential hush to
descend when they do – Dylan's face in performance registers fifty fleeting expressions
per second, so that when you hear, on the album, that line about watching out for
alien eggs in the mind, you can see in that mind's eye the delirious qui-viverie of
Dylan's face delivering it. The first review his work ever attracted, back in September
1961 in the *New York Times*, alluded to his Chaplinesque quality. It is a quality that
phases of ennui, bitterness and portentousness have occasionally suggested has vanished; but here it is again, rocking back on its heels, nimble and light.

When your heels are nimble and light is, in any case, the best time to be serious,
as the language of rhyme and song for children reminds us. And as I hope to have
shown, Dylan uses this nursery rhyme and fairy tale with an imaginative adult
intelligence, to re-walk the corridors of childhood psyche, to liberate some vivid
imagery from under the bushel of superficial riddle, and to give his songs the same
underpinning in eternal verities that he gets from folk and blues. The blues are still
here too, as we've also seen: sometimes such that you feel the presence of that other
great white blues singer, Elvis Presley (especially the 1960 Elvis of 'Feel So Bad' and
the "Elvis Is Back" album) at the back of "Under The Red Sky", as well as, as ever,
the language and agenda of the Bible. Dylan's passionate engagement with all these
elements synthesises them to inspired effect. 'Strap yourself to a tree with roots,' he
sang, so long ago that at the time those for whom he embodied the integrity of
restlessness thought he was joking. He wasn't, of course.

In all, alongside the innumerable quotes from and reminders of blues, R&B and rock'n'roll songs and the many allusions to biblical text, by my count "Under The Red Sky" (a very short album) makes direct raids on thirty-two nursery rhymes and game-songs, and offers demonstrable correspondence with three fairy tales and a further fifteen nursery rhymes, not counting variants. Even the sleeve note announcement that the album is 'for Gabby Goo Goo' represents an apt parting shot from the same eccentric armoury. In North American playgrounds, the chant 'Gabby gabby goo goo!' is used, rather like our own sing-song 'Naa na na naa naa!', as a mocking sneer – an accusation of babyishness.[71]

I end this chapter by looking at the way Bob Dylan ends the album. This reflects his continued interest in challenging dividing-lines between the song and the recording. As I've noted elsewhere, this was in evidence on "Oh Mercy" in 'What was it you wanted? / You can tell me, I'm back' when his vocal returned after an instrumental break, followed by the punning 'let's get it back on the track'. It is in evidence here too. A reminder to the listener that it *is* a recording is built into the whole structuring of "Under The Red Sky". Side 2 begins like a live recording: beginning before the song's beginning, by offering on the tape the ground-pawing noises musicians make just before they start to play, but without allowing you to feel certain if you've overheard genuine pawing or not. At the same time this sense of 'liveness' is undermined by the way that it begins with the smearing sound of this pre-song recording actually being switched on: to remind you that your LP, CD or tape is of a tape. As Side 2 begins, so it ends: like a live recording. For emphasis, every track on the album fades out except the last one. (The best thing about 'God Knows' is the way the shape of the song mocks the sermonising inside it, perhaps unintentionally, so that the singer has to rant more and more to squeeze the lines in as it works itself up like a sermon: and as soon as he starts to rant, they start fading him out. For the listener, it's as if you're slowly but surely closing the door on a Mormon or a Jehovah's Witness getting as much said as possible in his last few seconds' worth of your unwilling attention.) Only the last song on the album comes to a final end.

It's a challenge, though, a messy business: because while any pointing at *form* must distance the listener from *content*, Dylan's drawing attention to *this* form, this recording, stresses that the track has been done 'live', which is to make it, by rock's conventions, more 'real'. In turn the irony of this is that, unlike Dylan's early records, none of "Under The Red Sky" was done 'live': Dylan's vocals not only include drop-ins and overdubs but these are made as onto one big basic overdub. Dylan was still re-writing till the last possible moment so that his vocals were added at the mixing stage of the album. Dylan challenges every divide here. All the same, the device of coming to a 'live' finish on the last track of an album on which every other song fades

---

71. It may be Dylan's double-joke that he knows there is a precedent here too: for taking this chant and using it for pseudonyms. As we know, Dylan often lifts snatches of dialogue from Hollywood films of the 1930s to 1950s. At the end of the credits list for the W. C. Fields film *My Little Chickadee* [Universal, US, directed Edward Cline, written Mae West and W. C. Fields, starring both, 1939] two midgets are named as 'Gabby' and 'Goo Goo'. (Noted by reader Jeff Goodnow, Fayetteville, USA, *Telegraph*, no. 38, Spring 1991.)

There may be another, more personal term of endearment behind the dedication of the album to Gabby Goo Goo. Dylan was 49 when he recorded "Under The Red Sky". If this work were read for clues concerning the artist's private life at that time, we might have wondered, pruriently, if this compulsion to stalk nursery-rhyme-land under the red sky meant Bob Dylan had learnt he was going to become a grandfather. Meanwhile he and his cousin Beth Zimmerman were reported to have opened a baby-clothes shop in Hollywood, called 'Forever Young'.

out also dramatises the outrageous last-minute call across another such divide that is, in the lyric, the album's 'final end':

Goodnight my love, and may the Lord have mercy on us all.

That 'Goodnight my love' is so personal it leaps out at you, cutting not only clean through the recording but right out through the song itself. It is the most inspired, simple leave-taking I have ever heard on an album.

CHAPTER EIGHTEEN

Good as He's Been in a World Gone Wrong?

"Good As I Been To You", probably recorded in late July to early August 1992, and released on 2 November that year, was Bob Dylan's first solo acoustic album since 1964. But this was a surprise we might have seen coming ever since the extraordinary Never-Ending Tour began in 1988. I experienced an exhilarating flash of such a prospect when I saw him at Radio City Music Hall in New York in October 1988. I helped pay my way to seeing the shows by reviewing them for the *Independent*, and ended the review like this:

> if G. E. Smith's inspired playing has been a big factor in Dylan's current success, that success is due also to an old power Dylan has rediscovered within himself, as his fiery emphasis on pre-electric material shows. The long acoustic part of his set has been its highpoint, and it has seen Dylan re-embrace the strengths of traditional folksongs. After burning performances of 'Man Of Constant Sorrow', 'Trail of the Buffalo', 'Pretty Peggy-O' (all unperformed since 1962) . . . and the thrilling 'Eileen Aroon', Dylan's avid alignment with such material, for the first time in more than two decades, holds out tantalising possibilities as to where he might land next time he jumps.[1]

Speculation that solo acoustic work and a stress on traditional material were uppermost in Dylan's musical mind intensified after mid-1991. Until the middle of that year, Dylan had been relying on his lead guitarists to back him up even on the non-electric songs – but in Hamburg in June 1991 he reverted to *solo* performances for the first time since the mid-1980s (and the first song done this way was the ancient folk-ballad 'Barbara Allen').[2]

More recently still, Dylan's acoustic guitar-playing changed dramatically: he abandoned the very basic, raw (sometimes petulant, often incompetent) strumming he had insisted on for the previous twenty-five or more years – and went back to the deft, intricate picking style that was so strong a feature of his very early recordings.

---

1.   *Independent*, London, 21/10/88. The Never-Ending Tour began at Concord, California, on 7 June 1988. The New York City dates were 16–19/10/88. The performances of pre-electric material referred to come not from New York City but from earlier dates, and were débuted as follows: 'Man Of Constant Sorrow', Mountain View, California, 11/6/88; 'Trail Of The Buffalo', Holmdel, New Jersey, 25/6/88; 'Pretty Peggy-O', Mansfield, Massachusetts, 2/7/88; and 'Eileen Aroon', Denver, 15/6/88 (though quicker to circulate was the exquisite performance at Wantagh, New York, 30/6/88).

2.   Hamburg, 23/6/91.

At the same time, 1992 shows in Australia, North America and Europe treated audiences to solo performances (in some cases one-offs) of many pre-twentieth-century folksongs and pre-war country-blues songs. These included the eighteenth-century ballad 'The Golden Vanity', premiered in Kansas on Hallowe'en 1991 and performed again in Australia and Hawaii in April 1992; 'The Lady Of Carlisle' and the broadside 'The Female Rambling Sailor', performed in Australia the same month; and the turn-of-the-century black ballad 'Delia' (mentioned earlier vis à vis Blind Willie McTell), which Dylan was singing in his home state of Minnesota back in 1960, before ever he arrived in New York to try for a record deal, and which made a surprise reappearance exactly thirty-two years later in Hollywood.[3] It was to reappear on "World Gone Wrong", Dylan's second solo acoustic album of the 1990s.

First, though, there was "Good As I Been To You", showing Dylan making an emphatic full-circle. It compares with nothing so well as his début LP "Bob Dylan", released thirty years to the month beforehand. (And it's so *long*!: Side 1 is 33 minutes and Side 2 is 29. The whole of "Under The Red Sky" is only a little over 35 . . .)

After such a long time in between, in which Dylan changed the world of music, and the world changed the world of music too, for "Good As I Been To You" to achieve any equivalent distinction, its contents had to be rather different kettles of folk fish from the offerings of 1962. When "Bob Dylan" was released, its singer differed from those around him by cutting through the mimsy purity and the sacred cow divides between different cliques of folk performers, as well as by the cultivated uncultivatedness of his voice and the vibrant jittering energy he brought to what was largely a genteel coffee-house milieu. His eclectic mix of white and black song, his own two immaculate and very contrasting compositions, his brilliant pose of Ancient Geezer and his rock'n'roll irreverence – not to the material but to the conventions of the *Sing Out!* mind-set – added up to something that stood out and got noticed, though selling very poorly.

For "Good As I Been To You" Dylan returns to solo 'folk' performance in a context in which the *Sing Out!* mentality has been squeezed to the irrelevant sidelines (and even the saintly Pete Seeger has long since condescended to dabble with electric instruments). Dylan now needs none of his brilliance as a mimic to sound like an ancient cove, and the sub-divides between this kind of folk and that have been demolished. Yet there are still pricks to kick against – and one is the quest for the obscure and unusual. Dylan here exhibits his usual haughty disregard for the prevailing winds. If you were to get up at a folk club anywhere in the western world and start singing 'Frankie & Albert' (or 'Frankie & Johnny'), you'd be sneered right out of the place. It's too well-known, too obvious. Dylan's album makes it the opening track.

Not every track is solidly mainstream. Dylan has an ear for specific contemporary 'folk' recordings of numinous quality and is up for having a go at them, even knowing that now his is the voice encrusted with the detritus of years and with suspect habits of mannerism from too much public performance, so that he is hardly likely to

3.   Bob Dylan: 'The Golden Vanity', Melbourne, 6 & 7/4/92; Launceston, Australia, 10/4/92; and Waikiki, Hawaii, 24/4/92. 'Lady Of Carlisle', débuted Sydney, 14/4/92. 'The Female Rambling Sailor', débuted on this tour-leg's second date, Adelaide, 21/3/92. (There is a brief discussion of the historical phenomenon of female sailors and pirates later in this chapter.)
     'Delia', Hollywood, 14/5/92. 'Delia', amateur recording, St. Paul, Minnesota, May 1960.

compete successfully with their originators for freshness or authentic directness (nor for dexterity on the guitar). But Dylan is lining these songs up, not like Nic Jones, Mick Slocum or Paul Brady, against the rest of their own repertoires, but against the most well-known, the most 'obvious' folk standards there are.[4] He is not offering the result to folk club audiences but to the rest of us, and his purpose is to re-open the gate into the secret garden of the richly variegated past: into what Greil Marcus' fine book calls the *Invisible Republic* – the past of down-home pre-corporate, pre-Pentagon America and of the sometimes obscure inspired recording artists, black and white, who sang of and belonged to those faded-photo worlds – and into the past of English and Celtic history.[5]

There is immense multiplicity here, and re-opening these gates is, for someone in Bob Dylan's position, a far greater acting against the grain than could possibly be achieved with a rock album. "Good As I Been To You" and "World Gone Wrong" turn a radio telescope upon the past, retrieving that which seems light years away in the era of Microsoft, McDonald's and MTV. These albums are anthologies of individualism but they also champion the dignity of labour, the silenced and oppressed. They celebrate oral history, working-class history, history that struggled across oceans.

As "Bob Dylan" did, they also reject 'purity'. There are songs here of dodgy provenance – songs as likely to have been sanitised by nineteenth-century Irish clergymen as come down orally intact; songs that might be North American or Irish; songs with composers' names attached to them through accidents of publishing history; songs that may not be half the age they hint at. Above all, these collections embrace material that has belonged jointly to black America and white, as well as songs that have arisen in one camp or the other.

They are his Harry Smith anthology – a collection that was, as Greil Marcus writes, 'the founding document of the American folk revival' (but don't hold that against it) – and they include, inevitably, material from that wondrous collection.[6] As noted in Chapter 9, Dylan has been drawing on its mysterious waters since at least early 1960, before ever he arrived in Greenwich Village, and he is drawing on it still.

Yet Dylan's concern here is not a looking-back at himself and his own past but a shepherding us out into an older and wider world. It is not his early recordings that

4.   Nic Jones's immaculate album "Penguin Eggs", Topic 12TS411, London, 1980 (now deleted), CD-reissued Topic TSCD411, London, 1991, was the source for 'Canadee-i-o' [Nic Jones: 'Canadee-i-o', London, early 1980; it is the album's opening track; it is also on the Topic sampler-album "The Good Old Way", TPSS412, London, 1980]. The final track on "Penguin Eggs", 'Farewell To The Gold', was performed by Dylan in concert at Youngstown, 2/11/92. Nic Jones took this song from New Zealander Paul Metsers, who may have written it (or re-written it from a broadside) but who certainly made it available to Jones before recording it himself on "Caution To The Wind", Highway Records SHY 7014, New Zealand, 1981.

Mick Slocum (formerly of the group the Bushwackers) set the old convict song 'Jim Jones' to the melody Dylan used [Mick Slocum: 'Jim Jones', *nia*]; and Paul Brady tidied the old anti-militarist song 'Arthur McBride' into the order and exact shape Dylan recycles [Paul Brady: 'Arthur McBride', Wales, Autumn 1976; "Andy Irvine–Paul Brady", Mulligan Records LUN 008, Dublin, 1976; CD-reissue LUNCD008, Dublin, 1990]. All these appear on "Good As I Been To You".

5.   Greil Marcus: *Invisible Republic: Bob Dylan's Basement Tapes*, 1997.

6.   Harry Smith's "American Folk Music", set of 3 double-LPs (Vol. 1: Ballads; Vol. 2: Social Music; Vol. 3: Songs), Folkways Records FP251–253, NYC, 1952; CD-reissued as "Anthology Of American Folk Music" [6-CD box-set] with copious notes by many hands and including a CD-ROM of extras, Smithsonian Folkways Recordings SFW 40090, Washington, DC, 1997. Greil Marcus quoted from his introductory essay 'The Old, Weird America', included in the CD-reissue package. For more on Harry Smith, see Chapter 9, note 22.

give him the right to play the shepherd, but that his entire creative adult life has been a deeply inquiring, intelligent exploration of many kinds of popular and grass roots music, as this book has tried to attest. His perennial genius at telling stories is based upon his interest in other people's.

The story told in 'Frankie & Albert' is probably based on a nineteenth-century shooting. Harry Smith's anthology notes claim that 'Allen Britt shot Frankie Baker of 212 Targee Street, St. Louis, Missouri, October 15, 1899' and that the song 'was first sung by, and probably written by, "Mammy Lou", a singer at Babe Conner's Famous Cabaret in that city'. However, he doesn't explain why one of the names has been changed or why the sex-roles have been reversed, while other studies suggest an earlier origin. At any rate the song appears in many published collections, including three by the Lomaxes and Carl Sandburg's *An American Songbag* (1927). The first commercially published version seems to have been by one Hughie Cannon in 1904 under the title 'He Done Me Wrong'. As 'Frankie and Johnny' it also appears as a poem, authorship 'anonymous', in collections such as the *Penguin Book of American Verse*, with, as you'd predict, a few fanciful elaborations from some interfering enthusiast who stretches it to nineteen verses.[7]

The coupling Frankie and Albert probably pre-dates the more familiar Frankie and Johnny, though early recorded versions have been titled variously 'Frankie' (Mississippi John Hurt, and Dykes Magic City Trio), 'Frankie And Johnny' (both the white Jimmie Rodgers and the post-war black Jimmy Rogers), 'Frankie's Gamblin' Man' (Welby Toomey) and 'Frankie Dean' (Tom Darby & Jimmy Tarlton). Like a number of the songs on this Bob Dylan album, it has enjoyed widespread popularity among both blacks and whites, as even the short roster of disparate artists above must suggest.[8]

Its lyric varies almost as much as its musical genre. To take a white example by an important figure in the music's history, Charlie Poole With The North Carolina Ramblers' 'Leaving Home' is a lovely dance-hall version of the song, with banjo, guitar and fiddle, which stars Frankie and Johnny but in which the verses tell an only half-similar story – it begins with their having a quarrel, Johnny saying he's leaving and Frankie saying she knows *she* done *him* wrong but begging him to stay. The normal chorus is entirely missing, replaced by a hoe-downy 'Oh I'm goin' away, I'm goin' to stay, never coming home' which, given some prominence, as the song's title confirms, rather squanders the inherent appeal of the Frankie-and-whoever formula.[9]

7.   John A. Lomax and Alan Lomax, *American Ballads and Folk Songs* (1934); *Negro Folk Songs as Sung by Lead Belly* [sic] (1936); and *Folksong U.S.A.* (1941). Carl Sandburg's *An American Songbag*, published 1927, was reprinted 1970. He also published *New American Songbag: Broadcast Music* (1950). Hughie Cannon: *nia*, 1904. *The Penguin Book of American Verse* (1977).

8.   Mississippi John Hurt: 'Frankie', details below. Dykes Magic City Trio: 'Frankie', NYC, 9/3/27; "Dykes Magic City Trio", Old Homestead Records OHCS-191, Brighton, Michigan, late 1980s. Jimmie Rodgers: 'Frankie and Johnny', Dallas, 10/8/29. Jimmy Rogers: 'Frankie and Johnny', *nia*. Welby Toomey: 'Frankie's Gamblin' Man', Richmond, Indiana, c. 13/11/25. Tom Darby & Jimmy Tarlton: 'Frankie Dean', details below.

9.   Charlie Poole with The North Carolina Ramblers: 'Leaving Home', NYC, 18/9/26, CD-reissued on "White Country Blues 1926–1938", Columbia Roots N' Blues Series 472886 2, NYC, 1993. Judging by the Poole/Ramblers track adjacent to 'Leaving Home' on this CD, 'If The River Was Whiskey', NYC, 30/1/30 (a version of W. C. Handy's 'Hesitating Blues', itself based on older black floating couplets), this white outfit, led by a textile mill worker in the northern Piedmont area of North Carolina, born in 1892, who headed for New York in 1925 determined to make records, and succeeded, has been a marked, specific influence on the style of Taj Mahal, a black artist born in Massachusetts 50 years later. This influence is clear from Mahal LPs like "Oooh So Good 'n

'Frankie Dean' by Tom Darby & Jimmy Tarlton features Johnny rather than Albert but offers the kind of garbled narrative Bob Dylan sometimes manages on concert versions of 'Joey', in which Joey leaves jail before being sent to it. Here Frankie buys her gun and swears to kill Johnny before she finds 'with her surprise' that he's been cheating her. That aside, this white version is far closer to the song as we generally know it.[10]

Dylan already knew Mississippi John Hurt's 1928 recording of 'Frankie' before ever he arrived in New York. He knew it from its reissue on Harry Smith's anthology – and you might think that Dylan's own performance, decades later, confirms that specific familiarity, recapturing something of Hurt's approach to the song, which differs somewhat from the general flavour of Hurt's work.[11]

Hurt, born in 1894 in Teoc, Mississippi (too small to be on the map), lived and farmed in Avalon. He was one of those who recorded in 1928 – just twelve sides – and then not again for more than thirty years. His repertoire included 'Stack O'Lee Blues' and dance-tunes, some showing a nineteenth-century Spanish influence, like his 'Spanish Flangdang' (fandango). He made no attempt to become a professional singer and was unchanged as a performer when 'rediscovered' in March 1961 by a record collector from Washington, Tom Hoskins. Hurt played the Newport Folk Festival, campuses and clubs and his last recording session was in 1966. He died in Grenada, Mississippi, that November.

(An excellent piece by Stanley Booth, describing going to Mississippi John Hurt's funeral, includes this exchange about Hurt between Booth's companion and Furry Lewis:

' "I loved him," Christopher said. "He was such a sweet little man, and he was a wonderful guitar player."

"Yes," said Furry . . . "but he was sho ugly. I swear 'fore God he was." '[12])

At the same time as figuring in Mississippi John Hurt's repertoire, 'Frankie

---

Blues", CBS 65814, London, 1973, so it comes as no surprise to find that back in the mid-1960s, with Jesse Lee Kincaid and Ry Cooder, Mahal was one of the Rising Sons (who wowed them on the LA club scene in 1965), and that they recorded 'If The River Was Whiskey', Hollywood, 1/12/65 (though in this case not at all in Charlie Poole style!). Bob Dylan is reputed to have attended at least one session, while one Rising Son, Kevin Kelley, thereafter joined the Byrds. Only a single was issued at the time, so this track and the rest of the group's material (produced by Terry Melcher) remained unissued for 25 years until the CD "Rising Sons", Columbia Legacy 472865 2, NYC, 1993.

10. Tom Darby & Jimmy Tarlton: 'Frankie Dean', Atlanta, 16/4/30; "Old-Time Southern Dance Music: Ballads And Songs", Old Timey Records OT-102 [an Arhoolie Records subsidiary label], El Cerrito, *nia*; CD-reissued "White Country Blues 1926–1938", Columbia Roots N' Blues Series 472886 2, NYC, 1993.

Jimmy Tarlton, an important figure in hillbilly music, and the inventor of a pre-dobro way of playing guitar by using a comb to lift the strings off the fretboard, is credited as composer of 'Mexican Rag', the model for Dylan's early instrumental 'Suze', or 'The Cough Song', released on "Bootleg Series I–III" in 1991.

11. Mississippi John Hurt: 'Frankie', Memphis, 14/2/28, "American Folk Music" (see note 6). It was later issued on a Yazoo LP now CD-reissued, "Mississippi John Hurt: 1928 Sessions", Yazoo 1065, 1990. This also contains his 'Stack O' Lee Blues', NYC, 28/12/28 (mentioned below).

12. Stanley Booth: 'Been Here and Gone: The Funeral of Mississippi John Hurt', republished in the collection *Rythm Oil*, 1991.

It was first reported in 'In session: Dylan at Acme' by Blair Jackson, *Mix Magazine*, November 1992, that in 1992 at Acme Studio, Chicago, Dylan recorded 26 songs, including the Furry Lewis version of 'Kassie Jones' – yet *another* recording taken from the Harry Smith anthology. (Furry Lewis: 'Kassie Jones Part 1' and 'Kassie Jones Part 2', Memphis, 28/8/28; both parts CD-reissued "Furry Lewis: In His Prime 1927–1928", Yazoo 1050, New York, 1991, and on the compilation "Canned Heat Blues: Masters of the Delta Blues", RCA BMG Bluebird ND90648, 1992.)

& Albert' was being sung (not necessarily on record) by many other singers, especially the older ones, those all-round 'songsters' who knew nineteenth-entury material not least because they'd begun learning songs before the blues had grown into its own as a form. Some of these people were in their forties before they ever recorded at all, yet had been semi-pro musicians around their communities for perhaps as much as the preceding quarter-century. Charley Patton was one of these, and though most of his recordings are blues, he chose to include 'Frankie & Albert' at his second recording session, in 1929.[13]

The song was a western tune too. The same year Patton recorded it, Gene Autry cut it as 'Frankie & Johnny', and thirty years later, titled 'Frankie's Man Johnnie', Johnny Cash achieved a minor US hit with it, soon after leaving Sun Records for Columbia.[14]

As 'Frankie And Johnny' the song was also recorded at Sun by Jerry Lee Lewis, and by one of Dylan's favourite rock'n'roll stars, Gene Vincent, on his classic album "Gene Vincent Rocks! And The Bluecaps Roll". It was a minor hit in Britain for Brook Benton (1961), Mr. Acker Bilk (1962), Elvis Presley (1966: it was the title song of one of his most gruesome movies) and – more memorably – Sam Cooke (1963). Under the title 'Frankie & Albert' it was revived in the 1960s by Rolf Cahn & Eric von Schmidt and in the early 1970s on an album by Taj Mahal – whose next LP was named after another Hurt song, 'Satisfied And Tickled Too' – and, back as 'Frankie & Johnny', it was on Mike Bloomfield's "Analine" LP in 1977.[15]

Dylan takes the song far more seriously than Taj Mahal, though you might say that for just that reason, his arrangement is less resourceful; perhaps less ostentatious. Yet the voice is far from low-profile. On a solo album of just guitar, harmonica and voice – and especially one from an artist who has commanded so many different voices in his time – the one on offer here is bound to be under scrutiny. Our first encounter with it, on 'Frankie & Albert', is, by the nature of Dylan's performance, inconclusive.

What strikes the new listener, equally, however, on hearing Dylan's opening salvo,

---

13.   Charley Patton: 'Frankie & Albert', Grafton, Wisconsin, c. Oct. 1929.

14.   Gene Autry: 'Frankie & Johnny', NYC, 3/12/29, possibly vinyl-issued on a fan-club bootleg, *nia*. Johnny Cash: 'Frankie's Man Johnnie', Nashville, 8/8/58, issued on the single Columbia Records 41371, New York, 1959, LP-issued "Fabulous Johnny Cash", Columbia Records CL1253 [mono] and CS8122 [stereo], New York, 1959, CD-reissued on the 5-CD box-set "The Man In Black 1954–1958", Bear Family Records BCD 15517-EH, Vollersode, Germany, c. 1990.

15.   Jerry Lee Lewis: 'Frankie And Johnny', Memphis, March 1958, "Jerry Lee's Greatest", Sun 1265, Memphis [London-American HAS 2440, London], 1961. Gene Vincent: 'Frankie And Johnnie', LA, 9/12/57, "Gene Vincent Rocks! And The Blue Caps Roll", Capitol Records T970, Hollywood, 1958. Brook Benton: 'Frankie And Johnny', Mercury 71859, Chicago, 1961. Mr. Acker Bilk: 'Frankie And Johnny', *nia*. Elvis Presley: 'Frankie And Johnny', Hollywood, May 1965, RCA Victor 47–8780, New York, 1966. Sam Cooke: 'Frankie And Johnny', *nia*.

Rolf Cahn & Eric von Schmidt: 'Frankie And Albert', *nia*, "Rolf Cahn & Eric von Schmidt", Folkways FA 2417, NYC, 1967. (This LP also featured Dylan's 'He Was A Friend Of Mine' plus 'Make Me A Pallet On Your Floor' and 'Poor Lazarus'.)

Taj Mahal: 'Frankie & Albert', *nia*, "Oooh So Good 'n Blues", Columbia Records New York and CBS 65814, London, 1973, CD-reissued "Taj's Blues", Columbia/Legacy Roots N' Blues Series 52465, New York, c. 1991. In what may seem an excess of self-effacement, he gives the composer credit to Mississippi John Hurt. (There is an earlier Taj Mahal blues compilation, "Going Home", issued UK as CBS 31844, London, 1980, which includes his versions of 'Frankie & Albert', 'Satisfied 'n' Tickled Too', 'Dust My Broom', 'Sweet Home Chicago', McTell's 'Statesboro Blues', Chuck Berry's 'Brown-Eyed Handsome Man' and . . . 'Blackjack Davey'.)

Mike Bloomfield: 'Frankie & Johnny', "Analine", Takoma Records B-1059, USA, 1977.

his 'Frankie & Albert', is the unexpected *energy* of the guitar-work. The stripped-down ten-verse version he sings is not the Mississippi John Hurt version, though both begin with the same verse, starting with the ambiguous assertion that 'Frankie was a good girl, everybody knowed', and then go their largely separate ways.[16] Neither version gives the lyric lines an iota more emphasis than the decorative figures on the strings of the guitar: it's as if they are plaiting the words in among the guitar-strings. Yet the guitar-work of the two is very different. Hurt's is mournfully frisky, understated and neat as a box-hedge, and Dylan's is busy, bass-heavy (recorded as if we're inside the sound-box) and almost as dishevelled as somebody dragged *through* a hedge; but it's far from an incompetent dishevelment. Bursting with celebratory energy, it dashes up and down its runs with garrulous bonhomie, nudging you in the elbows and laughing.

'Frankie & Albert' shares common elements with 'Stack O'Lee' ('Staggerlee'), another old pre-blues song, not least in their endings. Mississippi John Hurt's 'Stack O'Lee' ends

> *Standing at the gallows*
> *Head way up high . . .*

while in Dylan's 'Frankie & Albert'

> *Frankie went to the scaffold*
> *Calm as a girl could be*
> *Held her eyes up t'wards the heavens*
> *Said 'Nearer My God To Thee'.*

Indeed they share so much that a couple of years before Mississippi John Hurt recorded either of them, Ma Rainey had already fused the songs together into one. Her 'Stack O'Lee Blues' ends each verse with the refrain 'He was her man / But he was doin' her wrong.'[17] There are additional similarities between this pair and another

16.   It's ironic that the song appends 'Everybody knows' to the claim that 'Frankie was a good girl', because not everybody knows the same thing here. To some, Frankie was a good girl in the same way that 'Lenny Bruce was bad': that is, with these terms embracing their own opposites. Stephen Calt, commenting on Robert Johnson's using the label 'a good girl' on 'I Believe I'll Dust My Broom', 1936, writes that it is 'A blues term for an obliging sex partner . . . As described by Gary Davis: ". . . she's very interested in your affairs and she likes you . . . she always looks out for you . . . You can call on her when you need it, you understand . . . She's not so regular with you but she's just good when you catch it."' [Stephen Calt: 'Idioms of Robert Johnson', *78 Quarterly*, Vol. 1, no. 4, 1989.] But granted the longevity of 'Frankie & Albert' I doubt if 'good girl' only has this resonance as 'a blues term'.

17.   Ma Rainey, 'Stack O'Lee Blues', NYC, c. Dec. 1925; "Classic Blues Sides", Riverside RLP 12–108, New York, 1956, "Ma Rainey's Black Bottom", Yazoo CD 1071, New York, 1985. This latter album title (after a 1927 recording) tells a tale. This seems my best opportunity to tell it.
   Ma Rainey's Black Bottom is a play by the modern black American playwright August Wilson (1984) about the humiliations of a typical early blues recording session, though in the play the artist suffers under a white producer, while Rainey had a black producer, Mayo Williams. He was no saint towards his artists and their royalties either. The song title the play uses might ordinarily have been 'Black Bottom', but there had already been instances where on this artist's early Paramount 78 rpm record labels the song title and artist are given in this fused, one-line way. Two 1924 Chicago recordings were thus billed as ' "Ma" Rainey's Lost Wandering Blues' and ' "Ma" Rainey's Dream Blues'. This way of putting it, which normally tends to stress the egocentrality of the artist, might have inspired her to the title ' "Ma" Rainey's Black Bottom', in this case having the opposite effect, as full of self-debunking as self-aggrandisement. The more prosaic explanation is that the dance's name, the Black Bottom, was always the cause of the same schoolboyish mirth as it was for my generation when we first came across it on the B-side of a Temperance Seven record, and that, then as now, Ma Rainey and/or her record company were not alone in trying to nudge-nudge the prospective punter in this way. Willie Scarecrow Owens managed to release

song, 'Duncan And Brady', which Bob Dylan recorded at his Chicago 1992 sessions with Dave Bromberg (from which nothing has been released) and which in turn can share at least one verse with 'Delia', included by Dylan on "World Gone Wrong".

There's also the curious way that Jimmie Rodgers' 'Blue Yodel No. 9' takes up the story of both 'Frankie & Albert' and of 'Stack O'Lee'. The latter, as told in the 1927 black version by Papa Harvey Hull and Long Cleve Reed, the so-called 'Original Stack O'Lee Blues', has this as its fifth verse:

> *Standing on the corner, well I didn't mean no harm.*
> *Well a policeman caught me, well he grabbed my arm.*
> *Well it's cruel Stack O'Lee.*

This reappears as the beginning of Jimmie Rodgers' 'Blue Yodel No. 9':

> *Standin' on the corner I didn't mean no harm*
> *Along came a po-lice, he took me by the arm.*
> *It was down in Memphis, corner of Beale and Main*
> *He says 'Big boy, you'll have to tell me your name'.*

The story continues with the narrator's refusal to give his name: but he could well have answered 'Albert' or 'Johnny', since a few lines later the lyric acts as a sort of 'answer' to the 'Frankie & Albert' narrative – telling the story from Albert's (or Johnny's) viewpoint:

> *My good gal loved me, everybody knowed*
> *And she paid a hundred cash dollars just for me a suit of clothes*
> *She come to the joint, a .44 in each hand*
> *She said 'Stand aside all you women and men,*
> *'Cos I'm looking for my man.'*

That's the end: which of course it would be.[18]

In strong contrast, 'Jim Jones' is one of the least popular of nineteenth-century

---

only the demure 'That Black Bottom Dance', but he recorded and then saw his record company fail to issue, 'I'm Going To Show You My Black Bottom', 'Everybody Wants To See My Black Bottom' and 'The World's Gone Crazy 'Bout My Black Bottom' – this last having at first been titled 'Come On And Show Me Your Black Bottom'. Which just about uncovers it.

August Wilson's next play (1986) was called *Joe Turner's Come and Gone*; another is titled *Two Trains Running* (1990).

Ma Rainey: 'Ma Rainey's Black Bottom', Chicago, c. Dec., 1927; "Ma Rainey's Black Bottom", Yazoo 1071. '"Ma" Rainey's Lost Wandering Blues' and '"Ma" Rainey's Dream Blues', both Chicago, c. March 1924; "Ma Rainey: Complete Recordings December 1923 to April 1924", VJM Records VLP 81, London, c. 1985.

Willie Scarecrow Owens: 'That Black Bottom Dance', Richmond, Indiana, 30/8/30; 'The World's Gone Crazy 'Bout My Black' Bottom', ditto but never issued; 'I'm Going To Show You My Black Bottom' and 'Everybody Wants To See My Black Bottom', Richmond, Indiana, 17/5/30, never issued.

18. Papa Harvey Hull & Long 'Cleve' Reed (as Long 'Cleve' Reed – Little Harvey Hull – The Down Home Boys): 'Original Stack O' Lee Blues', Chicago, c. May 1927, CD-reissued on "The Songster Tradition (1927–1935)", Document Records DOCD-5045, Vienna, 1991. Jimmie Rodgers: 'Blue Yodel No. 9', Hollywood, 16/7/30, "My Rough And Rowdy Ways", RCA Victor LPM 2112, New York, 1960.

The formulation 'I went down town, didn't mean no harm / Police grabbed me right by my arm', which Jimmie Rodgers dramatises by placing it at the start of his song, is a common one, also appearing, for example, in the version of 'Lost John' recorded by [Gus] Cannon's Jug Stompers as 'Feather Bed', Memphis, 9/9/28, and issued on Harry Smith's "American Folk Music" (see note 6).

broadside ballads (the words first collected by Charles Macalister), about a convict sent to Botany Bay, and it is a particular favourite of A. L. Lloyd, founding father of the British folk revival.[19] He regards it as unusual and admirable for 'its strong bloodshot defiance', stressing that unlike most songs of the period that deal with crime and punishment 'Jim Jones' implies no acceptance of the rules and divisions of society, rather justifying its denouement of avowed lawlessness on the grounds that it is society that is out of step with justice. This makes it eminently suitable as Bob Dylan material.

A version by Lloyd himself is on the album "The Great Australian Legend" (by Lloyd, Trevor Lucas and Martin Wyndham-Read, 1971); John Kirkpatrick and Sue Harris recorded it on their Sergeant Pepperishly titled "Among The Many Attractions At The Show Will Be A Really High Class Band" (1976) and Lawrence Hoy included it on his album "Beyond The Seas" (date unknown). North of England folk group the High Level Ranters sang it too, and it's on their LP "New High Level Ranters" (1982).[20]

Bob Dylan's version is more or less word for word the same as that collected in the 1964 *Penguin Australian Songbook* edited by John Manifold, but he has heard it, as we noted, from the version put together by Mick Slocum. It is as Bob Dylan takes this and runs with it that we are served notice of the regrettable condition his voice is in.

John Wesley Harding writes, in reviewing "Good As I Been To You":

19. Lloyd says that if the lyric is taken at face value then the song must have been written between September 1828 and 1830, the period in which Jack Donahue 'and Co.' were fugitives rebelliously at large in the Australian bush. Donahue was caught in 1830. He deplores the fact that 'such a well-made mettlesome piece' never became popular 'when flabbier creations on the same theme have ostentatiously survived'. (Lloyd is always regretting that the public isn't sufficiently communistic to appreciate the left's best tunes.) It was first collected in Charles Macalister, *Old Pioneering Days in the Sunny South* (1907), 'a book of reminiscences, mainly of the Sydney area in the 1840s'.

The commentary here by Lloyd is taken from his magnum opus, *Folk Song in England* (1967), as are his comments on 'Arthur McBride', below.

20. A. L. Lloyd: 'Jim Jones', London, c. 1970, "The Great Australian Legend", Topic 12TS203, London, 1971. Lloyd and Martin Wyndham-Read also collaborated on the album "Sea Shanties", Topic 12TS234, London, 1974, produced by Lloyd, on which Wyndham-Read sings the traditional song 'Haul Away The Bowline', the realism of which Dylan had mocked good-naturedly in 'Bob Dylan's 115th Dream': ' "Haul on the Bowline" / We sang that melody / Like all tough sailors do / When they're far away at sea.' Granted the seafaring ingredient in 'Jim Jones' and in 'Canadee-i-o', Dylan's 'straight' recordings of these songs nearly 30 years later is yet one more form of his 'bringing it all back home'. (Back further, Dylan and A. L. Lloyd momentarily come together as Lloyd, acting the communist thought-policeman, sits behind Dylan as Dylan performs at the Pindar of Wakefield pub, Grays Inn Road, London, 22/12/62; see the photo by Brian Shuel in *All Across the Telegraph*, ed. Michael Gray and John Bauldie, 1987.)

John Kirkpatrick & Sue Harris: 'Jim Jones At Botany Bay', London, March 1976; "Among The Many etc", Topic 12TS295, London, 1976. Lawrence Hoy: 'Jim Jones At Botany Bay', nia, "Beyond The Seas", nia.

The New High Level Ranters: 'Jim Jones', Newcastle, c. 1981; "The New High Level Ranters", Topic 12TS425, London, 1982. There is a Dylan connection here too. Louis Killen, the Northumbrian traditionalist, was a pal of the High Level Ranters. (They shared a home-base folk-club, The Bridge in Newcastle.) Killen moved to the States in the mid-1960s and became associated with the Clancy Brothers (who had earlier exposed Dylan to much British and Irish repertoire at their regular White Horse Tavern gigs at the time of Dylan's arrival in New York [the bar is still there, at 567 Hudson Street, Greenwich Village]) but as Karl Dallas reports, Dylan met Killen in 1967: '[When] Killen did a small concert at Woodstock at the height of Dylan's withdrawal from the music business, Dylan turned up disguised in dark glasses [!] and revealed afterwards to Killen that one of the reasons he had hidden himself away had been . . . folkdom's . . . over-enthusiastic move from acoustic to electric music – at his bidding, as they mistakenly thought.' (Karl Dallas: 'The Roots of Tradition', in *The Electric Muse: The Story of Folk into Rock*, Dave Laing, Karl Dallas, Robin Denselow and Robert Shelton, 1975.)

If we once admired Dylan for his age beyond his years, now we must listen to what that kind of age *really* sounds like. The voice that [Robert] Shelton described as 'anything but pretty' is a pure tenor compared to the craggy, bizarre, character-actor's constriction on evidence here. What was charming and old-sounding has become old and phlegm-constricted. What sounded effortless now sounds painful. These are the facts, and they do not stand in the way of making a great record . . . The beauty of the voice is found in the grain. The shape can tell you more than the purity of the note. Bob Dylan is one of the best singers in the world – always has been, always will be, and he used to be able to hold his breath three times as long . . . To listen to this album is to accept old age – Bob Dylan's and your own.[21]

This is all very well, but it rather relies on a notion that has hardly been current outside the Third World for well over fifty years: namely that to be 51, as Dylan barely was when this was recorded, is to have entered 'old age'. Nor, in any case, does 'old age' doom the singer to making 'phlegm-constricted . . . painful' noises. Listen, as I urged in Chapter 9, to the Skip James of "Skip James Today!", recorded when he was 15 years older than the Dylan of "Good As I Been To You": plenty of 'grain', no constriction; plenty of soul, no phlegm; street-cred absence of vocal training, no bum notes. This is not to say that Dylan fails, vocally, on these albums: he often pulls off noises of genius – but we are on notice, as we listen, that it is now a perilous business, that whereas Dylan once held total control of every syllable-sound he uttered, and 'grain' was achieved as much by that control as by direct intensity, now this under-repaired, over-strained and coaldust-choked old steam engine might fall right off the rails at any moment.[22]

Yet how intensely well Dylan performs 'Jim Jones', despite – not because of – the broke-down engine of his voice. The way he sings 'New South Wales' is as disarmingly particular, as yearningly expressive of the romance of place-names as he has ever been when he's been paying attention. He sings 'New South Wales' more under-statedly but as beautifully as in 'Boots Of Spanish Leather' he sings 'Barcelona'. Anyone who knows the studio version of the latter, from the early 1960s, will know that this is high praise indeed. His purpose this time, however, is not to stress romance, but to turn that level of poignancy to different effect.

In singing so savouringly of 'New South Wales' Dylan manages to bring out something of the extremity of aloneness of those sentenced to deportation – and something of the bitter irony of naming a place so far away after somewhere on the home side of the sea. As Gail Smith writes: 'In 1788 the first convicts arrived on the "fatal shore". Another world away, it might have been the moon – but as Robert Hughes so aptly observed, you could see the moon; you could not see Botany Bay. "It was 12,000 miles away, a desolate wilderness whose limits nobody knew, perched on the edge of a hypothetical map." '[23]

21.   John Wesley Harding: 'Good as he's been to us', *Stereofile*, February 1993. Robert Shelton is quoted from his catalytic review of Dylan's support-act performance in Greenwich Village, *New York Times*, 29/9/61.

22.   "Skip James Today!", NYC, January 1966, Vanguard VRS-9219, New York, 1967.

23.   Gail Smith, 'Bob Dylan on Botany Bay', *Who Threw the Glass?* [Dylan fanzine], no. 1, Autumn 1993. Her quotation from Robert Hughes is taken from his book *The Art of Australia* (1966).

In evoking such desolation by vocal caress as well as by stark and wayward strain, Dylan fully inhabits the song's world of a savage penal code in the old land, and of exile across a huge sea to further chains and cruelty, scrubland and thwarted desire.

The signficance of the very different, and immensely better-known, 'Blackjack Davey', 'Gypsy Davey' and 'The Raggle-Taggle Gypsies' (all versions of the same ancient ballad, Child no. 200) in relation to other work of Bob Dylan's, especially 'Boots Of Spanish Leather', was discussed in the previous chapter. It only needs noting here that this too is one of the songs you wouldn't dare sing in a contemporary folk club – too mainstream, too obvious. Which means, of course, that it has been immensely popular and widely recorded. Dylan gives a particularly good performance of it in concert (not folk club) in Holmdel, New Jersey, in 1993.[24]

The Carter Family and 1930s hillbilly Cliff Carlisle cut 'Black Jack David', and there's also a rockabilly version that teeters on the edge of the comically terrible by Warren Smith pretending to be Johnny Horton: a much foreshortened and moralising rewrite. Yet another variant, 'Gypsy Rover (The Whistling Gypsy)', was copyrighted in 1951 and performed at the 1960 Newport Folk Festival by Tommy Makem, whom Dylan has called 'the best ballad singer ever'. Dylan himself was taped singing a 'Gypsy Davey' version, Woody Guthrie style, at the home of the Gleasons in February or March of 1961. In those folk revival years 'Black Jack Davey' was also recorded by Dylan's friend from Minneapolis, the singer and music-writer Tony Glover. The act Koerner, Ray and Glover even performed it – in 'driving Carter Family-Guthriesque' style, according to witness Paul Nelson, at the 1964 Newport Folk Festival. Steeleye Span and the Incredible String Band also recorded it, as in the 1970s did the ubiquitous Taj Mahal.[25]

Like 'Jim Jones' (and unlike the 'Gypsy Davey' cycle of songs) 'Canadee-i-o' is a broadside, though it may have an earlier oral history. It was collected in Frank and Ethel Kidson's significant compilation *English Peasant Songs* (1929). As noted, Dylan's version feeds off English folkie guitarist Nic Jones's, on his 1980 album "Penguin Eggs", which was reissued on CD a few months before Dylan's album was released.

24. Francis James Child, *The English and Scottish Popular Ballads, 1882–98*, a standard work.
   Bob Dylan: 'Blackjack Davey', Holmdel, NJ, 14/9/93. (He gives a performance of 'Jim Jones' in Eindhoven, Netherlands, 17/2/93, that is worth hearing simply for the extraordinary mutinous desperation he evokes on 'into the bush I'll go—'.)

25. Carter Family: 'Black Jack David', Chicago, 4/10/40; "Country Sounds Of The Original Carter Family", Harmony Records HL7422 [a Columbia Records cheapo label], New York, 1967. Cliff Carlisle: 'Black Jack David', Charlotte, NC, 26/7/39; "Old-Time Southern Dance Music: Ballads And Songs", Old Timey Records OT-102 (see note 10).
   Warren Smith: 'Black Jack David', Memphis, August 1956; CD-reissued on "Warren Smith: Classic Sun Recordings", Bear Family BCD 15514-AH, Vollersode, Germany, c. 1992: a collection that rings other Bob Dylan bells – it includes 'Miss Froggie', 'Red Cadillac And A Black Moustache', 'Uranium Rock' and the Smith version of Slim Harpo's song 'Got Love If You Want It', which Dylan nearly released on his "Down In The Groove" LP in 1988 (it is on the version issued in Argentina). A line from Warren Smith's 'Miss Froggie' – 'gal shaped just like a frog' – is used as an item on the enormously long list of 'people' thanked on the sleeve of Dylan's 1986 album "Knocked Out Loaded".
   Tony Glover: 'Black Jack David', *nia*. Koerner, Ray and Glover: 'Black Jack Davy', Newport, RI, July 1964, issued "Newport Folk Festival, 1964, Evening Concerts Vol. 3", Vanguard VRS-9186 [m] and VSD-79186 [s], New York, 1965 [and Fontana Records TFL6052, London, 1965]. Paul Nelson quoted from *Sing Out!*, Vol. 15, no. 5, New York, November 1965.
   Steeleye Span's 'Black Jack Davy' is on their hit album "All Around My Hat", Chrysalis CHR1091, London, 1975. The Incredible String Band: *nia*. Taj Mahal: *nia*, issued "Mo' Roots", Columbia Records, New York, 1974 (now CD-reissued).

Dylan does not follow Jones' arrangement excessively closely. Jones begins with a long, sustained guitar part, whereas Dylan begins singing the story eight seconds into the recording. Jones' guitar part is quietly reflective, perambulating around its riffy figure as if half-remembering Bert Jansch's 'Angie';[26] it's unobtrusively dextrous and when the muted voice eventually arrives, it obeys the rules of British folk singing: it affects a well-bred expressionlessness and that flat East Midlands dialect that seems as *de rigueur* as phoney American used to be in British pop performance. The melodic range is very narrow, and Jones' voice never falters or gives anything away. Only later on in his album does his personality emerge. Any panel of A. L. Lloyds would give Nic Jones the prize here and recoil from Dylan's version in horror and distress.

Bob Dylan crashes into the song, making the guitar figure warmly enfolding yet impatient, nervy and rattlesome, as befits the narrative of a dangerous sea voyage and exile, a voyage among murderous scurvy rascals but ending in success. Dylan's guitar puts you right there among the ropes and sails and creaking decks, while his vocal walks a perilous gangplank between melodrama and real feeling – like the story's 'bold captain', he 'might prove true' – while physically his voice falls down painfully, even grotesquely, once or twice but always gets up and recovers itself and comes back warm and vivid. This is an extraordinarily cracked, husked, masculine voice to give to a woman's narrative, yet he makes it far clearer than Nic Jones that it is the woman of the song telling the story and speaking of herself in the third person, and his dodgy roughed-up voice has enough emotional range to convey key points with adept sensitivity. When Dylan sings for the first time that 'She longed to see that seaport town / Of Canadee-i-o' you hear that longing – the impetus of the whole story – in the way he sings the place name. You feel the coming and going of the dastardly crew, and at the same time the amused contempt of the 'fair and handsome girl' who survives their incompetent 'rage'. At the end, when the trade-mark of the broadsheet sails onto the horizon, the 'Come all of you fair and tender girls' formulation, Dylan's version evokes the smiling satisfaction of 'the finest of the ladies' as 'she cuts a gallant show' at having attained a version of what she wanted, albeit a version beholden to a simple twist of fate. And Dylan signs off, stepping back from the character he has just inhabited so well, to savour the story's irony: that while fate has toyed with this woman and as it happens has been kind, she urges 'fair and tender girls' to follow their 'own true love' as if sticking to your plan is the thing in life; and while she is promenading with the best of the genteel, 'dressed in silks and satins now', her position owing entirely to her husband, the moral she signs off with talks not of property and luck but of 'the honour' she 'has gained / By the wearing of the blue'.

In drawing out the story's unsavoury morality as well as its female narrator's personality and the genre's swashbuckling Captain Pugwash qualities, Dylan does not compete with Nic Jones, but he does lay a creative claim to the song.

This is exactly what he fails to do, it seems to me, with 'Sittin' On Top Of The World'. Since we know that Dylan has recorded it before, at the other end of his career, on harmonica and back-up vocals for Big Joe Williams in New York City in

---

26. Bert Jansch: 'Angie', *nia*, "Bert Jansch", Transatlantic Records TRA 125, London, 1965. On Jansch see also note 54, below.

1962 and that, as mentioned earlier in this book, Howlin' Wolf cut a great version for Chess in Chicago in 1957, we might ask what else, really, is there to know?[27] Well: that it was first recorded almost seventy years ago, by the Mississippi Sheiks, and by many blues artists (among them the Beale Street Rounders, Sam Collins, and Joe Evans & Arthur McClain); that Alan Lomax calls it 'the Delta favourite'; that it was recorded by Bill Monroe & His Blue Grass Boys in the 1950s (with composer credits given here to 'Henderson-Young-Lewis'), by Doc Watson in the 1960s and by the hobo-white-blues-pre-rockabilly artist Harmonica Frank Floyd in 1974. So here again we have Dylan building his album as a fusion of black and white repertoire – in this case with a song long-established as a standard in both.[28]

When I first heard the 1990s Dylan version, it seemed to me that the authenticating thing about it was that it wasn't quite as it might have been envisaged – but nor is it as good. Of all the songs on these two albums, this is the one that I'm quite sure Bob Dylan could do immensely better on another day. There's a strange rigidity to the rhythm, something Dylan is virtually never guilty of, and I puzzled as to what could explain this. I found the answer when I listened to the Mississippi Sheiks version. Dylan replicates it – at the same pace, and word for careful word! Everyone has sung this song, and everyone has personalised it; the lyric variations are boundless . . . and Bob Dylan stands aside from all that, and reproduces the Mississippi Sheiks version from early 1930. It's too scrupulous, too carefully exact. That's why it sounds so

27.   Big Joe Williams [acc. by Bob Dylan]: 'Sittin' On Top Of The World', NYC, 2/3/62, on "Three Kings & The Queen", Spivey Records LP 1004, New York, 1964.

28.   Mississippi Sheiks: 'Sitting On Top Of The World', Shreveport, Louisiana, 17/2/30; "Stop and Listen Blues: The Mississippi Sheiks", Mamlish S-3804, New York, 1974. Beale Street Rounders: 'I'm Sittin' On Top Of The World', Chicago, c. 13/10/30, CD-reissued "Memphis Harp & Jug Blowers (1927–1939)", RST Blues Documents BDCD-6028, Vienna, 1992. Sam Collins: 'I'm Still Sitting On Top Of The World', NYC, 8/10/31; "Sam Collins", Origin OJL-10, Berkeley, 1965. Joe Evans & Arthur McClain as The Two Poor Boys: 'Sittin' On Top Of The World', NYC, 21/5/31, issued "Early Country Music", Historical Records HLP-8002, Jersey City, NJ, nia, CD-reissued "The Two Poor Boys", Document DOCD-5044, Vienna, 1991.

   ('Sittin' On Top Of The World', nia, was also the title track of the Johnny Shines collection issued by Biograph in the 1960s, reissued Biograph BLP 12044, Canaan, NY, 1973.)

   Alan Lomax quoted from *The Land Where the Blues Began* (1993).

   Bill Monroe & His Blue Grass Boys: 'Sittin' On Top Of The World', nia; issued on "Knee Deep In Bluegrass", Stetson Records, USA, 1958; reissued Stetson HATC 3002, nia. (This track, plus other 1950s recordings including 'Poison Love', 'In The Pines', 'Blue Moon Of Kentucky' and 'House Of Gold', are collected on the 4-CD set "Blue Moon Of Kentucky (1950–1958)", Bear Family BCD 15423-DH, Vollersode, Germany, c. 1991; collected on the follow-up 4-CD set "Bluegrass 1959–1969", Bear Family BCD 15529-DH, are Monroe versions of 'Little Maggie', 'I'm So Lonesome I Could Cry', 'The Long Black Veil', 'The Dead March', 'Turkey In The Straw' and a song called 'Drifting Too Far From The Shore'.)

   Doc Watson: 'Sitting On Top Of The World', NYC, 25 or 26/11/63; "Doc Watson", Vanguard Records VRS-9152 [mono] and VSD-79152, New York, 1964 [an LP that also includes his 'St. James' Hospital', discussed in Chapter 15].

   Harmonica Frank: see note no. 50 re 'Step It Up And Go'.

   There's an interesting variant on 'Sittin On Top Of The World' by Bumble Bee Slim: 'Climbing On Top Of The Hill', Chicago, 10/9/34, covered within a year by the man who wrote 'Step It Up & Go', Blind Boy Fuller: 'I'm Climbing On Top Of The Hill', NYC, 23/7/35, this version now CD-issued on "Blind Boy Fuller: East Coast Piedmont Style", Columbia Roots N' Blues Series 467923 2, New York, 1991.

   Other songs using the melody and theme of 'Sittin' On Top Of The World' are Big Bill Broonzy's 'Worrying You Off My Mind', NYC, 29/3/32; "Do That Guitar Rag: 1928–1935", Yazoo L-1035, New York, 1973; CD-reissued "Big Bill Broonzy: Good Time Tonight", Columbia Roots N' Blues 467247–10, New York, 1990; Black Ace's lovely 'You Gonna Need My Help Someday', Dallas, 15/2/37; "New Deal Blues (1933–1939)", Mamlish S-3801, New York [and "Black Ace" EP XX Records Min701, Weybridge, UK], 1971; CD-reissued on Black Ace: "I'm The Boss Card In Your Hand", Arhoolie CD 374, El Cerrito, California, c. 1990; and Sonny Terry's 'One Monkey Don't Stop The Show', Englewood Cliffs, NJ, 26/10/60; "Sonny Is King", Bluesville BVLP 1059, c. 1963.

oddly rigid. It's a failure compounded by the way that while Dylan adds harmonica accompaniment – and the harp suffers from the same tentativeness that has been its fatal main characteristic for so long now – he offers no equivalent to the bluegrass flavour that makes the Sheiks' version attractive. The Sheiks have each other to raggedy it up and give it internal movement. Dylan, on his own, lacks this. The flaccid ending is like a giving up, an admission of failure.

The same absence is more greatly felt on 'Little Maggie'. 'Little Maggie (With A Dram Glass In Her Hand)' was first popularised by Whitter & Grayson, whose 'archaic' combination of vocal and violin was big in the early days of American country radio. (They also cut 'Omie Wise', another recording Dylan knew early on from Harry Smith's anthology, and that he was performing himself before he cut his first album.)

'Little Maggie' was a favourite in the Southern mountains. The repesentative traditional singer Obray Ramsey, from Marshall, North Carolina, was recorded performing it. It was handed down from Whitter & Grayson to the early 1930s stringband the Carolina Ramblers (who had a very bluesy violinist in Fiddlin' Steve Ledford) and to the bluegrass outfit the Stanley Brothers. Under the title 'Yonder Stands Little Maggie', it was recorded by Flatt & Scruggs. The ex-New Lost City Ramblers member Tom Paley, whom Dylan mentions as a source for songs on "World Gone Wrong", recorded 'Little Maggie' on an album of Southern Appalachian songs. Paul Clayton, another source of material for Dylan, recorded his own version, called 'The Hustling Gamblers'. Rather later 'Little Maggie' was cut by Barefoot Jerry, Area Code 615, the Grateful Dead and Eric Weissberg (a guitarist on "Blood On The Tracks").[29]

If there were any doubt that Dylan knew the song long before the likes of the Grateful Dead recorded it, this is removed by his own reference to it in his poem 'For Dave Glover', written for the programme notes to the 1963 Newport Folk Festival, in which he writes some interesting things about the value of old songs, but also writes

> I can't sing Little Maggie with a clear head
> I gotta sing Seven Curses instead.[30]

You might think from the performance on "Good As I Been To You" that Dylan (who uses a melody more or less unrelated to Whitter & Grayson's or the Stanley Brothers') is still rather tired of the song: and no wonder.

29.   Obray Ramsey: 'Little Maggie', nia, "Banjo Songs Of The Southern Mountains", Riverside Records RLP 12–610, New York, nia. Whitter & Grayson: nia. The Carolina Ramblers: nia. Flatt & Scruggs: 'Yonder Stands Little Maggie', collected on "20 Greatest Hits", Deluxe Records CD-1031, Markham, Ontario, 1986. The Stanley Brothers: nia. (For a note on the importance of the Stanley Brothers, see Chapter 9.)
   Tom Paley: 'Little Maggie', NYC, 1952–3, "Folk Songs From The Southern Appalachian Mountains", Elektra Records EKL12, New York, c. 1953. Paul Clayton: 'The Hustling Gamblers', nia, "Cumberland Mountain Folksongs", Folkways Records FA2007, New York, nia. 'Little Maggie' by Barefoot Jerry, Area Code 615, the Grateful Dead and Eric Weissberg, nia.
   Dylan may or may not know the David Grisman album "Early Dawg" [Sugar Hill Records SH-3713C, Durham, North Carolina, 1980] – which includes 'Little Maggie' and 'Little Sadie', nia – though he certainly knew Grisman in this period: Grisman made a guest appearance on 'To Ramona' at one of Dylan's concerts in Portland, Oregon, that December. Grisman, a bluegrass mandolin player since 1965, and sometime partner of Jerry Garcia, is also a member of Bluegrass Reunion, and the producer of their CD, details below.
30.   The Dave Glover referred to is also known as Tony Glover, mentioned elsewhere in this book. 'For Dave Glover' is one of many Dylan pieces excluded from Dylan's Lyrics 1962–1985 (1986, UK 1987).

His miscalculation is to concentrate on the lyric, rather than the hillbilly melody and music. Melodramatic and soppy in equal parts, the lyric makes it seem the sort of old-timey song that gives old-timey songs a bad name. Its best lyric ingredient is the common-stock sometimes-this-sometimes-that-and-sometimes-something-else format:

> *Well sometimes I got a nickel*
> *And sometimes I got a dime*
> *And sometimes I got ten dollars*
> *Just to pay Miss Maggie's fine*

which Dylan builds a whole song around in the 1963 'Baby I'm In The Mood For You', but which is far more dashingly applied than in 'Little Maggie' in Leadbelly's gorgeous 'Goodnight Irene', with its

> *Well sometimes I live in the country*
> *And sometimes I live in the town*
> *And sometimes I get a great notion*
> *To jump overboard and drown.*[31]

Anyway, by ignoring the hillbilly richness of the song and emphasising its nullity of a lyric, Dylan makes 'Little Maggie' very much the filler track on the album. It is also the only song on the collection that he had been singing in concert in the preceding period. A far more enjoyable outing for the song can be heard on "Bluegrass Reunion" by Bluegrass Reunion, where Herb Pedersen's singing, affectionately in debt to the great Roscoe Holcomb, reminds us of what Bob Dylan has clearly forgotten – that it's possible to hear why so apparently mediocre a number can have become such a standard item.

'Hard Times', on the other hand, is a near masterpiece. When the list of song titles for Dylan's "Good As I Been To You" collection came through, 'Hard Times' might have been any one of many numbers so called. It might have turned out to be the song that Uncle Dave Macon used to sing and play on banjo. It could have been a bluesy song normally known as 'Sweet Thing' or 'Crawdad Blues' but which sometimes gets called 'Hard Times' (recorded for instance by Big Bill Broonzy in 1951), or Barbecue Bob's 'We Sure Got Hard Times Now', Elder Curry's 1930 gospel song 'Hard Times', Scrapper Blackwell's 1931 'Hard Time Blues' or Skip James' 'Hard Time Killing Floor Blues' of the same year, Joe Stone's 1933 'It's Hard Time', Lane Hardin's 1935 'Hard Time Blues' (his only record), or one quoted earlier in this book, Lonnie Johnson's

---

31. Leadbelly: 'Goodnight Irene'; he cut this many times, often with the title simply as 'Irene'. Earliest is a one-part 'Irene', field-recorded for the Library of Congress at the State Penitentiary, Angola, Louisiana, 16–20/7/33, and a two-part 'Irene' cut at the same session; further two-part versions were also cut for the Library of Congress at Angola, c. 1/7/34, and at Wilton, Connecticut, 21/1/35; it is not known which of these two-parters is the one issued on the double-LP "Leadbelly: The Library of Congress Recordings: Recorded by John A. and Alan Lomax" [2 LPs], Elektra EKL301-2, New York, 1966.

Bluegrass Reunion (vocal by banjo-player Herb Pedersen, accompanists include Jerry Garcia; production by David Grisman, mentioned earlier): 'Little Maggie', San Rafael, California, 27–29/5/91, "Bluegrass Reunion", Acoustic Disc [sic] ACD-4, San Rafael (homebase of the Grateful Dead and hence location of the 1987 Dylan/Dead rehearsal tapes), 1992.

1937 'Hard Times Ain't Gone No Where', or more besides. It might just have been the beautiful, well-known Newfoundland song 'Hard Times', revived by Jim Joyce shortly before Dylan recorded his album.[32]

Least likely might have been thought to be Stephen Foster's 'Hard Times Come Again No More'. So of course this is the one it turns out to be.

Stephen Foster was born near Pittsburgh, on the 4th of July 1826, and he wrote his pseudo-black southerner songs from the north. Indeed he never saw the south till late on in his life, and perhaps didn't much care for black music. (Posterity's southern revenge is that an area of South Georgia swamp is now named after him.) Yet Foster created a series of massively influential as well as popular songs, all written while their black protagonists in the south were still slaves. His hits included 'Oh Susannah' (1848), 'Campdown Races' (the song from which the world picked up the phrase 'all of a doodah', 1850), 'Old Folks At Home' (1851), 'My Old Kentucky Home' (1853), 'Jeanie With The Light Brown Hair' (1854) and 'Old Black Joe' (1860).[33]

Though his work was hugely successful in his lifetime, Foster received very little financial reward until late on. When he did make money, he spent it and failed to support his wife and children. In 1860 he moved to New York City, where his debts increased and he started drinking heavily. His wife left him for the second and last time, after which he churned out many mediocre songs just for drinking money. Out of this period, however, came 'Beautiful Dreamer', written just a few days before his death. In the freezing bathroom of a cheap Bowery hotel in the winter of 1863–64, he hit his head on the edge of a sink, went into a coma and died in hospital next day, January 13th.

President Lincoln had emancipated the slaves the year before; the Civil War was still raging. Segregation laws were attempted in Mississippi immediately after the war in 1865 and after the period of Reconstruction were reinstated in 1888. By 1900

32.   The white old-timey star Uncle Dave Macon was born in 1870; his parents ran a theatrical boarding house in Nashville. He's an interesting figure because he learnt much of his wide repertoire before 1900. When the Grand Ole Opry started, on radio station WSM in Nashville, which had one of the south's biggest transmitters, its first star was Uncle Dave Macon. His last recordings were made in 1950 ("At Home, His Last Recordings, 1950", Bear Family Records BFX 15214, Vollersode, Germany, c. 1991). 'Sweet Thing/Crawdad Blues/Hard Times', collected by folklorists as 'Sweet Thing' in 1909, was performed for the BBC-TV series *The Devil's Music* (Maddalena Fagandini and Giles Oakley, BBC Continuing Education Dept., 1976 and 1979) by Memphis blues-singer Laura 'Little Bit' Dukes, who had been in Will Batts' Jug Band in the late 1930s to mid-1950s. Big Bill Broonzy: 'Crawdad', Chicago, 10/12/51, issued "Remembering Big Bill Broonzy", Mercury LP 20905, Chicago, *nia*. Barbecue Bob: 'We Sure Got Hard Times Now', Atlanta, 18/4/30; "Barbecue Bob, Masters of the Blues Vol. 10", Collector's Classics CC-36, Copenhagen, 1971. Elder Curry: 'Hard Times', Jackson, Mississippi, 16/12/30. Francis Scrapper Blackwell: 'Hard Time Blues', Richmond, Indiana, 24/11/31; "Scrapper Blackwell (1928–1934)", Yazoo L-1019, New York, 1970. Skip James: 'Hard Time Killing Floor Blues', c. February 1931; "Skip James: King of the Delta Blues Singers, 1928–1964", Biograph BLP-12029, Canaan, NY, 1971; CD-reissued on "Skip James (1931)", Document Records DOCD-5005, Vienna, 1990. Joe Stone: 'It's Hard Time', Chicago, 2/8/33; "St. Louis Blues, 1929–1935: The Depression", Yazoo L-1030, New York, 1972. Lane Hardin: 'Hard Time Blues', Chicago, 28/7/35; "Hard Time Blues: St. Louis: 1933–1940", Mamlish S-3806, New York, c. 1975; CD-reissued on "Backwoods Blues", Document DOCD-5036, Vienna, c. 1990. Lonnie Johnson: 'Hard Times Ain't Gone No Where', Chicago, 8/11/37; "The Blues Of Lonnie Johnson", Swaggie Records S-1225, Victoria, Australia, 1969. Jim Joyce's 1992 'Hard Times' is on the Various Artists collection "Another Time", Pigeon Inlet Records, Newfoundland, 1992.

33.   Foster's 'The Old Folks At Home' is the one that begins 'Way down upon the Swanee River'. This river would be less famous if Foster had stuck to his first draft, which proposed to use the Pee Wee River instead. I'm grateful for this nugget of information to William Least Heat-Moon's excellent book *Blue Highways* (1983), in which in effect he sets out to find what's left of the 'invisible republic' that Dylan examines in these two albums, and brings it back as memorably.

the Supreme Court had approved segregation laws and fourteen states possessed them.[34]

Foster's legacy is bound up in the history of the minstrel shows that were so popular in the nineteenth-century and have never quite been killed off since. The name of late-1960s pseudo-folk group the New Christy Minstrels (through which the world was brought the modest talent of Gene Clark, Kenny Rogers and Barry McGuire) refers back to the most famous of the nineteenth-century minstrel companies, Edwin P. Christy's. This was American, but it became internationally popular, and as it did so it came to rely less on the distinctive African-American input responsible for its initial appeal and to embrace far more European 'drawing-room song' material. However dodgily, the minstrel show movement brought black music and song to the ears of Europe, made it fashionable (so much so that at the turn of the century the future Edward VII, then Prince of Wales, took banjo lessons) and probably speeded up the rise in interest in genuine black music.

Such was the context in which Stephen Foster's songs became popular and influential. His work encouraged the black songwriter James Bland, who was 10 years old when Foster died, and who went on to write 'Carry Me Back To Old Virginny', and in 1871, seven years after Foster's death, the Fisk University Jubilee Singers conquered Britain with a repertoire that first popularised at least three other songs that have since become classics: 'Nobody Knows The Trouble I've Seen', 'Swing Low, Sweet Chariot' and 'Deep River'.

The impact of the Fisk Singers' European tour is difficult to exaggerate and its effect hard to pin down. Paul Gilroy, a pioneering black British writer in the field of cultural studies, notes that 'The musical authenticity of the Jubilee Singers has been explicitly challenged by Zora Neale Hurston, who refers to their work as "a trick style of delivery" and a "misconception of Negro Spirituals"', but he argues that in the light of their impact, their *vivant de la différence*, this seems a misplaced fastidiousness. Hurston's fastidiousness concerning the Fisk Jubilee Singers is shared by Robert Dixon and John Godrich, the authors of the classic blues listings book *Blues and Gospel Records 1902–1943*, which lists none of their recordings, preferring instead the prose entry: 'This group recorded extensively in the twenties and earlier, but their output was aimed principally at the white market, hence their recordings have little authentic gospel quality.'[35]

34. Negroes had been promised forty acres and a mule when the War was over; they didn't get them . . .

    A new system of slavery, sharecropping peonage, came into being. Labour costs were further cut by the iniquitous system of 'Convict-lease' in which teams of chained convicts were hired out to plantation owners; no one bothered if they were sick, beaten, mutilated or dead . . . [Moreover, southern blacks] were effectively disenfranchised. In 1883 the Supreme Court declared the Fourteenth Amendment was unconstitutional and deprived the Negro the right of appeal in law . . . the steep rise in the number of lynchings was no coincidence . . . In 1890 Mississippi made it constitutional to disenfranchise the Negro; Louisiana and South Carolina followed in 1895. In . . . the next fifteen years five more southern states . . . adopted new constitutions specifically aimed at limiting the Negro's power.

(Paul Oliver, *The Story of the Blues*, 1969.)

35. All quotations from Paul Gilroy here are from his essay 'Sounds Authentic: Black Music, Ethnicity and the Challenge of a *Changing* Same', London, unpublished, 1991. This work is now incorporated into Gilroy's book *The Black Atlantic* (1993). Zora Neale Hurston, a folklorist, published her influential book *Mules and Men* in 1935. Respected and befriended by Alan Lomax (they did fieldwork together the summer her book was published), her work is also recommended by the eccentric British writer Roy Kerridge, author of the light but readable travel book *In the Deep South* (1989). The Fisk University Singers have now been admitted to the fold in Dixon, Godrich and Rye's *Blues and Gospel Records 1890–1943*, the new 4th edition of this essential work (1997).

On the other hand, Gilroy's more detailed scrutiny of the impact of the Fisks yields a different picture. He writes: 'The world-wide travels of The Fisk Jubilee Singers provide . . . [an] important example of the difficulties that, from the earliest point, attended the passage of African-American "folk" forms into the emergent popular-cultural industries of the overdeveloped countries.' He quotes an unidentified contemporary American review of a concert by the group as saying that 'Those who have only heard the burnt cork caricatures of negro minstrelsy have not the slightest conception of what it really is', while in Europe a contemporary writer noted that 'the Jubilee music was more or less a puzzle to the critics . . . Some could not understand the reason for enjoying so thoroughly as almost everyone did these simple unpretending songs.'[36]

Gilroy adds: 'The Fisk troupe also encountered the ambivalence and embarrassment of black audiences unsure or uneasy about serious, sacred music being displayed to audiences conditioned by the hateful antics of Zip Coon, Jim Crow and their ilk. Understandably, blacks were protective of their unique musical culture and fearful of how it might be changed by being forced to compete on the new terrain of popular culture against the absurd representations of blackness offered by minstrelsy's dramatisation of white supremacy' while 'in the late nineteenth century, the status of the Jubilee Singers' art was further complicated by the prominence and popularity of minstrelsy'. Nevertheless, Gilroy emphasises: 'Black people singing slave songs as mass entertainment initiated and established new public standards of authenticity for black cultural expression.'[37]

The Fisk Jubilee Singers' European tour set up other lines of influence too. They had a big impact on the young English composer Samuel Coleridge-Taylor, whose father was a black West African doctor. 'These songs are the articulate message of the slave to the world,' he declared – and he used them as the basis of his own work *Twenty-Four Negro Melodies*. Inspired also by meeting the black American poet Paul Laurence Dunbar (one of whose poems gives us the title *I Know Why The Caged Bird Sings*), Coleridge-Taylor became a campaigner for black rights. At the same time it was possible for him to introduce his *Twenty-Four Negro Melodies* to the conservatory – to bring black music to the world of 'the classics' – because others were doing the same with different kinds of 'folk music'. Grieg, to take a prominent example, had already pushed Norwegian folk tunes into the conservatories of the 1880s. Coleridge-Taylor, therefore, could do the same for 'Wade In The Water' and 'Sometimes I Feel Like A Motherless Child', without being perceived as a black trouble-maker. At the turn of the century, indeed, he was able to play tennis in Croydon among the white middle classes.[38]

---

36. Gilroy quoting from J. B. T. Marsh's book *The Story of the Jubilee Singers with Their Songs* (1875).

37. Gilroy notes too that other factors were at work here. 'The role of music and song within the abolitionist movement is an additional and . . . little-known factor which must have pre-figured the Jubilees' eventual triumph' – a success that 'spawned a host of other companies who took to the road offering a similar musical fare in the years after 1871'. (He adds that the 'meaning of this movement of black singers for our understanding of Reconstruction remains to be explored'.)

38. Those Coleridge-Taylor played tennis with included the grandfather of the jazz writer and photographer Val Wilmer [see *Mama Said There'd Be Days Like This*, 1989].
  Samuel Coleridge-Taylor: *Twenty-four Negro Melodies*, nia. His best-known work remains *Hiawatha's*

Another English composer, the Yorkshireman Frederick Delius (1862–1934), may also have been influenced by the Fisks. His opera *Koanga* (written 1895–97) is essentially a love story set in Mississippi before the abolition of slavery and its big production dance number, 'La Calinda', includes a short passage for banjos – possibly the only use of this instrument in a symphony orchestra. On the other hand, before settling to composing, Delius had managed a Florida orange plantation and was very open to American influence in general.[39]

Meanwhile, songs like those popularised by the Fisks, such as 'Nobody Knows The Trouble I've Seen' and 'Swing Low, Sweet Chariot', plus the songs of Stephen Foster, in turn set the scene for later widely popularised songs like 'Ol' Man River' and 'That Lucky Old Sun' – songs that cross many boundaries and political eras and slide into the repertoires of people from Paul Robeson to Jerry Lee Lewis, the Isley Brothers to Frankie Laine, and Ray Charles to Bob Dylan.[40]

Scott Joplin's compositions were also deeply influenced by Foster's melodies, though Joplin was born four years after Foster's death, and in this way too, when Joplin's work spearheaded the turn-of-the-century ragtime craze, Foster's melodic legacy passed across to the Blind Blakes and Peg Leg Howells who inhabited the early blues world.

Alan Lomax, however, toiling in the field-recording part of this world, remained angered by the lingering legacy of minstrelsy behind all of this: 'The minstrel show [had] dominated the American consciousness for almost a century, and the curious and ironic result was that many blacks came to accept its racist distortions as their own, and often trotted out . . . [minstrel sketches] . . . when asked for black folklore.'[41]

Foster's politically least embarrassing songs were still being revived – in the country-pop market, on the whole – in the 1960s. 'Old Black Joe' was revived resplendently, one hundred years after its first publication, by Jerry Lee Lewis, who did not, as so

---

Wedding Feast, nia. He died of pneumonia in 1912.

Paul Laurence Dunbar (1872–1906), severely criticised towards the end of his life for sentimentalised depicting of the South. He felt that this was misunderstood. *I Know Why the Caged Bird Sings*, from a Dunbar poem, nia, is the title of Maya Angelou's first volume of autobiography (1969). Dunbar's first collection was *Oak and Ivy* (1893), his second *Majors and Minors* (1895), re-collected jointly as *Lyrics of a Lowly Life* (1896). His complete works were first published in Lida Keck Wiggins' *The Life and Works of Paul Laurence Dunbar* (1907).

39. Delius also composed the choral work *Appalachia* (1903), while his *Sea Drift* (1904) was based on Walt Whitman's poetry.

In France, the first 'serious composer' to put 'jazz' into concert music was Erik Satie, who, liking it for the way in which, as he put it, 'it shouts its sorrows', used it in the piece that re-vamped his reputation, the 1917 *Parade*, the programme notes for the first performance of which, written by Apollinaire, offered the first-ever use of the term *surréalisme*. (Until then, Satie had been able to complain – he said in a lecture [details unknown] – in terms that the present-day Bob Dylan might well relate to: 'I wrote my *Sarabandes* at 21 in 1887, my *Gymnopédies* at 22 . . . They are my only works that my detractors admire . . . Logically they might equally well like the works of my maturity . . . But no.' To his brother he wrote [again, details unknown] – at the same age Dylan is now – that 'I have had a good share of heckling in my life, but I was never so scorned. What had I been up to . . .? I used to write such charming things. And now! What a show-off! What cheek!' But then came *Parade*, a great success, after which younger composers sought him out and admired his modernity. (All quotations in this note taken from Roger Shattuck's great book *The Banquet Years: The Origins of the Avant-Garde in France, 1885 to World War I*, rev. edn, 1968.)

40. More or less all of these are 'cross-over artists' – even Frankie Laine, who had a big hit with 'That Lucky Old Sun' in 1949, nia. We may think of him as a sort of cowboy version of Tony Bennett, but the black 1950s R&B singer Ruth Brown, who worked with him, says he was considered almost an R&B artist back then, and as popular with black as with white audiences. (Ruth Brown was Atlantic Records' biggest-selling artist of the 1950s, outselling even Ray Charles and The Drifters.)

41. Alan Lomax, *The Land Where the Blues Began* (1993).

many did at the time, alter the title to the vaguer and supposedly more polite 'Poor Old Joe'. Marty Robbins (whose 'cowboy' hit 'El Paso' Bob Dylan clearly knew: 'Romance In Durango', as I've suggested elsewhere, is on one level a parodic tribute to it) cut Foster's 'Beautiful Dreamer' in 1963 and Roy Orbison also cut the same song in the early 1960s. Sam Cooke (who was nobody's Uncle Tom) recorded 'Jeanie With The Light Brown Hair' in the same period and, years later, as a result of hearing Cooke's record on the radio, Joan Baez cut a version of the song that she fused with 'Danny Boy', making the two songs one track on her "Diamonds And Rust" LP.[42]

'Hard Times', about the only Stephen Foster song now politically acceptable, was revived hideously in 1981 by academic revivalist Old Time Country Music outfit the Red Clay Ramblers, who once provided the soundtrack for a Sam Shepard film but seem preeningly smartypants and inappropriately soulless to me. On 'Hard Times' they sound as if they've never had any. The song has been recorded still more closely in front of Dylan's version by three acts with Dylan connections: Aaron Neville, Emmylou Harris and the modern US folk/pop singer Syd Straw.[43]

'Hard Times' is interesting for being a song-within-a-song – a splendid nineteenth-century example of the self-reflexive text, announcing and singing itself and even predicting its own future:

> *There's a song that will linger forever in our ears*
> *Oh Hard Times Come Again No More*

(except that 'Oh' is a sort of 'Aaow', as Dylan pronounces it, half-howling the pain of it to himself), and

> *Tis the song, the sigh of the weary:*
> *Hard Times, Hard Times, Come Again No More.*

As an imprecation it compares with Buddy Holly's immaculate blues 'Mailman Bring Me No More Blues', in which the self-reflexive quality is downplayed but implicit. If this had first been recorded for OKeh or Vocalion or Paramount in the 1930s, the label might well have given it as 'Mailman Bring Me No More Blues Blues'.[44]

Dylan's version of 'Hard Times', though I've heard it said that it doesn't fully exploit the nobility of Foster's melody, is a thrilling achievement. The voice! It breathes his affection for Foster's craft and his respect for its capacity to evoke, regardless of

42. Jerry Lee Lewis: 'Old Black Joe', Memphis, late 1959–early 1960, Sun Records 337, Memphis [London-American Records HLS 9131, London], 1960; CD-reissued on the 8-CD set "Classic Jerry Lee Lewis", Bear Family Records BCD 15420-HH, Vollersode, Germany, c. 1991. Marty Robbins: 'Beautiful Dreamer', Nashville, 7/8/63; reissued "Long Long Ago", Columbia Records CBS 40–88649, New York, 1984. Roy Orbison: 'Beautiful Dreamer', probably Nashville, 1963; CD-reissued "Roy Orbison: Best Loved Standards", Monument 463419 2, New York, 1992. Sam Cooke: 'Jeanie With The Light Brown Hair', NYC, 9/9/60; "Swing Low", RCA Victor LSP2293, New York [RCA RD 27222, London], 1961 [an album that also includes 'You Belong To Me', nia, the standard Dylan covered so beautifully at the same sessions as the "Good As I Been To You" tracks (Malibu, July–August 1992) and which he contributed to the soundtrack of Oliver Stone's movie *Natural Born Killers*, UNV Interscope Records ITSC-92460, US, 1994]. Joan Baez: 'I Dream Of Jeanie/Danny Boy', LA, 17–29/1/75, "Diamonds And Rust", A&M Records SP-3233, LA [AMLH 64527, London], 1975.

43. Aaron Neville: 'Hard Times', nia. Emmylou Harris: 'Hard Times', May 1991. Syd Straw: 'Hard Times', 1989, "Surprise", Virgin America VUSLP6 (and CD 91266–2), 1989. Her Dylan-connection is that she's married to Rolling Thunder Revuehead T-Bone Burnett.

44. Buddy Holly: 'Mailman Bring Me No More Blues', Clovis, New Mexico, 8/4/57, reissued on "The Complete Buddy Holly", 6-LP box-set, MCA Records CDSP 807, London, 1979.

political correctness, a mythic Old South that still has the power to shiver the imagination and to smoke its way inside the landscape we know from those writers and blues singers who inhabited the real terrain. The chorus of 'Hard Times' conjures up a world that Robert Johnson struggled to leave behind, and that the early Howlin' Wolf *lived*: it puts us right inside one of those cabins in the spooky backwoods where ghostly mists are in the trees and animals howl fitfully out there somewhere and oppression too can seem a creature that might be creeping under the door. And as with Johnson's 'Hellhound On My Trail' ('all around my door, all around my door . . .') and Howlin' Wolf's solo acoustic 'Ain't Goin' Down The Backroads (By Myself)', in Dylan's handling of the 'Hard Times' refrain the resonating wood that is the soundbox of the acoustic guitar is the perfect medium for putting us inside the woods of the lyrics.[45]

At the same time another world hovers in the words of the verses of 'Hard Times' – contemporaneous with Foster's American backwoods but a very different place: the England of the great Charles Dickens, with its waiflike victims of industrialism, its tattered urban poor. The two writers were near-contemporaries, Dickens being 14 when Foster was born, and touring America as a triumphantly successful novelist in 1841, while Foster was an educated, literate 15-year-old in middle class Pittsburgh. When Dickens' novel *Hard Times* was published, Foster was at the height of his powers, and by the time of Foster's death ten years later, Dickens had published all of his work except *Our Mutual Friend* and *The Mystery of Edwin Drood*. I don't suggest a relationship specifically between *Hard Times* the novel and 'Hard Times' the song (although I do note that both were published the same year, 1854), but on the evidence of that song alone, Foster has clearly been influenced by Dickens' compassionate vision and his concomitant reforming zeal. 'Let us . . . all sup sorrow with the poor' is both a characteristic sample of its Dickens-inspired expression and the stated theme of the song. Foster brings it to odd but vivid half-life, or after-life, showing us the hungry poor as 'frail forms fainting at the door'.

Foster obviously had a bit of a thing about these frail forms, this Victorian Gothic ghostliness that happens to suit the world he never knew, of cabins in the woods and mist on the bayou. A favourite word of his is 'vapors'. Even in 'Jeanie' we meet this ingredient right at the start of the song, where he dreams of Jeanie 'Borne like a vapor on the summer air'. In 'Beautiful Dreamer', very similarly, 'over the streamlets, vapors are borne' (or possibly 'born'). Later in 'Jeanie', he hears melodies 'like joys gone by . . . Sighing like the night wind and sobbing like the rain'. In 'Old Black Joe' it is the voices of the singer's long-dead friends he hears calling him, and he is left 'grieving for forms now departed long ago'. In 'My Old Kentucky Home' 'They sing no more by

---

45.   Robert Johnson: 'Hellhound On My Trail', Dallas, 20/6/37, CD-reissued "Robert Johnson: The Complete Recordings", Columbia Records Roots N' Blues Series CBS 467246, 1990s.
    Howlin' Wolf: 'Ain't Going Down That Dirt Road (By Myself)', Chicago, Nov. 1968, unissued till the 3-CD "The Chess Box", MCA Records CHD3–9332, 1992. This song, like several by Wolf, is an imaginative remodelling of an earlier one by the great Tommy Johnson: in this case 'Big Road Blues', Memphis, 3/2/28; "Blues Roots / Mississippi", RBF Records RBF-14, New York, 1966. It is not possible to know whether Johnson's was itself inspired by, or provided the inspiration for, Charley Patton's 'Down The Dirt Road Blues', Richmond, Indiana, 14/6/29. Both men were in the same place at the same time, performing long before they recorded. Either way, the ain't-going-down-the-road-alone theme is only a one-stanza ingredient in the many-themed Johnson and Patton songs, whereas Howlin' Wolf sees its possibilities for living and breathing over the long haul of an entire song.
    The *benign* side of nature outside the cabin door is represented in the Jimmie Rodgers song 'Miss The Mississippi And You' [NYC, 29/8/32], in which 'mockingbirds are singing around the cabin door'.

the glimmer of the moon / On the bench by the old cabin door / The day goes by like a shadow o'er the heart . . . By 'n' by hard times comes a-knockin' at the door.'

It would be easy to find in all this only the unacceptable face of its of-its-time sentimentality, but just as Dylan maximises the vividness of that 'all around my cabin door' in the refrain, because he's more interested in being alert to its imaginative pull than to its shortcomings as eternal truth poetics, so too in the verses Dylan brings out marvellously the song's lurid Dickensian darkness. How he lingers in fretful fascination (far more than on the word 'linger') over that mad, ghostly line 'There are frail forms fainting at the door', singing the nebulous, Victorian Gothic word 'forms' as if test-pushing against it, as if endeavouring by sheer concentration of will to make it materialise into something more human, less supernatural. And it is the most human of touches that he brings, in a moment of lovely articulation, to the pale maiden's 'sighin' all the day', enacting the sigh not on the word 'sighin'' itself but right across the four syllables he makes of 'all' in that phrase.

With its majestic incantatory length and the marvellous voice Dylan gives us, concentrated and sustained throughout, this is one of the finest performances on the two albums.

'Step It Up & Go' has no such claims to significance. It was originally recorded by the great Piedmont blues stylist Blind Boy Fuller (the man who recorded a 'Rag Mama Rag' thirty-odd years before The Band) in 1940, the year before his death.[46] By June that year Fuller, not at all well, returned to New York to record what were to be his last sides. Born Fulton Allen in Wadesboro, North Carolina in 1907, he moved to Rockingham at 18. He grew blind over the following five years. It used to be thought that he was blinded by a girlfriend (this is the story in Paul Oliver's classic work *The Story of the Blues*, 1969), but more recent, detailed research by Bruce Bastin has overturned this myth. Fuller played to workers coming off shift in the tobacco towns up and down Highway 70 and around Winston-Salem. He played a steel-bodied National guitar and was an influential singer. He worked and travelled with Sonny Terry, Gary Davis and Bull City Red, and made a successful version of 'Oh Red', written by Joe McCoy, the second husband of Bob Dylan's favourite female blues singer, Memphis Minnie. Fuller recorded well over a hundred sides, even though he died before he was 40.[47]

'Step It Up & Go' rapidly became as much a hillbilly property as a blues dance number: it was performed by nearly every bluesman south of Chicago in the 1940s and 1950s *and* became a standard repertoire item – one of those sort of test numbers, like 'Foggy Mountain Breakdown' – that every self-respecting hillbilly blues guitarist had to be able to play. To look at the history of this comparatively recent song is to encounter yet again the extraordinary commonality of American grass roots music, to see again how shared a musical heritage there so often was between, as Tony Russell's book has it, *Blacks, Whites and Blues*.

At the beginning of the 1960s, the Everly Brothers recorded 'Step It Up & Go',

46. Blind Boy Fuller: 'Step It Up & Go', NYC, 5/3/40, "Blind Boy Fuller with Sonny Terry and Bull City Red", Blues Classics BC-11, Berkeley, 1966. Fuller died 13/2/41.

47. A representative sample, but excluding 'Step It Up & Go' and 'Oh Red', is issued on CD on "Blind Boy Fuller: East Coast Piedmont Style", Columbia Roots N' Blues Series 467923, 1991 (insert-notes by Bruce Bastin).

and to look at their slim interweaving within the story is to see a representative illustration of how this music passes to and fro. Their 'Step It Up & Go' isn't on the album "Songs Our Daddy Taught Us", but Ike Everly would have been their source. Ike had been taught guitar by Arnold Schultz, a black who also taught the Monroe Brothers; in turn Ike taught the 14-year-old Merle Travis thumb-pick style, a style Travis developed . . . and showcased on 'Step It Up & Go'.[48]

Anthony Wall's BBC-2 TV profile of the Everly Brothers for *Arena* establishes that Ike Everly, who worked with two brothers of his own before developing the family show that featured Don and Phil as children, had a repertoire that was a typical mix of white and black. He was influenced by hillbilly acts like the Baile Brothers and York Brothers as well as the better known Delmores, and his relationship with Merle Travis was two-way (he performed Travis' 'Blue Smoke', for instance). At the same time we see Don Everly recalling going down Maxwell Street in Chicago with his father and saying that he was very aware of gospel and blues. Then we see the guitarist and RCA Victor producer Chet Atkins saying that most southern whites bought and identified with black artists' blues records. In another sequence in the same programme there occurs a most interesting illustration of both the truth and the limitations of this point. Don and Phil go back to Kentucky and call on a retired white coalminer and friend of their late father's, the revered amateur singer and guitar-picker Mose Rager. The song he starts performing for them in his living-room is Bessie Smith's 'Backwater Blues' . . . and Phil has to ask what it is![49]

'Step It Up & Go' was also in the repertoire of the populist cowboy outfit the Maddox Brothers And Rose, the pre-rockabilly artist Harmonica Frank Floyd (a figure championed by Greil Marcus in "Mystery Train") and John Hammond Jr, who includes it on his album "Frogs For Snakes".[50]

---

48.   Everly Brothers: 'Step It Up & Go', Nashville, autumn 1961; "Instant Party", Warner Brothers W (WS) 1430, Burbank, California, 1962. "Songs Our Daddy Taught Us", Nashville, August 1958, Cadence CLP 3016, New York, 1958 (reissued as "Folksongs By The Everly Brothers", Cadence CLP 3059 / CLP 23059, New York, 1962; CD-reissued on Ace CDCHM 75, London, 1990). To look back at the track-list for *this* album is to be reminded of how close was Bob Dylan's 'folk' repertoire of the early 1960s to the Everly Brothers' 'pop' repertoire of the late 1950s: the LP includes 'Roving Gambler', 'Who's Gonna Shoe Your Pretty Little Feet' and 'Barbara Allen'. ('Whose Gonna Shoe Your Pretty Little Feet' is the same song as 'Kingsport Town', Dylan's version of which, 1963, is on "Bootleg Series I–III".)
     Merle Travis: 'Step It Up & Go', nia, "Walking The Strings", Capitol Records nia, Hollywood, nia. Merle Travis also used the refrain of another Blind Boy Fuller song, 1935's 'Ain't It A Cryin' Shame?', in his 1946 West Coast radio broadcasts. Travis cut several songs also covered by Dylan, including 'Corrine Corrina', 'Blues Stay Away From Me' and, on "Merle Travis and Joe Maphis" (Capitol ST 2102, nia), a traditional song Dylan was airing on tour in 1992, 'Don't Let Your Deal Go Down': another show-off instrumental. This last has also been recorded by artists from Flatt & Scruggs (it's on the 4-CD set "Lester Flatt & Earl Scruggs 1948–1959", Bear Family BCD 15472-DH, Vollersode, Germany, c. 1990) to the Greenbriar Boys as well as latterly by Jerry Garcia. These songs do not need to have come to Dylan's attention via Garcia and the Grateful Dead. (The Everly Brothers' influential "Roots" album came out back at the end of 1968: a period in which we know Bob Dylan had them in mind: he cut the "Self Portrait" versions of their 'Let It Be Me' and 'Take A Message To Mary' in early 1969, shortly after submitting to them two of his own songs, 'Wanted Man' and 'Lay, Lady, Lay'. [Everly Brothers: "Roots", Nashville, Summer 1968, Warner Brothers W 1752, Burbank, California, 1968.])

49.   'The Everly Brothers: Songs of Innocence and Experience', Anthony Wall, for the *Arena* series, BBC-2 TV, London, first shown 2/11/94.

50.   Maddox Brothers And Rose: 'Step It Up And Go', nia, issued "Maddox Brothers And Rose 1946–1951 Volume 2" (along with 'Dark As The Dungeon', nia), Arhoolie 5017, El Cerrito, California, 1976.
     'Harmonica Frank . . . a white man with some life in him, whose music wasn't exactly blues but was too strange to peddle as anything else . . . was perhaps the first of the rock'n'roll vocal contortionists – like Buddy Holly, Clarence "Frogman" Henry and Bob Dylan – whose mission in life seemed to be the willful [sic] destruction

The song is of a type that crops up over and over again. The building blocks of the lyric are common-stock, in some cases shared with those in that other frisky classic of inconsequence, Tampa Red's 'Tight Like That'. 'Tight Like That', as remembered by Eugene Powell, for instance, includes

> *Had a little dog, his name was Ball*
> *Gave him a little taste and he want it all*

which Dylan puts in as the fourth stanza of 'Step It Up & Go':

> *Got a little girl, her name is Ball*
> *Give a little bit, she took it all.*[51]

At the same time we find the melody of 'Step It Up & Go' used everywhere from the Kansas City jazz-tinged boogie pianist-singer Julia Lee's 1946 'Gimme Watcha Got' to Elvis Presley's 1958 New Orleans pastiche 'Hard Headed Woman'. Another Blind Boy Fuller song, 'You've Got Something There', and Blind Willie McTell's 'Warm It Up To Me' are more or less the same, as is the Memphis Jug Band's 'Bottle It Up And Go' (cut in 1932 and 1934) and Tommy McClennan's 1939 'Bottle It Up And Go', later recorded by John Lee Hooker as 'Bundle Up And Go', 'Shake It Up And Go' and 'Bottle Up And Go'. Under that last title, it was also recorded in the late 1950s by Snooks Eaglin (at that time a street musician). Then there's 'Got The Bottle Up And Gone', a début session track by Sonny Boy Williamson I from 1937, and 'Touch It Up And Go', a track by Blind Boy Fuller's associates Sonny Terry & Jordan Webb, cut in New York a year after Fuller's death.[52]

of the mainstream tradition of popular singing, and the smooth and self-assured way of life it was made to represent', Greil Marcus, *Mystery Train*, 1975. Marcus recommends many of Floyd's multi-faceted sides, not least his post-rediscovery album "Blues That Made The Rooster Dance", Barrelhouse BH 05, US, 1974, which includes 'Sittin' On Top Of The World', *nia*. Floyd's 'Step It Up & Go' is on "The Great Original Recordings Of Harmonica Frank 1951–58", Puritan Records 3003, Evanston, Illinois, 1973.

John Hammond Jr's "Frogs For Snakes", *nia*, Rounder Records, *nia*, Somerville, Massachusetts, *nia*. (The phrase is also the name of a blues label founded by Ken Smith, the Dylan-fan proprietor of Red Lick Records mail-order records supplier, Porthmadog, Wales.) The title abbreviates the expression 'fattening frogs for snakes', meaning nurturing something or someone only for a third party to come along and get the benefit.

51.   Eugene Powell, 1930s Bluebird recording artist and veteran blues musician, interviewed in Alan Lomax's *The Land Where the Blues Began*.

52.   Julia Lee & Her Boyfriends: 'Gimme Watcha Got', Los Angeles, Sept. 1946, reissued "Tonight's The Night", Charly CRB 1039, London, 1982. Elvis Presley: 'Hard Headed Woman' [composed by Claude Demetrius, whose earlier 'Mean Woman Blues' also uses the same tune], Hollywood, 15/1/58; "King Creole", RCA LPM 1884, New York, 1958. Blind Boy Fuller: 'You've Got Something There', Memphis, 12/7/39, CD-reissued "Blind Boy Fuller: East Coast Piedmont Style", Columbia Roots N' Blues Series 467923, NYC, 1991. Blind Willie McTell: 'Warm It Up To Me', NYC, 14/9/33.

Fuller and McTell listened to each other's work. Fuller's 'Log Cabin Blues' of 1935 is virtually a cover of McTell's 1929 'Come On Around To My House Mama'. (Blind Boy Fuller: 'Log Cabin Blues', New York, 26/7/35; previously unreleased take issued on "Blind Boy Fuller: East Coast Piedmont Style", ibid.; Blind Willie McTell: 'Come On Around To My House Mama', Atlanta, 30/10/29; "King of the Georgia Blues Singers: Blind Willie McTell", Roots RL-324, Vienna, 1968.)

The Memphis Jug Band [billed the first time around as Picaninny Jug Band, and then as by Charlie Burse With Memphis Jug Band]: 'Bottle It Up And Go', Richmond, Indiana, 3/8/32, and Chicago, 7/11/34, both CD-reissued "Memphis Jug Band Complete Recorded Works 1932–1934", RST Blues Documents BDCD-6002, Vienna, *nia*. Tommy McClennan: 'Bottle It Up And Go', Chicago, 22/11/39, CD-reissued Travelin' Man TM CD-06, *nia*. John Lee Hooker: 'Bundle Up And Go', Chicago 10/6/58, unissued, and Detroit, April 1959, issued on Riverside LP 838, *nia*; 'Shake It Up And Go', Culver City, California, c. 1959, issued United Artists 3LP 127, *nia*; 'Bottle Up And Go', Chicago, 1963, issued VJ LP 1066, *nia*, and NYC, 23/11/65, issued Impulse LP 9103. Snooks Eaglin: 'Bottle Up And Go', New Orleans, 1959; "Country Boy In New Orleans", Arhoolie LP 2014, El Cerrito, California,

'Step It Up & Go' must owe its predominance to having the most accessible and familiar title. Like so many figures of speech, indeed like so much of the poetry of the blues, 'step it up and go' crossed over to the world of dancing from the world of work. It was what people said to their mules and horses. They still do, though it's now more common as an exhortation to the tourist trade horses drawing carriages in New Orleans than in the fields, where tractors now do the ploughing.

Dylan's version is unambitious, as befits someone who understands the tradition in which the song sits. Conscious that a bravura performance is for the young and brash, and that there's a hundred voices capable of matching up to what is a simple dance number, Bob Dylan settles quite rightly for something egolessly unexceptional. This is intelligent good-time, on which his robust and clumsy guitar work is countered by an alert, true-to-the-genre vocal. As John Wesley Harding notes, 'He screws up the riff at the end . . . so he goes through the whole sequence again, just for the hell of it.'[53]

There is, incidentally, another Blind Boy Fuller song sung by Dylan in the same period. At the Supper Club, New York City, in November 1993 he performed 'Weeping Willow', which Fuller recorded solo, also in New York, in 1937. Fuller's penultimate verse is one we already know from Skip James' 'Devil Got My Woman':

> *Lord I lay down last night, tried to take my rest . . .*
> *You know my mind got to rambling just like the wild geese in the west.*

Dylan avoids this verse altogether (the mourning dove is enough ornithology for one song, perhaps), and after singing Fuller's final verse, in which buying a bulldog (a little dog named Bull) is envisaged (though Dylan intends that it should 'watch you while you sleep' rather than 'watch you while I sleep'), Dylan ends by reprising the opening verse, or rather, his own tweaked version of it. Instead of Fuller's

> *Lord that weeping willow and that mourning dove*
> *That weeping willow and that mourning dove*
> *I got a girl up the country that I sure do love*

Dylan prefers the stranger, Baudelairean fusion

> *That weeping willow mourning like a dove.*

Either way, it would be impossible to hear Dylan croon that line without hearing behind it a line of his own from 1974's 'Shelter From The Storm': the line in which not weeping but wailing is heard to be 'like a mourning dove'.[54]

---

nia, CD-reissued Arhoolie CD348, El Cerrito, c. 1990. Sonny Boy Williamson I: 'Got The Bottle Up And Gone', Aurora, Illinois, 5/5/37; "Sonny Boy Williamson" [Treasury Of Jazz EP no. 22], RCA 75.722, Paris, 1963. Sonny Terry & Jordan Webb: 'Touch It Up And Go', NYC, 23/10/41; CD-issued "Good Time Blues", Columbia CK 46780, New York, 1991.

53. John Wesley Harding: 'Good as he's been to us' (see note 21).

54. Bob Dylan: 'Weeping Willow', NYC, 17/11/93. Blind Boy Fuller: 'Weeping Willow', NYC, 14/7/37, "Blind Boy Fuller On Down – Vol.1", Saydisc Records SDR143, Badminton, UK, c. 1967. Skip James: 'Devil Got My Woman', Grafton, Wisconsin, c. Feb. 1931; "Skip James, King of the Delta Blues Singers 1928–1964", Biograph BLP-12029, Canaan, NY, 1971.

An especially dreary version of 'Weeping Willow', which hardly gets beyond the line 'That weeping willow and that mourning dove', repeated ad tedium, is that by Bert Jansch (an enigmatic folk star of the 1960s over whom Black Sobranie-smoking Eng. Lit. students with Mary Travers hair used to drool): 'Weeping Willow Blues',

To return to the chronology of "Good As I Been To You" is to arrive at 'Tomorrow Night', written by Sam Coslow and Will Grosz in 1939, and recorded that year by gruesome, sickly outfits like Horace Heidt & His Orchestra (vocal by the Heidt-Lights). The song began its real life as a black market ballad hit by the blues great Lonnie Johnson, in 1948. He sold a million, and it kept him going for years. (Years later he and Dylan were on the same album, "Three Kings & The Queen".)[55]

Elvis Presley listened to many Mississippi blues singers, Lonnie Johnson included, and was 13 years old when Johnson had a hit with the song. It's been suggested that he would have been reminded of 'Tomorrow Night' by LaVern Baker, who put it on the B-side of her 1954 hit 'Tweedle-Dee' (which we know Elvis covered in live performance, as soon as it was a hit: a performance live at the Louisiana Hayride in Shreveport in 1955 is available on the misleadingly titled "Elvis: The First Live Recordings"). But in fact Elvis' 'Tomorrow Night', backed only by Scotty Moore's guitar, was cut at Sun on 10 September 1954, before LaVern Baker's was recorded, let alone issued. Elvis' version is in any case markedly similar to Lonnie Johnson's in sound, feel and delivery. It remained unissued till 1965, when it was doctored (a bridge cut out, many things overdubbed) and put out on a ragbag album called "Elvis For Everyone". In 1985 the proper version was issued on the "Reconsider Baby" album, and has most recently reappeared on the Elvis 1950s box-set, issued the same year as Bob Dylan's version on "Good As I Been To You".[56]

Big Joe Turner also recorded the song; Jerry Lee Lewis cut it at Sun in 1956; Sonny Burgess cut it there too; Mike Bloomfield cut it in 1973 and it appears on two Willie Nelson albums.

We know that Dylan admires the work of Willie Nelson (and indeed of Mike Bloomfield, at least as a guitarist) but to say, as Phil Sutcliffe did in Q magazine, that Dylan's version is 'culled from' this 'familiar source' is unreasonable and overrates Nelson and his influence.[57] It seems far more reasonable to say that Dylan would have

---

London, April 1967; "Nicola", Transatlantic Records TRA157, London, 1967; CD-reissued "Bert Jansch – Nicola + Birthday Blues", Demon Transatlantic DEMCD17, London, 1993. ('Weeping Willow' is also touched upon briefly in Chapter 9.)

There is another, much inferior song called 'Weeping Willow Blues', recorded by Bessie Smith (NYC, 26/9/24) and covered soon afterwards by a number of other early women 'classic blues' singers such as Monette Moore (NYC, c. Nov. 1924). This is the one Odetta chose to revisit rather dreadfully, emphasising the hollow vaudevillian character of the song, which Bessie Smith's unarguable artistry had done its best to counteract. Odetta: 'Weeping Willow Blues', *nia*, issued on "Odetta And The Blues", Prestige Bluesville R-9417 and then in the series Original Blues Classics OBC 509, Bergenfield, NJ, *nia*.

55. Lonnie Johnson: 'Tomorrow Night', Cincinnati, 10/12/47, LP-issued "Lonesome Road", King Records LP 520, Cincinnati, 1956, CD-reissued "Lonnie Johnson 1946–1963: Tomorrow Night", Blues Encore CD 52016, Italy, 1991 (along with 'See See Rider' and 'Blues Stay 'Way From Me'). Johnson re-recorded the song a few months later (Detroit, 1948) for the Paradise label, issued with a cut by George Dawson's Chocolateers on the B-side (Paradise 110, Detroit, *nia*); this excursion to Paradise seems odd, because it came in the midst of the many sessions Johnson did for King between 1947 and 1952.

56. Elvis Presley: 'Tomorrow Night', Memphis, 10/9/54, issued "Elvis For Everyone", RCA Victor LPM-3450, New York, 1965; issued properly on "Reconsider Baby", RCA Victor AFL1–5418, New York, 1985, CD-reissued on "The King Of Rock'n'Roll – The Complete 50s Masters", BMG/RCA Records PD90689(5), 1992. Elvis Presley: 'Tweedle Dee', Shreveport, 1955, "Elvis: The First Live Recordings", RCA International PG 89387, London, 1984.

LaVern Baker's 'Tomorrow Night' (and 'Tweedle Dee'), NYC, 20/10/54, have been reissued on the 8-CD compilation "Atlantic Rhythm and Blues 1947–1974", Atlantic Records 782305–2, New York, c. 1992. A touching piece on LaVern Baker's first visit to Britain in 1992 was published in the *Independent*, 24/10/92.

57. Jerry Lee Lewis: 'Tomorrow Night', Memphis, 1956, issued retrospectively on "Rockin' & Free", Phonogram 6467.029, London, 1974. Mike Bloomfield: 'Tomorrow Night', *nia*, unreleased till the CD version of his 1973 LP

known, but avoided any attempt to follow, Elvis Presley's version, and that he most certainly knew Lonnie Johnson's.

When Dylan performed this live in his exemplary concerts of early 1993, he varied his acoustic guitar intro enormously from one night to another; at least once he was using the guitar intro from *another* Lonnie Johnson ballad track, 'No Love For Sale', recorded by Johnson as late as 1960 – the very period in which Dylan was able to catch Johnson in and around Greenwich Village.[58]

Dylan's version is not perhaps for the uninitiated but it's a lovely thing: a performance that puts us right inside the poor-white-trash radio-romance world of Hank Williams, Elvis' boyhood and a lost working-class America. The value of such a performance is that Dylan avoids Ry Cooderish cleverness and the self-consciousness of dry curatorship here. His impassioned partisan understanding of the genre fleshes out its recreation on bones of love, allowing him to take the song seriously, as Elvis does. He's therefore free to sing the early, falling line of mistrust and future-gloom 'Will all the thrill be gone?' so that it also carries open, beguiling warmth. It's a reading with more than a hint of Dylan's interpretative genius.

It's quite a contrast to the track that follows, 'Arthur McBride'. This great Irish folk number is A. L. Lloyd's favourite song – 'that most good-natured, mettlesome and un-pacifistic of anti-militarist songs', he calls it – and it passed from him into the repertoire of the 1960s English folk scene. It was collected in Limerick from a Patrick W. Joyce in 1840, and, says Lloyd,

> around the same time George Petrie received a version from a Donegal correspondent. Sam Fone, the aging Dartmoor mason whom Baring-Gould found to be an inexhaustible fountain of songs, remembered it as his father's favourite in Devon in the 1830s . . . [The song] made its way to the Scottish north-east during the latter half of the century . . . More recently, a singer from Walberswick, Suffolk, recorded it for the BBC early in 1939.[59]

The recruiting sergeant was one of the most hated figures in Irish and British life, especially since poverty gave many men little alternative but to join up, though of course in the case of the Irish the army they were joining was not even their own. The roving recruiting sergeant encountered by Arthur McBride and his cousin had a function halfway between that of the earlier press-gang and the modern recruiting office, which still pulls in those with least education and fewest opportunities.

Like 'Jim Jones', this makes for a song readily understood within Bob Dylan's

---

"Try It Before You Buy", One Way Records A21265, New York, c. 1990. Willie Nelson: 'Tomorrow Night', *nia*, "There'll Be No More Teardrops Tonight", *nia*, and "Country Willie", *nia*.

Sonny Burgess: 'Tomorrow Night', Memphis, 1957–58, is one of several Elvis-associated items (like the Arthur Crudup song 'So Glad You're Mine' and 'One Night') on the 2-CD set "Sonny Burgess: The Classic Recordings 1956–1959", Bear Family BCD 15525-BH, Vollersode, Germany, 1991.

Phil Sutcliffe quoted from *Q* magazine, November 1992.

58. Bob Dylan: 'Tomorrow Night', London, 8/2/93 and 12/2/93. (The latter is the better performance.)

Lonnie Johnson: 'No Love For Sale' and 'I Don't Hurt Anymore', Englewood Cliffs, New Jersey, 8/3/60, "Blues By Lonnie Johnson", Bluesville LP 1007 and Original Blues Classics OBC 502, *nia*; CD-reissued Original Blues Classics OBCCD 502, *nia*. (Dylan included 'I Don't Hurt Anymore' on the Basement Tapes [Woodstock, June 1967].)

59. A. L. Lloyd, see latter part of note 19.

repertoire – and is as good an anti-militarist song as 'John Brown' is a bad one, being alive, spanning many moods and full of individual detail instead of being polemical and built upon lurid stereotypes to the exclusion of all real observation.

For 'Arthur McBride' Dylan owes a particular debt to an Irish singer he much admires, Paul Brady, who used to sing the song in the group Planxty and later as a solo performer. We know that when Dylan was in Ireland to play a 1984 concert he asked Brady to show him how he played his guitar accompaniment to another old song, 'The Lakes Of Pontchartrain', which Dylan then began to perform in the acoustic sections of his concerts in 1988. We also know that Dylan mentions Brady as one of his 'secret heroes' in the interview published in 1985's "Biograph" box-set. Brady himself had found the song 'Arthur McBride' in a 1973 American book, *A Heritage of Songs*, when living at the home of the 1960s folksinger Patrick Sky in Rhode Island, and had adapted it for his own recording of it in 1976. There is no doubting that Dylan knew this recording, nor that his own performance of it on "Good As I Been To You" is close – word for word, and melodically – to Brady's.[60]

This is hardly the whole story, however. Dylan brings his own knowledge and his own otherness to his recording. As Gavin Selerie puts it: 'I hear Brady's performance beneath Dylan's but there are other influences there as well . . . one can hear layers of musical experience in Dylan's work.' Moreover, Brady's phrasing and intonation may owe something to Dylan: 'notably a charged casualness of reference and an elasticity of syllabic emphasis'. Playing in Dublin, London and New York in his formative musical years, Brady can hardly have failed to absorb Dylan influences.[61]

Dylan's 'Arthur McBride', then, may be very close to Brady's but the voice is so strongly his own that he makes it seem an apt vehicle for expressing himself, and does so with a fond admiration for the song and a range of feeling that make this a highlight of the album.

The 8-bar blues 'You're Gonna Quit Me' is a remake of Blind Blake's 'You Gonna

60.   Dylan's concert at Slane, near Dublin, was 8/7/84. He débuted 'The Lakes Of Pontchartrain' at the first concert of the Never-Ending Tour, Concord, California, 7/6/88.

Paul Brady: 'The Lakes Of Pontchartrain', Dublin, March–April 1978; "Welcome Here Kind Stranger", Mulligan Records LUN 024, Dublin, 1978; live recording Dublin, 10/9/85, single release 1986, *nia*. Paul Brady: 'Arthur McBride', Wales, Autumn 1976; "Andy Irvine – Paul Brady", Mulligan Records LUN 008, Dublin, 1976; CD-reissue Mulligan Records LUNCD008, Dublin, 1990.

The account of Brady's finding and adapting 'Arthur McBride' is taken from a letter from Brady to Gavin Selerie, and quoted by Selerie in a published letter to the *Telegraph*, no. 54, Spring 1996. For an interesting exposition of the more complex route whereby 'The Lakes Of Pontchartrain' was learnt by Brady, see Gavin Selerie: 'Tricks and training: some Dylan sources and analogues (Part Two)', *Telegraph*, no. 51, Spring 1995. Selerie reports that Pontchartrain and its sister-lakes were a great flood nuisance to the citizens of nearby New Orleans. However, they were also a place for leisure. Val Wilmer [see note 38] notes that when the blues singer Roosevelt Sykes and his wife settled in New Orleans, around the end of the 1960s, they used to go fishing on the 13-mile-wide Lake Pontchartrain, while (see Chapter 9, note 93), Rabbit Brown had worked it as a singing boatman decades earlier.

'The Lakes Of Pontchartrain' is also on "Bayou Bluegrass" [an interesting-sounding category] by the Louisiana Honeydrippers, originally Folklyric LP 122, USA, 1961, now Arhoolie 5010, El Cerrito, California, *nia*, while 'On The Banks Of The Old Pontchartrain' is a recording by Hank Williams [Nashville, 4/8/47, MGM Records 10073, Hollywood, c. 1947].

Martin Carthy is another singer from the English folk scene from whom Dylan has learnt songs in the past, and 'Arthur McBride', sometimes called 'Arthur McBride and the Sergeant', is on Carthy's 1981 "Prince Heathen" LP, on his sometime-partner Dave Swarbrick's 1982 album "Swarbrick" and on John Kirkpatrick and Sue Harris' "Stolen Ground" (Topic, 1989). For a interview with Carthy that is thoughtful, warm and generous about Dylan, see 'A Chat with Martin Carthy', by Matthew Zuckerman, *Isis*, no. 83, February–March 1999.

61.   Gavin Selerie, *Telegraph*, no. 54, Spring 1996.

Quit Me Blues', recorded in Chicago in about October 1927, and its repeated line supplies the title for Dylan's album.[62]

Blind (Arthur) Blake – we think he was born between 1890 and 1895, and that he died about 1933 – is the man in the main picture on the cover of Paul Oliver's *The Story of the Blues* (with a smaller shot of Blind Willie McTell, whom Blake influenced, stuck on the corner). He came from Tampa, Florida to work in South Georgia and the east coast towns. He had a light, swinging guitar technique and a touchingly rueful way of singing, though this was balanced by a rough-edged quality (Ma Rainey liked him as an accompanist for this reason). His style suited dances and rags, and along with Peg Leg Howell's Gang (which included Henry ['Georgia Crawl'] Williams) Blake was a prominent early transmitter of nineteenth-century rags into the twentieth-century blues repertoire. Among much else he played guitar for Gus Cannon on 'Poor Boy', recorded 'Hastings Street' (which is in Detroit) with Charlie Spand and recorded with the writers of Bessie Smith's 'Gimme A Pigfoot', Leola B. Wilson and Welsey 'Kid Sox' Wilson. Josh White acted as Blind Blake's 'eyes' at one time. He was an important figure, and his playing was the main influence on the creator of 'Step It Up & Go', Blind Boy Fuller. His 'Southern Rag' was so well-known and of such lasting appeal that even musical *ingénue* Allen Ginsberg knew of Blind Blake as well as William: Ginsberg's 'Tear Gas Rag', about an anti-Vietnam War demo in Colorado in 1972, is based on what he calls Blake's 'Old Southern Rag'.[63]

'You're Gonna Quit Me' has also been recorded by Bob Dylan's old Greenwich Village acquaintance the Rev. Gary (or Blind Gary) Davis, from whom Paul Oliver suggests that Blind Boy Fuller also learnt much technique. They worked and travelled together, and Davis plays second guitar on Fuller's début recording session.[64]

'You're Gonna Quit Me' is the 'Corrina Corrina' of the album, although Dylan's performance is less numinous and caressive than on that early filler track. It isn't a very distinctive song but in terms of album programming it works, its simple structure and unhurried sense of space making it refreshing. The melody is always promising to become haunting, yet never quite manages it. The failure may come from its extreme simplicity; the promise arises from its sounding like one half of a melody that truly is haunting – that of Jimmie Rodgers' 'Waiting For A Train'.[65]

62. Originally issued on Paramount (the ones for which we have only approximate recording-dates are almost always on cheapskate, careless but good-at-talent-spotting Paramount Records); vinyl-issued "Guitar Wizards (1926–1935)", Yazoo L-1016, New York, 1969, now CD-reissued.
The line 'The day you quit me baby: that's the day you die' is used almost verbatim by Blind Blake as the ending to his earlier 'Early Morning Blues' [2 takes, NYC, c. September 1926; one issued "No Dough Blues: Blind Blake, Vol. 3", Biograph BLP-12031, Canaan, NY, 1971, the other on "Rope Stretchin' Blues: Blind Blake, Vol. 4, 1926–31", Biograph BLP-12037, Canaan, NY, 1972]. The same line recurs as the end of Barbecue Bob's 'Easy Rider Don't Deny My Name' [NYC, 16/6/27; "The Atlanta Blues", RBF Records RF-15, New York, 1966].

63. Blind Blake: 'Southern Rag', Chicago, c. October 1927; "Blind Blake: Foremost Fingerpicker", Yazoo L-1068, 1984, now CD-reissued.
'Tear Gas Rag', in *First Blues / Rags, Ballads & Harmonium Songs 1971–1974*, Allen Ginsberg, 1975.

64. Reverend Gary Davis: 'You're Goin' Quit Me Baby', recorded at Davis' NYC home, 1963 or 1968; "Let Us Get Together", Kicking Mule Records SNKF103, London, 1973.
I note that while Big Bill Broonzy says that Blind Blake was the best guitarist (Alan Lomax, *The Land Where the Blues Began*) Stefan Grossman knows better. His sleeve note to the Yazoo Gary Davis 1935–49 album says how inferior Blake was to Davis – though not as inferior as Blind Boy Fuller, who gets a thorough trashing.

65. There is a really fine recording of *that* song (aside, that is, from Rodgers' own) on the début album by Boz Scaggs, a neglected classic. Issued by Atlantic in 1969, it combines Scaggs' most plangent vocals with, on this track,

Next comes the splendid 'Diamond Joe'. There is another song about the same mean-spirited Texas cattle-boss, and also named after him, collected in John A. and Alan Lomax's book *Cowboy Songs*, and they report that it was popular in its home state in the 1880s. But the 'Diamond Joe' Bob Dylan sings is one within a complex of songs – often comic rather than dramatic – called 'State Of Arkansas', of which other examples are our old friend Henry Thomas's 'Arkansas' and the recording well-known to connoisseurs of the genre, Kelly Harrell's 'My Name Is John Johanna' – yet another item on the Harry Smith anthology. This has the same tune as 'Diamond Joe', includes some of the same lyric, and concerns the same boss. There's also a bluesy hillbilly song with the same name, of which a terrific 1920s version by the Georgia Crackers was reissued in the 1970s.[66]

At any rate the song Dylan sings is not very well-known, though it also seems very much of the genre of 'Trail of the Buffalo', a song Dylan has performed many times both in the very early 1960s and the late 1980s. 'Diamond Joe' seems to have surfaced at these times too. Ramblin' Jack Elliott used to perform 'Diamond Joe' in Greenwich Village, and has recorded it, while the contemporaneous Boston-based folkie Tom Rush put it on his 1963 album "Got A Mind To Ramble" – which Dylan's "Good As I Been To You" rather resembles, in being a collection of black and white folk material, some of which crosses over between the two. (The resemblance is more striking than that: Rush cut so many songs in a three-day recording period that it made for two albums' worth of these old songs – a "Good As I Been To You" and a "World Gone Wrong", you might say.) Elliott and Rush may have picked up the song from Cisco Houston, who includes a version on his "Cowboy Ballads" album that incorporates the verse about 'His bread it was corn-dodger / And his meat I could not chaw' – the verse that comes straight from the 'State Of Arkansas' ballad.[67]

an immaculate, unshowy slide guitar solo by Duane Allman. Boz Scaggs: 'Waiting For A Train', Muscle Shoals, Alabama, 1969, "Boz Scaggs", Atlantic K40419, London, 1969. This album was co-produced by Scaggs, Marlin Greene and *Rolling Stone* magazine editor Jann Wenner: surely the one act of his life that might redeem him. 'Waiting For A Train' reissued on "Let It Rock", Various Artists, Atlantic K40455, London, 1973.
    Jimmie Rodgers: 'Waiting For A Train', Atlanta, 22/10/28, is, along with the brilliant 'Blue Yodel [No. 1 (T For Texas)]', Camden, NJ, 30/11/27, collected with typically contemptuous lack of information by RCA on "20 Of The Best", RCA International NK89370, Brussels, 1984.

66. Henry Thomas: 'Arkansas', Chicago, 1/7/27; "Texas Country Music, Vol. 1", Roots RL-312, Vienna, 1968. Kelly Harrell: 'My Name Is John Johanna', Camden, NJ, 23/3/27; Harry Smith's "American Folk Music". The Georgia Crackers: 'Diamond Joe', Atlanta, 21/3/27; "Hell Broke Loose In Georgia: Georgia Fiddle Bands 1927–1934", County Records 514, USA, 1970s.

67. Bob Dylan: 'The Bay Of Mexico' [a variant of 'The Trail Of The Buffalo'/'Buffalo Skinners'], St Paul, Minnesota, May 1960; 'The Trail Of The Buffalo'/'Buffalo Skinners', East Orange, NJ, Feb.–March 1961; then débuted, back in New Jersey, at the early Never-Ending Tour concert at Holmdel, 25/6/88. There are fine versions three years later in Madison, Wisconsin, 5/11/91 and Louisville, Kentucky, 8/11/91.
    Ramblin' Jack Elliott: 'Diamond Joe', NYC, May 1963, "Jack Elliott", Vanguard VRS-9151 [mono] and VSD-79151 [stereo], NYC, 1964; CD-reissued (alongside versions of 'Roving Gambler', 'San Francisco Bay Blues', 'House Of The Rising Sun' and 'Don't Think Twice It's Alright', plus a version of 'Will The Circle Be Unbroken' that features Bob Dylan on harmonica, cut summer 1963 in New York) on "The Essential Ramblin' Jack Elliott", Vanguard VSD 89/90, NYC, 1976.
    Tom Rush: 'Diamond Joe', Boston, May 1963, issued with 10 other tracks on "Got A Mind To Ramble", Prestige/Folklore 14003, USA, 1964. A further 11 tracks cut over the same three-day period were issued on the later LP "Blues, Songs and Ballads", Prestige 7374, USA, 1965. The first collection included 'Duncan And Brady' (which Dylan recorded in Chicago, 1992), 'San Francisco Bay Blues', Merle Travis' 'Nine Pound Hammer' and Leroy Carr's 'Mobile-Texas Line', a variant of 'Corrine Corrina'. The second collection included 'Pallet On The

Dylan sings the song immaculately, while playing a quietly dextrous guitar part, and achieving a flowing cohesion between the two. By no means an immediate highlight of the album, it grows into one. It looks you in the eye and addresses you directly, without mannerism or flash, though there is a great deal of quiet artfulness in the presentation. There is the lovely delicacy of the way that on the phrase 'nearly starved to death, boys' voice and guitar slide down the scale together, as if with solicitous politeness. And though Bob Dylan on form is famously good at never singing a repeat line the same way twice, the various ways he finds here to breathe that closing 'Joe' at the end of each of the song's four verses is, even by his own standards, a delight. This is not a track on which you hear painful vocal difficulty. There is no striving to do it, no apparent effort and no sense of artifice; he varies the way he sings that small word with the most unobtrusive kind of aplomb, so that it comes across as thoughtful and as an expressively rueful looking-back.

That other small word, 'chaw', invites a different looking-back. It may sound very Cowboy – but there is nothing exclusive to this milieu about the word, or in using it with the rhyme 'jaw'. In the first book of Edmund Spenser's great poem *The Faerie Queen*, published in Elizabethan England, Spenser's description of the debilitating vice of envy seizes on the word at once:

> *And next to him malicious Envy rode*
> *Upon a ravenous wolfe, and still did chaw*
> *Between his cankred teeth a venomous tode,*
> *That all the poison ran about his jaw.*[68]

At least as old as Spenser's poetry, and probably older, is 'Froggie Went A-Courtin'', sung and played with real charm by Dylan, who keeps deftly away from both hammed-up comedy and song-archivist solemnity, enabling him to offer a version that is good-humoured and alert to the riches and full humanity of the song.

This is at base an ancient nursery rhyme/ballad, which also has a niche in the history of folk song recordings. The sleeve notes to the Harry Smith anthology begin by remarking that the most famous recording of the early 1900s was Uncle Josh's unaccompanied 'Frog Went A Courting'.

One collector, Theodore Raph, believes the song can be traced back to Wedderburn's book of around 1549, *The Complaynt of Scotland*, in which it appears as 'The Frog cam to the Myl Dur', a song he suggests was chiefly sung by shepherds.[69] Bruno Bettelheim, giving the publication date of *The Complaynt of Scotland* as the slightly earlier 1540, says that it includes mention of a pre-Grimms' version of their fairy tale

---

Floor', 'Stackerlee', Blind Boy Fuller's 'Rag Mama' and three other items that were in Dylan's early repertoire, 'Cocaine', 'Barb'ry Allen' and 'Baby Please Don't Go'. The whole lot is CD-reissued as "Songs, Blues and Ballads", Big Beat CDWIK 948, UK, *nia*.

   Cisco Houston: 'Diamond Joe', *nia*, "Cowboy Ballads", Folkways FA 2022, New York, 1957. When this version was published in *Reprints from* Sing Out! *Vol. 2*, 1992, it was given as copyrighted to Stormking Music, 1961 – which was odd as well as risible, because it had first been published in *Sing Out! Vol. 4, no. 4,* in March 1954.

68. Edmund Spenser (c. 1552–1599): *The Faerie Queen*, 1590, 1596 and 1609.

69. Theodore Raph, *The Songs We Sang: A Treasury of American Popular Music* (1965).

'The Frog King', called 'The Well of the World's End'. Since 'the well' is also the frog's location at the beginning of the earliest known versions of the 'Frog Went A Courting' song, this may suggest some conjunction between that thirteenth-century version of this 'animal groom' story and the 'Frog Went A Courting' song-group. But the Opies and Harry Smith both note that the earliest listing is the title 'A moste Strange weddinge of the ffrogge and the mowse', listed by Her Majesty's Stationery Office on 21 November 1580, and it seems generally agreed that the earliest extant version of the *song* is in Ravenscroft's *Melismata* of 1611.[70]

This version is called 'The Marriage of the Frogge and the Movse' and is a 13-verse text with tune, beginning:

> *It was the Frogge in the well . . .*
> *And the merrie Movse in the Mill*

and including

> *The Frogge would a woing ride . . .*
> *Sword and buckler by his side.*

In this version the frog and mouse are married by the rat, and the wedding supper ('three beanes in a pound of butter') is interrupted by the cat catching the mouse, a drake catching the frog and the rat escaping up the wall.

The song grew widespread as a nursery rhyme in the eighteenth century, and by the time we get to Kirkpatrick's *Ballad Book* (1824) it begins

> *There lived a puddy in a well,*

it has become 'Sword and pistol by his side' and they have to get Uncle Rotten's consent. (A variant that connects with other things, 'Squire Frog's Visit', has the chorus

> *Heighho! says Brittle*
> *With a namby pamby*
> *Mannikin pannikin*
> *Heigh! says Anthony Brittle.*)[71]

The Opies suggest that the nursery rhyme version is best known in the comparatively recent version called 'A Frog He Would A-Wooing Go', 'popularised first by Grimaldi and then by the comedian John Liston in the early nineteenth century'. (It

---

70.   Bruno Bettelheim, *The Uses of Enchantment* (1976). The later quotes from Bettelheim in the present chapter are also from *The Uses of Enchantment*.
    'The Well of the World's End' is republished in *A Dictionary of British Folk Tales*, 4 volumes, Katherine M. Briggs (1970). Iona and Peter Opie, *The Oxford Dictionary of Nursery Rhymes* (rev. edn, 1951).

71.   The line pairing the sword and the pistol occurs in other folksongs and game-chants. The poet and Blake scholar Kathleen Raine writes of her father that during his childhood in the north of England (County Durham) he had been 'initiated, unawares, into a tradition older than Christianity, surviving in the "guiser's play", handed down by the older to the younger boys in secrecy and by word of mouth . . . "Here comes in King George, / King George is my name, / With sword and pistol by my side / I hope to win the game." ' (Kathleen Raine, *Farewell Happy Fields*, 1973, collected in *Autobiographies*, 1991.)
    A 'guiser' is a mummer, usually one performed at Christmas (as was the one referred to here) or Hallowe'en. (The same 'guiser's play' verses also include the line 'Round the world and back again', which Dylan implants into 'Handy Dandy' on his nursery-rhyme-studded album "Under The Red Sky".)

was first published with a tune in about 1809 under the title 'The Love-Sick Frog'.) Its repeated chorus line 'Heighho! says Anthony Rowley' is not found before the nineteenth century. Earlier versions tend to have 'Humble-dum, humble-dum, tweedle tweedle wino', which, representing the humming of the wheel and the twiddling and winding of the thread, suggests that it may have started as a spinning song. 'Yes kind sir I sit and spin.'

As a song, always popular in America in both white and black folksong, it holds several Dylan connections. His version, substantially that in Cecil Sharp's *Nursery Songs from the Appalachian Mountains* (1921–23), is also included in the 1927 *American Songbag* collection by Carl Sandburg, whom Dylan went to visit in 1964.[72] A variant version is yet another song Dylan found on the 1952 Harry Smith anthology: the 1928 recording 'King Kong Kitchie Kitchie Ki-Me-O' by Chubby Parker & His Old Time Banjo ('vocal solo with 5-string banjo and whistling'). Parker was, in Tony Russell's phrase, 'up at the minstrel end of hillbilly'[73] but his performance on this track has a pleasantly clean-cut, straightforward quality: a light touch and no ingratiation.

It is not the version sung by Dylan, though it begins with the near-identical first line 'Frog went a-courtin' and he did ride', and does include 'With a sword and a pistol by his side', 'He rode till he came to Miss Mousie's door', 'He took Miss Mousie on his knee / And he said "Miss Mousie will you marry me?"'. However, it ends with the frog killing all comers (with his sword and his pistol) before honeymooning with his mousy wife.

The most authoritative study of the song in its American form is in *Ozark Folk Songs Volume 1: British Ballads and Songs*, by Vance Randolph, reissued in the 1980s. Randolph published huge amounts on the song and folklore of the Ozarks. It's interesting that the very young Bob Dylan was acquainted with some of Randolph's work. In Minneapolis in 1959, reports Robert Shelton's Dylan biography, Bob's friend Spider John Koerner had a room-mate called Harry Weber, 'a ballad scholar', who says: 'I did loan Bob a set of Randolph's *Folk Songs of Arkansas* [sic]. I wonder if he still has them.'[74]

While Sharp printed the first American version of 'Froggie' taken from oral tradition, the first version into print taken from black oral tradition was in Thomas

---

72. Carl Sandburg, *American Songbag* (1927).
 The Dylan news-item compiler Ian Woodward thinks that Dylan went to see Sandburg because of his folksong collecting more than his being a poet: 'There were plenty of poets he didn't go and see', as Woodward remarked (phone-call to the present writer, 1994). Robert Shelton's account, in *No Direction Home* (1986), implies the reverse, yet says that when visiting Sandburg, Dylan and his companions emphasised that they knew his *Songbag* book.
 'Froggie Went A-Courtin'' is also included in John A. Lomax and Alan Lomax's *American Ballads and Folk Songs* (1934) and in many others. In 1926 the Texas Folklore Society alone knew of 40 versions, and the *American Folklore Bibliography* of 1939 listed 22 American variants.

73. Tony Russell, a renowned authority on, and collector of, hillbilly music and the blues, in conversation with the present writer, 17/9/96.

74. Bob Dylan, interviewed by Cameron Crowe for "Biograph", 1985, says that Koerner himself knew many ballads: that by the time he was at the Ten O'Clock Scholar coffee-house in Dinkytown, Minneapolis, he 'was singing stuff like 'Ruby Lee' by the Sunny Mountain Boys . . .' and that 'Spider John Koerner . . . played mostly ballads and Josh White type blues. He knew more songs than I did. 'Whoa Boys Can't Ya Line 'M', 'John Hardy', 'Golden Vanity', I learned all those from him. We sounded great; not unlike the Delmore Brothers.' For a less enthusiastic view of Koerner's abilities, see note 99 below.

W. Talley's classic collection *Negro Folk Rhymes*, published in 1922 (republished 1949 and 1991).[75]

As with 'Black Jack Davey', Dylan's friend Tony Glover is one of the people who has recorded 'Froggie Went A-Courtin'' in more recent decades. So has Doc Watson, Wally Whyton and ex-Steeleye Span member Tim Hart.[76]

Of course, 'Froggie' might be said to be a deeply conservative song: nature is destiny and nature will out. The socialist experiment collapses because cats will be cats and ducks will be ducks. Yet its theme runs far deeper, and less judgementally, than that. The basic storyline, summarised in typical style by Harry Smith as 'ZOOLOGIC MISCEGENY ACHIEVED IN MOUSE FROG NUPTIALS, RELA- TIVES APPROVE', seems to be one European version of an archetypal human myth- wish. Colombian Indians have a ritual / ceremony 'wedding' of a condor to a bull: they strap an enormous condor on the back of a bull and set them running. In the nursery rhyme 'Hoddley, Poddley'

> *Hoddley, poddley, puddle and fogs*
> *Cats are to marry the poodle dogs*
> *Cats in blue jackets, and dogs in red hats*
> *What will become of the mice and rats?*

and in the fairy tale 'Thumbelina' the toad wants the heroine to marry her son, and the fieldmouse tries to make her marry the mole. Of course in the case of the pseudo- human Thumbelina, the archetype of 'zoologic miscegeny' shifts over into another, the 'animal groom' archetype – in which the human protagonist's sexual partner is first experienced as an animal.

Bettelheim, in *The Uses of Enchantment*, says that this motif 'is so popular worldwide that probably no other fairy-tale theme has so many variations'. His analysis is that these are tales

> which – without any reference to repression which causes a negative attitude to
> sex – simply teach that for love, a radical change in previously held attitudes
> about sex is absolutely necessary. What must happen is expressed, as always in
> fairy tales, through a most impressive image: a beast is turned into a magnificent
> person . . . Some fairy stories emphasise the long and difficult development which
> alone permits gaining control over what seems animalistic in us, while conversely
> other tales center on the shock of recognition when that which seemed animal
> suddenly reveals itself as the source of human happiness . . . 'The Frog King'
> belongs to the latter category.

A little of this might be felt to reverberate through 'Froggie Went A-Courtin'' (which may, as we've seen, share a common ancestry with that fairy tale), in which we readily identify with the story, especially in the early parleying between

---

75. As 'Frog Went A Courting' it was field-recorded for the Library of Congress in Frederica, Georgia, in June 1935, performed by Drusilla Davis and accompanying 'group of little girls'.

76. Tony Glover: 'Froggie Went A-Courtin''', *nia*. Doc Watson, *nia*, collected on "The Essential Doc Watson", Vanguard VMLP5038, New York, 1974, now CD-reissued. Wally Whyton, *nia*, "50 Children's Songs", *nia*. Tim Hart, *nia*, "The Drunken Sailor and Other Kids' Songs", Music For Pleasure Records, *nia*, London, 1983.

prospective groom and bride and authoritative relative, so that on one level it doesn't matter whether they are given as animals or people, while on another we never quite forget (whether we've read Anne Sexton or not) the 'ugly' animal potency of the frog: so deeply has the image of the frog-and-the-princess spoken to our psyches that it remains common currency between us all as subject matter for jokes – especially around the politics of gender – which surely confirms the gist of Bettelheim's analysis.

A different arc of psychological truth cuts through the song too. Behind the twinkling guitar that propels Dylan's version along like a rolling hoop, and via a melody line which parallels Blind Willie McTell's 'Hillbilly Willie's Blues', and at its centre also parallels Elvis' 'Paralyzed' (the deft lines of added detail like 'sword and pistol by his side' use the same tune as those like 'couldn't say a word for thinkin' of you' in 'Paralyzed'), we identify with the world in which the story's events unfold.[77] We recognise the truth of the shadow falling over the initially ideal, the chain of events darkening as the wedding feast collapses from exquisite and generous communal celebration, on a tiny and delicate scale, first into the black comedy of the grotesque, monstrously overlarge and clumsy intrusion of Mrs Cow (at the mention of whom we envisage at once the accidental squashing of many of the smaller guests). This is followed by the intrusion of evil, in the symbolically loaded figure of the black snake, and finally comes the effectively wanton destruction of the main protagonists. This is a timeless human story.[78] One way and another, therefore, 'Froggie Went A-Courtin'' seems to me an extraordinary song, and one that proves – insists on – the indivisibility between adult and children's song.

In this way, given the emphasis it enjoys by being the last song on "Good As I Been To You", it is a fine postscript to the "Under The Red Sky" album. And like that album, which bows out with 'Goodnight my love and may the Lord have mercy on us all', this one has a great sign-off, provided by the song's self-reflexive text of a last line: 'If you want any more you can sing it yourself'.[79]

There are striking changes of genre and oeuvre between one song and another – perhaps most spectacularly the wonderful switch of worlds between 'Tomorrow Night', that brilliant recreation of the American 1940s radio-romance poor-white-trash world (the world of Vernon and Gladys Presley and little boy Elvis in their shack in Tupelo, Mississippi, in fact), and the insouciant self-confident grace of the

77.   Blind Willie McTell: 'Hillbilly Willie's Blues', Chicago, 25/4/35, "The East Coast States Vol. 2", Roots RL-326, Vienna, 1969–70: a Various Artists compilation.
    Elvis Presley: 'Paralyzed', Hollywood, 2/9/56 (composed for Elvis by Otis Blackwell, later co-producer of the title-track on Dylan's 1981 album "Shot Of Love"); first issued on the "Elvis Volume One" EP, RCA Victor EPA-992, New York, 1956; re-released on the CD box-set "The King Of Rock'n'Roll – The Complete 50s Masters", BMG/RCA Records PD90689(5), 1992.

78.   It also has a certain biological accuracy, as with the wedding food 'fried mosquito'. From the port of Cochin, India, frogs' legs used to be an export until conservationists succeeded in banning them. An importer-exporter tells Alexander Frater that this has been a blessing because 'you need a thriving frog population to keep the mosquitoes down'. (*Chasing the Monsoon*, Alexander Frater, 1991.)

79.   The version of the song collected from black oral tradition by Talley in the 1920s has this ending instead: 'Now I don't know no mo' 'an dat / Now I don't know no mo' 'an dat / If you gits mo' you can take my hat, Uh-huh!!! Uh-huh!!! / An' if you thinks dat hat won't do / An' if you thinks dat hat won't do / Den you mought take my head 'long too, Uh-huh!!! Uh-huh!!!'

articulate working class in eighteenth-century Ireland evoked by 'Arthur McBride'. Yet these dramatic contrasts jostle inside a cohesive whole: for the unity of the collection is as marked as its contrasts.

There is, to begin with, that striking cavalcade of individual names: Frankie, Albert, Jim Jones, Blackjack Davey, Little Maggie, Arthur McBride, Diamond Joe and Froggie in the song-titles alone, and a comparable catalogue in the last song's narrative. Going far beyond this, however, is the songs' thematic unity.

Of course, we can demur – to some extent – from the idea that all their thematic common ingredients have been significantly in Dylan's mind in the compiling of the album. Stephen Scobie, reviewing it when it was almost new, wrote: 'I am about to argue that the songs on "Good As I Been To You" appear to be obsessed with the themes of infidelity and revenge – but if, say, you were to pick at random *any* thirteen songs out of the folk and blues tradition, wouldn't there be a good chance that you would come up with a fair number . . . about unfaithful lovers and avenging spouses?'[80]

Yet what Dylan assembles here involves the continual re-exploring of the same sets of themes and correspondences of expression – themes that range far wider than personal infidelity and revenge.

'I ain't gonna tell you no story', he sings in the opening track; 'If you want any more you can sing it yourself', he sings in the last. In between, we have more talk about talk: in the second song, 'Come and listen for a moment lads and hear me tell my tale'; in the seventh, 'There's a song that will linger forever in our ears'; in the tenth, 'Now mark what followed and what did betide . . . / And so to conclude and to finish this speech'; and in the fourth 'Well it's [i.e. my story is] all of a fair and handsome girl'.

The heroine of 'Blackjack Davey' is a 'pretty little miss' in her tender years; so too the heroine of the next is a girl 'all in her tender years'. At the end of her story is a matching exhortation to Jim Jones' 'Come and listen for a moment lads and hear me tell my tale' – 'Come all ye fair and tender girls, wheresoever you may be'. In this song, and also in the first and third, the heroine pursues her own true love (though all with differing results). In the same three songs there is a love triangle and a betrayal, while in the sixth there is a posited triangle and in the twelfth a betrayal.

In the first there is a shooting, a judge and a hanging; in the second there's a judge, a threatened hanging and a threatened shooting. In the tenth, a threatened execution; in the eleventh, a threatened killing. In the first there is 'a forty-four', in the sixth a rifle and a 'six-shooter'.

In the first there is jail, in the eleventh the threat of the jailhouse, in the second men in irons, and in the eleventh again, the chain-gang. Each of the first three songs features a folk-hero baddie, while 'Diamond Joe' centres around a notorious baddie (though not a folk-hero).

Three songs feature the sea; the second involves exile, the third a sort of exile and the sixth a posited exile. The second, third and tenth emphasise a rejection of ruling

80.   Stephen Scobie: 'As good as who's been to who?', *On the Tracks* 'premier issue', Summer 1993.

class values, while the harsh oppression of a colonial power comes into song two and ten, and in 'Hard Times' there is social injustice and oppression all around.

The fourth includes a captain and the wearing of a military (naval) uniform; the tenth includes a sergeant and the wearing of a military (army) uniform. In 'Blackjack Davey' fine clothes are sacrificed; in the adjacent 'Canadee-i-o' fine clothes are gained; in 'Arthur McBride' 'fine clothes' are offered and declined; in 'You're Gonna Quit Me' shoes and clothes are bought in vain. In the third song there are horses and an implied blanket ('wrapped up with Blackjack Davey'), and there are horses and blankets in 'Diamond Joe'. There are even neat, small conjunctions in the use of children's descriptive phrases, from the opening song's 'rooty-toot-toot', through another's 'rowdy-dow-dow' to the closing song's 'bumble-y-bee'.

In writing about 'Belle Isle', I once suggested that Dylan's taste for narrative ballads was for those tales that were 'of horses and daughters and hangings, exile and injustice'.[81] The songs on "Good As I Been To You" fit this pattern pretty well. In the end, what is so clear from this collection is not merely that it has the thematic unity of a concept-album without any of the potential self-importance, but that while Bob Dylan hasn't written a single one of these songs, the album could hardly be more Dylanesque.

If we felt that Dylan was signing off from such work with that self-reflexive last line, 'If you want any more you can sing it yourself', we were wrong. A year after "Good As I Been To You" came "World Gone Wrong", a second volume of old folk and blues songs, again performed solo by Dylan with just voice, guitar and occasional harmonica, and again offered without any precise recording session information – no where or when, nor anything to be learnt from others on hand (presumably no one else was), about how many takes had been attempted or how many other songs recorded and held back. (We have since gleaned that the sessions were again held at Dylan's Malibu home-studio, probably in May of 1993, and that at least four other songs were recorded but held back, including the lovely 1930s Carter Family song 'Hello Stranger' and Robert Johnson's '32–20 Blues', this last a revisit to a song that, like 'Sittin' On Top Of The World', he had also performed at the very beginning of his career.[82])

The songs on "World Gone Wrong" also share common themes – friendship and betrayal, murder and revenge, exile and disguise, and so on (themes common to both albums, in fact) but this time they seem to lend themselves to a different form of examination by their natural tendency to cluster in still broader thematic groups, addressing themselves, for example, to the story of America's railroads and the musical

81. 'Back To Belle Isle', *Telegraph*, no. 29, Spring 1988. An updated and revised version appeared as 'Grubbing For A Moderate Jewel: In Search of the Blooming Bright Star of Belle Isle', *Canadian Folklore canadien*, Vol. 8, nos 1–2, '1986', actually published 1988.

82. Carter Family: 'Hello Stranger', NYC, 17/6/37; "A Collection Of Favorites By The Carter Family", Decca Records DL4404, New York, c. 1963. Robert Johnson: '32–20 Blues', San Antonio, 26/11/36; "Robert Johnson: King Of The Delta Blues Singers", Columbia CL-1654, New York, 1961. (Johnson's song is an almost verbatim reworking of Skip James' '22–20 Blues', Grafton, Wisconsin, c. February 1931; "Skip James, King Of The Delta Blues Singers 1928–1964", Biograph BLP-12029, Canaan, NY, 1971.) Bob Dylan: 'Kind-Hearted Woman (32–20 Blues / Cornfield Holler)', Gaslight Café, NYC, October 1962.

transferences these made possible, and to the passions of the Civil War of the 1860s. These we shall reach.

The principal difference between the two albums, however, and one that shone out at once when "World Gone Wrong" was new, was that this time the collection came with sleeve notes (liner-notes), and that Dylan had written them. Dylan's title for these – 'ABOUT THE SONGS (what they're about)' – is, like so much of his work, ambiguous. It is, first, combative: a doubled insistence that his commentary will restrict itself to the songs' real subject-matter – in renewed rebuke to 'interpreters' like me. Yet it doesn't escape Dylan's notice that the word 'about', which his title insists on repeating, has no straightforwardness of meaning at all: means, indeed, 'inexactly', and is circumnavigatory. It's a self-reflexive word, confessing that it roams (round and about). Dylan has played on this before, in that *Playboy* interview of 1966, in which, asked if he knows what his 'songs are about', he retorts that 'some of them are about five minutes . . . some are about eleven or twelve'.[83] This time around, knowing most emphatically what these 'songs are about', he offers us a pseudo-stream-of-consciousness account far more wide-ranging and internalised than 'interpreters' could manage or than we could have anticipated from Bob Dylan, regardless of how he'd chosen to title it.

Still more unexpected, perhaps, are the raw, unambiguous remarks in the middle. What could be less Dylanesque than the very first sentence in this piece of 'Dylanesque' writing: 'BROKE DOWN ENGINE is a Blind Willie McTell masterpiece.'? At the same time, starting as he means to go on, the first thing Dylan says the first song is 'about' is in one way wholly untrue. 'Broke Down Engine' is *not* 'about trains', any more than Bessie Smith's 'You Been A Good Ole Wagon (But You Done Broke Down)' is about wagons.[84] Yet in attempting to set down the fleeting stuff that these songs put him in mind of as he hears them, sings them, perhaps performs them live (if and when), Dylan does us a greater service than any conventional annotation would.

These notes are also part of his armoury of insistence on the contemporary relevance of such material: the continuing value and pertinence of both the poetry of the old blues world and that of medieval balladry. The title character in 'Love Henry' is presented immediately by Dylan as 'Henry – modern corporate man'. He writes of the Civil War song 'Two Soldiers' something he clearly applies to all these songs: that they're about 'learning to go forward by turning back the clock, stopping the mind from thinking in hours, firing a few random shots at the face of time'. He changes the Mississippi Sheiks' title 'The World Is Going Wrong' into 'World Gone Wrong', deploying the past tense for present pertinence.

This contemporaneity of relevance is so clear from the album itself that Dylan hardly need underscore it in the liner-notes: yet they underscore other continuities. In

83. 'The *Playboy* Interview: Bob Dylan: a candid conversation with the iconoclastic idol of the folk-rock set', *Playboy*, March 1966.

84. Blind Willie McTell: 'Broke Down Engine Blues', Atlanta, 23/10/31; "Blind Willie McTell: The Early Years (1927–1933)", Yazoo L-1005, NYC, 1968. 'Broke Down Engine', NYC, 18/9/33; "The Atlanta Blues", RBF Records RF-15, New York, 1966. 'Broke Down Engine No. 2' [2 takes], NYC, 18/9/33; "Atlanta Blues 1933", JEMF-106, LA, 1979. 'Broke Down Engine Blues', Atlanta, Oct. 1949, Atlantic Records 891, 1950 and then "Country Blues Classics – Vol.3", Blues Classics BC-7, Berkeley, 1966. As so often, the first of these is the best.

Bessie Smith: 'You Been A Good Ole Wagon (But You Done Broke Down)', NYC, 14/1/25; "The Bessie Smith Story Volume 1: Bessie Smith With Louis Armstrong", Columbia CL-855, New York, 1950s.

reverting to offering us any notes at all, Dylan is reasserting a link between the now and the then of his own artistic career. And in the very mode of expression he chooses for the notes, he reasserts the timelessness of his own stances and styles. While we don't need the notes to show us the record's parallels between the world of the Mississippi Sheiks and the here and now, they are themselves a warp-zone leading back and forth between here and the world of "Highway 61 Revisited".

So are their multi-layered contents. Time and again Dylan slips into them small, quiet references to other old records, other old blues and hillbilly music, plus the odd bit of rockabilly, often with further connections to the songs on "World Gone Wrong" itself as well as more generally to Dylan's past and his musical inheritance. Look at the very first few lines:

> BROKE DOWN ENGINE *is a Blind Willie McTell masterpiece. it's about trains, mystery on the rails—the train of love, the train that carried my girl from town— The Southern Pacific, Baltimore & Ohio whatever—*

Beyond the features already noted – the un-Dylanesque first sentence, the 'untruth' of 'it's about trains' – these few lines build up, phrase by phrase, a pile of allusions. There's the reversing of the title of one of the *great* train songs, 'Mystery Train', whose provenance is at the heart of the beginning of it all for Dylan, at Sun Records in Memphis, on Highways 51 and 61, with Junior Parker and with Elvis, with the birth of rock'n'roll and the key to Dylan's sense of liberation. There's the adjacent reference to 'Train Of Love', an old Johnny Cash record (also on Sun) and, returning at once to the heart of things, there's the mention of 'the train that carried my girl from town'.

This, presented in apparently casual prose, is a very specific reference: to the first record by coalminer Frank Hutchison, whose hillbilly version of 'Stack A Lee' Dylan follows so closely – you might say recreates so affectionately – on the album. (Again, Dylan's note says so with un-Dylanesque plainness: 'STACK A LEE is Frank Hutchison's verion.') Hutchison's first record, cut in New York in the autumn of 1926, *was* 'The Train That Carried The Girl From Town' (the other side was 'Worried Blues'), while its later revival came from Doc Watson, who put it on his début album along with 'Lone Pilgrim', the song Dylan uses to close "World Gone Wrong".[85]

Then, rattling right along, his reference to the Baltimore & Ohio railroad, far from being cited randomly, as that disingenuous 'whatever – ' implies, consciously alludes to yet another train song: in this case another one that Blind Willie McTell cut, 'B And O Blues No. 2'. In itself it's an inconsequential little song, with the quirk of having every rhyme land on the same sound: the one that hovers halfway between

85.   Junior Parker: 'Mystery Train', Memphis, c. Oct. 1953, Sun Records 192, Memphis, 1953–54. Elvis Presley: 'Mystery Train', Memphis, 11/7/55, Sun 223, Memphis, 1955. Johnny Cash: 'Train Of Love', Memphis, 1956, Sun 258, Memphis [London-American Records HLS 8427, London], 1956. (I don't suppose Dylan had in mind 'Train Of Love' by Alma Cogan [& Ocher Nebbish], London, 1959–60, HMV Records POP 760, London, 1960, or that by the Lindys [London, 1960, Decca Records F11253, London, 1960] though these may have been cover-versions of Cash's record.) Frank Hutchison: 'Stack A Lee', NYC, 28/1/27, "American Folk Music", Folkways Records FP 251–253, NYC, 1952. Frank Hutchison: 'The Train That Carried The Girl From Town' and 'Worried Blues', NYC, 28/9/26; CD-reissued on "White Country Blues 1926–1938: A Lighter Shade Of Blue", Columbia Roots N' Blues 01–472886–10, New York, 1993. Doc Watson: 'The Train That Carried My Girl From Town', *nia*, "The Doc Watson Family", Folkways Records FA2366, NYC, 1963, and a re-recording, *nia*, on "The Essential Doc Watson Vol. 1", Vanguard Records VMLP 5038, 1973, CD-reissued VMCD 7308, New York, 1987.

'oh' and 'ore', commonly rendered as in the line 'can't stay home no mo''. Thus 'B & O' can be rhymed with 'Baltimore' and with 'O-hi-o', and when the theme of the song is effectively summed up by the couplet 'I never would have thought that my baby would have treated me so / Ah she broke my heart when she grabbed that B & O', the lines end, in performance, in perfect rhymes.

Yet the connections the song makes amount to a positive Chicago Junction of blues history. Walter Davis had a hit from his début session in 1930 with 'M & O Blues', which inspired Bumble Bee Slim's hit 'B And O Blues' a couple of years later, which Blind Willie McTell radically re-wrote as 'B And O Blues No. 2' the year after that (McTell cut two takes, with Curley Weaver on second guitar – and Weaver cut a version himself while they were at it – the same week that he had made his first two re-recordings of 'Broke Down Engine'). Making a full circle, Walter Davis eventually recorded this himself as 'New B & O Blues' in the immediate post-war period.

In the "World Gone Wrong" album booklet, then, Bob Dylan makes another full circle by taking the opportunity of writing about 'Broke Down Engine', which he terms another McTell 'train song', to allude in his typically quiet way to this one. This is still more resonant, since in fact 'one of the Willie Browns', as Dylan puts it in his notes (another casual confirmation that Dylan knows his blues), had started the whole song cycle rolling, cutting an 'M & O Blues' just a fortnight before Walter Davis cut his.[86]

As for the railway lines themselves, Dylan is again invoking rich layers of history. The Southern Pacific and the Baltimore & Ohio railroad companies operated some of the many migratory routes of the 1920s and 1930s – oddly, all east–west rather than south–north – the first running between New Orleans and Houston and on west, and the second running the line between St Louis and the east coast via Cincinnati, which linked up with its other line, the main route between Chicago and New York. Chicago was the centre of the rail routes: eleven major routes spread out from it and five rail companies competed on the routes from Chicago to New York City. Other famous lines, because named outright in cross-over hit songs, were the Rock Island Line, linking Oklahoma City with Kansas, and the Wabash, on which the Cannonball raced between Chicago and Detroit. This last offers yet another 'train song', a commemoration on record by many people – including, again, Blind Willie McTell, whose performance (from his last session, in 1956) mimics hillbilly vocal mannerisms with deft good humour.[87]

The history of the railways and the history of popular music ran together long before the migration of black workers from the south and the countryside to the cities of the north. The railroads were the first big, inter-state businesses in the USA, and

86.   Walter Davis: 'M & O Blues', Cincinnati, 12/6/30 (Davis also cut a version of 'Broke And Hungry' at the same session). Bumble Bee Slim: 'B And O Blues', NYC, 16/3/32. Blind Willie McTell: 'B And O Blues No. 2', NYC, 21/9/33; "Blind Willie McTell 1927–1935", Yazoo L-1037, NYC, 1973. Blind Willie McTell: 'B And O Blues No. 2' [2nd take], NYC, 21/9/33; "Atlanta Blues 1933", JEMF-106, LA, 1979. Walter Davis: 'New B & O Blues', Chicago, 12/2/46. Willie Brown: 'M & O Blues', Grafton, Wisconsin, 28/5/30.

87.   Blind Willie McTell: 'Wabash Cannonball', Atlanta, Sept. 1956; "Blind Willie McTell: Last Session", Prestige Bluesville 1040, Bergenfield, New Jersey, 1961 [in the UK "Blind Willie McTell: Last Session", Transatlantic Records, PR1040, London, 1966], CD-reissued Prestige Bluesville Original Blues Classics OBCCD-517-2 (BV-1040), Berkeley, California, 1992. This CD-reissue's 'bonus tracks' include the Atlanta 1949 'Broke Down Engine Blues'.

they boomed from the first big push at the end of the Civil War till the end of the nineteenth century. When everywhere west of the Mississippi was called 'the great American desert', they laid 1,800 miles of track to the west coast, and took just four years to build track coast-to-coast. They ran immigrant trains and colonised the western states, partly with farmers from Europe – still being brought in by the railroad companies as late as 1910 – and partly using Colonising Agents paid to recruit people from the eastern states and settle them on prairie land owned by the rail barons. They ran Education trains, teaching farmers as they went, so that produce became freight train business. All these immigrants were white.

Greed soured it. The companies raised billions of dollars in the 1870s alone, and rail company shares introduced 'ordinary people' to gambling on the stock market; but speculators and dodgy tycoons, and their ability to charge farmers what they liked because they held monopoly positions, turned public opinion against them. After a financial panic and mini-depression in 1893, railworkers went on strike in 1894 and the government sent in troops. As Dylan says in his notes on 'Broke Down Engine', 'it's about dupes of commerce & politics colliding on tracks.' By 1934, during the better-known and more severe Depression, one third of all US rail mileage was in bankruptcy. The last time most rail companies made a profit was in the 1950s, when they carried the concrete that built the interstate highways that killed them off.

But the railways succeeded, without intending it, at disseminating black song across the land and into mainstream American consciousness. When the railroad came through the Appalachian mountains in the mid-nineteenth century, it was built by blacks. They kept up their spirits by singing, and the white mountain men listened. The black song 'John Henry The Steel-Driving Man' became a white ballad.

There were also very strong, specific black influences on Appalachian music-making. In the case of fiddle-playing, Alan Lomax argues that it is black fluidity that gets the white performer's left hand sliding up and down the strings while the right hand is playing the bow, and sets his middle body jigging as he plays. One consequence is that when, now, you see these old Appalachian fiddlers – and indeed the younger dancers in their home community audiences – you recognise that the flat-foot shuffle they insist on derives, just as I think Chuck Berry's duck-walk does, from the flat-foot shuffle that is the fundamental of black dance.[88]

Our friend Paul Gilroy proceeds more circumspectly than Alan Lomax to the pros and cons of emphasising black performance strengths. He quotes from Edouard Glissant's book *Caribbean Discourse*: 'It is nothing new to declare that for us music, gesture, dance are forms of communication just as important as the gift of speech. This is how we first managed to emerge from the plantation: aesthetic form in our cultures must be shaped from these oral structures.' But while Gilroy is concerned to avoid what he calls 'the pernicious metaphysical dualism that identifies blacks with the body and whites with the mind' (which he says 'has roots in eighteenth and nineteenth century discussions of aesthetics') he also wants to give due weight to 'the

---

88.   This summary of remarks by Alan Lomax is taken from his TV documentary *Appalachian Journey*, produced by Dibbs Productions for Channel 4, London, 1990, issued as a video through Jane Balfour Films Ltd, London. This is also drawn upon and footnoted in Chapter 9, and again below.

traditions of performance which continue to characterise the production and reception of diaspora musics'. This orientation 'to the specific dynamics of performance has a wider significance in the analysis of black cultural forms than has so far been supposed. Its strengths are evident when it is contrasted with approaches to black culture that have been premised on textuality and narrative rather than say dramaturgy, enunciation and gesture.'

He notes too that 'The pre-eminence of music within the diverse black communities of the Atlantic diaspora is itself an important element in their essential connectedness.' Yet the ever-shifting 'complexity of black expressive culture alone supplies powerful reasons to resist the idea that an untouched, pristine Africanity resides inside these forms', though he also writes of 'the long shadow of our enduring traditions – the African ones and the ones forged from the slave experience which the black vernacular so powerfully and actively remembers'.[89]

Lomax, untroubled by such PC notions, has this to say about the overall black influence:

> A note of unconflicted happy eroticism rings out . . . all the little double- and triple-entendre rhymes of the ring games, of black minstrelsy, of ragtime, jazz, the blues, and rock – have gradually chiselled away at the starchy standards of nineteenth-century propriety . . . Nowadays the language of song employs the explicit argot of the streets. In all this, the driving force has been the sexually more permissive African cultural tradition, in which fertility rather than continence is a central value.[90]

James Baldwin is also untroubled by dangers of racial stereotyping when considering the question of black influence on music and language. Val Wilmer writes of attending a public meeting at which Baldwin spoke, I think in the early 1960s. She writes:

> One student asked him [Baldwin] how he could explain to unsympathetic whites that black people had earned the right to equal treatment through the history of their presence in America. Baldwin mused, 'Ask them how America would *sound* without us. How would the language sound? How would the music sound?' Everyone laughed. It was just so obvious, but exactly the kind of explanation that was resisted so strongly in England.

Back in the Appalachian mountains, it was, too, blacks who first used the fiddle as a rhythm instrument and who first put the fiddle and the banjo together. Later, there were the mountain communities where blacks and whites were neighbours, and, in Lomax's phrase, 'swapped favours, and stole each other's music', while the railways spreading out from Chicago made it possible for goods, including the new Sears Roebuck mail order guitars and radios and phonographs and records, to be supplied by rail to all over the country. Thus did Blind Lemon Jefferson become the favourite

89.   Paul Gilroy, see note 35.

90.   Alan Lomax, *The Land Where the Blues Began*. He argues the same points specifically of the influence of black culture on dance, too.

of, and a huge influence upon, many a white mountain man and woman, including so 'authentic' a 'folk' musician and singer as the great Roscoe Holcomb.[91]

In these ways a wide and deep distribution was achieved for the very songs that Bob Dylan offers on these albums – songs like 'Frankie & Albert', 'Stack A Lee' and 'Delia': the ballads that co-exist in white and black tradition, songs that have gripped the imagination of both, along with the blues that have been heard on the radio all across the Appalachians and been taken up by crackers who would play their instruments differently if it weren't for the African influence that had been, literally, railroaded in.

Bob Dylan's 'Stack A Lee' emphasises this duality perfectly. This is a classic black ballad, glorifying superhuman black fleetfootedness and an enviable, flamboyant mastery of the skills of escape. Yet Dylan chooses to copy – and copy he does, and says so – the version recorded by an important though much-neglected white artist: a man whose life was rooted not in the recording studio but in a mining community in West Virginia – a man who, in other words, was exactly the kind of peckerwood whose musical life was entwined with that of black America. Frank Hutchison, a contemporary of Blind Willie McTell, exemplifies the 'invisible republic' and stands buffeted by all the forces of history just sketched out above.

Hutchison, 'The first real white bluesman to record', in Charles Wolfe's words, 'came from a rough, isolated community in Logan County, West Virginia . . . where miners both black and white found themselves living in company towns, fighting with company thugs when they tried to unionize . . . In many ways, the miners led lives as desperate as sharecroppers in the Mississippi delta, and many . . . were drawn to the blues.' Hutchison learnt his from two local blacks, railroad worker Henry Vaughn (from whom he learnt to play slide guitar with a knife) and one Bill Hunt, who was also able to pass on to him a wealth of nineteenth-century songs.

Between 1926 and 1929 Frank Hutchison cut thirty-two sides for OKeh Records. In concentrating on slide-based blues, Hutchison offered white blues a grittily author-itative alternative seam to that so strongly hewn by Jimmie Rodgers. 'The Train That Carried The Girl From Town' alone influenced 'generations of hill country musicians'. As noted in an earlier chapter, another Frank Hutchison song about a train, his 'Cannon Ball Blues', includes lines Bob Dylan uses on 'Caribbean Wind' and 'Man Of Peace'.

Hutchison's own recordings of 'The Train That Carried The Girl From Town', 'Cannon Ball Blues' and 'Worried Blues' (plus the instrumental 'K.C. Blues': not another train song but a version of 'John Henry') are issued, along with the notes by Charles K. Wolfe, on the excellent double-CD "White Country Blues 1926–1938: A Lighter Shade Of Blue" in the Columbia Roots N' Blues series. Not included, however, is Hutchsion's version of 'Stack A Lee'. This *is* available, though, on – yes, you guessed it – the 1952 Harry Smith anthology "American Folk Music": and to hear this 1927 Hutchison side is to recognise just how closely Bob Dylan follows it, in

---

91. Karl Dallas writes that the banjo, rather than being straightforwardly 'African' in origin, as generally suggested, came via Africa from Arabia: 'The Africans did bring one instrument with them, the Arabian banjar, which was one side-benefit from the Arab involvement in the West African slave trade.' It was whites who gave the banjo its fifth string, and so, in Lomax's phrase, its 'high, constant whining note'. (Karl Dallas in *The Electric Muse*, see note 20. Alan Lomax in his TV documentary *Appalachian Journey*, see note 88.)

lyrics, melody, guitar-part, harmonica and, most importantly, in spirit, almost fifty years later. When you hear the Hutchison, you come to appreciate what a fine, affectionate, resourceful, knowledgeable, authoritative, live-wire thing the Dylan recording really is.[92]

There is one especially neat change Dylan makes – a change of the tiniest kind – in the lyric. Hutchison, singing before the world was familiar with the work of Jimmie Rodgers (Rodgers first recorded the same year Hutchison made 'Stack A Lee') uses the phrase 'waiting for the train'. Dylan, singing in the post-Rodgers era, amends this to 'waiting for a train', thus bringing into his own version a tipping of his John B. Stetson hat to one of the greatest of Rodgers' songs, while adding, in effect, to the list of train-song titles he mentions, one way and another, in the course of presenting us with this album.

Many other blues greats and not-so-greats also recorded versions of 'Stack A Lee', from Furry Lewis' 'Billy Lyons And Stack O'Lee' in 1927 and Mississippi John Hurt's 'Stack O'Lee Blues' from the same year he cut 'Frankie' (1928), through two mentioned earlier, by Ma Rainey and by Papa Harvey Hull & Long 'Cleve' Reed in 1925 and 1927, to Lucille Bogan (as Bessie Jackson), who cut an unissued 'Jim Stack O'Lee Blues' in 1934. Ivory Joe Hunter's only pre-war recording is 'Stackolee', cut for the Library of Congress at Wiergate, Texas (he was born there in 1914) in 1933. Roscoe McLean and some state farm convicts were field-recorded singing 'Stagolee', again for the Library of Congress, in 1936. The song's surprisingly resilient life flourishes all the way through to the terrific R&B hit by Lloyd Price at the end of the 1950s, 'Stagger Lee' (based, he said, on hearing it played years before in New Orleans by Professor Longhair), and the Boston folk scene version by Tom Rush in 1963, 'Stackerlee'.[93]

Who knows how many of these versions of the song Bob Dylan knew? We do know, though, that he heard the song not only from records but from performers who never made it into the studio: 'Nothing is new,' he says in the 1985 "Biograph" interview:

92.   Frank Hutchison: 'The Train That Carried The Girl From Town' and 'Worried Blues', see note 85; 'Cannon Ball Blues and 'K.C. Blues', NYC, 9/7/29: all CD-reissued on "White Country Blues 1926–1938: A Lighter Shade Of Blue", Columbia Roots N' Blues 01–472886–10, New York, 1993. Frank Hutchison: 'Stack A Lee', NYC, 28/1/27, "American Folk Music", see note 6.

Hutchison cut yet another train song, the splendid 'Hell Bound Train', in 1928 [NYC, 10/9/28; "Frank Hutchison", Rounder Records 1007, Somerville, Massachusetts, mid-1970s]. He also wrote, or at least recreated from the obscurely traditional, the lovely 'Coney Isle' [NYC, 28/1/27, also issued on "Frank Hutchison"]; altered unnecessarily to 'Alabam', the song was a hit for Cowboy Copas in 1961 – three years before it was properly revived, indeed exquisitely so, by Roscoe Holcomb. [Roscoe Holcomb: 'Coney Isle', *nia*, "The High Lonesome Sound", Folkways FA2368, New York, 1968. More on Roscoe Holcomb follows.]

Hutchison, born West Virginia, March 1897, died in Ohio, November 1945.

93.   Furry Lewis' 'Billy Lyons And Stack O'Lee', Chicago, 9/10/27, CD-reissued "Furry Lewis: In His Prime 1927–1928", Yazoo 1050, New York, 1991. Mississippi John Hurt: 'Stack O'Lee Blues', NYC, 28/12/28, CD-reissued "Mississippi John Hurt: 1928 Sessions", Yazoo 1065, 1990. Lucille Bogan (as Bessie Jackson): 'Jim Stack O'Lee Blues', NYC, 1/8/34. Ivory Joe Hunter: 'Stackolee', Weirgate, Texas, c. 11/7/33. Roscoe McLean: 'Stagolee', Raiford, Florida, 3/5/36. Lloyd Price: 'Stagger Lee', *nia*, 1958, ABC Paramount single 9927, New York, 1958; "The Exciting Lloyd Price", ABC-Paramount Records ABCS-277, 1959, CD-reissued with extra tracks on MCA Records MCD 32654, London, 1995. Tom Rush: 'Stackerlee', May 1963, issued on "Blues, Songs & Ballads", Prestige 7374, 1965.

There is a nifty section on this song in Greil Marcus' *Mystery Train*, 1975.

Even rap records. I love that stuff but it's not new, you used to hear that stuff all the time . . . there was this one guy, Big Brown, he wore a jail blanket, that's all he ever used to wear, summer and winter . . . he was like Othello, he'd recite epics like some grand Roman orator, really backwater stuff though, 'Stagger Lee', 'Cocaine Smitty', 'Hattiesburg Hattie'. Where were the record companies when he was around? Even him though, it's like it was done 30 years before that . . . and God knows when else.

Dylan's liner-notes to his own, or rather Frank Hutchison's, version of the song certainly amount to a rap:

> . . . *what does the song say exactly? it says no man gains immortality thru public acclaim. truth is shadowy. in the pre-postindustrial age, victims of violence were allowed (in fact it was their duty) to be judges over their offenders—parents were punished for their children's crimes (we've come a long way since then) the song says that a man's hat is his crown. futurologists would insist it's a matter of taste. they say 'let's sleep on it' but theyre already living in the sanitarium. No Rights Without Duty is the name of the game & fame is a trick. playing for time is only horsing around. Stack's in a cell, no wall phone. he is not some egotistical degraded existentialist dionysian idiot, neither does he represent any alternative lifestyle scam (give me a thousand acres of tractable land & all the gang members that exist & you'll see the Authentic alternative lifestyle, the Agrarian one) Billy didnt have an insurance plan, didnt get airsick yet his ghost is more real & genuine than all the dead souls on the boob tube—a monumental epic of blunder & misunderstanding. a romance tale without the cupidity.*

The ferocious desire to talk up the present-day relevance of such songs is undeniable here; but it puzzles me in seeming to deny the usual appeal of the song, which does make Stack A Lee the hero, the rebel who triumphs in chimes of freedom on behalf of every underdog. Dylan, though, urges that 'fame is a trick' and that Stack does not gain 'immortality thru public acclaim'. Surely this is exactly what 'Stack A Lee' has gained.[94]

Alan Lomax's book *The Land Where the Blues Began* is good on black admiration for speed and fleetfootedness, and on the rage, engendered in the workcamps, that needed these 'black ballads' – sometimes ballads adopted from Anglo-Irish originals – with heroes like Stack A Lee:

> Like their ancestors, who had herded cattle and hunted game on foot, blacks . . . depended on fleetness of foot to get them out of trouble, away from the walking boss, the patrollers, the high sheriff and the lynch mob. Br'er Rabbit was their first hero, the Travelin Man their next . . . Early on, blacks sang a few of the

---

94.   Dylan's liner-notes allude to the hat in the song: 'the song says that a man's hat is his crown', he says. 'That John B. Stetson hat', as the Hutchison/Dylan version of the song has it, was the crowning glory of its maker, John Batterson Stetson (1830–1906), who might even have lived to hear his name and hat celebrated in the song. His fortune was put to a surprising use by his son, worlds away from Stack A Lee's murderous brawling. John B. Stetson Jr became a significant collector of Oscar Wilde material; his important collection was dispersed after being auctioned in New York in 1922. (H. Montgomery Hyde, *Oscar Wilde*, 1976.)

Anglo-American ballads that pleased them, and as they did, they ... began to create their own.

Lomax goes on:

In this series of black ballads, we come close to the main concerns of Delta folk [though he needn't restrict his survey to the Delta in this regard] at the turn of the century, just before the blues began. The story of a magical Irish horse, the 'Noble Skew Skuball', was a favourite ... Out of that ballad came one of Bill Monroe's hits, a universal favourite ... [that] bears many marks of black style. Meantime, black prison gangs, with quick getaways always on their minds, filled the Southern bottomlands with roaring choruses about ol Stewball ... At night in the work camps ... continual humiliation turned to rage. The men needed ballad heroes ... At night in the shanties, when the fiddles and the guitars began to whine, they sang about ol Stagolee, about Frankie with a pistol under her red petticoat, about Duncan, the black bartender who had the nerve to blow police-man Brady away!

One of the black ballads Lomax mentions is 'Delia', though it doesn't really fit the pattern he's described. It features no fleetfooted superhero, nor any 'liberated heroine' like Frankie.

In print the song surfaced first in 1911 as 'One More Rounder Gone', collected by Howard W. Odum in Georgia in about 1907. Three variants collected in Alabama, Georgia and North Carolina by Newman Ivey White were published in his *American Negro Folk Songs* in 1928, the same year that the Library of Congress archivist Robert W. Gordon supposedly traced the song's origin to Savannah. Three more versions appeared in print in 1937.[95]

Yet as blues authority Tony Russell has pointed out to me, 'Delia' has always been far more popular among white revivalists than among black performers. This is certainly the case to judge by how few black *recordings* there are in the pre-war period and how many post-war white ones. A very early example of the former is that from 1923 by the obscure songster Reese DuPree (who cut six sides for OKeh, probably all in New York City, between November 1923 and June 1924, and then made it back to the studio only to make a further two sides, both remaining unissued, nearly five years later in September 1928). His version of 'Delia', titled 'One More Rounder Gone', and 'Delhia' [sic] by Jimmie Gordon, cut in 1939, are almost the only black American recordings of the song other than Library of Congress field-recordings: on one it is thrown into a performance of 'Frankie & Albert', and could well have been performed at the behest of Lomax, and on another, field-recorded by his father John Lomax, it is performed alongside 'Stagolee' and '[Duncan and] Brady'.[96]

95. 'One More Rounder Gone', published first by Howard W. Odum in *Journal of American Folklore*, nia, 1911; collected between 1906 and 1908 in Newton County, Georgia. The three versions published 1937 were collected by Chapman J. Milling and appeared in *Southern Folklore Quarterly*, nia, 1937. It is collected in G. Malcolm Laws Jr, *Native American Balladry* (rev. edn, 1964).

96. Reese DuPree: 'One More Rounder Gone', NYC, c. 7/2/23, *nia*. Jimmie Gordon: 'Delhia' [sic], NYC, 28/4/39, *nia*. Booker T. Saps: 'Frankie And Albert (Cooney And Delia)', field-recorded Belle Glade, Florida, June 1935; "Boot That Thing: 1935 Field Recordings From Florida", Flyright-Matchbox SDM 258, Bexhill-on-Sea, 1975, and also on "Negro Songs Of Protest Vol. 2", Rounder Records 4013, Somerville, Massachusetts, nia. 'All

The case of the Rev. Gary Davis is telling too. Perhaps 'Delia' was a song he'd always known, and he seems to have taught it to his guitar pupils like Stefan Grossman, but it obviously wasn't one of his own favourites. He was recorded live many times, yet in spite of working and performing in the white folk-blues-revivalist world, somehow this song was never present on such occasions until 1970, when he was recorded performing it at one of his last-ever gigs, at a summer camp in Connecticut. Even here, as the recording reveals, the song is performed only after a young white woman's voice repeatedly requests it (overriding a request for 'Cocaine Blues'). He responds, but you can hear from the lengthy guitar intro that he's trawling his memory to try to recall the song, which he manages only to a very modest extent, though he invests it with an affecting sadness that brings it closer to Dylan's 1993 version than most others – not least in using, as Dylan approximately does, the inherently poignant chorus-line 'All the friends I have is gone'.[97]

The shining exception to all this dutiful performance for whitey may reside in the transcendent figure of Blind Willie McTell. He recorded two versions, one pre-war, one post . . . and even in his case, the earlier version was recorded for Lomax's father, and may well have been chosen by some version of the process whereby the swooped-upon black street-singer offers the sort of thing he knows from experience that the big white chief wants to hear. Lomax was the great panjandrum of folksong collecting: he'd travelled the US exhaustively for this purpose, often with his son Alan, and 'discovered' Leadbelly, whom he used as his driver, signed to an outrageous management contract, wrote a book about, and recorded extensively.

When he met McTell, Lomax was in his seventies, and on his last go-round: testy, fierce, and with fixed ideas about what was collectable. He had favourite black folksongs and tended to prompt people into performing them. He was of a generation confidently interventionist in their work, where later folklorists sought to record without the distortion of their own supervision. Lomax several times interrupts McTell, even stopping his guitar-playing with a 'just a minute . . .', in order to talk himself. He has no qualm that he might inhibit or stifle the very things he seeks. The tactful, sensitive and alert McTell may or may not have chosen 'Delia' in other circumstances. Certainly he never recorded it commercially in his prolific sessions of the pre-war period.[98]

Post-war recordings, on the other hand, have proliferated, running to skiffle, trad jazz, folk-revival, country and rock versions. The 1957 'Delia's Gone' by the atrocious

The Friends I Got Is Gone' by Blind Jesse Harris, field-recorded by John Lomax for the Library of Congress at Livingston, Alabama, 24/7/37 (Harris also performs 'Stagolee' and '[Duncan and] Brady' at the same session). 'All De Friend I Had Dead An' Gone' by the McDonald Family, field-recorded by Herbert Halpert for the Library of Congress near Livingston, Alabama, 27/5/39.

NB. 'All I Got Is Gone' by Barrelhouse Buck MacFarland (Chicago, 17/7/35) and by Henry Townsend ('All I Got's Gone', Aurora, Illinois, 11/11/37) are nothing to do with 'Delia', but are versions of a standard old St Louis song.

97. Gary Davis: 'Delia', live at New Milford, Connecticut, 12/8/70, CD-issued on "Delia – Late Concert Recordings 1970–1971", American Activities [a sister-label to UnAmerican Activities] Records UACD103, Leeds, 1990.

98. Blind Willie McTell: 'Delia', Atlanta, 5/11/40; "Blind Willie McTell: 1940", Melodeon MLP-7323, Washington, DC, 1966 (Storyville 670.186 and SLP186 in Europe); CD-reissued "Blind Willie McTell: Complete Library of Congress Recordings In Chronological Order (1940)", RST Blues Documents BDCD-6001, Vienna, 1990.

'Little Delia', Atlanta, Oct. 1949; "Blind Willie McTell: Atlanta Twelve String", Atlantic Records SD 7224, NYC, 1972, CD-reissued Atlantic 7 82366–2, 1992. [A second take remains unissued.]

City Ramblers Skiffle Group (oh-so-1950s-British label-mates of the Alexis Korner Skiffle Group and of Ray Bush And The Avon Cities' Skiffle) was followed hotly by the 1958 cut 'Delia Gone' by Mr. Acker Bilk & His Paramount Jazz Band, who recorded the song around the same time as Pete Seeger. Bob Dylan was taped singing 'Delia' in May 1960 in St Paul, Minnesota. His friend from that state, Spider John Koerner, recorded it as 'Delia Holmes' (which, as noted below, was probably the song's original title, coined around 1900) on the mid-1960s album "Spider Blues". In 1968 Stefan Grossman recorded the song as 'All My Friends Are Gone', taking his chorus-line from his mentor Gary Davis.[99] Waylon Jennings took Delia into outlaw country territory in 1969, making the country charts Top 40 with another 'Delia's Gone'. In the two decades between then and Bob Dylan's putting the song on "World Gone Wrong", renewing its greatness in the process, other whiteys who have stumbled into the studios to try it for themselves range from Bobby Bare and Johnny Cash to Al Stewart and Ronnie Wood. Yep, it's even on Ronnie's "Gimme Some Neck". Truly, you can't swing a white hepcat for fear of hitting 'Delia'.[100]

Glen Dundas' book *Tangled up in Tapes Revisited* lists the song as by Blind Blake. The American songster and bluesman of that name neither wrote nor recorded it, but in the 1950s John Steiner of Chicago Music Publishing managed to renew the copyright on the song, and various others, in Blind Blake's name. To complicate things further, there's *another* Blind Blake, from the Bahamas, a sort of tourist souvenir version of Joseph Spence, and while he certainly didn't write the song either, it has always been 'a popular song among street musicians' in the Bahamas and remained so through to the 1960s (according to Alan Lomax in *The Penguin Book of American Folk Songs*) so that it is sometimes the Bahamian Blind Blake who is assumed to hold this composer credit. When *Sing Out!* magazine published the Pete Seeger version, the song was described as a 'honky-tonk Bahamas folksong'.[101] On Stefan Grossman's

99.   The City Ramblers Skiffle Group: 'Delia's Gone', London, 29/10/57; "The City Ramblers Skiffle Group" EP, Tempo Records EXA 77, London, 1958. (The EP's 'title' isn't really a title at all, since at least two other EPs by the same group on the same label also offer no other title than "The City Ramblers Skiffle Group", i.e. the earlier EXA 59, *nia*, and EXA 71, *nia*.) Mr. Acker Bilk & His Paramount Jazz Band: 'Delia Gone', London, 1958; reissued "A Golden Hour Of Trad Jazz", Knight Records KGHCD103, UK, c. 1990 [and at least two other CD compilations subsequently]. Pete Seeger: 'Delia', *nia*; "The Pete Seeger Sampler", a 10-inch LP, Folkways Records FA2043, New York, c. 1958. Bob Dylan: 'Delia', St Paul, Minnesota, May 1960, unissued. Spider John Koerner: 'Delia Holmes', *nia*; "Spider Blues", Elektra Records EKL-90 [mono] and EKS-7290 [stereo], New York, c. 1965 (an album that also offers a song called 'Need A Woman'). This album was slated memorably by Albert McCarthy, stalwart critic of *Jazz Monthly*, July 1965:

> Each country has its own way of finding room for the talentless, in Britain the traditional escape route for many years being the church or the army. It appears that the outlet in the USA . . . is for them to become folk singers . . . This is, without any doubt, one of the worst records I have had to review for many a long day . . . a passably competent guitarist, a poor harmonica player and a quite dreadful singer . . . the butchery of inoffensive blues verses is spread out remarkably evenly throughout . . . this grotesque blues kitsch.

Stefan Grossman: 'All My Friends Are Gone', London, 1968; "Aunt Molly's Murray Farm", Philips Records, *nia*, London, 1968 [reissued Sonet Records SNTF640, 1973].

100.   Waylon Jennings: 'Delia's Gone', *nia*, RCA Victor Records 0157, New York/Nashville, 1969. Bobby Bare, *nia*. Johnny Cash: 'Delia', *nia*; CD-reissued "Johnny Cash" [3-CD set], Reader's Digest Association Records 67006LJON, London, 1994. Al Stewart: 'Delia's Gone', *nia*, RCA LP 9001, London, 1981, CD-reissued "24 Carats", EMI Records CDP7800242, 1992. Ronnie Wood: 'Delia', *nia*; "Gimme Some Neck", Castle Communications Records TFOCD025, London, 1990.

101.   *Sing Out!*, republished in Sing Out! *Reprints*, Vol. 2, c. 1961.

Amelia Defries published the first Bahamian version in 1929, in *In a Forgotten Colony*; the Library of

recording, the composer credit reads 'traditional, adapted Rev. Gary Davis/Stefan Grossman' – whereas Gary Davis, or his manager, the folk-revival entrepreneur Manny Greenhill, copyrighted the song as a Davis composition. In Waylon Jennings' case, composer credits were claimed by Waylon and his brother Tommy. Bobby Bare has also registered the song for copyright purposes, under the same title. Dave Bromberg's version linked the song to Blind Willie McTell. Bob Dylan's "World Gone Wrong" album credits simply state, except for 'Lone Pilgrim': 'All songs traditional, arranged by Bob Dylan.' His own liner-notes add that his 'Delia' is 'two or more versions mixed into one'.

Many of the same names crop up again for 'Duncan And Brady'. So do some of the same words. Tom Rush's version includes this variant on a common-stock stanza often found inside 'Delia':

> *High-tailed carriages*
> *Rubber tired hacks*
> *Take King Brady* [or whoever] *to the graveyard*
> *Ain't gonna bring him back*

while on "World Gone Wrong", Dylan omits this carriages-hacks-graveyard-back stanza from 'Delia' – in order to include it in the very next song on the album, 'Stack A Lee'. Similarly, the version of 'Delia' in Lomax's *Penguin Book of American Folk Songs* includes this verse, which is also omitted from the Dylan version:

> *'Jailer, O Jailer*
> *How can I sleep?*
> *When all around my bedside*
> *My little Delia creeps.'*

yet closely parallels a verse he does include in 'Stack A Lee', in which

> *Stack A Lee turned to the jailer*
> *He said 'Jailer, I can't sleep*
> *Round about my bedside*
> *Billy Lyons began to creep.'*

As if to emphasise the close relations, the common-stock, between these different old black ballads, Dylan's version of 'Delia' begins in exact parallel to the opening of McTell's 1949 version of another song he recorded more than once, 'Dyin' Crap-shooter's Blues'. This opens

> *Little Jesse was a gambler*
> *Night and day;*

Dylan's 'Delia' begins with

Congress holds two Bahamian pre-war field-recordings and there are many post-war commercial recordings. I am grateful to the unpublished research of John H. Cowley for this information. I'm not sure which Blind Blake it is who appears on the blues label XX Records under the alluring pseudonym Gorgeous Weed.

Delia was a gambling girl
Gambled all around.

Meanwhile as noted already, Dylan too is among those who have recorded 'Duncan And Brady' – at his never-released Chicago sessions in 1992 with Dave Bromberg.

Dylanologist Ian Woodward writes that *he* associates the song 'with Spider John Koerner's storming version at Newport . . . 1965, when he was joined by Tony Glover' at a Sunday session. Nearly thirty years on, a recording of 'Duncan And Brady' by the Johnson Mountain Boys was voted top favourite in the 1993 *Bluegrass Unlimited* National Bluegrass Survey. The evidence suggests, then, that despite Lomax's eloquence, 'Duncan And Brady' is, like 'Delia', another of these 'black ballads' more beloved by whites than blacks.[102]

Nevertheless, the solid and pleasing fact is that Blind Willie McTell and Dylan share a piece of repertoire in 'Delia'. We don't know from whom McTell learnt this sinuously lovely song, but when he recorded it for Atlantic Records in 1949 he was about 50 years old – about the same age as Bob Dylan was when *he* recorded it.

There's another white revivalist version worth mentioning again, and it's one with a Dylan connection. Called 'Delia's Gone', it is a live performance by Dave Bromberg, recorded in New York City in 1970 – in which Bromberg breaks off in mid-performance to discuss Blind Willie McTell's version! (And this was released on the 1971 album "David Bromberg", on which Bob Dylan played harmonica on another track, the Bromberg composition 'Sammy's Song'.[103]) What Bromberg says in mid-performance – before speculating on whether 'Delia' is essentially a prison song told from the viewpoint of the man who has shot poor Delia down – is that McTell's version is unique for including the verse

Delia oh Delia, how could it be
You loved all those rounders but you never really did love me
She's all I got and gone.

The version cut by McTell in 1949, 'Little Delia', actually *opens* with this:

Delia oh Delia, how can it be
Say you loved all those rounders and don't love me
One more rounder gone.

Dylan gives it at least as great a prominence, *ending* his version of the song by singing this verse twice.

Unlike 'Broke Down Engine' – on which, despite Dylan's guitar being as good as it could be, he has no hope of matching the exquisite, transcendent McTell original,

102. Tom Rush: 'Duncan And Brady', Boston, May 1963; "Got A Mind To Ramble", see note 67. Blind Willie McTell: 'The Dyin' Crapshooter's Blues' ; "Blind Willie McTell: Atlanta Twelve String", Atlantic Records SD 7224, NYC, 1972, CD-reissued Atlantic 7 82366–2, 1992. Spider John Koerner (with Tony Glover): 'Duncan And Brady', Newport, Rhode Island, 25/7/65. Johnson Mountain Boys: 'Duncan And Brady', *nia*; "Blue Diamond", Rounder Records 0293, Somerville, Massachusetts, 1993. *Bluegrass Unlimited* 1993 National Bluegrass Survey results published *Bluegrass Unlimited*, August 1993 issue. Ian Woodward, quoted from *Isis*, no. 46, December 1992–January 1993; added information Ian Woodward, phone-call from the present writer 6/5/94.

103. Dave Bromberg: 'Delia's Gone', live in NYC, 1970; "David Bromberg", Columbia Records KC 31104, New York, 1971.

and it is brave of him to even attempt it – in the case of 'Delia' he improves upon, even transforms, the song as McTell presents it. McTell treats it as a throwaway number, a bit of vaudeville corn; Dylan stretches it out like velvet, giving it a sumptuous poignancy.

Clearly the most fundamental way in which Dylan achieves such gorgeous heightened compassion within his 'Delia' is via the simple expedient of singing the song slowly instead of fast. But slowing it down doesn't in itself achieve depth of feeling; it only makes the space in which depth of feeling can be created.

Dylan inhabits this space with cogent authority. He manages to tell this 'one sad tale' with so many luminous details that while the storyline might remain unclear – Who is who and who does what? Who are these treacherous, dangerous rounders? Who is the man in Atlanta tryin' to pass for white? Is the singer Curly? – the intimate particularities of the song are crystalline and bright, from the ringing, tinkling guitar notes that begin the track through its every beautifully realised constituent part. The way he sings the word 'gambling', which comes twice in the opening verse, gives it three syllables, so that the first time he might almost be making it one of those intuitive puns of his – 'Delia was a gambolling girl' – with the voice full of sadness that her lovable recklessness killed her, and the second time he has that 'gam-bl-ing girl' go tum-bl-ing down like the notes down the frets of the guitar, in a perfect unity of words, voice and music. When he is

> *High up on the rooftops, high as I can see*
> *Looking for them rounders looking out for me*

he sings that 'see' at line's end with such a long, lingering fading-away that it enacts what it describes: it peers out as far as it can and ends in a haze, out there in the nebulous distant air.

The entire song is unfolded so tenderly, so scrupulously, and with such a fine use of silence and space that Dylan deepens the song, holding an attentive compassion for everyone inside it, such that the repeated chorus-line at each verse's end – 'All the friends I ever had are gone' – speaks the grief and loneliness of different people in different verses. In the second verse, it is for Delia's mother, understanding that her grief is worsened by her having been away from home, on 'a little trip out west', when her daughter died, and having been robbed even of the funeral ritual, which took place in her absence. In the third verse, we spare a thought for the father's grief too, as he copes with his daughter's having never been at home anyway.[104]

In the seventh and eighth verses, even the judge appears to have some compassion.

---

104. The verse in question begins with a version of the formulaic 'X's daddy this, X's mama that', the X here being Delia. Dylan once said of 'Love Henry' that 'In the last couple of lines, it might just open up a door for another song. William Blake could have written that.' (Bob Dylan, interviewed by Gary Hill, San Diego, circulated by Reuters press agency, 13/10/93.) It interests me that he happened to say that, since actually here in this formulaic fragment of 'Delia' we do find William Blake's writing. 'Delia's daddy weeped, Delia's mama moaned' over her death; in Blake, it is birth not death, but 'My mother groan'd! My father wept / Into the dangerous world I leapt.' ('Infant Sorrow', *Songs of Innocence and Songs of Experience*, 1794.)

William Blake (1757–1827) and Rabbie Burns (1759–1796) were also contemporaries. The year before *Songs of Innocence and Experience* were published together (1794), Burns wrote the lyric 'Phillis the Fair', setting it to the older folk tune that turns up in Ireland as 'Eileen Aroon', performed by Dylan in 1988 (see note 1).

He still hands down a sentence of ninety-nine years, but he starts by asking for Curly's side of the story – that neat line

> *Judge says to Curly, 'What's this noise about?'*

implying that he is open-minded, that it may be that the other side's story has been much exaggerated – and even when sentencing him, and thereby dashing Curly's naïve hope that he might get away with a fine, the judge's heart seems to go out to him:

> *Curly says to the judge, 'What might be my fine?'*
> *Judge says, 'Poor boy, you got ninety-nine.'*

Again Dylan finds a pun here, on 'poor boy'. Instead of a snappy response from the judge meaning simply 'the rich pay fines; the poor go to jail, boy', Dylan's singing fills these lines with a world of humane regret, so that the judge as well as the singer speaks softly, in the knowledge of our common fallibility.

   This extends to that curious near-repetition at the end of the song. Is it not Curly, in the jail where he will die, who sings those last two verses, in which the questions he asks in vain of the woman he killed explain in effect why he killed her?:

> *Delia, oh Delia, how can it be*
> *Y'loved all them rounders, 'n' never did love me?*

and then, as if coming back for a second attempt to articulate the nub of it with a clarity befitting the end of the song – which is a very Dylanesque thing to do: a second-attempting we hear him do to attain a fit closure on guitar on 'Step It Up & Go', as we noted earlier – he asks here, in character, with the same heartfelt puzzlement and reproach but in slightly changed words

> *Delia oh Delia, how can it be*
> *You wanted all them rounders,'n' never had time for me?*

That rephrasing, that double-ending, which is Bob Dylan's creation, is such a truthful touch, and in two ways. As well as enacting what people do – trying to say what they mean when it's important to do so, and trying too to put themselves in the best light they can when they sign off – the rephrasing here *does* reveal what this character means: reveals the double burden of resentment felt – not only did she never love him, she never fancied him either, never included him when passing around her casual and reckless favours. It's a brilliant intuitive truth on Dylan's part that he places this complaint last, giving it the greater emphasis, understanding that this is the one the spurned lover resents more deeply. (It's a man thing.)

   And while the character may ask these questions rhetorically, as if to justify his having slain her, and we can demur from that, at the same time our compassion for all the protagonists remains fully engaged. Life is sad, life is a bust. *'does this song have rectitude? you bet.'*

   When Dylan comes to the work of the Mississippi Sheiks, here too he deepens it. This was a long way from the case with his 1992 version of 'Sittin' On Top Of The World', but with 'Blood In My Eyes' and 'World Gone Wrong' he reaches higher than the Sheiks did. He abbreviates their titles and extends their contents. In the case of 'Blood In My Eyes' he has gained, by gaining middle-age, the ability to sing so sour and 'adult' a love song without it either ringing false or glamorising the unglamorously cynical, as a more youthful performer, a more youthful Dylan, would surely do. His version stalks along with a predatory, loping menace, its quiet unhurried unstoppability sinister and brooding, the terrible calm of the guitar-work enacting some old, twisted animal's implacable pace. Early on, it even halts altogether for a moment – a moment in which anything might happen: and then it simply resumes its hunt. The words are just lies, snares, hooks, traps. The singer is asked 'Hey hey man, can't you wait a little while?' and he answers 'No, no, babe . . .' and even this is a lie. The long guitar-break comes in at this point, as if he can wait, and will wait, because waiting is part of the pleasure of the kill. He's like the treacherous judge in 'Seven Curses', whose 'old eyes deepened in his head'. And at the end, what is the last noise on the track? A cough! He coughs, like an old man. Like an old lion who has choked on his food. It is not the Bob Dylan I like best, but it's a vividly imagined, powerful performance, and as a reading of the Sheiks' song, indisputably up at the creative end of song-interpretation.[105]

With the song he chooses as the opening track, and the title track, of "World Gone Wrong", Dylan also does something special. His liner-notes describe them (perhaps surprisingly) straightforwardly, and he seems concerned to stress that their work needs no alteration:

> the Mississippi Sheiks, a little known de facto group whom in their former glory mustve been something to behold. rebellion against routine seems to be their strong theme. all their songs are raw to the bone & are faultlessly made for these modern times (the New Dark Ages) nothing effete about the Mississippi Sheiks.

Despite the insistence that all their songs are 'faultlessly made for these modern times', Dylan updates this one, making it the more perfectly suited to the present day by changing its title from the present tense into the past. For the Mississippi Sheiks, 'The World Is Going Wrong'; for Dylan it's already a 'World Gone Wrong' (though he retains their present tense version of the line in the repeated refrain – in fact singing it so that it's almost impossible to distinguish between the two).[106] And as with 'Delia',

105. The Mississippi Sheiks: 'I've Got Blood In My Eyes For You', Atlanta, 25/10/31; "Stop and Listen Blues: The Mississippi Sheiks", Mamlish S-3804, New York, 1974; CD-reissued "Stop And Listen", Yazoo Records 2006, New York, 1992.

   As to the expression used in the title, long or shortened, it is unusual but not unique. As mentioned in Chapter 9, J. T. Funny Papa Smith's 'Hungry Wolf' includes the beautifully 'Dylanesque', brooding 'With blood in my eye, and malice in my heart / In places I used to go . . .' [Chicago, c. April 1931; "'Funny Papa' Smith: The Original Howling Wolf", Yazoo L-1031, New York, 1972]. There's also a record by Bill Gaither, which I've not been able to hear, called 'Bloody Eyed Woman', Chicago, 22/10/39, and there's the book *Blood in My Eye* by George Jackson, his last work, written a few days before his death, according to the publisher. Jackson's text never explains the use of this title, but his meaning is clearly that blood – physical violence, revenge – is what he has his eye on. The book's dedication is 'To the black Communist youth – To their fathers – We will now criticize the unjust with the weapon.' Between the Sheiks' song from the 1930s and Jackson's title from the 1970s, therefore, it's clear that the phrase itself has had some currency in black America.

   (For more on Jackson and 1960s–1970s activism, see Chapter 5, note 25.)

106. The Mississippi Sheiks: 'The World Is Going Wrong', Atlanta, 24/10/31; "Stop and Listen Blues: The Mississippi Sheiks", Mamlish S-3804, New York, 1974; CD-reissued "Stop And Listen", Yazoo Records 2006, New York, 1992.

   I'm quite certain that Dylan knew these recordings in the 1960s, but I note that all three of the Sheiks songs used on these two Bob Dylan albums were reissued on this one Yazoo CD in 1992.

Dylan takes something jaunty and close to throwaway, something recorded in a few minutes back in 1931, and, as it were, restores it to a greatness it never knew it had.

It also makes the ideal opening statement for a Bob Dylan album, and with a flash of mischief about it too, as well as its mordancy – the mischief of following up an album called "Good As I Been To You" with a very similar album that begins 'I can't be good no more'.

The song's first phrase, too, makes such a good Bob Dylan opening statement, just as 'Lone Pilgrim' makes such a good closing statement: 'Strange things have happened . . .' is decidedly Dylanesque. And as he occupies the song, we find it far more poignant, far less of a sandwich-board song, than the rumours preceding its release had led us to expect, and he sings it so aptly, with a lovely, wriggling, burrowing delivery.

Better still is the blues that comes next on the album, with the wonderful white balladry of 'Love Henry' sandwiched between, the excellent 'Ragged & Dirty', which, in a surprising but unexceptionable piece of programming, begins a run of four consecutive 'black' tracks on this album. (It's suprising, too, and in all likelihood coincidence, but three of the blues originals that Dylan's album revisits were cut in the same town on three consecutive days: McTell's 'Broke Down Engine Blues' on 23 October 1931, the Sheiks' 'The World Is Gong Wrong' on the 24th, and their 'I've Got Blood In My Eyes For You' on the 25th, all in Atlanta.)

Dylan writes this of 'Ragged & Dirty':

> *RAGGED & DIRTY one of the Willie Browns did this—schmaltz & pickled herring, stuffed cabbage, heavy moral vocabulary—sweetness & sentiment, house rocking, superior beauty, not just standing there—the seductive magic of the thumbs up salute, carefully thought out overtones & stepping sideways, the idols of human worship paying thru the nose, lords of the illogical in smoking jackets, sufferers from a weak education, pieces of a jigsaw puzzle—taking stupid chances—being mistreated only just so far.*

This may be a moderately engaging piece of Dylan prose – a pale reminder of his "Planet Waves" sleeve note – but it could hardly give you a less likely picture of the world of the song in question.

The first recorded version of the song was by Blind Lemon Jefferson, but nobody else's version shares much in common with his. He goes his separate way after the opening verse, wandering through the rest of his recording plucking out ready-made verses as if at random from elsewhere: he even uses one from 'Careless Love'.[107]

A key recording after Jefferson is the one by Sleepy John Estes, whose vital influence on Bob Dylan's work was argued in Chapter 9. The very first track Estes recorded was his own version of Jefferson's 'Broke And Hungry', which he either misheard (it's easily done: poor Blind Lemon's recordings come to us through one of the worst aural fogs of all), or re-wrote, as 'broken-hearted', and which was given a characteristically lengthy Estes title, 'Broken-Hearted, Ragged And Dirty Too'. This

---

107. Blind Lemon Jefferson, 'Broke And Hungry', Chicago, c. November 1926; "Blind Lemon Jefferson Volume Two", Milestone Records MLP-2007, New York, c. 1968.

début recording, made in Memphis in mid-September 1929, remained unissued; he had another go at the same song just nine days later, and this time it gained release.[108]

The version Dylan performs on "World Gone Wrong" is far more similar to the Sleepy John Estes than to the 1940s Willie Brown version cited in Dylan's notes.[109] Dylan deploys a guitar-riff throughout that is an echo of the mandolin-riff played by James Yank Rachel on the Estes record, and uses a lyric that keeps almost parallel with Estes' for the first four verses of the song (which is to say for four out of six verses in Dylan's case and four out of five in Estes'). In the opening verse, the only differences are that of course Estes has it as 'broken-hearted', whereas Dylan restores it to 'broke and hungry', and Estes' 'pretty mama / may I' becomes 'sweet mama / can I' for Dylan. Dylan swaps the order of verses two and three, and, mystifyingly, takes the sexual betrayal out of the 'bed-springs' incident. Everyone else who has used this verse (including Willie Brown) renders it as Estes does:

> Now I went to my window, couldn't see through my blinds
> I heard the bed-springs poppin' an' I believe I heard my baby cryin'.

Granted that sexual betrayal is a main theme of Dylan's album, it's a puzzle why he eliminates it here, replacing it with the meaningless 'Heard my best friend coming and I thought I heard my baby crying' (in which the sexual import of that 'coming' is a mere accident of convergent vocabulary).

Both singers place the 'How can I stay here?' verse fourth, though Dylan makes no attempt to echo the autobiographical touches of geography Estes weaves into his own account. Dylan sings it straight:

> How can I live here baby, Lord and feel at ease?

(to ask which is, of course, to re-state the theme of the album's title track)

> When that woman that I got, man, she do just what she please.

Sleepy John Estes, being more specific, asks instead:

> How can I stay in Memphis, babe and feel at ease
> And have a woman in Brownsville an' she goin' with who she please?

(a sort of stuck inside of Memphis with the Brownsville blues again).[110] After the fourth verse on Dylan's recording, his brief but beautifully stubborn, struggling, faltered guitar-work is particularly reminiscent of Estes.

Both singers choose to bow out with a verse snatched from elsewhere yet certainly not at random. Sleepy John takes as his couplet

> Now sure as the stars all shine in the world above
> You know life's too short for to worry 'bout the one you love

108. Sleepy John Estes, 'Broken-Hearted, Ragged And Dirty Too', Memphis, 17/9/29; unissued. 'Broken-Hearted, Ragged And Dirty Too', Memphis, 26/9/29; "Sleepy John Estes, 1929–1940", RBF Records RF-8, New York, 1964.
109. Willie Brown, 'Ragged & Dirty', Sadie's Beck Plantation, Arkansas, 16/7/42, a Library of Congress field-recording.
110. Estes is from Brownsville, Tennessee, not the Texas Brownsville of Dylan's song, discussed in Chapter 16.

so ending the song – which is as much about the difficulties of leaving and staying as of poverty and hunger – with a philosophical concluding shrug. (In a neat departing touch, Estes actually omits that final word 'love', leaving it to hang implied, inside the listener's head, as Dylan does with 'snake', the unspoken last word of 'Man Gave Names To All The Animals'.)

Dylan's bought-in ending, as it were, on 'Ragged And Dirty', matching Estes for aptness, is a verse that turns up in Robert Johnson's 'Walking Blues':

> Well I'm leaving in the morning if I have to ride the blinds
> Well I bin mistreated an' I swear I don' mind dyin' –

which, in one of Dylan's flashes of quiet, weird inspiration, achieves the juxtaposing of this other meaning of 'blinds', redolent of menace and desperate travel, with the quite different, domestic one already there earlier in the lyric.[111]

The two main features of the album, as we have so far dealt with its repertoire, have been black balladry and the history of its infusion into American popular music, and the private dramas of a particular clutch of pre-war blues: the grand dustclouds of oral history and the small intensities of a particular milieu, both equally revitalised into a Bob Dylan vision of then and now and the world gone wrong. But there are two further main features within the album's repertoire, both of which contribute to its overall vision. There is the evocation of another great sweep of history, that of the American Civil War, with all its psychic divides, its North–South, then–now, slave–abolitionist flames never extinguished, the South's defeat still so real and fundamentally defining in the South that it might have happened in the 1980s rather than the 1860s (except for the veterans and their families directly involved, the Vietnam War seems longer ago and harder to remember).[112] And then, matching the private violence of those pre-war blues songs, there is the individual and private suffering Dylan brings so alive in those two 'white' songs 'Love Henry' and 'Lone Pilgrim'.

It is with 'Two Soldiers' and 'Jack-A-Roe', songs that Dylan has good reason to place adjacently – though it seems an inspired and intuitive placing – that he invokes the Civil War's foment. In many versions of 'Jack-A-Roe', not only does the disguised heroine claim that she *could* 'see ten thousand fall' but she participates in the warfare, and therefore there is much more common ground – common battleground – shared by the two songs than Dylan's version of the latter suggests. (In one 'Jack Munro', which starts her off in the English town of Chester: 'This maid she fought with courage, / With courage bold and true. / Two captains and one colonel / All in one day she slew'.) Other versions simply centre far more on the war that the heroine's lover has gone to fight than does the Dylan version.[113]

---

111. Robert Johnson: 'Walking Blues', San Antonio, 27/11/36, "Robert Johnson: King of the Delta Blues Singers", Columbia Records CL-1654, New York, 1961.

   Dylan adds in another verse to his version of 'Ragged And Dirty'. The one that runs 'You shouldn't mistreat me 'cos I'm young and wild / You should always remember you was once a child' is imported straight from Blind Lemon Jefferson's 'Stocking Feet Blues', Chicago, c. Nov. 1926; "Black Snake Moan: Blind Lemon Jefferson", Milestone Records MLP-2013, New York, 1970.

112. The modern plaque at the campus entrance to the University of Georgia (in Athens, home to 30,000 students and hometown of R.E.M. and the B52s) refers not to the American Civil War but to 'the War for Southern Independence'.

113. Dylan's liner-notes say that 'Jerry Garcia showed me TWO SOLDIERS (Hazel & Alice do it pretty similar)'

There is a stirring conjunction between these two adjacently placed songs on "World Gone Wrong" and the eloquent memorial to the defeated Confederate Army in Columbia, state capital of South Carolina – the state that led the breakaway from the Union – to which the writer V. S. Naipaul was directed by a judge he met in the South in the 1980s, who told him 'that the inscription of the memorial was something that should be studied. It was poetic and contained much of the South's idea of itself.' Naipaul writes:

> On one side of the monument was engraved: 'To South Carolina's dead of the Confederate Army 1861–1865.' On another side it said: 'Erected by the Women of South Carolina. Unveiled May 13, 1879.' There was rhetoric in that reference to women; monuments of grief and revenge, or grief and piety, are most unsettling when they depict women bowed in grief.[114]

---

and that 'JACK-A-ROE is another Tom Paley ballad (Tom, one of the original New Lost City Ramblers)'. Hazel & Alice were Hazel Dickens and Alice Foster, later Gerrard. For more on Tom Paley, see later in the present chapter.

'Two Soldiers' was published in *Sing Out!*, Vol. 14, no. 3, July 1964, an issue with Tom Paley's New Lost City Ramblers partner Mike Seeger on the cover and a feature on him inside by Bob's old friend Jon Pankake. Songs in the same issue include 'The Lonesome Death Of Hattie Carroll' and 'Danville Girl'. In the same month that we believe Dylan recorded "World Gone Wrong" he got together with Mike Seeger for a re-recording of his own 'Ballad Of Hollis Brown' (with Seeger on banjo): Los Angeles, 19/5/93; "Third Annual Farewell Reunion" [various-artists compilation], Rounder Records CD 0313, Somerville, Massachusetts, 1995.

The Chester-based version of 'Jack Monroe' is taken from *The Greig–Duncan Folk Song Collection*, Vol. 1, ed. Patrick Shuldham-Shaw and Emily B. Lyle (1981), which offers many variants.

'Jackaroe' is also released on the fourth Joan Baez album – the one for which Dylan contributed a sleeve note poem – and Dylan's 'Jack-A-Roe', 30 years later, uses the Baez version of the text. Baez, awful though she is in many ways, should not be discounted as a conduit of traditional material to Bob Dylan. Her first album includes 'East Virginia', 'Fare Thee Well', 'House Of The Rising Sun' and 'Little Moses', her second 'Wagoner's Lad', 'The Lily Of The West', 'Barbara Allen' and 'Railroad Boy', while 'The Trees They Do Grow High' is an alternative title for 'Young But Daily Growing'. On the third comes 'Copper Kettle' and 'House Carpenter' (plus 'Pretty Boy Floyd'), and in among the four Bob Dylan songs on the sixth ("Farewell Angelina") we find 'Will Ye Go, Laddie, Go' and 'Satisfied Mind'.

Many further connections and comparisons arise on the same albums. Her first album's 'John Riley', a broadside ballad collected by G. Malcolm Laws Jr, belongs with 'Belle Isle' in telling of a soldier or sailor returning in disguise to test his lover's fidelity, while 'Rake And Rambling Boy' has a final verse that melds the 'I'm Riding Old Paint' format discussed in Chapter 1 ('when I die, don't bury me at all / Place my bones in alcohol') and the ending of 'Railroad Boy' ('at my feet place a white snow dove / To tell the world I died for love'). This last formulation is found widely – as for instance in the Lincolnshire folksong 'Died For Love (I Wish My Baby It Was Born)', which not only ends the same way ('Dig me my grave long, wide and deep / Put a marble stone at my head and feet / But a turtle white dove put over above / For to let the world know that I died for love') but also offers this recognisable prefiguring of a portion of 'Bob Dylan's Dream': 'I wish, I wish, but it's all in vain / I wish I was a maid again'. (Published in the pamphlet 'Twenty-one Lincolnshire Folk Songs', from the Percy Grainger collection, ed. Patrick O'Shaughnessy, Lincolnshire & Humberside Arts, 2nd edition, 1983.) The third album's 'Matty Groves', a Child ballad, shares its theme with that other Child ballad 'Blackjack Davey', while 'Geordie', a part-Child and part-broadside ballad, reminds us of both 'Blackjack Davey' and Dylan's own 'Seven Curses': 'Ah my Geordie will be hanged . . . / Go bridle me my milk white steed / Go bridle me my pony / I will ride to London's court / To plead for the life of Geordie . . . / The judge looked over his left shoulder / He said fair maid I'm sorry'.

[Joan Baez: "Joan Baez", Vanguard VRS-9078, New York, 1960; "Joan Baez, Vol. 2", Vanguard VRS-9094, New York, 1961; "Joan Baez In Concert", Vanguard VRS-9112, New York, 1962; "Joan Baez In Concert, Part 2", Vanguard VRS-9113, New York, 1963; "Farewell Angelina", Vanguard VRS-9200 (stereo VSD-79200), New York, 1965. All these are CD-reissued on, respectively, Vanguard Records VMD 79078–2, 1995; VMD 79094–2, 1995; VMD 79112–2, 1996; VMD 79113–2, 1996; and VMD 79200–2, 1995. All these songs are published in *British Ballads and Folk Songs from the Joan Baez Songbook* (with illustrations by Eric von Schmidt), 1964 and 1967.]

Dylan débuted his own version of 'Two Soldiers' (with insignificant small variations in the lyric from the "World Gone Wrong" version of five years later) live in concert, Sacramento, 9/6/88; and his own version of 'Jack-A-Roe' (ditto variations), at the Supper Club 2nd Show, NYC, 16/11/93.

114. V. S. Naipaul, *A Turn in the South* (1989). Naipaul may be right to imply that this monument is unusual in depicting women's grief. Civil War memorials all over the South purport to do the same, but the first 'monument

The memorial reads:

This monument perpetuates the memory of those who, true to the instincts of their birth, faithful to the teachings of their fathers, constant in their love for the state, died in the performance of their duty: who have glorified a fallen cause by the simple manhood of their lives, the patient endurance of suffering, and the heroism of death, and who, in the dark hours of imprisonment, in the hopelessness of the hospital, in the short, sharp agony of the field, found support and consolation in the belief that at home they would not be forgotten.

The first half of this, of course – up to 'the heroism of death' – is the predictable clamour of patriotism and (white) male supremacy: but how striking and surprising, how enlivening for its candour and compassion, is the passage this official monu-mentese slides into, as into a confession: you do not expect a war memorial to address and meditate upon 'the dark hours of imprisonment . . . the hopelessness of the hospital' (that phrase seems especially subversive) and 'the short, sharp agony of the field'. It is this humane and feminine second half of the inscription that converges upon 'Two Soldiers' (and that the 'Two Soldiers' are blue-eyed Boston boys of the Yankee army only serves to make the common humanity of both sides reverberate the more poignantly) and 'Jack-A-Roe'.

In the latter, the disguised woman, having claimed that it wouldn't faze her 'to see ten thousand fall', finds her lover 'among the dead and dying': among those 'in the short, sharp agony of the field'. In the version Dylan sings, it is nicely ambiguous as to whether she finds her lover a wounded survivor among the dead and dying, or whether, as you might consider is more straightforwardly implied, she finds that he too is indeed 'among the dead and dying', after which the doctor tends his wounds but can do nothing to countermand their mortal effect, so that the marriage with which the song then ends so hastily is the deathbed marriage: the kind Barbara Allen is too late with her change of heart to offer Sweet William in the version Dylan sings of *that* ballad.

In 'Two Soldiers' – 'a battle song extraordinaire, some dragoon officer's epaulettes laying liquid in the mud, physical plunge into Limitationville . . . America when Mother was the queen of Her heart,' as Dylan puts it (with sumptuous muscularity) – the soldiers truly are preoccupied with seeking 'consolation in the belief that at home they would not be forgotten' by the women who do stay and wait.

In this case they wait in vain, for both of the soldiers are 'among the dead', and not among 'those whom death and doom had spared'. It is also in this simple phrase 'among the dead', and its extension 'and dying' – omitted but implicit here – that the songs 'Two Soldiers' and 'Jack-A-Roe' come together. There are not only common concerns but common-stock elements in each song, and that this is one they share is shown by those versions of 'Two Soldiers' brought together under varying titles in

---

to the women of the Confederacy', which was unveiled in Rome, Georgia, in 1910, seems rather to depict their gentle and uncomplaining womanhood than their grief: male soldiers lie wounded in their arms, which detracts from its claimed concentration on the women's suffering (this may be the typical depiction). Another sub-text of such monuments may be the message – a message that is as clear as day all over the South – that the Civil War matters far more than any other. In Blind Willie McTell's place of burial, Thomson, Georgia, the town's memorial statue plinth reads 'In Memory of the Women of the Sixties . . .' Everyone understands as if from birth that this means the 1860s.

G. Malcolm Laws' standard work *Native American Balladry*, when he comes to Civil War songs. In 'The Drummer Boy Of Shiloh' 'On Shiloh's dark and bloody ground / The dead and wounded lay around'; in 'A Soldier From Missouri' (sometimes called 'The Kansas Line') 'A soldier from Missouri / In early manhood's prime / Lay with the dead an' dyin' / In Mississippi's clime'.[115]

Yet 'Two Soldiers' ends not with their deaths per se but with the bleakness of their leaving a silence behind, with 'no one to write' to the women left stranded at home. They are the women who might have paid to raise such a memorial as the one to be found in Columbia, South Carolina.

Its inscription's end – envisaging that the dying soldiers would find 'consolation in the belief that at home they would not be forgotten' – is itself the lonely consolation of the women. The sensibility of these songs is such as to offer a sisterhood to these disruptive human whispers from within the carved stone: a fluid, oral guardianship of the past running alongside the fixity of its official text.

In the 19-verse version of 'Jack-a-Roe' called 'Jackie Frazier', collected in A. L. Lloyd's *Folk Songs of the Americas* (in which the song begins by telling us, 'There was a wealthy merchant, in London he did dwell / He had a daughter Polly, and the truth to you I'll tell', and in which she claims that 'They call me Jack Monroe', the false name from which we get the corruption 'Jackaroe'), her lover unambiguously recovers and the far less reverberative moral of the story is 'So parents let your children get married as they please'.[116] But as Roscoe Holcomb refashions the story in his *tour de force* recording 'Across The Rocky Mountain', in which the piercing vocal tumbles with unfaltering dexterity down lines almost as eccentric in syllabic distribution as are Bob Dylan's in 'Julius & Ethel', the song ends with the boast of the heroine (rendered at its most callous, as the feminine seeks to imitate the masculine), the subsequent discovery of her lover, and the pared-down ambiguity of a frantic dash to the doctor, its outcome left unsaid. The words duplicate those of 'Jack-A-Roe':

> *My cheeks are not too rosy, my fingers not too small*
> *No they would not change my conscience to see ten thousand fall*
> *. . . She's walking through the battlefield a-searching up and down*
> *It's all among the dead and wounded her darling Jack she found*
> *. . . She picked him up all in her arms, she carried him to the town*
> *She took him to the doctor for to quickly heal the wound.*[117]

---

115. Albert B. Friedman, writing in a 1956 collection of ballads he edited, *The Viking Book of Folk Ballads of the English-Speaking World*, says that 'Of the spate of cloyingly pathetic ballads that came out of the Civil War, this is one of the few to last in oral memory.' Laws (rev. edn, 1964) quotes an earlier collector's description of it as 'Patently "literary"', and himself describes the Ohio version that he reprints, 'The Last Fierce Charge', as 'a rather artless text in the idiom of the folk'.

116. A. L. Lloyd (ed.), *The Folk Songs of the Americas* (1965). The song is elsewhere found as 'Jack Went A-Sailing' (e.g. as collected from Mrs Gentry at Hot Springs, North Carolina, 26/8/16, by Cecil J. Sharp, published in Sharp and Karpeles' *English Folk Songs from the Southern Appalachians*, 1932, no. 65); as 'Jack Monroe'/'Jack Munro' (as in *The Greig–Duncan Folk Song Collection*, Vol. 1 (note 113); in Scottish form as 'The Bold Munro' (ditto); and under many other names, including 'Pretty Polly' (ditto again). A. L. Lloyd also recorded the song, as 'Jackie Monroe', on "English Street Songs", Riverside Records RLP 12–614, *nia*.

117. Roscoe Holcomb: 'Across The Rocky Mountain', Daisy, Virginia, 1959; "Mountain Music Of Kentucky", Folkways Records FA 2317, New York, 1960; CD-reissued [as 2-CD set with extra tracks] same title, Smithsonian-Folkways SFCD 40077, Washington, DC, 1996.

In the early days of the Folk Revival, Robert Shelton remembers, the Stanley Brothers (increasingly

The unreassuring finality is emphasised by Holcomb's rhyming of 'wound' with 'town': in effect one of those Ricksian double-rhyme endings, 'making a conclusive ending, that your conclusions can be more drastic'. That we cannot assume a happy ending from the mere invocation of the doctor is also pressed upon us by recalling that the same line – about the doctor, the healing and the wound – is an ingredient in the 'Unfortunate Rake' series of songs, in which despite the physician's attention, the outcome is death. ('Go send for the doctor to heal up my wounds' sings 'this young lady . . . cold as the clay' in 'One Morning In May'. In the James Iron Head Baker/ Doc Watson variant, the doctor is expected not to achieve recovery but mere cosmetic tidiness: 'Send for that doctor to come and heal up my body / And send for the preacher to come and pray for my soul'.)[118] They send for the doctor in Dylan's 'Stack A Lee' too, of course, and he comes not to repair but to rebuke.

With the happy ending refused in both the Holcomb and the Dylan versions of the 'Jackie Frazier' song, we're left to question the consolation the heroine receives for having refused to wait passively at home for news from the war, as wives and mothers and sisters more usually must.

Consolation was small either way. The American Civil War was the biggest in the western world in the hundred years between the end of the Napoleonic Wars and the start of World War I. It cost more American lives than the two world wars, Korea and Vietnam combined. It also introduced the special horrors of 'modern' warfare, the trenches, the prisoner-of-war camp and the first American conscription, plus ironclad ships, aerial observation, the Gatling gun and propaganda.

The travel writer William Least Heat-Moon describes one battle, at Spotsylvania, Virginia, in brief, succinct terms that illustrate the full wanton horror of the war:

> The fighting here in the wet spring of 1864 was so close that cannoneers, standing ankle deep in mud, fired at point-blank range; soldiers, slogging it out in a smoky rainstorm, fought muzzle to muzzle, stabbing with bayonets . . . clubbing each other into the mire from dawn to midnight, and trampling fallen men out of sight into the muck. The intense rifle fire cut in half oak trees two feet in diameter. One soldier, Horace Porter, wrote: 'We had not only shot down an army, but also a forest.' On that single day, May 12, nearly thirteen thousand men died fighting over one square mile of ground abandoned by both sides several days later. Yet,

acknowledged as an important influence by Dylan in the 1990s) were 'sponsored by Mike Seeger', just as 'Ralph Rinzler squired about Bill Monroe and Doc Watson, and John Cohen became Roscoe Holcomb's "discoverer" and good friend': this was at a time (Shelton specifies no dates) when 'it was as if each active city performer "adopted" a country performer to escort, tout and make popular'. (Robert Shelton in *The Electric Muse*, Laing, Dallas, Denselow and Shelton, 1975.)

John Cohen, who also has a great archive of Bob Dylan photographs and conducted the 1968 *Sing Out!* interview with Dylan, was a member of the New Lost City Ramblers with Mike Seeger and Tom Paley. The great Roscoe Holcomb is well worth checking out: he makes Bob Dylan sound as smooth as Cliff Richard, and his material has many Dylan-connections.

('I learnt this from Ralph Rinzler', Bob Dylan tells Cynthia Gooding on the radio-show tape that emerged thirty years late in 1992 [WBAI Radio, NYC, probably 13/1/62, broadcast 11/3/62] re 'Roll On John', a highlight of that tape. Rinzler died in 1994, while still working with Mike Seeger on the project to reissue the Harry Smith Anthology, see note 6.)

118. For details on these versions and a discussion of the 'Unfortunate Rake' cycle of songs, see Chapter 15.

had anyone been paying attention, the battle could have shown the futility of trench warfare.[119]

The first modern war-novel, Stephen Crane's *The Red Badge of Courage*, first published in 1895, also came out of the American Civil War, though the war was over before its author was born.[120] The novel is thought to centre around the real Battle of Chancellorsville of 1863, while the song 'Two Soldiers' focuses upon the Battle of Fredericksburg (the song is sometimes known as 'The Battle Of Fredericksburg' and also as 'The Last Fierce Charge'). The latter battle took place on 13 December 1862, demoralised the North and heartened the South, yet would prove to be almost the last significant Southern victory (and largely by default at that). The North lost over 12,000 men and the Confederate South had 5,000 killed or wounded. It was this battle, too, that brought home to people on both sides the sense that the war might be a remorseless, continuing conflict with no end ever in sight.

It was a battle of mad tactics and vast confusion; it took place in thick fog; and for the 'blue-eyed Boston boys' it was utterly futile. Douglas Welsh writes that 'The stubborn bravery of the Union soldiers was phenomenal. Time and time again they threw themselves into an attack which had no possible chance for success.' The plan had been 'to march to Fredericksburg, capture the city and from there launch an attack on Richmond'. The drawback was that the Union forces had to cross the Rappahannock River and seize the heights behind Fredericksburg – 'the heights that they could not gain', as the song has it – and to do so before Confederate General Robert E. Lee could retreat and escape. Greatly outnumbered, surprise was Union commander Burnside's only hope, and this he threw away. In the event, writes Welsh, 'Lee watched from his vantage point on the heights unable to believe the carnage which was resulting from Burnside's tactics.' Next morning, Burnside wanted to resume; his generals persuaded him it would be hopeless. 'Exhausted and disheartened the Army of the Potomac slipped back across the river two days later under cover of darkness.'[121]

Bob Dylan's richly concentrated, sombre and ineffably tender version of 'Two Soldiers' draws out of the song every last sorrowful morsel of its skilful encapsulation of this vast, doomed slaughter into the story of two individual doomed innocents and the repercussions of grief and silence that follow from their deaths. It works affectingly despite its historical inaccuracy – there was, for instance, no cavalry engagement at the Battle of Fredericksburg. And even though it is so very difficult to hear all the words as Dylan sings them, nevertheless you feel when you listen that he sings them extraordinarily well!

The pity with his 'Jack-A-Roe' is that suddenly, disruptively, the recording cranks up the amount of echo or reverb or both on the vocal track, giving it a wholly different sound from the rest of the album. It's a puzzling disruption and hard to 'hear past', as it were.

119. William Least Heat-Moon, *Blue Highways* (1984).

120. Stephen Crane was born 1 November 1871 and died aged twenty-eight, 5 June 1900.

121. This account is taken, as are the quotations, from Douglas Welsh, *American Civil War: A Complete Military History* (1981).

It is not hard, however, to hear *the* past, including a past the song incorporates from well before the American Civil War: the English and Scottish ballad past in which 'This lady she was courted / By many a lord and knight', and in which the dominant culture seems to have been more sexually flexible than is suggested by accounts of the history of sexual politics offered in our own times. How else to explain the remarkable ending to the Chester-based version of 'Jack Monroe'? Its final verse runs

> *They both got married in men's clothes,*
> *Lest anyone should know,*
> *While the officers stood gazing*
> *On their darling Jack Monroe.*[122]

Even without this surprising apparent fancying by heterosexual men of people they thought were other men, and apparent countenancing of male-on-male marriage, it tells us something interesting – that there has always been in this ballad tradition great popularity for songs not merely about women dressing up in men's clothes but for songs about such women going off to sea. It surely reflects their plentifulness, rather than some special interest of his own, that when Dylan turns back to traditional material in the early 1990s, he performs one such song live – 'Female Rambling Sailor' – and includes one on each of these two solo albums.

Certainly what he says of the third of these, 'Jack-A-Roe', in his liner-notes, picks out delightfully and deftly other areas of interest within the song rather than its cross-dressery: he comments that

> *the song cannot be categorized – is worlds away from reality but 'gets inside' reality anyway & strips it of its steel and concrete. inverted symmetry, legally stateless, travelling under a false passport. 'before you step on board, sir . . .' are you any good at what you do? submerge your personality.*

That ' "before you step on board, sir . . ." are you any good at what you do?' is so Dylanesque! Strictly speaking, the question in the lyric is not this one but 'your name I'd like to know'; the suggestion that 'Jack-A-Roe' might not be strong enough for the things that 'all tough sailors do when they're far away at sea' (to quote a different piece of Dylanesquerie) comes later. But Dylan's seeing this as coming down to the question 'are you any good at what you do?' sends us straight back down the years to the abrasive, impassioned dialogues he has in 1965 with people (the journalist and 'the science student') in the film *Don't Look Back*.[123]

Nevertheless, these 'female rambling sailor' songs come aboard the Dylan ship of this period sufficiently to reflect their popularity. In turn, though, such songs themselves reflect, as it were, an *un*sung part of the history of 'the people'. It's been said that in the early eighteenth century there were so many women dressed as men in the British army that they might have formed battalions of their own, and that similar numbers may have sailed the high seas. As the narrative of 'Jack-A-Roe' suggests, women dressed as men often transferred from sea to land fighting, participating in

---

122. *The Greig–Duncan Folk Song Collection*, Vol. 1 (note 113).

123. *Don't Look Back*, Leacock-Pennebaker, US, auteured by D. A. Pennebaker, 1967.

both. Some became famous, like the Englishwoman Mary Read and the Irishwoman Anne Bonny, who were among Calico Jack Rackam's pirates arrested and put on trial in Jamaica in 1720. While seventeen were hanged, these two surprised the court by pleading for clemency on the grounds that they were pregnant. They were jailed instead of hanged. It transpired that Mary Read had enlisted in the Navy at 15, sailed on a man-o'-war and later fought against the French in Flanders in both the cavalry and infantry. Anne Bonny, though her father was 'a wealthy farmer' (as in the case of 'The Girl I Left Behind', a song Dylan sang in 1961 that shows links with both 'Jack-A-Roe' and Roscoe Holcomb's 'Across The Rocky Mountain'), ran away to the Caribbean simply to seek adventure, and found it in piracy. Accounts of witnesses suggest that such women were known to be women ('by the largeness of their breasts'), that their pretence was an accepted convention, and that they were not merely tolerated but capable, if proving brave enough, of exercising authority and even leadership. Less a question, then, of 'submerge your personality', as Dylan suggests in his liner-notes, as express it.[124]

'Love Henry' is also about a tough mama: a 'fairy queen exploiter', Dylan calls her, in his commentary on this thrilling Child ballad, which is essentially number 68, 'Young Hunting', of which Child gives eleven versions (all from Scotland) but which is offered with over forty variants in Bronson's standard work *The Traditional Tunes of the Child Ballads, Vol. 2*. Dylan sings Bronson Variant 19 almost word-for-word with the addition of one verse from elsewhere.[125]

Bronson comments that this begins as a Scottish ballad – or that if it began in England it has left no trace there (which is odd, granted that one of the variants he includes is set firmly in Yorkshire) but seems to have passed straight from Scotland to the USA, 'where it has enjoyed a great vogue in our own century – at least in the Appalachians'. Its early history remains murky, as is its relationship to the ballads 'Lady Isabel' and 'The Elfin Knight'. However, we do know that versions called 'Young Redin' and 'Earl Richard' were in collections published as far back as 1827.

My own responses take no heed of the historiography of these ballads, nor of whether there are tiny discrepancies (as there are) between Cecil Sharp's manuscript transcriptions and the same versions when published under Maud Karpeles' editorship, nor of whether the melodies are hexatonic or heptatonic, nor of the scholarly dividing of all these versions into Story Types A to H by Tristram Potter Coffin.[126]

It is Dylan's version of the song that has sent me back to these variants, and while his treatment is dark, serious and fully committed to the mystery of traditional song, it doesn't detract from this to be able to enjoy the process of surveying the song's variants, which is an informal process of deconstruction. You see the elements retained

124. This historical sketching is based on the article 'Shiver her timbers!' by Dermot Purgavie, *Daily Mail*, 7/12/93, which cites as sources *A General History of the Pyrates*, by Captain Charles Johnson, published in the 1720s, and an interview with Marcus Rediker, 'a professor of history at Georgetown University who has studied pirate culture'.
    Bob Dylan: 'The Girl I Left Behind', *Oscar Brand's Folksong Festival*, WNYC Radio, NYC, 29/10/61.

125. Francis James Child, see note 24. Bertrand Harris Bronson, *The Traditional Tunes from the Child Ballads, Vol. 2* (1962).

126. Cecil Sharp and Maud Karpeles, *English Folk Songs from the Southern Appalachians*; Tristram Potter Coffin, *The British Traditional Ballad in North America* (1950).

and lost along the way, those distorted by design and accident: perhaps misheard and then passed on as in a game of Chinese Whispers. You see how common-stock ingredients drift in and out of the core narrative, and the relishable, comic ways in which the incandescent poetry of some versions collapses into ungainly, fatuous bathos in others.

This is the one Dylan sings so immaculately:

> Get down get down Love Henry she cried
> And stay all night with me
> I have gold chains and the finest I have
> I'll apply them all to thee
>
> I can't get down an' I shan't get down
> Or stay all night with thee
> Some pretty little girl in Cornersville
> I love far better than thee
>
> He laid his head on a pillow of down
> Kisses she gave him three
> With a penny knife that she held in her hand
> She murdered mortal he
>
> Get well, get well Love Henry she cried
> Get well get well said she
> Oh don't you see my own heart's blood
> A-flowing down so free
>
> She took him by his long yellow hair
> And also by his feet
> She plunged him into well water where
> It runs both cold and deep
>
> Lie there lie there Love Henry she cried
> Till the flesh rots off your bones
> Some pretty little girl in Cornersville
> Will mourn for your return
>
> Hush up hush up my parrot she cried
> Don't tell no news on me
> Oh these costly beads around my neck
> I'll apply them all to thee
>
> Fly down fly down pretty parrot she cried
> And light on my right knee
> The doors to your cage shall be decked with gold
> And hung on a willow tree
>
> I won't fly down and I can't fly down
> And light on your right knee

A girl who would murder her own true love
Would kill a little bird like me.

There are three moments where Dylan's voice allows a hint of variation from this version. As Dylan sings the second verse, it isn't clear whether he has Love Henry sing 'I won't fly down and I shan't fly down' or 'I won't fly down and I shouldn't fly down' – which would suggest his immediate wavering, thus preparing the way for his laying his head on her pillow. Then, Dylan sings that 'She plunged him into well water where' as if he's singing 'water wet', which ought to sound unhelpfully obvious, in effect a clumsy tautology; yet it somehow has a rightness that appeals by elucidating further her heightened instability of mind: she's so intensely aware of the feel and look and sound of everything at this point that a suggestion of her awareness of the water's wetness is all of a piece with her awareness of its coldness. Thirdly, Dylan sings her plea to the parrot such that you cannot tell for certain whether he sings 'Don't tell no news on me' or whether he makes it the even better 'Don't trill no news on me'.

At any rate, this version is a taut ellipse – taut even though it uses all those echoing repetitions that bounce back and forth within its dialogues: 'Get down, get down . . . I can't get down and I shan't get down'; 'Fly down, fly down . . . I won't fly down and I can't fly down'. But in omitting part of the story and simplifying a further part, it gives us a particular take on the motives and characters that fuller versions do not bear out.

These begin with the hero going hunting, and then returning to his lover, usually named as Lady Margaret. When she welcomes him back and invites him to her bed, he tells her he prefers another – the usual phrase here is the blunt one that he loves her 'far better than thee' – or even his wife: 'For I have a far better bride than you / To enjoy when I go home.' In any case, this already shifts the moral picture, showing the hero as faithless to the one rather than faithful to the other. And exceptionally tactless too. Then, adding arrogance to his other qualities, he no sooner tells her how much less attractive she is than the third party he's never told her about before, than he bends down from on high on his horse – a 'milk-white steed' in some variants – and kisses her. (Bob Dylan's brilliant updating of this in his liner-notes has Love Henry as 'career minded, limousine double parked'.) Enraged, she stabs him, and he realises that he is mortally wounded. Filled at once with remorse, she sobs out her imprecations that he should live. (' "Get well, get well, Love Henry," she cried . . .')

At this point two common-stock ingredients drift through the picture like character-actor stalwarts whose faces you recognise from a hundred films but whose names you don't feel a need to know.

First, the heroine promises that if he'll just hang on a while, she will summon a doctor and the doctor will heal the hero. Thus we are returned to exactly the formula met already in songs like 'Jack-A-Roe', 'Across The Rocky Mountain' and even 'The Unfortunate Rake',[127] and the same words too, with 'town' rhymed with 'wound':

For there's a doctor in yonder town
Can cure your mortal wound . . .

127. Bronson (see note 125) comments on the *tune* of a variant called 'Loving Henry' that it suggests some variants of 'Streets Of Laredo', which, as noted in Chapter 15, belongs to the 'Unfortunate Rake' song-cycle.

or

> *You shall have all the doctors in the whole round town*
> *For to heal and cure your wounds . . .*

to which the stabbed lover replies along the lines of

> *There hain't a doctor but God alone*
> *Can cure those wounded wounds.*

(In so many cases, these last two among them, there is this continual redoubling, as here with the doubled rhyme of 'round town' and then those 'wounded wounds'.)

Second, there are many versions in which the dead man is strapped back on his horse and sent riding off again so that the body will be found elsewhere, though somehow it always end up deep in water. (In a rare instance or two, she sends him off not to place the crime elsewhere but in the forlorn hope that he'll reach the doctor in time.) Within these stanzas it sometimes happens that when he's tied back on his steed and sent off, his murderess makes sure that, like Froggie, he goes 'with a sword and pistol by his side'.[128]

These stalwarts having made their brief appearances, the narrative continues with the disposal of the body, usually down a well. This is often achieved not by the heroine alone but with the help of her servants. Thus Dylan's version's one touch of bathos – when she picks him up by his hair 'and also by his feet' – has been inherited from older formulations in which there are staff to attend to these matters, so that

> *Some took him by the golden hair*
> *Some took him by the feet –*

a more seemly phrasing that yields another in the song's long pattern of repetitions.

Two main alternative resolutions follow this. In one, as with that Bob Dylan gives us, the heroine realises that the crime has been observed by the bird and either attempts to buy its silence or else, soon abandoning this ploy, tries to lure it within killing distance by crude coaxing and lavish promises. The bird is not as bird-brained as that, and states its suspicions and refusal with varying degrees of bluntness. When, as with the Dylan variant, the song ends there, it leaves the bird's power hovering over the heroine, and this might be thought a refined, unending punishment; but this is a foreshortened ending, omitting a further exchange between woman and bird, in which, just as suddenly as she switched with the hero from loving invitation to murder, so she drops her politesse toward Polly, switching abruptly to shouting straightforwardly at it that

> *If I had a bow all in my hand*
> *And an arrow to a string*

---

128. Two variants even manage to remind us of a third well-known story, that of 'Blackjack Davey'! One, known as 'Love Henry', 'Young Henry' or 'The Well Water', collected from one George Vinton Graham in San José, California, in 1938, but locating itself in Yorkshire nevertheless, has the hero ride a milk-white steed, and he's killed with a 'Spanish dart' concealed under a 'mantle cloak'. The other, 'Lord Henry', collected in Virginia, sings out the accusation 'Away, away to the wild match woods / Is where you stayed last night'; the murderess picks him up 'by his coal-black hair' and tells him 'You've rode your last to the wild match woods / To see that fairly dame'.

I'd shoot you through the very heart
Among the leaves so green . . .

This merely brings the bird more plainly to blackmail as it retorts along these lines:

If you had your bow arrow
Your bow arrow and string
I'd fly away to yonder green
And tell what I have seen.

This is usually the end of the song, so that it might be said that Dylan's variant merely says the same in fewer stanzas. Occasionally, though, this is still not the end, for the heroine then dies too. In Child's variant B8, ungainliness of form and content become one, as we come to the comic awkwardness of the penultimate line:

With her heart like a stone
She stood there alone
Then she walked to the side of the well
Soon she fainted and fell over sideways
And down she fell, fell, fell.

One or two examples have the heroine so filled with remorse that she commits suicide.
    Yet this is only one of two main endings. The other may or may not include a bird, but nemesis comes not by feathers but by blood and fire. The body being discovered by the authorities, the murderess then seeks to blame the servants. However, the victim's body remains inactive in their presence, his wounds by now

As white as a linen clout
But as the traitor she cam near
His wounds they gushéd out!

When they try to burn the servant all the same, the flames don't take. Trial by fire finally proves the guilt of the heroine. Verdict and punishment are one. In Child's first example, which gives us the full tale, the 'wylie' parrot's refusal to 'come doun, come doun' occurs in verse 14. It takes a further ten verses to reach the end of the song.
    There is altogether between these variants a great clamouring of elements wanting to be in the song. The Scots version just quoted begins with Young Redin out hunting. When he reaches 'his true-love's' home, with thirty-three lords accompanying him, the heroine tells him

Ye're welcome here, my young Redin
For coal and candle licht
And sae are ye, my young Redin
To bide wi' me the nicht.

That is to say, the woman is offering the civilities of shelter and accommodation to the hunting party, and extends her lover the politeness of asking if he will spend the night with her, instead of assuming he will. He, with the sensitivity of the boar he's been hunting, accepts the warming and lighting of the guest-rooms but tells her he's no intention of sleeping in *her* bed because

> *. . . thrice as fair a ladie as thee*
> *Meets me at Brandie's well.*

Having told her that, they go to their separate chambers, and then he comes sneaking along the corridor to her room (again it's stressed here that she is his 'true-love'), finds her crying and lies in her arms. He's stabbed with the penknife; she asks her chamber-maid Meggy (her 'bouer-woman') to take away the body and is told to sort it out herself. The heroine pleads

> *O heal this deed on me, Meggy*
> *O heal this deed on me*

and promises her a reward of silken finery. So they put his boots back on and throw him in the deepest part of the River Clyde. The parrot then causes its usual trouble and eventually the fire burns the bouer-woman's hands and then burns

> *. . . the fause, fause arms,*
> *That young Redin lay in.*

But in time and North America, the elements that introduce themselves include what may be seen as a sort of 'poetic' neatening-up: the heroine offers not hospitality but a bribe to lure the hero to her bed, in exactly similar terms to the bribe she then offers the servants and the third set of bribes she offers to the parrot. But form being inseparable from content, this change in the structural pattern of the song effects a reversal in our perception of who is the goodie and who the baddie in the tale. The version Dylan sings has lost the hunting and the servants but has retained the parallel bribing of man and bird, so that it has lost both the heroine's civility and ill-treatment from the beginning and the bribing of the servant in the middle, and therefore ends up retaining two bribings, which itself makes another of the many doublings contained within the song.

Despite the disappearance of the chamber-maid, an echo of the conversation between lady and servant is retained in Dylan's version. The lady's plea to the servant has been altered almost completely, and has become a plea to the parrot (a plea not there in 'Young Redin'), changing from 'Oh heal this deed on me' to 'Don't trill no news on me'. As we've seen, Dylan's version also retains the phrases that used to describe the help in moving the hero's body by the now-abolished servants. It retains too a vestige of the dialogue about whether the now-abolished doctors can make him well again when she is immediately sorry for what she's done and begs him to get well, as he responds with

> *Oh don't you see my own heart's blood*
> *A-flowing down so free,*

but has dropped the elaboration that only God can save him now.

In all probability, though, in dropping the doctors, the Dylan variant is dropping an ingredient that was never there in the first place and was introduced in North America only by mistake. Tristram P. Coffin points out that the sending for doctors 'is entirely absent from the Scots tradition that supplied all the texts in Child. It is distinctly possible, therefore, that it is derived from the "send for the king's duckers" episode that does appear in Child . . . Thus may the searching of the waters for the body – the duckers' function – have been transformed.'[129]

On the other hand, mishearing or transforming the by-then-meaningless 'duckers' may not be how the doctors got summoned into the song: we noted earlier that sending for the doctors (with the 'town'/'wound' pairing) is a common-stock ingredient. At any rate, by the time of Dylan's 'Love Henry' it has been introduced and dropped again. Meanwhile the other sweetheart, who shifts from 'Brandie's well' to 'the girl that I've left on the Arkansas line' to 'a girl in Yorkshire land' to 'in the Eden land' to 'that pretty little girl in Gospel Land' to 'a bonny lass in a merry green land', has become an inhabitant of Cornersville, Tennessee, due south of Nashville and twenty miles north of the Alabama border. This makes perfect sense, granted that the version Dylan sings is, with an extra verse added at the end, the one collected by Byron Arnold in his *Folksongs of Alabama*, published in 1950, from the singing of one Lena Hill of Lexington, Alabama five years earlier. Lexington is only *just* below the Tennessee state line, and the old highway runs north-east from there to Cornersville, less than forty miles away.

It's curious, then, that while these antiquated 'duckers' are amended, knights and lords become nicknamed lads called Henry, ladies and maidens become girls from Arkansas, and the parrot sits up in anything from a willow to a vine, or becomes a bird in the street outside a bar-room, or doesn't appear in the song at all, the weapon remains unchanged (except for that one Spanish dart), and this in spite of the arrays of weaponry available in North America. (Whether Dylan is singing the corruption 'penny-knife' is impossible to decide.)

We're left with none of the comic clumsiness of other variants – variants that yield, between them, such mishandlings of the power of words as these:

> *She called her housemaids three*
> *Saying 'Lord Bonnie he has died in my lap;*
> *I think it's time he was taken away.'*

(this from 'Lord Bonnie', collected in North Carolina: a version that has no parrot – no bird at all – and specifically has her say to the dead body 'Lie there, lie there, you false-hearted man');

> *I can't shut up and I won't shut up*

and

> *She picked him up all in her arms*
> *Being very active and strong*
> *And she throwed him into an old dry well*
> *About sixty feet.*

Leaving the depth unspecified is doubly wise. It allows the creation of yet another of the song's neat pairings: the penknife plunges 'deep' into his heart, and the body plunges 'deep' into the water. And it avoids bathos. As might be expected, once you start specifying how deep the well is, you're asking for risible variation, and this we

---

129. Coffin, see note 126.

get. 'About sixty feet' is the depth of the dry well. Most are full of water – in Yorkshire, aptly, the well is 'Where it rained so cold and deep' – and sometimes so deep that it is measured in fathoms, like the ocean: 'Sixteen fathoms deep'; 'Full thirty fathoms deep'; 'Some sixty fathoms deep'; plus the comically cautious 'Just about eighteen feet' and the splendidly incredible 'dew drop well' that is 'About forty-thousand feet deep'!

It may be that this Scottish dialect imprecation is seductively melodious, when sung, but seeing it on the page it's hard to imagine, even when the addressee is the parrot:

> *Come doon, come doon, my pretty parrot*
> *An pickle wheat aff my glue*[130]

and the equally Scottish version collected by Carl Sandburg, 'Little Scotch-ee' (which is also in Bronson), has the unwise addition of chickens:

> *Are the chickens a-crowing for the middle of the night*
> *Or are they a-crowing for day*
> *Or are they a-crowing for day?*[131]

While avoiding these dullard sore thumbs, Dylan's version inevitably dispenses too with a few attractive phrases available in other variants. Perhaps not everyone would like the usage that ties in with a blues phrase (noted in an earlier chapter) that Dylan uses of his own 'Tough Mama' – 'meat shakin' on your bones' – but I like the apt, murderous toughness of one version of 'Young Hunting' in which 'till the flesh rots off your bones' is replaced by 'till the meat drops off your bones'. Nor is anything wrong with the Dylan version's description of the hero's blood 'A-flowing down so free' – yet the more unusual and particular expressions chosen by others, though these too can become a risible list if stacked up alongside each other, offer an affecting poetic appeal considered singly, as in

> *For don't you see my own heart's blood*
> *Come twinkling down me knee?*

or

> *. . . don't you see my own heart's blood*
> *Is trinkling to my knees?*

while in one version a chic and nifty pun is achieved, as the lady uses her knife, with the simple phrase 'She pierced him heartilee'.

All in all, though, the version Dylan uses is as fine and sinuous a recreation of the song as could be wished for: a version full of mystery and poetry, loaded with menace and grace, and retaining vivid vestiges of ancientness – including, if you will, what Bronson calls 'a relic of belief in metempsychosis, the bird being the soul of the dead lover'.

---

130. This is taken from the 25-verse version 'The ladie stude in her bour-door', included as text V in Child (see note 24).

131. Carl Sandburg, *Songbag* (see note 7).

Dylan will have selected his version from among the several or more he must know. One of these is a recording on – you'll never guess – the Harry Smith anthology. It is in fact the opening track of the entire 84-track set, Dick Justice's 1929 recording 'Henry Lee': a version with a different melody, a plodding, dull strum for its guitar accompaniment and a voice of now-touching naïveté.[132] The song itself is summarised in Harry Smith's unmistakable, endearing style as 'SCORNING OFFER OF COSTLY TRAPPINGS, BIRD REFUSES AID TO KNIGHT THROWN IN WELL BY LADY'. This is, to say the least, an unusual twist on the customary narrative, and suggests a reading of the song that is eccentric even by Harry Smith's standards. Why would he think it is the dead 'Lovin' Henry Lee' who requests the bird's help (or then threatens to shoot it from a hundred feet down in the well), especially since the bird's response is the standard one, that

> *A girl would murder her own true love*
> *Would kill a little bird like me?*

Despite the yokel charm of the vocal, and touches such as 'the girl I have in that merry green land', this is in essence an urban version, bringing into the action 'you ladies in the town' and with phrasing delightfully more redolent of the cruel .44 than the ladylike weapon cited:

> *With the little penknife held in her hand*
> *She plugged him through and through.*

The singer's vocal gaucherie also belies his hard life. Born in 1906, he lived in West Virginia, worked down the coal mines and was a neighbour of . . . Frank Hutchison, with whom he sometimes played. Like Hutchison, he was influenced by black as well as white musicians (in person and on records) and his ten recordings mix ballads and the blues. Bob Dylan may not use Dick Justice's version but in this wide, important sense, he follows his example.

Other recordings include Peggy Seeger's 'Henry Lee' (probably learnt from the Dick Justice version); the unlistenable, tuneless, inauthentic and lute-playing collector John Jacob Niles' 'Lady Margot and Love Henry'; 'Lowe Bonnie' by Jimmie Tarlton and even a 'Henry Lee' by P. J. Harvey, Nick Cave & The Bad Seeds. I know none of these, but the Jimmie Tarlton one is bound to be terrific, and its text and melody is the final, 43rd version included in Bronson's *The Traditional Tunes of the Child Ballads, Vol. 2* – from which I know that it starts with 'a hunting young man', that he is offered 'white chocolate tea' but declines, saying endearingly (and rather like the White Rabbit) 'But I haven't got a moment to spare', and that the song includes doctors but avoids parrots: a very different lyric from Dylan's.

Dylan will have heard more than one of these. I'm sorry that I have heard June Tabor's version and Hedy West's (in each case the untitled Bronson Variant 22), both of which treat the song as a maypole-tripping throwaway to be pranced through unthinkingly, which I find as hard to understand as I do those people who dropped

132. Dick Justice: 'Henry Lee', Chicago, 20/5/29. Harry Smith's "American Folk Music" (see note 6).

acid at the drop of a hat, as if it were a cheap thrill, instead of treating it with respect and allowing its mystical depths to work on them.[133]

Dylan implies in his liner-notes that he takes his version from performances or a recording he remembers by Tom Paley, who is never careless in such matters. Dylan implies as much with the opening sentence of his liner-note: 'LOVE HENRY is a "traditionalist" ballad. Tom Paley used to do it.' Not, that is, a traditional so much as a traditionalist ballad: one of those taken up by the traditionalist faction in the Great Folk Revival Wars of the 1950s and early 1960s. 'Folk music was a strict and rigid establishment', Dylan says in the "Biograph" interview. 'If you sang Southern Mountain Blues, you didn't sing Southern Mountain Ballads and you didn't sing city blues. If you sang Texas cowboy songs, you didn't play English ballads . . . You just didn't. If you sang folksongs from the thirties, you didn't do bluegrass tunes or Appalachian ballads. It was very strict. Everybody had their particular thing that they did.'

This gives the atmosphere but rather exaggerates the divisions. Apart from anything else, the songs cannot be divided that rigidly, since the same ones crop up inside different genres, as Sharp and Karpeles' very title *English Folk-Songs from the Southern Appalachians* confirms. In the case of Tom Paley, while Dylan says that it is Paley from whom he took the traditional British ballad 'Love Henry' and the American broadside ballad 'Jack-A-Roe', Paley himself took 'Love Henry' from the book (mentioned earlier) of folksongs field-recorded in Alabama, recorded it at the English home of Ewan MacColl and Peggy Seeger, and is also an enthusiast for a music far more akin to the world of Frank Hutchison and pre-bluegrass. What Karl Dallas calls 'the first and . . . most sensational folk-based pop music of the electric age, the American "hillbilly" string bands of the twenties whose records sold by the million', is, he says, regarded 'with peculiar reverence by American revivalists like Mike Seeger and Tom Paley', though he adds that they 'appear to treat it as a kind of musical fossil rather than as a fertile and creative source'.[134]

Be that last as it may, it was no surprise that alongside the city bluegrass groups of the folk revival period, the New Lost City Ramblers trio (Paley, Mike Seeger and John Cohen) revived the pre-bluegrass music of the 1920s and 1930s. Robert Shelton notes that 'this proselytizing work . . . helped the rural musicians to come to the fore,

133. Peggy Seeger: 'Henry Lee', *nia*, Prestige Records PRS 13005, *nia*. John Jacob Niles: 'Lady Margot and Love Henry', *nia*, Tradition Records TRD 1046, *nia*. Darby and Tarlton [but this track is only Jimmie Tarlton]: 'Lowe Bonnie', Atlanta, 3/12/30; Folksong Society of Minnesota LP KB3796, Minneapolis/St Paul, 1960 [very rare: but Bob Dylan was in the right place at the right time to hear it]; first widely circulated on "Darby and Tarlton", Old Timey Records OT112, El Cerrito, California, 1970s; CD-reissued "On The Banks Of The Lonely River", County Records CTY 3503, Floyd, Virginia, 1994. P. J. Harvey, Nick Cave & The Bad Seeds: 'Henry Lee', *nia*, REP 46195. June Tabor: 'Love Henry' [demo], UK, March 1990, "Circle Dance", Hokey Pokey cassette, London, 1990. Hedy West: 'Love Henry' *nia*, "Ballads", *nia*, 1967.

134. Bob Dylan's liner-notes refer to Tom Paley but do not specify (as they do re Frank Hutchison and Doc Watson) that he is referring to *recordings*. Nevertheless there are Paley recordings of both songs. Tom Paley: 'Love Henry', Beckenham, Kent, 1964; "Peggy Seeger & Tom Paley: Who's Gonna Shoe Your Pretty Little Feet?", Topic Records 12T113, London, 1964. Tom Paley: 'Jack-A-Roe', NYC, 1952; "Folk Songs From The Southern Appalachian Mountains Sung By Tom Paley" [10-inch LP], Elektra Records EKL12, New York, 1953.

The information that Paley himself took 'Love Henry' from Byron Arnold's *Folksongs of Alabama*, 1950, and that he recorded it at the home of Ewan MacColl and Peggy Seeger, is from Paley [London, phone-conversation with the present writer, 22/4/99].

Karl Dallas: 'The Roots of Tradition' in *The Electric Muse* (see note 20).

while the city trio slid to the back of the stage'. This selfless form of activity, Shelton feels, 'is one of the little-known aspects of the folk revival that, in its strange irony, gave the whole interchange between city and country a glow of beauty, ethics and honour'.[135]

Despite the rigidities and internal squabblings, however, Bob Dylan all along recognised the power of traditional song itself. He has said so many times, and this book has quoted him on the subject more than once. In the same interview as his description of the great divides between one group of folk revival performers and another, he reasserts warmly the thrall in which he stands to traditional music: 'The thing about rock'n'roll is that for me anyway it wasn't enough . . . I knew that when I got into folk music it was more of a serious type of thing. The songs are filled with more despair, more sadness, more triumph, more faith in the supernatural, much deeper feelings.'

Extraordinarily, this was said the same year Dylan was creating "Empire Burlesque". But you could hardly look for a more exact summary of his approach to, and his valuing of, a song like the version he chooses of 'Love Henry'. It explains the seriousness he brings to it.

The wonder is that Paley took it from the book of Alabama folksongs mentioned earlier, and its compiler, Byron Arnold, field-recorded it from a woman in a tiny town in Alabama in 1945 who says that she arrived at her version of the text when she was young. What a brilliant poetic instinct she must have had, this unschooled [?] teenager [?]. As we've established, there are many looser, sloppier versions that have far less power and deep resonance, and many versions that have no special faults but no particular distinction or impact either. While we pay tribute to the middle-aged Bob Dylan for his intelligence of judgement in picking out a version of the ballad that compresses it into so rich and taut a form, we might also pause to admire the intelligence of judgement and the poetic maturity of Lena Hill of Lexington, Alabama, who told her field-recording collector that she had 'written' her version of the text 'when a girl'.[136]

Nigel Hinton summarises the effect of hearing Bob Dylan's great recording of it like this:

> Lyrically, 'Love Henry' is the most wonderful, I think. What a story of misplaced hope that riches will buy happiness. The poor girl can win neither her lover nor a mere parrot with her promises of riches – only killing them will get what she desires: killing for company and then killing for silence. Then the terrified regret after the deed, when she begs her victim 'Get well, get well' (four times). It *is* also her heart's blood that is being spilled. And the ghastly detail, like close-ups, of the flowing blood, yellow hair, feet, and the *plunge* (so visual and

135. Robert Shelton: 'Something happened in America' in Laing *et al.*
  Within the group itself, there developed a less roseate glow. Paley, a stickler for detail, didn't like starting a number until his guitar was precisely tuned. It came to be said that the group broke up because the others got tired of waiting. Paley now lives in London and has done for very many years. His son, Ben Paley Gould, is a folk-circuit performer.
136. The direct quotation here is from Bronson (see note 125), not Ms Hill. It is taken from the comments attached to Bronson's Variant 19, stating that this version is from Byron Arnold's *Folksongs of Alabama*.

onomatopoeic) into the cold, deep water that has splashed her or touched her hand (that's why she remarks its coldness) as the body sinks (that's why she remarks its depth). And then the horrified visualisation of that once warm and desired flesh rotting off the bones. It is so shudderingly real that it tips her over into a dreadful, and psychologically true, paranoid madness. The parrot! Oh my God! the parrot saw it all and will tell all, and so she goes back to the hopeless promises – as if a parrot would want any of these worthless riches anyway. She's judging others, even a parrot, by her own terms, so lost is she in the toils of the material world gone wrong. And the smiling cunning: *pretty* parrot, she pleads. And then the final craziness: she thinks the parrot replies – and oh, what a terrible reply, with its awful reminder of the conversation with her lover: he wouldn't get down and now the parrot 'won't fly down'. And in her brain the parrot tells the truth that she hoped he wouldn't know – she has murdered (oh God! he does know!) and he's seen through her subterfuge and he'll be there as a perpetual threat. Crime and Punishment. Dostoevsky eat your heart out, it's been done in thirty-six lines.[137]

Dylan treats the song accordingly. He begins with a guitar part that doesn't announce at once whether this is going to be a black song or a white: it doesn't trailer 'ballad', 'blues' or anything in the nature of a recognisable genre. It just pulls you into its musical well. Then the vocal comes in, more muttered than sung and yet most beautifully sung: a sustained and concentrated whole, nuzzlingly intimate, smouldering yet fastidious. And without anything so obtrusive as a vocal mannerism, he gives us the best breathing and dyings-away of any Bob Dylan vocal for many years, soaked in regret and consternation, mortal fear and supernatural dread. The unexpected extra two musical notes he adds at the end of the word 'deep', to make it 'dee-ee-eep', is done not only long after you assume that the first note and syllable will continue its long dying-out, but is effected with the most understated discretion you will ever hear: at lightyears' remove from easy pop cliché; the slightest possible pause on 'mourn' is likewise an irreproachable gesture, so subtly done as to be barely discernible, such that what we're offered is a performance that demands, and amply rewards, the closest possible attention.

This is itself the optimum matching of subject matter to approach: Dylan inhabits the character of the murderous heroine so well that it's as if her secret pathology, her suppressed jealousies and seething, quiet derangement have been kept so tightly clutched in her heart that the listener must put an ear close to the singer's chest to hear at all the rangey, fitful ebb and flow of an infantile anger, dark despair and spectral desperation.

The album closes with a song of matching spectral calm, and with another performance that aptly requires you to bend and put your ear close to in order to hear: 'Lone Pilgrim'. Dylan writes in his liner-notes that it 'is from an old Doc Watson record'. But long before Doc Watson recorded it, 'The Lone Pilgrim' was a piece of core repertoire of the always-unaccompanied and now-legendary Aunt Mollie Jackson. In 1939 a Jackson performance of this song was field-recorded by

137. Nigel Hinton (Mardens Hill, East Sussex, 2/12/93): letter to the author; used by permission.

the indefatigable Alan Lomax for the Library of Congress (and issued twenty-two years later).[138]

Aunt Mollie Jackson begins her performance by remarking that the song was always a favourite of her grandfather's as well as of her own. It might be assumed that, as with 'St. James Hospital', Doc Watson has been fed this repertoire directly by Alan Lomax, except that the sleeve notes to his record say that it was his father's favourite hymn. In any case, the lyric Doc Watson sings, and that Bob Dylan uses word for word, is both more poetic than Aunt Mollie Jackson's and at moments dangerously close to being more 'poetic' instead, and it has four lines that simply aren't there in the version Aunt Mollie Jackson performed for Lomax.

Jackson's version veers between creditable straightforwardness and the dully prosaic; the Watson/Dylan version just manages to avoid the faults of leaning the other way. This is surely a very old song either tampered with, or more likely written, by one of those nineteenth-century men of the church who so much enjoyed re-writing folksongs by a process of empurplement. When this is done to a very good, robust old ballad, as happened to so many of the songs of nineteenth-century Ireland, the new version gets put into print, played in the drawing-room for a few faddish years, and is soon dropped as dated, mannered and artificial. If we're lucky, the people who can't read go on singing the older, unempurpled version and it survives down the generations, oblivious to drawing-room tastes that come and go. But when a song that isn't so good in the first place gets set upon by a Victorian man of letters or hobbyist-poet of above-average instinct, or originates with such a person, it may be that versions of differing degrees of gentrification can co-exist more equably. 'The Lone Pilgrim' is surely such a song, and the gentleman in question may have been a John Ellis, a William Walker or a B. F. White.

White, a nineteenth-century folksong collector, singer and teacher from Georgia still given a composer credit on the Doc Watson and Bob Dylan albums, is first credited with its authorship in the 1911 edition of an anthology he had edited and first published back in 1844; but the song had not been included in the 1844 edition, and first saw publication three years after this, in the second edition of another anthology, *Southern Harmony and Musical Companion*, a collection of hymns edited by White's brother-in-law, William Walker. This had first been published in 1835, which seems slightly to pre-date the song's composition; it makes its first appearance in print in the edition of 1847, with Walker crediting the song to himself.[139]

138. Doc Watson: 'Lone Pilgrim', *nia*; "The Doc Watson Family", Folkways Records FA2366, New York, 1963. Aunt Mollie Jackson: 'The Lone Pilgrim', *nia*, 1939; "Aunt Mollie Jackson: Library of Congress Recordings Vol. 7, no. 4", Rounder Records 1002, Somerville, Massachusetts, 1961.

139. Watson and Dylan both attribute 'The Lone Pilgrim' to B. F. White and J. M. Pace; but Pace's is in fact only an arranger's credit, and B. F. White is claimed to be the sole composer. However, as the main text now suggests, the song has other origins.
    B. F. White's anthology *The Sacred Harp* (1844); song first credited to him in the 1911 edition. William Walker's anthology *Southern Harmony and Musical Companion* (1835; 2nd edn, 1847) gave first publication to the song. A reprint of the 1854 3rd edn was published in Los Angeles c. 1966.
    I am grateful to Gavin Selerie's article 'Tricks and Training: Some Dylan Sources and Analogues – Part 2' (see note 60), for almost all this information. Selerie writes that *Southern Harmony* sold 600,000 copies 'in the Southern states between 1835 and the Civil War'. William Walker was a popular figure, known as Singin' Billy.

The song's origins are older than this. Gavin Selerie suggests that aside from 'Jack-A-Roe' and 'Love Henry', 'Lone Pilgrim' is the oldest song on the album. He notes that the tune used for 'The Lone Pilgrim' has been identified as that of the Scottish melody 'The Braes O' Balquhidder', which may itself duplicate a still older tune, the Gaelic 'Brochun Buirn'. He notes too that the folklorist D. K. Wilgus argues that 'The Lone Pilgrim' is a variant of 'The White Pilgrim', whose text was written in 1838 by John Ellis, a preacher, after visiting the New Jersey grave of an evangelist, Joseph Thomas, who had been converted to the preaching life by meeting a 'believing jew' who wandered moneyless, dressed in a long robe and preaching. Thomas began to do the same in 1815, travelling throughout the East and South on foot, dressed in white. Ellis visited his grave when it was 'fresh made' and wrote 'The White Pilgrim' afterwards.[140]

John Ellis' text seems to have been revised by William Walker, making it, argues Selerie, 'more universal in reference and richer in imagery'. Did B. F. White then revise it again? Whoever fashioned which verses, all three of these men were of exactly the kind I described earlier: teacherly amateur collectors of a religious bent and with literary aspirations.

The pen that has replaced the pinched and desiccated 'came to the spot' (Aunt Mollie Jackson) with the rich nebulousness of 'came to the place' (Watson/Dylan) has done the song a favour in its very opening line, banishing the inevitability of things earthbound, and coming out at once in recognition of ethereal, weirder dimensions. It readies us for the delight, in the third line, of 'I heard something say' – not 'someone' but the occult 'something' – and so deepens our own receptivity as listeners to hearing from the realm of the dead: a prevalent possibility in the most moving kinds of folk ballad (in songs like 'Love Henry', in fact).

Similarly, Aunt Mollie Jackson's final line – 'Has quietly conducted me home' – has been improved in the Watson/Dylan version by the change to 'kindly assisted me home'. The former makes God sound like a tight-lipped male nurse, escorting you back to the ward whether you like it or not: certainly a process requiring no uplift or desire by the soul concerned. Changed to 'kindly assisted' instead, it evokes the narrator's own ardour and effort, while at the same time, paradoxically, it makes the Master's hand much more akin to the human, with its hint of a journey in which one old soul leans upon the other and they make their slow way together.

---

140. Again I summarise information from Gavin Selerie, but he writes that these details come (a) re the tune from G. P. Jackson (ed.): *Spiritual Folk Songs of Early America* (1953), and (b) re the texts from D. K. Wilgus: ' "The White Pilgrim": Song, legend and fact', *Southern Folklore Quarterly*, Vol. 14, no. 3, 1950. Selerie adds: 'Wilgus's argument is repeated, in abbreviated form, in his notes to the original Doc Watson Family album (Folkways FA2366). Here we are told that Doc's father learned 'The Lone Pilgrim' from William Walker's 'Christian Harmony' (1866 et seq.). But this text was, presumably, derived from 'Southern Harmony' (1854).'
  Selerie also notes (though his details are incorrect) that Buell Kazee recorded a version of 'The White Pilgrim', Kentucky, c. 1956; "Buell Kazee Sings & Plays", Folkways Records FS3810, New York, 1958. Kazee (1900–1976) had an extraordinary recording career, even by the standards of the re-discovered. He cut 58 tracks in 1927–29, and then the album for Folkways thirty years later. This was recorded at his home and he said later that he hadn't known it would be issued and wasn't happy. Hence it was a long time once more before he returned to recording, for the final [and in the event posthumous] album "Buell Kazee", various places and dates of recording but mostly Seattle, 1969; June Appal Records 009, Whitesburg, Kentucky, 1978. His 1928 recordings of 'The Butcher's Boy' and 'The Wagoner's Lad' are on the Harry Smith anthology. Bob Dylan's performances of these songs are detailed elsewhere in the present volume.

The lines immediately before this last are also less effective in the Jackson version. Her

> *The same hand that brought me*
> *Through all dangers and fears*

is replaced in Watson/Dylan by

> *The same hand that led me*
> *Through scenes most severe.*

Again 'brought me' is less participatory, more automated, than 'led me' – the one has no resonance of any kind, the other suggests being taken child-like by the hand: it's more humane and gives the imagination something to see; and although both 'dangers and fears' and 'scenes most severe' avoid specifics, the former has a hint of sermonly rhetoric about it that the latter avoids. That word 'scenes', suggesting distance, gives an apt hint of the inviolability the speaker believes that God-given protection affords, while the phrase taken as a whole is simply the less tired of the two.

One tiny change seems preferable on Aunt Mollie's version. Her pilgrim's body asks that the narrator tell her 'companions' and children not to weep; Dylan sings 'companion', which achieves a jarring dislocation of period, making it sound a present-day politically correct term like 'significant other' or 'partner' when you are avoiding 'wife'.

Aunt Mollie Jackson's version omits a verse that Watson uses, and therefore that Dylan uses too, that is actually a compression of *two* verses from the song as published in the 1950s in G. P. Jackson's [no relation] *Spiritual Folk Songs of Early America*. These two are:

> *The cause of my master compelled me from home,*
> *I bade my companions farewell;*
> *I blessed my dear children who now for me mourn, –*
> *In far distant regions they dwell.*
>
> *I wandered an exile and stranger from home*
> *No kindred or relative nigh;*
> *I met the contagion and sank to the tomb,*
> *My soul flew to mansions on high.*[141]

The compression that drops all but the first line from the first of these verses and the first line from the second seems entirely meet. It clears away a good deal of the empurplement that always lurks behind the drawing-room curtains of such songs. The only line that Dylan might have been tempted to retain, had he known of its availability, is that 'I wandered an exile and stranger from home' – a sentiment he so often expresses in his own songs, takes up in songs by others and appreciates for its biblical import.

---

141. G. P. Jackson, quoted in Selerie.

All three recordings also avoid the glutinous gilding of the religious lily offered by the extra final verse offered in G. P. Jackson's published text:

And there is a crown that doth glitter and shine,
That I shall for evermore wear;
Then turn to the Savior, his love's all divine,
All you that would dwell with me there.

Again, well worth avoiding. (In any case, I'm not sure how many people's notion of heaven would involve dwelling with Aunt Mollie Jackson, especially with a crown forever on her head.)

That Jackson sings none of these verses gives her version, for all its lyric inferiority to Watson's, a stripped-down quality, a narrative reticence, that matches her unaccompanied, uncompromising and inelegant delivery. As Gavin Selerie comments, 'her stark delivery, slow and stretched out, gives us a sense of a fiercely independent and unbroken tradition. Whatever consolation is offered through the words, there remains a fidelity to the tough circumstances of life.'

Bob Dylan's interest is more in the question of fidelity to self. He is uncharacteristically straightforward in writing of the song's appeal: 'what attracts me to the song is how the lunacy of trying to fool the self is set aside at some given point. salvation & the needs of mankind are prominent & hegemony takes a breathing spell. "my soul flew to mansions on high".'

This re-states a core position Dylan has long, probably always, held. He expressed it on an earlier occasion like this: 'if you try to be anyone but yourself, you will fail',[142] just as in 'The Groom's Still Waiting At The Altar' he sings of 'the madness of becoming what one was never meant to be'.

Among other things, these two albums are an investigation on Dylan's part as to how far he can remain true to, as it were, this folksong part of himself. The result of the investigation is that while he finds that his heart is still in the right place, and we find that the sheer fact that these records exist is itself an affirmation that not everything in the world has gone wrong, there is no shaking off the sad truth that for all his assertions that in youth he couldn't conduct himself fittingly like the old blues singers, and for all that he has claimed not to 'copy guys under fifty', his instincts for the felicitous handling of his material have been, if anything, dulled by the years, not sharpened, and his voice has deteriorated immensely in range and capability. Worse, his desire to communicate has fallen away so much. Age has made him less open, less direct, more introspective.

Set against this is a depth of real experience, and the invaluable asset of its authenticity in place of its inspired impersonation. However superbly he pretended in his early work to possess the experience of age, it was a pretence, and his youthfulness showed through – glowed through, indeed, giving some of these recordings incandescent impact and an untramelled creative felicity in drawing upon the same rich repertoire on his very first albums and out-takes as for "Good As I Been To You" and

---

142. Bob Dylan, interviewed by Ron Rosenbaum, Burbank, Nov. 1977, published in 'The *Playboy* interview', *Playboy*, March 1978: 'if you try to be anyone but yourself, you will fail; if you are not true to your own heart, you will fail.'

"World Gone Wrong". Play his début album's extraordinary version of Blind Lemon Jefferson's 'See That My Grave Is Kept Clean', or his muscular, contemplative, wistful 'Man Of Constant Sorrow', and you think anew how tremendous, how undimmed they are – so much so that you feel sure the 1990s material cannot stand up against it. Then play 'World Gone Wrong' and it does. The authentic patina of age has a reliable textural value, a rub and a complete credibility that the youthful imitation lacks, for all its energy, commitment and charm. Part of that charm lies in our hearing the sweetness of the *ingénue* trying so hard – so youthfully hard – to sound so old. And though it's cute, there's an unavoidable callowness within it that cannot but pale when set against the older Bob Dylan's authoritativeness.

Mostly. Not quite always, though. He may still wipe the floor with most performers, and the collective and cumulative richness of these two 1990s albums is a marvellous thing – but his tragedy is that he cannot compete against himself and win when you place the best of then against the best of now. Experience alone cannot triumph over imaginative truth. There are times when the young Dylan's burning desire to communicate propels him through performances where every syllable of sound he makes is perfectly judged, unfalteringly right and sears its way through to you, such that it's impossible to take your ears off him for a moment. He is combining intuitive excellence of execution with an intimacy of feeling that embraces shared hope, the optimisim of a world still young. In the world gone wrong, world-weariness and withdrawal, sheer lack of urgency in the act of communicating cannot hold up so well. This is why even such wonderful recorded performances as 'Hard Times', 'Diamond Joe', 'Love Henry' and 'Ragged & Dirty' cannot better the fully realised genius, the exquisite, gritty grace of that transcendent masterpiece 'Moonshiner', recorded in 1963, when Bob Dylan was 22 years old, or 'No More Auction Block', the traditional slavery (or anti-slavery) song, recorded in 1962, when the still younger Bob Dylan's moral imagination and sympathy were such that he attains a fiery scrupulousness that never tries cheap rhetorical delivery and never lapses from its concentrated, yearning calm.[143] I wish it wasn't the case that these early performances transcend the later ones, to which he brings decades of real experience. But it is.

---

143. 'Moonshiner', NYC, 12/8/63, and 'No More Auction Block', NYC, late 1962, were both issued on the 1991 "Bootleg Series I–III".

The latter song was, in the folk revival and civil rights movement period, associated with the black group the Freedom Singers, who sang it during a march on Washington, and with whom Dylan was rubbing shoulders. There's a well-known photo of Bob Dylan with the Freedom Singers and others linking arms on stage together at the end of the Newport Folk Festival of 1963.

[The Freedom Singers: 'Fighting For My Rights', 'Get On Board, Little Children' and 'I Love Your Dog, I Love My Dog' (all 27–28/7/63), plus Bob Dylan and Joan Baez: 'With God On Our Side' (28/7/63) and Bob Dylan and Pete Seeger: 'Ye Playboys And Playgirls' (27/7/63); all "Newport Broadside – Topical Songs", Vanguard Records VRS-9144 (mono) and VSD-79144, New York, 1964, and Fontana Records TFL6038, London, 1965. The Freedom Singers: 'Woke Up This Morning' and 'We Shall Overcome' plus Bob Dylan: 'Blowin' In The Wind', all 26/7/63; all "Evening Concerts At Newport Vol. 1 [1963]", Vanguard Records VRS-9148 (mono) and VSD-79148, New York, 1964, and Fontana Records TFL6041, London, 1965.]

A founder member of the Freedom Singers was Bernice Johnson Reagon, to whom Dylan originally addressed 'To Ramona'. She acquired her cracked country lips growing up in Albany, Georgia. In 1974, with the shortened name Bernice Reagon, she was one of those who formed the feminism-and-gospel group Sweet Honey In The Rock, and in this capacity is reunited with Bob Dylan on adjacent tracks on the 1987 Woody Guthrie–Leadbelly tribute album "Folkways: A Vision Shared".

[Sweet Honey In The Rock: 'Sylvie' and 'Gray Goose', nia, and Bob Dylan: 'Pretty Boy Floyd', LA, probably April, 1987; all "Folkways: A Vision Shared", Columbia Records OC 44034, New York (CBS Records 460905,

When we consider the way the songs on these two 1990s albums have themselves been used by the younger Dylan in his own songs – not in the large, undissectable, general way but for recognisable and particular nuts and bolts – nothing leaps out and shouts its debt, but several things on each album do make themselves known. Of course, such nuts and bolts may be common to many songs, traditional and contemporary. However, if you notice resemblances, they surely exist.

On "Good As I Been To You", the melody of 'Jim Jones' – which is said to be that of the song 'Irish Molly-O' – reminds me in a general way of the melody of 'If You See Her Say Hello', while a specific part of the melody of 'Arthur McBride' is to be found in 'Ballad In Plain D'. The tune of each verse's third line is the same in each song – so that 'Arthur McBride's 'Now mark what followed and what did betide' can be overlaid, syllable for syllable and note for note, by the 'Ballad In Plain D' line 'Noticing not that I'd already slipped' – while the next line, the fourth line of each four-line verse, would also be the same in both songs except that in 'Arthur McBride' the line in question alternates verse by verse between ending on the resolved tonic, as 'Ballad In Plain D' always does, and ending on a half-resolve, to hang over, awaiting the start of the next. The upshot is that half of every second verse of 'McBride' – and the melody-line of the guitar intro too – has the same tune as 'Ballad In Plain D'. Thus, for example, these 'McBride' lines (comprising the second half of verse two) –

> *And a little wee drummer intending to camp*
> *For the day being pleasant and charming –*

can be replaced, so far as the tune is concerned, by these, the second half of 'Plain D''s verse:

> *At the peak of the night, the king and the queen*
> *Tumbled all down into pieces.*

It was Paul Brady who introduced the half-resolves on alternate verses. That Dylan follows him in doing so is one of the things that establishes how closely Dylan's version is modelled upon Brady's. If it were not for this, then the second half of *every* verse of 'McBride' would parallel those of 'Ballad In Plain D'.

In 'Blackjack Davey', 'Saddle me up my coal-black stud' is the underlay to Dylan's 'Saddle me up a big white goose' in his 1969 'Country Pie', while the resemblances between 'Blackjack Davey' and/or 'Gypsy Davey' and Dylan's 'Boots Of Spanish Leather' have already been propounded. Parts of 'Sittin' On Top Of The World' sound like the 'somebody got lucky but it was an accident' bits of Dylan's own great blues song 'Pledging My Time' (though as noted in Chapter 9, these are also common to, and as likely come from, Skip James or Robert Johnson as from the Mississippi Sheiks). Dylan's 'Buckets of rain, buckets of tears / Got all them buckets comin' out of my ears' echoes, rhymes with and suggests he's heard plenty of 'Frankie & Albert''s 'bucket of beer', while the hanging of the woman at the end of the song is used at the end of another "Blood On The Tracks" song, 'Lily, Rosemary And The Jack Of

---

London) 1988.]

C. H. Nichols' study of slavery in America is called *Many Thousand Gone* (1963), in reference to the song 'No More Auction Block', and the second chapter (titled 'Auction Block') describes the routines and humiliations, and offers the statistics, involved in the slave auctions in the southern cities of the USA.

Hearts', which of course also features Diamond Jim, as opposed to 'Diamond Joe'. In 'Little Maggie' the repetitive staccato niggle of melody and even the opening rhetorical lyric phrase in the line 'How can, I ev, er stand it?' throws me back to Dylan's own 'How can, how can, you ask me again?' in 'Boots Of Spanish Leather'. The phrase 'life's pleasures' cannot appear in many popular songs, especially when suggesting that such pleasures are few; but the phrase does occur, and in such a context, in both 'Hard Times' and in Bob Dylan's "Nashville Skyline" song 'To Be Alone With You'. 'Step It Up & Go' features the bizarre, sudden appearance of 'the chief of police', to be reprised by Dylan in 'Man Of Peace'; perhaps it also has a bit of lyric and bare-bones tune that prefigure 'Silvio'.

In the phrases we hear on "World Gone Wrong" also, there are fragments we have heard in Bob Dylan songs, or phrases that Dylan can be said to have re-written. In the title song of the collection, the line 'Just tell her kindly, there is a front door' makes me think back to Dylan's 'If You Gotta Go, Go Now', which carries much the same ruthless message wrapped up in much the same exterior politeness. When, in 'Love Henry', we hear of Henry's murderess that after killing him

> *She took him by his long yellow hair*

we recollect two different moments in Dylan songs. There is that moment in 'Angelina' (1981) in which Dylan recollects 'blood dryin' in my yellow hair'; and there is Dylan's home-made ancient ballad 'As I Went Out One Morning' (1968), in which

> *She took me by the arm.*

The contrast between the two is then highlighted by Dylan's liner-note to 'Love Henry', in which he says that 'he mustve had a hearing problem', whereas in 'As I Went Out One Morning'

> *I knew that very instant*
> *She meant to do me harm.*

Casting us back too to 'Simple Twist Of Fate', not only does 'Love Henry' feature 'a parrot that talks' – but it suddenly reveals the double-meaning that has lurked unheeded in that phrase all along, as the ancient ballad describes the killer queen's attempt to coax the parrot down onto her knee in order to stop it talking. And then she hisses at murdered Henry

> *Lie there, lie there, Love Henry . . .*
> *Till the flesh rots off your bones;*

on Dylan's next studio-album, "Time Out Of Mind", his 'Standing In The Doorway' offers

> *Even if the flesh falls off-a my face . . .*

And as noted in an earlier chapter, when we hear Dylan singing Blind Willie McTell's line

> *She can really do the Georgia crawl*

in 'Broke Down Engine Blues', we know that we hear him sing it fourteen years earlier, on the "Slow Train Coming" track 'Gonna Change My Way Of Thinking', on which

> *She can do the Georgia crawl.*

If only these rich, difficult albums crawled, or there were more of them, teeming as they are with the history of North America and her immigrants and exiles from Europe and from Africa. They take their leave too soon. The last track of all, 'Lone Pilgrim', takes its leave too soon too, like the person who speaks from the tomb. But it provides yet another fine farewell from Bob Dylan, who is so very good at farewells at the ends of albums, and who has here provided us with so many pathways back into the ever-present past. As the song's conclusion has it,

> *The same hand that led me through scenes most severe*
> *Has kindly assisted me home.*

CHAPTER NINETEEN

Time Out of Mind

I am perhaps Dylan's worst listener: I'm the guy who expects him to continually be brilliant year after year. None of my peers or betters make this demand. I take it personally when Dylan does shoddy music . . .

David Bowman, novelist[1]

I find it astonishing that the general media world has taken "Time Out Of Mind" to its fickle bosom so fulsomely. The whole public mood of the 1980s and 1990s has been smile-smile-smile, never admit to gloom or despondency, never complain, and if you want to get ahead, be remorselessly *upbeat*! The Tina Turner Syndrome, in fact. In this climate, people were regarded as from the lunatic fringe if they insisted on saying that Bob Dylan was a seminal artist of the times and absolutely invaluable as a bulwark against Shopping Mall culture. Those of 'balanced' views and 'living in the contemporary world' spoke of Dylan with dismissive contempt as 1960s Man, a hopeless old has-been of no relevance whatever and whose talents, it went without saying, had vanished a good twenty years ago.

Then along comes "Time Out Of Mind", the gloomiest, most desolate, least Tina-Turner-Elton-John-Princess-Di-Chris-Evans-David-Letterman record in human history . . . and suddenly it's 'Well of course we've known all along that Bob Dylan was a genius and a Great American Institution who could come back at any time with a work that would snuggle straight into that special place in our hearts we've always kept open for him, and here it is.'

It was a pleasure to see Dylan on the front of *Newsweek* and giving such relaxed, honest and interesting interviews, standing behind this new work with unaccustomed straightforwardness – but I do find it exasperating to be preached at by *The Sunday Times* in 1997 about how important an artist Bob Dylan is, after they've spent the last twenty years deriding him and anyone who had kept faith with him.[2]

---

1.   David Bowman, reviewing "Time Out Of Mind", *Salon* online magazine, 19/9/97. Bowman's novels include *Modern Bunny* (1998).

2.   *Newsweek*, 6/10/97; cover photo by Richard Avedon (whose photos Greil Marcus once called 'the curse of rock'), making Dylan look like a hairy Leonard Cohen; plus interview by David Gates. The same issue also contained an interview with James Meredith, the first black student at the University of Mississippi, whose riot-causing enrolment in 1962 was the subject of Dylan's early song 'Oxford Town'; thirty-five years on he was

It was especially exasperating when the album was new and I didn't like most of it much at all, though the large amount of writing on the album was appreciated, and several songs seemed compelling at the outset: 'Standing In The Doorway', 'Tryin' To Get To Heaven', 'Highlands' and maybe 'Not Dark Yet'.

After five hearings I was still at that thrilling stage with a new album where you don't yet know which songs contain which bits – lines and phrases I liked straight away still came around again in unexpected places. They were all damn gloomy songs, though, and on a bright morning, the sun streaming in, with Dylan dishing out the way-past-midnight, weary-as-hell doom-merchandise, it seemed an odd business, sitting there grinning, enjoying the adventure of being led through this fresh Dylan landscape when what he was singing about was how barren everything is.

What made me deeply uneasy was that only here and there did Dylan seem authentic about this woe-is-me stuff. Mostly it seemed a posture, designed to claim a spurious gravitas. Too many lines boasted cheap defeatedness instead of evoking felt defeat. There was far too much of this sort of thing: 'Same old rat-race, life in the same old cage'. 'Well I'm tired of talkin' / I'm tired of tryin' to explain'. 'Sometimes my burden is more than I can bear.' 'The air burns / And I'm tryin' to think straight / And I don't know / How much longer I can wait'. 'Well I'm strollin' through the lonely graveyard of my mind.'

(Oh please – not another something-of-our-minds. The "Empire Burlesque" 'wasteland of your mind' is specious enough. Even back on 'Mr. Tambourine Man', it was the 'smoke-rings of my mind' that brought that magnificent song momentarily close to hippie risibility.)

Same old what? What sharp, alert phrase did the pre-eminent wordsmith find, and find truthful? 'Rat-race.' What ellipses of poetry were achieved, what tight, right phrases defined this much-declaimed sense of oppression?

> I feel like the whole world
> Got me pinned up against the fence.

These are not lines it is possible to admire: nothing pared down, nothing acute, nothing agile, nothing brave or raw. Nor is it honestly minimalist: it's too flabby for that. In instances like this, what he takes to be, or expects us to receive as, the glamorous honesty of declaring his soul's disenchantment and sickness seems mostly the grizzly, grisly pretence of someone who reckons he can probably get away with a hollow substitute for legitimate work. Lines like these suggest a Bob Dylan ducking out of being the serious artist while cynically pretending that his cynicism is profound.

Portentous self-aggrandisement seemed evident across much of "Time Out Of Mind", as lines claiming false gravitas wedged themselves between slices of self-imitation and cliché – though one of the crucial distinctions to be made (and this was obvious at once) was that not every familiar line was dismissable as self-imitation nor every old phrase as cliché. The first great graspable achievement of the album was the wit and intelligence and deft control, and the life-affirming fondness too, with which

---

working for the right-wing Republican Senator Jesse Helms and was a Fellow at the Leadership Institute, Washington, DC.

    Brian Appleyard, a regular contributor, *Sunday Times*, 28/9/97: 'Bob Dylan is one of the very greatest artists of our era, one of a handful of defining geniuses of the 20th century . . .'

Dylan wove into his songs whole lines and phrases from song, especially from folksong and the blues: more straightforwardly and purposively than ever before. Similarly, in one or two places echoes and half-repeats of earlier lines of his own were clearly used with dexterity to well-judged effect.

These moments were immediately seen to be very different from those more frequent ones where lack of authentic inspiration has had him resort to cheaper forms of prefabrication. At the low-point of the album, on 'Make You Feel My Love', one of these pre-formed chunks is actually used twice, the laziness noticeable not because the words are memorable but because the fit is awkward. You might get away with

> *No there's nothing that I wouldn't do*

once, at the end of a short list of extreme things you *would* do, such as Dylan offers in the song's best stanza (the fourth), where it tops out the disarming

> *I'd go hungry, I'd go black and blue*
> *I'd go crawling down the avenue.*

You might get away with it if the line that, as it were, tops out the topping out were less wretched than 'to make you feel my love' – a phrase that ineptly emphasises the febrile wish to compel, rather than any believable, patient wish to have a depth of passion noticed. But even without this inbuilt, gruesome bathos, you can't get away with *repeating* that 'nothing that I wouldn't do' two stanzas on, where, promoted uncomfortably to being the second line, it sits in the midst of a more enfeebled list of these herculean offers – offers that go through the motions of stating a love minus zero no limit but are doomed to sound a hollow horn:

> *I could make you happy, make your dreams come true*
> *Nothing that I wouldn't do*
> *Go to the ends of the earth for you*
> *To make you feel my love.*

The repetition, in fact, draws attention to itself by the sheer inattentiveness that has produced it. Yet while one minute's thought could have avoided the clumsiness of this enervated duplication and yielded a better line, no line could have saved the lyric at this point from constituting the kind of whole that even a greeting card company would baulk at.

'I could hold you for a million years,' he sings, also on 'Make You Feel My Love', with a straight face and the voice of a reptilian roué. Where have we heard this flaccid rhetoric before? Well, a few tracks earlier, actually, in the tetchy, disgruntled chorus-line 'Well I've tried to get closer but I'm / Still a million miles from you'. Ah, but where have we heard *that* before? We heard it thirty-odd years ago, on 'One Too Many Mornings', when the same theme was rendered creatively, with a wonderfully clear-sighted, calm-centred, complex compassion that conjured up in a few attentive, humane strokes the particularities and atmosphere of real people in real moments and real places: living individuals glimpsed in the living, breathing night, evoked without recourse to formula or filler-lines, sung out along a melody of infinite space with a consummate syllable-by-syllable accuracy, with grace, heart and head in balance, naked truth and art vaulting out of the speakers directly and accessibly to whoever wanted to listen. Nothing could be further downhill from there to the sour artifice of Dylan's pretence at snarling energy, as his bombastic, shrivelled, cheaply theatrical, echo-cranked voice bumps and grinds through the pinched, weary crabbiness of 'Well I've tried to get closer but I'm / Still a million miles from you'.

The melody is the sort of awful, finger-snapping cabaret-jazz that Dylan and the 1978 tour band parody so beautifully on a rehearsal of 'You're A Big Girl Now'. Then, though, the musicians so much enjoy what starts out as a merciless pastiche of the Mel Tormés that their exuberance keeps Dylan bothering, and therefore prolonging the performance from what might have been intended as a sixteen-bar joke into a full rendition. Between the musicians' freedom to contribute and Dylan's openness, it ends by turning into a near-equivalent to Elvis' 'Reconsider Baby': that sort of band, that sort of authenticity. 'Million Miles' is the same sort of musical sludge as the parodic start of that memorable 'You're A Big Girl Now' but takes itself seriously. This is what the *Daily Telegraph* calls the album's 'truly different . . . enthusiastic embrace of the blues'.[3]

As for that repeated chorus-line of lyric, it is enough to note that 'I'm one too many mornings and a thousand miles behind' is a far more effective evocation of distance felt between two people than 'I'm tryin' to get closer but I'm still a million miles from you'. The first makes you feel that distance, and makes you feel that the singer feels it; the second is arid hyperbole. Not only that: the first is trustingly subtle, rightly expecting the listener to pick up the implication of regret; the second over-explains this. The earlier lyric also hints at a judgemental complexity – suggests that the singer may be allocating blame to himself if to anyone; the later suggests only complaint.

Here's another:

> There's too many people
> Too many to recall
> I thought some of 'em were friends of mine
> I was wrong about 'em all.

New work? It seems another bleating about false friends, its repetition of this whining theme handled without expressive credibility, let alone flair. This writing-off is so much easier than real writing. You want Bob Dylan to have things to say, and if a topic he alights upon is among the common preoccupations of people of his own generation, so much the more potentially interesting, perhaps, provided he treats it conscientiously. If he raises the subject of friendship, then, it doesn't have to fulfil a specific attitudinal expectation; nor does it have to be profound. But how prescriptive is it to expect something considered? You listen in vain here for a nod towards the complexity of the ebb and flow of old friendships, the gains and losses we go through as youth's casual intimacies, with all their formative incandescence, give way to warier, more difficult intimacies that we may sometimes weary of, or wish for fresh equivalents of (while knowing their nurture might be too costly), yet that we dread to imperil, so that we tiptoe round old friends' increasingly fixed little habits, and lament

---

3.   Bob Dylan: 'You're A Big Girl Now', Santa Monica, 30/1/78 [unreleased rehearsal tape for 1978 tour]. Clark Collis: 'Old hat, but new rabbits' [review of "Time Out Of Mind"], *Daily Telegraph*, nia, 1997.

that we daren't any longer impose upon them too long at a time, nor they upon us . . . You listen in vain here equally for any contradictory experience to that one. You listen in vain for *any* alternative account of either retrospective or more immediate observation. There's plenty in the realm of friendship for the middle-aged heart and head to engage with, from any angle in the spectrum. Dylan avoids it all, preferring the all-too-easy option of a petulant, infantile 'you're-not-my-friend-anymore'.

Then there is the sheer dispiriting *disappointment* of his automatic, gridlocked concentration on Lurve as subject-matter (though concentration has seemed not much in evidence). In most of these songs this apparently exhausted topic demands our attention without offering one tangible feeling, evocative moment or observant sentence.

Even if you discount the Billy Joel song – and Billy Joel is the perfect exponent for its kind of turgidly formulaic, AOR-radio pop – even if you programme this out, its contemptible phoneyness must seep into the rest of the album's content, calling into question the artistic and personal sincerity of his apparent preoccupation with lost loves and old romances.

All this croaking phlegm about lost love, all this cocooned preoccupation with it, this trying to sound tragic about vanished impossible perfect loves: was there nothing else to engage the intelligent adult's interest, or to be written about? He *promises* something else, in the opening song, summing up the situation with admirable terseness:

> *I'm sick of love*
> *I hear the clock tick*
> *This kind of love –*
> *I'm lovesick*

yet for much of the album 'this kind of love' seems the only topic, and an awareness of time running out does not seem to concentrate its singer's mind on other matters. Far from sounding like the mature work of a major artist in middle age, dealing with the serious questions of life, or even with its small pleasures, all this crying in the doorway, calling out his baby's name, enchained and haunted by the ghost of an old love, all this wondering if you'll be true, sounded more like the posturing of a spoilt celebrity hamming up gravitas, and badly – so out of touch that he doesn't realise how flimsy a sham it is.

The production, for all Daniel Lanois' alchemical skills, sometimes accentuates this sense of a sham. Lanois explained exactly the *intention* behind the distorted vocal sound on the opening track, 'Love Sick': 'We treated the voice almost like a harmonica when you over-drive it through a small guitar amplifier.' That's spot-on: that distinctive-sounding distortion is familiar because it does recreate the harmonica sound on things like the King Biscuit radio shows of the early 1950s. But does it work? If it gives 'Love Sick', and therefore the album's opening moments, a sort of stark drama, it comes very close to contrived starkness and melodrama.

> *I'm walkin'* . . .

announces this sepulchral voice

> *. . . through streets that are dead*

and if Boris Karloff isn't lurking behind a lamp-post, Leonard Cohen surely is.

Nor is this aural theatricality helpful when this frail question hobbles into the frame:

> *Did I*
> *Hear someone's distant cry?*

The accompaniment ought to lend a steadying hand, a bit of solid, unobtrusive support, allowing the lyric to pass on quickly. Instead, an immediate musical 'cry' – a dweepling electronic ooh-ooh, ooh-ooh – comes up behind the singer's querulous wobble towards portentousness and kicks away any hope of it not sounding risible. It's so crass you can hardly believe you're hearing it. Its less processed prototype may sound fine on steel guitar at the beginning and the end of Santo & Johnny's 'classic' 1959 instrumental hit 'Sleep Walk', but in its 'Love Sick' context, it's gruesome.[4]

The sound is elsewhere unhelpful too, isn't it? Some tracks have Dylan so buried in echo that there is no hope whatever of hearing any of the detailing in his voice that was so central and diamond-like a part of his genius. 'Dirt Road Blues', which might under normal production circumstances be a heartening, even dextrous little rockabilly number, puts Dylan so far away and so tiny you just despair. It's as if the microphone was an audio telescope and he's using the wrong end of it. The voice on 'Cold Irons Bound' is so badly down in the mix that without clamping headphones to your ears the lyric comes and goes, recurrently offering indecipherable passages, while the contrived voodoo galumph of the music clatters across the foreground like donkeys on a tepid tin roof. This recording won a Grammy because 'Like A Rolling Stone' never did – and because when 'Cold Irons Bound' came out, Bob had just had a 'worryin' heart, worryin' heart, heart disease', to quote from Son House.

The tracks that aren't so distancing, so blatantly reductive of Dylan as these, are perversely reductive in a different way, bringing his voice forward with a crude excess of echo, as on ''Til I Fell In Love With You' – 'recorded in Lanois' proverbial echo-laden cyber-bunker', as David Bowman puts it – and, yes, 'Million Miles'. A bunker is where you retreat when you're desperate. Is Dylan's voice really so weak and weedy now, so pitiful a husk of its former self (of any of its former selves) that instead of recording it straightforwardly, up close, alertly, as on the very first albums he ever made, now Dylan's implausibly reconstituted voice must puff forward in a swollen simulated intimacy that bloats it up only to rob us of all its real detail, its truly distinctive power? No. It isn't.

I was wrong. Not about the bad lines scattered all through the songs to the detriment of the whole, nor about the irredeemable awfulness of 'Make You Feel My Lurve' in particular, nor about how badly or misguidedly produced the voice is on 'Dirt Road

---

4.   Santo & Johnny: 'Sleep Walk', NYC, 1959; Canadian-American Records 103, Winnipeg and New York, 1959; CD-reissued "The Golden Age Of American Rock'n'Roll Volume 5", Ace Records CDCHD 600, London, 1995. Perhaps the supposedly dream-like plangent echo in which this US No. 1 hit single is saturated is the core inspiration behind the Daniel Lanois sound.

Blues', 'Million Miles', ''Til I Fell In Love With You', 'Cold Irons Bound' and 'Can't Wait', nor in being absolutely clear that four songs stand way above the rest and that they are 'Standing In The Doorway', 'Tryin' To Get To Heaven', 'Not Dark Yet' and 'Highlands'. But I was way wrong about the spirit of the album, its special distinctions and the whole experience of having it. Not for the first time, I missed what wasn't there long before I appreciated what was.

The process of growing to appreciate "Time Out Of Mind" is a weird business – but at the core of it is something deeply familiar to me yet almost forgotten: the long-absent communing with a real Bob Dylan album – the inward thrill, the continuous inner dialogue, the repeated playing, cross-referencing, laughing aloud, floating on the moving sea of it and finding within it a cohesion of sound and purpose, an infinite play of fleeting, indefinable frissons and at the heart of it a Bob Dylan of absolute conviction, with no nervous corner of the eye directed at other people's approbation or taste.

It was different with "Good As I Been To You" and "World Gone Wrong", because Dylan didn't write them, so that however much he 'made the songs his own', as he did, the listener's inner exploration of the songs was necessarily not the same as with Dylan compositions. While not wishing to undervalue those albums, it's surely something different and richer again when you come to an album full of new Dylan writing: an album that coheres, that propels itself by belief in itself and sets you loose inside it as in a maze. "Time Out Of Mind" has that quality, no matter what its weaknesses. And in this respect I understand why people have hailed it as 'the best since "Blood On The Tracks"', much as I deplore the concomitant sweeping aside of albums as fine as "Desire", "Street Legal" and maybe even "Slow Train Coming".

Every real Bob Dylan album brings with it its own rules and its own demands, takes you along its own hallways and raises its own distinctive questions.

The album opens with an immediate challenge. 'I'm walking through streets that are dead', delivered in that sepulchral tone, distortedly recorded, at once shoves itself in your face as something to demur at. Yet what opens up here is fascinating. Is it supposed to be a genre song or raw personal statement? The answer seems to be that it's both. As implied earlier, it called Leonard Cohen to mind at once on first hearing, and if Cohen had done the song he would give it an ironic detachment that would neutralise the dodgy melodrama of that opening. Yet in Dylan's hands, it is clearly the very absence of ironic detachment that gives the track its power. So it works both ways.

It's most interesting that he can make you address this kind of dilemma so much: this has turned out to be one of the album's distinctive strengths. It happens all the way through. Is the narrator of 'Highlands' a persona – Greil Marcus heard it that way, as coming from a persona living in some cruddy apartment building in a dilapidated part of LA who doesn't get out much – or is it, as for instance David Bowman hears it, the song in which we come closer than we've ever come before to walking around the world inside Bob Dylan's head?[5]

---

5. Greil Marcus, *Interview*, July 1997: 'The song . . . is about an older man who lives in one of Ed Kienholz's awful furnished rooms in the rotting downtown of some fading city – Cincinnati, Hollywood, the timeless, all-

Is it persona or raw Bob Dylan? I'm with Bowman on this, though that's not to say that 'raw' means artless. On the contrary, 'Highlands' is a most artfully wrought achievement and of a very high order. But that the songs trigger off these queries and dialogues about the very nature of what sort of songs they are: this is a central richness of the album.

Similarly, the resistance felt, on first hearing the album, at his constant declarations of angst – a resistance that brings out an urge to give him a good shake and tell him to do the washing-up once in a while (feeling that it's little boy lost taking himself *so* seriously) – gives way to an acceptance of this declamatory gloom on its own terms as not only the single most recognisable element of the album but as one of its strengths. An acceptance that we really are on Desolation Row here and that Dylan's expressiveness about desolation is, cumulatively, resourceful and distinctive.

Again, how can he manage, as he does, to take you through some weird initiation from hearing 'Million Miles' as unlistenable Buddy Grecoland – finger-snapping cabaret-jazz of a kind that rock'n'roll was born to abolish if at all possible – to finding it tolerable and then to almost liking it? What quality does it have to make this possible?

Of course it does have one of Dylan's fine opening lines:

> *You took a part of me that I really miss,*

which seems clear, truthful, humane, direct, fresh and universal. Yet its effectiveness is besmirched and deflected at once by the turgid polyfilla quality of the line Dylan puts next –

> *I keep asking myself how long it can go on like this,*

by the horrible echo-primped production on the voice and by the tetchy-old-man quality of the voice itself – though if you want Kingsley Amis Sings Buddy Greco, you couldn't do better than the perfect way that Dylan delivers 'never did intend to do' to conclude the third verse line

> *Did so many things I never did intend to do.*

Similarly, buried in the aural torment of 'Cold Irons Bound', in which the voice floats in its own balloon of echo, sending it away into the obscuring clouds even as it pretends to make it fat and full, is a Dylanism as fine as anything from the people-just-get-uglier era: the hilarious and clever 'Reality as always had too many heads'. Or is it the slightly less alert 'Reality has always had too many heads'?

In fact there is interesting writing, and hints at themes one could wish him to expand on, inside all the songs on the album that I think of as musically unpleasant and unsympathetically produced. In the third verse of 'Million Miles' there is that engaging metaphor for trying to escape from guilt and regret, where he sings of

> *Throwin' all my memories in a ditch so deep –*

American Nowheresville you see in David Lynch's *Blue Velvet* – getting up and going for a walk, maybe for the first time in weeks . . . The song is someone else's dream, but as Dylan sings it, you are dreaming it.'

David Bowman (note 1) writes of hearing 'Bob finally share with us what it's like for Bob Dylan to be Bob Dylan'.

which is never expanded upon and so stands alone, a one-liner metaphor that draws us by its mix of stating so futile a task in so vivid a phrase. That vividness reveals the fervour of his desire to eliminate the past, while the *choice* of metaphor, 'a ditch so deep', draws upon the core psychological metaphors of pushing down, of suppression, of subterranean placement: the very metaphors by which Freud taught the twentieth century that thrusting memories out of sight is not at all the same thing as escaping them – that you cannot push, as it were, bad time out of mind. Dylan's choice of metaphor thus contains within it this sense of his proclaimed task's futility, achieving a neat poetic compression of meaning that would not be achieved were the metaphor different – if, for example, he had chosen to write of 'burnin' up my memories in a fire so fierce'.

Though this desire to escape memories is elaborated by the line that follows – 'Did so many things that I never did intend to do' – the metaphor that expresses it, the 'ditch so deep', stands alone, unexpanded upon. Yet it leaves a residual image of undergroundness, a state of mind that Dylan returns to expressing, though differently, in the next verse. This begins with one of the most lovely uses on the whole album of lines from other songs, in this case a highly resourceful, clever appropriation of imagery:

> I need your love so bad, turn your lamp down low
> I need every bit of it for the places that I go.

Leaving aside that 'I need your love so bad' is itself, despite its inherent anonymity, a phrase we might recognise from its prominence on the record 'Need Your Love So Bad' by Little Willie John and later by Fleetwood Mac, what we have here is that 'turn your lamp down low', an exhortation familiar to us from many an R&B song.[6] What Dylan achieves is to use the phrase unaltered while letting context transform its meaning. Here that love-light must be turned down low *to conserve it*, as Dylan takes it with him, a miner's lamp to light his way through the dark tunnels of 'the places that I go'. Clinched by that unobtrusively intense 'I need *every* bit of it', it takes a phrase from the common corpus of the blues only to revitalise it with the particularity of Dylan's usage. It's a beautiful appropriation.

The blues are also behind him, in spirit, as the sixth verse opens, with what I believe is Dylan's own invented blues-style joke – it is certainly in blues style, anyway:

> Yes the last thing you said before you hit the street
> 'Gonna find me a janitor to sweep me off my feet.'

It's an unexpected light touch in the midst of this dour, despairing song, and the only moment at which we glimpse the 'you' that it addresses. Here, with this departing pun, said over her shoulder as she leaves, we get human dialogue and remembrance:

6.   Little Willie John (aka William Edward John): 'Need Your Love So Bad', NYC, 20/9/55, King Records 4841 (c/w 'Home At Last', same session), Cincinnati, 1955. Fleetwood Mac: 'Need Your Love So Bad', *nia*, Blue Horizon BH57–3179, England, 1968.
    'Turn Your Lamp Down Low' is, for example, the title of a single by Dave Bartholomew (the blues and R&B band-leader and trumpet-player best known as leader of Fats Domino's band and the co-writer of many of Fats' hits). The Royal Hawks [aka Bartholomew and orchestra]: 'Turn Your Lamp Down Low', New Orleans, 20/3/56, Imperial Records 5390, Hollywood, 1956.

we get back to the turning point in the story of the song, the point at which she leaves. We hear the lie of his retort –

I said 'That's all right, mama, you – you do what you gotta do'

– which confesses its hollowness by its play on the cliché 'a man's gotta do what a man's gotta do'. He matches the woman's pun by this wordplay – but whereas her departing shot contains a put-down (she'd rather take up with anybody than remain with the singer), his does no more than shield him from the blow, and with a shield that confesses his bereft distance from her. In a different song, which is to say if it were surrounded by something less tetchy than the representative mood of 'Maybe in the next life I'll be able to hear myself think', this moment of their splitting-up would be the believable heart of a believable song about a creatively rendered relationship. As it is, these well-crafted and interesting moments loom out of the fog of the song like fleeting glimmers of light.

The same is true for the similarly finger-snapping, over-echoed ' 'Til I Fell In Love With You', the sort of song that people who care little for the blues describe as 'bluesy'. Like the repeated, title-enfolding chorus line of 'Million Miles', here we have the repetitious insistence that 'I was all right 'til I fell in love with you': another phrase that sounds more like Tin Pan Alley running on empty than a real creation that could take you anywhere particular. This cold, mechanical formulation is matched aptly by music like metal scraping metal and emitting brief muted squeaks for help ('oil me! oil me!'), while burbling cocktail lounge organ noises try to suffocate them. Yet this song too contains fragments of interest, the principal one being this absorbing, brave statement that God's support, while still believed in rather than rejected or questioned, is nevertheless not support enough. Dylan starts with a traditional sort of statement, in which the peril, or at least change, felt to be imminent by the singer is followed by the standard response of reaching out for God's protection:

I feel like I'm coming to the end of my way
But I know God is my shield and He won't lead me astray;

but here this is not the punch-line, and that 'But . . .' is not the closing turn-around. Another comes immediately:

Still I don't know what I'm gonna do
I was all right 'til I fell in love with you.

Once more, context is all – for this is the very same chorus couplet that ends every verse of the song: yet here, instead of being empty pop-songwriterliness, it becomes a most interesting deflation of the expected: a daring questioning of whether the comfort of God is much comfort at all. And as with so much else on this album, such a notion has a knock-on effect elsewhere. In this case it is one of the album's scattered statements that co-join with the more concentrated, sustained exploration of what it is to feel bereft of feeling, which is what is offered when we come to 'Not Dark Yet', the song that comes next (but which I discuss later).

The secondary point of interest in ' 'Til I Fell In Love With You' is a serendipitous accident of self-reflection in the text, and one made possible by singer and producer working together appropriately enough. Between the echo-drowned production and Bob Dylan's tendency to mumble, we get the happy way that when Dylan sings

If I'm still among the living

he really sounds as if he's singing 'If I'm still a-mumbling'. Because he is. This is a more pleasing example of production, music and singer coming together than we get on 'Cold Irons Bound' when Dylan reaches those sinking lines towards each verse's end where the voice almost disappears into the surrounding aural murk, so that the headphone-audible words he's a-mumbling on the first of these verses seem more pertinent to the recording itself than to the state of mind claimed by the narrative voice:

I'm waist-deep, waist-deep in the mist
It's almost like I don't exist.

There's an interesting tension, too, in 'Cold Irons Bound', perhaps more accurately an interesting inappropriateness between, on one side, the grinding electronic blizzard of the music and the cold, aircraft-hangar echo of the voice lamenting its sojourn across a lethal planet – fields turned brown, sky lowering with clouds of blood, winds that can tear you to shreds, mists like quicksand – and on the other side the recurrently stated pursuit of tenderness, in phrases that seem imported from another consciousness, another narrative mind, as well as from a gentler outside world. It's decidedly odd to hear, pitched against the scraping Lanois winds half tearing us to shreds, sentiments as obdurately 'romantic' as

I found my own, found my one in you

or

Lookin' at you and I'm on my bended knee

or

I tried to love and protect you

and to hear such a defensively bleak, exhausted old voice articulate the thought that

I'm gonna remember forever the joy we've shared.

'Cold Irons Bound' also returns us, perhaps, to that idea of the singer's downgrading of God's importance when it's asked to compete with that of unrequited love, or love involuntarily cancelled. We're given the almost comic, pleasing picture in the song's opening verse of Bob Dylan the upstanding parishioner:

I went to church on Sunday . . .

which he sings with a matter-of-factness that suggests the implicit suffix 'as usual'; yet what he actually adds is

. . . as she passed by,

making our perception shift at once, so that we see his going to church as nothing to do with religious feeling or ritual at all but rather, as in some Victorian novel, as the one opportunity left to him to catch a glimpse of 'her'. (This is, like '4th Time Around' or 'Tangled Up In Blue', a song with shifting personal pronouns.) Again, there is an implicit tenderness and constraint, a delicacy of sensibility, sketched here that ill-accords with the howling barbarity in which the singer seems stranded for the great majority of the song, twenty miles out of town and a thousand miles from this orderly, solicitous parish.

Exactly the same weird contrast obtains on the last of the album's clanking, finger-snapping, cold-wind tracks, the no doubt 'bluesy' 'Can't Wait'. (Richard Harrington in the *Washington Post* describes this song and 'Love Sick' as 'spooky voodoo blues – think Screamin' Jay Hawkins on downers . . .'[7]) Again, in general this is a tetchy elaboration of disgruntlement and gloom, mixed with a mournful sorrowing over lost love that hardly seems reasonable from a man in his fifties, a man beset by the growling dyspepsia of 'Well I'm strolling through the lonely graveyard of my mind' and the repeated brick wall of 'And I don't know how much longer I can wait' – to which one feels like saying 'Or else what?', since he growls this out over and over again in a vaguely threatening, blustering way, as if the listener had better watch out. As when the same pose is struck in the playground, it more or less provokes the reaction 'Oh yeah? Whaddaya gonna do about it?'

Yet somewhere inside this windy bluster, as on 'Cold Irons Bound', we find these ineffably timid and gentle, vulnerable confessions of the hopeless romantic:

> *I've tried to recover the sweet love that we knew . . .*
> *. . . my heart can't go on beating without you*

and

> *I'm thinkin' of you, and all the places we could roam together.*

We could what? Roam together? It's disarming in its quaintness. They might be going to roam together into the sunset, hand in hand like toddlers in Start-Rite shoes.

His third verse depiction of bleakness culminates with one of the album's most resonating lines:

> *Skies are gray . . .*
> *Night or day*
> *It doesn't matter where I go anymore, I just go*

(a fine articulation of a recognisable, particular state of desperation); but in the midst of this he switches back to calling upon a quaintness of expression, surprising us anew: it takes an apparently uncontaminated innocence of sensibility here to sing that

> *I'm looking for anything that will bring a happy glow.*

Of course there may be a voice at the back of the head saying 'Try some smack', but this is not the area of meaning suggested in the song itself. What the song itself seems to stagger to its knees to assert, then, in spite of all the encrustations of weariness, all the souring by time and experience and disappointment, is a belief in, and a yearning for, a 'sweet love' that is somehow one's rightful but involuntary destiny. 'I'm your

---

7.   Richard Harrington, 'This Dylan's No Wallflower', *Washington Post*, c. Oct. 1997.

man . . . I wish I knew what it was that keeps me loving you so . . . I'm doomed to love you.' This is a highly curious stance to take from inside the burning bowels of despair.

It is a despair, however, that yields in this song a single line that might be taken as the gist of the whole album: the vigorously plainspoken 'That's how it is when things disintegrate'.

Despite the ill-judged production of the voice on these musically unattractive tracks, the overall sound of the music on "Time Out Of Mind" still, as with "Oh Mercy", offers cohesion. One of its distinctive ingredients is Augie Myers' Farfisa organ, which David Bowman hears as coming 'from the soundtrack of some 1950s saucers-from-Mars drive-in movie' (he says he means this as a compliment) but which also throws me straight back to the eerie magic of the first Country Joe & The Fish album, "Electric Music For The Mind And Body", which used exactly the organ sound we confront at once on "Time Out Of Mind".[8] All these elements are stirred into Daniel Lanois' digitally plangent soup, which nourishes everything in an enveloping way – and in doing *that* it reminds me of nothing so much as the very different music on "Blonde On Blonde". As that does, this too carries you along all through the album, as if the songs were all one; and as that does, it binds together the weaker tracks with the strong.

What of the strongest? Four tracks are surely great, and Lanois, it must be said, helps them to be so. On these four, the vocals are not drenched in echo: not swollen forwards artificially as in Grecoland, nor recorded down the wrong end of an aural telescope as on 'Dirt Road Blues' (on which the Farfisa organ provides quite the wrong touch, if recreating the Sun Sound was the aim: the result is more Joe Meek than Sam Phillips), thus ruining what would have been an attractive minor song had it been recorded straight, like, say, 'Down Along The Cove'. On the album's Big Four, the voice is beautifully attended to, permitting the listener to attend to it in a way that, whatever has actually been done technically in the studio, is experienced as if directly, matching absolutely aptly the directness with which Dylan sings.

Again, there's plenty of artfulness here, but it stands in the service of direct communication. There isn't a moment on any of these four when you think 'Ah, if only Dylan were younger, or still in his prime, he could sing that line beautifully.' He does sing it all beautifully. Even that very rasping voice employed on 'Tryin' To Get To Heaven' – a voice that in concert tends to be a clumsiness Dylan lapses into when he's faking energy or meaning – is here deployed consummately. It's such a sustained achievement that it's misleading to single out one sound or phrase above the rest, but for instance the way that the whole world opens up only to hurtle out of reach on that gasping, long 'lost' in 'when you think that you've lost everything', while on the next line the voice lands on the very different and smooth sound of 'lose' as if with graceful resignation . . . well, Bob Dylan has lost not one iota of his genius as a vocalist here.

All through the song, this consummate delivery, flowing through in an inexhaust-

---

8. Country Joe & The Fish: "Electric Music For The Mind & Body", Berkeley, *nia*, Vanguard Records SVRL 19026, New York, 1967 [Fontana Records TFL 6081, London, 1967], CD-reissued Vanguard Records VMD 79244–2, New York, c. 1990 [London, c. 1994].

ible stream of fleeting nuance of meaning, and allied to the perfect match of melody and words, makes for a recording both unfailingly well-judged and moving – a creation of disciplined detachment, of found ingredients mostly, yet forged into something unmistakably by Bob Dylan, and saturated in impassioned regret and leave-taking fondness for the world and the world of human feeling, even as it takes its place on an album the thrust of which is to elaborate the loss of all such feeling.

As I mention elsewhere in the case of the word 'mysteriously', Dylan's occupation of the most common-property yet emotive words is quite extraordinary, and is achieved when the entire retinue of his attention and intelligence is applied to the task of yielding all the import of such words. We have another example with that small and omipresent word 'memory'. In 'Tryin' To Get To Heaven' Dylan sings the simple, touching couplet

> *Every day your memory grows dimmer*
> *It doesn't haunt me like it did before*

and once you've heard him sing this, it's quite impossible afterwards to encounter the word in any other poetic context without it coming through via the immaculately alluring mediation of Dylan's voice. Here's an instance: only after "Time Out Of Mind" had been out for a couple of months did I come across this terrific passage from John Ruskin's *Sesame and Lilies* (1865), which Edward Elgar inscribed at the end of his score of *The Dream of Gerontius*:

> This is the best of me; for the rest I ate and drank, and slept, loved and hated, like another; my life was as the vapour, and is not; but this I saw and knew; this, if anything of mine, is worth your memory.

Impossible to reach the crescendo of that passage, for me at least, without hearing its impassioned 'your memory' in the cadence of the Bob Dylan of 'Tryin' To Get To Heaven'.

The track is a demonstration, over and over again, of how deftly and alertly he wrests every hint of meaning he requires from a whole arsenal of individual weapons of words. In the first verse, along with 'your memory', there is the enactment of straining to keep above the rising waterline on the stretched-out word 'high' of 'wadin' through the high muddy water', and the inspired wading he enacts on 'walkin' through the middle of nowhere', which takes up a far greater length than you'd anticipate from either seeing the line written down or hearing the music that propels it – there's a pause before 'walkin'' and another for the long mimicry of travelling through the word 'through', such that the overall effect is precisely that of wading, in which your legs move more slowly, and require more deliberate propulsion, than on land.

In the second verse everything is sung so expressively that it isn't possible to single out one word or phrase. Yearning has never been better expressed. And after the first verse's 'wadin' through the high muddy water' and 'walkin' through the middle of nowhere', we arrive now at 'I been walkin' that lonesome valley', to which Dylan brings a fresh delivery, giving an unexpected distribution of the syllables along the rhythm of the line and bringing by its almost sprightly step a touch of something close to optimism to counter-balance the deathliness of the walk itself. He seems here to feel he has a decent chance, the pilgrim's chance, of getting to heaven before they close its door.

In the third verse there is the lovely and youthful Dylanesque relish as he lands on 'a-beatin'' in that fanciful passage in which, seeing

> *People on the platforms, waiting for the trains*

he

> *. . . can hear their hearts a-beatin'*
> *Like pendulums swingin' on chains:*

an odd and not quite satisfactory simile, but a neat moment of correspondence to the album's opening track, in which in parallel to hearing hearts beat like a grandfather-clock, he hears a smaller clock 'tick' while his own heart sickens. His delivery is superb here not only on that utterly charming 'a-beatin'' but also when he hurries through the three syllables of 'pendulums', drawing attention to the word not by making it enact its slow functioning but by rippling through it as if it's a sort of twiddle, pulling to the surface its nonsense-rhyme diddly-dum quality – and *then* evoking the one-two, tick-tock motion anyway, against all possible odds, by making the rhythm of his 'swingin' on' exactly echo that of his 'pendulums'.

The scene here on the platforms is doubly beguiling: beguiling for the other correspondence it sets up, this time sending us back to 'I And I', in which we see 'two men on a train platform . . . waiting for spring to come smoking down the track', but mainly so for its central conceit, the depiction of the singer's consciousness as so raw, so intensely attuned, that, like George Eliot envisaging our hearing 'the squirrel's heartbeat', he can hear the muffled beat of strangers' hearts on the platforms of the station.[9]

The flood of vulnerability the singer feels while burdened by this supernormal rawness of sympathy is the impetus not only to the restless travel the song describes – it is evoked as if it has been an anxiety state recollected in comparative tranquillity – but also makes for a fine psychological fit with the other main preoccupation of the song, the poignant desire to return to the just-as-rawly-tender but far sweeter world of childhood, when the world was safe and warm. This is not, of course, a politically correct feeling, but it's a human one, and Dylan explores it by revealing this desire in whispers of nursery-rhyme language.

After this third verse comes the most plaintive, still-small-voiced harmonica passage you could conceive of, sticking as nearly as possible to a rhythmic repeat on one note (and with a tone reminiscent of the harmonica on 'Jokerman'), colouring in with this different brush the mood of exquisite yearning that alternates with one of bleakness all through this turbulently aching song.

The voice that opens the fourth verse has, if possible, an even more heightened expressiveness than elsewhere in the song. Here the simple, ostensibly unelaborated description of his envisaged journey –

> *I'm goin' down the river, down to New Orleans –*

9.   This quotation from *Middlemarch* is given more fully in Chapter 6, note 3.

is given as riddled with painful desperation. The voice creates it, rather than merely asserting it with words. We hear this as desperation at the prospect of yet another random journey and we pick up on the undercurrent beneath the Mississippi's churning brown surface – the hint of being sold down the river. And Dylan sings 'down to New Orleans' with a kind of frantic bleakness that we register as lacking any of the hope or resonance that going to New Orleans ought to hold for the man who grew up at the other end of Highway 61, who has loved New Orleans from afar and up close, and through whose heart the blues has flowed so passionately.

This bleakness is immediately articulated in the words of the 'classic' lines that follow – lines that yield such a triumphant Bob Dylanism that they make you laugh to hear it even though its humour is that of black despair:

> They tell me everything's gonna be all right
> But I don't know what all right even means.

This is followed by the main batch of nursery rhyme borrowings, as he switches suddenly from the 'I'm going to' of the verse's beginning to 'I was ridin'', the apparent recollection of an earlier journey. It turns out to be a journey back in time, trying now not so much to get to heaven before they close the door as back to the paradise of early childhood – a theme re-opened in the last verse with its 'Gotta sleep down in the parlor and re-live my dreams'. (There is an added frisson of some sort here from the fact that it is so hard to make out whether Dylan is singing 'sleep down in the parlor' or 'harbor': he seems to me to sing 'parbor'. 'Gotta sleep down in the harbor' thus becomes one of those misheard lines one tends to prefer to the one that's really there; at any rate, in this instance 'harbor' would fit nicely with going down the river to where it meets the sea, bringing to mind another fateful moment, another departure point.) But before that there is the slyly delivered summation of all this travelling – 'I been all around the world boys' – in which Dylan once again plucks a quotation from elsewhere (in this case a common-stock line from many a folksong), with that 'boys' stuck on the end to emphasise the work-song feel, perhaps even adding a sea-shanty flavour, a me-hearties touch redolent of another kind of perilous hard travel. Dylan sings this line with a complex wicked smile, leaving hollow desperation playing at the corners of his mouth.

This desperation too is subsequently articulated in words after being vividly conveyed by sheer tones of voice. In one of the most effective of these statements – because expressed so simply and quietly, with a pleasing and appropriate diffidence rather than any self-glamorising, suffering heroics – he sings

> I close my eyes and I wonder
> If everything is as hollow as it seems.

When it's stated like this, with self-doubt not declaimed or self-absorbed but offered as tentative, muted curiosity about the outside world, it is moving.

Dylan follows it with a final ricochet around the walls of memory, internal journeying conveyed once more as external travel, with an entirely borrowed simile taken from the gospel song 'This Train', which Dylan knows will throw us back to Woody Guthrie, Dylan's own version of 'People Get Ready', sung on the soundtrack of *Renaldo & Clara*, and more besides.

Beyond the unremarkable change of 'this train' to 'some trains', which has the apt effect of distancing him from the hearty conviction of faith that 'This Train' is designed to convey, he does bring a neat touch of his own to these borrowings. Conventionally, if you sing

> *Some trains don't pull no gamblers*
> *No midnight ramblers*

and then add

> *. . . like they used to do*

you would mean that these people used to be carried and now they're not; but Dylan knows that we know that the point of 'This Train' is that it never did carry these 'hopeless sinners', so that his way of putting it is a quirky equivalent of a double-negative: saying that these trains don't carry these people just like they used to not carry them. The song closes with the beautifully expressive alliteration and internal rhyming of

> *I been to Sugartown, I shook the sugar down*

and the final return to the title line.

This title too is wholly borrowed, in fact; but Dylan of course makes it his own, in part by how it accords with themes he has spent his creative career pursuing – embodied, you might say, in 'Knockin' On Heaven's Door', the Bob Dylan song title that half-echoes behind this one, and which itself observes that he finds himself there 'just like so many times before'. The second means by which Dylan makes his own the entirely appropriated 'Tryin' to get to heaven before they close the door' is – just like so many times before – a matter of context. It is the theme of desolation, of isolation even from God and Jesus the Saviour, the album's most fundamental theme, that imbues these borrowed lines with the Dylanesque inference that even heaven may no longer be a refuge absolute in its timelessness and open-handedness: either that even the gates of heaven might have been taken over by the laws of supply and demand, by greed and an arbitary admissions policy, like a penthouse nightclub guarded by bouncers; or, just as horrendously, that even heaven might simply have closed.

The further admirable thing within 'Tryin' To Get To Heaven' is the series of half-rhymes that Dylan installs in the opening lines of every verse but one. It's a regrettable lack of rigour, I suppose, that has him indulge that one exception, as the poet on the page would not expect to do; but that leaves us with four verses out of five on which a quietly achieved and neatly made pattern of these half-rhymes is sewn into the fabric of the song. I represent them here with typographical emphasis to draw attention to them, but as Dylan presents them the point is that he avoids belabouring us with any such emphasis. In the first verse we find

> *The air is getting* hotter, *there's a rumbling in the skies*
> *I been wadin' through the high muddy* water
> *With the heat risin' in my eyes.*

The second verse equivalent is this:

> *When I was in Missouri, they would not let me be.*
> *I had to leave there in a hurry, I only saw what they let me see.*

In the third, the half-rhyme is the beautiful and unexpectedly delayed

> *People on the* platforms, *waitin' for the trains*
> *I can hear their hearts a-beatin'*
> *Like* pendulums *swingin' on chains*

and in the song's closing verse

> *Gotta sleep down in the* parlor, *and re-live my dreams*
> *I close my eyes and I wonder*
> *If everything is as hollow as it seems.*

It is a fine example of the poet quietly getting on with his job and the singer working in cahoots with him to deliver the effect with unshowy subtlety and flair.

Listen too to how Dylan sings 'Not Dark Yet' from start to finish. I demurred at this track on first hearing it because you can sing 'Something's Burning, Baby' over the intro, which is a bad start, and I found just a leetle hard to take seriously that 'Billy 7' voice on 'but it's [pause] gitt'n' there'; yet the more I play it the more perfect seems the fit between every element in the song, and Dylan's vocal proves immaculately felicitous. This is surely one of Bob Dylan's first-rate achievements: a song that can hold its own with those of earlier eras, in that it confronts a theme and pioneers a concentrated treatment of it.

If you were to ask for a work that expresses with dignity and fortitude the conviction that only decline lies ahead – decline of your powers and your capacity for openness to the world of colour and feeling – you could hardly ask for a better attempt than this: a better fusion of scrupulously concentrated singing, fittingly contemplative melody and resonant words.

If you're not busy singing 'Something's Burning, Baby', the song's complex sombreness is constructed first by a slow, smouldering musical intro – an intro described by Richard Harrington as establishing 'a soft-spun martial cadence (the muffled drums evoke a funeral cortège)' complete with 'churchy organ'.[10] Nineteen seconds in, presaged by a sketch of itself a few seconds earlier, a falling guitar-line comes in, laid across the top of the rest, that is straight out of the musical introduction to the revisit-version of that great early Everly Brothers song 'I Wonder If I Care As Much', the version included on their influential "Roots" album of 1968.[11]

This invoking of other songs is of course another of the album's most distinctive strengths (and remains to be discussed); but of the many such sub-texts that Dylan calls upon in the course of "Time Out Of Mind", none is more apposite or cleverly placed than this. It is especially beguiling that he should let the thought be whispered 'I wonder if I care as much / As I did before' in the introduction to a song that explores the depths of Dylan's desolation and dares to say that 'My sense of humanity has gone down the drain'.

---

10.   Richard Harrington, note 7.
11.   Everly Brothers: "Roots", Nashville, Summer 1968, Warner Brothers W 1752, Burbank, California, 1968.

This, the opening of the second verse, is so brave, clear and striking, and so attentively sung, that it combines with the stately pace and the stone steps of the descending chords in such a way as to seem like a sobered revisit to 'Like A Rolling Stone'. I wonder if I care as much. How does it feel? How does it feel?

What makes the words so resonant is that they mix powerful directness with subtle circuitousness. Balancing the clear-sighted confessional bluntness of

> *My sense of humanity has gone down the drain*

is the subtle complexity of feeling, two lines later, inside the couplet

> *She wrote me a letter and she wrote it so kind.*
> *She put down in writing what was in her mind.*

Dylan's delivery of these edgy lines rises above guiding us as to their moral weighting. He remains magnificently inscrutable here. Is he recognising that her intention was 'kind' in setting down her feelings in a letter (something the narrator himself does to the 'you' in 'When The Night Comes Falling From The Sky'), or is 'she wrote it so kind' gallows sarcasm? Is there a barb here to the effect that ending a relationship – if that is what she's doing – would be kinder in person than by letter? More centrally, is the matter-of-fact 'She put down in writing what was in her mind' to be taken as honesty or, on principle, extreme foolhardiness? Is he condemning it as rash and dangerous? Should we? Is it an open question?

And then having delivered the lines with such care, he falls back upon what may be the worst, because the deadest, response: 'I just don't see why I should even care.' Again, we are left to get a grip on this unaided by any hint in the way that the words are sung. If the line claims a numbness of response, a not caring, is this a defensive pose, a plain statement of the emotional inadequacy he's reduced to, or a plain statement of an indifference that just-happens-to-be-there-that's-all, for good or ill? Or is it, on the contrary, a protest at what he sees as the unreasonableness of finding that he *does* care? This is writing of great subtlety and strength, stripped of all adjectival elaboration. It can bear the weight of all the conjecture it prompts from the listener, because it is thought-out and all its ambivalence is plausible.

Working out the balance of probability of meaning in this way is demanded of us at several other points in the song. In the first verse, 'Feel like my soul has turned into steel': is this good or bad – toughened or dehumanised? If the latter, the truth of the lament is challenged in the line that follows: 'I've still got the scars . . .' is something only flesh or the psyche can claim. When the third verse opens with

> *Well I been to London and I been to Gay Paree,*

the effect is the opposite. It is not that the intrinsically ambivalent line gets no clarification from Dylan's delivery. On the contrary, it is more that the intensely expressive delivery belies the apparent neutrality of the line. This one is sung with shrivelling mordancy, conjuring a world of bleakness from this ostensible recitation of glamorous experience. It isn't as simple a snarl, on that long-drawn-out 'Gay— Paree', as to suggest mere seen-it-all ennui – is it? What does it express? Murderous contempt for the vacuousness of the ooh-la-la, can-can Paris? Sullen resentment at having arrived too late to catch any of this except the seedy huckster version – a crumbling

Moulin wearing too much Rouge? Despair at being unmoved even by this great chic European capital or by the contemplation of its immense and variegated cultural past?

Dylan's use of the word 'gay' is doubly insistent here – insistent because he holds the word on the note for so long, rolling it around in his mouth like a pretty poor sort of a toffee and then spitting it out into the waiting napkin of 'Paree', and because this is the second time he has used the word in the course of the album. It has been offered earlier, and in a phrase sufficiently surprising to draw attention to it, in the second verse of 'Standing In The Doorway', which finds him strumming on his 'gay guitar'. Does he do it to annoy, because he knows it teases? I think so. And I think the more purposive gesture that underlies this one is stubborn defiance of its appropriation by the thrash of sexual politics, and more generally an insistence upon not submitting to the thought-police of political correctness.

This defiance draws on several different weapons. In 'Standing In The Doorway' the first weapon is comedy:

> *I'm strummin' on my gay guitar,*
> *Smokin' a cheap cigar*

is inherently comic, partly by the joke of conceiving of such a thing as a homosexual guitar, partly by the notion of Bob Dylan playing one and partly because, while retrieving the word 'gay' so as to have it mean 'cheery' again, he sings these cheery lines about pleasure with all the glumness of a great comedian, a Max Wall. In 'Not Dark Yet' the first weapon is licence. 'Gay Paree' is a phrase of unarguable familiarity – what, therefore, can possibly be wrong with using it?

But Dylan's underlying weapon in both these cases is the weapon of song. If he has asserted anything as strongly in the course of creating radical song-forms as in the course of re-stating the strengths of old ones, it is that the language of popular song can embrace an unconstrained vocabulary, drawing at will on the phrases and cadences of the Bible, the blues, folk balladry, high-brow poetry and the street – vocabulary that can be crude and sophisticated, simple and complex, modish and ancient. This is what he taught us in the first place, on the pioneering work of the 1960s. This unconstrained, resourceful flexibility is one of the main things he brought to rock'n'roll. On "Time Out Of Mind" Dylan is asserting his defiant guardianship of the right – of everybody's right – to use and re-use an old word. Fighting with him he has all the old songs in which the word 'gay' means light-hearted or jolly, just as he has blues lyric poetry behind him when he wants to explore some other phrase that no one else might dream of deploying inside their contemporary composition. I don't see this as an especially reactionary foray. The fact that many deeply conservative people are always moaning about the appropriation of the word 'gay' doesn't make Bob Dylan one of them. He isn't moaning; he isn't trying to stop its PC usage. He's just insisting on its revivable capacity to say something else. Were he to succeed in sparking off this renewed usage among the rest of us, he would rescue Elvis Presley's smouldering and macho song 'Paralyzed' from the unintended high comedy attendant upon its lines

> *I'm gay every morning,*
> *At night I'm still the same.*

An uphill task.[12]

In any case, Dylan's citing of 'Gay Paree' in 'Not Dark Yet' is one of those parts of the recording in which the subtleties of what is conveyed by Dylan's undimmed expressiveness of delivery get no clarification from the ostensible neutrality, or undirectingness, of the line itelf. As we pass on through the lyrics, we return to writing that offers none of these complex weighings-up but offers instead a bleak straightforwardness – a plainspeaking this is how it is when things inside disintegrate:

> *I ain't lookin' for nothin' in anyone's eyes.*

> *I was born here and I'll die here against my will.*

> *Don't even hear the murmur of a prayer.*

The metaphoric title line itself, of course, is also plain and unmistakable in its import, even though we hear it first, as it closes the first verse, as a neat extension of the *non-*metaphor that ushers in the song's very first line. The first duty of 'It's not dark yet but it's getting there' is to round off a description of a particular day's end: to observe that dusk is drawing the curtains on a particular hot afternoon. The song's first lines are

> *Shadows are falling, and I been here all day*
> *It's too hot to sleep and time is running away.*

Only as that introductory particularity is, as it were, put to bed, should we accept the declared onset of darkness as the closing down of a life or a consciousness. As the line comes around again to conclude the other three verses, this metaphoric meaning is re-emphasised, of course, though whether the singer is looking forward to death as a release from this lingering, crepuscular shut-down, in which every nerve is 'vacant and numb', is again for the listener to try to put his or her finger on. When the line comes around for the last time, close listening reveals that it is amended to 'It's not dark yet *and* it's gettin' there' (my emphasis – Dylan gives it none). This has been taken by some as hinting more strongly than 'but' at relish or keener anticipation.

Whether the line announces an omnipresent consciousness of the comparative imminence of actual death or a consciousness that everything once worth savouring in life is losing its meaning, one of the things on offer here, as on 'Tryin' To Get To Heaven', is the sojourn of defeat. It is never more perfectly rendered than in the quiet achievement, in the song's concluding verse, of the line

> *I can't even remember what it was I came here to get away from,*

on which Dylan achieves some extraordinary equivalence to onomatopoeia, enacting as he sings the line the long weary journeying, physical and emotional, away from something and somewhere. This is perfect singing and inventiveness, and quietly done.

The least 'perfect' of the four major songs, both in terms of writing and singing, is I think 'Standing In The Doorway'. There are filler passages here, and the vocal performance is the least subtle and flexible of the four – there's a sort of blanket vocal stance, with an almost automatic expressive croak at each line's end (it's especially

12. Elvis Presley: 'Paralyzed', 1956; detailed in Chapter 18, note 77.

noticeable, which is to say especially questionable, in the middle of the first verse, on 'I got no place left to turn / I got nothin' left to burn') – though genuine yearning still breaks through repeatedly in the course of the performance, and Dylan's understated stateliness of control is still exquisite.

What it lacks in honed perfection, it almost makes up for in sheer generosity of text. The first thing that is striking on early playings is the bountiful *length* of the song. To generalise, it arrives sounding like a 'Shooting Star' sort of a song. You expect three verses and hope for four. That is, you hear the long first verse (ten lines long), the second comes in immediately (same shape, same length) and then comes what sounds as if it's going to be a verse-long instrumental break, and you assume that after this has unfolded there will be one more verse and the close-out. Instead you find that the instrumental break lasts only for the equivalent of two lines of verse before Dylan is back in, pressing the third verse upon us with what comes across as some urgency, precisely because, confounding expectations, this foreshortened instrumental passage and his precipitate vocal return suggest a hurrying on with things. After the third verse, the same thing happens again: the instrumental break is a mini-break, a mere fifteen seconds' worth, and a fourth verse is upon us . . . and then a fifth. We've had five 10-line verses instead of three: a pleasurable generosity.

If the instrumental passages are brief, they are not unimportant. The introductory one, before the vocal arrives in the first place, calls at once upon a sub-text song far more widely known (both in itself and because Bob Dylan himself has recorded it) than 'I Wonder If I Care As Much', the Everly Brothers song that lurks around the start of 'Not Dark Yet'. This time it is Elvis Presley's 'Can't Help Falling In Love', and its opening three notes of melody ('wise men say') are played here, with insistent clarity, on the bass-guitar that introduces 'Standing In The Doorway'. Andrew Muir writes of this that ' "Wise men say . . ." is what I hear each time it starts', and that therefore when he hears the opening lines of the *Dylan* song, which are

> *I'm a-walkin' through the summer nights*
> *The jukebox playin' low,*

'Elvis hasn't left my mind – so I can almost hear 'Can't Help Falling In Love' coming from the jukebox.'[13] More important, Dylan is using the whisper of this song's presence to confess that he is not among the 'wise men' but rather, as he complains in 'Love Sick', has lost the struggle to resist 'falling in love with you' – the 'you' here being placed when he comes to sing, in the second verse, that

> *The ghost of our old love has not gone away*
> *Don't look like it will any time soon,*

so that the sub-text of 'can't help falling in love with you' is especially apt in its use of the continuous present tense.

13.   Elvis Presley: 'Can't Help Falling In Love', Hollywood, 21–23/3/61; RCA Victor Records 47–7968, New York, 1961. (This became Presley's 29th gold record; it was from the soundtrack of the film [Hal B. Wallis/ Paramount, US, directed Norman Taurog, 1961], and therefore album, "Blue Hawaii", RCA Victor LPM/LSP-2426, New York [RCA RD27238 / SF 5115, London], 1961.)
    Andrew Muir, 'Time Out of Mind', *Isis*, no. 75, October 1997.

It is the second verse, in fact, that brings the song alive. The first has that obtrusive pair of lines

Don't know if I saw you if I would kiss you or kill you
It probably wouldn't matter to you anyhow.

Though that first line is a striking representation of the recognisable tension between ardour and anger, and Andrew Muir, in another piece, writes of 'the wonderful way the second line here tugs the carpet from under the feet of our preconceptions',[14] that second line is not entirely successful as an expression of the singer's own sense of insignificance to this 'old love'. Her indifference can't quite be envisaged as that absolute, cannot quite suppress the objection that the insignificant ex-lover is the last person you don't mind having come along and kill you. It's too demanding a pay-off line: it clamours too hard for the suspension of disbelief.[15]

The unwillingness to accept this on first hearing is all the greater because, as you hear the first verse of the song the first time around, you are still in the process of weighing up whether this is going to be a real song or a fake: an honourable creation or one of those money-making pop 'ballads' that Dylan throws in these days (one per album, it seems) like 'Make You Feel My Lurve'. It is, therefore, the second verse of 'Standing In The Doorway' that makes the song come alive and establishes its authenticity. The first verse could be empty pop with that dodgy pair of 'kiss you–kill you' lines thrown in; the second verse lets go of cagey artifice and gives generously of the writer's individuality. The reassurance comes that this is what is going on when we come to the fourth line here:

The light in this place is so bad
Makin' me sick in the head
All the laughter is just makin' me sad
The stars have turned cherry red.

Ah!, says the listener, now we're getting somewhere. We're getting, indeed, something particular and warmly human, something with the panache of surprise which, this time, has no sense of straining for its effect. It doesn't matter that 'Cherry Red' is another of the song titles thrown in all through this album – thrown in as never before in all of Dylan's work. It's deployed with brio and a sly smile. We're getting real observation here – not, of course, of the real sky but of a real narrative personality, his responses elucidated with a real articulacy. And we're getting the prospect, therefore, of more to come, as the song starts to deliver the goods: to deliver this liveliness, this creativity.

This promise starts to be fulfilled at once, as the couplet about the gay guitar and the cheap cigar comes right in, followed by the citing of the core of the song, that 'ghost of our old love' that is being grappled with. There are, here, several changes of

14. Andrew Muir: 'The Difference Between a Real Blonde on Blonde and a Fake', *Dignity*, no. 12, Sept.–Oct. 1997.

15.   So implausible a level of ineffectuality is much better exploited in comic put-down. In 1950s Soho (London), a woman called Hilary Bonner was approached in a bar by a particularly small male journalist who announced that he'd very much like to make love to her. 'If you do,' she said, 'and if I ever find out about it, I shall be very, very cross.' (Source unknown.)

mood, in rapid succession. There is no faltering between them, no implausibility in the way that the lyrics range through them. This implicit restlessness neatly contradicts the claim of the opening verse that

> *Yesterday everything was goin' too fast*
> *Today it's movin' too slow:*

neatly because the sense that things are moving too slow, that he's left 'standing', only makes more readily explicable the restless turmoil, the quick shifting of emotions 'in the head' as this torpor is defied and struggled with.

The effect of the foreshortened instrumental break between the second and third verse works, I've suggested already, to enhance this sense of pent-up urgency, and then as we enter the third verse itself, an extra ingredient is introduced, an extra and mysterious side of the singer's personality and situation is revealed, in the enigmatic opening lines

> *Maybe they'll get me and maybe they won't*
> *But not tonight and it won't be here.*

Not, then, a song only about being hounded by love but, by the sound of it, hunted by killers too. It comes like a breath of fresh air to the listener, even as it speaks of hideaways and doom. There's a welcome light touch to the fatalist fortitude here too, varying the emotional colours of the song, plus the nifty slide from the shoulder-shrugging *que sera, sera* in the first line to the confident predicting of the future straight afterwards.

One of the characteristic challenges of Bob Dylan songs is the recurrent working-out of whether a particular passage is there in illumination of its predecessor or whether the two are addressing separate themes. Such a challenge is presented here, immediately after these lines, lines that have opened up but not explained this new dimension to the narrator's situation. He has told us that 'they' are out to 'get' him, but not why, nor who they are. Is he commenting on this, then, when the next line gives us

> *There are things I could say, but I don't*

(a finely achieved self-reflexive text, if so) and commenting on the approach of the death 'they' might bring when he adds

> *I know the mercy of God must be near –*

or are these lines another switch of topic and mood? And are they another fragment of a different story or a return to the main theme of the song, the tale of the man standing in the doorway haunted by unending as well as unrequited love – the man who feels himself, or wishes himself, to be waiting at the doorway of heaven?

It may be a characteristic challenge to have to work this out, or else be kept wondering about it every time you hear the song, but there is nothing unsatisfactory about the way that a good Bob Dylan song puts you in this position. It isn't a matter of opacity or failure to communicate. Rather it is a part of Dylan's lifelong exploration of the ways in which truth exists on many levels and the inner life is complex. In this instance we may speculate as to whether these two lines are a fragment of a new story or an extension of the old because each of the two statements offered here veers away interestingly from the positions recurrently stated all through "Time Out Of Mind". Most of the album's comments about words and saying things are to the effect that there is nothing to be said and it is futile to try. This very song concludes with the loftily said

> *I see nothing to be gained by any explanation*
> *There's no words that need to be said;*

and this is re-stated many times in the other songs: 'Now you can seal up the book and not write any more' (or 'not write anymore') in 'Tryin' To Get To Heaven'; 'I'm tired of talkin', I'm tired of tryin' to explain' in ''Til I Fell In Love With You'; the strong implication in 'Not Dark Yet' that writing down 'what was in her mind' was fatally unwise; and in 'Highlands' either the party's over because 'there's less and less to say' or else 'there's less and less to say' because the party's over. In 'Dirt Road Blues' the only thing he hopes to hear from a human voice is his name hollered out, and he knows he won't hear that; and in 'Love Sick' the only human sounds are a distant cry and a lie. Only once on the whole album is the opposite sentiment expressed – that there might be some point to talking. This comes on 'Million Miles' when he declares despondently

> *Feel like talkin' to somebody but I just don't know who.*

Even here, this is more a confession of loneliness, suggesting the possible therapeutic value of talking rather than expressing faith in the communicative power of words. It is also slipped in between the irascible, implicit anti-talk remark 'Maybe in the next life I'll be able to hear myself think' and the concluding *explicit* anti-talk complaint that 'there's voices in the night trying to be heard / I'm sitting here listening to every mind-polluting word'.

It seems a different narrative position, therefore, on 'Standing In The Doorway', when Dylan sings that lovely

> *There are things I could say, but I don't.*

This voice knows all too well the communicative power of words. It's not that words are futile but that they are dangerous. The implication is that it is safer not to speak, and that those truths pressing to be said are the most dangerous.

Similarly, when this voice sings that

> *I know the mercy of God must be near*

it is an almost unique expression, on "Time Out Of Mind", of untrammelled faith and untroubled anticipation. As we've seen already, this quiet faith, akin to that of the Dylan of 'Every Grain Of Sand', is exactly what "Time Out Of Mind" seems unable to maintain: this is one of the ley lines of its distinctive despair. In ''Til I Fell In Love With You', as we saw, having God as his shield is not enough; in 'Cold Irons Bound' his church-going is little to do with faith; in 'Tryin' To Get To Heaven', Heaven cannot be trusted to stay open and the singer has been walking that lonesome valley not with the fearlessness of he who puts his faith in the Lord but with the isolation of one who has lost everything and is 'just going down the road feeling bad'.

In 'Not Dark Yet' 'the sun' can be taken as an aural pun on 'the Son', if we wish (and a large number of people do seem to), in which case we've a further statement of this new, and for the singer newly desolating, religious doubt, as he refers to still having 'the scars that the sun wouldn't heal'.[16] Less tendentiously, the singer can't even manage 'the murmur of a prayer'. Even the straining toward the 'Highlands', the holding on to its crumb of optimism with much difficulty, is a wish for a nebulous otherness, and more an act of will than of faith. Only in the inconsequential lyrics of 'Dirt Road Blues' do we find him chipper enough to be 'praying for salvation'. Only on 'Standing In The Doorway', then, do we find a voice avowing anything with the clear conviction of 'I know the mercy of God must be near'.

Whether or not these lines from the middle of the song's third verse comment on those that went before, or are the fragment of a different story, they articulate in their different ways moments of strong feeling before the narrative thrust slips back into deploring absence of feeling.

> *I been ridin' the midnight train*

(which seems a borrowed line that's too easy, too ready-made) is followed by

> *Got iced water in my veins.*

I don't know why I demur at this. Although it's fairly crude, the standard water-instead-of-blood metaphor for unfeelingness (or weakness) ought to seem satisfactorily personalised by Dylan's making it 'iced water'; and if 'iced water' strikes me, as a Briton, as being one of those contemptible self-indulgences that Americans persuade themselves are necessities of life, then Dylan's citing this one here should help things along, by acting as one of the fleeting touches we find all through the album that help colour in the narrator's isolation from real life, from meaningful human contact. Instead, I recoil from it with some unease, feeling, I suppose, that this is the voice of the Dylan who spends too much of his time in expensive, over-heated hotel suites where everyone is fussing about iced water trivialities, and that Bob Dylan should be getting a life instead of room-service.[17]

In contrast, what I especially do like about

> *There are things I could say, but I don't*

is that it concentrates into its spare frame a whole portrait of another side of Bob Dylan, the one who has always been a master both of saying things and of not: the one who, in Joan Baez's great line, is 'so good with words – and at keeping things vague'.[18] But it is not simply that the line's content portrays something central about Dylan, nor yet that the joke of its self-reflexiveness is typical of him. It is also that his

---

16. I dislike this. There should be a reason within the text to suggest that such a pun *is* intended; it shouldn't be jumped at for no better reason than that it is theoretically possible. In 'Standing In The Doorway' he refers to 'the dark land of the sun': we are surely not to conjecture that this may be Dylan's condemnation of a newly discovered great wickedness in Jesus and his entire domain.

17. An alternative is offered by a mishearing in a home-made transcript of the lyrics sent to me when the album was new; this makes the couplet 'I been ridin' the midnight train / But I'm swallowin' my pain'!

18. Joan Baez: 'Diamonds And Rust', Los Angeles, 17–29/1/75, "Diamonds And Rust", A&M Records SP 3233, LA [AMLH 64527, London], 1975.

timing and phrasing here are themselves a lovely demonstration of how he can say things and not say them. Taking the delivery of the line in isolation, it is timelessly Dylanesque in its sly, immaculately-measured long pause before 'but I don't', and taking it in the context of this song and this album, it both articulates and embodies a fine and dignified grace under pressure. Encompassing Dylan's undiminished skill at understatement, its quiet special flourish is that it states that understatement itself.

The verse then ends with the mild surprise of the singer musing on whether *he* should take *her* back. But it is artfully done, the simple

> *I would be crazy if I took you back*

capturing a moment of fantasy–speculation that giddies him: a flash of how it might feel to be the one to choose. He sings the line with a ruminative, exploratory hesitation, as if every time he puts the thought to himself, it thrills him, and he must calm himself, push this fantasy away again, by a no-no-no-that-would-never-do, which he puts as

> *It would go up against every rule.*

As he sings this, he lets the relish that he feels for this fantasy linger on, at odds with the self-restraining admonition, while the words he uses also recognise that the scenario he is toying with would go up against every rule of probability and realism.

As we press on into the penultimate verse, hurried along again by the foreshortened instrumental interlude, we come to one of the album's vocal low-points and one of the high-points in its writing. The opening lines are

> *When the last rays of daylight go down*
> *Buddy you'll roll no more*
> *I can hear the church bells ringin' in the yard*
> *I wonder who they're ringin' for.*

The vocal blemish here lies in sheer mispronunciation: a clumsiness of execution all too common in contemporary Dylan concerts but normally avoided by the special concentration demanded of the vocals on his studio recordings. This kind of carelessness marks one of the deteriorations time has effected from the immaculate standards set by the young Bob Dylan, to whom making exactly the right noise, indeed the best possible noise, on every syllable of an entire concert, and certainly on every breath of singing in the studio, was a part of the effortless precision of his intelligence and inspiration. It was a vocal equivalent of, say, Jimi Hendrix's supernatural abolition in concert of any gap whatever between the brain's conception and the fingers' immediate and fluent execution. The middle-aged Dylan, to whom much that 'came naturally' now involves some struggle, falters in just such ways as these. It is a faltering not merely of physical co-ordination but of instinct. In concert he often offers noises now that are simply not the lithe or fiery special creatures that all his articulation once comprised. In the studio, this slippage of vocal infallibility reveals itself here, as he smudges the singing of 'Buddy you'll roll no more' and 'I can hear the church bells' in two places. He sings 'na more' such that it simply sounds false, like no real person's dialect or accent at all. It jars, and it draws attention to itself by being unclear. On cheap speakers, or on a copy of a copy of a cassette, its offers the delightful but distracting mishearing 'Butter your own amour' (setting up a zinging dialogue with the 'Highlands' line 'You could say I was on anything but a roll'). And stumbling out of this ditch, he steps in another as he sings that he 'can her the church bells'. Again, this is no catastrophe; yet it cannot be heard as anything but regrettable, intrusive error.

This audible faltering distracts momentarily from the moving acuteness of the lines themselves:

> *I can hear the church bells ringin' in the yard*
> *I wonder who they're ringin' for.*

Andrew Muir writes that when 'he hears the church bells and wonders for whom they toll' he is aware that 'If it is not for him this time . . . [it] will be soon.'[19] This is part of what is at issue here – as Muir notes, the 'buddy' who'll roll no more is the singer himself – but the greatness of the lines lies in their inspired, quiet expression of the utter lack of human sympathy the singer feels, and the absolute isolation he feels instead. John Donne's majestic eloquence is nowhere more fundamentally embedded in our account of ourselves than in the ringing imperative of his that everyone knows:

> No man is an Island . . . any man's death diminishes me, because I am involved in Mankind; And therefore never send to know for whom the bell tolls; it tolls for thee.[20]

To sing, therefore, as Dylan does, 'I wonder who they're ringin' for' is to declare that he no longer feels this bedrock connection with his fellow man. Its greatness lies in its needing no overt explication and its yielding its meaning wholly by inference. Much commentary on "Time Out Of Mind" has revolved around Dylan's use of lines and phrases from blues and popular song; but here is an instance of his ability to make creative, deeply resonant use of literary allusion.

The verse ends with a return to the world with the mention of a touching moment, as Dylan sings the pleasing line

> *Last night I danced with a stranger*

– a moment at which it is impossible to picture the narrative persona as anyone but Dylan himself, precisely because it seems out of character for Dylan to go dancing, and the prospect beguiles. Sung with a shy, light confessionalism, which beautifully conveys that this uncharacteristicness is a tangible factor in what the line confesses – it offers a fleeting, filmic glimpse to charm the pants off anyone who's ever loved him for his Bob Dylanness: a charm that you sense would be powerfully present to the stranger during the dance. It is a more affecting, and seems a more intimate, moment in the song than the pay-off argument for which it is marshalled – the predictable 'but' of

> *But she just reminded me you were the one.*

We enter the song's final verse with one of his loveliest uses of second-hand song line. Back in 1963, a third of a century before he recorded 'Standing In The

19.   Andrew Muir, note 13.

20.   John Donne: Meditation XVII, 'Devotions upon Emergent Occasions', 1624, republished in *No Man Is an Island: A Selection from the Prose of John Donne*, edited by Rivers Scott, 1997.

Doorway', Dylan recorded the most exquisite version possible of the traditional song known as, among other things, 'Moonshiner': a version in which he so fully inhabits the persona of the Old Derelict narrator (the grace-kissed soul as well as the voice of the man) that it is eerie and certainly challenges any convenient notion that his youthful counterfeiting of age and world-weariness must sound shallow alongside his interpretative abilities with similar material when he has decades of authentic ageing and experience behind him, as on "Good As I Been To You" or "World Gone Wrong". Now, however, he revisits that song, pulling out of it lines that are a hymn to cynical pragmatism:

> Let me eat when I'm hungry, let me drink when I'm dry,
> Dollars when I'm hard-up, religion when I die.

Now, walking through the autumn nights of his 'Standing In The Doorway' persona, the jukebox plays these lines inside the writer's head, and he deploys them to delicate effect to declare at song's end that he has resolved to settle for the narrowed perspectives, the closed-down expectations those lines communicate:

> I'll eat when I'm hungry, drink when I'm dry
> And live my life on the square.

This is terrific writing. What was the old moonshiner's lifelong stance, his unapologetic all, is now the battened-down hatch of a once far richer, more open life that the singer of "Time Out Of Mind" feels reduced to. Entailed in this declared resolve, which is a form of cutting one's coat to suit one's cloth, is the decision to be more guarded from now on: the reductive defensiveness of the hurt person. Along with this is the other form of defence, embodied in the added part of the lines.

The resolve to 'live my life on the square' is his own take on another expression picked up ready-made: 'on the square'. To 'live my life on the square' is a nifty phrase, drawing on several different meanings of 'square': the sense of facing things squarely – head-on, straightforwardly, and the accompanying sense of living a straight, honest life, with no shady vices or double-dealings to come back on you later. Because 'on the square' is itself an old-fashioned American expression – last heard on a hit record before Bob Dylan recorded 'Moonshiner'[21] – it embraces aptly and self-reflexively the sense of the speaker becoming 'a square' (itself an old-fashioned American expression); and when you add, as Dylan does, *living* 'on the square', you insinuate the extra meaning of living right in the middle of your small town community – of living this steady, cautious life open to the gaze of your neighbours. To add it on, therefore, to 'I'll eat when I'm hungry, drink when I'm dry' is to make for a new whole: to take away from the moonshiner's lines any possibility of their suggesting the open, instinctive virtues of the wild animal, the natural creature in tune with its most basic

---

21.   Every American I've questioned is unfamiliar with the phrase 'on the square' as something used in real life, though it was common in the nineteenth century and lingered in song into the 1950s. 'You know my love for you is on the square,' sing Norm Foxx & The Rob-Roys on the doo-wop standard 'Tell Me Why' [*nia*, Backbeat Records, Texas, 1957], a record still so popular on NYC radio at the start of the 1960s that it was re-made by the group Dion DiMucci had just split from, the Belmonts: 'Tell Me Why', NYC, March 1961, Sabrina Records 500, New York [Pye International 7N 25094, London], 1961; CD-reissued "The Golden Age Of American Rock'n'Roll Volume 5" (note 4). (From its notes, by Rob Finnis, 1995, I take the details of the Norm Foxx antecedent.) The Belmonts' record was a US Top 20 hit in 1961.

needs, and to line them up with 'on the square', all militating in favour of the psychologically rash caution of the damaged person who is resolved to be narrower, more suspicious, more self-constructed, less spontaneous, less at peace with inner complexity and its contradictory desires: in short, less open to life.

Though the effect is particular to this song, the technique is exactly the same as in 1989's 'Where Teardrops Fall', in which Dylan adds on to the ready-made two-parter

> *Roses are red, violets are blue*

a third item that puts a new spin on these, the vigorous (and in this case hand-made)

> *Time is beginning to crawl.*

Time is beginning to crawl again as 'Standing In The Doorway' closes, and does so with the lovely and apposite final line (also hand-made, so far as I know)

> *You left me standing in the doorway cryin',*
> *Blues wrapped around my head.*

It could be taken as ammunition for those who believe that Bob Dylan cannot sing, but one of the more general features of Dylan's singing on the title line of the song, which comes round five times, is that he makes it sound as if that odd chord, arrived at on the emphatically delivered word 'cryin'', is not necessarily the same chord every time. This is a perplexing variant on his superb ability to be able and keen to sing a repeat line in a new way, however many times the challenge presents itself. This strange variant, his creating here of the aural illusion that 'cryin'' lands on several different chords (always odd, and therefore un-Dylanesque, chords – though anything beyond the most well-trod basic three chords is un-Dylanesque), is augmented by the more normal achievement of giving the word itself differing degrees of emphasis in different verses. (The third is especially soft and forgiving, the last especially and carefully impassioned.)[22]

The song takes its leave with an instrumental passage that extends beyond the inter-verse length (two lines of melody), reaching as far as the short fifth and sixth lines – the ones that in the lyric are occupied by clipped, insistent couplets ('I got no place left to turn / I got nothin' left to burn'), and though the whole passage is, like more or less all the instrumental part of the album, ensemble playing with a deliberate absence of solos, the poking insistence of the melody on these short mid-verse lines is repeated and dramatised here on the fade-out by a muted but splendidly clangy, old-fashioned guitar that sounds like Dylan himself dreaming of being Hubert Sumlin playing on Howlin' Wolf's 'Going Down Slow'.[23]

As for the concluding vocal line, the rueful, half ironic pride, half howl of woe

---

22.   On the topic of Dylan's taking a conscious interest in this ever-varying expressiveness, these remarks of his about the Egyptian singer Om Kalsoum (1904–1975) are pertinent: 'She was one of my favourite singers of all time. I don't understand a word she sings . . . And she'll sing the same phrase over and over and over again, y'know, in a different way every time. And there's no US or western singer I think, that's in that kind of category, y'know – except possibly me.' [Westwood One radio station interview, NYC, 30/7/84.]

23.   Howlin' Wolf: 'Goin' Down Slow', Chicago, Dec. 1961, Chess Records 1813, Chicago, 1962 [c/w 'Smoke-stack Lightnin'', Pye International 7N 25244, London, 1964].

'blues wrapped around my head' – well it's true, of course, and I hope to have dispelled any residual notion (a notion I have heard advanced by the odd aficionado) that when Dylan sings a line from the blues, from Woody Guthrie or 'Moonshiner', he is doing something lazy, or easier than writing his own 'new' line.

We shall come to all these adept and imaginative borrowings shortly, but first there are the creative heights of 'Highlands' to be scaled.

What a song! Some people say that sixteen-and-a-half minutes long is too long. I'm with those who say it's too short. The track never ends without sounding unfairly foreshortened, like an idyll snatched away. I always want more. Bob Dylan has always been a talking blues maestro, to achieve which requires being in infinitely intelligent control of timing and phrasing; and he displays 99.9 per cent of that control on the *tour de force* of 'Highlands' (there are two tiny, minor fluffs, neither of which matters). And displays it with the crowning touch of the genuine maestro, that of making it sound easy, as he steers us through its twenty stanzas, alternating without a microsecond's hesitation between the 'otherly', aspirational 'My heart's in the highlands' chorus sections, with their magnificent recourse to formal poetic strengths, and the 'here and now' sections that seem to walk you round Dylan's daily world as seen from inside his head, which offer the perfect illusion of spontaneous composition.

The all-encompassing sweep of 'Highlands' is constructed with genius, fusing into one three-dimensional portrait the high and black comedy, the Dylanesque sarcasms and off-the-wall observations – all of which are plentiful, authentic and delivered as faultlessly as anything in his back-catalogue – and, set against all these, the recurrent expressions of yearning for a better version of himself and of the world, for a renewed sense of moral cleanliness as well as an unsullied terrain of natural grandeur, while all but confessing that what his eyes are raised to is never-never land. All this is performed with an unshakeable, wise, good-humoured authority that trusts the form even as it achieves a large expansion of its possibilities, that acts in good faith and addresses itself to an intelligent audience – creditably belying its writer/composer's claims to have lost his conscience and sense of humanity. In doing this, 'Highlands' acts as the best possible conclusion to the album, achieving, just as the final lines of the song do, a farewell bow of dignified, painfully gained, limited optimism, dragged back from the turbulent labyrinths of despair and decay.

'Highlands' begins by, well, setting the scene – the scene the singer envisages, yearns for, dreams of, aspires to. It does so exhilaratingly:

> *Well my heart's in the Highlands, gentle and fair*
> *Honeysuckle blooming in the wildwood air*
> *Bluebells blazing where the Aberdeen waters flow*
> *Well my heart's in the Highlands*
> *I'm gonna go there when I feel good enough to go.*

One of the immediately striking things is how much better written it is than the Robert Burns poem it founds itself upon. Andrew Muir writes interestingly about the significance of 'My Heart's in the Highlands' for Burns' reputation, granted its 'triviality' yet its immense popularity, and about Burns having based his poem's beginning and end on 'a circulating folk source with a couple of stock traditional images thrown in'.[24] Whatever the reasons, the Burns poem opens (and closes) with nothing better than

> *My heart's in the Highlands, my heart is not here;*
> *My heart's in the Highlands a-chasing the deer;*
> *Chasing the wild deer and following the roe;*
> *My heart's in the Highlands, wherever I go.*

Its two middle verses offer nothing beyond a listing: 'Farewell to the' this 'and farewell to the' that, and the only imaginative or personal touch in the whole poem is the phrase 'wild-hanging' in 'Farewell to the forest and wild-hanging woods'.[25]

Dylan takes the framework of Burns' poem (a frame that Andrew Muir argues is taken in turn from Scottish folksong). He also effects a reversal of Burns' implicit theme, which is of yearning to return to a real place, inhabited in the Edenic past and in which he has left his heart – a heart formed by these known, loved, roamed-over, geographically specific as well as sentimentalised Scottish Highlands. Dylan instead yearns for are-they-aren't-they-Scottish? Highlands – its pseudo-geographic hints are contradictory – to which he makes no claim ever to have been, and which represent a dream future in time and space, and not an idealised past.

The main thing Dylan does, though, is write of it imaginatively: that is, so that we see the idealised fantasy place that calls to the contemporary, alienated, rootless citizen of urban/suburban USA, whose grasp of plant-life detail is shaky but whose ardour is real. Bluebells don't 'blaze' – especially in Scotland, where what are called bluebells are what the English call harebells: delicate meadow flowers, rather than the form of wild hyacinth that masses in the woods. But 'bluebells blazing' is not only a fine alliterative touch: 'blazing' sets the tone of how these Highlands are in the singer's mind. After the initial 'gentle and fair' the whole scene blazes with the singer's rapture (and to some extent with the restorative cleanliness that is next to godliness). The energising 'Aberdeen waters' must flow sparklingly clean and bracingly cold. Lest this is getting too hiking-bootedly wholesome, the heady scent of honeysuckle blooms in the air.

Here again, botanical realism is not all it might be. As the British sculptor Andrew Darke writes: 'In selecting [English] bluebells and honeysuckle he has two of the most transporting scents that might come to you on a woodland walk. They are so powerful that it is like total immersion – for a first, brief moment (and the brevity is part of the power) they overwhelm and immobilise the mind and spread a balm of pure pleasure. But . . . in actuality it is unlikely that one could experience both on the same day . . . honeysuckle is later in the season.' Similarly, the fourth stanza's gaze is on the buckeye trees, but 'the buckeye – American for the horse chestnut – is not likely to be seen in the Scottish Highlands'.[26] Moreover, Dylan's honeysuckle blooms inside that quintessential place of childhood mystery and of exciting danger, the 'wildwood'.

24. Andrew Muir, note 14.

25. Robert Burns (1759–96): 'My Heart's in the Highlands', 1790, quoted from Muir, note 14.

26. Andrew Darke, Gloucestershire, 11/4/99; personal correspondence answering my request for comments on what he considers probably his 'favourite Dylan track of all time, and emphatically too short'. I'm also grateful to my wife, Sarah Beattie, for bluebell information.

Impossible to have read Bruno Bettelheim and not take the wildwood too as the emblem of inner confusion, lostness and unresolved desires. One way and another, it is not so much that the bluebells are blazing but that the singer's yearning blazes for the redemptive power of these imagined Highlands.[27]

In accord with the aim of this opening stanza, the point about its last line –

> *I'm gonna go there when I feel good enough to go –*

is not that it stumbles into unintended bathos, as the reader of the isolated stanza (A. S. Byatt, perhaps) might assume, but that its descent into this near-comic ungainliness, into this prosaic conversational mode, both captures sympathetically the narrative tone of irresolution that makes clear how vague is his will actually to *go* to these Highlands, and guides us down into the unrarified air of the narrator's daily round, now introduced in the second stanza. Additionally, there is the neatly comic pun (a pun with a purpose, as good puns must have) that Dylan slips in with that 'when I feel good enough'. Behind the main meaning – 'when I feel cheerier, or more energetically healthy' – loiters the alternative, that of 'when I feel I'm a good enough person to deserve to go', furthering our sense of the spiritual, redemptive nature of these yearned-for Highlands.

He starts with the problematic lines

> *Windows were shakin' all night in my dreams*
> *Everything was exactly the way that it seems*
> *Woke up this mornin' and I looked at the same old page:*

are the windows shaking while he dreams, the noise intruding upon the dreaming, or are they shaking only in the dreams? Does everything seem the same in the dreams as in waking life (a fine touch) or does he, as the third line implies, wake more conventionally from twisted dreams to find tired normality restored? This latter is then expanded upon with the wrong kind of tiredness – not evoked by creative writing but enacted only by the tired writing of 'Same old rat-race, life in the same old cage' – and we move on to the second of the initial this-is-my-awful-life verses, which almost duplicates, but actually darkens, the 'Not Dark Yet' line about not looking for anything in anyone's eyes:

> *I don't want nothin' from anyone – ain't that much to take*

and then offers the precarious

> *Wouldn't know the difference between a real blonde and a fake.*

This is a distinctly unpromising start to the grim story of the speaker's shrivelled husk of a life, with nothing to suggest the riches that are to come, and which soon prove wholly capable of counter-balancing the Highlands choruses. If it's hard to feel that some of this lazy sourness is not a fake, the feeling is soon dispelled. The hopeless, doomed plea 'I wish someone'd come and push back the clock for me' is said with a rueful quietness that is affecting, and then comes the second chorus, in which the Highlands are given one of their two most explicit heavenly touches, on the line

---

27. Bruno Bettelheim, *The Uses of Enchantment* (1976), a book much referred to in Chapter 17.

> *That's where I'll be when I get called home*

(a nice use of an old-fashioned gospel-song stock phrase – as indeed he also manages for his second such Christian allusion, which is to

> *Big white clouds like chariots that swing down low*).

Then we begin to enjoy the surprises and sly wit that the song delivers, starting with the somehow innately comic prospect conjured by Bob Dylan singing 'I'm listening to Neil Young'. Part of the surprise here is a sort of stepping through the glass that normally divides the work from the person, or a breaking of some Dylan-imposed convention about what gets specified and what doesn't.

The last bad moment in the song's construction – and it only happens to British Empire ears – comes at the start of the next verse, when we get a disastrous pause after 'Insanity is smashing' and before 'up against my soul'. It's a poor line anyway, but only English jolly-hockey-stickism makes its first half comically incompetent. It gives way to the intentional sardonic comedy of the nicely put 'You could say I was on anything [pause] but a roll', with its funny, almost slapstick pun on drugs and bread rolls, and then the audacious lines about being so bereft of a conscience that all he can imagine he'd do with one if he had it would be to 'take it to the pawn shop'. At this point the third Highlands chorus comes in, winging us with soothing, balm-giving grace from this gritty, dirty Los Angeles of the soul to the cleansing break of dawn and the deeply inviting 'beautiful lake of the black swan': a transformation that enacts exactly the sense of catharsis that we recognise from city-clogged experience as one of the rescuing powers of Wordsworthian nature and benign landscape.

So far the established pattern of the song has been to have a Highlands chorus, two verses, chorus, two verses, chorus. Now comes an extraordinary shift of pattern, which only reveals itself in retrospect. We now get seven verses, all spinning the vivid, ridiculous yarn of an encounter between him and a waitress in a Boston restaurant. This is so off-the-wall, so riveting, so sublimely told, so funny and at the same time so inspired an evocation of how it might feel to be the 'artist' being told peremptorily that you must come up with some 'art'.[28]

The tactical manoeuvring in their odd, shifting relationship is delineated step by conversational step, as they jockey for advantage in an encounter that is partly a flirtation, partly a tale about the singer's myriad uncertainties having to gird themselves to repel the outsider's demanding intrusions, and partly, as its setting of the forlornly empty restaurant on a public holiday so brilliantly evokes, a momentary, unhopeful effort by both people to wrest a little diversionary human contact while marooned by the emptiness of their lives.

It would be unpalatable to go through it phrase by phrase applying the butterfly-pins of critical exegesis. I should just like to say that the many, many highlights include his saying that *she* studies *him* closely as he sits down but immediately making clear that it's been mutual with the observation 'She got a pretty face and long white shiny legs' – those legs so comically described, as if she's either a horse or from

---

28. As Richard Harrington perceives (see note 6), their encounter is 'also a caustic metaphor for the historically high expectations of critics'.

another planet. Then there's his choice of 'hard-boiled eggs' as *her* choice of what he probably wants to eat – with its hint of a put-down, perhaps even an ageist put-down – and the silly follow-up of there then not being any, or, rather, of her claiming that there aren't any. Another hint of contempt on her part is subtly achieved too in the battle over whether he must draw her on the napkin, when she hands it to him and says 'You can do it on that', as if *he*'s asked, and as if what he's asked is where he can relieve himself. Then there's the exquisitely made internal rhyme of 'napkin' and 'back an'' in

> *Well she takes the napkin, and throws it back an'*
> *Says 'That don't look a thing like me'.*

There's also the way that he brings in the language of the traditional white ballad to use as part of the elaborate push-and-pull of rudeness and politeness between them when he contradicts her brusque dissatisfaction with his 'Oh kind miss'. This would be nothing special as mere surface sarcasm: what makes it delightful is that its smiling aside invites a comparison between their crude contemporary skirmishes and the elaborate courtship rituals of old.

There are also the quite brilliant detonations set off on his hilarious self-put-down of a retort to her challenge 'You don't read women authors, do you?' (itself a refreshing, unpredictable capturing of the waitress' contemporary sensibility, 'made' in less than 'a few lines') when he says, like a reluctant schoolboy whose teacher has questioned his homework excuse: 'Read Erica Jong', pronouncing this 'Jong' instead of 'Yong' and still making for a long-suspended, joyously ludicrous half-rhyme with the other real name he threw into the song hours ago, 'Neil Young'.[29] The whole gift of Bob Dylan giving us a cameo of feminist debate, and wholly free of any unpleasant reactionary sneering, is a delightful surprise, totally outside the range of subject matter we expect from him. Then there's the slyly resourceful way that one of the many brushes with blues consciousness brought to this album occurs here, as he deploys, without the least elbow-nudging, one of the standard blues song *double entendres*, that of the pencil as the penis, with or without lead in it – which he takes into marvellous, surreal realms as the sparring moves from

> *. . . but I don't know where my pencil is at*

(which also resonates with his hard-boiled-egg agedness) to

> *She pulls one out from behind her ear.*

A conjuring-trick indeed.[30]

Andrew Darke comments that the entire exchange 'is so silly and unlikely that it has a strong ring of truth about it'. The song takes us through it word for word, and we're so entranced by its clever and very contemporary bleak dance of courtship – one

29. There's also the uncanny fact – drawn to my attention by Andrew Muir (e-mail, June 1999) – that Erica Jong's terrible novel *Any Woman's Blues* (1990) actually includes the line 'he had scribbled a rough sketch on a napkin . . . Not my style at all.' (Chapter 2.)

30. Of course 'lead in his pencil' belongs as much to English music-hall as to the blues world, but "Time Out Of Mind" owes little to English music-hall, and plenty to the blues, in which the image is used, for instance, by Bo Carter: 'My Pencil Won't Write No More', NYC, 4/6/31.

with real adversarial edge – and so transfixed by what strongly suggests itself as this unprecedented tour of the world of yer actual Bob Dylan, that the time goes by and the story unfolds and we quite forget the existence of the other side of the song and are taken by surprise when, after this six-minute spellbinding passage we're re-introduced to

> *Well my heart's in the Highlands . . .*

and we find ourselves transported once again, this time

> *. . . with the horses and hounds.*

As ever, the contrast of worlds is immense, wrought on this chorus specifically by the pre-twentieth-century atmosphere, perhaps the medieval British atmosphere of twang-ing arrows and snapping bows and the 'sport of kings': one more fanciful version of the Highlands, to which is added a new *geographical* dodginess, as he sings of being 'Way up in the border country'. The border country is not 'way up' but 'way down', below even the central lowlands, and thus as far from the Highlands as you can get without crossing the border and leaving Scotland altogether.[31] (Dylan never claims that he is singing of Scotland. There are many places called the Highlands, from Kentucky to Kenya, and there are Aberdeens in Mississippi, Idaho and Washington.)

With a relapse into the cornered gloom of

> *My heart's in the Highlands, can't see any other way to go*

we're back to the remorseless sameness of daily life, except that he feels

> *. . . further away than ever before,*

an expression of disconnectedness echoed later still in

> *I got new eyes: everything looks far away.*

Before that, however, there is the surprising common-sense candour of

> *Some things in life it just gets too late to learn,*

followed at once by one of those brief, affecting passages that it is impossible not to take autobiographically:

> *Well I'm lost somewhere – I must have made a few bad turns:*

a line that re-states the one touching, authentic-sounding passage that we find in 'Can't Wait', the shockingly direct, desolate

> *Oh honey, after all these years you're still the one*
> *. . . I left my life with you somewhere back there along the line.*

But the spiky black humour of 'Highlands' is not over. Lost, he sees, in a splendidly Dylanesque formulation,

---

31. Hunting may be first set down in verse as 'the sport of kings' in William Somerville's *The Chase*, Book 1, 1735, in which he calls it 'Image of war, without its guilt'.

> *. . . people in the park, forgettin' their troubles and woes*
> *They're drinkin' and dancin', wearin' bright-colored clothes.*

This is one of my favourite observations of this or any other Dylan album – the wonderful, strong-grain-of-truth perception that our culture's garish predeliction for brightly coloured clothes (rather than the muted options of the 1950s or the simple grace of the white or black robes of Arab countries even today) is just one long, pathetic attempt to escape our troubles. Playing further on this idiot vanity, as we trudge across the dreary street with him

> *. . . to get away from a mangy dog*

he envisages saying to himself ('in a monologue': another hilarious, clever small joke) the supremely withering

> *I think what I need might be a full-length leather coat.*

In a song that cascades with superlative vocal delivery, this is a high point of encapsulated contempt for the culture's emptiness. Adding a similarly clipped articulation of our common powerlessness, he gives a comparable but sadder withering treatment to

> *Somebody just asked me if I'm registered to vote.*

Four lines on and we swap it all, for the last time, for the metaphysical Highlands:

> *Well, my heart's in the Highlands at the break of day*
> *Over the hills and far away*
> *There's a way to get there and I'll figure it out somehow*
> *Well I'm already there in my mind and that's good enough for now.*

Dylan takes his bow of dignified yearning with one of the nattiest touches he has ever brought to anything. Throwing off the despairing 'further away than ever before', the deteriorated, stricken 'far away' of his 'new eyes' in the here and now, he regains the positive, glowing wonderment of that same phrase as it works in the lovely line from English nursery rhyme and folksong,

> *Over the hills and far away,*

singing *this* 'far away' incomparably beautifully – finding an infinitely delicate, fleeting tone that manages a sort of rhapsodic regret, a momentary lyrical sigh of grace and adieu. It is the most beautifully understated thing. It always means so much, this softest of touches. Confessing to the never-never land pull of these Highlands, it signals sad resignation that in truth he will never get there; but the warmth and tragic nobility that inform this sadness come from its also being his loving farewell to the real human world that once was ardently lovable and is now glimpsed again for a moment before receding, equally unreachable. To carry this admirable concentration of meaning so lightly and elegantly, he throws off, momentarily, the simple, relentless musical straight line that is so appropriate and right for the great unstoppable machine of the rest of the story, and with a fine enactment of ease gives this 'far away' a little rising and falling filigree of melody that floats off just a little way above the rest, like the curve of one of these faraway hills.

This nursery rhyme line is undeniably evocative by itself – you have only to use it without facetious knowingness to let its affectiveness come through. As noted in Chapter 17, the British writer G. K. Chesterton described it as one of the most beautiful lines in all English poetry, and Iona and Peter Opie add, in their pioneering *Oxford Dictionary of Nursery Rhymes*, that 'as if in confirmation, Gay, Swift, Burns, Tennyson [and] Stevenson . . . thought well enough of the line to make it their own'.[32]

Its spell, its conjuring of a simple, peaceable, unattainable Eden – its self-reflexive ability to transport us – comes partly from its having been, as the Opies put it, among the lines that form the 'first poetic memory' of childhood, so that *that* lost Edenic rapture throws its softening golden light upon the one evoked by the line itself. Bob Dylan's use of it, therefore, goes to the heart of his song: it distils the unfailing yearning for what is lost and catches the fleeting redemptive moment, a moment of contact with his better self, the self of loving, open hopefulness, which allows him – perhaps propels him – to end the song, and thus the album, on a note of good faith, albeit limited and fragile.

'Highlands' epitomises the best of "Time Out Of Mind". It deals with most of the album's prominent themes: endless, almost compulsive walking; desolation; lack of a sense of contact with other people; a suffocating sense of the hollowness of everything, and therefore the purposelessness of life; a looking forward to death, alternating with a wish that time was not running out; the conviction that long ago some crucial wrong turning was taken in life, one that meant the loss of true love; the conviction that there is little to say and ever less point to saying it; the exhaustion of feeling, mingled with a passionate sorrow for all this loss.

'Highlands' also epitomises the album in the way that one of its principal expressive techniques is the use of lines and phrases straight from other songs, plus phrases that may not duplicate but calculatedly remind us of other songs – in both cases songs by Bob Dylan and songs by other people in roughly equal proportions. And, as we've seen, not songs alone, but other works too: a religious meditation by John Donne, a poem by Robert Burns, a novel by Erica Jong at the very least.

We've also identified the Leonard Cohenishness of 'Love Sick', its intrusive Santo & Johnny steel guitar and its Country Joe & The Fish organ-sound; a Little Willie John record title; a lyric phrase from Norm Foxx & The Rob-Roys and/or The Belmonts; musical quotation from the Everly Brothers and Elvis Presley; and a line of lyric from Dylan's own back catalogue (from 'Moonshiner') and another, by associa-

---

32. ' "G. K. Chesterton," writes Ivor Brown, "observed that . . . 'Over the hills and far away' is one of the most beautiful in all English Poetry" ': Iona and Peter Opie, *The Oxford Dictionary of Nursery Rhymes*, 1951. The nursery rhyme that yields it, 'Tom, he was a piper's son' (Opie, no. 508), dates back at least as far as 1705, and it quotes the line itself as already being a song title: 'And all the tune that he could play / Was, "Over the hills and far away" '. (As noted in Chapter 17, the ending of Dylan's 'Percy's Song', 'And the only tune / My guitar could play / Was, "Oh The Cruel Rain And The Wind" ' duplicates this.) The Opies find the refrain 'Over the hills and far away' itself 'in a black-letter ballad, "The Wind hath blown my Plaid away, or, A Discourse betwixt a young Woman and the Elphin Knight" '. Aptly, for Dylan's purposes, this strongest candidate for having originated the line, publication of which the Opies date to about 1670 but note as having been 'possibly alluded to in 1549', comes from Scotland.

tion, back to 'Percy's Song'; plus an explicit reference to 'listening to Neil Young'. This is barely the beginning of the album's enormous juke-box sampler.

Of course, Dylan has always utilised other song titles within his own work. They crop up with differing degrees of obviousness, and when they are not obvious you're left to wonder not so much whether they are intended but rather whether they are intended to be recognised. Examples. It's odds on that Dylan knew quite well when he wrote 'Just Like Tom Thumb's Blues' that there is a Hank Williams song called 'Howlin' At The Moon', and that when he wrote 'Never Say Goodbye' he knew that there was a Bill Monroe record called 'Footprints In The Snow'.[33] But were *we* assumed to know that? If we were, should we have been expected to hear, underneath the reminiscence

> *Twilight on the frozen lake*
> *North wind about to break*
> *On footprints in the snow*
> *Silence down below*

the alternative remembrance of

> *Twilight on the frozen lake*
> *North wind about to break*
> *On 'Footprints In The Snow'*
> *Silence down below?*

Probably not: it doesn't help. It doesn't exactly *help* in the case of 'Just Like Tom Thumb's Blues' either – but granted that Hank Williams was Dylan's 'first idol', there is certainly a fascination, an opening up of playful ironic possibilities, to hearing the end of the third verse like this:

> *And she steals your voice*
> *And leaves you 'Howlin' At The Moon'.*

As Chapter 9 details, Dylan lyrics incorporate within them the Sonny Boy Williamson II title 'Nine Below Zero' in the mid-1960s, 'The Night Time Is The Right Time' at the end of the 1960s, and many more besides. The country gospel warhorse 'Mansion On The Hill' trots across the landscape of the 1980s Dylan song 'Sweetheart Like You'.[34] His repertoire has also included the occasional use of song-titles *as* song-titles, from 'Down The Highway' in the early 1960s, through 'Trouble In Mind' in the

---

33. Hank Williams: 'Howlin' At The Moon', Nashville, 16/3/51, MGM Records 10961, Hollywood, 1951; and on "Honky Tonkin'", MGM Records E242 (10-inch LP), Hollywood, 1954; reissued "The Legendary Hank Williams", K-Tel International Records NE1121, London, 1981.

Bill Monroe & The Blue Grass Boys: 'Footprints In The Snow', Nashville, 13/2/45, Columbia Records single, *nia*, New York, 1946. The song itself dates back to the turn of the century, perhaps earlier. Monroe's was not the first recording but was the first version of any significant popularity released post-war. It was revived in Britain in the 1950s by, and proved a minor hit for, Johnny Duncan & The Blue Grass Boys (not the same group). It was Duncan's follow-up but one to his big hit, 'Last Train To San Fernando'. [Johnny Duncan & The Blue Grass Boys: 'Footprints In The Snow', *nia*, Columbia Records DB 4029, London, 1957.]

34. For example Kitty Wells: 'Mansion On The Hill', *nia*; reissued "The Golden Years, 1949–1957", Bear Family Records BFX 15239, Vollersode, Germany, c. 1989.

late 1970s to the 1986 'Driftin' Too Far From Shore' (this last duplicating another Bill Monroe title).[35]

In the albeit limited output of the 1990s, however, while the duplicating of song titles *as* titles has remained almost negligible, the usage of song titles and phrases *within* Dylan's own work has increased exponentially, almost to Van Morrisonian proportions. First there was "Under The Red Sky", with its extraordinary inwardness with nursery rhymes and now here, the other side of the two acoustic solo albums of folk and blues placed in between, we have in "Time Out Of Mind" this banquet of, as it were, music made earlier, both by Bob Dylan himself and by earlier chefs.

To move beyond those examples already listed, and to begin at the beginning, the first vocal remark of the album, 'I'm walkin'', is the title of one of Fats Domino's greatest hits. Of course it's also a very anonymous remark, but as we know, Fats Domino whispers behind Bob Dylan many times down the years. He does so several times in the course of "Time Out Of Mind" while, as I suggested earlier, one of the spiritual homes of Dylan's album is New Orleans, which would not be the same place without Fats Domino, the most famous epitomiser and greatest populariser of New Orleans R&B. Everyone knows too that all his classic and hit recordings were made there and he names this, his hometown, in his lyrics – not least in the case of his big 1960 hit 'Walking To New Orleans'. In Dylan's line 'I'm goin' down the river, down to New Orleans', then, it is hard not to hear an allusion to Domino's early classic 'Going To The River'. Elsewhere on "Time Out Of Mind" we encounter the Domino title 'Sometimes I Wonder', and the allusion that seems to me the most subtle but the most certain – the line from ''Til I Fell In Love With You' where he sings that he's

>   ... *thinkin' about that girl who won't be back no mo'*.

This 'who won't be back no mo'' echoes in every way – the attractively bouncy distribution of the syllables, the accent on that 'no mo'', the mournful tone, as well as the words themselves – Fats Domino's singing about the girl who 'won't be back no mo'' (and left a note to say so) – in another 1960 hit song 'It Keeps Rainin''. I'm quite certain, therefore, that one of the girls Dylan is thinkin' about who won't be back no mo' is the one on Fats Domino's record.[36]

'Dirt Road Blues' is – like 'Trouble In Mind' – the core of the title of a classic blues song: or rather, a cluster of venerable blues songs, centred on Patton's 'Down The Dirt Road Blues', recorded at his début session, in 1929, but being performed, we can assume, much earlier and constructed from traditional lyrics. The great Tommy Johnson drew on them in 1928 for his 'Big Road Blues'. Arthur Crudup recorded 'Dirt Road Blues' in 1945 and as late as 1968 Howlin' Wolf was recording 'Ain't Goin' Down That Dirt Road'.[37]

35.   Details Chapter 18, note 28.

36.   Fats Domino: 'I'm Walkin'', New Orleans, 3/1/57, Imperial 5428, Hollywood, 1957; 'Walking To New Orleans', New Orleans, April 1960, Imperial 5675, Hollywood, 1960; 'Going To The River', New Orleans, Dec. 1952, Imperial 5231, Hollywood, 1953; 'Sometimes I Wonder', New Orleans, Feb. 1951, Imperial 5123, Hollywood, 1952; 'It Keeps Rainin'', New Orleans, Dec. 1960, Imperial 5753, Hollywood, 1961. For more on Domino in relation to Dylan, and re-release information, see Chapter 3.

37.   Charley Patton: 'Down The Dirt Road Blues', Richmond, Indiana, 14/6/29; "Charlie [sic] Patton No. 2" or "The Immortal Charlie Patton 1887–1934 Number 2", Origin Jazz Library OJL-7, Berkeley, 1964. Tommy Johnson: 'Big Road Blues', Memphis, 3/2/28; "Blues Roots/Mississippi", RBF Records RBF-14, New York, 1966.

Dylan's 'Dirt Road Blues' has two attractive verses – the one where he is 'Rollin' through the rain and hail looking for the sunny side of love' (a fine affirmative line amid the album's general gloom) and the one where he is 'Layin' around in a one-room country shack'. 'One Room Country Shack' is a 1953 record by the Texas-based pianist-vocalist Mercy Dee [Walton], a re-working of his 1949 début 'Lonesome Cabin Blues' (itself a re-working of Curtis Jones' 'Lonesome Bedroom Blues', which Dylan sang several times in concert in 1978).[38]

'Standing In The Doorway' similarly drops in a title, his line 'the stars have turned cherry red' calling up the 1939 and 1956 records of 'Cherry Red' by Big Joe Turner (in which the singer wants his face to turn cherry red). In the same Dylan song, his 'Smokin' a cheap cigar' comes from variants of the song we know best as Jimmie Rodgers' 'Waiting For A Train' (the line is used, for instance, on the version called 'The Georgia Hobo' by the Cofer Brothers); the phrase 'Buddy you'll roll no more' harks back to 'Roll On Buddy', a song and LP title by Ramblin' Jack Elliott and Derroll Adams, and perhaps also to 'Buddy Won't You Roll Down The Line', one of the Uncle Dave Macon tracks on the seminal Harry Smith anthology "American Folk Music", while the Dylan song's lovely last line, 'Blues wrapped around my head' carries a strong echo of the traditional blues line 'blues all around my bed'.[39]

'Million Miles' incorporates the Presley début title 'That's All Right' (so often known as 'That's Alright Mama', the phrase Dylan sings here, and which also began life as a blues record by our friend Arthur Crudup).[40]

In 'Tryin' To Get To Heaven', Dylan's 'I been walkin' that lonesome valley' alludes to a song recorded by the Carter Family, Woody Guthrie and others, '(You've Got To Walk That) Lonesome Valley'; his 'been all around the world, boys' quotes

Arthur 'Big Boy' Crudup: 'Dirt Road Blues', Chicago, 22/10/45, Victor Records 20–2757, New York, 1947. Howlin' Wolf: 'Ain't Goin' Down That Dirt Road', Chicago, Nov. 1968; unissued until the 3-CD set "The Chess Box", MCA Records CHD3–9332, New York, 1992.

38. Mercy Dee: 'One Room Country Shack', LA, 1953, Specialty Records 458, Hollywood, 1953. Bob Dylan: 'Lonesome Bedroom Blues', Tokyo, 20, 21 & 23/2/78.

39. Big Joe Turner: 'Cherry Red', NYC, 30/6/39; "The Original Boogie Woogie Piano Greats", Columbia KC32708, New York, 1974. Big Joe Turner: live NYC, 6/3/56; Atlantic Records LP 1234, New York, 1956. (Tommy Johnson's 'Big Road Blues', note 37, also mentions 'poor Cherry Red'.) The Cofer Brothers: 'The Georgia Hobo', Atlanta, 21/3/27; never reissued until the CD "Georgia Stringbands Vol. 1 (1927–1930)", Document DOCD-8021, Vienna, 1998. 'Danville Girl' / 'The Gambler' sometimes offers us the cheap cigar in a related variant – yielding this junction with "Time Out Of Mind" lyrics: 'Standing on a platform / Smoking a cheap cigar . . .': Cisco Houston: 'The Gambler', nia, "Railroad Songs", Folkways FA 2013, New York, c. 1961. ('A cheap cigar' also occurs in Peg Leg Howell's 'Coal Man Blues', Atlanta, 8/11/26; further detail Chapter 9, note 70.) Ramblin' Jack Elliott & Derroll Adams: 'Roll On Buddy', London, c. 1956, "Rambling Boys", Topic Records 10T14 (10-inch LP), London, 1957; reissued "Roll On Buddy", Topic Records 12T105 (12-inch LP), London, c. 1964; CD-reissued on "Ramblin' Jack", Topic Records TSCD477, London, 1996. For Dylan's familiarity with this, see Chapter 5, note 33. Uncle Dave Macon: 'Buddy Won't You Roll Down The Line', Chicago, 25/7/28; "American Folk Music", Folkways FP251–253, New York, 1952; CD-reissued as "Anthology Of American Folk Music" [6-CD box-set] with copious notes by many hands and a CD-ROM of extras, Smithsonian Folkways Recordings SFW 40090, Washington, DC, 1997.

40. Elvis Presley: 'That's All Right', Memphis, 5/7/54, Sun Records 209, Memphis, 1954. Arthur Crudup: 'That's All Right', Chicago, 6/9/46, Victor Records 20–2205, New York, 1946.
 And if you're train-spotting this kind of thing, 'Sometimes I Wonder' is the title not only of a Fats Domino record (see note 36) but also of an R&B hit single by the Drifters in 1960; and 'Do What You Gotta Do' was a hit by both the Four Tops and Nina Simone. The Drifters: 'Sometimes I Wonder', NYC, 27/10/60, Atco 6185, New York, 1962. The Four Tops: 'Do What You Gotta Do', nia, Tamla Motown TMG 710, London, 1969. Nina Simone: 'Do What You Gotta Do' [B-side of 'Ain't Got No – I Got Life'], NYC, 7/4/68, RCA Victor 9602, New York [RCA 1743, London], 1968.

the folkie repertoire item 'Hang Me, O Hang Me (Been All Around This World)' – which Dylan was performing live as the 1990s began; and his 'I'm just goin' down the road feelin' bad' tips his hat to Woody Guthrie's version of the traditional 'Lonesome Road Blues', namely 'Goin' Down That Road Feelin' Bad'.[41]

'Tryin' To Get To Heaven' also incorporates nursery rhyme cum folksong, including two that Alan Lomax quotes in his *Folk Songs of North America*, and several fragments of Spirituals, apparently taken from the same source. 'Miss Mary Jane' begins

> *Riding' in the buggy, Miss Mary Jane*
> *Miss Mary Jane, Miss Mary Jane*
> *Ridin' in the buggy, Miss Mary Jane*
> *I'm a long way from home*

and soon moves on to

> *Sally got a house in Baltimo',*
> *Baltimo', Baltimo'*
> *Sally's got a house in Baltimo'*
> *And it's three storeys high.*

while 'Buck-eye Rabbit' gives us

> *I wanted sugah very much*
> *I went to Sugah town*
> *I climbed up in that sugah tree*
> *An' I shook that sugah down.*

Dylan's song title can also be found inside the pages of the Lomax anthology. 'The Old Ark's A-Moverin'' gives him

> *Look at that sister comin' 'long slow*
> *She's tryin' to get to heaven fo' they close the do';*

a few songs further on and we get a version of that song we associate with the great Blind Willie Johnson and the great Son House, 'John The Revelator', which here includes the line

> *Seal up your book, John, and don't write any more,*

while three songs later what should we reach but 'This Train' with its

> *This train don't pull no gamblers, no midnight ramblers, this train!*

It is disappointing, perhaps, to think that Dylan has assembled this marvellous song not from the immense and erudite swirl of American song in his head but by flipping

---

41.   The Carter Family: 'Lonesome Valley', NYC, 8/5/35; "The Famous Carter Family", Harmony Records HL 7280, New York, c. late 1950s. Woody Guthrie: 'Lonesome Valley', *nia*, and 'Goin' Down That Road Feelin' Bad', *nia*, both CD-reissued "Woody Guthrie Library of Congress Recordings", Rounder Records 1041, Cambridge, Massachusetts, c. 1990.

   Bob Dylan: 'Hang Me, O Hang Me (Been All Around This World)' débuted New Haven, Connecticut, 12/1/90, five times on the January–March leg of the Never-Ending Tour, twice on the August–September leg and in Boone, North Carolina, 30/10/90 [third leg].

through an Alan Lomax book and pulling bits out more or less in order from every third or fourth song.[42] But as I have argued before, in discussing what it is that makes certain 'found lines' recommend themselves to the finder and others not, the interaction still reflects the particularity of the finder's imaginative sympathy. Just as important, the result is the finder's responsibility. The collage is necessarily made from pre-made things, but the collage artist assembles the picture. In this instance it is reasonable to credit Dylan with a familiarity with the majority of these songs that has been earned by a far longer and more inward process than thumbing idly through one folksong anthology, so that when he does so his creative imagination is not in fact idle at all, but applies itself with a heartfelt intelligence, holding in play a great many possibilities, discovering, as is usual in such a process, new exchanges of meaning and inter-weavings of resonance, and working by means of the usual exercise of discrimination and judgement towards what is a new creative whole: in this case a very fine one, and at the same time so very Dylanesque!

Dylan also pulls a line and a half from a well-known Spiritual in 'Cold Irons Bound'; but in this case it's easier to pin down what he does with it. The second verse begins

> *There's a wall of pride high and wide*
> *Can't see over to the other side;*

part of Dylan's evocation of doom and despair comes from the way that what was 'deep and wide / I got a home on the other side' in the Spiritual was the River Jordan; now it's the wall of his own ego. (An alternative slice of the traditional lyric is 'The river is deep and the river is wide, Hallelujah / Milk and honey on the other side, Hallelujah'.) The Spiritual is 'Michael, Row The Boat Ashore', an infuriatingly catchy song that most of us who are old enough were trying to resist as the 1960s dawned when it was thrust at us by the chart-topping Highwaymen (and in Britain by Lonnie Donegan), and which Dylan himself refers to in his early unrecorded composition 'Talkin' Folklore Center'. The song was venerable long before the Highwaymen prettified it and is likely to outlast 'Cold Irons Bound' by some decades yet. So is the other traditional song cited later in 'Cold Irons Bound', 'Whisky In The Jar', best remembered by many from the 1970s hit single by the Irish group Thin Lizzy.[43]

We stay with secular song as we move on through the remainder of the album, coming first to 'Make You Feel My Love', in which one of the least numbingly

42. Alan Lomax, *Folk Songs of North America* (1960) in which 'The Old Ark's A-Moverin'' is song no. 248, 'John The Revelator' no. 252, 'This Train' no. 255, 'Miss Mary Jane' no. 259 and 'Buck-eye Rabbit' no. 266. I am grateful to Andrew Muir for forwarding (e-mail 9/4/99) e-correspondence from Mike Daley and Anneke and Hans Derksen (date unstated) containing these details.

43. The Highwaymen: 'Michael', *nia* [HMV POP 910, London], 1961. Lonnie Donegan: 'Michael, Row The Boat', *nia*, Pye 7N 15371, London, 1961. The Highwaymen were part of the middle-of-the-road folk revival happening in a parallel universe that came into being with the Small Bang of the Kingston Trio's 1958 success with an Ivy League version of the traditional murder ballad 'Tom Dooley'. Others included the Brothers Four, the Limeliters, the Tarriers and the Rooftop Singers.

Bob Dylan: 'Talkin' Folklore Center', only known to have been performed at Gerdes Folk City, NYC, 16/4/62, as part of medley with 'Talkin' New York'.

Thin Lizzy: 'Whisky In The Jar', *nia*, 1972 [UK] Decca Records F 13355, London, 1972.

For pointing out Dylan's use of 'Michael, Row The Boat Ashore', and two or three other Dylan debts, I am grateful to John Way.

dreadful lines, that in which the storms are raging '. . . on the highway of regret', picks up its dubious poesy directly from an old Ralph Stanley bluegrass standard, 'Highway Of Regret' . . . which is to be found on the same 1959 Stanley Brothers album as the song 'Riding The Midnight Train' (used as a Dylan line in 'Standing In The Doorway').[44]

In 'Can't Wait' we have the singer 'tryin' to walk the line', 'I Walk The Line' being one of Johnny Cash's best known songs and hits and recorded, though not released, by Dylan and Cash together at the 1969 sessions that yielded their 'Girl Of The North Country' duet on "Nashville Skyline". We also have the Leonard Cohen title 'I'm Your Man', used as the opening phrase of the second verse, and the mention of 'stormy weather', a jazz standard song title, while you might feel that the phrases 'standing at the gate' and 'I can't wait' conspire to remind us of another Woody Guthrie title, 'Waiting At The Gate'.[45]

Dylan has said in interviews that the riff that runs through 'Highlands' (a model of restrained hypotic insistence) is based on an old Charley Patton record. This is hard to pin down; the closest echo I can find is in Patton's 'Dry Well Blues', his first 1930 recording. If so, then as with the musical figures borrowed from the Everly Brothers and Elvis, there is a sub-text appropriateness here, granted that one of the album's main themes – one inextricably linked, as so often in Dylan, with the search for, or loss of, love – is the search for, or loss of, the muse.[46] He has *not* said – he may not know, though it would make for a mildly eerie coincidence – that a significant part of the lyric of 'Highlands' also resembles a record by Terry Allen, 'The Beautiful Waitress', a song from the late 1970s, which features a dialogue with a waitress that involves both food and drawing on napkins. (In this one, they agree that legs are hard to draw and an attempt at horses is said to look more like sausages.[47])

In accordance with the album's more normal usage of other people's songs, 'Highlands' draws to a close with two more imported references, one direct and one indirect. The first is the use of the croonerish popular song 'The Party's Over', and the other, the line 'The sun is beginning to shine on me', sets up an adroit murmur, in the context of blues lyric poetry, with the lovely and well-known common-stock line expressing an equally unconvinced, fragile optimism, 'The sun's gonna shine in my back door some day.'

I'm quite sure I've missed some, but those explored above are at least some of the quotations of titles and phrases worked into the music and words of "Time Out Of Mind" from the songs of other people – so many of them songs that are a part of the consciousness of anyone who has ever been grabbed by the worlds of folksong, the

---

44.   'Highway Of Regret', written by Ralph Stanley and Don Chubby Anthony, and recorded by the Stanley Brothers, Live Oak, Florida, summer 1959, Starday Records 466, Nashville, 1959. The same sessions also included 'Riding The Midnight Train', Starday Records 494, Nashville, c. 1960. Both songs were on the album "Mountain Song Favorites", Starday LP 106, Nashville, 1959.

45.   Johnny Cash: 'I Walk The Line', Memphis, 1956, Sun Records 241, Memphis, 1956. Bob Dylan & Johnny Cash: 'I Walk The Line', Nashville, 18/2/69. Leonard Cohen: 'I'm Your Man', *nia*; title track of album, Columbia Records CBS CK 44191 [CD], New York, 1988. Woody Guthrie: 'Waiting At The Gate', *nia*; CD-reissued "Struggle", Smithsonian/Folkways Records SF 40025, Washington, DC, 1990s.

46.   Charley Patton: 'Dry Well Blues', Grafton, Wisconsin, c. 28/5/30; issue details as in note 37.

47.   Terry Allen: 'The Beautiful Waitress', Lubbock, 1977–78; "Lubbock On Everything", CD-reissued Sugar Hill Records, *nia* [LP first issued 1978].

blues, rock'n'roll and/or popular song. As we've seen, they work by calling up deep soundings of meaning and memory to boom and rumble and hum underneath the dark, churning surface of the album, setting up multi-layered resonances between themselves and between singer and listener. But just as important, and working in much the same way, are the many parallels and contrasts, the many echoes and dialogues, set up between the songs on the album and the vast Bob Dylan songbag of the past. As Andrew Muir puts it, 'allusions to his own songs play a crucial structural role throughout the album'.[48]

We have touched to some extent on such resemblances as between different songs within "Time Out Of Mind", and there are one or two more of these to mention. But they themselves cannot naturally be altogether separated from the resemblances they call to mind between themselves and songs from Dylan's magnificent, huge back catalogue. To begin with the one will inevitably slide us into the other.

That several "Time Out Of Mind" songs begin with a declaration of walking has been widely noted and thus in itself ties several of the songs together. That this walking has a hounded quality, almost suggesting the old-fashioned pyschiatric syndrome of fugue (where you forget your normal life, walk huge distances with a blank mind and 'come to', exhausted, a long way from home), is evoked by memorable lines from two different songs here: 'I can't even remember what it was I came here to get away from' on 'Not Dark Yet' and 'It doesn't matter where I go anymore, I just go' on 'Can't Wait', both delivered to maximise the sense of a hollow-eyed, haunted condition.[49] The related theme of pushing along through some form of mental or emotional blizzard, experienced like a physical one, is expressed very similarly in the 'Rollin' through the rain and hail' of 'Dirt Road Blues' and the 'Rollin' through stormy weather' of 'Can't Wait'. ('Rollin'' is an odd word to use here.)

There is also a striking similarity between the lurid anticipation of the flesh falling 'off of' his face in 'Standing In The Doorway' and 'my eyes feel like they're falling off my face' in ''Til I Fell In Love With You' – though both of these may strike us as inspired by the line 'till the flesh rots off your bones' sung so recently by Dylan in 'Love Henry' on "World Gone Wrong".

More importantly, the theme of looking with wistful envy at the normalcy and apparent tolerable happiness of other people's lives also finds expression in several "Time Out Of Mind" songs. In 'Love Sick', the opening song, he watches silhouettes in the window and lovers in the meadow; in 'Highlands', the closing song, he sees people in the park, dancing and drinking and forgetting their troubles. He'd change places with any of them and wishes someone would push back the clock so that he too could be like the 'young men with the young women lookin' so good'. And in between, he watches the boys and girls come out to play in ''Til I Fell In Love With You' (the light touch of nursery rhyme here making for another inter-song echo, this time with 'Tryin' To Get To Heaven', in which nursery rhyme abounds) and other people's laughter just makes him sad while he's marooned in the doorway crying. This

48. Andrew Muir: *Dignity* (see note 14).

49. For a riveting examination of fugue, and its importance to contentious ideas about the shifting nature of mental illnesses, see Ian Hacking's *Mad Travellers* (1999) and/or the review/discussion of it by Mikkel Borch-Jacobsen: 'What Made Albert Run', *London Review of Books*, Vol. 21, no. 11, 27/5/99.

last element, the strandedness behind a barrier, is a reminder too of something further back in Bob Dylan's work: instead of watching silhouettes in the window or being stranded in the doorway crying, the singer of 'I Dreamed I Saw St. Augustine' ends up with 'I put my fingers against the glass and bowed my head and cried'.

The final inter-song dialogue on "Time Out Of Mind" to mention here is that which centres upon the too-fast-too-slow and the moving-standing-still dynamic in 'Standing In The Doorway' and 'Not Dark Yet', though here again these do not keep themselves neatly to themselves but send us off elsewhere too, inside and outside Dylan's own repertoire. First, there are three of these slow-fast focuses on the album itself. Along with

> Yesterday everything was goin' too fast
> Today it's moving too slow

and

> I know it looks like I'm moving
> But I'm standing still

we have the more subtle and interesting contradiction in the scene-setting beginning to 'Not Dark Yet', in which

> It's too hot to sleep and time is runnin' away.

The usual experience is that if you can't sleep time passes with intolerable slowness, not with great speed. Thus it is that between them, these pieces of writing throw us back to 'If You See Her Say Hello' in which, with a similar challenge to our expectations,

> I know every scene by heart
> They all went by so fast.

As for the *less* subtle slow-fast, moving-standing-still contradictions, these too operate in an interesting way, to do with their very predictability. In the first instance, the fact that we've already had the line-end 'low' planted in our ears means that when we hear 'yesterday . . . too fast' and then 'today . . .' we know before he gets there that it's going to conclude with 'too slow'. This is, then, a neat proof of precisely what it diagnoses. We reach the line's conclusion before he does: he's moving too slow. Similarly, when we hear first the line end 'against my *will*', we are primed so that when we then embark upon 'I know it looks like I'm moving but . . .' we fill in 'standing still' at once, ahead of him again. The self-reflexiveness of the text triumphs again.

However, this would be no triumph at all if the context here was, say, modern poetry, or indeed any form of literary poetry. It would merely score low marks for its lumbering obviousness. The point is, though, that on "Time Out Of Mind" the context, the medium, is not literary poetry but the blues – and as we saw in Chapter 9, one of the ways in which *blues* lyric poetry functions as between performer and audience is by allowing in, to use the phrase that Pete Welding appropriates for it, the shock of recognition (which is actually no shock at all: in a way it's quite the opposite, more a reassurance of recognition), opening up for the listener other resonances from other experiences of having encountered the same formulation, the same motif or line or phrase before. Dylan's deep sympathy with the spirit of blues lyric poetry is what leads him into generating this particular form of, if you will, 'reassurance of recognition'. Just as hearing, in the blues (to repeat the example given in Chapter 9),

I lay down last night, tried to take my rest

gives you the strong hunch that what will come next will be

My mind got to ramblin' like the wild geese in the west,

so here too we know what is coming before it arrives. It makes space for us, it allows in one more part of our participation in making the work we are hearing.

This may be a fair part of the appeal too of our recurrent recognition of lines, phrases, fleeting echoes, from Dylan's enormous body of previous work when we attend to "Time Out Of Mind". The endless play of cross-referencing and dialogue is part of the huge speculative space that a great artist offers the listener/reader/viewer.

One example that fuses both a blues-recognition factor and a Dylan one is that when we hear him sing that he can hear the church bells, in 'Standing In The Doorway', this can yield for us the recollection of his 'listenin' to the church bells tone' and 'hearin' them church bells tone' in his "Blood On The Tracks" out-take 'Call Letter Blues', that of his 'listenin' to them church bells tone' too in his early 1960s song 'Ballad For A Friend', *and* the ringing of those bells in the ears from many an old blues song in which it is itself a formulaic ingredient.

The ears pick up Dylan parallels so easily, though of course the more of his work you know, and the more inwardly you know it, the more of these multi-layerings will be there for you to savour or push around. Even the small and innocuous 'rock me once / . . . rock me for a couple of months' is likely to take you back to 1981's 'Lenny Bruce' and 1986's 'Maybe Someday', in both of which he also rhymes 'once' with 'months' (in 'Lenny Bruce' with the identical phrase 'a couple of months'). To hear that lovely expression, on 'Tryin' To Get To Heaven', of the attempt to get back to an earlier, more childlike condition, 'Gotta sleep down in the parlor', is to hear it as a wish to return to that comparable moment set playing again in the head from 'Time Passes Slowly', when he remembers that 'We sat in her kitchen while her mama was cookin''.

The complaint about the grind of 'life in the same old cage' in 'Highlands' parallels another "Blood On The Tracks" out-take, 'Up To Me', in which he sings of 'the cage where I used to work'. More generally, the long dadaist brilliance of 'Highlands' is reminiscent of nothing so much as the wondrous 'Clothes Line' of the Basement Tapes. More generally still, it is impossible to encounter a long song called 'Highlands' at the end of a long Bob Dylan album without being put in mind of 'Sad-Eyed Lady Of The Lowlands', in its day an unprecedentedly long song at the end of "Blonde On Blonde". And if 'standing at the gate . . . can't wait' echoes a Woody Guthrie title, it also echoes 'Sad-Eyed Lady''s chorus-line 'Should I leave them by your gate / Or . . . should I wait?'

The Basement Tapes also echo in the mind when we hear, on ''Til I Fell In Love With You', 'I been hit too hard / Seen too much', because not only the words but the staccato melodic shape too parallels the much more vivacious, undefeated lines in 'Million Dollar Bash' in which 'I been hittin' it too hard / My stones won't take' – an example that shows one of the general ways in which these cross-references work between this album and those of the past. Not in every instance, but in most, one of the effects they have is to underline and deepen what the lyrics of "Time Out Of Mind" articulate again and again: loss – loss of youth, joie de vivre, love, intimations of immortality, human kindness, faith, trust and inspiration. In general, that is, the message of the cross-referencing between the older work and the newer – the 'it used to be like that and now it goes like this' – is that what used to be all right no longer is. That now he no longer knows what all right even means. Another small example is the re-treading of that rocky road in 'Cold Irons Bound'. Now,

> Well, the road is rocky and the hillsides mud
> Up over my head nothing but clouds of blood

whereas once upon a time he saw through to 'Paths Of Victory' and could sing that

> The trail is dusty and my road it might be rough

and

> The gravel road is bumpy, it's a hard old road to ride

but

> . . . I turned my head up high.
> I seen that silver linin' that was hangin' in the sky.

The only two instances on "Time Out Of Mind" that seem to me to involve a gratuitous trading on his back catalogue – a deliberate re-using of old nuggets to try to augment new rubble – are those he places inside 'Make You Feel My Love'. Here the vainglorious boast 'You ain't seen nothin' like me yet' wholly fails to crank itself up from, or trade upon, the far more appealing modesty of 'She should have caught me in my prime', a line in a variant version of 'Simple Twist Of Fate'. Likewise, in the preceding line of 'Make You Feel My Love', Dylan's distasteful attempt at a winsome recycling of 'when the winds of changes shift' from 'Forever Young' into the windbaggery of 'The winds of change are blowin' wild and free' does nothing to lessen the general sense of transparent sham that pervades the song from start to finish.

Actually it does do one other thing: it stirs a memory from when 'Forever Young' was new and itself elicited a frisson of disquiet as to its slight flirtation with sentimentality, and slight disquiet too at the fact that 'when the winds of changes shift' itself seemed perilously close to a suspect re-usage of the 'wind' in 'Blowin' In The Wind', and more particularly the idea of keeping in tune with shifts in the wind, an idea so memorably expressed – indeed patented, you might say – in that great 'Subterranean Homesick Blues' line 'You don't need a weatherman to know which way the wind blows'. But if 'Forever Young' prompted this fastidious disquiet about its possible sentimentality and its possible suspect recycling, well – it seems like *The Brothers Karamazov* looked back on from the Mills and Boonery of 'Make You Feel My Love'.

These are the exceptions, and they come from the one "Time Out Of Mind" song that is utterly inauthentic. One might dislike 'Million Miles' and its aircraft-hangar-production companions, one might discount 'Dirt Road Blues' as lightweight and a missed opportunity, a fudged attempt to contribute worthily to the rockabilly genre (one of Dylan's favourite genres) but only 'Make You Feel My Love' is entirely irredeemable, unworthy of any place at all in Bob Dylan's repertoire.

Nor is it always the case that the contrast offered by "Time Out Of Mind" is to work from decades earlier. In this respect the throwback to 1993's 'Love Henry' is not alone. The very last line of the very last song on the album,

> *And that's good enough for now,*

is a particularly neat repeat of the same self-reflexive sign-off he gave us at the finishing end of 1992's "Good As I Been To You", with its

> *If you want any more you can sing it yourself.*

And if the main distinguishing feature of 'Tryin' To Get To Heaven' is its warm handling of nursery rhyme ingredients (as it is), the back-catalogue song it urges upon us is the not-very-far-back 'Under The Red Sky', from 1990.

Of course, you might argue that even leaving 'Make You Feel My Love' aside, one of the ways in which this process of using allusions to Dylan's own past works as part of the "Time Out Of Mind" elaboration of 'how it is when things disintegrate', is that the old songs we're reminded of by the new tend to be superior imaginative works. In a number of cases this is undoubtedly true and the early part of this chapter addressed itself to this issue. But I hope the rest of the chapter has argued a rather different evaluation in the case of the four major songs on the album, so that on the whole when we ricochet between the old works and these new ones, it is by contrasts of treatment and tone, not by a contrast of quality, that the greater desolation and darkness of "Time Out Of Mind" establishes itself.

Moreover, labelling these things is often too crude. One of the most enticing examples of all the parallels that "Time Out Of Mind" invokes certainly involves conceding that the old song, a major work, is greatly superior to the new – but that is not, in this instance, the point at issue. What *is* the point is that the contrast serves to point up in a most skilful way the state of mind that "Time Out Of Mind" is intent upon addressing throughout. The old song is 'Mr. Tambourine Man', the new one is 'Can't Wait', and the unexpected contrast that functions so well lies here, in the perfect parallel form and rhythm of these two lines:

> *My weariness amazes me, I'm branded on my feet*

and

> *Your loveliness has wounded me, I'm reeling from the blow.*

This plays so unanswerably upon the irony that it is the line that speaks of weariness that dances with life's loveliness, and vice versa. It makes the clear fall from then to now a weapon of effectiveness for the now itself. Evoking the contrast, then, is an inspired, legitimate device whereby Dylan emphasises yet again, and with a dancing subtlety, one of the main themes of "Time Out Of Mind" – the fall from the joys and humanity of then to the wounded emptiness of now.

There is another, more general usefulness to being reminded of 'Mr. Tambourine Man' when letting "Time Out Of Mind" roam through the listener's mind. 'Mr. Tambourine Man' was Dylan's most sustained and successful early song of imprecation to the muse – or to put it less high-falutingly, about the conscious seeking for inspiration. It was itself an inspired work about that seeking, fashioning the seeking into the source of inspiration itself. And this is what Dylan seeks to pull off again, as he stands in the far more desperate straits of "Time Out Of Mind". And for a substantial portion of the album, he manages it. All through it, there are pleas for the return of inspiration. In many cases passages that are at first assumed to be lamentations for lost love can be heard also as lamentations for the loss of the muse that once loved him, that was around so reliably that it seemed an indivisible part of him. He'll keep on walkin' till he hears her holler out his name. As Christopher John Farley wrote in reviewing the album, 'Worse . . . than losing a lover is losing a muse . . . again and again, he hints at writer's block and creative barrenness, subtly linking it to his lost love . . . Turning the quest for inspiration itself into relevant rock – that is alchemic magic.'[50]

Dylan achieves this with partial success. It is not a sparkling story of transcendent triumph like 'Mr. Tambourine Man' and the careening creativity of the mid-1960s. There are scars of dreary cheapness and craters of barrenness all across the terrain of the album. But there is much imaginative achievement too, both in the unparalleled calling-up of dialogues and soundings from other works of song *and* in finding inspiration in the seeking for it, from the matchless evocation of 'Not Dark Yet' of how it is to see, without delusion, that what lies ahead is all downhill, to the disproving of that by the creation of these 'Highlands': something not only tremendous but new – genuinely new – work.

What comes stepping in too, when the writer and singer is inspired, is the impetus to the recipient's creativity. For Andrew Darke, and in contrast to the scars and craters in the album's terrain, the best thing about 'Highlands' lies here, in

> the *vast* speculative space that is laid out. The degree to which the participant's imagination is engaged in any artwork (in any artform) is a significant part of the power of a work. The most powerful experiences generated by artworks are those which bring one's own imagination and emotions into full play. A *new* thing is made, catalysed by the artwork but 'made' by oneself. A great work is one which has enough speculative space and possibility in it to go on stimulating the imagination in different ways each time you engage with it. A dense fabric of imaginative journeys is built up. You can choose to re-make one of those journeys or take a new turning. Sometimes you take a familiar route but holding the sense of all those other possibilities.[51]

I don't want to end with invidious comparisons between any Dylan albums – but in spite of its huge flaws "Time Out Of Mind" is up there somewhere, and that is because of the complex, multi-layered experience it offers as you listen and re-listen. The experience of grappling with a real Bob Dylan album.

50. Christopher John Farley, 'Dylan's lost highway', *Time*, 29/9/97.
51. Andrew Darke, note 26.

CHAPTER TWENTY

There Is Only Up Wing an' Down Wing

> They asked what effect Bob Dylan had on me. That's like asking how
> I was influenced by being born.
>
> Pete Townshend, 1985[1]

The Down Wing

In performance, the Bob Dylan of the 1990s may be continuing to revise or re-write the texts of the mid-1960s and 1970s: but wasn't it the Bob Dylan of back then who did most of the work? Is the Bob Dylan of here and now coming up with all that many new first drafts for the Bob Dylan of twenty years hence to be able to re-write in perpetuity?

Confronting these difficulties means acknowledging those areas of Dylan's activity as an artist over these last two decades that have given rise to much disquiet. It's no fun to go into it, and it wouldn't bear handling at all if it weren't for its pertinence to Dylan's art itself. I suppose I'm saying that it's a nasty business but somebody has to do it. To what extent other people share *my* disquiets over aspects of what Dylan has done to himself and his art over these last years, I can't say, but much of what follows arises from conversations with many people.

I make a distinction here between the well-intentioned unease of those who have appreciated Dylan's art over some kind of long haul, and the merely public disapprobation Dylan inevitably attracts in the media, when it notices him at all, and among people whose only awareness of his existence is through these occasional media blips. That public chorus is of no interest. It is the same chorus that once wanted Dylan to carry on singing folksongs, or writing protest songs, or staying pre-electric; the same chorus that wanted Elvis to stop singing black music and wiggling his hips; the same chorus that thinks it wants everyone to be 'normal'. So I'm not concerned here with whether Dylan 'behaves properly' at Live Aid, or on arrival at the airport, or anywhere else. The 1980s was a hard period to get through, and at least Dylan managed it without turning into one of the Stepford Wives of the American entertainment industry

---

1. Pete Townshend of the Who, 1985, quoted in Bill Flanagan's *Written in My Soul*, 1986.

like so many other public figures. Not for him the renouncing of the anti-materialist hard rains of the 1960s; not for him the joining of the Born-Again Body-Worshippers. (Look at us! We came through all that nonsense unscathed! . . . and great is our reward in the garden of showbiz: we have cleaned up in both senses.) Bob Dylan, the old spoilsport, shows no interest in aerobics, looks his age, is liable to sing about what will happen when we die, and generally makes himself far from the ideal guest on glitzy chat-shows or for opening that new shopping mall; you can't even trust him not to mention the role of American banks at a charity event for the starving of the Third World. Not for him the making of music that sounds like a Pepsi ad even before it gets turned into one.

So if Dylan managed to get through the awful 1980s partly by stumbling around on a bit too much alcohol and/or whatever (while the cameras snapping at him yielded pictures of scowling, bleary charmlessness), it's not hard to credit that this decline from the unerring, photogenic precision of youth was all of a piece with his struggle to retain a deeply unfashionable integrity.

Less easy to accept is another part of the same process: Dylan's growing of a more cynical outer shell, from which part of the cynicism – in the corrosive form of some kind of self-contempt, some denigration of his own artistry – has seeped inside. It damages the very integrity it was meant to protect. It makes for a whole series of ways in which he appears to give less, care less and respect his own talent less, and it delivers him into demeaning situations and tawdry dullnesses his best self would avoid. Indeed it was *by* his avoidance of shabbiness and ennui that his best self taught us in the beginning what unfaltering nimble grace was possible for the popular artist in the marketplace.

Among the ways this decline manifests itself is in the matter of the sheer technical quality of his recordings. Bob Dylan tells Bill Flanagan (in *Written in My Soul*) that 'When I hear my old stuff I just think of how badly it was recorded.' Yet this is the opposite of the truth. With the exception of "Oh Mercy" (to achieve which producer Daniel Lanois reputedly had to fight Dylan, almost literally, to get him to bother), the work Dylan recorded in the 1980s to 1990s is markedly inferior technically not only to what is and should be possible, but to what was achieved on his own earliest work.

The deleterious effect applies all round but especially in what happens to his vocals. Listen to the way the voice is recorded on any track on the first four albums, and it's right *there*: you hear the detail of the voice vividly as it chisels out each crystalline syllable; you hear every intake of breath and you hear how each exhalation is distributed along the lines he sings. You register every nuance, feel every surface, receive all that close-up intelligence of communication, the infinitely variable, fluid expressiveness. This is how it should be. This is how to bring out the genius of his singing, in which these intakes of breath, these chiselled inflections that change moment by moment, these almost silent sighs, are all integral: all alive, interdependent dynamics in his uniquely intensive vocal detailing. He wasn't joking when he famously described his songs as 'exercises in tonal breath control'. There's an equivalence here to what's meant in a remark about blues guitar-playing that Stanley Booth recounts in *Rythm Oil*: 'An old black Memphis musician stood one night in an alley beside a young white guitarist, pointed to the stars, and said, "You don't plays de notes – you plays de molecules." '[2]

This is how Dylan's voice is when it gives you goose bumps. So it demands close attention from the vocal mike, like a diamond under a magnifying glass: and on the early albums it gets it. It more or less gets it too on the solo 'Spanish Is The Loving Tongue', the "Folkways: A Vision Shared" track 'Pretty Boy Floyd' and 'Ring Them Bells' ('we've recaptured some of the quality that the early records had; you can really hear him in the foreground', said Lanois at the time); but on the whole it's absent, there's no such care and attention on the work of the 1980s and 1990s. Listen to the 3-D vividness, the shining, buoyant (pre-transistorised?) *presence* of the voice either in the studio on, say, 'To Ramona' or 'North Country Blues' (to cite two vocals that are in other ways stylistically quite different) or in concert on 1963's 'Tomorrow Is A Long Time'. And then listen to the dry, flattened out, wrong-end-of-a-megaphone recording the vocals get (incompetently tricked out with phoney echo) on "Empire Burlesque".[3]

Or listen to 'Maybe Someday', a song that would be terrific if the voice weren't halfway to sounding like a Chipmunks parody of Dylan recorded from the far side of a football field. The difference in recording quality between the vocal on a track like this (recorded in 1986) and on, say, 'Black Crow Blues' (1964) is pathetic. Or listen to the disparity between the recording quality of Arthur Alexander's 1959, *one*-track-tape-deck cut of 'Sally Sue Brown' and Bob Dylan's 1987, 24- or 48-track cut of the same song. Alexander's voice is, as Dylan's once was, right *there*; Dylan's seems to be flailing around inside the dishwasher.[4]

Dylan elsewhere acknowledges this deterioration himself, according to U2's axeman The Edge: 'Talking to Dylan, he was saying that the technology has improved but the recordings were still better in the Sixties, when they had more of whatever they had; and whatever they had is essential.' And interviewed by U2's Bono, Dylan elaborated:

> You know the studios in the old days were all much better, and the equipment so much better, there's no question about it in my mind . . . they were just big rooms, you just sang, you know, you just made records; and they sounded like the way they sounded there . . . You go into a studio now and they got rugs on the floor, settees and pinball machines and videos and sandwiches coming every ten minutes. It's a big expensive party and you're lucky if you come out with anything that sounds decent.[5]

Then there's the shift to digital recording, which swiftly dominated the market-place *and* proved a disappointment. Neil Young says we're living in the dark ages of

2.   Stanley Booth: *Rythm Oil*, 1991.

3.   'Tomorrow Is A Long Time', live NYC, 12/4/63, has been released on "Bob Dylan More Greatest Hits" and on the 3-LP set "Masterpieces".

4.   Arthur Alexander: 'Sally Sue Brown', Sheffield, Alabama, 1959; Judd Records, USA, 1960: his début single. He wrote his exquisite classic 'You Better Move On' while working as a bell-hop in the Muscle Shoals Hotel.

5.   The Edge, quoted in the *Melody Maker* Bob Dylan supplement, 3/2/90. Bono's interview with Dylan, Slane/ Dublin, 8/7/84, *Hot Press*, no. 26, 1984.
    Even the tape used in the 1950s and early 1960s was better. *Q* magazine (no. 70, July 1992) quotes Rhino Records remastering engineer Bill Inglot as saying that modern tape deteriorates more in storage than older tape: 'Most things from 1954 are in better condition than masters from 1974.'

audio because of CDs and digital recordings. He told Bob Colbourn's *Rock Line* listeners on the Global Network Satellite that digital recording meant

> people started hearing much less of the original sound, and all of . . . the universe of sounds available to the ear and to the brain to analyse and to feel were all gone . . . and those are the very things that stimulate the . . . body into reacting and feeling and enjoying music and . . . its therapeutic effects . . . it's all reduced, it's a surface sham, it's not the real thing. It's like . . . digital cameras, when you take a picture of a field full of cows . . . you take the same picture with a Kodachrome camera with a film in it and you look at the film picture . . . take a magnifying glass and . . . go way in and you look at the cows and it still looks like a cow . . . and you go to the digital picture and you go in with a magnifying glass and all you see is like three or four little black squares where the cow was. And that's what's happening to your ears and your heart and your brain when you listen to digital music.[6]

Even a decent guitar sound now seems out of reach – and seems so whether Dylan is floundering in one of these large professional studios or recording by himself in his Malibu home studio, as he did for the recent albums on which we're in a position to scrutinise his acoustic-guitar sound most easily, "Good As I Been To You" and "World Gone Wrong". César Díaz, for a time Dylan's Never-Ending Tour guitar-tuner and temporary guitarist, and 'an outspoken advocate of tube amps and vintage guitars', made these comments to *Guitar Player* magazine in 1993:

> Whoever [Dylan] learned to play the guitar from must have been very old, because his chording and approach to melody is so old-fashioned . . . For example, he plays a first-position Dm [D minor] by fingering F on the D string, A on the G string and D on the B string. He has this formula worked out where he plays these triadic shapes all up and down the neck.
>
>   I've seen Bob do some amazing ragtime and Travis-style fingerpicking. Listen to his first album, and you'll hear some incredible shit! And the tone of those Gibson guitars! The recorded sound of the acoustic guitar was defined by him. Listen to that original version of 'Don't Think Twice'. When he starts doing that flatpicking thing on the low strings – my God, not even Doc Watson had that kind of tone.[7]

6.   Neil Young, quoted in the fanzine *Broken Arrow*, no. 46. (There is more of this splendid rant therein.)
    Q, no. 70, July 1992, quotes hi-fi writer Alvin Gold as saying something less mystic but perhaps telling too: 'Engineers have discovered that a certain amount of background noise can enhance the recording.'
    Then again, there are those who feel we had a loss imposed upon us long before digitalisation, when transistors took over from valves. When Jackie Wilson's dazzlingly sung 'Reet Petite' (NYC, July 1957, Brunswick Records 55024, New York [Coral Records Q 72290, London], 1957) was a hit all over again in the 1980s (SMP Records SKM 3, UK, 1986), my son told me he'd got it on 12-inch; I told him I'd got it on 78. Playing his version on modern equipment and then playing the 78 on an old electric valve-driven radiogram, there was no doubting the extra warmth and beefiness of the older system. Since the early 1980s valve-driven recording consoles have been resuscitated in London (currently there is, for instance, Chiswick Reach Studio), deliberately catering to those who've felt there is this difference. There are a number of companies making (extremely expensive) valve-driven amps. Bob Dylan could afford to check into all this.
7.   César Díaz, *Guitar Player*, nia, 1993, quoted from *Isis*, no. 48, 1993.

Exactly! And all the more dissatisfying that he can't achieve it in the 1980s and 1990s, after the accretion of decades of professional experience and with access to far more expensive guitars – vintage Martins and all.

There may be spasmodic signs that Dylan can be bothered to fight for this: the main studio used on "Under The Red Sky" was Oceanway, which is dedicated to achieving an ambient old warmth and recognising the need to strive for one to compensate for digital, transistorised coldness – though the resulting production on "Under The Red Sky" has been as criticised as any other album of recent years, and you certainly can't blame all the deficiencies of recordings like 'Maybe Someday' or 'Sally Sue Brown' on tape storage, transistors or digits: they're inept productions by the standards of any audio regime.

In any case Dylan is never going to become an equipment expert; and granted his recent capacity for shooting himself in the foot from boredom, it seems hard to expect that if we stand on the threshold of a new recording era, Dylan will step across it. Look at the cheapness of his equipment for touring in 1991; his not seeming to care that he pays a technical crew uninterested in the new generation of mikes, DAT recorders and so on, uninterested even in keeping the heads clean on the cassette-machine on the mixing-desk. As Paul D. Lehrman wrote of a 1996 concert, '. . . he was only playing medium-size theaters, with a small band. How could the sound be bad there? . . . The guy at the mixing board, even though he had a clear path to the aisles, never moved, never walked away to see what it sounded like anywhere else.'[8]

It doesn't have to *be* like this. It's all of a piece with Dylan telling the Never-Ending Tour's fine original bass player Kenny Aaronson 'I don't give a shit who plays bass' when Aaronson, recovered from illness, asked (unsuccessfully) for his job back. Inertia kept the less interesting replacement bassist in the band instead. It's all of a piece with Dylan referring, in the "Biograph" interview, to 'my little voice'. With him telling Al Kooper with a shrug that "Knocked Out Loaded" didn't turn out right because it got handed over to producers and what can you do? With his saying something about how any one album is only an album, and there'll always be another one: a dispiriting way of replacing the previously held Dylan view, which was that each album was a unique step along an unknown road, a deliberate creation under the control of the artist, however much the chaos of the moment was allowed to feed into it. ("Blonde On Blonde" is exemplary in this respect, as in so many others.)

Dylan seems to have given up fighting to maintain that control – perhaps given up on that responsibility to his art. It may be a sign of this that even his judgement about the running-order of the tracks seems to have slipped. It would be absurd to say that the running-order of any of the albums of the 1960s or 1970s was 'wrong' or ill-judged; yet even without going into such perversities as "Shot Of Love"'s including 'Trouble' and excluding 'The Groom's Still Waiting At The Altar', or on "Oh Mercy" choosing 'Political World' as an opener instead of 'Dignity', it seems self-evidently wrong that on the second side of "Knocked Out Loaded" the running-order does its best to minimise the impact of 'Brownsville Girl' by putting it before the humdrum 'Got My Mind Made Up' and the unconvincing 'Under Your Spell', instead of allowing

---

8.   Paul D. Lehrman: 'Sounding off: what happened to the FOH mix?', in the recording sound magazine *Mix*, May 1996.

'Brownsville Girl' to be the long, impressive conclusion to the record, as 'Sad-Eyed Lady Of The Lowlands' and 'Every Grain Of Sand' had been on earlier collections.

Even the album cover art seems to get given up on in the 1980s. The covers used to give a clear, imaginative signal as to what sort of world was within. What a surprise it was to find that the five inner-sleeve photos on the vinyl version of "Bootleg Series I–III", and the front cover photograph of "Good As I Been To You", revert to this skilled panache, this intelligent accuracy of signalling. It was a surprise because of the opportunities flabbily squandered with such covers as "Shot Of Love", "Real Live" and "Down In The Groove".

Not caring to secure a decent vocal sound; accepting tacky artwork; excluding the best tracks; minimising the impact of the best of the rest – these are part of the new defensiveness, the 1980s if-I-don't-really-try-I-don't-really-fail posture which may seem inoffensively low-key, even charmingly fallible, but surely signals an aggressive distrust of the audience and of himself. In personal terms, this can't be criticised: if it's how he feels, it's how he feels – but in terms of his work, it is damaging, regrettable, self-destructive, 'and if you can't speak out against this kind of thing . . .'

Likewise, it seems an act of wilful artistic self-destruction that having made what was in effect the best video ever, the 'Subterranean Homesick Blues' film that opens *Don't Look Back*, in the 1980s Dylan made truly gruesome ones.[9] There are exceptions. 'Jokerman', from 1983, is good, though it courts uneasiness of the wrong kind: partly by putting Dylan straight back up there with Mona Lisa in the Louvre, and partly because his miming is so inept. In spontaneous performance, such incompetence at the artifices of showbiz can be funny – even glorious: witness his classic on-stage-guest routine of casting around him bemusedly, as if he's never met such people and can hardly credit that this activity they expect of him, this *performance*, is sane behaviour, but he'd best humour them (best go along with the charade until he can think his way out). This masterly piece of theatre can be savoured on the footage from the Seville Guitar Legends Festival in 1991, where he mimes faultlessly the high comedy of making out that he's woken to find himself on stage with certifiable lunatics (Keith Richards & Co.) and has never heard anything as mystifying as 'Shake Rattle & Roll' in his life. He's always done this (and more besides) to Roger McGuinn – see 'Mr. Tambourine Man' on the so-called *Roy Orbison Tribute Show* – and he manages a splendid variation on the act when the circumstances *are* bizarre, as on the Chabad Telethon charity TV performance of September 1989 with his awful son-in-law and Harry Dean Stanton, where he implies, with all his Chaplinesquerie intact, that in his experience life is usually as unknowable and grotesque as this.[10] You can imagine, therefore, a video in which Dylan's ineptness at miming might itself be transformed into incandescent, hilarious mime. (I'd like to have seen him making his script coach 'prompt' him on the set of *Hearts of Fire*, too.) But in the context of the

9.   'Subterranean Homesick Blues', filmed London, 8/5/65; included in *Don't Look Back*, Leacock-Pennebaker, US, auteured by D. A. Pennebaker, 1967.

10.   Bob Dylan, Keith Richards and others: 'Shake, Rattle & Roll', Guitar Legends Festival, Seville, 17/10/91; Bob Dylan & The Byrds: 'Mr. Tambourine Man', LA, 24/2/90, "The Byrds", Columbia Legacy Records CK46773, New York, 1990; Bob Dylan, Peter Himmelman & Harry Dean Stanton: 'Einsleipt Mein Kind Dein Eigalach', 'Adelita' and 'Hava Nagilah', LA, 24/9/89, telecast live on KCOP-TV, LA.

quick, cold close-ups on the 1983 'Jokerman' video, the ineptitude is no success at all: he's visibly put-upon, instead of effortlessly in charge.[11]

Far better is the 1993 video for 'Blood In My Eyes', where the imprecision of the miming is unimportant, because it is but a minor factor in a scheme that pursues an *idea*: that of watching Dylan set loose in all his mythic glory, and using the shabby charm of Camden street market in the 1990s much as in *Renaldo & Clara* he used the streets of Montreal in the mid-1970s, as a backdrop reminiscent of the 1960s Greenwich Village world, so that it offers the long-haul Dylan viewer a rich, multi-layered experience full of fleeting, playful allusions to the past without ever golden-oldifying it or pretending away the present.

'Most Of The Time', a 1990 'live' performance done in order to avoid miming, is a success by any standards, and in a traditionally radical Dylan way. Like the *Hard Rain* television performance, it strips away the packaging in which music and its images are customarily offered, and is instead a sort of punk kitchen-sink drama: you see all the grungy old amps and the wires, and you get a real sense of what it might be like to stand in the middle of all that and push out real music. In other words, the 'Most Of The Time' video isn't like a video at all.

At the opposite extreme, 'Series Of Dreams' (1991) (on which he co-operated for a few fragmentary feet of new footage) really uses cinematic possibilities to construct a rich, intelligent, sustained movie of the fleeting moment, using Dylan's iconic power and the grandeur of vérité to build an always alert dreamscape put together, without a doubt, by people who know Dylan's work intimately and are willing to put their own professional expertise in the service of that work, instead of imposing their professionalism upon him. This should be no remarkable occurrence: it should be the norm. They jump to it when knowing, modern artists know what they want and are interested in the possibilities of the medium. 'Series Of Dreams' and 'Blood In My Eyes' are the only modern instances of Bob Dylan getting similarly tailor-made attention to his art from people of real flair in the artistic support services.[12]

Look at the others. Or rather, it's best not to. 'Tight Connection To My Heart', made by one of those 15-minute cinema whizz-kids, commits every error of over-literal 'interpretation' of song possible; 'Sweetheart Like You' is abject; the ones with Dave Stewart on camera, well, what can you expect? The waste of time and money, as all these awful egos fritter away the days, desperately trying to disguise utter absence of purpose . . . it's horrible to divine all this so plainly from the end result, let alone to have to read all about the making of the video in the *Telegraph*. It's the sort of living death Bob Dylan once avoided.[13]

As long ago as 1985 he was saying 'Videos are out of character for me . . . I was just ordered around.'[14] He doesn't have to make them at all – Frank Zappa didn't

---

11. 'Jokerman' video, filmed NYC, March 1984, directed George Lois and Larry Sloman.

12. 'Series Of Dreams' video, USA, March 1991, directed Meiert Avis; 'Blood In My Eyes' video, London, 21/7/93, directed Dave Stewart.

13. 'Sweetheart Like You' video, LA, October 1983, directed Mark Robinson; 'Tight Connection To My Heart' video, Tokyo, May 1985, directed Paul Schrader; 'When The Night Comes Falling From The Sky' and 'Emotionally Yours' videos, LA, 22/8/85, directed Markus Innocenti and Eddie Arno.

14. Bob Dylan interview by Scott Cohen, *Spin*, vol. 1, no. 8, December 1985.

make promotional videos, nor does Neil Young – but if Dylan's going to make them, the only way to make them work for him is to take charge, to have a purpose and to accept responsibility. It's such a waste that he doesn't, that he doesn't seize the moment, either prompted by artistic curiosity or even merely to protect himself from the tangible indignities of being put upon. Instead he gives his weary, what-the-hell shrug, from inside what looks like some fog of self-contempt. It used to be that you could know, without a shadow of doubt, that footage of Bob Dylan, whatever he was doing, from walking onto a stage to rubbing his eyes, would be a fine thing to see. Now you have to hope against hope that a video won't be embarrassingly dreadful: that he won't be stuck in some terrible crap, down on his knees like an old bull elephant, suffering indignities all the more terrible because of the dignity his presence once guaranteed.

Something else to regret is Dylan's switch of policy towards interviews. He used to bother to give out, albeit often in the form of a wit that rubbed the questioner's face in the fatuousness of the question. Sometimes this went beyond dismissal and became a reaching out to the person inside the journalist: became Dylan trying to teach them something true. That's what he does in the so-called 'vicious' exchanges we see in *Don't Look Back* with the *Time* Magazine Man and the Science Student. As he says to the latter: 'I don't think you know when you're liked.'

The walls have gone up since then. You see it in the contrast between the end-of-1965 press conferences and the NFT press conference for *Hearts of Fire*.[15] In those early ones he radiates good humour, unguarded spontaneity, optimism; in the later he emanates a deadening boredom and a deeply cynical, self-lacerating dispiritedness. He breaks out of it twice, momentarily. Once is when he's first on the platform, before the formal event begins, when, spotting someone he knows near the front, he flashes an extraordinarily vibrant conspiratorial vamped grin, like a schoolboy on the dais on Speech Day, gleefully dissociating himself from all this pomp and circumstance to friends down below. The other moment is when Philip Norman is brave enough to keep on asking him why he isn't doing what he's best at, namely writing great songs, instead of proposing to waste his time on the set of a movie that is obviously going to be awful. Warming to this theme, Norman invites Dylan to imagine how bored he's going to be, and Dylan comes out of his already-bored-shitless shell just long enough to murmur: 'Oh, I don't know – maybe *you'll* be around': a put-down to compete against any from his own past.

But this was six seconds' worth of life and spirit in an hour of stultifying disaffection. It used to be more like the other way round. The six seconds' worth just points up how rare it is now that Dylan will ever allow himself to do that: to compete with his own past on any level. The rest of the event just proves Philip Norman right. As does the film.

In general, Dylan's policy switch on interviews has been from generous energy and acerbic soundbite to a disingenuous meanness of content: to saying, by recourse to unquotable, elaborate twaddle, absolutely nothing.

However, all this may be doom-mongering (it takes one to know one, he

---

15. Bob Dylan press conferences San Francisco, 3/12/65, telecast on KQED-TV, USA, 1965; LA, 16/12/65; cf. press conference London, 17/8/86, excerpts broadcast Capital Radio and TV-AM, London, 18/8/86.

grimaces). Among the dozens of 1980s and 1990s interviews he has done (it's always been a myth that Dylan interviews are rare: they average well over one a month for all four decades of his career) there have been a handful of valuable exceptions, which evidence a Dylan still disarmingly more real than any other 'celebrity' I can think of – a Dylan who still has his head and heart in the right places. These illuminating, and sometimes funny, exceptions include Bill Flanagan's 1985 interview for his book *Written in My Soul*; Scott Cohen's 1985 *Spin* magazine interview; the BBC-TV interviews given to Christopher Sykes in 1986 while on the set of *Hearts of Fire*; Sam Shepard's 1987 'play'/interview in *Esquire*; and an interview, again about songwriting, given to Paul Zollo for *Songtalk* magazine in 1991.[16]

These several exceptions offer a truthful, reflective Dylan who gives out at least as much as in the great *Playboy* interviews either of 1966 (*Tarantula* rides again) or of 1977 (the mature artist breaks his silence). Yet what could be more disquieting than the circumstances in which, it turns out, the *Songtalk* interview, for one, was conducted? When, in February 1992, the interviewer became the interviewed, we learnt that Dylan's publicist, Elliot 'Chewy' Mintz, had not only sat in on the entire Dylan interview but had tried to proscribe it beforehand and censor it afterwards.

Beforehand, Zollo reported, Mintz told him 'not to ask [Dylan] about songs that were so old that he would have to wrack his brain'. During the interview,

> Bob made a comment like 'People will burn their hair just because Jimi Hendrix burned his guitar' and Elliot wanted it cut out because he thought it offensive to Hendrix. After the interview Bob said he didn't mean anything against Hendrix and I agreed that it didn't come off as being negative towards Hendrix, so Elliot agreed to allow it but the next day he called me and said that he and Bob had talked it over and that Bob wanted it left out.
>
> Another time, the part where he said he didn't write lies, he mentioned the songs 'Feelings' and 'People' as the type of song that he wouldn't write. He actually started singing them for a few seconds and when he sang the line 'People who need people are the luckiest people in the world' he turned and said that that was bullshit . . . He then thought for a few seconds and said that maybe people who needed people *were* the luckiest people, and laughed. Elliot had that taken out because he thought it would offend the people who wrote the songs . . . I asked him about 'Idiot Wind' and he made the comment that not even Neil Young had written a song like that, not yet anyway. Elliot thought that too would be offensive, to Neil Young . . . he was in control of the whole scene.[17]

Do you often read anything quite so depressing? There ought to be a special hell for people like Mintz who sanitise and demean the very personality of the artist they

---

16. Bill Flanagan: *Written in My Soul*, 1986; Scott Cohen's interview, *Spin* magazine, see note 14; Christopher Sykes' interviews in Bristol and Toronto, Sept.–Oct. 1986, telecast in edited form on *Omnibus*, BBC-TV, London, 18/9/87; Sam Shepard's 'play'/interview 'True Dylan', *Esquire*, July 1987; and Paul Zollo's interview, Beverly Hills, 14/4/91, *Songtalk*, Vol. 2, no. 16, 1991.

17. *Telegraph*, no. 42, Summer 1992.

are supposed to look after. Eternal fire is too good for them. Eternal tape-loops of 'Feelings' and 'People', maybe.

But that Bob Dylan delivers himself into the hands of these ghouls: that is the disquieting thing, because of what it augurs for his work – because of how it threatens to diminish (*aims* to diminish) the autonomy of its author, pulling down and intruding upon his 'lone guitar and a point of view'.

Why does he tolerate these people? As well as Elliot Mintz, the 1980s saw him acquire a 'dresser', one Suzie Pullen, to swell his entourage and, for the 1986 tour for instance, to put on his fingerless gloves for him and strap up his over-elaborate boots. Why can't he put on his own?

Why can't he choose his own clothes? It's not as if she's proved, or could prove, sartorially convincing. His clothes have inevitably got dodgier under her influence, less straightforwardly reflective of Bob Dylan and more inclined to tiresome designerism. So why payroll yet another counter-productive courtier (in this case one who, as John Bauldie once wrote, 'couldn't dress a salad')?[18]

The Bob Dylan who toured Britain and Ireland almost single-handedly in 1965, as *Don't Look Back* illustrates, wouldn't have tolerated these people Mintzing around him for one minute. That the current Bob Dylan submits himself to them suggests a beleaguered, sorry figure. Tell me that it isn't true.

Along with the disproportionate amount of entourage is the ridiculous dodging of the press and public when they're not even after him. The present-day Bob Dylan acts as a parody of The Celebrity. He's to be seen dressed up in such ostentatious incognito costumes that everyone's attention is drawn to him. The truth is that if he didn't dress as if he came from Mars, he could pass unrecognised and unpestered almost every-where on earth except in a few central streets in a few Western capital cities.

A classic case, reported in the letters page of the *Telegraph*, no. 36, had Dylan, in London in February 1990, deliberately using the front exit to the Mayfair Hotel, for the first time ever, just at the moment when he and his long-term minder Victor Maimudes knew that photographers were there for the film star Julia Roberts. Upshot: 'Another hit! Dylan snaps as cameras start to roll' (*Daily Express*); 'Who's got the hump?' (*Daily Mirror*), along with a photo of a 'man in dark glasses attempting to hide his face under a leather hooded coat' and trying to hit a photographer with a rolled-up newspaper. This squalid publicity might be better than none, but it doesn't come about *in spite of* Dylan, and certainly doesn't suggest the hounded public figure unjustly denied his privacy.[19]

There are, unfortunately, other ways in which American showbiz goo – goo in which Bill Clinton and MTV swim equally happily, and against which Bob Dylan has traditionally set his face – now seems to be eroding his defences.

Dylan's live performances used to begin with Dylan walking on the stage. Now they begin with this glutinous cloned-American voice saying 'Ladies an' gennelmen, please welcome . . . Columbia recording artist BAAB DYLAN!' This is a clear step into the jaws of straight showbiz: and very unpleasant it is to hear. As well as

18. I can't locate where John Bauldie's remark is published.
19. *Telegraph*, no. 36, Summer 1990.

signalling some degree of capitulation to those jaws by Dylan, the underlying announcement is that Columbia Records *owns* Bob Dylan. There's also the condescending implication that this disembodied voice needs to intercede for Dylan before he can be wheeled out there. Even the 'Ladies an' gennelmen' is a piece of reactionary old blag. Bob Dylan's name was long and insistently synonymous with the overthrow of this kind of socially regressive supper-clubbery, as was Woody Guthrie's before him. It's hucksters' bullshit, however you look at it, and that it should now precede him onto the concert platform is repellent.

Dylan seems to collude with it. He could abolish that demeaning introduction, and once he would have done. Doesn't he notice how unsavoury it is? Is it weary indifference, or is there a slide towards taking on a more conventional showbiz mindset than once obtained? On a radio interview in the mid-1980s, Dylan was asked how he felt about a theatrical production someone was mounting based on his songs, and Dylan responded with some hostility to such a project, saying that 'We do our own show.' To read that on the page is to assume that some comic irony underlay Dylan's phrase: but there was none. Dylan seemed comfortable with the idea that what he did in live performance was a 'show'. My unease at this may be mere semantic squeamishness, but I was not alone among admirers of Dylan's work in feeling it. It could be that for those who grew up in the Reagan–Thatcher years, it *is* all showbiz, just as, for instance, being a student is routinely just a career move now. But it wasn't always so, and there was a very long period in which a Dylan live performance might have been an event, might have been a concert but was never merely a 'show'.

It is also a new development in the same reductive direction for Dylan to start being one of those celebrities who will endorse other people's work by giving them blurb quotes. It was one thing for him to write such a thing for Allen Ginsberg's *Collected Poems 1947–1980* (1985): it was a favour for a friend, a gesture of respect for a poet's work, a one-off; and perhaps it held the attraction for Dylan of offering him a modest writing exercise, as he tried out the language of conventional criticism. ('Ginsberg,' ran Dylan's wordbite, 'is both tragic and dynamic, a lyrical genius, con man extraordinaire, and probably the single greatest influence on the American poetical voice since Walt Whitman.' A splendidly un-Dylanesque composition, and fairly plausible stuff.) But by the end of 1991, this had been joined by the dubious company of two more Dylan book blurbs, one gruesome and the other vacuous. On *Lazarus and the Hurricane* by Sam Chaiton and Terry Swinton (1991):

> The first book [Carter's *The Sixteenth Round*, 1974] was a heartbreaker. This one is a mind-breaker, abolishing parts of the nervous system.

And on Minneapolis Rabbi Manis Friedman's book *Doesn't Anyone Blush Any More? Reclaiming Intimacy, Modesty and Sexuality in a Permissive Age* (1991), there is this back cover testimonial:

> Anyone who's either married or thinking of getting married would do well to read this book.

Is this an example of how Dylan keeps on doing the same thing but it comes across differently because he's grown older or the world has changed around him – as for instance you might argue is the case with Dylan's clothes: you could say that he's always had dodgy clothes but used to be young and beautiful enough to get away with them? In the case of the book blurbs, well, he endorsed Fender bass-guitars in 1965, didn't he? And he wrote the sleeve notes for "Joan Baez In Concert, Part 2", and for Peter, Paul & Mary's album "In The Wind"?[20]

Surely the more recent blurbs are something different. Dylan used those liner-notes as opportunities to publish 'some other kinds of songs', and to reach the large audiences of 'bigger' stars than he was, yet who had already performed his work, and therefore with whom he had some tangible artistic connection. And he did so in his own uncompromising style: they were liner-notes unlike any other. Whereas the recent excursions into book-blurbing are just Bob Dylan playing a conventional showbiz game, no differently from Bob Hope or Bob Roberts.

It's the same game as the pally music-biz tributes and mutually presented awards, which Dylan has also, after a lifetime's honourable opposition, begun to join in and play, to the immense disappointment of those who ardently admired his long-term contempt for such stuff.

Dylan knows all this. Weariness, getting worn down by the pressure: these surely are the sad defeats that have pushed him into this arena. He discusses it himself, or something parallel to it, when on the "Biograph" material he rails against artists letting their work get used for adverts; he's rightly proud of having *not joined in*; and he's conscious of how perilous it is.

He has, now, joined in the co-option of real music by advertising, the turning of his art into a tool for selling other things. On US television in the first week of January 1994, there appeared minute-long commercials for the mega-accountancy consulting agency Coopers & Lybrand, using a Richie Havens recording of 'The Times They Are A-Changin''.

If this were not shameful enough in itself, the fact is that Coopers & Lybrand is a deeply unsavoury organisation that it takes no special or batty idealism to wish to have no truck with. It was investigated in the case of its auditing of the notorious swindler Robert Maxwell's business affairs; the investigation began in 1993; in 1994 Coopers & Lybrand attempted, unsuccessfully, to have this investigation halted, and in February 1999, as a result of the investigation, it was announced that the company and four of its senior employees were to be fined a record amount with costs: nearly £3.5 million. The fine, detailed in a long-awaited report from the tribunal of the Accountants Joint Disciplinary Scheme, was accompanied by severe criticism of the firm.[21]

(Craig Jamieson, Keeper of Sanskrit Manuscripts at Cambridge University Library, commented wryly on the Internet newsgroup 'rec.music.dylan' that a lot of its members would be 'going to see Dylan at Woodstock whatever the rest of you think [i.e. Woodstock II, 1994, twenty-five years after Dylan's refusal to attend the first

20. The Fender ads were discreet and showed a photo of the 1965 leather-jacketed Dylan posing with a Fender electric bass guitar (an instrument he does not play); they appeared in Spring 1965 in the UK music papers and Fender sponsored Dylan's 1965 and 1966 tours. Joan Baez: "Joan Baez In Concert, Part 2", Vanguard Records VRS-9113, New York, 1964. Peter, Paul & Mary: "In The Wind", Warner Bros. Records WS1507, New York, 1963.

21. *Private Eye*, no. 847, 3/6/94.

one]. And now is the time to decide where to meet. So could I propose we all meet at the Coopers & Lybrand stand?')[22]

The year after Dylan's leasing out a song that was only heeded in the first place because of its political integrity, and only sought by the advertising industry for the kudos of this special credibility, he was grubbing around on much lower levels of gratuitous commerce. On the back of your ticket for his Edinburgh concert of 5 April 1995 was a 'Special Offer' for McChicken Sandwiches™.

How can it have come to this – Bob Dylan promoting battery chickens? Don't tell me it's nothing to do with him. Would that stance suffice if the ad was from the British Nazi Party? All it takes is a simple clause in his contract with the promoter prohibiting these sordid commercial tie-ins. The tickets were quite pricey enough, and the promoter sufficiently in profit, without demeaning Bob Dylan's name in this sorry way. This is entirely different from the relationship with Fender in 1965–66, which, being the discreet sponsorship of important concert tours by a maker of excellent guitars, seems irreproachable. Fender's name did not appear on the tickets.

In 1993, Dylan discarded his life-long eschewal of any political endorsement – a fastidiousness the young Bob Dylan had had the sense to maintain without a moment's hesitation – and threw one of his silliest hats into the ring to appear at the inaugural concert for clubbable wide-boy President Clinton, singing so risibly incomprehensible a version of his magnificent 'Chimes Of Freedom' that the whole First Family was smirking and fidgeting through it while the oleaginous Tony Bennett waited, puzzled and unable to believe his luck, in the wings. In February 1996, Dylan and his band were hired to give a private concert in Phoenix, Arizona, for 250 senior staff of something called Nomura Securities International. That October 'The Times They Are A-Changin'' was back on TV as a jingle, this time sung by a choir of children promoting the Bank of Montreal. And the following September, looking about as comfortable as he should have done, Dylan played gruesome versions of three songs for the Pope – one of the most pro-actively right-wing popes of recent decades.[23]

Dylan himself talks in the "Biograph" interview, and somewhere more recently still, about how 'Sometimes you feel you're walking around in that movie *Invasion of the Bodysnatchers* and you wonder if it's got you yet, if you're still one of the few or are you "them" now'.

In fact he talks a great deal about these very things – the take-over of real music by false, the traps of fame, the need to stand apart from it all: as with so many things that Dylan has done over the years, the "Biograph" interview is richer and more valuable in retrospect than perhaps it seemed when it was new. He talks generously and well about all these things, including the integrity of the past and the threats the present makes against it: talks about it at length and with passion, leaving no doubt that all these things matter greatly to him. He knows it more inwardly than you or I do, and he can articulate it in a more heartfelt way, since he is the artist, than this

22. Print-out faxed to me by Andrew Muir, London, 18/6/94.

23. Bob Dylan: 'Chimes Of Freedom', America's Reunion On The Mall, Lincoln Memorial, Washington, DC, 17/1/93. Namura Securities International private performance by Dylan in the Pavilion of the Biltmore Hotel, Phoenix, 2/2/96. Performance for Pope John Paul II at the World Eucharistic Congress, Bologna, Italy, 27/9/97. And in no case did these people even appreciate the spectacle.
  Bank of Montreal TV campaign using 'Times They Are A-Changin'', 1996–97.

critic ever can. But while Dylan can say, among much else, 'It's important to stay away from the celebrity trap . . . The media is a great meatgrinder, it's never satisfied and it must be fed', warning himself is not the same as remaining immune.

Much of what has become disappointing in how Bob Dylan comports himself these days *is* to do with 'the celebrity trap': what one deplores is precisely the decay into celebrity. Real people are always more interesting than celebrities, just as hillbilly singers are more interesting than pop singers. Dylan's early poems are about Bob Zimmerman discovering the world: discovering New York, discovering Hibbing once he's able to look back on it from elsewhere, and so on. What he has to say about Hibbing is far more interesting than what he might now say about Hollywood. What he feels about Johnny Cash when he's an adolescent out in Hibbing and Cash is out there in the public domain – this is far more interesting than what he has to say about Johnny Cash now they're good ole buddies, fellow artistes and liggers at other celebrities' parties.[24]

It's a slippery slope. Like the blurb for Allen Ginsberg leading into something worse, the awards ceremonies and the tribute-shows begin with the decent, honourable ones – the Guthrie Memorial Concert of January 1968; the *World of John Hammond* TV show in September 1975; and possibly the Martin Luther King Birthday Tribute, eighteen years to the day after the Guthrie one. Nor is it anything but curmudgeonly to complain if Dylan wants to do something as surprising, as splendidly un-Dylan-esque, as turn up at the Gershwin Celebration at the New York Academy of Music in Brooklyn, and sing (sweetly) a carefully selected, little-known item from the old pro songwriter's repertoire. And what could be more reasonable than Dylan performing at the Grammy Awards ceremony in February 1980 – especially since what he did was to hurl the chastising burn of 'Gotta Serve Somebody' at a glitzy audience that, having so clearly chosen to serve Mammon, was satisfactorily discomforted by a lyric that pierced through the whole sticky set of rules?[25]

I suppose he shouldn't be begrudged going along again and accepting his Lifetime Achievement Grammy either – especially since, by virtue of the inspired, on-the-edge timing of his acceptance 'speech', which was another piece of absolutely classic Dylan, he once again pushed the limits of the occasion, making people sweat over that mid-speech *tour de force* of a pause: making them wonder whether some awful puncturing of the whole ceremonial game wasn't about to happen. Even going back, in between

24.   The adolescent Dylan's views on Cash are expressed on the amateur tape-recording made with his childhood friend John Bucklen in Hibbing in 1958 (the earliest known extant recording of Bob Dylan's voice), first put into circulation when excerpts were broadcast on the TV documentary *Highway 61 Revisited*, produced by Anthony Wall, telecast BBC-TV, London, 8/5/93.

25.   Bob Dylan: 'I Ain't Got No Home', 'Dear Mrs. Roosevelt', 'Grand Coulee Dam', 'This Land Is Your Land' and 'This Train', Woody Guthrie Memorial Concert, NYC, 20/1/68 [first three titles with the Crackers, fourth and fifth titles with ensemble; first three and fifth titles issued "Tribute To Woody Guthrie (Vol. I)", Columbia Records KC31171, New York, 1972; fourth title issued "Tribute To Woody Guthrie (Vol. II)", Warner Bros. Records K46144, LA, 1972]. Bob Dylan: 'Hurricane', 'Oh Sister' and 'Simple Twist Of Fate', *World of John Hammond*, WTTW-TV, Chicago, 10/9/75, telecast PBS-TV, 13/10/75. Bob Dylan: 'The Bell Of Freedom Still Rings' [with Stevie Wonder], 'I Shall Be Released', 'Blowin' In The Wind' [with Peter, Paul & Mary] and 'Happy Birthday' [with ensemble], Martin Luther King Birthday, Washington, DC, 20/1/86. [In fact King's birthday is 15 January and in the USA is now observed on the 19th.] Bob Dylan: 'Soon', *The Gershwin Gala*, NYC, 11/3/87, telecast ZDF-TV, West Germany, 7/7/87. Bob Dylan: 'Gotta Serve Somebody' [with group] and acceptance speech, Grammy Awards, LA, 27/2/80, telecast CBS-TV.

these two occasions, to deal in yet more damn Grammys in front of yet another self-congratulatory celebrity audience – this time presenting some, along with Stevie Wonder, in 1984: I suppose that's OK too.[26] At any rate, Dylan disarmed any possible criticism when he told an interviewer:

> I know going on the Grammies is not my type of thing, but with Stevie it seemed like an interesting idea. I wasn't doing anything that night. I didn't feel I was making any great statement. For me, I was just going down to the place and changing my clothes.[27]

Point taken: but the sub-text of Dylan's point is that it was OK because it was a one-off, and it would be a different matter to start getting into the swing of this stuff. The trouble is, he seems in danger of doing just that. Accepting an award for achieving '25 years in the music business' (November 1985)? Is this what Bob Dylan has come to stand for? Accepting an ASCAP award, for being a wily old long-time member of a Tin Pan Alley trade union (March 1986)? The collecting of awards for yourself and the paying of tributes to others: these occasions, of dubious import at best, get more frequent and more tacky. A tribute message to Ian & Sylvia for broadcast on CBC-TV in September 1986? Presenting a Juno Award to Gordon Lightfoot, again on CBC, just two months later? Donating comments on Ritchie Valens as a puff for the routine bio-pic *La Bamba* in 1987 (used in the trailer)? And for God's sake: a Message of Congratulations to Willie Nelson, January 1986, for an ABC Television awards programme?[28]

Better the Bob Dylan we see in *Don't Look Back*:

Columbia Records official: I've got an award for him . . .
Dylan: No, man, I just don't want it.
Grossman: Should we have it mailed to you?
Dylan: I don't even want to see 'em.

and the Bob Dylan who, sixteen years later, sang of Lenny Bruce that he

> *Never did get any Golden Globe award . . .*

and the Bob Dylan who, even as he slides down this slope, can see what pernicious nonsense it is. Asked, in a 1995 interview, 'How do you feel about the idea of a rock hall of fame?', he responded at once with 'Nothing surprises me anymore.'[29]

Not only are all these repulsively named awards, these Grammys and Tonys and Junos, irrelevant to authentic personal or artistic stature; not only do they get bestowed

---

26. Bob Dylan: 'Masters Of War' [with group] and acceptance speech, Grammy Awards, NYC, 20/2/91. Bob Dylan and Stevie Wonder: introduction of nominees, Grammy Awards, LA, 28/2/84.

27. Interview by Scott Cohen, *Spin* (see note 14).

28. Bob Dylan: acceptance speech, Whitney Museum, NYC, 13/11/85; acceptance speech, ASCAP Awards, LA, 31/3/86; 'message' to Ian & Sylvia, *nia*, July–Aug. 1986, telecast CBC-TV, Canada, Sept. 1987; Juno Award presentation to Gordon Lightfoot, Toronto, 10/11/86, telecast CBC-TV, Canada; comment on Ritchie Valens during car-ride, California, 1987, for use in promotional trailer for *La Bamba*, New Visions/Columbia Pictures, US, directed Luis Valdez, 1987; congratulatory 'message' to Willie Nelson re an award for humanitarianism, LA, January 1986, telecast ABC-TV, New York, 27/1/86.

29. Dylan interviewed by John Dolen, Fort Lauderdale, c. 26/9/95; 'A midnight chat with Bob Dylan', *Fort Lauderdale Sun-Sentinel*, 28/9/95.

in a mendacious circus that would by its embrace put Mother Teresa's humility in doubt, and make the Holden Caulfield in any of us puke: but as Dylan himself implies there in 'Lenny Bruce', they are a public declaration that those to whom they're presented have been thoroughly co-opted by the system, like those who acquire peerages in England.

There's a further deeply conservative force at work here, as all this slides into the syndrome of picking up achievement trophies in inverse proportion to current achievements. Lifetime Achievement Oscars, for instance, are notoriously given to people not felt to be doing worthwhile current work – indeed, often to people barely alive at all – as a sort of apology for not having recognised the quality of work they once did, back in the safe mists of time.

This over-praising of minor current achievement because of the artist's major work of the past, or the less shifty but absurd alternative of presenting him with garlands of congratulation for work done twenty-five years earlier – this is not good for anyone's sense of reality. It must damage the antennae on which any artist depends for his or her present-day art. It certainly threatens Bob Dylan's.

Even at the level of audience response it's pernicious. In the solo acoustic halves of his 1966 concerts, he got polite applause for showering genius around: for singing with intensive precision sustained over the magical long hauls not only of songs as original and complexly structured as 'Visions of Johanna' but of a 'Just Like A Woman' slowed down and stretched out so far that it offered the listener a time-stopping world to fall into and reside within – and playing, too, the most lovely, risk-taking harmonica, crinkling along the synapses like golden light. Now, in unhealthy contrast, he gets whoops and wild applause between each verse, however blearily and absently he bluffs his way through untrusting, perfunctory versions of the same songs. The overkill of applause gets worse if he manages an alternating two-note harp twiddle in the right key. On 'Walls of Red Wing' live from the New York Town Hall in April 1963 he starts with a harmonica passage he then comments on as being 'bad harmonica': if he could play that same passage today it would be the virtuoso *tour de force* of the average evening's performance, since he seems recently to have forgotten how to play the harmonica altogether.[30]

This is inexplicable, but has certainly happened. There are signs, from some of the more recent of his concerts, that he may be re-learning it, though the best attempts have a horrible tentative quality to them, a painful timidity that it makes you fret just to hear. (You can hear it on such otherwise fine studio performances as 'Pretty Boy Floyd', 'Shenandoah' and 'This Old Man'.)

There have been, contemporaneously, periods of great dodginess on the guitar too. I don't mean on Dylan's technically hopeless, instinctively good electric guitar, which habitually flails around (sometimes wondering what key it's in) and still achieves a kind of curly reverie, as if it were being played with a hen's foot instead of a human hand: no, I mean that since 1987 there have been periods of dire acoustic guitar-playing. On the opening night at the Beacon Theatre in New York in 1989, he seemed obsessed with seeing how high up the neck he could play, and he got lost in this quest

---

30. Bob Dylan: 'Walls Of Red Wing', New York Town Hall, 12/4/63 [his first major concert], recorded but unreleased.

for the ultimate spartan chord slashed across the music's face. On and on he clawed, long after the vocal was over, till each real song disappeared behind him and you wondered whether the finishing end would ever be at hand. The crowd still responded as if the angel Gabriel had descended with a celestial concerto.[31]

This out-of-kilter enthusiasm, this smothering the reality of the present with adoration for the past, produces incongruities that we ask ourselves not to notice. At, say, Radio City Music Hall in late 1988, the incongruity was evident immediately he lit into 'Subterranean Homesick Blues' in a voice that was ungainly instead of fly, uncouth instead of chic, dull-minded instead of sharp. This voice couldn't have written those words.[32]

This credibility gap between the song and the singer's performance, the sense of defeat, the bowing to showbiz 'wisdom' – all these hit a low-point on *MTV Unplugged*™, for which Dylan ducked out of the opportunity to re-assert bravely his original unplugged power as the lone artist with the guitar and the point of view, even though he had just released two solo albums of folk and blues material he could have drawn upon for fresh performances of infinitely powerful songs. He could have stood there alone, looked the camera in the eye, lit into this material and thrilled anyone who ever cared about his work. Instead, he bowed to 'industry pressure' and settled for a tired parade of overworked greatest hits, propped up by every dissembling device there is, from the hired crowd at the start of things to the risibly airbrushed CD front cover photo of the end-product. The audience, partly hired to 'look good' (a hoary, hopeless device no more convincing than those people clapping with vacant, mad enthusiasm in the nightclub scenes of 1960s Elvis movies), whoops and hollers its indiscriminate keenness as Dylan sings so badly that, as Andy Gill comments about the version of 'Times They Are A-Changin'', it's 'as if he's tried to do so many different versions he's simply lost track of how best to sing it, accenting words and phrases almost randomly, as if successive words were set in different typefaces and font sizes', while those in the crowd 'applaud each successive indignity as a brilliant new interpretation'. As Gill goes on to ask: 'when every audience, too, is as suffused with sycophantic devotion as this, how on earth is Dylan to know when what he's done is good, bad or indifferent?' And he complains quite rightly of the 'shameful dullness of the country-rock arrangements and the yawnsome predictability of the material chosen'.[33]

It would be infinitely healthier for today's Bob Dylan voice to be singing today's Bob Dylan songs. That's what artists *do*. Painters who get the chance of a 1990s exhibition don't fill it up with their canvases from 1965. Miles Davis didn't spend his life playing 'Sketches Of Spain'. Duke Ellington is representative in saying: 'My favourite tune? The next one. The one I'm writing tonight or tomorrow. The new baby is always the favourite.' The poets who, along with Dylan, attended the Moscow Poetry Festival in the summer of 1985 read out their newest works, which is to say

---

31. NYC, 10/10/89.

32. NYC, 16–19/10/88.

33. Andy Gill, reviewing Bob Dylan's "MTV Unplugged™", *Q* magazine, no. 105, June 1995.

the ones that interested them. Only Dylan, then 44 years old, offered work he'd written when he was 21.[34]

All this Grammying around accepting awards a quarter of a century late can only encourage in Dylan the artist this deleterious change from don't-look-back to looking back all the time. Why isn't he, like any other authentic artist, bound up in his new work?

Instead, he's eating up his own back catalogue. His most significant releases of the last ten years have been box-sets trading in the past; even the brilliant video for 'Series Of Dreams' is constructed shamelessly from Bob Dylan the historical monument instead of Bob Dylan the living artist; and his concert repertoire stresses old songs all the time: a process that extends even to exhuming 'John Brown', a song that in 1963 was rightly considered too awful to release and which, when the first Great White Wonder bootlegs appeared in the late 1960s, was the cringe-making low-point of their contents. Is a truly wooden protest song from 1963 really more worth offering in 1990s concerts than contemporary material?[35]

He may consider his contemporary material hard to come by, and he may hate offering up work that will inevitably get compared to the old; but to duck out of that and keep on presenting the same eighteen or twenty old songs as the core of his repertoire, as he has done, with the honourable exception of 1979–80, every time he's toured since those songs were first no longer new – that is from 1974 right through to 1998 – can only make more and more rigid the process whereby only those old songs get any attention, and they rigidify more and more into deadweight classics from which the present-day artist cannot escape.[36]

34.   Miles Davis: "Sketches Of Spain", NYC, 20/11/59 and 10–11/3/60, Columbia Records CS 8271 [stereo] and CL 1480 [mono], New York, 1960/61; CD-reissued CBS Records 460604, London, 1990s. Duke Ellington: *Music Is My Mistress*, 1973, quoted in Val Wilmer: *Mama Said There'd Be Days Like This*, 1989. Bob Dylan: 'A Hard Rain's A-Gonna Fall', 'Blowin' In The Wind' and possibly 'The Times They Are A-Changin'', Moscow Poetry Festival, Moscow, 25/7/85.

35.   Bob Dylan: 'John Brown', NYC, Feb. 1963: in fact this was released, but only on "Broadside Ballads" Vol. 1, Broadside Records BR301, New York, 1963 [with Dylan billed as 'Blind Boy Grunt']. Another version, NYC, August 1963, studio-recorded as a demo for Witmark Music Publishing, was issued on the limited circulation untitled demo LP Warner Bros./7 Arts Music Records XTV221567, LA, 1969, and far more widely disseminated on the pioneering Great White Wonder bootlegs issued in the late 1960s. Dylan was performing the song by October 1962 (e.g. at the Gaslight Café, NYC that month) but didn't choose to try it at the sessions for either "The Freewheelin' Bob Dylan" (April 1962–April 1963) or "The Times They Are A-Changin'" (August, October 1963) in spite of the prevalence of 'protest songs' on both albums. By mid-1964 Dylan had dropped the song from his concert repertoire; he disinterred it under the encouragement of the Grateful Dead: rehearsals with them, San Rafael, California, March–April 1987, and in eleven concerts with them, e.g. Foxboro, Massachusetts, 4/7/87. It was then re-introduced on the Never-Ending Tour (1988 onwards) and eventually featured on the abject "MTV Unplugged™" album of 1995.

36.   The core songs are (to the end of 1998): 'All Along The Watchtower', 'Like A Rolling Stone', 'Maggie's Farm', 'It Ain't Me, Babe', 'Mr. Tambourine Man', 'Tangled Up In Blue', 'Ballad Of A Thin Man', 'Highway 61 Revisited', 'Blowin' In The Wind', 'Rainy Day Women Nos. 12 & 35', 'Masters Of War', 'Just Like A Woman', 'Silvio', 'Don't Think Twice, It's All Right', 'The Times They Are A-Changin'', 'I Shall Be Released', 'Gotta Serve Somebody', 'Knockin' On Heaven's Door', 'Simple Twist Of Fate', 'In The Garden', 'Forever Young', 'It's All Over Now, Baby Blue', 'Girl Of The North Country', 'Memphis Blues Again' and 'It's Alright Ma (I'm Only Bleeding)'. Occasionally, one of these gets a holiday, but never for long. Two are thirty-seven years old, the youngest other than 'Silvio' is twenty-five and the average age of these songs well over thirty.

   ('All Along The Watchtower' was finally given a sustained rest in 1997, after being played at 40 out of 40 concerts in 1974, 110 out of 114 concerts in 1978, 10 out of 19 of the 1980 semi-secular concerts, 35 out of 54 concerts in 1981, all 27 of the 1984 concerts, 11 out of 60 in 1986, 8 out of 36 in 1987, 39 out of 71 in 1988, 63 out of 99 in 1989, 81 out of 92 in 1990, 89 out of 101 in 1991, and 86 out of 92 concerts in 1992. From 20 August 1992 until 3 August 1997 it became the third song in every Bob Dylan concert (that night it came

Even these core repertoire songs disappear through repetition. For every fresh twist of interpretation or treatment, there are five, ten or twenty instances where the song dies from weariness, as Dylan stumbles through on automatic, fronting a clumsy pub rock band that makes *everything* sound like 'Shake Rattle & Roll'. Down that plughole goes, for instance, all the sly, lithe, comic insolence of 'Leopard-Skin Pill-Box Hat' on "Blonde On Blonde"; in its place is a turgid piece of 12-bar rockism interchangeable with 'Rainy Day Women Nos. 12 & 35' and more recently, to my especial regret, 'Watching The River Flow'. Indeed such is the enervating effect of this process that even a song as young as 'Everything Is Broken' could be plucked from the breast of "Oh Mercy"'s attentive particularity and put straight out into the rockist world without any individuality (something that can only reside in the words and their performance, since the music holds none), and left to fend for itself among the other 12-bar workhorses.

If you listen to 'Leopard-Skin Pill-Box Hat' from Manchester Free Trade Hall 1966 (the so-called 'Royal Albert Hall 1966' tape), when the song *was* fresh – indeed the audience had never heard it before, and "Blonde On Blonde" was as yet unreleased – it is a revolutionary blues performance on every level.[37] The intelligent hip modernity that transforms its tradition-based lyric is picked up and flown higher by a committed, cawing vocal that achieves both druggy sexual strut and energised venom: riding on inspired, hot, careening music inside which you hear not the familiar old chord structure but the dazzling, organic rise and fall of an ocean of sound from mutually alert, high-adrenalin musicians, the whole *is* revolutionary, *was* revolutionary. It transformed the psychic arena that electric, city blues singing inhabited.

Since then, hundreds of workaday performances with lesser bands have over-printed the individuality of the song and the inspirational experience of its fresh, live rendition so that both have disappeared and all that's left is a blurred old beat group's 12-bar churn-out that you could expect to hear just as satisfactorily from Bob Job & The Blobs in a pub in Wolverhampton, or from Keith Richards and his moribund old musos on stage in Seville.[38]

Again, is this more worth offering in concerts in the 1990s than contemporary material? If Bob Dylan hid in the chains of the old songs less, he might write more new ones. And if he didn't, so be it. There's no quota he has to fulfil. The American fanzine-contributor John Hinchey may write that 'you might even say he wrote more great songs then than he writes songs these days . . . an artist whose once miraculously unerring sense of what he was about is now half-buried in the soot of weariness and self-doubt': but writer's block goes away in the end, and is a condition that can be borne without shame.[39] Binding yourself to the work of years and years ago, work

---

fourth, was then dropped for a few days, reintroduced on 12 August and then dropped properly until resuscitated as the opening number at his forty-third concert of 1998) – and thus performed a further 76 times in 1993, 109 times in 1994, 118 times in 1995, 86 times in 1996, 38 times in 1997 and just 7 more in 1998. This totals a numbing 1033 performances in the last 25 years, 690 of them in the 1990s alone.)

These statistics and those given in later footnotes are extrapolated from the 3rd and 4th editions of Glen Dundas' *Tangled up in Tapes*, 1994 and 1999. If there are any errors, they are mine, not his.

37.   "Blonde On Blonde" was issued in the USA the day before this concert; in Britain, it didn't come out until August.

38.   Keith Richards & friends, Guitar Legends Festival, note 10.

39.   John Hinchey: 'Stealing home: Bob Dylan then and now', *Telegraph*, no. 32, Spring 1989.

that was produced in a different biological way – the several songs a day process that cannot be revisited – this can never blow away the soot. You can't roll away the 'Stone' if your hands are tied.

I thought of Dylan being tired of his same-old-songs but doing them again and again regardless when I came across a comment he had made in Japan in 1986. 'Somebody comes to see you for two hours or one and a half hours, whatever it is . . . I mean, they've come to see *you*. You could be doing anything up on that stage. You could be frying an egg or hammering a nail into a piece of wood.'[40] How *enormously* more riveting and magical it would be if he *did* come on stage and proceed to fry an egg. All that Chaplinesque panache! the comic possibilities! the *freshness* of such a performance! It would be so much more revealing, so much more of an artistic nakedness, at once dramatic and intimate, than the 700th posturing blitz through 'Tangled Up In Blue' – a song he's done so unfeelingly so often that it has spoiled, for many admirers of his work, even the early studio versions of what was once a major work of consequence and delight. As the *Monthly Film Bulletin* comments somewhere in a different context, 'It's not the familiar which breeds contempt but the debasement of the familiar.'

Standing by old songs because they're still valid is, of course, itself something it's valid to do. In 1992, in California, in the wake of the riots sparked off by a jury acquitting the policemen who gave Rodney King a savage beating the world saw on video, nothing could have been more apposite than Dylan's performance of 'The Lonesome Death Of Hattie Carroll' on the opening night of his San Francisco concerts: a timeless song about racial injustice made riveting once again by contemporary events. Dylan's 1991 Grammy choice, 'Masters Of War', sung during the Gulf War, was an apt one also: why write a new anti-war song when one he wrote in 1963 still speaks volumes?[41]

Yet it doesn't if no one can make out a word of it – if people genuinely can't tell what song he's singing, because he's actually too bored with it to sing it straight. And standing by old songs would be more distinct from merely regurgitating them if Dylan would also stand by the best of his *new* songs. Which he doesn't.

What are the truly great songs of the 1980s? There's bound to be disagreement here, but if it were possible to nominate only three, you might feel it understandable (even if not your own choice) for the three to be 'Jokerman', 'Blind Willie McTell' and 'Brownsville Girl'. Dylan abandoned 'Jokerman' for ten years after its début performances in 1984. He first played 'Blind Willie McTell' in August 1997, fourteen years after recording it and six years after its official release on CD. He never bothers with 'Brownsville Girl' at all. Meanwhile the numbingly undistinguished 'Silvio', co-written by Dylan and recorded in 1987, had received well over 500 performances by the end of 1998.[42]

---

40.   Bob Dylan, Tokyo, 10/3/86, quoted by Dave Thomas in 'Bigger than Elvis', *Isis*, no. 65, Feb.–March, 1996.

41.   Bob Dylan: 'The Lonesome Death Of Hattie Carroll', San Francisco, 4/5/92; 'Masters Of War' at the Grammy Awards, NYC, 20/2/91.

42.   'Jokerman' débuted on the European tour of 1984, Verona, Italy, 28/5/84; played each night of the 27-date tour; not played again until Sendai, Japan, 5/2/94. 'Blind Willie McTell' débuted Montreal, 5/8/97. Up to the end of 1998, 'Silvio' had been performed 543 times, making this miserable nonentity his 13th-most performed song of all time.

When he did sing 'Jokerman' on the 1984 tour, when it was newly released on album, he cut out the marvellous fourth verse, as he always cuts out verses from long songs these days. There is no reason for this, beyond the sheer shrugging-off of the task of full performance. There you are, say at the concert in Montreal in May 1990; Dylan launches into 'Desolation Row', which is fresh – having been performed only five times in the previous two decades: and he misses out five verses.[43] How can this not disappoint? Such short-changing of the audience, such short-changing of his own work, is in essence another expression of self-contempt. What other impression can it give except that he can't be bothered?

It's ironic that the decade in which this shabbiness of performance became the norm was, since he wrote comparatively little and toured so much, Dylan's perform-ance decade: especially since the 1980s performances were also those where he could hardly sing a song without fluffing it. There have been many times when the Never-Ending Tour has become the metaphor for Bob Dylan's descent into lostness – a ceaseless repetition bereft of cultural significance, creative inspiration or light.

Mind you, he's been fluffing it since . . . when? At least the Isle of Wight back in 1969, as that event's 'Like A Rolling Stone' makes clear on the "Self Portrait" release. And it's true that while it's mostly an annoyance that Dylan so often knows his lyrics less well than 80 per cent of the people he's singing them to (the irony of which soon loses its novelty) just occasionally it produces something good: the desertion of the words, for instance, on the 1984-tour Barcelona 'Lay, Lady, Lay' pushes him to summon up lovely aural noises – it goads the voice on to better things – and at Houston in 1981, singing 'The Times They Are A-Changin'' without concentrating, the mangling of words produced the irrational but splendid 'you'll be drenched like a bone'.[44] And it's an odd business: at Radio City Music Hall (19/10/88), after that clodhop through 'Subterranean Homesick Blues', and after fluffing his way through an array of the over-familiar, he lights into a never-sung-live-before, word-perfect, full-length version of the lengthy 'Bob Dylan's 115th Dream' from almost twenty-four years earlier. But however postmodernist you feel the more normal fluffing is, it isn't better than if he were sufficiently interested in the words to get them right.

If Bob Dylan says, well, I've given enough already, there is no new concert, or there is no new album, then so be it. That's wholly up to him. It may have been impossible to summarise these widely felt disquiets of the last decade-plus without sounding a begrudging old Stalinist, but no such he-ought-tos are offered as to whether he works or not. If he's going to work, then to work in good faith is only what's asked of any artist. Not to perform half-drunk, when half-drunk blurs and demeans – 'Lay, Lady, Lay' at Hamburg on 23 June 1991 is far more cruelly dreadful than any outsider's parody of Dylan ever is: it is as bad an advert for alcohol as the 1966 concerts were good adverts for drugs.

So no, not to perform half-drunk, when half-drunk numbs instead of inspiring;

---

43. Montreal, 29/5/90; the only previous performances since 1966 had been at St. Louis, 4/2/74, ten years later in Rome, 21/6/84, and at three 1987 concerts: Copenhagen, 21/9/87, Helsinki, 23/9/87, and Brussels, 8/10/87.

44. Bob Dylan: 'Like A Rolling Stone', Isle of Wight, 31/8/69; 'Lay, Lady, Lay', Barcelona, 28/6/84; 'The Times They Are A-Changin'', Houston, 12/11/81.

not to offer token renditions from which half the lyrics have been dumped out of soured laziness; not to get shrivelled down into a defensive not-trying. It seems the worst of both worlds to slide into the tired old bag of tricks of professional showbiz, and at the same time to lose all grip on the kind of professionalism that makes for honourable competence in performance and public life.[45]

Age is a reason for Bob Dylan 1999 to be different from Bob Dylan 1966; it is no reason for abandoning the dictum 'You do what you must do and you do it well'. Chuck Berry, at over 70, may tour round with the same core repertoire he has had for aeons; he may accept a second-rate band and then test their nerve by changing key on them in mid-song; he may do a shortish set and conserve his energy: but his core repertoire represents a fair cross-section of his admirable writing talents; he gives out while he's on stage by being alert and gracious, and he can be bothered to play his guitar and live sufficiently in the moment to get the words right. Every time.[46] Bob Dylan's genius, original on a massively wider scale than Chuck Berry's, is such that he wipes the floor with the sort of professionalism most performers and most songwriters swear allegiance to, but shambolic unprofessionalism is in itself no substitute for, nor affirmation of, that genius.

The Up Wing

Yet Bob Dylan still has genius, it was not inseparably linked to his long-gone youth, and he is still capable of being an inspired, fresh performer on a whole other level from everybody else, and a songwriter–poet of superlative richness.

There has been plenty of evidence of it since the beginning of the 1980s, though I'm not sure that evidence is what people notice about him. There's a process at work that I don't understand whereby, whatever Bob Dylan does now, only a relatively small coterie will pay it any attention. There are millions of people around today who listened to Dylan in the 1960s and gained great pleasure from it, yet who wouldn't dream of giving him a listen now, even though they do listen to some 'contemporary' music. It's as if one artist can only expect a quota of people's attention – and it really

---

45.   As if in summary of disquiets widely felt since the 1980s hove into view, I have had a series of dreams about Dylan (I don't remember dreaming about him at all in previous decades), though the first touched on an older disquiet at his adoption of a vengeful Christian orthodoxy in the late 1970s. From this dream, I only remember waking with the phrase 'The Preacherous and Treacherous Bob Dylan' in my mind. That visual word-play connection surprised me, but there it was. (My problem, not his.) The second dream touched on 'the celebrity trap'. I found myself walking through some college, where I noticed Elizabeth Taylor on a sofa chatting to some students in a smoky room. She asked me when Bob Dylan had died, and added 'How old was he, anyway?' Later in the dream I was telling John Bauldie about this, saying it just showed you couldn't trust media reports of celebrities' intimacy: all these pictures of Bob and Liz, and her reportedly hanging round the studio during the making of 'Wiggle Wiggle' (about the time the doorknob broke), yet she knew so little about him, she didn't even know he was still alive! Then, in the months after the awful concerts at Hammersmith in 1991 (8–10, 12, 13, 15–17 February), I had a number of dreams expressing anxieties about what can be expected of a contemporary Dylan concert performance. These involved going to see concerts where he didn't turn up at all, or where the seats in the hall were arranged so that the audience couldn't see the stage, or where he came on hours late and then stayed behind a pillar, finally emerging with his face transformed into Guy Mitchell's.

46.   Keith Richards complained that Berry had tried to change key on him when being 'helped' by Richards, as seen in the fine and fascinating documentary film *Chuck Berry Hail! Hail! Rock'n'Roll!*, US, produced Stephanie Bennett and Keith Richards, directed Taylor Hackford, 1987. On the evidence of Live Aid, however [Philadelphia, 13/7/85], Keith Richards' help is best avoided.

doesn't matter whether what the artist does later is good, bad or indifferent, they're simply on the wrong side of some time barrier and cannot get a hearing. Sometimes you can catch this process at work very quickly. The world listened to Tracy Chapman's first album as to some long-lost soul sister restored to its bosom; her second album was treated as if it simply did not exist.

In Bob Dylan's case, it makes you wonder why people still go and see him. Their reasons may have little to do with anything conducive to his capacity for the fresh or the richly creative.

One reason, indeed, is because he's musically 'safe'. Millions of 40-to-60-year-olds who liked rock music in the 1960s and were subsequently unimpressed by the coming of disco, punk, syntho-pop, rap/hip-hop/house, know that if they go to a Dylan concert, they'll find a good old guitars/bass/keyboards/drums-centred outfit, not a singer and three synth operators, nor a singer and two baggy-trousered men leaping about while a third tortures some albums on a turntable. This may seem a minimal reason for going to see Bob Dylan but it's a strong one and getting stronger. When *Radio Times* trailered the televising of the Seville Guitar Festival, it was along the lines of 'All the great old names associated with the guitar were there – Clapton, B. B. King, Dylan, Richard Thompson'. I'm sure Dylan was delighted to be seen as a guitar hero, but essentially what was expressed was an 'All-Star 60s Heroes Show' attitude, and it applies to Dylan as to, say, Lou Reed, Paul McCartney, the Stones and Springsteen; and it is very pervasive. After all, from about 1976 till about 1985, the only fashionable *chart* performers who played what could be called mainstream guitar-based rock were Dire Straits, so that people had to go to '60s (which is to say 1965–1974) acts for their music.

Nor is this attitude entirely reprehensible. A friend of mine remembers going to see the late Carl Perkins on Merseyside in 1962, when he'd never heard a record by him – he was just one of those old rockin' names (his name was about 7 years old at the time), whom you knew would be of interest. Today, if you have never seen him before, a concert by Dylan in, say, Helsinki, is probably rather wonderful if you're 15, have heard some of your mother's old tapes, liked them, and gone along to see who this strange old man is.

Yet for people to go to see a Bob Dylan concert because he's one of those 1960s heroes, or because he's a legend, does not encourage the legend to be a *living* legend, to go on creating, to be open to the present and unchained by the past. I remember seeing a Neil Young concert around the start of the 1990s, in the ghastly environs of Wembley Arena, throughout which he alternated bored, dutiful renditions of things like 'Heart Of Gold' and 'The Needle & The Damage Done' with engaged, vibrant performances of new material; the audience responded with lukewarm politeness to the new work and went apeshit for the indifferently performed old 'hits'. This cannot but send out an unhealthy message to the artist.

What makes it worse is that it's the message of the people who *quite* like the artist. Those really engaged by his or her work want to hear whatever work it interests the artist to perform. The revelation of that is one of the pleasures the artist's concert is going to yield them. If new material is offered, they welcome it. They do not want to browbeat the artist with the tyranny of old hits. In any case, these people who *quite* like the artist not only want the hits, they want them performed exactly as they were on the records, and since Dylan won't oblige with that, there really is no point their shouting the message at him at all.

It may be that Bob Dylan has done well to survive that constant message as obdurately as he has. What is certainly true is that recounting all these disquiets about his performances of the 1980s and 1990s obscures the central fact of the extraordinary variety of guises in which he has performed. We have witnessed extremes of contrast and myriad shadings between different tours: in terms of repertoire, style, voice, appearance and personnel, let alone mood and level of engagement.

His song-bag has varied from the all-new repertoire performed at the seventy-nine concerts on the untitled 1979/80 tour, to some Greatest Hits phases, as on the 1984 tour and some early 1990s legs of the Never-Ending Tour, to the incredible gunnery of repertoire on the 1987 'Temple Of Flames' tour and during the Never-Ending Tour's first three years, right from its beginning back in June 1988. Some statistics: on the North American section of the 'True Confessions' tour in the summer of 1986, Dylan performed 'only' fifty-eight different songs in the course of forty-seven concerts (a total of 999 song performances); on the early 1990 dates, up to and including the Hammersmith Odeon, in a mere fourteen concerts he sang eighty different songs (within a total of 246 song-performances). When he gave his two début performances in Israel in 1987, his repertoire was wholly different each night. What other performer could or would do that?[47]

Moreover, the balance of material from the deep past and the recent past has not always been either the same or as disproportionate as the list of core-songs (footnoted earlier) would suggest. The first of those Israeli dates, in Tel Aviv, offered six songs from the 1960s, the same number from the 1970s, four from the 1980s and one traditional song. At the Jerusalem concert, he performed more songs from the 1980s than from the 1970s.

Indeed, to see how broadly he reaches around his catalogue of songs you have to look at the broad picture. That Dylan goes through periods when he is at one with his work of the mid-1970s for example, and other periods when he feels estranged from it, itself suggests that he is not running on automatic but is open and receptive in ways only a real artist can remain. On the 1984 tour, he sang no traditional material whatever and no blues songs by other artists; on those first fourteen 1990 concerts (played to audiences in the USA, Brazil, France and England), he performed half a dozen traditional songs – and still no blues songs by other artists. On the first leg of the 1978 tour he had sung four different such blues songs, and in the course of that year sang Tampa Red's 1941 blues 'She's Love Crazy' forty-eight times, while the 1986 tours found him especially interested in 1950s rockabilly music and singing such Sun Records back catalogue items as Warren Smith's 'Uranium Rock'.[48]

47.   The untitled 1979/80 tour comprised 79 North American concerts 1/11/79 to 21/5/80, starting with 18 nights in San Francisco. The 1984 Europe tour was 28/5/84 to 8/7/84. The Never-Ending Tour began 7/6/88. The Temple Of Flames tour (starting with his two début performances in Israel) ran 5/9/87 to 17/10/87. The North American leg of the True Confessions tour was 9/6/86 to 6/8/86. The 14 early 1990 dates referred to, up to and including the Hammersmith Odeon, were 14 January to 8 February.

48.   The 1978 World Tour first leg was in the Far East, 20 Feb. to 1 April; the other two legs were USA and Europe, 1 June to 15 July (at Blackbushe Aerodrome) and North America 15 September to 16 December. Tampa Red's 'She's Love Crazy' is detailed in Chapter 9. The True Confessions tour first leg was Far East, 5/2/86 to

Even when an uninspired Dylan concert offers no oddity of repertoire and yields all the faults catalogued earlier – the muffed lines, the dull rockism, the over-declamatory delivery, the lot – you only have to listen to something like U2 performing 'All Along The Watchtower' (on the "Rattle & Hum" LP) to be reminded that there are all kinds of vulgarities and cheap posturings being committed by the supposedly modern and popular that Bob Dylan can still be relied upon not to countenance.[49] Indeed for all the aficionados' disquiet about slippages of integrity over recent years, and despite his toiling in the brothel of commercial popular music for nearly forty years, Dylan has retained plenty of integrity in ways often readily abandoned by supposedly more 'serious' artists. Thus James Galway indulges a shameless professional Irishness to propel him through hammy performances of inferior populist material, and André Previn is remembered as much for selling television sets as for his conducting or composing. (Not to mention the haircut, John.)

Dylan is also still capable, by virtue of a kind of undiminished playful waywardness, of surprising anew people who have followed him for decades. I have in mind things like his turning up in a 20-second cameo role as a sculptor in a hard hat, toting an electric saw, in the 1989 Denis Hopper film *Catchfire* (and not even securing a mention in the credits) and his having a letter published in 1990 in the pages of the deeply obscure feminist journal *Sister 2 Sister* and signing off (rather splendidly, and as if he's still writing *Tarantula*) with the daring deadpan wit of 'God bless you much, good luck and say hello to the boys'.[50]

I have in mind also things like his continued talent for soundbites that cut to the core of American cheapness, as when in 1991 he told a *Los Angeles Times* reporter: 'There used to be a time when the idea of heroes was important. People grew up

---

10/3/86; second leg as note 47. Warren Smith: 'Uranium Rock', Memphis, 23/2/58: "Sun Rockabillys [sic] #1", Phonogram/Sun 6467 025, London, 1972.

49.   So why does he join forces with such people? Why co-write a song with Bono? Or *Michael Bolton*? These people represent such numbing mediocrity that in the resulting co-written songs you can't even tell which bits Dylan may have contributed, while the end results, which probably took immensely more studio-time to achieve than 'A Hard Rain's A-Gonna Fall', are such that the young Bob Dylan who wrote and recorded *that* song would know better than to give one minute of his time to the co-written ones. Have you *heard* the Dylan–Bolton song 'Steel Bars'? Its only significance is as an object lesson in how the death grip of the music industry works. He must do it for the money. 'Steel Bars' probably brought in more than the whole of "Oh Mercy". But then why write 'Band Of The Hand' for the kind of film that makes *Hearts of Fire* feel like Bergman? Money doesn't explain cultural slumming like that.

[Co-composed by Bob Dylan and Bono of U2 (or Bobo, to use the delightful typo in Glen Dundas' *Tangled up in Tapes*, 3rd edn, 1994) and recorded by U2 with Dylan on harmonica: 'Love Rescue Me', Memphis, probably May 1987, "Rattle & Hum", Island Records 7 91003–1, USA, 1988. Co-composed with Michael Bolton and recorded by the latter: 'Steel Bars', *nia*. Bob Dylan with Tom Petty & The Heartbreakers: 'Band Of The Hand', Sydney, 8–9/2/86, MCA Records MCA-52811 (single) and MCA-6167 ('film sountrack album'), New York, 1986; the film *Band of the Hand*, RCA/Columbia Films, US, 1986. Dylan does not appear in the film. He performed the song 33 times in 1986 concerts.]

50.   *Flashback* aka *Catchfire*, Vestron/Precision Films/Mack-Taylor Productions, US, directed Alan Smithee, 1989.
      Sister 2 Sister, vol. 2, no. 10: 2nd anniv. issue, July 1990. Dylan's letter, to 'Jamie', is short and vague and is about time 'being a mind thing not a soul thing'. After signing off as quoted above, he adds 'PS. Congratulations on your second year. Bob Dylan.' When I enquired about this by phone (Feb. 1992) no one in the UK seemed to have heard of *Sister 2 Sister*, except possibly at the Women's Press. 'It's a radical feminist magazine,' their spokesperson told me, but could add no details. The US Embassy reference library in London said it wasn't listed in the *Standard Periodical Directory 1991*; the *Gale Directory of Publications and Broadcasting Media, 1990* or *Ulrich's International Directory of Periodicals*. Nor was it known to Compendium, Sisterwrite or Silver Moon bookshops, nor to the Women's Research Resources Centre, London, nor to the feminist library there, nor yet to *Spare Rib* magazine.

sharing myths and legends and ideals. Now they grow up sharing McDonald's and Disneyland.' Bruno Bettelheim couldn't have put it better. And I have in mind things like his lack of dilettanteism toward other art forms. He doesn't just paint, he attended regular painting classes in New York City week in and week out for months (as he did, in another time and place, with Bible study classes); and according to photographer Elliott Landy, while Dylan is not too good with a camera, he *is* a good painter, he's done some 'mind-blowing' sculpturing in clay, and some stained-glass of 'incredible . . . form and colour'.[51] *Drawn Blank*, a book of Dylan's drawings, mostly done on the road 'from about 1989 to about 1991 or '92 in various locations mainly to relax and refocus a restless mind', as Dylan puts it in his short foreword to the book, was published in the US by Random House in 1994. It's a modest achievement, likely to have gained publication only because Bob Dylan's name can be attached to it, yet it reveals a Dylan still curious about the outside world, still observing the real world and its ordinary detail: something his songwriting does not always show him doing.

Then there's his suddenly playing the saxophone (or at least, making oinking noises on one) at a concert in Boston in October 1981, and his ending a New York City concert in 1989 by jumping from the stage into the audience and dodging out by a side staircase – in effect calling down his own bolt of lightning to escape by – and leaving his band as surprised as the crowd. His living in a tent in a recording studio's back yard, as Eric Clapton says Dylan was doing in 1976. His getting off the plane at Cairo en route to Israel in 1987, with no word of goodbye, and then, after missing the soundchecks and rehearsals, turning up on the day of the first concert having made the journey from the Egyptian border by bus.[52]

At the 1990 sessions for "Under The Red Sky" he had this unexplained box in a corner of the studio day after day; then one day, producing from it a new accordion still in its sealed polythene bag, he unwrapped it and recorded the accordion part to 'Born In Time' in one take. No one knew it was an instrument he could even half-play.[53]

Many times on European legs of the Never-Ending Tour he cycled to work, wobbling up to the stage door of the concert hall while the support act played. He walked to his Dunkirk Festival appearance in June 1992: he was to be seen strolling along, following the crowd to find his way to the site.

At a festival in 1992, he swapped sets with Bryan Adams, going on before Adams instead of after, so that he could get to a favourite restaurant before it closed. And yet while he tends to stay in very agreeable hotels when he's touring Europe these days, in the USA it has often been rather different during the Never-Ending Tour. César Díaz says that 'the crew stay at Hyatt Regency and all the nice hotels, and Bob and the

51.   Elliott Landy, interviewed by Paul Williams in the *Telegraph*, no. 30, Summer 1986.

52.   The Dylan-on-saxophone concert was Boston, 21/10/81; the jump into the audience was during NYC, 10–13/10/89, I think on the second night. The description of Dylan's living in a tent outside Shangri-La Studios, Hollywood, while helping Eric Clapton to record part of the "No Reason To Cry" album in March 1976 [Polydor RSO RS-13004, New York, 1976] comes from the Clapton interview by Roger Gibbons, Surrey, May 1987, in *Telegraph*, no. 29, Spring 1988. Dylan's crossing out of Egypt by bus to Tel Aviv with his son Jesse, 4/9/87, after their flying in to Cairo from the USA two days earlier, was reported in an Israeli newspaper, *nia*, at the time.

53.   The relevant "Under The Red Sky" sessions were in LA, March 1990; the accordion story, reported by co-producer David Was in the *Telegraph*, no. 44, Winter 1992, doesn't seem borne out by the credits on the album-sleeve.

band stay at Motel Six at the side of the road away from town . . . he likes to see what the low life is like so he can get inspiration. So we would stay at all these places where you . . . would roll back the sheets to go to sleep and you could see that somebody had slept there the night before.'[54]

He is still, to appropriate a phrase that is either his or John Bauldie's, a funny wonder. He even goes from fat to thin and back again more radically than most of us: look at the pudgy, raddled Bob Dylan from Live Aid in mid-1985, the skinny-armed, lean-machine version on tour early the following year, and the bulky Old Testament prophet on stage with the Grateful Dead the year after that.

His chameleon ability as a performer is as noticeable as his bravery, and if there are concerts as poor as Hammersmith 1991 there are those as marvellous as Hammersmith 1990. You'd get neither from a performer less reliant on the spontaneity of the moment. Nor would you get to see songs reflected in so many different lights; you get this from Dylan because he is still open to being caught in such a wide sweep of moods. Sometimes he's not engaged; usually you can sense his getting into, and drifting away from, his material, often in mid-song, let alone mid-concert. The results can be extreme. Replaying, recently, a tape of a Dylan concert in Toulouse in 1993, it struck me with equal force that 'Born In Time' was the worst vocal performance of the worst 'ballad' I'd ever heard him offer, and that the same night's 'Hard Times' was magnificent – completely committed, vocally and on guitar. He was intensely interested in his guitar-lines, which were exploratory and deft, while he also had time to tease the other players; he guided the whole to a delicate ending that avoided any easy crowd-pleasing; and the entire creation was, too, dramatically different from the also-excellent studio version.

And who else ever offers radical re-writings of their songs, as Dylan did on tour in Europe in 1984 with 'Tangled Up In Blue', and in 1990 with the beautiful reverie, the glorious dancing shuffle, of a largely re-shaped 'You Angel You', suddenly thrown in on the last night at Hammersmith that February? The re-written 'Tangled Up In Blue' was less excellent than the earlier version of the lyric, but it was such a splendid thing to do. Who else has ever done such things?

At best, this free-spirited openness offers concerts that are still utterly un-showbiz, still heightened experiences for those who, all too briefly, stand there captivated in the same room as this major twentieth-century artist. At such times, he can call forth *numinous* revisits to his old songs.

By these standards, he gave pretty indifferent performances at Farm Aid in 1985, Farm Aid II in 1986, Toads Place in 1990 and the later Eurogigs of 1991 (though at Hamburg an immaculate and intimate 'When I Paint My Masterpiece' more than compensated for the horrible, drunken 'Lay, Lady, Lay' of earlier in the set).[55]

The *great* performances might be said to include:

---

54. Dunkirk, 30/6/92. Bryan Adams shared bill, details not to hand. César Díaz, interviewed by Derek Barker, Old San Juan, Puerto Rico, 23–25/3/99; 'A Chat with César Díaz, part 2', *Isis*, no. 84, April–May 1999.

55. Farm Aid, Champaign, Illinois, 22/9/85; Farm Aid II, Buffalo, New York, 4/7/86. Toads Place was a club in New Haven where Dylan, most unusually, did four sets in one evening, 12/1/90; 'the later Eurogigs of 1991' were actually in June (Hamburg was 23 June), but they were in strong contrast to the awful gigs that the year still brings to many fans' minds, especially those in Scotland and England in February (beginning Glasgow, 2 February, and ending London, 17th).

The Grammy Awards 'Gotta Serve Somebody' 27/2/80, as seen on American television; the evangelical concert in Denver in January 1980 and the fervent Toronto concerts that April; the 1981 concerts in Oslo in July and in Houston in November; the rehearsal as well as the performance for Dylan's first *David Letterman Show* TV appearance of 22/3/84; the Barcelona, Paris and Newcastle concerts of 1984; his filmed interview by Christopher Sykes in the Dylan film-set caravan that autumn, at which Dylan did one of his classic reversals of who-is-interviewing-who, on this occasion turning the interrogation round by studying and sketching the face of his interrogator (shown on BBC-TV's *Omnibus* 18/9/87); the Wembley 1987 concerts, other than the first night; likewise at the Birmingham NEC; the Glasgow SEC concert in June 1989 (which yielded, as Rob Flynn wrote in the *Guardian*, 'this extraordinary vision of a withered priest somehow plugging himself back into his unique, mystic jukebox of hits'); the magical residency at Hammersmith Odeon in February 1990 (not least because, as David Fricke noted in *Melody Maker*, it offered 'a unique opportunity to sample the vagaries of Dylan's peculiar genius over a long haul in close, sharp focus . . . a chance to witness the process, not just sample the product');[56] the already cited acceptance speech at the 1991 Grammy Awards; remarkable, soul music concerts that year at Ames, Iowa and Madison, Wisconsin; some of the California concerts of May 1992 and some of the European ones of 1995, beginning in Prague with a concert truly fit for that much put-upon capital city. Plus a substantial body of great individual song performances in the midst of less than inspired whole concerts – including the Martin Luther King Birthday Commemoration rendition of a re-written 'I Shall Be Released' on 20 January 1986; the Los Angeles Amnesty Concert performances of 'License To Kill' and 'Shake A Hand' that June; the compulsive, dream-like rendition of 'Soon' at the Gershwin Celebration at the New York Academy of Music in Brooklyn in 1987; a perfect revisit to the overworked 'It Ain't Me, Babe' in London in 1993; a 'Queen Jane Approximately' almost as lovely as you could wish for, in Berlin in 1996; and an immanent, turbulent, shining 'Tears Of Rage' of authority and heightened inspiration performed at Besançon, France, in 1994 that is, against all possible odds, a finer thing than the 1967 studio original.[57]

I don't have the space here for a detailed account of such a huge body of live performance work, but to try to suggest some of what's going on during a *good* concert, I want to describe just one such performance: Dylan's concert at Berkeley on 7 May 1992. I wasn't there – and if I had been, I'd have been too busy being there to make notes, and too aware of those layers of experience glimpsed when it's happening live in front of you but inexplicable afterwards. This, then, is a description of how it felt to hear, fresh, an audience-made tape of the event, which I offer as some approximation of responding to the event itself.

It starts, unpromisingly, with a throat-clearing, are-we-all-here, is-the-mixing-desk-manned, are-the-mikes-on, OK-well-um-here-we-go-then 'Rainy Day Women Nos. 12 & 35', as unheeding of whatever individuality the song once had as I was

56.   *Guardian*, 8/6/89, and *Melody Maker*, 3/2/90.

57.   The 1991 Grammys, the 1986 'I Shall Be Released' and the 1987 'Soon', see earlier notes. Amnesty Concert 'License To Kill' and 'Shake A Hand', LA, 6/6/86; Ames, Iowa, 2/11/91; Madison, Wisconsin, 5/11/91; 'It Ain't Me, Babe', London, 12/2/93; 'Queen Jane Approximately', Berlin, 17/6/96; 'Tears Of Rage', Besançon, 3/7/94.

suggesting earlier. Then the band starts up a jaunty little shuffle that sounds like an intro to 'If Not For You'. Dylan starts singing, and it *is* 'If Not For You', or at least, that portion of the song that he remembers. It's a song never sung live in earlier years, and from an album he's tended to neglect, so the fact that he's doing the song at all is interesting – in fact it is only the third time he's sung it live, the others having been in Sydney the previous month – and makes the vagaries of the composer's memory less irksome than if it were the four-hundredth time around.[58]

Less irksome than usual too, on the same grounds, is his apparent inability to come to the microphone and open his mouth until the moment for the opening vocal phrase has already passed. Dylan has made this particular shambolicism a trade-mark of recent years. You can almost rely on it, so that what we get now is a series of song openings like

> *Was a maid in the kitchen*

> *Ambassador to England or France*

> *Me, I don't have much to say*

and in this case

> *I couldn't find the door*

and while these last two might seem apt – even inspired ellipses – it's clear from the great majority of examples that unfortunately it's just disorganisation or laziness. Yet once the singer has emerged from the undergrowth of the song's beginning into the clearing of the sound system, he seems to be in a mood of benevolent delicacy of feeling, singing to express a heartfelt fragility and allowing himself to savour, unhurriedly, a wistful poignancy of recollection that infuses 'If Not For You' with far deeper emotion than it seemed to carry in the past. It is an open, sharing mood that fully endorses that 'Outlined Epitaph' pay-off line from nearly thirty years earlier, 'I "expose" myself / every time I step out / on the stage' – and as it turns out, it extends throughout the great majority of the concert. There is no dramatising bluster here, nor any of the bored guardedness into which he has often retreated.

Next comes 'Union Sundown', another song fresh to the live repertoire, and sung with such badly articulated, mumbled cascades of syllables that it takes half the opening verse before it's possible to recognise what song it is. Tonight's first verse becomes a tentative jumble of the original first and second verses: threatening, as with most of his 'list' songs, to be downgraded, if sung frequently in the future, to the gobbledegook treatment. The song's third verse comes second, its 'capitalism is above the law' changed to a dodgy 'capitalism is against the law', suggesting that Dylan is already not paying attention – or rather, since some endearing eloquence of regret is discernible in the singing, even if there is little outward decipherability or sense, that he is already struggling to hold himself together, mid-way through the third number. An instrumental break comes to his rescue, and he returns to offer a re-written fifth

---

58. 'If Not For You', débuted Sydney, 14/4/92, and repeated the next night, also in Sydney. By the end of 1998, however, it had become a common repertoire item, with 65 performances in seven years.

verse. Well, either it's re-written or Dylan is offering a bluff-through of pretend-words: it's impossible to tell, because nobody can quite catch them. You might think this minimises the point of a re-write, but Dylan doesn't worry about that, and he lands back on the track emphatically enough for the last two lines (the only ones not re-written), by giving them far more sung-out, humorously insistent clarity of articulation than he's sounded capable of mustering till now, and which finally offers this interesting song's lyric a musical frame worthy of it.

Then, opening with the observation that 'Body feels any pain', comes 'Just Like A Woman', a song that Dylan had, in general, sent on sabbatical for a while, after overworking it for years beforehand. It's a song that in live performance in 1966 created a timeless, sensuous journey through a landscape of mystery all its own, and that in live performance at the 1971 Concert for Bangla Desh yielded a very different treatment – one of intensive, exhilarating, high-register vocal beauty, on the highest point of which, the vaulting bridge of the song, Dylan in effect announced that from now on he could find innumerable inspired ways to time and phrase its wonderfully insistent shunting of rhyming and half-rhyming words – 'first', 'thirst', 'curse', 'hurts', 'whut's' and 'worse', and the intertangled 'came in here', 'pain in here', 'stay in here' and 'Ain't it clear' – followed by the glorious logic of that overhanging descent into the start of the final verse.[59]

It was to become, as it were, a fixed rendezvous for his masterly, never-the-same-way-twice spontaneity of delivery. Then, after a period in which the rest of the song's performance had long since lost its own allure but this regular date with inspirational delivery was still honoured, somewhere down the road Dylan started standing us up even on these occasions. Unhappily, here on this Berkeley tape, he sings the much-rested 'Just Like A Woman' as if he has no memory of ever having handled it with consummate skill. The only pleasurable touch he brings is on a piece of guitar playing at the end of the performance, which is not just beguilingly grungy, as ever, but sustained and on target, which is rather less common. The harmonica playing is atrocious.

Then it's 'The Drifter's Escape', another welcome newcomer to Dylan's live repertoire.[60] This is taken at a Hendrixian riffing lick, with Dylan finding early on one of those inspired melodic vocal phrases which, having been alighted on once, he recognises as worth alighting on again – so that the fleeting sunlit moment, first come upon by free extemporising, is caught and used again to light up other moments along the improvised journey of the song. For the listener, it works very much in-the-moment, as a way into Dylan's attunedness, rather than just as a passively received exhibition of his vocal skill. You hear him find one of these vocal riffs, these aural equivalents of a flick of the wrist that may be a momentary gesture of elegance or may unlock an unnoticed door into the song, and, liking its flair, being warmed by the sunlight it reveals, you wait to hear whether Dylan too has heeded it. He usually has.

This time, for 'The Drifter's Escape', it is a compulsive yet elegant end-of-line

59.   Concert for Bangla Desh [sic], NYC, 1/8/71.

60.   'Drifter's Escape' was débuted at Eugene, Oregon, 30/4/92; the Berkeley performance was its second. By the end of 1998 it had been performed 57 times.

melodic phrase that lends itself particularly well to being repeated – it's a kind of 'yoo-hoo!' that implies its own playful echo in the first instance. From here, Dylan tantalises with the odds-on chance that he'll regain the impassioned but undeclamatory mood of 'If Not For You'.

It's starting to be clear too how much improved the band is by the recently added steel guitarist Bucky Baxter and second drummer Charlie Quintana. Baxter adds range; Quintana covers up the awful clink-clink-clink of the first drummer, who, except for a rolling 'Peggy Sue'-ish beat achieved occasionally on 1991 performances (as on the Gordon Lightfoot song 'Early Morning Rain' at South Bend, Indiana that November 6th) has always been incapable of lope, fox-trot or anything but a cumbersome pace. Now, there's a new fluidity and textural density to the band and it's starting to sound like God's garage band.

Dylan says 'Thanks ev'ybody!' at the end of this one, which tends to be his current way to signal that he thinks it a decent performance himself. Then it's straight into a truly lovely, shy, tender reading of 'I Don't Believe You', with the lines mostly given soft-falling feminine endings, pitched lower melodically than on the standard version of the tune, though occasionally he ends the lines higher instead, and at these times the sweetness and delicacy are extraordinary. Redolent of the ethereal grace sometimes achieved by the very old, it is sung, not half-recited, as by an old guy on his porch remembering "Nashville Skyline". It's nearly great.

This is followed by the surprise of a fast-paced 'Tangled Up In Blue' that abandons tranquil reflection in favour of what is, at its best, a precision-drill vocal performance, deftly rat-a-tat-tatting the syllables into place in the nick of time along descending melodic lines foreshortened by the sheer speed of it: a display of Dylan's being fully on top of both the words and their placement. It fully hits its stride twice in the course of the song, and elsewhere it's a reading that's urgent yet also wasted and pained.

So I'm listening to this hard-working, alert, brilliant vocalising on a run of three consecutive songs – 'The Drifter's Escape', 'I Don't Believe You' and 'Tangled Up In Blue' – and I'm trying to square this with lurid rumours of the artist's physical and mental decline, purveyed to me by a long-term Dylan admirer on the telephone mere days beforehand. He told me that a doctor who'd seen the BBC-TV *Omnibus* interview in 1987 had pronounced Dylan to be showing clinical symptoms of alcohol-abuse brain damage; that someone else who'd seen footage of Dylan receiving his honour from the government of France in January 1990 had seen in Dylan's peculiar spasmodic neck-jerking comportment 'unmistakable' signs that he was beginning to suffer from some kind of Parkinson's disease, possibly Alzheimer's; and that these days he was obviously drinking more, looking old beyond his years and generally becoming a lost, tragic figure crying out for help, like Elvis in his last years.[61]

Of course this is a characteristic by-product of star-watching: it's the same morbid derangement that had the motorcycle-crash Bob Dylan horribly scarred for life, and you could find similarly gory, fantastical dooms rumoured about any artist over the age of 30. They're the basic commodity of papers like the *National Enquirer*. Yet

---

61. BBC-TV *Omnibus*, note 16. Dylan was made Commandeur des Arts et des Lettres at a presentation by French Culture Minister Jack Lang in Paris, 30/1/90, with footage being widely screened on TV in America and Europe.

Elvis *was* a lost, tragic figure crying out for help, and Dylan can certainly look that way too. The one fundamental difference between all photos of Dylan in the mid-1960s and of Dylan now is that in the 'then' photos we see a man who knows exactly who he is and what he's doing, and in the 'now' photos we see a man who doesn't. Which might be said to sum it all up. Yet cameras lie, of course. In the mid-1960s he had novelty value to the press, so their lenses smiled upon him; but he never became one of their celebrity pets, and now that he's old and he scowls at the press, their lenses scowl back at him. In real life, time and again people who find themselves up close to him these days report that he looks 'beautiful', with translucent skin and corrosive blue eyes, that he retains an aura the power of which knocks them back in surprise, and that part of that aura is a strong sense that he knows *exactly* who he is. So it isn't clear-cut. Meanwhile, the fact that you can even make out a case along the lines of 'Brain-Damaged Protest Star Tragedy: Bob Nearly Vegetable Say Boffins', shows how *much* muffing and word-forgetting and song-mauling and playing in the wrong key, and so on, there has been. And if all this medical macabrism is untrue, why *is* it that he can't get through a song without getting the words wrong?

The inescapable effect is that even when you're experiencing the reality of a run of three inspired, acute performances, you don't any longer trust him to keep it up.

Tonight he almost does. Next comes 'Love Minus Zero/No Limit', fast but with a deft, bluesy, voice-lowered delicacy. He loses concentration in the second verse, forgetting the line 'Some speak of the future' and substituting the next, 'My love speaks softly', while knowing it's not right, and therefore offering it with that embarrassing, embarrassed diffidence that so often signals such slippages, after which of course he's forced to repeat the line straight away. Perhaps it's the audience applauding and whooping after this mauled second verse, but briefly he loses concentration again after this and makes a mistake as he comes into the third.

He quickly corrects it – which is all you can do at that point – though the swift correction means that the opening line he sings is the unlooked for 'the bridge and dagger dangles'. He moves on, getting back into what he was doing before, seeing it through to the end, even to having a game go at a harmonica solo. It's clear that he is truly bothering here, because after years of relying on another guitarist to help him through the acoustic sections (which in itself makes him sound like some sort of invalid) he is now not only taking responsibility entirely by playing solo, but playing lovely, wholly professionally competent guitar – even throwing in a couple of moments of picking amid the strumming – and facing up to the challenge of playing harmonica solos that are not just alternating 2-note twiddles but to some degree limn a tune.

'Little Moses', an old Spiritual, has no harp but keeps the mood and the care of this performance. We are in timeless folk performance terrain now.[62] Dylan is playing

62. 'Little Moses' is yet another song to be found on the Harry Smith anthology "American Folk Music", Folkways FA251–253, New York, 1952; CD-reissued as "Anthology Of American Folk Music" [6-CD box-set] with copious notes by many hands and a CD-ROM of extras, Smithsonian Folkways Recordings SFW 40090, Washington, DC, 1997. Smith's notes read: ' "Little Moses" (A. P. Carter): The Carter Family (1932). Their 1927 records made in Maces Springs, Virginia, are among the very first electrical recordings; their instantly recognizable rhythm has influenced every folk musician for the past 25 years.' Dylan says [interview answers taped in California, June 1987, broadcast BBC Radio Scotland, 30/9 and 14 & 21/10/87] that one of the first things that attracted him to Woody Guthrie was his sound, and that this wasn't very different from the Carter Family's sound. (While Smith

the acoustic guitar better than I have heard him play it for many years: there is a tangible renewal of attentiveness and dedication here, and it's great to witness it.

Then the band comes in for a 'Visions Of Johanna' that isn't as inspired vocally as another night might find it but certainly has its moments, and it's the first time I've known a fast version of this song have a point to it. It shimmies with gypsy intensity, and it achieves what it does from having a clear interpretational stance, with Dylan again finding a strong, riff-like counter-melody that works beautifully on the piled-up repetitions that the song's long, multi-line verses comprise, while the instrumental section is made into something delightful – like a post-punk revisit to "Pat Garrett & Billy The Kid" territory – by the new guitar and mandolin player, who even dares to do a long, melodically definite solo: something Dylan allowed G. E. Smith to do when the Never-Ending Tour first began but which within a year had been more or less elbowed out of the way. Now the new player seems to have turned the band around, putting in a country accent that balances Dylan's punk quality to make for a richer, more complex outfit.[63]

They make a country song out of 'Don't Think Twice, It's All Right', playing it fast and flimsy, as if it were an old bluegrass classic. I think it's a hard song for Dylan to revisit, because the lyric content suits the straightforwardness of youth, and when the middle-aged Dylan tries to sing it 'sincerely', he ends up sounding shifty. Tonight's performance, however, with the emphasis entirely on music and musical genre, soars above all such problems, avoiding comparisons with the long-gone past. Bob strums, John Jackson does the picking – playing like Jerry Reed on the Presley recording of the song (on which Elvis remembers even fewer of the words than Dylan on a bad night) – while the steel-player stays at the back to send lazy, moody phrases smoking up into the air between the vocal lines. The music encourages Dylan to another committed performance, like a cross between "Nashville Skyline" and Johnny Horton. At the end we get a longer than expected harmonica solo, perfectly in sympathy with the rest of the music. It stops, but this turns out to be only a pause, and he comes back with more, including one of those great moments when the band falls silent and the harp carries on alone.

Next comes a fine 'Cat's In The Well', until he gets into a mess with the words after the instrumental break. Before this, he sings it marvellously. The 'barn is full o' the bull' verse is so cool, sneaky, feline, stretched out: wonderful stuff. Meanwhile the extra player makes such a difference, really *playing*, and keeping the others at it. After the first instrumental break, Dylan completely forgets the words, singing a verse of nothings and ending with a feeble repeat of a previous line. Then there's a second instrumental section, in which the new recruit holds it together – insists that it not fall apart – and Dylan comes back in with a decent ending. If he hadn't faltered, if he really *knew the words*, it would have been a terrific performance of what is Dylan's best blues since 'Blind Willie McTell'. I hope it won't end up turned into an 'Everything Is Broken': it's too good for that.

---

attributes the composition to 'Pa' Carter, Glen Dundas' *Tangled up in Tapes Revisited* attributes it to 'Williams-Jones'.)

63.   The band at this point comprised John Jackson on guitar, Bucky Baxter on pedal steel, dobro, mandolin and guitar, Tony Garnier on bass and Ian Wallace and Charlie Quintana on drums.

'Idiot Wind', reintroduced to Dylan's live repertoire for the first time in sixteen years (the first time since the Rolling Thunder Revue of 1976), here blows a perilous course between glorious genius and disaster. Genius wins out. The technical report would have to note that after the first verse (each verse has ten lines) he mangles the chorus by mixing up 'teeth' and 'mouth' (and not switching back, as he did on the *Hard Rain* TV concert when the same thing happened),[64] so that we never get the lovely line about 'blowing down the backroads headin' south', nor the terse poetic effects of the 'teeth/breathe' lines, because these are dissipated by their fudged and accidental repetition. Then he does the next verse and sings another chorus, this time inspiredly, with the most glorious melodic fragility that really does rework the song. After an instrumental passage, Dylan comes back in – to do a very curious thing. He sings the opening two lines of the scheduled next verse, then sings its eighth, ninth and tenth lines, adds the first two lines from the final verse, and then returns to the third verse's fourth and fifth lines to achieve the rhyme: an extraordinary route around the second half of the song, and one that has the lyric concluding with the precarious insistence that 'you'll find out when you reach the top, you're on the bottom', before the reconciliatory last chorus comes stepping in.

Yet the potential self-pity in the lyric is abolished here. Singing the first verse, Dylan climbs step by heartfelt, fragile step to a summit of regret and all-encompassing complexity. There's a whole world cradled here within the caressive, pampiniform cage of this majestic song. When he sings like this, with this intensity of possession of a song's structure and of the timeless moment's feelings and the spaces around both, Bob Dylan is at his unique best. He opens some golden gateway and you step through, to stand there moved and enthralled. The detail of the music becomes many things at once: becomes the terrain he takes you through, the different glints of the notes catching the sun like diamonds falling past you in space; becomes the echo of the singer's heartbeat, the discourse of stirrings in the breast and the leap across the synapses, as layers of memory and loss, love and aspiration interplay. This is great art: it's as close to the evocation of human complexity and its frailty as song and performance get.

The spell is broken with 'The Times They Are A-Changin'', in which Dylan doesn't seem sure he's interested. John Jackson plays something angularly energetic here, making it sound like an old Spanish folk club favourite. Dylan does a bit of fiery staccato strumming, instead of that wandering up the pathway of the neck, poking into the bushes for agonised, uninvented chords, and then plays a properly attentive harp solo: so that in the end, though he hasn't been engaged by the words, he has been engaged by the music. Then it's into a stately 'Like A Rolling Stone', beginning with some harmonica riffs and launching into a relaxed, tender, flexible vocal that shows the song altogether better for its recent well-earned rest. The whole thing is proceeding well . . . until, unfortunately, the harmonica at the end proves utterly hopeless. ('What key, what key?', as one of the musicians shouts audibly on Little Stevie Wonder's début single, the live 'Fingertips Part 2'.[65])

---

64. 'Idiot Wind' was reintroduced in Melbourne, 2/4/92, its first performance since the *Hard Rain* TV special, Fort Collins, Colorado, 23/5/76, televised NBC-TV, New York, 14/9/76, and BBC-TV, London, 28/9/76.

65. Little Stevie Wonder: 'Fingertips, Part 2', live Chicago, 1963, Tamla Records 54080, Detroit, 1963.

The encore consists of two electric songs, 'Absolutely Sweet Marie', a great song but not, here, a great performance, followed by a pleasantly slow, low-key 'All Along The Watchtower' that has a guitar solo after the first, delicately delivered verse, a second verse vocal that finds an insistent melody and sticks to it beautifully, and another break, cut short by Dylan's coming in early with the last verse. After that he leaves the stage again – and comes back to play, fairly unusually, a second encore. This final end is an acoustic *solo* 'Blowin' In The Wind', niftily and respectfully played and with a proper harmonica sequence before and after the last verse in the original trademarked Bob Dylan way. They may not be great harp passages but they show willing, and altogether it's an effective performance, full of restraint and empty of the sorts of embellishment that so often signal that his mind has wandered.

In ending with a lovely delicacy characteristic of much of the concert, Dylan stresses on what a fine, distinctive journey tonight's performance has taken us. It has been, approximately, his eight-hundredth concert.

And if, set against such glory, Dylan as often seems wrong-headed in his performance judgement, we're usually wrong too: the concerts that go down best at the time are often one-dimensionally raucous, or have an over-declamatory quality, a forced energy that is no convincing substitute for real artistic engagement when you hear the tapes afterwards. Reviewers and critics rave about all sorts of dross and likewise pan good stuff (as in the case of the Tel Aviv and Jerusalem concerts of 1987). My own experience certainly bears this out. Birmingham 1989 was, though less wonderful than Wembley a night or two later, pretty good to be at; John Bauldie referred to it afterwards as 'this quite marvellous concert' – each tape reveals something far more mundane.[66]

Of course all this begs the question, to some degree, as to whether the evidence of an amateur tape – which flattens out the vividness of the voice, and is in this respect more likely to be gruesome than tapes of earlier concerts that survive to us from an era of warm, ambient microphones – is any more 'real' than the evidence of the concert experienced in the moment or recollected in tranquillity. On a good night, there in the hall, it is impossible not to be reminded that there is an unmeasurable, unexplainable incandescence of experience, of heightened feeling and soaring glimpses at inarticulable possibilities, that Dylan gives out, whether a tape of such a concert communicates any of that or not.

And yet . . . listen to the acoustic half of one of the 1966 British tour concerts and whether you were there or not, all that hot spirit and magnesium thrill pours right out of the tape into your soul.

And yet . . . would it, if it only came bumping indistinctly towards us through the murk of most unofficial recordings? Unfortunately Frank Zappa was not one of Dylan's big fans. If he had been, we might have had a series of dazzlingly achieved, technically perfect bootlegs of things that instead exist only on mudpool recordings by blokes with no more idea how to wield their portable tape-recorders than how to curtsey or play the synclavier. And by the inexorable Sod's Law, the times when Dylan gives his best performances, and 'outs' rare slices of repertoire, tend to be the times

---

66. Bob Dylan: Tel Aviv and Jerusalem concerts, 5 & 7/9/87; Birmingham, 7/6/89; London (Wembley), 8/6/89. I've forgotten the source of John Bauldie's quoted comment.

when the only ones recording these for posterity are drunks with bespittled lumps of Golden Virginia gumming up their second-hand dictaphones and standing, for good measure, either far too close to the speakers at the front of the hall or else in the burger-bar of the foyer.

It is from these aural war-zones, therefore, that we must glean what we can of such things as: the first (and, as it has turned out so far, penultimate) performance of Dylan's cool-dude gospel song 'Ain't No Man Righteous, No Not One' from San Francisco, November 1979; his only live performance of 'Abandoned Love', which he 'tried out' on the 60-odd punters who happened to be at a Ramblin' Jack Elliott gig at the Other End Club in Greenwich Village when he popped in one evening in July 1975; a performance of the eighteenth-century ballad 'The Golden Vanity' at a concert in Wichita, Kansas in October 1991; and the still-unreleased dream-version of 'Blind Willie McTell', recorded by someone hiding in the air-conditioner at the "Infidels" sessions in New York City in the spring of 1983.[67]

When I first drafted this chapter, the comparatively recent tapes to have emerged included one of atrocious quality from the long-gone "Pat Garrett & Billy The Kid" sessions, which, though it includes the previously unheard song 'Sweet Amarillo' and a performance of Arthur Crudup's 'Rock Me Mama', is hopelessly user-unfriendly; a 1991 concert in Vienna, Virginia taped at the wrong speed; and some "Oh Mercy" out-takes that manage to be both under-recorded *and* distorted, and which wow and flutter gruesomely.[68] Indeed, there is a familiar collector's syndrome whereby when someone asks 'How would you like a never-before-circulated tape of Dylan singing this new stuff?' you're slavering to get it . . . and then when you've heard it once you put it straight up on the shelf with absolutely no inclination ever to play it again.

The telling thing about all this is that these dire technical results are the norm: so much so, in fact, that as every collector knows, the majority of Dylan tapes they acquire cannot be played at all to people other than their compadres in Dylanology. Even for the Dylan extremist, these performance tapes soon give you too much of a bad thing. As big Dylan fan Bob Willis wrote in an unpublished 1987 article: 'I find most of that underwater bathroom-material doesn't do much for me, really. The occasional thing, a new song or a song he didn't write that he slipped into a concert, or whatever, but . . . listening to a tape of a concert [like] Osaka '86: after half an hour, you know, you really need a break.'[69]

You have to cope as best you can with all this lamentable lo-fi, by waiting till you're in the mood, playing it loud, playing it very loud in the next room, or playing it on headphones. It's not a lot of fun, and a prolonged journey into this aural twilight zone will so much attenuate your own conception of what sound really sounds like, back in the world, that to switch from hours of this murk to an officially released Van

---

67.   Bob Dylan: 'Ain't No Man Righteous, No Not One', San Francisco, 16/11/79 (this was followed by Bob Dylan & Regina Havers, 'Ain't No Man Righteous, No Not One', Hartford, Connecticut, 7/5/80); 'Abandoned Love', NYC, 3/7/75; 'The Golden Vanity', Wichita, 31/10/91 (followed by 3 further 1991 performances and 4 in 1992); unreleased studio version of 'Blind Willie McTell', NYC, April–May 1983. This last has now been bootlegged in rather better quality.

68.   Bob Dylan: 'Sweet Amarillo' and 'Rock Me Mama' (could be said to be two takes of the latter), Burbank, Feb. 1973; Vienna, Virginia, 18 or 19/7/91; "Oh Mercy" out-takes, New Orleans, 7–24/3/89.

69.   Bob Willis, unpublished article, 1987; used by permission. Bob Dylan, Osaka, 9/3/86.

Morrison or Zappa album is the aural equivalent of how it must be to live all your life in the sewers of a city and then find yourself instantaneously transported to Senegal.

Yet just occasionally, a murky audience tape captures something not apparent from more professional scrutiny. One of the murkiest audience recordings of 'Mr. Tambourine Man' from a European concert of 1966 (in Dublin) captures the way the harmonica solos echoed around the hall like a Bach organ-work played by the phantom of the opera on LSD; the professional tape captures none of it.[70] In the case of the Berkeley 1992 concert described earlier, there's no such dramatic difference in effect as between the lo-fi tape I heard first and the infinitely clearer DAT-recorded audience tape I received later – but actually the lo-fi one has the band sounding an organic whole and the vocal sounding sweeter, and is in these ways preferable to the over-separated sounds, the brutal close-up effects, achieved on the DAT machine.

It may be that DAT machines are superseding the old murk with a new pseudo-clarity: a vividness that beguiles you into forgetting that it still captures only the narrow band of information directly in its path and not by any means the full sound and atmosphere of the concert.

At any rate, it's perhaps no wonder that there is so often a disparity between the experience of a concert and the tape of it. Another such disparity that touches on matters of judgement – Dylan's and ours – lies in the odd way that there's often no correlation between the great Dylan songs and the most popular hits and favourites: there is, for instance, a whole catalogue of neglected major songs from the 1970s, songs not only that Dylan doesn't stand by, or even sing now and then, but that no one ever shouts out for in the concert hall – 'Three Angels', 'Sign On The Window', 'Never Say Goodbye', 'Black Diamond Bay', 'Abandoned Love' and 'No Time To Think'.

This has always applied. Look at Dylan's preference for the comparatively didactic dullness of 'The Times They Are A-Changin'' over the richly sustained, symbolic power of 'When The Ship Comes In', or the way he kept the unique, marvellous achievement of 'Lay Down Your Weary Tune' as hidden in the 1960s as 'Blind Willie McTell' twenty years later.

There might be other ripostes to the idea that the 1980s saw some slippage in Dylan's judgement about his songs. First, most artists are atrocious judges of their own material. In 1955, according to Memphis DJ Dewey Phillips, Elvis Presley considered himself a country singer, and didn't expect his audience to find 'Good Rockin' Tonight' more exciting than 'Old Shep'.[71] The artist's is only one reading. And while it's easy to feel that Dylan was mad to hold back 'Blind Willie McTell', he might be right to hold back material like 'You Changed My Life', the release of which on the "Bootleg Series I–III" box-set reveals it as a disturbingly AOR (Adult Oriented Rock) song. Perhaps Dylan finds in 'John Brown' something interesting enough to compensate for its clumsy obviousness and graceless, spiteful piety. Certainly for him 'Masters Of War' seems to have stood the test of time – whereas for Aidan Day, writing that everyone 'has their favourite failure amongst the youthful offerings of

---

70. 'Mr. Tambourine Man', Dublin, 5/5/66.
71. Reported in Stanley Booth's *Rythm Oil*.

Dylan's "protest" phase', it is 'the earnest self-assertion and embarrassing directness of . . . 'Masters of War'' that he cannot take, adding that these characteristics 'are not redeemed by the lyric's blurting spasms of alliteration'.[72] I've never liked the I'm-just-a-saintly-youth stance, which recurs in other early songs, but I've never minded the directness or the blurting spasms.

In any event, if in concert Dylan has in some cases signalled more of an attachment to cruder songs than to subtler, as he has too often towards over-dramatised, mannered vocal performances and the inauthentic energy of songs tackled at frenetic pace rather than giving himself the time and space to let in the more effective power of nuance and understatement, this is not to say that he has abandoned his interest in small and quiet aspects of working. There is a good piece by John Lindley which notes the way that in concert Dylan has frequently applied himself to the finding of extra internal rhymes within the lines of his songs: for instance the way he has tidied up the chorus of 'Just Like A Woman', and secured the extra rhyme of 'do-yer' with 'Mis-ter' in 'Ballad Of A Thin Man'.[73]

I think, as some of this suggests, that very often Dylan ploughs his own quiet furrow, setting himself these modest, attentive tasks unfazed by whether people notice them or not: and often we don't. This is especially true of the general audience and the general reviewer, partly because what Dylan did in the 1960s knocked us all right between the eyes – and partly because that's the only effect sought in rock.

What also hinders us at times is our own tea-leaf-reading ingratitude. Was I alone in turning my nose up at 'I Shall Be Released', 'You Aint Goin' Nowhere' and 'Down In The Flood' on the "More Greatest Hits" album, just because they weren't the Basement Tapes versions, didn't bulge with the special energy of the "Bob Dylan" LP's acoustic material, and weren't mysteriously hip like "Blonde On Blonde"? This sort of stupidity is entangled in a process which is bound to underrate the strengths of Dylan's current output, always, as surely as stadium enthusiasm for Rockin' Greatest Hits overrates mediocre renditions of 'Maggie's Farm'. It's the process whereby it is easier to be open to work that is not his latest, because then it doesn't augur something for the future.

I should know by now that it doesn't anyway, but it's a rare listener who can resist feeling it. When "Self Portrait", "Saved" or "Down In The Groove" is the current offering, it's worrying; when it's dropped back into the long, richly diverse avenue of Dylan's total output, it can far more readily be appreciated for what it is, instead of resented for what it isn't or fretted over for what it might indicate for the future. I fretted over "Shot Of Love" because when it was new, in 1981, it didn't sound very new or very 1981, so that I had to feel on the defensive about giving my attention – once again, into yet another decade – to an artist who could himself be charged with occupying a time warp, albeit this time a sort of 1940s to 1950s zone he had not really visited before. I heard those voices on my shoulder tut-tutting and deploring its lack of contemporary relevance. Now, in the long back-projection of Bob Dylan's immense range of work, the album's evocation of a 1940s–1950s musical

---

72. Aidan Day, 'Escaping on the Run', *Wanted Man Study Series*, no. 3, 1984.
73. John Lindley, 'Reels of rhyme', *Telegraph*, no. 36, Summer 1990.

aesthetic remains one of the strengths of "Shot Of Love", and the fact that it offers no essential 1981-ism is either irrelevant or a good thing.

One's own perspective shifts down the years too. I used to hate voices that wobbled on the note. It seemed a leakage of old age, like incontinence. The first time Dylan did it – on the word 'pa' in 'have a bunch of kids who call me pa', aptly enough – it leapt out of the track at me. Now he does it recurrently and I'm so old myself I don't mind any more.

There's another experience of shift that must be pertinent here. Works of art don't stay still. A friend dropped me a note a while ago to say that he'd been re-listening to "Oh Mercy", and it had seemed wise and fine, a work of depth and maturity in ways that hadn't struck him in an earlier era of hearing the same album. That's how it is with art, isn't it, whether it's Dylan or Beethoven's Ninth Symphony or Miles Davis? The Ninth might sometimes seem oppressive, pompous, heavy; other times what oppressed is moving. Of course there are set achievements generally agreed upon – "Highway 61 Revisited", "Blood On The Tracks", whatever – but 'this was a major work of the 1960s' or 'of the 1970s': this has nothing to say at all about how the piece itself makes you feel, or how it excites or moves you, reveals things to you, thrills your intellect or anything else. And *those* effects are fluid for the individual, as well as between one and another.

I also think that for an artist so generally perceived to be as stuck in the past as Dylan is, he has done creditably well in carrying forwards into the 1980s and 1990s some residual capacity for ahead-of-his-time social relevance. In 1985 *New Society* ran a typically as-if-alert editorial on the subject of how machinery for social intervention that is intended to solve problems often creates them instead. As an example, it noted: 'Set up a riot police and they will seek a riot to police.'[74] This, offered in the mid-1980s, was an obvious truth: we have been watching riot police at work, at the very least on our TV screens, ever since the foment of 1968. Dylan had made the same observation two decades before *New Society*, when it did take alertness, because he was focusing on what was a budding phenomenon: 'And the riot squad they're restless / They need somewhere to go', he sang in 'Desolation Row' back in 1965. At the end of the 1970s, it might not have been prescient but it was six years before the Live Aid effort that Dylan was warning, on 'Slow Train', of

> *People starving and thirsting, grain elevators are bursting*
> *Oh, you know it costs more to store the food than it do to give it.*

On the same album, Dylan's disparaging equation of Karl Marx and Henry Kissinger, on 'When You Gonna Wake Up?', was taken at the time as one of his most deplorable reactionary comments – the very idea of attacking Marxism!, the sacrilegious muddle-headedness of equating such a towering intellectual, someone so permanently crucial, with someone whose temporary celebrity was as the initiator of the saturation bombing of Cambodia. Yet ten years after Dylan's disparagement, the Marx-inspired regimes of the world collapsed (in spite of the riot squads) and today it is very much part of new-wave cultural studies consciousness to pull back, after decades of struggle, from trying uncomfortably to accommodate women's concerns

74. *New Society*, London, *nia*, 1985.

and black concerns within Marxism, and to begin to see Marx as having only been capable of one 'reading' – to see that for all his impact on the late nineteenth century and all of the twentieth, he was just another old white patriarch.

In the 1990s there have loomed in prospect few battles larger than that over the genetic manipulation of food: over the way that big business is suppressing the huge variety of strains of old produce, while claiming that it needs to go into genetic engineering in order to increase the number of varieties and therefore the public's 'choice'. In Britain, for instance, it is possible to order any of two thousand varieties of apple tree from the National Collection – yet as Sarah Beattie comments, 'most people accept Garden Centre reluctance to offer much more than Golden Delicious clones', unaware of this rich gene bank.[75] The same richness of traditional choice, elbowed out of reach by big business interests, applies to many other fruits and vegetables. Meanwhile bureaucracy seeks to curtail variety of size and shape, since it hates the irregular, the quirky, the different; and lack of funds allotted to the National Collections means that many are under threat, though these are the only official keepers of what used to be – offering a public record of historical truth as well as the building blocks of the future in matters crucial to the diversity of the planet. At the same time, agro-business has bought the *copyrights* to certain gene patterns and it is already illegal to buy or sell large numbers of 'unapproved' seed varieties. It was as early as 1983 that Dylan was addressing these matters, remonstrating in 'Union Sundown' that

> *I can see the day coming when even your home garden*
> *Is gonna be against the law.*

Perhaps in Dylan's work of the 1980s to 1990s there's nothing as exhilaratingly *sharp* about greed, corruption, manipulation, ugliness and threats to the social fabric as in the work that tackles these themes in *Tarantula* and in songs contemporaneous with it. Nor as mercilessly funny. How deftly the youthful Dylan draws his vivid, quick picture, for instance, of the callous sadism that pitches welfare supplicants, who inevitably look grotesque because daily life drags them through a hedge or two backwards, against the intransigent uncompassion of officialdom, in the minor, 'throwaway' couplet 'Georgia Sam he had a bloody nose / Welfare Department wouldn't give him no clothes'. Maybe the best of recent equivalents, though less sharp and funny, are, all the same, quietly acute? The same sense of the grotesque chaos and bizarreness of life is surely present as the Dylan of 1990's 'TV Talkin' Song' rolls his eyes and remains master of the italicised delivery on the dark paranoia of 'Don't let an *egg* get laid in it by something you can't see'.

Whatever the debated detail, one overall graph has been called up time and again on our collective screen. That is, all through the 1980s and 1990s Bob Dylan has essentially been perceived as being in a down-cycle, with the occasional 'up' song, or clutch of songs, peaking amid the general slide. Yet though the poor work of the last twenty years has been worse than the poor work of previous decades – more ravaged by the diseases of quotidian pop and leaning more on the Ron Woodenisms of rock

---

75. Sarah Beattie, *Neither Fish nor Fowl: Meat-free Eating for Pleasure*, 1993.

cliché – when you list the 'up' songs, the ones that clamour for, and repay, proper attention, there are a couple of dozen of them:

'Yonder Comes Sin'; 'Let's Keep It Between Us'; 'Caribbean Wind', 'Angelina', 'Need A Woman', 'Every Grain Of Sand' and 'The Groom's Still Waiting At The Altar'; 'Jokerman', 'Lord Protect My Child', 'Blind Willie McTell' and, I suppose, 'I And I'; 'New Danville Girl' / 'Brownsville Girl'; 'Ring Them Bells', 'Most Of The Time', 'What Was It You Wanted?' and 'Dignity'; 'Under The Red Sky', 'Handy Dandy', 'Cat's In The Well'; and 'Standing In The Doorway', 'Tryin' To Get To Heaven', 'Not Dark Yet' and the magnificent 'Highlands'.

Way back in 1963 Dylan said that 'There's mystery, magic, truth and the Bible in great folk music. I can't hope to touch that. But I'm goin' to try.'[76] Contrary, then, to the common assertion that folk music was just his cynically taken route to stardom, he was thoughtfully appreciative of the value and strengths of folk music and oral culture – and was toweringly ambitious to be a *songwriter* in the face of it. 'I can't hope to touch that. But I'm goin' to try.' Try he certainly did. And *some* part of what he succeeded with has come from work achieved in the 1980s and 1990s: a small proportion of his whole, without question, but a part we'd be the poorer without. I wouldn't want not to have the songs just listed. I wouldn't want not to have 'Someone's Got A Hold Of My Heart', 'Foot Of Pride', 'Love Sick' or even 'Watered-Down Love'.

Twenty-four or more great songs. This is no small number by any sane standard, let alone from someone on a down-cycle with writer's block. Stephen Scobie's book[77] argues that if we only had Dylan's output from the 1970s – if the work of the 1960s didn't exist – it would still make him the greatest songwriter of the age. I believe this would still be true if we only had the work of the 1980s and 1990s.

Some of his incandescent greatness lies here, just as some of it can still be there in his concert performances – on occasion very powerfully, such that people who aren't 'fans', people who've never seen him before, can come out of one of his concerts certain that they've been in the presence of someone unique and great: someone still touched by mystery, magic and truth.

If you look at the video footage of Dylan at Woodstock II, he looks stiff, defensive, crucially withheld, as he did singing 'Restless Farewell' for Frank Sinatra's 80th Birthday.[78] It's regrettable that seeing him no longer enhances the experience of hearing him, as it used to do, but there it is. If you attend, instead, to the audio recordings, Dylan's greatness is still present.

It comes as a delight to re-encounter 'Restless Farewell' here as a sustained, considered performance, blotched only once by that posturing gargle he gives us sometimes – that short tour of the phlegm in his throat, which never fails to coarsen things – and its twin assassin, the silly sob, on the title phrase at the end of the first verse.

76. Bob Dylan, interview by Michael Iachetta, *Daily News*, NYC, 20/10/63, quoted in Robert Shelton, *No Direction Home* (1986).

77. Stephen Scobie, *Alias Bob Dylan* (1991).

78. Bob Dylan: 'Restless Farewell', LA, 19/11/95. Edited-down version televised ABC-TV, New York, 14/12/95; complete song televised in Europe, variously, first on Swedish TV, Stockholm, 12/12/95. Audio not officially released.

Throughout the rest, he's controlled, careful, discreet, alert to what he's on about: so much so that it makes you conjecture as to how it might have seemed if it were a new song, and on "Time Out Of Mind". Many's the person who would have rushed to say what a major work it was – a major work of retrospection, looking back down the long hallways of his life. Ironic, since it was not only a work of his youth but always regarded as a very minor work. One of the penalties he pays for our over-enthusiasm and under-discrimination these days is that when we step back, in this case, we're likely to stress that it *is* a minor and youthful work, rather than that what he achieves with this revisit is a refashioning that is expressive for the middle-aged artist. One or two of the lines do betray an immaturity, but in general his 1995 performance re-occupies and renews the material. Whoever would have guessed?

As for his Woodstock II performance of 1994, it is incontestably something I wouldn't want to be without – and it has an extraordinary highlight in 'Just Like A Woman': a song I never thought I'd want to hear 'live' again. Against all expectation, we get here one of his very most engaged, inspired, gloriously unloosed yet focused vocal performances in many years. And by far his best harp solo – almost "Blonde On Blonde"ish, no less. (Indeed when, before this, did Dylan last play three harmonica solos running, as here on 'Just Like A Woman', 'It Takes A Lot To Laugh, It Takes A Train To Cry' and 'Don't Think Twice, It's All Right'?)

The whole performance, with the sound so well-mixed and the band so good that night, argues that the mid-1990s Bob Dylan can stand in the same room with the Dylans of the past. He is alive, alert, fully into his jazz-improvisational vocals and making some wonderful noises: and not imitating himself but singing – phrasing – afresh. Woodstock II is a *real* performance.

The punkish, grungy music is good, complex, Tom Verlaineish, real: not remotely MTVAOR, and surprisingly resourceful. How interesting the rendition of 'Masters Of War' is – so very different from the brave, scrupulous version at Hiroshima earlier the same year, yet so fine, with the double-bass ominous but not overplayed. There's also the splendid bluegrass–folk of 'Don't Think Twice'; and, in yielding so fresh a milieu for 'It's All Over Now, Baby Blue', Dylan rises fully to the occasion, creating a whole that is concentrated and time-stopping – this last for the first time since live 1966 – and even, to hone in on a specific detail, devising something special for the repeated sound of the word 'home' in the 'seasick sailors' verse, just as he did so unerringly in 1966. Here is an example of Dylan in the mid-1990s offering brave singing, braver harp-playing and love.[79]

If I spend too much time seeking out these performances while not listening much to the live 1966 concert sound, if I'm more interested to hear a current, inevitably inferior Bob Dylan treatment of 'Like A Rolling Stone', that is not least because the 1966 Bob Dylan is intimately, deeply in my heart. I almost don't need to hear it, because internally I hear it all the time, as you could say one does with all the great formative voices of one's lifetime, be they George Eliot, Elvis, Jesus, Wagner, whoever. It's because Bob Dylan 1966 is in there that I'm compelled to go to the current Bob Dylan and to see how it is. And sometimes it's still transcendent. The Woodstock II 'Just Like A Woman', Besançon's 'Tears Of Rage': you can't match his warm reverie,

---

79. Woodstock II, Saugerties, NY, 14/8/94.

his grungy, authentic band, his attentiveness, his unpredictability, his obduracy, his perseverance, his grace, his creativity.

It's possible too to see Dylan's deteriorated voice sympathetically, as for instance in this lovely description by the blues critic Tom Freeland, written the day after seeing the Jackson, Mississippi, concert of October 1997: 'His voice is entirely shot, but he works around that pretty well, like an old dancer who uses gesture to substitute for things he's too old to do any more.'[80]

I'm charmed by that way of putting it, but not entirely persuaded that Dylan's age is so great that he cannot be expected to have a voice anymore – he was 56 years old at the time of that concert. And he used to give out more, which is not in any case a matter of the technical robustness of the voice: it is a matter of effort. Even at the tiniest level: the way he makes 'Judas Escariot' sound on 'With God On Our Side' is more vivid, full-blooded and outward-facing, galvanising greater energy and concentration, than, say, the way he makes 'New South Wales' sound on 'Jim Jones'. Lovely though that is, he's just that bit meaner about it. About projecting it, and about doing it best. In live performance, his focused determination to communicate is a lot less alive than it was in the 1960s and was again in the period 1978–1980. Not always (listen to 'Woodstock') but usually (listen to 'Unplugged').

My fervent hope is that, as he moves into the future, he refuses to settle for this comfortable descent, in an apparently inevitable smooth arc, into being a performer and writer of less and less artistic power. I look to his moving forwards in old age, as so many great artists have done – the Beethoven of the Last Quartets, the Monet of Giverny (or even the Matisse of the cut-outs), the 'rediscovered' Skip James – into a long period in which he gives out fully and is inspiredly alert.

The bottom line is: why hold back when time is running out? The artist who created brilliant songs about the concerns of youth and beyond it: about the city, the romance of the druggy visionary life, early love, the pull of the countryside, thirty-something love, the seductiveness of foreign places, estrangement, Christ – he must have new concerns crowding in now, as time presses. Impending old age is itself good raw material. Instead of clinging to his back catalogue, he could voice his real concerns, as once he did, and be glad to have an audience: 1997's "Time Out Of Mind" is a faltering step along this path.

I hope this is his destiny: that having given so wholeheartedly in his youth he will not duck from, but rise to, doing so again. Instead of resting on his incomparable laurels, may we find that he calls a halt to his reluctance, to his holding back . . . and then we shall gain, in the wintertime of Bob Dylan's work, extraordinary new songs that really speak to any audience, performed with grace and wit and ardour.

---

80. Tom Freeland, e-mail 26/10/97, re Bob Dylan concert Jackson, Mississippi, 25/10/97; used by permission.

Bibliography

Articles, essays and album notes are detailed in the text; books are detailed here. These are not always first, or best, editions/printings: they are those that were available to me. *Asterisked entries* are those that have been cited in my text (in some cases they are classic works on their subject) but that I have not used at first hand. Items of information that could not be located at the time of going to press are identified by *nia* (no information available).

Achebe, Chinua, *Things Fall Apart*, Oxford: Heinemann African Writers Series (paperbacks), 1986 [3rd UK edn]

Ackroyd, Peter, *Blake*, London: Quality Paperbacks Direct, 1995

Albery, N., Elliot, G. and Elliot, J. (eds), *The New Natural Death Handbook*, London: Rider Books, 1997

American Folklore Bibliography, nia, 1939

Angelou, Maya, *I Know Why the Caged Bird Sings*, New York: Random House, 1969

*Arnold, Byron, *Folksongs of Alabama*, Birmingham: University of Alabama Press, 1950

Arnold, Matthew, *Culture and Anarchy*, London: Cambridge University Press, 1966 [1st edn 1867]

Aubrey, John, *Brief Lives* [17th-century mss; ed. Oliver Lawson Dick, 1949], Harmondsworth: Penguin, 1976 [reprint]

Auster, Paul, *City of Glass*, Los Angeles: Sun and Moon Press, 1985 [reissued in *The New York Trilogy*, London: Faber & Faber, 1987]

Bane, Michael, *White Boy Singin' the Blues*, London: Penguin, 1982

*Barthes, Roland, *S/Z*, trans. Richard Miller, London: Cape, 1975

Barthes, Roland, *Image, Music, Text*, London: Fontana, 1977

Bastin, Bruce, *Crying for the Carolines*, London: Studio Vista, 1971

*Bateson, F. W., *English Poetry: A Critical Introduction*, nia, 1950

*Baudelaire, Charles, *La Fanfarlo*, 1847

*Baudelaire, Charles, *Les Fleurs du mal*, Paris: nia, 1857

*Baudelaire, Charles, *Les Paradis artificiels*, 1860

Bauldie, John, *The Ghost of Electricity*, Romford, Essex: self-published, 1989

*Bauldie, John, *Wanted Man: In Search of Bob Dylan*, London: Black Spring, 1990 [rev. paperback, Penguin, 1992]

Baxter, Doreen (ill.), *A Treasury of Grimm and Andersen*, London: Collins, 1959

Beattie, Sarah, *Neither Fish nor Fowl: Meat-free Eating for Pleasure*, London: Optima Books, 1993

Belsey, Catherine, *Critical Practice*, London: Routledge, 1991

Bennett, Alan, *Writing Home*, London: Faber & Faber, 1994

*Benson, Carl, *The Bob Dylan Companion: Four Decades of Commentary*, USA: Schirmer Books, 1998

Berendt, John, *Midnight in the Garden of Good and Evil*, London: Chatto & Windus, 1994

Berne, Eric, *What Do You Say after You Say Hello? The Psychology of Human Destiny*, New York: Grove Press, c. 1972

*Berne, Eric, *Games People Play: The Psychology of Human Relationships*, New York: Grove Press, 1977 [1964]

Bettelheim, Bruno, *The Uses of Enchantment*, London: Thames & Hudson, 1976

Bible, *King James Version*, London: Collins, *nia*

Bible, *New Testament, Revised Standard Version*, New York: American Bible Society, 1963

Bible, *Good News Bible: Today's English Version*, London: Bible Societies/Collins/Fontana, 1976

Blake, William, *Blake: Complete Writings*, ed. Geoffrey Keynes, London: Oxford University Press, 1969

Blake, William, *Songs of Innocence and Songs of Experience: Shewing the Two Contrary States of the Human Soul* [republication of 1794 edition], New York: Dover Thrift Editions, 1992

Bloomfield, Mike, with Summerville, S., *Me and Big Joe*, San Francisco: Re/Search Productions, 1980

Bloomsbury Book of Quotations, London: Bloomsbury, 1994

*Blumenstein, Gottfried, *Mr. Tambourine Man: Leben und Musik von Bob Dylan*, Berlin: Henschel Verlag, 1991 [1995]

Boardman, J., Griffin, J. and Murray, O. (eds), *The Oxford History of the Classical World*, Oxford: Oxford University Press, 1986

Booth, Stanley, *Rythm Oil*, London: Cape, 1991

Boswell, H., *Jingle Time*, London & Glasgow: Collins, 1960

Botkin, B. A., *A Treasury of American Folklore*, New York: Crown Publishers, 1994

Bowden, Betsy, *Performed Literature: Words and Music by Bob Dylan*, Bloomington: Indiana University Press, 1982

*Bowman, David, *Modern Bunny*, New York: Little, Brown & Co., 1998

Breese, Martin, *Breese's Guide to Modern 1st Editions*, London: Breese Books, 1993

*Bremser, Bonnie, *Troia: Mexican Memoirs*, New York: Croton, 1969

*Bremser, Ray, *Poems of Madness*, New York: Paperbook Gallery, 1965

*Bremser, Ray, *Angel*, New York: Tomkins Square Press, 1967

*Bremser, Ray, *Drive Suite*, San Francisco: Nova Broadcast Press, 1968

Brewer's Dictionary of Phrase and Fable, London: Cassell, 8th [rev.] edn, 1968

*Briggs, Raymond (ed.), *The Mother Goose Golden Treasury*, London: Hamish Hamilton, 1966

*Briggs, Katherine M., *A Dictionary of British Folk Tales* [4 vols], Bloomington: Indiana University Press, 1970

Bronson, Bertrand Harris, *The Traditional Tunes of the Child Ballads, Vol. 2*, Princeton: Princeton University Press, 1962

*Broonzy, Big Bill (as told to Yannick Bruynoghe), *Big Bill Blues*, London: Cassell, 1955

Broughton, Viv, *Black Gospel: An Illustrated History of the Gospel Sound*, London: Blandford Press, 1985

Browning, D. C., *Everyman's Dictionary of Literary Biography*, London: J. M. Dent & Co., rev. edn, 1969

Browning, Robert, *Poetical Works 1833–1864*, ed. Ian Jack, London: Oxford Standard Authors, 1970

Bryson, Bill, *The Lost Continent: Travels in Small Town America*, London: Abacus Books, 1990

Bryson, Bill, *Made in America*, London: Secker & Warburg, 1994

Bunyan, John, *The Pilgrim's Progress: From This World to That Which Is to Come*, London: Partridge, *nia* [Part 1 first published 1678, Part 2 1684]

*Bunyan, John, *The Life and Death of Mr. Badman* [1680]

Burroughs, William, *Nova Express*, New York: Grove Press, 1964

Cable, Paul, *Bob Dylan: His Unreleased Recordings*, London: Scorpion/Dark Star, 1978

Calasso, Roberto, *The Marriage of Cadmus and Harmony*, London: Vintage, 1994

Cantor, Louis, *Wheelin' on Beale*, New York: Pharos Books, 1992

Cantwell, Robert, *When We Were Good: The Folk Revival*, Cambridge, MA: Harvard University Press, 1996

Carey, John, *The Violent Effigy: A Study of Dickens' Imagination*, London: Faber & Faber, 1979

Carroll, Lewis, *Alice in Wonderland* and *Through the Looking-Glass*, Harmondsworth: Puffin Books, 1962, reprinted 1963

Carter, Angela (ed.), *The Virago Book of Fairy Tales*, London: Virago, 1990

*Carter, Rubin, *The Sixteenth Round: From Number 1 Contender to #45472*, New York: Viking Press, 1974

*Chaiton, Sam and Swinton, Terry, *Lazarus and the Hurricane*, London: Penguin, 1991

Chambers, Aidan, *The Reluctant Reader*, Oxford: Pergamon Press, 1969

Chambers, H. A. (ed.), *The Treasury of Negro Spirituals*, London: Blandford Press, 1964

Chandler, Raymond, *The Big Sleep*, Harmondsworth: Penguin, c. 1963 [1939]

*Charters, Samuel B., *The Country Blues*, New York: Reinhart, 1959 [Da Capo Press, rev. edn, 1975]

*Charters, Samuel B., *The Poetry of the Blues*, New York: Oak Publications, 1963

*Chesterton, G. K., *Robert Browning*, London: Macmillan, 1903

*Child, F. J., *The English and Scottish Popular Ballads, 1882–98*, 3 vols, New York: Cooper Square Publishing, 1965; or 5 vols, New York: Dover, 1965

Clarke, Adam, *Commentary on the Bible*, 7 vols, London: Thomas Tegg, 1844 [not the first edition]

Coffin, Tristram P., *The British Traditional Ballad in North America*, Austin: University of Texas Press, 1977 [1950]

Cohn, Lawrence (ed.), *Nothing But the Blues: The Music and the Musicians*, New York: Abbeville Press Publishers, 1993

Cohn, Nik, *Awopbopaloobopalopbamboom: Pop from the Beginning*, London: Weidenfeld & Nicholson, 1969 [Paladin, 1970]

Coleridge, S. T., *Complete Poems: Coleridge*, ed. William Keach, London: Penguin, 1993

Collins English Dictionary, Glasgow: HarperCollins, updated 3rd edn, 1994

Contemporary Authors, vols 17–18, Detroit: Gale Research, 1975

Cooke, Deryck, *Vindications*, London: Faber, 1982

Cooper, J. C., *Fairy Tales: Allegories of the Inner Life*, Wellingborough: Aquarian Press, 1983

Corrin, S. and S., *The Faber Book of Favourite Fairy Tales*, London: Faber, 1988

*Corso, Gregory, *Gasoline*, New York: New Directions, 1958

*Corso, Gregory, *The Happy Birthday of Death*, New York: New Directions, 1960

Cott, Jonathon, *Dylan*, New York: Dolphin/Doubleday, 1985

Cotten, Lee, *All Shook Up: Elvis Day-By-Day, 1954–1977*, Ann Arbor: Popular Culture Ink, 1993

Crane, Stephen, *The Red Badge of Courage*, Ware, Hertfordshire: Wordsworth, 1994 [first published 1895]

Cruden, Alexander, *Cruden's Complete Concordance to the Old and New Testaments*, London: Lutterworth, 1964

*cummings, e. e., *Complete Poems, 1913–1962*, New York: Harcourt, Brace, Jovanovich, 1973

Dahl, Linda, *Stormy Weather: The Music and Lives of a Century of Jazz Women*, New York: Pantheon Books, 1984

*Dante [Alighieri], *The Divine Comedy*, Italy: 14th century [written 1307–1321]

Darling, Charles W. (ed.), *The New American Songster: Traditional Ballads and Songs of North America*, Lanham, MD: University Press of America, 1992 [1st edn, 1983]

Davie, Michael, *The Titanic: The Full Story of a Tragedy*, London: Bodley Head, 1986

Dawson, Jim and Propes, Steve, *What Was the First Rock'N'Roll Record?*, Winchester, MD: Faber & Faber, 1992

Day, Aidan, *Jokerman: Reading the Lyrics of Bob Dylan*, Oxford: Blackwell, 1989

*de la Mare, Walter (ed.), *Come Hither*, London: Constable, 1923

de Silva, Anil and von Simson, Otto (eds), *Man through His Art: Vol. 1: The Human Face*, East Ardsley, Yorkshire: Educational Productions, 1963

Dean's New Gift Book of Nursery Rhymes, London: Dean & Son, 1971

Defries, Amelia, *In a Forgotten Colony*, London: Cecil Palmer, 1929

Dixon, Robert M. W. and Godrich, John, *Blues and Gospel Records 1902–1943*, Chigwell, Essex: Storyville, 3rd edn, 1982

Dixon, Robert M. W., Godrich, John and Rye, Howard W., *Blues and Gospel Records 1890–1943*, Oxford: Clarendon Press, 1997

Dixon, Willie, with Snowden, Don, *I Am the Blues: The Willie Dixon Story*, London & New York: Quartet Books, 1989

Donne, John, *A Selection of John Donne's Poetry*, ed. John Hayward, Harmondsworth: Penguin, 1950

Donne, John, *No Man Is an Island: A Selection from the Prose of John Donne*, ed. Rivers Scott, London: Folio Society, 1997

Drabble, Margaret (ed.), *The Oxford Companion to English Literature*, Oxford: Oxford University Press, 1985 [5th edn]

*Dunbar, Paul Laurence, *Lyrics of a Lowly Life* [comprising *Oak and Ivy* and *Majors and Minors*], New York: Dodd, Mead, 1896 [London: Chapman & Hall, 1897]

Dundas, Glen, *Tangled up in Tapes Revisited*, Thunder Bay, ON: SMA Services, 1990 [2nd edn of *Tangled up in Tapes*]

Dundas, Glen, *Tangled up in Tapes*, Thunder Bay, ON: SMA Services, 1994 [3rd edn]

Dundas, Glen, *Tangled up in Tapes*, Thunder Bay, ON: SMA Services, 1999 [4th edn]

Dylan, Bob, *Tarantula*, London: MacGibbon & Kee, 1971

Dylan, Bob, *Writings and Drawings*, London: Cape, 1972

Dylan, Bob, *The Songs of Bob Dylan from 1966 through 1975*, New York: Knopf, 1976

Dylan, Bob, *Lyrics 1962–1985*, London: Cape, 1987

Dylan, Bob, *Drawn Blank*, New York: Random House, 1994

*Edelman, Gerald, M., *The Remembered Present: A Biological Theory of Consciousness*, New York: Basic Books, 1989

*Edelman, Gerald, M., *Bright Air, Brilliant Fire: On the Matter of the Mind*, New York: Basic Books, 1992

Eliot, George, *Middlemarch*, Harmondsworth: Penguin, 1965 [first published in parts, 1871–72]

*Eliot, T. S., *Collected Poems 1909–35*, London: Faber & Faber, 1936

Eliot, T. S., *Selected Essays: 1917–1932*, London: Faber & Faber, 1932

Eliot, T. S., *Collected Poems 1909–62*, London: Faber & Faber, 1963

*Ellington, Duke, *Music Is My Mistress*, New York: Doubleday, 1973

*Ellis, E. J., *The Real Blake*, London: Chatto & Windus, 1907

Engel, Dave, *Dylan in Minnesota: Just Like Bob Zimmerman's Blues*, Rudolph, WI: self-published, 1997

Escott, Colin and Hawkins, Martin, *Sun Records: The Discography*, Vollersode, Germany: Bear Family Books, 1987

Escott, Colin and Hawkins, Martin, *Good Rockin' Tonight: Sun Records and the Birth of Rock'n'Roll*, New York: St Martin's Press, 1991

Evans, David, *Tommy Johnson*, London: Studio Vista, 1971

Farmer, David Hugh, *The Oxford Dictionary of Saints*, Oxford: Oxford University Press, 2nd edn, 1987

Fenton, David (ed.), *Shots: Photographs from the Underground Press*, London: Academy Editions, 1972 [New York: Douglas Book Corp., 1971]

*Ferlinghetti, Lawrence, *Pictures from the Gone World*, San Francisco: City Lights, 1955

Ferlinghetti, Lawrence, *A Coney Island of the Mind*, London: Hutchinson, 1958 [this incorporates *Pictures from the Gone World*]

Fitzgerald, F. Scott, *The Great Gatsby*, Harmondsworth: Penguin, c. 1964 [1925]

Fitzgerald, F. Scott, *The Beautiful and Damned*, Harmondsworth: Penguin, 1966 [1922]

Fitzgerald, F. Scott, *The Pat Hobby Stories*, Harmondsworth: Penguin, 1967

Fitzgerald, F. Scott, *The Letters of F. Scott Fitzgerald*, ed. Andrew Turnbull, Harmondsworth: Penguin, 1968

Flanagan, Bill, *Written in My Soul*, Chicago: Contemporary Books, 1986

Fleet, Thomas, *The New-England Primer*, Boston: Thomas Fleet, 1737

*Flores, Angel (ed.), *An Anthology of French Poetry from Nerval to Valéry*, New York: Anchor Books, 1958

Fong-Torres, Ben (ed.), *The Rolling Stone Rock'n'Roll Reader*, New York: Bantam, 1974

Foss, Michael, *Traditional Nursery Rhymes and Children's Verse*, London: Book Club Associates, 1976 [reprinted 1981 and 1983]

Fountain, Nigel, *Underground: The London Alternative Press 1966–1974*, London: Routledge, 1988

Fowler, H. W., *A Dictionary of Modern English Usage*, 2nd edn, revised by Sir Ernest Gowers, Oxford: Oxford University Press, 1965

Frater, Alexander, *Chasing the Monsoon*, London: Penguin, 1991

Freud, Sigmund, *The Interpretation of Dreams*, trans., ed. James Strachey, London: Allen & Unwin, 1961 [1900]

Friedman, Albert B. (ed.), *The Viking Book of Folk Ballads of the English-Speaking World*, New York: Viking, 1956

*Friedman, Manis, *Doesn't Anyone Blush Any More? Reclaiming Intimacy, Modesty and Sexuality in a Permissive Age*, nia, 1991

Gammond, Peter, *Scott Joplin and the Ragtime Era*, London: Abacus, 1975

*Gardner, Helen, *The Composition of 'Four Quartets'*, London: Faber, 1978

Gardner, Helen (ed.), *The Metaphysical Poets*, Harmondsworth: Penguin, 1963

Gardner, Helen (ed.), *New Oxford Book of English Verse*, Oxford: Clarendon Press, 1972

Garon, Paul and Beth, *Woman with Guitar: Memphis Minnie's Blues*, New York: Da Capo Press, 1992

*Genet, Jean, *The Balcony*, trans. Bernard Frechtman, New York: Grove Press, 1960

Genet, Jean, *Our Lady of the Flowers*, trans. Bernard Frechtman, New York: Grove Press, 1963 [Paris: 1944]

*Geronimo, *Geronimo's Story of His Life*, nia, 1906

Gerould, Gordon H., *The Ballad of Tradition*, New York: Oxford University Press, 1932

* *Gesta Romanorum*, England: late 13th century

*Gill, Andy, *Classic Bob Dylan 1962–69: My Back Pages, the Stories Behind Every Song*, London: Carlton, 1998

Gillett, Charlie, *The Sound of the City*, London: Sphere Books, 1971

Gilroy, Paul, *There Ain't No Black in the Union Jack*, London: Hutchinson, 1987

*Gilroy, Paul, *The Black Atlantic: Modernity and Double Consciousness*, London: Verso, 1993

Ginsberg, Allen, *Howl and Other Poems*, San Francisco: City Lights Pocket Poets Series, 1955

Ginsberg, Allen, *First Blues: Rags, Ballads & Harmonium Songs 1971–1974*, New York: Full Court Press, 1975

Ginsberg, Allen, *Collected Poems 1947–1980*, London: Viking, 1985

Glissant, Edouard, *Caribbean Discourse: Selected Essays* (trans. J. Michael Dash), Charlottesville: University Press of Virginia; London: Free Association Books, 1999

Goldman, Albert, *Elvis*, New York: McGraw-Hill, 1981

Goldrosen, John, *Buddy Holly: His Life and Music*, London: Charisma Books, 1975 [updated as *Remembering Buddy: The Definitive Biography* by John Goldrosen and John Beecher, New York: Da Capo Press, 1996]

*Goldstein, Kenneth S., *A Guide for Fieldworkers in Folklore*, Hatboro, PA: Folklore Associates, 1965

*Gomme, Alice B., *The Traditional Games of England, Scotland and Ireland* [2 vols], London: D. Nutt, 1894–98

Gordon, Robert, *It Came from Memphis*, Winchester, MA: Faber, 1995

Graves, Robert, *The White Goddess: A Historical Grammar of Poetic Myth*, London: Faber, 1952 [3rd edn]

*Graves, Robert, *The Greek Myths* [2 vols], Harmondsworth: Penguin, 1960

Gray, Michael, *Mother! The Frank Zappa Story*, London: Plexus, 2nd rev. edn, 1994

Gray, Michael and Bauldie, John (eds), *All Across the Telegraph: A Bob Dylan Handbook*, London: Sidgwick & Jackson, 1987

Gray, Michael and Osborne, Roger, *The Elvis Atlas: A Journey Through Elvis Presley's America*, New York: Henry Holt, 1996

*Grendysa, Peter A., *Atlantic Master Book #1*, Milwaukee: self-published, 1975

Greene, Graham, *Stamboul Train*, Harmondsworth: Penguin, 1963 [1st edn, London: Heinemann, 1932]

Greene, Graham, *Journey Without Maps*, Harmondsworth: Penguin, 1976 [1936]

Greenleaf, Elisabeth Bristol and Mansfield, Grace Yarrow (eds), *Ballads and Sea Songs of Newfoundland*, Hatboro, PA: Folklore Associates, 1968 [1933]

*Grossman, Stefan, *Country Blues Guitar* [foreword by Stephen Calt], New York: Oak Press, c. 1968

*Grover, Carrie B., *A Heritage of Songs*, Norwood, PA: Norwood Editions, 1973

Guralnick, Peter, *Feel Like Going Home*, New York: Outerbridge & Dienstfrey, 1971 [reissued in paperback, London: Penguin, 1992]

Guralnick, Peter, *Last Train to Memphis: The Rise of Elvis Presley*, London: Little, Brown, 1994

Guterson, David, *Snow Falling on Cedars*, London: Bloomsbury, 1995

*Guthrie, Woody, *American Folksong*, New York: Oak Publications, 1947

Guthrie, Woody, *Bound for Glory*, Garden City, NY: Dolphin, 1949

Guthrie, Woody, *Born to Win*, ed. Robert Shelton, New York: Macmillan, 1965

Haag, Michael, *Egypt*, London: Cadogan Books, 1993

Hacking, Ian, *Mad Travellers: Reflections on the Reality of Transient Mental Illnesses*, Charlottesville: University Press of Virginia, 1999

*Halliwell-Phillips, James O., *The Nursery Rhymes of England*, London: Percy Society, 1842 [rev. and enl. edns 1843, 1844, 1846, 1853 and c. 1860]

*Halliwell-Phillips, James O., *Popular Rhymes and Nursery Tales*, London: John Russell Smith, 1849

Hammett, Dashiell, *The Maltese Falcon*, Harmondsworth: Penguin, 1963 [1930]

Hardy, Phil and Laing, Dave (eds), *The Encyclopaedia of Rock, Vol. 1: The Age of Rock'n'Roll*, London: Panther Books, 1976

*Harris, Michael W., *Thomas A. Dorsey and the Rise of the Gospel Blues*, Oxford: Oxford University Press, 1992

Harris, Sheldon (ed.), *Blues Who's Who*, New Rochelle, NY: Arlington House, 1979 [New York: Da Capo Press, rev. edn, 1991]

Harrowven, Jean, *Origins of Rhymes, Songs and Sayings*, London: Kaye & Ward, 1977

Hatch, D. and Millward, S., *From Blues to Rock: An Analytical History of Pop Music*, Manchester: Manchester University Press, 1987

Haunton, Hugh (ed.), *The Chatto Book of Nonsense Poetry*, London: Chatto & Windus, 1988

Hayes, Cedric J. and Laughton, Robert, *Gospel Records 1943–1969: A Black Music Discography*, 2 vols (A–K, L–Z), London: Record Information Services, 1992

Hayter, Alethea, *Opium and the Romantic Imagination*, London: Faber & Faber, 1968

Haywood, Ernest (ed.), *The Song Satchel*, London: New World Publishers, 1944

Heller, Joseph, *Catch-22*, London: Corgi Books, 1965 [1961]

Heller, Joseph, *God Knows*, New York: Simon & Schuster, 1984

Herdman, John, *Voice Without Restraint: Bob Dylan's Lyrics and Their Background*, Edinburgh: Paul Harris Publishing, 1982 [USA: Delilah Books, 1982]

Herzberg, M. J. (ed.), *Reader's Encyclopedia of American Literature*, New York: Crowell, 1962

*Heylin, Clinton, *Bob Dylan: Stolen Moments*, Romford, Essex: Wanted Man, 1988

*Heylin, Clinton, *Bob Dylan Behind the Shades: A Biography*, London: Viking, 1991

*Heylin, Clinton, *Bob Dylan, the Complete Recording Sessions: 1960–1994*, New York: St Martin's Press, 1995

*Heylin, Clinton, *A Life in Stolen Moments: Bob Dylan Day by Day 1941–95*, New York: Schirmer Books, 1996

Hogan, Homer (ed.), *Poetry of Relevance 1*, Toronto: Methuen, 1970

Hoggard, Stuart and Shields, Jim, *Bob Dylan: An Illustrated Discography*, UK: Transmedia Express, 1977

Hollo, Anselm (ed.), *Negro Verse*, London: Vista Books, 1964

Honderich, Ted (ed.), *The Oxford Companion to Philosophy*, Oxford: Oxford University Press, 1995

Horowitz, David, *From Yalta to Vietnam*, Harmondsworth: Penguin, 1967

Houghton, Walter E., *The Victorian Frame of Mind*, New Haven: Yale University Press, 1964

*Hughes, Langston, *Tambourines to Glory*, New York: Hill and Wang, 1958

*Hughes, Robert, *The Art of Australia*, Sydney: Penguin, 1966

*Humphries, Patrick and Bauldie, John, *Oh No! Not Another Bob Dylan Book*, Brentwood: Square One Books, 1991 [*Absolutely Dylan: An Illustrated Biography*, New York: Viking Studio Books, 1991]

*Hurston, Zora Neale, *Mules and Men*, New York: HarperCollins, 1990 [1935]

*Huson, Paul, *The Devil's Picturebook: The Compleat Guide to Tarot Cards, their Origins and their Usage*, London: Abacus, 1972

Hutchings, David F., *RMS Titanic: 75 Years of Legend*, Southampton: Kingfisher Railway Productions, 1987

Huxley, Aldous, *The Doors of Perception*, New York: Harper, 1954

Hyde, H. Montgomery, *Oscar Wilde*, London: Eyre Methuen, 1976 [Mandarin paperback, 1990]

Hymns Ancient and Modern Revised, London: William Clowes, 1972 [1861]

Idle, Christopher (ed.), *The Lion Book of Favourite Hymns*, Tring: Lion Publishing, 1980

Jackson, Blair, *Goin' Down the Road: A Grateful Dead Traveling Companion*, New York: Harmony Books (paperback), 1992

Jackson, George, *Blood in My Eye*, Harmondsworth: Penguin, 1975

Jackson, George, *Soledad Brother: The Prison Letters of George Jackson*, London: Jonathan Cape, 1970 [Harmondsworth: Penguin, 1971]

Jackson, G. P. (ed.), *Spiritual Folk Songs of Early America*, New York: nia, 1953

Jacobs, Joseph, *English Fairy Tales*, London: Bodley Head, republished 1968

*Johnson, Captain Charles, *A General History of the Pyrates*, London: 1720s

Jong, Erica, *Any Woman's Blues: A Novel of Obsession*, New York: Harper & Row, 1990

Jung, Carl (ed.), *Man and His Symbols*, London: Picador, 1978

Keats, John, *The Complete Poems*, ed. John Barnard, London: Penguin, 1991

Kerouac, Jack, *On the Road*, London: Pan Books, 1963 [1957]

*Kerouac, Jack, *Mexico City Blues*, New York: Grove Press, 1959

*Kerouac, Jack, *The Subterraneans*, New York: Grove Press, 1958

*Kerouac, Jack, *Visions of Gerard*, New York: Farrar, Straus, 1963

Kerridge, Roy, *In the Deep South*, London: Michael Joseph, 1989

*Kidson, Frank and Ethel, *English Peasant Songs*, London: Ascherberg, Hopwood & Crew, 1929

King, Roma A., *The Bow and the Lyre: The Art of Robert Browning*, Ann Arbor: University of Michigan Press, 1957

Kingsley, Charles, *The Water Babies: A Fairy Tale for a Land Baby*, London: Dent, 1957 [1st edn in volume form, 1863]

Kirkpatrick, *Ballad Book*, nia, 1824

Kowl, Andrew (ed.), *High Times Encyclopedia of Recreational Drugs*, New York: Stonehill Publishing Co., 1978

Kramer, Daniel, *Bob Dylan*, New York: Citadel Press, 1991 [large format reissue of 1967 original]

Krivine, J., *Juke Box Saturday Night*, London: New English Library, 1977

Krogsgaard, Michael, *Twenty Years of Recording: The Bob Dylan Reference Book*, Copenhagen: Scandinavian Institute for Rock Research, 1981

*Krogsgaard, Michael, *Positively Bob Dylan*, Ann Arbor: Popular Culture Ink, 1991

Kureishi, Hanif, *The Black Album*, London: Faber & Faber, 1996 [2nd edn paperback]

Kurtz, Irma, *The Great American Bus Ride*, New York: Simon & Schuster, 1993; London: Fourth Estate, 1994

Laing, Dave, *One Chord Wonders*, Milton Keynes: Open University Press, 1985

Laing, D., Dallas, K., Denselow, R., and Shelton, R., *The Electric Muse: The Story of Folk into Rock*, London: Methuen, 1975

Langbaum, Robert, *The Poetry of Experience: The Dramatic Monologue in Modern Literary Tradition*, London: Chatto & Windus, 1957

Langland, William, *Piers the Ploughman*, trans. J. F. Goodridge, London: Penguin, 1990

Larkin, Colin (ed.), *The Guinness Encyclopedia of Popular Music* [4 vols], Enfield: Guinness Publishing, 1992

*Larkin, Philip, *All What Jazz? A Record Diary 1961–1971*, London: Faber, 1985

Lawless, Ray M., *Folksingers and Folksong in America*, New York: Duell Sloan Pearce, 1960

Lawrence, D. H., *Studies in Classic American Literature*, Harmondsworth: Penguin, 1971 [1923]

Lawrence, D. H., *The Complete Poems*, London: Heinemann, 1957 [3 vols]

Lawrence, D. H., *Sons and Lovers*, Harmondsworth: Penguin, c. 1963

Laws, G. Malcolm, Jr, *American Balladry from British Broadsides*, Philadelphia: American Folklore Society, 1957

Laws, G. Malcolm, Jr, *Native American Balladry*, Philadelphia: American Folklore Society, rev. edn, 1964

Leadbitter, Mike and Slaven, Neil, *Blues Records 1943–1970, Vol. 1: A–K*, London: Record Information Services, 1987

Leadbitter, M., Fancourt, L. and Pelletier, P., *Blues Records 1943–1970: The Bible of the Blues, Vol. 2, L–Z*, London: Record Information Services, 1994

Least Heat-Moon, William, *Blue Highways: A Journey into America*, London: Picador, 1984 [USA: 1983]

Leavis, F. R., *Revaluation: Tradition and Development in English Poetry*, Harmondsworth: Peregrine, 1964 [1936]

Leavis, F. R., *New Bearings in English Poetry*, Harmondsworth: Peregrine, 1963 [1932]

Leavis, F. R., *The Common Pursuit*, Harmondsworth: Peregrine, 1963 [1952]

Leavis, F. R., *The Great Tradition*, Harmondsworth: Peregrine, 1966 [1948]

Leavis, F. R., *D. H. Lawrence: Novelist*, Harmondsworth: Peregrine, 1964 [1955]

Leavis, F. R. (ed.), *A Selection from Scrutiny, Volume I* and *Volume II*, Cambridge: Cambridge University Press, 1968

Lee, C. P., *Like the Night – Bob Dylan and the Road to Manchester Free Trade Hall*, London: Helter Skelter, 1998

Leigh, Spencer and Firminger, John, *Halfway to Paradise: Britpop, 1955–1962*, Folkestone: Finbarr International, 1996

Lewis, Roger, *Outlaws of America*, Harmondsworth: Pelican, 1972

Lightfoot, Gordon, *I Wish You Good Spaces*, Boulder, CO: Blue Mountain Arts, 1977

Lipscomb, Mance, *I Say Me for a Parable: The Oral Autobiography of Mance Lipscomb as Told to Glen Alyn*, New York: Norton, 1993

Lloyd, A. L., *Folk Song in England*, London: Lawrence & Wishart, 1957

Lloyd, A. L. (ed.), *Folk Songs of the Americas*, London: Novello, 1965

Lomax, Alan, *The Folk Songs of North America*, Garden City, NY: Doubleday, 1960

Lomax, Alan, *The Penguin Book of American Folk Songs*, Harmondsworth: Penguin, 1964

Lomax, Alan, *The Land Where the Blues Began*, London: Methuen, 1993

*Lomax, John A., *Adventures of a Ballad Hunter*, New York: Macmillan, 1947

Lomax, John A. and Lomax, Alan, *American Ballads and Folk Songs*, New York: Macmillan, 1934

*Lomax, John A. and Lomax, Alan, *Negro Folk Songs as Sung by Lead Belly*, New York: Macmillan, 1936

*Lomax, John A. and Lomax, Alan, *Cowboy Songs*, New York: Macmillan, rev. edn 1941

*Lomax, John A. and Lomax, Alan, *Folksong U.S.A.*, New York: Sloan and Pearce, 1941

Mabey, Richard, *The Pop Process*, London: Hutchinson, 1969

*Macalister, Charles, *Old Pioneering Days in the Sunny South*, Goulburn, Australia: nia, 1907

MacGregor, Craig, *Bob Dylan: A Retrospective*, New York: Morrow, 1972 [reprinted as *Bob Dylan, the Early Years: A Retrospective*, New York: Da Capo Press, 1990]

Magi, Giovanni (ed.), *Egypt*, Florence: Casa Editrice Bonechi, 1993

Mailer, Norman, *Armies of the Night*, Harmondsworth: Penguin, 1970

Major, Clarence, *Juba to Jive: A Dictionary of African–American Slang*, London: Penguin, 1994

*Manifold, John (ed.), *The Penguin Australian Songbook*, Harmondsworth: Penguin, 1964

Marcus, Greil, *Mystery Train*, London: Omnibus Press, 1977 [1975]

Marcus, Greil, *Invisible Republic: Bob Dylan's Basement Tapes*, New York: Henry Holt, 1997

*Marsh, J. B. T., *The Story of the Jubilee Singers with Their Songs*, London: Hodder & Stoughton, 1875

Marx, Karl and Engels, Frederick, *Selected Works Vol. 2*, Moscow: Foreign Languages Publishing House, 1962

*McLuhan, Marshall, *The Gutenberg Galaxy: The Making of Typographic Man*, Toronto: University of Toronto Press, 1962

*McLuhan, Marshall, *Understanding Media*, London: Routledge & Kegan Paul, 1964

McLuhan, Marshall, *The Medium Is the Massage* [sic], Harmondsworth: Penguin, 1967

*McRobbie, Angela, *Postmodernism and Popular Culture*, London: Routledge, 1994

Mellers, Wilfrid, *A Darker Shade of Pale: A Backdrop to Bob Dylan*, London: Faber & Faber, 1984

Mendelson, Edward (ed.), *The English Auden: Poems, Essays and Dramatic Writings 1927–1939*, London: Faber & Faber, 1977

Mercer, Paul, *Newfoundland Songs and Ballads in Print 1842–1974*, St John's, Newfoundland: M.U.N. Folklore & Language Publications, 1979

*Mezzrow, Mezz and Wolfe, Bernard, *Really the Blues*, New York: Random House, 1946 [republished London: HarperCollins, 1993]

*Michel, Steve, *The Bob Dylan Concordance*, Grand Junction, CO: Rolling Tomes, 1992

Middleton, Richard and Horn, David (eds), *Popular Music, Vol. 1*, Cambridge: Cambridge University Press, 1981

Middleton, Richard and Horn, David (eds), *Popular Music, Vol. 4, Performers and Audiences*, Cambridge: Cambridge University Press, 1984

Miles, Barry, *Ginsberg: A Biography*, New York: Simon & Schuster, 1989

*Millay, Edna St Vincent, *The Buck in the Snow*, New York: Harper & Bros, 1928

*Millay, Edna St Vincent, *Collected Sonnets*, New York: Harper & Bros, 1941

Milton, John, *Paradise Lost*, ed. Robert Vaughan, London: Cassell, 1905 [written 1658–63; first published 1667, rev. edn, 1674]

Mitchell, Margaret, *Gone with the Wind*, London: Macmillan, 1936

*Monsarrat, Nicholas, *The Cruel Sea*, London: Cassell, 1951

Moore, Geoffrey (ed.), *The Penguin Book of American Verse*, Harmondsworth: Penguin, 1979

Morgan, Robert and Barton, John, *Biblical Interpretation*, Oxford: Oxford University Press, 1988

Naipaul, V. S., *A Turn in the South*, New York: Knopf, 1989

New Gift Book of Nursery Rhymes, London: Dean & Son, 1971

Nichols, C. H., *Many Thousand Gone*, Leiden, Holland: E. J. Brill, 1963

*Nimoy, Leonard, *We Are All Children Searching for Love*, Boulder, CO: Blue Mountain Arts, 1970s

Oakley, Giles, *The Devil's Music: A History of the Blues*, London: BBC Publications, 1976

Odum, H. W. and Johnson, G. B., *The Negro and His Songs: A Study of Typical Negro Songs in the South*, Chapel Hill: University of North Carolina Press, 1925

*Oldfield, Mike, *Dire Straits*, London: Sidgwick & Jackson, 1984

Oliver, Paul, *Blues Fell This Morning: Meaning in the Blues*, Cambridge: Cambridge University Press, 1990 [1st edn, as *Blues Fell This Morning: The Meaning of the Blues*, London: Cassell, 1960]

Oliver, Paul, *Conversation with the Blues*, London: Cassell, 1965

Oliver, Paul, *The Story of the Blues*, Harmondsworth: Penguin, 1972

Oliver, Paul, *Songsters and Saints: Vocal Traditions on Race Records*, Cambridge: Cambridge University Press, 1984

Oliver, Paul (ed.), *The Blackwell Guide to Blues Records*, Oxford: Blackwood, 1989

O'Neill, Eugene, *The Emperor Jones, Diff'rent, The Straw*, New York: Boni and Liveright, 1921

*Opie, Iona and Peter, *Children's Games in Street and Playground*, Oxford: Oxford University Press, 1969

*Opie, Iona and Peter, *The Classic Fairy Tales*, Oxford: Oxford University Press, 1974

Opie, Iona and Peter, *The Oxford Dictionary of Nursery Rhymes*, Oxford: Oxford University Press, rev. edn, 1951

Opie, Iona and Peter, *The Oxford Nursery Rhyme Book*, Oxford: Oxford University Press, 1955

Opie, Iona and Peter, *The Singing Game*, Oxford: Oxford University Press, 1985

Orwell, George, *Collected Essays, Journalism and Letters*, ed. Sonia Orwell and Ian Angus, London: Secker and Warburg, 1968 [4 vols]

Orwell, George, *Shooting an Elephant and Other Essays*, London: Secker & Warburg, 1950

Osborne, Charles (ed.), *Dictionary of Composers*, London: Bodley Head, 1977

*Oster, Harry, *Living Country Blues*, Hatboro, PA: Folklore Associates, 1969

*Otis, Johnny, *Upside Your Head: R&B on Central Avenue*, Boston: Wesleyan, 1993 [hardback and paperback]

Ousby, Ian (ed.), *The Cambridge Guide to Literature in English*, Cambridge: Cambridge University Press, 1993, corrected reprint 1995

Oxenbury, Helen, *The Helen Oxenbury Nursery Rhyme Book*, London: Heinemann, 1991 [1986]

Palmer, A. W., *Dictionary of Modern History 1789–1945*, Harmondsworth: Penguin, 2nd edn, 1964

Palmer, Roy (ed.), *Everyman's Book of British Ballads*, London: J. M. Dent, 1980

Palmer, Roy (ed.), *The Oxford Book of Sea Songs*, Oxford: Oxford University Press, 1986

Partridge, Eric, *A Dictionary of the Underworld, British and American*, London: Routledge & Kegan Paul, 1949

*Patchen, Kenneth, *The Journal of Albion Moonlight*, New York: New Directions, 1941

Patchen, Kenneth, *The Selected Poems of Kenneth Patchen*, New York: New Directions, 1957

Penguin Modern Poets 5: Corso, Ferlinghetti, Ginsberg, Harmondsworth: Penguin, 1963

Pennebaker, D. A., *Bob Dylan: Don't Look Back*, New York: Ballantine, 1968

Percival, Dave, *Love Plus Zero/With Limits*, Walton-on-Naze, Essex: self-published, 1993

Phillips, Bruce, *Starlight on the Rails and Other Songs*, New York: Wooden Shoe Press, 1973

Pichaske, David, *The Poetry of Rock: The Golden Years*, Peoria: Ellis Press, 1981

Plowman, Max, *An Introduction to the Study of Blake*, London: Frank Cass, 2nd edn, 1967

*Poe, Edgar Allan, *The Narrative of Arthur Gordon Pym of Nantucket*, New York: Hill and Wang, 1960 [1838]

Pope, Alexander, *Poetical Works*, London: Oxford Standard Authors, 1966

Porter, Peter, *Last of England*, Oxford: Oxford University Press, 1970

*Porterfield, Nolan, *Jimmie Rodgers*, Champaign, IL: University of Illinois Press, 1979

Pritzker, Pauline, *Magritte*, New York: Leon Amiel, *nia*

*Proust, Marcel, *Remembrance of Things Past*, New York: Random House, 1982

Quiller-Couch, Arthur (ed.), *Oxford Book of English Verse*, Oxford: Oxford University Press, 2nd edn reprint, 1943

Raine, Kathleen, *Blake and Tradition* [2 vols], London: Routledge & Kegan Paul, 1969

Raine, Kathleen, *William Blake*, London: Thames & Hudson World of Art Library Series, 1970

Raine, Kathleen, *Autobiographies*, London: Skoob Books, 1991

*Randolph, Vance, *The Devil's Daughter and Other Folk Tales*, New York: *nia*, 1955

*Randolph, Vance, *Ozark Folk Songs Vol. 1: British Ballads and Songs*, Columbia, MO, and London: University of Missouri Press, 1980/82 [1946]

Raph, Theodore, *The Songs We Sang: A Treasury of American Popular Music*, New Jersey: A. S. Barnes, 1965 [paperback 1978]

*Ravenscroft, Thomas, *Melismata: mvsicall phansies*, Amsterdam: Theatrum Orbis Terrarum, and New York: Da Capo Press, 1971 [1611]

Rees, D., Lazell, B., and Osborne, R., *40 Years of NME Charts*, London: Boxtree, 1992

Reynolds, Simon, *Blissed Out*, London: Serpent's Tail, 1988

Rhys, Ernest, *Browning & His Poetry*, London: Harrap, 1st edn 4th reprint, 1928

Ribakove, Sy and Barbara, *Folk-Rock: The Bob Dylan Story*, New York: Dell Paperbacks, 1966

Rice, Rice, Gambaccini and Read, *Guinness Book of British Hit Singles* (5th edn), Enfield: Guinness Superlatives, 1985

Ricks, Christopher, *The Force of Poetry*, Oxford: Clarendon Press, 1984

*Riley, Tim, *Hard Rain: A Bob Dylan Commentary*, New York: Alfred Knopf, 1995

*Ritson, Joseph (ed.), *Gammer Gurton's Garland or The Nursery Parnassus*, London: R. Christopher, 1784 [enlarged editions (Christopher and Jennett), c. 1799 and (R. Triphook), 1810]

Road Atlas: United States, Canada, Mexico (54th edn), Chicago: Rand McNally, 1978

*Robbins, Harold, *A Stone for Danny Fisher*, New York: Knopf, 1952

Robinson, Edwin A., *Collected Poems*, New York: Macmillan, 1921, 1929, 1937

Rogers, Kenny, with Epand, Len, *Making It with Music*, New York: Harper & Row, 1978

*Rosenberg, Neil V. (ed.), *Transforming Tradition: Folk Music Revivals Examined*, Urbana: University of Illinois Press, 1993

*Rossetti, Christina, *Goblin Market: The Prince's Progress and Other Poems*, London: Macmillan, 1875

*Roth, Philip, *The Anatomy Lesson*, New York: Farrar, Straus and Giroux, 1983

Rowe, Mike, *Chicago Breakdown*, London: Eddison Press, 1973

*Ruppli, Michel, *Prestige Jazz Records 1949–1969*, Denmark: Knudsen, 1972

*Ruppli, Michel, *The Prestige Label: A Discography*, Westport, CT: Greenwood Press, 1980

*Ruppli, Michel, *The Savoy Label: A Discography*, Westport, CT: Greenwood Press, 1980

Russell, Tony, *Blacks, Whites and Blues*, London: Studio Vista, 1970

Russell, Tony, *The Blues from Robert Johnson to Robert Cray*, London: Aurum Carlton, 1997

Samuel, Raphael, *Island Stories: Unravelling Britain – Theatres of Memory, Vol. 2*, London: Verso, 1998

*Sandburg, Carl, *An American Songbag*, New York: Harcourt Brace, 1927 [reprinted 1970, and in paperback by Harvest Books, 1970]

*Sandburg, Carl, *New American Songbag: Broadcast Music*, New York: Harcourt Brace, 1950

Santelli, Robert, *The Big Book of Blues: A Biographical Encyclopedia*, London: Pavilion Books, 1994

*Sartre, Jean-Paul, *La Nausée [Nausea]*, Paris: Gallimard, 1937 [and trans. by Lloyd Alexander, Norfolk, CT: New Directions, 1969]

Scaduto, Anthony, *Bob Dylan*, London: Abacus Books, 1972

*Scarborough, Dorothy, *On the Trail of Negro Folksongs*, Cambridge, MA: Harvard University Press, 1925

Scobie, Stephen, *Alias Bob Dylan*, Red Deer, AB: Red Deer College Press, 1991

*Service, Robert W., *The Complete Poems of Robert Service*, New York: Dodd, Mead, 1944

*Sexton, Anne, *To Bedlam and Part Way Back*, Boston: Houghton Mifflin, 1960

Sexton, Anne, *Transformations*, Boston: Houghton Mifflin, 1971

Shakespeare, William, *Hamlet, Prince of Denmark*, London: Signet Classics Edition, New English Library, 1963

Sharp, Cecil, *Folk-Songs from Somerset*, nia, 1906

*Sharp, Cecil, *Nursery Songs from the Appalachian Mountains*, nia, 1921–23

Sharp, Cecil and Karpeles, Maud, *English Folk-Songs from the Southern Appalachians*, Oxford: Oxford University Press, 1932

Shattuck, Roger, *The Banquet Years: The Origins of the Avant-Garde in France 1885 to World War I*, New York: Vintage Books, rev. edn, 1968

Shaw, Geoffrey (ed.), *Twice 44 Sociable Songs*, London: Hawkes & Son, 1927

Shelton, Robert, *No Direction Home*, London: Penguin, 1987

Shepard, Leslie, *The Broadside Ballad*, Hatboro, PA: Legacy, 1978

Shepard, Sam, *Rolling Thunder Logbook*, Harmondsworth: Penguin, 1978

*Shepard, Sam, *Fool for Love and Other Plays*, Toronto: Bantam Books, 1984

Shuldham-Shaw, Patrick and Lyle, Emily B. (eds), *The Greig–Duncan Folk Song Collection, Vol. 1*, Aberdeen: Aberdeen University Press, 1981

Solomon, Maynard (ed.), *British Ballads and Folk Songs from the Joan Baez Songbook*, New York: Ryerson, 1967

Somerville, William, *The Chase* (illustrated by Hugh Thompson), London: G. Redway, 1896 [reprinted from the original edition of 1735]

Spenser, Edmund, *The Faerie Queen*, ed. Thomas P. Roche Jr and C. Patrick O'Donnell Jr, Harmondsworth: Penguin, 1978 [1590, 1596 and 1609]

Spitz, Bob, *Dylan: A Biography*, London: Michael Joseph, 1989

Steinbeck, John, *The Grapes of Wrath*, Harmondsworth: Penguin, 1951 [1st edn, USA, 1939]

Steinbeck, John, *Travels with Charley: In Search of America*, London: Heinemann, 1962

Stevenson, Anne, *Bitter Fame: A Life of Sylvia Plath*, London: Penguin, 1990

Stevenson, Burton, *Stevenson's Book of Quotations Classical and Modern*, London: Cassell, c. 1958 [9th edn]

*Stevenson, T. G. (ed.), *Scottish Ballads and Songs*, Edinburgh: James Maidment, 1859

Taft, Michael, *Blues Lyric Poetry: An Anthology*, New York: Garland, 1983

Taft, Michael, *Blues Lyric Poetry: A Concordance* [3 vols], New York: Garland, 1984

Talley, Thomas W., *Negro Folk Rhymes*, ed. Charles K. Wolfe, Knoxville: University of Tennessee Press, 1991 [3rd edn] [1st edn, New York: Macmillan, 1922]

Thiele, Bob, *What a Wonderful World: A Lifetime of Recordings* (as told to Bob Golden), New York: Oxford University Press, 1995

*Thomas, Dylan (ed.), *So Early One Morning*, London: Dent, 1954

Thompson, Hunter S., *Fear and Loathing in Las Vegas: A Savage Journey to the Heart of the American Dream*, London: Granada, 1972

Thomson, Elizabeth M. (ed.), *Conclusions on the Wall*, Prestwich: Thin Man, 1980

Thomson, Elizabeth and Gutman, David (eds), *The Dylan Companion*, London: Macmillan, 1990

Tilling, Robert, *Oh! What a Beautiful City: A Tribute to Rev. Gary Davis 1896–1972*, Jersey, CI: Paul Mill Press, 1992

Tolkien, J. R. R., *The Lord of the Rings* [3 vols], London: Allen & Unwin, 1954–55

*Updike, John, *Concerts at Castle Hill*, Northridge, CA: Lord John Press, 1993

Usher, Bill (ed.), *For What Time I Am in This World*, London: Peter Martin, 1977

*van Gogh, Vincent, *My Life and Love Are One*, Boulder, CO: Blue Mountain Arts, 1970s

Vansittart, Peter, *Voices 1870–1914*, London: Jonathan Cape, 1984

*Vlach, John Michael, *Back of the Big House: The Architecture of Plantation Slavery*, Chapel Hill: University of North Carolina Press, 1993

*Vollers, Maryanne, *Ghosts of Mississippi: The Murder of Medgar Evers, the Trials of Byron De La Beckwith, and the Haunting of the New South*, New York: Little, Brown, 1995

*von Schmidt, Eric and Rooney, Jim, *Baby Let Me Follow You Down*, Garden City: Anchor Books, 1979 [rev. edn paperback, Boston: University of Massachusetts Press, 1994]

*Waite, A. E., *The Pictorial Key to the Tarot*, London: W. Rider, 1971

Walker, John (ed.), *Halliwell's Film Guide*, London: HarperCollins, 1995 [11th edn]

*Walker, William (ed.), *Southern Harmony and Musical Companion*, *nia*, 1835; 2nd edn, 1847; 3rd edn, 1854 [3rd edn reprint, ed. Glenn C. Wilcox, Los Angeles: *nia*, c. 1966]

Ward, Ed, *Michael Bloomfield: The Rise and Fall of an American Guitar Hero*, Port Chester, NJ: Cherry Lane Crooks, 1983

Watson, George (ed.), *New Cambridge Bibliography of English Literature*, Vol. 3, *1800–1900*, Cambridge: Cambridge University Press, 1969

Watson, J. and Hill, A., *A Dictionary of Communication and Media Studies*, London: Edward Arnold, 1984

Weberman, A. J., *My Life in Garbology*, New York: Stonehill, 1980

*Wedderburn, *The Complaynt of Scotland*, Edinburgh: Constable, 1801 [Paris?, c. 1549]

Welsh, Douglas, *The American Civil War: A Complete Military History*, London: Bison, 1981

Werner, Jane (ed.), *The Big Golden Book of Poetry*, New York: Golden Press, 1965

West, Nathanael, *Day of the Locust*, Harmondsworth: Penguin, 1963 [1939]

*White, B. F. (ed.), *The Sacred Harp*; *nia*, 1844; 1911

White, Edmund, *Jean Genet*, London: Chatto & Windus, 1992

White, George, *Bo Diddley: Living Legend*, Leatherhead: Castle Books, 1995

White, George R., *The Complete Bo Diddley Sessions*, Bradford: G. R. White, 1993

White, Newman I., *American Negro Folk-Songs*, Cambridge, MA: Harvard University Press, 1928 [facsimile reprint, Hatboro, PA: Folklore Associates, 1965]

White, Roger, *Walk Right Back: The Everly Brothers*, London: Plexus, 1984

Whitman, Walt, *The Complete Poems*, London: Penguin Classics, 1977

Widgery, David, *Preserving Disorder*, London: Pluto Press, 1989

*Wiggins, Lida Keck, *The Life and Works of Paul Laurence Dunbar: Containing His Complete Poetical Works*, Naperville, IL: J. L. Nichols, 1907 [reprint edn, New York: Kraus, 1971]

Williams, Oscar and Honig, Edwin (eds), *The Mentor Book of Major American Poets*, New York: Mentor, 1962

*Williams, Paul, *Performing Artist: The Music of Bob Dylan, Vol. 1, 1960–1973*, Novato, CA: Underwood-Miller, 1990

*Williams, Paul, *Performing Artist: The Music of Bob Dylan, the Middle Years: 1974–1986*, Novato, CA: Underwood-Miller, 1992

*Williams, Paul, *Watching the River Flow: Observations on Bob Dylan's Art-in-Progress, 1966–1995*, London: Omnibus Press, 1996

Williams, Richard, *Dylan: A Man Called Alias*, London: Bloomsbury Press, 1992

*Williams, William Carlos, *The Greater Trumps*, London: Gollancz, 1932

*Williams, William Carlos, *Paterson, Book I*, New York: New Directions, 1946

*Williams, William Carlos, *The Collected Later Poems*, New York: New Directions, 1950

*Williams, William Carlos, *The Collected Earlier Poems*, New York: New Directions, 1951

Willison, I. R. (ed.), *New Cambridge Bibliography of English Literature, Vol. 4, 1900–1950*, Cambridge: Cambridge University Press, 1972

Wilmer, Val, *Mama Said There'd Be Days Like This*, London: Women's Press, 1989, 1991

Wilson, Colin, *The Outsider*, London: Reader's Union/Gollancz, 1957

Wilson, Sloan, *The Man in the Gray Flannel Suit*, New York: Simon & Schuster, 1955

Wissolik, Richard D. (ed.), *Bob Dylan: American Poet and Singer: An Annotated Bibliography and Study Guide of Sources and Background Materials 1961–1991*, Greensburg, PA: Eadmer Press, 1991

Wissolik, Richard D. and McGrath, Scott (eds), *Bob Dylan's Words: A Critical Dictionary and Commentary*, Greensburg, PA: Eadmer Press, 1994

*Wolfe, Thomas, *You Can't Go Home Again*, Harper & Bros, 1940

Wolfe, Tom, *Radical Chic and Mau-Mauing the Flak-Catchers*, New York: Farrar, Straus & Giroux, 1970

Wolfe, Tom, *Mauve Gloves and Madmen, Clutter and Vine*, New York: Farrar, Straus & Giroux, 1976, Bantam Books, 1977

*Woliver, Robbie, *Bringing It All Back Home*, New York: Pantheon Books, 1986 [and as *Hoot: A 25-Year History of Greenwich Village*, New York: St Martin's Press, 1986]

Wordsworth, William and Coleridge, S. T., *Lyrical Ballads, with a Few Other Poems*, nia [1st edn, Bristol: Cottle, 1798]

Worth, Fred L. and Tamerius, Steve D., *Elvis: His Life from A to Z*, London: Corgi, 1989

*Yeats, W. B., *Essays*, New York: Macmillan, 1924

Whitman, Walt, The Complete Poems, London, Penguin Classics, 1975.

Wicke, Jennifer, Advertising Fictions, London, Pluto Press, 1988.

Wiggins, Dick, The Life and Works of Bob Dylan, a Dorsey Community Press.

Cornell, Peter J. Works, Emeryville, IL, Lake Claremont Press, Chicago, New York, Grove, 1971.

Williams, Oscar and Honig, Edwin (eds), The Mentor Book of Major American Poets, New York, Mentor, 1962.

Williams, Paul, Performing Artist: The Music of Bob Dylan, Vol. 1, 1960–1973, Novato, CA, Underwood Miller, 1990.

Williams, Paul, Performing Artist: The Music of Bob Dylan: The Middle Years, 1974–1986, Novato, CA, Underwood Miller, 1992.

Williams, Paul, Watching the Rare Bird (ed), Observations on Bob Dylan's Art in Progress, 1966–1993, London, Omnibus Press, 1996.

Williams, Richard Dylan: A Man Called Alias, London, Bloomsbury Press, 1992.

Williams, William Carlos, The Great American..., London, Collier, 1973.

Williams, William Carlos, Paterson, Book 1, New York, New Directions, 1946.

Williams, William Carlos, The Collected Later Poems, New York, New Directions, 1950.

Williams, William Carlos, The Collected Earlier Poems, New York, New Directions, 1951.

Wimsatt, W. K. (ed), New Criterion: a Bibliography of Critical Literature, Vol. 4, 1800–1814, Cambridge, Cambridge University Press, 1974.

Winter, Val, Sister, Sisterhood is Here: Long Way Days, London, Women's Press, 1984.

Wilton, Dana, The Outsider, London, Reader's Union/Collance, 1957.

Wilson, Sloan, The Man in the Grey Flannel Suit, New York, Simon & Schuster, 1955.

Wissolik, Richard D. (ed), Bob Dylan's Words and Images: An Annotated Bibliography and Study Guide of Sources and Background Materials 1960–1991, Greensburg, PA, Eadmer Press, 1991.

Wissolik, Richard D. and Scott McGrath (eds), Bob Dylan's Words: A Critical Dictionary and Commentary, Greensburg, PA, Eadmer Press, 1994.

Wolfe, Thomas, You Can't Go Home Again, Harper & Row, 1940.

Wolfe, Tom, Radical Chic and Mau-Mauing the Flak Catchers, New York, Farrar, Straus & Giroux, 1970.

Wolfe, Tom, Mauve Gloves and Madmen, Clutter and Vine and The Purple Decades, New York, Farrar, Straus & Giroux, 1976, Bantam Books, 1977.

Wolcott, Robbins, Review of Bob Rock Heroes, New York, Pantheon Books, 1986, fandango Dutch Mill, Neil Blue (ed), Greenwich Village, New York, fa St Martin's Press, 1966.

Wordsworth, William and Coleridge, S. T., Lyrical Ballads, with a Few Other Poems, ed. H. Littledale, Bristol, Gordo, 1798.

York, Fred L. and Lametrie, Steve W., Blues: the Life from A to Z, London, Cong., 1999.

Young, I. L., Poetry, New York, Macmillan, 1927.

Index

'Abandoned Love' 12, 22n, 166n, 213n, 221, 266, 465, 870f.
ABC Television 849
'Aberdeen Mississippi Blues' 302
Abrams, Harvey 278
'Absolutely Sweet Marie' 41, 44, 94, 109, 145–7, 367, 396, 550, 869
Achebe, Chinua 363, 686
acid-rock 7, 60, 119, 197, 201n, 300
'Across The Rocky Mountain' 761–2, 765, 767
Adams, Bryan 860
Adams, Derroll 189n, 825
Adler and Ross 406
'Advice For Geraldine On Her Miscellaneous Birthday' 80n, 560, 640
'Ain't Gonna Go To Hell For Anybody' 391, 440
'Ain't No Man Righteous, No Not One' 391, 407, 485, 870
'Ain't Nobody's Business' 306
Akers, Garfield 269–70, 514
'Alabama Woman Blues' 311
'Alberta' 164f.
Alexander, Arthur 315n, 652, 837
Alexander, Texas 305, 315
Alice Through the Looking-Glass 672n, 675n
Alice's Adventures in Wonderland 675n
Alien 699
Alk, Howard 22n
'All Along The Watchtower' 6, 10, 73, 159, 377, 600, 852n, 853n, 869
'All I Really Want To Do' 4, 42, 168, 644n
Allen, Terry 828
Allen, Woody 149n
Allison, Mose 288
Allman Brothers 342
Allsop, Kenneth 201n
'Alternatives To College' (poem) 80n, 560, 660
Altman, Robert 424
Alyn, Glen 38n
'Am I Your Stepchild?' 334f.
America, South and Central
   Dylan's performances in 434
   Guatemala 428
   literature of 435
   war zones 428
      CIA involvement in 428, 434

American Civil War 542, 740, 743, 758ff., 762f.
"American Folk Music (Anthology of)" 164n, 165n, 189n, 199n, 207n, 278f. 289, 328, 643n, 645n, 705–6, 707, 773, 825, 866n
American literature *see under* literature
American radio stations 88
'And All The Hills Echoéd' 609
Andersen, Hans Christian 641n, 661
'Angelina' 14, 215n, 333, 426, 432ff., 442–7, 502, 621, 638, 783, 875
'(Annie Been A-Working On The) Midnight Shift' 109
Anka, Paul 107, 113, 632
"Another Side Of Bob Dylan" 4, 116, 127f., 141n, 197n, 216n, 350
Anouilh, Jean 196n
Anthony, Don Chubby 828n
Anthony, Eddie 524, 649n
Apollinaire, Guillaume 201n, 226n, 629n, 653n, 721n
'Are You Ready?' 246n, 247, 410, 528
Area Code 615 716
Armatrading, Joan 117
Armstrong, Louis 288n, 675
Arnold, Byron 775
Arnold, Kokomo 311n, 331f., 345n, 353n, 357ff., 647
Arnold, Matthew 83, 203
'Arthur McBride' 15, 635, 729f., 730n, 738, 782
'As I Went Out One Morning' 330, 783
ASCAP award 849
Ashes and Sand (record label) 298, 525
Astaire, Fred 515
Atkins, Chet 89, 111n, 725
Atlantic Records 517, 527, 752
Auden, W. H. 75n, 568n
Augustine of Hippo, Saint 74
Auster, Paul 259–60
'Automobile Blues' 304
Autry, Gene 708

'Baby Let Me Follow You Down' 285
'Baby, I'm In The Mood For You' 12, 289, 717
'Baby Please Don't Go' 364

'Baby, Stop Crying' xvii, 15, 192, 217, 361, 549
Bacall, Lauren 553n, 554, 566, 622
Bachelors, The 400
'Back Door Man' 366
'Back-Water Blues' 275
Bacon, Houston 351n
'Bad Girl's Lament' 532, 533, 536, 537
'Bad Luck Is Killing Me' 324–5
Baez, Joan xvii–xviii, 22n, 29n, 43, 81n, 107n,
    110n, 142, 164n, 165n, 166n, 186n, 202, 397,
    429, 500n, 627f., 722, 759n, 781n, 810, 846
Bailey, Kid 354
Baker, Arthur 567, 573ff.
Baker, Ginger 114
Baker, James Iron Head 351n, 533n, 541, 762
Baker, LaVern 728
Baker, Willie 356
Bale Brothers 725
Ball, Kenny 675
'Ballad For A Friend' 378, 831
'Ballad In Plain D' 132, 216n, 429, 659, 782
'Ballad Of A Thin Man' 10, 65, 140f., 352, 468n,
    615, 872
'Ballad Of Frankie Lee And Judas Priest, The' 30,
    96, 366, 395, 398
'Ballad Of Hollis Brown, The' 25, 27, 125f., 140,
    292, 377, 429n, 653, 759n
Band, The see Crackers
'Band Of The Hand' 258, 558, 859n
'Barbara Allen' 642, 703
Barbecue Bob 282n, 317, 346, 354, 395n, 717
'Barcelona' 712
Bardot, Brigitte 560
Bare, Bobby 750
Barefoot Jerry 716
Barthes, Roland 258, 261, 382, 386–7, 388, 459
Barton, Ernie 355
Basement Tapes 7, 9, 15, 74n, 94, 98, 104, 108n,
    147, 160, 167n, 181, 211, 265, 297, 309, 339,
    342, 355, 383, 643, 661n, 665, 690, 696, 699,
    729n, 831, 872
Basie, Count 356
Batts, Will 294, 296
Baudelaire 201, 420, 429n, 727
Bauldie, John 85n, 250, 255–6, 267, 413f., 446,
    578, 644n, 711n, 844, 856n, 861, 869
Baxter, Les 85
'Bay Of Mexico, The' 732n
BBC (British Broadcasting Corporation) 87f., 112f.,
    286, 424n, 718, 725, 729, 843; see also
    Omnibus
Beale Street Rounders 715
Beale Street Sheiks 19
Beat Poets see under poetry
Beatles, The 17, 42n, 89, 91, 93n, 98, 119n, 120,
    129, 147, 173, 226n, 352n, 573, 595
Beattie, Sarah 816n, 874
Beauregard, Nathan 294
Bechet, Sydney 467
Beecher, Bonnie (aka Jaharana Romney) 309–10n
BeeGees, The 114

Beethoven, Ludwig Van 877
"Before The Flood" 8
Behan, Brendan 84n
Behan, Dominic 656
Belafonte, Harry 292
Bell, Anna 349n
Bell, Ed 338f., 371
'Bell Of Freedom Still Rings, The' 848n
'Belle Isle' 6, 26, 168ff., 170, 739
Belmonts, The 813n, 822
Belsey, Catherine 264, 381–2, 386ff.
Bennett, Tony 101, 406, 721n, 847
Bentley, Gladys 346
Benton, Brook 708
Bernstein, Joel 448
Berry, Chuck 53, 89ff., 94ff., 107, 116, 280n, 315,
    342, 578, 652, 743, 856
"Best Of Bob Dylan, The" 16
betrayal theme in Dylan's work 217–18, 220,
    223–4, 666, 738; see also Dylan, Sara
Bettelheim, Bruno 420, 634, 640–1, 689, 733,
    736–7, 817, 860
Bible, biblical allusions see under religion
Bible Belt 162
Bible in the Lyrics of Bob Dylan, The 392
Bicknell, Ed 448
Big Bang theory 424
Big Brother & The Holding Company 119
Big Joe Williams 279
Bigeou, Esther 301n
Bikel, Theodore 37n
Bilk, Acker 708, 750
Bill Monroe & His Blue Grass Boys 715, 823n; see
    also Monroe
Billboard (magazine) 85f.
'Billy' 105, 627
Billy Mack And Mary Mack 331
'Billy 7' 105, 627, 696, 802
Billy Ward & The Dominos 406
"Biograph" 2, 12, 17n, 22n, 83, 105n, 165n, 190n,
    197n, 202, 212n, 213n, 215n, 226n, 231n,
    259, 273n, 287, 288n, 289, 299, 336, 351n,
    358, 362, 383f., 425f., 447–8, 452ff., 494n,
    582, 631, 655, 665n, 695, 730, 735n, 746,
    774, 839, 846f.
Birkin, Jane 616n
Black ballads 747ff.
'Black Cross' 591
'Black Crow Blues' 309f., 330, 837
black culture 37, 102; see also civil rights
'Black Diamond Bay' 9, 185, 187, 465, 672, 871
black music
    blues 35, 395; see also blues
    gospel 212n; see also gospel
    Negro Spirituals 35, 307ff., 326n, 365, 610,
        826f., 866
    pop 99
    soul 102
'Black Pony Blues' 371
Black Power movement 178n
'Black Train Blues' 313

'Blackjack' 351–2
'Blackjack Blues' 351
'Blackjack Davey' 713, 739, 782
Blackwell, Scrapper 651n, 717
Blake, Blind (Arthur) 270, 282n, 299, 312, 321, 337, 370n, 522–3, 600, 721, 730, 750
Blake, William 2, 54ff., 64, 84n, 177, 194, 225n, 246, 258, 307, 412–18, 423, 464, 609, 620, 665, 733n, 753n
Bland, Bobby 92, 349
Bland, James 719
Blind Boy Fuller see Fuller
Blind Lemon Jefferson see Jefferson
Blind Willie Johnson see Johnson
'Blind Willie McTell' (song) 14, 274, 279f., 282, 517–47 passim, see esp. 541–5), 854, 875
"Blonde On Blonde" 5ff., 32n, 33, 39, 44f., 65, 68, 71, 90, 115n, 116, 119f., 129, 142–159 passim, 169–81 passim, 188n, 189ff., 196, 208, 241, 249, 262, 274, 300, 302, 303–4, 315, 324, 345f., 348, 489, 594, 623, 633, 661n, 797, 831, 839, 853, 872
'Blood In My Eyes' 342, 648n, 754, 841, (video) 841
'Blood On The Saddle' 28n, 551
"Blood On The Tracks" xvii, 8ff., 15, 30, 41, 56, 77, 111, 170, 181, 185, 187, 190n, 193, 209ff., 241, 248, 362, 375, 551, 633, 695, 716, 782, 791, 831, 873
Bloomfield, Mike 320, 708, 728
'Blowin' Down The Road' 36
'Blowin' In The Wind' 3, 10, 16, 22f., 111n, 116, 240n, 385, 432, 469, 781n, 832, 848n, 852n, 869
'Blue Moon' 92, 164
'Blue Yodel No. 12' 359
Blue-Belles 93
bluegrass 33n
Bluegrass Reunion 717
blues 35f., 39, 53, 139, 150f., 194, 268–379, 426, 663, 700, 704, 804, 831, 858
jazz-blues 303n, 467
recordings xxiii–xxvi
Blues Lyric Poetry see Taft
Blumenstein, Gottfried 255
Bob B. Soxx & The Blue Jeans 92
"Bob Dylan" (album) 3, 289, 705
"Bob Dylan At Budokan" 10, 131
"Bob Dylan In Concert" 197n
"Bob Dylan Live 1966: The Bootleg Series Vol. 4: The Royal Albert Hall Concert, 1998" 16
"Bob Dylan Unplugged" 431n, 877; see also MTV
"Bob Dylan: Highway 61 Interactive" 166n
'Bob Dylan's Dream' 43f.
'Bob Dylan's 115th Dream' 96, 104, 116, 140, 338, 711n, 855
"Bob Dylan's Greatest Hits" 5
"Bob Dylan's Greatest Hits Vol II" 7, 106n
"Bob Dylan's Greatest Hits Vol. 3" 431n
'Bob Dylan's New Orleans Rag' 662
Bobby Boris Pickett & The Crypt-Kickers' 92–3

Bodkin, Maude 491
Bogan, Lucille (Bessie Jackson) 684, 746
Bogart, Humphrey 551–4, 557–8, 563, 566, 624
Bolton, Michael 859n
Bonds, Son 303
Bono 112n, 837, 859n
Book of Common Prayer 242n, 485n
Booth, Stanley 294n, 325f., 328, 329, 334, 707, 836–7, 837n, 871n
"Bootleg Series I–III" xix, 14, 20f., 41n, 142n, 143n, 160n, 164n, 207n, 245n, 277n, 330, 356, 375, 391, 400, 413, 426, 429, 437n, 446, 470, 532n, 564, 601n, 607n, 627, 663, 666n, 684, 707n, 725n, 781n, 840, 871
"Bootleg Series Vol. 4: Bob Dylan Live 1966" 82n
'Boots Of Spanish Leather' 140, 168, 397, 530, 575, 657, 658–9, 712f., 782f.
'Born In Time' 14, 258, 672, 695, 697, 860f.
Bosch, Hieronymus 49, 144
Bowden, Betsy 251, 554
Bowie, David 117
'Boxer, The' 165
Boyd, Eddie 349, 350n
Bracey, Ishman 298, 313n, 347n, 357, 359f.
Brady, Paul 705, 730n
Brecht, Bertolt 84n, 196
Bremser, Ray 84
"Bringing It All Back Home" 4, 41n, 72, 80n, 98, 116, 129, 142n, 215, 243n, 292, 483, 485n, 560, 595
"Broadside Ballads" 245n, 852n
"Broadside Reunion" 126n
'Broke Down Engine' 752
'Broke Down Engine No. 2' 740n
'Broke Down Engine Blues' 520n, 524, 525, 740n, 742n, 756, 784
Bromberg, Dave 710, 751f.
Broonzy, Big Bill 84n, 275, 279, 300n, 302f., 303n, 313n, 314n, 332, 349, 647, 717, 731n
'Brother John & The Dungarees' 288
Brothers Grimm 420, 635n, 641f., 654, 667, 682, 733
Brothers Karamazov, The 832
Brown, Hi Henry 358, 649n
Brown, Hollis 523
Brown, Jonas 523
Brown, Richard Rabbit 309, 460, 684
Brown, Ruth 721n
Brown, Will Mae 368
Brown, Willie 337, 342, 757
'Brown Skin Girl' 317
Browning, Robert 2, 54, 64ff., 258, 459, 544
Browns, The 400
'Brownsville Girl' 13, 15, 19n, 83, 96n, 186n, 259, 262, 265f., 305n, 309, 329n, 369, 525n, 560–1, 566, 577ff., 586–8, 590ff., 602f., 621, 664, 839f., 854, 875
Bruce, Lenny 399, 697, 831, 849
Bryant, Boudleaux 167n, 664
Bryant's Jubilee Quartet 439n
Bryson, Bill 29n, 95n, 189n, 275n, 295n

'Buckets Of Rain' 39, 185, 215, 301, 664
'Buck-eye Rabbit' 826
Buddhism 602–3, 605
Buffy Sainte-Marie 63
Bull City Red 724
Bunn, Teddy 315, 649n, 650n
Bunyan, John 3, 47f., 51, 505–6, 623, 625
Burgess, Sonny 729n
Burnett, Chester Arthur 318; *see also* Wolf, Howlin'
Burns, Robert 754n, 815–16, 822
Burnt Norton 510
Burroughs, William 75
Burton, Richard 556–7, 560
Buster Carter & Preston Young 344
Butterbeans and Susie 355
Byatt, A. S. xviii, 817
Bygraves, Max 492n
Byrd, James 368
Byrds, The 119, 185n, 643f., 707n
Byron, George (Lord) 516n, 656, 661n

Cagney, Jimmy 560
Cahn, Rolf (& Eric von Schmidt) 708
Cahn, Sam 708
"Cahoots" 7
Calasso, Robert 491
'California' 41, 243, 341
'Call Letter Blues' 375ff., 377f., 831
Calloway, Blanche 354
Calt, Stephen 283n, 344–5, 353n, 359n, 645, 709n
Calvinism *see under* religion
Cambodia, war in 178n, 873
Campbell, Bob 311n, 360
Camus, Albert 84n
'Can *You* Please Crawl Out Your Window?' 7, 10, 129, 140, 142
'Canadee-i-o' 27n, 713, 739
'Candy Man' 313n
Canned Heat 274n
Cannon, Freddie 91
Cannon, Gus 290, 327f., 337, 731
'Cannon Ball Blues' 458, 745
Cannon's Jug Stompers 280n, 327, 710n
'Can't Help Falling In Love' 8, 106, 486n, 806
'Can't Wait' 16, 791, 796, 829, 833
Cantor, Louis 102n, 326
capitalism 135, 386, 434
'Car Car' 644
'Cardinal And The Dog, The' 69
'Careless Love' 756
Carey, Henry 684
Carey, John 511, 630
'Caribbean Wind' 12, 235n, 266, 358, 383f., 405, 426, 447–8, 449–52, 457–60, 462, 469, 507, 557, 576n, 745, 875
Carlisle, Cliff 713
Carlisle & Ball 363
Carlyle, Thomas 75
Carmichael, Hoagy 553–4, 670, 679n
Carolina Ramblers 716

Carr, Leroy 280n, 299, 303n, 311, 333, 339, 345n, 371, 732n
Carr, Wynona 652
Carroll, Lewis 70f., 672n, 675n
Carter, Betty 356
Carter, Bo 362n, 819n
Carter Family, The 460, 713, 739, 825, 866–7n
Cartwright, Bert 256, 359n, 392, 404, 408, 409, 562, 606ff., 646n
Casey, Smith 351n
Cash, Johnny 84n, 89, 93, 103n, 111, 163, 577n, 708, 741, 828, 848
Caston, Baby Doo 319
Catch-22 49, 558, 676
Catchfire see Flashback
Catherine of Alexandria, Saint 610n
Cathy Jean and the Room-Mates 98
Cat-Iron (William Carradine) 310n
'Cat's In The Well' 14, 324, 371, 455, 639, 649, 679–80, 681, 694, 696f., 867, 875
Cave, Nick (& The Bad Seeds) 773
Chandler, Raymond 554n, 559
'Changing Of The Guards' 15, 191, 215, 220ff., 359, 452
Channel, Bruce 92, 93n
Chaplin, Charlie 69, 700, 854
Chapman, George 671
Chapman, Tracy 857
Charles, Ray 91n, 92f., 349, 351–2, 575n, 721
Charlie, Pickett 293
Charters, Sam 18n, 280, 284, 288n, 328, 343, 346n, 519n, 546
Chatman, Bo 357, 361, 648n
Chatman, Lonnie 648n
Chaucer, Geoffrey 46, 638
Chenier, Clifton 304
'Cherry Red' 825
Chesterton, G. K. 65, 69, 636, 822
'Chimes Of Freedom' 4, 20, 79, 81, 116, 128, 221, 245n, 429, 468f., 594, 644n, 847
Christ, Jesus *see under* religion
Christian, Charlie 84n
Christianity *see under* religion
Church *see under* religion
Circuit (arts journal) 43n
Citizen Kane 622, 625
'City Of Gold' 562
Civil Rights movement 37, 102n, 781n
Clapton, Eric 108, 114, 172, 269ff., 857, 860
Clark, Gene 719
Clarke, Adam 406n, 407n, 438, 546n, 637–8, 690
Clayton, Paul 30, 84n, 716
'Clean-Cut Kid' 258, 263, 452, 560, 568n
Cline, Patsy 89, 111
Clinton, W. J. xxi, 844, 847
'Close Your Eyes, Close The Door' 70
'Clothes Line' 591, 670, 831
Coasters 90
Coburn, James 627
'Cocaine' 694n, 732n

Cochran, Eddie 91, 93, 100
Cofer Brothers 825
Cohen, John 762n
Cohen, Leonard 59, 189, 790f., 822, 828
Cohen, Scott 45n, 841n, 843, 849n
Cohn, Nik 46
'Cold, Cold Heart' 168
'Cold Irons Bound' 16, 264, 790–1, 792, 795f.,
    827, 832
Cold War (new) 247
Coleman, Lonnie 354
Coleridge, Samuel Taylor 47n, 55, 75, 200, 516
Coleridge-Taylor, Samuel (composer) 720
Collins, Sam 715
Collis, Clark 788n
Coltrane, John 84n
Columbia Records (CBS) 3, 22, 252, 708, 518, 845,
    849
'Come On In My Kitchen' 313, 345, 521n
Como, Perry 55, 327
"Complete Buddy Holly, The" 107n
Complexity Theory 424n
Concert for Bangladesh 864
Conley, Walt 289
Contours, The 93
Cooder, Ry 325n, 729
Cooke, Sam 18n, 90, 92, 615, 631–2, 675, 708,
    722
Copeland, Martha 533n
'Copper Kettle' 6, 26, 164, 168n, 400, 759n
Cornell, Lyn 93
Corso, Gregory 82ff.
Coslow, Sam 728
Costa, Sam 88
Costello, Elvis 55, 117, 146
Cott, Jonathon 251, 255
Cotten, Elizabeth 290
Country Joe & The Fish 119, 130f., 797, 822
'Country Pie' 29f., 104, 160, 661, 782
'Covenant Woman' 237, 241
cowboy culture 27, 35
cowboy music 32f.
cowboys 29n
Cowley, John H. 19n, 283n, 526n, 751n
Cox, Harry 531
Cox, Ida 354f., 378n
Crackers/Band, The 7ff., 12, 28, 92n, 109, 114n,
    162, 163n, 356n, 584n, 643f., 665, 724, 732
Cramer, Floyd 89, 92f., 103
Crane, Stephen 763
Cray, Robert 542
Cream 118, 274n
Credence Clearwater Revival 97
Crosby, Stills & Nash 172
Crowe, Cameron 2n, 165n, 273n, 285n, 286, 288n,
    351n, 447–8, 582, 665, 735n
Crudup, Arthur 98, 295, 298, 312n, 324–5, 357,
    371, 623f., 664n, 824f., 870
Cruel Sea, The 456, 557n
Crystals, The 92, 627n
Cuban Missile Crisis 122, 245n

cummings, e. e. 75, 80, 84n, 110n
Curry, Elder 299f., 717

da Vinci, Leonardo 412n
Dadaism 473n
Dali, Salvador 144
Dallas, Karl 48n, 308–9n, 530, 656n, 711n, 745n,
    774
Damon, Bill 162, 166, 168
Danny & The Juniors 90
Dante [Alighieri] 456
'Danville Girl' 19n, 584n, 759n, 825n
Darby, Tom 706–7
'Dark Eyes' 548, 568n, 569, 575
Darke, Andrew 816, 819, 834
'Darn Good Girl' 344
Darwin, Charles 410
Davies, Ray 698
Davis, Bette 560
Davis, Gary, Rev. (aka Blind Gary Davis) 279, 285,
    292, 341, 694, 724, 731, 749ff.
Davis, Miles 84n, 851, 852n, 873
Davis, Skeeter 89
Davis, Walter 369, 742
Day, Aidan 251, 256, 259ff., 374, 380, 497–8,
    510, 579ff., 871f.
Day, Texas Bill 311n
'Day Of The Locusts' 41, 75, 175
'Days Of '49' 6, 25, 164, 607n
de la Beckwith, Byron 37n
de la Mare, Walter 653
de Somogyi, Nick 256, 263, 380, 388, 430n, 499,
    500f.
'Dead Man, Dead Man' 394f., 498, 564n
Dean, James 560
'Dear Landlord' 140
'Dear Mrs. Roosevelt' 848n
'Death Cell Blues' 335
'Death Don't Have No Mercy' 285
'Death Is Not The End' 13, 441, 470, 593n
Decca (Records) 89, 93
'Delia' 15, 279, 525, 704, 710, 745, 748ff., 751–3
Delius, Frederick 721
Delmore Brothers 287, 725
'Denise' 429
Derrida, Jaques 258
'Desiderata' 424
"Desire" xvii, 9ff., 22n, 48, 77, 80, 84, 143, 158n,
    166n, 170, 185, 209f., 213ff., 218n, 242n,
    248, 263, 265, 499, 560, 590, 664, 791
'Desolation Row' 5, 22, 66–7, 74, 79, 83f., 135f.,
    139, 155, 15⚹, 223, 358, 460, 560, 660, 689,
    855, 873
'Devil Got My Woman' 345–6, 347, 727
Díaz, César 838, 860
Diamond, Neil 258
'Diamond Joe' 15, 27, 732, 738f., 781, 783
Dickens, Charles 511, 610, 630, 723
Dickinson, Jim 328–9
Dickson, Pearl 337

Diddley, Bo 107, 304n, 459, 652
Dietrich, Marlene 84n, 560, 623n
'Dignity' 15, 47n, 300, 357, 431n, 439n, 525, 616–20, 621ff., 631f., 839, 875
DiMucci, Dion (& The Belmonts) 90, 92, 813n
Dire Straits 448, 857
'Dirge' 54, 57, 81, 180, 208, 400, 623
'Dirt Road Blues' 790–1, 797, 801, 809, 824f., 829, 832
disco 857
'Disease Of Conceit' 597, 604f., 615, 626
Disney, Walt 33n, 860
Divine Comedy, The 456
Dixie Cups, The 176
Dixie Harmony Four 368
Dixie Jubilee Singers 439n
Dixon, Robert (& Godrich) xxvi, 332, 719
Dixon, Willie 299, 319, 325n, 460
'Do It Right' 301
'Do Right To Me Baby (Do Unto Others)' 42, 230n, 243–4
Dr John 300
Doe, Ernie K. 92
Domino, Fats 85n, 90, 94, 101, 104, 300n, 322, 343, 364, 514, 608n, 631n, 632, 793n, 824
Donegan, Lonnie 827
Donne, John 54ff., 571, 812, 822
Donovan 118
'Don't Fall Apart On Me Tonight' 262, 264, 336, 466, 468, 470, 560
'Don't Let Your Deal Go Down' 725n
Don't Look Back 41, 60, 113–14, 121, 189n, 243n, 245n, 249, 403, 764, 840ff., 844, 849
'Don't Start Me To Talkin' ' 318, 515n
'Don't Think Twice, It's All Right' 3, 10, 30, 50, 106, 111n, 165n, 179, 367, 679n, 838, 852n, 867, 876
Doors, The 119f., 274n
Dorsey, Thomas (Rev.) 255
Dorsey, Thomas A. (Georgia Tom) 299, 300n, 314, 326n, 522
Dos Passos, John 75
Douglas, Kirk 558
'Down Along The Cove' 6, 120, 168, 662, 797
'Down In The Flood (Crash On The Levee)' 7, 9, 111n, 309, 872
"Down In The Groove" 13, 343, 592–3, 840, 872
'Down The Highway' 337, 343, 397, 823
Drawn Blank 860
Drifters, The 90, 721n, 825n
'Drifter's Escape, The' 70, 109, 672n, 675, 696, 864–5
'Driftin' Too Far From Shore' 13, 557, 577, 824
'Drop Down Mama' 341n, 342–3
drugs/drug culture 3, 15, 194–205, 239, 250, 309, 369, 370, 855
Drummond, Tim 448n
Dryden, William 55
Duke Ellington *see* Ellington
Dukes, Laura 'Little Bit' 718n
Dumas, Alexandre (père et fils) 362

Dunbar, Aynsley 349
Dunbar, Paul Laurence 720
Duncan, Johnny (and The Blue Grass Boys) 116, 823n
'Duncan And Brady' 710, 732n, 748, 751f.
Dundas, Glen 94n, 165n, 251, 255, 513n, 576n, 648n, 750, 853n, 859n, 867n
Dunkirk Festival 860
Dupree, Champion Jack 299f.
'Dusty Old Fairgrounds' 542
'Dyin' Crapshooter's Blues, The' 319, 374, 523, 533ff., 538, 545, 546, 751–2
Dykes Magic City Trio 706
"Dylan" (album) 8, 15, 76, 104f., 167
Dylan, Sara 210–15, 220, 222, 265, 596
Dylan Concordance 56n, 372
"Dylan & The Dead" 13
Dylan Liberation Front 56n

Eaglin, Snooks 290, 726
'Early Morning Rain' 6, 164n, 575n
'East Virginia' 25
Eastwood, Clint 555
Eat the Document 60, 92n, 340n
Eddy, Duane 88, 90, 577, 631
Edward VII (as Prince of Wales) 719
Edwards, David Honeyboy 294
Edwards, Frank 364
Edwin Hawkins Singers 577n
Egan, Nick 568n
Egypt, Ancient 435–7
Ehrmann, Max 424n
'Eileen Aroon' 703
'11 Outlined Epitaphs' 80n, 84n, 201n, 429, 550, 560, 599–600, 628, 643, 863
Elgar, Edward 798
Eliot, George 70, 195, 606, 799, 876
Eliot, T. S. 2, 53f., 60, 66n, 71ff., 79n, 80n, 83, 139, 247n, 258, 342, 412n., 510, 578
Elkins-Payne Jubilee Singers 439n
Ellington, Duke 288n, 851
Elliott, Ramblin' Jack 22n, 38n, 212, 243, 289, 555n, 569, 732, 825, 870
Ellis, Shirley 652
Emerson, Ralph Waldo 75f., 206
'Emotionally Yours' 12, 263, 548, 568, 571–3, 575, 674, 841n
"Empire Burlesque" 12, 15, 383, 386, 548, 551–2, 556f., 563f., 566, 569, 571, 575, 576f., 633, 672, 775, 786, 837
Engel, Dave 254
Engels, Frederick 445n
English Romantics 194n
Eno, Brian 268, 269n
'Enough Is Enough' 316
Ernst, Max 473
Esquire (magazine) 249, 265, 843
Estes, Sleepy John 290, 292, 295, 302f., 305, 315n, 327n, 329n, 340ff., 348, 359f., 648, 756–7, 758
'Eternal Circle' 127, 429

Evans, David 227n, 375n, 518n, 520f., 525n, 538n
Evans, Joe 307n
Everly, Don 551n, 725
Everly, Ike 725
Everly, Phil 725
Everly Brothers, The 89f., 92, 166, 92ff., 108f., 164ff., 191, 724–5, 802, 806, 822, 828
Evers, Medgar 24, 36f., 320
'Every Grain Of Sand' 11, 64n, 377, 385, 391, 400–25, 461–2, 564, 606f., 641, 809, 840, 875
'Every Lady In The Land' 653
'Everything Is Broken' 594, 600, 602, 607, 611, 614f., 620, 631, 853
'Ev'rybody's Got To Die' 307
Exciters, The 93
Ezell, Will 650

fairy tales 634–702
   sexual psychology of 667
'Fame And Fortune' 632
Famous Hokum Boys 314n
Famous Myers Jubilee Singers 439n
'Fare Thee Well' 524–5
'Farewell Angelina' 128n, 129, 142f., 160n, 180, 435, 607n, 666, 759n
Farina, Dick (and Eric von Schmidt) 336, 694n
Farley, Christopher John 834
Farm Aid 861
Farm Aid II 861
Fats Domino *see* Domino
Faulkner, William 559
Felix, Julie 679n
Fellini, Federico 550
'Female Rambling Sailor, The' 704, 764
Ferlinghetti, Lawrence 80, 82f.
Fields, W. C. 701n
Fish, Stanley E. 375n
Fisk Jubilee Singers 719–20
Fitzgerald, Ella 85, 101, 303n
Fitzgerald, F. Scott 1, 52, 65, 68, 75, 151, 490
'Fixin' To Die' 280, 396
Flanagan, Bill 276n, 397, 421, 561n, 581, 835n, 836, 843
Flashback 212n, 859
Flatt, Lester 111n
Flatt & Scruggs xviii, 111, 570n, 716, 725n
Flaubert, Gustave 641n
Fleetwood Mac 793
Fleetwoods, The 90
Flower Power 119n
Flynn, Errol 560–1
folk art and culture 37, 44ff., 53
   American folk revival 705
   Anglo-American 639
folk music 17–44, 163, 573
   American 24
   Appalachian 26n
   black 24, 29n, 35, 36, 278
   Cowboy 24, 29
   English 695

influences in Dylan's songs 24, 36, 54, 700
   North American 532
   Southern Poor White 24ff., 278
   traditional 272
   Yankee 24
folk tales 635
folk-ballads 75, 804
folklore, European 638
folk-rock 60, 71, 116f., 137n, 435n, 465
folksong 637, 700, 704
"Folkways: A Vision Shared" 837
food, genetic manipulation of 874
'Fool Such As I, A' 8, 106
'Fools Like Me' 168
'Foot Of Pride' 14, 426, 438n, 441n, 470, 472–9, 560, 875
'Footprints In The Sand' 409
'Footprints In The Snow' 823
Ford, Tennessee Ernie 33, 85, 492n
'Fore Day Blues' 312n, 359
Forehand, Blind Mamie 439n
'Forever Young' 8, 12, 525n, 832, 852n
"40 Red, White And Blue Shoestrings" 226n
Foster, Stephen 718–9, 721–2
Fountain, Nigel 42n
'4 o'clock Blues' 316, 348n
Four Seasons 93
Four Tops, The 825n
'4th Time Around' 55, 68, 147–9, 796
Foxx, Norm & The Rob Roys 813n, 822
Francis, Connie 91
'Frankie & Albert' 704, 706, 707–8, 709f., 745, 748, 782
'Frankie & Johnny' 704, 708
'Frankie And Johnny' 706, 708
Franklin, Aretha 577n
Frater, Alexander 685
Frazier, Warren 439n
Freedom Singers, The 306
Freeman, Eddie 84n
"*Freewheelin' Bob Dylan, The*" 2n, 3, 123n, 207n, 245n, 281, 295, 306, 308, 532, 587n, 601n, 661n, 852n
'Freight Train Blues' 43
Freud, Sigmund 630, 793
Friedman, Albert B. 761n
French Symbolists 2, 194n, 201n
'Frisco Whistle Blues' 338
Frizzell, Lefty 108n
'Froggie Went A-Courtin' ' 15, 331n, 521, 533n, 642, 733ff., 736–7
'From A Buick 6' 42n, 96, 140, 151, 341f.
Frost, Robert 667n
'Fugitive, The' 166
Fuller, Blind Boy 292f., 303, 332, 346, 349n, 354, 371, 724, 726f., 731f.
Fuller, Jesse 3, 288f., 676
Fulmer, David 547
Fulson, Lowell 103
Fury, Billy 93, 349

Gable, Clark 560
Gainsbourg, Serge 616n
Gaither, Bill 338
Galway, James 859
Garcia, Jerry 290, 725n, 758n
Garon, Paul and Beth 302n, 305
'Gates Of Eden, The' 4, 49, 57, 61, 67, 134n, 246n, 439n, 482, 696
Gay, John 822
Gaye, Marvin 576
Gell, David 88
Genet, Jean 176n, 196n
George, Barbara 93
'George Jackson' 7, 10, 177
'Georgia Bound' 600
Georgia Crackers 732
'Georgia Crawl' 524–5, 649n, 731
'Georgia Rag' 524n, 684
Georgia Tom *see* Dorsey
Gershwin, George 694, 848
'Get Your Rocks Off' 649
Gibson, Clifford 337, 500n
Gibson, Don 89, 110f.
Gilbert and Sullivan 24, 443n
Gill, Andy 255, 851
Gilmore, Gene 319
Gilroy, Paul 719f.
Ginsberg, Allen 46, 78, 80, 82ff., 92n, 187, 279, 370, 414n, 416f., 551n, 609, 665, 731, 845, 848
'Girl I Left Behind, The' 605, 765
'Girl I Love, She Got Long Curly Hair, The' 341–2
'Girl Of The North Country' 3, 140, 185, 525n, 653, 655, 828, 852n
Gladys Knight & The Pips 93
Gleason, Ralph J. 42n
Glover, Tony 284, 713, 736
'Go Down Moses' 564n
'Go Way Little Boy' 576
'God Knows' 359, 667n, 673, 676f., 701
Godrich, John 719
'Goin' Down Slow' 329, 460–1, 814
'Goin' To Acapulco' 383
'Going Country' 166
'Going, Going, Gone' 178ff., 299, 600n
'Going To The River' 824
Goldberg, Steven 177, 195ff., 204f.
Golden Gate Jubilee Quartet 439n
'Golden Vanity, The' 704, 870
Goldsmith, Olver 443n
Gone With The Wind 559
'Gonna Change My Way Of Thinking' 39, 208, 244, 246, 524, 677, 784
Good, Jack 349
"Good As I Been To You" 14f., 26f., 635, 657, 703f., 705, 711f., 716f., 727, 730, 732, 736, 739, 756, 780, 782, 813, 833, 838, 840
Gordon, Jimmy 748
Gordon, Robert W. 748
gospel (music) 7, 13, 23, 162, 173n, 206, 216, 231,

239n, 288, 308, 326n, 331, 359n, 364f., 394f., 522, 624, 690–1, 800, 818
country gospel 527, 823
recordings of xxiv–xxv
'Gospel Plow' 18, 359, 600
'Got My Mind Made Up' 13, 561, 577, 839
'Gotta Serve Somebody' 10, 15, 26, 212n, 231, 234, 240, 246n, 307, 564n, 575n, 594, 848, 852n
'Gotta Travel On' 164
Grainger, Porter 533n
Grammy, Lifetime Achievement 848–9
Grammys xxi, 109n, 848, 850, 854, 862
'Grand Coulee Dam' 848n
Grand Ole Opry 167n, 718n
Grant, Cogi 85
Grape, Moby 119
Grapes Of Wrath, The see Steinbeck
Grateful Dead, The 13, 165n, 173n, 290, 327, 343, 716, 725n, 852n, 861
Graves, Blind Roosevelt 365
Graves, Robert 82n, 488n, 490, 636
Great Pop Protest Craze 117–18
Great Society, The 3
Great White Wonder bootlegs 852
"Greatest Hits II" 15
"Greatest Hits Volume 3" 15f., 626
Greek mythology 499, 642
Greek tragedy 590
Green, Lil 366, 370n
Green, Peter 349
Greene, Graham 273n, 468
Greenhill, Manny 751
Greenwich Village 3, 17f., 22n, 28n, 56n, 60, 213n, 228, 243n, 252f., 278, 284, 286, 288, 291, 296, 328, 378n, 705, 729, 731f., 841, 870
'Grievin' Me Blues' 314
Grimm Brothers *see* Brothers Grimm
'Groom's Still Waiting At The Altar, The' 11, 15, 235n, 322, 384f., 426–63, 555n, 780, 839, 875
Grossman, Albert 21n, 252
Grossman, Stefan 749ff.
Grosz, Walter 728
grunge-rock 304
guitar, Dylan's playing of 39, 131, 141, 714, 733, 752, 757, 776
Gulf War 854
Gunfighter, The 560ff., 579ff.
Gunter, Arthur 308
Guralnick, Peter 89n, 344–5, 347, 348n, 353n, 375n
Guterson, David 602n
Guthrie, Woody 3, 19ff., 36, 44n, 46, 51f., 75, 83, 110n, 126, 163, 206, 212, 241n, 276n, 283, 299, 362, 468, 503n, 526, 555n, 644, 650, 658, 664, 713, 781n, 800, 815, 825f., 828, 831, 845, 848
Gutman, David 250
Guy, Buddy 652n
'Gypsy Davey' 713

'Had A Dream About You Baby' 13, 316
Hagan, Sean 607
Haggard, Merle 108n
Haley, Bill 85f.
Halliwell-Phillips 634, 660
Hammett, Dashiel 559
Hammond, John 3, 268
Hammond, John, Jnr 725
Handy, W.C. 301, 319, 326
'Handy Dandy' 14, 337, 668, 672f., 691, 694ff., 699, 734, 875
'Hang Me, O Hang Me (Been All Around This World)' 826
"Hanging In The Balance" 131n
Hank Ballard & The Midnighters 675
Hank Penny & His Radio Cowboys 664
'Happy Birthday' 848n
Hard Hearted Papa' 333
'Hard Rain's A-Gonna Fall, A' 2f., 79, 80n, 122–4, 201n, 207, 247, 249, 380, 469, 617, 637, 653, 852n, 859n
"Hard Rain" (album) 9, 11
Hard Rain (TV film) 10n, 502, 841, 868
'Hard Times' 15, 717, 722–4, 739, 783, 861
'Har Times Ain't Gone No Where' 339
Hardin, Lane 717
Harding, John Wesley 711, 727
Hardy, Thomas 203, 567
harmonica, Dylan's playing of 39, 239, 284n, 586, 594, 614–15, 876
Harmonica Frank Floyd 715, 725
Harrell, Kelly 732
Harris, Blind Jesse 749n
Harris, Emmylou 722
Harris, Peppermint 349
Harrison, George 94n, 114, 147n, 172
Harrison, Wilbert 274n
Harvey, P. J. 773
Havens, Richie 846
Hawkins, Jack 456
Hawkins, Walter Buddy Boy 316
Hawks 16
Hayes, Bill 33n, 492n
'Hazel' 161, 180
'He Was A Friend Of Mine' 80
'Heart Of Mine' 12
'Heartland' 702
Hearts of Fire 13, 316, 840, 842f., 859n
Heat-Moon, William Least 29n, 52n, 718n, 762–3
Heller, Joseph 49, 558n, 676
Helm, Levon 95n
Hemingway, Ernest 30, 554, 559
Henderson, Hamish 536n
Henderson, Joe 93
Henderson, Rosa 533n
Hendrix, Jimi 811, 843, 864
Henry, Clarence Frogman 92
Hercules (Heracles) 488, 491, 493f.
Herdman, John 256, 381n
'Hero Blues' 550
Hester, Carolyn 284

'Hey Lawdy Mama – The France Blues' 29n, 319, 364–5, 396
'Hey, Little Richard' 110n
Heylin, Clinton 250, 254, 276f., 383
Hicks, Minnie 355
'Hide Me In Thy Bosom' 528
Higginbotham, Thomas 652
High Level Ranters 711
'Highlands' 16, 79, 82, 591, 636, 786, 791f., 810f., 812, 815, 820, 822, 828f., 831, 834, 875
'Highway 51' 281
'Highway 51 Blues' 281
Highway 61 294 *passim*
'Highway 61 Revisited' (song) 96, 140, 477–8, 699, 852n
"Highway 61 Revisited" (album) 5, 8–9, 12, 60f., 71, 80n, 98, 111, 120, 129, 151, 155, 181, 196, 215, 248f., 293, 560, 628, 661n, 699, 741, 873
'Highway 61 Revisited' (TV *Arena* film) 286
Hill, King Solomon 316
hillbilly 23, 25, 27, 31n, 36, 98, 102, 287, 344, 362, 390, 521, 577, 645, 717, 724f., 732, 735, 741, 774
    recordings xxiv–xxv
Hinchey, John 266, 853
Hinton, Nigel 563, 568–9, 575ff., 579, 621, 775
Hitchcock, Alfred 550
Hogan, Homer 491, 500n
Hokum Boys 395n, 522
Hokum Jug Band 395n
Holcomb, Roscoe 717, 745f., 761–2, 765
'Hold On' 600–1
Holly, Buddy 90f., 94, 101, 106ff., 116, 270, 343, 448n, 578, 601, 632, 652, 722
Hollywood 23, 465, 502, 543, 551, 556, 561–2, 566, 580, 583
    film industry, influences in Dylan's work 550–63, 589, 701n
Holmes, Winston 648
Holy Rollers 23
Homer, the slut 255, 617n, 627n, 630n, 672n, 687n, 688
'Honey Just Allow Me One More Chance' 281f., 587n
'Honeymoon Blues' 315f.
Hooker, John Lee 286, 329, 726
Hopkins, Lightnin' 150n, 304f., 368n, 581n
Hopper, Denis 859
Horace Heidt & His Orchestra 728
Horovitz, David 122–4, 125–6
Horovitz, Michael 43n
horses 396–7
house (music) 857
House, Son 290, 292, 298, 341, 347n, 359f., 367f., 372, 378n, 790, 826
'House Carpenter' 164n, 759n
Housemartins, The 508
Houston, Cisco 19n, 526, 732, 825n
'How Blue Can You Get?' 334
'Howling At The Moon' 823

Howard, Rosetta 467
'Howdido' 644
Howell, Peg Leg (Joshua Barnes) 280n, 355, 721, 825n
Hoy, Lawrence 711
Hull, Papa Harvey (& Long 'Cleve' Reed) *see* Papa Harvey Hull
Humble Pie 114
Hunter, Alberta 317
Hunter, Ivory Joe 746
Hunter, Robert 13, 344
Hurley, Michael 519n
'Hurricane' 15, 80, 185, 260, 272, 848n
Hurston, Zora Neale 719
Hurt, Mississippi John 38, 290, 306, 330, 365, 706ff., 746
Huston, John 551n, 554, 559n
Hutchison, Frank 458, 460, 533n, 741, 745ff., 773f.
Huxley, Aldous 194f.

'I Ain't Got No Home' 848n
'I Am A Lonesome Hobo' 207
'I And I' 11, 243n, 408, 485, 799, 875
'I Ain't Superstitious' 232
'I Believe' 400–1
'I Believe I'll Dust My Broom' 352–3
'I Believe In You' 234f.
'I Don't Believe You' 12, 108, 116, 140, 429, 865
'I Don't Hurt Anymore' 167n
'I Dreamed I Saw St. Augustine' 6, 9, 58, 74, 226, 830
'I Forgot More' 92, 162f.
'I Got To Cross The River Jordan' 528–9
'I Have To Do My Time' 333–4, 335
'I Love You Porgy' 137n
'I Pity The Poor Immigrant' 6, 232n, 392n
'I Saw A Man With No Eyes' 653
'I Saw A Peacock With A Fiery Tail' 653, 668
'I Shall Be Free' 1, 19n, 55, 306, 327n, 359n, 383, 526, 560, 650, 661n, 672n
'I Shall Be Free No. 10' 1, 19n, 327n, 397n, 495, 527, 659, 673, 698
'I Shall Be Released' 7, 9, 28n, 92n, 200, 208, 261, 848n, 852n, 862, 872
'I Threw It All Away' 32, 103, 209
'I Wanna Be Your Lover' 12, 226, 322, 336
'I Want A Good Woman' 363
'I Want It Awful Bad' 361
'I Want You' 7, 10, 16, 109, 115, 144
'I Was Young When I Left Home' 276–7, 278, 280, 283f., 291
'I Wonder If I Care As Much' 802, 806
'Idiot Wind' 10, 14, 73, 183, 211, 213, 465, 575, 843, 868
'If Dogs Run Free' 83n, 330
'If Not For You' 171, 174, 863
'If You Gotta Go, Go Now' 7, 140, 783
'If You See Her, Say Hello' 185, 356
Ikettes 93
'I'll Be Your Baby Tonight' 6, 68, 110f., 120

'I'll Keep It With Mine' 12, 465
'I'll Remember You' 358, 554, 571, 575
'I'm A-Ridin' Old Paint' 29, 365
'I'm Movin' On' 167n
'I'm Not There (1956)' 342
Impressions, The 212n
'In My Time Of Dyin' ' 165n, 269n, 365
'In Search Of Little Sadie' 163
'In The Garden' 211n, 236, 241, 506, 564n, 852n
'In The Summertime' 694n
Incredible String Band 347, 713
Industrial Revolution 46, 48n
    technology 51
"Infidels" 11, 13, 211, 262, 386, 392, 426, 429, 458, 464f., 470–1, 480, 508, 513, 551, 556f., 563, 684, 870
Interpretation of Dreams 630
"Invasion Of The Bodysnatchers" 699, 847
Iron Butterfly 119
'Is Your Love In Vain?' 191, 217, 361, 497
'Isis' 9, 12, 167, 186, 213, 216, 261f., 340n, 437, 490
Isis (journal) 74n, 84n, 167n, 255, 752n
Isle of Wight Festival 42n, 92n, 114, 499, 855
Isley Brothers 93, 721
Israel, performances in 858, 869
'It Ain't Me, Babe' 4, 30f., 54, 92n, 111n, 342, 348, 465, 852n, 862
'It Hurts Me Too' 168n
'It Keeps Rainin'' 824
'It Takes A Lot To Laugh, It Takes A Train To Cry' 14, 40ff., 44, 80, 103, 310–13, 876
'It's All Over Now, Baby Blue' 4, 12, 23, 41, 49, 140, 479, 676, 852n, 876
'It's Alright Ma (I'm Only Bleeding)' 4, 133f., 234n, 338, 340n, 462n, 483, 852n

Jack Kelly & His South Memphis Jug Band 293
'Jack Monroe' 764
'Jack Munro' 758
'Jack-A-Roe' 758f., 760f., 763ff., 767, 774, 778
'Jack O'Diamonds Blues' 350–1
Jackson, Aunt Mollie 776–7, 778–80
Jackson, Bessie (Lucille Bogan) 684n, 746
Jackson, George 177n., 330, 525n, 606, 755n
Jackson, Jack 88
Jackson, Jim 19n, 199n, 270, 327
Jackson, John 867n, 868
Jackson, Papa Charlie 299, 348n, 354, 648
Jackson, Wanda 315n
Jacobs, Joseph 635
Jacobs, Walter 648n
Jagger, Mick 98, 117f., 332
James Alley Blues 279n, 309
James, Elmore 319, 352f., 522
James, Etta 350, 652
James, Henry 54
James, Jesse (blues singer) 293, 648f.
James, Skip 274n, 290, 298f., 316, 344ff., 354, 712, 717, 727, 739n, 782, 877
Jansch, Bert 714, 727–8n

Jaxon, Frankie Half-Pint 395n
Jay & The Americans 93
jazz 84n, 303, 356, 467, 744
Jefferson, Blind Lemon 3, 18, 279f., 282n, 299,
    312n, 315, 319, 330, 339, 342, 350, 354,
    356ff., 366, 368n, 371, 378, 396, 518f., 522,
    744, 756, 759n, 781
Jefferson Airplane 119f., 173n, 274n
Jennings, Waylon 750, 751
Jenny Clayton & The Memphis Jug Band 278f.
'Jericho' 164
'Jesus Make Up My Dying Bed' 165n, 269n, 365
'Jesus Met The Woman At The Well' 285, 680
'Jet Pilot' 12
Jewish roots, Dylan's 437n, 566
'Jim Jones' 712f., 730, 738, 782, 877
'Jinx Blues Part I, The' 360, 372n
Joe Evans & Arthur McClain 715
Joel, Billy 789
'Joey' 80, 185, 242n, 333, 560, 707
'John Brown' 730, 852
John Kirkpatrick & Sue Harris 711
John Paul II, Pope 847
'John The Revelator' 165n, 269n, 279n, 372n, 826,
    827n
'John Wesley Harding' (song) 34f., 160
"John Wesley Harding" (album) 6, 8f., 30, 33ff.,
    48, 58, 70, 110f., 120, 159f., 170, 181, 196,
    207, 209, 215, 226, 248, 392, 601
Johns, Glyn 11
Johnson Mountain Boys 752
Johnson, Bessie 691n
Johnson, Blind Willie 165n, 207n, 269f., 280, 285,
    372n, 521, 826
Johnson, Lonnie 18n, 280n, 288, 305, 314, 333,
    335, 339, 370n, 624, 717, 728f.
Johnson, Robert 37n, 229n, 274n, 277, 278, 280,
    282f., 292, 297, 299, 312n, 313, 315–6,
    317ff., 322n, 330f., 345–6, 353n, 354, 358ff.,
    375n, 517–18, 600n, 651f., 723, 739, 758,
    782
Johnson, Tommy 293n, 319, 325n, 357, 360n,
    824n
'Jokerman' 11, 47n, 64n, 211n, 224n, 232n, 234n,
    237n, 263f., 359n, 381n, 426, 452, 464–516,
    586, 676, 799, 840f., 854, 855, 875
Jones, Alberta 346
Jones, Curtis 281, 825
Jones, Floyd 274n
Jones, Jake 354
Jones, Nic 705, 713f.
Jones, Richard 302
Jong, Erica 819, 822
Joplin, Janis 252
Joplin, Scott 721
Jordan, Louis 334n, 355n
Jordanaires, The 164, 326n
Joyce, Jim 718
'Julius & Ethel' 470, 472, 761
Jumpin' Judy 336
Jung, Carl 491–3, 495, 496n, 500, 631

Junior Walker & The All-Stars 356
'Just A Dream (On My Mind)' 302
'Just As Well To Get Ready, You Got To Die' 528
'Just Like A Woman' 5, 57, 149, 454, 850, 852n,
    864, 872, 876
'Just Like Tom Thumb's Blues' 7, 10, 41, 83, 115n,
    163, 301, 584, 661, 823

Kant, Immanuel 53, 244n
Kantner, Paul 162, 173n
'Kassey Jones' 325
Keaton, Buster 590
Keats, John xviii, 64n, 489f., 505, 656, 693n
Kennedy Center Award xxi
Kermode, Frank 249
Kerouac, Jack 53, 75, 80, 82ff., 297, 566
Kerridge, Roy 21n, 719n
Kid Stormy Weather 370n
Kidson, Frank and Ethel 713
Kind-Hearted Woman 739n
King, B.B. 292n, 326, 334, 489, 857
King, Carole 55
King, Claude 93
King, Martin Luther 178n, 848, 862
King, Rodney 854
Kingsley, Charles 244n
'Kingsport Town' 14, 277n, 643
Kinks, The 118
Kirkpatrick, John (& Sue Harris) 711
Kissinger, Henry 873
"Knocked Out Loaded" 12, 224n, 300, 463, 551,
    557–8, 560–1, 563, 577, 672, 713n, 839
'Knockin' On Heaven's Door' 8, 528, 801, 852n
Knopfler, Mark 448, 470, 596
Knox, Buddy 89
Koerner, Ray and Glover 713
Koerner, Spider John 284, 289, 735, 750, 752
Kooper, Al 839
Koran, the 638
Korner, Alexis 328n, 750
Kramer, Daniel 251
Kristofferson, Kris 13, 577
Krogsgaard, Michael 251, 255
Ku Klux Klan 178n, 542

Lacey, Rube 347n
'Lady Of Carlisle, The' 704
Laine, Frankie 400, 721
'Lakes Of Pontchartrain' 730
Lancaster, Burt 558
Landau, John 120
Landy, Elliott 521, 860
Langbaum, Robert 64
Langland, William 46, 671
Lanois, Daniel 13, 614, 626f., 789, 795, 797, 836
Larkin, Philip 699
'Lass From The Low Country, The' 502
'Last Thoughts On Woody Guthrie' 14, 20f., 340n,
    362, 560
Lawrence, D. H. 48f., 54, 58, 69n, 75, 140, 382,
    657, 659n

'Lay Down Your Weary Tune' 12, 75f., 193,
   197–9, 200, 202, 203–4, 327n, 429, 631, 871
'Lay, Lady, Lay' 92, 103, 160, 166n, 239, 466,
   526n, 725n, 855, 861
Leadbelly 18n, 278, 282n, 292, 299, 312n, 333,
   336, 378n, 518, 522, 526, 533, 644, 650, 717,
   749, 775n, 781n
Lear, Edward 480n, 672, 693n
Leary, Timothy 118, 195
'Leaving Home' 706
'Leaving Of Liverpool, The' 525n
Leavis, F. R. 46–7, 59, 71n, 79, 382–3
Ledford, Fiddlin' Steve 716
Lee, Brenda 86, 91, 98, 632
Lee, C. P. 254
Lee, Julia 726
'Legend In My Time' 111n
'Legionnaire's Disease' 299
Lehrman, Paul D. 839
Leiber & Stoller 325
Lennon, John 114, 117, 147n, 250, 340n, 581
'Lenny Bruce' 11, 831, 850
'Leopard-Skin Pill-Box Hat' 68f., 150–1, 169,
   173f., 302, 304, 853
Lester, Ketty 93
'Let It Be Me' 6, 31, 166, 525n, 725n
'Let Me Die In My Footsteps' 245n, 461–2
'Let Me Squeeze Your Lemon' 361
'Let's Keep It Between Us' 306, 384f., 875
'Let's Learn To Live & Love Again' 111n
Letterman, David 318, 362n, 464n, 515n, 862
Levy, Jacques 185, 590f.
Lewis, Archie 282n
Lewis, Furry 6, 32, 168, 229n, 270, 290, 292n,
   294, 326, 329, 360, 364, 368, 395n, 746
Lewis, Jerry Lee 6, 32, 89, 91, 103n, 111, 168,
   174, 459, 519, 708, 721, 728
Lewis, Noah 327–8
Lewis, Richard 393n
Lewis, Smiley 680
Lewis, Willie 439n
'License To Kill' 464n, 465f., 470f., 515n, 862
Lick the Tins 689n
Lifetime Achievement Grammy 848
Lifetime Achievement Oscars 850
Lightfoot, Gordon 164, 849, 865
Lightnin' Hopkins see Hopkins
'Like A Rolling Stone' 5, 55, 111n, 116, 139f., 161,
   164, 170, 196, 273n, 293, 596n, 661, 696,
   790, 803, 852n, 855, 868, 876
'Lily, Rosemary And The Jack Of Hearts' 185,
   591n, 782
Lincoln, Abraham (US President) 718
Lincoln, Charley 354
Lindley, John 551, 555n, 560, 872
Lipscomb, Mance 38, 290f., 349f., 518
literature/literary influences 45–84
   American 74ff.
'Little Laura Blues' 343–4
'Little Maggie' 716f., 783
Little Milton 297n

'Little Moses' 866
'Little Queen Of Spades' 316, 360
Little Richard 89ff., 97, 101, 108f., 268, 270,
   314n, 315n, 348, 646f., 649, 675
'Little Sadie' 163, 168n, 525n
Little Walter 367
Little Willie John 793
Live Aid 12, 112n, 835, 856, 861, 873
'Living The Blues' 168
Lloyd, A.L. 84n, 529, 531, 711, 714, 747–8, 761
'Lo And Behold' 98, 696
Lockwood, Robert Junior 651f.
Lofton, Cripple Clarence 317, 355, 361, 650
Lomax, Alan 21ff., 26, 29n, 48n, 137n, 199n, 273,
   281, 293f., 303n, 308, 321, 325n, 326n, 334,
   336, 350, 357n, 532, 631, 645, 647, 674, 706,
   719n, 721, 731n, 732, 735n, 743–4, 749f.,
   777, 827
Lomax, John A. 336, 523n, 526, 533, 706, 732,
   735n, 748f.
Lomax, Ruby T. 523n, 533
'Lone Pilgrim' 15, 751, 756, 758, 776–80, 784
'Lonesome Bedroom Blues' 281, 825
'Lonesome Death Of Hattie Carroll, The' 24, 39,
   55, 134, 140, 507, 631, 759n, 854
'Lonesome House Blues' 315
'Lonesome Town' 601n, 632
'Long Ago, Far Away' 128f., 429n
'Long Lonesome Blues' 371
'Long Time Gone' 645f.
'Long Time Man Feel Bad' 164n
Longfellow, Henry W. 75, 76–7, 605n, 665
Lord Buckley 591n
'Lord Protect My Child' 14, 266, 470–1, 875
Lord's Prayer, The 650
Lost Generation, The 75
Loudermilk, John D. 89
'Love Henry' 15, 575, 666, 740, 753n, 756, 758,
   765–76, 778, 781, 783, 829, 833
'Love Is Just A Four-Letter Word' 550
'Love Minus Zero/No Limit' 5, 58f., 128n, 140,
   188, 263, 429, 866
'Love Rescue Me' 859n
'Love Sick' 789f., 796, 806, 809, 829, 875
Lovelle, Herb 303n
Lovin' Spoonful 698
Lowell, Robert 667n
Lucas, Jane 300n, 647
Lucas, Trevor 711
Lunsford, Bascom Lamar 358n
Lynch, David 792n
lyrics, of Bob Dylan
   rhyming schemes 421, 427f., 433, 446, 475–6,
      487f., 503–4, 617–21, 801ff.
   rhythm 415
Lyrics 1962–1985 41n, 129n, 141n, 143n, 147n,
   207n, 231n, 238n, 243n, 296, 305, 321, 334,
   363, 378, 383ff., 391, 401n, 411, 429–30,
   448, 456, 463, 482n, 661n, 716n

Mabey, Richard 117
Macalister, Charles 711
McCarthyism 472
McCartney, Paul 7, 172, 857
McClennan, Tommy 280n, 315, 319, 338, 364,
    518, 522n, 726
McCloud, Green 347
MacColl, Ewan 65, 465, 529, 531, 774
McCollum, Mother 365
McCormick, Mack 38
McCoy, Joe 293, 337, 724
McCoy, Viola 355, 533n
McDaniels, Harry 301
McDonald's 705, 860
MacDonogh, Steve 67
McDowell, Fred 290, 294, 325
McFarland, Barrel House Buck 317n
McGhee, Brownie 279, 290
McGrath, Scott 82n, 251
McGuinn, Roger 840
MacGuire, Barry 465, 719
McKinney, Mamie 533n
McLean, Roscoe 746
MacLeish, Archibald 667n
McLuhan, Marshall 45, 53, 373, 388, 454n
McMullen, Fred 315
Macon, Uncle Dave 302, 717, 825
McTell, Blind Willie 11, 298ff., 313, 317, 319, 321,
    335, 337, 345, 369n, 374, 453, 490–1,
    517–47, 648, 684, 704, 726, 731, 737, 740ff.,
    745, 749, 751ff., 756, 760n, 783–4, 854–5
McTell, Ralph 519n
McVie, John 349
Maddox Brothers and Rose 725
'Maggie's Farm' 5, 188, 367, 852n, 872
Magritte, René 144, 226, 631
Mailer, Norman 45n, 65, 75, 113, 174
'Make You Feel My Love' 16, 605, 790, 787, 807,
    827, 832f.
Makem, Tommy 711n, 713; see also Clancy
    Brothers
Malcolm X 178n
'Mama You Been On My Mind' 111n
'Man Gave Names To All The Animals' 231f.,
    675–6, 758
'Man In Me, The' 171, 174, 176
'Man In The Long Black Coat, The' 558, 570,
    603ff., 614
'Man In The Wilderness, The' 660
'Man Of Constant Sorrow' 43f., 703, 781
'Man Of Peace' 263, 317, 323, 458, 469, 555n,
    564n, 745, 783
'Man On The Street' 652
Manchester Free Trade Hall xx, 16, 115n, 853
Manfred Mann 115
Mann, Woody 519
Marcels, The 92, 94
Marcus, Greil xx, 9n, 28n, 56, 57n, 89n, 101n,
    108f., 252, 325, 665, 705, 725, 746n, 785n,
    791
Marcuson, Alan 42n

Mariposa Folk Festival 290, 539n, 569
Márquez, Gabriel García 435
Marsden, Beryl 93
Martha, Saint 610n
Martin, Carl 354
Martin, Dean 85
Martin, Sara 355
Marvelettes, The 92
Marvell, Andrew 545, 571
Marvin, Lee 104
Marx, Karl 445n, 873f.
Marx Brothers 550
Marxism 387–8, 445n
"Masterpieces" 10
'Masters Of War' 3, 22, 125f., 134, 206, 266, 679,
    849n, 852n, 854, 871, 876
Maurice Williams & The Zodiacs 93, 98
Maxwell, Robert 846
May, Brian 574
May, Hannah 300n
Mayall, John 349
'Maybe Someday' 13, 224n, 563, 578, 831, 837,
    839
'Me And My Chauffeur Blues' 274n, 302–4
Mayfield, Curtis 44n, 212n
'Meet Me In The Morning' 39, 185
Mellers, Wilfrid 36, 39, 45, 119, 250
Melody Maker 114, 389, 862
Melville, Herman 83n
'Memphis Blues Again' 5, 81, 96, 151f., 156, 179,
    189, 208, 301, 330, 357, 499, 598, 852n
Memphis Jug Band 282, 297, 320, 349n, 368,
    649n, 726
Memphis Minnie 270, 282, 297, 293, 299, 301ff.,
    305, 314n, 337, 357, 364, 648n, 663, 724
Memphis Slim 307–8
Mercedes-Benz, as symbol of western
    corruption 434
Mezzrow, Mezz 467
Michel, Steve 251
Michelangelo (Buonarroti) 502–4, 575
Mickey & Sylvia 352
Microsoft 705
'Milk Cow Blues' 311–12, 331, 341f., 359–60, 647
'Milkcow Blues Boogie' 104
Mill, John Stewart 244n
Millay, Edna St Vincent 457–8n
Miller, Arthur 75
Miller, Lillian 313
Miller, Mitch 85
'Million Dollar Bash' 9, 69, 55, 831
'Million Miles' 16, 788, 790–1, 792, 794, 809, 825
Milton, John 441n, 456, 507
'Minstrel Boy' 112, 499, 653
Mintz, Elliot 'Chewy' 843f.
Miracles, The 92
Mirroneau, Serge 372
'Miss Mary Jane' 826
Mississippi Sheiks 357, 715f., 740–1, 754f., 782
'Mr. Bojangles' 8
'Mr. Tambourine Man' 4f., 28n, 111n, 119, 141n,

142, 152n, 195f., 260, 452, 480, 490, 511, 644n, 693n, 786, 833f., 840, 852n, 871
Mitchell, Joni 326, 429
Mitchell's Christian Singers 366n, 439n
Mitchum, Robert 558
'Mixed-Up Confusion' 7, 10, 12
Modigliani, Amedeo 84n
Mohammed 365
Monet, Claude 631, 877
Monitor (pop journal) 389
Monk, Thelonius 84n
'Monkey Man Blues' 355, 361
Monroe, Bill 33n, 762n, 823f.
Monroe Brothers (Bill and Charlie) 725
Monsarrat, Nicholas 456
Montgomery, Eurreal Little Brother 298, 367
Monty Python 473
'Moonshiner' 14, 781, 813, 815, 822
Moore, Alice 366
Moore, Merrill 652
Moore, Whistlin' Alex 651, 688
"More Bob Dylan's Greatest Hits" 7, 872
Morrison, Van 266f., 269, 288, 310, 417n, 824, 870f.
Moscow Poetry Festival 852
Moss, Buddy 299f., 518n
Moss, Wayne 32n
'Most Likely You Go Your Way (And I'll Go Mine)' 68, 150, 507
'Most Of The Time' 14, 263, 559, 595–6, 602, 614, 626, 841, 875
'Mother Earth' 307–8
'Motherless Children Have A Hard Time' 269, 285, 521
Mothers of Invention *see* Zappa
'Motorpsycho Nightmare' 97, 116, 189, 527, 550, 560, 659
Motown 11, 92, 431
MTV 467, 592, 605, 672, 705, 844
"MTV Unplugged™" (album) 15, 431n, 626
'MTV Unplugged™' (video) 851f., 877; *see also* "Bob Dylan Unplugged"
Muddy Waters 243, 274n, 279ff., 283n, 291, 306n, 319f., 322, 338, 342, 363, 369n, 517
Muir, Andrew 255n, 671f., 806f., 812, 815f., 819n, 827n, 829, 847n
Murray, Pete 8
Musical Retrospective tour 391
'My Back Pages' 4, 119, 177, 266
'My Blue Eyed Jane' 166n
'My Handy Man' 367
'My Heart's In The Highlands' 815–16
'My Life In A Stolen Moment' 283, 335, 520n
Myers, Augie 797
mysticism 194–205; *see also* drugs

Naipaul, V.S. 275n, 759
'Naomi Wise' 164n
Napier, Simon 519
Narváez, Peter 271, 273, 349, 367
Nashville 103, 110f., 162, 166, 595, 615

"Nashville Airplane" 111n
"Nashville Skyline" xvii, 6, 29ff., 70, 92, 110f., 120, 159ff., 166n, 170, 174, 177, 181, 204f., 209, 215, 248, 349, 783, 828, 865, 867
'Nashville Skyline Rag' 111n
National Film Theatre (NFT) 842
'Nearer, My God To Thee' 459–60
'Need A Woman' 14, 352, 384, 447, 666, 875
'Need Your Love So Bad' 793
Negro Spirituals *see under* black music
'Neighborhood Bully' 436, 469, 470, 472
Nelson, Paul 347, 425, 713
Nelson, Ricky 87, 89, 91, 100, 601, 632
Nelson, Romeo 650
Nelson, Sister Mary, Rev. 365
Nelson, Willie 596, 728, 849
'Never Go Wrong Blues' 367
'Never Gonna Be The Same Again' 556, 568, 575, 640
'Never Say Goodbye' 8, 41, 126, 180, 208, 465, 823, 871
Never-Ending Tour 112n, 703, 730n, 839, 855, 858, 860, 867
Neville, Aaron 722
New Christy Minstrels 719
'New Danville Girl' 19n, 83, 525n, 560, 580, 582n, 584f., 586–8, 590, 592, 602–3, 759n, 875
'New Huntsville Jail' 307
New Lost City Ramblers 716
"New Morning" xvii, 6ff., 75, 77, 105f., 170ff., 176–7, 181, 190, 226, 385, 633
'New New Minglewood Blues' 327
'New Pony' 39, 191, 215f., 316, 370, 372
Newman, Paul 550, 555
Newman, Randy 395
Newport Folk Festival 23, 117, 212n, 273, 290, 306, 320, 325, 328, 347, 372, 378n, 644n, 707, 713, 716, 752, 781n
Newton, Isaac 424
NFT (National Film Theatre) 842
Nickerson, Charlie Bozo 371
'Night Time Is The Right Time' 349–50, 823
Niles, John Jacob 348, 773
'Nine Below Zero' 316–17, 823
'1913 Massacre' 20n
'No More Auction Block' 781
'No Time To Think' 78, 192, 215, 220, 223ff., 441n, 509, 602, 871
Noble, George 331f.
'Nobody 'Cept You' 356–7, 663
Norman, Philip 842
North Carolina Ramblers 706
'North Country Blues' 25, 128n, 134f., 140, 264, 347, 452, 465, 837
Norton, George A. 301
'Not Dark Yet' 16, 786, 791, 794, 802, 804ff., 809f., 829f., 834, 875
'Not Fade Away' 109n
'Nothing Was Delivered' 104
nursery rhyme 272, 634–702, 826

O'Brien, Brendan 626
'Obviously 5 Believers' 151, 302ff.
'Odds And Ends' 108n, 297
Odetta 292, 332, 350
Odum, Howard W. 748
"Off The Top Of My Head" 560
'Oh Babe It Ain't No Lie' 290
"Oh Mercy" xvii, 13ff., 77, 108, 300, 343, 357,
    431n, 530, 558–9, 570, 593f., 597, 600ff.,
    614, 616, 622, 626f., 631ff., 665, 679, 701,
    797, 836, 839, 853, 859n, 870, 873
'Oh Sister' 186f., 392n, 848n
'Old Ark's A-Moverin', The' 826
Oldfield, Mike (music journalist) 448n
Oliver, Paul 25n, 38f.
Olsson, Bent 328
Om Kalsoum 437n, 814n
Omnibus (BBC-TV) 843n, 862, 865
'On A Night Like This' 466
'On The Road Again' 96, 109, 140, 297, 330, 527
'One Grain Of Sand' 644
'One More Cup Of Coffee' 435
'One More Night' 32, 103
'One More Weekend' 173f.
'One Morning In May' 532f., 536f., 762
'One Of Us Must Know (Sooner Or Later)' 9, 68,
    151–2
'One Too Many Mornings' 3, 31, 128, 174, 357,
    429, 787
O'Neill, Eugene 196n, 468
'Only A Hobo' 80
'Only A Pawn In Their Game' 24, 36f., 133, 272
'Open The Door, Homer' 355
'Open The Door, Richard' 355
Opie, Iona 634
Opie, Peter 634
Orbison, Roy 6, 92f., 108n, 163, 325, 401, 722,
    840
Orwell, George 40
Oscar Brand's Folk Song Festival 605n
Oscars, the *see* Lifetime Achievement
Otis, Johnny 325, 351
O'Toole, Peter 560
'Outlaw Blues' 41, 151, 243n, 316–17, 341, 364
Owens, Willie Scarecrow 710n
'Oxford Town' 22, 785n

Pace, Kelly 336
Paine, Tom (Award) 56, 700
Paley, Tom 716, 774f.
Palmer, Robert 652
Pankake, Jon 278f., 290, 347, 759n
Papa Harvey Hull & Long Cleve Reed 29n, 319,
    364f., 710, 746
Paradise Lost 441n, 456, 477
'Paralyzed' 737, 804
Parker, Chubby 735
Parker, Colonel Tom 167n, 325, 542
Parker, Fess 33n, 492n
Parker, Junior 287, 320, 350, 741
Parry, Hubert 58n

'Pastures Of Plenty' 20n, 679n
"Pat Garrett & Billy The Kid" (album) 7, 105, 867,
    870
Pat Garrett & Billy The Kid (film) 243n, 627
Patchen, Kenneth 79ff.
'Paths Of Victory' 132, 567, 832
Patton, Charley 274n, 282, 294, 318ff., 325n, 354,
    360, 371f., 518, 708, 723n, 824n, 828
Peace News (journal) 123n
Peck, Gregory 558, 560f., 582f., 604
Pederson, Herb 717
'People Get Ready' 212n, 366, 800
Percival, Dave 251
'Percy's Song' 12, 507, 655, 822n, 823
Perkins, Carl 18n, 103n, 325, 857
Peter, Saint 610n
Peter, Paul & Mary 17f., 22, 212n, 368n, 846,
    848n
Petty, Norman 107n, 615
Petty, Tom (& The Heartbreakers) 163n, 560,
    558n
Petway, Robert 338
Phillips, Bruce 569–70
Phillips, Dewey 88f., 871
Phillips, Sam 89n, 287, 319, 325, 355n
Phillips, Washington 691n
Piaf, Edith 84n, 400
piano, Dylan's playing of 39, 173n, 615
Picasso 629n
Pickett, Charlie 293ff., 361
'Piers Plowman' 46
'Pig Meat Mama' 333
Pilgrim's Progress, The see Bunyan
Piltdown Men 91
Pinewood Tom (Josh White) 300n
'Piney Woods Money Mama' 358
Pirandello, Luigi 196
Pitchford, Lonnie 652
Pitney, Gene 562
Pittman, Sampson 293
"Planet Waves" 8, 41, 50, 54, 77, 147, 161, 178,
    181f., 190, 201n, 208ff., 220, 234n, 248, 320,
    322, 357, 392, 600n, 633, 756
Plath, Sylvia 215, 667n
Platters, The 89
Playboy (magazine) 2n, 137n, 169n, 201n, 299,
    435, 642, 740, 843
'Please Mrs. Henry' 9, 147
'Pledging My Time' 39, 151, 297, 325, 330, 345,
    782
Plugz, The 361, 464n, 515
Poe, Edgar Allan 75, 77–8, 79, 201n, 226n
Polanski, Roman 429
'Political World' 593, 616
polyrhythm 574
'Pony Blues' 371, 372
Poole, Charlie 706
'Poor Wind (That Never Change)' 396
Pope, Alexander 55, 410–11, 486n, 671n
Porter, Cole 23, 101

'Positively 4th Street' 7, 54, 68f., 129, 140f., 180, 184, 228, 367, 666
post-feminism 425
postmodernism 196, 249, 258, 261f., 373, 380, 386, 422, 425, 435, 515, 579, 612, 627, 855
post-structuralism 266, 373, 375n
Potter, Beatrix 676
Pound, Ezra 66n, 74f., 84n, 370n
Powell, Eugene 726
'Precious Angel' 10, 230ff., 238, 246, 307, 416, 441n
'Precious Memories' 13, 577
Preminger, Otto 550n
Presley, Elvis 7, 33, 40f., 46, 55, 84n, 85ff., 98ff., 112f., 116, 119, 173n, 176n, 250, 274n, 283n, 291, 308, 311ff., 319f., 324, 326, 328, 390, 394, 400, 407, 486n, 518, 528, 542, 545, 561, 577n, 578, 632, 700f., 726n, 728f., 736, 788, 804, 806, 822, 835, 851, 865, 871, 876
'Pressing On' 11, 41, 231, 234n, 239, 242f., 465, 485
'Pretty Boy Floyd' 22, 241n, 759n, 781n, 837, 850
'Pretty Peggy-O' 25, 27, 703
Previn, André 859
Price, Lloyd 89, 652n
Prince Buster 619.
Princeton University, Dylan receives honorary doctorate from 385
Prine, John 243
'Prison Wall Blues' 316
Procul Harum 119
Proffitt, Frank 321
protest songs/movement 3, 12, 22, 26, 37, 39, 119, 130, 134, 177, 185, 207, 248, 272, 340, 343, 367, 465, 472, 521, 643, 656, 835, 852n, 872
Prothro, Allen 336
Proust, Marcel 229n
Pullen, Suzie 844
punk 112, 173, 857

quantum physics 425
'Queen Jane Approximately' 13, 176n, 192, 435, 862
'Quinn The Eskimo (The Mighty Quinn)' 12, 104f., 115, 164, 665
'Quit Your Low-Down Ways' 26, 206f., 330f., 353n

R&B xix, 93, 390, 426
Rabelais, François 673
Radio City Music Hall 703, 855
Radio Luxembourg 88
Raft, George 553
Rager, Mose 725
'Ragged & Dirty' 15, 756-8, 781
'Raggle-Taggle Gypsies, The' 713
'Rags To Riches' 406-7
railroad (in US culture) 39f., 43f., 739-40, 742-4
Rainey, Ma 299, 301, 519n, 709, 746
'Rainy Day Women Nos. 12 & 35' 111n, 151, 352, 626, 694n, 852n, 853, 862

Raitt, Bonnie 325n, 384
'Ramblin' Gamblin' Willie' 653
Ram's Horn Music 662
Ramsey, Obray 716
Randolph, Vance 634, 735
Raney, Wayne 287ff.
'Rank Strangers To Me' 356
Ransom, John Crowe 621
rap 747, 857
"Rare Batch Of Little White Wonder, A, Volume 3" 197n
Ratner, Jon 42n
Rattigan, Terence 559
rave 574f.
RCA Victor (Nashville recording studio) 103
Reagan, Ronald 178n, 216, 247n, 573f., 845
"Real Live" 11, 316, 840
Rechy, John 84n
Red, Tampa see Tampa
Red Clay Ramblers 722
Reed, Jimmy 287, 291, 297n, 329, 351
Reed, Lou 581, 857
Reeves, Jim 111n
Regal (record label) 527
religion
    Bible 6, 28, 47, 50, 69, 132n, 160, 190, 194, 200n, 215, 272, 307, 323, 359, 391n, 392f., 398-9, 401-4, 407ff., 418, 426, 431f., 438f., 444, 457, 461-2, 467, 472f., 477, 479ff., 497, 499, 502-4, 513, 542, 544, 546, 548-9, 561-2, 565ff., 606f., 609, 611, 624, 637f., 640f., 645, 668-9, 673, 677, 683, 686, 690, 693n, 700f., 804
        as part of poor white and black culture 392, 543
    Born-again Christian(ity) xix, 10, 30, 37, 44, 49, 162, 196, 207, 210, 217, 232, 236, 239, 392, 593
    Calvinism 3, 6, 25f., 47f.
    Catholicism 381, 434-5, 603
    Christ, Jesus 44, 132n, 207, 209, 213, 217, 220, 230, 238, 242n, 402ff., 426, 437, 439, 447, 461, 478f., 481f., 489, 495, 496-7, 499f., 502, 509f., 513-14, 564, 601n, 607, 611, 663, 677, 684, 685, 801, 876
        persona of, in Dylan's songs 2n, 435, 455, 877
        parallels between Dylan and 210-11, 217, 220, 222, 224, 227, 236, 486, 488, 502
        second coming of 444
    Christian period, Dylan's xix, 398, 597
    Christianity 37, 44, 70, 211, 220, 231, 245, 248, 265, 393, 404-5, 473, 598, 818, 856n
        conversion to 210n, 215, 392, 527, 561, 563, 625n
        evangelical/evangelism 384, 485, 528
        retreat from 391-9
        forgiveness 62
        sin 62
    Gnostic Gospels 444, 446n, 447

God 81, 196, 199, 205, 207, 210, 265, 393, 402ff., 419ff., 437, 542, 606, 794, 801
  existence of 424, 483
  science v. God debate 424
  good v. evil 62
  institutionalised religion (the Church) 58n
  materialism v. spirituality 62
  Methodism 471n
  Puritanism 381
Renaldo & Clara 22n, 44n, 60, 212, 214, 397, 414n, 416n, 453, 464, 550n, 609, 663, 800, 841
'Restless Farewell' 30, 127, 602, 660, 875–6
Reynolds, Simon 389
Rhodes, Edward 523, 533, 546
rhyme schemes *see under* lyrics
rhythm 'n' blues (R&B) xxiii, 93, 390, 426
Richard, Cliff 87, 99
Richards, Keith 840, 853, 856
Richmond Jazz Quartet 355
Ricks, Christopher xx, 227n, 239n, 242n, 247n, 267n, 322, 478, 508, 545–6, 621, 762
Riddle, Nelson (Orchestra) 85, 101
Riley, Billy Lee 355
Riley, Tim 250
Rimbaud, Arthur 201n, 259f., 459
'Ring Them Bells' 14f., 132n, 365, 594, 600, 607–8, 609–10, 615, 631f., 696, 837, 875
'Rita May' 10, 316
Ritter, Tex 551
'Road Runner' 356
Robbins, Marty 89, 111, 186, 722
Robertson, Robbie 320, 400
Robeson, Paul 721
Robinson, Edward Arlington 75
Robinson, Edward G. 554
Robinson, Mabel 303
Robinson, Smokey 93n, 431
'Rock Me Mama' 870
'Rock, Salt And Nails' 569
'Rocks And Gravel' 41, 308
Rockwell, George Lincoln 550
Rodgers, Jimmie 166n, 279, 359, 362n, 521, 706, 710, 723n, 731, 745f., 825
Rogers, Jimmy 706
Rogers, Roy 551
Rogers, Weldon 615
Roland, Walter 371
Rolling Stone (magazine) 42n, 106n, 114, 118, 121, 162, 166n, 170n, 251, 425n, 732n
Rolling Stones 120n, 178n, 320, 857
Rolling Thunder Revue tour 9, 11f., 107n, 165, 272, 550n, 868
'Romance In Durango' 9, 12, 185n, 186f., 435, 591n, 676, 722
Romantic movement, influence of on ideas of 'great art' 386
Ronettes, The 92
Rooftop Singers 328
Rossetti, Christina 240n
Rosten, Norman 644n

'Rough Alley Blues' 526
Rousseau, Henri 629
'Royal Canal, The' 28n
Royal Hawks, The 793n
Runyan, Damon 75
Rush, Tom 732, 746, 751
Ruskin, John 798
Russell, Tony 102, 288n, 338n, 347n, 724, 735, 748

'Sad-Eyed Lady Of The Lowlands' 5, 73, 151f., 155f., 158, 213, 253, 274, 452, 480, 503n, 831, 840
Sager, Carole Bayer 300
St Augustine, Confessions of 74
'Sally Sue Brown' 837, 839
'Salty Dog' 313, 328, 346
salvation *see under* religion
Sam Price's Blusicians 303
'San Francisco Bay Blues' 288, 289
Sandburg, Carl 29n, 706, 735
Santo & Johnny 790, 822
'Sara' 77, 78, 143, 158, 210f., 215n, 218n, 604–5, 664, 685
Sartre, Jean-Paul 182n
Satie, Erik 227n, 641n, 721n
Savage, Joe 334, 335
"Saved" xvii, xix, 11, 15, 30, 41, 49, 135, 161f., 170, 193, 211n, 215, 220, 230f., 237, 239, 242, 244ff., 391f., 425, 440, 498, 528, 597f., 872
'Saving Grace' 70, 162, 231, 236, 238
Scaduto, Anthony 249
Scaggs, Boz 731n
Schultz, Arnold 725
Scobie, Stephen 251, 259f., 262f., 264–5, 274, 374, 382f., 388, 579, 685, 738
Scott, Jack 11, 111n
Scruggs, Earl 111n
Sebastian, John 698
Sedaka, Neil 89, 92
'See That My Grave Is Kept Clean' 2, 18, 279, 319, 378, 525n, 780
Seeger, Charles 290
Seeger, Mike 762n
Seeger, Peggy 773f.
Seeger, Pete 21n, 37n, 84n, 245n, 555n, 584n, 643f., 704, 750
'Seeing The Real You At Last' 338, 552, 554f., 568n
"Seems Like A Freeze Out" 197n, 226n
Selerie, Gavin 75n, 443n, 730, 777–8, 780
"Self Portrait" xvii, 6, 25ff., 30, 32, 94, 104, 106, 161ff., 177, 204, 464, 550, 725n, 855, 872
Sellers, Brother John 288, 350f.
'Sending Up My Timber' 528
'Señor (Tales Of Yankee Power)' 208, 216, 218, 435, 545, 564n, 625n, 697
"Sgt. Pepper's Lonely Hearts' Club Band" 119f.
'Series Of Dreams' (song) 14, 15, 626ff., 630ff., 852

'Series Of Dreams' (video) 841
Sermon on the Mount 241n, 444, 576n, 599, 668n
Service, Robert 591n
'Sesame And Lilies' 798
'Seven Curses' 507, 659, 676, 755
Seville Guitar Legends Festival 840, 853n, 857
sex and sexuality 100, 101–3, 152, 216, 250, 339, 361, 476, 592, 629, 630, 645, 650, 667, 736
   lust 396, 501, 524
   orgasm 56
   sexual betrayal 757
   sexual imagery/symbolism 32, 282n, 300n, 651, 657f.
   sexual innuendo 54f., 147, 376, 645ff., 663–4, 819
   sexual jealousy 455
Sexton, Anne 667, 737
Shade, Will 366, 649n
'Shake A Hand' 862
shaker music 36
Shakespeare, William 46f., 410–11, 531n, 562, 671, 673, 676n, 686
Shannon, Del 91
Sharp, Cecil 47f., 636n, 643, 735, 765
'She Belongs To Me' 5, 140, 164, 310
'She's Love Crazy' 858
Sheila E 689n
Shelley, Percy Bysshe 59, 490n
'Shelter From The Storm' 16, 61, 81, 211, 322, 575n, 725n
Shelton, Robert 21n, 37n, 110n, 165n, 176n, 201n, 243n, 250, 252–4, 284, 285, 289, 290, 352, 499, 712, 735, 774
'Shenandoah' 850
Shepard, Sam 13, 257, 265, 550n, 552n, 566, 579, 581, 590, 591, 722, 843n
'She's Your Lover Now' 14, 333, 442, 465, 575, 611
Shines, Johnny 296n, 715n
Shirelles 93
Shirley & Lee 585–6
Shoot the Piano Player (Tirez sur le Pianiste) 550–1, 559n, 560
'Shooting Star' 511, 599, 593–4, 598–9, 603–4, 627, 631, 632, 806
'Shot Of Love' (song) 217n, 333, 368, 388, 840, 872–3
"Shot Of Love" (album) xix, 11, 12, 266, 384, 391, 394, 425f., 430, 464, 470, 498, 640, 839
Siegel, Don 550
'Sign On The Cross' 172, 211, 690
'Sign On The Window' 172, 174, 176, 337, 465, 871
'Silvio' 15, 593n, 783, 852n, 854
Simon, Paul 7, 79n, 164f., 653f.
Simon & Garfunkel 79n, 165n
Simone, Nina 315n, 825n
'Simple Twist Of Fate' 15, 183, 783, 832, 848n, 852n
Sinatra, Frank 17, 85, 101, 102n, 875

Sing Out! (journal) 168n, 348n, 368n, 502f., 577n, 644n, 704, 750, 762n
'Sinking Of The Titanic' 309n, 460
'Sissy Man' 331–2
Sister 2 Sister (magazine) 859–60
'Sittin' On Top Of The World' 285n, 319, 321, 342, 345, 714–16, 739, 754, 782
'Sitting On A Barbed-Wire Fence' 41, 98, 341
'Sixteen Snow White Horses' 2
"Sketches Of Spain" 851
Slim, Bumble Bee 742
Slocum, Mick 705, 711
'Slow Train' 10, 53, 230n, 231, 234–5, 564n, 873
"Slow Train Coming" xix, 10, 30, 42, 44n, 49, 135, 161f., 193, 208, 220, 228, 230f., 233, 238, 240, 243, 245, 248, 317, 366, 385, 392f., 485n, 528, 784, 791
Smith, Bessie 3, 275, 279, 314, 345n, 725, 728n, 731, 740
Smith, Clara 378n
Smith, G. E. 703
Smith, Harry 163, 165, 189n, 199n, 207n, 269n, 280, 289, 301–2, 309, 326n, 328, 358n, 378n, 460, 481ff., 643n, 645, 691n, 705n, 710n, 716, 732ff., 737, 745, 762n, 773, 778n, 825, 866n, 867
Smith, J. T. Funny Papa 318, 333, 651, 755n
Smith, Mamie 370n
Smith, Patti 576
Smith, Stuff 467
Smith, Warren 297n, 713, 858
'Smokestack Lightnin'' 324
Snow, Hank 167n, 365
Snyder, Gary 84n
'So Long, Good Luck & Goodbye' 615
'Solid Rock' 235f., 441n
'Some Other Kinds Of Songs' 80n, 141n, 350, 429
'Someone's Got A Hold Of My Heart' 14, 446, 470, 563f., 566, 684, 875
Somerville, William 820
'Something There Is About You' 8, 179f., 209
'Something's Burning, Baby' 83, 363f., 548, 568, 802
Song of Solomon 457–8, 563, 564
'Song To Woody' 3, 19f., 23, 27, 110n, 126, 284, 355, 525n
Songs of Experience 412f., 415–6, 609n, 753n
Songs of Innocence 412f., 416, 609, 753n
Songtalk (magazine) 843
'Soon' 694, 862
Sopwith Camel 119
'Southern Can I Mine' 298, 525
Southern Poor White *see under* folk music
Spand, Charlie 731
'Spanish Harlem Incident' 4, 116, 129, 132, 435, 571–3, 575, 644n
'Spanish Is The Loving Tongue' 7, 10, 432, 615, 676, 837
Spann, Otis 306
'Special Agent (Railroad Police Blues)' 280n, 341n, 343

Special Rider Music 298, 344
Speckled Red (Rufus Perryman) 294
Spector, Phil 92, 117, 352, 627
Spence, Joseph 317n
Spenser, Edmund 733
Spin (magazine) 843; *see also* Cohen, Scott
spirituals *see under* black music
Spitz, Bob 82, 250, 254
Spivey, Victoria 284f., 292, 299, 367
Spoelstra, Mark 288
Springs, Helena 317
Springsteen, Bruce 120, 448n, 699, 857
'Stack A Lee' 741, 745f., 748, 751, 762
'Stack O'Lee' (and variant titles) 289n, 707,
    709–10
Stagolee (and variant names) (mythic hero) 336,
    747
'Standing In The Doorway' 16, 605, 783, 786, 791,
    804ff., 809f., 812–13, 814, 825, 828ff., 875
Stanley, Ralph 828
Stanley Brothers 716, 828
Stanton, Harry Dean 581n, 840
Staple Singers 212
Starr, Kay 85
Starr, Ringo 85, 352n
'Statesboro' Blues' 280, 517, 519, 546, 708n
Steele, Tommy 86f., 266f., 332, 553n
Steeleye Span 713, 736
Steinbeck, John 20, 25, 36, 75, 295, 458n
'Step It Up & Go' 726–7, 754, 783
Stevens, Vol 299f., 314
Stewart, Al 750
Stewart, Dave 841
Stewart, James 557
'Still A Fool'/'Two Trains Running' 279, 320, 322,
    339
Stills, Stephen 674n
'Stocking Feet Blues' 356, 758n
Stokes, Frank 19n, 301, 306, 327, 331, 526, 650
Stone, Joe 717
'Stop Breaking Down Blues' 361
'Stop Crying' 361
Strachwitz, Chris 38
'Straight A's In Love' 576
Straw, Syd 722
"Street Legal" 10, 30, 44n, 56, 190, 192f., 208,
    215f., 223, 229n, 230, 233ff., 248, 265, 299,
    359, 361, 370, 602, 697, 791
Strickland, Napoleon 321
'Strike Up The Band' 694
Stuckey, Henry 346–7
'Subterranean Homesick Blues' 5, 64–5, 72, 83, 97,
    116, 140, 314, 388, 492n, 611, 672n, 696,
    832, 848, 851, 855
'Sugaree' 290
Sumlin, Hubert 320, 326, 329, 814
Sun Records 13, 93, 106, 324f., 632, 728, 858
Sunday Times, The 785, 786n
Sunny & The Sunglows 406
Sunnyland Slim 294n
surrealism 144, 159, 190, 473n, 630–1, 721n

Sutcliffe, Phil 728
'Sweet Amarillo' 870
'Sweetheart Like You' (song) 362, 466f., 470, 557,
    823
'Sweetheart Like You' (video) 841
Swimme, Brian 424
Swift, Jonathan 475, 661n, 822
Sykes, Roosevelt 290, 293, 295, 337, 349, 362n
syntho-pop 857

Tackett, Fred 400
Taft, Michael 276, 298, 301, 369, 372–5, 378, 664
Tagg, Philip 574–5
'Tail Dragger' 323f., 366–7, 679
Taj Mahal 706–7, 708, 713
'Take A Message To Mary' 166, 725n
'Take Me As I Am (Or Let Me Go)' 164, 167f.
'Talkin' Folklore Center' 827
'Talkin' John Birch Paranoid Blues' 22, 550, 672n
'Talkin' New York' 3, 207n, 241n, 591
'Talkin' World War III Blues' 96, 122, 527
'Talking Bear Mountain Picnic Massacre Blues' 20
Tamla-Motown *see* Motown
Tampa Red 282, 290, 299, 302, 305, 314n, 315,
    368, 374, 395n, 522, 726, 858
'Tangled Up In Blue' 11, 14f., 122, 182f., 230n,
    259, 261f., 264, 356, 366n, 373, 380, 796,
    852n, 854, 861, 865
'Tangled Up In Tapes' 533n
Tarantula 76, 81f., 83n, 130n, 176n, 369, 453,
    492n, 553, 661, 679, 698, 843, 859, 874
Tarlton, Jimmy 522, 706–7, 773
Tarot 82n, 225, 499–500
Tawney, R. H. 381
Taylor, Edward 75
Taylor, Elizabeth 551n, 556–7, 560, 856n
Taylor, Koko 297
'Tears Of Rage' 9, 48, 484, 862, 876
Teddy Bears 90
Telegraph, The (journal) 26n, 56n, 75n, 185n,
    227n, 239n, 245n, 251, 255–7, 260n, 261n,
    263n, 264n, 266n, 268, 277n, 279n, 310n,
    312n, 340n, 359n, 372, 373n, 388n, 430n,
    443n, 464n, 521n, 551n, 553n, 562n, 563n,
    578, 653n, 665n, 675n, 693n, 701n, 730n,
    739n, 843f., 853n, 860n, 872n
Television (band) 515
'Tell Him I Said Hello' 356
'Tell Me' 234n, 429, 470, 483, 485
'Tell Me Mama' 296
'Tell Me, Momma' 55n, 192, 296, 314, 383
'Tell Me That It Isn't True' 103
Temple, Johnny 346
'Temple Of Flames' (tour) 858
'Temporary Like Achilles' 66, 144f., 149, 174, 315
10cc 595
'10,000 Men' 337, 677, 680, 693ff.
Tennyson, Alfred, Lord 75, 459, 822
Terry, Sonny 19, 286f., 290, 349n, 526, 644n, 724,
    726
'That's All Right' 33, 98, 103, 110, 312n, 825

The Edge (of U2) 837
'There Was A Time When I Was Blind' 285
'There'll Be Some Changes Made' 353
Thin Lizzy' 827
'Think You Need A Shot' 369
Third World 469, 836
'This Land Is Your Land' 848n
'This Old Man' 673, 850
'This Train'/'This Train Is Bound For Glory' 212n, 366, 801, 826, 848n
'This Wheel's On Fire' 9
Thomas, Elvie 298
Thomas, Henry 274n, 281f., 395n, 587n, 678, 732
Thomas, James 294
Thompson, Hunter S. 75, 568
Thompson, Richard 857
Thoreau, Henry David 83n
Thornton, Big Mama 304, 315, 325
'Three Angels' 81, 176, 247n, 871
'Three Woman Blues' 453
'Tight Connection To My Heart (Has Anybody Seen My Love?)' 408, 456, 566, 549, 552, 556, 562–3, 568n, 576
''Til I Fell In Love With You' 16, 790–1, 794, 809, 824, 829, 831
'Time Is Drawing Near' 340, 341n, 343
Time magazine 245n, 842
"Time Out Of Mind" xix, xxi, 16, 77, 109n, 131n, 189n, 212n, 300, 328, 591, 601n, 605, 783, 785–834, 876f.
'Time Passes Slowly' 175, 831
'Times They Are A-Changin', The' 3, 10, 22, 25, 30–1, 109, 111n, 116, 128, 130ff., 197, 207, 467, 469, 523, 846f., 851ff., 855, 868, 871
Tin Pan Alley 6, 23, 119, 175, 533n, 594f., 794, 849
'Tiny Montgomery' 696
'Titanic Blues' 358
Titanic, R. M. S. 136–7, 460
'To Be Alone With You' 349, 783
'To Ramona' 4, 50, 52, 92n, 716n, 781n, 837
Tokens, The 92
Tolkien, J. R. R. 202ff.
Tom Petty & The Heartbreakers 558, 859n
'Tombstone Blues' 66, 96, 212n, 560
'Tomorrow Is A Long Time' 7, 54n, 106, 164n, 837
'Tone The Bell Easy' 365
'Tonight I'll Be Staying Here With You' 31, 43, 160f., 397, 455
Tonys, the 849
'Too Much Of Nothing' 45, 74n, 339, 484
Toomey, Welby 706
Tormé, Mel 101, 788
Touch of Evil, A 622
'Tough Mama' 147, 180–1, 220, 357, 470n, 772
Townsend, Henry 337
Townshend, Pete 99, 835
'Trail Of The Buffalo' 703, 732
'Train A-Travelin' ' 126n, 127
'Travelin' Blues' 526–7

Travelin' Wilburys 353
'Traveling Riverside Blues' 361
Travellers, The 679n
Travis, Merle 725
Travis, Randy 108n
troubadours 45, 519
'Trouble' 99, 104f., 839
'Trouble In Mind' 231f., 238, 242n, 317, 393, 823f.
'Trouble No More/Someday Baby Blues' 342
Troy, Doris 576
True Confessions tour 858, 859n
'True Love Tends To Forget' 16, 190, 217f.
Truffaut, Francois 550n, 559n
'Trust Yourself' 640
'Tryin' To Get To Heaven' 786, 791, 797–8, 801, 805, 809, 825f., 829, 831, 833, 875
Tull, Jethro 178n
'Turn Your Lamp Down Low' 793
Turner, Big Joe 728, 825
Turner, Ike 320
Turner, Tina 785
'TV Talkin' Song' 672, 696, 874
TV-AM 842n
'Tweeter And The Monkey Man' 353
Twitty, Conway 88, 632
'2 x 2' 672, 693n, 694, 696, 697
'Two Soldiers' 15, 740, 758, 759ff., 763
Two Trains Running (play) 710n
'Two Trains Running' (song) *see* 'Still A Fool'
Tyler, Wat 46

U2 112n, 837, 858
'Ugliest Girl In The World, The' 13, 343f., 593n
'Unbelievable' 14, 257, 258, 673, 675, 694ff.
Uncle Dave Macon *see* Macon
'Under The Red Sky' (song) 640f., 651, 669, 683–5, 688–90, 833, 875
"Under The Red Sky" (album) 14, 15, 257f., 263, 265, 323f., 337, 371, 420n, 634–701, 704, 734n, 737, 824, 839, 860
'Under Your Spell' 13, 300, 463, 578, 839
'Unfortunate Rake, The' 529–33, 576ff., 767
'Union Sundown' 264, 339f., 343, 468–9, 471, 863, 874
'Up To Me' 12, 190n, 259, 362, 695, 831
'Uranium Rock' 858

Valens, Ritchie 90, 107, 849
Van Halen 574
Van Ronk, Dave 284
Vee, Bobby 85, 101
Velvet Underground, The 119, 515
Verlaine, Tom 515, 876
Vietnam War 123n, 178n, 216, 758, 762
"Villager, The" 197n
Villon, François 84n, 201n, 560
Vincent, Gene 88, 91, 99, 708
'Viola Lee Blues' 328n
'Visions Of Johanna' 5, 12, 33, 72f., 83, 96, 151f.,

154ff., 264, 330, 416, 425, 465, 489, 499, 661, 850, 867
von Franz, M.-L. 493
von Schmidt, Eric 336, 694n, 708

'Wade In The Water' 694n
Wagner, Richard 876
'Waiting To Get Beat' 576
'Walking Blues' 277, 278n, 283n, 372n, 758
'Walking To New Orleans' 824
Wall, Anthony 725
Wall, Max 804
Wallace, Sippie 350
Wallace, Will Shade-Minnie 366
'Walls Of Red Wing' 14, 128, 428, 532, 601, 850
Walter Vincson & The Mississippi Sheiks 319, 356
Walton, Lorraine 467
Walton, Mercy Dee 825
'Wanted Man' 96, 166
Wardlow, Gayle 347
Warhol Factory 304
Warnes, Jennifer 400
Was, Don and David 14, 692
Washboard Sam 316, 330, 357n
Washington Post 796
'Watcha Gonna Do' 206f.
'Watching The River Flow' 7, 162, 266n, 301, 575n, 602, 853
'Watered-Down Love' 11, 430, 462n, 605, 875
Waters, Ethel 353
Waters, Muddy *see* Muddy Waters
Watson, Doc 164n, 532, 541, 715, 736, 741, 762, 776f., 838
Wayne, James 300
'We Better Talk This Over' 190, 218–19
Weaver, Curley 282n, 337, 354, 366, 518n, 522, 648, 742
Weaver, Sylvester 299
Webb, Jordan 726
Weberman, A. J. 56, 254
Wedderburn 634, 733
'Wedding Song' 50, 76, 180, 209f., 243n
'Weeping Willow' 346, 727
Weinberger, Sybil 286
Weissberg, Eric 716
Welch, Lenny 406
Welding, Pete 374f., 378, 830
Weldon, Will 337, 349n, 368
Welles, Orson 622
Wells, Kitty 823n
Wells, Mary 93, 576
Wenner, Jann 42n
'Went To See The Gypsy' 8, 105, 174f., 226
Wesley, Charles 471–2
Wesley, John 471n
West, Nathanael 75
West, Mae 701n
'What Can I Do For You?' 11, 231, 237, 239, 242
'What Good Am I?' 597, 606, 611, 615, 626, 631
'What Kind Of Friend Is This?' 297

'What Was It You Wanted?' 14, 224n, 343, 611–14, 615, 626, 875
'Whatcha Gonna Do' 207n
'When He Returns' 10, 231, 235, 238, 240f., 441n
'When I Paint My Masterpiece' 7, 346, 366, 490, 861
'When The Night Comes Falling From The Sky' 258, 429, 452, 548, 552, 556, 567, 665, 803, 841n
'When The Ship Comes In' 27, 29, 109, 131f., 199f., 207, 263, 465, 469, 575, 871
'When Things Go Wrong With You' 168n
'When You Gonna Wake Up?' 243, 247, 441n, 873
'When You Got A Good Friend' 362
'Where Are You Tonight? (Journey Through Dark Heat)' 41, 191, 215, 220, 228, 230, 493, 664
'Where Teardrops Fall' 14, 108, 530, 601, 605, 606–7, 615, 632f., 655, 679, 814
'Which Side Are You On?' 137n
White, B. F. 777
White, Bukka 3, 279, 280, 288f., 299f., 302, 313, 396
White, Georgia 359, 664
White, Josh 299, 331f., 731
White, Newman Ivy 748
Whitfield, David 400, 406
Whitman, Walt 75, 78f., 83, 416, 453, 459, 721n, 845
Whittaker, Dave 82n, 278
Whitter & Grayson 716
'Who Killed Davey Moore?' 185, 644n, 645, 656
'Who Loves You More? (Baby I Do)' 576
'Wiggle Wiggle' 14, 257, 282n, 525, 673ff., 678, 686, 694ff., 700, 856
'Wigwam' 6
Wilber, Bill 316
'Wild Mountain Thyme' 92
Wilde, Marty 99n
Wiley and Wiley 336
Wiley, Geeshie 298
Wilkins, Robert 364
Will Batts' Jug Band 718n
Williams, Big Joe 273n, 282f., 285, 290, 292, 318f., 331, 364, 371, 518, 647, 714
Williams, Ellis 679n
Williams, Hank 13, 22, 32, 43, 85, 110, 166n, 287, 729, 823
Williams, Henry 524, 649n, 731
Williams, Jesse 537
Williams, Joe (not "Big") 361
Williams, Paul 251, 257, 628
Williams, Richard 13, 250
Williams, Roger 85
Williams, Rowan 424
Williams, Tennessee 550, 559
Williams, William Carlos 79n, 510n
Williamson I, Sonny Boy 299, 303, 317ff., 325n, 361, 726f.
Williamson II, Sonny Boy 287n, 301, 317f., 353n, 361, 464n, 651, 823
Williamson, Robin 347

ob 870
, August 709–10
n, Jackie 108, 838n
on, Kid Wesley 301
son, Leola B. 731
lson, Wesley 'Kid Sox' 731
Winterlude' 8, 172, 174f.
Wissolik and McGrath 693n
Wissolik, Richard 251
'With God On Our Side' 4, 25, 35, 224n, 428, 611, 656, 877
Witherspoon, Jimmy 306
Wobblies, The 569
Wolf, Howlin' 274n, 287n, 315, 318ff., 329, 343, 366, 396, 460, 518, 679, 715, 723, 814, 824
Wolfe, Charles K. 745
Wolfe, Thomas 53, 83
Wolfe, Tom 158n
Wonder, Little Stevie 869
Wonder, Stevie 849
'Won't You Buy A Postcard?' 542
Wood, Hally 532n
Wood, Ronnie 750
Woods, Hosea 316
'Woodstock' (song) 877
Woodstock (festival) 94n, 131n, 167n, 212n, 356, 392, 569, 711n, 729n, 847
Woodstock II 676, 846, 875f.
Woodward, Ian 752
'Woogie Boogie' 550, 674
Wordsworth, William 75, 83, 174, 199f., 203, 818
"World Gone Wrong" 15, 22n, 26, 80n, 279, 342, 348, 458, 524f., 533n, 648n, 666, 704f., 710, 716, 732, 739, 740ff., 750f., 754f., 757, 759, 778f., 783, 791, 813, 829, 838
'World Is Going Wrong, The' 648n
'Worried Blues' 14

Writings and Drawings by Bob Dylan 43n, 163, 207n, 299
Wyndham-Read, Martin 711

Yancey, Jimmy 378n
Yardbirds, The 118
Yates, Blind Richard 299f.
'Ye Shall Be Changed' 391
'Yea! Heavy & A Bottle Of Bread' 160
Yeats, W.B. 61n, 245n, 412
Yevtushenko, Yevgeny 84n
'Yonder Comes Sin' 354, 391, 393, 395, 397–8, 400, 875
Yorke Brothers 725
'You Ain't Goin' Nowhere' 7, 17, 872
'You Angel You' 234n, 861
'You Can Never Tell' 96
'You Changed My Life' 391, 560–1, 871
'You Don't Know Me' 575n
'You Wanna Ramble' 13, 561
Young, Neil 823, 837, 842, 857
'(Your'e The) Devil In Disguise' 394
'You're A Big Girl Now' 12, 159, 183, 193, 215n, 216, 353, 495n, 666, 788
'You're Goin' Quit Me Baby' 285
'You're Gonna Make Me Lonesome When You Go' 30, 184
'You're Gonna Need Somebody On Your Bond' 207n
'You're Gonna Quit Me' 15, 730f., 739
'You're No Good' 289
'You've Got To Walk That Lonesome Valley' 624
Yuro, Timi 93

Zappa, Frank 118ff., 130n, 841–2, 869, 871
Zephaniah, Benjamin 508
Zimmerman, Hermes 366
Zuckerman, Matthew 74n, 730n